# EXAMKRACKERS MCAT®

# PHYSICS

## 8TH EDITION

# OSOTE
PUBLISHING

ISBN 10: 1-893858-63-4 (Volume 5)
ISBN 13: 978-1-893858-63-3 (5 Volume Set)


8th Edition

To purchase additional copies of this book or the rest of the 5 volume set,
call 1-888-572-2536 or fax orders to 1-859-255-0109.

Examkrackers.com

Osote.com

Audioosmosis.com

Cover/inside layout design/illustrations: Examkrackers' staff

**FAIR USE NOTICE.** This book is an independent educational guide for students who are preparing to take the Medical College Admission Test® exam, also known as the MCAT® exam. This book has been prepared and published by Examkrackers, Inc. and is not endorsed or sponsored by, or otherwise affiliated with, the Association of American Medical Colleges (AAMC), which publishes the MCAT exam and owns the foregoing trademarks. A small number of questions and answers from the "MCAT Practice Test" and "MCAT Practice Items" as published by AAMC are used in this book for purposes of teaching, scholarship and commentary pursuant to the Fair Use Doctrine of the U.S. Copyright Act (17 USC §107). The trademarks owned by AAMC are used for information and identification only, and are not intended to claim or suggest any affiliation with AAMC.

Printed and bound in the United States of America.

# Acknowledgements

Although I am the author, the hard work and expertise of many individuals contributed to this book. The idea of writing in two voices, a science voice and an MCAT voice, was the creative brainchild of my imaginative friend Jordan Zaretsky. I would like to thank Scott Calvin for lending his exceptional science talent and pedagogic skills to this project. I also must thank thirteen years worth of ExamKrackers students for doggedly questioning every explanation, every sentence, every diagram, and every punctuation mark in the book, and for providing the creative inspiration that helped me find new ways to approach and teach physics. Finally, I wish to thank my wife, Silvia, for her support during the difficult times in the past and those that lie ahead.

I also wish to thank the following individuals:

## Contributors

Jennifer Birk-Goldschmidt
Patrick Butler
Dr. Scott Calvin
Sam Crayton
Spencer Lewis
Steven Ngai
Jeffrey Peacock
Shuo Song
Vinita Takiar
Steven Tersigni
Ruopeng Zhu

# Read This Section First!

This manual contains all the physics tested on the MCAT® and more. It contains more physics than is tested on the MCAT® because a deeper understanding of basic scientific principles is often gained through more advanced study. In addition, the MCAT® often presents passages with imposing topics that may intimidate the test-taker. Although the questions don't require knowledge of these topics, some familiarity will increase the confidence of the test-taker.

In order to answer questions quickly and efficiently, it is vital that the test-taker understand what is, and is not, tested directly by the MCAT®. To assist the test-taker in gaining this knowledge, this manual will use the following conventions. Any term or concept which is tested directly by the MCAT® will be written in **red, bold type**. To ensure a perfect score on the MCAT®, you should thoroughly understand all terms and concepts that are in **red, bold type** in this manual. Sometimes it is not necessary to memorize the name of a concept, but it is necessary to understand the concept itself. These concepts will also be in **bold and red**. It is important to note that the converse of the above is not true: just because a topic is not in **bold and red**, does not mean that it is not important.

Any formula that must be memorized will also be written in **red, bold type**.

If a topic is discussed purely as background knowledge, it will be written in *italics*. If a topic is written in italics, it is not likely to be required knowledge for the MCAT® but may be discussed in an MCAT® passage. Do not ignore items in italics, but recognize them as less important than other items. Answers to questions that directly test knowledge of italicized topics are likely to be found in an MCAT® passage.

Text written in orange is me, Salty the Kracker. I will remind you what is and is not an absolute must for MCAT. I will help you develop your MCAT intuition. In addition, I will offer mnemonics, simple methods of viewing a complex concept, and occasionally some comic relief. Don't ignore me, even if you think I am not funny, because my comedy is designed to help you understand and remember. If you think I am funny, tell the boss. I could use a raise.

Each chapter in this manual should be read three times: twice before the class lecture, and once immediately following the lecture. During the first reading, you should not write in the book. Instead, read purely for enjoyment. During the second reading, you should both highlight and take notes in the margins. The third reading should be slow and thorough.

The 24 questions in each lecture should be worked during the second reading before coming to class. The in-class exams in the back of the book are to be done in class after the lecture. Do not look at them before class.

**Warning:** Just attending the class will not raise your score. You must do the work. Not attending class will obstruct dramatic score increases. If you have Audio Osmosis, then listen to the appropriate lecture before and after you read a lecture.

If you are studying independently, read the lecture twice before doing the in-class exam and then once after doing the in-class exam. If you have Examkrackers *MCAT® Audio Osmosis With Jordan and Jon*, listen to that before taking the in-class exam and then as many times as necessary after taking the exam.

A scaled score conversion chart is provided on the answer page. This is not meant to be an accurate representation of your MCAT score. Do not become demoralized by a poor performance on these exams; they are not accurate reflections of your performance on the real MCAT®. The thirty minute exams have been designed to educate. They are similar to an MCAT® but with most of the easy questions removed. We believe that you can answer most of the easy questions without too much help from us, so the best way to raise your score is to focus on the more difficult questions. This method is one of the reasons for the rapid and celebrated success of the Examkrackers prep course and products.

If you find yourself struggling with the science or just needing more practice materials, use the Examkrackers 1001 Questions series. These books are designed specifically to teach the science. If you are already scoring 10s or better, these books are not for you.

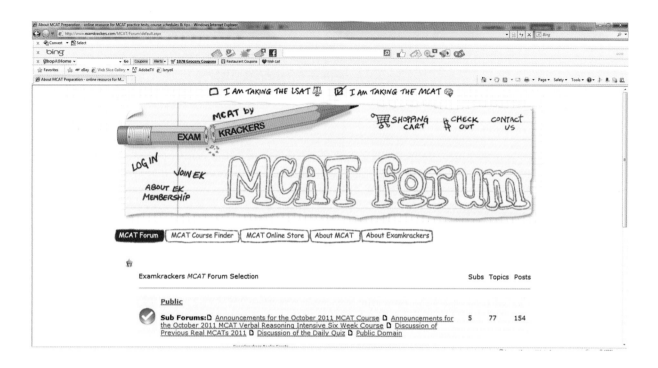

You should take advantage of the forums at www.examkrackers.com. The bulletin board allows you to discuss any question in the book with an MCAT® expert at Examkrackers. All discussions are kept on file so you have a bank of discussions to which you can refer to any question in this book.

Although we are very careful to be accurate, errata is an occupational hazard of any science book, especially those that are updated regularly as is this one. We maintain that our books have fewer errata than any other prep book. Most of the time what students are certain are errata is the student's error and not an error in the book. So that you can be certain, any errata in this book will be listed as it is discovered at www.examkrackers.com on the bulletin board. Check this site initially and periodically. If you discover what you believe to be errata, please post it on this board and we will verify it promptly. We understand that this system calls attention to the very few errata that may be in our books, but we feel that this is the best system to ensure that you have accurate information for your exam. Again, we stress that we have fewer errata than any other prep book on the market. The difference is that we provide a public list of our errata for your benefit.

Study diligently, trust this book to guide you, and you will reach your MCAT® goals.

# Table of Contents

# PHYSICAL SCIENCES

**DIRECTIONS.** Most questions in the Physical Sciences test are organized into groups, each preceded by a descriptive passage. After studying the passage, select the one best answer to each question in the group. Some questions are not based on a descriptive passage and are also independent of each other. You must also select the one best answer to these questions. If you are not certain of an answer, eliminate the alternatives that you know to be incorrect and then select an answer from the remaining alternatives. A periodic table is provided for your use. You may consult it whenever you wish.

---

## PERIODIC TABLE OF THE ELEMENTS

| 1 H 1.0 | | | | | | | | | | | | | | | | | | 2 He 4.0 |
|---|---|---|---|---|---|---|---|---|---|---|---|---|---|---|---|---|---|---|
| 3 Li 6.9 | 4 Be 9.0 | | | | | | | | | | | | 5 B 10.8 | 6 C 12.0 | 7 N 14.0 | 8 O 16.0 | 9 F 19.0 | 10 Ne 20.2 |
| 11 Na 23.0 | 12 Mg 24.3 | | | | | | | | | | | | 13 Al 27.0 | 14 Si 28.1 | 15 P 31.0 | 16 S 32.1 | 17 Cl 35.5 | 18 Ar 39.9 |
| 19 K 39.1 | 20 Ca 40.1 | 21 Sc 45.0 | 22 Ti 47.9 | 23 V 50.9 | 24 Cr 52.0 | 25 Mn 54.9 | 26 Fe 55.8 | 27 Co 58.9 | 28 Ni 58.7 | 29 Cu 63.5 | 30 Zn 65.4 | 31 Ga 69.7 | 32 Ge 72.6 | 33 As 74.9 | 34 Se 79.0 | 35 Br 79.9 | 36 Kr 83.8 |
| 37 Rb 85.5 | 38 Sr 87.6 | 39 Y 88.9 | 40 Zr 91.2 | 41 Nb 92.9 | 42 Mo 95.9 | 43 Tc (98) | 44 Ru 101.1 | 45 Rh 102.9 | 46 Pd 106.4 | 47 Ag 107.9 | 48 Cd 112.4 | 49 In 114.8 | 50 Sn 118.7 | 51 Sb 121.8 | 52 Te 127.6 | 53 I 126.9 | 54 Xe 131.3 |
| 55 Cs 132.9 | 56 Ba 137.3 | 57 La* 138.9 | 72 Hf 178.5 | 73 Ta 180.9 | 74 W 183.9 | 75 Re 186.2 | 76 Os 190.2 | 77 Ir 192.2 | 78 Pt 195.1 | 79 Au 197.0 | 80 Hg 200.6 | 81 Tl 204.4 | 82 Pb 207.2 | 83 Bi 209.0 | 84 Po (209) | 85 At (210) | 86 Rn (222) |
| 87 Fr (223) | 88 Ra 226.0 | 89 Ac⁼ 227.0 | 104 Unq (261) | 105 Unp (262) | 106 Unh (263) | 107 Uns (262) | 108 Uno (265) | 109 Une (267) | | | | | | | | | |

| * | 58 Ce 140.1 | 59 Pr 140.9 | 60 Nd 144.2 | 61 Pm (145) | 62 Sm 150.4 | 63 Eu 152.0 | 64 Gd 157.3 | 65 Tb 158.9 | 66 Dy 162.5 | 67 Ho 164.9 | 68 Er 167.3 | 69 Tm 168.9 | 70 Yb 173.0 | 71 Lu 175.0 |
|---|---|---|---|---|---|---|---|---|---|---|---|---|---|---|
| ⁼ | 90 Th 232.0 | 91 Pa 231) | 92 U 238.0 | 93 Np (237) | 94 Pu (244) | 95 Am (243) | 96 Cm (247) | 97 Bk (247) | 98 Cf (251) | 99 Es (252) | 100 Fm (257) | 101 Md (258) | 102 No (259) | 103 Lr (260) |

# TRANSLATIONAL MOTION

## 1.1 Salty's Five Step Never-Fail Method for Solving Physics Problems

Whether they realize it or not, any good physics student has a system to solve physics problems. Some problems are so trivial that the entire system is done without conscious thought in a fraction of a second. Other times, each step is given careful and deliberate consideration. The following is my system that you should use to solve every single physics problem on the MCAT. For easy problems you will be able to do the entire system in your head in seconds or less, but the moment you feel any hesitation you should begin writing with your pencil.

**Step 1: Be confident.**

Don't be intimidated by any MCAT question. Remember the MCAT only tests basic physics. After reading this manual, you will know all the physics necessary to handle any MCAT problem.

**Step 2: Draw a well-labeled diagram.**

A good diagram takes the question out of the 'MCAT environment', and puts it on your terms. Also, the act of drawing a diagram provides you with new insight into the problem.

**Step 3: Narrow your focus to only the system of bodies in which you're interested.**

This may be the most obvious step in physics but it is the one most often forgotten. You must learn to concentrate upon only the body or bodies about which the question asks, and ignore all extraneous information.

**Step 4: Find a formula that uses the variables in your diagram.**

Write down several formulas, and then eliminate until you find the useful one. Actually write your formulas out on your scratch paper. It doesn't take much time and it increases accuracy.

**Step 5: Plug in values and calculate the answer.**

Note: This last step is often unnecessary on the MCAT.

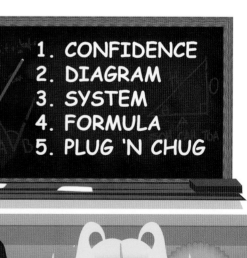

1. CONFIDENCE
2. DIAGRAM
3. SYSTEM
4. FORMULA
5. PLUG 'N CHUG

## 1.2 Vectors and Scalars

Appreciating the difference between vectors and scalars will help you solve MCAT physics problems. A **scalar** is a physical quantity that has magnitude but no direction. A **vector** is a physical quantity with both magnitude and direction. A vector can be represented by an arrow. The direction of the arrow reveals the direction of the vector; the length of the arrow reveals the magnitude of the vector.

## 1.3 Adding and Subtracting Vectors

In order to add vectors, place the head of the first vector to the tail of the second vector, and draw an arrow from the tail of the first to the head of the second. The resulting arrow is the vector sum of the other two vectors. Notice that the magnitude of the sum of two vectors must be smaller than or equal to the sum of their magnitudes and greater than or equal to the difference of their magnitudes. In other words, the sum of two velocity vectors that are 10 m/s and 7 m/s will be greater than or equal to a velocity vector of 3 m/s, but smaller than or equal to a velocity vector of 17 m/s.

To subtract vectors place the heads of the two vectors together and draw an arrow from the tail of the first to the tail of the second, or add the negative of the vector to be subtracted. The new vector is the vector difference between the two vectors.

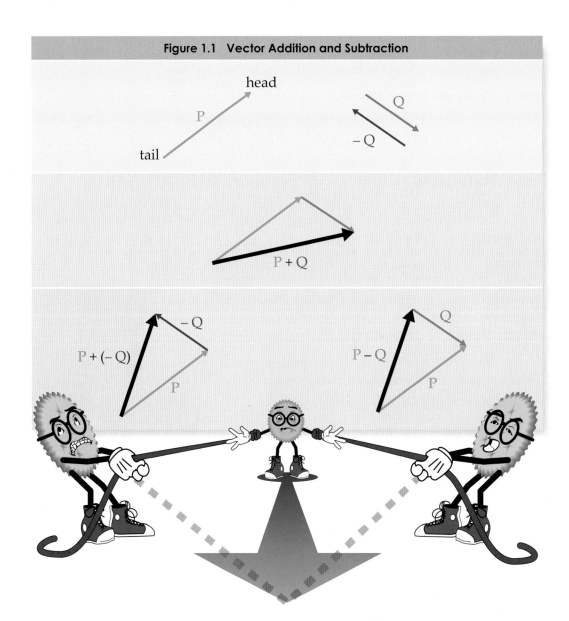

**Figure 1.1 Vector Addition and Subtraction**

## 1.4 Multiplying Vectors

Vectors cannot be added to nor subtracted from scalars or vice versa. However, vectors can be multiplied or divided by scalars. When a vector is multiplied or divided by a scalar the direction of the original vector is retained but the magnitude changes in proportion to the scalar.

*For example:*

$$5 \text{ m/s}^2 \text{ rightward} \quad \times \quad 5 \text{ s} \quad = \quad 25 \text{ m/s}^2 \text{ rightward}$$
$$\text{(vector)} \qquad\qquad \text{(scalar)} \qquad\qquad \text{(vector)}$$

Technically, one vector cannot be multiplied by another. Instead there is something called *dot product* and *cross product*. Although neither product is required by the MCAT, you will be required to predict the results when certain vector quantities are multiplied together. When multiplying two vectors, first check to see if the resulting physical quantity is a scalar or vector. If a vector, then the vector must point perpendicularly to both of the original two vectors, and the magnitude of the new vector is the product of the magnitude of the original vectors times the sine of the angle between them. ($V_{product} = V_1 V_2 \sin\theta$). There will always be two possible directions that are perpendicular to both of the original two vectors. The **right hand rule** is used to decide between these two directions. Although the *MCAT Student Manual* lists the Right Hand Rule as being tested by the MCAT, it is unlikely that it will be. If the product of the two vectors is a scalar, the magnitude of the scalar is equal to the product of the magnitudes of the two vectors times the cosine of the angle between them. ($S_{product} = V_1 V_2 \cos\theta$). Since there are only a few instances on the MCAT that require multiplication of vectors, students often prefer to memorize each case separately rather than memorize the above rules. This book will cover all possible MCAT occurrences of vector multiplication on a case by case basis.

A vector times a scalar is a vector. The product of two vectors may be either a scalar or a vector. For instance, if we multiply vectors A and B as shown and the product is a vector, it will point into or out of the page depending upon the right hand rule. For the MCAT you just need to know that the vector will point perpendicularly to both A and B. The magnitude of the product vector will be AB sinθ. If the product is a scalar, it will have a value equal to AB cosθ.

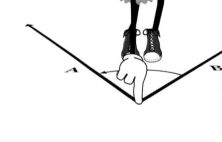

---

**Figure 1.2   Vector Multiplication**

*a*

*ma*

'*m*' is a scalar
$m = 2$

Multiplication

---

*Notes:*

## 1.5 Component Vectors

Any vector can be divided into two perpendicular **component vectors** whose vector sum is equal to the original vector. This is often convenient, since vectors acting perpendicularly to each other sometimes don't affect each other, or affect each other only in a limited fashion. We shall examine this more closely in projectile motion, circular motion, and other areas. In addition, any vector has an infinite number of possible component vectors, offering great versatility in solving vector problems.

**Figure 1.3 Component Vectors**

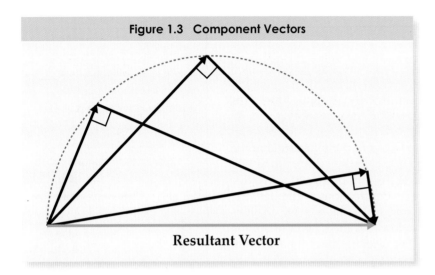

**Resultant Vector**

Figure 1.3 shows three possible pairs of components for the resultant vector. Each component is perpendicular to its partner and sums with its partner to equal the resultant. Each of the infinite number of points on the semi-circle represents a pair of possible component vectors.

The lengths of the component vectors are found through simple trigonometry such as the **Pythagorean Theorem** and **SOH CAH TOA**.

**Figure 1.4 Simple Trigonometry**

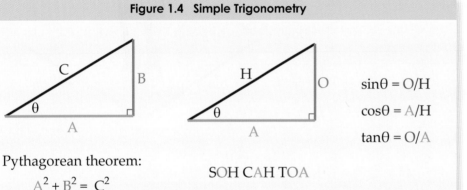

$$\sin\theta = O/H$$
$$\cos\theta = A/H$$
$$\tan\theta = O/A$$

Pythagorean theorem:
$$A^2 + B^2 = C^2$$

SOH CAH TOA

As long as we're thinking about the Pythagorean theorem, we might as well remember one of the most common triangles used on the MCAT: the 3-4-5 triangle, and a less common cousin: the 5-12-13 triangle.

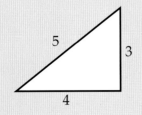

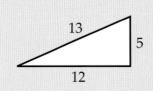

PythagoSaltoras

## 1.6 Distance-Displacement, Speed-Velocity, Acceleration

Distance and displacement are scalar and vector counterparts, as are speed and velocity. In other words, displacement is distance with the added dimension of direction, and velocity is speed with the added dimension of direction. The definitions of speed and velocity are given by the following formulae:

$$\text{speed} = \frac{\text{distance}}{\text{time}} \qquad \text{velocity} = \frac{\text{displacement}}{\text{time}}$$

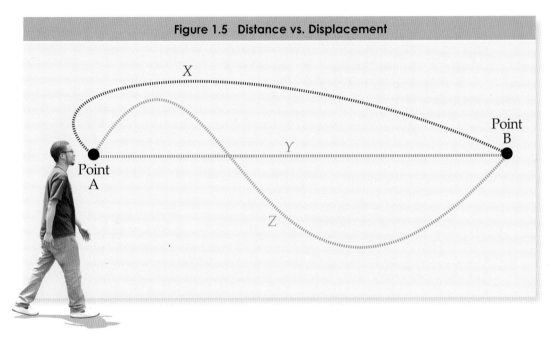

**Figure 1.5  Distance vs. Displacement**

If a man walks from Point *A* to Point *B*, his distance traveled can be measured by the number of steps that he takes. His displacement is his position relative to his starting point or his *net* distance. If Point *A* and Point *B* are 10 meters apart, the man's displacement is 10 meters to the right; however, the distance that he has traveled is unknown, because he may have taken path *X, Y,* or *Z*. If the entire trip took 100 seconds, the man's average velocity is his displacement divided by the time or 0.1 m/s to the right. Notice that the average velocity is independent of the path chosen. The man's average vertical velocity during the trip was zero. Since the man's distance is unknown, his speed or instantaneous velocity at any moment during the trip is unknown. Even if the man took path *Y*, he may have covered the first half of the trip in 99 seconds and the second half in 1 second, thus, not maintaining a constant velocity or speed.

Acceleration is a vector, and is defined as the rate of change in velocity.

$$\text{acceleration} = \frac{\text{change in velocity}}{\text{time}}$$

Any change in velocity, in either magnitude or direction, is acceleration. This means that a particle must accelerate in order to change the direction of its motion. An object traveling at 10 m/s north one moment and 10 m/s east the next moment has accelerated even though it is moving at the same speed. This also means that a particle moving at constant velocity has no acceleration.

You have a natural intuition about velocity, but not about acceleration. For instance, we all know what it feels like to move at a velocity of 55 miles/hour, but what does it feel like to accelerate at 55 miles/hour$^2$? Are we thrown to the back of our seats, or do we become impatient waiting to reach a good speed? We can understand 55 miles/hour$^2$ as a change in velocity of 55 miles/hour every hour. In other words, starting from zero by the side of the highway, it would take us one hour to reach a velocity of 55 miles/hour, and still another hour to reach 110 miles/hour. Now you know what it feels like to accelerate at 55 miles/hour$^2$.

One more point about acceleration: Velocity and acceleration do NOT have to be in the same direction. A particle can be moving to the left while accelerating to the right, or moving up while accelerating down. For instance, a ball thrown upwards is accelerating downwards even while moving upwards. In fact, it is even accelerating the moment it reaches its maximum height where its velocity is zero.

1. A weather balloon travels upward for 6 km while the wind blows it 10 km north and 8 km east. Approximately what is its final displacement from its initial position?

   A. 7 km
   B. 10 km
   C. 14 km
   D. 20 km

2. Which of the following gives the average velocity of an athlete running on a circular track with a circumference of $\frac{1}{2}$ km, if that athlete runs 1 km in 4 minutes?

   A. 0 m/s
   B. 2 m/s
   C. 4.2 m/s
   D. 16.8 m/s

3. A man entered a cave and walked 100 m north. He then made a sharp turn 150° to the west and walked 87 m straight ahead. How far is the man from where he entered the cave? (Note: sin 30° = 0.50; cos 30° = 0.87.)

   A. 25 m
   B. 50 m
   C. 100 m
   D. 150 m

4. The Earth moves around the sun at approximately 30 m/s. Is the Earth accelerating?

   A. No, because acceleration is a vector.
   B. No, because the net displacement is zero.
   C. Yes, because the speed is not constant.
   D. Yes, because the velocity is not constant

5. An airliner flies from Chicago to New York. Due to the shape of the earth, the airliner must follow a curved trajectory. How does the curved trajectory of the airliner affect its final displacement for this trip?

   A. The displacement is less than it would be if the airliner flew in a straight line to New York.
   B. The displacement is greater than it would be if the airliner flew in a straight line to New York.
   C. The displacement is the same as it would be if the airliner flew in a straight line to New York.
   D. The final displacement of the airliner is zero.

6. An automobile that was moving forward on a highway pulled over onto the exit ramp and slowed to a stop. While the automobile was slowing down, which of the following could be true?

   A. The velocity was positive and the acceleration was positive.
   B. The velocity was negative and the acceleration was negative.
   C. The velocity was positive and the acceleration was negative.
   D. The velocity and acceleration had the same sign, either positive or negative.

7. All of the following describe the magnitude and direction of a vector EXCEPT:

   A. 10 m/s West
   B. 10 m/s in a circle
   C. 20 m to the left
   D. 20 m straight up

8. An elephant runs at a speed of 36 km/hour. Based on this information, how far can the elephant run in 10 seconds?

   A. 10 m
   B. 50 m
   C. 100 m
   D. 200 m

7

**STOP.**

# Uniformly Accelerated Motion and Linear Motion

**Uniformly accelerated motion** is motion with constant acceleration. Since acceleration is a vector, constant acceleration means that both direction and magnitude of acceleration must remain constant. A particle in uniformly accelerated motion will accelerate at a constant rate regardless of the path traveled by the particle. The most common example of uniformly accelerated motion on the MCAT is a projectile. However, before we examine projectile motion we will examine the rules for the simpler case of uniformly accelerated motion along a straight line.

For a particle in uniformly accelerated motion on a linear path, there are four basic variables that will describe its motion completely: displacement $(x)$, velocity $(v)$, acceleration $(a)$, and time $(t)$. The first three of these are vectors and the last one is a scalar. The values for these variables can be found through three basic equations. These equations can be derived with calculus, but it is far better for you to memorize them. We will refer to these equations as the linear motion equations. However, remember that constant acceleration is required for all of them. The equations are:

The equations on this page require constant acceleration.

$$x - x_\text{o} = v_\text{o}t + \tfrac{1}{2}at^2$$

$$v - v_\text{o} = at$$

$$v^2 = v_\text{o}^2 + 2a(x - x_\text{o})$$

The subscript $_\text{o}$ indicates a starting value. Note that $x - x_\text{o} = \Delta x$ and $v - v_\text{o} = \Delta v$, where '$\Delta$' means *change in*. Accordingly, substitutions may be made to alter the equations. In order to use these equations, there must be constant acceleration and linear motion. When choosing which equation to use, pick the one for which you know the value of all but one of the variables.

The velocities above are instantaneous velocities, or velocities at a given moment in time. Another concept that is useful on the MCAT is average velocity. Average velocity in a uniformly accelerated motion problem is given by:

$$v_\text{avg} = \tfrac{1}{2}(v + v_\text{o})$$

# Graphs of Linear Motion

Most graphs of linear motion will be plotted as displacement, velocity, or acceleration, versus time. Keep in mind that the graph gives information only about position and motion along one line in space. For instance, a linear motion graph describing a particle's north and south position or movement would not indicate anything about the particle's position or movement with respect to east and west. For graphs of linear motion, you should know the significance of the slope, the line, and the area under each curve.

On a displacement versus time graph, the slope at any point is the instantaneous velocity at that time. An upward slope indicates positive velocity; a downward slope, negative velocity (velocity in the reverse direction). A straight line indicates that the slope is constant and, thus, the velocity is constant as well. A straight *horizontal* line indicates that the particle is not moving. A curved line represents a changing slope, which indicates a changing velocity and thus acceleration. (Acceleration is the rate of change in velocity.) The area beneath the curve has no meaning for a displacement versus time graph.

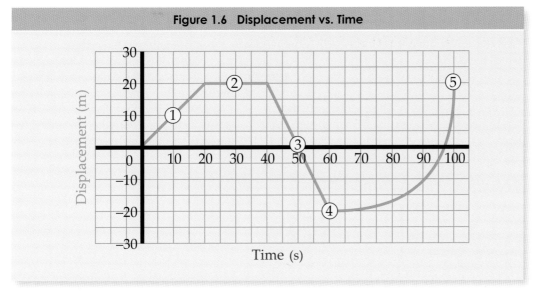

**Figure 1.6 Displacement vs. Time**

Sometimes students look at these graphs and imagine that the particle follows a path that somehow resembles the line. This is incorrect. On the displacement versus time graph, if the slope is positive, the particle is moving in the positive direction (let's say to the right). If the slope is negative, the particle is moving in the opposite direction. Notice also that the graph tells us nothing about any perpendicular motion (up or down, in or out) that the particle may have.

If the graph above describes the position of a particle with respect to north and south only, and we arbitrarily choose north as positive, we can make the following observations about its motion:

① Between zero and 20 seconds, the particle has a velocity of 1 m/s to the north because the slope of the line is one. (Its east or west velocity or up or down velocity cannot be determined from the information given.)

② Between 20 and 40 seconds, the particle remains exactly 20 meters to the north of its original position. It is stationary with respect to movement along a north-south axis. (Note that it may or may not be stationary with respect to movement east or west. We simply do not have any information about its movement in those directions.)

③ At 50 seconds, the particle is back where it started (with respect to its north-south coordinates), but it is moving at 2 m/s to the south because the slope of the line is -2 . It has traveled a total distance of 40 meters; 20 meters north and 20 meters south. Its total displacement, however, is zero (assuming it is not moving east or west).

④ At 60 seconds, the particle changes direction and begins to accelerate north.

⑤ The average north-south velocity of the particle after 100 seconds is 20 m/100 s or 0.2 m/s to the north.

If you just read through this very quickly, go back now and examine the graph at each step and try to derive the values for yourself.

**Figure 1.7 d/t Graph Machine**

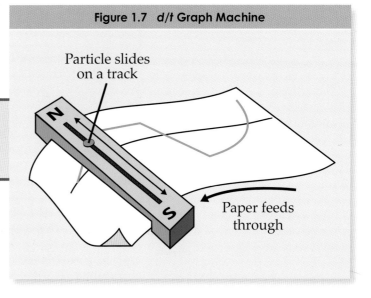

Particle slides on a track

One way to visualize the movement on a d/t graph is to imagine this machine:

Paper feeds through

On a velocity versus time graph, the slope at any point is the instantaneous acceleration at that time. An upward slope indicates positive acceleration; a downward slope, negative acceleration. Negative acceleration is not necessarily slowing down. It is acceleration in the reverse direction, which means slowing down if the velocity is already in the positive direction, or speeding up if the velocity is already in the negative direction. A straight line indicates that the slope is constant and, thus, the acceleration is constant as well. A curved line represents a changing slope, which indicates a changing acceleration. The area beneath the curve can represent distance or displacement. If we label all the area between the curve and zero velocity as positive, the area represents distance. If we label the area below zero velocity as negative, the total area represents displacement.

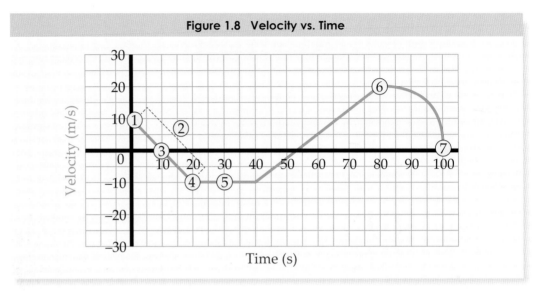

**Figure 1.8   Velocity vs. Time**

If, again, the graph above describes the position of a particle with respect to north and south only, and we arbitrarily choose north as positive, we can make the following observations about its motion:

1. The particle begins with a velocity of 10 m/s to the north. (Remember, the particle could also be moving up, down, east, or west; we just don't know.)

2. For the first 20 seconds, the particles acceleration is -1 m/s² because the slope of the line is -1. The negative just means that it is accelerating to the south. Notice that for the first 10 seconds it is moving north but decelerating (slowing down), and for the second 10 seconds it is moving south and accelerating (speeding up).

3. At exactly 10 seconds, the particle has traveled 50 meters to the north (not zero meters).

4. At 20 seconds, the particle has a displacement of zero meters. It is at its starting point with respect to north and south. However, it has travelled 100 meters.

5. Between 20 and 40 seconds, the particle has no acceleration and is moving at a constant velocity to the south.

6. At 80 seconds, the particle begins decelerating; it is moving north but slowing down. The deceleration, or negative acceleration, is not constant as is indicated by the curved line.

7. At 100 seconds, the particle has a positive, nonzero displacement.

Calculating the displacement requires subtracting the area under the x-axis and above the curve from the area above the x-axis and below the curve. To find the total distance traveled requires adding these areas. Area beneath the x-axis is negative displacement, but, since distance is a scalar and has no direction, the area above and beneath the curve is positive distance.

If you just read through this very quickly, go back now and examine the graph at each step and try to derive the values for yourself.

The linear motion equations can be used on any of the straight-line sections of the velocity versus time graph because acceleration for those sections is constant.

Want a fast, easy way to solve linear motion problems without using the equations? Use a v/t graph as follows. Draw a line and label the left end with the initial velocity and the right end with the final velocity. If the acceleration is constant, this line represents the line on a v/t graph. The exact middle of the line is always the average velocity. Since the displacement is the average velocity times the time, you know the displacement. If you don't know the time, it is the change in velocity divided by the acceleration, or the difference between the two ends of your line divided by the rate of change in velocity. Remember to always think of acceleration as how fast velocity is changing.

It's not as complicated as it sounds. Watch.

What is the distance traveled by a particle that starts at 30 m/s and accelerates to 50 m/s in four seconds? What is the acceleration?

1) draw and label your line

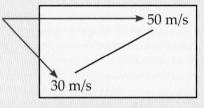

2) find the average velocity exactly at the middle

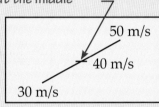

3) average velocity times time is 160 m

4) the acceleration is 50 minus 30 divided by four = 5 m/s$^2$

An object is dropped from a plane and falls for 5 seconds. How far does it fall?

1) vertical velocity for a projectile changes by 10 m/s each second so final velocity is 50 m/s

2) draw and label your line

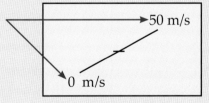

3) find the average velocity exactly at the middle

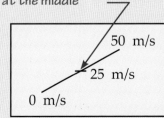

4) average velocity times time is 125 m, which is the distance it falls

9. Which of the following graphs best represents a particle with constant velocity?

**A.**

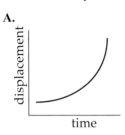

**C.**

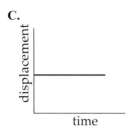

**B.**

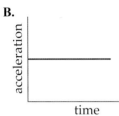

**D.**

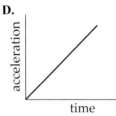

10. The graph below represents a particle moving along a straight line. What is the total distance traveled by the particle from $t = 0$ to $t = 10$ seconds?

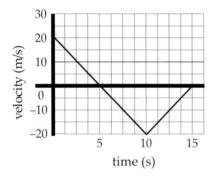

A. 0 m
B. 50 m
C. 100 m
D. 200 m

11. Which of the following is the most probable description of the motion of the object depicted by the graph below?

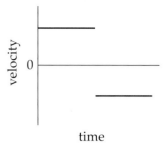

A. A person on a bike accelerating in a straight line, and then decelerating.
B. A baseball thrown by a pitcher and hit by a batter.
C. A planet in orbit.
D. One swing on a pendulum.

12. A car accelerates at a constant rate from 0 to 25 m/s over a distance of 25 m. Approximately how long does it take the car to reach the velocity of 25 m/s?

A. 1 s
B. 2 s
C. 4 s
D. 8 s

13. A particle moving in a straight line slows down at a constant rate from 50 m/s to 25 m/s in 2 seconds. What is the acceleration of the particle?

A. $-12.5 \text{ m/s}^2$
B. $-25 \text{ m/s}^2$
C. $-50 \text{ m/s}^2$
D. $-100 \text{ m/s}^2$

14. The graph below shows the displacement of a particle over time.

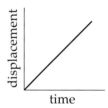

The particle exhibits increasing:

I. displacement
II. velocity
III. acceleration

A. I only
B. II only
C. I and II only
D. I and III only

**15.** A driver moving at a constant speed of 20 m/s sees an accident up ahead and hits the brakes. If the car decelerates at a constant rate of –5 m/s², how far does the car go before it comes to a stop?

   **A.** 10 m
   **B.** 20 m
   **C.** 40 m
   **D.** 100 m

**16.** The graph below represents a particle moving in a straight line. When $t = 0$, the displacement of the particle is 0.

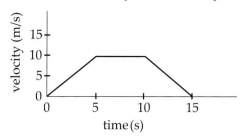

All of the following statements are true about the particle EXCEPT:

   **A.** The particle has a total displacement of 100 m.
   **B.** The particle moves with constant acceleration from 0 to 5 seconds.
   **C.** The particle moves with constant velocity between 5 and 10 seconds.
   **D.** The particle is moving backwards between 10 and 15 seconds.

## 1.9  Projectile Motion

Projectile: a body projected by an external force and continuing in motion by its own inertia. Because projectile motion is not linear motion, we cannot apply the linear motion equations directly. However, we can separate projectile motion into perpendicular components and analyze it as two distinct linear motion problems. Separate the motion into vertical and horizontal components. For the vertical motion, acceleration is constant and due to gravity (10 m/s²). For ideal situations with no air resistance (as on most MCAT problems) the horizontal acceleration is a constant zero.

In Figure 1.9 a projectile experiencing no air resistance is launched with a velocity $v$ at an angle $\theta$. In order to describe this motion with the linear motion equations, we must separate the motion into perpendicular components. For convenience we choose the horizontal and vertical directions. Using SOH CAH TOA we find that the initial vertical velocity is always $v\sin\theta$ and the horizontal velocity remains constant at $v\cos\theta$. Notice that there is no acceleration in the horizontal direction, and therefore no change in horizontal velocity throughout the flight. Notice that the vertical acceleration throughout the flight remains constant at $g$. At its peak height ($h$), the projectile has no vertical velocity but is still accelerating downwards at 10 m/s².

### Figure 1.9  Projectile Motion

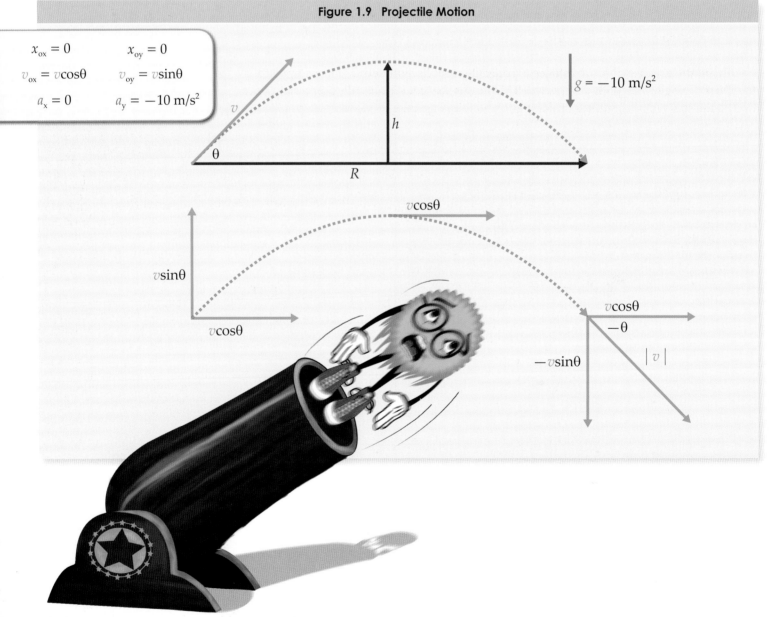

$$x_{ox} = 0 \qquad x_{oy} = 0$$
$$v_{ox} = v\cos\theta \qquad v_{oy} = v\sin\theta$$
$$a_x = 0 \qquad a_y = -10 \text{ m/s}^2$$

$$g = -10 \text{ m/s}^2$$

The peak height of the projectile can be found from the equation:

$$v_o \sin\theta = \sqrt{2gh}$$

where $g$ is positive 10 m/s$^2$. By substituting $v\sin\theta$ for $v_o\sin\theta$, this equation gives the final velocity $v$ of a projectile when dropped from a height $h$. Notice that $v\sin\theta$ gives us the vertical component of the velocity of the projectile. Beginning at its peak, the vertical velocity is zero and changing at a rate of $g$ in the downward direction. This means that $v_o$ is zero and choosing the downward direction as positive gives $g$ a positive value. Solving for $h$ or $v$ results in a convenient positive value as well.

Notice that the path of a projectile not experiencing air resistance is independent of the mass of the projectile. In a vacuum, a bowling ball will follow the same path as a ping pong ball if their initial velocities are the same.

In the absence of air resistance, the projectile follows a parabolic path. Its vertical velocity decreases as it moves toward its peak and increases as it moves away from its peak.

You should also know that vertical velocity alone dictates the time of flight for a projectile. The range (horizontal distance) is the horizontal velocity times the time in flight; thus the range is dictated by both horizontal and vertical velocities.

Finally, in the absence of air resistance a projectile exhibits symmetry: its path upward is the mirror image to its path downward. This means that for a projectile over a flat plane time is the same for both halves of the flight, and initial speed is equal to final speed.

Understand projectile motion qualitatively and quantitatively. In other words, don't just rely on the equations. Stop right now and contemplate projectile motion. Even though the projectile moves both up and down in the same flight, its acceleration is constant. Even while the projectile is motionless at the instant it reaches its peak, acceleration is still –$g$. How can a motionless object have acceleration? The answer lies in the definition of acceleration.

Use the symmetry of projectile motion to help you solve problems. For instance, if we use only the second half of the trip, vertical $v_o$ will always equal zero, making calculations easier.

Understand that vertical velocity dictates time of flight. If two projectiles leave the Earth with the same vertical velocity, they will land at the same time, regardless of their horizontal velocities. For example, a bullet shot horizontally from a gun and a rock dropped from the same height will both land at the same time.

And, of course, always remember that, in the absence of air resistance, mass does not affect projectile motion.

As shown above, in a vacuum the billiard ball and the feather fall at the same rate. Outside a vacuum, air resistance will cause the feather to fall more slowly.

Factors that change air resistance are: velocity, surface area, and shape.

Mass changes the effect of air resistance, but does not change air resistance.

## 1.10    Air Resistance and Drag

Air resistance is a type of friction called drag. (We will discuss friction in Lecture 2.) For the MCAT, you need to understand air resistance only qualitatively. In other words, you don't need to memorize or be familiar with any formulae. Drag occurs when any object moves past a nonideal gas or liquid. (We will discuss nonideal gases and liquids in Lecture 5.) In the case of projectile motion, the fluid is air. As an object (or a projectile) moves through a fluid (such as air), or as a fluid moves past an object, fluid molecules collide with and drag past the object. These interactions act to impede the motion between the fluid and the object. In other words, if the object is a projectile, drag slows the projectile; if the object is a pipe, drag slows the fluid moving through the pipe. The more molecular collisions that occur each second, the greater the effect of drag.

Since drag is increased with the number of collisions of air molecules on an object, **shape**, **surface area**, and **velocity** of a projectile affect drag. Streamlined objects experience fewer collisions with fluid molecules and thus experience less drag. Fluid molecules slip by smoother objects more easily than rougher objects, and thus smoother objects experience less drag. Smaller surface area also means fewer collisions and therefore less drag. Faster moving objects collide with more fluid molecules each second and thus experience more drag. As a rough rule of thumb, the drag on a projectile in air is proportional to its velocity, and the drag on an object moving through water is proportional to the square of its velocity. At high speeds, these rules break down due to erratic behavior of the fluid flow.

**Mass** doesn't change the force of air resistance, but it does change the path of the projectile experiencing the air resistance. Since the force of air resistance remains constant for any mass, then, from $F = ma$, we see an inverse relationship between mass and acceleration; acceleration must decrease as mass increases. This acceleration is not $g$; it is only the deceleration due to air resistance. Thus, larger masses experience less deceleration due to air resistance because they are less affected by the same force of air resistance.

To understand how air resistance affects a projectile, compare a bowling ball (a massive projectile) with a volley ball (a less massive projectile). Propel both of them down a bowling alley at bowling pins. The bowling pins represent the air molecules that create air resistance. Both experience the same resistance, but the volley ball is deflected to the side while the bowling ball moves through the pins like they're not there. Air resistance has less effect on a more massive object.

## 1.11 Equation Summary

$$v = \frac{d}{t} \qquad \vec{v} = \frac{\vec{d}}{t} \qquad \vec{a} = \frac{\Delta \vec{v}}{t}$$

| | |
|---|---|
| $d$ = distance | $\vec{v}$ = velocity |
| $v$ = speed | $t$ = time |
| $\vec{d}$ = displacement | $\vec{a}$ = acceleration |

$$x - x_o = v_o t + \tfrac{1}{2}at^2$$

$$v - v_o = at$$

$a$ must be constant

$$v^2 = v_o^2 + 2a(x - x_o)$$

| |
|---|
| $t$ = time |
| $x$ = displacement |
| $h$ = height |
| $v$ = velocity |
| $a$ = acceleration |

$$v_{avg} = \tfrac{1}{2}(v + v_o)$$

$$v = \sqrt{2gh} \quad \left| \begin{array}{l} v_o \text{ must} \\ \text{be zero} \end{array} \right.$$

## 1.12 Terms You Need to Know

| | |
|---|---|
| Component Vectors | SOH CAH TOA |
| Drag | Uniformly Accelerated Motion |
| Pythagorean Theorem | Vector |
| Right Hand Rule | Velocity |
| Scalar | |

**17.** If an apple that is dropped from an altitude of 100 m reaches an altitude of 80 m after falling for $t = 2$ seconds, what altitude will it be at in $t = 4$ seconds?

    **A.** 60 m
    **B.** 40 m
    **C.** 20 m
    **D.** 0 m

**18.** Two skydivers are playing catch with a ball while they are falling through the air. Ignoring air resistance, in which direction should one skydiver throw the ball relative to the other if the one wants the other to catch it?

    **A.** above the other since the ball will fall faster
    **B.** above the other since the ball will fall more slowly
    **C.** below the other since the ball will fall more slowly
    **D.** directly at the other since there is no air resistance

**19.** If an antelope is running at a speed of 10 m/s, and can maintain that horizontal velocity when it jumps, how high must it jump in order to clear a horizontal distance of 20 m?

    **A.** 5 m
    **B.** 10 m
    **C.** 20 m
    **D.** 45 m

**20.** Ignoring air resistance, if the initial height of a body in free fall is increased by a factor of 4, the final velocity when it hits the ground will increase by a factor of:

    **A.** 2
    **B.** 4
    **C.** It depends upon the value of the initial height.
    **D.** The velocity will remain the same.

**21.** A projectile is launched at an angle of 30° to the horizontal and with a velocity of 100 m/s. How high will the projectile be at its maximum height?

    **A.** 100 m
    **B.** 125 m
    **C.** 250 m
    **D.** 500 m

**22.** Two balls are dropped from a tall tower. The balls are the same size, but Ball $X$ has greater mass than Ball $Y$. When both balls have reached terminal velocity, which of the following is true?

    **A.** The force of air resistance on either ball is zero.
    **B.** Ball $X$ has greater velocity.
    **C.** Ball $X$ has greater acceleration.
    **D.** The acceleration of both balls is 9.8 m/s$^2$.

**23.** A hiker throws a rock horizontally off a cliff that is 40 meters above the water below. If the speed of the rock is 30 m/s, how long does it take for the rock to hit the water? (Ignore air resistance, g = 10 m/s$^2$).

    **A.** 3 sec
    **B.** 4 sec
    **C.** 5 sec
    **D.** 6 sec

**24.** A golfer hits a ball with an initial speed of 30 m/s at an angle of 40° to the horizontal. If the ball is in the air for 6 seconds, which of the following expressions will be equal to the horizontal distance traveled by the ball? (Ignore the effects of air resistance.)

    **A.** $(15)(6)^2(\cos 40°)$ m
    **B.** $(30)(6)(\cos 40°)$ m
    **C.** $(15)(6)^2(\sin 40°)$ m
    **D.** $(30)(6)(\sin 40°)$ m

# FORCE

## 2.1 Mass and Weight

Whether moving or at rest, all objects tend to remain in their present state of motion. This tendency of an object to remain in its present state of motion is called **inertia**. **Mass** is the quantitative measure of an object's inertia. An object's mass tells us how much that object will resist a change in its motion. On the MCAT, mass is measured in kilograms (kg).

**Weight** is the gravitational force an object experiences when near a much larger body such as the Earth. On the MCAT, weight is measured in newtons (N). An object's weight at the surface of the Earth is given by the product of its mass and the gravitational constant $g$. Thus, the weight of any object at the surface of the Earth is '$mg$'. Weight and mass are proportional to each other, but they are not the same physical quality.

On Earth, I have weight.

Here in space I am virtually weightless. Yet, my mass is the same as it is on Earth. Regardless of where I go, my mass does not change.

## 2.2 Center of Mass

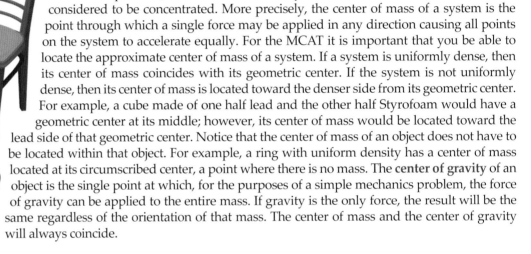

Center of mass

When solving mechanics problems it is often convenient to consider an object as a single particle with its mass concentrated at a single point. This can be done without error as long as the point chosen is the **center of mass** and all forces move through the chosen point. The center of mass of a system is the single point at which, for the purposes of a simple mechanics problem, all the mass of that system can be considered to be concentrated. More precisely, the center of mass of a system is the point through which a single force may be applied in any direction causing all points on the system to accelerate equally. For the MCAT it is important that you be able to locate the approximate center of mass of a system. If a system is uniformly dense, then its center of mass coincides with its geometric center. If the system is not uniformly dense, then its center of mass is located toward the denser side from its geometric center. For example, a cube made of one half lead and the other half Styrofoam would have a geometric center at its middle; however, its center of mass would be located toward the lead side of that geometric center. Notice that the center of mass of an object does not have to be located within that object. For example, a ring with uniform density has a center of mass located at its circumscribed center, a point where there is no mass. The **center of gravity** of an object is the single point at which, for the purposes of a simple mechanics problem, the force of gravity can be applied to the entire mass. If gravity is the only force, the result will be the same regardless of the orientation of that mass. The center of mass and the center of gravity will always coincide.

> On the MCAT, center of mass questions will be intuitive or they will involve symmetrical objects. Just look for the perfect balancing point.

The center of mass is the point where, if you could hang your system by a string, your object would be perfectly balanced in any orientation. But center of mass isn't limited to systems with only one object. A system with any number of objects also has a center of mass.

For instance, if the planets in Figure 2.1 were of uniform density, the center of mass would be in the point shown. If a spaceship were far away, the planets would appear as a single small dot. The ship would be affected by their gravitational force as if their entire mass were concentrated at the center of mass of the system.

**Figure 2.1   Center of Mass of a Group of Objects**

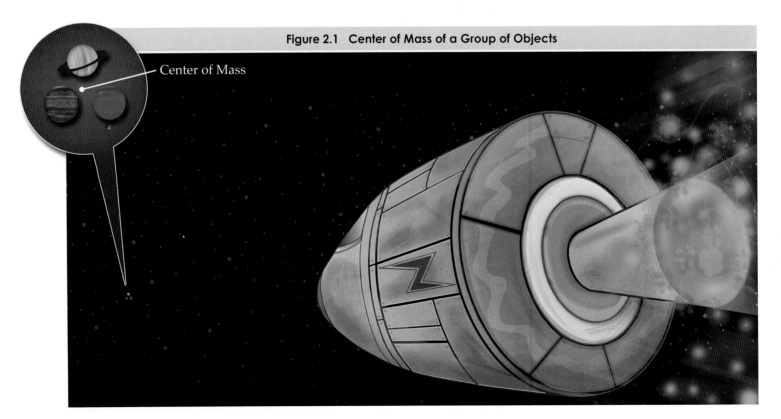

Center of Mass

There are only four forces in nature. They are:

1. the *strong nuclear force*;
2. the *weak nuclear force*;
3. **gravitational force**; and
4. **electromagnetic force.**

The first two are not on the MCAT. Thus, all forces on the MCAT will be gravitational or electromagnetic. This would make identifying forces very easy except for one problem: some electromagnetic forces are difficult to identify. For instance, if a person pushes a book with his finger, this force is actually electromagnetic.

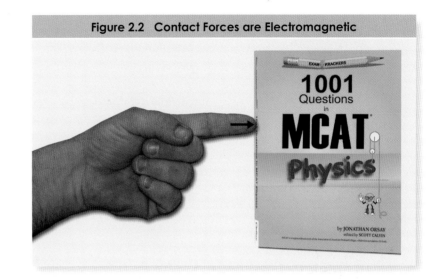

**Figure 2.2   Contact Forces are Electromagnetic**

The electrostatic repulsion between the atoms in the person's finger and the atoms in the book create a force that we naturally think of as being created by contact. Since it is difficult to think of such *contact forces* as electromagnetic, we will label all such forces as 'contact forces' instead of electromagnetic.

Thus, for any MCAT problem, there are only three possible forces:

1. gravitational;
2. electromagnetic; and
3. contact.

Only gravitational and electromagnetic forces act at a distance. These forces are easy to identify. Gravity is usually just *mg*. Electromagnetic forces require a charged object or a magnet. In order for any other force to be acting on a system, something must be making visible contact with the system.

Contact forces must act in at least one of two directions:

1. perpendicular to a surface; and/or
2. parallel to a surface.

(An exception is tension, which is a contact force that can act in any direction away from the object. Tension will be discussed later in this lecture.)  The perpendicular force is also called the normal force. The parallel force requires friction. Both the normal force and friction will be discussed later in this lecture.

*Notes:*

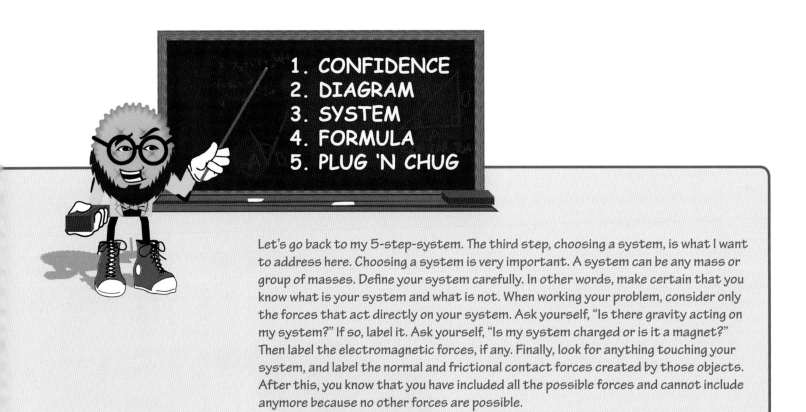

1. CONFIDENCE
2. DIAGRAM
3. SYSTEM
4. FORMULA
5. PLUG 'N CHUG

Let's go back to my 5-step-system. The third step, choosing a system, is what I want to address here. Choosing a system is very important. A system can be any mass or group of masses. Define your system carefully. In other words, make certain that you know what is your system and what is not. When working your problem, consider only the forces that act directly on your system. Ask yourself, "Is there gravity acting on my system?" If so, label it. Ask yourself, "Is my system charged or is it a magnet?" Then label the electromagnetic forces, if any. Finally, look for anything touching your system, and label the normal and frictional contact forces created by those objects. After this, you know that you have included all the possible forces and cannot include anymore because no other forces are possible.

For instance, if we are interested in the movement of the box in the diagram to the right, we should consider only the forces acting on the box. The top diagram contains all kinds of force vectors and is nearly useless. The dark red vectors in the bottom diagram represent only forces acting on the system (the box) and are the only forces that should be considered. So, first draw the weight forces, then any electromagnetic forces, and then any contact forces, which can only be due to something making direct physical contact with your system.

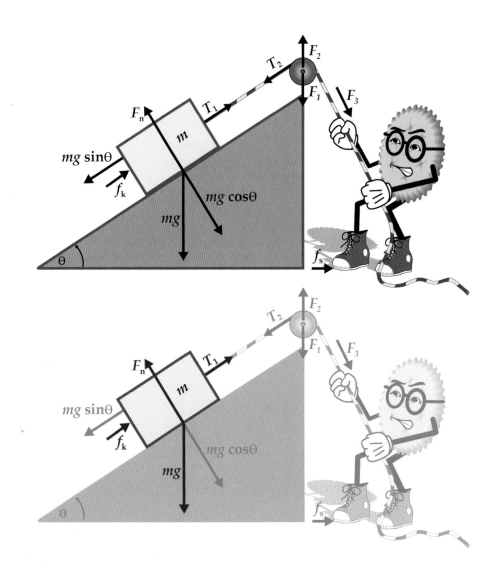

## 2.4 Newton's Laws

**Newton's First Law** is the law of inertia: an object in a state of rest or in a state of motion will tend to remain in that state unless it is acted upon by a net force.

**Newton's Second Law** tells us quantitatively that, when an object is acted upon by a net force, the change in that object's state of motion will be inversely proportional to the mass ($m$) of the object and directly proportional to the net force ($F$) acting upon the object. Written as an equation, Newton's second law is:

$$F = ma$$

**Newton's Third Law** states that, for every action, there exists an equal and opposite reaction. This simply means that when object A applies a force to object B, object A experiences a force of equal magnitude but in the opposite direction. Newton's third law forces never act on the same system.

### Thought Provoker

Notice that Newton's Second Law is an explanation of the 'if' part of Newton's First Law. Newton's First Law tells us what will happen 'if' there is <u>no</u> net force. His Second Law tells us what will happen 'if' there <u>is</u> a net force.

So, according to Newton's Third Law, forces come in equal and opposite pairs. Well then, for a block resting on a table, what is the Newton's Third Law equal and opposite force to gravity acting on the block?

*Hint: it's not the normal force exerted by the table on the block.*

Answer: See page 39.

Figure 2.3   Systems Approach to Newton's Third Law

It will never work, Isaac.

How can the horse accelerate the cart? No matter how hard the horse pulls, the cart pulls back just as hard. How can it possibly move?

*Force on the cart due to the horse*

*Force on the horse due to the cart*

For the answer, choose your system to be the cart only and then draw only the forces acting on the cart. Notice that the equal and opposite force to the horse pulling on the cart, is the cart pulling on the horse. When we choose our system to be the cart, we ignore this force because it is acting on the horse. Now we see that there is a net force on the cart.

25. An astronaut on the moon applies a 100 N horizontal force to a 10 kg mass at rest on a table. At what rate does the mass accelerate? (Note: the gravitational constant at the moon's surface is 1.6 m/s$^2$. Ignore friction.)

    A.  5 m/s$^2$
    B.  8 m/s$^2$
    C.  10 m/s$^2$
    D.  16 m/s$^2$

26. A bottle rocket is launched into the air. The black powder, which propels it, burns, leaving an exhaust trail mainly consisting of $CO_2$ gas. If the force propelling the rocket is constant, the rate of change in its velocity: (Note: ignore air resistance).

    A.  remains constant.
    B.  decreases.
    C.  increases.
    D.  is zero.

27. A 10 kg mass is in free fall with no air resistance. In order to slow the mass at a rate equal to the magnitude of $g$, an upward force must be applied with magnitude:

    A.  0 N
    B.  10 N
    C.  100 N
    D.  200 N

28. A 50 kg skydiver and a 100 kg skydiver open their parachutes and reach a constant velocity. The net force on the larger skydiver is:

    A.  equal to the net force on the smaller skydiver.
    B.  twice as great as the net force on the smaller skydiver.
    C.  four times as great as the net force on the smaller skydiver.
    D.  half as great as the net force on the smaller skydiver.

29. If $F$ is the force of air resistance on an object with mass $m$ moving at a constant velocity, which of the following best describes the acceleration of the object when the force of air resistance is reduced by a factor of 4?

    A.  $F/m$
    B.  $\frac{1}{2} F/m$
    C.  $\frac{1}{4} F/m$
    D.  $\frac{3}{4} F/m$

30. The system below consists of three spheres of equal mass $m$.

    The center of mass of the system is located at point:

    A.  3
    B.  4
    C.  5
    D.  6

31. An airplane's propellers exert a force on the plane of 2500 N to the east. Wind resistance of 500 N acts to the west. If the weight of the plane is 40,000 N, what is the acceleration of the plane?

    A.  0.5 m/s$^2$ to the east
    B.  0.5 m/s$^2$ to the west
    C.  0.05 m/s$^2$ to the east
    D.  0.05 m/s$^2$ to the west

32. An automobile with a mass of 3000 kg is traveling down a straight flat road at a constant speed of 20 m/s. The coefficient of friction between the tires and the road is 0.5. The net force acting on the automobile is:

    A.  0 N
    B.  30,000 N
    C.  60,000 N
    D.  90,000 N

# The Law of Universal Gravitation

**Newton's Law of Universal Gravitation** states that every mass in the universe exerts an attractive force on every other mass in the universe, and that the force is proportional to both of the masses $m_1$ and $m_2$ and inversely proportional to the square of the distance $r$ between their centers of mass. Note that the distance is from the center of one mass to the center of the other, and not the distance between their surfaces. The formula representing the law of gravitation is given as follows:

$$F = G\frac{m_1 m_2}{r^2}$$

where G is $6.67 \times 10^{-11}$ m$^3$ kg$^{-1}$ s$^{-2}$. This formula gives the magnitude of the force but not the direction. The direction is from the center of mass of one object to the center of mass of the other. According to Newton's third law, both masses experience a force of the same magnitude. Since this is true, the Earth pulls you toward its center with a force equal to your weight, and you, in turn, pull the Earth toward your center of mass with a force also equal to your weight. When we use the gravitational acceleration constant $g$, we consider the force that the object exerts on the Earth as negligible and assume the Earth to be stationary. Of course, due to the large difference in mass, this is a very good assumption. However, if we examined the two bodies below, and were asked to find how fast they would accelerate toward each other, we would have to apply Newton's second law to each mass, and then add the magnitudes of their accelerations.

The Earth pulls down on the 400 pound barbell, but the barbell also pulls up on the earth with the same force. To separate the barbell from the Earth, the weightlifter gets between them and pushes up on the barbell with a 400 pound force, but also must push down on the Earth with a 400 pound force.

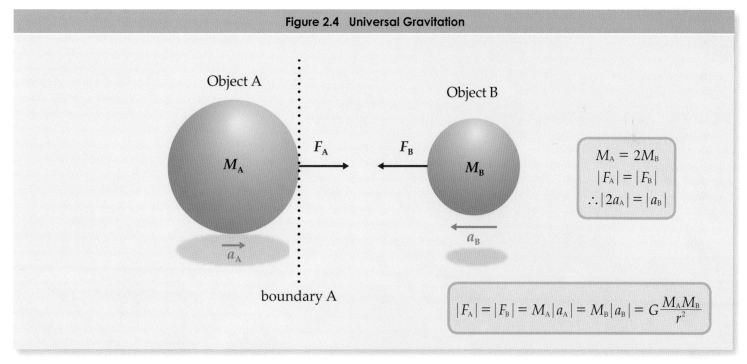

**Figure 2.4   Universal Gravitation**

Object A

Object B

$F_A$

$F_B$

$M_A$

$M_B$

$M_A = 2M_B$
$|F_A| = |F_B|$
$\therefore |2a_A| = |a_B|$

$a_B$

$a_A$

boundary A

$$|F_A| = |F_B| = M_A|a_A| = M_B|a_B| = G\frac{M_A M_B}{r^2}$$

In other words, suppose that the gravitational force on object A caused it to accelerate 10 m/s$^2$ in the direction of object B. Assuming object B is half as massive as object A, although the gravitational force on B is of equal magnitude, object B accelerates at 20 m/s$^2$. These values represent the separate accelerations of the objects, but the two bodies are accelerating toward each other at a faster rate. To find out how fast the bodies are accelerating toward each other, we must add the magnitudes of their individual accelerations for a value of 30 m/s$^2$. In other words, object B is accelerating relative to object A at 30 m/s$^2$, but it is accelerating relative to a stationary boundary A at only 20 m/s$^2$.

Notice that big $G$, the Universal Gravitational Constant, and little $g$, the acceleration due to gravity, are not the same thing. Big $G$ is a constant anywhere in the universe, while little $g$ is a constant only near the surface of the Earth. Notice also that big $G$ is a very small number, on the order of $10^{-11}$.

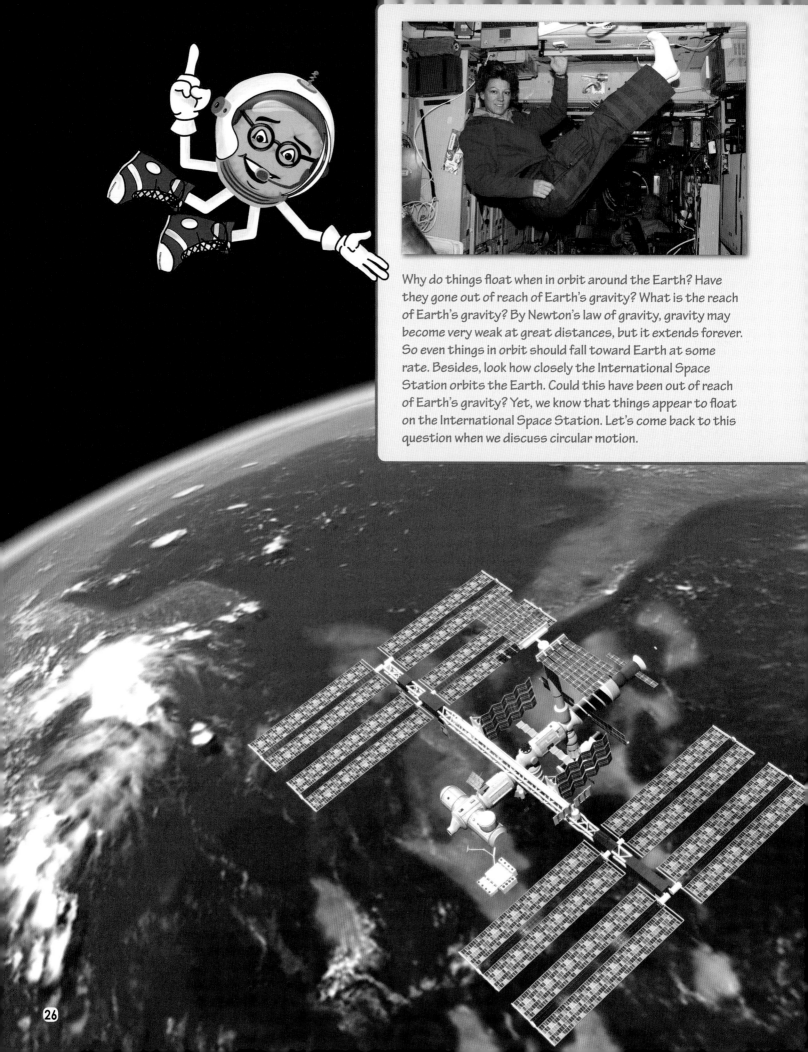

Why do things float when in orbit around the Earth? Have they gone out of reach of Earth's gravity? What is the reach of Earth's gravity? By Newton's law of gravity, gravity may become very weak at great distances, but it extends forever. So even things in orbit should fall toward Earth at some rate. Besides, look how closely the International Space Station orbits the Earth. Could this have been out of reach of Earth's gravity? Yet, we know that things appear to float on the International Space Station. Let's come back to this question when we discuss circular motion.

The **inclined plane** is a specific topic often tested by the MCAT. There are certain basic characteristics that exist for all inclined planes. Once we understand these characteristics, all inclined plane problems become trivial.

In the simplest, ideal case (no friction and nothing attached to the block), the only forces acting on a block on an inclined plane are gravity pushing straight downward, and the inclined plane pushing back. The force of the inclined plane pushing back against the gravitational force is called the **normal force** ($F_n$). The normal force is always perpendicular to the surface that applies it. Your diagram of a block on a frictionless inclined plane should look like Figure 2.5.

Since gravity and the normal force are the only forces acting on the block, their sum is called the **net force**. It is the net force that should be plugged into Newton's second law to find the acceleration of your system. Notice from Figure 2.6 that vector addition of gravity and the normal force creates a right triangle. Notice also that this triangle is similar to the triangle of the inclined plane. Similar triangles have equal corresponding angles. By SOH CAH TOA we find that the resultant vector has a magnitude of $mg \sin\theta$. Thus the force due to gravity and the normal force of an inclined plane is always equal to $mg \sin\theta$ for any inclined plane and points directly along the plane.

Remember that $mg \sin\theta$ is the vector sum of the weight and the normal force. You may not label your system with both $mg \sin\theta$ and weight or the normal force, since this would be redundant.

Notice also from Figure 2.6 that, by the rules of SOH CAH TOA, the normal force is always equal to $mg \cos\theta$.

**Figure 2.5 $mg$ and the Normal Force with an Inclined Plane**

**Figure 2.6 Deriving the Net Force on an Object on an Inclined Plane**

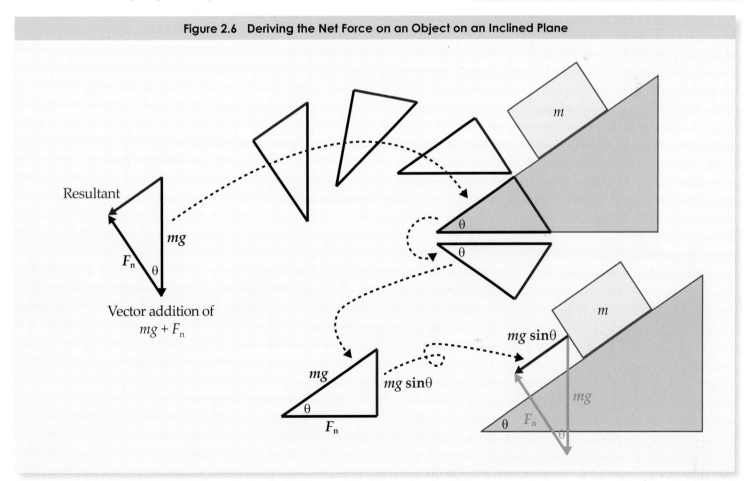

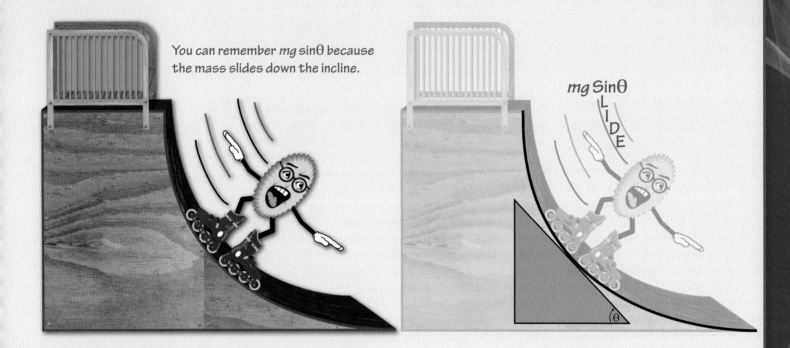

You can remember *mg* sinθ because the mass slides down the incline.

*mg* Sinθ SLIDE

Whenever you see an inclined plane, think *mg* sinθ. This is always the net force down any inclined plane due to gravity and the normal force. Likewise, *mg* cosθ is always the normal force. These formulas work regardless of the angle of the plane. Even curved surfaces can be thought of as an infinite number of inclined planes, and the force along the inclined plane at any given instant is as if the mass were on an inclined plane with a surface tangent to the circle.

**Be careful!** The normal force for a mass moving down a curved surface has two jobs:

1. a portion (*mg* cosθ) counters some gravitational forces, and

2. the rest ($mv^2/r$) must create the centripetal acceleration to change the direction of the velocity.

The normal force in this situation is therefore *mg* cosθ plus the centripetal force, which is our next topic.

---

By the way, the extreme cases of inclined planes are 90° and 0°. At 90°, *mg* sinθ = *mg*; at 0°, *mg* sinθ = 0. Therefore, an object on a frictionless incline with any angle between 0° and 90° will accelerate at some fraction of *g*.

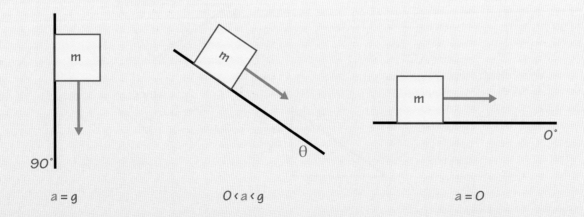

## 2.7 Circular Motion and Centripetal Force

*Angular velocity* (ω) and *angular acceleration* (α) are not tested on the MCAT. We shall address them briefly for completeness. Angular velocity is a measure of the speed at which an object spins and is given by the equation:

$$\omega = v/r$$

where $r$ is the radius at which the velocity $v$ is measured. Angular velocity is given in radians per second. The following formula converts angular velocity into frequency ($f$):

$$f = \omega/2\pi$$

The frequency is the number of full rotations per second.

Angular acceleration is simply the rate of change in angular velocity and is given by:

$$\alpha = a/r$$

The equations above are given only for clarification and are not on the MCAT. We will refer back to these equations from time to time to improve our understanding of certain concepts that are on the MCAT.

Okay, the stuff below is what you really need to know about circular motion on the MCAT.

The cyclist is circling the track at a constant speed but is accelerating because his direction is continually changing. The force causing this acceleration is the centripetal force.

$$a_c = \frac{v^2}{r}$$

$$F_c = \frac{mv^2}{r}$$

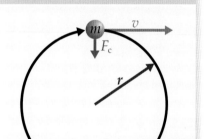

**Figure 2.7   Circular Motion**

**Circular motion** on the MCAT deals with concepts in translational motion applied to objects spinning or moving in circles. Examine Figure 2.7. An object moving in a circle at a constant speed has an instantaneous velocity $v$ at any given moment. The magnitude of this velocity remains constant but the direction continually changes at a constant rate. The rate of this change in velocity is acceleration. So, the object's speed never changes, yet the object is continually accelerating. This type of acceleration is called **centripetal acceleration** ($a_c$). Centripetal acceleration always points toward the center of the circle that is circumscribed by the motion. Since, when an object moves in a circle, the direction of centripetal acceleration is constantly changing, only the magnitude of centripetal acceleration is constant. By Newton's second law we know that an acceleration must be accompanied by a net force. The net force in this case is called **centripetal force** ($F_c$). Of course, centripetal force always points toward the center as well. The formulae for centripetal force and centripetal acceleration are shown next to Figure 2.7.

An easy way to remember that centripetal force must be created by another force is by thinking about a car on ice. A fast moving car on ice cannot turn or drive in a circle because there is nothing to create the centripetal force. What would normally cause the centripetal force that allows a fast moving car to turn on pavement? That is our next topic.

Recall from section 2.3 that there are only four forces in nature, and that centripetal force is not one of them. For MCAT we reclassified force into three types: gravitational, electromagnetic, and contact forces. Centripetal force will always be the result of one or more of these forces. Whenever centripetal force exists, there is always some other force responsible for it. Most centripetal force problems on the MCAT can be solved by equating the centripetal force with the responsible force. For instance, the gravitational force of the earth causes the moon to move around it. In this case we simply set the centripetal force equation equal to the Newton's gravitational force equation. We do not add the two forces together. These two forces are the same force, and thus are equal. An object being swung in a circle by a string is another example. Here, the centripetal force is created by the tension in the string. Whenever there is a centripetal force, there will always be a force causing it.

International Space Station

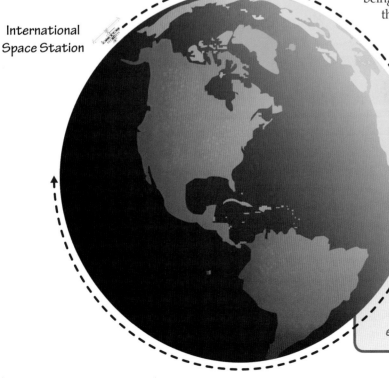

But first, back to "Why do things float when in orbit about the Earth?" The answer is that they don't. Something in orbit about the Earth is actually constantly falling toward the earth due to gravity. Remember, there must be a force causing the centripetal force. Gravity creates the centripetal force that makes a satellite orbit the Earth rather than fly off in the direction of its velocity. So, a satellite is constantly falling toward the center of the Earth but its velocity makes it continually miss the ground, and always by the same distance. Thus, to someone falling in a circular orbit with the satellite, the satellite and everything in it appear to be floating.

33. If $M$ is the mass of the Earth, $m$ is the mass of the moon, and $d$ is the distance between their centers, which of the following gives the instantaneous velocity of the moon as it orbits the Earth? (The universal gravitational constant is given by $G$.)

A. $\sqrt{\dfrac{GM}{d}}$

B. $\sqrt{\dfrac{GMm}{d}}$

C. $\sqrt{\dfrac{Gm}{d}}$

D. $\sqrt{\dfrac{GM}{md}}$

34. The owner of a warehouse asks an engineer to design a ramp which will reduce the force necessary to lift boxes to the top of a $\frac{1}{2}$ m step. If there is only room enough for a 4 m ramp, what is the maximum factor by which the lifting force could be reduced?

A. $\frac{1}{2}$
B. 2
C. 4
D. 8

35. If the radius of the orbit of a satellite orbiting the Earth is reduced by a factor of 2, the gravitational force on the Earth will:

A. decrease by a factor of 2.
B. remain the same.
C. increase by a factor of 2.
D. increase by a factor of 4.

36. Which of the following is true of the magnitudes of velocity and acceleration as the ball rolls down the slope as shown? Note: Please ignore any centripetal acceleration.

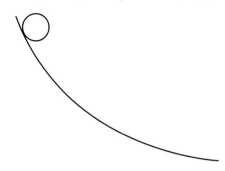

A. The velocity and the acceleration increase.
B. The velocity and the acceleration decrease.
C. The velocity increases and the acceleration decreases.
D. The velocity decreases and the acceleration increases.

37. A box starts from rest and slides 40 m down a frictionless inclined plane. The total vertical displacement of the box is 20 m. How long does it take for the block to reach the end of the plane?

A. 1 s
B. 2 s
C. 4 s
D. 8 s

38. An object of mass $m$ resting on the surface of the Earth experiences a force equal to its weight $mg$, where $g$ is the acceleration due to gravity. If $M$ is the mass of the Earth, $G$ is the universal gravitation constant, and $R$ is the radius of the Earth, which of the following expressions is equal to $g$?

A. $\dfrac{GMm}{R^2}$

B. $\dfrac{GM}{R^2}$

C. $\dfrac{GMm}{R}$

D. $\dfrac{GM}{R}$

**39.** A jogger is running on a circular track with a radius of 30 meters. If the jogger completes one trip around the track in 63 seconds, what is her average speed?

  **A.** 0 m/s
  **B.** 1 m/s
  **C.** 2 m/s
  **D.** 3 m/s

**40.** A box rests on an incline. Which of the following describes the forces on the box as the angle of inclination is increased?

  **A.** The force parallel to the ramp increases and the force perpendicular to the ramp decreases.
  **B.** The force parallel to the ramp increases and the force perpendicular to the ramp also increases.
  **C.** The force parallel to the ramp decreases and the force perpendicular to the ramp also decreases.
  **D.** The force parallel to the ramp and the force perpendicular to the ramp remain constant.

Any object that contacts your system may apply forces in two directions:

1. the normal force is always perpendicular to the contact surface;

2. a frictional force is always parallel to the contact surface.

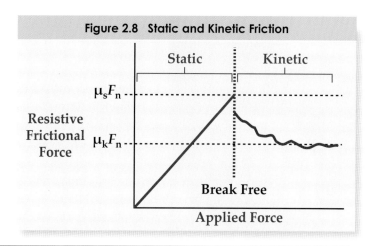

**Figure 2.8 Static and Kinetic Friction**

Friction does NOT oppose motion; it opposes relative motion. Always draw a frictional force vector pointing in the direction that would prevent surfaces from sliding past each other. For instance, the frictional force on the front tires of an accelerating front wheel-drive car points in the direction of motion of the car because the force prevents the tires from sliding backwards on the road.

**Friction** is caused by the attractive molecular forces between contiguous surfaces. Since the forces are attractive, friction opposes the relative motion between contiguous surfaces.

There are two important types of surface-to-surface friction on the MCAT: static and kinetic friction. **Static friction** ($f_s$) is the force opposing motion when two contiguous surfaces are not moving relative to each other. If you lay a block on an inclined plane and the block does not slide down the plane, it is the static frictional force that prevents it from sliding. **Kinetic friction** ($f_k$) is the force resisting motion once the two contiguous surfaces are sliding relative to each other. A block of wood sliding down an inclined plane moves more slowly than a block of ice sliding down the same plane, because the kinetic frictional force is greater on the wooden block.

For any two surfaces, there are two **coefficients of friction** ($\mu_s$ **and** $\mu_k$), which represent the fractions of the normal force that will equal the maximum static and the kinetic frictional forces. Thus the formulae for static friction and kinetic friction are respectively:

$$f_s \leq \mu_s F_n \qquad \text{and} \qquad f_k = \mu_k F_n$$

Static friction          Kinetic friction

Note the less-than-or-equal-to sign in the formula for static friction. This inequality indicates that the maximum static frictional force is $\mu_s F_n$. In other words, any 'applied' force up to and including this maximum amount that tries to set the object in motion will be exactly opposed, not by a static frictional force equal to $\mu_s F_n$, but by a static frictional force equal and opposite to the 'applied' force. Any 'applied' force greater than the maximum static frictional force will cause the object to 'break free' of the static friction and to accelerate. Once an object 'breaks free' of static friction and is moving, a kinetic frictional force equal to $\mu_k F_n$ will oppose the objects motion regardless of the strength of the 'applied' force. See Figure 2.8.

The maximum static frictional force on this anvil is proportional to its weight and the weight of the elephant sitting on it. If I apply a small force, $F_{applied}$ to the anvil with one finger, obviously the anvil does not push back with a force proportional to the weight of the elephant. Instead, it pushes back with a small force fs that is equal and opposite to $F_{applied}$.

From the formula for kinetic friction, $f_k = \mu_k F_n$, we can see that the kinetic frictional force is proportional to the normal force, so if you push down on sand paper, you increase the kinetic frictional force.

Since friction is usually a fraction of the normal force, the coefficients of friction generally have a value less than one. In addition, $\mu_s$ is greater than $\mu_k$. Imagine pushing a heavy object. Once the object is moving, it is usually easier to push. This is due to $\mu_s$ being greater than $\mu_k$.

When faced with a friction problem on the MCAT, first decide if your system is moving relative to the surface creating the friction. If it is, then use kinetic friction. If not, then use static friction. If you don't know, then calculate the component of the net force (excluding friction) on your system that is parallel to the surface creating the friction. Next, compare that *calculated* net force to $\mu_s F_n$. If the *calculated* net force is smaller than $\mu_s F_n$, then your system is probably* not sliding along the surface; static friction holds it in place. In this case, since there is no acceleration, the static friction is equal and opposite to the *calculated* net force. Notice that the static friction could never be greater than the *calculated* net force. If the *calculated* net force is greater than $\mu_s F_n$, then your system must be sliding along the surface. In the later case, ignore the static friction and subtract the magnitude of the kinetic frictional force from the *calculated* net force to arrive at a new net force that includes friction.

There are other types of friction, such as drag (i.e. air resistance), which is fluid resistance to an object's motion through that fluid, and viscosity, which is a fluid's resistance to motion through itself. On the MCAT these other types of friction will be dealt with only qualitatively or else a formula will be provided for plug-n-chug calculations. We will discuss the qualitative effects of drag and viscosity in Physics Lecture 6.

* We say "probably" because if the surfaces were already sliding relative to one another, the calculated net force could still be less than $\mu_s F_n$. Remember $\mu_k$ is usually less than $\mu_s$.

---

## 2.9 Tension

For the MCAT, think of **tension** as a force acting through a flexible object with no mass, such as a string or rope. (We shall refer to all these objects as simply ropes.) Tension is equal throughout a rope as long as there is no friction acting on the rope. At any point in a rope there is a tension force pulling in equal and opposite directions. We only use the force pulling away from our system. Tension requires an equal force at both ends of the rope, and the tension in the rope is equal to only one of the forces, not both. This is tricky, but remember, the rope has no mass. Thus, if a net force were applied to only one end of a rope, it would accelerate at an infinite rate.

### Thought Provoker

*To see where the confusion may result, take a look at the mass hanging from the rope in Figure 2.9. We know that the tension in the rope is mg. But is it really mg, or do we need to add the force of the ceiling pulling up on the rope with a force mg and the box pulling down on the rope with a force mg? And if we add these forces do we get zero or 2mg?*

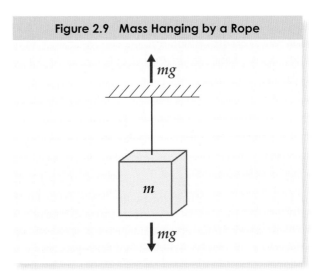

**Figure 2.9 Mass Hanging by a Rope**

Tension is actually beyond the scope of the MCAT. However, they test it in exactly the way explained above. When you see tension on the MCAT, just replace the rope with a force vector acting on your system.

One more important force on the MCAT is the force due to a compressed or stretched object following **Hooke's law**. When deformed, solids tend to 'remember' their shape and re-form to it. Hooke's law describes the force applied by most objects against a deforming force. This force is directly proportional to the amount of deformation or, more precisely, the change in position ($\Delta x$). Hooke's law is given by the following equation:

$$F = -k\Delta x$$

where $k$ is a constant unique to a given object. The negative sign indicates that the force is in the opposite direction of the displacement. Most solids follow Hooke's law to some extent. All solids violate Hooke's law at some limit of displacement, unique to that object. The point of violation is called the yield point. When an object is deformed beyond its *yield point*, it loses some of its 'memory' and will not regain its original shape. At some greater displacement, the object will reach a *fracture point* and break.

On the MCAT, Hooke's law is most often applied to springs. The force $F$ is really the tension in the spring and $\Delta x$ is the change from its rest position. For instance: the spring shown in Figure 2.10 has a spring constant $k = mg/\Delta x$.

> The most common MCAT questions concerning Hooke's law deal with springs. '$k$' is often referred to as the 'spring constant'. The negative sign in the formula can usually be ignored for the MCAT.

**Figure 2.10  Hooke's Law**

Assuming that my head follows Hooke's law, the force that it produces against this vise is equal to the change in its thickness, $\Delta x$, times some constant, $k_{salty}$, which is specific to my head. The change in the thickness of my head is negative because I'm getting thinner. If I were being stretched, the change in my thickness would be positive and the force I create would be in the other direction. According to Newton's third law, the vise applies an equal but opposite force against me. That's the one that hurts.

$$F = -k_{salty}\Delta x$$

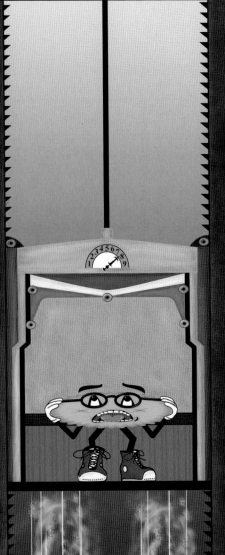

## 2.11 Reference Frames

When working a physics problem, measurements are given based upon the perspective of some single observer. As long as the observer is moving at a constant velocity, the reference frame is considered to be an *inertial reference frame*. All observers in all inertial reference frames will measure the same acceleration for any particle. In other words, two observers moving at different constant velocities will measure the same acceleration for any particle. Additionally, although some physical quantities will have different values in different inertial reference frames, the laws of physics will hold true for all inertial reference frames. For instance, observers in different inertial reference frames may measure different velocities and thus different kinetic energy changes (different work) for the same particle; however, the kinetic energy theorem will still hold true in both reference frames.

Occasionally, the MCAT may ask you to predict what an observer in a non-inertial reference frame might feel. Examples of such questions include those concerning **apparent weight** or centrifugal force. To answer these questions, you put yourself in an inertial reference frame and find the net force on the observer. Since, from the observer's frame of reference, he is not accelerating, he perceives a 'pseudo-force' opposite to the net force. For instance, if there is a net force accelerating him upward, rather than feeling the acceleration, he feels this force as additional weight pushing him downward; his apparent weight is that much greater. If there is a net force to the right (perhaps centripetal force), he feels this as a force of unknown origin pushing him to the left.

You may see 'apparent weight' on the MCAT. This is weight measured from some non-inertial reference frame. It is usually equal to the weight that would be measured by a bathroom scale. It is NOT always equal to *mg*. For instance, if you stand on a scale in an elevator accelerating upwards, the scale supports your real weight, *mg*, plus it accelerates you upward with an additional force, *ma*. Thus the scale would give an apparent weight equal to *mg* plus *ma*. (This situation is equivalent to an elevator moving faster and faster upward, or moving slower and slower downward.) The person in the elevator (a non-inertial reference frame) would feel heavier than he really was. Likewise, if the elevator accelerated downward, the scale would give an apparent weight of *mg* minus *ma*. (This situation is equivalent to an elevator moving faster and faster downward, or moving slower and slower upward.) The person in the elevator would feel lighter than he really was.

**Figure 2.11   Centrifugal Force**

You may have heard of centrifugal force and you may have also heard that it is a pseudo-force. This doesn't mean that you won't see it on the MCAT. On the contrary, MCAT often requires you to apply basic science knowledge in a novel or unfamiliar setting. Centrifugal force is the effect of centripetal force viewed from a different frame of reference (a non-inertial reference frame). Imagine that you are in a room with no windows. You believe the room is stationary, however it is actually moving forward in a straight line. A pendulum dangles via a string from the ceiling. It is motionless (from your point of view). The room makes a sharp turn to the left. You do not know the room is moving. Instead, you feel thrown to the right (to the outside of the turn) by some unexplained force. The pendulum also swings right due to some unexplained force. From your point of view, there is one, and only one force acting. This force is pushing you and the pendulum to the right. This force is quite real from your perspective. You could even measure it based upon the angle of the string and the weight of the pendulum. This is centrifugal force. An outside observer, on the other hand, views the room as moving left and, in turn, forcing you to the left and dragging the pendulum to the left via the string. This leftward force is centripetal force. To the outside observer in a non-inertial reference frame, there is no centrifugal force.

## 2.12 Equation Summary

| | Equations |
|---|---|
| **Newton's Second Law** <br><br> $F = ma$ | The net force applied to the center of mass of a system always equals the mass of the system times its acceleration. |
| **Gravity** <br><br> $F = G\dfrac{m_1 m_2}{r^2}$ | The force of gravity is proportional to the mass of each body and inversely proportional to the square of the distance between their centers of gravity. $G$ is a universal constant. |
| **Inclined Planes** <br><br> $F = mg\sin\theta$ <br><br> $F_n = mg\cos\theta$ | The sum of the normal force and the force of gravity is $mg\sin\theta$. <br><br> The normal force is $mg\cos\theta$. |
| **Circular Motion** <br><br> $a_c = \dfrac{v^2}{r}$ <br><br> $F_c = \dfrac{mv^2}{r}$ | An object moving in a circle at constant speed $v$ experiences a centripetal acceleration that is proportional to the square of its speed and inversely proportional to the radius of the circle which it circumscribes. <br><br> Some force $F_c$ must be applied to an object in order to give that object a centripetal acceleration. |
| **Friction** <br><br> $f_s \leq \mu_s F_n$ <br><br> $f_k = \mu_k F_n$ | Contiguous surfaces may exert equal and opposite forces against each other parallel to their contiguous surfaces. If the surfaces do not slide relative to each other, this force is static friction. If the surfaces slide relative to each other, this force is kinetic friction. |
| **Hooke's Law** <br><br> $F = -k\Delta x$ | When deformed, objects obeying Hooke's Law will exert a force proportional to their deformity. $k$ is a constant unique to the object. |

## 2.13 *Terms You Need To Know*

| Terms | |
|---|---|
| Apparent Weight | Inertia |
| Center of Gravity | Kinetic Friction ($f_k$) |
| Center of Mass | Mass |
| Centripetal Acceleration ($a_c$) | Newton's First Law |
| Centripetal Force | Newton's Law of Universal Gravitation |
| Circular Motion | Newton's Second Law |
| Coefficients of Friction ($\mu_k$ and $\mu_k$) | Newton's Third Law |
| Electromagnetic Force | Normal Force ($F_n$) |
| Friction | Net Force |
| Gravitational Force | Static Friction ($f_s$) |
| Hooke's Law | Tension |
| Inclined Plane | Weight |

### *Thought Provoker Answers*

*Answer from page 23:*

*Newton's Third Law equal and opposite force to gravity acting on the block is actually gravity acting on the Earth. See section 2.5 for more detail.*

*Answer from page 34:*

*The answer is that the tension in this case is simply mg.*

**41.** If the rear wheels of the truck pictured below drive the truck forward, then the frictional force on the rear tires due to the road is:

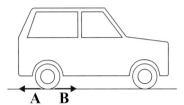

**A.** kinetic and in the direction of A.
**B.** kinetic and in the direction of B.
**C.** static and in the direction of A.
**D.** static and in the direction of B.

**42.** If a rope capable of withstanding 900 newtons of tension is attached to a wall as shown, what is the maximum force that can be applied in the direction of *F* before the rope will break?

**A.** 300 N
**B.** 450 N
**C.** 900 N
**D.** 1800 N

**43.** In many harbors, old automobile tires are hung along the sides of wooden docks to cushion them from the impact of docking boats. The tires deform in accordance with Hooke's law. As a boat is brought to a stop by gently colliding with the tires, the rate of deceleration of the boat:

**A.** is constant until the boat stops.
**B.** decreases until the boat stops.
**C.** increases until the boat stops.
**D.** increases and then decreases before the boat stops.

**44.** On a particular stretch of wet pavement, the kinetic coefficient of friction μ for a particular car with mass *m* is 0.08. If the car is moving at a velocity *v*, and suddenly locks its wheels and slides to a stop, which of the following expressions gives the distance that it will slide?

**A.** $\dfrac{v^2}{mg\mu}$

**B.** $\dfrac{v^2}{2mg\mu}$

**C.** $\dfrac{v^2}{2g\mu}$

**D.** $\dfrac{v}{2g\mu}$

**45.** In order to test the strength of a rope, one end is tied to a large tree and the other end is hitched to a team of 2 horses. The horses pull as hard as they can, but cannot break the rope. If the rope is untied from the tree and attached to another team of 2 horses with equal strength, and the two teams pull in opposite directions, the tension in the rope will:

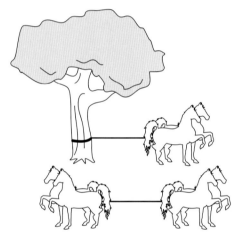

**A.** decrease by a factor of 2.
**B.** remain the same.
**C.** increase by a factor of 2.
**D.** increase by a factor of 4.

**46.** A child on a sled is sliding down a hill covered with snow. The combined mass of the child and sled is *m*, the angle of inclination of the hill is θ, and the coefficient of kinetic friction between the snow and the sled runners is μ. Which of the following expressions gives the frictional force on the sled?

**A.** μ*mg* cosθ
**B.** μ*mg* sinθ
**C.** μ*mg*
**D.** *mg*

47. The diagram below shows two different masses hung from identical Hooke's law springs. The Hooke's law constant k for the springs is equal to:

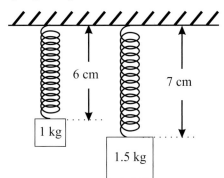

A. 2 N/cm
B. 5 N/cm
C. 10 N/cm
D. 20 N/cm

48. In a very tall building, an elevator with weight $W$ moves quickly upward at a constant speed. The entire weight of the elevator is supported by a single cable. The tension in the cable is:

A. greater than $W$.
B. less than $W$.
C. equal to $W$.
D. dependent on the speed of the elevator.

*Notes:*

# Equilibrium, Torque and Energy

## 3.1   Equilibrium

**Equilibrium** is a fancy word for no translational (straight line) or angular (rotational) acceleration. Stated another way, a system is in equilibrium if the translational velocity of its center of mass and angular velocities of all its parts are constant (i.e. it is moving and rotating at a constant velocity). If all velocities are zero, then the system is in **static equilibrium**. If any velocities are nonzero, but all velocities are also constant, then the system is in **dynamic equilibrium**. Remember, equilibrium does not mean motionless; it means constant velocity.

Notice that static and dynamic equilibrium both mean unchanging velocity. The only difference is that static equilibrium means the velocity is zero as well. Problems involving static or dynamic equilibrium are solved exactly the same way.

**Force due to gravity**

**Static Equilibrium:**
**Velocity is a constant zero.**

**Normal Force**

**Force due to gravity**

**Force due to gravity**

**Force of air resistance**

**Dynamic Equilibrium:**
**Velocity is constant and not zero.**

For all systems in equilibrium, the sum of all the forces acting on the system equals zero. In other words, the net force acting on a system in equilibrium is zero. A reliable and simple method of viewing systems in translational equilibrium on the MCAT is as follows: The sum of the magnitudes of the upward forces equals the sum of the magnitudes of the downward forces, and the sum of the magnitudes of the rightward forces equals the sum of the magnitudes of the leftward forces. This method allows you to use only positive numbers for all your forces; it is no longer necessary to decide if $g$ is positive or negative 10. $g$ is always positive with this method.

This is not the method that you learned in physics class, but it is faster and more intuitive for simple problems. More importantly, it is an effective method for MCAT. Thus two formulae that you must know for a system in equilibrium are:

> For any system in translational equilibrium the upward forces equal the downward forces and the rightward forces equal the leftward forces.

$$F_{upward} = F_{downward}$$
$$F_{rightward} = F_{leftward}$$

> These equations are for translational equilibrium. For rotational equilibrium see Physics Lecture 3.3.

> Notice that an object traveling in a circle at constant speed is NOT in equilibrium (it requires an external force to maintain its motion); however, an object rotating around its own center of gravity, like a top, is in equilibrium if it is rotating at a constant rate and its center of mass is moving at a constant speed.

---

## 3.2 Systems Not in Equilibrium

If a system is not in equilibrium, it simply means that the center of mass is accelerating translationally or its parts are accelerating rotationally. The MCAT does not test angular acceleration (where parts are accelerating rotationally), so a system not in equilibrium on the MCAT must be exhibiting only translational acceleration. For a system not in equilibrium, the sum of the forces equals the mass of the system times the acceleration of the system or $\Sigma F = ma$. However, on the MCAT there is a faster and more effective way to solve nonequilibrium problems. When faced with any system not in equilibrium, follow these five steps:

Step 1: Assume that you have the knowledge to solve the problem.

Step 2: Draw your diagram.

    A. Ignore the acceleration and lay out the problem as if it were in equilibrium.

    B. Predict the direction of acceleration and verify that one of your axes is parallel to the direction of acceleration.

Step 3: Choose your system.

Step 4: Find your formulae.

Step 5: Plug and chug.

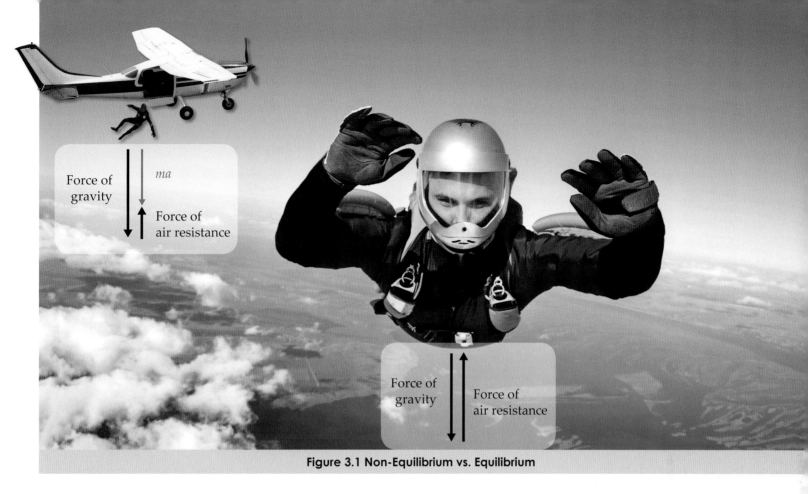

Figure 3.1 Non-Equilibrium vs. Equilibrium

As an example, we can solve for the acceleration of the skydiver in Figure 3.1. Immediately after the skydiver jumps from the plane, he is not in equilibrium. The downward force on him due to gravity is greater than the upward force due to air resistance. In order to find his acceleration, we pretend he is in equilibrium by putting all upward forces on one side of the equation and all downward forces on the other. Since he is not in equilibrium, the two sides are not equal.

$$F_{\text{upward}} \neq F_{\text{downward}}$$

Now we must decide which side has greater force. Since he is accelerating downward, the downward force must be greater. In order to balance the two sides of our equation, we must add '$ma$' to the side with less force.

$$F_{\text{upward}} + ma = F_{\text{downward}}$$

Now the two sides are equal and we can solve for acceleration.

After a few seconds, the skydiver reaches terminal velocity where the gravitational force downward is equal to the force of air resistance upward. At this point, he is in equilibrium and his acceleration is zero.

Note again that our method is not the method that you learned in physics class. In physics class recall that you assign opposite directions a positive and negative value and label your forces accordingly. Then you set the sum of these positive and negative forces equal to $ma$. If your acceleration is positive, your object is accelerating in the positive direction; if negative, then in the negative direction. In our method, all numbers are positive. Our method helps you think about the problem more intuitively. Since MCAT tends to test your science intuition as opposed to your ability to recall formulae and to plug and chug, our method tends to be fast and effective on the MCAT. Of course, the physics class method works perfectly and is even the preferred method if you are an engineer building a bridge. However, you have to be careful when using it on the MCAT. MCAT expects you to use the physics class method and has developed questions designed to confuse you when you use it.

**49.** A circus tightrope walker wishes to make his rope as straight as possible when he walks across it. If the tightrope walker has a mass of 75 kg, and the rope is 150 m long, how much tension must be in the rope in order to make it perfectly straight?

    **A.**   0 N
    **B.**   750 N
    **C.**   1500 N
    **D.**   No amount of tension in the rope could make it perfectly straight.

**50.** A rescue helicopter lifts a 50 kg rock climber by a rope from a cliff face. The rock climber is accelerated vertically at 5 m/s². What is the tension in the rope?

    **A.**   350 N
    **B.**   500 N
    **C.**   750 N
    **D.**   1500 N

**51.** The pulley shown below is old and rusted. When the 50 kg mass is allowed to drop, the friction in the pulley creates a constant 200 N force upward. What is the tension in the rope?

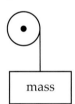

    **A.**   0 N
    **B.**   200 N
    **C.**   400 N
    **D.**   600 N

**52.** A skydiver jumping from a plane will accelerate up to a maximum velocity and no greater. This constant velocity is known as terminal velocity. Upon reaching terminal velocity, the net force on the skydiver is:

    **A.**   zero and the skydiver is in equilibrium.
    **B.**   zero and the skydiver is not in equilibrium.
    **C.**   equal to the weight of the skydiver and the skydiver is in equilibrium.
    **D.**   equal to the weight of the skydiver and the skydiver is not in equilibrium.

**53.** The arrows shown below represent all the force vectors that are applied to a single point. Which of the following could NOT be true of the point? (Note: $\sin 150° = 0.5$; $\cos 150° = -\frac{\sqrt{3}}{2}$)

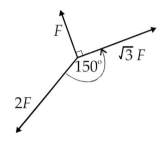

    **A.**   The point is moving at a constant velocity.
    **B.**   The point is not moving.
    **C.**   The point is accelerating at a constant rate.
    **D.**   The point is not accelerating.

**54.** There are 3 forces acting on an object. Two of the forces are of equal magnitude. One of these forces pulls the object to the north and one pulls to the east. If the object undergoes no acceleration, then in which direction must the third force be pulling?

    **A.**   northeast
    **B.**   northwest
    **C.**   southeast
    **D.**   southwest

**55.** Which of the following describes a situation requiring no net force?

    **A.**   A car starts from rest and reaches a speed of 80 km/hr after 15 seconds.
    **B.**   A bucket is lowered from a rooftop at a constant speed of 2 m/s.
    **C.**   A skater glides along the ice, gradually slowing from 10 m/s to 5 m/s.
    **D.**   The pendulum of a clock moves back and forth at a constant frequency of 0.5 cycles per second.

**56.** A child pushes a block across the floor with a constant force of 5 N. The block moves in a straight line and its speed increases from 0.2 m/s to 0.6 m/s. Which of the following must be true?

    **A.**   The force applied by the child is greater than the force of kinetic friction between the block and the floor.
    **B.**   The force applied by the child is less than the force of kinetic friction between the block and the floor.
    **C.**   The force applied by the child is greater than the force due to the weight of the block.
    **D.**   The force applied by the child is less than the force due to the weight of the block.

## 3.3 Torque

**Torque** (τ) is a twisting force (MCAT definition). Although torque is a vector, the MCAT allows you to think of torque as being clockwise or counter-clockwise. Torque is the vector product of both a force vector $F$ and a position vector $r$. Since this is vector multiplication and the result is a vector, the magnitude of the resultant vector must include the sine of the angle between the original two vectors (see Physics Lecture 1). The magnitude of torque is given by the following equation:

$$\tau = Fr \sin \theta$$

where θ is the angle between the force and the position vectors. In this equation, the position vector is the distance from **the point of rotation** to the point of application of the force. The point of rotation is any fixed point of your choosing. It is convenient to choose the position vector to be from the point of rotation to the point where the force acts at 90°. Such a position vector is called a **lever arm** (l). When the lever arm is used, the equation for torque becomes:

$$\tau = Fl$$

Compare $r$ and $l$ in Figure 3.2.

Any problem on the MCAT involving torque will be a statics problem. Therefore, use the following three formulae in the order given to solve any MCAT torque problem:

$$F_{\text{upward}} = F_{\text{downward}}$$
$$F_{\text{rightward}} = F_{\text{leftward}}$$
$$\tau_{\text{clockwise}} = \tau_{\text{counter-clockwise}}$$

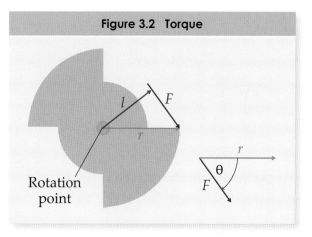

**Figure 3.2  Torque**

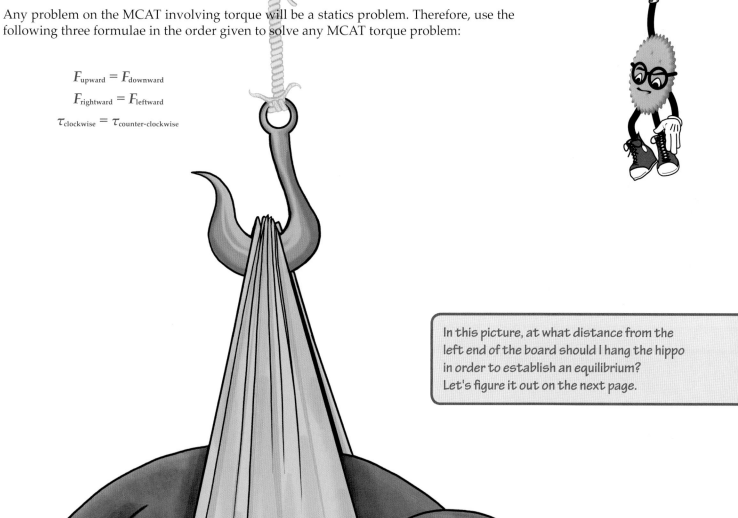

In this picture, at what distance from the left end of the board should I hang the hippo in order to establish an equilibrium? Let's figure it out on the next page.

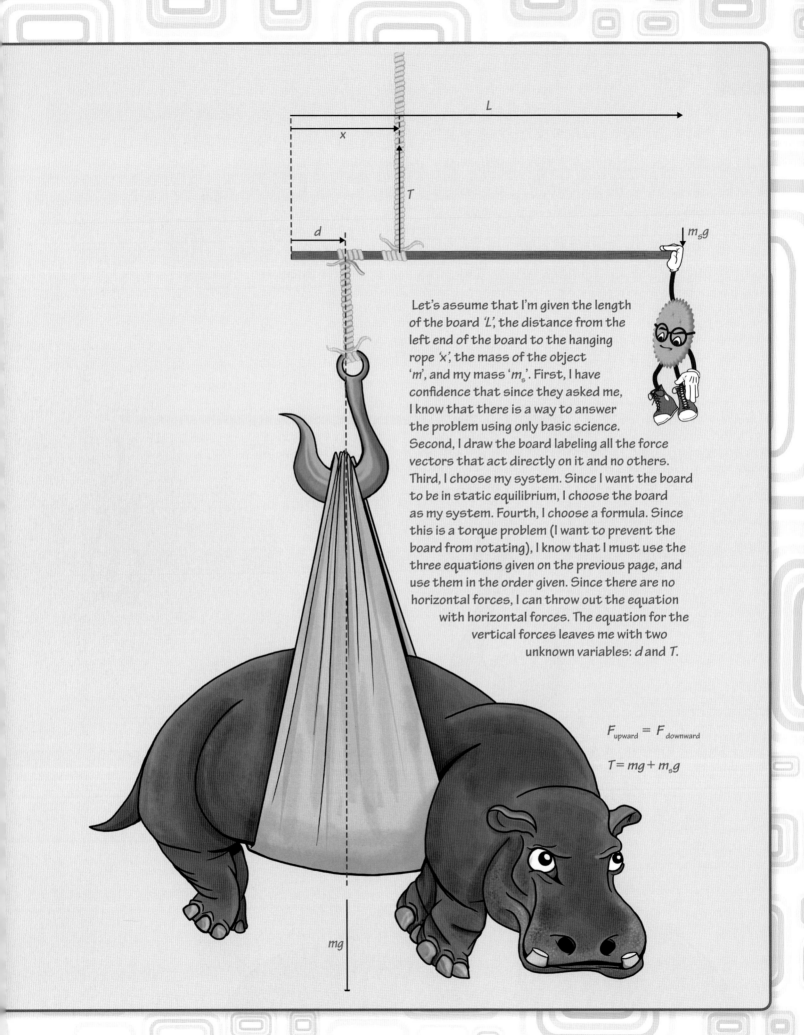

Let's assume that I'm given the length of the board 'L', the distance from the left end of the board to the hanging rope 'x', the mass of the object 'm', and my mass '$m_s$'. First, I have confidence that since they asked me, I know that there is a way to answer the problem using only basic science. Second, I draw the board labeling all the force vectors that act directly on it and no others. Third, I choose my system. Since I want the board to be in static equilibrium, I choose the board as my system. Fourth, I choose a formula. Since this is a torque problem (I want to prevent the board from rotating), I know that I must use the three equations given on the previous page, and use them in the order given. Since there are no horizontal forces, I can throw out the equation with horizontal forces. The equation for the vertical forces leaves me with two unknown variables: $d$ and $T$.

$$F_{upward} = F_{downward}$$

$$T = mg + m_s g$$

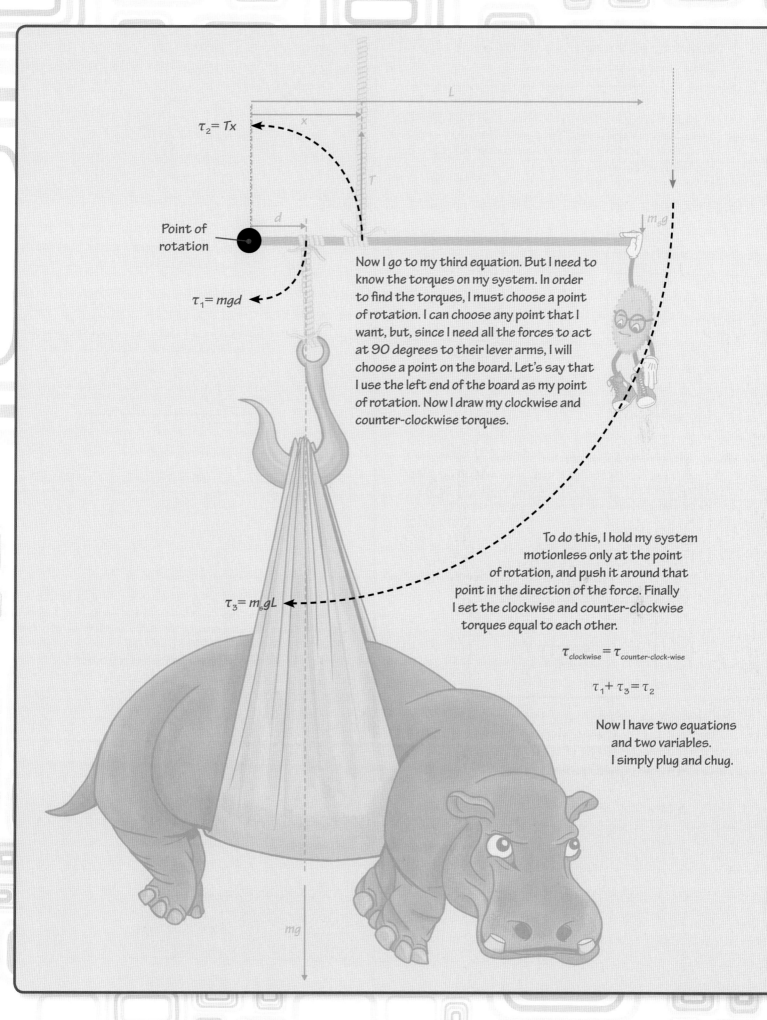

$\tau_2 = Tx$

Point of rotation

$\tau_1 = mgd$

$\tau_3 = m_sgL$

Now I go to my third equation. But I need to know the torques on my system. In order to find the torques, I must choose a point of rotation. I can choose any point that I want, but, since I need all the forces to act at 90 degrees to their lever arms, I will choose a point on the board. Let's say that I use the left end of the board as my point of rotation. Now I draw my clockwise and counter-clockwise torques.

To do this, I hold my system motionless only at the point of rotation, and push it around that point in the direction of the force. Finally I set the clockwise and counter-clockwise torques equal to each other.

$$\tau_{clockwise} = \tau_{counter-clock-wise}$$

$$\tau_1 + \tau_3 = \tau_2$$

Now I have two equations and two variables. I simply plug and chug.

$mg$

**57.** A telephone pole stands as shown below. Line A is 4 m off the ground and line B is 3 m off the ground. The tensions in line A and line B are 200 N and 400 N respectively. What is the net torque on the pole?

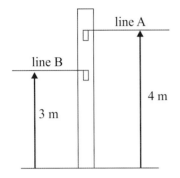

A. 0 Nm
B. 400 Nm
C. 800 Nm
D. 2000 Nm

**58.** A sign hangs by a rope attached at 30° to the middle of its upper edge. It rests against a frictionless wall. If the weight of the sign were doubled, what would happen to the tension in the string? (Note: sin 30° = 0.5; cos 30° = 0.87)

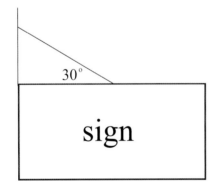

A. It would remain the same.
B. It would increase by a factor of 1.5.
C. It would increase by a factor of 2.
D. It would increase by a factor of 4.

**59.** If all of the forces below have equal magnitude, which one creates the most torque?

A.

C.

B.  

D.

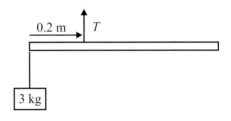

**60.** A one meter board with uniform density hangs in static equilibrium from a rope with tension $T$. A weight hangs from the left end of the board as shown. What is the mass of the board?

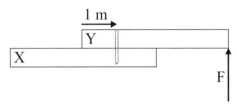

A. 1 kg
B. 2 kg
C. 3 kg
D. 4 kg

**61.** Boards X and Y are both massless and 4 m in length. A 4 N force $F$ is applied to board Y as shown. Board X is held stationary. The two boards are nailed together at 1 m from the left end of board Y. If the boards do not move, what is the static frictional force between the nail and board X?

A. 4 N
B. 8 N
C. 12 N
D. 16 N

**62.** A person pushes on a door and it swings open. Where should the force be applied in order to make the door swing open as quickly as possible?

   A. On the edge of the door nearest the hinges.
   B. At the center of the door.
   C. On the edge farthest from the hinges.
   D. A force anywhere on the door will have the same effect.

**63.** A student with a mass of 40 kg sits on the end of a seesaw with a total length of 10 meters as shown in the picture.

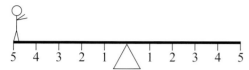

How far to right of the center of the seesaw should a student with a mass of 50 kg sit to achieve the best balance?

   A. 1 m
   B. 2 m
   C. 4 m
   D. 5 m

**64.** A carpenter who is having a difficult time loosening a screw puts away his screwdriver and chooses another with a handle with a larger diameter. He does this because:

   A. increasing force increases torque.
   B. decreasing force decreases torque.
   C. increasing lever arm increases torque.
   D. decreasing lever arm decreases torque.

Look inside most basic physics textbooks and you will find the statement "**Energy** is the capacity to do work." This statement, which is inaccurate, is an attempt to define energy. It is inaccurate because a system can have energy and still have no capacity to do work. There is no satisfactory definition of energy. Energy is a man-made concept designed to assist us in understanding our universe. The best way to understand energy is to work physics problems. For now, think of energy as you have always thought about it. For instance, you have an intuitive idea of what is meant by the statement "He is full of *energy* today." Use that intuition about energy when you work physics problems.

> You already have an intuitive sense about what energy is. Like, if I say "I am full of energy this morning!", you know just what I mean. This intuitive sense is the best way to think about energy when solving a physics problem. If, instead, you think of energy as 'the capacity to do work', I can write an MCAT problem that will probably fool you.

The unit of energy used on the MCAT is the **joule (J)**. One joule is 1 kg m²/s², which is the same thing as 1 N m. For microscopic systems, you may also see the **electron volt (eV)**. The electron volt is the energy necessary to move one electron through a potential drop of 1 V. It is equal to $1.6 \times 10^{-19}$ J.

> You don't need to memorize the conversion between electron volts and joules—the MCAT will give it to you if you need it. All you need to know is that an electron volt is a unit of energy that is very small compared to a joule.

Energy is a scalar. Thus energy usually provides the most convenient method by which to solve mechanics problems. Whenever you have a mechanics problem on the MCAT, always check first to see if you can solve it using conservation of energy, which we shall discuss below.

Energy can be divided into mechanical and nonmechanical energies. **Mechanical energy ($\Delta E_m$)** is energy of a macroscopic system. A macroscopic system is a system that you can examine without a microscope.

**Kinetic energy ($K$)** is the energy of motion. Any moving mass has a kinetic energy given by the equation:

$$K = \tfrac{1}{2}mv^2$$

> Keep it simple here. For now remember that there are two kinds of energy: Mechanical and non-mechanical. Mechanical energy is the energy of macroscopic objects, while non-mechanical energy is the energy of microscopic objects.

**Potential energy ($U$)** is the energy of position. All potential energies are position dependent. There are several types of potential energy. The most important types on the MCAT are gravitational potential energy ($U_g$) and elastic potential energy ($U_e$). (Electrical potential energy will be discussed in Physics Lecture 7.)

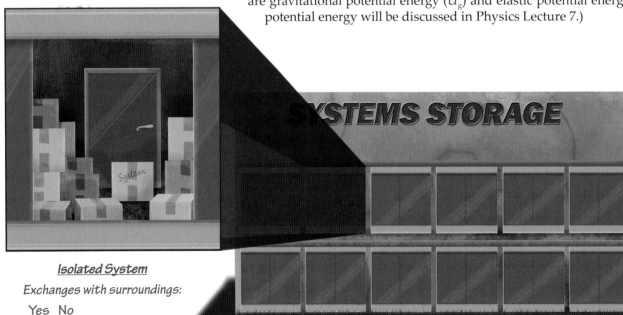

**Isolated System**

Exchanges with surroundings:

| Yes | No | |
|-----|-----|-----|
| ☐ | ☑ | Work and Heat |
| ☐ | ☑ | Mass |

**Gravitational potential energy ($U_g$)** is the energy due to the force of gravity. Gravitational potential energy between any two masses is given by $U_g = -Gm_1m_2/r$, where $G$ is the universal gravitational constant, $m_1$ and $m_2$ are the two masses, and $r$ is the distance between their centers of gravity. The negative sign indicates that energy decreases as the distance between objects that are attracted to each other decreases. A limited form of this equation, more useful on the MCAT, gives the gravitational potential energy of an object near the earth's surface. This formula is:

$$U_g = mgh$$

where $m$ is the mass of the object, $g$ is the free-fall acceleration at the surface of the earth, and $h$ is the height of the object or system above some arbitrary point.

**Elastic potential energy ($U_e$)** is the energy due to the resistive force applied by a deformed object. The elastic potential energy for objects following Hooke's law is given by the formula:

$$U_e = \tfrac{1}{2}k\Delta x^2$$

where $k$ is the Hooke's Law constant for the object (See Physics Lecture 2), and $\Delta x$ is the displacement of the object from its relaxed position.

Some MCAT questions will be solvable with either vectors or conservation of energy. It will be much faster to solve them using conservation of energy. So when faced with a mechanics problem, always consider conservation of energy first.

## 3.5  Systems

Before we can talk about energy transfer, we need to have some understanding of systems. A *system* is any defined area that we choose to consider separately from the rest of the universe. The rest of the universe is called the *surroundings*. Together, mass and energy define the three basic systems in physics: the *open system*, where energy and mass are exchanged with the surroundings; the *closed system*, where energy is exchanged with the surroundings but mass is not; and the *isolated system*, where neither energy nor mass is exchanged with the surroundings. By definition, although the form of energy in an isolated system may change, the energy of an isolated system is conserved. For instance, in the First Law of Thermodynamics when we say that the energy in the universe remains constant, we are defining the universe to be an isolated system.)

Conservation of energy does not say that a certain type of energy (i.e. kinetic or potential) must be conserved; instead it says that the sum of all energy types must remain constant in an isolated system. In a closed system, the change in the sum of all energy types must equal the energy leaving or entering the system. Energy can enter or leave a closed system only as work or heat. (Work is discussed next. Heat is discussed in Chemistry Lecture 3.)

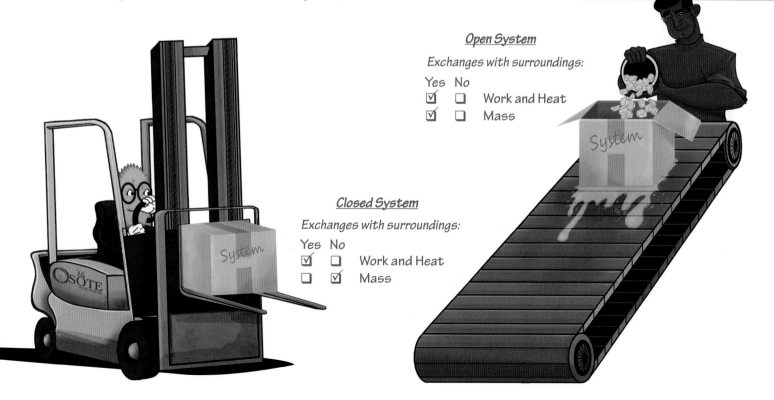

**Open System**

Exchanges with surroundings:

Yes No
☑ ☐  Work and Heat
☑ ☐  Mass

**Closed System**

Exchanges with surroundings:

Yes No
☑ ☐  Work and Heat
☐ ☑  Mass

## 3.6 Work

There are only two types of energy transfer: work and heat. **Work (W)** is the transfer of energy via a force. **Heat** is the transfer of energy by natural flow from a warmer body to a colder body. (See Chemistry Lecture 3 for more on heat.) Thus all work is energy transfer, but not all energy transfer is work. By 'transfer', we mean transfer from the system to the surroundings or vice versa.

The amount of work done will depend upon what we choose for our system. [This Lecture will not consider pressure-volume work (*PV* work). *PV* work is discussed in Chemistry Lecture 3.]

Work is a scalar and is measured in units of energy (**joules**).

The work done by any force other than friction is:

$$W = Fd \cos\theta \text{ (for all forces except friction)}$$

where $F$ is the force on some system, $d$ is the displacement of the system, and $\theta$ is the angle between $F$ and $d$. This equation gives the energy transferred into a system due to a force. The force may be one of many forces acting on the system or it may be the net force.

**Frictional forces** are an exception to the equation above because frictional forces change internal energy as well as mechanical energy. (Internal energy is the energy of individual molecules. Unfortunately, the MCAT will probably call this 'heat energy' or, worse, just 'heat'. Internal energy is discussed in Chemistry Lecture 3.)

A second way of looking at work is from **The First Law of Thermodynamics** which states that the total change in energy ($\Delta E_{total}$) of a closed system is due to work ($W$) and heat ($q$). The First Law of Thermodynamics for a closed system can be expressed in an equation as:

$$W + q = \Delta E_{total}$$

You have probably seen the formula for work:

$$W = Fd$$

This formula is an abbreviation for $W = Fd \cos\theta$. $F\cos\theta$ is the force in the direction of displacement, so when you see $W = Fd$, $F$ is understood to be the force in the direction of displacement.

The work done by the frictional force as the match is dragged across the matchbox increases the internal energy of the match enough to cause combustion.

**Something is wrong here.**

This looks like a nice example of work plus energy is equal to the change in my energy throughout the day, but a closer analysis will show that this doesn't work as an example of $W + q = \Delta E$. Can you find three reasons why?

Since there are only two kinds of energy, and if we assume no heat transfer, we can rewrite this equation under conditions of no heat as:

$$W = \Delta E_m + \Delta E_i \text{ (no heat)}$$

Since mechanical energy ($E_m$) can be divided into kinetic and potential energy, we can rewrite this equation as:

$$W = \Delta K + \Delta U + \Delta E_i \text{ (no heat)}$$

Friction is the only force that changes internal energy, so if there is no friction the equation is simplified to:

$$W = \Delta K + \Delta U \text{ (no heat, no friction)}$$

where $K$ is kinetic energy, $U$ is any potential energy, and $E_i$ is internal energy. This makes sense in terms of conservation of energy. Since work and heat are the only two types of energy transfer, when there is no heat, work must be responsible for any net energy change, and therefore must equal the sum of all energy changes. If there is no friction, all energy change is in the form of mechanical energy.

In any physics textbook you will also see:

$$W = \Delta K$$

This is the *Work-Energy Theorem*. It is <u>only</u> true when all energy transfer results only in a change to kinetic energy. In other words, it is a very limited case of the previous equations, and is not very useful for the MCAT.

The simplest way to understand work is to remember the first law of thermodynamics: energy is always conserved, or

$$\Delta E = W + q$$

where $q$ is heat and $\Delta E$ is the total change in energy of a closed system. This simply says that there are only two ways that energy can leave or enter a system: work and heat.

Now, if you want to know if work is done, do the following: define your system. If your system is the same temperature as its surroundings, then there can be no heat. Any energy change to such a system must be accomplished through work. Sum the change in energy and you have the work done on the system. If your system is not the same temperature as the surroundings, then heat must be considered and you have a thermodynamics problem. {Caveat: *Change in temperature is not the same thing as heat.*}

Answer: 1. The work being done is transferring energy into the surroundings, while the heat is transferring energy into me. 2. The sun beating down on me is transferring heat into me, but that doesn't make me feel more energized as this example suggests. 3. The change in energy should be final energy minus initial energy, so in this case, my final energy is greater than my initial energy; my energy has increased. It doesn't make much sense if my energy increases after doing work on the surroundings. So this example is wrong in at least three ways. We can fix all this by doing the following: 1. Recognize the work that since I am doing work on the surroundings, the work is negative. 2. I can sit on ice and heat the surroundings, so that my heat is now negative. 3. I reverse the energy pictures so that my initial high energy state is subtracted from my final low energy state where I am in bed, and the net energy change is negative. Now it's correct.

## 3.7 Conservative and Nonconservative Forces

Conservative forces are called conservative because the mechanical energy is conserved within the system. If a force acts on a system as the system moves from point A to point B and back, and the total work done by the force is zero, the force is a **conservative force**. Thus, the net work done by any conservative force on an object moving around any closed path is zero. A second way to recognize a conservative force is that the energy change is the same regardless of the path taken by the system.

It is a necessary but not a sufficient condition that conservative forces be functions of position only. In other words, the strength of a conservative force is dependent solely upon its position. For instance, the conservative force of gravity upon an object is dependent upon its position within a gravitational field; the conservative Hooke's law force is dependent upon the position of the spring or object creating it.

Conservative forces have potential energies associated with them. Conservative forces do not change the mechanical energy of a system. Thus the **Law of Conservation of Mechanical Energy** states that when only conservative forces are acting, the sum of the mechanical energies remains constant:

$$K_1 + U_1 = K_2 + U_2 \text{ (conservative forces only, no heat)}$$

Written another way:

$$0 = \Delta K + \Delta U \text{ (conservative forces only, no heat)}$$

**Warning:** If a question asks, "How much work is done by gravity?" (or any other conservative force), the question itself implies that gravity is not part of the system. There are three methods to answer such a question: 1) use $Fd \cos\theta$; 2) simply calculate the change in $\Delta U_g$; or 3) use: $W = \Delta K + \Delta U + \Delta E_i$ but do not include gravitational potential energy in your calculation of $\Delta U$. Technically speaking, a conservative force doesn't do work because energy is never lost nor gained by the system.

Conservative forces do not change the temperature or the internal energy of an object to which they are applied. Gravitational forces, Hooke's law forces and electric and magnetic field forces, are the conservative forces that you're likely to see on the MCAT.

Maximum potential energy, minimum kinetic energy

Maximum kinetic energy, minimum potential energy

The work done against conservative forces is conserved in potential energy; the work done against nonconservative forces is not conserved.

**Nonconservative forces** are forces that change the mechanical energy of a system when they do work. Examples of nonconservative forces are kinetic frictional forces and the pushing and pulling forces applied by animals. For instance, if a human lifts an object from rest to a height '$h$', the total mechanical energy of the object has changed. On the other hand, if an object were propelled by its kinetic energy to a height '$h$', its total mechanical energy would remain constant.

Except for frictional forces, the work done by all nonconservative forces equals the change in the mechanical energy of the systems upon which they are applied. This result is described by the equation:

$$W = \Delta K + \Delta U \quad \text{(nonconservative forces other than kinetic friction, no heat)}$$

Notice that this is the same equation as given for one of the definitions of work. This is because conservative forces don't do work. Compare this equation to the equation for the change in mechanical energy when only conservative forces act.

Animal forces are nonconservative. In this picture the force applied to the cart by the horses is a nonconservative force.

This is a tough topic. A famous physicist once wrote "There are no nonconservative forces," meaning that, of the four possible forces in nature, all are conservative. However, on a macroscopic scale, mechanical energy is changed when certain forces are acting. These forces we call nonconservative. It is possible that the MCAT might ask you to identify conservative and nonconservative forces. But the most important thing to understand is how they affect work. If you already understand work, and can do most MCAT problems involving work, then it may be best not to worry too much about conservative and nonconservative forces.

*Notes:*

## 3.8 Work and Friction

Kinetic frictional forces increase the internal energy of the systems to which they are applied. Thus, only a portion of the work done by friction goes into changing mechanical energy. When you rub your hands together to warm them, you are doing work, via kinetic friction, which increases their internal energy. There is no heat because your two hands are at an equal temperature throughout.

In order to find the work done by a kinetic frictional force, we must consider the internal energy. Imagine a box sliding to a stop along a tabletop. Kinetic friction has done negative work on the box; the force decreases the kinetic energy of the box. The mechanical energy change of the box is given by:

$$f_k d \cos\theta = \Delta K + \Delta U$$

From this formula it appears that work done by friction is equal to mechanical energy change. But this is not the case. The box and table increased their internal energy. They both warmed up. That energy came from the box, so the net energy loss of the box (or work done by friction) is more than just $f_k d \cos\theta$. (You may want to attribute some of the energy transfer as heat, but there is no heat transfer in this problem. The box and table begin at the same temperature. Heat must move from a warmer body to a cooler body, so no heat transfer is possible here.) The energy change of the box (the work done by friction) is the sum of the change in its kinetic energy, which is negative, and the change in its internal energy, which is positive. The work done on the box is $W = \Delta K + \Delta U + \Delta E_i$

> Work done by friction is not likely to be on the MCAT. It is explained here because we have seen it used as a practice question leading to confusion and brain melt downs. The explanation is also a valuable exercise in understanding conservation of energy and work.

Notes:

**Figure 3.3   Work and Friction**

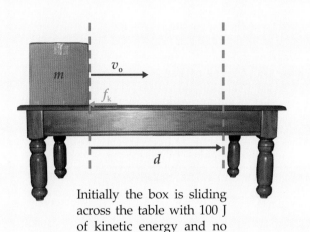

Total energy of the isolated system of the table and box is conserved. The energy transfer into the closed system of the box is equal to the work done on the box (in this case it is negative). Notice that work done by friction is NOT *Fd* and can only be found if the change in internal energy is known.

Initially the box is sliding across the table with 100 J of kinetic energy and no internal energy.

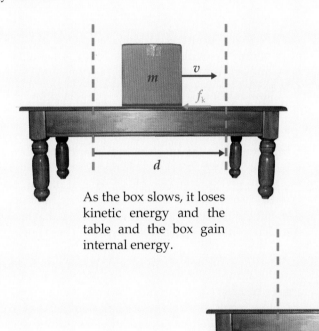

$d = 10 \text{ m}$

$m_{\text{of the box}} = 2 \text{ kg}$

$f_k = 10 \text{ N}$

$v_o = 10 \text{ m/s}$

As the box slows, it loses kinetic energy and the table and the box gain internal energy.

$E_{\text{i final of table}} = 30 \text{ J}$

$E_{\text{i final of box}} = 70 \text{ J}$

$E_{\text{i initial of table}} = 0 \text{ J}$

$E_{\text{i initial of box}} = 0 \text{ J}$

$K_{\text{initial}} = \frac{1}{2}mv^2 = 100 \text{ J}$

$K_{\text{final}} = \frac{1}{2}mv^2 = 0 \text{ J}$

The box stops with no kinetic energy remaining, but now has 70 J of internal energy. The table now has 30 J of internal energy.

$W_{\text{done by friction}} = \Delta E_{\text{total for either system}} = 30 \text{ J}$

$W_{\text{done on box}} = \Delta K + \Delta E_{\text{i of box}} = -30 \text{ J}$

$W_{\text{done on table}} = \Delta E_{\text{i of table}} = 30 \text{ J}$

$\Delta E_{\text{total}} = \Delta E_{\text{i of box}} + \Delta E_{\text{i of table}} + \Delta K = 0 \text{ J}$

In this example, friction did 30 J of work on the table and -30 J of work on the box. The box began with 100 J of energy and finished with 70 J; the table began with 0 J of energy and finished with 30 J. (The internal energy values cannot be calculated from the information provided. They have been chosen arbitrarily.)

Note: Although due to the internal energy increase the box and the table are warmer than when they started, this is NOT heat, nor is it the result of heat. Heat is the transfer of energy from a warmer body to a cooler body. The energy transfer in this example is entirely due to work done by friction.

## 3.9 Examples of Work

If we look at the Figure below, we have the following:

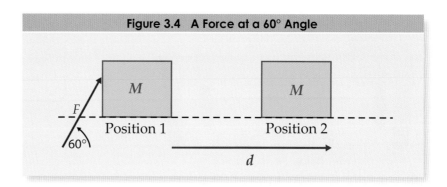

**Figure 3.4 A Force at a 60° Angle**

A force $F$ acts on mass $M$ along a frictionless surface resulting in a displacement $d$. It is important to realize that the force is acting through the entire displacement. The mass moves from position 1 to position 2. Many concepts can be appreciated by this simple display. First, since a force is applied resulting in a transfer of energy from the applicator of the force (whomever or whatever that might be) to the mass, work is done. The vertical component of the force was apparently too small to move the mass off the horizontal line. Thus the vertical displacement is zero, and the vertical force component does no work. Gravity and the normal force are 90° to the displacement and also do no work. The horizontal component of the force, however, moves the mass a displacement of $d$. To find the work done by the force, we would use $W = Fd \cos 60°$. (Notice that $F \cos 60°$ is the horizontal component of the force.) The mass does not change height, so there is no change in potential energy, $U$. Thus, the work done goes completely into changing kinetic energy. The change in kinetic energy is equal to the work.

Consider the physical manifestations of work in the example above. In other words, since work is a transfer of energy, what are the physical changes to a mass as a result of this energy transfer? To test yourself, imagine the same force acting on the box at an angle of 30°. How would this affect the work done on the box? Would one force do more work than the other? If a different amount of work is done in each case, then we should be able to see this difference in physical quantities. What would be the physical manifestations of the difference in work done?

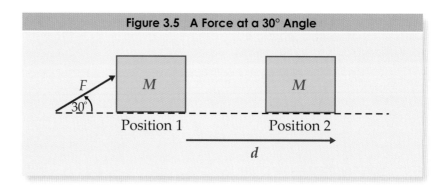

**Figure 3.5 A Force at a 30° Angle**

Since the force applied at 30° has a greater horizontal component, it does more work. This greater work would manifest itself in greater acceleration throughout the displacement, greater velocity at the end of the displacement, and less time required to achieve the displacement.

## 3.10 Summary of Work

When faced with a problem involving work, follow my 5 step system given at the beginning of Physics Lecture 1. Once you have defined your system, decide what energy transfers are taking place. If there is heat or pressure-volume change, you have a thermodynamics problem. See Chemistry Lecture 3. Otherwise, all energy transfer is work. The work done will be $W = Fd \cos\theta$ unless friction is acting, but can always be found by $W = \Delta K + \Delta U + \Delta E_i$ if information on internal energy change is available. Remember, if you want to consider a conservative force as doing work, you have three methods:

1. $Fd \cos\theta$;

2. $\Delta U$;

3. everything but $\Delta U$.

## 3.11 Power

**Power (P)** is the rate of energy transfer. The unit of power is the **watt (W)**, which is equivalent to J/s. Do not confuse the unit W with the concept $W$ for work.

Power is given by the following equation:

$$P = \frac{\Delta E}{t}$$

where $t$ is the time during which energy is transferred and $\Delta E$ is the energy change of the system, which equals work $W$ plus heat $q$. A more narrow definition of power, but one that is often used, is the rate at which a force does work:

$$P = \frac{W}{t}$$

The instantaneous power due to a force is:

$$P = Fv \cos\theta$$

where $\theta$ is the angle between $F$ and $v$. The $\cos\theta$ indicates that the force is in the direction of the velocity, and, like the equation for work ($W = Fd$) you may see this equation written as $P = Fv$ where it is understood that $F$ is the force in the direction of the velocity. We can see by these equations that power is a scalar.

Digesting a cracker releases five times as much energy per gram as exploding dynamite, but the dynamite releases it in much less time. Thus, the power of the dynamite is greater. That's why we don't make bombs out of crackers.

## 3.12 Equation Summary

| Equations | |
|---|---|
| **Equilibrium (no acceleration)** | **Non-equilibrium (acceleration)** |
| $F_{\text{upward}} = F_{\text{downward}}$ <br> $F_{\text{rightward}} = F_{\text{leftward}}$ <br> $\tau_{\text{clockwise}} = \tau_{\text{counter-clockwise}}$ | $F_{\text{upward}} = F_{\text{downward}} \pm ma$ <br> $F_{\text{rightward}} = F_{\text{leftward}} \pm ma$ <br> Add $ma$ to the weaker side. |
| **Torque** | **Energy** |
| $\tau = Fl$ | $K = \frac{1}{2}mv^2$ <br> $U_{\text{g}} = mgh$ <br> $U_{\text{e}} = \frac{1}{2}k\Delta x^2$ |
| **Work** | **Power** |
| $W = Fd\cos\theta$ (for all forces except friction) <br> $W = \Delta K + \Delta U + \Delta E_{\text{i (no heat)}}$ | $P = \dfrac{\Delta E}{t}$ <br> $P = Fv\cos\theta$ |

## 3.13 Terms You Need to Know

| Terms | |
|---|---|
| Conservative Force | Lever Arm ($l$) |
| Dynamic Equilibrium | Mechanical Energy ($\Delta E_{\text{m}}$) |
| Elastic Potential Energy ($U_{\text{e}}$) | Nonconservative Forces |
| Electron-volt (eV) | Potential Energy ($U$) |
| Energy | Power ($P$) |
| Equilibrium | Static Equilibrium |
| First Law of Thermodynamics | The Point of Rotation |
| Frictional forces | Torque ($\tau$) |
| Heat | Watt (W) |
| Joule (J) | Work ($W$) |
| Kinetic Energy ($K$) | |
| Law of Conservation of Energy | |
| Law of Conservation of Mechanical Energy | |

65. A meteor with a mass of 1 kg moving at 20 km/s collides with Jupiter's atmosphere. The meteor penetrates 100 km into the atmosphere and disintegrates. What is the average force on the meteor once it enters Jupiter's atmosphere? (Note: ignore gravity)

    A. $2 \times 10^3$ N
    B. $4 \times 10^3$ N
    C. $8 \times 10^3$ N
    D. $2 \times 10^5$ N

66. If 1 kg blocks were stacked one upon the other starting at the surface of the earth and continuing forever into space, the blocks near the bottom of the stack would have:

    A. less gravitational potential energy than blocks at the middle or blocks near the top of the stack.
    B. less gravitational potential energy than blocks at the middle and the same gravitational energy as blocks near the top of the stack.
    C. the same gravitational potential energy as all other blocks.
    D. more gravitational potential energy than blocks at the middle or blocks near the top of the stack.

67. Objects A and B are placed on the spring as shown. Object A has twice as much mass as object B. If the spring is depressed and released, propelling the objects into the air, object A will:

    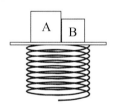

    A. rise one fourth as high as object B.
    B. rise half as high as object B.
    C. rise to the same height as object B.
    D. rise twice as high as object B.

68. A spring powered dart-gun fires a dart 1 m vertically into the air. In order for the dart to go 4 m, the spring would have to be depressed:

    A. 2 times the distance.
    B. 3 times the distance.
    C. 4 times the distance.
    D. 8 times the distance.

69. A 100 N force is applied as shown to a 10 kg object for 2 seconds. If the object is initially at rest, what is its final velocity? (Ignore friction: sin 30° = 0.5; cos 30° = 0.87)

    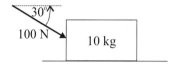

    A. 8.7 m/s
    B. 1 m/s
    C. 17.4 m/s
    D. 34.8 m/s

70. A large rock is tied to a rubber band and dropped straight down. As the rock falls, the rubber band gradually stretches, eventually bringing the rock to a stop. Which of the following energy transfers is taking place in this process?

    A. Kinetic to gravitational potential to elastic potential
    B. Kinetic to elastic potential to gravitational potential
    C. Gravitational potential to elastic potential to kinetic
    D. Gravitational potential to kinetic to elastic potential

71. Energy consumption in the home is generally measured in units of kilowatt hours. A kilowatt hour is equal to:

    A. 3,600 J
    B. 6,000 J
    C. 3,600,000 J
    D. 6,000,000 J

72. A winch is used to lift heavy objects to the top of building under construction. A winch with a power of 50 kW was replaced with a new winch with a power of 100 kW. Which of the following statements about the new winch is NOT true?

    A. The new winch can do twice as much work in the same time as the old winch.
    B. The new winch takes twice as much time to do the same work as the old winch.
    C. The new winch can raise objects with twice as much mass at the same speed as the old winch.
    D. The new winch can raise objects with the same mass at twice the speed of the old winch.

*Notes:*

# MOMENTUM, MACHINES, AND RADIOACTIVE DECAY

## 4.1 Momentum

A baseball, when thrown by a major league pitcher, has approximately the same energy as a bowling ball thrown by a professional bowler. Why, then, can the baseball be knocked out of the park with a swing of a bat, when the same swing would only deflect the motion of the bowling ball? The answer is **momentum** ($p$). The momentum of the bowling ball is much greater. Momentum is a measure of a moving object's tendency to continue along its present path. By increasing either an object's velocity or its mass, and thus its momentum, it becomes more difficult to change its path. Momentum is given by the equation:

$$p = mv$$

The units of momentum are kg m/s. Momentum is closely related to inertia (Physics Lecture 2).

There are two important points to know about momentum for the MCAT. The first is that in an isolated system **momentum is always conserved**. This law is as inviolable as the law of conservation of energy. The second important point is that **momentum is a vector**. When we put these two points together, we find that the initial momentum of the center of mass of an isolated system is always equal to its final momentum in both magnitude and direction. In other words, the momentum of the center of mass of an isolated system is constant in direction and magnitude.

> Momentum of an isolated system is always conserved.

## 4.2 Collisions

A collision occurs in the following manner: Two bodies come into contact and are momentarily or permanently deformed while doing so. From Hooke's law we know that the force generated by the deformed bodies is proportional to the degree of the deformity. If the bodies follow Hooke's law perfectly, the force is conservative and the all energy is transferred (via $W = Fd \cos\theta$) back to the motion of the bodies. If the bodies do not follow Hooke's law perfectly, some or all of the energy is dissipated as internal energy. The two types of collisions just described are called elastic collisions and inelastic collisions, respectively.

This crash is an example of an inelastic collison. Some of the initial kinetic energy is dissipated as internal energy, which can result in permanent deformation of the objects.

**Elastic collisions** are collisions where the mechanical energy is conserved. In an elastic collision, no energy is dissipated to internal energy. When very small hard objects with no internal parts collide, the energy has no place to dissipate. This is an elastic collision. Atomic collisions approximately follow this model. Two magnets may slide into each other's magnetic field and repulse each other without ever touching. Their kinetic energies would be conserved momentarily in their magnetic fields. This represents a perfectly elastic collision. A rubber ball dropped from 1 meter bounces off a hard surface and returns to the same height. This is another elastic collision. In all these collisions, only conservative forces are at work resulting in conservation of mechanical energy.

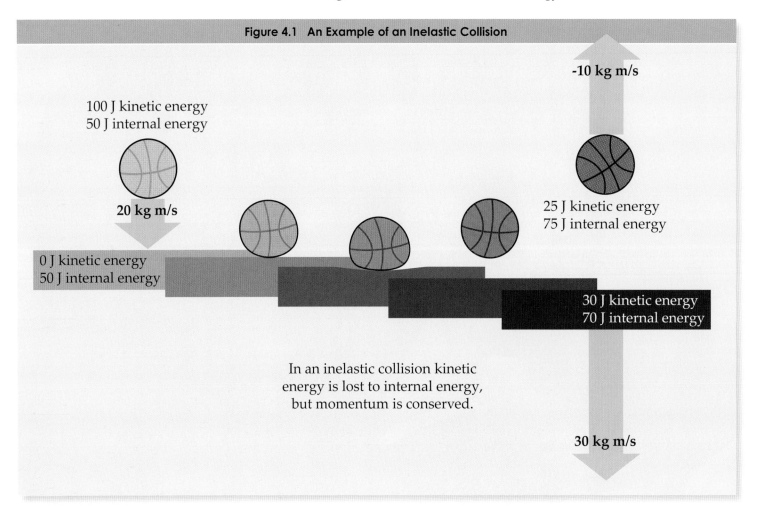

**Figure 4.1   An Example of an Inelastic Collision**

-10 kg m/s

100 J kinetic energy
50 J internal energy

20 kg m/s

25 J kinetic energy
75 J internal energy

0 J kinetic energy
50 J internal energy

30 J kinetic energy
70 J internal energy

In an inelastic collision kinetic energy is lost to internal energy, but momentum is conserved.

30 kg m/s

Elastic collision problems are easy to solve because the sum of the mechanical energies before the collision is equal to the sum of the mechanical energies after the collision.

$$U_{initial} + K_{initial} = U_{final} + K_{final}$$

Since energy is a scalar, even the directions of the colliding objects are irrelevant.

**Inelastic collisions** occur when the colliding objects lose some of their mechanical energy to internal energy. Any collision that is not elastic is inelastic. Stated another way, if any mechanical energy is lost, the collision is inelastic. A *completely* inelastic collision occurs when the colliding objects stick together upon collision. Since mechanical energy is not completely conserved in any inelastic collision, we must use conservation of momentum to solve inelastic collision problems. The formula for solving inelastic collision problems is simple enough:

$$p_{initial} = p_{final}$$

The initial momentum of an isolated system equals the final momentum of an isolated system. However, because momentum is a vector, we must pay close attention to its direction. For instance in the inelastic collision diagram in Figure 4.1, we see that by adding the momentum vectors of the final system, we arrive at a 20 kg m/s vector pointing downward, the same as the initial momentum. In multidimensional systems, the vector nature of momentum may require several equations. For instance, in a 2 dimensional system, if we have momentum in both the $x$ and $y$ directions, one equation is required for each direction. Thus a 2 dimensional collision may require the following equations:

$$p_{(x)initial} = p_{(x)final}$$

$$p_{(y)initial} = p_{(y)final}$$

When solving a collision problem on the MCAT, be sure that your chosen system in step 3 of my Never-Fail Method is an isolated system. Repeat step 2, drawing two diagrams of your system. The first should be a diagram of the system immediately before the collision and the second a diagram immediately after the collision. Then, for elastic collisions, set the total mechanical energy in the first diagram equal to the total mechanical energy in the second diagram. For inelastic collisions, set the initial and final momentums equal.

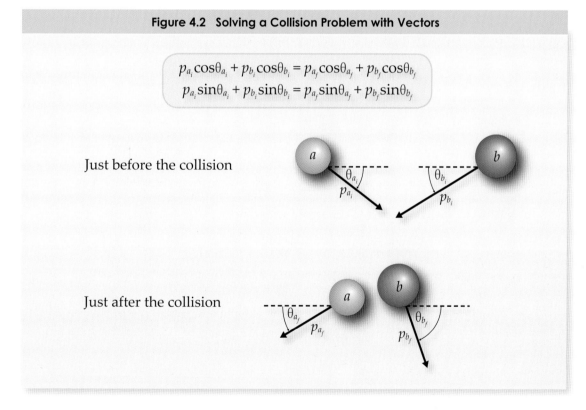

**Figure 4.2   Solving a Collision Problem with Vectors**

$$p_{a_i}\cos\theta_{a_i} + p_{b_i}\cos\theta_{b_i} = p_{a_f}\cos\theta_{a_f} + p_{b_f}\cos\theta_{b_f}$$
$$p_{a_i}\sin\theta_{a_i} + p_{b_i}\sin\theta_{b_i} = p_{a_f}\sin\theta_{a_f} + p_{b_f}\sin\theta_{b_f}$$

Just before the collision

Just after the collision

The $x$ and $y$ components are found by using the cosine and sine of the angles as shown in the example in Figure 4.2. Since this involves lengthy calculations, the MCAT probably will not test it in this manner. Instead, the MCAT is likely to ask only about the momentum in the $x$ direction or only about the momentum in the $y$ direction.

## 4.3 Reverse Collisions

Imagine watching a short film of two objects colliding and sticking together. This is a completely inelastic collision. The final momentum equals the initial momentum. If the objects stop when they collide, the final momentum is zero, so the initial momentum must have been zero as well. Now play the film again, only this time run it backwards. The two objects start together and suddenly burst apart. This is a reverse collision. Of course, just running the film backwards didn't change the momentums. The final and the initial momentums must still be zero. This is true of any explosion or radioactive decay where the pieces start from rest. Notice that the vector nature of momentum dictates that, in a two-piece explosion, the two pieces must separate in exactly opposite directions.

**Figure 4.3   An Explosion is a Reverse Collision**

$m_1 + m_2$

$m_1v_1$

$m_2v_2$

Why can't this happen?

Answer: Because momentum is not conserved.

Now imagine a cat standing on a board on top of a frozen, frictionless lake. The momentum of the cat and the board together is zero. If the cat tries to jump to the right, the board must be pushed to the left in order to conserve momentum.

**Figure 4.4  Pushing Off is a Reverse Collision**

$m_1v_1$

$m_2v_2$

## 4.4 Intuition About Collisions

Collisions will be fully elastic, partially elastic, or fully inelastic. If you study the table and the graph below, you will be able to make simple predictions concerning such collisions. Knowing this table and graph is by no means crucial for the MCAT, but it will provide you with a deeper understanding concerning collisions. Don't try to memorize the table!

**Figure 4.5 Collision Equations (not required for the MCAT)**

| | Elastic | | Partially Elastic | | Inelastic |
|---|---|---|---|---|---|
| | $v_1$ | $v_2$ | $v_1$ | $v_2$ | $v_{combined}$ |
| **Equations** | $\dfrac{v_1}{v_o} = \dfrac{m_1 - m_2}{m_1 + m_2}$ | $\dfrac{v_2}{v_o} = \dfrac{2m_1}{m_1 + m_2}$ | $\dfrac{v_1}{v_o - v_2} = -\dfrac{m_2}{m_1}$ | $\dfrac{v_2}{v_o - v_1} = \dfrac{m_1}{m_2}$ | $\dfrac{v_c}{v_o} = \dfrac{m_1}{m_1 + m_2}$ |
| $m_1 < m_2$ | $-v_o < v_1 < v_o$ | $0 < v_2 < v_o$ | $-v_o < v_1 < \dfrac{v_o}{2}$ | $0 < v_2 < v_o$ | $0 < v_c < \dfrac{v_o}{2}$ |
| $m_1 = m_2$ | $v_1 = 0$ | $v_2 = v_o$ | $0 < v_1 < \dfrac{v_o}{2}$ | $\dfrac{v_o}{2} < v_2 < v_o$ | $v_c = \dfrac{v_o}{2}$ |
| $m_1 > m_2$ | $0 < v_1 < v_o$ | $v_o < v_2 < 2v_o$ | $0 < v_1 < v_o$ | $\dfrac{v_o}{2} < v_2 < 2v_o$ | $\dfrac{v_o}{2} < v_c < v_o$ |

The table above is based upon a collision between a mass $m_1$ moving at velocity $v_o$ and a stationary mass $m_2$. The velocities $v_1$ and $v_2$ represent the respective velocities of the masses after the collision. The velocity $v_c$ represents the velocity of the combined mass after a fully inelastic collision.

The graph in Figure 4.6 represents the information in the table. If you understand the graph, it is an excellent guide to answering collision questions qualitatively. If you don't understand the graph, don't sweat it. It won't be on the MCAT.

Here is an example using the graph in Figure 4.6: a partially inelastic collision occurs when an object moving with velocity $v_o$ collides with a stationary object of equal mass. We examine the $y$-axis of the graph because the masses are equal along the $y$-axis. We see that the stationary object must have a velocity in the darkly shaded region along the $y$-axis, so it must have a final velocity less than $v_o$ but greater than $v_o/2$. The first object must have a velocity in its original direction, greater than zero but less than $v_o/2$.

The graph also shows that in order for the first object to bounce backwards, it must have a mass less than the object it strikes.

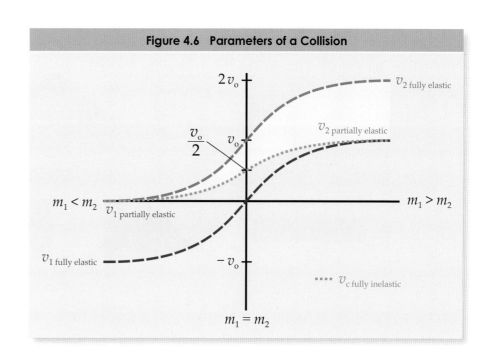

**Figure 4.6 Parameters of a Collision**

# Impulse

**Impulse (J)** is equal to the change in momentum.

$$J = \Delta p$$

If you examine any collision, you will notice that, if the materials approximately follow Hooke's law, the force during the time of contact is not constant. The average force on either colliding body can be found from the equation:

$$J = F_{avg} \Delta t$$

To find the average force from the change in momentum simply put the two impulse equations together to make:

$$\Delta mv = F_{avg} \Delta t$$

Impulse shows us that if the time over which the force acts is increased, the same change in velocity can be achieved with a lower force. For instance, air bags on an automobile don't change the momentum, but they increase the time over which the collision occurs, and thus decrease the force on the driver. The graphs below show three separate ways that the same particle might change its velocity.

The area under the curve represents impulse or change in momentum. Since the particle is the same each time, the mass remains constant, and the initial and final velocities are the same for each graph. However, the way that the final velocity is achieved is very different in each graph. If the particle were an egg, which graph represents the conditions under which the egg would be least likely to break?

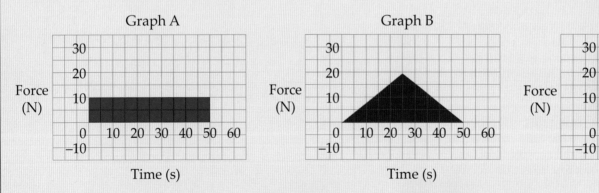

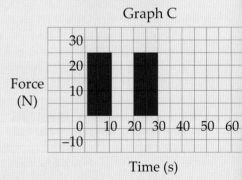

The answer is graph B because the force builds up slowly.

**73.** A rocket with a mass of $7.2 \times 10^4$ kg starts from rest in outer space and fires its thrusters until it is moving with a velocity of 100 m/s. What was the average force on the rocket due to the thrusters?

- **A.** $7.2 \times 10^3$ N
- **B.** $7.2 \times 10^4$ N
- **C.** $7.2 \times 10^6$ N
- **D.** The average force cannot be determined with the information given.

**74.** A boy is sliding down a long icy hill on his sled. In order to decrease his mass and increase his velocity, he drops his heavy winter coat and heavy boots from the sled while he is moving. Will his strategy work?

- **A.** No, because he loses the potential energy of the objects that he leaves behind.
- **B.** No, because although his kinetic energy increases, his momentum decreases.
- **C.** Yes, because although his kinetic energy decreases, his momentum increases.
- **D.** Yes, because although his momentum decreases, his kinetic energy decreases.

**75.** Ball A moving at 12 m/s collides elastically with ball B as shown. If both balls have the same mass, what is the final velocity of ball A? (Note: sin 60° = 0.87; cos 60° = 0.5)

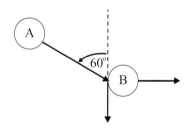

- **A.** 3 m/s
- **B.** 6 m/s
- **C.** 9 m/s
- **D.** 12 m/s

**76.** The chemical potential energy in gasoline is converted to kinetic energy in cars. If a car accelerates from zero to 60 km/h, compared to the energy necessary to increase the velocity of the car from zero to 30 km/h, the energy necessary to increase the velocity of the car from 30 to 60 km/h is:

- **A.** half as great.
- **B.** the same.
- **C.** twice as great.
- **D.** three times as great.

**77.** A 3 kg cat sitting on a 1.5 kg piece of cardboard on a frozen lake wants to jump to shore without touching the ice. If there is no friction between the cardboard and the ice, when the cat jumps, the cardboard will move in the opposite direction with a velocity:

- **A.** half as great as the cat's velocity.
- **B.** equal to the cat's velocity.
- **C.** twice as great as the cat's velocity.
- **D.** four times as great as the cat's velocity.

**78.** A block of mass $m_1$ slides across a frictionless surface with speed $v_1$ and collides with a stationary block of mass $m_2$. The blocks stick together after the collision and move away with a speed $v_2$. Which of the following statements is (are) true about the blocks?

- **I.** $m_1 v_1 = (m_1 + m_2)v_2$
- **II.** $\frac{1}{2}m_1 v_1^2 = \frac{1}{2}(m_1 + m_2)v_2^2$
- **III.** $v_1 = v_2$

- **A.** I only
- **B.** II only
- **C.** I and II only
- **D.** I, II and III

**79.** Two 1 kg carts with spring bumpers undergo a collision on a frictionless track as shown in the before and after pictures below.

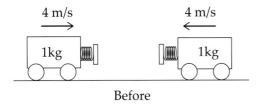

Before

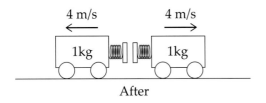

After

The total momentum of the system is equal to:

A. 0 kg m/sec before the collision and 0 kg m/sec after the collision.
B. −4 kg m/sec before the collision and 4 kg m/sec after the collision.
C. −8 kg m/sec before the collision and 8 kg m/sec after the collision.
D. 8 kg m/sec before the collision and 0 kg m/sec after the collision.

**80.** A trapeze artist who accidentally falls builds up a great deal of momentum before he is brought safely to rest by a safety net. The safety net serves to:

A. increase the force of the collision by decreasing the collision time.
B. decrease the force of the collision by decreasing the collision time.
C. increase the force of the collision by increasing the collision time.
D. decrease the force of the collision by increasing the collision time.

## 4.6 Machines

Now that we've covered the more simple topics in classical mechanics, let's examine one of the ways these topics may appear on the MCAT; let's examine machines. **Machines** are mechanical devices that reduce force when doing work. Every time that you see a machine on the MCAT, remind yourself that ideal machines reduce force but don't change work. (Nonideal machines increase work because they increase internal energy through friction.) Remembering that ideal machines don't change work can make some otherwise difficult MCAT problems fast and simple. In this lecture we will examine the **ramp**, **lever**, and **pulley**. In Physics Lecture 5 we will examine one more simple machine called a hydraulic lift.

This ramp is a simple machine. The men use less force to lift the piano into the truck because the ramp increases the distance over which the force is applied. The work done remains the same.

## 4.7 The Ramp

A **ramp** is simply an inclined plane (see Physics Lecture 3). If we examine the work necessary to lift a mass $m$ to a tabletop of height $h$, we find that it is the force $mg$ times the distance $h$, or $mgh$.

By building a frictionless ramp, we can achieve the same result with a reduced force. To push the mass up the inclined plane, we must only overcome the force that is pushing the mass down the plane, which is $mg \sin\theta$. Since the sine of any angle is a fraction, we know that this force is only a fraction of $mg$ and thus is reduced by the machine. To prove that the work is still the same we can multiply the force times the distance. From SOH CAH TOA, we know that the distance along the ramp is the opposite, or $h$, divided by $\sin\theta$. Thus, $W = mg \sin\theta \times h/\sin\theta$. This reduces to $W = mgh$, the same work as without the machine. From this it becomes clear that the fraction by which we want to *reduce* the force must be the same as the fraction by which we *increase* the length of the ramp. In other words, if we want to reduce the force to ½ $mg$, we must make a ramp with length $2h$. This is the same as saying that, when work is held constant in $W = Fd$, force and distance are inversely proportional to each other.

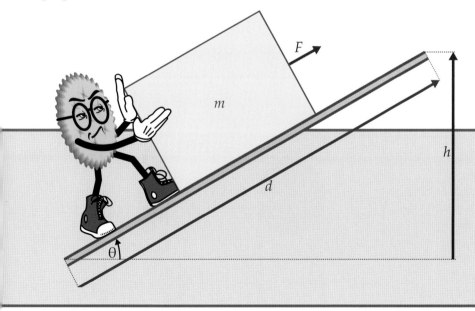

$$\sin\theta = \frac{h}{d} \qquad\qquad W = Fd$$

$$F = mg \sin\theta \qquad\qquad \therefore W = mg\frac{h}{d}d$$

$$\therefore F = mg\frac{h}{d} \qquad\qquad \therefore W = mgh$$

## 4.8 The Lever

The **lever** is based on the principle of torque. Again, let's examine lifting a mass $m$ to a height $h$. Like the ramp, the lever simply allows us to increase the distance through which our force acts. Since we want to move the mass at a constant velocity, we want to establish a dynamic equilibrium. This means that the clockwise torques must be equal to the counter-clockwise torques. Torque is force times lever arm. So, by doubling the length of the lever arm, we reduce the force necessary by a factor of two. We can do this by placing our fulcrum twice as far from our force as from our mass. By the diagram below, we can see that the curve traveled by the mass to reach height $h_1$ is only half as long as the curve traveled by the force-bearing end of the lever. Once again, the force is inversely proportional to the distance, and the work is the same with or without the machine. (Notice that as soon as the lever begins to move, the lever arm shortens. However, as long as both gravity and the force point downward, the lever arms remain in the same proportions.)

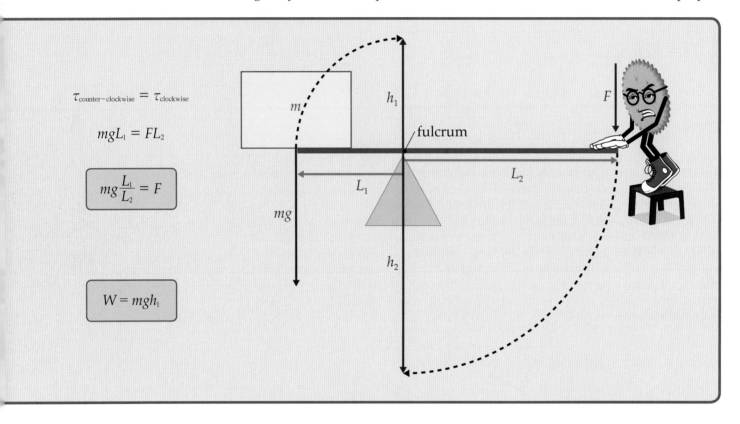

$$\tau_{\text{counter-clockwise}} = \tau_{\text{clockwise}}$$

$$mgL_1 = FL_2$$

$$mg\frac{L_1}{L_2} = F$$

$$W = mgh_1$$

### Figure 4.7  Modified Levers

Although these machines appear to be pulleys, they are actually modified levers. They work on the principle of torque. In each, the lever arm acted upon by force $F$ is greater than the lever arm acted upon by $mg$, thus the force necessary to lift $mg$ is reduced. Of course, the work remains the same. Notice that the tension is not the same throughout these ropes as it is throughout the ropes of a true pulley.

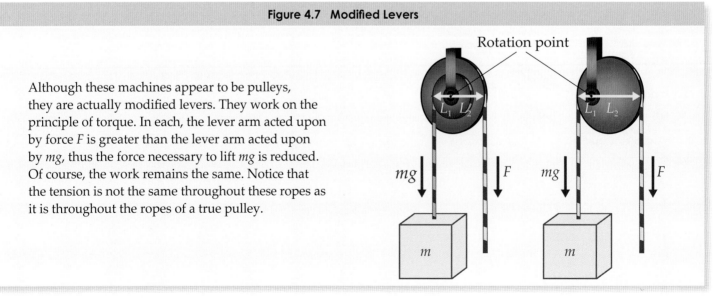

## 4.9 The Pulley

A **pulley** acts on the same principle as the ramp and lever; it allows force to act over a greater distance and thus do the same amount of work with less force. The key to understanding a pulley is remembering that tension throughout a massless rope attached to a frictionless, massless pulley is constant. In other words, in the diagram below, the tension $T$ is the same at every point in the rope.

Now, in our 5-step-system, let's choose our system to be pulley number 1. We choose pulley number 1, because pulley number 1 will move exactly as the mass moves. (If you have trouble visualizing this, imagine that the rope attaching pulley number 1 to the mass is a solid, inflexible bar. It won't change the problem.) If you first chose the mass as your system, you would not get the problem wrong, you would simply arrive at the conclusion that the rope connecting the mass to pulley number 1 has a tension of $mg$. Then you would be forced to choose a new system. Eventually, you would have to find a system on which your unknown, $T$, was acting directly. This system is pulley number 1.

Like the lever, we wish to create a dynamic equilibrium where our mass has a constant velocity upward. To do this, we want the upward forces to equal the downward forces. The downward force is $mg$. The upward forces are the two tensions in the rope attached to the pulley. The tension throughout a rope in an ideal pulley is the same at every point, so the two tensions here must be equal. Setting upward forces equal to downward forces gives us $mg = 2T$, or $T = \frac{1}{2}\,mg$.

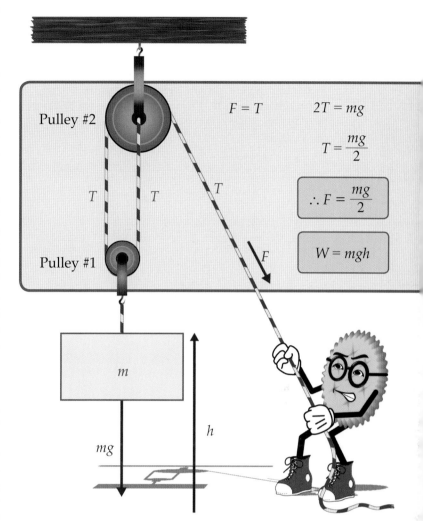

Of course the work necessary to lift the mass to the table has not changed. So, since the force is halved, how is the force applied over twice the distance? If we look closely at the pulley system and imagine that the mass is raised one meter, we see that in order for the rope to lift evenly, one meter must come off of both sides of the pulley rope. Since it is all one rope, this amounts to pulling the rope a distance of two meters where the force $F$ is applied. Thus we have reduced the force by two and increased the distance over which it acts by two as well. Again, when work is held constant, force and distance are inversely proportional.

*Notes:*

81. The frictionless pulley system below reduces the force necessary to lift any mass by a factor of 3. How much power is required to lift a 30 kg object 2 meters in 60 seconds using this pulley system?

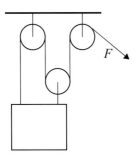

    **A.**    4 W
    **B.**    10 W
    **C.**    24 W
    **D.**    120 W

82. An eccentric pulley can be used on a compound bow to increase the velocity of an arrow. The pulleys pivot around the dots as shown. Below is a compound bow in two positions. The tension at point A compared to point B is most likely:

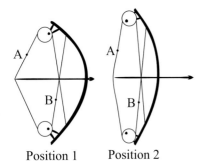

    Position 1    Position 2

    **A.**    less in both position 1 and position 2.
    **B.**    less in position 1 and greater in position 2.
    **C.**    greater in both position 1 and position 2.
    **D.**    greater in position 1 and less in position 2.

83. A crate is to be lifted to a height of 3 meters with the assistance of an inclined plane. If the inclined plane is a non-ideal machine, which of the following statements is most likely true?

    **A.**    The non-ideal inclined plane increases the force required and decreases the work that has to be done.
    **B.**    The non-ideal inclined plane decreases the force required and increases the work.
    **C.**    The non-ideal inclined plane increases the force and the work required.
    **D.**    The non-ideal inclined plane decreases the force and the work required.

84. A girl riding her bicycle up a steep hill decides to save energy by zigzagging rather than riding straight up. Ignoring friction, her strategy will:

    **A.**    require the same amount of energy but less force on the pedals.
    **B.**    require the same amount of energy and the same amount of force on the pedals.
    **C.**    require less energy and less force on the pedals.
    **D.**    require less energy and more force on the pedals.

85. An inventor designs a machine that he claims will lift a 30 kg object with the application of only a 25 N force. If the inventor is correct, what is the shortest possible distance through which the force must be applied for each meter that the object is raised?

    **A.**    5 m
    **B.**    8 m
    **C.**    12 m
    **D.**    15 m

**86.** The pulley system shown below operates as a modified lever. Pulley A and pulley B turn together, so when a person pulls on rope A the mass attached to rope B will be lifted. Which of the following changes to the system will reduce the force needed to lift the mass?

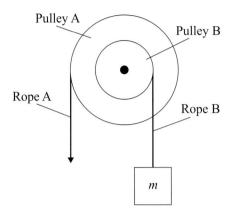

A. Increase the length of rope A.
B. Increase the length of rope B.
C. Increase the diameter of pulley A.
D. Increase the diameter of pulley B.

**87.** The mechanical advantage for a machine is defined as the output force divided by the input force. Since the output force is typically greater than the input force, this value is normally greater than one. For an ideal machine, what would be another way of representing the mechanical advantage?

A. (output distance)/(input distance)
B. (input distance)/(output distance)
C. (output distance) × (input distance)
D. (input distance) + (output distance)

**88.** A wheelchair access ramp is to be designed so that 1000 N can be lifted to a height of 1 meter through the application of 50 N of force. The length of the ramp must be at least:

A. 5 m
B. 10 m
C. 20 m
D. 100 m

**Table 4.1 Radioactive Particles**

| Particle | Symbol |
|----------|--------|
| alpha | $\alpha_2^4$ |
| beta | $^-\beta$ or $_{-1}\beta$ or $_{-1}^0e$ |
| positron | $^+\beta$ or $_{+1}^0e$ |
| gamma | $\gamma_0^0$ |

## 4.10 Radioactive Decay

**Radioactive decay** concerns atoms that spontaneously break apart. All atoms other than hydrogen are subject to some type of spontaneous decay. However, the rate at which decay occurs varies dramatically. Atoms with a high decay rate are said to be radioactive. Of the 2000 known nuclides (atoms and their isotopes), only 266 are stable. Atomic stability can be reasonably predicted by an atom's neutron to proton ratio. No atoms with more than 83 protons are considered stable. In smaller atoms, a stable neutron to proton ratio is 1:1. As atoms get heavier, they require a larger number of neutrons for stability and the ratio increases to as much as 1.5:1.

## 4.11 Half-Life

There is no way to predict how long a single atom will take to spontaneously decay. However, since atoms are small, we are usually concerned with millions of them at a time. Thus we can apply the rules of probability and make predictions concerning large groups of atoms. Any substance (a large group of identical atoms) has a predictable rate of decay. This predictable rate of decay is usually given in terms of a half-life. A **half-life** is the length of time necessary for one half of a given amount of a substance to decay.

In any half-life problem, there are 4, and only 4, possible variables. They are the initial amount of substance, the final amount of substance, the length of the half-life, and the number of half-lives (often given as a time period, in which case you simply divide by the length of a half-life). Any MCAT half-life question will provide you with some form of three of these, and ask you to find the fourth. Any half-life question on the MCAT should be a fast, free point. To answer a half-life question on the MCAT, count the number of half-lives on your fingers. For instance, if after 5 years, 12.5% of a substance remains, what is the half-life? The initial amount is, of course, 100%. The final amount is 12.5%. The number of half-lives is found by dividing the initial amount by 2 until you arrive at the final amount. Keep track on your fingers of the number of times that you divide by 2. 50% is once, 25% is twice, 12.5% is thrice. That's three half-lives. In another example: how long will it take for 500 grams of a substance with a half-life of 2 years to decay to 62 grams? The initial amount equals 500, the final amount equals 62, the half-life is 2 years. Divide the initial amount by 2 until you arrive at the final amount. Keep track of the number of half-lives on your fingers. 250 is one, 125 is two, 62.5 is three. Rounding off numbers is the rule on the MCAT, so the answer is 3 half-lives or 6 years. Whatever the combination, look for the 3 variables and solve for the fourth by counting half-lives on your fingers.

There goes one half-life.

## 4.12 Types of Radioactive Decay

There are five types of radioactive decay on the MCAT: alpha decay, beta decay, positron emission, electron capture, and gamma ray production. (Positron emission and electron capture are actually types of beta decay.) If you remember how each particle is written and on which side of the equation it belongs, solving a decay problem on the MCAT becomes a very simple math problem. Simply be sure that the sum of the atomic numbers and the sum of the mass numbers on the left side of the equation equal the sum of the atomic numbers and the sum of the mass numbers on the right side, and look up the proper elements in the periodic table.

**Alpha decay** (or $\alpha$-decay) is probably the easiest to remember. An alpha particle is a helium nucleus. Thus, it contains 2 protons and 2 neutrons. In alpha decay, an alpha particle is lost. An example of alpha decay is:

$$^{238}_{92}\text{U} = {}^{4}_{2}\alpha + {}^{234}_{90}\text{Th}$$

**Beta decay** ($\beta$-decay) is the expulsion of an electron. (Some books include positron emission as a type of beta decay.) A beta particle is an electron or positron. (A positron is like an electron with a positive charge.) Notice that beta decay is not the destruction of an electron; instead, it is the creation of an electron and a proton from a neutron, and the expulsion of the newly created electron. An example of beta decay is:

$$^{234}_{90}\text{Th} \rightarrow {}^{234}_{91}\text{Pa} + {}^{0}_{-1}\text{e}$$

A *neutrino* (not shown) is also emitted during beta decay. A neutrino is a virtually massless particle. A neutrino is typically represented with the Greek letter nu ($\nu$).

**Positron emission** is the emission of a positron when a proton becomes a neutron. In positron emission, a proton is transformed into a neutron and a positron is emitted. An example of positron emission is:

$$^{22}_{11}\text{Na} \rightarrow {}^{0}_{1}\text{e} + {}^{22}_{10}\text{Ne}$$

**Electron capture** is the capture of an electron along with the merging of that electron with a proton to create a neutron. In electron capture, a proton is destroyed and a neutron is created. An example of electron capture is:

$$^{201}_{80}\text{Hg} + {}^{0}_{-1}\text{e} \rightarrow {}^{201}_{79}\text{Au} + {}^{0}_{0}\gamma$$

A **gamma ray** is a high frequency photon. It has no charge and does not change the identity of the atom from which it is given off. Gamma ray emission often accompanies the other decay types. An example of gamma ray emission is when an electron and positron collide:

$$^{0}_{-1}\text{e} + {}^{0}_{1}\text{e} \rightarrow {}^{0}_{0}\gamma + {}^{0}_{0}\gamma$$

This is a matter-antimatter collision called *annihilation*. Mass is destroyed, releasing energy in the form of gamma rays.

The gamma knife targets brain tumors with a high dose of radiation.

## 4.13 Mass Defect

The matter-antimatter collision between an electron and positron brings up an interesting question. Did the energy exist before the collision occurred? Is this a violation of the conservation of energy? Einstein had the answer with:

$$E = mc^2$$

This equation gives the *rest mass energy* of an object. For the MCAT just think of rest mass energy as latent energy within the mass of an object. It will only appear on the MCAT if mass is created or destroyed. Otherwise, never even think about rest mass energy. If mass is created or destroyed, always use $E = mc^2$ to find the answer, where $m$ represents the amount of mass created or destroyed and c is the speed of light ($3 \times 10^8$ m/s). The forces holding the nucleons (protons and neutrons) together are the result of a change in the rest mass energy of the individual nucleons. In other words, if we measured the mass of the nucleons before forming the nucleus of an atom, and then measured the mass of the nucleus, there would be a discrepancy; the nucleus would have less mass than the sum of the masses of its individual parts. The difference in the masses is called the **mass defect**. To find the binding energy holding the nucleons together, plug the mass defect into $E = mc^2$.

**Figure 4.8   A Nucleus Has Less Mass Than the Sum of the Masses of Its Individual Parts**

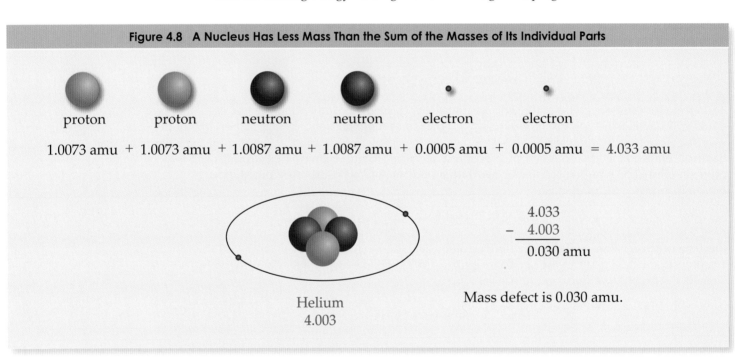

proton        proton        neutron        neutron        electron        electron

1.0073 amu  +  1.0073 amu  +  1.0087 amu  +  1.0087 amu  +  0.0005 amu  +  0.0005 amu  =  4.033 amu

Helium
4.003

$$\begin{array}{r} 4.033 \\ -\ 4.003 \\ \hline 0.030 \text{ amu} \end{array}$$

Mass defect is 0.030 amu.

*Notes:*

## 4.14 Fission and Fusion

**Fusion** is the combining of two nuclei to form a single heavier nucleus. **Fission** is the splitting of a single nucleus to form two lighter nuclei. How can large amounts of energy be released in both processes? The energy comes from the mass defect. If we think of the binding energy as a bond, we know that energy must be added in order to break a bond (including ATP bonds). Thus, when we make a bond in fusion, we can see from where the energy can come; energy is always released when a bond is formed. The energy comes from the bonds between the nucleons in the new nucleus. These new bonds are stronger and more stable than those of the nucleus that was just divided. Thus more energy was released in the formation of the stronger bonds than was absorbed in the breaking of the weaker bonds.

The most stable nuclei have the strongest binding energy per nucleon. Both fission and fusion produce more stable nuclei. The graph in Figure 4.9 shows an approximation.

**Figure 4.9  Stronger Binding Energy Per Nucleon Makes for a More Stable Nucleus**

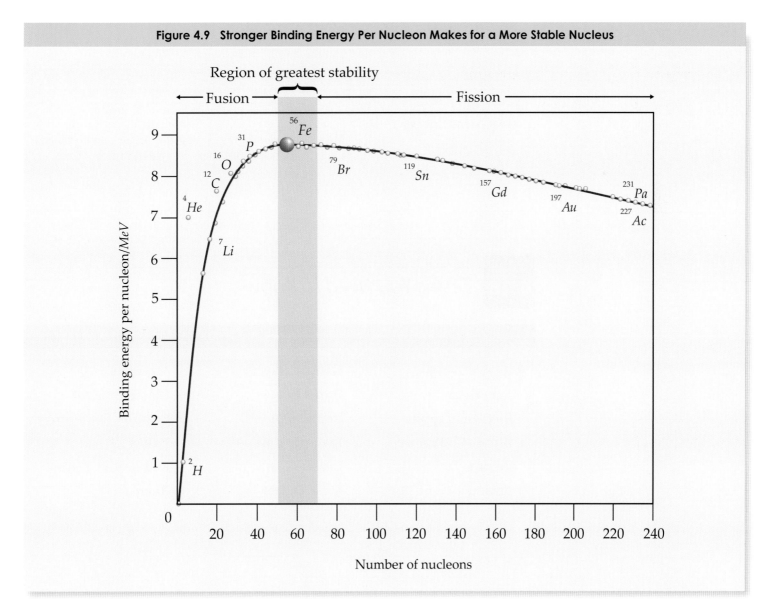

## 4.15 Equation Summary

| | Equations |
|---|---|
| **Momentum** $$p = mv$$ | Momentum is a measure of a moving object's tendency to continue along its present path. |
| **Elastic Collisions** $$U_{intitial} + K_{intitial} = U_{final} + K_{final}$$ | Mechanical energy is conserved. In an elastic collision, no energy is dissipated to internal energy. |
| **Inelastic Collisions** $$p_{initial} = p_{final}$$ | Mechanical energy is not conserved. In an inelastic collision, some energy is dissipated to internal energy. |
| **Impulse** $$J = \Delta p$$ $$J = F_{avg}\,\Delta t$$ $$\Delta mv = F_{avg}\,\Delta t$$ | The average force on either colliding body. To find the average force from the change in momentum simply put the two impulse equations together. |
| **Rest Mass Energy** $$E = mc^2$$ | This is the latent energy within the mass of an object. Only think about it if mass is created or destroyed. |

## 4.16 Terms You Need to Know

| Terms | | |
|---|---|---|
| Alpha Decay | Gamma Ray | Machines |
| Beta Decay | Half-Life | Momentum ($p$) |
| Electron Capture | Impulse ($J$) | Positron Emission |
| Elastic Collision | Inelastic Collision | Pulley |
| Fission | Lever | Radioactive Decay |
| Fusion | Mass Defect | Ramp |

**89.** The half-life of substance X is 45 years, and it decomposes to substance Y. A sample from a meteorite was taken which contained 1.5% of X and 13.5% of Y by mass. If substance Y is not normally found on a meteorite, what is the approximate age of the meteorite?

- **A.** 45 years
- **B.** 100 years
- **C.** 140 years
- **D.** 270 years

**90.** When $^{224}$Ra undergoes alpha decay an alpha particle is emitted at $1.0 \times 10^7$ m/s. What is the velocity of the other particle?

- **A.** $1.6 \times 10^4$ m/s
- **B.** $1.8 \times 10^5$ m/s
- **C.** $1.8 \times 10^6$ m/s
- **D.** $5.4 \times 10^6$ m/s

**91.** In nuclear fission, a uranium nucleus combines with a neutron, becomes unstable, and splits into Ce and Zr plus two neutrons. The change in the mass of the interacting parts is 0.211 amu. How much energy is released in this reaction? (Note: $c^2 = 931.5$ MeV/amu)

- **A.** 98 MeV
- **B.** 130 MeV
- **C.** 157 MeV
- **D.** 197 MeV

**92.** $^{216}$Po undergoes two alpha decays and two beta decays to form:

- **A.** $^{208}$Tl
- **B.** $^{224}$Ra
- **C.** $^{212}$Pb
- **D.** $^{208}$Pb

**93.** Which of the following graphs best represents the radioactive decay of $^{238}$U?

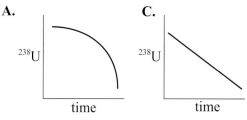
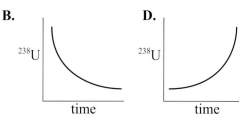

**94.** A diagram showing the changing mass of an unstable isotope undergoing radioactive decay over time is shown below. What is the half-life of the isotope?

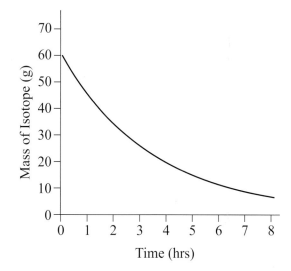

- **A.** 1.5 hours
- **B.** 2.5 hours
- **C.** 4.0 hours
- **D.** 6.0 hours

**95.** Which of the sequences below could describe the decay process from $^{210}$Bi to $^{206}$Pb?

    **A.**    alpha, beta
    **B.**    beta, beta
    **C.**    alpha, alpha
    **D.**    beta, beta, beta

**96.** The mass number of an atom undergoing radioactive decay will remain unchanged in all of the processes below EXCEPT:

    **A.**    alpha decay.
    **B.**    beta decay.
    **C.**    electron capture.
    **D.**    gamma emission.

# FLUIDS AND SOLIDS

## 5.1    Fluids

Most substances can be classified as either a solid or a fluid. The molecules of a solid are held in place by molecular bonds that can permanently resist a force from any direction. A **fluid** is a liquid or gas. Unlike a solid, any existing molecular bonds in a fluid are constantly breaking and reforming due to the high kinetic energy of the molecules. Since the molecules of a fluid are not arranged with any order or structure, but move about in random directions relative to each other, a fluid has only temporal (impermanent) resistance to forces that are not perpendicular to its surface. However, since fluid molecules require room to move, collectively they can create a permanent force outward from within the fluid. This outward force allows a fluid to permanently withstand forces perpendicular to its surface. In other words, the only permanent force that a resting fluid can exert is one normal to its surface. Thus, a fluid is pushed and molded until its surface matches the shape of its container exactly. When the fluid comes to rest, it experiences only the normal force from the surface of its container and the force of gravity. (A liquid takes on a flat upper surface so that the gravitational force is also perpendicular. In a gas, gravity has an insignificant effect on the path of an individual molecule due to the high average velocity of the molecules, and a gas will fill an enclosed container.)

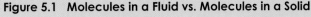

**Figure 5.1    Molecules in a Fluid vs. Molecules in a Solid**

Molecules of a fluid bond weakly and rotate, spin, and move past each other.

Molecules of a solid bond strongly and vibrate in a fixed position.

In other words, a fluid conforms to the shape of its container. The ocean, a fluid, will withstand the weight of a motionless battleship forever by conforming its surface to that of the battleship's so that all forces are normal to its surface. However, the ship can move through the water propelled by a much smaller force than its own weight. This is because the net force from the moving ship is not perpendicular to the surface of the water and thus the water provides only temporal resistance. (The forces shown in the diagram are the forces on the water due to the ship, and are not meant to represent the forces on the ship.)

In particle mechanics we discussed mass and energy. These properties were useful because we knew exactly how much substance with which we were dealing. <u>Ex</u>ternally, we could view the entire object and measure these properties. Properties such as these, which are concerned with quantity, are called *extensive properties*. Extensive properties change with the quantity of a substance. In fluid mechanics, we often don't know how much there is of a given fluid, thus we cannot measure its mass or energy. In order to analyze such fluids we use *intensive properties* or properties that are concerned with the intrinsic nature of a substance. Intensive properties do not change with the quantity of a substance. The two intensive properties that are analogous to mass and energy are, respectively, density and pressure.

## 5.2    Density

**Density (ρ)** is the 'heaviness' of a fluid; it is how much mass it contains in a specified volume (*V*). The formula for density is:

$$\rho = \frac{m}{V}$$

The S.I. units of density are kg/m³. Notice that changing the amount of a given substance will not change the density of that substance. Compression of a fluid changes its volume without changing its mass, and therefore will change density. Since gases compress more easily than liquids, the density of a gas is easily changed while that of a liquid is not. Unless otherwise indicated, for the MCAT, assume that all liquids and solids are totally incompressible, and thus have constant density. In reality, gases are far more compressible than liquids, and liquids are far more compressible than solids. Gases on the MCAT change their volume (and thus their density) as per the ideal gas law: $PV = nRT$.

We have a strong intuition about the concept of mass because we use it everyday; however, few of us have a strong sense of density. For instance, you can appreciate how it feels to lift a 13 kg mass (about 29 pounds), but can you lift a bucket full of mercury, which has a density of about 13,600 kg/m$^3$? Most of us have no idea. We just don't know density well enough.

In order to make density a more intuitive concept, specific gravity was created. The **specific gravity (S.G.)** of a substance is the density of that substance ($\rho_{substance}$) compared to the density of water ($\rho_{water}$).

$$\text{S.G.} = \frac{\rho_{substance}}{\rho_{water}}$$

Notice that a specific gravity of less than one indicates a substance lighter than water; a specific gravity of one indicates a substance equally as heavy as water; a specific gravity greater than one indicates a substance heavier than water. Since we all have an intuitive feel for the heaviness of water, we can relate this to a substance if we know its specific gravity. The specific gravity of mercury is 13.6, so lifting one bucket of mercury would be equivalent to lifting 13.6 buckets of water.

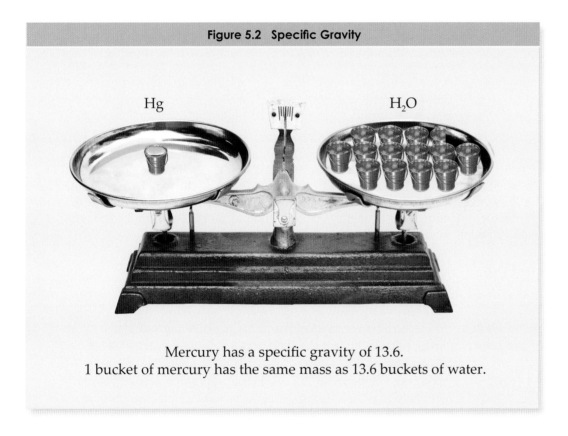

**Figure 5.2 Specific Gravity**

Hg                    H$_2$O

Mercury has a specific gravity of 13.6.
1 bucket of mercury has the same mass as 13.6 buckets of water.

For the MCAT you should memorize the density of water in the following two forms:

$$\rho_{water} = 1000 \text{ kg/m}^3$$

$$\rho_{water} = 1 \text{ g/cm}^3$$

## 5.3 Pressure

Recall our discussion about impulse from Lecture 4. Impulse is the change in momentum, or the force of a collision multiplied by the duration of the collision ($F\Delta t$).

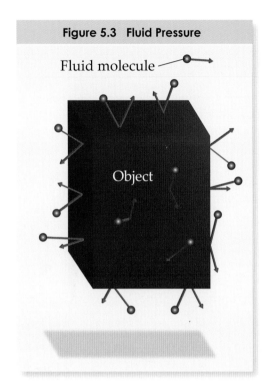

**Figure 5.3 Fluid Pressure**

Fluid molecule

Object

Since the millions of molecules in a fluid are moving rapidly in random directions, some will collide with an object submerged in that fluid. In any given time $t$, such a submerged object will experience millions of collisions. If we measure the magnitude of the impulse of each collision and divide it by the time over which the collisions occur, we arrive at the average magnitude of force created by the collisions. Since the molecules are moving in random directions and at random speeds, no single direction or speed will be more likely than any other, and the force on one side of the object will be exactly countered by the force on its other side. (We will ignore gravity for the moment and we will also assume that if the fluid is moving, the object is moving at the same velocity as the fluid.) If we take the average magnitude of the force and divide it by the area over which the collisions are taking place (the surface area of the object), we have the pressure experienced by the object. This is the **fluid pressure**. Fluid pressure results from the impulse of molecular collisions. It is the average of the magnitudes of the change in momentum of these collisions divided by the time duration of the collisions and the area over which these collisions occur. Pressure ($P$) is defined as force ($F$) per unit area ($A$).

$$P = \frac{F}{A}$$

The S.I. unit of pressure is the **Pascal (Pa)**. Pressure is a scalar; it has no direction. Pressure exists in a fluid whether or not an object is immersed in that fluid.

Another way to think of fluid pressure is as a measure of the kinetic energy due to the random velocities of molecules within a fluid distributed over the fluid volume. The units of pressure are equivalent to energy per unit volume. So pressure can be thought of as a type of 'stored' energy per unit volume.

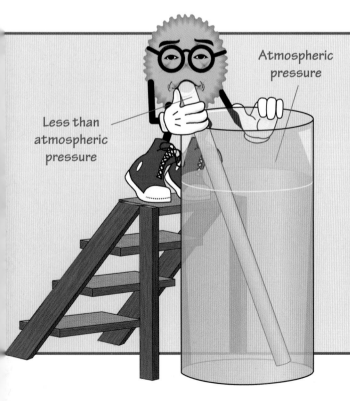

Atmospheric pressure

Less than atmospheric pressure

Biologists often talk about negative pressure created in your chest when you suck in air. If you think of the molecular collision model of pressure (Chemistry Lecture 2), you will realize that negative pressure is impossible. It would indicate less than zero collisions; an absurdity. The negative pressure that biologists refer to in the chest cavity is **gauge pressure**. Gauge pressure is a measure of the pressure compared to local atmospheric pressure. In other words, local atmospheric pressure is arbitrarily given a value of zero. So when a biologist says there is negative pressure inside your chest, there is still pressure in your chest; it is just less pressure than atmospheric pressure. The higher pressure of the atmosphere pushes air into your lungs. The same thing happens when you 'suck' fluid through a straw. You create a partial vacuum inside the straw. But a vacuum doesn't really 'suck' anything into it. The atmospheric pressure pushes down on the fluid outside the straw pushing up the fluid inside the straw. Without atmospheric pressure, a straw would not work. Just remember, in real life, **physics never sucks**.

# *Fluids at Rest*

A fluid at rest is one that is experiencing forces only perpendicular to its surface. At any given depth, the pressure is equal to the weight of the fluid above a disk with area *A* divided by the area of the disk. Notice from the diagram that the pressure is independent of the area chosen.

For a fluid at rest with uniform density in a sealed container, pressure *P* is given by:

$$P = \rho g y$$

where ρ is the density of the fluid, *g* is the gravitational constant, and *y* is the depth of the fluid.

**Figure 5.4   The Weight of a Fluid Creates the Fluid Pressure**

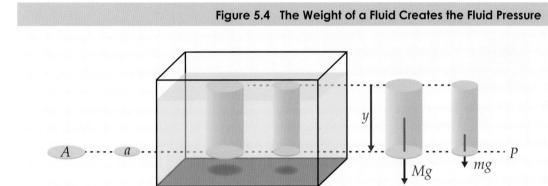

$$P = \frac{Mg}{A} = \frac{mg}{a} = \rho g y$$

Since fluid pressure is simply weight divided by area, additional fluids on top of the first fluid simply add their weight toward the total pressure. The total pressure can be found by summing the pressures due to each fluid as shown in Figure 5.4.

Air is a fluid. If we open our sealed container and expose it to the atmosphere, we must add atmospheric pressure to any point in our fluid. In any fluid open to the atmosphere, the pressure can be found from $P = \rho g y + P_{atm}$. (Note: If you are using meters and kilograms, you must measure the atmospheric pressure in pascals (Pa). $P_{atmospheric} = 101{,}000$ Pa)

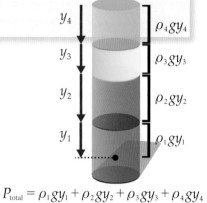

$$P_{total} = \rho_1 g y_1 + \rho_2 g y_2 + \rho_3 g y_3 + \rho_4 g y_4$$

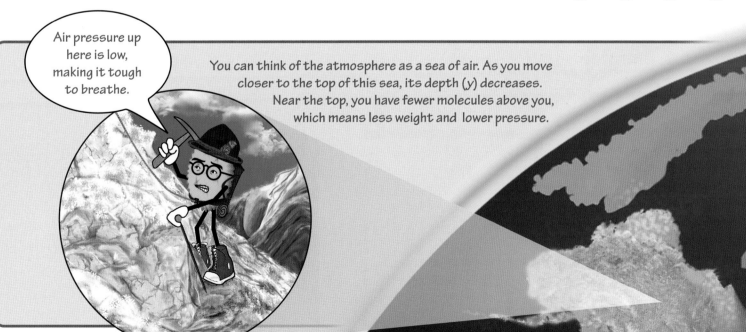

Air pressure up here is low, making it tough to breathe.

You can think of the atmosphere as a sea of air. As you move closer to the top of this sea, its depth (*y*) decreases. Near the top, you have fewer molecules above you, which means less weight and lower pressure.

Since fluid pressure is a function of depth, the shape of the container does not affect it. The pressure everywhere at a given depth in the same resting fluid will be constant.

Just as each block in a stack of blocks must bear the weight of all the blocks above it, each point in an enclosed fluid must bear any increase in pressure.

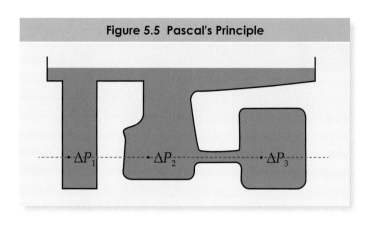

**Figure 5.5  Pascal's Principle**

This is called **Pascal's principle**. Pascal's principle states that pressure applied anywhere to an enclosed incompressible fluid will be distributed undiminished throughout that fluid. Notice that Pascal's principle does not apply to a gas because a gas is compressible.

## 5.5  Hydraulic Lift

The **hydraulic lift** is a simple machine that works via Pascal's principle. A force on piston 1 acts to apply a pressure on the incompressible fluid. This pressure is transferred undiminished to piston 2. Since piston 2 has a greater area than piston 1, the force on piston 2 is proportionally greater. However, recall that an ideal machine does not change work. Thus, the distance through which the force is applied is proportionally less.

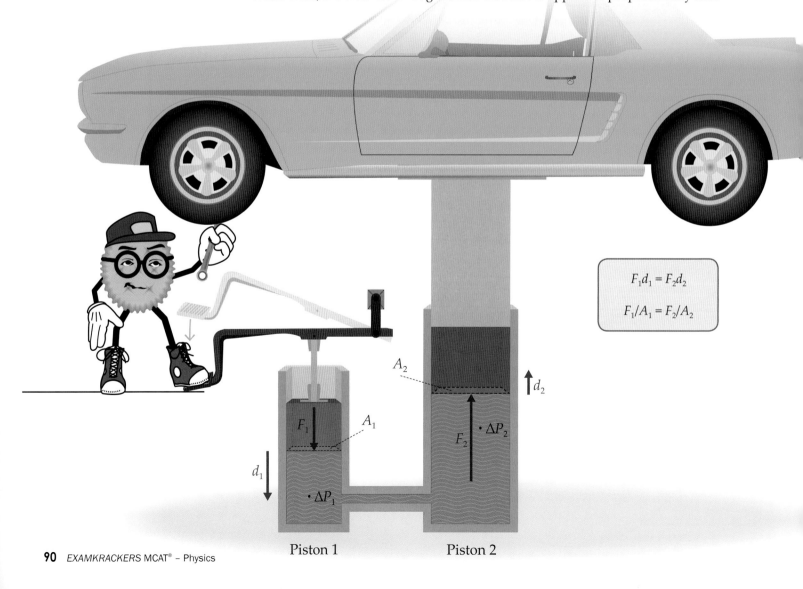

$$F_1 d_1 = F_2 d_2$$

$$F_1/A_1 = F_2/A_2$$

## 5.6 Archimedes' Principle

In the 3$^{rd}$ century B.C., the king of Syracuse was given a crown and told that it was solid gold. Archimedes was given the task of proving or disproving that the crown was solid gold. Archimedes knew the density of gold and decided to find the density of the crown. To find the volume of the crown, he submerged it into a bucket of water and measured the amount of water displaced. He then weighed the crown and divided its mass by its volume. The density of the crown was not the density of gold; Archimedes had proven that the crown was a fake.

This story reminds us that an object submerged in a fluid displaces a volume of fluid equal to its own volume. Before the object is submerged, the upward force on the fluid that it will displace must equal the weight of that fluid ($F_{\text{buoyant}} = mg_{\text{water}}$). Once the object is submerged, the net upward force remains, but the fluid is gone, replaced by the object. Thus the upward force acts on the submerged object. This force is called the buoyant force. Archimedes' principle says that the **buoyant force ($F_b$)** is an upward force acting on a submerged object, and is equal to the weight of the fluid displaced by the submerged object. The buoyant force is given by:

$$F_b = \rho_{\text{fluid}} V g$$

where $V$ is the volume of the displaced fluid. The buoyant force is always equal to the weight of the displaced fluid. In Figures 5.6 and 5.7 the buoyant force is $F_{\text{buoyant}}$.

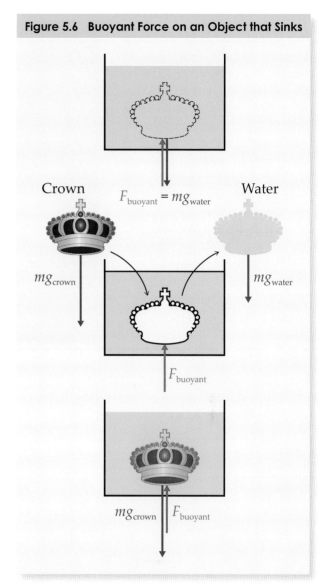

**Figure 5.6   Buoyant Force on an Object that Sinks**

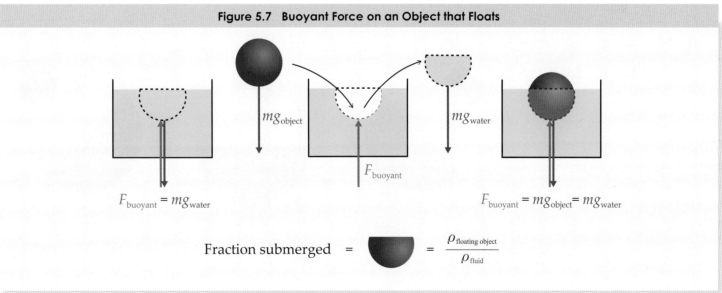

**Figure 5.7   Buoyant Force on an Object that Floats**

A *floating* object displaces an amount of fluid equal to its own weight. The *floating equation* says that the submerged fraction of a floating object is equal to the ratio of the density of the object to the density of the fluid in which it is floating. If the object is floating in water, this ratio is the specific gravity of the floating object.

Another way to understand the buoyant force is as a result of the pressure difference between the upper and lower surfaces of a submerged object. Since pressure increases with depth, the lower surface of an object experiences greater pressure than the upper surface. This pressure difference multiplied by the upper or lower surface area is equal to the buoyant force.

A fully submerged object displaces its volume in fluid; a floating object displaces its weight in fluid.

$$F_b = \rho V g$$
$$V = A\Delta h$$
$$\therefore F_b = \rho g A \Delta h$$
$$\frac{F_b}{A} = \rho g \Delta h$$
$$\Delta P = \rho g \Delta h$$

Make sure that you understand that since the buoyant force is due to the 'difference' in pressure, the buoyant force does not change with depth.

If we consider an object to be a single particle, the buoyant force acts at the *center of buoyancy*. The center of buoyancy is the point where the center of mass would be if the object had a uniform density. If the object is not uniformly dense, the center of mass and the center of buoyancy will not coincide. This could create a torque on the object and cause it to spin as shown in Figure 5.8. Center of buoyancy explains why a fishing bobber always floats upright.

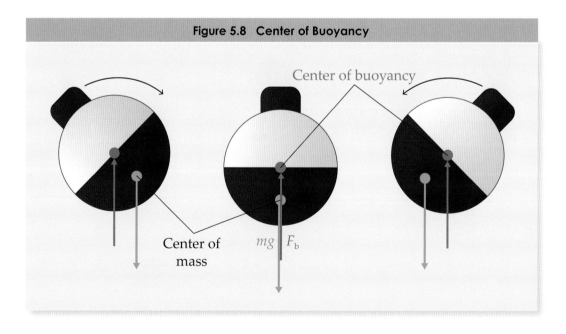

**Figure 5.8   Center of Buoyancy**

**97.** Mercury has specific gravity of 13.6. The column of mercury in the barometer below has a height $h = 76$ cm. If a similar barometer were made with water, what would be the approximate height $h$ of the column of water?

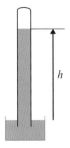

- A.    5.6 cm
- B.    76 cm
- C.    154 cm
- D.    1034 cm

**98.** Two identical discs sit at the bottom of a 3 m pool of water whose surface is exposed to atmospheric pressure. The first disc acts as a plug to seal the drain as shown. The second disc covers a container containing nearly a perfect vacuum. If each disc has an area of 1 m², what is the approximate difference in the force necessary to open the containers? (Note: 1 atm = 101,300 Pa)

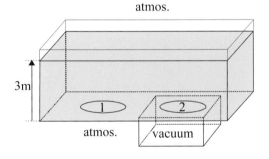

- A.    There is no difference.
- B.    3000 N
- C.    101,300 N
- D.    104,300 N

**99.** A brick with a density of $1.4 \times 10^3$ kg/m³ is placed on top of a piece of Styrofoam floating on water. If one half the volume of the Styrofoam sinks below the water, what is the ratio of the volume of the Styrofoam compared to the volume of the brick? (Assume the Styrofoam is massless.)

- A.    0.7
- B.    1.4
- C.    2.8
- D.    5.6

**100.** A helium balloon will rise into the atmosphere until:

- A.    The temperature of the helium inside the balloon is equal to the temperature of the air outside the balloon.
- B.    The mass of the helium inside the balloon is equal to the mass of the air outside the balloon.
- C.    The volume of the helium is equal to the volume of the air it displaces.
- D.    The density of the helium in the balloon is equal to the density of the air surrounding the balloon.

**101.** A child's bathtub toy has a density of 0.45 g/cm³. What fraction of the toy floats above the water?

- A.    5%
- B.    45%
- C.    55%
- D.    95%

**102.** The diagram below shows a hydraulic lift. A force is applied at side 1 and an output force is generated at side 2. Which of the following is true?

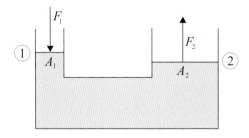

- A.    The force at side 1 is greater than the force at side 2.
- B.    The force at side 1 is less than the force at side 2.
- C.    The pressure at side 1 is greater than the force at side 2.
- D.    The pressure at side 1 is less than the pressure at side 2.

**103.** The pressure at the bottom of a cylindrical tube filled with water was measured to be 5000 Pa. If the water in the tube were replaced with ethyl alcohol, what would be the new pressure at the bottom of the tube? (The density of ethyl alcohol is 0.8 g/cm$^3$.)

A.   4000 Pa
B.   4800 Pa
C.   5000 Pa
D.   6250 Pa

**104.** Three containers are filled with water to a depth of 1 meter. At the bottom of which container is the pressure the greatest?

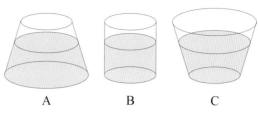

A B C

A.   Container A
B.   Container B
C.   Container C
D.   The pressure is the same at the bottom of all the containers.

## 5.7 Fluids in Motion

The molecules of a moving fluid can be thought of as having two types of motion:

1.  the **random translational motion** that contributes to fluid pressure as in a fluid at rest and;
2.  a **uniform translational motion** shared equally by all the molecules at a given location in a fluid.

The uniform translational motion is the motion of the fluid as a whole. This motion does not contribute to fluid pressure. If we recall our molecular model of fluid pressure, an object moving along with the fluid will not experience additional collisions due to this uniform translational motion. Thus, it will not experience any additional pressure. In fact, the energy from the two types of motion can be converted back and forth; some of the random translational motion can be converted to uniform translational motion and vice versa. For instance, if we remove a portion of the wall of a container holding a fluid at rest, the fluid will move through the opening. This happens because the molecules moving in the direction of the opening do not collide with anything, but instead continue in their present direction. Some of the random motion has changed to uniform motion. Since there are fewer collisions in the fluid moving through the opening, there is less pressure. We will come back to this point later in this lecture.

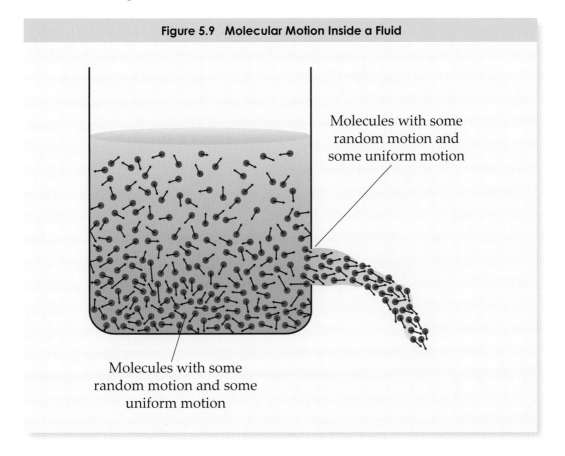

**Figure 5.9 Molecular Motion Inside a Fluid**

Molecules with some random motion and some uniform motion

Molecules with some random motion and some uniform motion

## 5.8 | Ideal Fluid

Because moving fluids are very complicated, it is useful to create a hypothetical fluid which lacks certain characteristics of real fluids. This hypothetical fluid is called **ideal fluid**. Ideal fluid differs from real fluids in the following four ways:

1. Ideal fluid has **no viscosity**. Viscosity is a measure of a fluid's temporal resistance to forces not perpendicular to its surface. (More precisely, viscosity is the rate of shear stress divided by the rate of strain.) For the MCAT, think of a fluid's viscosity as its tendency to resist flow. For example, syrup has greater viscosity than water. A closely related concept to viscosity is drag. *Drag* is a force, similar to friction, created by viscosity and pressure due to motion. Drag always opposes the motion of an object through a fluid.

2. Ideal fluid is **incompressible**; it has uniform density. This is the same assumption that we make for any liquid on the MCAT unless otherwise indicated, but not for gasses.

3. Ideal fluid lacks *turbulence*; it experiences steady (or *laminar*) flow. Steady flow means that all fluid flowing through any fixed point will have the same velocity. Remember, velocity specifies magnitude and direction. Turbulence means that, at any fixed point in the fluid, the velocity may vary with time.

4. Ideal fluids experience *irrotational flow*. This means that any object moving with the ideal fluid will not rotate about its axis as it flows, but will continue to point in one direction regardless of the direction of flow. The MCAT is not likely to touch this one.

No ideal fluid actually exists. However, we can use ideal fluid to make crude predictions about real fluids. We do this by imagining how ideal fluid would behave in a given situation, and then considering how the above characteristics would affect this behavior. On the MCAT, all liquids are ideal, unless otherwise indicated.

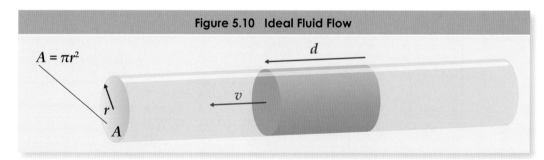

**Figure 5.10   Ideal Fluid Flow**

Since ideal fluids are incompressible, their volume remains constant. The volume of a fluid moving through a section of pipe is given by the cross-sectional area ($A$) of the pipe times the distance ($d$) of the pipe section. If this same volume of fluid moves completely through this pipe section in a given time ($t$), the rate ($Q$) at which volume passes through the pipe is $Ad/t$. Since the fluid moves a distance $d$ in time t, its velocity is $v = d/t$. Putting these two equations together we get the **continuity equation**:

$$Q = Av$$

where $Q$ is called the '**volume flow rate**'. Flow can be given in terms of mass as well. For the mass flow rate ($I$) multiply the volume flow rate by density:

$$I = \rho Q = \rho Av$$

**In an ideal fluid, flow rate is constant.** Notice from these equations that area is inversely proportional to velocity; the narrower the pipe, the greater the velocity.

A second important equation that you must memorize for the MCAT is **Bernoulli's equation**:

$$P + \rho g h + \frac{1}{2}\rho v^2 = K$$

Where $K$ is a constant specific to a fluid in a given situation of flow, and $P$, $h$, and $v$ refer to the pressure, height, and velocity of the fluid at any given point. (**Warning**: $h$ is not the same as $y$ in $P = \rho g y$. $h$ is the distance *above* some arbitrary point; $y$ is the distance beneath the surface.) Bernoulli's equation states that, given one continuous ideal flow, the sum of its three terms is a constant at any point in the fluid. If we look closely at Bernoulli's equation, we see that it is actually a restatement of conservation of energy. Notice that if we multiply any of the terms by volume, we get units of energy. In fact, the second term gives the gravitational potential energy per unit volume ($mgh/V$). The third term gives the kinetic energy from the uniform translational motion of the molecules per unit volume (($\frac{1}{2}mv^2)/V$). The first term, pressure, is the energy per volume from the random motion of the molecules. Because energy is conserved in ideal fluid flow, the total energy must remain constant; thus, the sum of the three terms is constant throughout the fluid. This is an easy method for remembering Bernoulli's equation. This also aids our understanding of the terms. For instance, the h in the second term is similar to the $h$ in gravitational potential energy; the zero value for $h$ can be chosen arbitrarily. Like the $h$ term in gravitational potential energy, it is measured from bottom to top. Notice this is the opposite direction of measurement for the $y$ term in hydrostatic pressure: $P = \rho g y$. Also, recall the equation that predicts the velocity of a body in free fall when all of its potential energy is converted to kinetic energy. You may see that Bernoulli's equation predicts the same result for a fluid. If a spigot attached to a tank of fluid is opened, and we choose $h = 0$ to be the point of the spigot, the velocity of the fluid coming from the spigot can be derived from Bernoulli's equation as:

$$v = \sqrt{2gh}$$

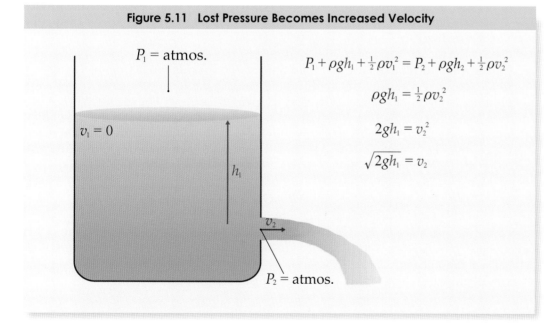

**Figure 5.11   Lost Pressure Becomes Increased Velocity**

A helpful analogy might be to think about a swarm of bees. Imagine that the swarm represents a fluid with each bee as a fluid molecule. Bee stings represent pressure-causing collisions. Now if I stand still in the swarm, it's going to hurt. The bees can swarm around and sting me at their leisure. I'm going to get stung a lot; this is analogous to lots of molecular collisions and high pressure. But if I run, each bee must use some of its swarming energy to keep up with me. Therefore, they can't swarm as much, and I won't get stung as often. Fewer stings is analagous to less pressure. The same is true with molecules in a fluid; uniform translational kinetic energy is achieved by borrowing energy from the random translational kinetic energy, thus pressure decreases.

From Bernoulli's equation we can derive an important (and possibly counter-intuitive) notion about the relationship between pressure and velocity in ideal fluid flow. As velocity increases, pressure decreases.

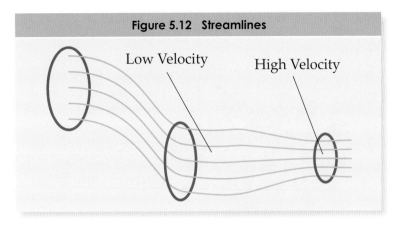

**Figure 5.12 Streamlines**

Low Velocity

High Velocity

The concept of *streamlines* was created to assist in the visualization of an ideal fluid. A streamline is a path followed by a hypothetical fluid particle. This particle follows only the uniform translational motion of the moving fluid. The magnitude and direction can change from one point to the next, but its velocity at any fixed point will remain the same. The velocity of the particle at any point along a streamline is tangent to the curve made by the streamline. The magnitude of the velocity is inversely related to the distance between streamlines; the closer the streamlines, the greater the velocity. Streamlines can never intersect, since this would indicate two possible velocities for the same fixed point. A group of streamlines three-dimensionally encompass a *tube of flow*.

## 5.9 Non-ideal Fluids (Real Fluids)

All real fluids are **non-ideal**. The MCAT only requires that you understand non-ideal fluids qualitatively. This means that you must predict the general deviation to ideal fluid when we add the first three of the four lacking characteristics. (Irrotational flow will not be on the MCAT.)

*Drag* and viscosity are like friction and always act to impede flow. Increasing viscosity increases drag. Drag occurs at the fluid-object interface and is a force working against flow. As we move away from the fluid-object interface the effect of drag lessens. In a real fluid flowing through a pipe, the greatest velocity would be at the center of the pipe, the spot furthest from the fluid-object interface. You can remember this general rule about drag by recalling the dusty blades of a well-used fan. The dust on the fan blade remains despite the high speed of the fan. This is because the air immediately adjacent to the fan moves extremely slowly or not at all due to drag. Because the sides of the pipe create the greatest drag, the longer the pipe, the greater the amount of fluid-object interface, and the greater is the resistance to flow. Also notice that if the radius of a pipe is reduced by a factor of 2, the fluid volume ($V = \pi r^2 d$) is reduced by a factor of 4, but the surface area is only cut in half ($A = 2\pi r d$). Thus, the more narrow the pipe, the greater the effect of drag.

Notice from the tube of flow that fluid does not necessarily move from high pressure to low pressure. Pressure has no direction. The driving force behind the direction of fluid flow is the fluid's tendency to find its greatest entropy. For the MCAT, just use common sense. Ask yourself in which direction you would expect the fluid to flow. If all other things are equal, fluid will move from high pressure to low pressure. In a horizontal pipe of constant cross-sectional area, fluid will flow from high pressure to low pressure according to the following equation:

$$\Delta P = QR$$

where $R$ is the resistance to flow. In Physics Lecture 7, we will discuss the similarity of this equation to Ohm's law for voltage and the analogy of pressure to voltage. The volume flow rate for real fluid in a horizontal pipe with constant cross-sectional area can also be given in terms of pressure, viscosity ($\eta$), pipe length ($L$), and pipe radius ($r$):

$$Q = \Delta P \frac{\pi r^4}{8\eta L}$$

This equation is known as *Poiseuille's Law*. It is given here because it is a common equation and you should recognize that it is concerned with real fluids, not ideal fluids.

**Warning:** a non-ideal fluid does not behave in an opposite manner to an ideal fluid. Narrowing a pipe increases the velocity of an ideal fluid. It will probably increase the velocity of a non-ideal fluid as well. However, with a non-ideal fluid you must also consider drag, which impedes flow. Thus, if you narrow the pipe in a non-ideal fluid, velocity will probably increase, but not as much as if there were no drag.

# 5.10 A Method for Greater Understanding of Fluid Flow

As stated earlier, Bernoulli's equation describes conservation of energy within an ideal fluid. If each term in Bernoulli's equation is divided by the specific weight $\rho g$ of the fluid, the units of each new term become meters. Each new term is referred to as a '*head*'. $\rho g h$ becomes $h$, and is called the *elevation head*. ½ $\rho v^2$ becomes ½ $v^2/g$, and is called the *velocity head*. $P$ becomes $P/(\rho g)$, and is called the *pressure* head. We shall refer to the original terms by the heads, but, for simplicity, we shall not divide by the specific weight.

If we examine the figure below, a hypothetical fluid particle at the top of the tank is stationary. Its energy is completely contained as gravitational potential energy. The height of the fluid at this point is its elevation head. The zero point is arbitrary, so we will choose the floor. The velocity and pressure heads are zero because the particle is at zero velocity and zero gauge pressure. Since energy is conserved in ideal fluid flow, the sum of the three heads (the *piezometric head*) always measures to this same value. An *energy line (EL)* can be drawn horizontally at this level. The *piezometer tube* measures the piezometric head. A *static pressure tap* measures the pressure head and the elevation head, but not the velocity head. The *hydraulic gradient line (HGL)* can be drawn along the top of the static pressure taps.

With this knowledge, you can use the continuity equation ($Q = Av$) to better understand fluid flow. The difference between the piezometric tube and the static pressure tap is the velocity head. The top of the elevation head is at the center of mass of the moving fluid. In Figure 5.13, the displacement from where the elevation head ends to where the velocity head begins is the pressure head. If that displacement is downward, there is negative guage pressure. Notice if a static pressure tap were placed at a position where there is negative guage pressure, atmospheric pressure would push air into the fluid.

In a real fluid, the energy line drops as the fluid progresses.

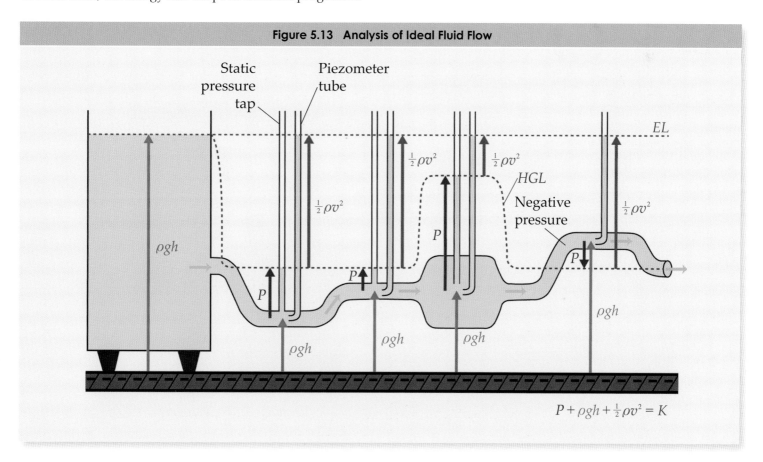

**Figure 5.13  Analysis of Ideal Fluid Flow**

$$P + \rho g h + \tfrac{1}{2}\rho v^2 = K$$

## 5.11 | *Surface Tension*

You should understand surface tension qualitatively for the MCAT. Any formula will be provided with a passage.

Although more dense than water, a tiny needle can be made to float on the surface of water. The force supporting the needle is not the buoyant force; no water is displaced. The force supporting the needle is created by surface tension. **Surface tension** is the intensity of the intermolecular forces per unit length. Much like a spring, when the molecules at the surface of the water are pushed downward by the weight of the needle, the intermolecular bonds of the water are stretched, and pull upward. Surface tension is also responsible for the formation of water droplets. The **intermolecular forces** pull inward tending to minimize the surface area by creating a more spherical shape. (A sphere has the least surface area per volume of any shape.) Since surface tension is a function of the intermolecular forces, it is dependent upon the temperature of the fluid (the higher the temperature, the weaker the surface tension) and upon the fluid with which it is interfacing.

Related to surface tension is the phenomenon of *capillary action*, where a fluid may be pulled up a thin tube. For capillary action, recognize that there are two types of forces acting: the intermolecular forces responsible for surface tension (*cohesive forces*), and the forces between the molecules of the tube and the fluid molecules (*adhesive forces*). If the cohesive forces are stronger, a convex meniscus is formed and the fluid is pulled downward by the vertical component of the surface tension. If the adhesive forces are stronger, a concave meniscus is formed and the fluid is pulled upward by the vertical component of the surface tension. In Figure 5.14, the adhesive forces between water and glass are stronger than the cohesive forces between water molecules, so the water is pulled upward. In the other tube, the adhesive forces between mercury and glass are weaker than the cohesive forces between mercury molecules, so the mercury is pulled downward.

The surface tension in this water droplet is determined by the strength of its intermolecular forces, such as hydrogen bonds. These forces pull inward, minimizing the surface area and creating a spherical shape.

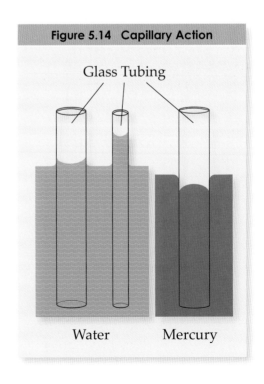

Figure 5.14 Capillary Action

Glass Tubing

Water          Mercury

Questions 105 through 112 are **NOT** based on a descriptive passage.

**105.** An ideal fluid with pressure $P$ flows through a horizontal pipe with radius $r$. If the radius of the pipe is increased by a factor of 2, which of the following most likely gives the new pressure?

- **A.** $P$
- **B.** $4P$
- **C.** $16P$
- **D.** The new pressure cannot be determined without more information.

**106.** If the container pictured below is filled with an ideal fluid, which point in the fluid most likely has the greatest pressure?

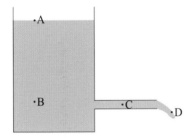

- **A.** A
- **B.** B
- **C.** C
- **D.** D

**107.** Water in moist soil rises through capillary action. The intermolecular forces between water molecules are:

- **A.** weaker than the intermolecular forces between water and soil molecules.
- **B.** equal to the intermolecular forces between water and soil molecules.
- **C.** stronger than the intermolecular forces between water and soil molecules.
- **D.** The comparative strength between the intermolecular forces cannot be determined with the information given.

**108.** All of the following would increase the volume flow rate of a fluid being pumped through a pipe EXCEPT:

- **A.** increasing the pressure difference between the ends of the pipe.
- **B.** decreasing the fluid viscosity.
- **C.** increasing the pipe radius.
- **D.** increasing the length of the pipe.

**109.** A spigot is to be placed on a water tank below the surface of the water. Which of the following gives the distance of the spigot below the surface $h$ compared to the velocity with which the water will run through the spigot?

**A.** 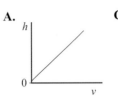   **C.**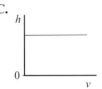

**B.** 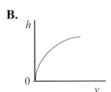   **D.**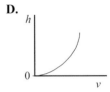

**110.** Two drops of equal volume of different substances were placed on the same flat surface. A side view of drop A and drop B is shown below.

Compared to drop B, drop A has:

- **A.** stronger intermolecular forces and lesser surface tension.
- **B.** stronger intermolecular forces and greater surface tension.
- **C.** weaker intermolecular forces and lesser surface tension.
- **D.** weaker intermolecular forces and greater surface tension.

111. The diagram below shows a cross-sectional view of a cylindrical pipe of varying diameter.

If an ideal fluid is flowing through the pipe, all of the following statements are true EXCEPT:

A.  The cross-sectional area is greater at point A than at point B.
B.  The pressure is lower at point B than at point A.
C.  The volume flow rate is greater at point A than at point B.
D.  The flow speed is greater at point B than at point A.

112. A spigot was opened at the bottom of a barrel full of water and the water was allowed to run through the spigot until the barrel was empty. Which of the following describes the speed of the water flowing through the spigot as the barrel emptied?

A.  Always decreasing
B.  Always increasing
C.  Constant
D.  Decreasing, then increasing

In Chemistry Lecture 4, we discussed the different structures of a solid. In general, atoms or molecules tend to be held together rigidly. However, all solids are, to some extent, elastic. In other words, they can change their dimensions by stretching or compressing, but not breaking, these rigid bonds. To discuss the elasticity of solids we must understand two concepts: stress and strain.

Stress is the force applied to an object divided by the area over which the force is applied. It has the same units as pressure but by convention we use $N/m^2$ and not Pa in order to distinguish it from pressure.

$$\text{Stress} = \frac{F}{A}$$

Strain is the fractional change in an object's shape. Strain is a ratio of change in dimension compared to original dimension, and has no units.

$$\text{Strain} = \frac{\Delta \text{dimension}}{\text{original dimension}}$$

Stress is what is done to an object, and strain is how the object responds.

Like force and displacement in Hooke's law, stress and strain are proportional to each other. This proportionality can be given as a ratio known as the **modulus of elasticity**.

$$\text{Modulus of elasticity} = \frac{\text{stress}}{\text{strain}}$$

Up to some maximum stress, the modulus of elasticity is a constant for a specific substance. This constant is arrived at through experiment. Like Hooke's law, the maximum stress point is called the *yield point*. An object strained to its yield point will regain its shape once the stress is removed. Up to this point, the ratio of stress to strain is described accurately by the modulus of elasticity. Beyond the yield point an object will remain intact, but will not regain its original shape. The stress-strain ratio is not described accurately by the modulus when the stress exceeds the yield point. When a stress is applied that is significantly greater than the yield point, the object will break. This is called the *fracture point*.

The pig is stressed out, but we are not concerned with that kind of stress. On the MCAT, we are concerned with the stress aplied to the diving board.

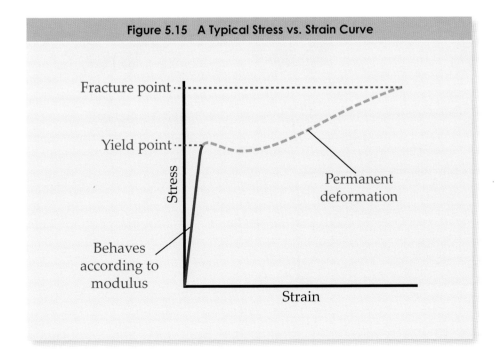

**Figure 5.15   A Typical Stress vs. Strain Curve**

Fracture point

Yield point

Permanent deformation

Stress

Behaves according to modulus

Strain

There are three separate moduli that you should know for the MCAT:

1. **Young's modulus** ($E$) for tensile stress;
2. the **shear modulus** ($G$) for shear stress; and
3. the **bulk modulus** ($B$) for compression and expansion.

All moduli work in both directions. For instance, Young's modulus works for tensile compressive forces and tensile stretching forces. Also, in each case, the force used in the equation is not the sum of the forces, which would be zero, but the magnitude of one of the forces.

**Figure 5.16   The Three Moduli of Elasticity**

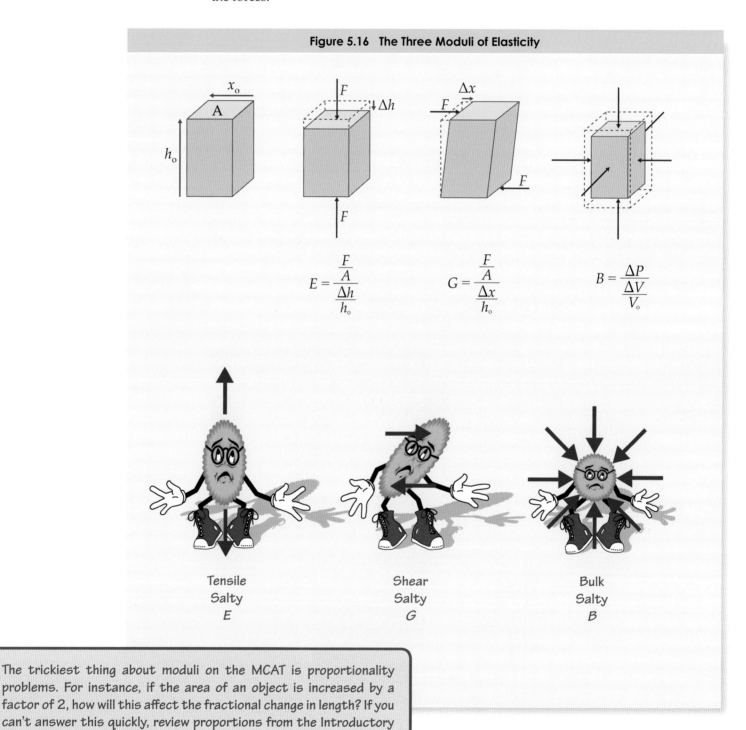

$$E = \frac{\frac{F}{A}}{\frac{\Delta h}{h_o}}$$

$$G = \frac{\frac{F}{A}}{\frac{\Delta x}{h_o}}$$

$$B = \frac{\Delta P}{\frac{\Delta V}{V_o}}$$

Tensile
Salty
E

Shear
Salty
G

Bulk
Salty
B

The trickiest thing about moduli on the MCAT is proportionality problems. For instance, if the area of an object is increased by a factor of 2, how will this affect the fractional change in length? If you can't answer this quickly, review proportions from the Introductory Lecture of this course.

## 5.13 Thermal Expansion

Solids typically expand when heated. As their molecules absorb energy, their vibrations require more room. Expansion is typically considered in one dimension (linear expansion) or three dimensions (volume expansion). The formula for linear expansion is:

$$\Delta L = L\alpha\Delta T$$

where $L$ is the original length of the object, $\Delta T$ is the change in temperature, and $\alpha$ is a constant unique to the particular substance. Notice that the change in temperature is proportional to the change in length.

The formula for volume expansion is:

$$\Delta V = V\beta\Delta T$$

where $V$ is the original volume and $\beta$ is a constant unique to the particular substance. It is a simple exercise to show that $\beta = 3\alpha$.

As this sphere is heated, the vibrations of the ball's molecules require more room to move around. This leads to expansion of the sphere.

## 5.14 Equation Summary

| Equations |
| --- |

**Fluids at Rest**

$$\rho = \frac{m}{V} \qquad \text{S.G.} = \frac{\rho_{\text{substance}}}{\rho_{\text{water}}} \qquad P = \rho g y \qquad P = \frac{F}{A}$$

**Fluids in Motion**

$$Q = Av \qquad K = P + \frac{1}{2}\rho v^2 + \rho g h \qquad v = \sqrt{2gh} \qquad \Delta P = QR$$

**Solids**

$$\text{Stress} = \frac{F}{A}$$

**Buoyant Force**

$$F_b = \rho_{\text{fluid}} V g$$

$$\text{modulus of elasticity} = \frac{\text{stress}}{\text{strain}} \qquad \text{Strain} = \frac{\Delta \text{dimension}}{\text{original dimension}}$$

## 5.15 Terms You Need to Know

| Terms |
| --- |

Bernoulli's equation

Bulk Modulus (*B*)

Buoyant Force (*F*$_b$)

Continuity Equation

Density ($\rho$)

Fluid

Fluid Pressure

Hydraulic Lift

Ideal Fluid

Modulus of Elasticity

Non-ideal

Pascal (Pa)

Pascal's Principle

Random Translational Motion

Shear Modulus (*G*)

Specific Gravity (S.G.)

Strain

Stress

Surface tension

Uniform Translational Motion

Volume Flow Rate

Young's Modulus (*E*)

**113.** If a solid will buckle under pressure greater than 12 atm, and that solid has a specific gravity of 4, what is the maximum height of a circular column made from the solid that can be built at the earth's surface? (Note: 1 atm = 101,000 Pa.)

    **A.**   4 m
    **B.**   12 m
    **C.**   24 m
    **D.**   30 m

**114.** Which of the following gives the percent change to the Young's Modulus for a substance, when its cross-sectional area is increased by a factor of 3?

    **A.**   0%
    **B.**   33%
    **C.**   300%
    **D.**   900%

**115.** The Young's modulus for bone is $9 \times 10^9$ N/m$^2$. What is the percent change in length of a tibia with a cross-sectional area of 6 cm$^2$, if it experiences a compressive force of $5.4 \times 10^3$ N?

    **A.**   0.001%
    **B.**   0.1%
    **C.**   1%
    **D.**   10%

**116.** A single steel column is to support a mass of $1.5 \times 10^8$ kg. If the yield strength for steel is $2.5 \times 10^8$ N/m$^2$ and safety regulations require the column to withstand five times the weight it presently holds, what should be the approximate cross-sectional area of the base of the column?

    **A.**   0.6 m$^2$
    **B.**   3 m$^2$
    **C.**   6 m$^2$
    **D.**   30 m$^2$

**117.** The sole of a certain tennis shoe has a shear modulus of $4 \times 10^7$. If the height of the sole is doubled, the strain will:

    **A.**   decrease by a factor of two.
    **B.**   remain the same.
    **C.**   increase by a factor of two.
    **D.**   increase by a factor of four.

Questions 118 through 119 are based on the table of Young's moduli shown below.

| Substance | Young's modulus (N/m$^2$) |
|---|---|
| Copper | $1.0 \times 10^{11}$ |
| Aluminum | $7.0 \times 10^{10}$ |
| Magnesium | $4.1 \times 10^{10}$ |
| Lead | $1.5 \times 10^{10}$ |
| Glass | $6.0 \times 10^{10}$ |

**118.** If all of the substances listed are subjected to the same stress, which one will undergo the smallest fractional change in length?

    **A.**   Copper
    **B.**   Aluminum
    **C.**   Lead
    **D.**   Glass

**119.** A glass rod is subjected to a stress and undergoes a fractional change in length of 1.0%. If a lead rod is subjected to the same stress, it will undergo a fractional change in length of:

    **A.**   0.25%
    **B.**   0.50%
    **C.**   1.0%
    **D.**   4.0%

**120.** The bulk modulus for a substance would be most important to a researcher who is testing material that will be:

    **A.**   used in high tension cables.
    **B.**   submerged deep in the ocean.
    **C.**   subjected to high temperatures.
    **D.**   transported at great speeds.

*Notes:*

# WAVES

## 6.1 Wave Characteristics

A **wave** is the transfer of momentum and energy from one point to another. There are three types of waves: mechanical, electromagnetic, and matter. Although many of the concepts discussed early in this lecture are applicable to electromagnetic and *matter* waves, these waves have some special features that will be discussed toward the end of this lecture and in Physics Lecture 8.

**Mechanical waves** obey the laws of classical physics and **require some medium** through which to travel. The medium, if it is perfectly elastic, is momentarily displaced by a wave and then returned to its original position. Such a medium is called *nondispersive* because a wave maintains its shape and does not disperse as it travels. Nondispersive waves can be considered *ideal waves*. On the MCAT assume all media to be nondispersive unless otherwise indicated.

Mechanical waves can be further separated into transverse and longitudinal waves. A **transverse wave** is one in which the medium is displaced perpendicularly to the direction of wave propagation, such as waves on a string. A **longitudinal wave** (also called a sound wave) is one in which the medium is displaced parallel to the direction of wave propagation, such as a sound wave in air.

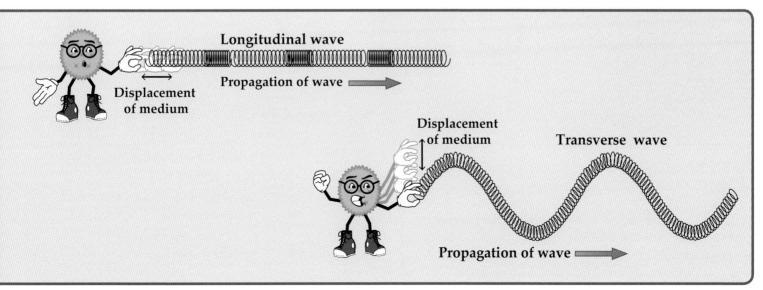

This structure is built to resemble a transverse wave.

Simple transverse and simple longitudinal waves can be represented mathematically by the sine function. For a transverse wave, the sine function represents vertical displacement of the medium with respect to time or displacement of the wave. For a longitudinal wave, a phase-shifted sine function represents either the change in pressure or the horizontal displacement of the medium with respect to the time or displacement of the wave.

If we examine this mathematical representation of a wave, when the x-axis is displacement of the wave, the **wavelength (λ)** is measured from any point in the wave to the point where the wave begins to repeat itself. For a simple sine function, the wavelength can be measured from trough to trough, or peak to peak. For any other function, a wavelength is measured from any point to the next point where the function begins to repeat itself. Wavelength has units of meters.

The **frequency (f)** of a wave is the number of wavelengths that pass a fixed point in one second. Frequency is measured in **hertz (Hz)**, or cycles per second. It is often written simply as 1/s.

The product of wavelength and frequency is velocity.

$$v = f\lambda$$

The reciprocal of frequency is called the **period (T)**. The period is the number of seconds required for one wavelength to pass a fixed point. When the x-axis is time, the period is from any point on the wave function, to the next point where the function begins to repeat itself.

$$T = \frac{1}{f}$$

The **amplitude** A of a wave is its maximum displacement from zero. Amplitude is always positive.

**Figure 6.1   Properties of a Wave**

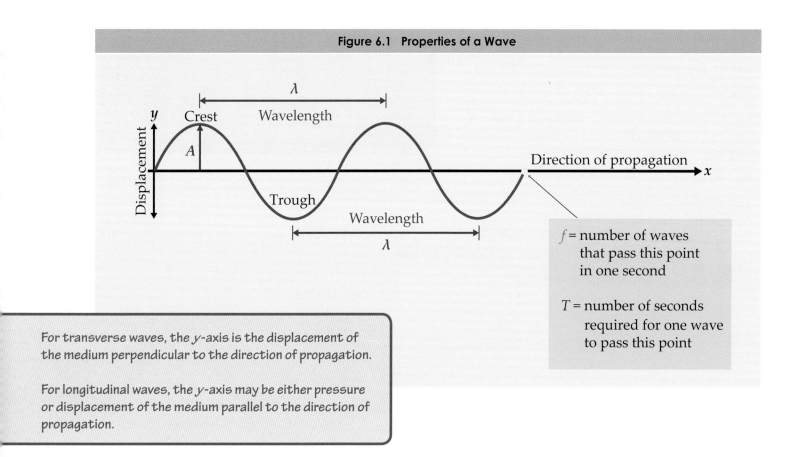

For transverse waves, the y-axis is the displacement of the medium perpendicular to the direction of propagation.

For longitudinal waves, the y-axis may be either pressure or displacement of the medium parallel to the direction of propagation.

Be aware that the wave function can be plotted against either displacement or time. For a sinusoidal wave moving along a string in the $x$ direction, the transverse displacement $y$ is given by:

$$y(x,t) = A \sin(kx - \omega t)$$

where $k$ is the *angular wave number*, and $\omega$ is the angular frequency (see Physics Lecture 2). This equation will not be useful on the MCAT, but understanding it helps to understand waves.

Although the velocity of a wave is always given by the product of the wavelength and frequency, the **velocity is dictated by the medium** through which the wave travels. A change in frequency or wavelength does not change the velocity of a wave in a given *nondispersive* medium. Nor does the velocity of the wave source affect the velocity of the wave itself. In other words, the sound waves made by a speeding jet travel at the same speed as the sound waves made by a crawling turtle. Only the medium affects the velocity.

**Two aspects of the medium affect the velocity:**

1.  the medium's resistance to change in shape (or elasticity); and
2.  the medium's resistance to change in motion (or inertia).

For instance, the velocity of a wave traveling along a perfectly elastic string is:

$$v = \sqrt{\frac{T}{\mu}} \quad \text{(Here, $T$ is tension not period.)}$$

where $T$ is the tension in the string (not the period), and $\mu$ is the mass per unit length of the string. From this equation, we see that we change the medium without changing the string, but by increasing the tension on the same string.

The velocity of a sound wave is given by:

$$v = \sqrt{\frac{B}{\rho}}_{\text{(small pressure variations only)}} = \sqrt{\frac{P}{\rho}}_{\text{(isothermal gases only)}}$$

where $B$ is the bulk modulus of the medium and $P$ is the pressure of the gas. It is not important to memorize these equations, but it is important to be able to predict how a change in medium might change the wave velocity. For instance, if the tension is equal, a wave will travel faster on a lighter string than a heavier one. However, notice that, when comparing sound waves in water and air, we cannot predict the relative velocities without actual values. Since water is heavier than air, it should slow the sound waves. But actually, water more than makes up for its higher density with a much greater bulk modulus, and sound waves travel significantly faster in water.

> The velocity of sound waves in a gas is limited by the average speed of the molecules within that gas. Thus, sound waves move more quickly through hot gases than through cold gases.

You should also be aware that **for a gas, the velocity increases with temperature** according to the equation:

$$v = \sqrt{\frac{\gamma RT}{M}} \quad \text{(Here, $T$ is temperature.)}$$

where $\gamma$ is a constant for a specific gas (about 1.4 for air) which compensates for temperature changes during contractions, $R$ is the universal gas constant, and $M$ is the molecular mass. This indicates that the random velocity of the gas molecules is a limiting factor for the velocity of a sound wave. The greater the temperature, the greater the random velocity, the greater the sound wave velocity. In fact, the velocity of a sound wave through a gas is on the order of magnitude of (but slightly less than) the random velocity of its molecules.

> Hold on! Too many formulas! Don't memorize all of these formulas; just the ones given in the equation summary at the end of each Lecture. Instead of memorizing, look at the relationships each formula implies.

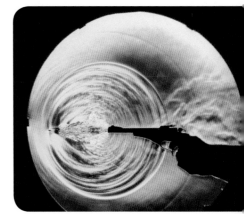

This photograph demonstrates the shockwaves produced by the explosion of a firing gun.

> Notice that heavier mediums tend to slow waves down, while stiffer mediums tend to speed waves up. Since a wave must move the medium in order to pass through it, the inertia of the medium (its resistance to motion) tends to slow it down. On the other hand, the greater the elasticity of the medium, the faster it snaps back to position moving the wave along. The elastic component stores potential energy; the inertial component stores kinetic energy. Wave velocity is a constant in a nondispersive medium; it is independent of frequency, wavelength, and amplitude.

*Surface waves*, such as waves on the surface of water, have some special properties. They are neither completely transverse nor completely longitudinal. If the MCAT were to test your knowledge of surface waves, it would probably give you a formula in a passage. Surface waves are also called *gravity waves*, because gravity acts as the elastic component. Because gravity acts as the elastic component, just like a projectile, the mass (or density) of the liquid does not change the rate at which a surface wave rises and falls. Thus, the velocity of wave propagation is not changed by the density of the liquid. In shallow liquid, where the depth $y$ is much smaller than the wavelength $\lambda$, the velocity of a surface wave is given approximately by:

$$v = \sqrt{gy} \qquad (y \ll \lambda)$$

Notice that the velocity increases as the depth increases. Although not shown by this approximation, the velocity also increases slightly with amplitude.

In deep liquid, a *dispersive* medium, the velocity increases with the wavelength as follows:

$$v = \sqrt{\frac{g\lambda}{2\pi}} \qquad (y \gg \lambda)$$

Power is the rate at which a wave transfers energy. Power in waves is typically discussed in terms of **intensity (*I*)**. It has units of W/m². Intensity of a sound wave is given by:

> Know that intensity increases with the square of the amplitude and the square of the frequency for all waves.

$$I = \tfrac{1}{2}\rho\omega^2 A^2 v$$

where $\rho$ is the density of the medium, $\omega$ is the angular frequency, $A$ is the amplitude, and $v$ is the wave velocity. For a wave on a string, simply replace $\rho$ with $\mu$. Recall from Physics Lecture 2 that $\omega = 2\pi f$, so intensity is proportional to the square of the frequency. Dependence of intensity (or power) on the square of frequency and square of amplitude is true for all types of waves. Notice that frequency and amplitude depend upon the wave source, while density and velocity are factors of the medium.

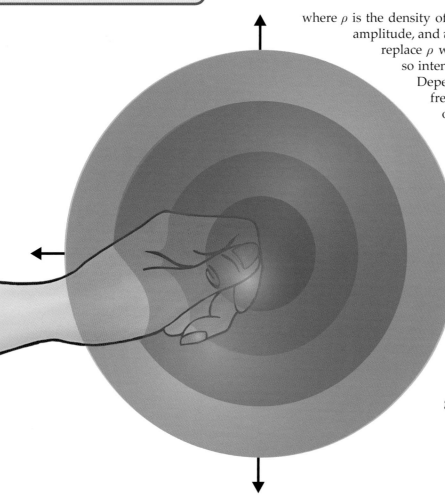

Intensity is a useful way to discuss the rate of energy transfer of waves because a wave may travel in several directions at once. For instance, if you snap your fingers in the air, some of the energy is transferred away from your fingers in the form of a sound wave moving in all directions. Although this energy remains constant, it is moving away from your fingers and spreading out over the surface area of an ever enlarging sphere. The increase in area means that the intensity of the sound is decreasing. Here, the intensity at any given radius r is the power divided by the surface area of a sphere and given by:

$$I = \frac{P}{4\pi r^2}$$

This is not a useful equation to memorize because it is applicable only under very limited circumstances.

Although intensity for sound waves is a measure of energy rate transfer per area, humans do not perceive intensity on a linear scale. For instance, the sound waves created by the rustling of leaves are about 10 times more intense than those created by normal breathing; yet, we don't perceive them as 10 times louder. In order to compensate for this and to make intensity more intuitive, an artificial scale for **intensity level ($\beta$)** has been created, based upon a logarithmic scale of intensities. The units of this scale are **decibels (dB)**. The relationship between $\beta$ and $I$ is given by:

$$\beta = 10 \log \frac{I}{I_0}$$

where $I_0$ is the threshold intensity of human hearing (the lowest intensity audible by the typical human).

The decibel system was created to provide an intuitive system that reflects how our human brain perceives the varying intensity of sound.

| | $\Delta I$ | $\Delta \beta$ |
|---|---|---|
| All you need to understand about decibels on the MCAT is that, if the intensity increases by a factor of 10, the decibels increase by the addition of 10 decibels. In other words, an increase in intensity from 30 W/m2 to 3000 W/m$^2$ is equivalent to an increase of 20 decibels; I added 2 zeros to intensity, so I add 20 decibels to the decibel level. If I had added 3 zeros to the intensity, I would have added 30 decibels to the decibel level, and so on. | $\times 10 = +10$ <br> $\times 10^2 = +20$ <br> $\times 10^3 = +30$ <br> $\times 10^4 = +40$ | |

*Notes:*

121. If an ocean wave hits a particular beach once every four seconds, and the wave peaks are 12 meters apart, with what velocity are the waves coming into shore?

   A.   3 m/s
   B.   4 m/s
   C.   12 m/s
   D.   48 m/s

122. Waves generally travel faster in solids than in gases because:

   A.   The density of solids is generally greater than the density of gases.
   B.   The density of gases is generally greater than the density of solids.
   C.   Solids are less compressible than gases.
   D.   Gases are less compressible than solids.

123. One end of a string is shaken each second sending a wave with an amplitude of 10 cm toward the other end. The string is 5 meters long, and the wavelength of each wave is 50 cm. How many waves reach the other end of the string in each 10 second interval?

   A.   2
   B.   5
   C.   10
   D.   50

124. The sound level of the chirping made by a bird at a distance of 5 meters is measured at 30 dB. When the same bird is 50 meters away the sound level is measured at 10 dB. How many times greater is the amplitude of the sound wave at 5 meters away compared to 50 meters away?

   A.   3 times greater.
   B.   10 times greater.
   C.   20 times greater.
   D.   100 times greater.

125. Sound waves are an example of:

   A.   longitudinal waves because the medium moves perpendicularly to the propagation of the wave.
   B.   longitudinal waves because the medium moves parallel to the propagation of the wave.
   C.   transverse waves because the medium moves perpendicularly to the propagation of the wave.
   D.   transverse waves because the medium moves parallel to the propagation of the wave.

126. When the frequency of a sound wave is increased, which of the following will decrease?

   I.    Wavelength
   II.   Period
   III.  Amplitude

   A.   I only
   B.   III only
   C.   I and II only
   D.   I and III only

127. A ship uses a depth finder to discover the depth of water beneath it at any time. The depth finder operates by sending a sound wave towards the bottom of the ocean and measuring the time it takes for the wave to be reflected off the bottom and return to the ship. At a certain point, it takes 1 second for the wave to return. What is the depth at that point? (The speed of sound in water is 1500 m/s).

   A.   750 m
   B.   1500 m
   C.   3000 m
   D.   4500 m

128. If the intensity of a sound is doubled, the decibel level will increase by:

   A.   less than 10 dB.
   B.   exactly 10 dB.
   C.   more than 10 dB.
   D.   exactly 20 dB.

## 6.2 Superposition, Phase & Interference

The **phase** of a wave relates to its wavelength, frequency, and place and time of origin. In a nondispersive medium, the phase is constant and given by:

$$kx - \omega t = \text{the wave phase}$$

The angular values in this equation are beyond the MCAT. Don't memorize this equation. It is sufficient for the MCAT to think of phase as a horizontal shift of a wave on a Cartesian graph as shown below. Each wavelength represents 360°. So half a wavelength represents 180°. Two waves that are the same wavelength, and begin at the same point, are said to be in phase with each other. Two waves that are the same wavelength but travel different distances to arrive at the same point, will be out of phase if that distance is not some multiple of the wavelength. The angle by which two waves differ is called their *phase constant*.

Two or more waves can occupy the same space. When this happens, if the waves are transverse, their displacements add at each point along the wave to form a new wave. This superposition of waves is called interference. Interference can be constructive or destructive. **Constructive interference** occurs when the sum of the displacements results in a greater displacement. **Destructive interference** occurs when the sum of the displacements results in a smaller displacement. After passing through each other, waves that interfere will revert to their original shape, unaffected by the interference.

Any waveform, no matter how irregular, can be created by superposition of a sufficient number of sine waves with the correct amplitudes and wavelengths.

**Figure 6.2  Constructive and Destructive Interference**

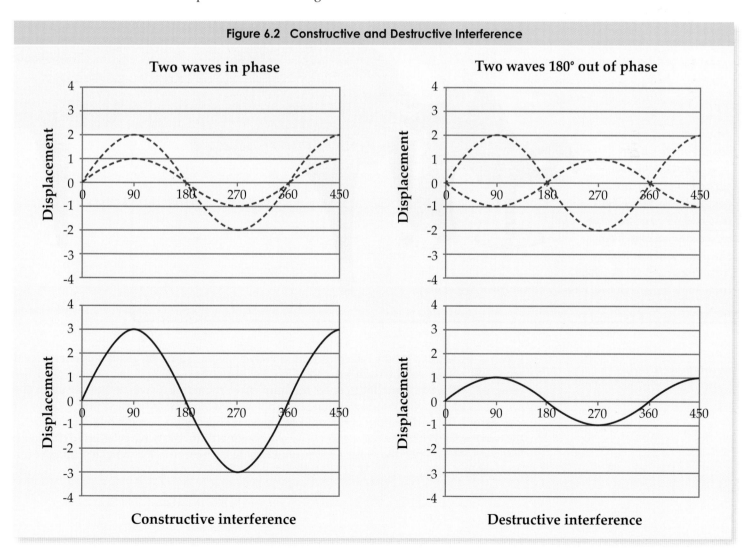

A special case of superposition of waves is the phenomenon known as beats. **Beats** occur when two waves with slightly different frequencies are superimposed. At some points they will be nearly in phase and experience constructive interference. At other points they will be out of phase and experience destructive interference. These points will alternate with a frequency equal to the difference between the frequencies of the original two waves. This difference is called the beat frequency.

$$f_{Beat} = |f_1 - f_2|$$

Notice the lines below. They occur at slightly different frequencies. Your eye perceives equally spaced light and dark spots, which correspond to the beat frequency.

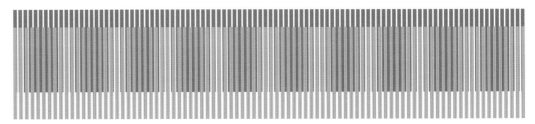

A good way to remember the beat frequency is to think about tuning a piano. It is impossible to tune a piano perfectly. The piano tuner listens to the beat frequency of the tuning fork and the piano note. In order to bring the piano into perfect tune, the beat frequency must be zero. The tuner would have to wait forever while the beats get farther and farther apart until they are infinitely separated. By the way, the beat frequency is an alternating increase and decrease in the intensity of the noise. How "high" or "low" a note sounds is called the pitch. The frequency creating the pitch would be an average of the frequencies from the piano and the tuning fork. Pitch correlates with frequency; a high note has high pitch and high frequency.

When a wave reaches an interface between two media, some or all of the energy and momentum will reflect back into the first medium. Any energy and momentum not reflected will *refract* into the second medium. Any refracting wave will continue in the same orientation with the same frequency but with a smaller amplitude and a different wavelength. The orientation of the reflected wave will depend upon the relative density of the two media. When the wave reflects off a denser medium, the wave is inverted (Its phase is shifted 180°). When the wave reflects off a less dense medium, it is reflected upright (no phase shift occurs).

The reflection of a wave is most easily visualized by examining a wave pulse. A *wave pulse* is a single wavelength. If you imagine a string attached to a thread, and then imagine sending a wave pulse down the string, some of the energy would continue into the thread (the light medium) as an upright wave pulse, and the rest of the energy would reflect back as an upright wave pulse. Now imagine the same string attached to a heavy rope. The reflected wave is inverted.

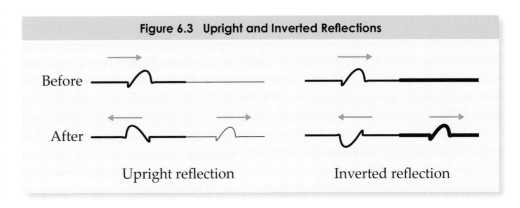

**Figure 6.3  Upright and Inverted Reflections**

Before

After

Upright reflection          Inverted reflection

Now let's look at two sine waves with the same wavelength traveling in opposite directions on the same perfectly elastic string. As shown in Figure 6.4, when they pass through each other something interesting happens. The point where they collide is never displaced. It doesn't move at all. This point is represented by the black dot in the diagram and is called a **node**. Notice also that only the points intersected by the two vertical lines experience maximum constructive interference. These points are called **antinodes**. Now imagine two endless rows of sine waves traveling in opposite directions on the same string. The string would hold perfectly still at the nodes and move violently up and down at the antinodes. This condition is known as a **standing wave**.

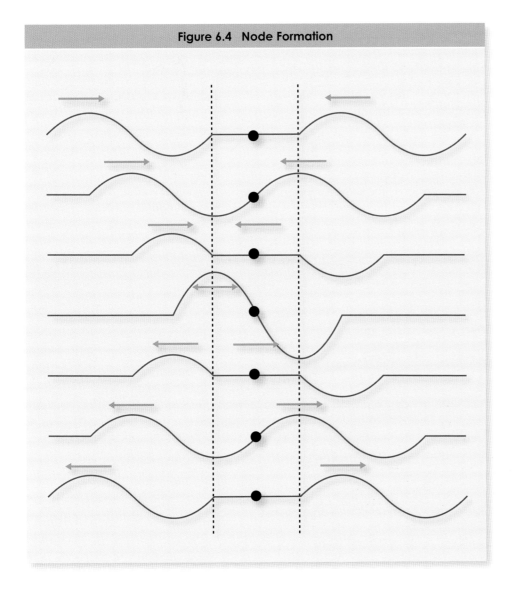

**Figure 6.4  Node Formation**

The strings on a guitar create standing waves when plucked. Changing the length and thickness of the string will alter the pitch.

What would happen if we locked both ends of the string at zero displacement by tying them to a wall and then generated a row of sine waves on the string? Let's assume that at the string-wall interface, the entire wave is reflected back to the string and no energy is refracted into the wall. In this situation, since two nodes, one at each wall, are already specified, only certain wavelengths would create a standing wave. All other wavelengths would create very small, irregular oscillations of the string. A list of the wavelengths from largest to smallest of the possible standing waves for a given situation is called a **harmonic series**. The harmonics are numbered from longest to shortest wavelength. The longest wavelength, called the **first harmonic** ($\lambda_1$) or **fundamental wavelength**, is created with the fewest number of nodes: two. This means that the distance from one wall to the other is half a wavelength. The **second harmonic** ($\lambda_2$) is created by adding another node. This makes the wavelength of the second harmonic equal to the distance between the walls. Each successive harmonic is created by adding a node.

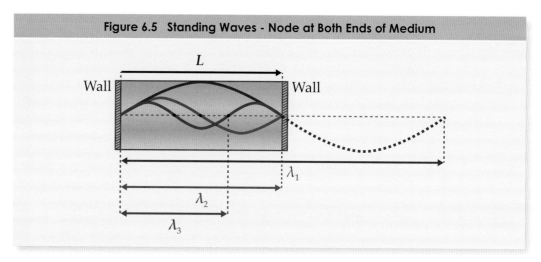

**Figure 6.5  Standing Waves - Node at Both Ends of Medium**

The equation for the harmonic series where each end is tied down as a node or where each end is loose creating an antinode is:

$$L = \frac{n\lambda_n}{2} \ (n = 1, 2, 3, ...)$$

where $L$ is the distance between the two ends of the string and $n$ is the number of the harmonic. This equation is the same for longitudinal waves such as sound. A pipe closed or open at both ends with sound waves inside will follow this equation. If only one end of the string is tied down, or only one end of a pipe is open, the untied or open end is an antinode.

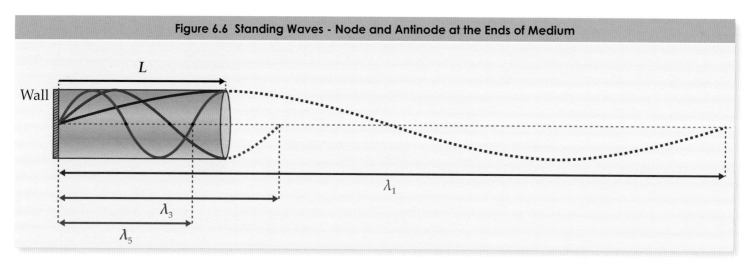

**Figure 6.6  Standing Waves - Node and Antinode at the Ends of Medium**

For a string tied at only one end, or a pipe open at only one end, the equation changes to:

$$L = \frac{n\lambda_n}{4} \ (n = 1, 3, 5, ...)$$

Notice when one end is an antinode, the even numbered harmonics are missing.

The standing waves described on the previous page cause the string to **resonate** or vibrate at its **natural frequency** or **resonant frequency**. Since velocity is constant for a given medium, the resonant frequency can be found for any given harmonic from the equation $v = f\lambda$.

All mechanical structures have natural frequencies at which they resonate. If an outside driving force is applied to a structure at the resonant frequency, the structure will experience maximum vibration velocities and maximum displacement amplitudes. The condition where the natural frequency and the driving frequency are equal is also called **resonance**. An examination of the resonating string discussed above will reveal the driving force to be the reflected wave. This demonstrates that both definitions of resonance are the same. In a non-ideal situation, energy is lost to some *damping effect* at the resonant frequency, and must be replaced by some outside driving force at the same frequency. A maximum displacement is produced resulting in a standing wave.

The phenomenon of sympathetic resonance can be demonstrated by blowing across a bottle top and listening to an identical bottle held near. The sound will be repeated although at a lower pitch.

*Notes:*

**129.** How many wavelengths are shown between the dotted lines in the wave form below?

- **A.** 1
- **B.** 2
- **C.** 3
- **D.** 4

**130.** When two waves are superimposed, the resulting wave can be found by summing their:

- **A.** frequencies
- **B.** periods
- **C.** wavelengths
- **D.** displacements

**131.** In order for two sound waves to have an audible beat frequency, the two waves must be:

- **A.** in phase.
- **B.** out of phase.
- **C.** close in frequency.
- **D.** of the same wavelength.

**132.** All of the following statements are true about a resonating string EXCEPT:

- **A.** A resonating string forms a standing wave.
- **B.** The wavelength of a resonating string must coincide with one of its harmonics.
- **C.** Some spots on a resonating string will not move at all.
- **D.** If left alone, the amplitude of a wave on a resonating string will grow infinitely large.

**133.** If a guitar string is 0.5 m long, what is the wavelength of its third harmonic?

- **A.** 0.25 m
- **B.** 0.33 m
- **C.** 0.5 m
- **D.** 1 m

**134.** Two violinists are playing together, slightly out of tune. If one violinist produces a frequency of 883 Hz and the other produces a frequency of 879 Hz, beats would be heard with a frequency of:

- **A.** 2 Hz.
- **B.** 4 Hz.
- **C.** 881 Hz.
- **D.** 1762 Hz.

**135.** A vibrating string has consecutive harmonics at wavelengths of 2.0 m and 4.0 m. What is the length of the string?

- **A.** 1.0 m
- **B.** 2.0 m
- **C.** 4.0 m
- **D.** 8.0 m

**136.** Waves A and B, pictured below, may or may not be in phase. If wave A and wave B are superimposed, the range of possible amplitudes for the resulting wave will be:

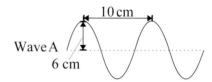

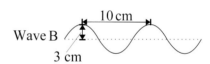

- **A.** from 0 cm to 3 cm.
- **B.** from 0 cm to 9 cm.
- **C.** from 3 cm to 6 cm.
- **D.** from 3 cm to 9 cm.

## 6.3 Simple Harmonic Motion

Any motion that repeats itself is called periodic or harmonic motion. If we stand directly in front of someone who is steadily peddling a stationary bicycle, and we watch the peddles, they appear to move straight up and down. They move faster in the middle of the motion and slow down at the top and bottom. If we recorded this up and down motion on paper as the paper was pulled to our right, we would draw a perfect sine wave. This type of motion is a specific type of harmonic motion. It is called **simple harmonic motion**, which means that it is a **sinusoidal function** in time. Objects in simple harmonic motion exhibit similar properties of which you must be aware for the MCAT.

The function that gives the displacement $x$ of an object in simple harmonic motion with respect to time is a simplified form of the equation for a wave moving along a string. It is:

$$x(t) = A \cos(\omega t + \phi)$$

where $A$ is the maximum displacement, $\omega$ is the angular frequency ($\omega = 2\pi f$), and $\phi$ is the phase constant that depends on what displacement $x$ we call t = 0 (when $x$ = A at $t$ = 0, then $\phi$ = 0). You will never need this equation on the MCAT. By taking the first and second derivatives of this equation we get the velocity and acceleration of the object in simple harmonic motion. Although these equations are not required for the MCAT, by combining the displacement and the acceleration equations we arrive at:

$$a(t) = -\omega^2 x(t)$$

*Notes:*

This simple relationship identifies two important properties of simple harmonic motion; the acceleration is directly proportional to the displacement, but opposite in sign, and the acceleration and displacement are related by the square of the frequency.

If we multiply both sides of $[a(t) = -\omega^2 x(t)]$ by mass m, we get Hooke's law! $F = -m\omega^2 x$, and we can see that the spring constant $k$ is $m\omega^2$. Therefore, since a spring follows Hooke's law, a mass bouncing on the end of a massless spring exhibits simple harmonic motion. If we lay the mass and spring on a frictionless horizontal table, stretch the spring, and release it, we get the same motion, and we can examine it without the complication of gravity. When the spring is fully stretched or fully compressed, the restoring force is at a maximum. Since the force is at a maximum, the acceleration is also at a maximum. Since displacement is at a maximum, the elastic potential energy, $\frac{1}{2}kx^2$, is also at a maximum. At this point the velocity is zero because the mass is reversing directions. Since the velocity is zero, the kinetic energy, $\frac{1}{2}mv^2$, is also zero. When the mass is crossing the equilibrium point of the spring (the length of the spring at rest), the net force on the mass is zero because $\Delta x$ is zero ($F = -k\Delta x$). The potential energy is zero for the same reason. The velocity, however, is at a maximum, which means that kinetic energy is also at a maximum. Of course, no force means that acceleration is zero. So we see that another characteristic of most systems in simple harmonic motion is an oscillation between kinetic energy and potential energy. No energy is lost to the surroundings.

**Figure 6.7 Harmonic Motion and Hooke's Law**

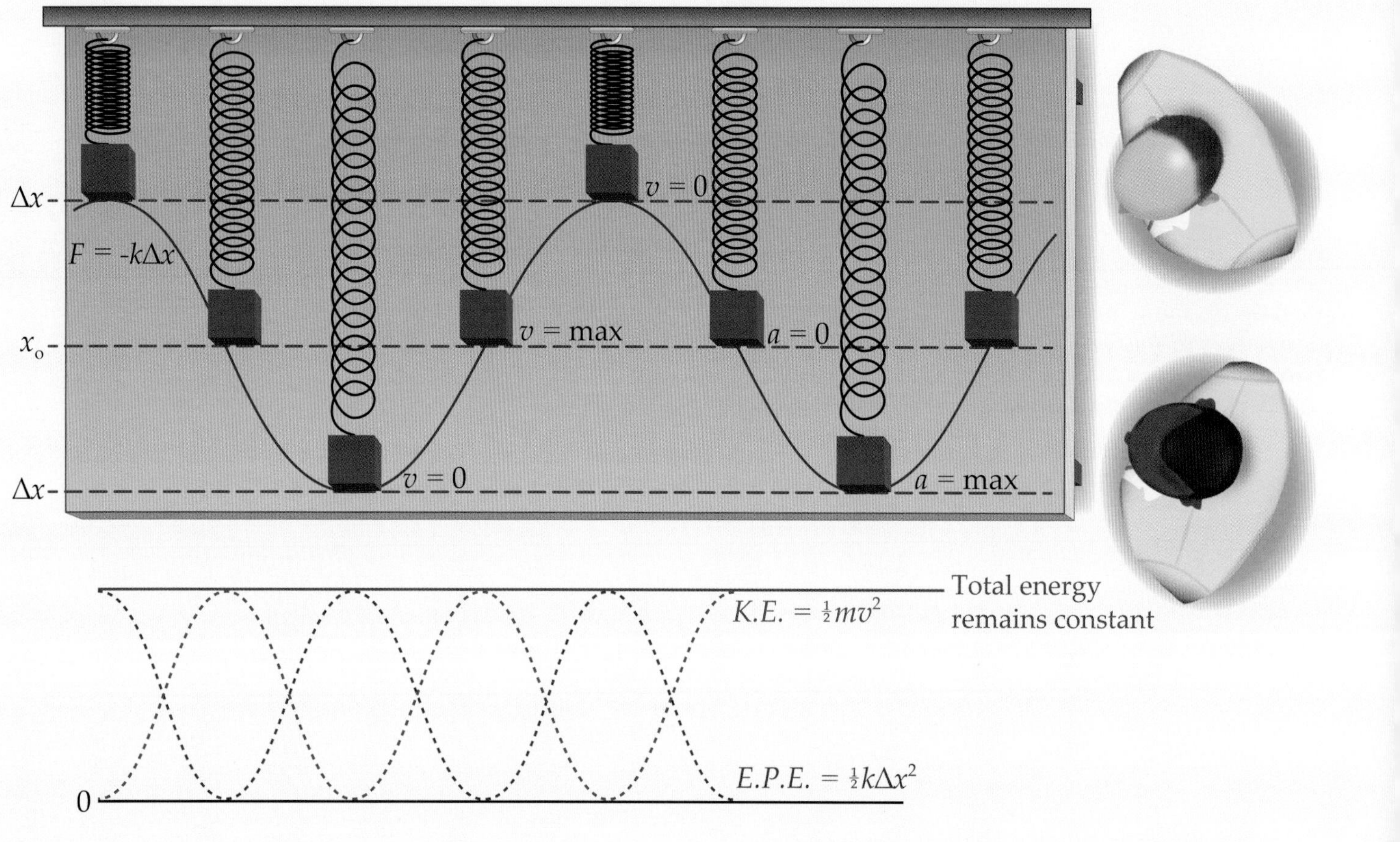

Since $k = m\omega^2$, and $\omega = 2\pi f$, the period of the motion for the mass on a spring is given by:

$$T = 2\pi \sqrt{\frac{m}{k}}$$

Notice that the inertial factor is on top and the elastic factor is on the bottom. Since period is inversely proportional to velocity, this is what we would expect from a wave phenomenon.

Another apparatus that simulates simple harmonic motion is a **pendulum** swinging at a small angle. (A 5 degree angle equals approximately 0.1% deviation from simple harmonic motion. For the MCAT, assume simple harmonic motion on all pendulums unless otherwise indicated.) Just like the mass on a spring, the pendulum exchanges energy forms between potential and kinetic. A pendulum has total gravitational potential at the top of its swing and total kinetic at the bottom. The period of a pendulum is given by:

$$T = 2\pi\sqrt{\frac{L}{g}}$$

Simple harmonic motion can take many forms and is easily disguised on the MCAT. For example: the orbit of a planet viewed from the side; a tetherball spinning around a pole viewed from the side; and electrons oscillating back and forth in AC current are all forms of simple harmonic motion.

Use Hooke's law to help you remember that the acceleration of any system in simple harmonic motion is proportional to the displacement of that system. Also, remember that it is proportional to the square of the frequency.

Recognize that for most systems in simple harmonic motion, energy oscillates between kinetic and one or more forms of potential.

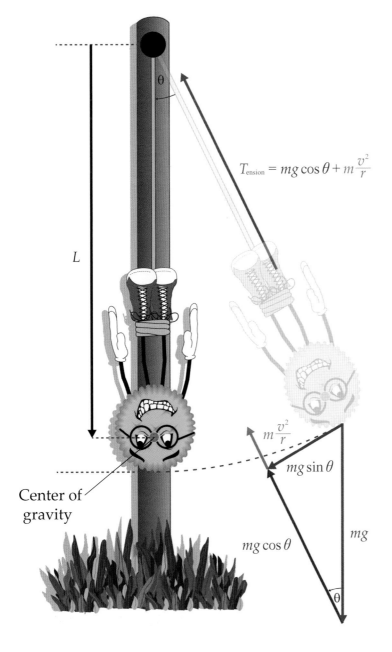

$$T_{\text{ension}} = mg\cos\theta + m\frac{v^2}{r}$$

Note that for the mass-spring system, the period is independent of the displacement. Likewise, for the pendulum, the period is independent of the displacement. That means that no matter how high you raise the pendulum, the time it takes for one full swing remains the same. (Of course, that assumes simple harmonic motion.)

Finally, I can't resist giving this mnemonic. To remember the angular frequencies for a mass on a spring and for a pendulum, just remember WACK'EM and WIGGLE:

$$\omega = \sqrt{\frac{k}{m}} \qquad \omega = \sqrt{\frac{g}{L}}$$

Wack'em & Wiggle

Even though these formulas will not be on the MCAT, they can help you remember things like the period of a pendulum is independent of the mass.

## 6.4 The Doppler Effect

**The Doppler effect** results because waves are unaffected by the speed of the source which produces them. If the source moves relative to the receiver of the waves (here called 'the observer'), each wave will travel a different distance in order to reach the observer, and therefore the observer will not receive them at the same frequency as they were emitted. For instance, if the source were to move toward the observer as fast as the waves, all the waves would arrive at the observer at the same time; obviously this would not be the frequency with which they were emitted. If we are talking about sound waves, where pitch changes with frequency, the observer would not hear the same pitch that the source emitted. With light, the observer would not observe the same color that was emitted.

You can simulate the Doppler Effect by allowing a tennis ball serving machine to pelt you with tennis balls. If you stand still, tennis balls come at you with a certain frequency, say one ball per second. If you run away from the machine, they still leave the machine at one ball per second, but as you run, they hit you with a lower frequency. If you run toward the machine, the balls hit you with a higher frequency.

Because tennis balls are particles and not waves, there is an important difference. Waves travel at the same speed through a medium regardless of whether or not the source moves. The tennis balls, on the other hand, if shot from a moving server, will travel at their original speed plus the speed of the server. This means that the frequency of tennis balls is different depending upon who is moving, the source or the observer. In a true Doppler Effect, the frequency change depends upon relative motion only, and who is actually moving cannot be distinguished.

If needed, the formula for the Doppler Effect for mechanical waves will be given to you on the MCAT as:

$$f_s = f_o \left( \frac{v \pm v_s}{v \pm v_o} \right)$$

This formula is unlikely to be useful on the MCAT. The difficult aspect of this formula is to understand when to use the plus sign and when to use the minus sign. The easy way to solve this problem is to follow these steps: 1) assume that the observer is not moving; 2) if the source is moving toward the object, label that direction negative and use the minus sign for $v_s$; 3) now check the direction that the observer is moving. If the direction is the same, use the same sign for $v_o$; if not, use the opposite sign for $v_o$. This system is possible because velocity is a vector and once you label a direction positive for one vector it must be so for all vectors.

For all waves, the Doppler Effect can be approximated by:

$$\frac{\Delta f}{f_s} = \frac{v}{c} \quad \text{and} \quad \frac{\Delta \lambda}{\lambda_s} = \frac{v}{c}$$

($c$ is not neccessarily the speed of light)

You should always use these formulae for any Doppler MCAT problem, and not the more complicated formula from page 122. These formulae approximate the Doppler Effect when the relative velocity $v$ of the source and the observer are much smaller than the wave velocity $c$. $\Delta f$ and $\Delta \lambda$ are the change to the source frequency $f$ and the source wavelength $\lambda$.

$$|\Delta f| = |f_o - f_s| \qquad |\Delta \lambda| = |\lambda_o - \lambda_s|$$

Notice that you must make a qualitative judgement as to the direction of the change in frequency and wavelength. This is simple: when the relative velocity brings the source and observer closer, observed frequency goes up and observed wavelength goes down; in the opposite case, the opposite is true. If the objects are getting farther apart as time passes, subtract $\Delta f$ from $f_s$ or add $\Delta \lambda$ to $\lambda_s$; if they are approaching each other as time passes, add $\Delta f$ to $f_s$ or subtract $\Delta \lambda$ from $\lambda_s$.

The relative velocity $v$ is sometimes difficult to grasp. It is simply the net speed at which the source and object are approaching each other. For objects moving in the same direction, subtract their individual speeds; for objects moving in opposite directions, add their individual speeds.

**Table 6.1**

| | source | observer | relative velocity $v$ |
|---|---|---|---|
| Same direction | ← 5 m/s | ← 6 m/s | 1 m/s |
| Same direction | → 5 m/s | → 6 m/s | 1 m/s |
| Opposite directions | → 5 m/s | ← 6 m/s | 11 m/s |
| Opposite directions | ← 5 m/s | → 6 m/s | 11 m/s |

In the diagram below, the train's velocity tends to make me hear the whistle with a higher pitch. Notice that the wave peaks to the right of the train are closer than those to the left. The movement of the train pushes the peaks closer together. By running to the right, I tend to spread the wave peaks back out again as they strike me. However, since I'm not as fast as the train, the net result is that the train is closing in on me. This makes me hear the train's whistle at a higher frequency and a higher pitch. This is evident from the closer wavelengths.

$v_{train}$

$v_{Salty}$

Notice that if the train were to approach and then reach the speed of sound, the wave fronts would bunch closer and closer together until they overlapped. They would then constructively interfere with each other resulting in a sonic boom. As the train continued faster than sound, the wave fronts would separate again with the new waves in front of the old waves.

Be sure to remember that, for light, when the source and observer are approaching each other, the wavelength shortens creating a blue shift. When they separate, a red shift is created.

Also remember that for objects moving in the same direction at the same speed, there is no Doppler Effect; the relative velocity is zero, so the change in frequency is zero.

## 6.5 Equation Summary

| Equations | |
|---|---|
| **Waves** | **The Doppler Effect** |
| $v = f\lambda$ | $\dfrac{\Delta f}{f_s} = \dfrac{v}{c}$ |
| $T = \dfrac{1}{f}$ | $\dfrac{\Delta \lambda}{\lambda_s} = \dfrac{v}{c}$ |
| **Sound** | |
| $\beta = 10 \log \dfrac{I}{I_0}$ | $L = \dfrac{n\lambda_n}{2} \; (n = 1, 2, 3, \ldots)$ |
| $f_{\text{Beat}} = \lvert f_1 - f_2 \rvert$ | $L = \dfrac{n\lambda_n}{4} \; (n = 1, 3, 5, \ldots)$ |

## 6.6 Terms You Need to Know

| Terms | |
|---|---|
| Antinodes | Mechanical Waves |
| Beats | Natural Frequency |
| Constructive Interference | Node |
| Decibels (dB) | Pendulum |
| Destructive Interference | Phase |
| Doppler Effect | Period ($T$) |
| First Harmonic ($\lambda_1$) | Resonance |
| Frequency ($f$) | Resonant Frequency |
| Fundamental Wavelength | Second Harmonic ($\lambda_2$) |
| Harmonic Series | Simple Harmonic Motion |
| Hertz (Hz) | Standing Wave |
| Intensity ($I$) | Transverse Wave |
| Intensity Level ($\beta$) | Wave |
| Longitudinal Wave | |

**137.** If the mass on the bob of a pendulum is increased by a factor of 3, the period of the pendulum's motion will:

A. be increased by a factor of 2.
B. remain the same.
C. be decreased by a factor of 2.
D. be decreased by a factor of 4.

**138.** Which of the following would most accurately demonstrate the kinetic energy of a pendulum?

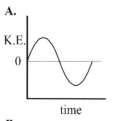
A.

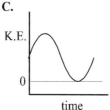
C.

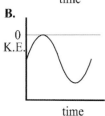
B.

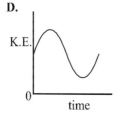
D.

**139.** If the amplitude of a sine wave is doubled, the intensity:

A. remains the same.
B. increases by a factor of 2.
C. increases by a factor of 4.
D. increases by a factor of 16.

**140.** Which of the following factors by itself will increase the frequency at which an observer hears a sound emanating from a source?

A. A wind blows from the source to the observer.
B. The source and the observer move away from each other at the same speed.
C. The source and the observer move in the same direction at the same speed.
D. The source moves away from the observer more slowly than the observer moves toward the source.

**141.** A piano creates a musical note when a metal wire stretched between two fixed ends is struck by a hammer, creating a standing wave. As the force with which the hammer strikes the string is increased, the amplitude of the string's motion is increased. Which of the following properties of the wave on the string will remain the same as the force of the hammer is increased?

I. frequency
II. wavelength
III. velocity

A. I only
B. I and II only
C. II and III only
D. I, II, and III

**142.** As a pendulum pictured below swings through point A, which of the following is at a maximum?

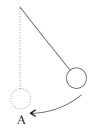

A. tangential acceleration
B. displacement from rest
C. kinetic energy
D. gravitational potential energy

**143.** A clock uses the motion of a pendulum to keep time. If the clock were placed at a height several thousand kilometers above the earth's surface, it would run:

A. faster than it would on the surface of the Earth.
B. slower than it would on the surface of the Earth.
C. at the same speed that it would at the surface of the Earth.
D. at a speed that can't be determined from its speed at the surface of the Earth.

**144.** All of the following are examples of harmonic motion EXCEPT:

A. a pendulum moving back and forth
B. a skydiver falling through the atmosphere
C. a car moving around a circular track
D. a string vibrating on a musical instrument

# ELECTRICITY AND MAGNETISM

## 7.1 Electric Charge

Like energy, **charge** is an entity that defies definition. Yet, all of us have an intuitive idea about what it is; we've all experienced a shock from static electricity, for instance. Charge is intrinsic to the nature of some subatomic particles; it is part of their identity. Most of us are aware that there is positive charge and negative charge. The 'positive' and 'negative' signify nothing more than that these charges are opposite to each other. Instead of positive and negative, they could have been called up and down, black and white, or even had their names reversed to 'negative' and 'positive'. It is an accident of science that electrons were labeled negative and not positive, and, as a result of this accident, current runs in the opposite direction of electrons. Charge ($q$) is given in units of **coulombs (C)**.

Just as there is a universal law of conservation of energy, there is a **Universal Law of Conservation of Charge**. The universe has no net charge. In the majority of situations (and for the MCAT), net charge is created by separating electrons from protons. If we were to put all the positive and negative charges in the universe together, they would cancel each other out, right down to the last electron and proton. Thus, anytime a negative charge is created, a positive charge is created, and vice versa. Charge is quantized. This means that any charge must be at least as large as a certain smallest possible unit. The smallest possible unit of charge is one electron unit ($e = 1.6 \times 10^{-19}$ C), the charge on one electron or one proton.

**Opposite charges attract each other; like charges repel each other.** The formula describing the magnitude of the force of the repulsion or attraction between two charged objects is called **Coulomb's law**, and is analogous to the formula for gravitational force:

$$F = k\frac{q_1 q_2}{r^2}$$

where $k$ is the Coulomb constant ($k = 8.988 \times 10^9$ N·m²/C²), $q$ represents the respective charges, and $r$ is the distance between the centers of charge.

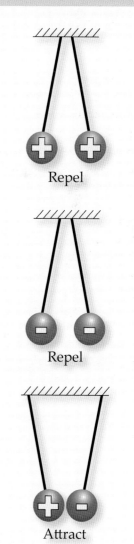

**Figure 7.1  Like Charges Repel, Opposite Charges Attract**

Repel

Repel

Attract

## Figure 7.2 Electric Force

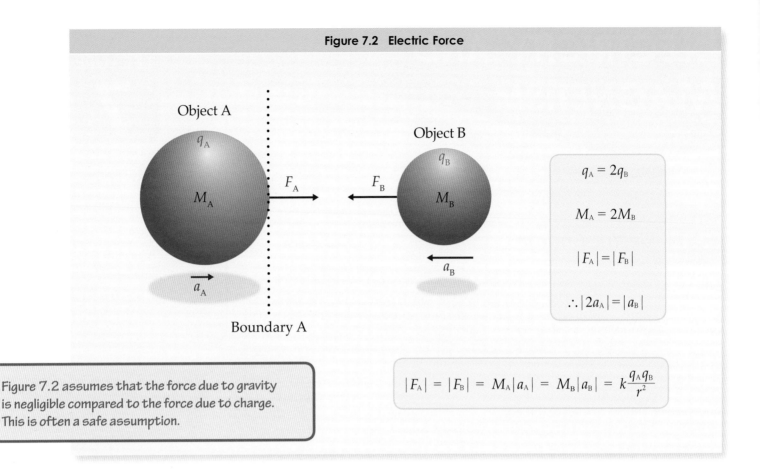

$$q_A = 2q_B$$

$$M_A = 2M_B$$

$$|F_A| = |F_B|$$

$$\therefore |2a_A| = |a_B|$$

Figure 7.2 assumes that the force due to gravity is negligible compared to the force due to charge. This is often a safe assumption.

$$|F_A| = |F_B| = M_A|a_A| = M_B|a_B| = k\frac{q_A q_B}{r^2}$$

To compare electrical forces with gravitational forces, imagine the following. Place two tiny grains of sand 30 meters apart. Not much gravitational force between them, right? What if all the charged parts of one grain were negatively charged and all the charged parts of the other grain were positively charged so that the electric forces were entirely attractive rather than balanced. The resulting force pulling the two grains of sand together would be about three million tons.

Notice that the diagram above is the same as that used for gravity in Lecture 2. We want to emphasize the similarity between these two forces. Both gravitational and electric forces change inversely with the square of the distance between the centers of mass or charge. One major difference is that gravitational forces are always attractive while electrical forces may be either attractive or repulsive.

Also notice that the force due to gravity in the diagram above is ignored. Coulomb's forces are usually of a far greater magnitude than gravitational forces, and, unless the masses are very large, gravitational forces are negligible.

In defining Coulomb's law, we used the phrase 'center of charge'. Similar to center of mass, the **center of charge** is a point from which the charge generated by an object or system of objects can be considered to originate. For example, the charges on a hollow, positively charged sphere made from conducting material will repel each other so that they move

### Figure 7.3  Center of Charge

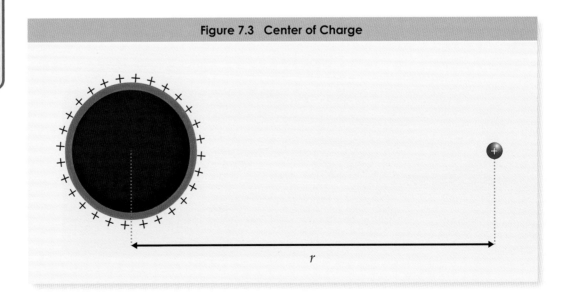

$r$

as far apart as possible. This results in the positive charge spreading uniformly along the outer surface of the sphere. Due to the symmetry, the center of charge exists at the center of the sphere, even though there is no actual charge at the center of the sphere. The electrostatic force on a charged object placed outside the sphere can be found using Coulomb's Law, where $r$ is the distance between the object and the center of the sphere.

Note the same is true for gravity.

The similarities between gravity and electricity stem from the fact that both mass and charge create fields. A **field** is some type of distortion or condition in space that creates a force on a charge (or mass, if it is a gravitational field; or magnet, if it is a magnetic field [A magnetic field and an electric field are really the same field.)] Recall that on the MCAT, any force that acts on your system must be physically contiguous to it, except for the forces of gravity, electricity, or magnetism. This is because these forces are created by fields and can act at a distance.

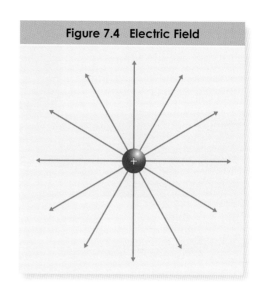

**Figure 7.4  Electric Field**

> *Good luck finding a more satisfying definition for a 'field'. The consensus among scientists is that a 'field' actually exists and is real; however, no one seems to be able to give it a definition that you can sink your teeth into. For our purposes, just think of a field as a made up concept to explain action at a distance, or, if you prefer, as a force per unit charge (or mass) located in space.*

Any field can be represented by **lines of force**. Lines of force point in the direction of the field (**positive to negative** for electric fields, towards the mass creating the field for gravitational fields). The relative distance between lines indicates the strength of the field; the closer the lines, the stronger the field. Lines of force can never intersect, as this would indicate a field pointing in two different directions from the same location, an impossibility. The lines of force for a single positive point charge are shown in Figure 7.4.

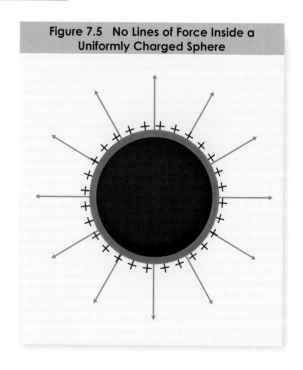

**Figure 7.5  No Lines of Force Inside a Uniformly Charged Sphere**

Examine the lines of force for the field created by the positively charged, hollow sphere in Figure 7.5. Notice that the inside of the sphere has no electric field. A negatively charged sphere would produce the same result. This is because the lines of force must begin on a positive charge and end on a negative charge. This is an impossibility for lines entering the sphere. Thus there can be no lines of force inside a uniformly charged sphere. Again, the same is true for a gravitational field.

An electric field is defined as the electrostatic force per unit charge. The symbol for any **electric field** is $E$. $E$ is a vector pointing in the direction of the field and has units of N/C or V/m. For a point charge, the electric field is found by dividing Coulomb's law by $q$ giving:

$$E = k\frac{q_1}{r^2}$$

The electric field for a system of point charges is found by summing the fields due to each charge. Remember that $E$ is a vector and you must use vector addition when summing fields.

Because I am inside the car, a hollow conductor, there is no electric field and I am safe from the lighting strike.

The symbol for the gravitational field near the surface of the earth is the familiar $g$. When we wish to discuss the gravitational force on any object at the surface of the earth, we normally use '$mg$' and not '$F = Gmm/r^2$'. This is because we are very familiar with the gravitational field near the surface of the earth, and thus we have created a shorthand method for describing the gravitational force for any mass; that method is the mass times the field, $mg$. Similarly, the force on a charge ($q$) in an electric field ($E$) is

$$F = Eq$$

To find the potential energy of a mass in the earth's gravitational field relative to some other position, we multiply this force times the displacement in the direction opposite the field, $mgh$. Similarly, the **potential energy (U)** of a charge in an electric field is the force times the displacement ($d$):

$$U = Eqd$$

where $d$ is measured from a zero point of our own choosing, similar to $h$ in gravitational potential energy. Since this particular electric potential energy is dependent upon position, it is also a type of potential energy.

If the electric field is created by a point charge, we can derive the electric potential energy from Coulomb's law:

$$U = k\frac{q_1 q_2}{r}$$

Notice that according to this formula, electric potential is zero for particles separated by an infinite distance. Since energy is a state function, its value can be arbitrarily assigned, and it is given a zero value in this case by convention.

**Figure 7.6  Work Done by a Field is Path Independent**

Field

Mass or charge

Any Path

$h$ or $d$

$W = mgh$  or  $W = qEd$

Mass or charge

Recalling our study of gravity, if we wanted to create a function for the work required to move any given mass along any frictionless path near the surface of the earth, what would this function be? In other words, we are looking for a function intrinsic to the gravitational field, which is independent of any mass. What function would give us the 'potential' of the field in terms of work gained or lost per unit mass? The answer is $gh$, the field times the displacement in the direction opposite the field. If we multiplied any mass times $gh$, we would have the work done by the field in moving that mass. This is called the potential of the field. In electricity, potential has a special name, voltage. **Voltage (V)** is the potential for work by an electric field in moving any charge from one point to another.

$$V = Ed$$

Voltage is given in units of **volts (V)**, and is a scalar. You should also recognize voltage in units of J/C.

The voltage due to a point charge is:

$$V = k\frac{q_1}{r}$$

Since voltage is a scalar, when finding the voltage due to a group of point charges, the voltages due to each individual charge can be summed directly.

Notice from Figure 7.6 that, like the work done by gravity, the work done by an electrostatic field is independent of the path. This is because both fields are conservative; they both conserve mechanical energy. As we will see when we discuss magnetism, this is not true of all electric fields.

Within an electric field, movement perpendicular to the field does not result in a change in potential, just as a mass moving along the surface of the earth does not experience a change in its gravitational potential. In any electric field we can define a surface normal to the field that describes a set of points all with the same potential. Examples of such surfaces are shown as dashed lines in Figure 7.7. They are called **equipotential surfaces**. All points on an equipotential surface are at the same voltage. An equipotential surface can be drawn at any point in the field.

Also shown in the diagram are the field lines of an electric dipole. An **electric dipole** is created by two opposite charges with equal magnitude. An *electric dipole moment (p = qd)* is a vector whose magnitude is the charge $q$ on one of the charges times the distance $d$ between the charges. In physics, this vector points in the opposite direction to the electric field, from the negative charge to the positive charge.

In chemistry the vector points from positive to negative. At large distances the electric field of a dipole varies by $1/r^3$.

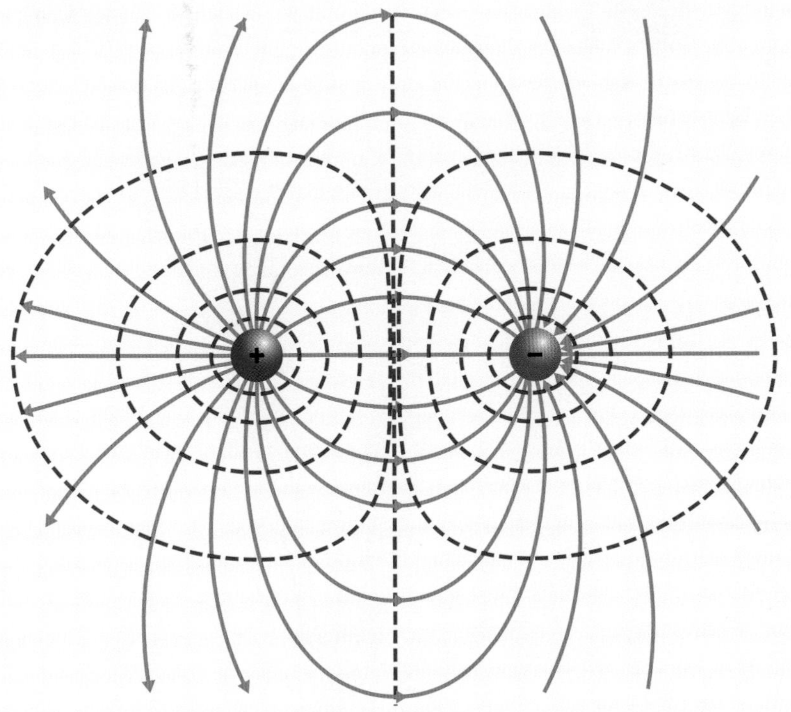

## Table 7.1 Formulas for an Electric Field Created by a Point Charge

| Equations | Units |
|---|---|
| $F = k\dfrac{q_1 q_2}{r^2}$ | N |
| $E = k\dfrac{q_1}{r^2}$ | N/C or V/m |
| $U = k\dfrac{q_1 q_2}{r}$ | J |
| $V = k\dfrac{q_1}{r}$ | V or J/C |

When working electricity problems be sure to know what type of electric field you're working with. The formulas in Table 7.1 refer to an electric field created by a point charge. Point charges create electric fields that change with *r*. If your electric field is constant, like the field inside a parallel plate capacitor, you should NOT use the formulas in Table 7.1. If your field is created by a point, you should be careful about using formulas other than those in Table 7.1.

### Figure 7.7 Electric Dipole Field Lines and Equipotential Surfaces

### Figure 7.8 A Dipole in an Electric Field

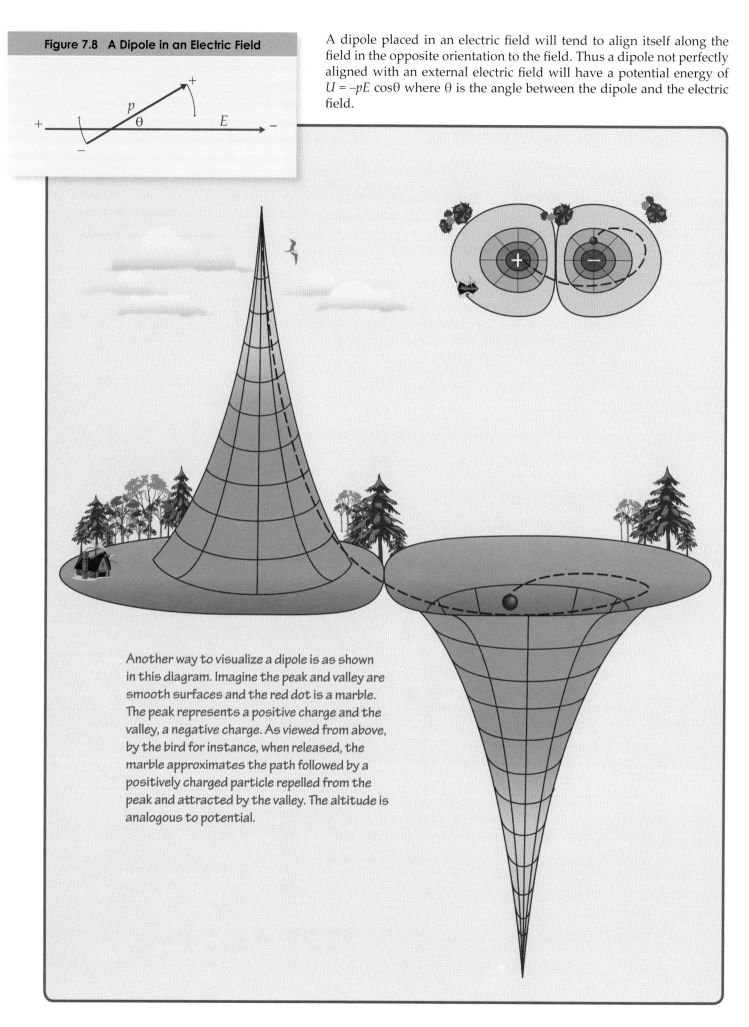

A dipole placed in an electric field will tend to align itself along the field in the opposite orientation to the field. Thus a dipole not perfectly aligned with an external electric field will have a potential energy of $U = -pE\cos\theta$ where $\theta$ is the angle between the dipole and the electric field.

Another way to visualize a dipole is as shown in this diagram. Imagine the peak and valley are smooth surfaces and the red dot is a marble. The peak represents a positive charge and the valley, a negative charge. As viewed from above, by the bird for instance, when released, the marble approximates the path followed by a positively charged particle repelled from the peak and attracted by the valley. The altitude is analogous to potential.

Questions 145 through 152 are **NOT** based on a descriptive passage.

145. Two charged metal plates are placed one meter apart creating a constant electric field between them. A one-coulomb charged particle is placed in the space between them. The particle experiences a force of 100 newtons due to the electric field. What is the potential difference between the plates?

    A. 1 V
    B. 10 V
    C. 100 V
    D. 1000 V

146. How much work is required to move a positively charged particle along the 15 cm path shown if the electric field E is 10 N/C and the charge on the particle is 8 C? (Note: Ignore gravity.)

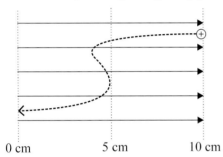

    0 cm          5 cm          10 cm

    A. 0.8 J
    B. 8 J
    C. 12 J
    D. 1200 J

147. If the distance between two point charges is increased by a factor of 3, the new force on either charge will:

    A. decrease by a factor of 9.
    B. decrease by a factor of 3.
    C. remain the same.
    D. increase by a factor of 3.

148. If the distance between a point charge and an infinitely large charged plate is increased by a factor of 2, the new force on the point charge will:

    A. decrease by a factor of 4.
    B. decrease by a factor of 2.
    C. remain the same.
    D. increase by a factor of 2.

149. A positively charged particle starts at rest 25 cm from a second positively charged particle that is held stationary throughout the experiment. The first particle is released and accelerates directly away from the second particle. When the first particle has moved 25 cm, it has reached a velocity of 10 m/s. What is the maximum velocity that the first particle will reach?

    A. 10 m/s
    B. 14 m/s
    C. 20 m/s
    D. Since the first particle will never escape the electric field of the second particle, it will never stop accelerating and will reach an infinite velocity.

150. The electric field for the two point charges A and B is shown below. Which of the following is true?

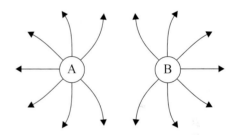

    A. Both charges are positive.
    B. Both charges are negative.
    C. The charges have opposite signs.
    D. The signs of the charges cannot be determined.

**151.** Two particles are held in equilibrium by the gravitational and electrostatic forces between them. Particle A has mass $m_a$ and charge $q_a$. Particle B has mass $m_b$ and charge $q_b$. The distance between the charges is $d$. Which of the following changes will cause the charges to accelerate towards one another?

   **A.**   $m_a$ is doubled and $m_b$ is doubled.
   **B.**   $m_a$ is doubled and $m_b$ is halved.
   **C.**   $q_a$ is doubled and $q_b$ is doubled.
   **D.**   $d$ is doubled.

**152.** When –10 C of charge are moved from point A to point B in the diagram below, 90 J of work is done.

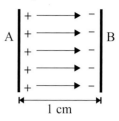

The voltage between point A and point B is:

   **A.**   0.9 V
   **B.**   9 V
   **C.**   90 V
   **D.**   900 V

## 7.2 Movement of Charge

When charge moves along an object (usually in the form of electrons), that object is said to be conducting electricity. At the same time that it is conducting electricity, the object also resists the movement of charge. All substances conduct electricity to some extent, and all substances resist movement of charge to some extent (superconductors excluded). Substances resist and conduct charge to different degrees. However, it turns out that the vast majority of substances either conduct charge very well or very poorly. Thus, we can safely classify most substances as conductors or resistors. Good **conductors**, such as metals, allow electrons to flow relatively freely. Poor conductors (good **resistors**) hold electrons tightly in place. Poor conductors are represented by, among other substances, network solids such as diamond and glass.

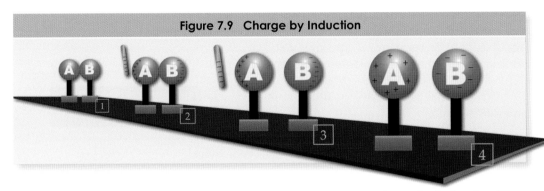

**Figure 7.9  Charge by Induction**

Since electrons flow easily along conductors, we can charge a conductor by **induction**. If we move a negatively charged object close to an electrically insulated conductor, the electrons on that conductor will be repelled to its opposite side. If we then touch a second conductor to the first, the electrons will move still further from the charged object by moving onto the second conductor. Once the second conductor is removed, the first conductor is left with fewer electrons than protons, and thus has an induced positive charge.

Moving charge is called **current**. Current is given in **amps (A)**, or C/s. Current is a scalar, but we describe its flow to be in the direction of the movement of positive charge. Unfortunately, Ben Franklin designated electrons to be negative without realizing it. Because of this, current, which is usually created by flowing electrons, is in the opposite direction to the flow of electrons.

The flow of electrons resembles the flow of a fluid. Like molecules in a moving fluid, electrons move very fast in random directions, while there is a much slower uniform translational movement (called *drift speed)* opposite the direction of the current.

When I rub electrons off my socks, I become positively charged.
My positively charged finger pulls electrons from the doorknob.

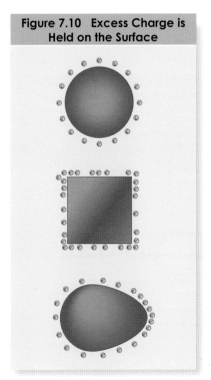

**Figure 7.10  Excess Charge is Held on the Surface**

## 7.3 Circuits

A **circuit** is a cyclical pathway for moving charge.

As we learned earlier, all substances resist the flow of charge. The quantitative measure of this property is called **resistivity (ρ)**. The quantitative measure of an object of a particular shape and size to resist the flow of charge is called its **resistance (R)** and is measured in **ohms (Ω)**. If an object is made from a homogeneous conductor, the resistance of the object when a voltage is applied uniformly to its ends is related to the resistivity of the material that it is made from by:

$$R = \rho \frac{L}{A}$$

This formula demonstrates that if the length of a wire is doubled or its cross-sectional area is cut in half, its resistance is also doubled. This is similar to what we would expect for fluid flowing through a pipe. Many useful analogies can be made between fluid flow and electron flow.

The product of the resistance ($R$) and the current ($i$) gives the voltage.

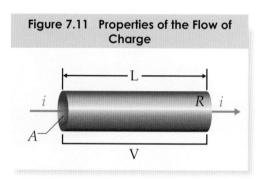

**Figure 7.11 Properties of the Flow of Charge**

$$V = iR$$

This is known as **Ohm's law**. Ohm's law is a very useful formula for analyzing circuits. This law also reveals another useful analogy between fluids and electricity. Recall from Lecture 5 that the change in pressure in a real fluid moving through a horizontal pipe with constant diameter is given by the product of the volume flow rate and the resistance ($\Delta P = QR$). Because we are probably more intuitive about fluids, it is often helpful to think of current as flow through a constant diameter pipe, and voltage as the difference in height between points in the pipe. (More precisely, voltage is analogous to $gh$.)

If we grasp this analogy, it makes a useful aid in remembering Kirchoff's two rules. **Kirchoff's first rule** states that the amount of current flowing into any node must be the same amount that flows out. A **node** is any intersection of wires. If we imagine current as fluid, it becomes obvious that the rate at which fluid flows into an intersection must match the rate at which fluid flows out. Otherwise, a pipe would burst. **Kirchoff's second rule** states that the voltage around any path in a circuit must sum to zero. If we imagine voltage as the height difference between two points, this rule states the obvious that the height of the starting point does not change when we go around some path (regardless of the path) and end up back where we started.

A battery adds energy to a circuit by increasing the voltage from one point to another. In our analogy to fluids, a battery pumps the fluid to a greater height. Batteries are rated with an **electromotive force (EMF)**. EMF is not a force at all, but is simply a fancy word for voltage. In fact, it is a mistake. EMF was named before scientists really understood voltage.

Real batteries have internal resistance. Most of the time on the MCAT, there will be no internal resistance. Always assume that there is no internal resistance unless otherwise indicated. To account for internal resistance, simply redraw the battery and place behind it, or in front of it, a resistor the size of the internal resistance.

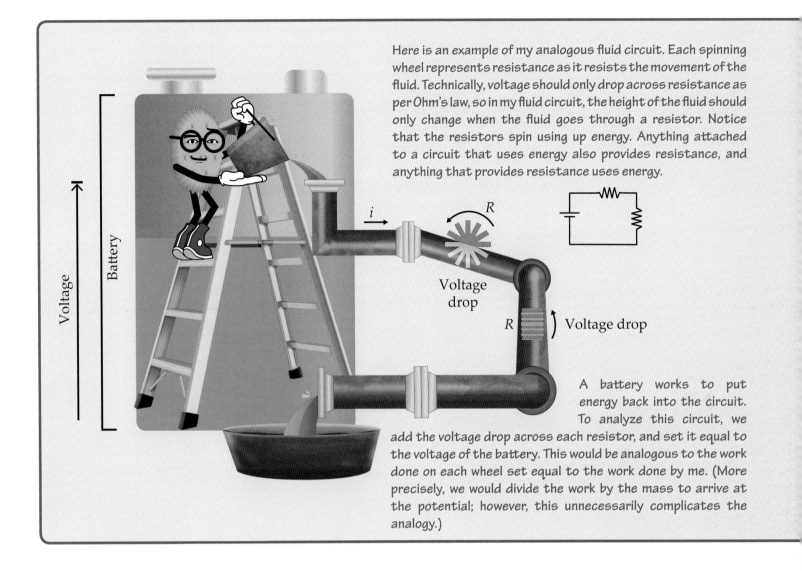

Here is an example of my analogous fluid circuit. Each spinning wheel represents resistance as it resists the movement of the fluid. Technically, voltage should only drop across resistance as per Ohm's law, so in my fluid circuit, the height of the fluid should only change when the fluid goes through a resistor. Notice that the resistors spin using up energy. Anything attached to a circuit that uses energy also provides resistance, and anything that provides resistance uses energy.

A battery works to put energy back into the circuit. To analyze this circuit, we add the voltage drop across each resistor, and set it equal to the voltage of the battery. This would be analogous to the work done on each wheel set equal to the work done by me. (More precisely, we would divide the work by the mass to arrive at the potential; however, this unnecessarily complicates the analogy.)

A **capacitor** is used to temporarily store energy in a circuit. It stores it in the form of separated charge. In a **parallel plate capacitor**, two plates made from conductive material are separated by a very small distance. On a charged capacitor, one plate holds positive charge, and the other plate holds the exact same amount of negative charge. This separation of charge creates an electric field that is constant everywhere between the plates. The electric field is given by:

$$E = \frac{1}{\kappa} \frac{Q}{A\varepsilon_\text{o}}$$

Notice that this $\kappa$ is not Coulomb's constant. This is the dielectric $\kappa$, which we will discuss below. $Q$ is the charge on either plate. The $\varepsilon_\text{o}$ term is derived from Coulomb's constant $k$. It is related to $k$ by:

$$k = \frac{1}{4\pi\varepsilon_\text{o}}$$

Note that in the electric field equation, $E$ and $Q$ are directly proportional, which means that $V$ and $Q$ are also directly proportional. That is, as the applied voltage increases, so too does the amount of stored charge. By definition, capacitance is the ability to store charge per unit voltage. In other words, something with a high capacity can store a lot of charge at low voltage.

$$C = \frac{Q}{V}$$

In a parallel plate capacitor, since the charge sits on the surface of the plates, the taller and wider the face of each plate, the more charge each plate will be able to store. Recall that charge sits on the surface of a charged conductor. In a charged capacitor, the charge sits on only the inside face of each plate. Therefore, the thickness of the plates of a capacitor will not increase their ability to store charge. Recall also that voltage is defined by distance ($V = Ed$). Thus, the farther the plates are separated, the greater the voltage, and the lower the capacitance. The physical makeup of a parallel plate capacitor in terms of plate area ($A$) and separation distance ($d$) is given by:

$$C = \kappa \frac{A\varepsilon_{\circ}}{d}$$

A capacitor's job is to store energy (generally for quick use in the future). The energy ($U$) stored in any shape capacitor is given by:

$$U = \frac{1}{2}QV \quad \text{or} \quad U = \frac{1}{2}CV^2 \quad \text{or} \quad U = \frac{1}{2}\frac{Q^2}{C}$$

If you know any one of these equations, the others can be derived from $Q = CV$.

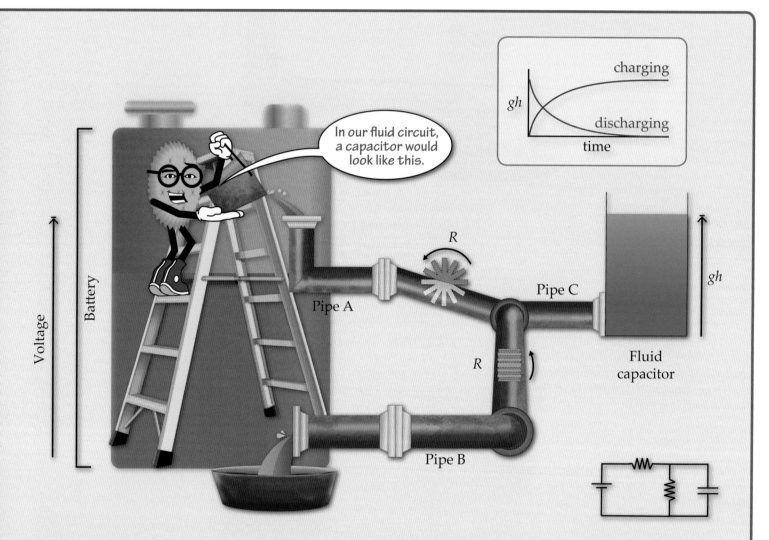

As the fluid comes to the fork at pipe B and C, some fluid would move in each direction. As the fluid capacitor fills, the fluid flow through pipe C would eventually come to a stop and all the fluid would move through pipe B. In order to maintain the fluid capacitor at height h, fluid flow through pipe A would have to have kinetic energy equal to the gravitational potential of the fluid capacitor. This results in the equation $v = \sqrt{2gh}$. The fluid capacitor now stores energy for the circuit. If flow through pipe A is suddenly blocked, the capacitor would empty with an initial velocity of $v = \sqrt{2gh}$. You should recognize the shape of the voltage vs. time graphs for charging and discharging a capacitor. Since gh is analogous to voltage, the gh vs. time graph is the same shape.

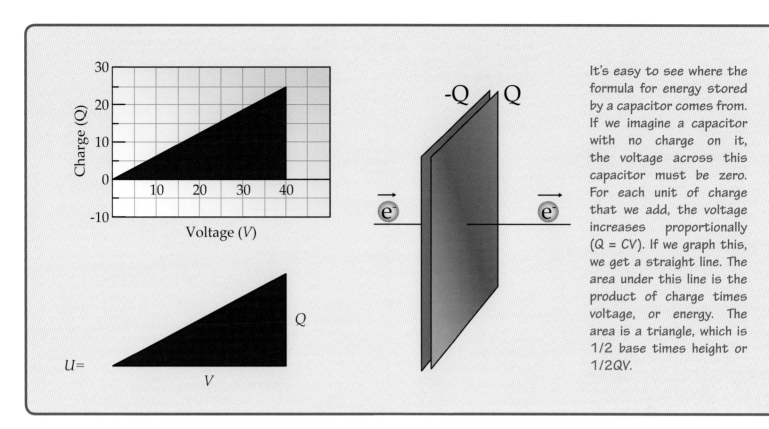

It's easy to see where the formula for energy stored by a capacitor comes from. If we imagine a capacitor with no charge on it, the voltage across this capacitor must be zero. For each unit of charge that we add, the voltage increases proportionally ($Q = CV$). If we graph this, we get a straight line. The area under this line is the product of charge times voltage, or energy. The area is a triangle, which is 1/2 base times height or 1/2QV.

The **dielectric constant**, κ, refers to the substance between the plates of a capacitor. The substance between the plates must be an insulator, otherwise it would conduct electrons from one plate to the other not allowing any buildup of charge. A dielectric acts to resist the creation of an electric field, and thus allow the capacitor to store more charge (to have greater capacitance). Usually a dielectric contains dipoles oriented in random directions. Recall that a dipole in an external electric field has potential energy depending upon its orientation. When the electric field begins to build up between the plates of a capacitor, the dipoles are rotated to point in the direction of the electric field (from a physics not a chemistry sense). This rotation requires energy in the form of work done on the dielectric. The work is conserved in the field, thus the capacitor is able to store more energy. Another way to look at it is from the standpoint that each dielectric creates its own electric field that reduces the overall electric field within the capacitor. The more charge required to build an electric field, the more energy stored within a capacitor. The dielectric constant of a vacuum is defined to be unity (one). Air is very close to one, and all other dielectric constants increase from there.

**Figure 7.12   Dielectric within a Capacitor**

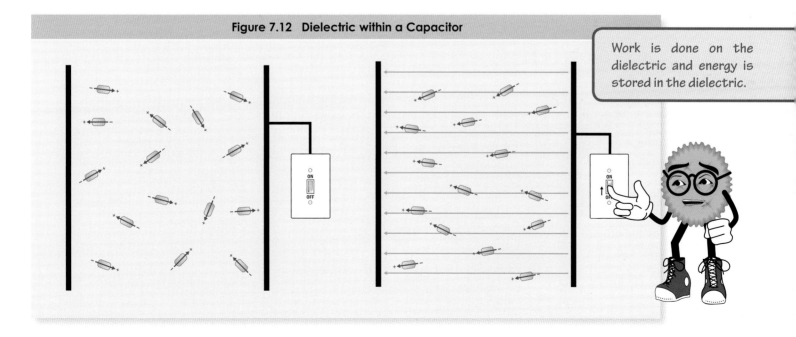

Work is done on the dielectric and energy is stored in the dielectric.

One other effect of a dielectric is to limit the value of the possible voltage across the plates. At some maximum voltage, the dielectric will break down and conduct electricity. This value of a dielectric is called the *dielectric strength*. If dielectric strength appears on the MCAT, it will be explained in a passage.

In order to analyze a circuit you must recognize the **symbols for a resistor, capacitor and a battery.**

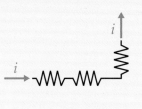
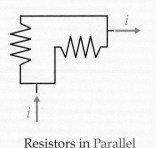
### Figure 7.14 Important Symbols in Circuits

Resistor        Capacitor        Battery

Lines connecting components should be considered completely non-resistive wires.

You also must be able to recognize when these components are in parallel and when they are in series. This has nothing to do with their orientation in space; parallel components are not always pointing in the same direction. Components lined up in a row, like train cars, are in **series**. More precisely, any two components not separated by a node are in series. Single components in alternate paths connecting the same nodes are in **parallel**.

When resistors are in series, their total resistance (effective resistance, $R_{eff}$) is the sum of their resistances.

$$R_{eff} = R_1 + R_2 + \ldots \qquad \textbf{(Resistors in series)}$$

When they are in parallel, their effective resistance can be arrived at through the following equation:

$$\frac{1}{R_{eff}} = \frac{1}{R_1} + \frac{1}{R_2} + \ldots \qquad \textbf{(Resistors in parallel)}$$

When we add a second bridge parallel to a first bridge, we improve traffic flow allowing for a greater 'current' of traffic.

Capacitors are exactly opposite. In parallel, their capacitance sums directly to give an effective capacitance:

$$C_{eff} = C_1 + C_2 + \text{...} \qquad \text{(Capacitors in parallel)}$$

in series, they follow the equation below:

$$\frac{1}{C_{eff}} = \frac{1}{C_1} + \frac{1}{C_2} + \text{...} \qquad \text{(Capacitors in series)}$$

To solve any circuit on the MCAT, we must simplify it as shown in Figures 7.16 and 7.17. We begin by replacing components in parallel and series with their corresponding effective components. We continue this process until we have our simplified circuit; one of each element. Next we use Ohm's law to find the missing quantity. For more complicated circuits we would have to use Kirchoff's rules. The solutions to more complicated circuits will not be required on the MCAT.

## Figure 7.15  Simplifying Circuits That Have Multiple Resistors

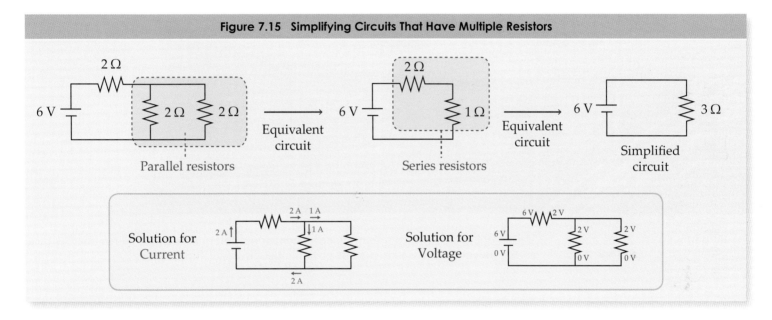

## Figure 7.16  Simplifying Circuits That Have Resistors and Compacitors

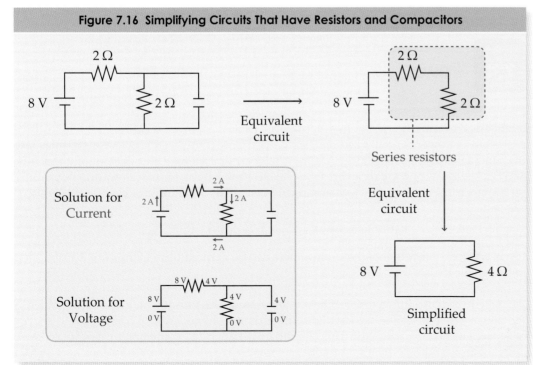

This is the solution for this circuit once it has been on for a long time.

If the circuit contains a capacitor, initially, for the first tiny fraction of a second, the capacitor behaves like a bare wire with no resistance. Once the capacitor is fully charged (likely to be a fraction of a second later), the capacitor behaves like a break in the circuit. It is most likely that you would be asked to solve the circuit after it has been on for a while.

These turbines at the Hoover Dam change gravitational potential energy of water into electrical energy. This energy is used to provide power to people across three states.

## 7.4 Power

Electrical **power** is the same quality as mechanical power, just as electric energy is the same quality as mechanical energy. In other words, power is power regardless of what source produced it. Power is often used on the MCAT to integrate electricity and mechanics into the same question. For instance, you may be given the voltage and current of a machine and be asked how quickly it can lift a mass to a certain height. In such a problem you would set the electrical power equal to mechanical power. The equations for electric power are:

$$P = iV \quad \text{and} \quad P = i^2R \quad \text{and} \quad P = \frac{V^2}{R}$$

If you remember any one of these, the others can be derived from Ohm's law by plugging in for $V$, $i$, or $R$.

As current goes through a resistor, heat is generated. The rate at which heat is generated is the power dissipated. The second and third equation shown are applicable only to energy dissipated as heat by a resistor. This is unlikely to cause any confusion on the MCAT.

**153.** What is the net force on the dipole inside the capacitor if the plates are separated by 1 cm?

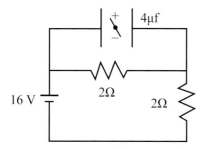

A. 0 N
B. 4 N
C. 8 N
D. 16 N

**154.** Each resistor in the circuit below has a resistance of 2 Ω. The battery is a 12 volt battery. What is the current across resistor B?

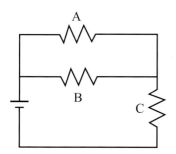

A. 1 A
B. 2 A
C. 3 A
D. 4 A

**155.** Which of the following changes to a parallel plate capacitor would not increase its capacitance?

A. decreasing the distance between the plates
B. increasing the area of the plates
C. increasing the dielectric constant
D. increasing the voltage across the plates

**156.** Each of the resistors in the circuits below represents a light bulb. If all three circuits use the same size battery, which circuit will produce the most light?

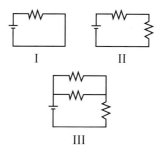

A. I only
B. II only
C. III only
D. I, II, and III will produce the same amount of light.

**157.** If all the resistors in the circuit pictured below have equal resistances, and the current flowing into resistor A is 4 amps, what is the current flowing into resistor F?

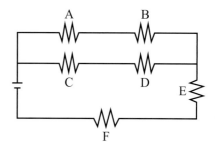

A. 2 A
B. 4 A
C. 8 A
D. 16 A

**158.** What is the energy required to operate a 60 W light bulb for 1 minute?

A. 1 J
B. 60 J
C. 360 J
D. 3600 J

**159.** The circuit shown below has three resistors connected in parallel to a battery.

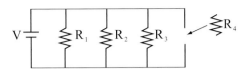

When an additional resistor, R4, is added to the circuit:

A. the voltage produced by the battery will be increased.
B. the voltage produced by the battery will be decreased.
C. the current produced by the battery will be decreased.
D. the power produced by the battery will be increased.

**160.** All of the following expressions are equal to an Ohm EXCEPT:

A. $\dfrac{V\ sec}{C}$

B. $\dfrac{W}{A^2}$

C. $\dfrac{A}{V}$

D. $\dfrac{V^2}{W}$

## 7.5 AC Current

Up to now, we have considered only **direct current (dc current)**, where the net movement of electrons is in one direction around the circuit. Since movement of the electrons creates power regardless of direction, electrons do not have to be driven in one direction. **Alternating current (ac current)** is created by oscillating electrons back and forth in simple harmonic motion. This is the current that is commonly used in home outlets in the U.S. Since it is simple harmonic motion, the voltage or the current can be described by a sine wave. Maximum current occurs when the electrons are at maximum velocity. This means that the value of the current is not steady, but varies with time. Since power and voltage also depend on current, they vary with time as well. At first this may appear as an unwelcome complication in calculations dealing with ac circuits; however, we can simplify things by using an average for ac current, and for the power and voltage generated by ac current. We use a special average called the *root mean square (rms)*. The rms is the square root of the average of the square. We use this fancy average because if we take the simple arithmetic mean of a sine function, we get zero. However, if we square the sine function first, and then take the average we get ½. Now, we take the square root and we get the $\sqrt{2}/2$. Thus, if the maximum value of the voltage is 170 V, the rms value is $\left(\sqrt{2}/2\right) \times 170\text{V} = 120\text{V}$. So for any maximum value of current, voltage, or power generated by ac current, the average value is given by:

$$V_{rms} = \frac{\sqrt{2}}{2} V_{max}$$

$$i_{rms} = \frac{\sqrt{2}}{2} i_{max}$$

The rms voltage in the US is typically 120 V.

> By switching to *rms* current, we can compute the average rate of energy dissipation (average power) for ac circuits just as we do for dc circuits.

## 7.6 Magnetism

A magnet creates a **magnetic field**. Magnetic field strength is measured in units of **tesla**, T. A magnetic field is part of the same entity as an electric field; however, the entity behaves differently with magnets. It is easier to understand and deal with this single entity (the electro-magnetic field) if we treat magnetic fields and electric fields as two distinct yet linked entities. **A static electric field produces no force on a magnet, and a static magnetic field produces no force on an electric charge.**

Like the positive and negative of electric charges, a magnet comes with a north and south pole, where **like poles repel and opposite poles attract**. Unlike electric charges, magnetic poles have never been found to exist separately; one pole always accompanies the other. Similar to the electric field, the magnetic field can be represented by lines of force. The lines of force in a magnetic field point from the north pole to the south pole of the magnet that created the field. Magnets placed within a magnetic field experience a force pulling their south pole opposite to the direction of the lines of force while pushing their north pole in the same direction as the lines of force. Earth itself is a magnet. Interestingly the Earth's poles are named for the poles on the compass magnet that points toward them, and not for the poles on the actual magnet that is Earth. Thus, the lines of force made by the magnet Earth point from the geographic South Pole to the geographic North Pole; what is called the North Pole is really the south pole of the Earth's magnetic dipole. (The actual magnetic poles are also 11.5° away from the geographic poles and constantly shifting very slowly.)

Unlike charges which can be separated, magnetic poles have never been found individually. If you try to separate magnetic poles by breaking a magnet, you just get more magnets with more poles.

**Figure 7.17 The Earth is a Magnet**

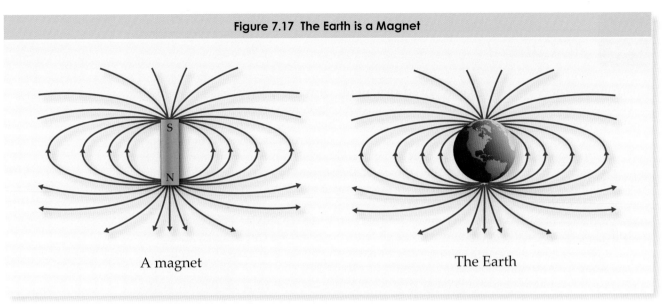

A magnet                    The Earth

Of course, since electric and magnetic fields are really the same entity that we are merely treating as two distinct fields, we would expect a change in either field to coincide with a change in the other, and it does. **Changing an electric field induces a magnetic field**, and, vice versa, **changing a magnetic field induces an electric field**. Thus, a stationary charge does not induce a magnetic field, while **a moving charge does induce a magnetic field**.

> By 'induce' we mean 'create'. A changing electric field creates a magnetic field and a changing magnetic field creates an electric field.

Current is moving charge. Thus any and all current creates a magnetic field. The magnetic field $B$ created at a displacement $r$ by a current $i$ moving through a small section of wire with length $L$ is given by:

A small magnet out pulls the entire Earth: magnetic force is stronger than gravitational force.

$$B = \frac{\mu_\circ}{4\pi} \frac{iL \sin\theta}{r^2}$$

where $\mu_0$ is a constant, called the permeability constant, and $\theta$ is the angle between the direction of the current and the displacement $r$. This equation (a form of the Biot-Savart Law) should not be memorized for the MCAT. It should be noted, however, that, like electric fields, magnetic field strength follows the inverse square law.

If we apply the Biot-Savart Law to a very long, straight wire the equation becomes:

$$B = \frac{\mu_\circ i}{2\pi r}$$

**Figure 7.18 Right-Hand Rule for Current (only option)**

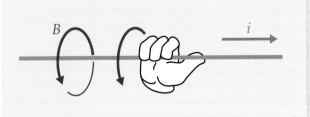

Notice that for a very long straight wire the magnetic field varies inversely with the displacement and not by its square. In other words, the magnetic field in this case varies with $r$, not $r^2$.

The direction of the magnetic field due to a current carrying wire is predicted by the right hand rule. If, using the right hand, we place our thumb in the direction of the current and grab the wire, the direction in which our fingers wrap around the wire is the direction of the magnetic field.

A charge moving through a magnetic field experiences a force. The force ($F$) on a charge ($q$) moving with velocity ($v$) through a magnetic field ($B$) is:

$$F = qvB \sin\theta$$

where $\theta$ is the angle between the magnetic field and the velocity of the charge. You must know that **the force is directed perpendicularly to both the velocity and the magnetic field.** This leaves only two possible directions for the force. The right hand rule also predicts which of these two directions is correct. The MCAT is unlikely to ask you to use the right hand rule, but it will require that you understand that the force is perpendicular to both the velocity and the magnetic field. To find the force with the right hand rule, using your right hand, again point your thumb in the direction of the moving positive charge, and point your fingers in the direction of the magnetic field. Your palm will point in the direction of the force. For a negative charge moving in the same direction, the direction of the force is reversed. In Figure 7.20, a positive charge moves to the left through a magnetic field pointing downward. The right hand rule predicts that the force will be directed out of the page.

Since this force is always perpendicular to the velocity, it does no work ($W = Fd \cos\theta$). It changes the direction, but never the magnitude of the velocity. Thus, this force always acts as centripetal force and can be set equal to $mv^2/r$ to find the radius of curvature of the path of the particle.

## Figure 7.19  Right Hand Rule for a Charge Moving Through a Magnetic Field

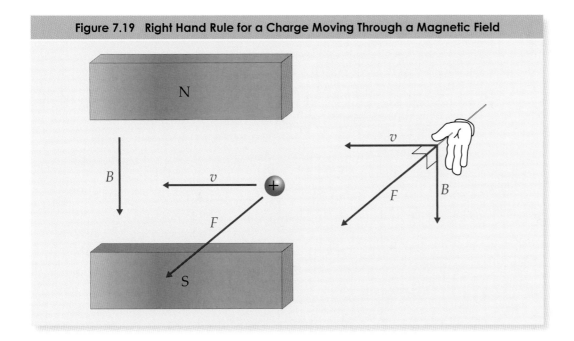

We still haven't seen a question on the MCAT that required you to know the right hand rule. However, you do need to understand that the force will be at a right angle to both the velocity and the magnetic field. That gives you exactly two possible directions for the force. The right hand rule predicts which of these two directions. You must know that it is either one or the other, but we haven't seen the MCAT ask you to choose between the two. Likewise, you must know that a current creates a magnetic field that circles the wire carrying it. We have not seen the MCAT ask you to identify the direction of the current.

In MCAT science, there are only two instances where the right hand rule is applicable. They are: 1. identifying the direction of a magnetic field around a current carrying wire, and; 2. the force on a charge moving through a magnetic field.

**Figure 7.20 The Magnetic Field Exerts a Centripetal Force on the Charged Particle**

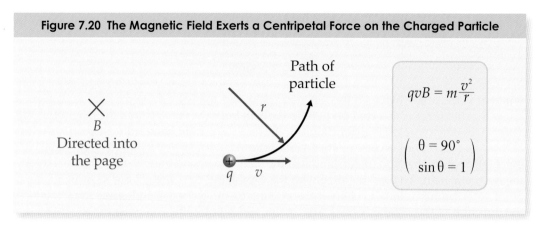

$$qvB = m\frac{v^2}{r}$$

$$\left(\begin{array}{c} \theta = 90° \\ \sin\theta = 1 \end{array}\right)$$

The force on a current-carrying wire placed in a magnetic field is: $F = iLB\sin\theta$, where $L$ is the length of the wire within the field and $\theta$ is the angle between the wire and the magnetic field. The direction of the force can be found using the right hand rule, and will be perpendicular to both the wire and the magnetic field.

As stated before, **a changing magnetic field creates an electric field.** However, unlike the electric field created by a stationary charge, this field is non-conservative. The mechanical energy creating the electric field is not conserved, but is dissipated as heat in the charged object. Thus, electric potential has no meaning for electric fields induced by changing magnetic fields.

Imagine a loop of wire pulled out of a magnetic field. As the magnetic field around the wire changes, an electric field is created and a current develops in the wire. The current created in the wire as it moves out of the external magnetic field creates its own magnetic field. A force is required to remove the loop at a constant velocity. The work done by this force is not conserved, but, instead, creates thermal energy in the loop.

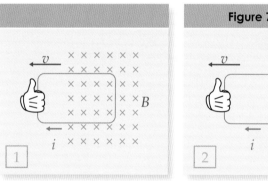

**Figure 7.21 Magnetic Flux Induces an emf**

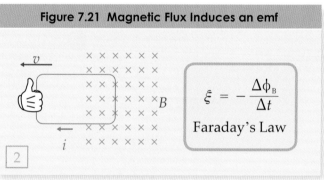

$$\xi = -\frac{\Delta\phi_B}{\Delta t}$$

Faraday's Law

This effect is simply stated in *Faraday's law of induction*, which says that a changing *magnetic flux* ($\Delta\Phi_B/\Delta t$) induces an emf ($E$). The magnetic flux is the number of magnetic field lines running through the loop shown above. Since the number of these lines changes as the loop is removed from the magnetic field, an electric field and a current are produced inside the wire. By the way, the electric field is induced even if the loop is not there.

**Figure 7.22 Magnetic Field Lines in the Wire Loop**

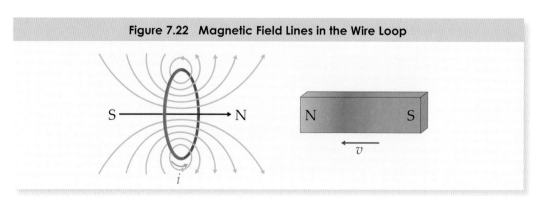

*Lenz's law* states that the induced current will create a magnetic field opposing the inducing magnetic field. Imagine a magnet moved toward a loop of wire. The magnetic flux through the loop changes, inducing a current in the wire. The current in the wire creates a magnetic field that opposes the magnetic field created by the magnet. The energy used to move the magnet becomes thermal energy in the ring.

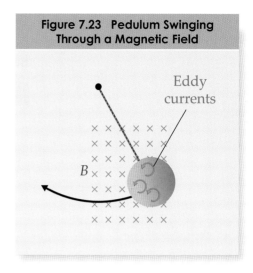

**Figure 7.23 Pedulum Swinging Through a Magnetic Field**

Eddy currents

Since an induced electric field is not dependent upon the presence of a loop, small eddies of current result when a conductor is moved through a magnetic field. Imagine a pendulum made from a conducting material swinging into and out of a magnetic field. *Current eddies* develop in the pendulum due to its electrons swinging through the magnetic field. The resistivity of the pendulum absorbs energy as internal energy (heat energy on the MCAT), thus changing the kinetic energy of the pendulum into internal energy. The swinging pendulum will stop swinging more quickly due to the magnetic field.

Notice that in each example of an induced electric field, mechanical energy is transferred to internal energy. This is because the forces due to the induced electric fields are nonconservative.

Hold on! Don't get bent here. Most of this information on magnetism is background trivia that, if it shows up at all, is likely to be explained in a passage. Concentrate on the basics. Here's what you must know:

1. a magnetic field is generated by a moving charge, and
2. a moving charge experiences force when moving through a magnetic field.

From number 2, remember how to find the circular path of a charged particle moving through a magnetic field. Like poles repel; opposites attract. The only formula that you need to remember about magnetism for the MCAT is:

$$F = qvB$$

Don't forget that the direction of the force is perpendicular to both the velocity of the charge and the direction of the magnetic field.

*Notes:*

| Equations |
| --- |

### Electric fields due to a point charge

$$F = k\frac{q_1 q_2}{r^2} \qquad U = k\frac{q_1 q_2}{r} \qquad E = k\frac{q_1}{r^2} \qquad V = k\frac{q_1}{r}$$

### Constant electric fields

$$F = Eq \qquad U = Vq \qquad U = qEd \qquad V = Ed$$

### Resistors

$$P = iV$$

$$R_{eff} = R_1 + R_2 + \dots \quad \text{(Resistors in series)}$$

$$V = iR$$

$$\frac{1}{R_{eff}} = \frac{1}{R_1} + \frac{1}{R_2} + \dots \quad \text{(Resistors in parallel)}$$

$$P = \frac{V^2}{R}$$

$$P = i^2 R$$

### Capacitors

$$U = \frac{1}{2}QV$$

$$\frac{1}{C_{eff}} = \frac{1}{C_1} + \frac{1}{C_2} + \dots \quad \text{(Capacitors in series)}$$

$$C = \frac{Q}{V}$$

$$U = \frac{1}{2}\frac{Q^2}{C}$$

$$C_{eff} = C_1 + C_2 + \dots \quad \text{(Capacitors in parallel)}$$

$$U = \frac{1}{2}CV^2$$

### Alternating current

$$V_{rms} = \frac{\sqrt{2}}{2}V_{max} \qquad i_{rms} = \frac{\sqrt{2}}{2}i_{max}$$

### Magnetism

$$F = qvB\sin\theta$$

## 7.8 Terms You Need to Know

| Terms | |
|---|---|
| Alternating Current (ac current) | Kirchoff's Second Rule |
| Amps (A) | Lines of Force |
| Capacitor | Magnetic Field |
| Center of Charge | Node |
| Charge | Ohm's Law |
| Circuit | Ohms ($\Omega$) |
| Conductors | Parallel Plate Capacitor |
| Coulomb's Law | Positive to Negative |
| Coulombs (C) | Potential Energy ($U$) |
| Current | Power |
| Dielectric Constant, ($\kappa$) | Resistance ($R$) |
| Direct Current (dc current) | Resistivity ($\rho$) |
| Electric Dipole | Resistors |
| Electric Field | Series |
| Electromotive Force (emf) | Tesla, (T) |
| Equipotential Surfaces | Universal Law of Conservation of Charge |
| Field | |
| Induction | Voltage ($V$) |
| Kirchoff's First Rule | Volts (V) |

Notes:

Questions 161 through 168 are **NOT** based on a descriptive passage.

**161.** If the AC current delivered to a home by the electric company is delivered at 120 V$_{rms}$, what is the maximum voltage across an outlet?

    **A.** 86 V
    **B.** 120 V
    **C.** 170 V
    **D.** 220 V

**162.** The north pole of the earth's magnetic field is at the geographic south pole. A compass is a small magnet whose north pole end is drawn in the approximate direction of:

    **A.** the geographic south pole along the lines of the magnetic field.
    **B.** the geographic north pole along the lines of the magnetic field.
    **C.** the geographic south pole against the lines of the magnetic field.
    **D.** the geographic north pole against the lines of the magnetic field.

**163.** A charged particle moves horizontally through a magnetic field which points directly upward. The force on the particle due to the magnetic field is:

    **A.** perpendicular to the magnetic field and parallel to the velocity of the particle.
    **B.** parallel to the magnetic field and perpendicular to the velocity of the particle.
    **C.** parallel to the magnetic field and parallel to the velocity of the particle.
    **D.** perpendicular to the magnetic field and perpendicular to the velocity of the particle.

**164.** The magnetic field created by a long straight current carrying wire:

    **A.** decreases in strength proportionally with the distance from the wire.
    **B.** decreases in strength with the square of the distance from the wire.
    **C.** increases in strength proportionally with the distance from the wire.
    **D.** increases in strength with the square of the distance from the wire.

**165.** A charged oil drop is allowed to fall through the electric field created by the plates as shown. In order to give the oil drop a straight trajectory, a magnetic field should be established with field lines pointing:

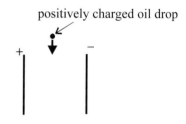

    **A.** right to left.
    **B.** directly upward.
    **C.** out of the page.
    **D.** The charged oil drop will not be affected by a magnetic field.

**166.** A positively charged particle is moving through a magnetic field of strength B as shown below.

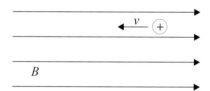

The force experience by the particle due to the magnetic field is:

    **A.** to the right.
    **B.** to the left.
    **C.** into the page.
    **D.** equal to zero.

**167.** A stationary loop of wire is placed in a magnetic field directed into the page as shown below.

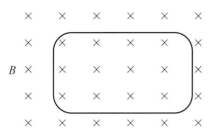

The current in the loop of wire is:

A. clockwise if the magnitude of the magnetic field is decreasing.
B. clockwise if the magnitude of the magnetic field is increasing.
C. clockwise if the magnitude of the magnetic field is increasing or decreasing.
D. No current will flow through the loop if the magnetic field is increasing or decreasing.

**168.** A particle of mass $m$ is fired into a magnetic field of strength $B$ at a speed $v$. The particle travels in a circular path inside the field with a radius $r$. Which of the following expressions gives the magnitude of the charge on the particle?

A. $\dfrac{vB}{mr}$

B. $\dfrac{mv}{Br}$

C. $\dfrac{mr}{v^2 B}$

D. $\dfrac{mv^2}{Br}$

*Notes:*

# LIGHT AND OPTICS

## 8.1 Light

In Lecture 7 we learned that a changing electric field creates a magnetic field and vice versa. An **electromagnetic wave** is the traveling oscillation of an electric and a magnetic field. The fields are perpendicular to each other and the direction of propagation is perpendicular to both fields. An electromagnetic wave is a transverse wave.

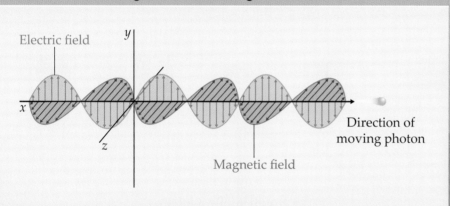

**Figure 8.1  Electromagnetic Wave**

Electric field

Magnetic field

Direction of moving photon

The speed ($c$) at which an electromagnetic wave propagates through free space is constant and is always equal to the ratio of the magnitudes of the electric field and the magnetic field:

$$c = \frac{E}{B}$$

Although the electric field is much larger when compared in SI units, the energies of the two fields are exactly equal. The above equation is useless for the MCAT. It is given here to remind you of the nature of electromagnetic radiation.

It is interesting to note that all electromagnetic waves are generated by the acceleration of electric charge. If a charge oscillates with frequency $f$, it radiates energy in the form of electromagnetic radiation at the same frequency. The rate and the direction in which an electromagnetic wave is transporting energy per unit area is described by a vector $S$, called the *Poynting vector*. The Poynting vector is always perpendicular to both $E$ and $B$, and has a magnitude of $EB \sin\theta$.

Electromagnetic waves are produced by the acceleration of charges.

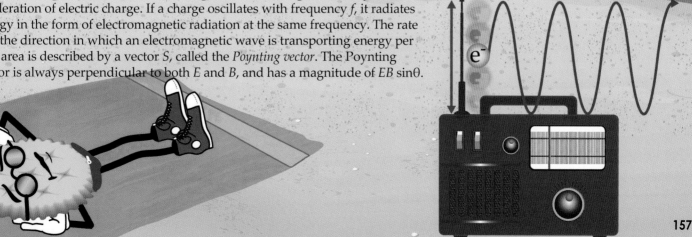

Electromagnetic radiation exists in all wavelengths. **Light** is a tiny sliver from the electromagnetic spectrum. For the MCAT you should memorize that visible light includes all wavelengths from $390 \times 10^{-9}$ m to $700 \times 10^{-9}$ m. You should also know that the shorter wavelengths correspond to violet light and the longer wavelengths to red light. Just beyond the visible spectrum is **ultraviolet** (beyond violet) light on the smaller wavelength side, and **infrared** (beyond red) on the longer wavelength side.

Just remember, Roy G. Biv invented the rainbow. O.K., not really, but Roy G. Biv is an acronym for the order of the colors in the visible spectrum (Red, Orange, Yellow, Green, Blue, Indigo, Violet). You can remember that wavelengths toward violet light have more energy because ultraviolet light has so much energy that it gives you sunburn.

Notice that each wavelength has a corresponding frequency. This is because the speed of light in a vacuum is constant ($3 \times 10^8$ m/s), which means that we can derive frequency $f$ from wavelength $\lambda$. From our wave equation, $v = f\lambda$, we have:

$$c = f\lambda$$

Light is slower when propagating through a medium. The speed of light propagating through some medium is found using a constant for that medium, called the **index of refraction ($n$)**. The index of refraction compares the speed $c$ of light in a vacuum to the speed $v$ of light in a particular medium.

$$n = \frac{c}{v}$$

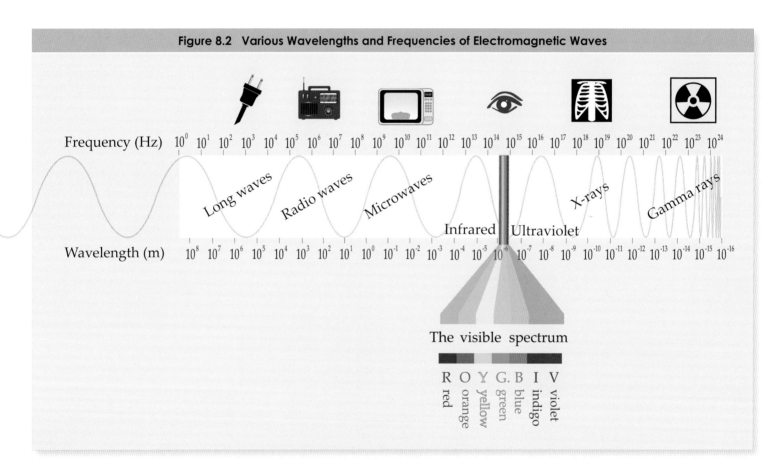

**Figure 8.2   Various Wavelengths and Frequencies of Electromagnetic Waves**

Since nothing exceeds the speed of light in a vacuum, all media have a refractive index greater than one. The greater the index of refraction for a medium, the slower light moves through that particular medium. Typically used on the MCAT are the indices of refraction for water and glass: 1.3 and 1.5 respectively. It helps to be familiar with these.

Glass blocks both ultraviolet light and infrared light, but is transparent to visible light. The electrons in glass resonate in the range of the frequency of ultraviolet light. When light strikes glass, the electrons begin to vibrate strongly and the vibrations dissipate through the glass as heat, preventing the ultraviolet light from continuing through. At the lower frequencies of visible light, the electrons don't resonate and so pass on the wave in phase, preserving the original wave. The visible light wave proceeds through the glass unchanged. However, the transfer creates a slight delay which accounts for slower speed of light through glass. The low frequency of infrared light causes entire glass atoms to vibrate, warming the glass and preventing infrared light from passing through.

When light strikes opaque objects it is absorbed as random kinetic energy or heat. (See Chemistry Lecture 3.3 for random kinetic energy and heat.)

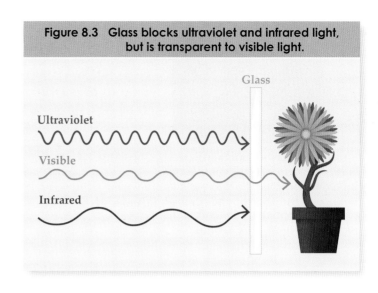

**Figure 8.3   Glass blocks ultraviolet and infrared light, but is transparent to visible light.**

Light is made up of photons. Each photon represents an electromagnetic wave. Recall from Chemistry Lecture 1.17 that a photon can strike an electron of an atom and be absorbed, exciting that electron to a higher energy level, or, vice versa, an excited electron may fall from a higher energy level to a lower energy level and emit a photon. The electron may move up or down to either the next closest energy level or it may skip one or more energy levels. The emitted photon has a frequency which corresponds exactly to the change in energy of the electron via $E = hf$. When that frequency falls within the visible spectrum, the resulting photon will have the corresponding color.

Each element has a unique pattern of electron energy levels. This pattern can be visualized when the excited electrons of a particular element drop to their ground state emitting light with the corresponding combination of wavelengths. A spectroscope separates these wavelengths via diffraction and refraction (discussed below) into an **emission spectrum** of the element. Since each element has a unique emission spectrum, an emission spectrum acts like a fingerprint to identify any given element.

Of course, the same electron transition that emits a photon with a particular wavelength can also absorb a photon when the electron is bumped to a higher energy level. When white light shone through an elemental gas is viewed with a spectroscope, an *absorption spectrum* is produced with dark lines appearing where the corresponding the wavelengths have been captured rather than emitted. These dark lines, called *Fraunhofer lines*, of the absorption spectrum exactly match the bright lines of the emission spectrum.

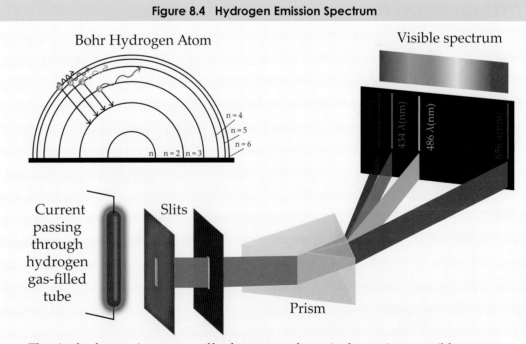

**Figure 8.4   Hydrogen Emission Spectrum**

The single electron in an atom of hydrogen may be excited to various possible energy levels. When the excited electron drops to a lower energy level, energy is released in the form of a photon. Of the many possible drops, only four produce visible light. When hydrogen gas is stimulated to produce light in this manner, the light appears white. When this light is shone through a spectroscope, the four bands of the hydrogen emission spectrum are produced. In this manner, each element produces its own unique emission spectrum.

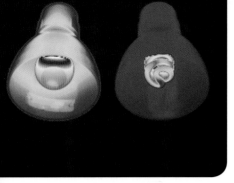

Shown here is a thermogram of two lamps, with an incandescent light bulb on the left and a fluorescent bulb on the right. The bulbs produce about the same amount of visible light, but compared to the incandescent bulb, the fluorescent bulb is several times more efficient and produces less wasted heat.

Another way an electron may be excited to a higher energy level is through atomic collisions. Recall from Chemistry Lecture 2.5 that the rate and energy of collisions increases with temperature. Thus, at higher temperatures, a substance has more excited electrons. When excited electrons drop to lower energy levels, visible light may be produced. This light has the property of *incandescence*. Incandescent light contains a continuous spectrum with an infinite number of wavelengths because electrons jump to energy levels of neighboring atoms as well as energy levels of their own atom. Incandescent light depends upon temperature; the dominant frequency of emitted light is directly proportional to the temperature. Therefore the temperature of an incandescent body can be measured by its color.

In some substances, an energy source may bump electrons up more than one energy level. The excited electron may then drop back down in smaller energy level steps releasing visible light. This phenomenon is called **fluorescence**. An example of fluorescence is when ultraviolet light excites electrons in a substance that then produces visible light as the electrons return to lower energy levels.

The excited state of an electron is temporary, typically lasting only for a fraction of a second. However, in some substances, the delay between excitation and de-excitation of an electron is longer than normal, anywhere from seconds to hours. In such cases, the atoms is said to be in a metastable state. Substances whose atoms are able to achieve *metastable states* are said to have phosphorescence. Phosphorescent substances may glow long after their source of electron excitation is removed.

## 8.2 Polarization, Coherence, and Lasers

Each photon represents an electromagnetic wave. If we examine only the electric fields of these electromagnetic waves, in typical visible light emanating from a point source (called *isotropic light*), the fields are oriented in random directions. If we use a device to screen out all photons not having an electric field in one particular direction, the resulting light

Nonpolarized light vibrates in all directions

Horizontal and vertical components

The vertical component passes through the first polarizer...

...and the second

The vertical component does not pass through this second polarizer.

with all electric fields oriented in the same direction is called **plane-polarized light**. When isotropic light is polarized, it loses one half of its intensity, since it loses from its electric field all components in one direction and keeps all components perpendicular to that direction.

An incandescent light bulb emits photons with infinite frequencies and infinite phases. Such light is *incoherent light* and is also called extended source light. *Spatially coherent light* is light where the photons are in the same phase. *Point source light* is spatially coherent. Sphere waves and plane waves behave as if they were emitted from a point source and are spatially coherent. Sunlight is considered incoherent or only partially coherent (i.e. approximately coherent when comparing two points that are close together). Starlight is coherent. The difference is that a star is so far away that it behaves like a point source. *Temporally coherent light* is light where the photons have the same frequency, making the light monochromatic. When MCAT uses the word coherent, they will probably define it, and they will probably use it to describe a beam of photons having the same frequency, phase, and direction.

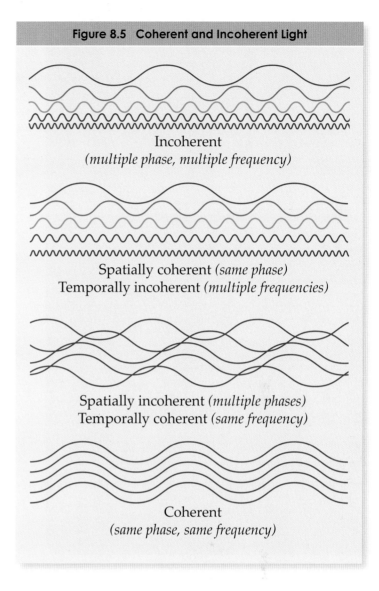

**Figure 8.5   Coherent and Incoherent Light**

Incoherent
*(multiple phase, multiple frequency)*

Spatially coherent *(same phase)*
Temporally incoherent *(multiple frequencies)*

Spatially incoherent *(multiple phases)*
Temporally coherent *(same frequency)*

Coherent
*(same phase, same frequency)*

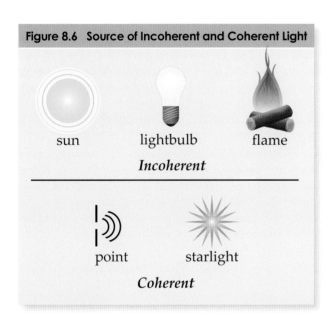

**Figure 8.6   Source of Incoherent and Coherent Light**

sun          lightbulb          flame

*Incoherent*

point          starlight

*Coherent*

*Notes:*

A solid-state sodium laser guidestar used at a telescope in Mauna Kea, Hawaii. The laser enables astronomers to observe celestial bodies at a higher resolution.

Light that is both spatially and temporally coherent can be forced into a parallel beam that spreads and weakens very little over great distances. **Lasers** emit such light. L.A.S.E.R. is an acronym for Light Amplification by Stimulated Emission of Radiation. This just means that a laser: (1) bumps electrons to a higher energy level; (2) <u>stimulates</u> those electrons to <u>emit</u> their energy as coherent photons (<u>radiation</u>); (3) and collects a small portion of those photons into a single <u>amplified</u> beam of <u>light</u>. The source of atoms in which the excitable electrons are found is called the *active medium* of the laser. The active medium must possess electrons that are capable of achieving a more stable excited state than normal called a *metastable* state. The active medium can be gas, liquid, or solid. An external energy source excites and re-excites the electrons in the atoms of the active medium until a majority of atoms are in a metastable state, called a *population inversion*. As we learned in Chemistry Lecture 1, when an electron falls back to a lower state it releases a photon of a particular frequency and wavelength. This gives the laser beam its characteristic color. When the photon comes near or collides with another atom in a similar metastable state, it induces the electrons in that atom to fall to its ground state and release a photon with the same direction, phase, wavelength, and even polarization. Now the two photons continue through the active medium stimulating still more atoms to release still more coherent photons. This is called *laser gain*. Laser gain amplifies the energy of the laser beam. Mirrors at either end of the laser trap some of the photons causing them to bounce back and forth within the medium stimulating still more photons, amplifying the beam further, increasing laser gain. One of the mirrors will be slightly transparent allowing for a small percentage (typically about 1%) of the trapped energy to escape in the form of a laser beam.

A laser does not produce energy; it transforms and sometimes concentrates energy from an external energy source into a narrow beam of light. The external energy source cannot be heat; it is impossible for heat alone to create a population inversion. Because of their higher frequency, laser beams can carry more information than radio waves.

**Figure 8.7  Laser Gain**

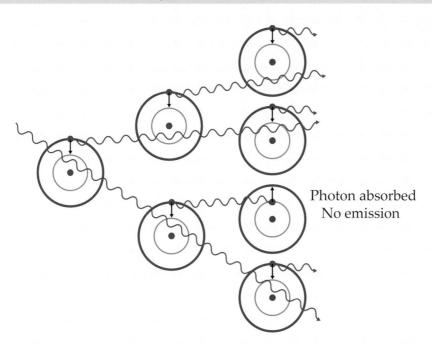

Photon absorbed
No emission

**Figure 8.8  Schematic of a Laser**

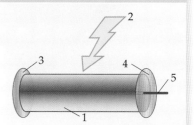

1. Active medium
2. External energy source
3. Reflective mirror
4. Partially transparent mirror
5. Laser beam

In laser gain each photon travels down the active medium stimulating electrons in metastable states to drop an energy level and release an identical photon with the same direction, phase and wavelength. An external energy source maintains a population inversion, where there are more metastable states than not.

The MCAT lists lasers as one of the topics it may test. If you were asked any question about a laser at all, it is most likely that it would be based upon a passage and/or entirely upon basic principles of science such as conservation of energy, speed of light, angles of reflection, refraction, diffraction, etc. When choosing the best answer, always keep in mind that the MCAT is a basic science test and that answers requiring advanced science knowledge cannot be correct.

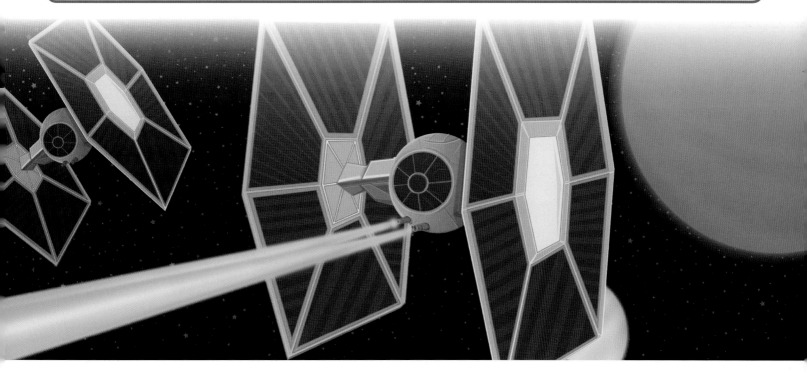

An interesting feature about Snell's law is that, at first glance, it seems to violate the conservation of energy. Since the frequency of the light wave does not change from one medium to the next, both the reflected light and the refracted light must have the same energy. This appears to be twice the energy with which the light started. The trick is that the light still has the same energy per photon. However, some of the photons have reflected and some have refracted. Thus, the sum of the intensities of the refracted and reflected beam equals the intensity of the incident beam. Energy is conserved.

Refraction does NOT change the phase of the wave at the interface between two media.

## 8.3 Refraction and Dispersion

Light has a **dual nature**. It acts like both a wave and a particle. The propagation properties of light can be described with wave theory, while the energy transformation properties of light are usually best described by particle theory. Neither wave nor particle theory alone explains the phenomenon of light.

We can approximate light as a ray moving in a straight line, and represent it as an arrow. This is called *geometrical optics*.

Like any other wave, when light meets an interface between two media, some of its energy reflects and some may also refract. The angles made by a light ray when it reflects or refracts are measured from a line normal to the interface. The angle at which the light ray strikes the interface is called the **angle of incidence**. The angle at which it reflects is called the **angle of reflection**. The angle at which it refracts is called the **angle of refraction**. The angle of incidence is equal to the angle of reflection. You can remember this because the collision of photons against the interface is completely elastic; the photons lose no kinetic energy.

$$\theta_{incidence} = \theta_{reflection}$$

The angle of refraction is given by **Snell's law**:

$$n_1 \sin \theta_1 = n_2 \sin \theta_2$$

where the subscripts 1 and 2 specify the respective interfacing media. Notice that in Snell's law, the angle of incidence and refraction are not specified; it makes no difference if light is moving from medium 1 to medium 2 or from medium 2 to medium 1.

Notice that all angles are measured from the normal; they are measured from an imaginary line that is perpendicular to the surfaces that interface.

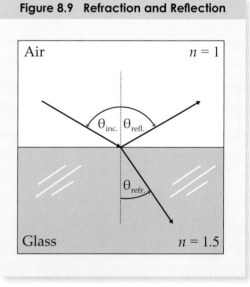

**Figure 8.9   Refraction and Reflection**

When light crosses into a new medium, the frequency remains the same and the wavelength changes. If the medium's index of refraction is higher, the wavelengths become shorter; if the index is lower, then the wavelengths become longer. The phase of the wave does not change due to refraction at an interface.

The energy of a single photon is given by:

$$E = hf$$
**(E is energy not electric field.)**

where h is Planck's constant (discussed in Chemistry Lecture 6). This equation shows that higher frequencies, such as violet and blue light, have more energy than lower frequencies. (**Warning:** Do not be mislead by this equation: This equation gives the energy per photon. It turns out that if we double the frequency, we also double the number of photons increasing the intensity by a factor of four as expected.)

## Figure 8.10 A Method for Visualizing Refraction

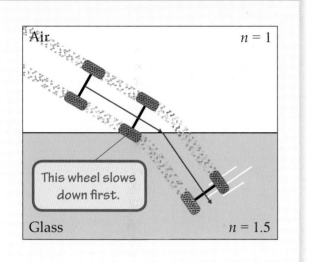

Air       n = 1

This wheel slows down first.

Glass       n = 1.5

Another simple way to choose the direction that light will bend is to imagine a pair of wheels on an axle. The wheels move fastest where light moves fastest and they always straddle the light ray. When the wheels hit the interface, the first wheel to make contact will either speed up, if light would speed up ('n' decreases), or slow down if light would slow down ('n' increases). Since the wheels hit the interface at different times, the axle will turn as the wheels move at different speeds. The direction in which the axle turns is the direction in which light will bend.

When light is coming from a medium with a higher index of refraction, the angle of incidence can be so great as to cause **total internal reflection**. In other words, if the angle of incidence is large enough, the entire amount of photons will be reflected at the angle of reflection, and none will refract. This angle is called the **critical angle**. The critical angle is derived from Snell's law by recognizing that the angle of refraction is 90° and that sin90° = 1:

$$\theta_{\text{critical}} = \sin^{-1}\left(\frac{n_2}{n_1}\right)$$

The concept of the critical angle is used in fiber optics, where a beam of light is trapped inside a glass tube and signals are sent using the energy of the beam.

## Figure 8.11 Total Internal Reflection

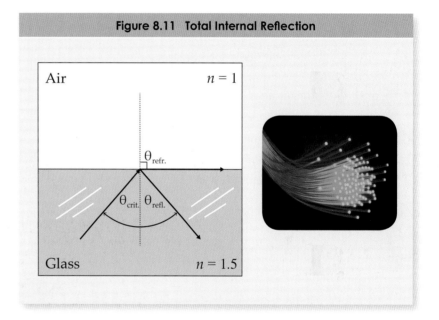

Air       n = 1

$\theta_{\text{refr.}}$

$\theta_{\text{crit.}}$   $\theta_{\text{refl.}}$

Glass       n = 1.5

The path that light travels between any two points is the shortest possible path for light in terms of time. This should help you decide which way light will bend at any interface. Imagine that I must rescue a fair maiden floundering in a swimming pool. She and I are both several feet from the edge of the pool. I must approximate at what point I should enter the water in order to reach her the fastest. I could either find a pen and paper and calculate Snell's law based upon my velocity on land and in the water, or I could just guess that since I am faster on land, I should travel farther on land. Just like light, I am looking for the shortest path in terms of time and I will bend my path in the same direction at the edge of the pool.

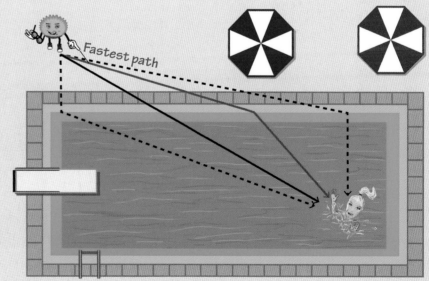

Fastest path

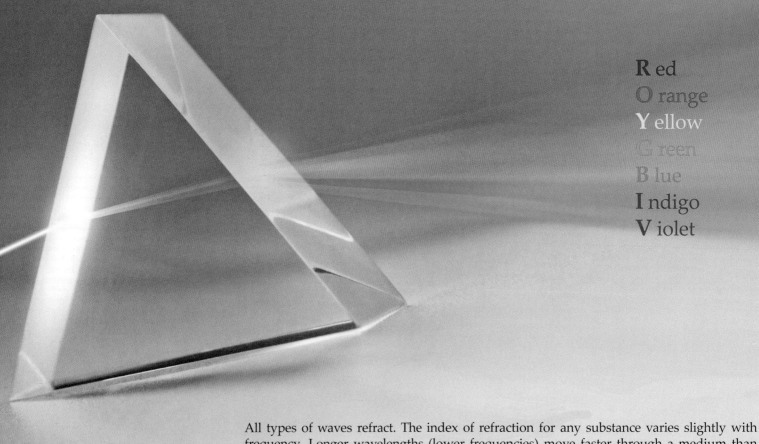

R ed
O range
Y ellow
G reen
B lue
I ndigo
V iolet

All types of waves refract. The index of refraction for any substance varies slightly with frequency. Longer wavelengths (lower frequencies) move faster through a medium than shorter wavelengths (higher frequencies), and therefore bend less dramatically at the media interface. As a result, white light, which is made up of all the frequencies in the visible spectrum, is split by a prism in a phenomenon known as **chromatic dispersion**.

We have assumed that our light ray is striking a smooth surface. When light strikes a rough surface it still follows the law of reflection, but a rough surface is actually microscopically uneven causing parallel rays of light to reflect away in different directions. This is called **diffuse reflection**. Diffuse reflection occurs when the distance between successive elevations are less than about ⅛ of a wavelength apart. If successive elevations are more than about ⅛ of a wavelength apart, the surface is considered polished for those waves and diffuse reflection does not occur.

> Chromatic dispersion is the result of refraction only. In a given medium, different wavelengths move at slightly different speeds resulting in slightly different angles of refraction.

**Figure 8.12   Reflection of parallel light rays**

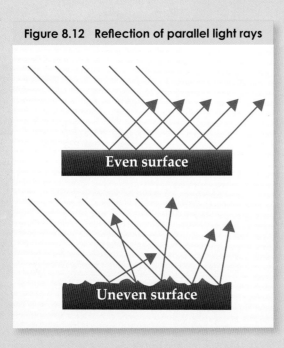

Even surface

Uneven surface

This satellite dish is a diffuse reflector for light rays, but is a polished detector for longer radio waves.

Thin film interference can also cause white light to disperse into colors. To create thin film interference, we sandwich a thin layer of one substance between two layers of another substance. The two substances must have different indices of refraction, for example soapy water and air as shown in Figure 8.13. The thin layer should be approximately as thick as the wavelength of incident light (i.e. $L \approx \lambda$). Following Figure 8.13, when light ray $i_2$ strikes the surface of soapy water, it both reflects ($r_\alpha$) and refracts ($r_\gamma$). Recall from Physics Lecture 6 that waves reflecting off a denser medium (in this case a medium with a greater index of refraction) change phase by one half of a wavelength, while refracted waves never change phase. As the refracted ray $r$ travels through the soapy water it has a shortened wavelength due to the larger index of refraction of water. The refracted ray strikes the back surface of the thin layer and reflects ($r_\delta$) (without phase change since the index it is reflecting off of has a lower index of refraction) and refracts ($r_\zeta$). Ignoring the refracted ray, we follow the reflected ray ($r_\delta$) back to the front surface where it reflects ($r_\varepsilon$) and refracts ($r_\beta$) again. Refracted ray $r_\beta$ follows the same path as the reflection of incident ray $i_3$ and thus the two rays interfere. This interference creates the light and dark portions. Although the wavelength of the ray $r_\beta$ is back to its original length, it may be out of phase with the reflection of $i_3$ because ray $r_\beta$ has: (1) followed a different path; (2) changed its wavelength during part of its trip; and (3) reflected without changing its phase. Constructive interference creates bright areas while destructive interference creates dark areas. The color is the result of different colors having different wavelengths and thus are out of phase to different extents due to length of their path through the soap bubble.

The equations for thin film interference maxima (bright portion) and minima (dark portion), respectively, are:

$$2L = (m + \tfrac{1}{2})\frac{\lambda}{n_2} \qquad for\ m = 0, 1, 2...$$

$$2L = (m)\frac{\lambda}{n_2} \qquad for\ m = 0, 1, 2...$$

where air with an index of refraction of 1 is assumed to surround the thin layer, $n_2$ is the index of refraction of the thin layer, $\lambda$ is the thickness of the thin layer, $L$ is the wavelength in air, and $m$ is an integer. Each value of $m$ that we plug into the equation returns a wavelength and thickness combination that creates a bright or dark portion. The constant ½ represents the reflective phase change that occurs at the first interface but not at the second.

In Figure 8.13, thin film interference would also occur if the back layer of air were changed to a substance with a higher index of refraction than water.

**Figure 8.13   Thin Film Interference**

Parallel light rays ($i_1, i_2, i_3, i_4, i_5$) from the same source strike a soap film. (The red rays indicate possible paths taken by photons arriving along incident ray $i_2$. Of course, all incident rays ($i_1, i_3, i_4, i_5$) have similar possible paths [not shown]. Assume θ to be approaching zero.) Some of the photons from incident light ray $i_3$ reflect off the soap bubble and follow path $r_\beta$. Some photons from incident light ray $i_2$ refract into the soap film, reflect off the back side, and refract back out along path $r_\beta$. Path $r_\beta$ is then travelled by photons that have originated from different paths and, as a result, the photons interfere with each other destructively or constructively depending upon the phase difference.

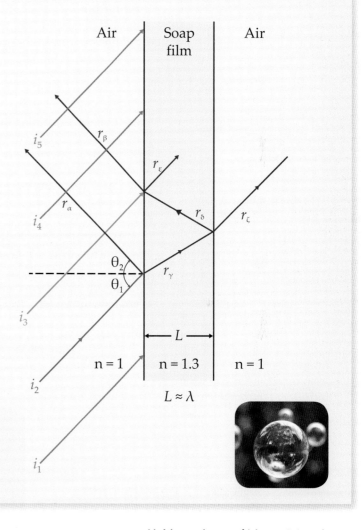

Hold your horses! Memorizing these equations will get you exactly zero extra points on the MCAT. The MCAT would give you this equation and you still probably wouldn't need it. Instead, maybe understanding the significance of the 'm' and the '½' will help you answer a question more quickly, but, much more importantly, understand the concept of thin film interference.

Such a case would cause $r_\delta$ to be inverted upon reflection. Since in the thin film interference equations given on the previous page the "½" reflects the absence of a phase change at the back interface, the equations would remain the same but the top equation would apply to minima while the bottom equation would apply to maxima.

If, in Figure 8.13, width $L$ of the soap film is much thinner than the wavelength of the incident light (i.e. $L < 0.1\ \lambda$), the phase difference is due only to the reflective phase shift. In such a case, the phase difference is approximately one half of a wavelength and the two waves are completely out of phase; destructive interference occurs and the film is dark.

## 8.4 Diffraction

When a wave moves past the edge of an object it bends around that object. This is called **diffraction**. All types of waves diffract, and waves diffract around all objects. Diffraction is most significant when waves pass through small openings or move around large objects. Significant diffraction occurs when the size of the opening or object is on the order of the wavelength or smaller. The smaller the opening and the larger the wavelength, the greater the bending of the wave.

Diffraction is a limiting factor for geometric optics. If we attempt to create a sharply defined ray of light by shining light through a small circle, diffraction occurs and the light spreads out, frustrating our efforts. The smaller we make the circle, the greater the spreading of the light. The light shone through a small circle doesn't only spread out; light spreading from one edge interferes with the light spreading from the other edge forming concentric light and dark rings around a central light circle (See Figure 8.15). To reduce diffraction, electron microscopes use electron beams which have smaller wavelengths than visible light.

Light bends in only three ways: 1. refraction; 2. reflection; and 3. diffraction. Notice that longer wavelengths diffract more than shorter wavelengths and refract less than shorter wavelengths

### Figure 8.14 Diffraction

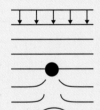

Light waves will bend around the corner of a slit or an object if the size is on the order of the wavelength.

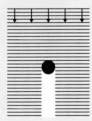

Minimal diffraction occurs when the wavelength is short compared to the slit or object.

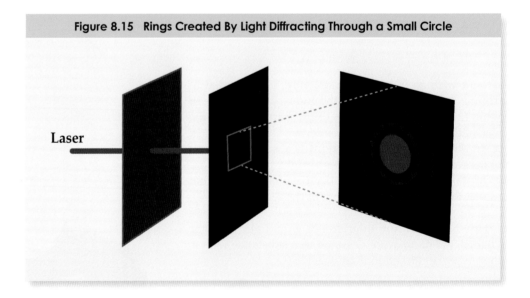

**Figure 8.15   Rings Created By Light Diffracting Through a Small Circle**

Laser

In **Young's double slit experiment**, coherent, monochromatic light is projected onto a screen with two small slits. The light waves diffracting through the two slits interfere with one another and produce a predictable pattern of alternating light and dark bands (maxima and minima) onto a detector screen. The waves from each slit start out in phase but travel different path lengths to meet at the same point on the detector. The difference in path length brings them alternately in and out of phase up and down the detector, causing them to interfere either constructively to form maxima or destructively to form minima. Each maximum is given an order so that The equation for the maxima is:

$$2d \sin\theta = m\lambda, \text{ for } m = 1, 2, 3...$$

where $d$ is the distance between the slits, $m$ is the order of the maxima, $\theta_m$ is the angle between the zero[th] order maximum and the m[th] order maximum, and $\lambda$ is the wavelength of the incident wave.

**Figure 8.16   Young's Double Slit Experiment**

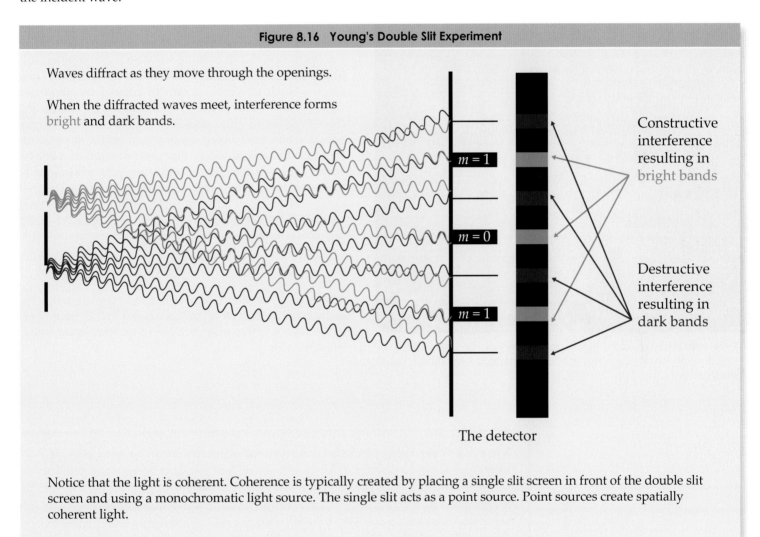

Waves diffract as they move through the openings.

When the diffracted waves meet, interference forms bright and dark bands.

$m = 1$

$m = 0$

$m = 1$

Constructive interference resulting in bright bands

Destructive interference resulting in dark bands

The detector

Notice that the light is coherent. Coherence is typically created by placing a single slit screen in front of the double slit screen and using a monochromatic light source. The single slit acts as a point source. Point sources create spatially coherent light.

A **diffraction grating** is a series of many small slits that diffracts a light source into its component colors. The slits are called *rulings*. A grating may contain as many as several thousand rulings per millimeter. Rulings may be perforations that allow light to pass through, or they may be grooves that reflect light. Either way, the diffraction pattern is the same. Like double slit diffraction a diffraction grating creates maxima and minima. For each maximum other than the zeroth order maximum the component parts of the light source are spread in a spectrum from shorter wavelengths (violet) to longer wavelengths (red). Higher order maxima exhibit a wider spread. The spread may be made up of discrete vertical lines or a smear of blended color depending upon whether the source light is made up of a few discrete wavelengths or a continuous spectrum. The more rulings that a grating has, the narrower and more defined each maximum and the wider the darker regions between the maxima. The formula for the diffraction grating is the same as the equation for the double slit experiment shown earlier: $d \sin\theta = m\lambda$., for $m = 0, 1, 2, \ldots$.

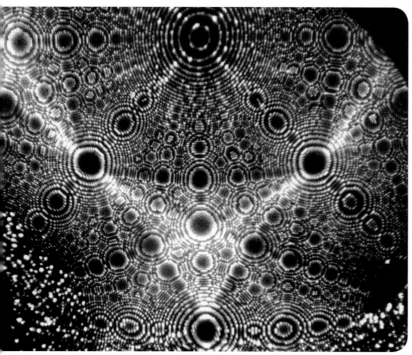

X-ray diffraction is used in crystallography to find the shape or structure of a molecule. This is a color enhanced x-ray diffraction of platinum crystal.

X-rays are electromagnetic radiation with wavelengths on the order of 1 Å. This is about 5000 times smaller than the wavelength for visible light and about the size of the diameter of an atom. Since diffraction works best when the opening is the size of the wavelength or smaller, it is impossible to mechanically construct a diffraction grating for x-rays. However, the atoms of crystals are about the right distance apart to act as a natural diffraction grating for x-rays. **X-ray diffraction** is unlike the diffraction that occurs when light bends around and object or opening. In x-ray diffraction, x-rays that are projected at a crystal scatter and create regular interference patterns unique to the structure of the crystal. X-ray diffraction is visualized as rays reflecting off different surfaces (or reflecting planes) created within the crystal. Bragg's law describes x-ray diffraction as follows:

$$2d \sin\theta = m\lambda, \text{ for } m = 1, 2, 3\ldots$$

where $d$ is the distance between reflecting planes, $\theta$ is the angle from the reflective plane to the ray (NOT the normal to the ray), $m$ is the order number of the maximum, and $\lambda$ is the wavelength of the x-ray.

Please don't spend your precious time memorizing Bragg's law. If, by some outside chance, you get one question on x-ray diffraction, and you need Bragg's law, it will be given. Even the fact that the angle is measured from the surface will be given to you. We discussed it here so that you have been exposed to it and won't be surprised or confused if you see it again. What do you need to know to answer an MCAT question on x-ray diffraction? Understand normal diffraction and the principles behind diffraction gratings; understand what an x-ray is; understand that x-ray diffraction is used to analyze crystalline structure.

**169.** A ray of light strikes a flat window as shown. Which ray most closely approximates the path of light as it exits the window?

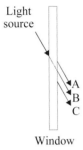

Light source

A
B
C

Window

A. A
B. B
C. C
D. Some light will follow all three paths.

**170.** Compared to humans, bees perceive a slightly higher frequency of electromagnetic waves. Based on only this information, to which of the following flower colors is a bee more likely to be attracted?

A. green
B. red
C. yellow
D. blue

**171.** The Coma Cluster is a galaxy approximately $2.7 \times 10^{15}$ km away from earth. How many years does it take for light from the Coma Cluster to reach earth? (Note: light travels at approximately $3 \times 10^8$ m/s)

A. $\dfrac{2.7 \times 10^{15}}{1} \times \dfrac{1}{3 \times 10^8} \times \dfrac{1}{60} \times \dfrac{1}{60} \times \dfrac{1}{24} \times \dfrac{1}{365} \times \dfrac{1000}{1}$

B. $\dfrac{2.7 \times 10^{15}}{1} \times \dfrac{1}{3 \times 10^8} \times \dfrac{1}{60} \times \dfrac{1}{24} \times \dfrac{1}{365} \times \dfrac{1000}{1}$

C. $\dfrac{2.7 \times 10^{15}}{1} \times \dfrac{3 \times 10^8}{1} \times \dfrac{1}{60} \times \dfrac{1}{60} \times \dfrac{1}{24} \times \dfrac{1}{365} \times \dfrac{1000}{1}$

D. $\dfrac{1}{2.7 \times 10^{15}} \times \dfrac{3 \times 10^8}{1} \times \dfrac{60}{1} \times \dfrac{60}{1} \times \dfrac{24}{1} \times \dfrac{365}{1} \times \dfrac{1000}{1}$

**172.** All of the following are indicative of the wave nature and not the particle nature of light EXCEPT:

A. diffraction
B. interference
C. dispersion
D. reflection

**173.** A piece of glass shaped as shown, with a refractive index of 1.5 allows light to pass through it striking point B. In order to make the light strike point A, the piece of glass should be:

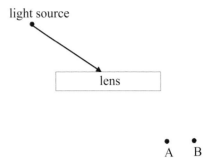

light source

lens

A   B

Note: diagram not drawn to scale

A. raised.
B. lowered.
C. made thicker from top to bottom.
D. made thinner from top to bottom.

**174.** If a light on a dimmer switch is gradually turned down, it will generally show a red glow at the moment before it is turned off. This is because red light:

A. moves more slowly through air than light of any other color.
B. moves more quickly through air than light of any other color.
C. has more energy than light of any other color.
D. has less energy than light of any other color.

**175.** The index of refraction of glass is 1.5. How long does it take for light to pass through a plate of glass that is 1 cm thick?

A. $5 \times 10^{-8}$ sec
B. $5 \times 10^{-11}$ sec
C. $2 \times 10^{-8}$ sec
D. $2 \times 10^{-11}$ sec

**176.** All of the following are examples of wave diffraction EXCEPT:

A. A light wave bends when passing from air to water.
B. Music is audible around a corner from the source.
C. The shadow cast by statue is blurred at the edges.
D. Ripples in water become semicircular after passing through a small space.

## 8.5 | Images

Mirrors reflect light; lenses refract light. In both cases light rays are bent. The mind may use reason and visual cues such as size and *parallax* to compensate, but the eye by itself cannot detect whether or not light rays have been bent. Without other visual cues, the mind assumes that light travels in a straight line. As a result, the mind traces straight back along the path of the light rays entering the eye and perceives an image. To the person in Figure 8.17, the fish appears to be where the image is formed because the person's eyes cannot detect the bending of the light.

**Figure 8.17  Your Eyes Cannot Detect the Bending of Light**

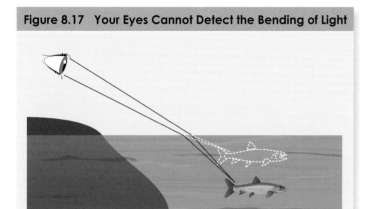

An image may or may not exist. A **virtual image** does not actually exist outside the mind of the observer; no light rays emanate from a virtual image. If a sheet of white paper is placed at the position of a virtual image, no image will appear on the paper. A **real image** exists separately from the observer. Rays of light actually intersect and then emanate from the point of intersection to form a real image. If a sheet of white paper is placed at the position of a real image, the image will appear on the paper.

Your reflection in a flat mirror is an example of a virtual image. Your reflection appears to be behind the mirror, but if you go behind the mirror and look for it, you won't find it. On a warm day, light from the sky enters the hot air just above the pavement, refracts, and shines into a driver's eyes, forming an image that may appear like water. This image is called a mirage. If you went to the pavement at the position of the mirage, you would not find the image of the sky. The mirage is a virtual image. The image of the fish in the diagram above is also a virtual image.

## 8.6 | Mirrors and Lenses

There are two types of mirrors: **convex** and **concave**. There are also two types of lenses: **diverging** (*concave*) and **converging** (*convex*). You should recognize both names for each lens type, but think of them as diverging and converging because a diverging lens acts like a convex mirror and a converging lens acts like a concave mirror.

This mirror from a school bus is an example of a convex mirror.

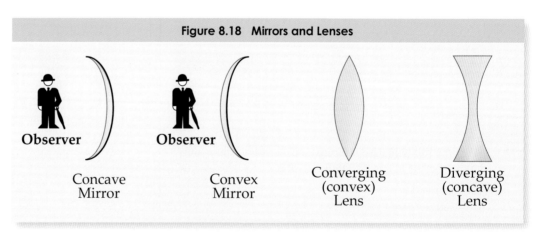

**Figure 8.18  Mirrors and Lenses**

Observer — Concave Mirror    Observer — Convex Mirror    Converging (convex) Lens    Diverging (concave) Lens

Generally the light from the object originates from some other source and reflects off the object. However, to avoid confusion, when working with mirrors or lenses, always assume that light originates from the object.

Here's a little trick to help identify a converging lens. Just remember the three C's: A thick center converges light.

Thi**c**ker

**c**enter

**c**onverges

**Figure 8.19   A Thicker Center Converges Light, A Thinner Center Diverges Light**

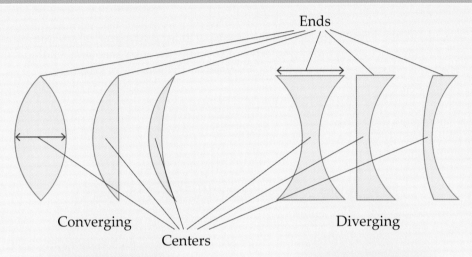

Ends

Converging

Centers

Diverging

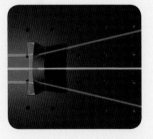

If the center of a lens is thicker than its ends, it will *converge* light, regardless of its shape or which direction light moves through the lens. If the center is thinner, it will diverge light.

A small enough section of any curve can be extended to form a perfect circle. The **radius of curvature** for that small section of the curve is the radius of the extended circle. Figure 8.20 shows the radii of curvature for two sections of a curved line. Notice that a smaller radius of curvature indicates a sharper curve. The straighter the line, the larger the radius of curvature. A straight line has an infinitely large radius of curvature.

**Figure 8.20   Radius of Curvature**

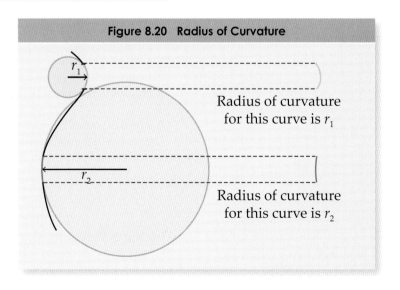

$r_1$

Radius of curvature for this curve is $r_1$

$r_2$

Radius of curvature for this curve is $r_2$

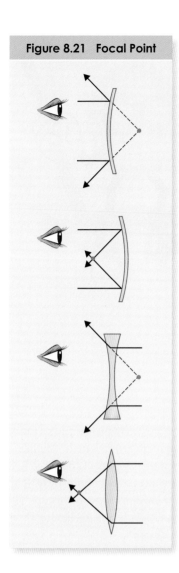

**Figure 8.21 Focal Point**

Although the mirrors in this lecture are called **spherical mirrors**, only a parabolically curved surface will focus all parallel lines to a single focal point. In other words, the equations for the rest of the chapter are only approximations for spherical mirrors, and they require that the rays of light are at small angles. For the same reasons, spherical lenses produce flawed images in a phenomenon called spherical aberration. This can lead to confusion if you are drawing ray-diagrams to find an image.

Light from horizontal rays is reflected by concave mirrors (or refracted by converging lenses) to focus on a single point called the **focal point**. For convex mirrors and diverging lenses, horizontal rays of light are reflected and refracted outward from a single point called the focal point. The focal point of convex mirrors and diverging lenses is found by tracing back along the reflected or refracted rays.

The focal point for any mirror or lens is separated from the mirror or lens by the **focal length**. The focal length ($f_{mirror}$) for a mirror is related to the radius of curvature ($r$) as follows:

$$f_{mirror} = \frac{1}{2}r$$

The focal length for a lens is affected by the refractive index of the lens ($n_1$) and the refractive index of the substance surrounding the lens ($n_2$). (Usually the substance surrounding the lens is air, $n = 1$.) The focal length of a lens ($f_{lens}$) is given by the *lens maker's equation*:

$$\frac{1}{f_{lens}} = \left(\frac{n_1}{n_2} - 1\right)\left(\frac{1}{r_1} - \frac{1}{r_2}\right)$$

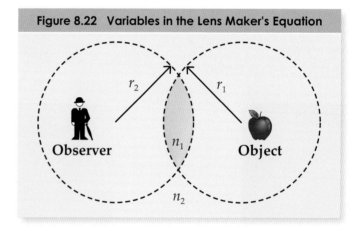

**Figure 8.22 Variables in the Lens Maker's Equation**

In the Figure 8.19, $r_2$ is negative. Notice that this equation indicates that a lens immersed in a fluid with an equal index of refraction will not bend light. In other words, when $n_1 = n_2$, a lens will not refract light.

You should be aware that since the index of refraction varies for different frequencies, the focal point of a lens also varies with frequency resulting in *chromatic aberration*. This is an entirely separate phenomenon from *spherical aberration* mentioned earlier in this lecture.

A lens has something called **power**. This power is not the same as the power in mechanics. The power of a lens is measured in **diopters**, which has equivalent units of $m^{-1}$. The power of a lens is simply the inverse of the focal length.

$$P = \frac{1}{f}$$

The rest of the equations in this lecture apply equally to both mirrors and lenses.

*Ray-diagrams* are a useful tool in understanding mirrors and lenses. They help locate the position of an image. However, they are not useful on the MCAT since they are time consuming and inaccurate. Later, Salty will offer a preferable alternative to ray-diagrams for solving optics problems on the MCAT, but for now, you should learn to draw them. When drawing a ray diagram for a mirror or lens, imagine the object emitting three photons from a single point. In the example below, this point is the tip of the candle flame. Each photon takes a different path. For simplicity, lenses will be considered infinitely thin, so refraction occurs at the center of the lens. The first photon (1°) moves parallel to the ground, strikes the mirror or lens and reflects or refracts so that its path can be traced back through the focal point. By definition, all rays of light parallel to the ground will reflect or refract through the focal point or so that their paths can be traced back through the focal point. The second photon (2°) moves through, directly away from, or directly toward, a focal point and reflects or refracts parallel to the ground. The third photon (3°) strikes the mirror or lens at the exact middle and reflects back and at an angle equal to the angle of incidence, or, in the case of a lens, moves straight through without being affected. (This is possible because the lens is considered to be infinitely thin and both sides of the lens are parallel at the middle). We follow the paths of the photons until they meet. Where the photons meet is where the image of the tip of the candle is formed. If the photons diverge, we trace their paths backwards from the mirror or lens to where they would meet.

### Figure 8.23 Ray-diagrams

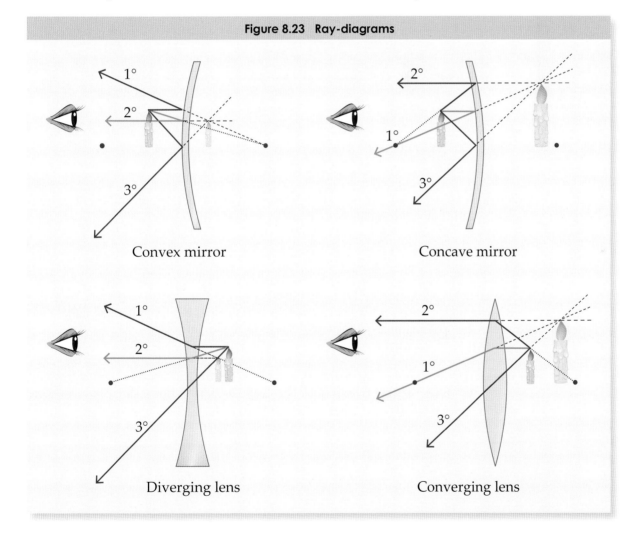

Convex mirror

Concave mirror

Diverging lens

Converging lens

Since light always travels the path that takes the least amount of time, although all our intersecting photons in the ray diagram travel different distances, all rays take the same amount of time for their trip. This can be explained as follows: Because light travels more slowly while in the lens, the ray that travels the farthest, travels the shortest distance through the lens. (In very strange cases where the lens has a lower index of refraction, the opposite is true.)

A mirror or a lens may magnify an image. The **lateral magnification (m)** is the ratio of the size of the image to the size of the object. For simplicity, we can compare only the height of the image $h_i$ with the height of the object $h_o$. The magnification is also equal to the negative of the ratio of the distance of the image $d_i$ and distance of the object $d_o$ from the mirror or lens. The negative sign indicates that, if both distances are positive, the image is inverted.

$$m = -\frac{d_i}{d_o} = \frac{h_i}{h_o}$$

Another way to measure magnification is **angular magnification**. The closest an object can be to an individual while that individual can still focus clearly on the object is called that individual's *near point*. The angle occupied by the object $\theta_{np}$ when at the near point, compared to the angle occupied by an image $\theta_i$ of the object when in front of a lens is called the angular magnification $m_\theta$:

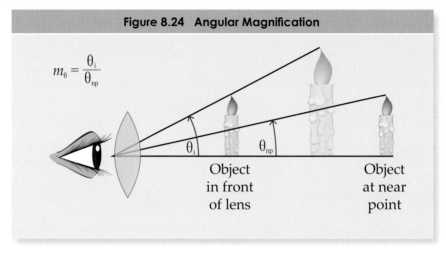

**Figure 8.24   Angular Magnification**

$$m_\theta = \frac{\theta_i}{\theta_{np}}$$

Object in front of lens

Object at near point

For any mirror or lens, distance of the image is related to the focal length and the distance of the object by the following equation:

$$\frac{1}{f} = \frac{1}{d_o} + \frac{1}{d_i}$$

This equation is called the **thin lens equation**; however, it applies to mirrors as well. It is called the thin lens equation because it assumes that the lens is so thin that the light bends only once when passing through the lens (instead of at both interfaces).

Objects, images, focal points, and radii of curvature are all given positive or negative values based upon their position relative to the mirror or lens. The difficult aspect of optics problems is identifying when a variable is positive or negative. The next section is devoted to a system for solving optics problems.

*Notes:*

**177.** The focal distance on a mirror cut from a glass sphere with a radius of 10 cm is:

    **A.** 2.5 cm
    **B.** 5 cm
    **C.** 10 cm
    **D.** 20 cm

**178.** When an object is 10 cm from a certain converging lens, the image is magnified by a factor of 1.5. What is the distance of the image?

    **A.** 3.3 cm
    **B.** 6.6 cm
    **C.** 10 cm
    **D.** 15 cm

**179.** A glass magnifying-lens is submerged in water to view an underwater object. Compared to viewing the object with the magnifying-lens out of water, this will:

    **A.** increase the magnification.
    **B.** decrease the magnification.
    **C.** not change the magnification.
    **D.** The magnifying glass will not work at all under water.

**180.** Which of the following statements is (are) true?

    **I.** Virtual images can be projected onto a screen.
    **II.** Real images can never be seen.
    **III.** Real images can only be created by converging lenses and concave mirrors in a single lens or single mirror system.

    **A.** III only
    **B.** I and II only
    **C.** I and III only
    **D.** I, II, and III

**181.** Which of the following is not a possible path for a light ray through a glass lens?

    **A.**      **C.**

    **B.**      **D.**

**182.** The image seen in a flat bathroom mirror is a:

    **A.** real image that appears behind the mirror.
    **B.** real image that appear in front of the mirror.
    **C.** virtual image that appears behind the mirror.
    **D.** virtual image that appears in front of the mirror.

**183.** An increase in which of the following lens properties will increase the power of a lens?

    **I.** Index of refraction
    **II.** Focal length
    **III.** Radius of curvature on one side of the lens.

    **A.** I only
    **B.** I and II only
    **C.** II and III only
    **D.** I, II, and III

**184.** A concave mirror has a focal length of 4 cm. What is its radius of curvature?

    **A.** 2 cm
    **B.** 4 cm
    **C.** 8 cm
    **D.** 16 cm

## 8.7 A System for Mirrors and Lenses

Mirrors and lenses may seem tricky, but, luckily, I have a system. The tough part of mirrors and lenses is deciding what's negative and what's positive. After that, it's just plug and chug with only three equations to memorize. My system, with only three rules and one exception, finds the positives and negatives.

1. Begin by drawing your mirror or lens and an eye on the side on which the observer will stand. I will draw all four possibilities on the next page. Now comes the first of three rules: "I (Eye) am positive that real is inverted." You must memorize this sentence. On the side which the eye is drawn, write 'positive, real, inverted'. Images and focal points on this side will always be positive, real, and inverted. Images and focal points on the other side will be always be negative, virtual, and upright. No exceptions.

2. Of course, everyone knows that you must stand in front of a mirror to see anything, so the front is the side that I (eye) am on. Lenses are just the opposite, but you can also remember that a camera is a lens, and I (eye) stand behind a camera to view an object. Label the front and back of your mirror or lens. Now comes the second rule: Objects are always positive when they are in front of a lens or a mirror and always negative when they are behind a lens or a mirror. For single lens systems or single mirror systems, the object must be placed in front, so the object must be positive.

3. Rule number three states: As long as the object is in front, convex mirrors and diverging lenses make negative, virtual, upright images. As long as the object is in front, concave mirrors and converging lenses make positive, real, inverted images EXCEPT when the object is within the focal distance, in which case they make negative, virtual, upright images.

In the case of a double lens or mirror system, simply find the image for the first lens or mirror, and use that image as the object of the second lens or mirror. Caveat: For a two lens or two mirror system, you must be careful with rule number 3 because the image of the first lens or mirror may be behind the second lens or mirror. This results in a negative object distance for the second lens or mirror.

Now we can label f, $d_o$, and $d_i$ positive or negative depending upon which side they are on. For a convex mirror and a diverging lens, f is always negative. For a concave mirror and a converging lens, f is always positive. Memorize the three formulas on the bottom of the next page. Any other formula for optics will be provided on the MCAT, including the lens maker's equation.

That's it. I have drawn one image for each mirror or lens to show you how the light rays are traced. However, if you are tracing light rays on the MCAT, you are wasting your time.

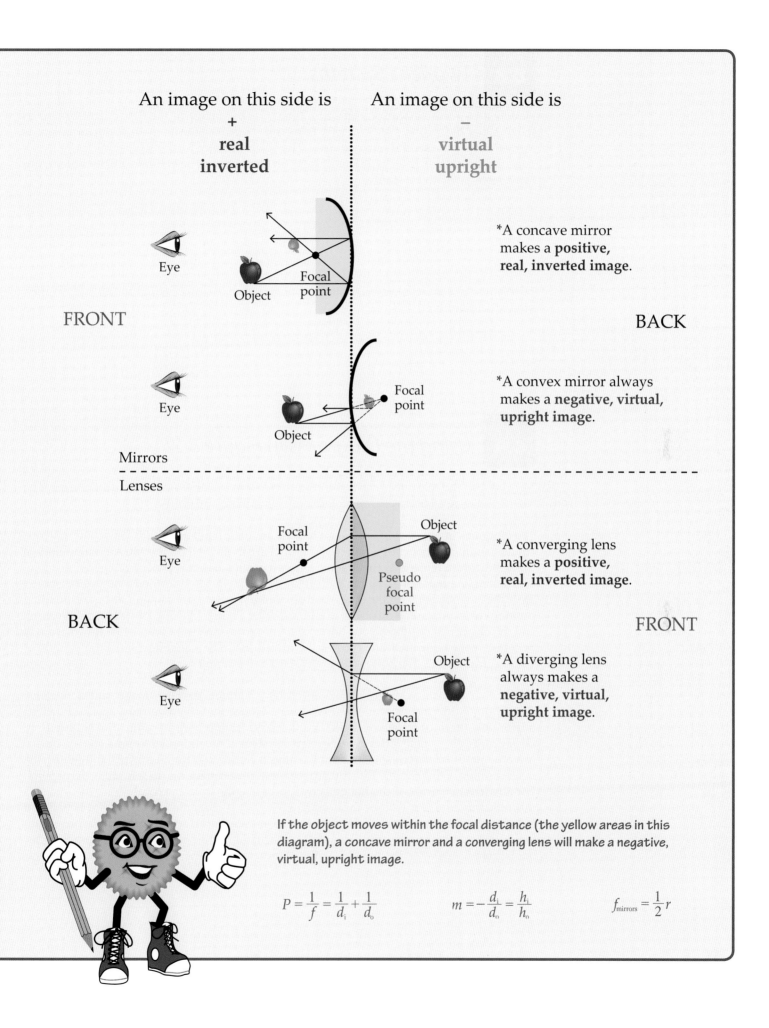

An image on this side is
+
**real**
**inverted**

An image on this side is
–
**virtual**
**upright**

*A concave mirror makes a **positive, real, inverted image**.

Eye

Object    Focal point

FRONT

BACK

Eye

*A convex mirror always makes a **negative, virtual, upright image**.

Object    Focal point

Mirrors
- - - - - - - - - - - - - - - - - - - - - - - - - - - - - - - - - -
Lenses

Eye

Focal point    Object

Pseudo focal point

*A converging lens makes a **positive, real, inverted image**.

BACK

FRONT

Eye

Object

Focal point

*A diverging lens always makes a **negative, virtual, upright image**.

If the object moves within the focal distance (the yellow areas in this diagram), a concave mirror and a converging lens will make a negative, virtual, upright image.

$$P = \frac{1}{f} = \frac{1}{d_i} + \frac{1}{d_o} \qquad m = -\frac{d_i}{d_o} = \frac{h_i}{h_o} \qquad f_{\text{mirrors}} = \frac{1}{2}r$$

## 8.8 | Two-lens Systems

Handle a two lens system one lens at a time. Use the image of the first mirror or lens as the object of the second mirror or lens. Sometimes the image from the first mirror or lens is formed behind the second mirror or lens. The object distance for the second mirror or lens is negative in this case. In a single lens system, an object cannot be behind a mirror or lens, nor can it have a negative distance.

The lateral magnification of a two lens system is the product of the lateral magnification of each lens:

$$M = m_1 m_2$$

Two lenses in contact with each other have an effective power equal to the sum of their individual powers:

$$P_{eff} = P_1 + P_2$$

## 8.9 | Using the Diagrams in Figure 8.25

Microscopes and telescopes can be built from two lens systems as well as from mirrors. The MCAT will give all necessary formulae concerning these apparatus.

The diagrams in Figure 8.25 are meant to increase your familiarity with lenses and mirrors. Understanding them is not a requirement in order to do well on the MCAT. The solid line in each diagram represents the magnification when the object is placed at a given distance. The dotted line represents the magnification when the image is formed at a given distance. Since the magnification for the image and object must match, you can find the corresponding positions of an image and an object as follows: draw a horizontal line anywhere on the graph and the object will be where your horizontal line crosses the solid line, while the image will be where your horizontal line crosses the dotted line. The magnification is the y-value of your horizontal line. The bottom diagram gives two examples.

Notice that a positive magnification indicates a virtual, upright image and a negative magnification indicates a real, inverted image. Notice that the diverging lens and convex mirror only produce smaller images for all object positions in front of the mirror or lens. In other words, in a single lens or single mirror system, a diverging lens and a convex mirror can only produce images smaller than the object. Notice that for all mirrors and lenses, the magnification of the image is directly proportional to the image distance from the focal point. For any lens or mirror, if the image is two focal lengths from the focal point, the image is magnified by two; if it is three focal lengths away, it is magnified by three; if it is half of a focal length away, it is magnified by one half (or reduced); and so on. Notice that converging lenses and concave mirrors produce smaller images while the object is outside 2 focal lengths, but larger images when the object is within 2 focal lengths.

**Figure 8.25  Lens and Mirror Diagrams**

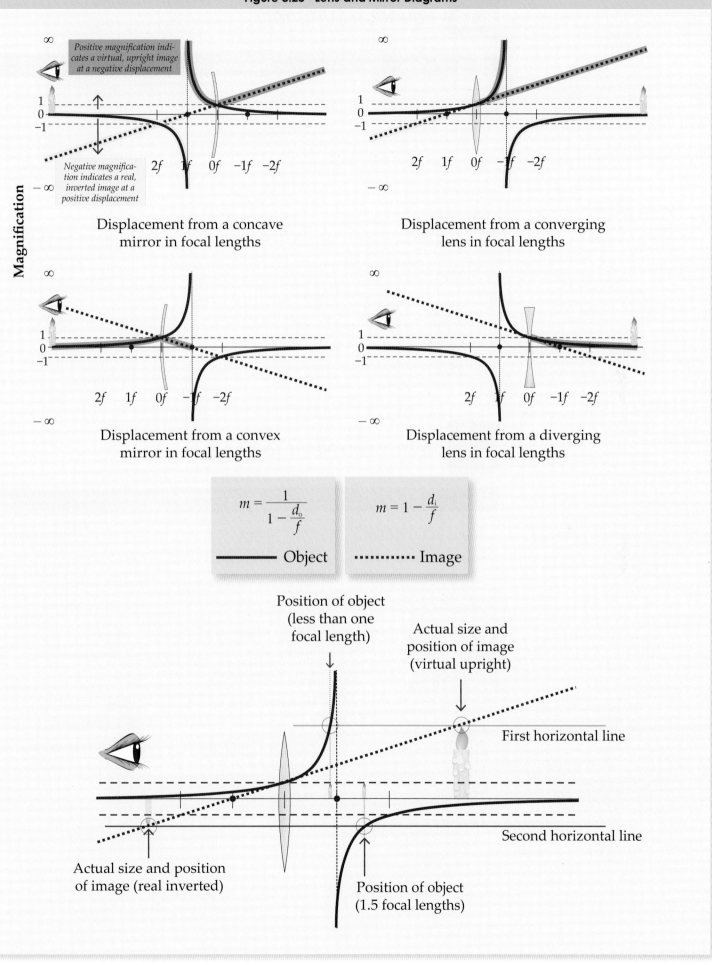

Positive magnification indi-cates a virtual, upright image at a negative displacement

Negative magnifica-tion indicates a real, inverted image at a positive displacement

**Magnification**

Displacement from a concave mirror in focal lengths

Displacement from a converging lens in focal lengths

Displacement from a convex mirror in focal lengths

Displacement from a diverging lens in focal lengths

$$m = \frac{1}{1 - \frac{d_o}{f}}$$

$$m = 1 - \frac{d_i}{f}$$

——— Object          ·········· Image

Position of object (less than one focal length)

Actual size and position of image (virtual upright)

First horizontal line

Second horizontal line

Actual size and position of image (real inverted)

Position of object (1.5 focal lengths)

## 8.10 Equation Summary

| Equations |
| --- |

**Electromagnetic radiation**

$$c = f\lambda \qquad\qquad\qquad n = \frac{c}{v}$$

$$E = hf \qquad\qquad\qquad n_1 \sin\theta_1 = n_2 \sin\theta_2$$

**Mirrors and lenses**

$$f_{\text{mirror}} = \frac{1}{2}r \qquad P = \frac{1}{f} \qquad m = -\frac{d_i}{d_o} = \frac{h_i}{h_o} \qquad \frac{1}{f} = \frac{1}{d_o} + \frac{1}{d_i}$$

## 8.11 Terms You Need To Know

| Terms |
| --- |

| | | |
| --- | --- | --- |
| Angle of Incidence | Dual Nature | Radius of Curvature |
| Angle of Reflection | Electromagnetic Wave | Real Image |
| Angle of Refraction | Emission Spectrum | Snell's Law |
| Angular Magnification | Fluorescence | Spherical Mirrors |
| Chromatic Dispersion | Focal Length | Total Internal |
| Concave | Focal Point | Reflection |
| Converging | Index of Refraction ($n$) | Ultraviolet |
| Convex | Infrared | Virtual Image |
| Critical Angle | Lasers | X-ray Diffraction |
| Diffraction Grating | Lateral Magnification ($m$) | Young's Double Slit |
| Diffuse Reflection | Light | Experiment |
| Diopters | Plane-polarized Light | |
| Diverging | Power | |

**185.** An object stands 4 cm in front of a converging lens. If the lens has a focal distance of 1 cm, where is the image formed?

    **A.** 0.75 cm in front of the lens
    **B.** 0.75 cm behind the lens
    **C.** 1 cm behind the lens
    **D.** 1.33 cm behind the lens

**186.** An inverted image is created 5 m in front of a mirror. Which of the following could be true about the mirror and the object?

    **A.** The mirror is convex with less than a 5 m focal distance.
    **B.** The mirror is concave with less than a 5 m focal distance.
    **C.** The mirror is convex with more than a 5 m focal distance.
    **D.** The mirror is concave with more than a 5 m focal distance.

**187.** A 1 cm candle stands 4 cm in front of a concave mirror with a 2 cm focal distance. The image is:

    **A.** inverted and 1 cm tall.
    **B.** inverted and 2 cm tall.
    **C.** upright and 1 cm tall.
    **D.** upright and 2 cm tall.

**188.** The focal distance of a lens is –3 m. The lens is a:

    **A.** 1/3 diopter converging lens.
    **B.** –1/3 diopter converging lens.
    **C.** 1/3 diopter diverging lens.
    **D.** –1/3 diopter diverging lens.

**189.** A lens is manufactured in such a way as to allow the object and the image to be at the same distance from the lens. If the lens is not flat, the only way this could be true is if the lens were:

    **A.** a diverging lens with the object at the focal distance.
    **B.** a diverging lens with the object at twice the focal distance.
    **C.** a converging lens with the object at the focal distance.
    **D.** a converging lens with the object at twice the focal distance.

**190.** An object is placed at the focal point of a converging lens. The image will appear:

    **A.** on the surface of the lens.
    **B.** at the focal point.
    **C.** at a distance of twice the focal length.
    **D.** not at all.

**191.** Light from the moon passes through a converging lens on the surface of the earth. If the lens has a focal length of 20 cm, at what distance from the lens will the image appear?

    **A.** 10 cm
    **B.** 20 cm
    **C.** 40 cm
    **D.** at infinity

**192.** The diagram below shows an object placed in front of an unknown optical device and the image produced.

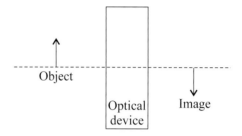

The optical device is a:

    **A.** convex mirror.
    **B.** concave mirror.
    **C.** converging lens.
    **D.** diverging lens.

*Notes:*

# STOP!

DO NOT LOOK AT THESE EXAMS UNTIL CLASS.

**30-MINUTE IN-CLASS EXAM FOR LECTURE 1**

## Passage I (Questions 1-6)

In 1939 Emanuel Zacchini, a circus entertainer, had himself shot from a cannon over three 18 m tall Ferris wheels. He reached a velocity of 27 m/s and sailed to a height of nearly 24 m landing safely in a net on the other side of the Ferris wheels. The cannon muzzle and the net were 3 m above the ground. Zacchini's initial trajectory was at an angle of 53° above the horizontal.

Zacchini had two concerns about his flight. First, he could not be completely certain of the effects of air resistance and air currents. Second, the force on him while inside the cannon was so great that he would momentarily lose consciousness during the stunt. The second problem he solved by training himself to wake quickly.

Projectile motion near the surface of the earth can be approximated by the following three equations:

$$x = x_o + v_o t + \frac{1}{2} at^2$$

$$v = v_o + at$$

$$v^2 = v_o^2 + 2a(x - x_o)$$

where $x$ is displacement, $v$ is either the horizontal or vertical velocity, $t$ is time in flight, and $a$ is either 0 or equal to the gravitational constant $g$ which can be approximated at 10 m/s². The subscript denotes initial values. These equations do not take into account the effects of the medium through which the projectile moves. (Note: sin 53° = 0.8, cos 53° = 0.6)

1. Using the above equations and adjusting the net for the effects of air resistance, Zacchini should place the center of the net at a displacement:

    A. exactly equal to $x$.
    B. exactly equal to $x_o$.
    C. greater than $x$.
    D. less than $x$.

2. From the information in the passage, which of the following factors most likely plays the greatest role in Zacchini's loss of consciousness during the flight?

    A. velocity
    B. height
    C. acceleration
    D. momentum

3. Which of the following is true of a projectile in a vacuum when it reaches its maximum height?

    A. Both its kinetic and potential energies are at a maximum.
    B. Both its kinetic and potential energies are at a minimum.
    C. Its kinetic energy is at a maximum and its potential energy is at a minimum.
    D. Its potential energy is at a maximum and its kinetic energy is at a minimum.

4. What is the vertical component of Zacchini's velocity when he exits the cannon?

    A. 16.2 m/s
    B. 21.6 m/s
    C. 23.8 m/s
    D. 27.0 m/s

5. At which of the following points during the stunt is Zacchini's acceleration the greatest?

    A. While he is still inside the muzzle of the cannon.
    B. The moment he exits from the muzzle.
    C. The moment before he lands in the net.
    D. Acceleration is constant throughout the stunt.

6. Ignoring the effects of air resistance, Zacchini would have flown farthest if his initial trajectory had been:

    A. 30°
    B. 45°
    C. 53°
    D. 60°

## Passage II (Questions 7-13)

Two boys, Tom and Jim, are at the local pool playing a game. They take turns dropping from the diving board and throwing each other a ball. Sometimes the boy dropping from the board throws the ball to the other who is waiting at the edge of the pool. Sometimes the one at the edge of the pool throws the ball to the one dropping from the board. They always drop straight down from the end of the board, and never jump upward.

The diving board is 10 m above the surface of the water and 10 m from the edge of the pool as shown in Figure 1. Tom has a mass of 60 kg and Jim has a mass of 50 kg. The ball has a mass of 1 kg.

Tom is bigger than Jim and is able to throw the ball faster. Tom throws the ball with an initial velocity of 10 m/s, whereas Jim throws the ball with an initial velocity of 8 m/s.

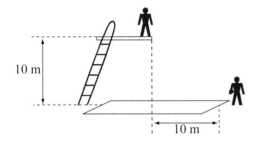

**Figure 1**

As the boys play the game, they vary the distance that they stand from the edge of the pool. (Note: the gravitational constant $g = 10$ m/s². Ignore air resistance unless otherwise indicated.)

7. If Tom throws the ball at the instant Jim leaves the board, in order to hit Jim, Tom should aim:

   A. slightly below Jim.
   B. directly at Jim.
   C. slightly above Jim.
   D. Where Tom should aim will depend upon how fast Tom throws the ball.

8. From the moment he leaves the board, approximately how long will it take Tom to hit the water?

   A. 1 s
   B. 1.4 s
   C. 2 s
   D. 4 s

9. Which of the following accurately describes Tom's fall from the board compared to Jim's fall?

   A. Tom's velocity will change faster and Tom will hit the water with greater velocity.
   B. Tom's velocity will change faster and Tom will hit the water with less velocity.
   C. Jim's velocity will change faster and Jim will hit the water with greater velocity.
   D. Both Tom and Jim will hit the water with the same velocity.

10. Tom throws the ball horizontally the moment he leaves the board. If Jim lets the ball hit the ground, Tom will be in the air:

    A. 1/5 as long as the ball.
    B. the same amount of time as the ball.
    C. 5 times as long as the ball.
    D. 25 times as long as the ball.

11. If Tom throws the ball to Jim releasing it at the moment Jim leaves the board, and Jim catches the ball at the moment he hits the water, approximately what is the maximum height achieved by the ball?

    A. 0 m
    B. 2.5 m
    C. 5 m
    D. 10 m

12. If Tom throws the ball horizontally the moment he leaves the board, approximately how far from the edge of the pool must Jim stand in order to catch it?

    A. 4 m
    B. 10 m
    C. 14 m
    D. 20 m

13. If the boys use a 2 kg ball instead of the 1 kg ball, and Tom wants the ball to follow the same projectile path, Tom must throw the ball with an initial velocity:

    A. half as great as the 1 kg ball.
    B. the same as the 1 kg ball.
    C. twice as great as the 1 kg ball.
    D. four times as great as the 1 kg ball.

**GO ON TO THE NEXT PAGE.**

## Passage III (Questions 14-19)

Students conduct an experiment to study projectile motion. A projectile is launched from a spring-loaded gun. The gun launches the projectile from a hill and with the same speed each time. The gun is aimed so that the initial velocity of the projectile has an angle $\theta$ from the horizontal. The angle $\theta$ is increased by $15°$ each time the projectile is launched. The horizontal displacement $d$ traveled by the projectile as well as the time $t$ spent in flight is measured and recorded. The results are shown in Table 1.

| angle $\theta$ | displacement d | time t |
|:---:|:---:|:---:|
| 0° | 14.0 m | 1.4 s |
| 15° | 16.4 m | 1.7 s |
| 30° | 17.3 m | 2.0 s |
| 45° | 16.2 m | 2.3 s |
| 60° | 12.6 m | 2.5 s |
| 75° | 6.9 m | 2.7 s |

**Table 1** Horizontal displacement and time of flight for a projectile shot from a spring-loaded gun

**14.** Approximately how high above the ground is the spring-loaded gun held when it releases the projectile?

- **A.** 1 m
- **B.** 5 m
- **C.** 10 m
- **D.** 14 m

**15.** Which of the following statements is true concerning the projectile in the experiment?

- **A.** The longer the projectile remained in the air, the greater was its horizontal displacement.
- **B.** The higher the projectile went, the greater was its horizontal displacement.
- **C.** The speed of the projectile was greatest just after it left the spring-loaded gun.
- **D.** The speed of the projectile was greatest just before hitting the ground.

**16.** Each time the projectile is launched, it leaves the spring-loaded gun with an initial speed of:

- **A.** 1 m/s
- **B.** 5 m/s
- **C.** 10 m/s
- **D.** 20 m/s

**17.** The projectile would reach its maximum height when fired from which of the following angles?

- **A.** 30°
- **B.** 45°
- **C.** 60°
- **D.** 90°

**18.** Which of the following graphs most accurately represents the relationship between the horizontal displacement of the projectile and the angle $\theta$?

A.
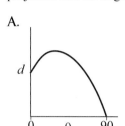

C.
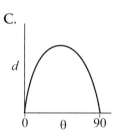

B.
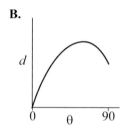

D.
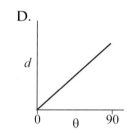

**19.** Which of the following statements is true concerning the flights of the projectile in the experiment?

- **A.** At its maximum height, the speed of the projectile was zero for every flight.
- **B.** All projectiles reached maximum acceleration just before hitting the ground.
- **C.** The speed of the projectile changed at a constant rate throughout the experiment.
- **D.** The distance traveled through the air by the projectile was smallest when launched at 0° from the horizontal.

Questions 20 through 23 are **NOT** based on a descriptive passage.

20. A man takes two strides each second. The same man walks at a rate of 1 m/s. How long are his strides?

  A.   ¼ m
  B.   ½ m
  C.   1 m
  D.   2 m

21. The moon has no atmosphere, and has less gravity than earth. How will the path of a golf ball struck on the earth differ from one struck on the moon?

  A.   Both the earth's atmosphere and gravity will act to lengthen the projectile path of the ball.
  B.   Both the earth's atmosphere and gravity will act to shorten the projectile path of the ball.
  C.   The earth's atmosphere will act to shorten the path of the ball but its gravity will act to lengthen the path.
  D.   The earth's atmosphere will act to lengthen the path of the ball but its gravity will act to shorten the path.

22. All of the following will affect the time of flight for a projectile experiencing no air resistance EXCEPT:

  I.    the mass of the projectile
  II.   the initial horizontal velocity of the projectile
  III.  the initial vertical velocity of the projectile

  A.   I only
  B.   III only
  C.   I and II only
  D.   I and III only

23. A ball is rolled down a 1 m ramp placed at an angle of $30°$ to the horizontal. The same ball is rolled down a 1 m ramp placed vertically. Which of the following statements is true? (Note: $\sin 30° = 0.5$, $\cos 30° = 0.87$)

  A.   The ball required the same amount of time for both trips.
  B.   The ball had the same displacement at the end of both trips.
  C.   The ball accelerated at the same rate for both trips.
  D.   The ball reached approximately 1.4 times the speed on the second trip as it did on the first trip.

---

**STOP.** IF YOU FINISH BEFORE TIME IS CALLED, CHECK YOUR WORK. YOU MAY GO BACK TO ANY QUESTION IN THIS TEST BOOKLET.

---

**STOP.**

# 30-MINUTE IN-CLASS EXAM FOR LECTURE 2

Statistically speaking, traveling on U.S. highways is more dangerous than airplane travel. At the high speeds achieved by vehicles on the highway, turns must be very gradual. As a safety precaution, highway turns are banked toward the inside. Federal guidelines specify highway curve speed limits based upon the angle of the bank, the average coefficient of friction between a vehicle and the pavement, and the radius of curvature of the turn. The radius of curvature of a turn is the radius of a circle that would be circumscribed by the vehicle if the vehicle were to complete a full circle.

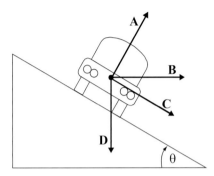

**Figure 1**

The diagram above shows a vehicle on a highway curve moving in a direction out of the page and turning to the driver's left.

24. Which of the following statements is most likely false concerning the federal guidelines on highway curve speed limits?

    A.  The speed limit increases with the radius of curvature.
    B.  The bank angle θ increases with the radius of curvature.
    C.  A greater bank angle θ allows for a greater speed limit.
    D.  A smaller radius of curvature leads to a greater bank angle.

25. If the vehicle in Figure 1 is moving very fast, but not slipping off the bank, the frictional force on the vehicle is most likely:

    A.  static and in the direction of vector C.
    B.  static and in the direction of vector B.
    C.  kinetic and in the direction of vector C.
    D.  kinetic and in the opposite direction of vector C.

26. The centripetal force on the vehicle is:

    A.  in the direction of B.
    B.  in the direction opposite to B.
    C.  in the direction of C.
    D.  in the direction opposite to C.

27. If the vehicle in Figure 1 were stationary, the net force on the vehicle would be:

    A.  zero.
    B.  in the direction of A.
    C.  in the direction of C.
    D.  in the direction of D.

28. If the speed of the vehicle were doubled, the centripetal force required to turn the vehicle would:

    A.  decrease by a factor of 2.
    B.  remain the same.
    C.  increase by a factor of 2.
    D.  increase by a factor of 4.

29. If the bank angle θ were increased to 90° and the vehicle did not fall, the frictional force on the vehicle would be:

    A.  less than the weight of the vehicle.
    B.  equal to the weight of the vehicle.
    C.  greater than the weight of the vehicle.
    D.  The laws of physics dictate that the vehicle must fall if the bank angle is increased to 90°.

30. Which of the following would require the bank angles which currently exist on highways to be increased?

    A.  The average mass of vehicles on the highways increases.
    B.  The average mass of the vehicles on the highways decreases.
    C.  Curve speed limits are increased.
    D.  Curve speed limits are decreased.

## Passage II (Questions 31-37)

A student imagines an astronaut sitting in his space vehicle as it orbits an unknown planet sometime in the future. His space vehicle is pressurized so he is able to remove his helmet. The astronaut has a plastic bag of juice. He opens the bag and squeezes the juice out into the air in front of himself. The juice does not pour into his lap but remains as an amorphous blob wiggling in the air in front of him. He puts his mouth to the juice and slurps it in completely. Finished with the juice, he gently tosses the empty bag toward a garbage receptacle. Then the astronaut removes his pen from his pocket and finds that it floats perfectly in the air.

He looks over at his grandfather clock that runs on a pendulum system, and notices that it is time to radio earth. He radios Earth, which is $3 \times 10^{13}$ km away, that he is done with breakfast. Earth replies that he must change the radius of his orbit. Earth asks him to decrease his present velocity by a factor of four, which he does. Soon afterwards he discovers that he is following the same orbital trajectory as a small moon.

The circular motion of the craft is governed by the equation below:

$$r = \frac{GM}{v^2}$$

where $v$ is the speed of the space ship, $r$ is the orbital radius, $M$ is the mass of the Earth ($5.98 \times 10^{24}$ kg), and $G$ is the gravitational constant ($6.67 \times 10^{-11}$ m$^3$/kg-s$^{-2}$).

31. The space ship experiences centripetal acceleration while orbiting the planet. According to Newton's laws of motion, if the spaceship encounters no resisting force in the course of its circular orbit, what will be its future path?

    A. It will orbit in a circle forever.
    B. It will gradually spiral inward.
    C. It will gradually spiral outward.
    D. It will break from the orbit to travel in a straight line.

32. If the plastic bag misses the garbage receptacle, from the astronaut's point of view, will it continue straight along its present path at a constant velocity?

    A. Yes, because space is a vacuum.
    B. Yes, because the net force on the bag is zero.
    C. No, because the gravity of the unknown planet will change the trajectory of the bag.
    D. No, because the air molecules in the spacecraft will create air resistance and slow it down.

33. From the astronaut's point of view, along what trajectory should he send his projectile if he wants it to reach the garbage receptacle?

    A. a perfect parabolic path that ends exactly at the receptacle
    B. a parabolic path that ends at the receptacle but is adjusted for air resistance
    C. a perfect parabolic path that ends just above the receptacle
    D. a straight line to the receptacle

34. How many hours will the astronaut's message take to reach earth?

    A. $3 \times 10^{13} \times 3 \times 10^8 \times 60 \times 60$
    B. $(3 \times 10^{16})/(3 \times 10^8) \times 1/60 \times 1/60$
    C. $(3 \times 10^{16})/(3 \times 10^8) \times 60 \times 60$
    D. $(3 \times 10^8)/(3 \times 10^{16}) \times 1/60 \times 1/60$

35. When the astronaut changes his velocity, the radius of his orbit:

    A. increases by a factor of 16.
    B. decreases by a factor of 2.
    C. decreases by a factor of 4.
    D. decreases by a factor of 16.

36. Which of the following is true concerning the spacecraft and the moon when they are in the same orbit? (Assume that neither is using a propulsion system to maintain its orbit.)

    A. They both must be at the same speed.
    B. They both must have the same mass.
    C. They both must have the same mass and speed.
    D. They must have different masses.

37. The passage comes from the imagination of a student. A real pendulum on the clock in orbit would:

    A. swing more slowly than it would if it were on the planet below.
    B. swing more swiftly than it would if it were on the planet below.
    C. swing at the same rate as it would if it were on the planet below.
    D. not swing on the orbiting spacecraft.

The earth does not move around the sun in a perfect circle. Not only is the path very slightly elliptical, but the moon creates a wobble in the orbit. It is actually the center of gravity of the earth-moon system, called the *barycenter*, that follows the smooth elliptical path around the sun. Nevertheless, the earth's orbit is so nearly a circle that it can be treated as such for most calculations. The average distance between the earth and the sun is called an astronomical unit, AU.

The moon moves once around the earth every 27.3 days. The moon does not rotate relative to the earth, so the same side of the moon is always facing earth.

Table 1 gives the mass, radius, and orbital radius of the sun, earth, and moon. The universal gravitational constant is: $G = 6.67 \times 10^{-11}$ N m$^2$/kg$^2$

| | Mass | Radius (km) | Orbital radius (km) |
|---|---|---|---|
| Sun | $1.9 \times 10^{30}$ | 696,000 | – |
| Earth | $5.97 \times 10^{24}$ | 6,378 | 149,600,000 |
| Moon | $7.5 \times 10^{22}$ | 1,738 | 384,400 |

**Table 1** Astronomical statistics

38. A light second is the distance that light moves in one second. How many light seconds is the moon from the earth?

   A. $5.8 \times 10^{-6}$ light seconds
   B. $1.2 \times 10^{-3}$ light seconds
   C. $5.8 \times 10^{-3}$ light seconds
   D. 1.28 light seconds

39. A lunar day is defined as the time that elapses from sunrise to the following sunrise on the moon at a given location. How long is one lunar day?

   A. 12 earth hours
   B. 24 earth hours
   C. 27.3 earth days
   D. one earth year

40. Which of the following expressions gives the approximate speed of the earth moving through its orbit?

   A. $\sqrt{\dfrac{G \times 1.5 \times 10^{11}}{1.9 \times 10^{30}}}$

   B. $\sqrt{\dfrac{G \times 1.9 \times 10^{30} \times 5.9 \times 10^{24}}{1.5 \times 10^{11}}}$

   C. $\sqrt{\dfrac{G \times 1.9 \times 10^{30}}{1.5 \times 10^{11}}}$

   D. $\sqrt{\dfrac{1.5 \times 10^{11}}{G \times 1.9 \times 10^{30}}}$

41. How much would a 100 kg man weigh on the moon?

   A. 17 N
   B. 100 N
   C. 170 N
   D. 1000 N

42. If $F$ is the gravitational force created on the moon by the earth, which of the following expressions is equal to the gravitational force created on the earth by the moon?

   A. $F$

   B. $\dfrac{(5.97 \times 10^{24}) \times F}{(7.5 \times 10^{22})}$

   C. $\dfrac{(7.5 \times 10^{22}) \times F}{(5.97 \times 10^{24})}$

   D. $\dfrac{(1,738)^2 \times F}{(5.97 \times 10^{24})(7.5 \times 10^{22})}$

**43.** In a 'tug of war' two groups of men pull in opposite directions on either end of a rope. Each group applies 2000 N of force. What is the tension in the rope?

   **A.**   0 N
   **B.**   1000 N
   **C.**   2000 N
   **D.**   4000 N

**44.** A 50 kg box is moved across the floor at a constant velocity of 5 m/s. The coefficient of friction between the box and the floor is 0.1. What is the net force on the box?

   **A.**   0 N
   **B.**   50 N
   **C.**   250 N
   **D.**   2500 N

**45.** The earth spins on its axis flattening its spherical shape from pole to pole and bowing out at the equator. An object is placed on a scale at the equator. How does the centrifugal force and the distance from the center of gravity affect the weight (as measured by the scale) at the equator?

   **A.**   Both the increased distance and the centrifugal force act to decrease the weight of the object.
   **B.**   The increased distance tends to decrease the weight of the object while the centrifugal force tends to increase its weight.
   **C.**   The increased distance tends to increase the weight of the object while the centrifugal force tends to decrease its weight.
   **D.**   The increased distance tends to decrease the weight of the object and the centrifugal force does not affect the weight of the object.

**46.** A 5 kg mass hangs from a spring distending it 10 cm from its resting point. What is the spring constant k of the spring?

   **A.**   50 N/m
   **B.**   100 N/m
   **C.**   250 N/m
   **D.**   500 N/m

---

**STOP.** IF YOU FINISH BEFORE TIME IS CALLED, CHECK YOUR WORK. YOU MAY GO BACK TO ANY QUESTION IN THIS TEST BOOKLET.

---

# 30-MINUTE IN-CLASS EXAM FOR LECTURE 3

## Passage I (Questions 47-51)

Puncho was a circus clown whose act consisted of juggling five 0.5 kg balls while riding a unicycle across a tightrope.

Puncho is shown in Figure 1 riding his unicycle while juggling and then riding his unicycle on a tight rope.

Puncho has a mass of 50 kg.

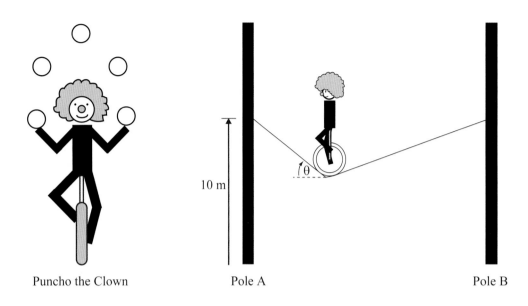

Puncho the Clown    Pole A    Pole B

**Figure 1**

47. If the radius of the wheel on Puncho's unicycle is 0.25 m, and Puncho is riding with a velocity of 10 m/s, how many revolutions does the wheel make each second?

    A.  $\pi/20$ revolutions
    B.  $\pi/10$ revolutions
    C.  $20/\pi$ revolutions
    D.  $20\pi$ revolutions

48. If the angle $\theta$ in Figure 1 is 60°, and Puncho is 2 m from Pole A, what is the net torque on Pole A? (Note: sin 60° = 0.87, cos 60° = 0.5)

    A.  0 N m
    B.  250 N m
    C.  2500 N m
    D.  5000 N m

49. If the distance between Pole A and Pole B in Figure 1 is doubled and the angle $\theta$ remains the same, the tension in the tightrope will:

    A.  decrease by a factor of 2.
    B.  remain the same.
    C.  increase by a factor of 2.
    D.  increase by a factor of 4.

50. Puncho throws each ball 5 m into the air. He throws one ball every half second with a velocity of 10 m/s. At any moment when all the balls are in the air, how much greater is their total energy than when all the balls are at rest?

    A.  50 J
    B.  125 J
    C.  250 J
    D.  500 J

51. Why is it easier for Puncho to balance on his unicycle if he carries a long heavy pole centered horizontally at his chest?

    A.  The pole decreases his rotational inertia.
    B.  The pole increases his rotational inertia.
    C.  The weight of the pole increases the frictional force between the unicycle and the tightrope.
    D.  The weight of the pole increases his momentum when he isn't moving.

### Passage II (Questions 52-58)

A student performed two experiments to investigate the nature of tension.

Experiment 1

The student used the apparatus shown in Figure 1 to measure the tension in a string when different masses (*M*) were hung from its end. The experimental results showing how the tension changed with *M* are given in Table 1.

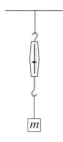

**Figure 1**

| Trial | *M* (kg) | *T* (kg) |
|---|---|---|
| 1 | 0.10 | 1.0 |
| 2 | 0.15 | 1.5 |
| 3 | 0.20 | 2.0 |
| 4 | 0.25 | 2.5 |

**Table 1**

Experiment 2

The student attached one end of a string to a 0.1 kg mass resting on a smooth table. The student attached the other end of the string over a pulley to a hanging mass (*m*). The apparatus is shown in Figure 2. The hanging mass was allowed to fall and the tension in the string as it fell was measured. Several different hanging masses were used and the results recorded in Table 2. (Note: Assume massless pulleys for all questions unless otherwise indicated.)

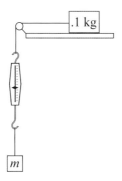

**Figure 2**

| Trial | *m* (kg) | *T* (N) |
|---|---|---|
| 1 | 0.10 | 0.50 |
| 2 | 0.15 | 0.60 |
| 3 | 0.20 | 0.67 |
| 4 | 0.30 | 0.75 |

**Table 2**

**52.** If the smooth table in Experiment 2 is frictionless, during the experiment the mass *m* is:

**A.** in static equilibrium.
**B.** in dynamic equilibrium.
**C.** initially not in equilibrium but may achieve equilibrium if the string and table are long enough.
**D.** not in equilibrium and does not achieve equilibrium during the experiment.

**53.** If the smooth table in Experiment 2 is frictionless, what is the maximum tension that can be achieved?

**A.** 0.1 N
**B.** 1 N
**C.** 10 N
**D.** As long as the string does not break, there is no limit to the tension that can be achieved.

**54.** What is the net force exerted on mass *M* in Experiment 1 Trial 3?

**A.** 0 N
**B.** 0.1 N
**C.** 1 N
**D.** 10 N

**55.** If the string in Experiment 2, Trial 1, were cut, and mass *m* were allowed to fall freely, what would be the tension in the string?

**A.** 0 N
**B.** 0.1 N
**C.** 10 N
**D.** 100 N

In-Class Exams

**56.** Which of the diagrams below most accurately represents the speed of the block in Experiment 2 after the block begins to slide? (Note: Assume that the tension and friction forces are constant.)

**A.**

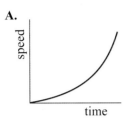

**C.**

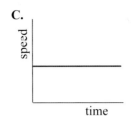

**B.**

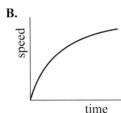

**D.**

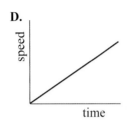

**57.** How does friction between the 0.1 kg mass and the table in Experiment 2 affect the results of the experiment?

    **A.**    The tension in the string is decreased by friction.
    **B.**    The tension in the string is increased by friction.
    **C.**    Friction decreases as mass $m$ increases.
    **D.**    Friction increases as mass $m$ increases.

**58.** Based on the results in Table 2, if another trial were attempted in Experiment 2 using a mass $m$ of 0.4 kg, what would be the approximate tension in the string?

    **A.**    0.80 N
    **B.**    0.83 N
    **C.**    1.3 N
    **D.**    4.0 N

**Passage III (Questions 59-66)**

In the early part of World War I (WW I) the science of aeronautics was in its infancy. Primitive propeller planes reached top horizontal speeds of 30 m/s. If a plane didn't come apart, greater speeds were possible in a dive. Initially airplanes were used only for reconnaissance. Enemy pilots would often salute each other with a friendly wave as they passed in the sky. However, as the war progressed, pilots began throwing bricks and other objects at each other. The first bombs were literally dropped from the pilots hands as he flew. In order to hit his target, a pilot would have to take into account his own velocity, wind velocity, and air resistance.

Modern warplanes fire jet-propelled missiles. Such missiles take air in through the front, heat and compress it, and force it out the back along with combusted fuel. Nevertheless, the same factors for dropping a projectile must also be considered when aiming a modern missile. (Note: Ignore air resistance unless otherwise indicated.)

**59.** If a WW I pilot flying horizontally at top speed dropped a 2 kg bomb from an altitude of 300 m, what would be the kinetic energy of the bomb just before hitting the ground?

    **A.**    900 J
    **B.**    1800 J
    **C.**    6000 J
    **D.**    6900 J

**60.** If a modern jet-propelled missile with a mass of 300 kg is designed to move vertically upward at 1200 m/s, how much power must be delivered by the propulsion system?

    **A.**    $3.6 \times 10^5$ W
    **B.**    $3.6 \times 10^6$ W
    **C.**    $2.2 \times 10^{10}$ W
    **D.**    $2.2 \times 10^{14}$ W

**61.** If a WW I pilot dropped a 2 kg bomb from an altitude of 300 m, which of the following would result in the greatest kinetic energy for the bomb just before it hit the ground? ($\sin 30° = 0.5$)

    **A.** The pilot releases the bomb while flying straight up at a velocity of 10 m/s.
    **B.** The pilot releases the bomb while climbing at an angle 30° above the horizontal at a velocity of 20 m/s.
    **C.** The pilot releases the bomb while flying straight down at a velocity of 20 m/s.
    **D.** The pilot releases the bomb while flying horizontally at a velocity of 25 m/s.

**62.** The gravitational potential energy of WW I propeller planes increased with altitude. Since energy is always conserved, from where did this energy most likely come?

    **A.** kinetic energy achieved on the runway
    **B.** kinetic energy of air molecules lifting the plane
    **C.** chemical potential energy from the airplane's fuel
    **D.** kinetic energy of the wind

**63.** When a WW I airplane went into a dive, it might reach a constant terminal velocity due to air resistance. Which of the following is true concerning a diving plane that has reached terminal velocity?

    **A.** The net force on the plane is zero.
    **B.** The plane is accelerating at 10 m/s$^2$.
    **C.** The plane is in static equilibrium.
    **D.** The air resistance is equal to the force of the propulsive produced by the planes engines.

**64.** While pulling out of a dive, a pilot's apparent weight:

    **A.** increases
    **B.** decreases
    **C.** remains the same
    **D.** The pilot is weightless while pulling out of a dive.

**65.** A WW I pilot increases his altitude at an angle of 30° to the horizontal and a velocity of 20 m/s. If he takes a 2 kg bomb with him, starting from rest on the ground, how much work has been done on the bomb when the plane reaches an altitude of 200 m? (Note: ignore air resistance. $\sin 30° = 0.5$)

    **A.** 2000 J
    **B.** 2400 J
    **C.** 4000 J
    **D.** 4400 J

**66.** A WW I pilot flying north at top speed and an altitude of 180 m wishes to drop a bomb on a trench. At how many meters before he is over the trench should he drop the bomb? (Ignore air resistance.)

    **A.** 60 m
    **B.** 120 m
    **C.** 180 m
    **D.** 360 m

**GO ON TO THE NEXT PAGE.**

**67.** A rocket is launched from Earth to explore our solar system and beyond. As the rocket moves out of the Earth's atmosphere and into deep space, the gravitational constant $g$ decreases and approaches zero, and the gravitational potential energy of the rocket:

   **A.** also decreases and approaches zero.
   **B.** continually increases.
   **C.** remains constant.
   **D.** increases at first and then decreases and approaches zero.

**68.** From the right end of a massless meter stick hangs a 5 kg mass. 20 cm from its left end the meter stick is attached to the ceiling by a string. What downward force $F$ should be applied to the left end of the meter stick to balance it horizontally and in rotational equilibrium?

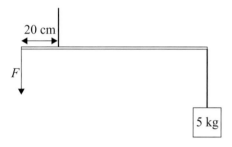

   **A.** 20 N
   **B.** 50 N
   **C.** 100 N
   **D.** 200 N

**69.** The Earth is approximately 80 times more massive than the moon. The average distance between the Earth and the moon is just less than 400,000 km. If the radius of the Earth is 6370 km, the center of gravity of the Earth-moon system is located:

   **A.** at the center of the Earth.
   **B.** just beneath the Earth's surface.
   **C.** just above the Earth's surface.
   **D.** exactly between the Earth and the moon.

---

**STOP.** IF YOU FINISH BEFORE TIME IS CALLED, CHECK YOUR WORK. YOU MAY GO BACK TO ANY QUESTION IN THIS TEST BOOKLET.

---

# 30-MINUTE IN-CLASS EXAM FOR LECTURE 4

Four examples are shown below to demonstrate the properties of collisions. All four examples take place on a frictionless horizontal surface at room temperature.

*Collision 1*

Block A, with mass 2 kg slides towards Block B with a speed of 4 m/s. Block B is at rest and its mass is unknown. After the collision, Block A remains at rest and Block B moves forward at angle $x$ relative to Block A's original motion with a speed of 4 m/s.

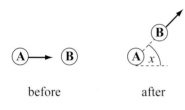

before                           after

**Example 1**

*Collision 2*

Block A with mass 1 kg slides towards Block B with a speed of 4 m/s. Block B is at rest and has a mass of 1 kg. After the collision, the two blocks stick together and move forward at an angle $y$ relative to Block A's original motion at an unknown speed.

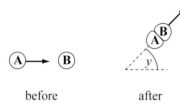

before                           after

**Example 2**

*Collision 3*

Block A with mass 3 kg is initially at rest. An explosion breaks the blocks into three pieces, each with mass 1 kg. The three pieces each move away at unknown speeds at the angles shown.

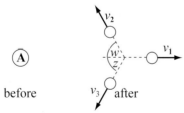

before                    after

**Example 3**

*Collision 4*

Block A with mass 2 kg slides towards Block B with unknown speed and Block B with mass 1 kg slides towards Block A with unknown speed. After the collision, the two blocks stick together at rest.

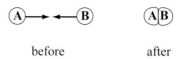

before                           after

**Example 4**

70. Which of the following statements must be true regarding angles $x$ and $y$ in *Collision 1* and *Collision 2*?

    **A.**    $x = 2y$
    **B.**    $2x = y$
    **C.**    $x = y = 90°$
    **D.**    $x = y = 0°$

71. What is the speed of the combined blocks after *Collision 2*?

    **A.**    1 m/s
    **B.**    2 m/s
    **C.**    4 m/s
    **D.**    8 m/s

72. What is the mass of Block B in *Collision 1*?
    **A.**    0.5 kg
    **B.**    1 kg
    **C.**    2 kg
    **D.**    4 kg

73. After *Collision 4*, what has happened to the kinetic energy initially present in the motion of the blocks?

    **A.**    It remains unchanged.
    **B.**    It is converted into elastic potential energy.
    **C.**    It is converted into gravitational potential energy.
    **D.**    It is converted into heat energy.

74. Which of the following must be true about *Collision 3*?

    **A.**    $v_1 = v_2 + v_3$
    **B.**    $v_2 = v_3$
    **C.**    $v_2 \cos(w) = v_3 \cos(z)$
    **D.**    $v_2 \sin(w) = v_3 \sin(z)$

**75.** Which of the collisions is perfectly elastic?

A. Collision 1
B. Collision 2
C. Collision 3
D. Collision 4

**76.** If $v_A$ is the speed of Block A and $v_B$ is the speed of Block B before Collision 4, which of the following must be true?

A. $v_A = v_B$
B. $v_A = 2v_B$
C. $2v_A = v_B$
D. $4v_A = v_B$

**Passage II (Questions 77-82)**

Two small nuclides can join together via nuclear forces to release energy. This process is called *fusion*. However, nuclear forces are only effective at relatively close range, and, in order for this reaction to occur, the particles must overcome the electrostatic repulsion between their positively charged nuclei. These repulsive forces make up the *Coulomb barrier*. For two protons, the height of the Coulomb barrier is about 400 keV.

One way that successful collisions can occur is through high temperatures. This is called thermonuclear fusion. Temperature in thermonuclear studies are reported in terms of the *most probable* kinetic energy $K$ of the interacting particles via the relation:

$$K = kT$$

where $k$ is Boltzmann constant ($8.62 \times 10^{-5}$ eV/K) and $T$ is the temperature in kelvins. Using this method, the temperature at the core of the sun is 1.3 keV; room temperature is approximately 0.03 eV; and the peak temperature for particles to overcome the Coulomb barrier is 400 keV.

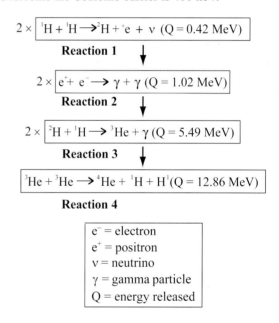

**Figure 1** Thermonuclear fusion at the sun's core

Thermonuclear fusion occurs in the sun via the reactions given in Figure 1. Fusion occurs despite the low temperature for two reasons: (1) some particles move at much greater speeds than the most probable speed; (2) some barrier tunneling can occur at temperatures lower than 400 keV. (Note: An electron carries a charge of $1.6 \times 10^{-19}$ C.)

**GO ON TO THE NEXT PAGE.**

77. The heat from thermonuclear fusion inside the sun's core comes from:

    **A.**    kinetic energy
    **B.**    chemical energy
    **C.**    mass energy
    **D.**    electrostatic potential energy

78. What is the approximate temperature of the sun's core in kelvins?

    **A.**    $4.6 \times 10^3$ K
    **B.**    $1.5 \times 10^4$ K
    **C.**    $4.6 \times 10^6$ K
    **D.**    $1.5 \times 10^7$ K

79. According to Figure 1, the net products of thermonuclear fusion in the sun's core are:

    **A.**    helium, hydrogen, neutrinos, and energy.
    **B.**    helium, neutrinos, and energy.
    **C.**    hydrogen, neutrinos, and energy.
    **D.**    helium, hydrogen, and neutrinos.

80. If an electron and a positron have the same mass then, according to Reaction 2 in Figure 1, what is the approximate mass of a positron?

    **A.**    $10^{-37}$ kg
    **B.**    $10^{-30}$ kg
    **C.**    $10^{-25}$ kg
    **D.**    $10^{-15}$ kg

81. In nuclear fission one high-mass nuclide is split into two middle-mass nuclides and energy is released. The nucleons (protons and neutrons) in both nuclides are held together by the nuclear binding energy $Q = \Delta mc^2$. The binding energy per nucleon of the high-mass nuclide:

    **A.**    is greater than the binding energy per nucleon of the middle-mass nuclides.
    **B.**    is less than the binding energy per nucleon of the middle-mass nuclides.
    **C.**    is equal to the binding energy per nucleon of the middle-mass nuclides.
    **D.**    may be either greater or less than the binding energy per nucleon of the middle-mass nuclides.

82. Which of the following is a requirement in order for energy to be released in a fusion reaction?

    **A.**    The resulting nucleus must be at a higher energy state than the colliding nuclides.
    **B.**    The nuclides must collide at a temperature of 400 keV or greater.
    **C.**    The number of nucleons in the fusing nuclides must be large.
    **D.**    The number of nucleons in the fusing nuclides must be small.

An important function of many mammalian bones is to act as a lever arm, transmitting an in-force to an out-force via a center of rotation or fulcrum. Three orders of lever arms exist: *first order* where the fulcrum separates the in-force and the out-force, *second order* where the in-force and out-force are on the same side but the out force is nearest to the fulcrum, and *third order* where both forces are also on the same side but the in-force is nearest the fulcrum. In mammalian bone lever systems the in-force is supplied by a muscle, one end of which is attached to the bone at the point where the in-force is applied and the other end anchored to a separate bone closer to the body.

Mammalian bones have evolved divergently to meet the requirements of different mammals. Figures 1 and 2 show the lever system in the forelimbs of two different mammals. Each lever system allows for a ratio of out-force to in-force and velocity of limb movement that best suits its respective user. Swift running mammals take advantage of third order lever systems to reduce bulky limbs and extend limb movements. Large muscles can be kept close to the body requiring less energy expenditure on unnecessary movements; short contractions can be translated into long strides. In order to further maximize velocity, the mass of the proximal portion of the limb has been reduced in these swift running mammals.

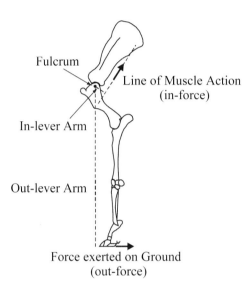

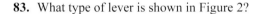

**Figure 1**

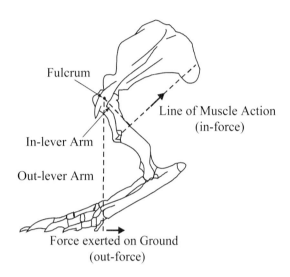

**Figure 2**

83. What type of lever is shown in Figure 2?

A.  first order
B.  second order
C.  third order
D.  It can not be determined from the figure.

84. Assuming the figures are drawn to scale, if the same in-force is applied to each lever system, which lever system will have the greatest out-force?

A.  The lever system in Figure 1.
B.  The lever system in Figure 2.
C.  The out-force would be the same in both lever systems.
D.  The answer cannot be determined from the information given.

85. If the out-lever arm in Figure 1 is 1 m and the in-lever arm is 10 cm, and the mammal applies an in-force of 10 N, what will be the approximate out-force?

A.  1 N
B.  10 N
C.  40 N
D.  100 N

86. The animal in Figure 2 is well adapted for rapid digging. If we assume ideal conditions for the lever system in Figure 2, compared to the in-force supplied by the muscle, the out-force must:

A.  do less work.
B.  do more work.
C.  be less than the in-force.
D.  be greater than the in-force.

**87.** According to the passage, which of the following conditions would most likely make the animal in Figure 1 a faster runner?

A.  increasing the length of the in-lever arm and decreasing length of the out-lever arm

B.  decreasing the length of the in-lever arm and increasing length of the out-lever arm

C.  increasing both the length of the in-lever arm and the out-lever arm

D.  decreasing both the length of the in-lever arm and the out-lever arm

**88.** Which position has the greatest in-lever arm?

A.

C.

B.

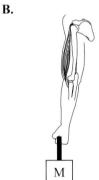

D.

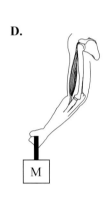

Questions 89 through 92 are **NOT** based on a descriptive passage.

**89.** The rate at which the thyroid gland absorbs iodine can be measured using the radio nuclide $^{128}$I. The half life of $^{128}$I is 25 min. A patient is administered 800 µg of $^{128}$I. If no $^{128}$I is absorbed by the thyroid, approximately how much will remain in the patient's blood after 2 hours?

A.  0 µg

B.  27 µg

C.  55 µg

D.  800 µg

**90.** $^{218}$Po undergoes two alpha decays and four beta decays to become:

A.  $^{210}$Bi

B.  $^{226}$Ra

C.  $^{210}$Pb

D.  $^{210}$Po

**91.** A pulley system is attached to a massless board as shown below. The board pivots only at the pivot point. A 10 kg mass $M$ sits exactly in the middle of the board.

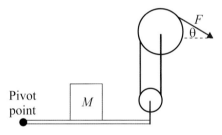

If the angle $\theta$ is 30°, what is the force $F$ necessary to lift the 10 kg mass? (Note: sin30° = 0.5)

A.  12.5 N

B.  25 N

C.  50 N

D.  100 N

**92.** If the two objects shown below collide and remain together without spinning, what will be their final velocity? (sin 60° = 0.87; cos 60° = 0.5)

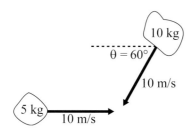

A.   5 m/s
B.   5.8 m/s
C.   8.7 m/s
D.   10 m/s

---

**STOP.** IF YOU FINISH BEFORE TIME IS CALLED, CHECK YOUR WORK. YOU MAY GO BACK TO ANY QUESTION IN THIS TEST BOOKLET.

---

**STOP.**

# 30-MINUTE IN-CLASS EXAM FOR LECTURE 5

Because heating a solid increases the vibrational energy of its molecules resulting in an increase in space required by each molecule, a typical solid will expand when heated. For such solids, the fractional change in their length per unit temperature is given by a *coefficient of linear expansion*, which is specific for each solid. Although the change in length varies slightly with temperature for any solid, the following equation gives a good approximation.

$$\Delta L = L\alpha\Delta T$$

where $L$ is the original length of the solid, $\Delta L$ is the change in length, $\alpha$ is the coefficient of linear expansion for the particular substance, and $\Delta T$ is the change in temperature.

Of course, any solid that increases in length when heated will also expand in both other directions. The change in volume $V$ for such a solid is given by:

$$\Delta V = V\beta\Delta T$$

where $\beta$ is the coefficient of volume expansion which is exactly 3 times the coefficient of linear expansion. The equation for the change in volume can be applied to most liquids as well as solids. Water, however, has a maximum density at $4°C$.

A list of the coefficients of linear expansion for some common substances is provided in Table 1.

| Substance | $\alpha$ ($10^{-6}/°$ C) |
|---|---|
| Ice (at $0°$ C) | 51 |
| Aluminum | 23 |
| Brass | 19 |
| Steel | 11 |
| Glass (ordinary) | 9 |

**Table 1**

93. What is the coefficient of volume expansion for glass?

    **A.**    $9 \times 10^{-18}/°C$
    **B.**    $27 \times 10^{-18}/°C$
    **C.**    $9 \times 10^{-6}/°C$
    **D.**    $2.7 \times 10^{-5}/°C$

94. A bimetal strip consisting of brass and steel is welded together lengthwise as shown.

As the temperature increases:

    **A.**    the brass will contract and the steel will expand, bending the rod to the left.
    **B.**    the steel will contract and the brass will expand, bending the rod to the right.
    **C.**    the brass will expand faster than the steel, bending the rod to the right.
    **D.**    the steel will expand faster than the brass, bending the rod to the left.

95. If a piece of brass is slowly heated from $25°C$ to $35°C$, by approximately what percent will its length be increased?

    **A.**    0.0019 %
    **B.**    0.019 %
    **C.**    0.19 %
    **D.**    1.9 %

96. Which of the following substances contracts the most when cooled?

    **A.**    aluminum
    **B.**    brass
    **C.**    steel
    **D.**    glass

97. A bottle is half filled with water at $4°C$ and sealed shut. The bottle is placed on a scale and put into a freezer. As the water nears $0°C$, the water level in the bottle:

    **A.**    falls and the reading on the scale remains constant.
    **B.**    rises and the reading on the scale remains constant.
    **C.**    rises and the reading on the scale decreases.
    **D.**    rises and the reading on the scale increases.

**98.** Which of the following is true concerning an aluminum buoy that floats in a lake all year round? (Note: The volume coefficient of expansion for water is $2 \times 10^{-3}/°C$.)

A. The buoy floats *higher* in the winter because the density of water changes *more* than the density of aluminum.

B. The buoy floats *higher* in the winter because the density of water changes *less* than the density of aluminum.

C. The buoy floats *lower* in the winter because the density of water changes *more* than the density of aluminum.

D. The buoy floats *lower* in the winter because the density of water changes *less* than the density of aluminum.

---

**Passage II (Questions 99-105)**

The pipe shown in Figure 1 holds a fluid with a specific gravity of 5.0. The top of the pipe at end A is sealed so that only a negligible amount of vapor pressure exists above the fluid surface. A narrow flexible section extends as shown from end A and is sealed at end D. Both ends of the pipe can be opened so that fluid flows from point A to D.

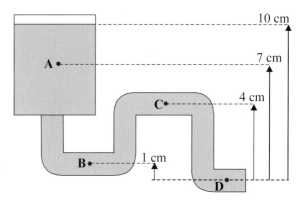

**Figure 1** Pipe with unknown fluid

The points A, B, C, and D and the surface of the liquid are measured from an arbitrary point as shown. Assume that the unknown fluid behaves ideally unless otherwise indicated.

**99.** When both ends are sealed shut, the pressure is the greatest at point:

A. A
B. B
C. C
D. D

**100.** When both ends are open, the flow rate is the greatest at point:

A. A
B. B
C. D
D. The flow rate is the same at all points.

**101.** What is the pressure at point C when the pipe is closed and the fluid is at rest?

A. 2000 Pa
B. 3000 Pa
C. 2000 Pa + 1 atm
D. 3000 Pa + 1 atm

**GO ON TO THE NEXT PAGE.**

**102.** What is the approximate velocity of the fluid at point D when the pipe is opened at both ends?

- **A.** 0.9 m/s
- **B.** 1.1 m/s
- **C.** 1.4 m/s
- **D.** 2.0 m/s

**103.** A 2 kg object submerged in the unknown fluid has an apparent loss of mass of 0.5 kg. What is the specific gravity of the object?

- **A.** 1
- **B.** 1.25
- **C.** 5
- **D.** 20

**104.** If both ends of the pipe were opened, all of the following would decrease significantly at point B as the unknown fluid drained from the pipe EXCEPT:

- **A.** volume flow rate
- **B.** fluid velocity
- **C.** fluid density
- **D.** fluid pressure

**105.** The pipe is closed at both ends and the fluid is at rest. Compared to the pressure at point A, the pressure at point C is:

- **A.** half as great.
- **B.** twice as great.
- **C.** ⅟₂ as great.
- **D.** ¼ as great.

**Passage III (Questions 106-111)**

The flight of a golf ball does not strictly follow the rules of projectile motion. The reason for this deviation is that the golf ball experiences a force called "lift" $F_L$. The lift force is directly proportional to the difference in pressure above and below the ball caused the ball's rotation during its flight. Lift can be roughly explained using Bernoulli's theorem.

$$\Delta P = \frac{1}{2}\rho v_2^2 - \frac{1}{2}\rho v_1^2$$

where $\Delta P$ is the pressure difference, $\rho$ is the density of the air surrounding the golf ball ($\rho = 1.2$ kg/m$^3$), and $v_2$ and $v_1$ are the effective airspeeds above and below the ball.

As the golf ball flies through the air, air moves past the ball at speed $u$. But as the ball spins, it drags some air along its surface. If the surface of the ball is moving at speed $w$, then the *effective airspeed* above the ball is $u + w$ and the *effective airspeed* below the ball is $u - w$.

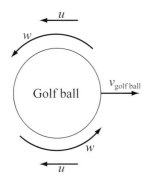

Golf ball manufacturers are continually experimenting with different surface patterns to improve lift properties. The mass of a typical golf ball is 45 grams and the diameter is 4.3 cm. The volume of a golf ball is 42 cm$^3$.

**106.** Assuming the spin on a golf ball has no effect on its horizontal acceleration, how does the flight of a ball undergoing the lift force compare to the flight of a ball that experiences no lift?

A. The ball that experiences lift will go higher, but not as far horizontally.

B. The ball that experiences lift will go higher and farther horizontally.

C. The ball that experiences lift will not go as high but will travel farther horizontally.

D. The ball that experiences lift will not go as high or as far horizontally.

**107.** The air very close to the surface of the ball is dragged along by a golf ball's spinning motion so that it moves at the same speed as the surface of the ball. If a golf ball in flight spins with a frequency of 60 Hz, what is the approximate speed $w$ of the air at its surface?

A. 1 m/s

B. 4 m/s

C. 8 m/s

D. 20 m/s

**108.** Which of the following changes would NOT serve to increase the lift force $F_L$ exerted on a golf ball in flight?

A. Weather conditions cause an increase in the density of air.

B. A golf ball with a lower density is used.

C. The golf ball is struck harder, causing it to move with greater speed.

D. The golf ball is struck with an angled club, causing it to spin more rapidly.

**109.** When a golf ball like the one described in the passage lands in a lake, which of the following will be true?

A. The ball will sink.

B. The ball will float with 96% of its volume submerged.

C. The ball will float with 93% of its volume submerged.

D. The ball will float with 87% of its volume submerged.

**110.** If a golf ball in flight spins in the direction opposite the one shown in Figure 1, the ball will experience:

A. a downward force because the pressure will be greater below the ball.

B. a downward force because the pressure will be greater above the ball.

C. an upward force because the pressure will be greater below the ball.

D. an upward force because the pressure will be greater above the ball.

**111.** Which of the following expressions is equal to the difference between the *effective airspeeds* above and below a golf ball while it is in flight?

A. $u$

B. $w$

C. $2u$

D. $2w$

112. A 5 liter container weighing 2 kilograms is thrown into a lake. What percentage of the container will float above the water? ($1 \text{ L} = 1 \text{ dm}^3$)

    **A.**    10%
    **B.**    40%
    **C.**    60%
    **D.**    90%

113. A brick sits on a massless piece of Styrofoam floating in a large bucket of water. If the Styrofoam is removed and the brick is allowed to sink to the bottom:

    **A.**    the water level will remain the same.
    **B.**    the water level will fall.
    **C.**    the water level will rise.
    **D.**    the density of the brick must be known in order to predict the rise or fall of the water level.

114. A water tower is filled with water to a depth of 15 m. If a leak forms 10 m above the base of the tower, what will be the velocity of the water as it escapes through the leak?

    **A.**    10 m/s
    **B.**    14 m/s
    **C.**    17 m/s
    **D.**    20 m/s

115. What is the approximate absolute pressure 5 m below the surface of a lake that is 20 meters deep?

    **A.**    50,000 Pa
    **B.**    150,000 Pa
    **C.**    200,000 Pa
    **D.**    300,000 Pa

**STOP.** IF YOU FINISH BEFORE TIME IS CALLED, CHECK YOUR WORK. YOU MAY GO BACK TO ANY QUESTION IN THIS TEST BOOKLET.

# 30-MINUTE IN-CLASS EXAM FOR LECTURE 6

**Passage I (Questions 116-122)**

Due to the large volume of traffic between Manhattan and Boston, a group of engineers proposed a tunnel that would allow a train to carry passengers along a perfectly straight path between the two cities. The engineers reasoned that the train could operate without consuming any energy because the force of gravity would pull the train down the first half of the tunnel. As the train accelerated during the first half of the journey, it would acquire exactly enough momentum to carry through the second half of the journey against the gravitational force. If friction is neglected and the gravitational constant $g$ is assumed to be constant throughout the trip, a one-way trip would be one-half of a cycle of simple harmonic motion similar to the swinging of a pendulum from one side to the other. (The radius of the earth is 6370 km. $g = 10$ m/s$^2$. Assume ideal conditions unless otherwise instructed.)

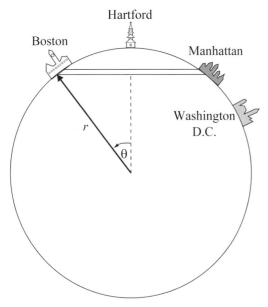

**Figure 1** Tunnel train (not drawn to scale)

**116.** Which of the following equations gives the acceleration of the train at the beginning of the trip?

- **A.** $g \sin\theta$
- **B.** $g \cos\theta$
- **C.** $Gm_{earth}/r^2$
- **D.** $g$

**117.** A similar tunnel was proposed to be built from Boston to Washington DC. Based upon Figure 1 compared to the travel time for the trip from Boston to Manhattan, the travel time for the trip from Boston to Washington DC would be:

- **A.** greater because the distance is greater.
- **B.** the same because the distance is greater but the train would go faster.
- **C.** shorter because the train would go faster.
- **D.** shorter because the trip would be downhill all the way.

**118.** Given ideal conditions, which of the following expressions most closely represents the time necessary for a trip from Boston to Manhattan?

- **A.** $2\pi\sqrt{\dfrac{r}{g}}$

- **B.** $\pi\sqrt{\dfrac{r}{g}}$

- **C.** $2\pi\sqrt{\dfrac{g}{r}}$

- **D.** $\pi\sqrt{\dfrac{g}{r}}$

**119.** Which of the following diagrams shows the change in the speed of a train as it travels on a one-way trip from Boston to Manhattan?

**A.**

**C.**

**B.**

**D.**

**120.** Which of the following best describes the net force and the acceleration on the train during the trip?

    **A.** The net force and acceleration are zero when the train is directly beneath Hartford.

    **B.** The net force and acceleration are at a maximum when the train is directly beneath Hartford.

    **C.** The net force is at a minimum when the train is directly beneath Hartford but the acceleration is constant throughout the trip.

    **D.** The net force and acceleration are constant throughout the trip.

**121.** Because the train goes downhill, then uphill, the shape of the track must be:

    **A.** a smooth constant curve along the entire length.

    **B.** a straight track along the entire length.

    **C.** a straight track with one bend exactly beneath Hartford where the train turns uphill.

    **D.** a successive series of straight track and curved track.

**122.** The engineers assumed that acceleration of gravity would remain constant during the trip. If we consider that the force of gravity gets smaller as the train nears the center of the earth, how will this affect the trip?

    **A.** The trip will require more energy than calculated by the engineers.

    **B.** The trip will require less energy than calculated by the engineers.

    **C.** The trip will require more time than calculated by the engineers.

    **D.** The trip will require less time than calculated by the engineers.

**Passage II (Questions 123-127)**

Because bats are nocturnal hunters, they rely upon sound waves to locate their prey. A horseshoe bat emits ultrasonic waves from its nostrils that reflect off its prey and return to the bat. When a horseshoe bat detects flying prey, it adjusts the frequency of the waves until the frequency of the waves rebounding off the prey is 83 kHz, the frequency at which the bat hears best. From the difference in the frequencies, the bat can judge the position of its prey and capture it.

The frequency at which the moth receives and reflects the waves emitted by the bat is given by the Doppler effect equation:

$$\frac{f_m}{f_b} = \frac{340 \pm v_m}{340 \pm v_b}$$

where $f_b$ is the frequency of the waves emitted by the bat, $f_m$ is the frequency at which the waves reflect off the moth, $v_b$ is the velocity of the bat, $v_m$ is the velocity of the moth. The sign conventions are chosen in accordance with the Doppler effect.

Certain moths can avoid being captured by bats by either flying directly away from the ultrasonic waves, or *clicking* to create a jamming frequency and confuse the bat.

A horseshoe bat flies at approximately 10 m/s. Assume that the moth flies at 5 m/s. The velocity of an ultrasonic wave in air is 340 m/s.

**123.** By flying directly away from the ultrasonic waves, the moth most likely avoids capture because:

    **A.** the sound waves reflect away from the bat.

    **B.** the frequency of the reflected waves is decreased so that it approaches the frequency of the emitted waves and the bat may not detect the moth.

    **C.** the frequency of the reflected waves is increased so that it approaches the frequency of the emitted waves and the bat may not detect the moth.

    **D.** the frequency of the reflected waves is increased so that it separates from the frequency of the emitted waves and the bat may not detect the moth.

**GO ON TO THE NEXT PAGE.**

**124.** If the bat and moth fly directly toward each other, and the bat sends ultrasonic waves at 66 kHz, at what frequency do the waves reflect off the moth?

A.  63 kHz
B.  65 kHz
C.  67 kHz
D.  69 kHz

**125.** Which of the following will decrease the frequency of the waves detected by the bat?

I.   The moth flies toward the bat.
II.  The bat flies toward the moth.
III. The moth flies away from the bat.

A.  I only
B.  III only
C.  I and II only
D.  II and III only

**126.** As the humidity of air is increased, there is less time between the moment when a bat sends a signal and the moment when the bat receives the signal from its prey. This is most likely because the addition of water vapor to air:

A.  increases the speed of sound in air by decreasing the density of the air.
B.  increases the speed of sound in air by increasing the density of the air.
C.  decreases the speed of sound in air by decreasing the density of the air.
D.  decreases the speed of sound in air by increasing the density of the air.

**127.** Which wavelength does the horseshoe bat hear best?

A.  $2 \times 10^{-3}$ m
B.  $4 \times 10^{-3}$ m
C.  2 m
D.  4 m

## Passage III (Questions 128-134)

A piano creates sound by gently striking a taut wire with a soft hammer when a key on the piano is pressed. All piano wires in a given piano are approximately the same length. However, each wire is tied down at two points, the *bridge* and the *agraffe*. The length of the wire between the the bridge and the agraffe is called the *speaking length*. The speaking length is the part of the wire that resonates. The point of the wire struck by the hammer is displaced perpendicularly to the wire's length. A standing wave described by Equation 1 is generated by the hammer strike, where *v* is the velocity, *T* is the tension in the wire, and μ is the mass per unit length of the wire.

$$v = \sqrt{\frac{T}{\mu}}$$

**Equation 1** Velocity of a wave on a piano wire

Different notes are created by using wires of different lengths, and masses. Most piano strings are actually three parallel wires; however, some lower notes are made by two or even a single wire.

Tuning a piano involves adjustment of the tension in the wires until just the right pitch is achieved. Correct pitch is achieved by listening to the beat frequency between the piano and a precalibrated tuning fork.

**128.** A piano wire with a *speaking length* of 120 cm is displaced 0.5 cm when struck by the piano hammer. What is the length of the first harmonic resonating through the wire?

    **A.**    60 cm
    **B.**    120 cm
    **C.**    180 cm
    **D.**    240 cm

**129.** A piano with which of the following properties would deliver a note with the lowest pitch?

    **A.**    100 cm speaking length; 800 N tension
    **B.**    120 cm speaking length; 800 N tension
    **C.**    100 cm speaking length; 700 N tension
    **D.**    120 cm speaking length; 700 N tension

**130.** The following are characteristics of a wave on a piano wire. Doubling which one will have the LEAST effect on the intensity of the sound produced?

    **A.**    μ
    **B.**    period
    **C.**    speaking length
    **D.**    amplitude

**131.** A piano note is compared to a tuning fork vibrating at 440 Hz. Three beats per second are discerned by the piano tuner. When the tension in the string is increased slightly, the beat frequency increases. What was the initial frequency of the piano wire?

    **A.**    434 Hz
    **B.**    437 Hz
    **C.**    443 Hz
    **D.**    446 Hz

**132.** Sound waves move through air at approximately 340 m/s. A piano wire with a 90 cm speaking length resonates at a frequency of 360 Hz. What is the wavelength of the resulting sound wave?

    **A.**    0.94 m
    **B.**    1.06 m
    **C.**    4 m
    **D.**    40 m

**133.** The wave on a piano wire is NOT an example of a:

    **A.**    transverse wave.
    **B.**    longitudinal wave.
    **C.**    standing wave.
    **D.**    harmonic wave.

**134.** If, when the hammer strikes the piano wire, the displacement of the wire increases, which of the following properties of the wave on the wire also increases?

    **A.**    the frequency
    **B.**    the wavelength
    **C.**    the amplitude
    **D.**    the velocity

**GO ON TO THE NEXT PAGE.**

**135.** A 5 kg mass bounces in simple harmonic motion at the end of a spring. At which point is the acceleration of the mass the greatest?

    **A.** when the spring is fully compressed and when the spring is fully extended

    **B.** when the spring is at its rest length

    **C.** when the spring is halfway between its rest length and its fully extended or compressed length

    **D.** the acceleration is constant

**136.** Two waves are traveling toward each other on the same string. If wave A has an amplitude of 3 cm and a wavelength of 10 cm, and wave B has an amplitude and wavelength twice that of wave A, what will be the maximum displacement of the string when the waves interfere with each other?

    **A.** 0 cm

    **B.** 3 cm

    **C.** 6 cm

    **D.** 9 cm

**137.** The period $T$ of a pendulum is given by:

$$T = 2\pi\sqrt{\frac{L}{g}}$$

where $L$ is the length and $g$ is the free fall acceleration near the surface of the earth. In order to increase the period of a pendulum by 42%, the length must be:

    **A.** decreased by 51%

    **B.** decreased by 20%

    **C.** increased by 42%

    **D.** increased by 102%

**138.** Identical wine glasses A and B contain water. If gently struck with a spoon, the water and the glass will vibrate at the same frequency. Which glass will ring at the higher pitch when struck?

A    B

    **A.** glass B because more air in the glass will create resonance at a longer wavelength

    **B.** glass B because less water in the glass results in less inertia which allows the glass to vibrate at a higher frequency

    **C.** glass A because less air in the glass will create resonance at a shorter wavelength

    **D.** glass A because more water in the glass lowers the frequency at which the glass can vibrate

---

**STOP.** IF YOU FINISH BEFORE TIME IS CALLED, CHECK YOUR WORK. YOU MAY GO BACK TO ANY QUESTION IN THIS TEST BOOKLET.

---

# 30-MINUTE IN-CLASS EXAM FOR LECTURE 7

**Passage I (Questions 139-145)**

If the velocity of a charged particle moving through a uniform magnetic field has a component parallel to that field the particle will move in a helical path as shown in Figure 1. The net force F on the particle can be described by the equation:

$$F = qvB\sin\theta$$

where $q$ is the charge on the particle, $v$ is the velocity of the charge, $B$ is the magnetic field strength, and $\theta$ is the angle between the velocity and the magnetic field. The pitch $p$ of the helix is the distance between adjacent turns. The radius $r$ of the helix is determined by the component of velocity of the charge perpendicular to the magnetic field and is independent of the component of the velocity parallel to the magnetic field.

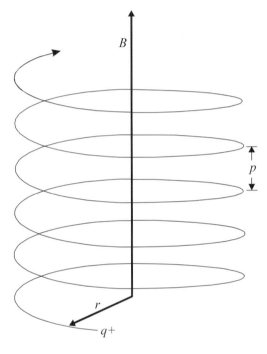

**Figure 1** Path of a charged particle
moving through a uniform magnetic field

A nonuniform magnetic field that is stronger at its ends than at its middle can trap a charged particle by reflecting it back and forth between its ends. Such a situation is shown in Figure 2.

In a similar phenomenon, electrons and protons above the atmosphere are reflected back and forth between the north and south poles of the Earth's magnetic field forming the two *Van Allen belts* high above the atmosphere. Occasionally a solar flare shoots additional electrons and protons into the *Van Allen belts* creating an electric field at the point where the electrons normally reflect. The electric field drives the electrons along the Earth's magnetic field lines into the atmosphere where they collide with the electrons of air molecules forcing them to a higher energy level. The energized electrons quickly drop back to their lower energy level emitting photons. Oxygen atoms emit green light and nitrogen atoms emit pink light. This light forms the curtain of lights in the sky known in the northern hemisphere as the *aurora borealis* and in the southern hemisphere as the *aurora australis*.

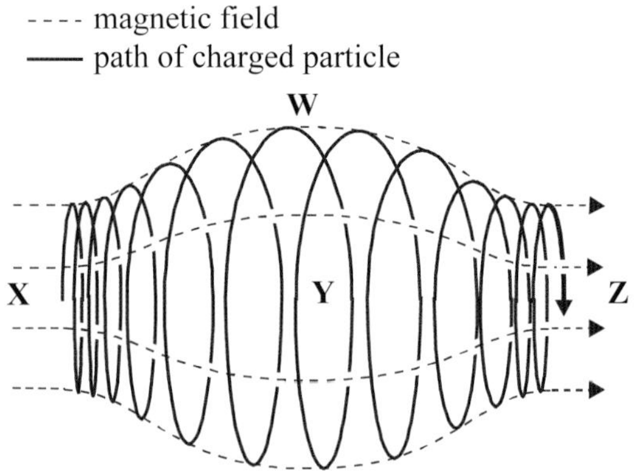

---- magnetic field
—— path of charged particle

**Figure 2** Path of a charged particle trapped
in a changing magnetic field

**139.** If the magnetic field in Figure 2 represents a portion of the Earth's magnetic field, at which labelled point would you expect to find the aurora borealis?

**A.** W
**B.** X
**C.** Y
**D.** Z

**140.** Which of the following most accurately describes the change in the pitch and period of the helical path traveled by a negatively charged particle moving through a magnetic field that is gradually strengthening?

**A.** The pitch increases and the period decreases.
**B.** The pitch increases and the period increases.
**C.** The pitch decreases and the period remains the same.
**D.** Both the pitch and the period decrease.

**141.** The diagram below shows five paths travelled by charged particles through a uniform magnetic field. If path X is the path of a proton, which path would most closely represent the path of an electron moving with the same speed?

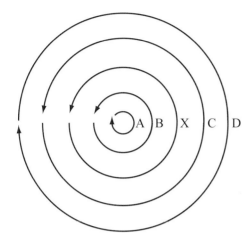

    **A.**   A
    **B.**   B
    **C.**   C
    **D.**   D

**142.** If the following particles move at the same speed and travel a helical path through a magnetic field which one is likely to experience the greatest net force?

    **A.**   a proton with a pitch $p$
    **B.**   an electron with a pitch $2p$
    **C.**   an alpha particle with a pitch $p$
    **D.**   an alpha particle with a pitch $2p$

**143.** The electrons and protons caught in the Van Allen belts reflect from one pole to the other. Looking up from the North pole, electrons rotate counterclockwise. Protons rotate:

    **A.**   counterclockwise both when looking up from the North Pole or when looking up from the South Pole.
    **B.**   clockwise both when looking up from the North Pole or when looking up from the South Pole.
    **C.**   clockwise when looking up from the North Pole but counterclockwise when looking up from the South Pole.
    **D.**   counterclockwise when looking up from the North Pole but clockwise when looking up from the South Pole.

**144.** Which of the following most accurately describes the work done by the Earth's magnetic field on an electron trapped in the Van Allen belts?

    **A.**   No work is done because the force is always perpendicular to the motion of the electron.
    **B.**   Work is done only by the component of the field that is parallel to the velocity of the electron.
    **C.**   Work is done only by the component of the magnetic field that is perpendicular to the velocity of the electron.
    **D.**   The work done is equal to the force on the electron times the distance traveled by the electron.

**145.** In order for the Van Allen belts to form, the magnetic field created by the earth must be:

    **A.**   weakest near the North Pole.
    **B.**   weakest near the South Pole.
    **C.**   weakest around the equator.
    **D.**   the same strength throughout.

**GO ON TO THE NEXT PAGE.**

Under normal conditions an electric field exists in the air near the surface of the Earth with an average strength of approximately 100 V/m. Since the human body is a relatively good conductor of electricity it remains at the same potential as the ground and the electric field in the air adjusts around the body accordingly as shown in Figure 1.

The atmosphere is about 50,000 m deep and the total potential difference between the ground and the top of the atmosphere is approximately 400,000 V. Air is a poor conductor and thus the average current is only about $10^{-12}$ A/m$^2$.

A lightning strike occurs when the bottom of a cloud has a negative electric charge that is greater than the negative charge below it on the ground. This temporarily reverses the electric field between the ground and the cloud, allowing electrons to flow from the cloud to the ground. The current in a lightning strike is about 10,000 amperes and a typical strike will deliver a charge of 20 coulombs.

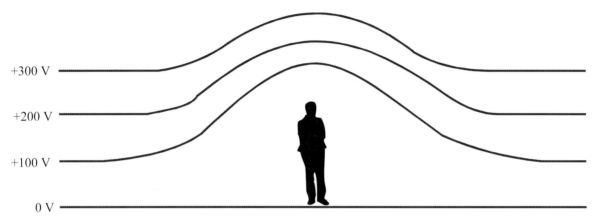

+300 V

+200 V

+100 V

0 V

**Figure 1** Potential gradient near the surface of the earth

146. The electric potential of the ground was measured at the top of a hill. If the height of the hill is 20 meters above the level of the surrounding plain, what will be the measured voltage?

   A.   0 V
   B.   5 V
   C.   200 V
   D.   2000 V

147. What is the approximate duration of the lightning strike described in the passage?
   A.   2 seconds
   B.   0.5 seconds
   C.   $2 \times 10^{-3}$ seconds
   D.   $5 \times 10^{-6}$ seconds

148. What is the average resistance of the atmosphere?

   A.   $0 \ \Omega(\text{m}^2)$
   B.   $4 \ \Omega(\text{m}^2)$
   C.   $4 \times 10^7 \ \Omega(\text{m}^2)$
   D.   $4 \times 10^{17} \ \Omega(\text{m}^2)$

149. Which of the following best describes the electric field vectors above a flat plain at the Earth's surface?

   A.   perpendicular to the ground and pointing upward
   B.   perpendicular to the ground and pointing downward
   C.   parallel to the ground and pointing north
   D.   parallel to the ground and pointing south

150. If the total electric current reaching the Earth's surface is nearly constant at 1800 A, approximately how much electrical energy is dissipated each second by the atmosphere?

   A.   $4 \times 10^{-7}$ J
   B.   $4 \times 10^5$ J
   C.   $7.2 \times 10^8$ J
   D.   $1.3 \times 10^{24}$ J

151. Which of the following describes the direction of current flow during a lightning strike?

   A.   From a cloud at high potential to the ground at lower potential.
   B.   From a cloud at low potential to the ground at higher potential.
   C.   From the ground at high potential to a cloud at lower potential.
   D.   From the ground at low potential to a cloud at higher potential.

## Passage III (Questions 152-157)

In 1879 Edwin Hall demonstrated that conducting electrons in a copper wire are deflected by a magnetic field. This phenomenon is now known as the Hall effect. The Hall effect also predicts the charge of the conduction carriers inside the copper wire.

To demonstrate the Hall effect, a copper strip carrying a current $i$ is placed in a magnetic field with field strength $B$ directed into the page as shown in Figure 1. The magnetic field and the average velocity of the electrons $v$ result in a force which pushes the electrons to one side of the copper strip. This in turn creates an electric field $E$ inside the strip which pushes the electrons in the opposite direction. An equilibrium quickly builds up to where the force on the electrons due to $E$ and $B$ are equal and in opposite directions. The Hall potential difference $V$ is proportional to the strip width $d$ and can be measured with a voltmeter.

When the electric and magnetic forces are in balance the number density of charge carriers $n$ (number of electrons per unit volume) is given by the following equation:

$$n = (Bi)/(Vle)$$

where $e$ is the charge on one electron and $l$ is the thickness of the strip and equals the cross-sectional area divided by the strip width; $l = A/d$.

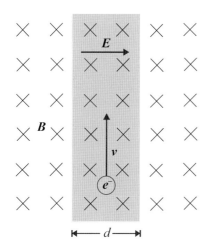

**Figure 1** Electrons moving through a copper strip in a magnetic field

The average velocity of the electrons can also be measured using the Hall effect. If the copper strip is moved in a direction opposite to the electron velocity, the Hall potential difference will be zero when the strip velocity equals the electron velocity. ($e = 1.60 \times 10^{-19}$ C)

152. In Figure 1, the force on the moving electron due to the magnetic field is in which direction?

   A.   to the left
   B.   to the right
   C.   into the page
   D.   toward the top of the page

153. Which of the following will be true if the direction of the magnetic field in Figure 1 is reversed and the system is allowed to establish equilibrium?

   A.   The electric field $E$ will be reversed.
   B.   The electron velocity $v$ will be reversed.
   C.   The Hall potential difference will be zero.
   D.   The magnetic field in Figure 1 cannot be reversed because the current creates a magnetic field directed into the page.

154. Which of the following is true when the copper strip in Figure 1 is moved in the direction opposite to the elctrons with a velocity greater than the average electron velocity $v$?

   A.   The electric field $E$ is equal to the magnetic field $B$.
   B.   The electric field $E$ is in the opposite direction of the electric field in Figure 1.
   C.   The magnetic field $B$ is in the opposite direction of the magnetic field in Figure 1.
   D.   The Hall potential difference will be zero.

155. If the copper strip is held stationary, the net force on the copper strip is:

   A.   zero.
   B.   directed into the page.
   C.   directed to the right.
   D.   directed to the left.

**GO ON TO THE NEXT PAGE.**

**156.** If an electron were to break free from the surface of the copper strip, which of the following would most accurately represent its path from the moment it breaks free?

A.

C.

B.

D.

**157.** Which of the following describes the Hall potential difference where $R$ is the effective resistance of the copper strip?

A. $evB$
B. $iR$
C. $evR$
D. $Ed$

Questions 158 through 161 are **NOT** based on a descriptive passage.

**158.** The capacitor shown below is fully charged. Both resistors have a 2Ω resistance. When the switch is opened, what is the initial current through resistor A?

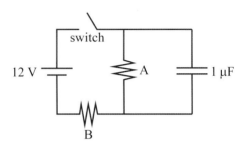

A. 2 A
B. 3 A
C. 6 A
D. 12 A

**159.** What is the charge on the capacitor in the circuit below after the circuit has been on a long time?

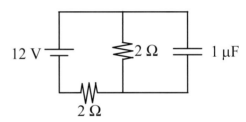

A. $1.2 \times 10^{-5}$ C
B. $2.5 \times 10^{-6}$ C
C. $6.0 \times 10^{-6}$ C
D. $1.7 \times 10^{-7}$ C

**160.** Charges A, B, C, and D are charged particles forming a square as shown. A and D have a charge of +2 C; B and C have a charge of –4 C. If $q$ is a particle with a charge of +1 sitting directly in the middle of the square, what is the net force on $q$ due to the other particles?

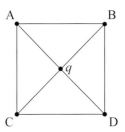

**A.** 0 N
**B.** 1 N
**C.** 1.4 N
**D.** 4 N

**161.** A particle possessing a charge of +2 C and a mass of 1 g is exposed to an electric field with strength 5 N/C. How far will the particle move in 10 seconds?

**A.** $1 \times 10^3$ m
**B.** $2 \times 10^5$ m
**C.** $5 \times 10^5$ m
**D.** $1 \times 10^6$ m

**STOP.** IF YOU FINISH BEFORE TIME IS CALLED, CHECK YOUR WORK. YOU MAY GO BACK TO ANY QUESTION IN THIS TEST BOOKLET.

**STOP.**

# 30-MINUTE IN-CLASS EXAM FOR LECTURE 8

## Passage I (Questions 162-167)

A physicist performed the following experiments to investigate the wave nature of light.

Experiment 1: Single Slit

Monochromatic light with frequency $f$ is incident on a diaphragm in which there is a single slit of width $W$. The light shining through the slit falls on a detector located a distance $D$ to the right of the slit. $D$ is much greater than $W$. The detector measures the energy delivered by the scattered wave as a function of the distance $x$. The entire apparatus is shown in Figure 1.

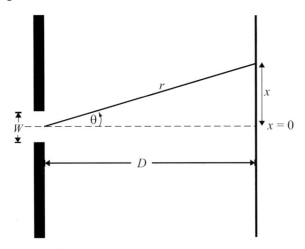

**Figure 1** Single-slit apparatus
(not drawn to scale)

The light falling on the detector reveals a series of dark and light fringes. These results are shown in Figure 2.

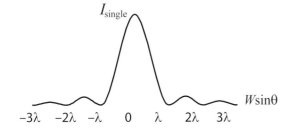

**Figure 2** Intensity vs. $W\sin\theta$ for Experiment 1

The intensity, $I_{single}$, at any given point near the center of the detector is a function of the phase difference $\phi$ between the rays at the top and bottom of the slit the moment they strike the same point on the detector. The intensity is given by the following equation:

$$I_{single} = I_m (\sin \tfrac{1}{2}\phi)/\tfrac{1}{2}\phi$$

where $I_m$ is the intensity of light striking the detector directly across from the slit.

Experiment 2: Double Slit

In Experiment 2 another slit also of width $W$ is made in the diaphragm at a distance $s$ from the first slit and the diaphragm is recentered as shown in Figure 3. $s$ is large compared to the wavelength of light $\lambda$. Again the physicist shines a monochromatic beam of light of frequency $f$ on the diaphragm. This time a different fringe pattern forms. The results of Experiment 2 are shown in Figure 4.

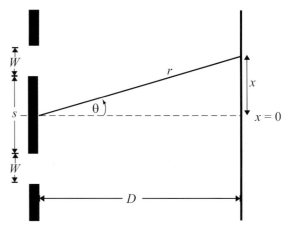

**Figure 3** Double-slit apparatus
(not drawn to scale)

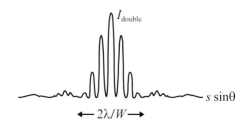

**Figure 4** Intensity vs. $s\sin\theta$ for Experiment 2

The intensity, $I_{double}$, striking near the center of the diaphragm in Experiment 2 is given by the following equation:

$$I_{double} = 4I_{single} \cos^2(\tfrac{1}{2}\psi)$$

where $\psi$ is the phase difference between rays of light from the different slits the moment they strike the detector at the point in question.

**162.** What wave phenomenon or phenomena are demonstrated by the two experiments?

    **A.** Experiment 1 demonstrates only interference and Experiment 2 only diffraction.
    **B.** Experiment 1 demonstrates only diffraction and Experiment 2 only interference.
    **C.** Both experiments demonstrate interference and diffraction.
    **D.** Neither experiment demonstrates interference or diffraction.

**163.** In Experiment 1, which of the following equations represents the time necessary for light to travel from the slit to any point on the detector? ($c$ = speed of light)

    **A.** $x/c \sin\theta$
    **B.** $x/c$
    **C.** $D/c \sin\theta$
    **D.** $D/c$

**164.** If light were purely a particle phenomenon, which of the following would best describe the results the physicist could expect from either experiment?

    **A.** The graph in Figure 2 would have more peaks.
    **B.** The graph in Figure 4 would have more peaks.
    **C.** The graph in Figure 2 would have 1 peak.
    **D.** The graph in Figure 4 would have 1 peak.

**165.** If white light were used in Experiment 1, the outermost fringes of light on the detector would appear:

    **A.** blue
    **B.** red
    **C.** white
    **D.** green

**166.** If the same light source is used for both experiments, the brightest fringe in Experiment 2 will have an intensity:

    **A.** half as great as the brightest fringe in Experiment 1.
    **B.** equal to the brightest fringe in Experiment 1.
    **C.** twice as great as the brightest fringe in Experiment 1.
    **D.** four times as great as the brightest fringe in Experiment 1.

**167.** If the amplitude of the light wave in Figure 1 were doubled, which of the following would be true?

    **A.** $I_{single}$ would increase by a factor of 2.
    **B.** $I_{single}$ would increase by a factor of 4.
    **C.** The distance between the peaks in Figure 2 would increase by a factor of 2.
    **D.** The distance between the peaks in Figure 2 would decrease by a factor of 2.

**GO ON TO THE NEXT PAGE.**

## Passage II (Questions 168-174)

The compound microscope (Figure 1) uses two convex lenses in order to magnify small objects at short distances. The lens nearest the object is called the *objective*; the lens nearest the observer is called the *ocular* or *eyepiece*. The distance between the two lenses minus the sum of the magnitudes of their focal lengths is called the *tube length L*.

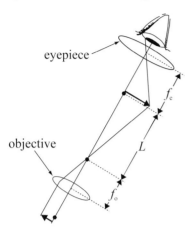

**Figure 1** A compound microscope

If a small object is placed just outside the focal point of the objective, an enlarged image is formed just inside the focal point of the eyepiece. The lateral magnification $m_o$ of this image is given by the equation:

$$m_o = -\frac{L}{f_o}$$

where $f_o$ is the focal length of the objective.

The eyepiece acts as a simple magnifier on the image formed by the objective. The angular magnification of the eyepiece $M_e$ is given by the equation:

$$M_e = -\frac{25\text{cm}}{f_e}$$

where $f_e$ is the focal length of the eyepiece, and 25 cm is the closest point to the eye for which a sharp image may be formed; this distance is called the *near point* or the *distance of most distinct vision*.

The total magnification of the microscope is given by the product of the lateral magnification of the objective and the angular magnification of the eyepiece.

$$M_{\text{total}} = m_o M_e$$

---

**168.** A certain compound microscope magnifies an image 1200 times. If the eyepiece is replaced with a lens with twice the power, the image will be magnified by a factor of:

- **A.** 600
- **B.** 1800
- **C.** 2400
- **D.** 4800

**169.** The image of the object in Figure 1 created by the objective is:

- **A.** virtual and inverted
- **B.** virtual and upright
- **C.** real and upright
- **D.** real and inverted

**170.** If the eyepiece on a compound microscope has a power of 25 diopters, what is the focal length of the eyepiece?

- **A.** 0.25 cm
- **B.** −0.25 cm
- **C.** 4 cm
- **D.** −4 cm

**171.** A 2 mm object is magnified 500 times by a compound microscope. The magnitudes of the focal lengths of the eyepiece and the objective are 1 cm and 0.5 cm respectively. What is the distance between the two lenses when the object is in focus?

- **A.** 8.5 cm
- **B.** 10.0 cm
- **C.** 11.5 cm
- **D.** 15.0 cm

**172.** What would happen if the object were placed just inside the focal point of the objective?

- **A.** The objective would form a virtual, upright image of the object on the object side of the lens.
- **B.** The objective would form a virtual, upright image of the object on the side of the lens opposite to the object.
- **C.** The objective would form a real, inverted image of the object beyond the eyepiece.
- **D.** The objective would form a real, inverted image of the object behind the object.

**173.** The word 'READ' is placed under the microscopic in the upright position. Which of the following represents the word when viewed through the microscope?

   **A.**  READ
   **B.**  ᴚE∀D
   **C.**  ᗡ∀Ǝᴚ
   **D.**  ᗡ∀Ǝᴚ

**174.** Which of the following describes how a compound microscope magnifies an image?

   **A.**  Light reflects off an object and diffracts through the lenses.
   **B.**  Light disperses off an object and reflects through the lenses.
   **C.**  Light reflects off an object and refracts through the lenses.
   **D.**  Light refracts off an object and reflects through the lenses.

**Passage III (Questions 175-180)**

A refracting telescope can be made from two convex lenses separated by a tube length $s$. The focal points of the two lenses must coincide in order for the telescope to focus on distant objects. Although Figure 1 shows two simple lenses, in practice, each lens is usually a compound lens. The lens nearer the observer is called the eyepiece, and the other lens is called the objective.

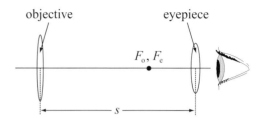

**Figure 1** A telescope

The angular magnification of a telescope is given by the following equation:

$$M = -\frac{f_{obj}}{f_{eye}}$$

where $f$ is the focal distance of the respective lenses.

Since a telescope is used to view distant objects, it requires *light-gathering power*. Light-gathering power determines how bright the image will be, and is increased by increasing the diameter of the objective. *Resolving power*, the ability to distinguish between two distant points, is also important for a telescope.

Refracting telescopes may have two flaws, *spherical and chromatic aberration*. Spherical aberration results in a blurred image because true spherical lenses do not focus all parallel light rays exactly on the focal point. This can be fixed by using parabolic lenses. Chromatic aberration occurs because different wavelengths refract at different angles.

**175.** Which of the following must be true in order for a refracting telescope to magnify distant images?

   **A.**  The focal length of the eyepiece must be greater than the focal length of the objective.
   **B.**  The focal length of the objective must be greater than the focal length of the eyepiece.
   **C.**  Only the eyepiece must be a compound lens.
   **D.**  Both the eyepiece and the objective must be compound lenses.

**GO ON TO THE NEXT PAGE.**

**176.** Where will the objective form the image of a very distant object?

    **A.**    in front of the objective
    **B.**    behind the objective but in front of the focal point of the objective
    **C.**    at the focal point of the objective
    **D.**    behind the eyepiece

**177.** If all lenses shown below are made from the same type of glass, which lens will have the greatest positive power in diopters?

    **A.**      **C.**

    **B.**      **D.**

**178.** Which of the following helps to explain chromatic aberration in a refracting telescope?

    **A.**    When light enters the lens, the frequency is lowered in a greater proportion for blue light than for red light.
    **B.**    When light enters the lens, the wavelength is shortened in a greater proportion for red light than for blue light.
    **C.**    When light enters the lens, the wavelength is lengthened in a greater proportion for blue light than for red light.
    **D.**    When light enters the lens, the wavelength is shortened in a greater proportion for blue light than for red light.

**179.** If the eyepiece of the telescope shown in Figure 1 has a power of 100 diopters, and the magnification of the telescope is −9, what is the focal length of the objective?

    **A.**    9 cm
    **B.**    −9 cm
    **C.**    10 m
    **D.**    −10 m

**180.** If the space between the lenses in the telescope in Figure 1 were filled with water, which of the following changes to the tube length would bring the image back into focus. (index of refraction for glass = 1.5, index of refraction for water = 1.3, index of refraction for air = 1)

    **A.**    increasing the tube length to compensate for the longer focal lengths of the lenses in water
    **B.**    increasing the tube length to compensate for the increased power of each lens
    **C.**    decreasing the tube length to compensate for the decrease in focal lengths of the lenses in water
    **D.**    decreasing the tube length to compensate for the decreased power of each lens

Questions 181 through 184 are **NOT** based on a descriptive passage.

181. Although waves in the open ocean propagate in all directions, waves washing into any shore usually move nearly perpendicular to the shore. Which of the following best explains the reason for this phenomenon?

   A. The shallow water decreases the speed of the waves causing them to refract.
   B. The shallow water increases the speed of the waves causing them to refract.
   C. The shallow water decreases the speed of the waves causing them to diffract.
   D. The shallow water increases the speed of the waves causing them to diffract.

182. A mirror has a radius of curvature of 8 cm and makes a real inverted image 20 cm from its surface. Where is the object?

   A. 4 cm
   B. 5 cm
   C. 10 cm
   D. 20 cm

183. A 3 cm object is placed 15 cm in front of a convex mirror. The image forms 5 cm behind the mirror. How big is the image?

   A. 1 cm
   B. 3 cm
   C. 5 cm
   D. 9 cm

184. On a hot day, a driver on the highway may see a *mirage* that appears as a puddle of water far ahead on the hot pavement. The mirage is actually a virtual image of the sky caused by light rays bending as shown below. Which of the following helps to explain the formation of the *mirage*?

   A. Hot pavement is an efficient reflector.
   B. The thin layer of warmer air acts as an aperture through which light diffracts.
   C. As air warms the speed of light decreases.
   D. As air warms the speed of light increases.

**STOP.** IF YOU FINISH BEFORE TIME IS CALLED, CHECK YOUR WORK. YOU MAY GO BACK TO ANY QUESTION IN THIS TEST BOOKLET.

**STOP.**

# ANSWERS & EXPLANATIONS

## FOR

## 30-MINUTE IN-CLASS EXAMINATIONS

# ANSWERS FOR THE 30-MINUTE IN-CLASS EXAMS

| Lecture 1 | Lecture 2 | Lecture 3 | Lecture 4 | Lecture 5 | Lecture 6 | Lecture 7 | Lecture 8 |
|-----------|-----------|-----------|-----------|-----------|-----------|-----------|-----------|
| 1. D | 24. B | 47. C | 70. D | 93. D | 116. A | 139. D | 162. C |
| 2. C | 25. A | 48. A | 71. B | 94. C | 117. B | 140. D | 163. A |
| 3. D | 26. A | 49. B | 72. C | 95. B | 118. B | 141. A | 164. C |
| 4. B | 27. A | 50. B | 73. D | 96. A | 119. A | 142. C | 165. B |
| 5. A | 28. D | 51. B | 74. D | 97. B | 120. A | 143. C | 166. D |
| 6. B | 29. B | 52. D | 75. A | 98. A | 121. B | 144. A | 167. B |
| 7. B | 30. C | 53. B | 76. C | 99. D | 122. C | 145. C | 168. C |
| 8. B | 31. A | 54. A | 77. C | 100. D | 123. B | 146. A | 169. D |
| 9. D | 32. D | 55. A | 78. D | 101. B | 124. D | 147. C | 170. C |
| 10. B | 33. D | 56. D | 79. B | 102. C | 125. D | 148. D | 171. C |
| 11. B | 34. B | 57. B | 80. B | 103. D | 126. A | 149. B | 172. A |
| 12. A | 35. A | 58. A | 81. B | 104. C | 127. B | 150. C | 173. C |
| 13. B | 36. A | 59. D | 82. D | 105. B | 128. D | 151. C | 174. C |
| 14. C | 37. D | 60. B | 83. C | 106. B | 129. D | 152. B | 175. B |
| 15. D | 38. D | 61. D | 84. B | 107. C | 130. A | 153. A | 176. C |
| 16. C | 39. C | 62. C | 85. A | 108. B | 131. C | 154. B | 177. A |
| 17. D | 40. C | 63. A | 86. C | 109. A | 132. A | 155. A | 178. D |
| 18. A | 41. C | 64. A | 87. B | 110. B | 133. B | 156. B | 179. A |
| 19. D | 42. A | 65. D | 88. A | 111. D | 134. C | 157. D | 180. A |
| 20. B | 43. C | 66. C | 89. B | 112. C | 135. A | 158. B | 181. A |
| 21. B | 44. A | 67. B | 90. D | 113. B | 136. D | 159. C | 182. B |
| 22. C | 45. A | 68. D | 91. B | 114. A | 137. D | 160. A | 183. A |
| 23. D | 46. D | 69. B | 92. B | 115. B | 138. B | 161. C | 184. D |

## MCAT PHYSICS

| Raw Score | Estimated Scaled Score |
|-----------|------------------------|
| 21 | 15 |
| 20 | 14 |
| 19 | 13 |
| 18 | 12 |
| 17 | 11 |
| 15-16 | 10 |
| 14 | 9 |
| 12-13 | 8 |

## MCAT PHYSICS

| Raw Score | Estimated Scaled Score |
|-----------|------------------------|
| 11 | 7 |
| 9-10 | 6 |
| 8 | 5 |
| 6-7 | 4 |
| 5 | 3 |
| 3-4 | 2 |
| 1-2 | 1 |

# EXPLANATIONS TO IN-CLASS EXAM FOR LECTURE 1

## Passage I

1. **D is correct.** The value $x$ in the equation gives the distance the projectile would travel in the absence of air resistance. Like all frictional forces, air resistance creates a force in the opposite direction of motion, so Zacchini should expect to fly a shorter distance than $x$.

2. **C is correct.** The passage says that it is the "propulsion" that causes the loss of consciousness. In other words, the force on Zacchini causes him to accelerate at a rate so great that he loses consciousness.

3. **D is correct.** Total energy is conserved throughout the flight. At maximum height gravitational potential energy $mgh$ is maximized, so kinetic energy $\frac{1}{2} mv^2$ is minimized.

4. **B is correct.** The vertical component is $v\sin\theta$ or $27 \times 0.8$.

5. **A is correct.** While in the cannon muzzle, gases build up behind Zacchini and force him through the muzzle of the cannon. During this time, Zacchini goes from zero velocity to maximum velocity. The acceleration is so great that it makes him unconscious. This is the greatest change in velocity in the shortest distance or time. Acceleration is rate of change in velocity. At the moment he exits the cannon muzzle the gases dissipate in all directions and there is no longer a net force accelerating Zaccini. He now becomes a pure projectile carried forward by only his momentum.

6. **B is correct.** For a projectile without air resistance, the range is maximized at $45°$. This is a fact that you should memorize for the MCAT. Subtracting or adding to the angle of trajectory from $45°$ by equal amounts results in equal ranges. For instance, $30°$ and $60°$ are both $15°$ from $45°$ and result in the same range.

## Passage II

7. **B is correct.** Without air resistance, both Jim and the ball will accelerate downward at the same rate, $10$ m/s$^2$. This is the same situation as if Tom and Jim were two astronauts in a spaceship orbiting earth. An orbiting spaceship and everything inside it fall toward earth at the same rate. Everything in the spaceship appears to float from the perspective of the two astronauts, Tom and Jim. In this case, it is obvious that Tom should throw the ball directly at Jim. In the diagram shown on the left, the ball moves with a constant horizontal velocity, and both Jim and the ball accelerate downward at the same rate. Notice that the ball moves along a straight line with respect to Jim, but moves in a parabolic path with respect to Tom. At every moment, the ball appears to Jim as if it were coming straight toward him along the dotted line. This effect is independent of the speed of the ball, and independent of where Jim catches the ball.

8. **B is correct.** The equation is $x = \frac{1}{2} gt^2$. $x$ equals $10$ m. You should probably know without calculating that an object starting from rest falls $5$ m in one second and $20$ meters in two seconds.

9. **D is correct.** The velocity of a projectile experiencing no air resistance is independent of its mass.

10. **B is correct.** Only vertical velocity dictates the time of flight for a projectile. When Jim throws the ball from the board, both Jim and the ball have an initial vertical velocity of zero. Again, the velocity of a projectile experiencing no air resistance is independent of its mass.

11. **B is correct.** Look at the diagram for question 7. Jim will travel a vertical distance of $10$ m starting from zero m/s and constantly accelerating. The ball will start with an initial vertical velocity upward, slow to zero, and then reverse direction to arrive at the same point and at the same time as Jim. Thus the ball could not possibly travel as far as Jim. $10$ m and $5$ m are out. The ball definitely rises above $0$ m. Thus B is correct. Another way to figure this out is to recognize that Jim's trip requires $1.4$ seconds (see question 8). This means that the ball must reach its peak at $0.7$ seconds due to the symmetry of projectile motion. From the formula $x = \frac{1}{2} gt^2$ we have approximately $2.5$ m.

12. **A is correct.** Since Tom's fall lasts $1.4$ seconds, the ball's flight also lasts $1.4$ seconds. (See question 8. Tom's flight time is the same as Jim's. Mass is irrelevant; they have the same initial vertical velocity.) The distance traveled by the ball is its horizontal velocity ($10$ m/s from the passage) times its flight time. This is $14$ m. Notice that the edge of the pool is already $10$ m from the board, so the answer is four meters.

13. **B is correct.** Mass is irrelevant to the path of a projectile experiencing no air resistance. Now, in order to achieve that velocity, Tom must use more force on the 2 kg ball, but that's a different question.

## Passage III

14. **C is correct.** This can be deduced from any trial, but the easiest is from the $0°$ trial. Since the vertical velocity is zero in this trial, the height is found from the equation $x = \frac{1}{2} gt^2$. This gives $x = 10$ m.

15. **D is correct.** A projectile launched across a level plane will reach its greatest horizontal displacement when launched at $45°$ above the horizontal. You need to know this for the MCAT. Table 1 shows that the projectile in the passage reached its greatest horizontal displacement when launched at a $30°$. Therefore, it must not be on a level plane. More evidence is given from the displacement when launched at $0°$. Unless the projectile is launched from above the ground, it will immediately strike the ground when launched at $0°$. Thus, the projectile in this experiment is launched from a platform above the ground. Since it is launched from a platform, and because projectile motion is symmetrical (the upward flight mirrors the downward flight) when it reaches the altitude of the platform on its way down, it will reach its launching speed. As it continues lower than the platform, it will increase its speed. Thus D must be correct. A is wrong because from Table 1 the displacement of the projectile does not increase with time. B is wrong because when a projectile is shot at greater angles, its altitude increases, yet from Table 1 the projectile's displacement does not continue to increase as the angle increases.

16. **C is correct.** Again, the first trial is the easiest to examine. From the first trial, we have $d = vt$, which gives us $v = 10$ m/s.

17. **D is correct.** This should be intuitive. $v \sin\theta = \sqrt{2gh}$. Sin $90°$ is 1, so is maximized at 90 degrees.

18. **A is correct.** This is the only graph that isn't zero when $\theta$ is zero.

19. **D is correct.** The distance through the air is not the horizontal displacement. This is best solved by process of elimination: A is wrong because only vertical velocity is zero at maximum height. B is wrong because acceleration was constant for all projectiles. C is wrong because only the velocity changed at a constant rate; as the projectile climbed, speed decreased; as it fell, speed increased.

## Stand Alones

20. **B is correct.** Use units. 1 m/s $\div$ 2 strides/s = $\frac{1}{2}$ m/stride

21. **B is correct.** The atmosphere will create air resistance, shortening the path of the ball, and the gravity will reduce the time of flight, also shortening the path of the ball.

22. **C is correct.** Only the vertical velocity affects the time in flight of a projectile experiencing no air resistance.

23. **D is correct.** The velocity is proportional to the square root of the initial height of a ball rolling down an inclined plane: $v^2 = 2ax$ or $v = \sqrt{2gh}$. The ball falls twice as far in the second trial. Thus the ball has $\sqrt{2}$ times the velocity. Eliminate A by taking the example to extremes. If the ball falls straight down, it will obviously take less time to travel one meter than if the ball rolls down at a very slight angle. Displacement is a vector; direction matters, so B is wrong. C is wrong because the acceleration down an inclined plane is $g \sin\theta$. You also should have known C is wrong because if A is wrong, speed is distance over time, C would be wrong as well.

## EXPLANATIONS TO IN-CLASS EXAM FOR LECTURE 2

### Passage I

24. **B is correct.** B and D are opposites so one must be the false statement. The larger the radius of curvature, the straighter the curve. A straight line would require no bank angle. (Radius of curvature is discussed in Physics Lecture 8).

25. **A is correct.** Friction is always parallel to the surfaces that create it, and it always opposes sliding motion between the two surfaces. In this case, the car is going very fast and, if the bank were made of ice (had no friction), the car would slide up the bank. The friction is static because the vehicle has no motion relative to the bank in the direction of friction (i.e., the tires do not slide along the pavement).

26. **A is correct.** If we were to draw a circle representing the path of the car, arrow B would point to the center of that circle. The centripetal force always points to the center of the circle.

27. **A is correct.** A stationary object experiences no net force. We will discuss this more in Physics Lecture 3.

28. **D is correct.** Centripetal force is given by $F_c = mv^2/r$. Doubling $v$ requires that $F$ quadruples.

29. **B is correct.** Since there is no vertical acceleration, the net vertical force would have to be zero ($F = ma$). The only vertical force downward would be the weight of the vehicle, so the frictional force would have to be equal and opposite. The normal force is the centripetal force of the wall on the vehicle. The car must be moving fast enough for the frictional force to be equal to gravity. So $f_s = \mu_s N = \mu_s mv^2/r$. $\mu_s mv^2/r = mg$.

30. **C is correct.** The mass of the vehicles will not affect the required bank angle because the centripetal force, the frictional force and the force down the incline due to gravity are all proportional to mass. A greater speed limit on the curves would require a greater bank angle in order to keep the cars from sliding off the road.

## Passage II

31. **A is correct.** As long as there are no resisting forces like friction, the centripetal force will always have the same magnitude and will always be perpendicular to the spaceship's motion, so the speed of the spaceship will never change. The ship will continue to travel with the motion dictated by the equation in the passage unless another force causes it to change.

32. **D is correct.** The passage says the ship is pressurized, thus there are air molecules in the ship. The passage also says that there is air in the cabin. The man has his helmet off and is still alive so there must be air in the ship. Air molecules create air resistance, which will slow any projectile. The gravity of the planet acts equally on the ship, the astronaut, and the projectile, so relative to the astronaut, the bag will move along a straight line.

33. **D is correct.** The bag will move in a straight line relative to the astronaut. (See question 32.)

34. **B is correct.** $t = d/v$. Convert seconds to hours. You must know that radio waves are electromagnetic, and electromagnetic waves move at the speed of light or $3 \times 10^8$ m/s.

35. **A is correct.** Centripetal force equals gravitational force. $GmM/r^2 = mv^2/r$. Thus $v^2$ is inversely proportional to $r$.

36. **A is correct.** Their orbits are related only to their velocities because both gravitational and centripetal force are proportional to mass. (See the equation in question 35.)

37. **D is correct.** The ship is in orbit. Thus, the ship and everything in it is in free fall. Since the clock housing and the clock pendulum are already falling at the same rate, the pendulum does not swing relative to the clock housing.

## Passage III

38. **D is correct.** Light travels $3 \times 10^8$ m each second, so a light second is equal to $3 \times 10^8$ m. The distance in light seconds is the orbital radius of the moon (found in Table 1), converted to meters (384,400,000 m), divided by meters per light second ($3 \times 10^8$ m/light second). Using scientific notation, this comes out to something slightly greater than 1.

39. **C is correct.** The passage states that the same side of the moon always faces the Earth and that the moon moves around the Earth once every 27.3 days. Thus the moon revolves once on its axis every 27.3 days. Yes, you probably would be expected to know what defines a day on a given planet.

40. **C is correct.** These are not lengthy calculations, so use your pencil! To solve this problem we set the gravitational force of the sun on the Earth equal to the centripetal force.

$$F = G\frac{M_{sun}m_{Earth}}{r^2_{orbital}} = m_{Earth}\frac{v^2}{r}$$

solving for $v$ we get: $v = \sqrt{\dfrac{GM_{sun}}{r}}$

41.     **C is correct.** The quickest way to solve this problem is by proportions. The radius of the earth is a little less than 4 times as large as the radius of the moon. According to $F = Gmm/r^2$, this would lead to an *increase* in relative gravity on the moon by a factor of something less than 16. From Table 1 we see that the Earth is about 80 times more massive than the moon. This would lead to a *decrease* in relative gravity on the moon by a factor of 80. Multiplying the man's weight on the earth (1000 N) by 16 and dividing by 80 we get: 16,000/80 = 200 N. This is easily closest to 170. Don't be afraid to round off. OR, you can solve this problem the long way: From Table 1, plug into $F = Gmm/r^2$ for the moon and solve.

42.     **A is correct.** This is Newton's 3rd law: for every force there is an EQUAL and opposite force.

## Stand Alones

43.     **C is correct.** Just as if we suspended a 200 kg mass from the rope, the ceiling would pull upward with a force of 2000 newtons and the mass would pull downward with 2000 newtons, but the tension in the rope would still be mg or 2000 newtons.

44.     **A is correct.** Since there is no acceleration, the net force is zero.

45.     **A is correct.** From the $F = Gmm/r^2$ equation, we know that the weight is reduced by increasing $r$. The flattened shape of the Earth makes the equator further from the center of gravity of the earth. Secondly, if there were no gravity, objects along the equator would be thrown away from the earth by the centrifugal force. More precisely, they would continue straight in the direction of their present velocity instead of turning with the earth's surface. Thus, some of the force of gravity is used up as centripetal force to turn the direction of the velocity of the objects. This results in a decrease in the weight of the object.

46.     **D is correct.** $F = -kx$ and $F = mg$. Thus $mg = -kx$. Ignore the negative which only indicates that the force is in the opposite direction of the displacement. $5 \times 10 = 0.1k$. Don't forget to convert centimeters to meters.

# EXPLANATIONS TO IN-CLASS EXAM FOR LECTURE 3

## Passage I

47.     **C is correct.** Each revolution moves Puncho $2\pi r$ meters, which equals $0.5\pi$ m/revolution. If we examine the units, we see that dividing the velocity 10 m/s by $0.5\pi$ m/rev gives us $20/\pi$ revolutions/second. The question asks for revolutions in one second, so the answer is $20/\pi$ revolutions.

48.     **A is correct.** Since the pole is stationary, the net torque must be zero Newton meters.

49.     **B is correct.** As shown by the equations below, the angle is related to the mass of Puncho and the tension in the rope, and is not related to the length of rope.

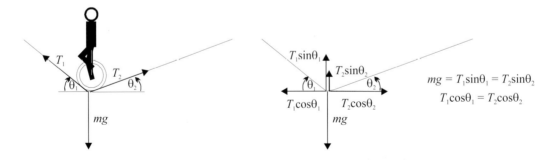

50.     **B is correct.** Since gravity is the only force acting on a ball while it is in the air, and because gravity is a conservative force, while in the air, the total energy of each ball remains constant. Each ball has an energy equal to the initial kinetic energy given to it by Puncho, $\frac{1}{2} mv^2 = 25$ J. Five balls gives a total energy of 125 J. Or each ball has an energy equal to the maximum potential energy which is P.E. = $mgh = 0.5 \times 10 \times 5 = 25$ J. Five balls gives a total energy of 125 J.

51. **B is correct.** When Puncho is on his unicycle, he doesn't want to move laterally. Inertia is the tendency for an object to resist change in its present state of motion. Mass is a measure of inertia, so a massive pole increases inertia. As an object's mass is spread from its center of gravity, more torque is required to rotate that object; its rotational inertia is increased.

## Passage II

52. **D is correct.** The mass $m$ pulls downward with a force of $mg$. This translates through the string to a horizontal force on the 0.1 kg mass. Without friction, this is the only horizontal force on the 0.1 kg mass. Thus, the 0.1 kg mass has a constant net force horizontally and therefore a constant acceleration.

53. **B is correct.** Think of the extreme case. If the mass $m$ is much, much larger than 0.1 kg, the greatest acceleration is still only equal to $g = 10$ m/s². In order to accelerate 0.1 kg at the rate of $g$, we would only need 1 N of tension in the string. ($F = ma$)

54. **A is correct.** The mass in Experiment 1 is in static equilibrium; there is no net force.

55. **A is correct.** Mass $m$ would fall at a rate of $g = 10$ m/s². Any tension in the string would slow this rate and mass $m$ would no longer be in free fall. The tension in the string must be zero.

56. **D is correct.** The mass $m$ pulls downward with a force of $mg$. This translates through the string to a horizontal force on the 0.1 kg mass. Without friction, this is the only horizontal force on the 0.1 kg mass. Thus, the 0.1 kg mass has a constant net force horizontally and therefore a constant acceleration. A constant positive acceleration is represented by a straight line with a positive slope on a speed vs. time graph. This is choice D.

57. **B is correct.** Friction is a force opposing motion, which is in the opposite direction of tension, increasing the tension. Changing mass $m$ does not change the friction. The friction is given by $f = \mu N$, where $N$ is the normal force which in this case is the weight of the 0.1 kg block.

58. **A is correct.** You should use Table 2 to figure this out quickly. You can see from the table that there is not a linear relationship between mass $m$ and tension $T$. From trial 1 to 3 the mass was doubled increasing the tension by 0.17 N; from trial 2 to 4 the mass was doubled increasing the tension by 0.15 N. Thus, you would expect that if we double the mass of trial 3 we would get an increase in tension of less than 0.15 N. A is the only answer that satisfies this criterion.

| Trial | $m$ (kg) | $T$ (N) |
|-------|----------|---------|
| 1 | 0.10 | 0.50 |
| 2 | 0.15 | 0.60 |
| 3 | 0.20 | 0.67 |
| 4 | 0.30 | 0.75 |

0.17 N increase
0.15 N increase
Increase should be less than 0.15 N, so $T$ should be less than 0.83.

The long way to figure this out is as follows: Assuming no friction, first look at the 0.1 kg mass. $T = ma \Rightarrow T = 0.1a$. For the other block $mg = T + ma \Rightarrow 0.4(10) = T + 0.4a$. Putting both equations together we get $0.4(10) = T + 0.4(T/0.1) \Rightarrow 4 = 5T \Rightarrow T = 4/5 = 0.8$.

## Passage III

59. **D is correct.** Once the bomb is in the air, gravity is the only force acting upon it. Since gravity is a conservative force, total mechanical energy is conserved. Just before the bomb hits the ground, all the energy would be kinetic. The initial potential energy of the bomb is $P.E. = mgh = 2 \times 10 \times 300 = 6000$ J. The initial kinetic energy of the bomb is $K.E. = \frac{1}{2}mv^2 = \frac{1}{2} \times 2 \times 30^2 = 900$ J. The total energy is the sum of these two.

60. **B is correct.** The power required is $P = Fv$. Where the force is the weight of the rocket $mg$, and $v$ is the velocity of the rocket. Thus, $1200 \times 300 \times 10 = 3.6 \times 10^6$ W.

61. **D is correct.** Energy is a scalar and is conserved. The total initial energy will equal the final energy in every case. Also, in every case gravitational potential energy will be completely converted to kinetic energy. Since energy is a scalar, the direction of the plane does not affect its initial energy. (Notice that in question 59 we were not concerned with the direction in which the plane was flying.) The initial potential energy is the same in each case. Thus the initial energy and the final energy are greatest where the initial velocity is the greatest.

62. **C is correct.** The plane is not a glider. It receives its energy from fuel.

63. **A is correct.** Terminal velocity is constant velocity, so the net force must be zero. The forces acting on the plane are its propulsive force, the air resistance, and gravity. The sum of these forces is zero.

64. **A is correct.** The apparent weight of the pilot is the reading on a scale if he were sitting on the scale during his dive. When he pulls out of the dive, he is decelerating. This means that the scale underneath him would have to push up with more force than his weight. His apparent weight increases.

65. **D is correct.** Don't use vectors to solve this problem. The work done is equal to the change in potential and kinetic energy. $W = \Delta K.E. + \Delta P.E.$ $W = \frac{1}{2}mv^2 + mgh = \frac{1}{2} \times 2 \times 400 + 2 \times 10 \times 200 = 400 + 4000$.

66. **C is correct.** The time for the bomb to reach the ground is found from the equation $x = \frac{1}{2}gt^2$. $t = 6$ seconds. The horizontal velocity of the bomb is the same as the plane, 30 m/s. In 6 seconds, the bomb will move 180 meters horizontally.

## Stand Alones

67. **B is correct.** Energy is required to separate attracting bodies. The rocket is attracted to Earth by gravity. Gravity gets smaller with distance of separation, but it never goes to zero. So, more and more energy is required to continue to separate the rocket from Earth. Gravity is a conservative force, so the energy is conserved as gravitational potential energy. The $g$ is presented in the question to distract you in the hopes that you will use the equation $U = -Gmm/r$ and be confused as to whether $U$ increases or decreases with $r$, or perhaps you will forget the negative sign.

68. **D is correct.** The left end is 4 times closer to the balancing point than the right end, and thus has a lever arm four times smaller. A lever arm four times smaller requires a force four times greater or $4mg$.

69. **B is correct.** Finding the center of gravity can be done like a torque problem. To find the center of gravity, we find the balancing point. The lever arm for the moon must be 80 times longer than the lever arm for the Earth because the Earth is 80 times heavier. We should divide the distance from the Earth to the moon into 81 equal parts, but it is easier to use 80. $400,000/80 = 5,000$. Thus $400,000/81 < 5,000$. The center of gravity is less than 5,000 km from the center of the Earth, which is just beneath the surface of the Earth.

# EXPLANATIONS TO IN-CLASS EXAM FOR LECTURE 4

## Passage I

70. **D is correct.** In order for momentum to be conserved, the initial horizontal momentum must equal the final horizontal momentum, and the initial vertical momentum must equal the final vertical momentum. There is no vertical momentum before either *Collision 1* or *Collision 2*, so there can be none afterwards. In order to have zero vertical momentum, angles $x$ and $y$ must be equal to zero.

71. **B is correct.** In order for momentum to be conserved, The momentum $m_1v_1$ (before) must equal $(m_1 + m_2)v$ (after). So, (1 kg)(4 m/s) = (2 kg)($v$). Thus, $v = 2$ m/s.

72. **C is correct.** To conserve momentum, $m_Av_A$ (before) must be equal to $m_Bv_B$ (after). Therefore (2 kg)(4 m/s) = $m$(4 m/s). So m – 2 kg.

73. **D is correct.** There is no motion after the collision, so there is no kinetic energy. The blocks are permanently deformed and all of the collisions take place on a horizontal surface, so there is no elastic or gravitational potential energy. So the kinetic energy must be converted into heat energy during the collision.

74. **D is correct.** The vertical momentum before the explosion is zero, so it must be zero after the explosion. The momentum going up the page is (1 kg)$v_2$sin($w$), and the momentum down the page is (1 kg)$v_3$sin($z$). These two must be equal if they are to add up to zero. The other particle has no vertical motion and thus has no effect on the overall vertical momentum.

75. **A is correct.** In order for a collision to be perfectly elastic, mechanical energy must be conserved. Mechanical energy is not conserved in explosions or in collisions where the colliding objects stick together, so only *Collision 1* can be perfectly elastic.

76. **C is correct.** The two blocks come to a stop after the collision, so their momenta must have been equal and opposite before the collision. Therefore (2 kg)$v_A$ = (1 kg)$v_B$. So $2v_A = v_B$.

## Passage II

77.  **C is correct.** Energy from a fusion reaction comes from rest mass energy: $E = mc^2$.

78.  **D is correct.** The equation is given in the passage. The temperature at the sun's core is given as 1.3 keV. We divide this by Boltzmann's constant to get D. Don't forget the *kilo* in keV.

79.  **B is correct.** The net reaction found by adding all the reactions together is:  $4^1H + 2e^- \rightarrow {}^4He + 6\gamma + 2\nu$.

80.  **B is correct.** The energy for the reaction came from the annihilation of an electron and a positron. This energy equals $mc^2$, where $m$ represents the mass of both the electron and positron. But first we must convert to joules by multiplying 1.02 MeV (don't forget that Mega = $10^6$) times coulombs/electron (given at the end of the passage). This is the energy in $E = mc^2$. We divide energy by the speed of light squared to get the mass of the electron and the positron. We divide by two for the mass of the positron. The answers are given to the nearest magnitude of 10, so, as usual, round your numbers and do calculations quickly: $10^6 \times 10^{-19} = m \times 9 \times 10^{16} \Rightarrow m = 10^{-13}/10^{17} = 10^{-30}$. The true mass of a proton or electron is $9.1 \times 10^{-31}$ kg.

81.  **B is correct.** If energy is released then stronger bonds must be formed. As stated in the question, the strength of the bonds comes completely from the binding energy.

82.  **D is correct.** Choice A is a violation of the conservation of energy. B is contradicted twice in the passage. C is contradicted in the passage and you should know that large nuclei undergo fission and small nuclei undergo fusion.

## Passage III

83.  **C is correct.** Both forces act on the same side of the fulcrum and the in-force is nearer to the fulcrum. From the passage, this is a third order lever system. The passage also states that running mammals take advantage of a third order lever system. Although Figure 1 shows a running mammal, and Figure 2 a digging mammal, the two lever systems are the same.

84.  **B is correct.** The lever in Figure 2 has a greater in-lever arm to out-lever arm ratio and thus applies greater leverage and more force.

85.  **A is correct.** The out-lever arm is 10 times greater than the in-lever arm, so the force applied by the out-lever arm must be 10 times smaller. As stated in the passage, the advantage to this system is speed not strength.

86.  **C is correct.** The same formula as the previous question applies. The shorter lever arm requires the greater force. Work is not changed by an ideal machine.

87.  **B is correct.** Decreasing the in-lever arm while increasing the out-lever arm creates greater relative velocity between the fulcrum and the point of out-force application. The animal in Figure 2 is a digger and the animal in Figure 1 is a runner; notice the lever arm proportions. The passage also explains this. The passage tells us that swift runners take advantage of third order lever systems. In other words, swift runners take advantage of having the in-force closer to the fulcrum and the out-force further away.

88.  **A is correct.** The elbow is the fulcrum. The distance from the elbow to the point where the force due to the muscle is $90°$ is greatest in A. This is the in-lever arm.

## Stand Alones

89.  **B is correct.** 2 hours is approximately 5 half-lives. $2^5 = 32$. 800/32 = 25. But you should just count on your fingers. Starting with 800 µg, after one half life, there is 400 µg left; after two half lives, 200 µg; after three half lives, 100 µg; after four half lives, 50 µg; and after five half lives, 25 µg. Choice B is the closest answer.

90.  **D is correct.** Two alpha decays indicate a loss of eight in mass number and four in atomic number. Four beta decays indicate an increase of four in atomic number. The element remains the same and the mass number goes to 210.

**91.** **B is correct.** The angle is irrelevant. Both the lever and the pulley system reduce the force necessary by a factor of 2 each. The total reduction is by a factor of 4.

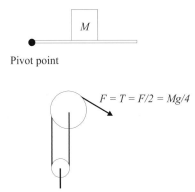

**92.** **B is correct.** The initial horizontal momentum of the two rock system is zero, so the final horizontal momentum will be zero as well. Since they stick together, in order to make their horizontal momentum zero, their horizontal velocity must also be zero. The initial vertical momentum of the system is 87 kg m/s downward, thus the final vertical momentum is 87 kg m/s downward. Dividing by the total mass (15 kg) leaves a final vertical velocity of 5.8 m/s.

## EXPLANATIONS TO IN-CLASS EXAM FOR LECTURE 5

### Passage I

**93.** **D is correct.** The passage states that the coefficient of volume expansion is 3 times $\alpha$. Use the value of $\alpha$ from the table. Don't forget that the table gives $\alpha$ in magnitudes of $10^{-6}$.

**94.** **C is correct.** Steel has a lower $\alpha$ than brass and increases more slowly to temperature change.

**95.** **B is correct.** Plug in $19 \times 10^{-6}$ for $\alpha$, 10 for $\Delta T$, and solve for $\Delta L/L$. $\Delta L/L$ is the fractional change in length. Multiply this times 100 to get the percent change in length.

**96.** **A is correct.** Aluminum has the highest $\alpha$, and thus has the greatest change in length or volume per change in temperature.

**97.** **B is correct.** Since the density of water is greatest at $4°$ C, water expands when cooled below $4°$ C. The weight does not change with expansion or contraction. There are the same number of water molecules; only the space between them has changed.

**98.** **A is correct.** The easy way to solve this problem is to take things to the extremes. Since the aluminum has a much smaller volume coefficient of expansion, imagine that the aluminum doesn't change volume at all. The buoy must displace enough water to equal its mass. The mass of the buoy doesn't change with temperature. So in our extreme example only the volume of water is changing with temperature. When the water gets warm, it expands. The same mass of water fills more volume. The buoy sinks in the summer, in order to displace enough water to equal its weight.

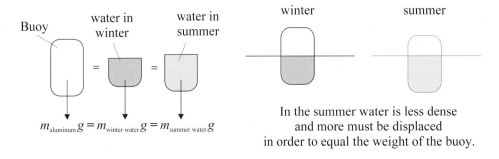

In the summer water is less dense and more must be displaced in order to equal the weight of the buoy.

The more difficult way to solve this problem is as follows: $\rho_{buoy}V_{buoy}g = \rho_{water}V_{water\ displaced}g \Rightarrow \rho_{water\ displaced}g = \rho_{buoy}g(V_{buoy}/V_{water\ displaced})$. Because aluminum changes volume much more slowly than water when heated, $V_{buoy}/V_{water}$ gets smaller as temperature increases.

## Passage II

99. **D is correct.** This is a fluid at rest. The pressure is greatest where the depth is the greatest. $P = \rho g y$; where $y$ is measured from the surface.

100. **D is correct.** In an ideal fluid, flow rate is the same at all points.

101. **B is correct.** $P = \rho g y$. $\rho$ is 5 times that of water, thus $\rho$ is 5000 kg/m$^3$. Measure $y$ from the surface of the fluid: 6 cm. $P = 5000 \times 10 \times 0.06 = 3000$ Pa. The pipe is sealed shut so there is no atmospheric pressure.

102. **C is correct.** Choose $h_0 = 0$ to be point D, so $h = 0.1$ m, and we have $v = v = \sqrt{2gh} = 1.4$ *m/s*. **Important:** Notice that the velocity at C and B will also be 1.4 m/s because $Q = Av$. We can only use $v = \sqrt{2gh}$ at point D because the pressure is the same at point D as at the surface of the fluid.

103. **D is correct.** The volume of fluid displaced by the object is equal to the volume of the object. The mass of the fluid displaced by the object is equal to the apparent loss of mass of the object (weight = 5 N). Since the specific gravity of the fluid is 5, the same volume of water would weigh 1 N. Thus, the object weighs 20 times more than water giving it a specific gravity of 20.

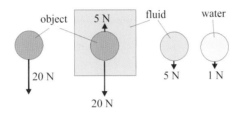

104. **C is correct.** As $y$ decreases, the pressure ($P = \rho g y$) decreases, velocity ($v = h = y$ in this case) decreases, and flow rate decreases ($Q = Av$ [since $v$ decreases, $Q$ decreases]). The density does not decrease. At first glance, this appears to violate the rule that $Q$ is constant everywhere in an ideal fluid. The reason that it doesn't violate this rule is because the rule says $Q$ is constant everywhere in space, not in time. In other words, $Q$ can change with time, but not with position; at any given moment, $Q$ is constant in any given cross-section of an ideal fluid.

105. **B is correct.** Point C is twice the depth as point A, so the pressure is twice as great ($P = \rho g y$). This question is really just asking "Do you measure $y$ from the top, or from the bottom?" Of course, you measure $y$ from the top.

## Passage III

106. **B is correct.** Since lift acts against gravity, the ball will undergo less downward acceleration, so it will go higher and stay in the air longer. The horizontal distance is given by the horizontal velocity times the time in the air. Since time in the air increases, it will also go farther horizontally.

107. **C is correct.** The speed of a point on the surface of a rotating object can be found by multiplying the frequency of rotation by the circumference. Don't forget to convert centimeters to meters. So $w = (3.14)(0.043 \text{ m})(60 \text{ Hz}) = 8.1$ m/s. 60 Hz has one significant digit, so the answer can have only one significant digit. The answer is 8 m/s.

108. **B is correct.** The density of the ball has nothing to do with the force exerted on it. A less dense ball might experience greater acceleration for a given force, but it will not change the actual lift force. All of the other choices will increase the pressure difference as shown in the equation in the passage.

109. **A is correct.** The density of the ball is $(45 \text{ g})/(42 \text{ cm}^3)$. Since the density is greater than 1 g/cm$^3$ (the density of water), the specific gravity is greater than 1 and the ball will sink in water.

110. **B is correct.** If the spin is reversed, the relative airspeed will be decreased above the ball, causing the pressure above the ball to be greater than the pressure below.

111. **D is correct.** Subtract the airspeed below the ball $u - w$ from the airspeed above the ball $u + w$ to get the difference $2w$.

112. **C is correct.** The density of the container is 2 kg/ $5 \times 10^{-3}$ m$^3$ = 400 kg/m$^3$. The specific gravity is 0.4 which means that 60% floats above the water. Or even simpler, the bottle weighs 2 kg, while 5 liters of water would weight 5 kg, so the specific gravity of the bottle is 2/5 = 0.4.

113. **B is correct.** When the brick is on the Styrofoam, the brick-Styrofoam combination floats, so it displaces an amount of water equal to the weight of the brick (Recall that the Styrofoam is weightless). When the brick is at the bottom, it only displaces an amount of water equal to the volume of the brick. Since the brick is heavier (more dense) than water, more water is required to match the weight of the brick than the volume of the brick. Since more water is displaced when the brick is floating, more water is pushed upward; the water level is higher when the brick floats on the Styrofoam than when the brick sinks to the bottom.".

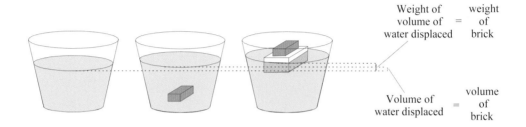

114. **A is correct.** The leak is 5 m below the surface. We use $v = \sqrt{2gh}$ where $h = 5$ m.

115. **B is correct.** 10 meters of water produces approximately 1 atm or 10$^5$ Pa of pressure ($P = \rho g h$). 5 m produces half of that. Add atmospheric pressure (10$^5$ Pa) to get 150,000 Pa.

# EXPLANATIONS TO IN-CLASS EXAM FOR LECTURE 6

## Passage I

116. **A is correct.** As shown in the diagram below, this is an inclined plane. The acceleration of any object down an inclined plane with no friction is $g \sin\theta$.

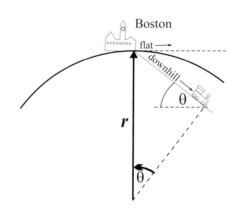

117. **B is correct.** The motion duplicates a pendulum with a length equal to the radius of the Earth. One period is equal to a round trip on the train. The equation for the period of a pendulum is $T = 2\pi\sqrt{\dfrac{L}{g}}$. Notice that the period is independent of the distance that the pendulum swings. Since the periods are equal, the top speed must be greater for the longer trip.

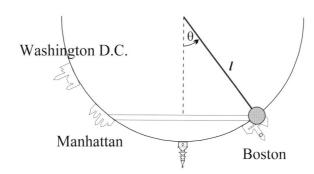

118. **B is correct.** The passage says that the motion is similar to a pendulum. The period of a pendulum is given by $T = 2\pi\sqrt{\dfrac{L}{g}}$. Here, $L$ is the same as $r$, and we only want half the period because it is a one way trip. See the diagram above.

119. **A is correct.** Simple harmonic motion can be graphed as a sine curve. Since a trip from Boston to Manhattan is half a cycle, Choice A is correct answer.

120. **A is correct.** At the midpoint in the trip, the train is on a flat plane perpendicular to the radius of the earth. The forces on the train are gravity acting straight toward the center of the earth, and the normal force acting straight away from the center of the earth. Since the train is obviously not accelerating in either or these directions, these two forces are equal, and the net force is zero. Newton's second law, $F = ma$, tells us that the acceleration must also be zero.

121. **B is correct.** See Figure 1. The track is straight. It is our perception of *uphill* and *downhill* that is the problem. We perceive *downhill* as any vector with some component in the direction toward the center of the earth, and uphill as any vector with some component in the direction away from the center of the earth. Because we are so small compared to the earth, we are accustomed to thinking of the direction of the center of the earth as being constant. This is not the case. In the example of the tunnel train, it is the direction toward the center of the earth that changes and not the direction of the track.

122. **C is correct.** Gravity decreases as we move toward the center of the earth from the surface, so acceleration decreases, and maximum velocity will be less. The trip will require more time.

**Passage II**

123. **B is correct.** Only B gives the correct prediction of change in frequency when the moth flies away from the bat. The Doppler effect predicts that when the source moves away from the observer, the observed frequency goes down. In this case, the bat is observing the frequency reflected off the moth.

124. **D is correct.** The waves reflect off the moth at the same frequency that it receives them. This is the Doppler effect. Don't use the equation in the passage. To find the frequency at which the bat receives the waves use $\Delta f/f = v/c$ where $f = 66$ kHz, $v = 15$ m/s (the relative velocity), and $c = 340$ m/s. Since they are moving toward each other, the frequency will increase. Thus, to find the frequency at which the waves reflect off the moth we add $\Delta f$ to 66 kHz.

125. **B is correct.** Only movement that separates the pair will decrease the frequency.

126. **A is correct.** If the signal takes less time, then it must be going faster. The speed of sound in a medium increases with decreasing density. You may think that humid air is heavier, but this is incorrect. There is a decrease in density as water vapor is added to air that occurs because the molecular mass of water (18 g/mol) is less than that of nitrogen (28 g/mol) or oxygen (32 g/mol) gases, the main constituents of air.

127. **B is correct.** This is just $v = \lambda f$. The numbers from the passage are: $f = 83$ kHz; $v = 340$ m/s. Don't forget the <u>kilo</u>hertz.

128.  **D is correct.** The length of the first harmonic is the longest possible standing wavelength, which is simply twice the length between the fastened ends of the wire.

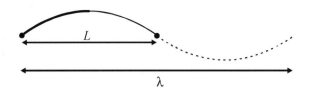

129.  **D is correct.** Pitch correlates with frequency; $f\lambda = v$. We can set this equation equal to the one in the passage to see that increased tension raises frequency, and increased length lowers frequency. (From question 128 we know that speaking length $L$ is proportional to wavelength $\lambda$.)

130.  **A is correct.** Intensity is given by $I = f_i \mu \omega^2 A^2 v$. Doubling $\mu$ increases intensity by a factor of only 2. Since $\omega = 2\pi f = 2\pi/T$, doubling $T$ would decrease intensity by a factor of 4. The speaking length is directly proportional to the fundamental wavelength. From $v = f\lambda$, doubling the speaking length doubles $\lambda$ and reduces $f$ by a factor of 2, reducing intensity by a factor of 4. Doubling amplitude increases intensity by a factor of 4. Thus, changing $\mu$ has the least effect.

131.  **C is correct.** 3 Hz is the beat frequency. The beat frequency is the difference between the frequency of the tuning fork and the frequency of the piano, so we know that the original frequency must be 3 Hz away from 440. We just don't know which direction. Tightening the string increased the beat frequency. This means that tightening the string moved us away from the tuning fork. Tightening the string increases the frequency, so when we increase the frequency we are moving away from 440 Hz. The original frequency of the piano note must be 443 Hz.

132.  **A is correct.** This is just $v = \lambda f$. The speaking length is extraneous information.

133.  **B is correct.** The piano wire moves up and down while the wave moves along the string; the medium is moving perpendicular to the propagation of the wave. This is a transverse, not a longitudinal, wave.

134.  **C is correct.** This is the definition of amplitude. The velocity is dictated by the medium. The wavelength is dictated by the speaking length. The frequency is dictated by the velocity and wavelength. How hard or far you strike the string only affects the amplitude.

## Stand Alones

135.  **A is correct.** When the spring is fully compressed or fully extended is when the Hooke's law forces are the greatest, and this indicates that the acceleration is the greatest. $F = ma$.

136.  **D is correct.** The maximum amplitude will result from constructive interference. This is the sum of the amplitudes.

137.  **D is correct.** The period is increasing by a factor of 1.42 (about the square root of 2)... From $T = 2\pi\sqrt{\dfrac{L}{g}}$ we see that the square of the period is proportional to the length. $L$ increases by a factor of 2, or a 100% increase.

138.  **B is correct.** Only B and C allow for a higher frequency, which would explain a higher pitch. Heavier objects vibrate more slowly. The water in the glass increases the inertia of the system and creates a lower frequency.

## EXPLANATIONS TO IN-CLASS EXAM FOR LECTURE 7

**Passage I**

139.  **D is correct.** The Earth's magnetic field points from the geographic South to the geographic North. From the passage, the aurora borealis is in the north.

140. **D is correct.** The easy way to answer this question is to look at Figures 1 and 2. From the passage and Figure 1 we see that pitch is the distance between the spirals. From Figure 2, we see that pitch is decreasing as the spirals move toward the stronger magnetic field. (The magnetic field lines are the horizontal lines. Closer field lines indicate a stronger field.) This leaves answer choice C or D. The period is the length of time necessary for the particle to make one rotation. You should know that the force on a moving particle due to a magnetic field is perpendicular to the velocity of the charge. This means that a magnetic field can do no work on a moving charge, which, in turn, means that it cannot change its kinetic energy or its speed. If the speed is the same, and from Figure 2 we see that the spirals are getting smaller, then the length of time to make each spiral is also decreasing. Thus, the period is decreasing.

141. **A is correct.** The electron has a negative charge, so it will be turned by the magnetic field in the opposite direction of the positively charged proton. The electron has less mass than the proton, so it will turn in a smaller circle than the proton. You can use the equation for centripetal force: $F = mv^2/r$. When m increases, $r$ must also increase.

142. **C is correct.** From $F = qvB$ we know that charge increases force, so the alpha particle will experience the greatest force. Only the velocity perpendicular to the magnetic field will create a force on a charged particle. Any velocity in the direction of the pitch does not increase the force. Thus the smaller the pitch, the greater the force.

143. **C is correct.** The protons rotate in the opposite direction to the electrons because they have an opposite charge. As per Figure 2, the particles continue rotating in the same direction when they reflect from one pole to the other. However, the perspective changes from one pole to another. Imagine a two headed coin. The noses on either side point in opposite directions. When the coin spins, if we view the front side and the head appears to tilt downward, the head on the opposite side would appear to tilt upward. If the coin continued spinning in the same direction as it followed the magnetic field lines from the North Pole to the South Pole, we would see the opposite side of the coin. From our point of view at the South pole, the opposite side would appear to be spinning counter-clockwise.

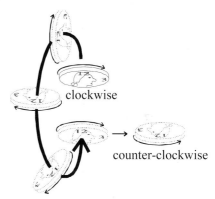
clockwise

counter-clockwise

144. **A is correct.** The force on any moving charged particle due to a magnetic field can only be perpendicular to the movement of the particle, and can therefore do no work. This is why the speed of the electron doesn't change.

145. **C is correct.** According to Figure 2, in order for the particles to bounce from pole to pole, the magnetic field at the poles must be stronger than at the equator.

## Passage II

146. **A is correct.** Use the same logic as that used in the passage to explain why the human body remains at the same potential as the ground. The ground is a conductor, so it will be at the same potential at any height.

147. **C is correct.** Use the definition of current. A = C/sec. So sec = C/A = 20/10,000 = $2 \times 10^{-3}$ seconds.

148. **D is correct.** $V = IR$ : From the passage: $400,000 = 10^{-12} \times R$.

149. **B is correct.** An electric field vector points from positive to negative potential. Figure 1 shows the electric field gets more positive as we move upward.

150. **C is correct.** This question concerns the rate of energy transfer, or power. $P = IV$. The answer is given in joules because the question asks for energy.

151. **C is correct.** Current always flows from high potential to low potential, so B and D are wrong. During a lightning strike, electrons flow from the cloud to the ground, so current must flow in the opposite direction, from the ground to the cloud.

**Passage III**

152. **B is correct.** The passage states that the electric field force is in opposition to the magnetic force. Electrons want to move against an electric field. The electric field pushes the electron to the left. You can also use the right hand rule: point your thumb in the direction of the current, down the page (opposite to movement of electrons), point your fingers in the direction of the magnetic field, and push in the direction of your palm. Your palm should be facing to the right. This is the force on the electrons due to the magnetic field.

153. **A is correct.** The passage states that at equilibrium "the force on the electrons due to $E$ and $B$ are equal and in opposite directions." Thus the direction of $B$ creates the direction of $E$ and reversing $B$ will reverse $E$. B and D concern the current which can be adjusted independently of the magnetic field. A Hall potential difference will be established regardless of the direction of current, so C is wrong.

154. **B is correct.** Moving the strip in the direction of the current is the same as moving the strip in the opposite direction to the electrons. If the strip is moved at the same speed as the electrons, the electrons are stationary with respect to the magnetic field and there is no Hall Effect. (This is explained in the passage.) When the strip is moved faster than the electrons, the relative velocity of the electrons with respect to the magnetic field is reversed. Thus the force on the electrons due to the magnetic field is also reversed. The Hall Effect is established in the opposite direction from the original.

155. **A is correct.** If the copper strip is held stationary then the sum of the forces or the net force must be zero. No acceleration; no net force.

156. **B is correct.** The electric field $E$ created by the magnetic field pushing the electrons to the right demonstrates the direction of force on the electrons due to the magnetic field $B$. Also, the right hand rule applies for the same result. Since the force is constant and perpendicular to the velocity, the magnitude of the velocity cannot change but the direction changes at a constant rate. The particle follows a circular path.

157. **D is correct.** The potential difference is the electric field times the distance. Choice B is the potential difference along the length of the strip, not the Hall effect, which is the potential difference across the width of the strip.

**Stand Alones**

158. **B is correct.** After the circuit has been on for even a short time, the capacitor is fully charged and behaves like a break in the circuit. The voltage across the capacitor is 6 V. $IR = V$ so 3 amps = 6 V / 2 Ω. See the diagram below.

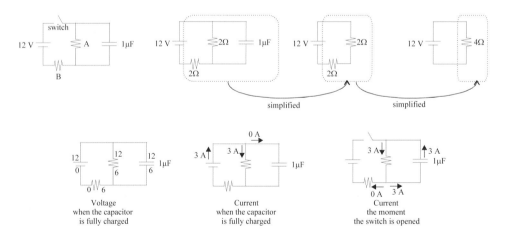

Voltage when the capacitor is fully charged

Current when the capacitor is fully charged

Current the moment the switch is opened

159. **C is correct.** The charge is equal to the voltage times the capacitance. See the diagram above for the solution of the circuit.

160. **A is correct.** According to Coulomb's law ($F = kqq/r^2$), A and D apply equal and opposite forces on $q$, and so do C and B.

161. **C is correct.** First set the force equal to mass times acceleration $Eq = ma$. Then use the uniform accelerated motion equation $x = \frac{1}{2} at^2$

# EXPLANATIONS TO IN-CLASS EXAM FOR LECTURE 8

## Passage I

**162.** **C is correct.** Diffraction is demonstrated by the light waves bending as they move through the opening. This happens in both experiments. Interference is demonstrated in both experiments where the path length traveled by light rays differs creating alternating high and low intensity bands due to constructive and destructive interference.

**163.** **A is correct.** From SOH CAH TOA, $x/\sin\theta$ is equal to $r$. From distance divided by velocity equals time, $r/c$ is the time light takes to travel to any given point on the detector.

**164.** **C is correct.** There would be no diffraction. In experiment 1, all the light would go directly to the detector at the level of the slit to form 1 peak on the graph. In experiment 2, two peaks would be formed.

**165.** **B is correct.** Longer wavelengths are diffracted the most. Red has the longest wavelength, so red would appear on the outermost fringes of the detector.

**166.** **D is correct.** The question is comparing the greatest intensity on the detector in Experiment 1 to that of Experiment 2. The intensity striking the detector in Experiment 1, is $I_{single}$, while in Experiment 2, it's $I_{double}$. The maximum value of cosine is 1; the maximum value of cosine squared is one as well. From the second equation we see that $I_{double}$ will have a maximum value of 4 $I_{single}$

**167.** **B is correct.** Intensity is proportional to energy, and energy is proportional to the square of the amplitude.

## Passage II

**168.** **C is correct.** From the passage we know that $m_o m_e = M_{total}$ and $m_e = -25cm/f_e$. Thus, the focal length is inversely proportional to the magnification. Since $P = 1/f$, power is inversely proportional to the focal length. Therefore, doubling the power doubles the magnification.

**169.** **D is correct.** The object is outside the focal length of a converging lens and thus creates a real inverted image.

**170.** **C is correct.** The focal length of a converging lens is positive. A diopter is the reciprocal of the focal length in <u>meters</u>. Thus, $\frac{1}{25}$ equals 0.04 meters.

**171.** **C is correct.** Just plug and chug. $M_{total} = m_o m_e = 500 \times 0.01 \times 0.005/0.25 = L$. $L = 10$ cm. Then add the focal lengths to get 11.5 cm.

**172.** **A is correct.** An object inside the focal point of a converging lens makes a virtual upright image on the same side as the object.

**173.** **C is correct.** The objective inverts the first image. This first image is within the focal point of the eyepiece so the eyepiece creates a virtual image WITHOUT changing the orientation. The final image is an inverted image of the object. An inverted image is inverted up and down, and left and right. When you push the slide left, it looks to be moving to the right under the microscope. When you push the slide up, it looks to be moving down. So, left is right and up is down on an inverted image. Answer choice C has these characteristics. Choice C is the inverted image.

**174.** **C is correct.** Go back to lecture 8 for an explanation of refraction and reflection.

## Passage III

**175.** **B is correct.** From the equation in the passage we can see that this is true.

**176.** **C is correct.** Although this is an approximation, it is the best answer. Light rays from distant objects will be approximately parallel and thus converge on the focal point. Since the rays aren't truly parallel, they would form slightly behind the focal point but this is not an answer choice.

**177.** **A is correct.** A thicker center converges more. Only converging lenses have positive power.

**178.** **D is correct.** When light enters the lens, velocity slows, frequency remains constant, and wavelength must shorten. This effect is greater on blue light than red light. This is called chromatic dispersion.

**179.** **A is correct.** $P = 1/$focal length. This means the focal length of the eyepiece is 0.01 m. The focal length of the objective must be nine times greater, or 9 cm. It is positive by the equation or because converging lenses have positive focal lengths.

**180.** **A is correct.** Light bends less moving from glass to water and thus the focal lengths of the lenses would lengthen. The tube length must be increased so that the two new focal points will coincide as per the passage.

## Stand Alones

**181.** **A is correct.** The waves are not moving through an aperture, so they are refracted, not diffracted. Since the waves are moving nearly perpendicular to the shore they must be turning toward the normal, which means their speed must be decreasing. Waves refract toward the normal when a new medium slows their progress. The new medium is water that is more shallow.

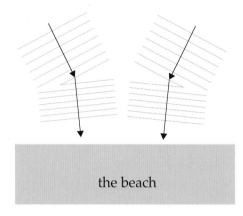

**182.** **B is correct.** The mirror is concave since it makes a real inverted image. The focal length is positive and half the radius of curvature. From the thin lens equation ($1/f = 1/d_i + 1/d_o$) we get $d_o = 5$ cm.

**183.** **A is correct.** Magnification $= -d_i/d_o$.

**184.** **D is correct.** The mirage is created by refraction of light. The light enters the warmer air and speeds up. The lines below show the wave fronts as they cross the boundary between warm air and warmer air. The lower portion of the wave front in the warmer air speeds up and passes the upper portion of the wave front causing the wave to turn upward.

# ANSWERS & EXPLANATIONS

## FOR

## QUESTIONS IN THE LECTURES

# ANSWERS TO THE LECTURE QUESTIONS

| Lecture 1 | Lecture 2 | Lecture 3 | Lecture 4 | Lecture 5 | Lecture 6 | Lecture 7 | Lecture 8 |
|-----------|-----------|-----------|-----------|-----------|-----------|-----------|-----------|
| 1.  C | 25.  C | 49.  D | 73.  D | 97.  D | 121.  A | 145.  C | 169.  A |
| 2.  A | 26.  C | 50.  C | 74.  A | 98.  C | 122.  C | 146.  B | 170.  D |
| 3.  B | 27.  D | 51.  B | 75.  B | 99.  C | 123.  C | 147.  A | 171.  A |
| 4.  D | 28.  A | 52.  A | 76.  D | 100.  D | 124.  B | 148.  C | 172.  D |
| 5.  C | 29.  D | 53.  C | 77.  C | 101.  C | 125.  B | 149.  B | 173.  C |
| 6.  C | 30.  B | 54.  D | 78.  A | 102.  B | 126.  C | 150.  A | 174.  D |
| 7.  B | 31.  A | 55.  B | 79.  A | 103.  A | 127.  A | 151.  A | 175.  B |
| 8.  C | 32.  A | 56.  A | 80.  D | 104.  D | 128.  A | 152.  B | 176.  A |
| 9.  C | 33.  A | 57.  A | 81.  B | 105.  D | 129.  B | 153.  A | 177.  B |
| 10.  C | 34.  D | 58.  C | 82.  B | 106.  B | 130.  D | 154.  B | 178.  D |
| 11.  B | 35.  D | 59.  A | 83.  B | 107.  A | 131.  C | 155.  D | 179.  B |
| 12.  B | 36.  C | 60.  B | 84.  A | 108.  D | 132.  D | 156.  A | 180.  A |
| 13.  A | 37.  C | 61.  D | 85.  C | 109.  D | 133.  B | 157.  C | 181.  B |
| 14.  A | 38.  B | 62.  C | 86.  C | 110.  B | 134.  B | 158.  D | 182.  C |
| 15.  C | 39.  D | 63.  C | 87.  B | 111.  C | 135.  B | 159.  D | 183.  A |
| 16.  D | 40.  A | 64.  C | 88.  C | 112.  A | 136.  D | 160.  C | 184.  C |
| 17.  C | 41.  D | 65.  A | 89.  C | 113.  D | 137.  B | 161.  C | 185.  D |
| 18.  D | 42.  C | 66.  A | 90.  B | 114.  A | 138.  C | 162.  B | 186.  B |
| 19.  A | 43.  C | 67.  C | 91.  D | 115.  B | 139.  C | 163.  D | 187.  A |
| 20.  A | 44.  C | 68.  A | 92.  D | 116.  D | 140.  D | 164.  A | 188.  D |
| 21.  B | 45.  B | 69.  C | 93.  B | 117.  B | 141.  D | 165.  C | 189.  D |
| 22.  B | 46.  A | 70.  D | 94.  B | 118.  A | 142.  C | 166.  D | 190.  D |
| 23.  A | 47.  B | 71.  C | 95.  A | 119.  D | 143.  B | 167.  A | 191.  B |
| 24.  B | 48.  C | 72.  B | 96.  A | 120.  B | 144.  B | 168.  B | 192.  C |

# EXPLANATIONS TO QUESTIONS IN LECTURE 1

1. **C is correct.** The balloon travels in three perpendicular directions. These can be considered three displacement vectors. The total displacement is the vector sum of the three. If you notice, two of the vectors have lengths of 8 and 6, multiples of 4 and 3 respectively. These are the components of a 3-4-5 triangle. Thus, the displacement from the tail of the 6 km vector to the head of the 8 km vector is 10 kilometers. This 10 km vector is perpendicular to the other 10 km vector. Using the Pythagorean theorem with the two 10 km vectors gives a total displacement of approximately 14 km.

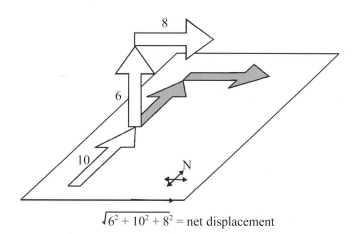

$$\sqrt{6^2 + 10^2 + 8^2} = \text{net displacement}$$

2. **A is correct.** Because the athlete is on a circular track, he will return to his starting position and, although he will have run a net distance, his displacement will be zero. Velocity is displacement over time, so his average velocity will be zero as well.

3. **B is correct.** The man is making a 30-60-90 triangle. Where he turns represents the 30° angle in the triangle. The distance back to the entrance is half the hypotenuse or 100 sin30°. You can either recognize the proportions of a 30-60-90 triangle or, if you have a lot of extra time on your hands while taking the MCAT, use the law of cosines: $A^2 = B^2 + C^2 - 2BC \cos(a)$.

4. **D is correct.** Acceleration is the rate of change of velocity. Since velocity is a vector it specifies direction. The direction of the earth's motion is constantly changing.

5. **C is correct.** Because the start and end points of the trip do not change regardless of the path taken, the displacement for the trip does not change.

6. **C is correct.** Because the car is slowing down, the velocity and the acceleration are in opposite directions and must have opposite signs. Only choice C meets this requirement.

7. **B is correct.** The direction for a vector must specify a straight line at a specific point. You couldn't draw an arrow to represent "in a circle."

8. **C is correct.** You need to convert your units.

$$\left(\frac{36 \text{ km}}{1 \text{ hr}}\right)\left(\frac{1000 \text{ m}}{1 \text{ km}}\right)\left(\frac{1 \text{ hr}}{3600 \text{ sec}}\right) = 10 \text{ m/s}$$

In 10 seconds, the elephant can run 100 m.

9. **C is correct.** Velocity is the slope on a $d/t$ graph. Constant velocity requires only a straight line on a $d/t$ graph. Any acceleration represents a change in velocity and so can not represent constant velocity.

10. **C is correct.** Since we are looking for distance and not displacement, we add up the total area between the line and the $x$-axis. We could also use our linear motion equations since there is constant acceleration.

11. **B is correct.** The graph shows an object moving in one direction at a constant velocity and suddenly changing directions. There is no gradual acceleration. The baseball is the only object that suddenly changes direction. A is wrong because the description describes gradual acceleration, and there is no gradual acceleration in the graph. C is constantly changing velocity. D is a gradual change in velocity.

12. **B is correct.** This problem may be tricky because the question only implies a necessary variable. That variable is initial velocity. The initial velocity is zero. The average velocity of any constantly accelerating object that starts with zero velocity is the final velocity divided by two. This is from $v_{avg} = (v + v_0)/2$. Then the average velocity times time equals displacement, $v_{avg}t = x$. Thus, $25/12.5 = 2$. Or, by Salty's method:

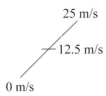

Average velocity times time equals distance: $12.5 \times 2 = 25$.

13. **A is correct.** This is a plug and chug problem. The correct formula is $v = v_0 + at$, which results in $25 = 50 + a2$. Thus $a = -12.5$. You also could reason that if it had taken only one second to slow from 50 to 25 m/s then the acceleration would have been $-25$ m/s$^2$. But it took more than one second so the acceleration must be less.

14. **A is correct.** The graph clearly shows that displacement increases with time. Since the displacement graph is a straight line, the particle must be moving at constant velocity, so neither velocity nor acceleration are increasing.

15. **C is correct.** The deceleration is 5 m/s$^2$, so the velocity is reduced by 5 m/s each second. After 1 second the velocity is 15 m/s; after 2 seconds, 10 m/s; after 3 seconds, 5 m/s; and after four seconds, 0 m/s. So the car stops in 4 seconds. The average velocity for motion with constant acceleration is the midpoint between the starting and ending velocities. The midpoint between 20 m/s and 0 m/s is 10 m/s. The average velocity times the time is 10 m/s $\times$ 4 s = 40 m.

$$v_f^2 = v_0 2 + 2ax$$

The car comes to a stop, so $v_f = 0$. If we plug in $v_0 = 20$ and $a = -5$, we'll get $x = 40$ m.

16. **D is correct.** In order for the particle to move backwards, the velocity graph would have to dip below zero. Between 10 and 15 seconds, the particle is slowing down, but not going backwards.

17. **C is correct.** The best way to answer this question is to plug 4 seconds into the linear motion equations $s = s_0 + v_0 t + \frac{1}{2}at^2$. This results in $s = \frac{1}{2}at^2$. The distance traveled by the apple is 80 m so it reaches 20 m in altitude. You could solve this problem using proportions. The square of the time is proportional to the distance. If we double the time, we multiply the distance by 4.

18. **D is correct.** Since both the ball and the skydivers are accelerating at the same rate, each skydiver should aim for the other's chest.

19. **A is correct.** You should use Salty's system in every single physics problem. However, sometimes the problem is easy enough for you to imagine the diagram in your head. This problem probably requires actually drawing a diagram. Once you have your diagram, you may notice that the antelope needs to be in the air for 2 seconds at 10 m/s to clear 20 meters. So now you have $t$. You know that the upward trip equals the downward trip, so the downward trip lasts one second. You also know that the downward trip starts at zero because a projectile at its peak has zero velocity. The question is now simplified to "How far does a free falling body starting from rest travel in one second?" At the end of one second the body is traveling at 10 m/s, thus its average velocity is 5 m/s. The object travels 5 meters. Alternatively, once you have 2 seconds, you can plug 2 seconds into $s = s_0 + v_0 t + \frac{1}{2}at^2$, with s and so as zero. Doing the math gives you the initial velocity of 10 m/s. The velocity at the top is zero. Using $v^2 = v_0^2 + 2ax$ gives you $x = 5$.

20. **A is correct.** This is a proportions question. The correct equation is $v_0 \sin\theta = \sqrt{2gh}$. Remember, due to the symmetry of projectile motion, the velocity in this equation can be initial or final depending upon the direction of motion. Multiplying the height by four only doubles the velocity.

21. **B is correct.** You can use $v_o \sin\theta = \sqrt{2gh}$. The sine of 30° is ½. Thus the vertical velocity is 50 m/s. $50^2$ is 2500. Divide this by $g = 10$, and by 2 gives 125. Practice doing problems like this in your head to save time, build your confidence, and most of all, to sharpen your skills. The initial vertical velocity is 50 m/s; the final at max height is zero. This is a change in velocity of 50 which takes 5 seconds at 10 m/s². Draw your line and multiply the average velocity by 5 seconds.

50 m/s

25 m/s

0 m/s

22. **B is correct.** At terminal velocity, acceleration is zero. The force of air resistance counters gravity exactly so the force is equal to the weight for both balls. Ball X requires more collisions with air molecules to compensate for the larger force of gravity. More collisions means greater air resistance.

23. **A is correct.** The horizontal speed has no effect on the length of time that a projectile is in the air, so you don't need it here. Because the initial vertical speed is zero, you can use the equation below.

$$x = (½)gt^2 \text{ with } x = 40 \text{ and } g = 10$$

$$t = \sqrt{8} \approx 2.8$$

Since there is only one significant figure in the numbers in the problem we round the answer up to 3.

24. **B is correct.** The horizontal distance traveled for a projectile is given by $vt\cos\theta$. In this case, $v = 30$, $t = 6$, and $\theta = 40°$.

## EXPLANATIONS TO QUESTIONS IN LECTURE 2

25. **C is correct.** This is a straight forward $F = ma$ plug-n-chug problem. The moon is thrown in to confuse you. The gravitational force of the moon acts perpendicularly to the horizontal force and is countered by a normal force. It has no effect on the motion.

26. **C is correct.** Since the mass of the rocket is decreasing, and the force remains constant, the rate of change in velocity (acceleration) must be increasing.

27. **D is correct.** The downward force is $mg = 100$ N. The first 100 N upward counters this to give a net force of zero and thus a constant velocity. We want a net force of $mg = 100$ N upwards. This requires adding 100 more newtons for a total of 200 N.

28. **A is correct.** Since both skydivers are at constant velocity, they must both experience a net force of zero.

29. **D is correct.** Since the projectile is at constant velocity when the force of air resistance is $F$, the force propelling the projectile must have a magnitude $F$ as well. When the air resistance is reduced by a factor of 4, the net force must be $F - ¼ F = ¾ F$. Thus $¾ F = ma$.

30. **B is correct.** Because the masses are all on a line, you can just average the distance of the masses from the origin to get the central point. The average distance is $(2 + 3 + 7)/3 = 4$.

31. **A is correct.** The net force on the plane is 2500 N − 500 N = 2000 N to the east. The mass of the plane will be the weight divided by $g$. That's 40,000/10 = 4000 mg. Acceleration is $F/m = 2000/4000 = 0.5$ m/s² to the east.

32. **A is correct.** If the car is moving in a straight line at a constant speed, then it is not accelerating. From Newton's second law, you know that if there is no acceleration, then there is no net force. Friction is irrelevant.

33. **A is correct.** Earth's gravitational force on the moon acts to pull the moon in a circle. Setting this gravitational force equal to centripetal force gives:

$$F = G\frac{Mm}{r^2} = m\frac{v^2}{r}$$

34. **D is correct.** The work done will remain the same. $W = Fd$. The distance is increased from ½ to 4. This is an increase by a factor of 8. Since work remains constant, force must decrease by a factor of 8.

35. **D is correct.** The fact that the satellite moves does not affect the answer; gravity is not affected by movement. This is a proportions problem. Using Newton's law of gravity, $F = G(mm/r^2)$, we see that gravitational force ($F$) is inversely proportional to the square of the distance between two objects ($r$). Thus, if we reduce the distance (the orbital radius in this case) by a factor of 2, we increase force by a factor of 4.

36. **C is correct.** The acceleration is $g \sin\theta$; however, $\theta$ is constantly decreasing and with it, the sine of $\theta$. Thus, the acceleration is decreasing. Since there is some acceleration throughout the drop, the velocity is increasing.

37. **C is correct.** The force down the incline is $mg \sin\theta$. The acceleration down the incline is $g \sin\theta$. The sine of $\theta$ is opposite over hypotenuse which is 20/40 = ½. Thus the acceleration is ½ $g$ or 5 m/s². If we plug this into our linear motion equation we have $x = \frac{1}{2}(\frac{1}{2}g)t^2$. x is the length of the incline. Thus $40 = \frac{1}{2}(\frac{1}{2}g)t^2$. $16 = t^2$. $t = 4$ seconds.

38. **B is correct.** Set the weight equal to Newton's law of universal gravitation.

$$mg = \frac{GMm}{R^2}, \text{ $m$ cancels, so } g = \frac{GM}{R^2}$$

39. **D is correct.** $v - d/t$. Once around a circular track is the same as the circumference, so $d = 2\pi r$. So $v = 2\pi r/t = (6.28)(30)/63 = (0.1)(30) = 3$ m/s.

40. **A is correct.** The force parallel to the ramp is the same as the net force, $mg \sin\theta$. As $\theta$ increases, $\sin\theta$ increases and so does the net force. The force perpendicular to the ramp is the same as the normal force, $mg \cos\theta$. As $\theta$ increases, $\cos\theta$ decreases, and so does the normal force.

---

41. **D is correct.** If we look at the point on the tire that makes contact with the road, that point does not move relative to the road or else the tires would spin in place. Since there is no relative movement, the friction must be static. The force of friction is in the direction opposite to the way the tires are trying to slide against the road. This is the force that accelerates the vehicle. So the only way that the truck can move forward is if the force on the tires is in this direction.

42. **C is correct.** Tension in a static system is defined by the force in one direction. The rope will also experience a force from the right, but that does not double the tension. That force is necessary to make the tension equal to 900 N.

43. **C is correct.** The force changes with the displacement of the tires. The greater the displacement, the greater the force, the greater the magnitude of acceleration as per the formula $F = k\Delta x = ma$.

44. **C is correct.** Since the frictional force is constant, this is a linear motion problem with constant acceleration. The normal force is $mg$, so the frictional force is $mg\mu$. The acceleration is just $g\mu$. Using $v^2 = v_0^2 + 2ax$ and plugging in $g\mu$ for the acceleration, gives us answer C.

45. **B is correct.** The tension could only be as great as the force at one end. Thus, the tension could not be greater than the force applied by the first team.

46. **A is correct.** On an inclined plane $F_n = mg\cos\theta$. So the force of friction is equal to $\mu mg\cos\theta$.

47. **B is correct.** The difference in mass between the two situations is 0.5 kg, so the difference in force is 5 N. The difference in displacement is 1 cm. These are the numbers we plug into Hooke's law. $k = F/x = (5 \text{ N})/(1 \text{ cm}) = 5$ N/cm. By the way, we can do this because we are really subtracting one equation from the other.

$$F_{1.5} = - k\Delta x_{1.5}$$

$$- F_1 = - k\Delta x_1$$

$$F_{1.5} - F_1 = - k\Delta x_{1.5} - - k\Delta x_1 \Rightarrow \Delta F_{1.5} = - k(\Delta x_{1.5} - - \Delta x_1)$$

48. **C is correct.** If the elevator is moving at constant speed, then there is no acceleration and no net force, so the tension in the cable must exactly balance the weight of the elevator.

# EXPLANATIONS TO QUESTIONS IN LECTURE 3

49. **D is correct.** When the tightrope walker stands in the middle of the rope, he is in static equilibrium. The vertical and the horizontal net force must equal zero. The force downward is the weight of the tightrope walker, 750 N. The force upward must also equal 750 N. The upward force must come from the vertical component of the tension in the rope. If the rope is perfectly straight, there is no vertical component.

50. **C is correct.** If we begin by examining the problem as a static equilibrium problem, the tension in the rope with no acceleration would be 500 N. If we want to pull the climber upward, we must increase the tension by $ma$, which is 250 N.

51. **B is correct.** The force upwards is defined by the question to be 200 N. The force on either end of a massless rope must be the same. The tension in the rope must be 200 N. This question answers itself and then attempts to confuse the issue by discussing a rusted pulley. The 500 Newton gravitational force downward on the mass is resisted by the 200 Newton force upward by the pulley. The mass is accelerated downwards by the remaining 300 Newton difference, but that part is irrelevant to the question.

52. **A is correct.** The skydiver has a constant velocity so the net force must be zero, and by definition, this means the skydiver is in dynamic equilibrium.

53. **C is correct.** You can use the Pythagorean Theorem to test if the choice A is true as follows: If choice A were true, then the sum of the forces would have to equal zero, and the vectors would form a right triangle. $F^2 + [\sqrt{(3)}F]^2 = (2F)^2$. Solving leaves $1^2 + \sqrt{(3)}^2 = 2^2 \Rightarrow 1 + 3 = 4$. The equation is true, so the forces add to zero. When the sum of the forces equals zero, the object is in equilibrium and cannot be accelerating. Choice C is false and therefore the correct answer. You may have noticed that you don't have to look at the diagram to answer this question. The question asks "Which CANNOT be true?" Choices A, B, and D all have no acceleration, so if C is true, they must all be false. Therefore, if C were NOT the correct answer, they would all have to be correct. C must be the correct answer.

54. **D is correct.** The third force must have equal components pulling to the south and west to counter the other two forces. Since the two components are equal, the third force will be directed exactly to the southwest.

55. **B is correct.** The bucket is moving at constant speed, so there is no acceleration. If there is no acceleration, then the system is in dynamic equilibrium. All of the other situations described include accelerated motion.

56. **A is correct.** The block is accelerating across the floor, so the force applied by the child must be greater than any force that is resisting the motion. The weight of the block acts vertically, so it is not directly involved in the horizontal motion. It is true that the frictional force is likely to be less than the weight, but that doesn't indicate whether the force applied by the child is greater or less than the weight.

---

57. **A is correct.** The pole is not rotating, so the net torque must be zero. The ground must be exerting a torque on the pole.

58. **C is correct.** The sign is not moving so it is in static equilibrium. There are only 3 forces acting on the sign – the tension in the rope, the normal force of the wall, and gravity. The tension in the rope must exert a force with an upward component equal to and opposite gravity and a horizontal component equal to and opposite the normal force exerted by the wall. The upward component of the tension is $T\sin30°$. Using just the equation for the vertical forces we have $T\sin30° = mg$. Doubling $mg$ doubles $T$.

59. **A is correct.** The longest lever arm is on A. The entire wrench is the lever arm on A.

60. **B is correct.** This is a straight forward torque problem. If we choose our point of rotation to be the point on the board where the string attaches to the board, and we understand that the weight of the board acts at the center of gravity which is the center of the board in this case, the counter-clockwise torque is 3 kg × 0.2 m. The clockwise torque is the weight of the board times 0.3 m. Setting these equal, we have the mass of the board at 2 kg.

**61.** **D is correct.** The net torque must be zero. If we choose the rotation point to be the end of board Y, then $1 \text{ m} \times F = 4 \text{ m} \times 4 \text{ N}$. The forces up equal forces down. The forces left and right are zero. The clockwise torques equal the counter clockwise torques.

A little tip for torque problems: Find a force that is neither known nor asked for, and choose the point where this force acts to be your rotational point.

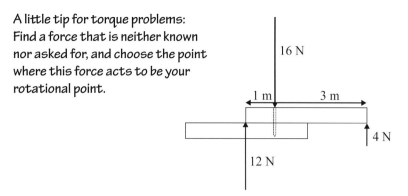

**62.** **C is correct.** If you push on the edge farthest from the hinges, you'll have the greatest lever arm, which will give you the greatest torque.

**63.** **C is correct.** For the best balance, the torques should be equivalent. $(400 \text{ N})(5 \text{ m}) = (500 \text{ N})(x)$. So $x = 4$ m

**64.** **C is correct.** Increasing the diameter of the screwdriver handle increases the lever arm for the force applied by his grip. Increased lever arm gives more torque to turn the screw.

---

**65.** **A is correct.** The frictional force applied by Jupiter's atmosphere times the distance along which it is applied equals the change in mechanical energy of the meteor. If we ignore the gravitational force of Jupiter, the change in the mechanical energy is a loss of all kinetic energy which equals $\frac{1}{2} mv^2$. We set this equal to force times distance and solve for force.

**66.** **A is correct.** The potential energy increases as you go up the stack. This may seem obvious if you are thinking about '$mgh$'; however, you would be thinking about this problem incorrectly because $g$ does not remain constant. If you use Newton's law of gravitation to solve for $g$ at any altitude and then plugged it into '$mgh$'($g = Gm/r^2$, $r = h$), you would get the reverse answer that potential energy decreases to zero. A fast and easy way to understand this problem is to think of work. Your system is the stack of blocks. Each time you add a block, you do work on the system. In other words, you transfer energy to your system.

**67.** **C is correct.** A simple technique for solving this and many other physics problems is to "take the examples to extremes". Here the examples are reasonably close in mass. What if object A were one million times as massive as object B? In other words, imagine that object A is a piano and object B is a dime. Now we place them on a spring and propel the piano one inch into the air. Will the dime be propelled one million inches into the air at the same time? Of course not. Thus we know that mass is not proportional to the height. Since all the answers are given as such, only C can be correct. We could also look at this problem and ask ourselves, "When do the masses become projectiles?" They must become projectiles the moment the spring stops pushing. From $F = ma$, we know that this is the moment the spring stops accelerating. This means that the masses become projectiles at the same moment and with the same velocity. As we learned in Lecture 1, mass is irrelevant to projectile paths.

**68.** **A is correct.** This is a proportions problem. We set the initial elastic potential energy equal to the final energy, $\frac{1}{2} kx^2 = mgh$, and we see that the square of the displacement of the spring is proportional to the height, $x^2 = h$. Thus, to increase the height by a factor of four, we must increase the displacement of the spring by a factor of 2.

**69.** **C is correct.** The horizontal component of the force is 87 N. To find the acceleration we use $F = ma$. $a = 8.7 \text{ m/s}^2$. We use $v = v_0 + at$ and arrive at $v = 17.4 \text{ m/s}$.

**70.** **D is correct.** The rock starts out with gravitational potential energy. As it falls, it loses gravitational potential energy and gains kinetic energy. As the rubber band stretches, the rock slows to a stop and kinetic energy is transferred to the elastic potential energy of the rubber band.

71.     **C is correct.**   $1\text{kW} - \text{hour}\left(\dfrac{3600\text{ sec}}{1\text{ hour}}\right) = 3600\text{kW} - \text{sec} = 3{,}600{,}000 \text{ W} - \text{sec}$

A Watt is a J/sec, so a W-sec = (J/sec)(sec) = Joule

So 3,6000,000 W-sec = 3,600,000 J

72.     **B is correct.** $P = W/t$. If the power is increased, more work can be done in less time. Choice B says the reverse of this.

---

# EXPLANATIONS TO QUESTIONS IN LECTURE 4

73.     **D is correct.** Impulse is equal to change in momentum, $F\Delta t = \Delta mv$. We know the change in momentum but not $F$ or $t$. We do not have enough information to solve for $F$.

74.     **A is correct.** This is easily visualized if we take the example to extremes. If the boy were somehow able to make himself nearly weightless, would he travel at some extremely high velocity? This is actually similar to a projectile problem. The boy receives his kinetic energy from his initial potential energy. When he drops his coat and boots, he is leaving that potential energy unused at the point where he dropped them.

75.     **B is correct.** The initial and final momentums must be equal. The initial vertical momentum is $mv\cos60°$. Since ball B has no vertical momentum, all the vertical momentum remains in ball A. Ball A has no horizontal momentum after the collision, so all of its momentum is represented by $mv\cos60°$.

76.     **D is correct.** To answer this question, we simply compare the total energy of the car at zero, 30, and 60 km/h. All the energy is kinetic energy. $K = \frac{1}{2}mv^2$. Without doing too much math we can see that if you double the velocity you increase energy by a factor of four. The question asks for the difference in the energies, $4 - 1 = 3$.

77.     **C is correct.** The initial momentum of the cat-cardboard system is zero, so the final momentum must be zero. Since the cat has twice the mass as the cardboard, the cardboard will have twice the velocity.

78.     **A is correct.** Choice I represents conservation of momentum, which is always true. Choice II is conservation of kinetic energy. In an inelastic collision, kinetic energy is not conserved. As for Choice III, if the masses are different before and after the collision and momentum is conserved, then the velocities before and after must be different.

79.     **A is correct.** Momentum is a vector quantity, so the two vectors with the same magnitude and opposite directions will add up to zero both before and after the collision.

80.     **D is correct.** We can use the impulse equation, $Ft = mv$, to answer this question. The trapeze artist is brought gradually to a stop in the safety net, so the change in momentum takes place over a longer time than if the person hit the floor. The increase in time means that less force is required to achieve the same change in momentum, which makes the fall less dangerous.

---

81.     **B is correct.** Like all ideal machines, the pulley does not change the amount of work done, nor does it change the time during which the force is acting. Power is work divided by time. Since neither work nor time is changed, the power is not changed.

82.     **B is correct.** The eccentric pulley does not work on the principles of a normal pulley but, instead, works on the same principle as a lever. The lever arm for the string at point A in position 1 is greater than that for point B in position one. In position 2, the reverse is true. The lever is stationary, so the sum of the torques must equal zero, or the clockwise torque equals the counter-clockwise torque. Where the lever arm is greater, the tension force must be less. (See Physics 4.8 Levers for more on eccentric pulleys.)

83.     **B is correct.** Machines are used because they decrease the force required to perform a task. An ideal machine requires the same work as would be done without the machine, but a non-ideal machine requires more work because frictional forces must be overcome.

84. **A is correct.** By zigzagging, she is basically using a ramp. Her path is not as steep, but it is longer. Ignoring friction, the work remains the same, but the force is lessened.

85. **C is correct.** The work cannot be changed by an ideal machine. Therefore, $W = Fd = mgh$. From here, $mgh/F = d \Rightarrow 300/25 = 12$.

86. **C is correct.** For a lever $F_1 l_1 = F_2 l_2$. The radii of the two pulleys act as the lever arms for the system, so increasing the diameter of pulley A will decrease the force required to pull rope A. Changing the lengths of the ropes will have no effect on the machine.

87. **B is correct.** The formula for machines is $F_{input}d_{input} = F_{output}d_{output}$, where $d$ is the distance over which the forces act. If mechanical advantage is equal to (output force)/(input force) , then it must also be equal to (input distance)/(output distance).

88. **C is correct.** For an inclined plane, $Fd = mgh$, so $(50 \text{ N})d = (1000 \text{ N})(1 \text{ m})$ and $d = 20$ m.

---

89. **C is correct.** Since Y is not normally found in the meteorite, we assume that all the Y came from the decomposition of X. Thus, the percentage of the sample that was X at the birth of the meteorite must have been the sum of the percentages of Y and X, or 15% (1.5% + 13.5% = 15%). Since the percentage of the sample that is X is now only 10% of that (or 1.5%), we can count on our fingers how many half lives is required to get to 10%. After the first half life there is 50% left; After the second half life, 25% left; after 3 half lives, 12.5% left. Thus, a little more than 3 half lives is required to reduce a substance to 10% of its original amount. Each half life is 45 years. 45 years times 3 half lives gives 135 years. A little more than three half lives are used, so the answer is a little more than 135 years.

90. **B is correct.** This is a reverse collision. The initial momentum is zero, so the final momentum must be zero. The momentum of the alpha particle is approximately $mv = 4 \times 10^7$. The momentum of the other particle, Rn-220 must be equal in magnitude and opposite in direction. Thus, the velocity of Rn equals $(4 \times 10^7)/220$. This quickly rounds to $4 \times 10^7/2.2 \times 10^2$ which is slightly less than $2 \times 10^5$ or choice B.

91. **D is correct.** This is a simple exercise in plug-n-chug. Whenever there is some mysterious missing mass, $E = mc^2$.

92. **D is correct.** First count the change in protons in order to discover the identity of the final atom. In this case, each alpha decay results in the loss of 2 protons, and each beta decay results in the gain of one proton. (Remember, create a negative, create a positive.) Thus, we have a net loss of 2 protons, and we know that our resulting atom is Pb. Now we track the change in the mass number. Each alpha decay loses 4 mass units and each beta results in no change in the mass units. (Beta decay is an exchange of a proton for a neutron.) This means a total loss of 8 mass units for a new mass number of 208.

93. **B is correct.** This is the shape of a half life curve; for equal units of time, the amount is divided by 2.

94. **B is correct.** The half life is the amount of time it takes for half of the isotope to decay. The graph decreases from 60 g to 30 grams in 2.5 hours, so the half life must be 2.5 hours.

95. **A is correct.** $^{210}_{83}\text{Bi} \rightarrow ^{206}_{82}\text{Pb} + ^4_2\alpha + ^0_{-1}\beta$.

96. **A is correct.** In alpha decay, a particle identical to a helium nucleus is released, so the mass number will change by 4. None of the other processes will change the mass number.

---

## EXPLANATIONS TO QUESTIONS IN LECTURE 5

97. **D is correct.** Atmospheric pressure supports the column of fluid. The pressure at the bottom of the column must be equal to atmospheric pressure. The pressure is equal to $\rho g h$. If $\rho$ is decreased by a factor of 13.6, the height must be increased by the same factor. Notice that, given the choices, there is no need to do the math. Every other answer is less than 10 times as tall.

98. **C is correct.** The only difference between the two discs is what they are covering. Ignore everything else. The first disc has atmospheric pressure pushing upward; the second disc does not. This is the difference between the forces necessary to lift them.

99. **C is correct.** The density of the brick is 1400 kg/m$^3$. The density of water is 1000 kg/m$^3$. In order to float, the brick must displace an amount of water equal to its weight. The density of the brick is 1.4 times that of water, so an amount of water 1.4 times the volume of the brick must be displaced. One half of the Styrofoam block is required to displace this water, so the volume of the water displaced is equal to half the volume of the Styrofoam and is also equal to 1.4 times the volume of the brick. Thus: $0.5\,V_{\text{Styrofoam}} = 1.4\,V_{\text{brick}}$. Multiplying both sides by 2, we get: $V_{\text{Styrofoam}} = 2.8\,V_{\text{brick}}$.

100. **D is correct.** The balloon rises because the buoyant force is greater than the weight. When these forces are equal, the balloon will stop rising. Thus the balloon stops rising when: $\rho_{\text{air}}Vg = \rho_{\text{helium}}Vg$. The volumes are always equal because the balloon is always fully submerged in the atmosphere. Another way to look at this problem is to see that the balloon is fully submerged in the fluid atmosphere. We want the balloon to float, not rise or sink, so we use the floating equation: Fraction submerged = $\rho_{\text{object}}/\rho_{\text{fluid}}$. The entire balloon is submerged, so the fraction submerged is equal to one. Choice A is incorrect because the temperature of the air and helium can be equal while their densities are not equal. Choice B is incorrect because the mass of the air outside the balloon is undefined. (Are we talking about all the air in the universe, or what?) Choice C is incorrect because the volumes of the helium and the displaced air are equal at all times (as is true for any submerged object).

101. **C is correct.** If you have forgotten the floating equation, the quickest way to do this problem is to take the example to the extremes. If the specific gravity of the toy were 0.999, the toy would be almost the same weight as water and, of course, only a very small part would float above the water; $0.001/1 = 0.1\%$. The specific gravity must be how much is under the water. Now we look at the example in the question. 45% must be under water so 55% must be above. To solve this problem mathematically, we set the buoyant force equal to the weight of the toy,

$$\rho_{\text{water}}V_{\text{submerged fraction of the toy}}\,g = \rho_{\text{toy}}V_{\text{toy}}\,g.$$

We end up with the ratio:

$$V_{\text{submerged fraction of the toy}}/V_{\text{toy}} = \rho_{\text{toy}}/\rho_{\text{water}}$$

The right side of this equation is the specific gravity, and the left side is the fraction of the toy submerged. To find the fraction of the toy above water, subtract the submerged fraction from 1.

102. **B is correct.** The pressure on both sides is the same. Force is equal to the product of pressure and area, so the force will be larger on the side with the greater area.

103. **A is correct.** The formula for fluid pressure is $P = \rho gh$. If the density is changed, the pressure will change by the same ratio. Since the specific gravity of ethyl alcohol is 0.8, the pressure will decrease by a factor of 0.8.

104. **D is correct.** Pressure depends only on depth and density, not on the shape of the container.

---

105. **D is correct.** The cross sectional area $A$ is increased by a factor of 4 when $r$ is doubled: $A = \pi r^2$. Since $Q$ remains constant, the velocity decreases by a factor of 4, $Q = Av$. From Bernoulli's equation, we see $K = P + \frac{1}{2}\rho v^2$. We know that the $\frac{1}{2}\rho v^2$ term decreases by a factor of 16, however, we don't know the amount and thus we don't know by how much P increases.

106. **B is correct.** The fluid at A and D are exposed to the atmosphere, so they must be at atmospheric pressure. The fluid at C is at the same level and velocity as the fluid exposed to the atmosphere and just leaving the pipe near point D, so the fluid at C must also be at atmospheric pressure. The fluid at B is at atmospheric pressure plus the weight of the fluid above it. The pressure at B is 1 atmos + $\rho gh$.

107. **A is correct.** Since the water is rising, it is *somehow* pulled up against gravity. The answer choices allow for only one explanation: the water must be grabbing the walls (the soil) around it and pulling itself upward. This 'grabbing' is an intermolecular bond between water and the soil. If it were weaker than the bond between water and water, then the water would be pulled back down onto itself.

108. **D is correct.** Because $\Delta P = QR$, an increase in pressure difference ($\Delta P$) or a decrease in resistance ($R$) increases flow ($Q$). Increasing pipe length increases resistance to flow and decreases flow rate.

109. **D is correct.** The equation for velocity of fluid from a spigot is derived from Bernoulli's equation. The relationship is $2gh = v^2$, and $h$ is proportional to $v^2$, which is reflected in the graph in answer choice D.

110. **B is correct.** The drop with stronger intermolecular forces will have greater surface tension, which will cause it to bead up more.

111. **C is correct.** For ideal flow, volume flow rate is constant at all points, so the volume flow rate will be equal at points A and B.

112. **A is correct.** The equation governing the speed is $v = \sqrt{2gh}$. As $h$ decreases, so does $v$.

---

**113.** **D is correct.** The pressure at the bottom of the column is given by $\rho gh$. Setting this equal to maximum pressure we get $12 \times 10^5 = 4000 \times 10 \times h$.

**114.** **A is correct.** The Young's modulus for any substance is a constant.

**115.** **B is correct.** Using the formula for Young's modulus we have:
$$\text{strain} = (5.4 \times 10^3/6 \times 10^{-4})/9 \times 10^9.$$
Thus strain equals $10^{-3}$. This is 0.1%.

**116.** **D is correct.** The weight per unit area cannot exceed one fifth of the yield strength. $1.5 \times 10^8$ kg weighs $1.5 \times 10^9$ N. Divide the yield strength by 5 and set this equal to the weight per unit area.
$$(0.5 \times 10^8 \text{ N/m}^2) = (1.5 \times 10^9 \text{ N})/A$$
$$A = (1.5 \times 10^9 \text{ N})/(0.5 \times 10^8 \text{ N/m}^2) = 30 \text{ m}^2$$

**117.** **B is correct.** The strain must remain the same. The deformity of the shoe will double with the height because F/A does not change. This keeps the strain ($\Delta x/h_o$) the same.

**118.** **A is correct.** Copper has the largest value for Young's modulus, so it will undergo the least strain for a given stress.

**119.** **D is correct.** Young's modulus for lead is one-fourth the modulus for glass. So the fractional change in lead will be four times the change for glass.

**120.** **B is correct.** The bulk modulus describes a substance's resistance to pressure applied from all sides, which is the same as the stress encountered under water.

---

# EXPLANATIONS TO QUESTIONS IN LECTURE 6

**121.** **A is correct.** The period of each wave is 4 seconds so the frequency is ¼ Hz. The wavelength is 12 meters. $v = f\lambda$.

**122.** **C is correct.** The formula for this problem is $v = \sqrt{\dfrac{\beta}{\rho}}$. Although densities of solids are usually greater than the density of gases, this would make waves move more slowly. Thus, the answer must be that solids are less compressible than gasses. This means that they have a higher bulk modulus $\beta$.

**123.** **C is correct.** The frequency of the waves being sent is equal to the frequency of waves being received. Everything else is irrelevant information. Every second one wave is sent. In 10 seconds, 10 waves are sent.

**124.** **B is correct.** Sound level ($\beta$) is related to intensity ($I$) by $\beta = 10 \log (I/I_o)$, so a change of 20 dB in sound level means that $I$ is 100 times greater at 5 meters. The intensity of a sound wave is proportional to the square of the amplitude, so to change the intensity by a factor of 100 requires a change in amplitue by a factor of only 10. This question requires you to consider two relationships. Although you should know both relationships for MCAT, that's probably one step more than a real MCAT question would require.

**125.** **B is correct.** By definition. (See the first page of this lecture)

**126.** **C is correct.** Frequency is related to both wavelength and period by inverse relationships. There is no direct mathematical relationship between amplitude and frequency.

**127.** **A is correct.** If it takes 1 second for the wave to go to the bottom and back, it must take 0.5 seconds for the wave to reach the bottom. We know that $vt = x$, and $x$ is the depth in this case. So, $(1500 \text{ m/s})(0.5 \text{ sec}) = 750 \text{ m}$.

**128.** **A is correct.** A 10 dB increase means that the intensity is increasing by a factor of 10, so if the intensity is only doubled, there will be less than a 10 dB increase (actually, it's about a 3 dB increase).

---

**129.** **B is correct.** The pattern repeats twice between the dotted lines.

**130.** **D is correct.** This is the definition of interference. The displacements of two superimposed waves are summed all along the wave.

**131.** **C is correct.** An audible beat frequency requires that the two sound waves have close frequencies.

132.    **D is correct.** When energy is added to a structure at one of its natural frequencies, the amplitude reaches some maximum value. At this point, damping effects create an energy loss at the same rate at which energy is absorbed, and the total energy of the structure is constant. A standing wave is produced.

133.    **B is correct.** The formula for the third harmonic closed on both sides is $L = 3\lambda/2$. Here, $L$ is 0.5 m. Thus $\lambda = 0.33$ m.

134.    **B is correct.** When two slightly different frequencies are sounded at the same time, they will create beats with a frequency equal to the difference. So 883 Hz – 879 Hz = 4 Hz.

135.    **B is correct.** The first and second harmonics are the only consecutive harmonics that have a ratio of 1 to 2. The second harmonic is the length of the string. Alternatively, use the harmonic series formula, $L = \dfrac{n\lambda_n}{2}$, to find $n$. $\dfrac{n(4.0)}{2} = \dfrac{(n+1)(2.0)}{2}$  From this you can find that $n = 1$. Now plug $n = 1$ back in to find $L$. $L = \dfrac{(1)(4.0)}{2} = 2.0$.

136.    **D is correct.** If there is perfect constructive interference, the amplitudes will add (6 + 3 = 9). If there is perfect destructive interference, they will subtract (6 – 3 = 3).

137.    **B is correct.** The period of a pendulum is not related to the mass of the bob. It is similar to projectile motion in this respect. It is possible to think of a pendulum like a 'guided' body in free fall. Remember 'wiggle', $\omega = \sqrt{\dfrac{g}{L}}$

138.    **C is correct.** As shown earlier in the lecture, kinetic energy of a pendulum can be described by a sine wave with energy fluctuating between zero and some maximum.

139.    **C is correct.** The square of the amplitude is proportional to the intensity.

140.    **D is correct.** For the frequency to increase, the relative velocity must move the source and observer toward each other. Be careful. The relative velocity does not dictate at what frequency the sound is heard. A wind can also change the frequency by changing the velocity of the sound, but, even with a wind, the source and the observer must have a relative velocity.

141.    **D is correct.** The velocity of the wave on a string is a function of the properties of the string, so it will remain constant. The wavelength of a standing wave is determined by the length of the string, so it will remain constant. If the velocity and wavelength are constant, then frequency is constant too.

142.    **C is correct.** The pendulum is at its greatest speed at point A, so it will be at it's greatest kinetic energy. All of the other quantities are at zero at this point.

143.    **B is correct.** Remember, frequency of a pendulum is related to the square root of $g/l$. High above the earth, the acceleration due to gravity will decrease. If $g$ decreases, the frequency will decrease. If the frequency of the timekeeper decreases, the clock will slow down.

144.    **B is correct.** Harmonic motion is motion that is repeated over and over again. There is no repeated action in the fall of a skydiver.

## EXPLANATIONS TO QUESTIONS IN LECTURE 7

145.    **C is correct.** This is a units question. 100 N/C is equivalent to 100 V/m. The one coulomb experiences 100 Newtons of force. This is a measure of the strength of the electric field: 100 N/C. Another way to say 100 N/C is 100 V/m. The plates are one meter apart, so they must have a 100 volt potential difference.

146.    **B is correct.** The forces are conservative so if we turn the picture 90°, this is just like gravity, *mgh*; the vertical distance *h*, and not the horizontal distance, is what matters. Likewise, in the question, the total length of the path does not matter because some of the movement is not against the electric field. Work is done only when the particle moves in the 10 cm direction against the electric field. The work required is the force times the distance parallel to the field or *Eqd*.

147.    **A is correct.** The force is given by Coulomb's law, $F = k\, qq/r^2$. The electrostatic force changes with the square of the distance between the centers of charge.

148.  **C is correct.** The electric field above an infinitely large electric plate remains constant with distance. You can visualize this by imagining the electric field lines. The lines are perpendicular to the plate and have nowhere to spread. By bending in one direction or another, they would increase their distance from one line, only to decrease their distance from another line. Since the lines would remain at an equal distance from one another, the electric field would remain constant.

149.  **B is correct.** This problem is about energy. The system has a total electric potential energy of $U = kqq/r$. Remember, the forces acting are conservative so mechanical energy is conserved. Thus, as the first particle is propelled away from the second, electric potential energy is converted to kinetic energy. When the first particle moves 25 cm, it has doubled its distance of separation. From $U = kqq/r$, we know that the first particle has lost half of its potential energy to kinetic energy when $r$ is doubled.

$$U_{\cancel{2}} = k\,\frac{qq}{\cancel{r}^{\,2}}$$

When the first particle is infinitely far from the second particle, it will have lost the rest of the electric potential energy to kinetic. In other words, it will have twice the kinetic that it had at 25 cm. We know from $K.E. = \frac{1}{2}mv^2$ that if we multiply the $K.E.$ by 2, we must multiply the velocity by the square root of 2 or approximately 1.4. 1.4 times 10 equals 14 m/s.

$$K.E. = \frac{1}{2}mv^{\overset{1.4}{\cancel{2}}} \quad \overset{2}{\cancel{\phantom{K}}}$$

150.  **A is correct.** The field lines are directed away from both charges, so by definition they are both positively charged.

151.  **A is correct.** Since gravitational force is attractive, the electric force must be repulsive. Doubling both masses will increase the attractive gravitational force. Choice C is wrong because doubling both charges will increase the repulsive electrical force. Choices B and D will not change the forces at all.

152.  **B is correct.** Electrostatic forces are conservative, so the work done by a force against them is conserved in potential energy. A volt is a joule/coulomb, so you can get voltage by dividing work by charge. (90 J)/(10 C) = 9 J/C = 9 V.

---

153.  **A is correct.** The electric field inside a capacitor is constant. By definition, a dipole has equal but opposite charges on either end. The force on each end of the dipole is $Eq$ and in opposite directions. The net force is zero.

154.  **B is correct.** The effective resistance is 3 Ω. The voltage divided by the effective resistance gives 4 amps coming out of the battery. The 4 amps split evenly at the node before A and B; 2 amps through each resistor.

155.  **D is correct.** Increasing the voltage across the plates would increase the amount of charge on the capacitor but not the capacitance of the capacitor. Capacitance is defined by $C = Q/V$.

156.  **A is correct.** The energy for the light comes from the battery. The rate at which the energy is released is the power. $P = i^2R$. Since the voltage remains constant, the change in the current will produce the greatest change in the power. Where more light bulbs are attached, the resistance goes up and the current goes down; thus the power goes down and less light is produced.

157.  **C is correct.** This is Kirchoff's first rule: current flowing into a node must also flow out. Since the resistors have equal resistances, the current is the same in both parallel branches. Thus 4 amps flow into the node from both branches. Therefore 8 amps must flow out of the node.

158.  **D is correct.** A Watt is a joule/sec. So you can get Joules by multiplying power and time. Don't forget to convert time to seconds. So (60 W)(60 sec) = 3600 J.

159.  **D is correct.** Adding a resistor in parallel decreased the overall resistance, which will increase the current and the power. The voltage of the battery is not affected by changes in the circuit.

**160.** **C is correct.** Choice A comes from $V = IR$, with $I$ replaced by C/sec. Choice B comes from $P = I^2R$. Choice D comes from $P = V^2/R$.

---

**161.** **C is correct.** The maximum voltage is given by $V_{max} = \sqrt{2}\, V_{rms}$.

**162.** **B is correct.** A magnetic field runs from magnetic north to magnetic south. The north pole of a compass needle points to the south pole of the earth's magnetic field, which is near the geographic North Pole.

**163.** **D is correct.** You must remember that the force is perpendicular to both the velocity and the magnetic field. You may recall from Lecture 1 that since velocity and the magnetic field are both vectors, and their product, force, is a vector, the product will always be perpendicular to the other two vectors.

**164.** **A is correct.** We can either memorize the Bio-Savart law, $B = \mu_o i/2\pi r$, or visualize how the energy of the field is spread from the wire. As we move away from the wire, the energy spreads out over a cylinder surrounding the wire. The circumference of this cylinder increases directly with the radius. In other words, if we double the radius, or distance from the wire, there is twice as much room over which to spread the energy.

**165.** **C is correct.** The electric field between the plates will push a positive charge to the right. The magnetic field must push the drop the opposite direction to counter this force. The right hand rule shows that a magnetic field coming out of the page will push a falling positively charged drop to the left. This will counter the action by the electric field. Note that this question does not require you to know right hand rule. Simply knowing that the oil drop will be pushed at a 90° angle to its motion and at a 90° angle to the magnetic field means that the magnetic field must be oriented either into or out of the page. That leaves only one possible answer choice. This is how MCAT is likely to test you without requiring direct knowledge of the right hand rule.

**166.** **D is correct.** A charged particle moving parallel to magnetic field lines experiences no force. Remember, $F = qvB\sin\theta$. If $\theta$ is zero, then $F$ is zero.

**167.** **A is correct.** Lenz's law states that current will flow in a loop of wire to oppose the changes of the magnetic field inside the loop. If the magnetic field is decreasing, current will flow to increase it. If we use the right hand rule and grab the wire, our fingers point in the direction of the magnetic field increase while our thumb points in the direction of the current. In order to orient our fingers so that they point into the page inside the loop, we must point our thumb in a clockwise direction along the loop. Yes, this question requires you to know the right hand rule and, consequently, will probably not appear on the MCAT with this wording. However, we want you to know the right hand rule because we think it will help you on the MCAT, so we asked this question anyway.

**168.** **B is correct.** Since the path is circular, the particle must be traveling at 90 degrees to the magnetic field (otherwise the path would be helical). The centripetal force is equal to the magnetic force. So, $qvB = mv^2/r$. If you solve for $q$, you get $mv/Br$.

---

## EXPLANATIONS TO QUESTIONS IN LECTURE 8

**169.** **A is correct.** The ray will turn toward the normal as it enters the glass and away from the normal as it exits the glass.

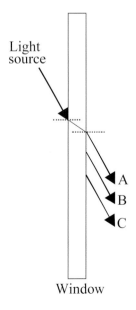

www.Examkrackers.com
Answers & Explanations For Questions In The Lectures **271**

170.    **D is correct.** Blue has the highest frequency of the given choices. Remember, ROY G. BIV.

171.    **A is correct.** We are given 'km'; we want 'years'. We work with the units as follows:

$$\text{km} \times \frac{\text{s}}{\text{m}} \times \frac{\text{min}}{\text{s}} \times \frac{\text{hrs}}{\text{min}} \times \frac{\text{days}}{\text{hrs}} \times \frac{\text{yrs}}{\text{days}} \times \frac{\text{m}}{\text{km}}$$

172.    **D is correct.** Reflection is indicative of either wave or particle theory.

173.    **C is correct.** Light passes through the piece of glass as shown below. Only the thicker glass directs the light toward A.

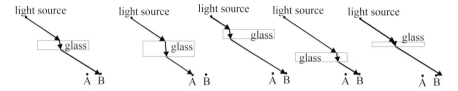

174.    **D is correct.** As the light is dimmed, less and less energy is available to the light bulb until, at the last moment, there is only enough energy to produce red light.

175.    **B is correct.** We can find the speed of light through glass by using the index of refraction.

$$n = \frac{c}{v}, \text{ or } v = \frac{c}{n} = \frac{(3 \times 10^8)}{1.5} = (2 \times 10^8)$$

Once we know the speed of light in glass, we can use $x = vt$. Rearrange the equation to solve for $t$ and change cm into meters.

$$t = \frac{(1 \times 10^{-2})}{(2 \times 10^8)} = 0.5 \times 10^{-10} = 5 \times 10^{-11}$$

176.    **A is correct.** Choice A describes refraction, not diffraction. Roughly speaking, diffraction occurs when waves bend around corners.

---

177.    **B is correct.** Focal distance is equal to one half the radius of curvature, $f = \frac{1}{2} r$.

178.    **D is correct.** $m = d_i/d_o$.

179.    **B is correct.** According to the lens maker's equation, as the refractive indices of the lens and the surrounding medium approach one another, the lens will lose its effect. However, you don't need the lens maker's equation to visualize this. If we use our technique of taking examples to their extremes, we can imagine a lens made out of water. When we use the lens in the air, it acts as a magnifying glass; when we use it in water, it doesn't work. If the water were at a slightly different temperature to change the index only slightly, the water lens would bend light only slightly under water.

180.    **A is correct.** Virtual images are called 'virtual' because they are not really there, so they cannot be projected on to a screen. Real images can be seen if they are focused into the eye or projected onto a screen. Diverging lenses and convex mirrors, by themselves, can only create virtual images.

181.    **B is correct.** Choice B is a diverging lens. It should diverge parallel light rays. It is shown converging a light ray, so it is drawn incorrectly.

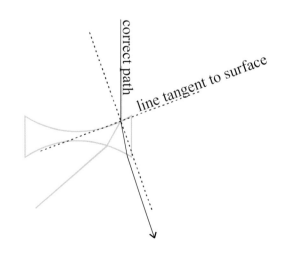

182. **C is correct.** The image is behind the mirror and it is upright, so it must be virtual.

183. **A is correct.** An increase in the index of refraction of a lens will increase the bending of the light rays, which will increase the power of the lens. Alternatively, you can look at the lens maker's equation to see that increasing $n_1$ will increase $1/f$. Increasing the radius of curvature of one side will flatten the lens and reduce the amount that it refracts light, thus decreasing its power. Since $P = 1/f$, an increase in $f$ will decrease the power.

184. **C is correct.** $f = r/2$. So if $f$ is 4, then $r$ is 8.

185. **D is correct.** The thin lens equation is $\frac{1}{f} = \frac{1}{d_o} + \frac{1}{d_i}$. The object distance is always positive. This results in a value of $\frac{4}{3}$ for $d_i$. Since this value is positive, the image is behind the lens where the 'eye' is. Remember, I (eye) am positive that real is inverted.

186. **B is correct.** This one is tricky. First of all, a convex mirror can't make an inverted image so A and C are out. Secondly, The focal point on a concave mirror is positive. Thus, from the thin lens equation, $\frac{1}{f} = \frac{1}{5} + \frac{1}{d_i}$. Since the image and the focal distance are positive, the focal distance must be less than 5 (which is the same as saying $\frac{1}{f}$ must be greater than $\frac{1}{5}$).

187. **A is correct.** The object is outside the focal distance of a converging mirror; the image will be positive, real, and inverted. The thin lens equation gives $\frac{1}{2} = \frac{1}{4} + \frac{1}{d_i}$. The image distance is four, so the magnification is negative 1. The negative means that the image is inverted.

188. **D is correct.** The focal distance is negative so the lens is diverging and the power is $\frac{1}{f}$.

189. **D is correct.** See question 187. If the lens is diverging then the image and the object cannot be at the same distance, $\frac{1}{f} = \frac{1}{d_o} + \frac{1}{d_i}$. Since $d_i$ is negative, the focal distance would have to be infinite; meaning the lens would be flat. Therefore, the only way an image and an object can be at the same distance is if the lens were converging with a focal distance equal to half the distance of the object.

190. **D is correct.** When an object is placed at the focal point of a lens, the rays will emerge parallel on both sides of the lens. If the rays never intersect, then no image is formed. If you use the thin lens equation, you'll get an image distance of infinity.

$$\frac{1}{f} = \frac{1}{f} + \frac{1}{\infty}$$

191. **B is correct.** If an object is placed at a very large distance from a lens, we can think of it as being placed at infinity. For an object placed an infinite distance from a lens, the image will appear at the focal point.

$$\frac{1}{f} = \frac{1}{\infty} + \frac{1}{f}$$

192. **C is correct.** A converging lens is the only one of the choices that produces an inverted image on the side opposite the object.

# PHOTO CREDITS

## Covers

Front cover, Outside Looping Roller Coaster:
© iStockphoto.com/KJimages
Back cover, Launch of Endeavour STS-134:
© iStockphoto.com/Celso Diniz

## Chapter 1

Pg. 5, Student walking: © Dana Kelley
Pg. 15, Projectile follows a parabolic path: © Ted Kinsman/
Photo Researchers, Inc
Pg. 16, Air resistance: © Erich Schrempp/Photo Researchers,
Inc
Pg. 16, Bowling: © iStockphoto.com/Neil Pope
Pg. 16, Volleyball: © Dana Kelley

## Chapter 2

Pg. 20, Gold Ring: © Dana Kelley
Pg. 21, Figure 2.2, Hand and book: © Dana Kelley
Pg. 23, Table and block of wood: © Dana Kelley
Pg. 25, 400 pound barbell image,: © Mike Powell/Getty
Images
Pg. 26, Floating Astronaut: © NASA/Photo Researchers, Inc
Pg. 26, Figure 2.2, International Space Station : © Roger
Harris/Photo Researchers, Inc
Pg. 29, Cyclist: © Istockphoto.com/Mlenny Photography
Pg. 30, Winter Driving: © iStockphoto.com/Brandon
Laufenberg
Pg. 30, Moon and Earth: © iStockphoto.com/tombonatti
Pg. 33, Wheel on yellow racecar: © iStockphoto.com/Steve
Mcsweeny
Pg. 34, Sanding wood: © iStockphoto.com/CandyBox
Images

## Chapter 3

Pg. 44, Spinning top: © iStockphoto.com/Greg Brookes
Pg. 45, Airplane Jump: © iStockphoto.com/Drazen Vukelic
Pg. 45, Skydiver: © iStockphoto.com/Aleksander Trankov
Pg. 54, Matchstick: © iStockphoto.com/Sunnybeach
Pg. 57, Cowboy with wagon: © iStockphoto.com/ Doug
Berry
Pg. 59, Cardboard box on wood table: © Dana Kelley

## Chapter 4

Pg. 66, Crash testing: © TRL Ltd. / Photo Researchers, Inc
Pg. 73, Piano Moving: © iStockphoto.com/Frances Twitty
Pg. 79, Gamma knife: © iStockphoto.com/Alexander
Gatsenko
Pg. 81, Nuclear power station: © iStockphoto.com/Vojtech
Soukup

## Chapter 5

Pg. 86, Cruiser: © iStockphoto.com/Nasowas
Pg. 87, Small buckets: © Dana Kelley
Pg. 87, Scale: © Veer.com/cjan
Pg. 100, Dripping faucet: © iStockphoto.com/Eric Delmar
Pg. 103, Pig on diving board: © Image Source/ Gettyimages.
com
Pg. 105, Metal spheres images: © Charles D. Winters/Photo
Researchers, Inc

## Chapter 6

Pg. 109, Neurospin MRI Research Center: © Philippe Psaila/
Photo Researchers, Inc
Pg. 110, Liberty Elementary School: © Dana Kelley
Pg. 111, Muzzle blast: © Gary S. Settles/Photo
Researchers, Inc
Pg. 113, Five young people grimacing at something they
hear: © iStockphoto.com/Don Bayley
Pg. 117, Guitar: © Dana Kelley
Pg. 119, Sympathetic resonance: © Efran/Gettyimages.com

## Chapter 7

Pg. 129, High voltage: © iStockphoto.com/Vladimir Popovic
Pg. 138, Firefighter fighting a fire: © iStockphoto.com/
Tatiana Belova
Pg. 138, Car battery: © iStockphoto.com/Carlos Gawronski
Pg. 144, Turbines of Hydroelectricity Power Generator at
Hoover Dam: © iStockphoto.com/YinYang

## Chapter 8

Pg. 160, Thermogram of incandescent and compact
fluorescent lamps: © GIPhotoStock/Photo
Researchers, Inc
Pg. 162, Solid-state sodium laser guidestar: © Stephen &
Donna O'Meara/Photo Researchers, Inc
Pg. 164, Sigmund Freud: © iStockphoto.com/Georgios
Kollidas
Pg. 165, Fiber optics: © iStockphoto.com/Henrik Jonsson
Pg. 166, Prism: © Dimitri Vervitsiotis/Gettyimages.com
Pg. 166, Satellite: © iStockphoto.com/TebNad
Pg. 167, Bubble: © iStockphoto.com/Mikkel William Nielsen
Pg. 170, X-ray diffraction of platinum crystal: © Erwin
Mueller, Pennsylvania State University/Science Source/
Photo Researchers, Inc/Colorization by: Mary
Martin
Pg. 172, Mirror from a school bus: © iStockphoto.com/Paul
Fries
Pg. 173, Refraction images: © David Parker/Photo
Researchers, Inc.

# INDEX

friction 33, 34, 55, 58, 59
fundamental wavelength 118
fusion 81

## G

gamma ray 79
gauge pressure 88, 90, 99
geometrical optics 164
gravitational force 19–21, 25, 27, 30, 31, 45, 85, 130–132
gravitational potential energy 53
gravity 14, 20–28, 30, 31, 43–45, 53, 56, 63, 74, 85, 87, 88, 91, 93, 107, 112, 122, 123, 130–133, 135
gravity waves 112

## H

half-life 78, 83
harmonic series 118
heat 52–54, 58–59
Hooke's law 35, 40, 41, 53, 56, 66, 103, 122–123
hydraulic gradient line 99
hydraulic lift 73, 90, 93

## I

ideal fluid 96–99, 101–102
impulse 70, 88
inclined plane 27–28, 31, 33, 73, 76
index of refraction 158, 164–167, 171, 174, 175
induction 137, 150
inelastic collisions 67, 69
inertia 14, 19, 23, 65, 111
infrared 158–159
intensity 112–114, 116, 128, 164
intensity level 113
intermolecular forces 100, 101
internal energy 54–56, 58–59, 61, 66, 67, 73, 82, 151
irrotational flow 96
isotropic light 160

## K

kinetic energy 52, 55–60, 66, 71, 85, 88, 97, 111, 122, 128, 140, 151, 159
kinetic friction 33–34, 40, 46, 57, 58
Kirchoff's first rule 138
Kirchoff's second rule 138

## L

laminar 96
laser 162–163, 168
lateral magnification 176, 180
law of conservation of energy 66, 129
Law of Conservation of Mechanical Energy 56
lenses 172–175, 177, 178, 180–182
lens maker's equation 174, 178
Lenz's law 151
lever 47–49, 51, 73–75, 77
lever arm 47, 51, 74
light 124–126, 145, 158, 157–178
lines of force 131, 147

longitudinal wave 109, 110

## M

machines 73–74
magnetic field 131, 147–151, 154, 155
magnetic flux 150–151
mass 16, 19, 20, 23, 25, 34, 52–53, 65, 79–80, 131–132
mechanical energy 52
mirrors 162, 172–174, 178, 180–181
modulus of elasticity 103–104
momentum 65–72, 88, 109, 116

## N

near point 176
net force 23, 24, 27–29, 34, 36, 44, 46, 54, 86, 122, 145
Newton's First Law 23
Newton's Law of Universal Gravitation 25
Newton's second law 23, 25, 27, 29
Newton's third law 23, 25, 35
node 117, 118, 138, 142
nonconservative forces 57
nondispersive 109, 111, 115
nondispersive medium 111, 115
normal force 21, 23, 27, 28, 33, 34, 60, 85

## O

Ohm's law 98, 138–139, 143–144

## P

parallax 172
Pascal 88, 90
Pascal's principle 90
pendulum 12, 37, 46, 123, 128, 151
period 110–111, 114, 122–123
phase 110, 115, 116, 120, 121, 159, 161–164, 167–169
phase constant 115, 121
piezometer tube 99
piezometric head 99
positron emission 79
potential energy 52, 53, 55, 56, 60, 63, 71, 97, 99, 111, 122, 128, 132, 134, 141
power 61, 63, 76, 112, 144, 146, 147, 174, 177, 180
Poynting vector 157
pressure head 99
projectile 4, 8, 11, 14–16, 18, 112
projectile motion 4, 8, 14–16
pulley 46, 73- 77
Pythagorean Theorem 4

## R

radioactive decay 78
radius of curvature 149, 173–174, 177
ramp 7, 31, 32, 73–75, 77
ray diagram 175
real image 172, 177, 178-180
reference frames 36
resistivity 138, 151
resistors 137, 139, 142, 145, 146

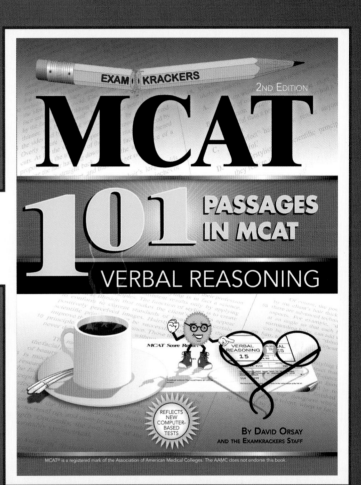

*Notes:*

*Notes:*

*Notes:*

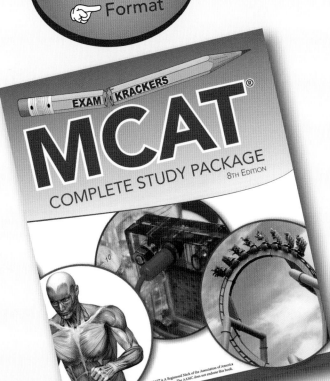

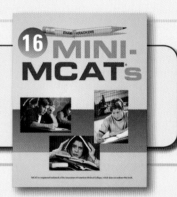

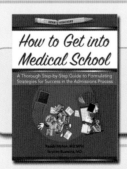

# An Unedited Student Review of This Book

The following review of this book was written by Teri R—. from New York. Teri scored a 43 out of 45 possible points on the MCAT. She is currently attending UCSF medical school, one of the most selective medical schools in the country.

*"The Examkrackers MCAT books are the best MCAT prep materials I've seen-and I looked at many before deciding. The worst part about studying for the MCAT is figuring out what you need to cover and getting the material organized. These books do all that for you so that you can spend your time learning. The books are well and carefully written, with great diagrams and really useful mnemonic tricks, so you don't waste time trying to figure out what the book is saying. They are concise enough that you can get through all of the subjects without cramming unnecessary details, and they really give you a strategy for the exam. The study questions in each section cover all the important concepts, and let you check your learning after each section. Alternating between reading and answering questions in MCAT format really helps make the material stick, and means there are no surprises on the day of the exam-the exam format seems really familiar and this helps enormously with the anxiety. Basically, these books make it clear what you need to do to be completely prepared for the MCAT and deliver it to you in a straightforward and easy-to-follow form. The mass of material you could study is overwhelming, so I decided to trust these books—I used nothing but the Examkrackers books in all subjects and got a 13-15 on Verbal, a 14 on Physical Sciences, and a 14 on Biological Sciences. Thanks to Jonathan Orsay and Examkrackers, I was admitted to all of my top-choice schools (Columbia, Cornell, Stanford, and UCSF). I will always be grateful. I could not recommend the Examkrackers books more strongly. Please contact me if you have any questions."*

*Sincerely,*
*Teri R—*

# About the Author

Jonathan Orsay is uniquely qualified to write an MCAT preparation book. He graduated on the Dean's list with a B.A. in History from Columbia University. While considering medical school, he sat for the real MCAT three times from 1989 to 1996. He scored in the 90 percentiles on all sections before becoming an MCAT instructor. He has lectured in MCAT test preparation for thousands of hours and across the country. He has taught premeds from such prestigious Universities as Harvard and Columbia. He was the editor of one of the best selling MCAT prep books in 1996 and again in 1997. He has written and published the following books and audio products in MCAT preparation: "Examkrackers MCAT Physics"; "Examkrackers MCAT Chemistry"; "Examkrackers MCAT Organic Chemistry"; "Examkrackers MCAT Biology"; "Examkrackers MCAT Verbal Reasoning & Math"; "Examkrackers 1001 questions in MCAT Physics", "Examkrackers MCAT Audio Osmosis with Jordan and Jon".

EXAMKRACKERS MCAT®

# VERBAL REASONING & MATHEMATICAL TECHNIQUES

## 8TH EDITION

OSOTE
PUBLISHING

ISBN 10: 1-893858-66-9 (Volume 2)
ISBN 13: 978-1-893858-66-4 (5 Volume Set)

8th Edition

To purchase additional copies of this book or the rest of the 5 volume set,
call 1-888-572-2536 or fax orders to 1-859-255-0109.

Examkrackers.com

Osote.com

Audioosmosis.com

Cover/inside layout design/illustrations: Examkrackers' staff

Printed and bound in the United States of America.

# PHOTOCOPYING & DISTRIBUTION POLICY

The illustrations and all other content in this book are copyrighted material owned by Osote Publishing. Please do not reproduce any of the content, illustrations, charts, graphs, photos, etc., on email lists or websites.

Photocopying the pages so that the book can then be resold is a violation of copyright.

Schools and co-ops MAY NOT PHOTOCOPY any portion of this book. For more information, please contact Osote Publishing: email: support@examkrackers.com or phone 1.888.KRACKEM.

# Acknowledgements

Although I am the author, the hard work and expertise of many individuals contributed to this book. The idea of writing in two voices, a science voice and an MCAT voice, was the creative brainchild of my imaginative friend Jordan Zaretsky. I would like to thank David Orsay for his help with the verbal passages. I wish to thank my wife, Silvia, for her support during the difficult times in the past and those that lie ahead.

Finally, I wish to thank my daughter Julianna Orsay for helping out whenever possible.

I also wish to thank the following individuals:

## Contributors

Jennifer Birk-Goldschmidt
Timothy Peck
Steven Tersigni
Sara Thorp
Michelle Young

# Table of Contents

# INTRODUCTION TO MCAT INCLUDING MCAT MATH

**LECTURE**

**i**

## i.1  MCAT Format

The MCAT consists of four sections:

1. Physical Sciences
2. Verbal Reasoning
3. Biological Sciences
4. Voluntary Unscored Trial Section

**Table i.1  The MCAT Format**

| Test Section | Questions | Time Allotted | Time/Question |
|---|---|---|---|
| Tutorial | (Optional) | 10 minutes | |
| Exam Agreement | | 10 minutes | |
| Physical Sciences | 52 | 70 minutes | ~1.35 minutes (81s) |
| Break | (Optional) | 10 minutes | |
| Verbal Reasoning | 40 | 60 minutes | 1.5 minutes (90s) |
| Break | (Optional) | 10 minutes | |
| Biological Sciences | 52 | 70 minutes | ~1.35 minutes (81s) |
| Score/Void Exam | | 5 minutes | |
| Break | (Optional) | 10 minutes | |
| Voluntary Section | 32 | 45 minutes | ~1.41 minutes (84s) |
| Survey | (Optional) | 10 minutes | |
| Total Content Time | | 4 hours, 5 minutes | |
| Total Test Time | | 4 hours, 40 minutes | |
| **Total Appointment Time** | | **5 hours, 10 minutes** | |

> Additional time is required for test center check-in.

### Physical Sciences Section

The Physical Sciences Section is 70 minutes. It covers topics from undergraduate physics and inorganic chemistry. Passages average approximately 200 words in length and are often accompanied by one or more charts, diagrams, or tables. Generally there are 6-10 questions following each passage, as well as 3 sets of stand-alone multiple-choice questions, for a total of 52 questions. The top score on the Physical Sciences Section is a 15.

### Verbal Reasoning Section

The Verbal Reasoning Section is 60 minutes long and consists of 40 questions with answer choices A through D. There are 9 passages followed by 4-10 questions each. Passages average approximately 600 words in length. There is a wide variety of passage topics ranging from economics and anthropology to poetic analysis, and most are intentionally soporific. The top score on the Verbal Reasoning Section is also 15.

### Biological Sciences Section

The Biological Sciences Section is 70 minutes and covers science topics from a wide range of undergraduate biology topics, organic chemistry and genetics. Like the Physical Sciences section, there are 6-10 questions following each passage, as well as 3 sets of stand-alone multiple-choice questions, for a total of 52 questions. The top score on the Biological Sciences Section is a 15.

### Voluntary Unscored Trial Section

The Voluntary Unscored Trial Section has replaced the Writing Sample Section for tests taken in 2013 and 2014. These questions will test content that will be added to the MCAT in 2015. It covers psychology, sociology, and biochemistry. It is 45 minutes and consists of 32 questions and will be administered after the three other sections are completed. Scores will not be reported for this section but if you put forth a good effort on the section, you will be compensated.

## i.2 | How to Approach Science Passages

The following guidelines should be followed when working on an MCAT science passage:

1. **Read the passage first.** Regardless of your level of science ability, you should read the passage. Passages often give special conditions that you would have no reason to suspect without reading and which can invalidate an otherwise correct answer.

2. **Read quickly; do not try to master the information given in the passage.** Passages are full of information both useful and irrelevant to the adjoining questions. Do not waste time by attempting to gain complete understanding of the passage.

3. **Quickly check tables, graphs, and charts.** Do not spend time studying tables, graphs, and charts. Often, no questions will be asked concerning their content. Instead, quickly check headings, titles, axes, and obvious trends.

4. **Pay close attention to detail in the questions.** The key to a question is often found in a single word, such as "**net** force" or "**constant** velocity".

5. **Read answer choices immediately, before doing calculations.** Answer choices give information. Often a question that appears to require extensive calculations can be solved by intuition or estimation due to limited reasonable answer choices. Sometimes answer choices can be eliminated for having the wrong units, being nonsensical, or other reasons.

6. **Don't be afraid to skip questions that are taking you too long to finish.** If you usually do not finish a science section, then make sure that you at least answer all of the easy questions. In other words, guess at the difficult questions. Be sure to make time to answer all of the free-standing questions. The free-standing questions are usually easier than those based on passages. By the time you have finished the Examkrackers Comprehensive Review, you should not need to skip any questions.

## i.3    MCAT Math

MCAT math will not test your math skills beyond the contents of this book. The MCAT *does* require knowledge of the following up to a second year high school algebra level: ratios, proportions, square roots, exponents and logarithms, scientific notation, quadratic and simultaneous equations, graphs. In addition, the MCAT tests: vector addition, subtraction; basic trigonometry; very basic probabilities. The MCAT *does not* test dot product, cross product or calculus.

Calculators are neither allowed on the MCAT, nor would they be helpful. From this moment until MCAT day, you should do all math problems in your head whenever possible. Do not use a calculator, and use your pencil as seldom as possible when you do any math.

If you find yourself doing a lot of calculations on the MCAT, it's a good indication that you are doing something wrong. As a rule of thumb, **spend no more than 3 minutes on any MCAT physics question**. Once you have spent 3 minutes on a question with no resolution, you should stop what you're doing and read the question again for a simple answer. If you don't see a simple answer, you should make your best guess and move to the next question.

Practice doing MCAT math quickly in your head.

## i.4    Rounding

Exact numbers are rarely useful on the MCAT. In order to save time and avoid errors when making calculations on the test, **use round numbers**. For instance, the gravitational constant *g* **should be rounded up to 10 m/s$^2$** for the purpose of calculations, even when instructed by the MCAT to do otherwise. Calculations like $23.4 \times 9.8$ should be thought of as "something less than $23.4 \times 10$, which equals something less than 234 or less than $2.34 \times 10^2$." Thus if you see a question requiring the calculations $23.4 \times 9.8$ followed by these answer choices:

  **A.** $1.24 \times 10^2$
  **B.** $1.81 \times 10^2$
  **C.** $2.29 \times 10^2$
  **D.** $2.35 \times 10^2$

**Wrong way**

Answer is something less than $23.4 \times 10 = 234$.

**Right way**

answer choice C is the closest answer under $2.34 \times 10^2$, and C should be chosen quickly without resorting to complicated calculations. Rarely will there be two possible answer choices close enough to prevent a correct selection after rounding. If two answer choices on the MCAT are so close that you find you have to write down the math, it's probably because you've made a mistake. If you find yourself in that situation, look again at the question for a simple solution. If you don't see it, guess and go on.

This is me after I hurt myself with complicated calculations on my first MCAT.

It is helpful to **remain aware of the direction in which you have rounded**. In the example just given, since answer choice D is closer to 234 than answer choice C, you may have been tempted to choose it. However, a quick check on the direction of rounding would confirm that 9.8 was rounded upward so the answer should be less than 234. Again, assuming the calculations were necessary to arrive at the answer, an answer choice which would prevent the use of rounding, like $2.32 \times 10^2$ for instance, simply would not appear as an answer choice on a real MCAT. It would not appear for the very reason that such an answer choice would force the test taker to spend time making complicated calculations, and those aren't the skills the MCAT is designed to test.

If a series of calculations is used where rounding is performed at each step, the rounding errors can be compounded and the resulting answer can be useless. For instance, we may be required to take the above example and further divide "23.4 × 9.8" by 4.4. We might round 4.4 down to 4, and divide 240 by 4 to get 60; however, each of our roundings would have increased our result, compounding the error. Instead, it is better to round 4.4 up to 5, dividing 235 by 5 to get 47. This is closer to the exact answer of 52.1182. In an attempt to increase the accuracy of multiple estimations, **try to compensate for upward rounding with downward rounding in the same calculations**.

Notice, in the example, that when we increase the denominator, we are decreasing the entire term. For instance:

$$\frac{625}{24} = 26.042 \qquad \frac{625}{25} = 25$$

Rounding the denominator of 24 up to 25 results in a decrease in the overall term.

**When rounding squares remember that you are really rounding twice.** $(2.2)^2$ is really 2.2 × 2.2, so when we say that the answer is something greater than 4 we need to keep in mind that it is significantly greater because we have rounded down twice. One way to increase your accuracy is to round just one of the 2.2s, leaving you with something greater than 4.4. This is much closer to the exact answer of 4.84.

Another strategy for rounding an exponential term is to remember that difficult-to-solve exponential terms must lie between two easy-to-solve exponential terms. Thus $2.2^2$ is between $2^2$ and $3^2$, closer to $2^2$. This strategy is especially helpful for square roots. The square root of 21 must be between the square root of 16 and the square root of 25. Thus, the MCAT square root of 21 must be between 5 and 4 or about 4.6.

$$\sqrt{25} = 5$$
$$\sqrt{21} = ?$$
$$\sqrt{16} = 4$$

For more complicated roots, recall that any root is simply a fractional exponent. For instance, the square root of 9 is the same as $9^{1/2}$. This means that the fourth root of 4 is $4^{1/4}$. This is the same as $(4^{1/2})^{1/2}$ or $\sqrt{2}$. We can combine these techniques to solve even more complicated roots:

It's worth your time to memorize:

$$\sqrt[3]{27} = 3$$
$$4^{\frac{2}{3}} = \sqrt[3]{4^2} = \sqrt[3]{16} = ? \approx 2.5$$
$$\sqrt[3]{8} = 2$$
$$\sqrt{2} \approx 1.4 \text{ and } \sqrt{3} \approx 1.7.$$

The MCAT is likely to give you any values that you need for trigonometric functions; however, since MCAT typically uses common angles, it is a good idea to be familiar with trigonometric values for common angles. Use the paradigm below to remember the values of common angles. Notice that the sine values are the reverse of the cosine values. Also notice that the numbers under the radical are 0, 1, 2, 3 and 4 from top to bottom for the sine function and bottom to top for the cosine function, and all are divided by 2.

| Table 1.1 | Sines and Cosines of Common Angles | |
|---|---|---|
| θ | sine | cosine |
| 0° | $\frac{\sqrt{0}}{2}$ | $\frac{\sqrt{4}}{2}$ |
| 30° | $\frac{\sqrt{1}}{2}$ | $\frac{\sqrt{3}}{2}$ |
| 45° | $\frac{\sqrt{2}}{2}$ | $\frac{\sqrt{2}}{2}$ |
| 60° | $\frac{\sqrt{3}}{2}$ | $\frac{\sqrt{1}}{2}$ |
| 90° | $\frac{\sqrt{4}}{2}$ | $\frac{\sqrt{0}}{2}$ |

Rounding is an effective tool for solving MCAT math. Practice it.

Less practiced test takers may perceive a rounding strategy as risky. On the contrary, **the test makers actually design their answers with a rounding strategy in mind**. Complicated numbers can be intimidating to anyone not comfortable with a rounding strategy.

*Notes:*

· For science passages, read first, read quick.

## Practice Problems

*Solve the following problems by rounding. Do not use a pencil or a calculator.*

1. $\dfrac{5.4 \times 7.1 \times 3.2}{4.6^2}$

   A. 2.2
   B. 3.8
   C. 5.8
   D. 7.9

2. $\dfrac{\sqrt{360 \times 9.8}}{6.2}$

   A. 9.6
   B. 13.2
   C. 17.3
   D. 20.2

3. $\dfrac{\sqrt{2} \times 23}{50}$

   A. 0.12
   B. 0.49
   C. 0.65
   D. 1.1

4. $\dfrac{(2 \times 45)^2}{9.8 \times 21}$

   A. 11
   B. 39
   C. 86
   D. 450

5. $\sqrt{\dfrac{2 \times 9.8^2}{49}}$

   A. 0.3
   B. 0.8
   C. 1.2
   D. 2

**Answers**

1. C is correct. The exact answer is 5.7981.

2. A is correct. The exact answer is 9.5802.

3. C is correct. The exact answer is 0.65054.

4. B is correct. The exact answer is 39.359.

5. D is correct. The exact answer is 1.9799.

## i.5 | Scientific Notation

One important math skill tested rigorously by the MCAT is your ability to use scientific notation. In order to maximize your MCAT score, you must be familiar with the techniques and shortcuts of scientific notation. Although it may not seem so, scientific notation was designed to make math easier, and it does. You should practice the following techniques until you come to view scientific notation as a valuable ally.

This manual will define the terms in scientific notation as follows:

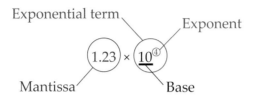

Exponential term, Exponent, $1.23 \times 10^{④}$, Mantissa, Base

**Magnitude:** You should try to gain a feel for the exponential aspect of scientific notation. $10^{-8}$ is much greater than $10^{-12}$. It is 10,000 times greater! Thus, when comparing one solution whose concentration of particles is $3.2 \times 10^{-11}$ mol/L with a second solution whose concentration of particles is $4.1 \times 10^{-9}$ mol/L, you should visualize the second solution as hundreds of times more concentrated than the first.

Pay special attention to magnitudes when adding. For example try solving:

$$
\begin{array}{r}
3.74 \times 10^{-15} \\
+ \ 6.43 \times 10^{-3} \\
\hline
\end{array}
$$

On the MCAT, the answer is simply $6.43 \times 10^{-3}$. This is true because $6.43 \times 10^{-3}$ is so much greater than $3.74 \times 10^{-15}$ that $3.74 \times 10^{-15}$ is negligible. Thus you can round off the answer to $6.43 \times 10^{-3}$. After all, the exact answer is 0.00643000000000374. Try solving:

$$
\begin{array}{r}
5.32 \times 10^{-4} \\
\times \ 1.12 \times 10^{-13} \\
\hline
\end{array}
$$

The MCAT answer is something greater than $5.3 \times 10^{-17}$. We cannot ignore the smaller number in this case because we are multiplying. **In addition or subtraction, a number 100 times smaller or more can be considered negligible. This is not true in multiplication or division.**

**The fastest way to add or subtract numbers in scientific notation is to make the exponents match.** For instance:

$$
\begin{array}{r}
2.76 \times 10^{4} \\
+ \ 6.91 \times 10^{5} \\
\hline
\end{array}
$$

The MCAT answer is something less than $7.2 \times 10^5$. To get this answer quickly we match the exponents and rewrite the equation as follows:

$$\begin{array}{r} 2.76 \times 10^4 \\ + \quad 69.1 \ \times 10^4 \\ \hline \end{array}$$

This is similar to the algebraic equation:

$$\begin{array}{r} 2.76y \\ + \quad 69.1y \\ \hline \end{array}$$

where $y = 10^4$. We simply add the coefficients of $y$. Rounding, we have $3y + 69y = 72y$. Thus $72 \times 10^4$, or $7.2 \times 10^5$ is the answer.

When rearranging $6.91 \times 10^5$ to $69.1 \times 10^4$, we simply multiply by 10/10 (a form of 1). In other words, we multiply 6.91 by 10 and divide $10^5$ by 10.

$$6.91 \times 10^5 \overset{\times 10}{\underset{\div 10}{=}} 69.1 \times 10^4$$

A useful mnemonic for remembering which way to move the decimal point when we add or subtract from the exponent is to use the acronym LARS,

$$\text{L}_{\text{eft}} \text{ A}_{\text{dd}}, \text{ R}_{\text{ight}} \text{ S}_{\text{ubtract}}$$

## i.6 Multiplication and Division

When multiplying similar bases with exponents, add the exponents; when dividing, subtract the exponents. $10^4 \times 10^5 = 10^9$. $10^4/10^{-6} = 10^{10}$.

When multiplying or dividing with scientific notation, we deal with the exponential terms and mantissa separately, *regardless of the number of terms*. For instance:

$$\frac{\left(3.2 \times 10^4\right) \times \left(4.9 \times 10^{-8}\right)}{\left(2.8 \times 10^{-7}\right)}$$

should be rearranged to:

$$\frac{3 \times 5}{3} \times \frac{10^4 \times 10^{-8}}{10^{-7}}$$

giving us an MCAT answer of something greater than $5 \times 10^3$. (The exact answer, $5.6 \times 10^3$, is greater than our estimate because we decreased one term in the numerator by more than we increased the other, which would result in a low estimate, and because we increased the term in the denominator, which also results in a low estimate.)

When taking a term written in scientific notation to some power (such as squaring or cubing it), we also deal with the decimal and exponent separately. The MCAT answer to:

$$(3.1 \times 10^7)^2$$

is something greater than $9 \times 10^{14}$. Recall that **when taking an exponential term to a power, we multiply the exponents.**

The first step in taking the square root of a term in scientific notation is to make the exponent even. Then we take the square root of the mantissa and exponential term separately.

$$\sqrt{8.1 \times 10^5}$$

**Make the exponent even.**

$$\sqrt{81 \times 10^4}$$

**Take the square root of the mantissa and exponential term separately.**

$$\sqrt{81} \times \sqrt{10^4} = 9 \times 10^2$$

Notice how much more efficient this method is. What is the square root of 49,000? Most students start thinking about 700, or 70, or something with a 7 in it. By using the scientific notation method, we quickly see that there is no 7 involved at all.

$$\sqrt{49,000} = \sqrt{4.9 \times 10^4} \approx 2.2 \times 10^2$$

Try finding the square root of 300 and the square root of 200.

## Practice Problems

*Solve the following problems without a calculator. Try not to use a pencil.*

1. $\dfrac{2.3 \times 10^7 \times 5.2 \times 10^{-5}}{4.3 \times 10^2}$

   A. $1.2 \times 10^{-1}$
   B. $2.8$
   C. $3.1 \times 10$
   D. $5.6 \times 10^2$

2. $(2.5 \times 10^{-7} \times 3.7 \times 10^{-6}) + 4.2 \times 10^2$

   A. $1.3 \times 10^{-11}$
   B. $5.1 \times 10^{-10}$
   C. $4.2 \times 10^2$
   D. $1.3 \times 10^{15}$

3. $[(1.1 \times 10^{-4}) + (8.9 \times 10^{-5})]^{1/2}$

   A. $1.1 \times 10^{-2}$
   B. $1.4 \times 10^{-2}$
   C. $1.8 \times 10^{-2}$
   D. $2.0 \times 10^{-2}$

4. $\frac{1}{2}(3.4 \times 10^2)(2.9 \times 10^8)^2$

   A. $1.5 \times 10^{18}$
   B. $3.1 \times 10^{18}$
   C. $1.4 \times 10^{19}$
   D. $3.1 \times 10^{19}$

5. $\dfrac{1.6 \times 10^{-19} \times 15}{36^2}$

   A. $1.9 \times 10^{-21}$
   B. $2.3 \times 10^{-17}$
   C. $1.2 \times 10^{-9}$
   D. $3.2 \times 10^{-9}$

**Answers**

1. B is correct. The exact answer is 2.7814.

2. C is correct. The other numbers are insignificant.

3. B is correct. The exact answer is $1.4107 \times 10^{-2}$.

4. C is correct. The exact answer is $1.4297 \times 10^{19}$.

5. A is correct. The exact answer is $1.8519 \times 10^{-21}$.

On the MCAT, proportional relationships between variables can often be used to circumvent lengthy calculations or, in some cases, the MCAT question simply asks the test taker to identify the relationship directly. When the MCAT asks for the change in one variable due to the change in another, they are making the assumption that all other variables remain constant.

In the equation $F = ma$, we see that if we double $F$ while holding $m$ constant, $a$ doubles. If we triple $F$, $a$ triples. The same relationship holds for $m$ and $F$. This type of relationship is called a **direct proportion**.

$$\overset{\times 2}{F} = m\overset{\times 2}{a}$$

$F$ and $a$ are directly proportional.

Notice that if we change the equation to $F = ma + b$, the directly proportional relationships are destroyed. Now if we double $F$ while holding all variables besides $a$ constant, $a$ increases, but does not double. **In order for variables to be directly proportional to each other, they must both be in the numerator or denominator when they are on opposite sides of the equation, or one must be in the numerator while the other is in the denominator when they are on the same side of the equation. In addition, all sums or differences in the equation must be contained in parentheses and multiplied by the rest of the equation. No variables within the sums or differences will be directly proportional to any other variable.**

If we examine the relationship between $m$ and $a$, in $F = ma$, we see that when $F$ is held constant and $m$ is doubled, $a$ is reduced by a factor of 2. This type of relationship is called an **inverse proportion**. Again the relationship is destroyed if we add $b$ to one side of the equation. **In order for variables to be inversely proportional to each other, they must both be in the numerator or denominator when they are on the same side of the equation, or one must be in the numerator while the other is in the denominator when they are on opposite sides of the equation. In addition, all sums or differences in the equation must be contained in parentheses and multiplied by the rest of the equation. No variables within the sums or differences will be directly proportional to any other variable.**

$$F = m\overset{\times 2}{\underset{\div 2}{a}}$$

$m$ and $a$ are inversely proportional.

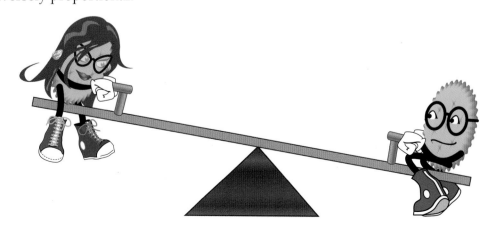

If we examine a more complicated equation, the same rules apply. However, we have to take care when dealing with exponents. One method to solve an equation using proportions is as follows. Suppose we are given the following equation:

$$Q = \frac{\Delta P \pi r^4}{8\eta L}$$

This is Poiseuille's Law. The volume flow rate $Q$ of a real fluid through a horizontal pipe is equal to the product of the change in pressure $\Delta P$, $\pi$, and the radius of the pipe to the fourth power $r^4$, divided by 8 times the viscosity $\eta$ and the length $L$ of the pipe.

Water ($\eta$ = 1.80 × 10$^{-3}$ Pa s) flows through a pipe with a 14.0 cm radius at 2.00 L/s. An engineer wishes to increase the length of the pipe from 10.0 m to 40.0 m without changing the flow rate or the pressure difference. What radius must the pipe have?

    **A.**    12.1 cm
    **B.**    14.0 cm
    **C.**    19.8 cm
    **D.**    28.0 cm

**Answer:** The only way to answer this question is with proportions. Most of the information is given to distract you. Notice that the difference in pressure between the ends of the pipe is not even given and the flow rate would have to be converted to m$^3$/s. To answer this question using proportions, multiply $L$ by 4 and $r$ by $x$. Now pull out the 4 and the $x$. We know by definition, $Q = \Delta P \pi r^4/8\eta L$; thus, $x^4/4$ must equal 1. Solve for $x$, and this is the change in the radius. The radius must be increased by a factor of about 1.4. 14 × 1.4 = 19.6. The new radius is approximately 19.6 cm. The closest answer is C.

$$Q = \frac{\Delta P \pi r^4}{8\eta L}$$

$$Q = \frac{\Delta P \pi (xr)^4}{8\eta (4L)}$$

$$Q = \frac{\Delta P \pi r^4}{8\eta L} \times \frac{x^4}{4}$$

$$4 = x^4$$

$$x = \sqrt{2}$$

## Practice Questions:

1. The coefficient of surface tension is given by the equation $\gamma = (F - mg)/(2L)$, where $F$ is the net force necessary to pull a submerged wire of weight $mg$ and length $L$ through the surface of the fluid in question. The force required to remove a submerged wire from water was measured and recorded. If an equal force is required to remove a separate submerged wire with the same mass but twice the length from fluid $x$, what is the coefficient of surface tension for fluid $x$? ($\gamma_{water} = 0.073$ mN/m)

   A. 0.018 mN/m
   B. 0.037 mN/m
   C. 0.073 mN/m
   D. 0.146 mN/m

2. A solid sphere rotating about a central axis has a moment of inertia

$$I = \frac{2}{3}MR^2$$

   where $R$ is the radius of the sphere and $M$ is its mass. Although Callisto, a moon of Jupiter, is approximately the same size as the planet Mercury, Mercury is 3 times as dense. How do their moments of inertia compare?

   A. The moment of inertia for Mercury is 9 times greater than for Callisto.
   B. The moment of inertia for Mercury is 3 times greater than for Callisto.
   C. The moment of inertia for Mercury is equal to the moment of inertia for Callisto.
   D. The moment of inertia for Callisto is 3 times greater than for Mercury.

3. The force of gravity on an any object due to earth is given by the equation $F = G(m_o M/r^2)$ where $G$ is the gravitational constant, $M$ is the mass of the earth, $m_o$ is the mass of the object and $r$ is the distance between the center of mass of the earth and the center of mass of the object. If a rocket weighs $3.6 \times 10^6$ N at the surface of the earth what is the force on the rocket due to gravity when the rocket has reached an altitude of $1.2 \times 10^4$ km? ($G = 6.67 \times 10^{-11}$ Nm$^2$/kg$^2$, radius of the earth = 6370 km, mass of the earth = $5.98 \times 10^{24}$ kg)

   A. $1.2 \times 10^5$ N
   B. $4.3 \times 10^5$ N
   C. $4.8 \times 10^6$ N
   D. $9.6 \times 10^6$ N

4. The kinetic energy $E$ of an object is given by $E = \frac{1}{2}mv^2$ where $m$ is the object's mass and $v$ is the velocity of the object. If the velocity of an object decreases by a factor of 2 what will happen its kinetic energy?

   A. Kinetic energy will increase by a factor of 2.
   B. Kinetic energy will increase by a factor of 4.
   C. Kinetic energy will decrease by a factor of 2.
   D. Kinetic energy will decrease by a factor of 4.

5. Elastic potential energy in a spring is directly proportional to the square of the displacement of one end of the spring from its rest position while the other end remains fixed. If the elastic potential energy in the spring is 100 J when it is compressed to half its rest length, what is its energy when it is compressed to one fourth its rest length?

   A. 50 J
   B. 150 J
   C. 200 J
   D. 225 J

---

**Answers**

1. B is correct. $\gamma$ and $L$ are inversely proportional.

2. B is correct. Since the bodies are the same size and Mercury is 3 times denser, Mercury is 3 times more massive. Mass is directly proportional to moment of inertia.

3. B is correct. If you are good with scientific notation, it is easy to see that $r$ is tripled. $r$ is the distance from the center of the Earth to the earth's surface. The Satellite is two Earth radii from the surface of the Earth, so it is three Earth radii from the center of the earth. Since the square of $r$ is inversely proportional to F, $F$ must be divided by 9.

4. D is correct. $E$ is directly proportional to $v^2$.

5. D is correct. If we imagine a spring 100 cm long at rest (We can use any spring length but 100 is always a good choice.) then the initial displacement is 50 cm and the final displacement is 75 cm. The displacement is increased by a factor of 1.5, thus the energy is increased by a factor of $1.5^2$. $1.5^2$ is greater than $1.4^2$ or greater than 2. Thus the energy is greater than $2 \times 100$.

## i.8 Graphs

The MCAT requires that you recognize the graphical relationship between two variables in certain types of equations. The three graphs below are the most commonly used. You should memorize them. The first is a directly proportional relationship, the second is an exponential relationship, and the third is an inversely proportional relationship.

Note: *n* is greater than zero for the graph of $y = nx$, and *n* is greater than one for the other two graphs.

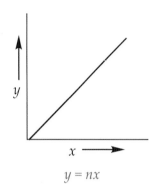
$$y = nx$$

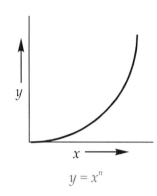
$$y = x^n$$

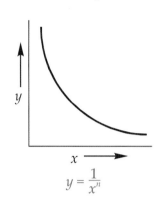
$$y = \frac{1}{x^n}$$

Notice that, if we add a positive constant $b$ to the right side, the graph is simply raised vertically by an amount $b$. If we subtract a positive constant $b$ from the right side, the graphs are shifted downwards.

As long as the value of *n* is within the given parameters, the general shape of the graph will not change.

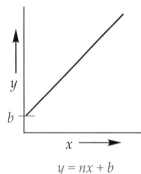
$$y = nx + b$$

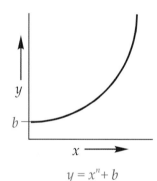
$$y = x^n + b$$

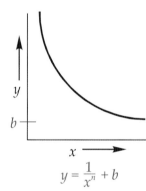
$$y = \frac{1}{x^n} + b$$

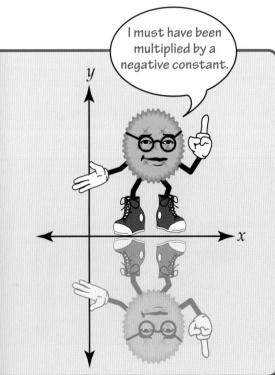

I must have been multiplied by a negative constant.

When graphs are unitless, multiplying the right side of an equation by a positive constant will not change the shape of the graph. If one side of the equation is negative, or multiplied by a negative constant, the graph is reflected across the $x$ axis.

**Whenever the MCAT asks you to identify the graphical relationship between two variables you should assume that all other variables in the equation are constants unless told otherwise.** Next, manipulate the equation into one of the above forms (with or without the added constant $b$, and choose the corresponding graph.

If you are unsure of a graphical relationship, plug in 1 for all variables except the variables in the question and then plug in 0, 1, and 2 for $x$ and solve for $y$. Plot your results and look for the general corresponding shape.

## Practice Questions

1. The height of an object dropped from a building in the absence of air resistance is given by the equation $h = h_o + v_o t + \frac{1}{2} g t^2$, where $h_o$ and $v_o$ are the initial height and velocity respectively and $g$ is $-10$ m/s$^2$. If $v_o$ is zero which graph best represents the relationship between $h$ and $t$?

A.

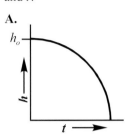

B.

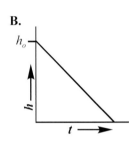

C.

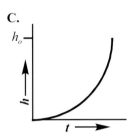

D.

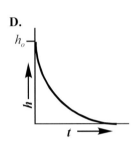

2. Which of the following graphs best describes the magnitude of the force ($F$) on a spring obeying Hooke's law ($F = -k\Delta x$) as it is compressed to $\Delta x_{max}$?

A.

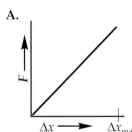

B.

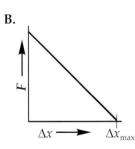

C.

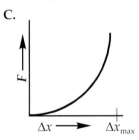

D.

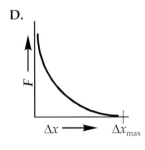

3. Which of the following graphs shows the relationship between frequency and wavelength of electromagnetic radiation through a vacuum? ($c = \nu \lambda$)

A.

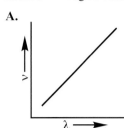

B.

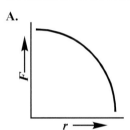

C.

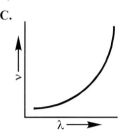

D.

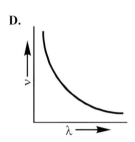

4. Which of the following graphs best describes the magnitude of the electrostatic force $F = k(qq)/r^2$ created by an object with negative charge on an object with a positive charge as the distance $r$ between them changes?

A.

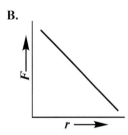

B.

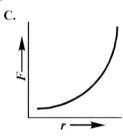

C.

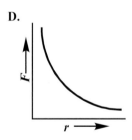

D.

**5.** Which of the following graphs demonstrates the relationship between power $P$ and work $W$ done by a machine? ($P = W/t$)

**A.**

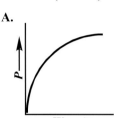

**C.**

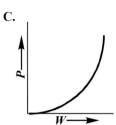

**B.**

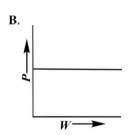

**D.**

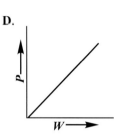

---

# STRATEGY AND TACTICS

## 1.1 The Layout of the Verbal Reasoning Section

The Verbal Reasoning Section of the MCAT is composed of seven passages, averaging 600 words per passage. Generally, a passage discusses a topic from the humanities, social sciences, or natural sciences. Six to ten multiple-choice questions follow each passage for a total of 40 questions. Answers to these questions do not require information beyond the text of the passage. The test taker has 60 minutes to complete the entire section.

## 1.2 Other Verbal Strategies

Dogma about the Verbal Section is abundant and free, and that's an accurate reflection of its value. There are many cock-a-mamie verbal strategies touted by various prep companies, academics, and well-wishers. **We strongly suggest that you ignore them.** Some test prep companies design their verbal strategy to be marketable (to make money) as opposed to being efficient (raise your score); the idea being that unique and strange will be easier to sell than commonplace and practical. Desperate techniques such as note taking and skimming are prime examples.

Some colleges offer classes designed specifically to improve reading comprehension in the MCAT Verbal Section. Typically, such classes resemble English 101 and are all but useless at improving your score. They are often taught by well-meaning humanities professors who have never even seen a real MCAT verbal section. Being a humanities professor does not qualify you as an expert at the MCAT Verbal Section. The emphasis in such classes is usually on detailed analysis of what you read rather than how to eliminate wrong answers and find correct answers. Improvements are predictably miserable.

There are those who will tell you that a strong performance on the verbal section requires speed-reading techniques. This is not true. Most speed-reading techniques actually prove to be an impediment to score improvements by shifting focus from comprehension to reading technique. It is unlikely that you will improve both your speed and comprehension in a matter of weeks. As you will soon see, speed is not the key to a good MCAT verbal score. Finishing the Verbal Section is within the grasp of everyone, if they follow the advice posited by this book.

If your college professor hasn't taken the MCAT, why would you take his advice on it?

"Reading a lot" isn't going to get you a better score on the Verbal section. Using the *EK method* will.

A favorite myth of MCAT students is that copious amounts of reading will improve scores on the Verbal Section. This myth originated years ago when one prep company having insufficient verbal practice materials suggested that their students "read a lot" rather than use the other companies' materials. The myth has perpetuated itself ever since. "Reading a lot" is probably the least efficient method of improving your verbal score. If you intend to take the MCAT four or five years hence, you should begin "reading a lot". If you want to do well on the Verbal Reasoning Section this year, use the strategies that follow.

## 1.3 Take Our Advice

Most smart students listen to advice, then pick and choose the suggestions that they find reasonable while disregarding the rest. This is not the most efficient approach for preparing to take the MCAT Verbal Section. In fact, it is quite counter-productive. Please abandon all your old ideas about verbal and follow our advice to the letter. Don't listen to your friends and family. They are not experts at teaching students how to score well on the MCAT Verbal Reasoning Section. We are.

## 1.4 Expected Improvement

Taking the MCAT verbal section is an art. (Not exactly what a science major wants to hear!) Like any art form, improvement comes gradually with lots of practice. Imagine attending a class in portraiture taught by a great artist. You wouldn't expect to become a Raphael after your first lesson, but you would expect to improve after weeks of coaching. The verbal section is the same way. Follow our directions to the letter, and with practice you will see dramatic improvements over time.

## 1.5 The Examkrackers Approach to MCAT Verbal Reasoning

We shall examine the verbal section on two levels: strategic and tactical. The strategic point of view will encompass the general approach to the section as a whole. The tactical point of view will explain exactly what to do, passage by passage, and question by question.

### Strategy

There are four aspects to strategy:

1. Energy

2. Focus

3. Confidence

4. Timing

## Energy

**Pull your chair close to the table. Sit up straight. Place your feet flat on the floor, and be alert.** This may seem to be obvious advice to some, but it is rarely followed. Test-takers often look for the most comfortable position to read the passage. Do you really believe that you do your best thinking when you're relaxed? Webster's Dictionary gives the definition of relaxed as "freed from or lacking in precision or stringency." Is this how you want to be on your MCAT? Your cerebral cortex is most active when your sympathetic nervous system is in high gear, so don't deactivate it by relaxing. Your posture makes a difference to your score.

Sit up straight young man!

One strategy of the test writers is to wear you down with the verbal section before you begin the biology section. You must mentally prepare yourself for the tremendous amount of energy necessary for a strong performance on the verbal section. Like an intellectual athlete, you must train yourself to concentrate for long periods of time. You must improve your reading comprehension stamina. **Practice! Practice! Practice!** always under timed conditions. **And always give 100% effort when you practice.** If you give less than 100% when you practice, you will be teaching yourself to relax when you take the verbal section, and you will be lowering your score. It is more productive to watch TV than to practice with less than complete effort. If you are not mentally worn after finishing three or more verbal passages, then you have not tried hard enough, and you have trained yourself to do it incorrectly; you have lowered your score. Even when you are only practicing, sit up straight in your chair and attack each passage.

## Focus

The verbal section is made up of seven passages with both interesting and boring topics. It is sometimes difficult to switch gears from "the migration patterns of the Alaskan tit-mouse" to "economic theories of post-Soviet Russia." In other words, sometimes you may be reading one passage while thinking about the prior passage. You must learn to **focus your attention on the task at hand**. We will discuss methods to increase your focus when we discuss tactics.

During the real MCAT, it is not unlikely that unexpected interruptions occur. People get physically ill, nervous students breathe heavily, air conditioners break down, and lights go out. Your score will not be adjusted for unwelcome interruptions, and excuses will not get you into med school, so learn to focus and **ignore distractions**.

## Confidence

There are two aspects to confidence on the Verbal Section: 1) **be confident of your score** and 2) **be arrogant when you read**.

Imagine taking a multiple choice exam and narrowing 50% of the questions down to just two answer choices, and then guessing. On a physics exam, this would almost certainly indicate a very low grade. Yet, this exact situation describes a stellar performance on the Verbal Section of the MCAT. Everyone of whom we know that has earned a perfect score on the Verbal Section (including many of our own students) has guessed on a large portion of the answers. The test writers are aware that most students can predict their grade on science exams based upon their performance, and that guessing makes science majors extremely uncomfortable. The Verbal Section is the most dissatisfying in terms of perceived performance. You should realize that even the best test takers finish the Verbal Section with some frustration and insecurity concerning their performance. A perceived dissatisfactory performance early in the testing day is likely to reflect poorly in scores on the Biology Section. You should assume that you have guessed correctly on every answer of the verbal section and get psyched to ace the Biological Sciences Section.

You the man!

The second aspect of confidence concerns how you read the passage. Read the passages as if you were a Harvard professor grading high school essays. Read critically. If you are confused while reading the passage, assume that it is the passage writer, and not you, who is at fault. If you find a contradiction in the reasoning of the argument, trust your reasoning ability that you are correct. The questions will focus on the author's argument and you must be confident of the strong and weak points. In order to identify the strong and weak points, you must read with confidence, even arrogance.

Timing

If you want a 10 or better on the Verbal Section, you must read every passage and attempt to answer every question. If you want to go to medical school, you should attempt to score 10 on the Verbal Section. Therefore, **read every passage in the order given, and attempt every question**.

Skipping around in the Verbal Section to find the easiest passages is a marketable strategy for a prep company but an obvious waste of time for you. It is a bad idea that makes a lot of money for some prep companies because it's an easy trick to sell. 'Cherry picking' is an unfortunate carry over from SAT strategy where it works because the questions are prearranged in order of difficulty. On the MCAT, some passages are difficult to read, but have easy questions; some passages are easy to read, but have difficult questions. Some passages start out difficult and finish easy. You have no way of knowing if a passage is easy or difficult until you have read the entire passage and attempted all the questions, so 'cherry picking' lowers your score.

If you begin reading a passage and are asking yourself "Should I continue, or should I move on to the next passage? Is this passage easy or difficult?", then you are not reading with confidence; you are not concentrating on what the author is saying; and you are wasting valuable time. Your energy and focus should be on doing well on each passage, not on trying to decide which passage to do first.

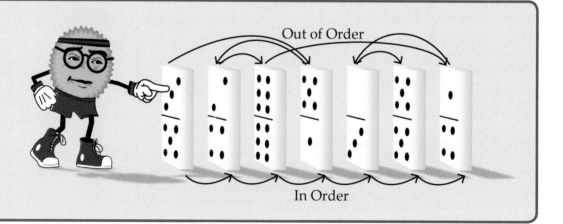

Hmmm. Let's see. I must knock down all seven dominos. Is it faster and more efficient to knock them down in order, or is it faster to decide which one is heaviest and then run back and forth and knock them down out of order?

Out of Order

In Order

Check your time only once during the Verbal Section. Constantly checking your time is distracting and not very useful since some passages take longer to finish than others. Instead, **check your time only once, and after you have finished the 4th passage**. You should have about 25 minutes left. A well-practiced test taker will develop a sense of timing acute enough to obviate looking at the time at all.

Don't spend too much time with the difficult questions. **Guess at the difficult questions and move on.** Guessing is very difficult for science students, who are accustomed to being certain of the answer on an exam or getting the answer wrong. Test writers are aware of this, and use it to their advantage. You should learn to give up on difficult questions so that you have more time on easier questions. Accurate guessing on difficult questions is one of the keys to finishing the exam and getting a perfect score. To accurately guess, you must learn to use all your tools for answering the questions. We will discuss this when we discuss tactics.

**Finish the entire section with two minutes to spare**, no more, no less. If you have more than two minutes to spare, you missed questions on which you could have spent more time. The stress of exam taking actually makes you more perspicacious while you take the exam. When you finish an exam, even if you intend to go back and check your work, you typically breathe a sigh of relief. Upon doing so, you lose your perspicacity. The best strategy is to use your time efficiently during your first and only pass through the exam.

Some people have difficulty finishing the exam. These people often think that they can't finish because they read too slowly. This is not the case. In tactics, we will discuss how finishing the exam does not depend upon reading speed and that anyone can finish the exam.

## 1.6 Tactics

Although, at first glance, it may not appear so, the following techniques are designed to increase your pace and efficiency. Tactics is where many students begin to pick and choose a verbal method that they think best suits their own personality. Please don't do this. Follow these steps exactly for each passage and after much practice your verbal score will move to a ten or above.

- **Take a five second break**

- **Read every word**

- **Construct a main idea**

- **Use all four tools to answer the questions:**

    1. going back;

    2. the main idea;

    3. the question stems; and

    4. the answer choices.

### The Five Second Break

If we went back to when the MCAT used to be a paper and pencil exam, and we observed a room full of MCAT test takers just after the sentence "You may break the seal of your test booklet and begin," we would see a room full of people frantically tear open their test booklets, read for 20 to 30 seconds, pause, and then begin rereading from the beginning. Why? Because as they race through the first passage, they are thinking about what is happening to them ("I'm taking the real MCAT! Oh my God!"), and not thinking about what they are reading. They need a moment to become accustomed to the idea that the MCAT has actually begun. They need a moment to focus. However, they don't need 20 to 30 seconds! They take so much time because they are trying to do two things at once; calm themselves down and understand the passage. They end up accomplishing neither. This loss of concentration may also occur at the beginning of each new passage, when the test-taker may still be struggling with thoughts of the previous passage while reading the new passage.

Many test-takers are able to guess on difficult questions during a practice exam, but when it comes to the real MCAT, they want to be certain of the answers. This meticulous approach has cost such students dearly on their scaled score. Learn to guess at difficult questions so you have time to answer the easy questions.

Finish the entire section with two minutes to spare.

Your brain needs breaks, and will take them regardless. If you schedule them yourself, you won't risk breaking your concentration in the middle of a passage.

If we continued to observe the test-takers, we would see them in the midst of a passage suddenly stop everything, lift up their head, stretch, yawn, or crack their knuckles. This is their beleaguered mind forcing them to take a break. No one has an attention span 60 minutes long. If you don't allow yourself a break, your mind will take one. How many times have you been reading a passage when suddenly you realize that you weren't concentrating? You're forced to start the passage over. More time is wasted.

There is a simple method to prevent all this lost time. Instead of taking breaks at random, inconvenient moments, plan your breaks. **Before each passage, including the first passage, take five seconds to focus your thoughts.** Remind yourself to forget the last passage and all other thoughts not related to the task at hand. Remind yourself to sit up straight, concentrate, and focus. For these five seconds, look away from the page, stretch your muscles and prepare to give your full attention to the next passage. Then begin and don't break your concentration until you have finished answering all the questions to that passage. The five second break is like a little pep-talk before each passage.

Unfortunately, most students will not take the five second break. Understand one thing. All students will take breaks during the verbal section. Most will take them without realizing it, and most will take them at inopportune moments. If your goal is to get the highest verbal score of which you are capable, you should take the five second break at planned intervals.

## Reading the Passage

Most test takers have difficulty finishing the verbal section in the 60 minutes allowed. Strangely enough, any premed without a reading disorder is capable of reading 4200 words in around 20 minutes. A very slow reader can easily read every word of a 600 word passage in 3 minutes. Try it! It's true! This leaves about 40 minutes to answer the questions, or around one minute per question to answer the questions. In other words, about two thirds of your time is spent answering questions on the MCAT Verbal Section, and less than one third is spent reading. If you read TWICE as fast as you do now, you would have about 70 seconds, instead of 60 seconds, to answer each question. **So increasing your reading speed has very little effect on your verbal score.** If you're not finishing now, you won't finish by reading faster.

| ← 60 minutes → | |
| --- | --- |
| Time spent reading | Time spent answering questions |

It's not your reading speed that you need to improve; it's your efficiency at answering the questions.

Improving your efficiency at answering questions will be more profitable than increasing your reading speed. Improving your efficiency at answering the questions will also allow you more time to read the passage. If you increase your reading speed by 10%, a strong improvement, you will only gain 2 minutes on the entire exam. Spread over 40 questions, this allows you an additional 3 seconds per question. Not too fruitful. If you increase your efficiency at answering questions by 10%, a rather simple task as you will soon see, you gain 4 minutes. This is easily enough time to read one entire additional passage!

Work on your efficiency at answering the questions, not your reading speed.

So why do so many test-takers fail to finish the verbal section? The answer is because they spend too much time hunting for the answer in the passage, and end up reading the passage many times over. We'll talk more about "looking back" at the passage when we discuss where to find the answer choice. For now, just believe us that **you can read every word in the verbal section and easily finish the exam**, so you should.

Have you ever tried skimming through a novel, not reading every word? Try it and see how much you understand. If you don't usually understand much when you skim, then why would you skim on the most important test of your life; especially when doing so won't give you much more time to answer the questions? **Don't skim.**

Have you ever mapped out a novel by writing a brief synopsis alongside each paragraph as you read? Try it. We think you will fall asleep from boredom. You will understand less of what you read, not more. Passages are intended to be read in their entirety as a single work presenting one overriding theme. MCAT expects you to understand this theme. The details within this theme are far less important. **Don't distract yourself by taking notes.**

The people that write the MCAT know that most of us are scientists. They know that we like to find the exact answer to things. Give us a mysterious powder and let us analyze it, and we will tell you exactly what it is. Show us the exact words in a passage as an answer choice and we will probably choose it. Don't fall for this trap. The Verbal Section tests your ability to detect and understand ambiguities and gray areas, not details. Rely heavily on your main idea and give little weight to details. If you are highly certain of all your answers on the Verbal Section, then you probably have fallen for all its traps. **Mastering this section is as much an art as a science.** With practice, you will develop a 'feel' for a good MCAT answer. Learn to use this 'feel' to help you move faster through the Verbal Section. If you teach yourself not to expect the concrete certainty that you get with science questions, you will become more comfortable with the Verbal Section and your score will increase.

The biggest mistake you can make on the verbal section is to consciously attempt to remember what you are reading. The vast majority of the questions will not concern the details of the passage and will not be answerable by searching the passage for facts. Most questions are about the main idea of the passage. The main idea will not be found in a list of details. In order to learn the main idea, the passage as a whole must be understood. Read the passage the way you would read an interesting novel; **concentrate on the main idea, not the detail**.

**An often posited tactic is to read the questions first; don't do it!** You will not remember even one question while you read the passage, much less the 6 to 10 questions that accompany every passage. In fact, a short term memory can contain 5 items; that may be why the passages are followed by six or more questions. Not only that, reading the questions first will force you to read for detail and you will never learn the main idea. You will probably end up rereading the passage many times but never straight through. This results in a tremendous waste of time.

When I create a great soup, you do not taste the salt, and each spice separately. You must experience the whole soup as a single, wonderful consommé.

Create an image of the author in your mind to help you understand the passages.

Some of the Verbal topics will fascinate you and some will bore you. The challenge will be to forget the ones that fascinate you as soon as you move to the next passage, and to pay close attention to the ones that bore you. **Train yourself to become excited and interested in any and every passage topic.** This will increase your comprehension. However, don't become so engrossed in a passage that you slow your pace.

**Don't use fancy speed reading techniques** where you search for meaningful words or try to read entire phrases in one thought. This will only distract you from your goal. Read the way you normally read. Your reading speed is unlikely to change significantly in 10 weeks, and your reading speed is not the problem anyway. Finishing the entire section depends upon how long you spend on the questions, not how long it takes you to read the passages. You also cannot assume that the passages are written well enough so that you can read just the first and last sentence of each paragraph. They are sometimes barely intelligible even when you read every word. You must read every word, read quickly and concentrate.

**Read each passage like you are listening to a friend tell you a very interesting story. Allow the details (names, dates, times) to slip in one ear and out the other**, while you wait with bated breath for the main point. The funny thing about this type of reading is that, when you practice it, you can't help but remember most of the details. Even if you were to forget some of the details, it only takes about 5 seconds to find a name, number, or key word in a 600 word passage. Thus, when you run into a rare question about a detail that you've forgotten, it is easy to find the answer. Another convenient aspect of this type of reading is that you are trying to accomplish exactly what the verbal section will be testing: your ability to pick out the main idea. The best thing about this type of reading is that you have practiced it every day of your life. This is the way that you read novels, newspapers and magazines. Read the passages the way that you read best; read for the main idea.

When you read, ask yourself, "What is the author trying to say? What is his point? Is he in favor of idea A or against it? If this author were sitting right in front of me, would he want to discuss idea A or is his real interest in idea B?" **Creating an image of the author in your mind will help you understand him.** Use your life experiences to stereotype the author. This will help you make quick, intuitive decisions about how the author might answer each MCAT question about his passage. Make careful mental note of anything the author says that may not fit your stereotype. Use the stereotype to help guide your intuition on the questions.

### The Main Idea

When you have finished reading a passage, take twenty seconds and construct a main idea in the form of one or two complete sentences. Verbal Reasoning Lecture 3 will cover how to construct a main idea. On a timed MCAT, writing the main idea requires too much time, so you should **spend 20 seconds mentally contemplating the main idea before you begin the questions**. After you have completed an entire timed practice exam, scored yourself, and taken a break, it is a good idea to go back to each passage and write out the main idea for practice.

### Answering the Questions

Answering the questions will be covered thoroughly in Verbal Reasoning Lecture 2. For now, attempt to answer the questions based upon the main idea and not the details.

# ANSWERING THE QUESTIONS

## 2.1 Tools to Find the Answer

For most students, the Verbal Reasoning Section is literally a test of their ability to comprehend what they have read. Such students read a question and choose the correct answer based upon what was said in the passage. If they do not arrive at an answer, they eliminate answer choices based upon what was said in the passage. If they still don't arrive at an answer, they search the passage for relevant information that they may have missed or don't recall. If they still don't arrive at a single answer choice, which is likely to be about 50% of the time with this method, they repeat the process until they give up and make a random guess in frustration. This method uses only about 50% of the information provided by the test. When you consider that a portion of the questions on a multiple choice test will be answered correctly by luck, it's no coincidence that the national mean score on the MCAT is attainable by answering only about 61% of the questions correctly. When you can't identify an answer, 'thinking harder' (whatever that means) is not an effective solution. Nor is an effective solution to search the passage until the answer jumps out at you. However, both methods consume your precious time.

In addition to your understanding of the passage, there are four tools that you should use to help you answer the questions. These four tools go beyond your understanding of the passage. They force you to consider additional information presented to you in the question stems and answer choices that is often overlooked or otherwise noticed only on a subconscious level.

The four tools are:

1. Looking Back,
2. The Main Idea,
3. The Question Stems, and
4. The Answer Choices.

You need to do more than just find the answer from what you read in the passage.

Just thinking harder won't work.

Use your four tools.

## Looking Back

'Looking back' refers to actually rereading parts of the passage to search for an answer. 'Looking back' should be **used only when:**

1. you are regularly finishing an exam on time,
2. you know what you're looking for, and
3. you know where you can find the answer.

'Looking back' is the most time consuming and least useful of the four tools. Unfortunately, it is the tool most often relied upon by inexperienced test takers. It is true that forgotten details can be found by rereading parts of the passage. However, most questions require an understanding of the main idea, not your memory of details. The main idea cannot be found by rereading parts of the passage.

'Word-for-word' and other traps have been set for the unwary test taker looking for the 'feel-good' answer. The 'feel-good' answer is an answer where a section of the passage seems to unequivocally answer the question so that the test taker *feels good* when choosing it. The 'feel-good' answer choice may even use a phrase from the passage word-for-word. This is often a trap. Remember, the Verbal Section is ambiguous and a simple clear answer is rarely the correct answer.

You should learn to use 'Looking Back' as seldom as possible. Most of the time, you should force yourself to choose the best answer without looking back at the passage. This is a difficult lesson to accept, but it is extremely important to achieving your top score. Looking back at the passage for anything but a detail will take large amounts of your testing time, and allow the test writers to skew your concept of the main idea by directing you toward specific parts of the passage. **If you are unable to finish the test in the time given, it is because you are overusing the 'Looking Back' tool.** If you are not finishing, you should not look back at all until you can regularly finish an entire verbal section with time left over.

Your number one goal should be to finish the Verbal Section. Difficult questions are worth no more than easy questions. **Don't sacrifice five easy questions by spending a long time answering a single difficult question. If you usually finish the Verbal section with time to spare, you can 'look back' to the passage more often; if you don't usually finish the Verbal section, you should stop looking back to the passage until you begin finishing within the allotted time on a regular basis.**

"Looking back" is a useful tool. Just use it wisely.

## Main Idea

The Main Idea is the most powerful tool for answering MCAT verbal questions. We will discuss The Main Idea in Verbal Reasoning Lecture 3.

---

If you're not finishing, then you are using the 'looking back' tool too long and too often.

If you usuallly don't have time to finish the verbal section, try taking a practice exam by reading the passage once through and then not allowing yourself to look back at the passage no matter what. You will finish with time left to spare, and your score will probably go up.

Now, you know you read fast enough to finish the exam. (Everyone reads fast enough; that's never the problem.) On the next practice exam, you can use the extra time that you know you will have at the end to take an occasional look back at the passage. But don't look too often or too long. Looking back is why you weren't finishing the exam in the first place.

It's not bad to use your 'Looking Back' tool; just don't over use it.

## Question Stems

The **question stems hold as much information as the passage.** Read these question stems taken from an actual AAMC MCAT passage and see how much you can learn about the passage from just the question stems.

The questions give as much information as the passage. You just have to learn to recognize and use this information.

1. The author of the passage believes that the fiction written by the current generation of authors:

2. The overall point made by the passage's comparison of movies to fiction is that:

3. According to the passage, John Gardner concedes that preliminary good advice to a beginning writer might be, "Write as if you were a movie camera." The word *concedes* here suggests that:

4. The fact that the author rereads *Under the Volcano* because it has been made into a movie is ironic because it:

5. The passage suggests that a reader who is not bored by a line-by-line description of a room most likely:

6. The passage suggests that if a contemporary writer were to write a novel of great forcefulness, this novel would most likely:

7. The passage places the blame for contemporary writers' loss of readers on the:

Ask yourself some questions about the author. What does he do for a living? How does he dress? What does he/she like to eat? How does he vote? How old is he? Is the author a he or a she? Look closely at each question stem and see what kind of information you get from it. Why are certain adjectives used? Who is John Gardner? What can I learn about the passage from these question stems?

Now, in the space below, write down everything that you can think of that is revealed about the passage from each stem. Include an answer to each of the seven question stems. (**Warning:** If you read on without writing the answers, you will miss an important opportunity to improve your verbal skills. Once you read on, the effect of the exercise will be ruined.)

1. _____

   _____

2. _____

   _____

3. _____

   _____

4. _____

   _____

5. _____

   _____

6. _____

   _____

7. _____

   _____

Information that can be gained from the seven previous question stems:

1.  The author of the passage believes that the fiction written by the current generation of authors:

From the first question stem, we immediately know that the passage was about the writing of fiction. The word 'current' suggests a comparison between authors of fiction from the past and the present.

2.  The overall point made by the passage's comparison of movies to fiction is that:

From the second question stem we learn that there is a comparison between movies and fiction. We also know that this was central to the author's point. The movies are a 'current' medium, while 'written fiction' might be considered older or in the past. Hmmm. What is the significance of this?

3.  According to the passage, John Gardner concedes that preliminary good advice to a beginning writer might be, "Write as if you were a movie camera." The word concedes here suggests that:

In question stem three, you need to wonder "Who is John Gardner?" You know he is not the author of the passage because on the MCAT, you never know the name of the author. Thus, a named identity will likely be someone whom the author used either to support his point or as an example of someone who has a bad idea. You should decide which. Now, even if the question didn't ask this, you should have asked yourself about the word 'concedes'. When you concede, you give in. So 'concedes' here indicates that Mr. Gardner is giving in to a point when he says "Write as if you were a movie camera." Mr. Gardner's argument must be that written fiction is not good when it's like the movies, but it is okay to write like a movie camera when you are a beginning writer. Notice how hesitant the wording is. 'Beginning' is emphasized by the use of both words 'preliminary' and 'beginning', and the word 'might' is also used.

At this point, you should begin forming a feeling of what this passage was about: movies versus fiction, current fiction versus past fiction, someone implying that movies don't make for good fiction. The author believes something about current fiction and makes a point about fiction and movies. Three question stems with no passage and not even answer choices to the questions, and we can already get a sense of the passage. The remaining question stems will confirm what the passage is about.

4.  The fact that the author rereads Under the Volcano because it has been made into a movie is ironic because it:

The fourth question stem indicates that a movie makes the author read a book. The question states that this is ironic. That means the actual result is incongruous with the expected result. Apparently, according to the author's argument, watching a movie should not make him read the book. Thus, part of the author's argument in the passage must be that movies make people less interested in reading. It is also reasonable to assume from this that the author used John Gardner in question stem #3 to support his argument, so the author probably believes that fiction written like a movie is not good fiction. Extrapolating further from the comparison of movies to fiction and the stated dichotomy between current and past fiction, the author is probably arguing that current fiction is not as good as old fiction.

5.  The passage suggests that a reader who is not bored by a line-by-line description of a room most likely:

The fifth passage compares the phrase 'line-by-line description' with the idea of boredom. It is a simple logical jump to equate 'line-by-line description' with past fiction as opposed to current fiction or movies. From our conclusions thus far about the author's argument, it would be logical to conclude that someone who is NOT bored by 'line-by-line descriptions' would NOT be bored by past fiction, but would, in fact, appreciate it as the author obviously does.

6. The passage suggests that if a contemporary writer were to write a novel of great forcefulness, this novel would most likely:

Question stem #6 reinforces our conclusion about the author's argument. The 'if' indicates that 'contemporary writers' do not 'write novels of great forcefulness'. Instead, they must be writing novels that resemble movies. The only question is "What would a novel of great forcefulness do?" Answering this question is as simple as seating the author in front of you and asking him. The amazing thing is that we already have a stereotypical idea of this author just by reading six question stems! This guy is a college English professor fed up with the quick fix satisfaction offered by movies. He would love a novel of great forcefulness. Does he think that we would appreciate it? Be careful here. He appreciates the novel because he truly believes that the novel itself is great, and not because he thinks he is great or better than everyone else. The answer is yes, he thinks that we would appreciate a novel of great forcefulness as well.

7. The passage places the blame for contemporary writers' loss of readers on the:

This last question stem answers the previous question. The seventh question stem says that current fiction is losing readers. It asks for the explanation. Of course, the author's whole point is to explain why current fiction is losing readership. It is because it is like movies and not forceful like past fiction.

What should be revealing and even shocking to you is that we can accurately answer every question on this actual AAMC passage without reading the passage. In fact, on this particular passage, we can accurately answer every question without reading the passage OR the answer choices. Most MCAT passages are like this. Did you realize that there was this much information in the question stems alone? Have you been using this information to answer the questions on the MCAT? If you haven't, you are capable of scoring many points higher on the MCAT Verbal Section. You can't expect to always be able to answer questions without the passage or the answer choices, but you can expect to gain much information about the passage from the question stems.

---

**1.**

    **A.** lacks the significance of fiction written by previous generations.

    **B.** is, as a whole, no better and no worse than fiction written by previous generations.

    **C.** brilliantly meets the particular needs of contemporary readers.

    **D.** is written by authors who show great confidence in their roles as writers.

**2.**

    **A.** contemporary authors have strengthened their fiction by the application of cinematic techniques.

    **B.** the film of Under the Volcano is bound to be more popular than the novel.

    **C.** great fiction provides a richness of language and feeling that is difficult to re-create in film.

    **D.** contemporary authors would be well advised to become screenwriters.

**3.**

    **I.** Gardner's approach to writing has been influenced by the competing medium of film.

    **II.** Gardner must have written screenplays at one point in his life.

    **III.** Gardner dislikes the medium of film.

    **A.** I only

    **B.** II only

    **C.** I and II only

    **D.** II and III only

**4.**

    **I.** seems to go against the overall point of the passage concerning fiction and film.

    **II.** implies that the film version was a box-office failure.

    **III.** hints that the author was dissatisfied with the novel.

    **A.** I only

    **B.** II only

    **C.** III only

    **D.** II and III only

**5.**

    **A.** prefers the quick fix of the movies.

    **B.** would be bored by a single shot of a room in a film.

    **C.** has no tolerance for movies.

    **D.** displays the attitude demanded by good fiction.

**6.**

    **I.** confuse and anger lovers of great literature.

    **II.** exist in stark contrast to the typical contemporary novel.

    **III.** win back some of the readers contemporary writers have lost.

    **A.** I only

    **B.** II only

    **C.** I and II only

    **D.** II and III only

**7.**

    **I.** competition presented by movies.

    **II.** writers themselves.

    **III.** ignorance of the public.

    **A.** I only

    **B.** II only

    **C.** I and II only

    **D.** I, II, and III

---

**STOP.** IF YOU FINISH BEFORE TIME IS CALLED, CHECK YOUR WORK. YOU MAY GO BACK TO ANY QUESTION IN THIS TEST BOOKLET.

---

## Answers to the Questions

### Question 1

Choice A, the answer to question #1 is exactly what we expected: past fiction is better than current fiction. Notice that we can simplify the choices to:

- **A.** Current fiction is not as good as past fiction.
- **B.** Current fiction is equal to past fiction.
- **C.** Current fiction is good.
- **D.** Current fiction is good.

Simplifying the question and the answer choices can make the correct answer easier to find. We'll discuss simplification later in this lecture. The main idea is all you needed to answer this question.

### Question 2

Choice C, the answer to question #2 is also exactly what we expected. The choices can be rephrased to:

- **A.** Movies have been good for fiction.
- **B.** Movies are more likeable than fiction.
- **C.** Movies aren't as good as good fiction.
- **D.** Authors of fiction should make movies.

When we put these questions to our author, the choice is obvious.

### Question 3

The answers to question #3 are not what we expected. We expected a more sophisticated question pertaining to the use of the word 'concedes'. Although the question told us much about the passage, the answer choices match a much simpler question than we anticipated, "Who is John Gardner?" The choices can be rephrased as:

- **I.** John Gardner has been influenced by movies.
- **II.** John Gardner wrote movies.
- **III.** John Gardner dislikes movies.

Clearly John Gardner has been influenced by movies if he is suggesting that writing like a movie might be good advice for a beginning writer. From the answer choices, we can see that if I is correct, then III is likely to be incorrect. If Gardner dislikes movies, it would be unlikely that he would be influenced by them. II is incorrect because Gardner would not have to have written movies in order to be influenced by them. Even if III were an option, and even if Gardner is like the author, liking good fiction more than movies isn't the same as disliking movies. Choice A is correct.

### Question 4

The answer to question #4 is exactly what we expected. The choices can be rephrased to:

- **I.** Seeing the movie shouldn't have made the author read the book.
- **II.** The movie flopped.
- **III.** The author didn't like the book.

Only choice I addresses the 'irony' suggested in the question. Only choice I pertains to the main idea. The answer is A.

### Question 5

Choice D, the answer to question #5 is exactly what we expected. The choices can be rephrased to:

- **A.** If you're patient, you'll prefer the fast pace of movies.
- **B.** If you're patient, you won't like waiting for action.
- **C.** If you're patient, you won't have the patience for the fast pace of movies.
- **D.** If you're patient, you'll like the careful pace of good fiction.

Choices A, B, and C seem to be self contradictory.

### Question 6

Choice D, the answer to question #6 is exactly what we expected. Remember that 'a novel of great forcefulness' describes past fiction to our author, and our author would expect us to like past fiction. This describes choices II and III.

### Question 7

Choice C, the answer to question #7 is exactly what we expected. Choice I restates the main idea that movies have hurt fiction. Certainly, our author is criticizing current authors, so choice II is also true. Choice III is not true based upon our idea that the author would expect us to like a forceful novel. The answer here is C.

---

For practice, try this exercise again on an Examkrackers' passage. Read these question stems and answer them in the blank lines given.

1. The passage suggests that most medieval thinkers of the 13th century were:

2. In the late 15th century, Christopher Columbus proposed an alternate passage to the Indies which would take him around the Earth. According to the passage, most of his educated contemporaries probably believed:

3. Based upon the information in the passage, which of the following events most likely occurred before 1300 A.D.?

4. The author probably believes that science in the 13th century:

5. Based upon the information in the passage, an educated person of the 13th century might explain the perpetual motion of the planets as:

6. The 13th century friar Roger Bacon argued that the progress of human knowledge was being impeded by excessive regard for ancient authorities. This information:

7. "Aristotle taught that natural science should be based on extensive observations, followed by reflection leading to scientific generalizations." (lines 3-5) The author would most likely agree with which of the following statements concerning this scientific method proffered by Aristotle?

1. _____

_____

2. _____

_____

3. _____

_____

4. _____

_____

5. _____

_____

6. _____

_____

7. _____

_____

## Discussion:

1. The passage suggests that most medieval thinkers of the 13th century were:

From the first question stem, we immediately know that the author gives us some opinion about "thinkers of the 13th century". Do not ignore the adverb "most". It doesn't tell us much, but it does hint of some moderation as to the tone of the passage. Compare the tone if we were to replace the word "most" with "all": "The passage suggests that all medieval thinkers of the 13th century were:"

Of course, we cannot yet answer the question with any accuracy, but let's just consider some possibilities. Does the author suggest that 13th century thinkers were naïve, well informed, foolish, clever, careful, brash, guided by religion, guided by reason, or what? Keep this in mind.

2. In the late 15th century, Christopher Columbus proposed an alternate passage to the Indies which would take him around the Earth. According to the passage, most of his educated contemporaries probably believed:

The second question stem tells us that we are not dealing with just the 13th century, but with a broader era of history that spans at least until the 15th century.

The question stem refers to a well known person from history. Certainly we all know something about Christopher Columbus. Do we dare use outside knowledge to answer an MCAT question? Of course we should! Use every ounce of knowledge you can muster to answer all questions on the MCAT. So, what things might contemporaries have believed about Columbus' journey? Columbus was sailing into the unknown, so the questions are likely to be about what he might find.

The question stem also repeats the theme of 'thinkers' with the words "educated contemporaries." We now know not only that the author is, at least, discussing educated thinkers from medieval times, but that he is giving his opinion as to how they thought. He is suggesting something about what these educated contemporaries probably believed about Columbus sailing around the Earth.

'Educated' is a key word. Imagine the question stem without the word 'educated'. "According to the passage, most of his contemporaries probably believed:" How does it change the answer? What is the difference between a 'contemporary'

and an 'educated contemporary'? Does the author suggest that *educated* contemporaries believed Columbus would fall off the edge of the world, or does he suggest that they believed that Columbus would find the new world? Because the question specifically mentions "around the Earth", this draws attention to the question of whether or not the world was thought to be round. Perhaps you are aware that Eratosthenes calculated the circumference of the Earth in 222 B.C. If so, you know that most educated people in the 15th century A.D. did not believe the Earth was flat. Even if you were not aware of this fact, the word 'educated' still strengthens the argument that the author is making the point that the 15th century thinker's thoughts may have been more accurate than most believe.

So we are expecting an answer that says 'educated contemporaries probably had reasonable expectations about Columbus' journey.

3. Based upon the information in the passage, which of the following events most likely occurred before 1300 A.D.?

Since we are asked to predict the chronology of certain events, the author must be discussing not just educated thought, but the progression of educated thought.

Additionally, we can begin to narrow in on the time period beginning before the 13th century and ending around 1500 A.D. (Remember that the 13th century is during the 1200s.) If you know your history, you know the author is discussing the late middle ages and early renaissance. How was educated thought progressing during this time? If you don't know your history, don't worry. It won't prevent you from answering the questions. However, you should at least know that educated thought was progressing.

Because the question asks about the early part of the progression of educated thought, (before the 13th century) and not the later part, (the 15th century) the answer choice should be an event that reflects less highly developed educated thought. Keep in mind that this is the MCAT and not a high school exam. The answer isn't likely to be as simple as "Thinkers were naïve in the 13th century and brilliant by the 15th century."

4. The author probably believes that science in the 13th century:

From this question stem, we see that the author is not just discussing educated thought, but science.

Like question 3, this question asks about the early part of the progress discussed in the passage. Again, we will choose an answer choice with this in mind.

Although we can assume that science in the 13th century was less like modern science than science in the 15th century, we still don't have enough information from the question stems alone to know how science changed.

5. Based upon the information in the passage, an educated person of the 13th century might explain the perpetual motion of the planets as:

This is almost the same question three times in a row. We might rephrase them as "Which of the following reflects a way of thinking early during or prior to the progress in thinking discussed in the passage?" However, we are still waiting to see the aspects and the extent of the change. One thing that we know is the explanation will be something different than a modern scientific explanation because there must be a progression to modern science.

6. The 13th century friar Roger Bacon argued that the progress of human knowledge was being impeded by excessive regard for ancient authorities. This information:

Finally we are given a clue about the aspect of change. Roger Bacon was a famous thinker from the 13th century. If you know anything about Roger Bacon, do not be afraid to use that knowlege. Assuming we have no outside knowledge, the stem tells us that Bacon thought thinkers of the 13th century relied too heavily upon ancient thinkers. You should ask yourself, "13th century thinkers relied on ancient thinkers as opposed to relying on what?" In other words, instead of just believing whatever ancient thinkers say, they should have done what? The answer should be obvious to any modern science student: You should investigate and think for yourself!

From our analysis thus far it appears that Bacon was used to support the author's argument.

The answer to this question is likely to go something like "This information supports the author's argument because it is evidence that 13th century thinkers were relying too much on ancient thinkers rather than thinking for themselves."

7. "Aristotle taught that natural science should be based on extensive observations, followed by reflection leading to scientific generalizations." (lines 3-5) The author would most likely agree with which of the following statements concerning this scientific method proffered by Aristotle?

As an MCAT student with a strong science background you should see that the method proposed is not only practical, but is the method currently in use by today's scientists. Even though, using the reasoning from question 6, we might be tempted to say that the author would disagree with an ancient source, we cannot override common sense. We must assume that the author would agree with this common sense statement made by Aristotle and that there is some kind of twist to this question that we are unable to predict from the question stem alone. We know the author thought early thinkers relied too heavily on ancient sources, but, in this case, it must have been a good thing. The MCAT is tricky like this.

---

We now have enough information to revisit and answer the earlier questions.

1. Revisited: Based on question 6, The passage suggests that most medieval thinkers of the 13th century were: too trusting of the work of the ancient thinkers and this impeded progress.

2. Revisited: We have already answered this to some extent, but the new information confirms: In the late 15th century, Christopher Columbus proposed an alternate passage to the Indies which would take him around the Earth. According to the passage, most of his educated contemporaries probably believed: his trip was at least possible.

3. Revisited: We still have no clue as to what events the answer choices will include, so we can only give a general answer. Based upon the information in the passage, the event that most likely occurred before 1300 A.D. was: one that, though perhaps more impressive than many modern students would expect, did not require too much advanced science.

4. Revisited: The author probably believes that science in the 13th century: was not completely primitive but not advanced either, or (from question 6) it relied upon ancient knowledge with few innovations.

5. Revisited: If we know about Aristotle's theory that objects like to be at rest, we will look for an answer that has something pushing the planets. Otherwise, we will need to be more general. Based upon the information in the passage, an educated person of the 13th century might explain the perpetual motion of the planets as: similar to the way ancient thinkers would have explained it, which is also somehow less scientific than renaissance science or modern science.

6. Revisited: As previously stated the answer to this question is likely to go something like "This information: supports the author's argument because it is evidence that 13th century thinkers were relying too much on ancient thinkers rather than thinking for themselves."

7. Revisited: As stated previously we must assume that The author would most likely agree that natural science should be based on extensive observations, followed by reflection leading to scientific generalizations and that there is some kind of twist to this question that we are unable to predict from the question stem alone.

**1.**

    **A.**    impractical mystics.
    **B.**    good empirical scientists.
    **C.**    somewhat superstitious.
    **D.**    confident of the veracity of Aristotelian physics.

**2.**

    **A.**    Columbus would fall off the edge of the earth.
    **B.**    the trip was possible in theory.
    **C.**    the sun was the center of the universe.
    **D.**    in Aristotelian physics.

**3.**

    **A.**    Spectacles for reading were invented.
    **B.**    Nicholas of Cusa conceived the idea of an infinite universe.
    **C.**    Scientists abandoned Aristotelian physics.
    **D.**    Raw sugar was refined.

**4.**

    **A.**    laid the ground work for modern science.
    **B.**    was the beginning of a scientific revolution.
    **C.**    is underestimated by modern historians.
    **D.**    was more practical than theoretical.

**5.**

    **A.**    propelled by a mysterious prime mover.
    **B.**    *impetus* resulting from an initial, tremendous push.
    **C.**    movement due to lack of any opposing force.
    **D.**    a violation of Aristotelian physics.

**6.**

    **A.**    weakens the claims made by the author because it is an example of a direct criticism of Aristotle's scientific presuppositions.
    **B.**    weakens the claims made by the author because it demonstrates that religion still dominated science in the 13th century.
    **C.**    strengthens the claims made by the author because it is evidence that 13th century thinkers were not questioning the scientific suppositions of Aristotle.
    **D.**    strengthens the claims made by the author because Aristotle was Greek, not Roman.

**7.**

    **A.**    This method had a stultifying effect on medieval science.
    **B.**    This method was faithfully practiced by most thirteenth century thinkers.
    **C.**    Practice of this method led to the *first major break with Aristotelian physics* (line 40) in the fourteenth century.
    **D.**    Extensive scientific observations of the thirteenth century resulted in gross inaccuracies in the interpretation of Aristotelian physics.

**STOP.** IF YOU FINISH BEFORE TIME IS CALLED, CHECK YOUR WORK. YOU MAY GO BACK TO ANY QUESTION IN THIS TEST BOOKLET.

## Answers to Questions

You should notice here that, although there was less information in the question stems in this passage than in the real AAMC passage, nevertheless that lack of information was made up for by information in the answer choices. In other words, in this passage, much of the information was in the answer choices. Still, the point is that you need to use all the information to answer a question and not just the words in the passage. In the next section we will discuss extraction of information from the answer choices. Now back to the answers to this passage.

### Question 1

Choice D is just what we thought: too much trust in ancient sources.

### Question 2

Choice B is, again, exactly what we might predict. Notice that choices C and D are what we expect from early thinkers, not later thinkers. Also choices C and D do not answer the question as precisely. Choice A does not represent the theme that 15th century thinkers were advancing in educated thought.

### Question 3

Choice A is correct. Our limited knowledge of only the question stem allows us to narrow the answer to A or D, but perhaps not choose between the two. It turns out that the author discussed pseudo-science of alchemy predating the 13th century. This makes choice D a poor choice, but we would have had to have read the passage to know this. On the MCAT, reading the passage is a good thing and recommended because it sometimes helps you answer the questions. Choice B is a theoretical advance. Recall from question #6 that early thinkers were relying on ancient thinkers rather than innovative thought. Choice C is wrong since the question refers to early thinkers. Again question #6 tells us that early thinkers weren't abandoning the ancient thinkers, but embracing them.

### Question 4

This one is very tough. Choice D is correct, and makes sense given our idea that there was little innovative thinking going on. However, choices A and B seem to be possibilities. Choice A is less of a possibility because 'modern' science does not arrive by the 15th century, so perhaps we can eliminate choice A. The weakness of choice B is the word 'revolution', but it is still not a bad answer based upon only the information in the question stems. Choice C doesn't seem to have any evidence for it.

We shouldn't be too concerned if we can't answer a question with absolute certainty based upon only the question stems. We still have the passage and the answer choices to consider. A close reading of all the answer choices of all the questions in this passage will reveal an underlying theme that is simply not in the question stems. That underlying theme is that science at the beginning of this period of scientific progression was more practical than theoretical. This theme is, of course, even more apparent with the reading of the passage.

### Question 5

Choice A is correct and probably, but not certainly, the best choice given our earlier conclusion. It is especially clear if you are familiar with Aristotelian physics where objects want to come to rest and require a force to remain in motion. Choices B and C are close to how we would explain it today, and thus wrong answers for how an early thinker would explain it. It turns out that choice B is actually specifically stated in the passage to be 14th century thought and thus clearly a wrong answer. Choice D contradicts the idea that 13th century thinkers were relying on ancient thinkers without thinking for themselves.

### Question 6

Choice C is correct and fits well with what we predicted.

### Question 7

Choice C is correct. This choice makes the most sense given our conclusion that the method was sound and used today and that there is some kind of twist. The twist is that Aristotle's own advice to base knowledge on observation led to the evidence that his physics was wrong. Thus, by following Aristotle's advice, the late thinkers were breaking with Aristotle. An irony that makes for a tricky MCAT question.

Each MCAT question has four possible answer choices. One of these will be the correct answer and the other three we will call *distracters*. Typically, when a verbal question is written, the correct answer choice is written first and then distracters are created. Because the correct answer is written to answer a specific question and a distracter is written to confuse, the two can often be distinguished without even referencing the question. In other words, with practice, a good test-taker can sometimes distinguish the correct answer among the distracters without even reading the question or the passage. This is a difficult skill to acquire and is gained only through sufficient practice.

Begin by learning to recognize typical distracter types. Among other things, effective distracters may be: a statement that displays a subtle misunderstanding of the main idea, a statement that uses the same or similar words as in the passage but is taken out of context, a true statement that does not answer the question, a statement that answers more than the question asks, or a statement that relies upon information commonly considered true but not given in the passage.

Think of 'Round-abouts' as the kind of answer a politician would give; it sounds really good but it doesn't answer the question.

In order to help you recognize distracters, we have artificially created five categories of **suspected distracters**. It is unlikely, but not impossible that the correct answer choice might also fall into one of these categories. Thus, you must use this tool as a guide to assist you in finding the correct answer, and not as an absolute test.

- **Round-About:** a distracter that moves around the question but does not directly answer it

- **Beyond:** a distracter whose validity relies upon information not supplied by (or information *beyond*) the passage

- **Contrary:** a distracter that is contrary to the main idea

- **Simpleton:** a distracter that is very simple and/or easily verifiable from the passage

- **Unintelligible:** a distracter that you don't understand

## The Round-About

Round-about distracters simply don't answer the question as asked. They may be true statements. They may even concur with the passage, but they just don't offer a direct answer to the question. A Round-about is the answer you expect from a politician on a Sunday morning polital talk show; a lot of convincing words are spoken but nothing is really said.

## Beyonds

Often times, a distracter will supply information beyond that given in the question and passage without substantiating its veracity. These distracters are called beyonds. When you read a beyond, you typically find yourself wondering something like "This answer sounds good, but this passage was on the economics of the post Soviet Union, I don't remember anything about the Russian revolution."

Beyonds can also play upon current events. A passage on AIDS may have a question with an answer choice about cloning. Cloning may be a hot topic in the news, but if it wasn't mentioned in the passage or in the question, you should be very suspicious of it being in an answer choice.

Don't confuse a *beyond* with an answer choice that directly asks you to assume information as true.

## Contraries

A *contrary* distracter contradicts the main idea. If the question is not an EXCEPT, NOT or LEAST, the answer choice is extremely unlikely to contradict the main idea. **Most answer choices support the main idea in one form or another.**

## Simpletons

If the correct answers on the Verbal Section were simple, direct, and straight forward, then everyone would do well. Instead, the correct answers are vague, ambiguous, and sometimes debatable. This means that an answer choice that is easily verifiable from a reading of the passage is highly suspect and often incorrect. These answer choices are called *simpletons*. Simpletons are not always the wrong answer choice, but you should be highly suspicious when you see one.

"I always never pick the simpleton answer!"

**Typical of simpletons is extreme wording like *always* and *never*.**

Here's a manufactured example of a simpleton:

13. In mid-afternoon in December in Montana, the author believes that the color of the sky most closely resembles:

   **B.**   cotton balls floating on a blue sea.

If this were the answer, everyone would choose it. This is unlikely to be the correct answer.

## Unintelligibles

Unintelligibles are answer choices that you don't understand. Whether it's a vocabulary word or a concept, avoid answer choices that you don't understand. These are likely to be traps. Strangely enough, many test takers are likely to choose an answer that confuses them. This is apparently because the MCAT is a difficult test so students expect to be confused. Test writers sometimes purposely use distracters with obscure vocabulary or incomprehensible diction in order to appeal to the test taker who finds comfort in being confused. As a general rule, don't choose an answer that you don't understand unless you can positively eliminate all other choices. Be confident, not confused.

## 2.3 Identifying the Correct Answer

Besides identifying distracters, you should become familiar with the look and feel of a typical correct answer choice.

Typical correct answer choices contain *softeners*. Softeners are words that make the answer true under more circumstances, such as *most likely, seemed, had a tendency to*, etc. An answer choice with a softener is not necessarily correct; it is just more likely to be correct.

## 2.4 Simplification of the Question and Answer Choices

It is often helpful to simplify the question and answer choices in terms of the main idea. For instance, reexamining the questions and answer choices from our original seven AAMC question stems, we have a passage with the following main idea:

"Great fiction provides a richness of language and feeling that is difficult to recreate in film. Contemporary authors emulating film have lost this richness and their audience with it."

This is a nice complete main idea but can be difficult to understand all at once. It is helpful to simplify it as follows: past fiction, current fiction, and movies.

- Past fiction is good;

- Current fiction is bad;

- Current fiction is like movies.

When analyzing the questions and answer choices, restate them in terms of these ideas, keeping in mind that this is a simplification. For instance, a reference to 'a great, forceful novel' or 'a line-by-line description' can be replaced by 'past fiction'. 'The passage suggests' can be replaced by 'the author thinks'. This is much like using the concept of an ideal gas to approximate the behavior of a real gas and then adding the characteristics of a real gas for the detailed work.

*Notes:*

Compare the following restatements with the original seven AAMC questions:

| Restatement | Original Question |
|---|---|

**Restatement**

1. The author believes current fiction is:

   A. not as good as past fiction.
   B. equal to past fiction.
   C. good.
   D. good.

2. The author compares movies to fiction in order to show that:

   A. movies have been good for fiction.
   B. movies are more likeable than fiction.
   C. movies aren't as good as good fiction.
   D. authors of fiction should make movies.

3. John Gardner says, "Write like the movies," therefore:

   I. he has been influenced by movies.
   II. he wrote movies.
   III. he dislikes movies.

4. The author sees a movie that causes him to read a book, this:

   I. weakens his argument.
   II. means the movie was bad.
   III. means the author didn't like the book.

**Original Question**

1. The author of the passage believes that the fiction written by the current generation of authors:

   A. lacks the significance of fiction written by previous generations.
   B. is, as a whole, no better and no worse than fiction written by previous generations.
   C. brilliantly meets the particular needs of contemporary readers.
   D. is written by authors who show great confidence in their roles as writers.

2. The overall point made by the passage's comparison of movies to fiction is that:

   A. contemporary authors have strengthened their fiction by the application of cinematic techniques.
   B. the film of Under the Volcano is bound to be more popular than the novel.
   C. great fiction provides a richness of language and feeling that is difficult to re-create in film.
   D. contemporary authors would be well advised to become screenwriters.

3. According to the passage, John Gardner concedes that preliminary good advice to a beginning writer might be, "Write as if you were a movie camera." The word concedes here suggests that:

   I. Gardner's approach to writing has been influenced by the competing medium of film.
   II. Gardner must have written screenplays at one point in his life.
   III. Gardner dislikes the medium of film.

4. The fact that the author rereads Under the Volcano because it has been made into a movie is ironic because it:

   I. seems to go against the overall point of the passage concerning fiction and film.
   II. implies that the film version was a box-office failure.
   III. hints that the author was dissatisfied with the novel.

## Restatement

5. The author says that if you like past fiction:

    A. you'll like movies.
    B. you'll be bored by past fiction.
    C. you won't like movies.
    D. you'll like past fiction.

6. If a new novel were like old fiction:

    I. people who like old fiction wouldn't like the novel.
    II. the novel would not be like current fiction.
    III. people would like to read it.

7. No one reads current fiction because:

    I. movies are as good.
    II. current fiction writers write bad fiction.
    III. people are ignorant.

## Original Question

5. The passage suggests that a reader who is not bored by a line-by-line description of a room most likely:

    A. prefers the quick fix of the movies.
    B. would be bored by a single shot of a room in a film.
    C. has no tolerance for movies.
    D. displays the attitude demanded by good fiction.

6. The passage suggests that if a contemporary writer were to write a novel of great forcefulness, this novel would most likely:

    I. confuse and anger lovers of great literature.
    II. exist in stark contrast to the typical contemporary novel.
    III. win back some of the readers contemporary writers have lost.

7. The passage places the blame for contemporary writers' loss of readers on the:

    I. competition presented by movies.
    II. writers themselves.
    III. ignorance of the public.

## 2.5  Summary

You have four tools for finding the correct answer: going back, main idea, question stems, and answer choices. In order to get your best MCAT score, you should use all of them. Your fourth tool is the most difficult to master. When evaluating the answer choices for distracters, keep in mind that there are no absolutes, just suspects. When necessary, restate complicated questions using the simplified concepts from the main idea.

To demonstrate how this works we use the questions and answer choices from a real AAMC passage.

## Passage I (Questions 1–7)

1. According to the passage, an image is a versatile tool that:

   A.  is always visual, never abstract.
   B.  can be either abstract or visual.
   C.  is always abstract, never visual.
   D.  is neither visual nor abstract.

2. An experiment found that dogs can remember a new signal for only five minutes, whereas six-year-old children can remember the same signal much longer. Based on the information in the passage, this finding is probably explained by the fact that:

   A.  a human being possesses a larger store of symbolic images than a dog possesses.
   B.  the human brain evolved more quickly than the brain of a dog.
   C.  the children were probably much older than the dogs.
   D.  most dogs are color-blind.

3. In order to defend poets from the charge that they were liars, Sidney noted that "a maker must imagine things that are not" (line 38). Sidney's point is that:

   A.  a true poet must possess a powerful imagination.
   B.  in order to create something, one must first imagine.
   C.  poets are the most creative people in our society.
   D.  imagination is not a gift unique to poets, but is possessed by all creative people.

4. In the context of the passage, the statement "if thereby we die a thousand deaths, that is the price we pay for living a thousand lives" (lines 52—54) is most likely meant to suggest that:

   A.  we must guard against using our imaginations toward destructive ends.
   B.  although imagination sometimes causes pain, its positive aspects outweigh its negative ones.
   C.  it is possible to be too imaginative for one's own good.
   D.  without imagination, the uniquely human awareness of death would not exist.

5. Which of the following findings would most weaken the claim that the use of symbolic imagery is unique to humans?

   A.  Chimpanzees are capable of learning at least some sign language.
   B.  Certain species of birds are able to migrate great distances by instinct alone.
   C.  Human beings have larger frontal lobes than do other animals.
   D.  Some animals have brains that are larger than human brains.

6. It has been said that language does not merely describe reality but actually helps to bring reality into existence. Which of the points made in the passage would best support this claim?

   A.  To imagine means to make images and move them about in one's head.
   B.  The tool that puts the human mind ahead of the animal's is imagery.
   C.  There is no specific center for language in the brain of any animal except the human being.
   D.  Images play out events that are not present, thereby guarding the past and creating the future.

7. According to the author, the most important images are:

   A.  words.
   B.  poetic images.
   C.  images of the past.
   D.  images of the future.

---

**STOP.** IF YOU FINISH BEFORE TIME IS CALLED, CHECK YOUR WORK. YOU MAY GO BACK TO ANY QUESTION IN THIS TEST BOOKLET.

---

## Answers to Questions

Before you look at the answers, let's discuss them.

Question 1:

If we look at this question and use common sense, we know that an image can be both abstract and visual. The word "versatile" in the question also helps us find the answer.

Question 2:

Ask yourself "Why might a child remember a signal longer than a dog?" B, C, and D don't seem like reasonable answers. For answer B, what does it mean for a human's brain to evolve more quickly? This answer is somewhat unintelligible. Choice C compares the age of a human child with a dog in terms of memory as if they were equivalent. This doesn't seem to be reasonable. At best, it calls for outside information about a dog's ability to remember based upon its age. For answer choice D, the question doesn't say anything about vision. Where does color-blind come in? Choice D is a beyond.

Question 3:

Notice that the question asks what is meant by the quote. For this type of question, just match the answer to the quote. Choice B is a paraphrase of the quote. Sidney himself is superfluous information.

Question 4:

This is the same type of question as the last. Match the answer to the quote. Notice answer choice D. This is for those who want to see things in black and white, and take the quote very literally. It also does not match the quote.

Question 5:

What would weaken the claim that the use of symbolic imagery is unique to humans? Answer: An example of a non-human using symbolic imagery. Choice A is correct.

Question 6:

Here we are asked to interpret a paraphrase. Just match the paraphrase to the answer choice. "bringing reality into existence" is the same as "creating the future".

Question 7:

This is difficult to answer without the passage. However, look at the other questions. Ask yourself, "What is the main idea of this passage?" It is certainly about images, symbols, and language. Which answer fits most closely? Notice that the word image is in all the answers except the correct one. This makes choices B, C, and D simpletons. A is correct.

The correct answers are: 1. B, 2. A, 3. B, 4. B, 5. A, 6. D, 7. A.

# STOP HERE UNTIL CLASS!

(DO NOT LOOK AT THE FOLLOWING QUESTIONS UNTIL CLASS.

IF YOU WILL NOT BE ATTENDING CLASS, GIVE YOURSELF 30
MINUTES TO COMPLETE THE FOLLOWING SET OF QUESTIONS.)

**Passage I (Questions 1–7)**

1.  When a beaver senses danger, it will instinctively slap its tail on the water, warning other beavers. According to the passage, this is not "a true form of communication" because it:

    A.  is instinctive.
    B.  is not language.
    C.  is unidirectional.
    D.  lacks emotion.

2.  According to the passage, which of the following are reasons that apes are better communicators than monkeys?

    I.   Apes are capable of a greater variety of facial expressions.
    II.  Apes are capable of a greater variety of sounds.
    III. Apes have a greater intelligence with which to interpret signals.

    A.  I and II only
    B.  I and III only
    C.  II and III only
    D.  I, II, and III

3.  Assume researchers were to select three adult chimpanzees from a wild troop and teach them sign language. Based upon information in the passage, if the researchers returned to the same troop four years later, which chimpanzees in the troop might they expect to be using sign language?

    A.  Only the chimpanzees that were originally taught sign language
    B.  Only the chimpanzees that were originally taught sign language and their offspring
    C.  All chimpanzees in the troop
    D.  No chimpanzees in the troop

4.  According to the passage, the most important difference between humans and chimpanzees explaining why humans developed language and chimpanzees did not is:

    A.  genetic make up
    B.  personal relationships
    C.  intelligence
    D.  ability to produce a variety of sounds

5.  Which of the following would most weaken the author's claim that chimps are the most intelligent communicators in the animal world?

    A.  Through whistling and clicking alone, two dolphins are able to work together to perform coordinated movements.
    B.  A wolf's howl can be heard by another wolf from several miles away.
    C.  Ants have more developed chemical messages than any other animal.
    D.  A honey bee instinctively performs a complicated series of movements which signals the location of a pollen source to the rest of the hive.

6.  The author most likely believes that by studying chimpanzee behavior, humans may learn:

    A.  that chimpanzees communicate as effectively as humans.
    B.  new ways of communication.
    C.  how ancestors of humans developed speech.
    D.  why chimpanzees can't speak.

7.  The author claims "The modern chimp may be making the first steps toward language." (Lines 32-33) Based upon the context of this claim in the passage, with which of the following statements might the author also agree?

    A.  Modern chimps will one day develop their own spoken language.
    B.  Given the right training, modern chimps are capable of speech.
    C.  Specific social behaviors of chimpanzees may prevent them from developing a universal chimp language.
    D.  Modern chimps are evolving more fluid communication skills.

## Passage II (Questions 8–16)

8. According to the passage, a universally accepted scientific theory:

   A. cannot be proven wrong.
   B. is not a fundamental truth.
   C. usually replaces a religious belief.
   D. is no better than a religious belief as a predictor of natural phenomena.

9. The author believes that the view that "You can't argue with science" is:

   A. not scientific.
   B. held only by top scientists.
   C. generally correct.
   D. true concerning matters outside religion.

10. The author mentions the Scopes Monkey Trial in order to support the claim that:

    A. religion and science are contradictory.
    B. the functions of science and religion are often misunderstood.
    C. science will eventually triumph over religion.
    D. when science and religion are in conflict, most people will believe religion.

11. Einstein once said "Whether you can observe a thing or not depends on the theory which you use. It is the theory which decides what can be observed." This quote best supports the author's claim that:

    A. science is an imperfect description of nature.
    B. science is not based upon fact.
    C. religion is more reliable than science.
    D. religion and science are similar.

12. Dawkins claims, "Religion is, in a sense, science; it's just bad science." (line 51) Dawkins' point is that:

    A. religion attempts to answer the wrong questions.
    B. religion does not provide answers.
    C. the answers provided by religion are unreliable.
    D. religious people are less honest than scientists.

13. If during a speech Dawkins said, "The argument that religion and science answer different types of questions is just false," which of the following statements made by Dawkins in the same speech would most weaken his own claim?

    A. Religions throughout history have attempted to answer questions that belong in the realm of science.
    B. Religion is science; it's just bad science.
    C. Science, then, is free of the main vice of religion, which is faith.
    D. Most religions offer a cosmology and a biology, a theory of life, a theory of origins, and reasons for existence.

14. According to the passage, which of the following properly belongs to the realm of science, but NOT to the realm of religion?

    A. healthy skepticism
    B. reliable prediction
    C. close observation
    D. peer review

15. With which of the following statements might the author agree?

    A. Science proves that God does not exist.
    B. Science proves the existence of God.
    C. God responds to prayer with a gentle guiding hand.
    D. God reveals himself through the lawful harmony of the universe.

16. According to the author, science and religion:

    A. ask the same questions, and provide conflicting answers.
    B. ask the same questions, and provide compatible answers.
    C. ask different questions, and provide conflicting answers.
    D. ask different questions, and provide compatible answers.

## Passage III (Questions 17–23)

17. The author of the passage believes that the modern art held in high esteem by today's art critics:

    A. has a weaker impact on contemporary society than did classical art.
    B. should not be judged in the same context as classical art.
    C. makes a clear statement about today's society.
    D. is a testament to the extraordinary skills of modern artists.

18. The comparison of sculpture and architecture (lines 31-35) best supports the author's claim that:

    A. modern artists have had to use new technologies in order to stay connected to their audience.
    B. modern art is more recognizable than classical art.
    C. art must address the social problems faced by contemporary society.
    D. function restrains novelty and dictates beauty.

19. The author would most likely agree that truly great works of art:

    A. comment on important contemporary social issues.
    B. are beautiful to look at.
    C. express the inner feelings of the artist.
    D. stimulate novel thoughts.

20. It has been said that art not only mimics reality, but reality mimics art. Which of the assertions from the passage would best support this claim?

    A. Beauty is not in the eye of the beholder, but an absolute reality to be discovered by the artist.
    B. Great men in history have been inspired to great deeds by great art.
    C. No mere child could recreate The Statue of David.
    D. Classical artwork was carefully planned and crafted.

21. Artwork resembling modern abstract art but painted by a chimpanzee recently sold alongside famous works at a prestigious London auction house for over $25,000. Based on this information, the author might agree with which of the following statements?

    A. Chimpanzees are capable of expressing emotion.
    B. Some chimpanzees may be great artists.
    C. Some modern art resembles the scribbling of a chimpanzee.
    D. Great artwork doesn't require great minds.

22. Picasso is credited with saying "If there were only one truth, you couldn't paint one hundred canvasses on the same theme." This statement best supports which of the following assertions from the passage?

    A. If we find classical art beautiful, it is because we see hints of perfection in otherwise common and familiar forms.
    B. The modern artist invites us to share a reality that is uniquely his own.
    C. There is beauty in truth.
    D. Upon a closer inspection, we see that the Diskobolus by Miron portrays the discus throw rather than the discus thrower.

23. The passage places the blame for the average person's lack of interest in modern art on:

    I. not enough talented modern artists
    II. obtuse subject matter
    III. ignorance of the average person

    A. I only
    B. II only
    C. I and II only
    D. I, II, and III

---

**STOP.** IF YOU FINISH BEFORE TIME IS CALLED, CHECK YOUR WORK. YOU MAY GO BACK TO ANY QUESTION IN THIS TEST BOOKLET.

---

Don't look at the answers yet, just read on.

## Passage I

### Question 1

From a layman's perspective, the beaver is 'communicating' to other beavers. Thus, we know that the word 'true' here is going to be important. The author has apparently distinguished 'true communication' from our everyday understanding of the word. From question 2 we see that apes and monkeys both 'communicate' according to the passage. Apes and monkeys don't have language, thus we assume that 'true communication does not require language. We can get rid of choice B. Choice D seems poor as well, since it would seem that a beaver in danger would not be emotionless. Of course you might make the argument that all animals lack emotion, but then there is question 2 again, where apes are animals and apes arc communicating, so communication is possible for animals. So now we are left with choice A or C. The tail slap is instinctive, as per the question, and it seems to be unidirectional. So which one seems to be a reason that it is NOT 'true' communication. We can think of many examples of communication that are unidirectional: television, a smile, a letter, etc… This weakens choice C. Choice A is correct.

### Question 2

Common sense tells us that being better at sound, facial expressions, and intelligence would make us better communicators, so the question is really asking, at which of these is an ape better than a monkey. From question stem 5 we see that chimps, which are apes, are "the most intelligent communicators in the animal world, so we know that III must be part of the answer. A is incorrect. We don't know for certain about sound or facial expressions, so it is difficult to narrow this one down just yet.

### Question 3

This question is basically asking us "In the wild, which other chimps, if any, does the author think a signing chimp would teach sign language? And would the signing chimp even retain his sign language?" This question is about social interactions within the troop. We don't have enough information to answer it yet.

### Question 4

At first glance, all the answers seem to be possible. As usual, it is important to read the question stem carefully. The stem does not ask for 'the only reason' why humans developed language and chimps didn't; it is asking for the 'most important' reason, and the most important reason 'according to the passage'. So all the answers may be legitimate reasons why chimps didn't develop language and humans did, but which one does the author believe is the most important? Is this author most concerned with genetics, social relationships, intelligence, or ability to produce sounds? Question 3 clearly lends support to choice B. Question 5 seems to strengthen choice C. Question 2 mentions sound in an answer choice, but perhaps that is a wrong answer choice. Genetics seems to have no support from any other question, so choice A seems wrong.

### Question 5

This question can be answered with common sense. The question asks about intelligence. Which answer choice has to do with intelligence? Only choice A.

### Question 6

Choice A is simply false. Choice B seems highly unlikely. Choice D is wrong because the author's interest lies in communication not in chimps themselves; when it comes right down to it, he wants to learn about communication, not about chimps. Choice C satisfies this criterion. Notice that this question also emphasizes behavior. This passage is looking more and more to be about communication as it is affected by social interactions. This is more support for choice B in question 4.

### Question 7

It is important to keep your common sense. Does the author really believe that chimps will be speaking one day? No, of course not. Choices A and B are incorrect. That leaves choices C and D. Choice D is far less practical than choice C; do we really believe that the author is saying that we are watching chimps evolving into a species with language as we speak? No. It is far more likely that the author is saying chimps are making the first steps and then their social behavior is preventing them from advancing further. But greater evidence than that for choice C is that the social behavior aspect for choice C fits so neatly with the rest of the questions. Choice C tells us almost for sure that the answer to question 4 is B.

## Question 2 revisited

We know that choice III is true. The only hint for choosing I or II, and it is quite a small hint, is the sense in the questions that the passage was concerned with signs, supporting choice I and not really concerned as much with sounds, lacking support for II. It would be difficult to be confident of this without reading the passage, but, hey, that's why you read the passage. Choice B is correct.

## Question 3 revisited

Now that we understand the passage is about social behavior as well as communication, and that via question 7 the social behaviors prevent chimps from developing a universal language, we know that the chimps are not going to teach all their troop mates to use sign language. Choice C is wrong. There is no reason in the question stems to assume that the chimp would lose his ability to use sign language, so choice D is unlikely. The question is "Would the adults teach signing to their offspring?" This is very tough to answer without reading the passage, but there is a hint. What are the "first steps toward language" that the author is talking about in question 7. The chimps are teaching their offspring, but not their peers. Choice B is correct.

## Question 4 revisited

From questions 6 and 7 we see that the answer must be choice B.

---

## Passage II

### Question 8

As an MCAT student strong in the sciences, you know that choice A is false and that choice B is true. Choice C is possible. Choice D seems unlikely. The answer is probably choice B, but we'll have to come back.

### Question 9

Again, as an MCAT student strong in the sciences, you know that choice B, C, and D are false. Choice A is correct. Now it is easy to go back and answer question 8.

### Question 8 revisited

In the light of question 9, the correct answer is choice B. Also, since we now know that choice D is wrong, we know that the author is taking a kind of middle ground between science and religion.

### Question 10

Choices A and C do not represent the tone that questions 8 and 9 present. They are incorrect. Choice B seems most closely related to the middle-ground tone of the questions and answers to 8 and 9. The Scopes Monkey trial refers to the trial of John Scopes for illegally teaching evolution in public school. He was convicted. Obviously, it was discussed in the passage, so being familiar with it before MCAT is unnecessary. The trial was a conflict between science and religion but in no way supports the conclusion drawn by choice D. However, it could support an argument that the roles of religion and science are misunderstood. Choice B is correct.

### Question 11

Choice B implies that a quote from Einstein is used to support a claim that science is not based upon fact. It also implies that the author believes science is not base upon fact. The incorrect choice D from Question 8 tells us that the author probably would find choice B to be incorrect. Choice C is incorrect for the same reasons. The question doesn't draw any connection between religion and science so choice D seems unlikely. Choice A seems to be a middle-ground again and works especially well with the assertion in question 8 that a scientific theory is not a fundamental truth. Choice A is correct.

### Question 12

Dawkins is not the author, or he wouldn't have been named. Dawkins is used either to support the author's point or to demonstrate why those who disagree with the author are mistaken. The aggressive confrontational tone of Dawkins comment is in strong contrast to the moderate tone of the author as revealed by the questions so far. Still, since this question is about Dawkins, and not the author, it is difficult to answer without reading more questions. We'll have to come back.

### Question 13

This question is a logical question that can be answered by common sense alone. Choice A most weakens Dawkins claim. Dawkins claims in the question stem that religion and science don't answer different questions, so they must either answer the same questions or no questions at all. Choice A indicates that Dawkins believes that certain questions belong in the realm of science and not in the realm of religion. This means that he believes that religion and science don't answer the same questions. This is a contradiction and weakens his argument. The correct answer is A.

## Question 12 revisited

From question 13 we see that Dawkins does not believe choice A. Question 12 also seems to indicate that Dawkins believes religion does provide answers, just answers that are somehow not as good as those provided by science. This fits best with choice C. The honesty of religious people is not addressed leaving no evidence for choice D. Choice C is correct.

## Question 14

Choice B fits nicely with choice D in Question 1 being incorrect. Skepticism, close observation, and peer review are not addressed by any other question, so choices A, C, and D are not supported.

## Question 15

Based upon questions 8 and 9, the author would have difficulty arguing that science proves anything. Choices A and B are incorrect. Also weakening them as answer choices is the fact that they are stated much more strongly than the moderate tone of the other questions and correct answers. Choice C might be possible, but choice D goes much better with question 14. Based upon questions 8 and 14, the author seems to feel that science is a reliable predictor. Choice D allows for such predictions and for God, while choice C seems that it might necessarily interfere with the predictive powers of science.

## Question 16

Question 14 tells us that the author believes that science and religion ask different questions. The tone of the questions tells us that he believes the answers are compatible. Question 15, choice D is an example of the compatibility of science and religion. Choice D is correct.

---

## Passage III

### Question 17

Why does the question include the modifying phrase "held in high esteem by today's art critics"? To what other kind of modern art might the question refer? Is there modern art that today's art critics consider bad? Is there bad modern art? Apparently, the question writer wants to be clear that he is talking about only good modern art and not bad modern art. Choice A is the only answer choice that makes sense using this distinction. With this distinction, choice A can be rephrased as "Even good modern art is worse than classical art", while the importance of the distinction is lost with choices B, C, and D: For instance, choice B: "Even good modern art should not be judged in the same context as classical art." Choice C. "Even good modern art makes a clear statement about today's society." Choice D: "Even good modern art is a testament to the extraordinary skills of modern artists." For the MCAT, it is important to develop this sense or feeling of whether or not the answer choice fits the question stem. Choice A is correct because it fits with the question stem while the other choices do not. Based upon this answer we have learned quite a bit about the author. Now we know the author has something against modern art and in favor of classical art. Since choices B, C, and D are incorrect, we can assume that the author thinks it is acceptable to judge modern art and classical art in the same context, that modern art does not make a clear statement about today's society, and that modern art is not a testament to the skills of the modern artist.

### Question 18

The question asks about a comparison. The correct answer should address a comparison. Choice D indicates that function behaves two different ways: 1) It restrains novelty and 2) It dictates beauty. How might this work with sculpture and architecture? How does function apply to architecture? Architecture has a specific function as housing or shelter. Might this function restrain novelty (or new ideas) in architecture? It seems logical. A roof can be made to look differently, but it still must have certain characteristics in order to function like a roof. Might this function also dictate beauty in architecture? Perhaps since the roof is required, what is beautiful in architecture must include a roof. On the other hand, sculpture doesn't seem to have a function in the same sense. Could a comparison to sculpture and architecture demonstrate how function restrains novelty and dictates beauty? It would seem so. D is a possibility. Choices A, B, and C do not address the comparison as well. In addition, choices A and B seem to favor modern art, contradicting the negative feel toward modern art in the first question. D seems to be correct, but we cannot be certain yet.

## Question 19

The word 'truly' is important here. It indicates that the author distinguishes between great works of art and 'truly' great works of art. Might that mean that he disagrees with art critics about what is and is not great art? This would support our answer for question 17. Since the author does not seem to be enamored with modern art, and he does seem to like classical art, it seems unlikely that he would think that 'truly' great art must comment on important contemporary social issues. Choice A is probably out. We will revisit this question after the next question.

## Question 20

This question can be answered by common sense. Only choice B answers the question. Only choice B is an example of reality mimicking art. The other choices simply don't address the premise of the question. Choice B is correct. This question is important because it gives us four examples of what the author thinks in the four answer choices. Even if we will have read the passage, these answer choices sum up the author's ideas in the question writer's words. What the question writer thinks the author said is even more important than what the author thinks he said. Choice A tells us that the author believes that beauty is a reality and not a matter of opinion. This verifies choice B for question 19.

## Question 19 revisited

From question 20, choice A, we know that the author believes that beauty is not a matter of opinion. This indicates that choice B in question 19 must be correct.

## Question 21

Clearly choices A and B are wrong; this passage is not about chimps, it is about art. Choice D would indicate that the author thinks that modern art by chimps is 'great artwork'. Instead, common sense and the author's attitude toward modern art in question 17 tell us that the correct answer is choice C.

## Question 22

The quote says there is more than one reality and art is the painter's idea of reality. Only choice B matches the quote. Choice B is correct. Again we have four examples of what the author thinks in the four answer choices. Especially revealing is choice A which verifies that the author likes classical art, and tells us why. This strongly supports choice B in question 19.

## Question 23

From previous questions we know that the author likes classical art more than modern art. Choice A in question 22 tells us that classical art is beautiful because of the true beauty discovered in its common and familiar subject matter, while choice B tells us that the modern artist is sharing his own reality that is 'uniquely his own', i.e. not a common familiar subject matter. Therefore subject matter of modern art must be a key reason why the author finds modern art less beautiful. Choice II must be one of the answer choices. On the other hand, there is no hint that the author has an issue with the talent of the modern artist. Everywhere that it might be an answer, it is a wrong answer. This leaves only choice B.

| | | | | |
|---|---|---|---|---|
| | | 20. B | 16. D | 12. C | 8. B | 4. B |
| 23. B | 19. B | 15. D | 11. A | 7. C | 3. B |
| 22. B | 18. D | 14. B | 10. B | 6. C | 2. B |
| 21. C | 17. A | 13. A | 9. A | 5. A | Answers 1. A |

This exercise is not to convince you not to read the passage. You should always read the passage. It should show you that there is a large amount of information in the questions and answer choices. If you scored higher without reading the passage, then you probably haven't been taking advantage of the wealth of information in the questions and answer choices.

# THE MAIN IDEA

## 3.1    The Main Idea

The main idea is a summary of the passage in one or two sentences. It should reflect the author's opinion (if presented or implied), and it should emphasize minor topics to the same extent as they are emphasized in the passage. It is not a list of topics discussed in the passage nor an outline of those topics. It is a statement about the passage topics, and includes the author's opinion.

**In one form or another, 90% of the Verbal Section questions will concern the main idea.** Notice that the main idea cannot be found by going back to the passage and searching for details. You must concentrate on the main idea while you read the entire passage. If you read for detail, if you try to remember what you have read rather than process what you are reading, you will have to guess at 90% of the questions.

It is important to have a clear concept of the main idea before reading any questions. MCAT Verbal Section questions are designed to take your inchoate thoughts concerning the passage and subtly redirect them away from the true main idea. Each successive question embellishes on insidious pseudo-themes steering unwary followers into an abyss from which there is no return. Like a faithful paladin, your clearly stated main idea unmasks these impostors and leads you toward the holy grail of Verbal Section perfection.

Writing the main idea on paper is an important step toward improving your ability to find the main idea; however, it requires too much time while taking the exam. Instead, a few days after taking a practice exam, go back to each passage and write out the main idea. While taking the exam, make a 20 second pause after reading a passage, and construct the main idea in your head.

Most students resist writing out their main idea until they are halfway through the course and the materials. At this point they begin to realize how important the main idea is. Unfortunately, they must start from scratch and begin writing out the main idea with only four weeks until the MCAT. Don't do this. Start now by going back to used passages and writing out the main idea. **It's very painful at first, but it will get easier, and it will dramatically improve your score.**

## 3.2 Constructing the Main Idea

A good main idea can be formed as follows:

1. After reading the passage, write down the main topics. Each topic should be from one to four words.

2. From these topics, choose the most important ones two or three at a time and write a short phrase relating them to each other and the passage.

3. Now connect the phrases into one or two sentences which still concern the most important topics but incorporate the other topics as well. Be sure to include the author's opinion if it was given or implied. Try to emphasize each topic to the same extent to which it was emphasized in the passage. This is your main idea. Over time, you will be able to construct the main idea in your head.

> Because I'm good enough, I'm smart enough and doggone it, people like me.

## 3.3 Confidence

Often on the MCAT, passages seem incomprehensible. Don't get bent! Remember, most questions are answered correctly by 60% or more of test-takers, and only two or three are answered incorrectly by less than 40%, so no group of questions will be that difficult. Have the confidence to keep reading. **Don't reread a line or paragraph over and over until you master it.** If a line or paragraph is incomprehensible to you, then it is probably incomprehensible to everyone else, and understanding it will not help your score. Instead, continue reading until you get to something that you do understand. Just get the general sense of what the author is trying to say. Chances are good that this will be enough to answer all the questions. Remember, after you read the passage you have four tools beyond your understanding of the passage to help you answer the questions.

## 3.4 Know Your Author

You must become familiar with the author. Who is he or she? Is the author young or old; rich or poor; male or female; conservative or liberal? Do you love or hate this author? Take a guess. Create a picture of the author in your mind. Use your prejudices to stereotype the author. Your harsh judgment of the author is everything to understanding what he is trying to say. The better you understand the author, the easier the questions will be. Read with emotion and judge harshly.

Now that you know the author intimately, when you get to a question, ask yourself "If this author were right here in front of me, how would he answer this question?" The way that the author would answer the question is the correct answer.

## 3.5 Ignore the Details and See the Big Picture

There is no reason to remember the details of a passage. They can be found in seconds, and are rarely important to answering a question. Instead, focus on the big picture. Ask yourself "What is the author trying to say to me? What's his beef?" The author's 'beef' will be the main idea, and the key to answering 90% of the questions.

# STOP!

DO NOT LOOK AT THE FOLLOWING PASSAGE AND
QUESTIONS UNTIL CLASS.

IF YOU WILL NOT BE ATTENDING CLASS, READ THE PASSAGE IN
THREE MINUTES AND ANSWER THE QUESTIONS WHICH FOLLOW.

## Passage I

It is roughly a century since European art began to experience its first significant defections from the standards of painting and sculpture that we inherit from the early Renaissance. Looking back now across a long succession
5 of innovative movements and stylistic revolutions, most of us have little trouble recognizing that such aesthetic orthodoxies of the past as the representative convention, exact anatomy and optical perspective, the casement-window canvas, along with the repertory of materials and
10 subject matters we associate with the Old Masters—that all this makes up not "art" itself in any absolute sense, but something like a school of art, one great tradition among many. We acknowledge the excellence which a Raphael or Rembrandt could achieve within the canons of that school;
15 but we have grown accustomed to the idea that there are other aesthetic visions of equal validity. Indeed, innovation in the arts has become a convention in its own right with us, a "tradition of the new," to such a degree that there are critics to whom it seems to be intolerable that any two
20 painters should paint alike. We demand radical originality, and often confuse it with quality.

Yet what a jolt it was to our great-grandparents to see the certainties of the academic tradition melt away before their eyes. How distressing, especially for the
25 academicians, who were the guardians of a classic heritage embodying time-honored techniques and standards whose perfection had been the labor of genius. Suddenly they found art as they understood it being rejected by upstarts who were unwilling to let a single premise of the inherited
30 wisdom stand unchallenged, or so it seemed. Now, with a little hindsight, it is not difficult to discern continuities where our predecessors saw only ruthless disjunctions. To see, as well, that the artistic revolutionaries of the past were, at their best, only opening our minds to a more global
35 conception of art which demanded a deeper experience of light, color, and form. Through their work, too, the art of our time has done much to salvage the values of the primitive and childlike, the dream, the immediate emotional response, the life of fantasy, and the transcendent symbol.

40 In our own day, much the same sort of turning point has been reached in the history of science. It is as if the aesthetic ground pioneered by the artists now unfolds before us as a new ontological awareness. We are at a moment when the reality to which scientists address themselves comes
45 more and more to be recognized as but one segment of a far broader spectrum. Science, for so long regarded as our single valid picture of the world, now emerges as, also, a school: a *school of consciousness*, beside which alternative realities take their place.

50 There are, so far, only fragile and scattered beginnings of this perception. They are still the subterranean history of our time. How far they will carry toward liberating us from the orthodox world view of the technocratic establishment is still doubtful. These days, many gestures of rebellion
55 are subtly denatured, adjusted, and converted into oaths of allegiance. In our society at large, little beyond submerged unease challenges the lingering authority of science and technique, that dull ache at the bottom of the soul we refer to when we speak (usually too glibly) of an "age of anxiety,"
60 an "age of longing."

Answer the following questions without going back to the passage. If you don't know the answer, guess.

*YOU MAY NOT LOOK AT THE PASSAGE!*

- Is the author male or female?
- Does the author have long or short hair?
- How old is the author?
- What political party is the author a member of?
- Would the author prefer a wild party or a night at the opera?
- Do you think you would like the author?
- What does the author do for a living?

These are the types of questions that you should be able to answer with prejudice if you have read the passage the way you should. If you can answer these questions, you have compared the author to people of your past and categorized the author accordingly. This means that you have a better understanding of who the author is, and how he would answer the MCAT questions about his own passage.

The previous questions were asked to make you realize how you should be trying to understand the author. You should not be asking yourself these questions on a real MCAT. Here are some questions that you should ask yourself on a real MCAT:

*YOU MAY NOT LOOK AT THE PASSAGE!*

- If the author were sitting in front of you, would he or she want to discuss science or art?
- What emotion, if any, is the author feeling?
- Is the author a scientist?
- Is the author conservative, liberal, or somewhere in the middle?

The answers to these questions are unequivocal. This author is discussing science, not art. Art is used as a lengthy, nearly incomprehensible introduction to make a point about science. The author doesn't even begin discussing the main idea until the beginning of the third paragraph. "In our own day, much the same sort of turning point has been reached in the history of science." When you read this, you should have been startled. You should have been thinking "Where did science come from? I thought we were talking about some esoteric art history crap that I really wasn't understanding." This one sentence should have said to you "Ahaa! That other stuff was appetizer, now the author is going to discuss his real interest." Notice that it is at the beginning of the third paragraph that the writing actually becomes intelligible. In other words, the second two paragraphs are much easier to read. This is because the author is interested in this topic and knows what he wants to say. The art stuff was a poorly written introduction and the author had not thought it through with any clarity. If you spent lots of time rereading the first two paragraphs, trying to master them, you wasted your time. The author didn't even master them; how could you?

The author is frustrated and possibly even bitter. He is so angry, that he is name-calling. For instance, he calls the scientific community "the technocratic establishment". The tone of the passage is like that of a whining child. He blames scientists for being too conservative and thus creating "an age of anxiety", as if the anxiety of most people would be relieved if scientists were less practical. In the last sentence, he even blames us, his reader, for not taking *his* issue more seriously. The author is positively paranoid. Notice that his adversaries move against him "subtly" as if trying to hide their evil intentions. They take "oaths of allegiance" like some Nazi cult. This is way overdone when you consider that the guy's only complaint is that science isn't liberal enough in its approach.

The author is certainly not a scientist. First of all, he writes like a poet not a scientist: "orthodox world view of the technocratic establishment", "subterranean history of our time", "gestures of rebellion subtly denatured". Secondly, his whole point is that he is upset with scientists. (An entire separate argument can be made that his point results from his misunderstanding of how science progresses.) And finally, he talks like a member of some pyramid cult, not a scientist: "alternative realities" and "ontological awareness". This author probably flunked high school physics and just can't get over it.

The author is certainly liberal, or anti-establishment. He talks about "liberating us" and "rebellion" among other things.

Now, with this understanding of the author, answer the questions on the next page.

*YOU MAY NOT LOOK AT THE PASSAGE!*

## Passage I (Questions 1–9)

1. The author believes that in "the subterranean history of our time" (line 56-57) we find the beginnings of a:

   A. renewal of allegiance to traditional values.
   B. redefinition of art.
   C. redefinition of science.
   D. single valid picture of the world.

2. The author compares art and science mainly in support of the idea that:

   A. the conventions of science, like those of art, are now beginning to be recognized as but one segment of a far broader spectrum.
   B. aesthetic orthodoxies of the past, unlike scientific orthodoxies of the present, make up only one tradition among many.
   C. artistic as well as scientific revolutionaries open our minds to a more global conception of art.
   D. artists of the past have provided inspiration to the scientists of the present.

3. The two kinds of art discussed in the passage are the:

   A. aesthetic and the innovative.
   B. dull and the shocking.
   C. traditional and the innovative.
   D. representative and the traditional.

4. The author's statement "How far [new perceptions of science] will carry toward liberating us from the orthodox world view of the technocratic establishment is still doubtful" (lines 57-59) assumes that the:

   A. technocratic establishment is opposed to scientific inquiry.
   B. traditional perception of science is identical to the world view of the technocratic establishment.
   C. current perceptions of science are identical to those of art.
   D. technocratic establishment has the same world view as the artistic revolutionaries of the past.

5. Which of the following concepts does the author illustrate with specific examples?

   A. Scientific innovations of the present
   B. Scientific innovations of the past
   C. Aesthetic innovations of the present
   D. Aesthetic orthodoxies of the past

6. The claim that the unease mentioned in line 62 is "submerged" most directly illustrates the idea that:

   A. our great-grandparents were jolted by the collapse of academic certainty.
   B. we have grown accustomed to the notion that there is more than one valid aesthetic vision.
   C. so far, new perceptions of science are only fragile and scattered.
   D. the authority of science is rapidly being eroded.

7. Based on the information in the passage, the author would most likely claim that someone who did NOT agree with his view of science was:

   A. dishonest.
   B. conformist.
   C. rebellious.
   D. imaginative.

8. Based on information in the passage, which of the following opinions could most reasonably be ascribed to the author?

   A. It is misguided to rebel against scientific authority.
   B. The world views of other disciplines may have something valuable to teach the scientific community.
   C. Art that rebels against established traditions cannot be taken seriously.
   D. The main cause of modern anxiety and longing is our rash embrace of new scientific and artistic theories.

9. Adopting the author's views as presented in the passage would most likely mean acknowledging that:

   A. it is not a good idea to accept traditional beliefs simply because they are traditional.
   B. we must return to established artistic and scientific values.
   C. the future is bleak for today's artists and scientists.
   D. the scientific community has given us little of benefit.

_____

**STOP.** IF YOU FINISH BEFORE TIME IS CALLED, CHECK YOUR WORK. YOU MAY GO BACK TO ANY QUESTION IN THIS TEST BOOKLET.

_____

Don't worry about the correct answers yet.

## *YOU MAY NOT LOOK AT THE PASSAGE YET!*

The first thing to notice is that only question 5 requires any information from the first two paragraphs, and question 5 was a question about detail, not concept. This is because the first two paragraphs are not about the main idea.

The second thing to notice is that none of the questions require us to go back to the passage, even though some refer us to specific line numbers. All but question 5 are answerable directly from the main idea. Question 5 is a detail question, but before you run back to the passage to find the answer, look at the possibilities. The chances are that you remembered Raphael and Rembrandt from the first paragraph. These are specific examples of "aesthetic orthodoxies of the past".

Notice that many of the questions can be rephrased to say "The author thinks _____." This is typical of an MCAT passage, and that's why you must "know your author".

**Question 1:** Forget about the quote for a moment. Simplify the question to say "The author thinks that we find the beginnings of a:". Answer C is the main idea. Certainly the author would disagree with A, B, and D.

**Question 2:** "The author thinks:" that science is like art, and that conventions of both are but part of a larger spectrum. B says science is not like art; the opposite of what the author thinks. C says that scientific revolutionaries are changing science; the author is frustrated because this is not really happening. D says scientists of the present are opening their minds to new ideas; the author complains that they are not.

**Question 3:** The main idea of the passage contains the theme of traditional vs. innovative.

**Question 4:** Ignore the quotes until you need them. Without the quotes, the question says "The author's statement assumes that the:". In other words, "The author thinks _____." C and D are exactly opposite to what the author thinks. Answer A plays a common game on the MCAT. They take the author's view too far. They want you to think "the author doesn't like the scientists; therefore, he thinks the scientists can't even do science." Even this author wouldn't go that far. A is incorrect. Answer B requires you to realize that the "technocratic establishment" is conservative.

**Question 6:** Answer D is out because it disagrees with the main idea, and C is the only answer that supports the main idea. However, this question is best answered by comparing the answer choices with the question. The question asks for an example of "submerged unease". "Jolted" in answer choice A certainly doesn't describe submerged unease. "Grown accustomed" in answer choice B certainly does not describe submerged unease. Answer choice C could describe submerged unease, and it does describe the main idea. It is the best answer.

**Question 7:** The author is rebellious and imaginative. If you disagree with him, he thinks you are a conformist, which, by the way, is worse than dishonest as far as he's concerned.

**Question 8:** "The author thinks _____." The whole point of the intro is to say that the scientific community should learn from the discipline of art.

**Question 9:** "The author thinks ." The author is a rebel. He thinks you should always question authority. Notice choice D is another example of taking things too far. No sane individual could argue that science has provided little benefit. Answer choice C would be incorrect even if it had not included 'artists'. It would have been too extreme.

## NOW YOU MAY LOOK AT THE PASSAGE.

Hopefully, we have demonstrated the power of knowing the author and understanding the main idea. Remember to use all four of your tools, and, most importantly, read and answer questions with confidence.

If you have problems, go back to the basics of this manual. Figure out what part of our strategy and tactics you aren't using, and use it.

*Notes:*

*Notes:*

# How to Study for the Verbal Reasoning Section

## 4.1 How to Study for the Verbal Reasoning Section

One might think that studying the correct answers to many verbal questions in order to discover why they are correct would be a helpful exercise toward improving your score. On the contrary, it's probably a waste of your precious time. It is rarely useful to go back to old tests and learn the logic used to explain why the correct answers are correct. By doing so, you may learn something about the topic of the passage, but you do not learn what you can do differently next time to improve your score. Since most explanations justify answers by pointing to a specific place in the passage that is claimed to support or even prove the correct answer, such practices can even lower your MCAT score by giving you the false impression that answers can be found in a specific place in the passage. Most MCAT answers require an understanding of the passage as a whole and cannot be proven correct by reading from one place in the passage. In most verbal materials, explanations tend to be too brief and not particularly insightful. It is doubtful that reading them will increase your reading comprehension skills.

One method for increasing your reading comprehension skills is to join a book club or organize a reading group, and discuss things that you have read. This is not particularly practical for most premeds, and even this idea is only effective if there are strong, insightful readers in your club or group. The often posited advice of reading lots of magazine and newspaper articles on your own is a significantly less effective method for improving your reading comprehension skills. At the very least, you should be spending your reading time doing verbal passages followed by questions and not just articles without questions.

Book clubs, reading, and study groups are a good way to increase your reading comprehension, but are not effective tools for increasing your MCAT Verbal Reasoning score in a short amount of time.

The most effective method of study to improve your MCAT verbal score is to do the following:

1. Take a verbal test under strict timed conditions and score yourself.

2. Take a break from verbal for at least one day.

3. Take the set of questions for the first passage in the verbal exam that you recently finished and examine the questions and each answer choice as if you had never read the passage, as was done in Lecture 2 of this book. If this step takes you less than 30 minutes per passage, then do it again because you missed quite a bit.

4. Repeat step 3 for each passage.

5. Take a break from verbal for at least one day.

6. Carefully read the first passage in the same verbal test, and write out a precisely worded main idea in one or two complete sentences being certain that your main idea expresses the author's opinion or stance on the issues.

7. Match your main idea to each question and all the answer choices and see what insights you gain into answering MCAT questions as was done in Lecture 3 of this book.

8. Repeat steps 6 and 7 for each passage.

# STOP!

## DO NOT LOOK AT THESE EXAMS UNTIL CLASS.

**30-MINUTE IN-CLASS EXAM FOR LECTURE 1**

## Passage I (Questions 1-7)

Philosophers Immanuel Kant and David Hume both spent their professional careers searching for a universal principle of morality. Considering that they began their searches with seemingly irreconcilable ideas of where to look, the similarity
5 in the moral systems they constructed is surprising. ...

Hume decided at the outset that a moral system must be practical, and maintained that, since reason is only useful for disinterested comparison, and since only sentiment (emotion) is capable of stirring people to action, the practical study of
10 morality should be concerned with sentiment. Hume begins with the assumption that whether something is judged moral or praiseworthy depends on the circumstances. He says, "What each man feels within himself is the standard of sentiment." ...

By contrast, Kant begins by assuming that, while
15 some time should be devoted to studying practical morality ("ethics"), it is also valuable to have an *absolute* system of morality based solely on reason, to be called "metaphysics". That forms the core of his laborious exploration of pure logic, called *Grounding for the Metaphysics of Morals*.

20 For both authors, the problem of subjectivity threatened to prevent unbiased analysis of morality. So both invented systems of "moral feedback," in which the philosophic actor tries to imagine the results of his actions as if someone else were performing them. Still, the final evaluation of the action's
25 worth must, in the end, be subjective. Kant's ultimate standard of morality is the "categorical imperative". It is phrased, "[To follow your] duty, act as if the physical act of your action were to become a universal law of nature." This means that, before one does anything, one should forget one's own motives for a
30 moment, and ask if he would want everyone to do as he does. If the answer is no, then his subjective desire is different from his objective assessment, and the action is contrary to duty.

Hume says that moral actions are those that create agreeable sentiments in others, as well as in oneself. You can therefore
35 judge what kind of sentiments your actions may cause others to feel by imagining someone else performing that action, and thinking about what kind of sentiments it would inspire in you. To make both of these constructions possible, there is a notion of some kind of uniformity in people's reason or emotion in
40 both works; Kant's reason for using pure logic was precisely to bypass empirical differences between people and individual circumstances, and ... he has the belief that people using only logic must inevitably reach the same conclusions about the morality of their own actions. Hume also admits
45 that "the notion of morals implies some sentiment common to all mankind." ...

Some Marxist theorists have speculated that Marx would tar both Kant and Hume as "bourgeois" philosophers. Answering why is an extremely difficult question. ... It may
50 lie in this sentence from *Marx's Manuscripts of 1844:* "The interests of the capitalist and those of the workers are therefore, *one and the same*, assert the bourgeois economists." ... In the directly preceding passage, Marx explained how capitalists try to mask the class struggle and exploitation inherent in
55 capitalist production, by monopolizing cultural institutions to establish hegemonic control over the working class. This is why, he explains, workers are actually conditioned to be grateful to the factory owner for allowing them to produce goods, only to have these taken away and sold. Based on
60 these writings, Marx would probably see any system that sought out a universal theory of morality as ignoring the opposing economic classes in society, and easily adapted to give the workers a false perception of the unitary interest of them and their oppressors.

1. The word *tar* (line 48) is used in the sense of:

   A. asphalt.
   B. suggest.
   C. label.
   D. stick.

2. According to the passage, Marx would have disagreed with Kant and Hume over which of the following ideas?

   A. What each man feels within himself is the standard of sentiment.
   B. There is uniformity in people's reason or emotion.
   C. The interests of the capitalists and the workers are one and the same.
   D. Morality is dependent upon the class struggle.

3. Assume that a universal principle of morality can be proven to exist. Which of the following hypotheses does this assumption suggest?

   A. The author is correct; despite their genesis, it is not surprising that Kant and Hume constructed similar systems.
   B. The author is correct; Marx, Hume, and Kant all constructed similar systems.
   C. The author is incorrect; Marx, Hume, and Kant did not all construct similar systems.
   D. The author is incorrect; despite their genesis, it is not surprising that Kant and Hume constructed similar systems.

4. According to the author, in creating his moral system, Hume equated:

   A. circumstances with disinterested comparison.
   B. circumstances with absolutism.
   C. practicality with stirring people to action.
   D. practicality with reason.

5. Based upon passage information, Marx most likely believed that:

   A. there is no universal theory of morality.
   B. philosophers were part of the bourgeois.
   C. the workers could be easily fooled.
   D. Kant's book supported capitalist exploitation.

6. Based upon passage information, Kant's system of "moral feedback" (line 22) differed from Hume's in that it might result in a situation wherein:

   A. one realized that his action might be 'right' so long as it didn't become a universal law of nature.
   B. one realized that a universal law of nature was unnecessary in determining duty.
   C. one realized that his action might be 'wrong' even though it created agreeable sentiments in others, as well as in oneself.
   D. one realized that his action might be illogical if sentiment was not further considered.

7. According to the passage, Hume's ideas evolved to the point where he:

   A. realized that reason was an inseparable part of a universal system of morality.
   B. was considering the sentiments of others as well as himself.
   C. chose to essentially agree with Kant on a universal system of morality.
   D. decided that sentiment without action was a necessary component of his morality system.

**GO ON TO THE NEXT PAGE.**

## Passage II (Questions 8-14)

In the Bible, when Jesus Christ was queried by skeptical Israelites on how Christians could continue to pay taxes to support the (pagan) Roman governors of Israel, he counseled, "Render unto Caesar what is Caesar's; render unto God what is
5　God's". The basic meaning of this guidance was that Christians may practice their faith while coexisting with the secular government. ... Later Christian theorists followed this example, often urging peaceful coexistence even with governments which violated every precept of Christian teachings. ...

10　The early Catholic bishop (St.) Augustine of Hippo and the Protestant dissident leader Martin Luther both advocated submission to the rule of tyrants, employing the analogy of a *dual* city or government, where earthly rule is often oppressive, yet is balanced by the assurance of brotherly love in the
15　kingdom of heaven. ...

According to Luther, true Christians should be willing to suffer persecution, without seeking to resist it by the anti-Christian methods of taking up arms in violent revolt, or seeking redress in the courts of the unbelievers. Luther even
20　took the analogy so far as to suggest that it is the Christians themselves who most benefit from harsh secular laws, which protect *them* from exploitation and persecution by false Christians and heathen. In fact, when commenting on popular "Christian" uprisings, Luther lays more blame on
25　self-righteous Christian rebels (such as various German peasant rebels of the age) than upon their oppressors, teaching that, regardless of their rulers' faults, rebels immediately cease to be Christians upon taking up arms, and incur further displeasure from God by blasphemously arrogating
30　His name and scriptures for an un-Christian cause. Luther claims that this is furthermore exacerbated because what the rebels often want is material benefit rather than religious freedom. ... According to Luther, it is the role of God alone to punish rulers, and rebels' usurpation of that authority for
35　themselves adds another sin to the list of charges against them; they effectively revolt against God's justice.

St. Augustine would have agreed. His *Confessions* and other theological writings maintained that God grants earthly rule to Christians and pagans alike, but that His
40　inscrutable will is always just. In the case of a revolt, Luther claimed, *both* sides inevitably incur divine punishment, since "God hates both tyrants and rebels; therefore He sets them on each other". Luther's vision of God raising up the peasants to punish their tyrants perfectly matches
45　Augustine's frequent portrayal of the Germanic "barbarians" who finally sacked Rome as the brutal instruments of God, sent to crush the corrupt Romans' arrogance. Augustine never considers the individual fate of these living tools, but Luther maintains that God sends the devil to stir them
50　up with lies, and afterwards they go to eternal torment.

Both of these theologians would hold that uprisings generally occur for the wrong reasons (i.e. worldly ambitions), because no tyrant can keep a true Christian from salvation, which should be all Christians' only concern in life.
55　For Luther, salvation lies in faith emanating from personal understanding of Biblical teachings, and "it is impossible that anyone should have the gospel kept from him...for it is a public teaching that moves freely." In Augustine's understanding, salvation is granted through the mercy of
60　God, who sends hardship and death to test men's faith. The true Augustinian Christian would maintain his faith through any ordeal, and even if his body perishes, God will save him for his conviction.

8. Which of the following statements, if true, would most directly *challenge* the principles of Martin Luther?

   A. The Bible's Old Testament refers to a period before the birth of Jesus.
   B. The Bible alone contains only a small part of what Jesus intended for his followers.
   C. The German "barbarians" who sacked Rome had been previously converted.
   D. Augustine's understanding of salvation granted through the mercy of Christ was flawed.

9. Some theologians believe that killing and violence are acceptable when used in self-defense. An appropriate clarification of the passage would be the stipulation that:

   A. both Luther and Augustine would have disagreed with this belief.
   B. both Luther and Augustine would have agreed with this belief.
   C. only Augustine might have agreed with this belief.
   D. only Luther might have agreed with this belief.

10. If the information in lines 37-54 is correct, one could most reasonably conclude that, compared to Luther, Augustine was:

   A. much more reasonably inclined.
   B. more prepared to define God's will.
   C. less eager to send people to eternal torment.
   D. less willing to announce God's final judgment on those who had sinned.

11. The author's attitude toward the theories of Augustine and Luther in the passage is most accurately described as:

A. disapproving.
B. mistrustful.
C. neutral.
D. favorable.

12. What is the meaning of the phrase; "The true Augustinian Christian would maintain his faith through any ordeal, and even if his body perishes, God will save him for his conviction" (lines 60-63)?

A. This Christian would end up in heaven because of his beliefs.
B. God would save this Christian for judgment at the end of the Christian's ordeal.
C. God would save this Christian from his ordeal and judge him.
D. It was not necessary for this Christian to die for him to be convicted.

13. The author's primary purpose in the passage is apparently:

A. to clarify the differences between the ways in which the early Catholics and Protestants dealt with persecution.
B. to justify the persecution of early Christians by secular governments.
C. to consider the similarities between the ways in which the early Catholics and Protestants dealt with persecution.
D. to question the passive practices of the early Catholics and Protestants when faced with persecution.

14. What is the most serious apparent weakness of the information described?

A. While implying that Christians may coexist with a secular government, it differentiates between Catholics and Protestants.
B. While implying representation of Augustine and Luther, its conclusions are based primarily on information according to Luther.
C. While implying representation of all Christian theorists, only Augustine and Luther are mentioned.
D. While implying agreement between Augustine and Luther, their attitudes were clearly opposed.

**GO ON TO THE NEXT PAGE.**

## Passage III (Questions 15-21)

Of all the bizarre and melancholy fates that could befall an otherwise ordinary person, Mary Mallon's has to be among the most sad and peculiar. ...Like millions before and since, she came to this country from Ireland, seeking a
5 better life. Never "tried" in any sense, instead, she was forced by public health officials to live for a total of 26 years on a tiny island in the East River, isolated from and shunned by her fellow humans. And, while she was not the only one of her kind, her name became synonymous with
10 disease and death. She was Typhoid Mary, and her story really begins on Long Island.

In the summer of 1906, Mallon, was working as a cook for a wealthy New York banker, Charles Henry Warren, and his family. The Warrens had rented a spacious
15 house in Oyster Bay, "in a desirable part of the village," for the summer. From August 27 to September 3, six of the eleven people in the house came down with typhoid fever, including Mrs. Warren, two daughters, two maids and a gardener. Two investigators were unable to find contaminated water or food
20 to explain the outbreak. Worried they wouldn't be able to rent the house unless they figured out the source of the disease, the owners, in the winter of 1906, hired George Soper, a sanitary engineer.

Soper soon dismissed "soft clams" and other potential
25 contaminants as the cause and began to focus on the family. He later wrote, "It was found that the family had changed cooks about three weeks before the typhoid epidemic broke out ... She remained with the family only a short time, leaving about three weeks after the outbreak occurred ... [and]
30 seemed to be in perfect health." Soper became convinced that this woman was a healthy carrier of the disease, and, in so doing, was the first to identify a healthy typhoid carrier in the United States. Although his deduction was undoubtedly brilliant, his handling of Mallon was not.

35 Soper tracked Mallon down to a home on Park Avenue in Manhattan where she was a cook. Appearing without warning, Soper told her she was spreading death and disease through her cooking and that he wanted samples of her feces, urine, and blood for tests. In a later description,
40 Soper wrote, "It did not take Mary long to react to this suggestion. She seized a carving fork and advanced in my direction. I passed rapidly down the narrow hall through the tall iron gate."

Convinced by Soper's information, the New York City
45 health inspector in March 1907, carried Mallon off, screaming and kicking, to a hospital, where her feces did indeed show high concentrations of typhoid bacilli. She was moved to an isolation cottage on the grounds of the Riverside Hospital, between the Bronx and Rikers Island.

50 ... She stayed there for three years, in relative isolation. It was during that time that she was dubbed Typhoid Mary. Mallon despised the moniker and protested all her life that she was healthy and could not be a disease carrier. As she told a newspaper, "I have never had typhoid in my life and have
55 always been healthy. Why should I be banished like a leper and compelled to live in solitary confinement ...?"

After a short period of freedom in which Mallon failed to comply with the health inspector's requirements, she was eventually sent back to North Brother Island, where
60 she lived the rest of her life, alone in a one-room cottage. In 1938 when she died, a newspaper noted there were 237 other typhoid carriers living under city health department observation. But she was the only one kept isolated for years, a result as much of prejudice toward the Irish and
65 noncompliant women as of a public health threat.

---

**15.** The author probably mentions that Mallon was "never 'tried' in any sense" (line 5) in order:

A. to demonstrate the power of the wealthy at that time.
B. to provide a comparison with people who have actually committed a crime.
C. to illustrate the persistence of Soper's investigations.
D. to support the claim that she deserved at least a hearing.

**16.** According to the passage, the first two investigators were unable to find the cause of the outbreak (lines 18-20). The information presented on typhoid makes which of the following explanations most plausible?

A. They focused too closely on the "soft clams" that Soper later discredited.
B. Typhoid is not really passed through contaminated food or water.
C. They never considered that typhoid could be carried by a healthy person.
D. By this time, Mallon was no longer employed by the Warren family.

17. The author's argument that Mallon's isolation was "a result as much of prejudice … as of a public health threat" (lines 64-65) is most weakened by which idea in the passage?

    A. Mallon's primary occupation was as a cook.
    B. Mallon did not believe that she was a carrier of the disease.
    C. Mallon would not abide by the health inspector's requirements.
    D. Mallon actually was the source of the typhoid outbreak in the Warren home.

18. Which of the following statements is the most reasonable conclusion that can be drawn from the author's description of the typhoid outbreak in the house at Oyster Bay?

    A. The Warren family did not hire Soper.
    B. The two investigators were hired by the Warrens.
    C. The Warren family hired Soper.
    D. The owners were anxious to sell the house.

19. Passage information indicates that which of the following statements must be true?

    A. Mallon had probably not infected anyone prior to the Warren family.
    B. Mallon was almost certainly not washing her hands prior to preparing the Warren's meals.
    C. Being labeled 'Typhoid Mary' by the press was the primary reason for her confinement.
    D. The health inspector was doubtless prejudiced toward the Irish.

20. According to passage information, Mallon worked for the Warren family for approximately:

    A. two weeks.
    B. three weeks.
    C. five weeks.
    D. six weeks.

21. The contention that in "1938 when [Mallon] died, ... there were 237 other typhoid carriers living under city health department observation. But she was the only one kept isolated for years" (lines 61-64), can most justifiably be interpreted as support for the idea that:

    A. Mallon was unfairly treated by the city health department.
    B. Mallon's isolation might have stemmed from the health department's early ignorance of the disease.
    C. The "other" 237 typhoid carriers were all kept isolated at one time or another.
    D. The "other" 237 typhoid carriers were much like Mallon.

---

**STOP.** IF YOU FINISH BEFORE TIME IS CALLED, CHECK YOUR WORK. YOU MAY GO BACK TO ANY QUESTION IN THIS TEST BOOKLET.

---

# 30-MINUTE IN-CLASS EXAM FOR LECTURE 2

Polling research shows that the ideal speaking voice should be clear and intelligible, of moderate volume and pace, and inflected to suggest the emotions expressed. To suggest credibility, the voice's tone should be pitched as
5 low as is naturally possible... A low pitch is desirable in both genders, since it is popularly associated with truth-telling. However, an artificially lowered voice can sacrifice intelligibility, which is irritating to listeners. Thus, speakers should experiment to find their optimal level, which will be
10 at their lowest intelligible pitch. ... To deepen the pitch, speakers should make an extra-deep inhalation before speaking, and then exhale fully as they speak.

Habits to be avoided (because they irritate most listeners) include monotony, mumbling, grating, pretension, high-
15 pitched whining, and breathiness. ... Among the best practitioners of mainstream vocal "propriety" are famous news anchors, like Walter Cronkite, Dan Rather, and Jane Pauley, for whom vocal image is a key component of their job success. However, everyone who communicates should
20 be aware that their voice is a critical component of their audience's perceptions of them, comprising about 38% of the overall impression imparted by their presentation. (By comparison, appearance accounts for about 50% of the speaker's impact, and the quality of content accounts for a
25 mere 6%.) ...

For those not born with naturally pleasant voices, or worse still, those with naturally unpleasant ones, speech training can be invaluable in improving impressions. No voice teacher is necessarily required, since practice alone
30 can produce significant improvements. However, some special equipment is needed. Because talking always causes cranial resonance, which distorts the speaker's hearing, no one can hear what his voice really sounds like to a listener. Thus, some sort of tape recorder or other feedback is a
35 virtual necessity.

Speaking begins with breathing, since speech is just exhaled air that sets the vocal cords to resonating. If insufficient air is inhaled before speaking, the words formed must necessarily be strained and breathless. ...
40 Diaphragmatic breathing results in a deeper voice than upper-lung breathing. People tend to stick out their chests and inhale shallowly with the upper lungs, resulting in a high-pitched voice, which must also be rapid to avoid running out of breath before the sentence ends. In diaphragmatic
45 breathing, the lower abdomen moves out, inflating the bottom two-thirds of the lungs fully, but the shoulders do not rise. To practice switching from shallow breathing to deep, diaphragmatic inhalations, it helps to lie on the floor and breathe naturally, since diaphragmatic breathing is
50 natural when prone. ... Increasing lung capacity will also deepen the voice and permit longer sentences without pausing. ... One method to increase lung capacity is to inhale fully, then count out loud slowly, while enunciating each number clearly, aiming for a count of 60.

55 Loudness, or volume, is distinct from pitch, though the remedy for overly soft-spoken people is similar. They can manage to speak louder by first inhaling more deeply, which allows them added lungpower to project their sentences. Alternately, they can pause more often, say fewer words in every
60 breath, and thus leaving more air power for each. There are those who speak too softly not because of improper breathing, but due to psychological factors: they may be shy and not wish to be obtrusive, or may not hear that their words are too soft to be intelligible at a distance. ... For them, one useful exercise
65 is to recognize the five basic volume levels (whisper, hushed, conversation, loud, and yelling) by practicing speaking a word in each of these modes. ...

22. According to the passage information, which of the following would be most likely if a person who was talking to you attempted to make their voice sound unusually low?

   A. You might think that they were lying.
   B. They could be irritated with you.
   C. They might well sound monotonous.
   D. You could find them difficult to understand.

23. The author most likely believes that one of the main purposes of speaking during a face-to-face meeting should be to:
   A. convey a favorable impression.
   B. effectively transmit your ideas.
   C. gain leverage.
   D. communicate as naturally as possible.

24. The author provides a list of "habits to be avoided" (lines 13-15). Which of the habits would the suggestions in this passage not help a speaker to curb?

   A. monotony
   B. breathiness
   C. pretension
   D. high-pitched whining

25. The term ideal speaking voice (line 1-2) refers implicitly to a voice that is:

   A. the most pleasant to listen to.
   B. the most persuasive.
   C. the least irritating.
   D. the most natural.

26. Passage information indicates that a person speaking in a high-pitched voice might be doing all of the following EXCEPT:

   I. Breathing with their upper lungs
   II. Breathing deeply
   III. Lying

   A. I only
   B. II only
   C. III only
   D. I and III only

27. Which of the following assertions is most clearly a thesis presented by the author?

   A. Speakers can gain by improving their speaking voices.
   B. The tone of the ideal speaking voice should be pitched as low as possible.
   C. What you are saying is more important than how you are saying it.
   D. Emotional inflections can be an irritating aspect of a speaker's voice.

28. The ideas discussed in this passage would likely be of most use to:

   A. A doctor
   B. A journalist
   C. A radio show personality
   D. A television commentator

**GO ON TO THE NEXT PAGE.**

A great deal of international conflict arises from border disputes. Throughout history, particularly along borders which have been "artificially" defined, rather than utilizing more natural pre-existing cultural and geographical
5 demarcations, there has been a constant ebb and flow as nations have sought to consolidate their borders and their security. However, with ever-increasing economic disparity between many bordering countries, these conflicts have changed and now center more around issues of immigration.
10 ... Such situations are prevalent today in countries such as New Zealand, the Colombian-Peruvian border, and the U.S.'s Mexican border. These instances ... exemplify the problems caused by such disputes.

Presently, New Zealand's conflict stems from illegal
15 immigration into its territory, mostly from the Chinese island-province Fujian. ... Fujian is situated on China's southern coast, near Taiwan. Many Fujianese immigrants use New Zealand, because of its location, as a stepping-stone to their final goal, the U.S. Their transport is usually a smuggling boat's hold,
20 where living conditions are inadequate and sometimes dangerous, with insufficient food, sanitation, and ventilation. Within the past year, U.S. officials found three Chinese immigrants in a smuggling boat's sealed cargo container, dead from suffocation. ... Recently, New Zealand attempted to deal with these aliens
25 by enacting new immigration laws which hasten the process required to deport them.

The reasons for the Chinese immigrant's journey stems from both "push" and "pull" factors relative to the countries of origin and destination. For example, the
30 Fujianese feel compelled ("pushed") to leave because of the area's low standard of living. The poor wages, bad housing, and lack of political freedom can also be seen as "pull" factors, due to the idea that the Fujianese understand that life would be better in other countries. The U.S. and New
35 Zealand offer much higher wages, a better standard of living, and political freedom. ... These push and pull factors are powerful incentives. ... What keeps New Zealand from experiencing an even more profound illegal immigration problem is that the immigrants often do not settle there. ...

40 The border issue between Colombia and its neighbors is another illustration of international conflict. Colombia lies along a corridor from South to Central America. This region has historically been politically unstable, partially due to regional narcotics trafficking, and the wars this engenders.
45 Colombia, itself, is notorious for its export of drugs, especially cocaine. This reputation forces neighboring countries to strengthen patrols over adjoining borders. Recently, Peru deployed additional soldiers to its border with Colombia. Although Peruvian President Fujimori denied any diplomatic
50 problems and stated his troops were there "to guarantee the sovereignty and integrity of Peruvian territory", their mission is both to keep guerrillas *and* drugs out of Peru. ... Though understandable, this has in turn, pushed Columbia to respond in kind with more Columbian border troops facing Peru. This

55 brinksmanship seriously depletes resources from these needy countries which might be better spent elsewhere.

Traditionally, these two countries might have been attempting to secure their borders from invading countries, or even seeking to expand their own territories and acquire
60 additional resources. However, Ecuador and Peru are protecting their borders from rogue drug traffickers and guerillas, not Colombia's government. ... Neither side is attempting to acquire new territory, but rather to secure and protect that which they already hold. ...

29. The author's discussion of "push" and "pull" factors (line 28) most accurately implies that:
   A. "pull" factors compel someone to leave, while "push" factors induce someone to come.
   B. "pull" factors induce someone to come, while "push" factors also induce someone to come.
   C. "push" factors require someone to leave, while "pull" factors also compel someone to leave.
   D. "push" factors compel someone to leave, while "pull" factors induce someone to come.

30. Given the information in the passage, if "'artificially' defined" borders (line 3) were eliminated throughout the world, which of the following outcomes would most likely occur?
   A. People would naturally immigrate to areas with higher standards of living.
   B. Nations would encounter less traditional border strife.
   C. Nations would require greater border security measures.
   D. People would live more harmoniously.

31. Which of the following assertions does the author support with an example?

    A. Transportation methods used by illegal immigrants are sometimes dangerous.
    B. Peru and Columbia are seeking to expand their own territories.
    C. New Zealand has enacted laws that hasten deportation proceedings.
    D. The mission of the Peruvian troops is to keep guerillas and drugs out of Peru.

32. The passage as a whole suggests that in order for a nation to slow the exodus of its inhabitants to other countries, it must:

    A. become more attractive to those who are leaving.
    B. abandon the traditional methods of guarding borders.
    C. respond in some way to the conflicts arising from border disputes.
    D. answer the challenges set forth by adjoining countries.

33. If the passage information is correct, what inference is justified by the fact that virtually no immigration from West Berlin to adjoining East Berlin occurred, over the 40 years before the period described?

    A. Crossing the heavily guarded borders between West and East Berlin was very dangerous.
    B. It was understood that life would be better in East Berlin.
    C. The inhabitants of both 'Berlins' were happy to remain where they were.
    D. The economic conditions of West Berlin were much more favorable than those of East Berlin.

34. The author implies that which of the following is not one of the reasons that Peruvian President Fujimori deployed soldiers to its borders with Columbia?

    I. Fujimori is attempting to keep drugs out of his country.
    II. Fujimori fears that Columbia is seeking to expand its territories.
    III. Fujimori is probably concerned that Columbia wants to acquire additional resources.

    A. I only
    B. II only
    C. III only
    D. II and III only

35. It seems likely that New Zealand may be suffering less from immigration issues than the United States for which of the following reasons:

    I. The U.S. offers higher wages than New Zealand.
    II. New laws enacted in New Zealand allow faster deportation proceedings.
    III. Immigrants often do not settle in New Zealand.

    A. II only
    B. III only
    C. II and III only
    D. I, II, and III

GO ON TO THE NEXT PAGE.

Perhaps the greatest problem with the law of personal injury is its uncertainty about its own purpose—does it exist to compensate victims fully, or to deter careless wrongdoers fully? It must choose, because these two aims are
5 mutually exclusive: tort awards cannot *fully* compensate and *correctly* deter, as long as there are administrative costs involved in obtaining an award. Assume a plaintiff's lawyer charges a 30% contingency fee upon winning a case (or the equivalent flat fee). If the plaintiff is awarded 100% of the
10 damages suffered, she only receives compensation for 70% of her injuries. If she is paid in full, then the defendant is paying 130% of the actual harm caused, and is over-deterred.

In reality, compensation tends toward inadequacy, and
15 not just because of administrative costs. There is no compensation unless the plaintiff proves "negligence", meaning a person may cause any amount of harm, but be excused from paying because she acted "reasonably" rather than carelessly. The hurdle of proving negligence also tends toward inadequate
20 deterrence, because even negligent injurers escape liability if plaintiffs cannot collect convincing proof of negligence.

On the other hand, in a few cases, both compensation and deterrence are exorbitant, especially when a single jury award tries to be both. Consider the following permutation
25 on actual events. A tanker passing through a residential neighborhood leaks acrylonitrile, destroying several homes and poisoning one. Angry residents sue the company for designing its tanker cars negligently. At trial, the company's counsel—a good economist, but a poor lawyer—admits
30 safer tankers were available, but the cost is prohibitive. After extensive cost-benefit analyses, he says, the company found it cheaper just to pay victims for their losses, as it now offers to do. Sound fair? The company would be lucky to escape punitive damages! Remember, these have been
35 applied where judges deemed that even full compensation is inadequate deterrence; generally when the plaintiff's conduct is seen as malicious. However, they may also be awarded when there is "a conscious and deliberate disregard of ... others." ... In this case, the company's cost-
40 benefit analysis is economically "correct" and justifiable: if the new tanker costs more than it saves, it is inefficient. On the other hand, how many juries—or even judges—will see this very analysis as anything but a cold and calculating balancing of profits against the costs of
45 human life? If (arbitrary) punitive damages are granted, plaintiffs emerge overcompensated, and defendants pay out of proportion to harm. Since repeated punitive awards are allowed, the company may be forced to buy the expensive tankers. This is unfortunate, because it results in a waste of
50 resources.

Tort law, gradually realizing the difficulty of proving negligence, has moved towards allowing recovery with ever less proof of negligence. ... Potentially, the most promising development in tort (personal injury) law has been the advent
55 of strict liability, which waives plaintiffs' need to prove the defendant's carelessness in certain instances where the carelessness is obvious, or could have resulted from no factor other than negligence. Unfortunately, the *application* of strict liability is severely constrained by legal doctrine, which limits
60 its application to a small range of "unusually hazardous activities".

Sometimes, the criteria for imposing strict liability seem arbitrary. ... For example, the law permits strict liability only when the expected damage—a product of risk and
65 probable harm—is high. ... Yet it is equally appropriate when the damage is *slight*. Consider the same tanker spilling toxic chemicals along a 200-mile stretch of farmland. Imagine the total cost of decontamination is $1,000,000, but the costs are borne by 150 small farmers.
70 In this scenario, the total damage is high, but comes to only $6,667 per plaintiff. Since just proving negligence may cost more, few will actually sue. The same applies for small harms; there is neither compensation nor deterrence, because plaintiffs bear the loss, and defendants effectively have no
75 incentive to prevent small harms. ...

**36.** What is the author's response to the standard story about the woman who spills hot McDonald's coffee in her lap, sues and gets several million dollars?

A. This story does not reflect that compensation is usually insufficient.
B. This story is a good example of just the right amount of compensation.
C. This story does not reflect that deterrence is costly.
D. In this story, the woman was malicious.

37. Which of the following assertions is the most effective argument *against* the author's opinion that personal injury law cannot satisfactorily compensate and deter "as long as there are administrative costs involved in obtaining an award" (lines 1-7)?

A. These administrative costs are inconsequential.
B. Attorneys are a necessary part of the judicial system and should be compensated for their work.
C. The administrative costs should be added to the compensation received by the plaintiff.
D. The administrative costs should be subtracted from the compensation received by the plaintiff.

38. The passage indicates that its author would NOT agree with which of the following statements?

A. Tanker companies are a good example of defendants who are under-deterred.
B. Negligence on the part of the defendant is generally not difficult for the plaintiff to prove.
C. The costs associated with suing and defending against suits can be tremendous.
D. In many situations, over-deterrence results in primarily economic ramifications.

39. Assume that since the 9-11 terrorist attacks on the World Trade Center (WTC) buildings, all lawsuits have been settled by the WTC insurance companies, who have now mandated that they will no longer insure any building in the world that is over five stories tall. The author's comments suggest that this situation could reasonably be interpreted as evidence that:

A. the insurance companies were over-deterred.
B. the insurance companies were under-deterred.
C. the plaintiffs were under-compensated.
D. the plaintiffs were overcompensated.

40. Suppose that a study found that police agencies routinely set aside large amounts of money in their yearly budgets, which they expect to pay out in lawsuits against their agency. Which of the following statements is an assumption of the author about the effects of lawsuit awards that would be called into question?

A. Simply proving negligence can be a very costly process.
B. Many people will not sue because the process is too costly.
C. If a plaintiff receives full compensation and administrative costs, the defendant is over-deterred.
D. Depending upon the size of the award, a defendant police agency might not be deterred at all.

41. Which of the following conclusions can justifiably be drawn from the experience of the tanker company's counsel mentioned in the passage?

A. Good economists make for poor attorneys.
B. Costs should never be considered prohibitive where safety is concerned.
C. Toxic materials should not be shipped through residential neighborhoods.
D. Honesty is not always the best policy for an attorney.

42. The author argues that, "Potentially, the most promising development in tort (personal injury) law has been the advent of strict liability" (lines 53-55). These beliefs imply that:

A. the use of strict liability has become increasingly popular for defendants.
B. the uses of strict liability should remain limited in scope.
C. the author approves of waiving the requirement for proof, where carelessness is evident.
D. the author approves of compensation where carelessness is evident.

---

**STOP.** IF YOU FINISH BEFORE TIME IS CALLED, CHECK YOUR WORK. YOU MAY GO BACK TO ANY QUESTION IN THIS TEST BOOKLET.

---

STOP.

# 30-MINUTE IN-CLASS EXAM FOR LECTURE 3

**Passage I (Questions 43-49)**

For most people, gender and gender identity go hand-in-hand. In other words, a female acts like a "woman". The fact that Gender Identity Disorder exists in the DSM IV [the official handbook of psychiatric disorders] as a diagnosis

5 is an admission on the part of psychologists that our society has clearly defined gender roles. These contribute to what it is generally considered "normal". Implied in the name of the disorder is an incongruity between assigned sexual organs and gender identity.

10 The most comprehensive case study of the disorder is the recently published case history of "Chris," a female patient who identified more closely with males, and stated a wish to become a male. In response, Chris adopted masculine mannerisms such as wearing men's clothes, deepening her

15 voice, sporting a masculine haircut, playing sports against male teams, etc. Chris believed she was born the wrong sex; she was a man inside a woman's body. The incongruity is undisputed; she did everything that was within her means to have her peers recognize her as a man.

20 It is important to stress when looking for causal factors for Chris' disorder that Chris was in no way confused about her identity. In some ways, this makes Chris an ideal subject for studying the causes of the disorder. She is described as a relatively well-adjusted individual who did well in school, was relatively

25 well liked among her peers, and seemed capable of creating long-term intimate relationships with others. Because the disorder is clearly present (Chris is aware of it herself), basic defects in personality (i.e. maladjustment, inability to make friends) can be more or less ruled out as causes of her uneasiness with her assigned sex. One must

30 then ponder the age-old question of society as the cause.

The notion of gender identity is so heavily dependent on societal norms that, in this case, many psychologists may believe society is the culprit. Similar to the ideas advanced in labeling theory, the mere labeling of some

35 behaviors as "masculine" and others as "feminine" may have created the criteria for this disorder to be labeled as deviant or abnormal. In another culture, where the labeling is different, would Chris have even felt the need to identify herself as distinctly male? Along the same lines of thinking, would the

40 incongruity even be considered a "disorder" in another culture?

Evidence varies regarding the two sides of the issue. Upbringing and/or some biochemical abnormalities could account for the etiology of the disorder, indicating that it is not simply due to societal labels. Indeed, it may seem

45 convincing to argue that Chris strongly identified with males very early in her life, and that this was reflected in her interest in "male" activities (e.g. sports) and unease in using girls' bathrooms and playing on girls' teams. Yet one could also argue that certain activities were labeled male, and

50 Chris molded her interests to include them, so she would be considered "male." It is virtually impossible to unravel which came first, the labeling of her favored activities as "male" or her interest in them. Almost certainly, there is a complex interaction between the two.

55 Remaining, however, is the question of treatment for Chris. Although she is currently a well-adjusted individual, she acknowledges a desire to change her sexual assignment to match her gender. One might ask if this is really necessary, since she is already well adjusted. Part of what we

60 strive for as psychologically healthy individuals is an acceptance of ourselves in a "natural" state. It is often the case that, through psychotherapy, one learns that one may not necessarily have to change oneself as much as one's perception of self. ... The effect of a physical sex reassignment

65 operation on Chris' happiness cannot be foretold with complete certainty.

In conclusion, it is interesting to note that Chris' desire to have the anatomy of a man is considered part of a "disorder," while a small-breasted woman's desire for breast implants

70 would usually be construed as a desire to increase her femininity and not be labeled as such. Perhaps Chris is somewhere on a male-female continuum and, like the woman who desires the breast augmentation, is pushing herself toward the closer end of the spectrum into our neatly constructed gender dichotomy.

**43.** The passage suggests that its author would probably *disagree* with which of the following statements?

  **A.** It is possible that Chris participated in "male" activities in order to be considered male.

  **B.** It is possible that Chris naturally participated in "male" activities.

  **C.** Chris was not confused about her identity.

  **D.** Most cultures have clearly defined gender roles.

44. Implicit in the passage is the assumption that:

 I. one should be happy in one's "natural" state.
 II. one can be well-adjusted, yet unhappy with one's "natural" state.
 III. one's perception of self is most important.

 A. I only
 B. II only
 C. III only
 D. I and III only

45. The author of the passage would be most likely to agree with which of the following ideas expressed by other psychologists?

 A. A DSM IV 'disorder' may not actually be a disorder at all.
 B. The DSM IV is a poor descriptor of abnormal behavior and desires since it is easily influenced by societal norms.
 C. Some DSM IV 'disorders' are simply an attempt to characterize socially abnormal behavior and desires.
 D. Behavior and desires must fall within the parameters of the DSM IV to be considered normal by society.

46. The author hints that the fact that Chris is well-adjusted indicates that her "uneasiness with her assigned sex" (lines 24-29):

 A. is a problem which should be overcome through psychiatry.
 B. is due to the culture she lives in.
 C. can be overcome through surgery.
 D. is a basic personality defect.

47. Suppose it is discovered that prescription medication allows Chris to become somewhat more comfortable with her "natural" state. Does this discovery support the author's argument?

 A. Yes; it confirms it.
 B. No; it does not affect it.
 C. No; it weakens it.
 D. No; it disproves it.

48. The author admits that, "The effect of a physical sex reassignment operation on Chris' happiness cannot be foretold with complete certainty" (lines 64-66). The author most likely believes that:

 I. it is just as likely that psychotherapy would help Chris to change her perception of self.
 II. in our society, in the body of a woman, Chris will not be happy.
 III. a "sex reassignment operation" would make Chris happier.

 A. I only
 B. II only
 C. III only
 D. II and III only

49. The author's attitude toward "our" societal norms is most accurately described as:

 A. favorable.
 B. neutral.
 C. distrustful.
 D. disapproving.

83     GO ON TO THE NEXT PAGE.

## Passage II (Questions 50-56)

Human values—these 'ends', which are generally viewed as "desirable"—are not static. They change according to certain factors surrounding the people who create them. One of the more significant of these factors is technology. Due to
5  this, people must continually question the reasons for the use of technology in their own surroundings; in their "information ecologies".

Just as "freedom of speech" is not clearly defined, the purpose of some technology is ambiguous. To decide
10 whether a certain technology is a good fit for a certain "ecology," one must use critical analysis. [Analysts] Nardi and O'Day create a three-pronged format for analyzing technology's worth. ... These methods include working from core values, paying attention, and asking strategic
15 questions.

Making sure that technology fits with a person's or group's "core values"—its essential function/purpose—is the first step in examining its use. If technology doesn't assist in promoting these values, then it cannot be considered
20 useful. For example, a for-profit business' core value is profit maximization; any technology which does not increase revenues or reduce costs should be viewed with suspicion. ... Paying attention keeps people from taking a technology for granted. If the technology is taken for
25 granted, the actual purpose for using it can become clouded. Finally, asking strategic and open-ended questions fosters a discussion about all uses for the technology. Asking who, what, why, where, and how questions is the best method in analyzing the use for technology in an information ecology. If,
30 by examining the situation, it becomes evident that the existing technology is not useful, then the person or group that expects to use it should have direct input into finding a replacement. This ensures that technology will be used for the right purposes.

Technology may force people away from their own
35 values. This idea, presented by theorists Neil Postman and Jacques Ellul, creates a disturbing image of a world where technology itself becomes the center of a society without values. One example is "information glut", a term coined by Postman. He states that the rapid flow of information
40 allowed by automation and Internet/email provides vast amounts of data to many users quickly and simultaneously, but doesn't allow humans to understand its meaning fast enough to keep up. He goes on to say that much of the information we receive does not pertain to us, so it is at best
45 an irrelevant distraction rather than the useful news it was intended as. This may create a problem when, for example, images of violence in the Middle East do not affect us because they are "here today, gone tomorrow" and are too far away to influence us. However, this view is somewhat
50 one-sided. It is argued that too much information is bad, yet it can also be argued that more information is good. By giving people more information, they have a wider basis from which to make decisions and form opinions. No one can argue that giving additional and different perspectives is
55 inherently bad. Yet, Postman does have a valid point that the

information is useless unless it is thoroughly examined. Simply put, the challenge is not necessarily to reduce the amount of information available, but to allow it to be better tailored to individual recipients' needs. Thus, we as a
60 society must consciously attempt to not only obtain information, but to analyze it for meaning and relate this back to our own values. ...

50. The author of the passage would be most likely to agree with which of the following ideas expressed by other technology theorists?

   A. Soliciting further ideas and diverse ideas is not always wrong.
   B. Obtaining additional and differing perspectives is always beneficial.
   C. For information to be of value, it must challenge our human values.
   D. A great deal of the information which we receive is useless because it does not pertain to us.

51. The passage argument suggests that information recipients might benefit from:

   I. a more rapid flow of information.
   II. thoroughly examining their information.
   III. limiting non-pertinent information.

   A. I only
   B. II only
   C. III only
   D. II and III only

52. In describing Neil Postman's "information glut", the author uses the example of "images of violence in the Middle East [that] do not affect us" (lines 47). The author's point is that:

   A. the Middle East is at best an irrelevant distraction.
   B. the Middle East is poorly understood by us.
   C. these images should affect us.
   D. these images should not be so easily accessible.

53. If the following statements are true, which would most weaken the argument of the author?

   A. The degree to which technology determines human values is questionable.
   B. Information must be analyzed for its relevance to human values.
   C. Human values are unchanging.
   D. Human values are culturally dependent.

54. The author argues, "more information is good" (line 51). Unlike Neil Postman, the author does not consider which of the following to be a factor that might limit the usefulness of information?

   A. Space
   B. Distance
   C. Frequency
   D. Time

55. According to the passage, one drawback of technology is that it can:

   A. supersede all other values.
   B. be used to destroy human values.
   C. subtly change people's values.
   D. become an irrelevant distraction.

56. Suppose it could be established that technology is most efficient when it performs its function unobtrusively, without being noticed. The author of the passage would be most likely to respond to this information by:

   A. suggesting that this determination ratifies his thesis.
   B. proposing that we must still analyze the information for meaning.
   C. asserting that efficiency is usually degraded when a technology is taken for granted.
   D. explaining that we must still remain aware of the technology and its intended purpose.

**GO ON TO THE NEXT PAGE.**

From its very beginning, ... the New York City Opera production of "Mephistopheles" deserves high marks for visual excellence. It begins with an audiovisual show featuring stars, religious images projected onto swirling mist, and very, very loud brass winds, intended for drama and only slightly corny.

The scene then shifts to Hell, where a naked, disheveled Mephisto, singing from his broken throne, sarcastically apologizes for not being up to Heavenly standards of singing, providing the proof that harmony is still a longer way off in some places than in others. In the director's vision, the characterization of Mephisto is akin to Milton's rebellious, but somewhat sympathetic anti-hero, a dissident angel who dares to fight a vastly superior power to preserve his vision of the world. Accordingly, this production features a Mephisto who is flippant but clever, blasphemous but thought provoking, and possessed of both sympathy and contempt for human weaknesses. He strikes a balance between his boldness and his cowering before Heaven.

A chorus presents the essential plot of Faust, reduced from its several incarnations. When the angels point out the mortal Dr. Faust, as God's incorruptible servant on earth, the devil Mephisto promises to turn him from God through temptation. Thus, this version presents temptation as essentially a wager, or struggle, between God and the Devil (which, at one time, was a remarkably blasphemous notion, as it contradicted the dogma that God is all-powerful over evil). As the divine host departs, Mephisto regains his mocking manner, singing, "It's nice to see the Eternal Father talking with the Devil—in such a human way!"

Mephisto tempts Faust in the middle of a country fair thronged with revelers, which is meant to symbolize the worldly pleasures. This symbolism hearkens back to the ancient morality play *Vanity Fair*, which also featured a bazaar extolling sins. Mephisto, garbed in virtue as a gray robed beggar monk, finally announces himself to be Mephisto. In a good aria, much of which is delivered while dancing or rolling on the ground, the devil again introduces himself sympathetically as God's constructive critic, one who "thinks of evil/ but always achieves the good," singing menacingly of how he wages an eternal dissent against God:

"Light has usurped my power,
seized my scepter in rebellion;
I hurl forth this single syllable—NO!"

In this version of *Faust*, it is Faust who seizes the devil's bargain: Mephisto must furnish him with a single moment so lovely it deserves to last forever.

In Scene II, Faust is transformed into a younger man, who courts the young woman of his dreams, a commoner named Margaret. At this point, the play devolves into stock characters and slapstick. Faust and Margaret sing very forgettable arias about the supremacy of feeling over reason, a theme which is not really congruent with the Faust myth. The shallowness of the libretto's throwaway lyrics is compounded by Margaret's emotionless singing.

Those who read the book know the next scene as the Witch's Sabbath on Walpurgis Night, though the libretto itself offers little explanation for the abrupt change of scene. Mephistopheles now appears as the leader of hedonistic sinners, calling them with the aria "Come on, onward, onward". Again, the portrayal of his character is less evil than rebellious and hedonic, he recognizes the power of mankind's pursuit of earthly pleasures, singing, "Here is the world, round and empty" while holding the globe. It is unclear whether it is his effort, or human nature itself, which is responsible for sin. At one point, he laments *mankind's* cruelty and cunning, concluding, "How I laugh when I think what's in store for them!/Dance on; the world is lost." ...

**57.** Assume that several others who had attended the same opera were interviewed. If they remarked that Margaret sang with tremendous passion, these remarks would weaken the passage assertion that:

A. Mephisto had rendered her irresistible to Faust.
B. the lyrics which she sang were "throwaway".
C. the young woman of Faust's dreams sang without emotion.
D. the young woman of Faust's dreams was a commoner.

**58.** On the basis of the passage, it is reasonable to conclude that:

   **A.** Faust lost his soul to the devil.
   **B.** the "country fair thronged with revelers" was not in the book.
   **C.** the operatic interpretation differed from the book.
   **D.** the author did not enjoy the performance.

**59.** According to the passage, the author felt that the New York City Opera production of "Mephistopheles":

   **A.** was plagued with a poor characterization of Mephisto.
   **B.** suffered from noticeable weaknesses beginning in Scene II.
   **C.** was enhanced by Dr. Faust's singing.
   **D.** could have been improved in Scene III.

**60.** According to the passage, the author seems to have most enjoyed:

   **A.** the music of the opera.
   **B.** the singing of the opera.
   **C.** the plot of the opera.
   **D.** the images of the opera.

**61.** Which of the following does the author suggest was a component of the original "Faust myth" (lines 53-54)?

   **I.** Reason triumphing over feeling
   **II.** A more evil Mephisto
   **III.** A more powerful God

   **A.** I only
   **B.** II only
   **C.** III only
   **D.** II and III only

**62.** According to the passage, through what primary means is the fundamental plot transmitted to the audience?

   **A.** Via visual imagery
   **B.** Via Faust's musings
   **C.** Via the chorus
   **D.** Via Mephisto

**63.** Regarding the devil's bargain with Faust, the passage strongly implies that:

   **A.** it is Faust who got the better deal.
   **B.** it is the devil who got the better deal.
   **C.** in other versions, the bargain was with Margaret.
   **D.** in other versions, it is Faust who does the bargaining.

---

**STOP.** IF YOU FINISH BEFORE TIME IS CALLED, CHECK YOUR WORK. YOU MAY GO BACK TO ANY QUESTION IN THIS TEST BOOKLET.

---

**STOP.**

# ANSWERS & EXPLANATIONS

## FOR
## 30-MINUTE IN-CLASS EXAMINATIONS

# ANSWERS TO THE IN-CLASS EXAMS

| Exam 1 | Exam 2 | Exam 3 |
|--------|--------|--------|
| 1. C | 22. D | 43. D |
| 2. B | 23. A | 44. B |
| 3. D | 24. C | 45. C |
| 4. C | 25. A | 46. B |
| 5. A | 26. B | 47. B |
| 6. C | 27. A | 48. D |
| 7. B | 28. C | 49. D |
| 8. B | 29. D | 50. A |
| 9. A | 30. B | 51. B |
| 10. D | 31. A | 52. C |
| 11. C | 32. A | 53. C |
| 12. A | 33. D | 54. D |
| 13. C | 34. B | 55. C |
| 14. B | 35. C | 56. D |
| 15. B | 36. A | 57. C |
| 16. C | 37. B | 58. C |
| 17. C | 38. B | 59. B |
| 18. A | 39. A | 60. D |
| 19. B | 40. C | 61. A |
| 20. D | 41. D | 62. C |
| 21. B | 42. C | 63. D |

# MCAT VERBAL REASONING AND MATH

| Raw Score | Estimated Scaled Score |
|-----------|------------------------|
| 21 | 15 |
| 20 | 14 |
| 19 | 13 |
| 18 | 12 |
| 17 | 11 |
| 15-16 | 10 |
| 14 | 9 |
| 12-13 | 8 |
| 11 | 7 |
| 9-10 | 6 |
| 8 | 5 |
| 6-7 | 4 |
| 5 | 3 |
| 3-4 | 2 |
| 1-2 | 1 |

# EXPLANATIONS FOR 30-MINUTE IN-CLASS EXAM 1

## Passage I (Questions 1–7)

1. The word tar (line 48) is used in the sense of:

   "Some Marxist theorists have speculated that Marx would tar both Kant and Hume as "bourgeois" philosophers" (lines 47-48).

   **A.** asphalt.
   WRONG: This is not the intended sense, or meaning, of the word. "Tar" is not used literally.

   **B.** suggest.
   WRONG: This is not the intended sense, or meaning, of the word. This is not strong enough.

   **C.** label.
   **CORRECT:** This is the intended sense, or meaning, of the word. The reference harkens to a literal "tarring and feathering" of individuals for the purpose of ridiculing and labeling them as collaborators. However, this knowledge was not necessary in order to answer the question. In the context of the passage, the author clearly theorizes that Marx would strongly disagree with Hume and Kant. Substituting the word "label" for "tar" is appropriate.

   **D.** stick.
   WRONG: This is not the intended sense, or meaning, of the word. This word is not specific enough.

2. According to the passage, Marx would have disagreed with Kant and Hume over which of the following ideas?

   The correct answer requires the embodiment of an idea which is 1. shared by Kant and Hume, and 2. disagreed with by Marx.

   **A.** What each man feels within himself is the standard of sentiment.
   WRONG: This is not an idea that Kant and Hume share. This is Hume's idea only (lines 12-13).

   **B.** There is uniformity in people's reason or emotion.
   **CORRECT:** First, this is an idea that Kant and Hume share; "To make both of [Kant's and Hume's] constructions possible, there is a notion of some kind of uniformity in people's reason or emotion in both works" (lines 38-40). Second, according to the passage, this is clearly an idea with which Marx would have disagreed. "Based on these writings, Marx would probably see any system that sought out a universal theory of morality as ignoring the opposing economic classes in society ..." (lines 59-62).

   **C.** The interests of the capitalists and the workers are one and the same.
   WRONG: This is not clearly an idea that Kant and Hume share. It is outside the scope of information in the passage.

   **D.** Morality is dependent upon the class struggle.
   WRONG: This is not an idea from the passage.

3. Assume that a universal principle of morality can be proven to exist. Which of the following hypotheses does this assumption suggest?

   A. The author is correct; despite their genesis, it is not surprising that Kant and Hume constructed similar systems.
   WRONG: This hypothesis is not suggested by the assumption in the question. "Considering that they began their searches with seemingly irreconcilable ideas of where to look, the similarity in the moral systems they constructed is surprising" (lines 3-5).

   B. The author is correct; Marx, Hume, and Kant all constructed similar systems.
   WRONG: This hypothesis is not suggested by the assumption in the question. The author never suggests that all three of these people did construct similar systems.

   C. The author is incorrect; Marx, Hume, and Kant did not all construct similar systems.
   WRONG: This hypothesis is not suggested by the assumption in the question. The author never suggests that *all three* of these people did construct similar systems.

   D. The author is incorrect; despite their genesis, it is not surprising that Kant and Hume constructed similar systems.
   CORRECT: This hypothesis is suggested by the assumption in the question. "Considering that they *began their searches with seemingly irreconcilable ideas* of where to look, the similarity in the moral systems they constructed *is surprising*" (lines 3-5). It is not so surprising once given the assumption that a universal principle of morality can be proven to exist. Hume and Kant simply arrived at this "Truth" by different paths.

4. According to the author, in creating his moral system, Hume equated:

   A. circumstances with disinterested comparison.
   WRONG: There is no support for this answer in the passage.

   B. circumstances with absolutism.
   WRONG: The two are diametrically opposed in the passage and not equated by Hume.

   C. practicality with stirring people to action.
   CORRECT: "Hume decided at the outset that *a moral system must be practical*, ... and since only sentiment (emotion) is capable of *stirring people to action*, the practical study of morality should be concerned with sentiment" (lines 6-10).

   D. practicality with reason.
   WRONG: Hume was not much impressed with reason. He focused on sentiment.

5. Based upon passage information, Marx most likely believed that:

   A. there is no universal theory of morality.
   CORRECT: This is Marx's most likely belief. "Marx would probably see any system that sought out a universal theory of morality as ignoring the opposing economic classes in society ...[which he felt were involved in a class struggle]" (lines 64-66).

   B. philosophers were part of the bourgeois.
   WRONG: Based upon passage information, this is not Marx's most likely belief. This is a vast generalization without any real support. We have no way of knowing what Marx thought about philosophers in general.

   C. the workers could be easily fooled.
   WRONG: Based upon passage information, this is not Marx's most likely belief. This is a vast generalization without any real support.

   D. Kant's book supported capitalist exploitation.
   WRONG: Based upon passage information, this is not Marx's most likely belief. There is no passage information that would tell us whether Kant's book had ever been read by Marx, whether it was written before Marx's time, or written well afterwards. This is outside the scope of the available passage information.

6. Based upon passage information, Kant's system of "moral feedback" (line 22) differed from Hume's in that it might result in a situation wherein:

  **A.** one realized that his action might be 'right' so long as it didn't become a universal law of nature.
  WRONG: Hume did not consider "universal laws of nature". Further, and more importantly, the idea of a "universal law of nature" (line 28) was all important to Kant.

  **B.** one realized that a universal law of nature was unnecessary in determining duty.
  WRONG: It was Hume who did not consider "universal laws of nature". Further, and more importantly, the idea of a "universal law of nature" (line 28) was all important to Kant.

  **C.** one realized that his action might be 'wrong' even though it created agreeable sentiments in others, as well as in oneself.
  CORRECT: Unlike Hume, Kant's system relied upon reason and logic [think Vulcan]; "before one does anything, one should forget one's own motives for a moment, and ask if he would want everyone to do as he does. If the answer is no, then his subjective desire is different from his objective assessment, and the action is contrary to duty" (lines 28-32). Sentiment was not a factor for Kant. A "subjective desire" that might, in the short term please himself and others, might in the long term not be best established as a "universal law of nature" (line 28).

  **D.** one realized that his action might be illogical if sentiment was not further considered.
  WRONG: Sentiment was not a factor for Kant.

7. According to the passage, Hume's ideas evolved to the point where he:

  Note that the correct answer *requires* that you know and understand where Hume's ideas stood when he began formulating them. "Hume's ideas *evolved* …". You must consider the paragraph beginning, "Hume decided at the outset …" (lines 6-13).

  **A.** realized that reason was an inseparable part of a universal system of morality.
  WRONG: Hume did not think much of reason (lines 6-8), but based his ideas upon sentiment (emotion).

  **B.** was considering the sentiments of others as well as himself.
  CORRECT: As indicated by the question, Hume's ideas *evolved*. They changed from the time he first began formulating them to the end. At first, Hume says "What each man feels within himself is the standard of sentiment" (lines 12-13 ); others are not considered. Later, "Hume says that moral actions are those that create agreeable sentiments in *others*, as well as in oneself" (lines 33-34).

  **C.** chose to essentially agree with Kant on a universal system of morality.
  WRONG: This is not correct. Even in the end, the two differed in their reliance on reason/logic as opposed to sentiment/emotion.

  **D.** decided that sentiment without action was a necessary component of his morality system.
  WRONG: Hume chose sentiment specifically because he felt that it was only sentiment which elicited action. "Hume decided at the outset that a moral system must be practical, … and since only sentiment (emotion) is capable of stirring people to action …" (lines 6-9).

## Passage II (Questions 8-14)

8. Which of the following statements, if true, would most directly *challenge* the principles of Martin Luther?

    **A.** The Bible's Old Testament refers to a period before the birth of Jesus.
    WRONG: This does not most directly challenge the principles of Martin Luther. This answer is way outside of the scope of the passage.

    **B.** The Bible alone contains only a small part of what Jesus intended for his followers.
    **CORRECT:** This most directly challenges the principles of Martin Luther. This is within the scope of the passage and relates directly to information provided in the passage on the beliefs of Martin Luther; "For Luther, salvation lies in faith emanating from personal understanding of Biblical teachings" (lines 54-56).

    **C.** The German "barbarians" who sacked Rome had been previously converted.
    WRONG: This does not most directly challenge the principles of Martin Luther. Whether they had been converted or not is irrelevant. Either way, they would have been considered "living tools" of God by both Luther and Augustine.

    **D.** Augustine's understanding of salvation granted through the mercy of Christ was flawed.
    WRONG: This does not most directly challenge the principles of Martin Luther. It has little bearing on the principles of Martin Luther. If anything, this information would *strengthen* Luther's ideas and principles.

9. Some theologians believe that killing and violence are acceptable when used in self-defense. An appropriate clarification of the passage would be the stipulation that:

    **A.** both Luther and Augustine would have disagreed with this belief.
    **CORRECT:** This stipulation would be an appropriate clarification. "Both of these theologians would hold that … salvation, … should be all Christians' only concern in life" (lines 51-54). There is no evidence in the passage that either theologian made exceptions to their explanations of Christ's teachings wherein "killing and violence" are acceptable.

    **B.** both Luther and Augustine would have agreed with this belief.
    WRONG: This stipulation would not be an appropriate clarification. There is no evidence in the passage that either theologian made exceptions to their explanations of Christ's teachings wherein "killing and violence" are acceptable.

    **C.** only Augustine might have agreed with this belief.
    WRONG: This stipulation would not be an appropriate clarification. "In Augustine's understanding, [God] sends hardship and death to test men's faith. The true Augustinian Christian would maintain his faith [and presumably his passivity] through any ordeal, and even if his body perishes, God will save him for his conviction" (lines 60-63).

    **D.** only Luther might have agreed with this belief.
    WRONG: This stipulation would not be an appropriate clarification. See above.

10. If the information in lines 37-54 is correct, one could most reasonably conclude that, compared to Luther, Augustine was:

    **A.** much more reasonably inclined.
    WRONG: This is not a reasonable conclusion. This is a fuzzy value judgment based solely upon personal opinion. Unless the passage itself provided direct evidence regarding the "reasonableness" of someone's inclinations or ideas, this type of answer would be a poor choice.

    **B.** more prepared to define God's will.
    WRONG: This is not a reasonable conclusion. There is no evidence in support of this. What does "more prepared" mean? This answer approaches the vagueness of Answer A.

**C.** less eager to send people to eternal torment.
WRONG: This is not a reasonable conclusion. This answer is attractive. Particularly given the last sentence of the quote, "Augustine never considers the individual fate of these living tools, but Luther maintains that … they go to eternal torment" (lines 48-50). However, neither of the theologians is "sending people to eternal torment". According to the passage and the information it is God who decides who is 'sent' to hell, not Luther or Augustine.

**D.** less willing to announce God's final judgment on those who had sinned.
CORRECT: This is the only reasonable conclusion based on the information. "Augustine never considers the individual fate of these [barbarians], but Luther maintains that … they go to eternal torment" (lines 48-50). This answer choice more correctly defines the role that Luther or Augustine might play as theologians in relation to God. The theologians can only "announce" what God has decided; if they think they know. They themselves do not have the power to "send" anyone to heaven or hell.

**11.** The author's attitude toward the theories of Augustine and Luther in the passage is most accurately described as:

This type of question must usually be gleaned from the overall impression given by the author as the passage is read. There is no 'going back' to the passage. The reader must ask if there were any derogatory, sarcastic, praiseworthy, or other type of information or words used that provide clues to the author's attitude. If the passage did not try to persuade or argue, then it is probably neutral.

**A.** disapproving.
WRONG: This is not the most accurate description of the author's attitude.

**B.** mistrustful.
WRONG: This is not the most accurate description of the author's attitude.

**C.** neutral.
CORRECT: This is the most accurate description of the author's attitude. This type of passage is not persuasive, but purely informative.

**D.** favorable.
WRONG: This is not the most accurate description of the author's attitude.

**12.** What is the meaning of the phrase; "The true Augustinian Christian would maintain his faith through any ordeal, and even if his body perishes, God will save him for his conviction" (lines 60-63)?

Unfortunately, passages and sentences are not always provided in their clearest form. The tortured syntax of this sentence begs for clarification. Particularly where the word "conviction" is used in its less common form; 'belief'. We are used to thinking of a prosecuting attorney seeking a criminal's 'conviction'.

**A.** This Christian would end up in heaven because of his beliefs.
CORRECT: This is the meaning of the phrase. Restated in other words, 'The true Christian would maintain his faith through any ordeal, and even if he physically died, God will save him *because of his belief*.

**B.** God would save this Christian for judgment at the end of the Christian's ordeal.
WRONG: This is not the meaning of the phrase. This answer mistakenly equates "for his conviction" with 'for his judgment'.

**C.** God would save this Christian from his ordeal and judge him.
WRONG: This is not the meaning of the phrase. First, this Christian will not be saved from his ordeal. It is clear that God is not going to save this Christian from his 'earthly' ordeal. "[E]ven if his body perishes …" means the Christian *will* probably die. Secondly, this answer mistakenly equates "for his conviction" with 'for his judgment'.

**D.** It was not necessary for this Christian to die for him to be convicted.
WRONG: This is not the meaning of the phrase. First, this Christian will not be saved from his ordeal. It is clear that God is not going to save this Christian from his 'earthly' ordeal. "[E]ven if his body perishes …" means the Christian *will* probably die. Secondly, though this answer is not completely clear, it seems to mistakenly equate "for his conviction" with "finding him guilty".

**13.** The author's primary purpose in the passage is apparently:

These questions are less value judgments on the word "primary" than they are accuracy questions. On these types of questions the "primary purpose" usually means the answer choice which accurately restates passage information. Generally, three are inaccurate and one is accurate. However, if two answer choices are accurate, one will clearly be more all encompassing (primary) than the other.

- **A.** to clarify the differences between the ways in which the early Catholics and Protestants dealt with persecution.
  WRONG: This is not the author's primary purpose. There seem to be *no* differences in the passage regarding the way in which the early Catholics and Protestants dealt with persecution. The only differences were in their understandings of how to achieve salvation and pronouncing God's judgment on others.

- **B.** to justify the persecution of early Christians by secular governments.
  WRONG: This is not the author's primary purpose. The only justification of persecution in the passage comes indirectly from Augustine's writings "that His inscrutable will is always just" (lines 39-40), and that "God ... sends hardship and death to test men's faith" (line 60).

- **C.** to consider the similarities between the ways in which the early Catholics and Protestants dealt with persecution.
  **CORRECT:** This is the author's primary purpose. A topic sentence in the first paragraph is, "Later Christian theorists followed this example, often urging peaceful coexistence even with governments which violated every precept of Christian teachings" (lines 7-9). The author then goes on to support this idea with Augustine and Luther by considering their "similarities". Though Luther's ideas predominate in the passage, "St. Augustine would have agreed" (line 37), and "Both of these theologians would hold that ..." (line 51), etc.

- **D.** to question the passive practices of the early Catholics and Protestants when faced with persecution.
  WRONG: This is not the author's primary purpose. The author is not questioning the practices, but explaining the reasoning behind them in a rather objective manner.

**14.** What is the most serious apparent weakness of the information described?

These types of questions are not necessarily the value judgments that they might first seem to be. At least two of the answer choices will inaccurately restate conclusions or passage information. Of the remaining two, one will obviously weaken the passage, while the other may even strengthen it.

- **A.** While implying that Christians may coexist with a secular government, it differentiates between Catholics and Protestants.
  WRONG: This is not the most serious apparent weakness of the information described. What little differentiation there is *strengthens* the passage by supporting the idea that "Later Christian theorists ..." (i.e. supporting the topic sentence).

- **B.** While implying representation of Augustine and Luther, its conclusions are based primarily on information according to Luther.
  **CORRECT:** This is the most serious apparent weakness of the information described. The author chooses the Catholic pillar St. Augustine and the Protestant representative Martin Luther to stand for later "Christian theorists". However, the second paragraph merely paraphrases the two of them. The large third paragraph is all Luther. Finally at line 37, "St. Augustine would have agreed" but by the next sentence we are back to Luther. The passage does not even come close to equally representing the two Christian theorists and is therefore weakened when attempting to use both men's theories in support of the topic.

- **C.** While implying representation of all Christian theorists, only Augustine and Luther are mentioned.
  WRONG: This is not the most serious apparent weakness of the information described. If you felt that there were other Christian theorists from that time you would be bringing in outside information. For instance, Fundamentalists, Mormons, and other sects did not exist at that time, for one thing.

- **D.** While implying agreement between Augustine and Luther, their attitudes were clearly opposed.
  WRONG: This is not the most serious apparent weakness of the information described. This is inaccurate and there is no support for this answer.

15. The author probably mentions that Mallon was "never 'tried' in any sense" (line 5) in order:

    A. to demonstrate the power of the wealthy at that time.
    WRONG: This is not the probable reason for the author's mentioning. Though the privilege of the wealthy is an underlying theme of the passage, there is no evidence that the "wealthy", nor their power, had anything to do with Mallon's confinement.

    B. to provide a comparison with people who have actually committed a crime.
    CORRECT: This is the most probable reason for the author's mentioning. This answer supports the fact that the author obviously feels that Mallon's treatment was unjust. This is evidenced in the first and last sentences of the passage: "Of all the bizarre and melancholy fates that could befall an otherwise ordinary person, Mary Mallon's has to be among the most sad and peculiar," and "But she was the only one kept isolated for years, a result as much of prejudice toward the Irish and noncompliant women as of a public health threat." This is the best answer.

    C. to illustrate the persistence of Soper's investigations.
    WRONG: This is not the probable reason for the author's mentioning. There is no evidence that Soper's investigations were 'persistent' in the first place.

    D. to support the claim that she deserved at least a hearing.
    WRONG: This is not the probable reason for the author's mentioning. There is no "claim" by the author that she "deserved at least a hearing".

16. According to the passage, the first two investigators were unable to find the cause of the outbreak (lines 18-19). The information presented on typhoid makes which of the following explanations most plausible?

    A. They focused too closely on the "soft clams" that Soper later discredited.
    WRONG: This explanation is not the most plausible. There is no evidence or information that the investigators focused on "soft clams" at all.

    B. Typhoid is not really passed through contaminated food or water.
    WRONG: This explanation is not the most plausible. It seems that typhoid is passed through contaminated food or water.

    C. They never considered that typhoid could be carried by a healthy person.
    CORRECT: This explanation is the most plausible. We know that Soper "was the first to identify a healthy typhoid carrier in the United States" (lines 30-33). Also, Soper's investigation and discovery occurred after the two investigators came to the Warren house. Therefore, this answer is the most likely.

    D. By this time, Mallon was no longer employed by the Warren family.
    WRONG: This explanation is not the most plausible. There is no timeframe given regarding the "two investigators", thus this is purely speculative. Further, since, Soper was the first person to identify a healthy typhoid carrier in the United States, it is unlikely that the two investigators would have suspected Mallon had she been even directly interviewed by them..

17. The author's argument that Mallon's isolation was "a result as much of prejudice … as of a public health threat" (lines 64-65) is most *weakened* by which idea in the passage?

Note that the correct answer must satisfy two criterions. It must 1) be an idea in the passage, and 2) weaken the author's argument.

- **A.** Mallon's primary occupation was as a cook.
  WRONG: The author's argument is not weakened by this idea, *to the extent that Answer C weakens it.* First, though it does seem that this answer is promoted in the passage, it is an assumption. If Answer C were not available this might be a good choice. However, it is not the fact that Mallon was a cook which doomed her, but it was the fact that she "failed to comply with the health inspector's requirements" (lines 57-58), which presumably would have precluded her from preparing meals. C is the better answer.

- **B.** Mallon did not believe that she was a carrier of the disease.
  WRONG: The author's argument is not weakened by this idea, *to the extent that Answer C weakens it.* If Answer C were not available this might be a good choice. However, similarly to Answer A, it is not the fact that Mallon did not believe that she was a carrier which doomed her, but it was the fact that she "failed to comply with the health inspector's requirements" (lines 57-58). C is the better answer.

- **C.** Mallon would not abide by the health inspector's requirements.
  CORRECT: The author's argument is weakened by this idea. Ultimate, this is the explicitly provided reason for Mallon's reincarceration. "After a short period of freedom in which *Mallon failed to comply with the health inspector's requirements,* she was eventually sent back to North Brother Island, where she lived the rest of her life, alone in a one-room cottage" (lines 57-60).

- **D.** Mallon actually was the source of the typhoid outbreak in the Warren home.
  WRONG: The author's argument is not weakened by this idea, *to the extent that Answer C weakens it.* Had Mallon complied with the "health inspector's requirements" (lines 57-58), she might well not have been reincarcerated.

18. Which of the following statements is the most reasonable conclusion that can be drawn from the author's description of the typhoid outbreak in the house at Oyster Bay?

- **A.** The Warren family did not hire Soper.
  **CORRECT:** This is a reasonable conclusion. "Worried they wouldn't be able to rent the house unless they figured out the source of the disease, *the owners … hired George Soper …"* (lines 20-22).

- **B.** The two investigators were hired by the Warrens.
  WRONG: This is not a reasonable conclusion. It is *not* certain who it was who hired the two investigators. Why not the owners, or the city health department, for instance?

- **C.** The Warren family hired Soper.
  WRONG: This is not a reasonable conclusion. "Worried they wouldn't be able to rent the house unless they figured out the source of the disease, *the owners … hired George Soper …"* (lines 20-22).

- **D.** The owners were anxious to sell the house.
  WRONG: This is not a reasonable conclusion. The owners were worried that they wouldn't be able to rent the house. "Worried they wouldn't be able to rent the house unless they figured out the source of the disease, *the owners … hired George Soper …"* (lines 20-22).

19. Passage information indicates that which of the following statements must be true?

**A.** Mallon had probably not infected anyone prior to the Warren family.
WRONG: There is no information that this *must* be true.

**B.** Mallon was almost certainly not washing her hands prior to preparing the Warren's meals.
**CORRECT:** We know that Mallon's feces "did indeed show high concentrations of typhoid bacilli" (lines 46-47). Therefore, there are only a few unlikely alternatives to the idea that the bacilli were being transferred from the feces to Mallon's hands, to the food she prepared, and then to those becoming sick. None of the grotesque alternatives is really plausible.

**C.** Being labeled 'Typhoid Mary' by the press was the primary reason for her confinement.
WRONG: There is no information that this *must* be true.

**D.** The health inspector was doubtless prejudiced toward the Irish.
WRONG: There is no information that this *must* be true.

20. According to passage information, Mallon worked for the Warren family for approximately:

**A.** two weeks.
WRONG: See explanation for Answer D.

**B.** three weeks.
WRONG: See explanation for Answer D.

**C.** five weeks.
WRONG: See explanation for Answer D.

**D.** six weeks.
**CORRECT:** According to Soper's own words describing Mallon's tenure in Oyster Bay, which are quoted in the passage, "It was found that the family had changed cooks about *three weeks before* the typhoid epidemic broke out ... She remained with the family only a short time, *leaving about three weeks after* the outbreak occurred" (lines 28-29).

21. The contention that in "1938 when [Mallon] died, ... there were 237 other typhoid carriers living under city health department observation. But she was the only one kept isolated for years" (lines 61-64), can most justifiably be interpreted as support for the idea that:

**A.** Mallon was unfairly treated by the city health department.
WRONG: This idea is not justifiably supported by the contention. "Fairness" requires a comparative analysis of some sort. Mallon was the "first" of her kind to be identified. The contention regards 1938, decades after Mallon's discovery. Her treatment cannot be compared to the 237 other typhoid carriers.

**B.** Mallon's isolation might have stemmed from the health department's early ignorance of the disease.
**CORRECT:** This idea is justifiably supported by the contention. This answer might be gleaned through process of elimination also. However, the key "*early* ignorance" is a giveaway given that the contention regards 1938, decades after Mallon's discovery and isolation.

**C.** The "other 237 typhoid carriers were all kept isolated at one time or another.
WRONG: This idea is not justifiably supported by the contention. Though this is tempting because the contention provides that "she was the only one *kept isolated for years*", this is not a strong interpretation of the contention. It is entirely possible that at least one of the 237 "other" carriers was never isolated at all, negating this answer.

**D.** The "other" 237 typhoid carriers were much like Mallon.
WRONG: This idea is not justifiably supported by the contention. This is very weak. For one thing, the contention regards 1938, decades after Mallon's discovery. Further, it can be presumed, based upon the passage, that those who were free had at least agreed and cooperated in not cooking and serving food, unlike Mallon.

## ANSWERS & EXPLANATIONS FOR 30-MINUTE IN-CLASS EXAM 2

### Passage I (Questions 22–28)

22. According to the passage information which of the following would be most likely if a person who was talking to you, attempted to make their voice sound unusually low?

    **A.** You might think that they were lying.
        WRONG: This would not be most likely. The key is *"unusually* low". Though a speaker who was lying, might be aware that in order to successfully lie, or "suggest credibility, the voice's tone should be pitched as low as is naturally possible" (lines 4-5), this is a much more 'tortured' answer choice. In other words, in contrast to the straightforward aspect of Answer D, this answer requires several assumptions that are outside the scope of the question.

    **B.** They could be irritated with you.
        WRONG: This would not be most likely. First, it is lack of "intelligibility" that is irritating. Second, it is the listener who is irritated, not the speaker.

    **C.** They might well sound monotonous.
        WRONG: This would not be most likely. There is no passage link between monotony and pitch. Monotony has to do with inflection, not pitch.

    **D.** You could find them difficult to understand.
        **CORRECT:** This would be most likely. The key is *"unusually* low". "[A]n artificially lowered voice can sacrifice intelligibility" (lines 7-8).

23. The author most likely believes that one of the main purposes of speaking, during a face-to-face meeting, should be to:

    **A.** convey a favorable impression.
        **CORRECT:** This is not the most likely belief of the author. Almost the entire passage is about conveying favorable *impressions,* not ideas or concepts. The author admits that "the quality of content accounts for a mere 6%" (lines 24-25) of the overall impression given by the speaker.

    **B.** effectively transmit your ideas.
        WRONG: This is not the most likely belief of the author. There is no support for this answer within the passage. The author admits that "the quality of content [i.e. ideas] accounts for a mere 6%" (lines 24-25) of the overall impression given by the speaker.

    **C.** gain leverage.
        WRONG: This is not the most likely belief of the author. There is no support for this answer within the passage.

    **D.** communicate as naturally as possible.
        WRONG: This is not the most likely belief of the author. For instance, the author would not be a proponent of communicating "as naturally as possible" if you *naturally* 1. were shy, 2. spoke with a high-pitched whine, 3. were 'breathy', etc.

24. The author provides a list of "habits to be avoided" (lines 13-15). Which of the habits would the suggestions in this passage *not* help a speaker to curb?

Notice that, of the four answer choices, Answer C. "pretension" differs in 'kind' from the other choices. In other words, if you had a list of only these four choices with a new question asking, 'Which one of the following items doesn't belong with the others?', you would still choose "pretension".

**A.** monotony
WRONG: There is information within the passage which would help a speaker to curb "monotony". Speech should be "inflected to suggest the emotions expressed" (line 3).

**B.** breathiness
WRONG: There is information within the passage which would help a speaker to curb "breathiness". See lines 36-54.

**C.** pretension
**CORRECT:** There is no information within the passage which would help a speaker to curb "pretension". Though we may make some assumptions, the passage does not convey how "pretension" is conveyed. Since the symptoms of 'pretension' are not defined, there is little in the way of help which can be gleaned from the passage for the person who suffers from 'pretension'.

**D.** high-pitched whining
WRONG: There is information within the passage which would help a speaker to curb "high-pitched whining". "To deepen the pitch, speakers should make an extra-deep inhalation before speaking, and then exhale fully as they speak" (lines 10-12).

25. The term *ideal speaking voice* (line 1) refers implicitly to a voice that is:

**A.** the most pleasant to listen to.
CORRECT: This is not the most strongly implied answer. The author gives us our first clue when describing a voice which might "sacrifice intelligibility, which is *irritating* to listeners. Thus, speakers should experiment to find their *optimal level*, which will be at their lowest intelligible pitch" (lines 8-10). At this point, we might assume that, thus, the "optimal level" or ideal speaking voice is the "least irritating" (Answer C.). However, overall, the implication of the passage is seeking to be the *best*, not (forgive the tortured syntax) the "least" worst of the worst.

**B.** the most persuasive.
WRONG: This is not the most strongly implied answer. This has to do with 'content'. We can surmise that since "the quality of content accounts for a mere 6%" (lines 24-25) of the overall impression given by the speaker, "most persuasive" is not a characteristic of the ideal speaking voice.

**C.** the least irritating.
WRONG: This is not implied. The author seeks the *best*, not (forgive the tortured syntax) the "least" worst of the worst.

**D.** the most natural.
WRONG: This is not implied. For instance, the author would not be a proponent of the idea speaking voice being the "most natural" if your *"most natural"* speaking voice was 1. shy sounding, 2. a high-pitched whine, or 3. 'breathy', etc.

**26.** Passage information indicates that a person speaking in a high-pitched voice might be doing all of the following EXCEPT:

  I.   Breathing with their upper lungs
       WRONG: This is not an exception. A person speaking in a high-pitched voice might be "breathing with their upper lungs". "Diaphragmatic breathing results in a deeper voice than upper-lung breathing" (lines 40-41).

  II.  Breathing deeply
       **CORRECT:** This *is* an exception. A person speaking in a high-pitched voice would probably not be "breathing deeply". For instance, "To deepen the pitch, speakers should make an extra-deep inhalation before speaking, and then exhale fully as they speak" (lines 10-12).

  III. Lying
       WRONG: This is not an exception. A person speaking in a high-pitched voice might be "lying". "To suggest credibility, the voice's tone should be pitched as low as is naturally possible… A low pitch is desirable in both genders, since it is popularly associated with truth-telling" (lines 5-7).

  **A.** I only

  **B.** II only
       **CORRECT:** See above answer explanations.

  **C.** III only

  **D.** I and III only


**27.** Which of the following assertions is most clearly a thesis presented by the author?

  **A.** Speakers can gain by improving their speaking voices.
       **CORRECT:** This is clearly a thesis presented by the author. It is presented through the negative aspects associated with having a 'poor' speaking voice, such as "irritating" the listener. It is presented through the examples of "famous news anchors" who had great speaking voices. And, it is presented through statistics within the passage; "everyone who communicates should be aware that their voice is a critical component of their audience's perceptions of them, comprising about 38% of the overall impression imparted by their presentation" (lines 19-22).

  **B.** The tone of the ideal speaking voice should be pitched as low as possible.
       WRONG: This is not clearly a thesis presented by the author, and inaccurately paraphrases the passage. Speakers are admonished to find their "lowest *intelligible* pitch" (line 10), and to pitch their voices as "low as it *naturally* possible" (line 5), else they will risk irritating their listeners.

  **C.** What you are saying is more important than how you are saying it.
       WRONG: This is not clearly a thesis presented by the author. It is an antithesis. "[T]he quality of content accounts for a mere 6%" (lines 24-25) of the audience's perception of the speaker.

  **D.** Emotional inflections can be an irritating aspect of a speaker's voice.
       WRONG: This is not clearly a thesis presented by the author. The ideal speaking voice "*should* be … inflected to suggest the emotions expressed" (lines 1-3).

28. The ideas discussed in this passage would likely be of most use to:

   **A.** A doctor
   WRONG: This is not most likely.

   **B.** A journalist
   WRONG: This is not most likely. There is no reason to believe that the ideal speaking voice is of more particular use to a journalist who writes for a living, than to anyone else.

   **C.** A radio show personality
   **CORRECT:** This is most likely. The passage is almost solely on the "ideal speaking *voice*". Unlike the "famous [television] news anchors" used by the author as examples, 'radio show personalities' would not require coaching and advice on their visual appearance.

   **D.** A television commentator
   WRONG: This is not most likely. The passage is almost solely on the "ideal speaking *voice*". Despite the author's use of "famous [television] news anchors" which might make this answer seem attractive, clearly, television relies at least somewhat, if not just as much, on visual components and appearance, as it does on the speaking voice. However, beyond mentioning that "appearance accounts for about 50% of the speaker's impact" (lines 23-24), there is no further discussion of these ideas within the passage. Nor is there any advice given regarding improving the "appearance". Thus, this passage would *not* be as completely useful to a 'television commentator' as it would to a 'radio show personality' to whom his speaking voice is his entire persona.

## Passage II (Questions 29–35)

29. The author's discussion of "push" and "pull" factors (line 28) most accurately implies that:

   **A.** "pull" factors compel someone to leave, while "push" factors induce someone to come.
   WRONG: This is not the most accurate implication.

   **B.** "pull" factors induce someone to come, while "push" factors also induce someone to come.
   WRONG: This is not the most accurate implication.

   **C.** "push" factors require someone to leave, while "pull" factors also compel someone to leave.
   WRONG: This is not the most accurate implication.

   **D.** "push" factors compel someone to leave, while "pull" factors induce someone to come.
   **CORRECT:** This is the most accurate implication. "For example, the Fujianese feel compelled ("pushed") to leave because of the area's low standard of living. The poor wages, bad housing, and lack of political freedom can also be seen as "pull" factors, due to the idea that the Fujianese understand that life would be better in other countries" (lines 28-34).

30. Given the information in the passage, if "'artificially' defined" borders (line 3) were eliminated throughout the world, which of the following outcomes would most likely occur?

    **A.** People would naturally immigrate to areas with higher standards of living.
        WRONG: This outcome is not the most likely to occur. Though the author does provide that people do tend to immigrate to areas with higher standards of living, there is no particular reason to believe that elimination of artificially defined borders would increase or decrease this tendency, *without more information* from the question.

    **B.** Nations would encounter less traditional border strife.
        **CORRECT:** This outcome is the most likely to occur. The key here is "traditional" border strife. In contrast to the immigration problems predominantly focused upon in the passage, this type of strife is characterized by nation/states "attempting to secure their borders from invading countries, or even seeking to expand their own territories and acquire additional resources" (lines 57-60). <u>Why?</u> Because they would be separated by natural "geographical" boundaries (such as wide rivers, mountain ranges, and oceans), or by cultural boundaries. One can presume that these are boundaries where people sharing the same cultural characteristics, such as language, religious beliefs, etc., have chosen to live together.

    **C.** Nations would require greater border security measures.
        WRONG: This outcome is not the most likely to occur. Natural "geographical" boundaries such as wide rivers, mountain ranges, and ocean would be separating peoples who shared the same cultures.

    **D.** People would live more harmoniously.
        WRONG: This outcome is not the most likely to occur. This is possible. However, this answer is vague when compared with Answer B.

31. Which of the following assertions does the author support with an example?

    **A.** Transportation methods used by illegal immigrants are sometimes dangerous.
        **CORRECT:** This assertion is supported with an example. "Within the past year, U.S. officials found three Chinese immigrants in a smuggling boat's sealed cargo container, dead from suffocation" (lines 21-23).

    **B.** Peru and Columbia are seeking to expand their own territories.
        WRONG: This assertion is not supported with an example. Presumably because it is not a passage assertion or an assertion of the author's!

    **C.** New Zealand has enacted laws that hasten deportation proceedings.
        WRONG: This assertion is not supported with an example.

    **D.** The mission of the Peruvian troops is to keep guerillas and drugs out of Peru.
        WRONG: This assertion is not supported with an example.

32. The passage as a whole suggests that in order for a nation to slow the exodus of its inhabitants to other countries, it must:

**A.** become more attractive to those who are leaving.
**CORRECT:** This is suggested by the passage as a whole. The information regarding the "push" and "pull" factors suggests that poor conditions in the native country 'push' the immigrant, while higher standards in an adjoining country 'pull' the immigrant. Presumably, by becoming "more attractive to those who are leaving" a nation might slow the leaving of its inhabitants. Though "more attractive" might seem vague, it encompasses a variety of options and changes such as higher pay, better standards of living, better political system, more political freedom, etc., that make this the best answer.

**B.** abandon the traditional methods of guarding borders.
**WRONG:** This is not suggested by the passage as a whole. We don't even really know what the "traditional methods of guarding borders" refers to. What was it? How are borders guarded now? "Traditional" refers to the types of borders which countries shared, not the methods by which they were guarded.

**C.** respond in some way to the conflicts arising from border disputes.
**WRONG:** This is not suggested by the passage as a whole. This really has nothing to do with the inhabitants leaving or staying.

**D.** answer the challenges set forth by adjoining countries.
**WRONG:** This is not suggested by the passage as a whole. This really has nothing to do with the inhabitants leaving or staying. One might infer that by "challenges", this answer refers to "economic challenges" and rising to meet the standards of the more attractive neighboring country. However, this is a stretch. "Challenges" might just as well mean challenges to war, or sporting challenges.

33. If the passage information is correct, what inference is justified by the fact that virtually no immigration from West Berlin to adjoining East Berlin occurred, over the 40 years before the period described?

**A.** Crossing the heavily guarded borders between West and East Berlin was very dangerous.
**WRONG:** This inference is not justified by the new "fact." There is no passage information to support the premise that more 'heavily guarded borders' would be effective in an effort to prevent or slow immigration. Or, that a "very dangerous" situation would prevent immigration. On the contrary, the example of the suffocated Chinese immigrants indicates that danger would not stop a motivated person from attempting to immigrate.

**B.** It was understood that life would be better in East Berlin.
**WRONG:** This inference is not justified by the new "fact." Just as the Fujianese migrated to countries and areas where the conditions were more favorable, if this answer were accurate, the question would provide that 'a great deal of immigration has taken place from West Berlin to East Berlin.'

**C.** The inhabitants of both 'Berlins' were happy to remain where they were.
**WRONG:** This inference is not justified by the new "fact." The use of the word 'happy' is simplistic and should alert you that this is probably not the best choice. The passage heavily incorporates economics as causal "push" and "pull" factors. Further, you assume that there is no immigration from East Berlin to West Berlin. Notice that this possibility is left open in the question's factual premise. This is not the best answer.

**D.** The economic conditions of West Berlin were much more favorable than those of East Berlin.
**CORRECT:** This inference is justified by the new "fact." Again, it is certainly in the realm of possibility that there is immigration taking place from East Berlin to West Berlin. But whether this is true or not, this answer incorporates passage economic ideas in advancing a reason why there would be "virtually no immigration from West Berlin to East Berlin."

34. The author implies that which of the following is *not* one of the reasons that Peruvian President Fujimori deployed soldiers to its borders with Columbia?

The question requires an implication of the author's, <u>not</u> the *absence* of an implication. Notice that this type of question differs dramatically from one reading: "The author implies that Peruvian President Fujimori deployed soldiers to its borders with Columbia for all of the following reasons EXCEPT:"

   I.   Fujimori is attempting to keep drugs out of his country.
        WRONG: The author implies that this is one of the reasons the soldiers were deployed.

   II.  Fujimori fears that Columbia is seeking to expand its territories.
        **CORRECT:** The author implies that this is not one of the reasons the soldiers were deployed. "Traditionally, these two countries might have been attempting to secure their borders from invading countries, or even seeking to expand their own territories and acquire additional resources. However, Ecuador and Peru are protecting their borders *from rogue drug traffickers and guerillas, not Colombia's government"* (lines 61-62).

   III. Fujimori is probably concerned that Columbia wants to acquire additional resources.
        WRONG: This is not an implication of the author's. The question requires an implication of the author's, not the absence of an implication. This is not an 'exception' type of question. Notice that this type of question differs dramatically from one reading: "The author implies that Peruvian President Fujimori deployed soldiers to its borders with Columbia for all of the following reasons EXCEPT:"

   A.   I only

   B.   II only
        **CORRECT:** See above answer explanations.

   C.   III only

   D.   II and III only

35. It seems likely that New Zealand may be suffering less from immigration issues than the United States for which of the following reasons:

   I.   The U.S. offers higher wages than New Zealand.
        WRONG: There is no support for this answer in the passage.

   II.  New laws, enacted in New Zealand, allow faster deportation proceedings.
        **CORRECT:** This answer choice "seems likely". "Recently, New Zealand attempted to deal with these aliens by enacting new immigration laws, which hasten the process required to deport them" (lines 24-26).

   III. Immigrants often do not settle in New Zealand.
        **CORRECT:** This idea not only "seems likely", it is provided in the passage as a reason. "What keeps New Zealand from experiencing an even more profound illegal immigration problem is that the immigrants often do not settle there" (lines 37-39).

   A.   II only

   B.   III only

   C.   II and III only
        **CORRECT:** See above answer explanations.

   D.   I, II, and III

## Passage III (Questions 36-42)

**36.** What is the author's response to the standard story about the woman who spills hot McDonald's coffee in her lap, sues and gets several million dollars?

Since this story is not actually in the passage, the author is not actually responding to it. However, corollaries can be drawn from within the passage. The author's response can be predicted. This type of question is very similar to others found on the MCAT such as, "The author would argue that …", "On the basis of the passage, it is reasonable to conclude that …", and "The author would be most likely to respond by …".

**A.** This story does not reflect that compensation is usually insufficient.
**CORRECT:** This is the most likely response to the "standard story". Remember that the author emphasizes that, "In reality, compensation tends toward *inadequacy*" (line 14). He gives several reasons, one of which is the "hurdle" of proving negligence. Thus, the author would not believe that the woman's case was indicative of most other torts.

**B.** This story is a good example of just the right amount of compensation.
**WRONG:** This story is *not* a good example of anything that the author promotes. We certainly have no way of knowing if the compensation was "just the right amount".

**C.** This story does not reflect that deterrence is costly.
**WRONG:** This is way outside of the scope of the passage. Deterrence is costly? The only information we have regarding the cost of deterrence is for the defendant. Finally, the question has to do with the woman's *compensation*, not deterrence.

**D.** In this story, the woman was malicious.
**WRONG:** This makes little sense given the abbreviated information in the question. It has nothing to do with the passage.

**37.** Which of the following assertions is the most effective argument *against* the author's opinion that personal injury law cannot satisfactorily compensate and deter "as long as there are administrative costs involved in obtaining an award" (lines 1-7)?

**A.** These administrative costs are inconsequential.
**WRONG:** This is not the most effective argument against the author's opinion. First, one must realize that the author has essentially *defined* 'administrative costs' as 'attorney's fees' (lines 6-13). Then, one must ask if it is reasonable to argue that attorneys should be compensated for their work. It is reasonable to argue that anyone should be compensated for their work (we are not saying how much or how little), and thus, yes, it is reasonable that attorneys should be compensated for their work. This answer is not reasonable. Further, if the costs are around "30%" of the awards, that is probably not considered by anyone to be "inconsequential".

**B.** Attorneys are a necessary part of the judicial system and should be compensated for their work.
**CORRECT:** This is the most effective argument against the author's opinion. First, one must realize that the author has essentially *defined* 'administrative costs' as 'attorney's fees' (lines 7-15). Then, one must ask if it is reasonable to argue that attorneys should be compensated for their work. It is reasonable to argue that anyone should be compensated for their work (we are not saying how much or how little), and thus, yes, it is reasonable that attorneys should be compensated for their work. Finally, unlike some of the other answer choices, this argument is one that the author has not responded to in the passage. This is the best answer.

**C.** The administrative costs should be added to the compensation received by the plaintiff.
**WRONG:** This is not the most effective argument against the author's opinion. The author responds to this idea in the passage. In the example, "If she is paid in full [i.e. administrative costs are added to the full compensation], then the defendant is paying 130% of the actual harm caused, and is *over-deterred*" (lines 11-13). This cannot be the *best* argument because it is answered already in the passage.

**D.** The administrative costs should be subtracted from the compensation received by the plaintiff.
**WRONG:** This is not the most effective argument against the author's opinion. The author responds to this idea in the passage. In the example, "If the plaintiff is awarded 100% of the damages suffered, she only receives compensation for 70% of her injuries" (lines 9-11). This cannot be the *best* argument because it is answered already in the passage.

38. The passage indicates that its author would NOT agree with which of the following statements?

    **A.** Tanker companies are a good example of defendants who are under-deterred.
    WRONG: There is no basis from which to judge whether the author would agree or not agree with this answer. The story of the tanker company is a "permutation on actual events"; it is a fabrication.

    **B.** Negligence on the part of the defendant is generally not difficult for the plaintiff to prove.
    **CORRECT:** The author would not agree with this statement. The author argues in several ways the "hurdle" (line 18) of proving negligence. Besides that fact that 'hurdle' connotes difficulty in surmounting, the author also tells us that "compensation tends toward inadequacy" (line 14) specifically because negligence is so hard to prove.

    **C.** The costs associated with suing and defending against suits can be tremendous.
    WRONG: There is no basis from which to judge whether the author would agree or not agree with this answer. The only dollar amounts provided are in the last paragraph. The idea of "tremendous" costs is relative and opinions between Bill Gates and a homeless person might vary.

    **D.** In many situations, over-deterrence results in primarily economic ramifications.
    WRONG: The author would probably agree. Over-deterrence "results in a waste of resources" (lines 48-49).

39. Assume that since the 9-11 terrorist attacks on the World Trade Center (WTC) buildings, all lawsuits have been settled by the WTC insurance companies, who have now mandated that they will no longer insure any building in the world that is over five stories tall. The author's comments suggest that this situation could reasonably be interpreted as evidence that:

    **A.** the insurance companies were over-deterred.
    **CORRECT:** A reasonable interpretation of the situation, based upon the author's information in the passage could lead one to this conclusion. This idea parallels the 'tanker trial' example offered by the author. Here, after settling the lawsuits from the WTC torts, the insurance companies have mandated a very extreme policy by anyone's estimation. Perhaps the WTC people were at fault which resulted in huge payments to the plaintiffs. Nevertheless, it seems that the WTC insurance companies were, in fact, "over-deterred", resulting in "a waste of resources" (lines 49-50).

    **B.** the insurance companies were under-deterred.
    WRONG: This is not a reasonable interpretation of the situation, based upon the author's information in the passage. "Under-deterrence" results in a defendants "effectively hav[ing] no incentinve" to change or prevent future harms. Here, after settling the lawsuits from the WTC torts, the insurance companies have mandated a very extreme policy by anyone's estimation.

    **C.** the plaintiffs were under-compensated.
    WRONG: This is not a reasonable interpretation of the situation, based upon the author's information in the passage. This is possible, but very unlikely. There *might* have been so many plaintiffs that their rather *small* compensatory damage awards simply overwhelmed the insurance companies. However, it is not probable. It is not even as probable as Answer D, which is also not the best answer. Review the explanations for Answer D and Answer A.

    **D.** the plaintiffs were overcompensated.
    WRONG: This is not a reasonable interpretation of the situation, based upon the author's information in the passage. This is possible. With a poor understanding of the author's concepts from the passage, this answer might seem to go hand-in-hand with Answer A; it might seem just as "correct". It is not. We have no way of knowing if the plaintiffs were overcompensated. Every one of the plaintiffs *might* have been making billions of dollars a year, yet rendered helpless quadriplegics requiring full-time 24-hour care which was *not* completely compensated by the lawsuits. There *might* have been so many plaintiffs that their rather small compensatory damage awards simply overwhelmed the insurance companies. We have no way of knowing based upon the information provided. Consider that, as mentioned, it is conceivable that over-deterrence and under-compensation occur simultaneously, to the benefit of no one. This is not the best answer.

40. Suppose that a study found that police agencies routinely set aside large amounts of money in their yearly budgets, which they expect to pay out in lawsuits against their agency. Which of the following statements is an assumption of the author about the effects of lawsuit awards that would be called into *question*?

The correct answer *must* satisfy *two* criteria. It must 1. be an assumption of the author about the effects of lawsuit awards, and 2. be called into question by the given supposition.

A. Simply proving negligence can be a very costly process.
WRONG: This statement is not a clear assumption of the author, and is not clearly called into question by the supposition.

B. Many people will not sue because the process is too costly.
WRONG: This is an implication of the author's since the idea was brought up in an example (lines 71-72), though the word "many" makes it highly questionable. Further, the supposition clearly states that the 'set aside' money is *not* for *defending* against lawsuits, but in order to "pay out" the awards.

C. If a plaintiff receives full compensation and administrative costs, the defendant is over-deterred.
CORRECT: This statement is very clearly an assumption of the author's (lines 11-13). Further, this statement is called into question by the supposition. If the police agency "routinely" sets aside/budgets the money it will have to pay out in awards, then it seems that this is just a business-as-usual approach. The author's definition of over-deterrence results in a "change". There is an "incentive to prevent [harm]".

D. Depending upon the size of the award, a defendant police agency might not be deterred at all.
WRONG: This is not clearly an assumption of the author, since it specifies police agencies, though it does somewhat parallel the idea that in situations where there is no award "defendants effectively have no incentive to prevent small harms" (lines 74-75). However, this statement is actually *supported* by the supposition. It is certainly not questioned by it.

41. Which of the following conclusions can justifiably be drawn from the experience of the tanker company's counsel mentioned in the passage?

A. Good economists make for poor attorneys.
WRONG: This conclusion cannot be justifiably drawn from the experience of the counsel (i.e. attorney). This answer is attractive because of the author's reference to "the company's counsel — a good economist, but a poor lawyer" (lines 28-29). However, there is no indication that *being* a good economist made this person a poor attorney.

B. Costs should never be considered prohibitive where safety is concerned.
WRONG: This conclusion cannot be justifiably drawn from the experience of the counsel (i.e. attorney). This is outside the scope of the question. The question does not ask about the tanker *incident in general*, but the tanker company's counsel *specifically*.

C. Toxic materials should not be shipped through residential neighborhoods.
WRONG: This conclusion cannot be justifiably drawn from the experience of the counsel (i.e. attorney). This is outside the scope of the question. The question does not ask about the tanker *incident in general*, but the tanker company's counsel *specifically*.

D. Honesty is not always the best policy for an attorney.
CORRECT: This conclusion can be justifiably drawn from the experience of the counsel (i.e. attorney). The author has already informed the reader that the tanker lawyer is a "poor lawyer". Thus, his actions would not be an example for others to follow. The lawyer "*admits* safer tankers were available, but the cost is prohibitive. After extensive cost-benefit analyses, he says, the company found it cheaper just to pay victims for their losses, as it now offers to do" (lines 30-33). The author emphatically (!) announces that the company would be lucky to "escape punitive damages" (lines 33-34). Apparently, the attorney was simply being honest, which (at least from the standpoint of his clients) was probably not the best idea.

42. The author argues that, "Potentially, the most promising development in tort (personal injury) law has been the advent of strict liability" (lines 53-55). These beliefs imply that:

Note that you must understand what "strict liability" is.

A. the use of strict liability has become increasingly popular for defendants.
WRONG: This is not implied by the beliefs in the author's argument.

B. the uses of strict liability should remain limited in scope.
WRONG: This is not implied by the beliefs in the author's argument. According to the passage, strict liability *is* limited in scope. The author believes that, "Unfortunately, the application of strict liability is severely constrained by legal doctrine, which limits its *application* to a small range of 'unusually hazardous activities'" (lines 58-61).

C. the author approves of waiving the requirement for proof, where carelessness is evident.
CORRECT: This answer is implied by the beliefs in the author's argument. "Potentially, the most promising development in tort (personal injury) law has been the advent of strict liability, which waives plaintiffs' need to prove the defendant's carelessness in certain instances where the carelessness is obvious, or could have resulted from no factor other than negligence" (lines 53-58).

D. the author approves of compensation where carelessness is evident.
WRONG: This is not implied by the beliefs in the author's argument. This answer may be accurate information according to the passage. However, that differs from specifically answering the question. You cannot simply choose an answer that provides accurate information to the question. It must be accurate *and* the most responsive answer to the question.

## ANSWERS & EXPLANATIONS FOR 30-MINUTE IN-CLASS EXAM 3

### Passage I (Questions 43–49)

43. The passage suggests that its author would probably *disagree* with which of the following statements?

A. It is possible that Chris participated in "male" activities in order to be considered male.
WRONG: The author would *not* disagree with this statement. From paragraph (lines 41-54) the author discusses the "two sides of the issue"; this statement being one of the sides. "Almost certainly, there is a complex interaction between the two" (lines 53-54).

B. It is possible that Chris naturally participated in "male" activities.
WRONG: The author would *not* disagree with this statement. From paragraph (lines 42-55) the author discusses the "two sides of the issue"; this statement being one of the sides. "Almost certainly, there is a complex interaction between the two" (lines 53-54).

C. Chris was not confused about her identity.
WRONG: The author would *not* disagree with this statement. "Chris was in no way confused about her identity" (lines 21-22).

D. Most cultures have clearly defined gender roles.
**CORRECT:** The author would disagree with this statement. The word, "most", in this statement renders it disagreeable. The author alludes to *other* cultures where Chris might not have felt the need "to identify herself as distinctly male" (lines 38-39). The culture/society wherein Chris lives is clearly defined as "our" (line 5 and 74) culture/society, implying that there are others. There is simply no way of quantifying this statement. This answer choice can also be arrived upon through process of elimination since the other answers the author would clearly *not* disagree with.

**44.** Implicit in the passage is the assumption that:

    **I.**    one should be happy in one's "natural" state.
        WRONG: This is not implied. Though we may strive for "an acceptance of ourselves in a 'natural' state" (lines 60-61), and psychotherapy may help us to arrive at this point, there is not value-judgment-type "should" or "should not" implication in the passage from which to choose this answer. The author seems to have no problem with the idea that Chris would want a sex change operation.

    **II.**    one can be well-adjusted, yet unhappy with one's "natural" state.
        CORRECT: This is clearly implied. We know from the passage that Chris "is described as a relatively well-adjusted individual" (lines 23-24). Additionally, we know that Chris felt "she was a man in a woman's body" (lines 16-17). "Unhappiness" can be used to describe this state because of the information at lines 64-66 "The effect of a physical sex reassignment operation on Chris' happiness cannot be foretold with complete certainty". Apparently, Chris' "happiness" was an issue.

    **III.**    one's perception of self is most important.
        WRONG: This is not implied. This assumption is defined by the quote from the passage that "through psychotherapy, one learns that one may not necessarily have to change oneself as much as *one's perception of self*" (lines 64-65). There is no indication or implication in the passage that this is "most important", or *more* important than *changing* the "natural state" to fit our perception of self.

    **A.**    I only

    **B.**    II only
        CORRECT: See above answer explanations.

    **C.**    III only

    **D.**    I and III only

**45.** The author of the passage would be most likely to agree with which of the following ideas expressed by other psychologists?

    **A.**    A DSM IV 'disorder' may not actually be a disorder at all.
        WRONG: The author would not *most likely* agree with this idea. This idea is perhaps a second best choice. But it is much more vague than Answer C. It is clear from the passage that the DSM is a *reflection* of societal norms. In *this* society, in "*our*" society, even the author admits that Gender Identity Disorder is a disorder.

    **B.**    The DSM IV is a poor descriptor of abnormal behavior and desires since it is easily influenced by societal norms.
        WRONG: The author would not *most likely* agree with this idea. Though it seems that the DSM is influenced by societal norms, there is no indication that it is "easily" influenced, or that overall it is a "poor descriptor" of abnormal behavior. It may actually be a very accurate descriptor of behavior that society has determined is abnormal.

    **C.**    Some DSM IV 'disorders' are simply an attempt to characterize socially abnormal behavior and desires.
        CORRECT: The author would most likely agree with this idea. The author argues that in another culture, Chris' disorder *might* not even be a disorder. "The fact that Gender Identity Disorder exists in the DSM IV [the official handbook of psychiatric disorders] as a diagnosis is an admission on the part of psychologists that our society has clearly defined gender roles. These contribute to what it is generally considered "normal"" (lines 2-7). In *this* society, in "*our*" society, even the author admits that Chris' is considered to have a disorder.

    **D.**    Behavior and desires must fall within the parameters of the DSM IV to be considered normal by society.
        WRONG: The author would not most likely agree with this idea. First, behavior falling "*within*" the parameters of the DSM IV is considered *abnormal*, not normal. Second, it is societal norms which the author believes have determined the DSM parameters. Not the other way around.

46. The author hints that the fact that Chris is well-adjusted indicates that her "uneasiness with her assigned sex" (line 29):

    **A.**    is a problem which should be overcome through psychiatry.
        WRONG: This is not hinted at by the author. This is too strong. The author admits that the treatment of Chris is still a *"question"* (line 55). There is no implication that she "should" overcome her problem through psychiatry. "Psychologically healthy individuals" accept themselves in a "natural" state (lines 60-61). However, the author seems to believe that the "natural" state may just as easily be altered, as one's perception of self.

    **B.**    is due to the culture she lives in.
        **CORRECT:** This is hinted at by the author. Paragraph 31-40, in its entirety, *strongly* argues this answer; beginning with, "in this case, many psychologists may believe society is the culprit" (lines 32-33).

    **C.**    can be overcome through surgery.
        WRONG: This is not hinted at by the author. This is too strong. The author admits that the treatment of Chris is still a *"question"* (line 55). There is no implication that she "can" overcome her problem through surgery.

    **D.**    is a basic personality defect.
        WRONG: This is not hinted at by the author. There is no support for this answer in the passage.

47. Suppose it is discovered that prescription medication allows Chris to become somewhat more comfortable with her "natural" state. Does this discovery support the author's argument?

What is the author's argument? This passage is *not* a completely objective representation of a psychological case study. His main argument is that "society is the culprit". "One *must* ... ponder the age-old question of society as the cause" (lines 29-30).

    **A.**    Yes; it confirms it.
        WRONG: This discovery does not support the author's argument. For this to be a correct answer choice, the author would have to be arguing that there is a psychological or neurological "causal factor". However, the author finds that Chris is "well-adjusted" and dismisses this idea and posits that, "One *must* ... ponder the age-old question of society as the cause" (lines 29-30).

    **B.**    No; it does not affect it.
        **CORRECT:** This discovery supports the author's argument. This passage is *not* a completely objective representation of a psychological case study. His argument is that "society is the culprit". "One *must* ... ponder the age-old question of society as the cause" (lines 29-30). He implies in paragraph 31-40 that in another culture, Chris might not even be suffering from a disorder. Her unhappiness can be linked to society's unwillingness to accept her. Therefore, even if drugs help her become *"somewhat"* more comfortable with her "natural" state, the author's argument is not affected by this discovery.

    **C.**    No; it weakens it.
        WRONG: This discovery does not support the author's argument. The author's argument that "society is the culprit", is *not* weakened by an unspecified *dosage* and *type* of "prescription medicine" rendering Chris only *"somewhat* more comfortable". The supposition in the question is vague enough to assume that she was on a very strong dosage of a very powerful psychotropic drug. This is not the best answer.

    **D.**    No; it disproves it.
        WRONG: This discovery does not support the author's argument. This answer and Answer A are the poorest of the four choices. See the explanations to Answer B.

48. The author admits that, "The effect of a physical sex reassignment operation on Chris' happiness cannot be foretold with complete certainty" (lines 63-66). The author most likely believes that:

    **I.**    it is just as likely that psychotherapy would help Chris to change her perception of self.
        WRONG: This is not what the author most likely believes. The author believes that Chris is "well-adjusted" and that "society is the culprit" (lines 24 and 33). The author's nod to psychotherapy is lukewarm at best and provided only in the spirit of seeming to be objective (lines 59-64).

II. in our society, in the body of a woman, Chris will not be happy.
**CORRECT:** The author most likely believes this. This passage is *not* a completely objective representation of a psychological case study. His argument is that "society is the culprit". "One *must* ... ponder the age-old question of society as the cause" (lines 29-30). He implies in paragraph 31-40 that in another culture, Chris might not even be suffering from a disorder. Her unhappiness can be linked to society's unwillingness to accept her acting as a man in the body of a woman.

III. *a "sex reassignment operation" would make Chris happier.
**CORRECT:** The author most likely believes this. This answer is tantamount to Answer II. See the above explanation.

A. I only

B. II only

C. III only

D. II and III only
**CORRECT:** See the above answer explanations.

49. The author's attitude toward "our" societal norms is most accurately described as:

A. favorable.
WRONG: This is not an accurate description.

B. neutral.
WRONG: This is not an accurate description.

C. distrustful.
WRONG: This is not an accurate description because it is not strong enough. Further, "trust" or "distrust" are poor descriptors for the author's attitude in the passage. See the explanation for Answer D.

D. disapproving.
**CORRECT:** This passage is *not* a completely objective representation of a psychological case study. The author's argument is that "society is the *culprit*" (line 33). "One *must* ... ponder the age-old question of society as the cause" (lines 29-30). He implies in paragraph lines 46-47 that in another culture, Chris might not even be suffering from a disorder. Her unhappiness can be linked to society's unwillingness to accept her acting as a man in the body of a woman. "Our" societal norms are described disparagingly as a "neatly constructed gender dichotomy" (line 74).

## Passage II (Questions 50–56)

50. The author of the passage would be most likely to agree with which of the following ideas expressed by other technology theorists?

A. *Soliciting further ideas and diverse ideas is not always wrong.
**CORRECT:** The author would be most likely to agree with this idea. This answer is restating the rather stilted statement from the passage, "No one can argue that giving additional and different perspectives is inherently bad" (lines 53-54).

B. Obtaining additional and differing perspectives is always beneficial.
WRONG: The author would not be likely to agree with this idea. The word "always" in this idea is extreme. This idea is certainly not the same as the rather stilted statement from the passage, "No one can argue that giving additional and different perspectives is inherently bad" (lines 53-54). At most the author offers that "it *can* also be argued that more information is good" (line 51). However, conspicuous by its absence is the necessary "*always*" good.

**C.** For information to be of value, it must challenge our human values.
WRONG: The author would not be likely to agree with this idea. This is an antithesis. According to Nardi and O'Day, whom the author seems to agree with, "If technology doesn't assist in promoting ... [our human] values, then it cannot be considered useful" (lines 18-20).

**D.** A great deal of the information which we receive is useless because it does not pertain to us.
WRONG: The author would not be likely to agree with this idea. He certainly would not be as likely to agree with this idea as the idea given in Answer A. Answer D is actually an idea of Postman's, not the author's; "[Postman] goes on to say that much of the information we receive does not pertain to us" (lines 43-44). First, the author does not agree with some of what Postman posits (lines 49-55). Further, even Postman does not say that this renders the information "useless". He refers to it as "at best an irrelevant distraction" (lines 44-45).

51. The passage argument suggests that information recipients might benefit from:

**I.** a more rapid flow of information.
WRONG: This is not suggested. Though the author does not completely agree with everything that Postman says, even the author seems to think that recipients are receiving all the information that they can handle at this point.

**II.** thoroughly examining their information.
CORRECT: This is suggested. The author argues that "information is useless unless it is thoroughly examined" (line 56) and "we as a society must consciously attempt to not only obtain information, but to analyze it for meaning" (lines 59-61). There are no counterpoints offered in the passage to this argument.

**III.** limiting non-pertinent information.
WRONG: This is not suggested. The idea is only implied as counterpoint to the main passage arguments. Only Postman, whom the author does not completely agree with, says that "much of the information we receive does not pertain to us [and that] this may create a problem ..." (lines 43-46). Yet, the reader is left only to assume that Postman would go on to 'limit non-pertinent information'; this is not stated. However, the author then argues (lines 49-55) that Postman's view is too extreme. The author sees Postman as wanting to "reduce the amount of information available" (lines 57-58) and is against this.

**A.** I only

**B.** II only
CORRECT: See above answer explanations.

**C.** III only

**D.** II and III only

52. In describing Neil Postman's "information glut", the author uses the example of "images of violence in the Middle East [that] do not affect us" (line 47). The author's point is that:

**A.** the Middle East is at best an irrelevant distraction.
WRONG: This is not the author's point. Perhaps Postman would suggest this. However, the author, who does *not* want to "reduce the amount of information available" (lines 57-58), would not agree.

**B.** the Middle East is poorly understood by us.
WRONG: This is not the author's point, and neither is it suggested in the passage.

**C.** these images should affect us.
CORRECT: This is the author's point. The author prefaces his example of the Middle East categorizing it as a *"problem"* (line 46) that we are *not* affected by these images.

**D.** these images should not be so easily accessible.
WRONG: This is not the author's point. The author would not limit "access" to information, which is tantamount to limiting the amount of information available. Instead, he would better tailor the information "to individual recipient's needs" (lines 58-59).

**53.** If the following statements are true, which would most *weaken* the argument of the author?

**A.** The degree to which technology determines human values is questionable.
WRONG: This statement would not most weaken the argument of the author. This answer/statement admits that technology determines human values. It is only a question of the "degree" of change. To paraphrase the author: human values "are not static", but change according to certain factors, one of the most significant being technology. Based solely upon passage information and this statement it is difficult to determine if there is any disagreement at all.

**B.** Information must be analyzed for its relevance to human values.
WRONG: This statement would not most weaken the argument of the author. This is the thesis of the passage.

**C.** Human values are unchanging.
**CORRECT:** This statement would most weaken the argument of the author. The author argues that "Human values … are not static [i.e. unchanging]" (lines 1-2). His thesis rests upon this idea since he considers technology to be a "significant" factor affecting human values.

**D.** Human values are culturally dependent.
WRONG: This statement would not most weaken the argument of the author. It would matter little to the author's arguments whether they were culturally dependent or not.

**54.** The author argues, "more information is good" (line 51). Unlike Neil Postman, the author does not consider which of the following to be a factor that might limit the usefulness of information?

The correct answer must be one that Postman considers a "limiting factor", but the author does not.

**A.** Space
WRONG: This is not implied as a limiting factor by Postman, and is not alluded to by the author.

**B.** Distance
WRONG: This is not implied as a limiting factor by Postman, but is offered as an example of Postman's 'information glut' idea *by the author*. Providing this example *of Postman's ideas*, the author writes "for example, images of violence in the Middle East do not affect us because they are … too far away to influence us" (lines 46-49). Further, the author never responds to this idea of distance as a limiting factor.

**C.** Frequency
WRONG: This is not implied as a limiting factor by Postman, and is not alluded to by the author. "Frequency" cannot be assumed to be the same as 'quantity', or 'amount'.

**D.** Time
**CORRECT:** This is implied as a limiting factor *by Postman*, and is alluded to by the author, who does not seem to agree that it might limit the usefulness of information. Postman "states that the rapid flow of information allowed by automation and Internet/email provides vast amounts of data to many users *quickly* and *simultaneously*, but doesn't allow humans to understand its meaning *fast enough to keep up*" (lines 39-43). In other words, they don't have time to process the information. However, the author apparently doesn't think that this is a problem. He seems to believe that people generally have all the time in the world. "By giving people *more* information [*which admittedly takes more time for them to process it*], they have a wider basis from which to make decisions and form opinions. No one can argue that giving additional and different perspectives is inherently bad [*except that we usually don't have the time*]" (lines 53-55).

55. According to the passage, one drawback of technology is that it can:

**A.** supersede all other values.
WRONG: This is not a drawback of technology. First, technology is not implied to be a "value". The "other" in this answer clearly implies that technology is a value. Though the passage provides that, "Technology may force people away from their own values [which] creates a disturbing image of a world where technology itself becomes the center of a society *without values*" (lines 34-35). This idea still does not make technology a value.

**B.** be used to destroy human values.
WRONG: This is not a drawback of technology. Though the passage provides that, "Technology may force people away from their own values [which] creates a disturbing image of a world where technology itself becomes the center of a society *without values*" (lines 34-38), there is no inference that "the technology can be used to destroy human values". The two do not have the same meaning.

**C.** subtly change people's values.
**CORRECT:** This is a drawback of technology. Notice the use of the 'softener' "subtly" which makes this answer even more palatable. We know that technology is a "significant factor" that *can* change people's values (lines 1-4). "Technology may force people away from their own values" (lines 34-35). This is a drawback illustrated by Ellul's "disturbing image" (lines 36-38). The passage provides that technology should fit with the values and not vice versa. One way to ensure this is the "three-pronged format" posited by Nardi and O'Day.

**D.** become an irrelevant distraction.
WRONG: This is not a drawback of technology. It is *"information"* that can become an "irrelevant distraction rather than the useful news it was intended as" (lines 45-46).

56. Suppose it could be established that technology is most efficient when it performs its function unobtrusively, without being noticed. The author of the passage would be most likely to respond to this information by:

This is a classic MCAT question. Consider your best answer choices those that would allow the author to either *support* or, in the worst case, *resurrect* or *rehabilitate* his main arguments and thesis. No author would be likely to admit he was completely wrong or abandon his thesis.

**A.** suggesting that this determination ratifies his thesis.
WRONG: The author would not be most likely to respond in this way. The supposition in the question is *somewhat* in opposition to his thesis. The author agrees with Nardi and O'Day that, "If the technology is taken for granted, the actual purpose for using it can become clouded" (lines 24-25). The author would be required to do some explaining to resurrect his ideas.

**B.** proposing that we must still analyze the information for meaning.
WRONG: The author would not be most likely to respond in this way. Though the entire second half of the passage is about information, this is tangential to the overall thesis on technology. It begins with the example of 'information glut' and snowballs. However, this answer is not really responsive to the supposition. *Information* technology would be only one small aspect of *technology*.

**C.** asserting that efficiency is usually degraded when a technology is taken for granted.
WRONG: The author would not be most likely to respond in this way. The supposition in the question is *somewhat* in opposition to his thesis. The author agrees with Nardi and O'Day that, "If the technology is taken for granted, the actual purpose for using it can become clouded" (lines 24-25). However, it is a leap of logic to assume that what the author and these analysts specifically mean is that "efficiency is usually degraded".

**D.** explaining that we must still remain aware of the technology and its intended purpose.
**CORRECT:** The author would be most likely to respond in this way. The supposition in the question is *somewhat* in opposition to his thesis. The author agrees with Nardi and O'Day that, "If the technology is taken for granted, the actual purpose for using it can become clouded" (lines 24-25). Therefore, by responding in the fashion of Answer D, the author has responded to the seemingly opposing-supposition without losing ground in his own arguments.

## Passage III (Questions 57–63)

**57.** Assume that several others who had attended the same opera were interviewed. If they remarked that Margaret sang with tremendous passion, these remarks would *weaken* the passage assertion that:

**A.** Mephisto had rendered her irresistible to Faust.
WRONG: This answer is not a "passage assertion", which is a requirement for a correct answer.

**B.** the lyrics which she sang were "throwaway".
WRONG: This answer is a "passage assertion". However, it is not weakened by the assumption in the question. The remarks have to do with the "tremendous passion" of Margaret's singing, not the *"lyrics"*. This answer is not as responsive to the question as Answer C.

**C.** the young woman of Faust's dreams sang without emotion.
**CORRECT:** This answer is a "passage assertion". First, the young woman of Faust's dreams is a "commoner named Margaret" (lines 50-51). Second, the passage asserts and alludes to "Margaret's *emotionless* singing" (line 56).

**D.** the young woman of Faust's dreams was a commoner.
WRONG: This answer is a "passage assertion". The young woman of Faust's dreams *is* a "commoner named Margaret" (lines 50-51). However, the remarks do not weaken this assertion because they have no relation to it.

**58.** On the basis of the passage, it is reasonable to conclude that:

**A.** Faust lost his soul to the devil.
WRONG: This is not a reasonable conclusion. There is no sure way of knowing this from the passage.

**B.** the "country fair thronged with revelers" was not in the book.
WRONG: This is not a reasonable conclusion. There is no sure way of knowing this from the passage.

**C.** the operatic interpretation differed from the book.
CORRECT: This is a reasonable conclusion. There are several instances which allude to and support this conclusion: "In the director's vision ..." (lines 11-12), and "A chorus presents the essential plot of Faust, *reduced* from its *several incarnations* ..." (lines 20-21), and "... this version presents ..." (line 24 and line 46), and "a theme which is not really congruent with the Faust myth ..." (line 54).

**D.** the author did not enjoy the performance.
WRONG: This is not a reasonable conclusion. This is certainly arguable. Though the author indicates that at Scene II the opera was not particularly to his liking, he begins the passage by asserting that "the New York City Opera production of "Mephistopheles" deserves high marks for visual excellence" (lines 1-3).

**59.** According to the passage, the author felt that the New York City Opera production of "Mephistopheles":

**A.** was plagued with a poor characterization of Mephisto.
WRONG: This is not supported by passage information. The author actually seems to have liked Mephisto's characterization.

**B.** suffered from noticeable weaknesses beginning in Scene II.
**CORRECT:** "In Scene II, ... the play devolves into ... very forgettable arias [and] ... a theme which is not really congruent with the Faust myth" (line 54).

**C.** was enhanced by Dr. Faust's singing.
WRONG: This is not supported by passage information. There are no allusions to Faust's singing.

**D.** could have been improved in Scene III.
WRONG: This is not supported by passage information. There are no allusions to Scene III.

60. According to the passage, the author seems to have most enjoyed:

   A.   the music of the opera.
        WRONG: This is not supported by passage information. It is not clear if the author really enjoyed the music. He said that the music was "only slightly corny" (lines 5-6). He certainly did not like the music as much as the "visual excellence" of the production.

   B.   the singing of the opera .
        WRONG: This is not supported by passage information. The author cared little for Margaret's "emotionless singing", for instance.

   C.   the plot of the opera.
        WRONG: This is not supported by passage information. All this we know from the passage, is that this operatic version differed from the book and other versions which the author was familiar with. Further, at Scene II, and at the "Walpurgis night" scene, the author seems not have cared for the way in which the opera was presented.

   D.   the images of the opera.
        CORRECT: "… the New York City Opera production of "Mephistopheles" deserves high marks for visual excellence" (lines 1-3).


61. Which of the following does the author suggest was a component of the original "Faust myth" (line 54)?

   I.   Reason triumphing over feeling
        CORRECT: This is clearly suggested. From the passage we know that in the opera "Faust and Margaret sing very forgettable arias about the supremacy of feeling over reason, a theme which is not really congruent with the Faust myth" (lines 51-54).

   II.  A more evil Mephisto
        WRONG: This is not clearly suggested. The second paragraph, for one, describes the character of Mephisto in the operatic production, and does give the impression that he has been portrayed/characterized differently in other versions. However, the author gives no indication that "a more evil Mephisto" "was a component of the original 'Faust myth'". There is not enough specificity in the passage information for one to draw this conclusion.

   III. A more powerful God
        WRONG: This is not clearly suggested. This answer *seems* attractive because of the passage statement, "Thus, this version presents temptation as essentially a wager, or struggle, between God and the Devil (which, at one time, was a remarkably blasphemous notion, as it contradicted the dogma that God is all-powerful over evil)" (lines 24-28). However, it is not at all clear that the phrase "at one time" refers to the "Faust myth" or about people's attitudes and belief in God *in general*. This is not the best answer.

   A.   I only
        CORRECT: See the above answer explanations.

   B.   II only

   C.   III only

   D.   II and III only

62.    According to the passage, through what primary means is the fundamental plot transmitted to the audience?

   A.    Via visual imagery
         WRONG: This is not described as a means of transmitting the 'fundamental' plot to the audience.

   B.    Via Faust's musings
         WRONG: This is not described as a means of transmitting the 'fundamental' plot to the audience.

   C.    **Via the chorus**
         **CORRECT:** This is *specifically* described as a means of transmitting the 'fundamental' plot to the audience. "*A chorus presents the essential plot* of Faust, reduced from its several incarnations" (lines 20-21).

   D.    Via Mephisto
         WRONG: This is not described as a means of transmitting the 'fundamental' plot to the audience.


63.    Regarding the devil's bargain with Faust, the passage strongly implies that:

   A.    it is Faust who got the better deal.
         WRONG: This is not implied.

   B.    it is the devil who got the better deal.
         WRONG: This is not implied.

   C.    in other versions, the bargain was with Margaret.
         WRONG: This is not implied.

   D.    in other versions, it is Faust who does the bargaining.
         **CORRECT:** This is implied. "In this version of *Faust*, it is Faust who seizes the devil's bargain …" (lines 46-47).

# PHOTO CREDITS

*Notes:*

*Notes:*

*Notes:*

*Notes:*

# 11 FULL-LENGTH
# MCAT®
## VERBAL EXAMS

### In the NEW MCAT® format

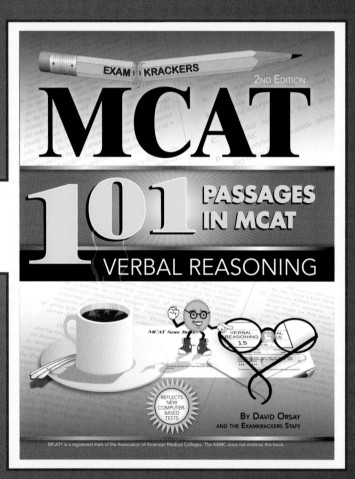

- 674 MCAT® Verbal questions in total

- 16 solid hours of MCAT® Verbal testing

- 2,696 explanations for correct and incorrect answer choices

- 101 MCAT® Verbal Reasoning passages

- 12 tear-out answer sheets for simulation accuracy

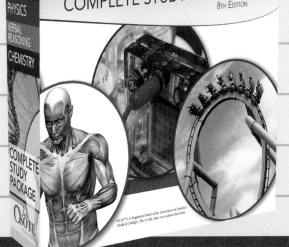

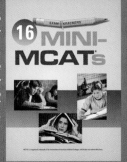

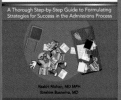

# An Unedited Student Review of This Book

The following review of this book was written by Teri R—. from New York. Teri scored a 43 out of 45 possible points on the MCAT. She is currently attending UCSF medical school, one of the most selective medical schools in the country.

*"The Examkrackers MCAT books are the best MCAT prep materials I've seen-and I looked at many before deciding. The worst part about studying for the MCAT is figuring out what you need to cover and getting the material organized. These books do all that for you so that you can spend your time learning. The books are well and carefully written, with great diagrams and really useful mnemonic tricks, so you don't waste time trying to figure out what the book is saying. They are concise enough that you can get through all of the subjects without cramming unnecessary details, and they really give you a strategy for the exam. The study questions in each section cover all the important concepts, and let you check your learning after each section. Alternating between reading and answering questions in MCAT format really helps make the material stick, and means there are no surprises on the day of the exam- the exam format seems really familiar and this helps enormously with the anxiety. Basically, these books make it clear what you need to do to be completely prepared for the MCAT and deliver it to you in a straightforward and easy-to-follow form. The mass of material you could study is overwhelming, so I decided to trust these books—I used nothing but the Examkrackers books in all subjects and got a 13-15 on Verbal, a 14 on Physical Sciences, and a 14 on Biological Sciences. Thanks to Jonathan Orsay and Examkrackers, I was admitted to all of my top-choice schools (Columbia, Cornell, Stanford, and UCSF). I will always be grateful. I could not recommend the Examkrackers books more strongly. Please contact me if you have any questions."*

*Sincerely,*
*Teri R—*

# About the Author

Jonathan Orsay is uniquely qualified to write an MCAT preparation book. He graduated on the Dean's list with a B.A. in History from Columbia University. While considering medical school, he sat for the real MCAT three times from 1989 to 1996. He scored in the 90 percentiles on all sections before becoming an MCAT instructor. He has lectured in MCAT test preparation for thousands of hours and across the country. He has taught premeds from such prestigious Universities as Harvard and Columbia. He was the editor of one of the best selling MCAT prep books in 1996 and again in 1997. He has written and published the following books and audio products in MCAT preparation: "Examkrackers MCAT Physics"; "Examkrackers MCAT Chemistry"; "Examkrackers MCAT Organic Chemistry"; "Examkrackers MCAT Biology"; "Examkrackers MCAT Verbal Reasoning & Math"; "Examkrackers 1001 questions in MCAT Physics", "Examkrackers MCAT Audio Osmosis with Jordan and Jon".

EXAMKRACKERS MCAT®

# INORGANIC CHEMISTY

8TH EDITION

OSOTE

PUBLISHING

# Acknowledgements

Although I am the author, the hard work and expertise of many individuals contributed to this book. The idea of writing in two voices, a science voice and an MCAT voice, was the creative brainchild of my imaginative friend Jordan Zaretsky. I would like to thank Scott Calvin for lending his exceptional science talent and pedagogic skills to this project. I also must thank the ExamKrackers students for doggedly questioning every explanation, every sentence, every diagram, and every punctuation mark in the book, and for providing the creative inspiration that helped me find new ways to approach and teach chemistry. Finally, I wish to thank my wife, Silvia, for her support during the difficult times in the past and those that lie ahead.

I also wish to thank the following individuals:

## Contributors

Jennifer Birk-Goldschmidt
Patrick Butler
Dr. Scott Calvin
Sam Crayton
Spencer Lewis
Steven Ngai
Mark Pederson
Ahmed Sandu
Shuo Song
Vinita Takiar
Steven Tersigni
Ruopeng Zhu

# Read This Section First!

This manual contains all the inorganic chemistry tested on the MCAT and more. It contains more inorganic chemistry than is tested on the MCAT because a deeper understanding of basic scientific principles is often gained through more advanced study. In addition, the MCAT often presents passages with imposing topics that may intimidate the test-taker. Although the questions don't require knowledge of these topics, some familiarity will increase the confidence of the test-taker.

In order to answer questions quickly and efficiently, it is vital that the test-taker understand what is, and is not, tested directly by the MCAT. To assist the test-taker in gaining this knowledge, this manual will use the following conventions. Any term or concept which is tested directly by the MCAT will be written in **red, bold type**. To ensure a perfect score on the MCAT, you should thoroughly understand all terms and concepts that are in **red, bold type** in this manual. Sometimes it is not necessary to memorize the name of a concept, but it is necessary to understand the concept itself. These concepts will also be in **bold and red**. It is important to note that the converse of the above is not true: just because a topic is not in **bold and red**, does not mean that it is not important.

Any formula that must be memorized will also be written in **red, bold type.**

If a topic is discussed purely as background knowledge, it will be written in *italics*. If a topic is written in italics, it is not likely to be required knowledge for the MCAT but may be discussed in an MCAT passage. Do not ignore items in italics, but recognize them as less important than other items. Answers to questions that directly test knowledge of italicized topics are likely to be found in an MCAT passage.

Text written in orange is me, Salty the Kracker. I will remind you what is and is not an absolute must for MCAT. I will help you develop your MCAT intuition. In addition, I will offer mnemonics, simple methods of viewing a complex concept, and occasionally some comic relief. Don't ignore me, even if you think I am not funny, because my comedy is designed to help you understand and remember. If you think I am funny, tell the boss. I could use a raise.

Each chapter in this manual should be read three times: twice before the class lecture, and once immediately following the lecture. During the first reading, you should not write in the book. Instead, read purely for enjoyment. During the second reading, you should both highlight and take notes in the margins. The third reading should be slow and thorough.

The 24 questions in each lecture should be worked during the second reading before coming to class. The in-class exams in the back of the book are to be done in class after the lecture. Do not look at them before class.

**Warning:** Just attending the class will not raise your score. You must do the work. Not attending class will obstruct dramatic score increases. If you have Audio Osmosis, then listen to the appropriate lecture before and after you read a lecture.

If you are studying independently, read the lecture twice before doing the in-class exam and then once after doing the in-class exam. If you have Examkrackers *MCAT Audio Osmosis With Jordan and Jon*, listen to that before taking the in-class exam and then as many times as necessary after taking the exam.

A scaled score conversion chart is provided on the answer page. This is not meant to be an accurate representation of your MCAT score. Do not become demoralized by a poor performance on these exams; they are not accurate reflections of your performance on the real MCAT. The thirty minute exams have been designed to educate. They are similar to an MCAT but with most of the easy questions removed. We believe that you can answer most of the easy questions without too much help from us, so the best way to raise your score is to focus on the more difficult questions. This method is one of the reasons for the rapid and celebrated success of the Examkrackers prep course and products.

If you find yourself struggling with the science or just needing more practice materials, use the Examkrackers 1001 Questions series. These books are designed specifically to teach the science. If you are already scoring 10s or better, these books are not for you.

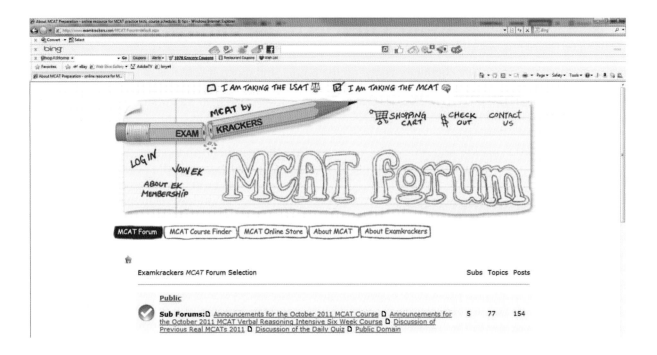

You should take advantage of the forums at www.examkrackers.com. The bulletin board allows you to discuss any question in the book with an MCAT expert at Examkrackers. All discussions are kept on file so you have a bank of discussions to which you can refer to any question in this book.

Although we are very careful to be accurate, errata is an occupational hazard of any science book, especially those that are updated regularly as is this one. We maintain that our books have fewer errata than any other prep book. Most of the time what students are certain are errata is the student's error and not an error in the book. So that you can be certain, any errata in this book will be listed as it is discovered at www.examkrackers.com on the bulletin board. Check this site initially and periodically. If you discover what you believe to be errata, please post it on this board and we will verify it promptly. We understand that this system calls attention to the very few errata that may be in our books, but we feel that this is the best system to ensure that you have accurate information for your exam. Again, we stress that we have fewer errata than any other prep book on the market. The difference is that we provide a public list of our errata for your benefit.

Study diligently, trust this book to guide you, and you will reach your MCAT goals.

# Table of Contents

## PHYSICAL SCIENCES

**DIRECTIONS.** Most questions in the Physical Sciences test are organized into groups, each preceded by a descriptive passage. After studying the passage, select the one best answer to each question in the group. Some questions are not based on a descriptive passage and are also independent of each other. You must also select the one best answer to these questions. If you are not certain of an answer, eliminate the alternatives that you know to be incorrect and then select an answer from the remaining alternatives. A periodic table is provided for your use. You may consult it whenever you wish.

---

## PERIODIC TABLE OF THE ELEMENTS

| 1<br>**H**<br>1.0 | | | | | | | | | | | | | | | | | 2<br>**He**<br>4.0 |
|---|---|---|---|---|---|---|---|---|---|---|---|---|---|---|---|---|---|
| 3<br>**Li**<br>6.9 | 4<br>**Be**<br>9.0 | | | | | | | | | | | 5<br>**B**<br>10.8 | 6<br>**C**<br>12.0 | 7<br>**N**<br>14.0 | 8<br>**O**<br>16.0 | 9<br>**F**<br>19.0 | 10<br>**Ne**<br>20.2 |
| 11<br>**Na**<br>23.0 | 12<br>**Mg**<br>24.3 | | | | | | | | | | | 13<br>**Al**<br>27.0 | 14<br>**Si**<br>28.1 | 15<br>**P**<br>31.0 | 16<br>**S**<br>32.1 | 17<br>**Cl**<br>35.5 | 18<br>**Ar**<br>39.9 |
| 19<br>**K**<br>39.1 | 20<br>**Ca**<br>40.1 | 21<br>**Sc**<br>45.0 | 22<br>**Ti**<br>47.9 | 23<br>**V**<br>50.9 | 24<br>**Cr**<br>52.0 | 25<br>**Mn**<br>54.9 | 26<br>**Fe**<br>55.8 | 27<br>**Co**<br>58.9 | 28<br>**Ni**<br>58.7 | 29<br>**Cu**<br>63.5 | 30<br>**Zn**<br>65.4 | 31<br>**Ga**<br>69.7 | 32<br>**Ge**<br>72.6 | 33<br>**As**<br>74.9 | 34<br>**Se**<br>79.0 | 35<br>**Br**<br>79.9 | 36<br>**Kr**<br>83.8 |
| 37<br>**Rb**<br>85.5 | 38<br>**Sr**<br>87.6 | 39<br>**Y**<br>88.9 | 40<br>**Zr**<br>91.2 | 41<br>**Nb**<br>92.9 | 42<br>**Mo**<br>95.9 | 43<br>**Tc**<br>(98) | 44<br>**Ru**<br>101.1 | 45<br>**Rh**<br>102.9 | 46<br>**Pd**<br>106.4 | 47<br>**Ag**<br>107.9 | 48<br>**Cd**<br>112.4 | 49<br>**In**<br>114.8 | 50<br>**Sn**<br>118.7 | 51<br>**Sb**<br>121.8 | 52<br>**Te**<br>127.6 | 53<br>**I**<br>126.9 | 54<br>**Xe**<br>131.3 |
| 55<br>**Cs**<br>132.9 | 56<br>**Ba**<br>137.3 | 57<br>**La***<br>138.9 | 72<br>**Hf**<br>178.5 | 73<br>**Ta**<br>180.9 | 74<br>**W**<br>183.9 | 75<br>**Re**<br>186.2 | 76<br>**Os**<br>190.2 | 77<br>**Ir**<br>192.2 | 78<br>**Pt**<br>195.1 | 79<br>**Au**<br>197.0 | 80<br>**Hg**<br>200.6 | 81<br>**Tl**<br>204.4 | 82<br>**Pb**<br>207.2 | 83<br>**Bi**<br>209.0 | 84<br>**Po**<br>(209) | 85<br>**At**<br>(210) | 86<br>**Rn**<br>(222) |
| 87<br>**Fr**<br>(223) | 88<br>**Ra**<br>226.0 | 89<br>**Ac**⁼<br>227.0 | 104<br>**Unq**<br>(261) | 105<br>**Unp**<br>(262) | 106<br>**Unh**<br>(263) | 107<br>**Uns**<br>(262) | 108<br>**Uno**<br>(265) | 109<br>**Une**<br>(267) | | | | | | | | | |

| | 58<br>**Ce**<br>140.1 | 59<br>**Pr**<br>140.9 | 60<br>**Nd**<br>144.2 | 61<br>**Pm**<br>(145) | 62<br>**Sm**<br>150.4 | 63<br>**Eu**<br>152.0 | 64<br>**Gd**<br>157.3 | 65<br>**Tb**<br>158.9 | 66<br>**Dy**<br>162.5 | 67<br>**Ho**<br>164.9 | 68<br>**Er**<br>167.3 | 69<br>**Tm**<br>168.9 | 70<br>**Yb**<br>173.0 | 71<br>**Lu**<br>175.0 |
|---|---|---|---|---|---|---|---|---|---|---|---|---|---|---|
| * | | | | | | | | | | | | | | |
| ⁼ | 90<br>**Th**<br>232.0 | 91<br>**Pa**<br>(231) | 92<br>**U**<br>238.0 | 93<br>**Np**<br>(237) | 94<br>**Pu**<br>(244) | 95<br>**Am**<br>(243) | 96<br>**Cm**<br>(247) | 97<br>**Bk**<br>(247) | 98<br>**Cf**<br>(251) | 99<br>**Es**<br>(252) | 100<br>**Fm**<br>(257) | 101<br>**Md**<br>(258) | 102<br>**No**<br>(259) | 103<br>**Lr**<br>(260) |

# ATOMS, MOLECULES AND QUANTUM MECHANICS

## 1.1 Atoms

All mass consists of tiny particles called **atoms**. Each atom is composed of a **nucleus** surrounded by one or more electrons. The radius of a nucleus is on the order of $10^{-4}$ angstroms (Å). One angstrom is $10^{-10}$ m. The nucleus contains **protons** and neutrons, collectively called *nucleons*, held together by the *strong nuclear force*. Protons and neutrons are approximately equal in size and mass. (Neutrons are very slightly heavier.) Protons have a positive charge and neutrons are electrically neutral.

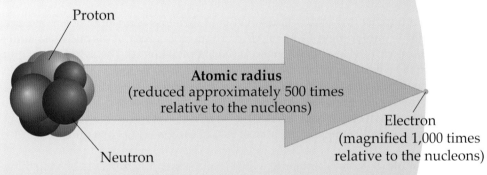

Proton

**Atomic radius**
(reduced approximately 500 times relative to the nucleons)

Electron
(magnified 1,000 times relative to the nucleons)

Neutron

Surrounding the nucleus at a distance of about 1 to 3 Å are **electrons**. The mass of one electron is over 1800 times smaller than the mass of a nucleon. Electrons and protons have opposite charges of equal magnitude. Although for convenience we often think of the charge on an electron as 1– and the charge on a proton as 1+, we should remember that this charge is in electron units '*e*' called the *electronic charge*. A charge of 1 *e* is equal to $1.6 \times 10^{-19}$ coulombs, the SI unit. An atom itself is electrically neutral; it contains the same number of protons as electrons.

**Table 1.1 Composition of an Atom**

| *Particle* | *Charge* | *Mass* (amu) |
|---|---|---|
| Proton | Positive (1+) | 1.0073 |
| Neutron | Neutral | 1.0087 |
| Electron | Negative (1-) | $5.5 \times 10^{-4}$ |

*Of course, you want to know the charges on the particles, but don't memorize the masses in the table shown. Instead, recognize the disparity in size between electrons and nucleons. Also, notice that protons and neutrons have nearly the same mass, about one amu.*

Since the nucleons are so small compared to the size of the atom, the atom itself is composed mostly of empty space. If an atom were the size of a modern football stadium, it would have a nucleus the size of a marble.

Any given atom must be one of just over 100 **elements**. Elements are the building blocks of all compounds and cannot be decomposed into simpler substances by chemical means. Any element can be displayed as follows in Figure 1.1 where **A** is the **mass number** or number of protons plus neutrons, and **Z** is the **atomic number** or number of protons. The atomic number is the identity number of any element. If we know the atomic number, then we know the element. This is not true of the mass number or the number of electrons. Any element may have any number of neutrons or electrons, but only one number of protons.

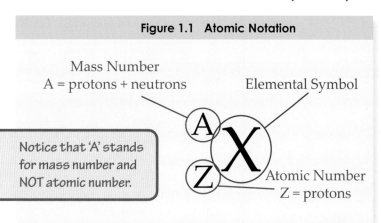

**Figure 1.1  Atomic Notation**

Mass Number
A = protons + neutrons

Elemental Symbol

$$\begin{smallmatrix} A \\ Z \end{smallmatrix}X$$

Atomic Number
Z = protons

Notice that 'A' stands for mass number and NOT atomic number.

Two or more atoms of the same element that contain different numbers of neutrons are said to be **isotopes**. A nucleus of a specific isotope is called a *nuclide*. Isotopes have similar chemical properties. Hydrogen has three important isotopes: $^{1}H$ (*protium*), $^{2}H$ (*deuterium*), and $^{3}H$ (*tritium*). 99.98% of naturally occurring hydrogen is protium. Examples of three isotopes for carbon are:

$$^{12}C, \ ^{13}C, \text{ and } ^{14}C.$$

Each of carbon's isotopes contains 6 protons. Six protons define carbon. $^{12}C$ (carbon-12) contains 6 neutrons, $^{13}C$ (carbon-13) contains 7 neutrons, and $^{14}C$ (carbon-14) contains 8 neutrons.

The number of protons identifies the element. For a given element, the number of neutrons identifies the isotope.

Although the mass number is a good approximation of the mass of an atom, it is not exact. The **atomic weight** or **molar mass** (**MM or M**) of an atom is given in **atomic mass units** (abbreviated **amu** or with the less commonly used SI abbreviation **u**). The atomic weight of an element is actually a mass (or in some books a ratio) and not a weight. An amu is defined by carbon-12. By definition, one atom of $^{12}C$ has an atomic weight of 12 amu. All other atomic weights are measured against this standard. Since carbon naturally occurs as a mixture of its isotopes, the atomic weight of carbon is listed as the weighted average of its isotopes or 12.011 amu. (This is very close to 12 amu because almost 99% of carbon occurs in nature as $^{12}C$.)

Think of an amu as approximately the mass of one proton or one neutron.

Biochemists call an amu a dalton.

$^{12}C$ also defines a **mole**. A mole is similar to a dozen or a score. A dozen is 12 of something and a score is 20 of something. So 3 dozen eggs means 3 × 12 = 36 eggs and "four score and seven years ago" means 4 × 20 + 7 = 87 years ago. A mole is just 6.022 × 10²³ of something, where **6.022 × 10²³** is **Avogadro's number**, the number of carbon atoms in 12 grams of $^{12}C$. Keeping in mind the relationship between an amu and a gram can be useful:

$$6.022 \times 10^{23} \text{ amu} = 1 \text{ gram}$$

We can read atomic weights from the periodic table as either amu or g/mol.

If we are given the amount of an element or compound in grams, we can divide by the atomic or molecular weight to find the number of moles in that sample.

$$\text{moles} = \frac{\text{grams}}{\text{atomic or molecular weight}}$$

If you can't find moles from molecular or atomic weight, then you better get crackin'. This is basic stuff, but you need to have it down cold!

One mole of carbon.

# *The Periodic Table*

The **periodic table** lists the elements from left to right in the order of their atomic numbers. Each horizontal row is called a **period**. The vertical columns are called **groups or families**. There are at least two methods used to number the groups. The newer method is to number them 1 through 18 from left to right. An older method, which is still used, is to separate the groups into sections A and B. These sections are then numbered with Roman numerals as shown below.

The periodic table below divides the elements into three sections: 1) nonmetals on the right (green), 2) metals on the left (yellow gold), and 3) metalloids along the blue-shaded diagonal separating the metals from the nonmetals.

**Metals** are large atoms that tend to lose electrons to form positive ions or form positive oxidation states. To emphasize their loose hold on their electrons and the fluid-like nature of their valence electrons, metals are often described as atoms in a sea of electrons. The easy movement of electrons within metals gives them their metallic character. Metallic character includes ductility (easily stretched), malleability (easily hammered into thin strips), thermal and electrical conductivity, and a characteristic luster. Metal atoms easily slide past each other allowing metals to be hammered into thin sheets or drawn into wires. Electrons move easily from one metal atom to the next transferring energy or charge in the form of heat or electricity. All metals but mercury exist as solids at room temperature. Metals typically form ionic oxides such as BaO. (BeO is one exception that is not ionic.)

One characteristic of metals is malleability. Here, hot iron is hammered into a different shape by a blacksmith.

> *Know the characteristics of metals: lustrous, ductile, malleable, thermally and electrically conductive.*

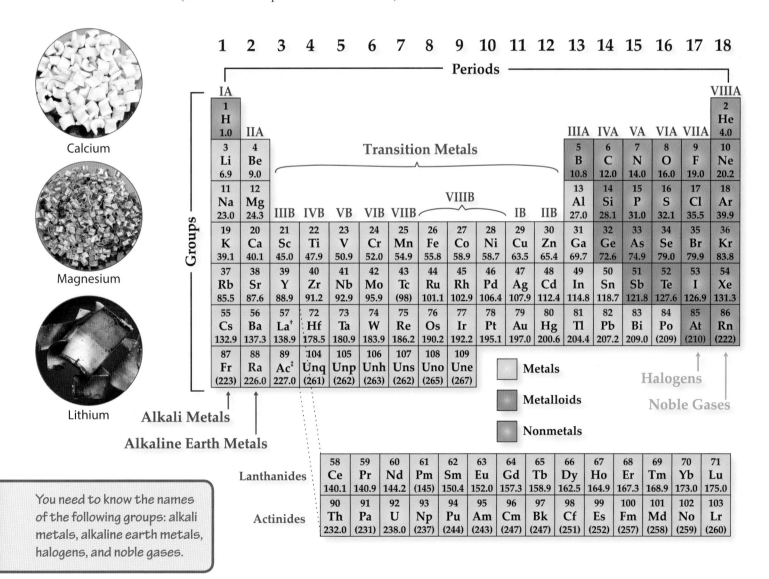

Calcium

Magnesium

Lithium

**Alkali Metals**

**Alkaline Earth Metals**

**Lanthanides**

**Actinides**

> *You need to know the names of the following groups: alkali metals, alkaline earth metals, halogens, and noble gases.*

**Nonmetals** have diverse appearances and chemical behaviors. Generally speaking, nonmetals have lower melting points than metals. They form negative ions. Molecular substances are typically made from only nonmetals. Nonmetals form covalent oxides such as $SiO_2$ or $CO_2$.

**Metalloids** have some characteristics that resemble metals and some that resemble nonmetals.

You should also recognize the names of the following four groups: alkali metals, alkaline earth metals, halogens, and noble (or rare) gases. The section A groups are known as the *representative* or *main-group elements* and the section B groups are called the **transition metals**.

Elements in the same family on the periodic table tend to have similar chemical properties. For example, they tend to make the same number of bonds and exist as similarly charged ions.

> Elements in the same family have similar chemical properties. Hydrogen is an exception to the rule.

## 1.4 *Characteristics Within Groups*

Hydrogen is unique and its chemical and physical characteristics do not conform well to any family. It is a nonmetal. Under most conditions, it is a colorless, odorless, diatomic gas.

As pure substances, Group 1A or alkali metals are soft metallic solids with low densities and low melting points. They easily form 1+ cations. They are highly reactive, reacting with most nonmetals to form ionic compounds. Alkali metals react with hydrogen to form hydrides such as NaH. Alkali metals react exothermically with water to produce the metal hydroxide and hydrogen gas. In nature, alkali metals exist only in compounds.

Group 2A or alkaline earth metals are harder, more dense, and melt at higher temperatures than alkali metals. They form 2+ cations. They are less reactive than alkali metals. Heavier alkaline earth metals are more reactive than lighter alkaline earth metals.

> You can remember that alkali metals are Group 1 and alkaline earth metals are Group 2 because alkali comes before alkaline in alphabetical order.

All the 4A elements can form four covalent bonds with nonmetals. All but carbon can form two additional bonds with Lewis bases. Of the 4A elements, only carbon forms strong π-bonds to make *strong* double and even triple bonds.

Group 5A elements can form 3 covalent bonds. In addition, all 5A elements except nitrogen can form five covalent bonds by using their *d* orbitals. These elements can further bond with a Lewis base to form a sixth covalent bond. Nitrogen forms strong π-bonds to make double and triple bonds. Phosphorous can form only weak π-bonds to make double bonds. The other 5A elements cannot make π-bonds. Nitrogen can also form four covalent bonds by donating its lone pair of electrons to form a bond.

Group 6A elements are called the *chalcogens*. Oxygen and sulfur are the important chalcogens for the MCAT. Oxygen is the second most electronegative element. Oxygen is divalent and can form strong π-bonds to make double bonds. In nature, oxygen exists as $O_2$ (*dioxygen*) and $O_3$ (ozone). Oxygen typically reacts with metals to form metal oxides. Alkali metals form peroxides ($Na_2O_2$) and *super oxides* ($KO_2$) with oxygen. The most common form of pure sulfur is the yellow solid $S_8$. Metal sulfides, such as $Na_2S$, are the most common form of sulfur found in nature. Sulfur can form two, three, four, five or even six bonds. It has the ability to pi-bond making strong double bonds.

Phosphorus is a multivalent nonmetal of Group 5A and is commonly found in inorganic phosphate rocks.

Granulated mineral sulfur

The radioactively stable Group 7A elements (called halogens) are fluorine, chlorine, bromine, and iodine. Halogens are highly reactive. Fluorine and chlorine are diatomic gases at room temperature; bromine, a diatomic liquid; iodine, a diatomic solid. Halogens like to gain electrons. However, halogens other than fluorine can take on oxidation states as high as +7 when bonding to highly electronegative atoms like oxygen. When in compounds, fluorine always has an oxidation state of −1. This means that fluorine makes only one bond, while the other halogens can make more than one bond. Hydrogen combines with all the halogens to form gaseous hydrogen halides. The hydrogen halides are soluble in water forming the hydrohalic acids. Halogens react with metals to form ionic halides (example NaCl).

Noble gases are nonreactive. They are sometimes called the **inert gases**. Only the noble gas elements are normally found in nature as isolated atoms. They are all gases at room temperature.

The elements that tend to exist as diatomic molecules are hydrogen, oxygen, nitrogen, and the halogens. Typically, when these elements are discussed, it is assumed that they are in their diatomic form unless otherwise stated. In other words, the statement "nitrogen is nonreactive" refers to $N_2$ and not N.

Notice that the size of an atom has a significant effect on its chemistry. If we examine the smallest element in a Group, we can sometimes see deviations in its behavior due to its size. Small atoms have less room to stabilize charge by spreading it out. This makes them bond more strongly to water resulting in greater heats of hydration. Because beryllium in its ionic form is not large enough to stabilize its charge, it forms a covalent oxide, whereas other alkaline earth metals make ionic oxides. This means that BeO is amphoteric whereas other alkaline earth metal oxides are basic. Small atoms don't have $d$ orbitals available to them for bond formation. Atoms without $d$ orbitals cannot form more than four bonds. Oxygen typically forms two bonds, while the larger sulfur can form up to six. On the other hand, the $p$ orbitals on atoms that are too big don't overlap significantly, so large atoms can't easily form π-bonds. The second period elements carbon, nitrogen, and oxygen are small enough to form strong π-bonds while their larger third row family members form only weak π-bonds, if they form π-bonds at all.

Flasks containing bromine ($Br_2$) and iodine ($I_2$).

### Figure 1.2  Orbital Illustration

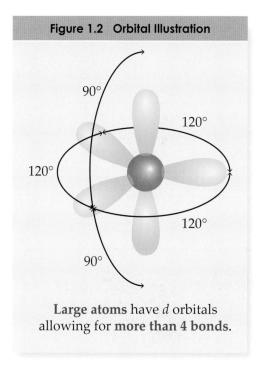

**Large atoms** have $d$ orbitals allowing for **more than 4 bonds.**

### Figure 1.3  Pi (π) Bonds

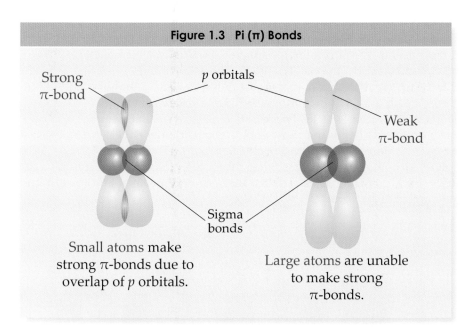

Small atoms make strong π-bonds due to overlap of $p$ orbitals.

Large atoms are unable to make strong π-bonds.

This is a lot of detail! Knowing some of details of the characteristics of each group on the periodic table will be helpful, but is not required by the MCAT. Don't be too concerned with all this detail.

## 1.5 Ions

When an element has more or fewer electrons than protons, it becomes an ion. Positive ions are called cations; negative ions, anions. The representative elements make ions by forming the closest noble gas electron configuration. (Electron configurations are discussed later in this Lecture.) Metals form cations; nonmetals form anions. When the transition metals form ions, they lose electrons from their $s$-subshell first and then from their $d$-subshell. (Subshells will be discussed later in this lecture.) Below are some common ions formed by metals.

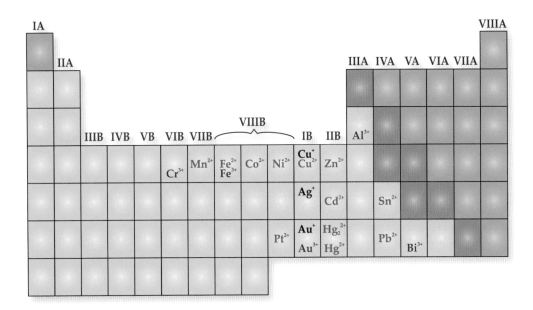

The periodic table to the left shows some of the more common ions formed by the transition metals. Notice that Group 1B makes three 1+ ions. There are five 3+ ions $Cr^{3+}$, $Fe^{3+}$, $Au^{3+}$, $Al^{3+}$, and $Bi^{3+}$. The other transition metal ions are 2+.

Cations are significantly smaller than their neutral atom counterparts. For instance, sodium's outermost electron is located by itself on an outer shell. When this outer electron is removed, the sodium cation is significantly smaller because the remaining electrons are located in inner shells. The reverse is true for anions. The additional electrons are added to an outer shell making the anion much larger than its neutral atom counter part. Isoelectronic ions (ions with the same number of electrons) tend to get smaller with increasing atomic number because more protons pull inward on the same number of electrons. The sizes of the oxygen, fluorine, sodium and magnesium ions in Figure 1.4 reflect this trend.

In Figure 1.4 the purple spheres represent the atoms oxygen, fluorine, neon, sodium, and magnesium. The pink and blue spheres show an isoelectronic series. The pink spheres represent the anions $O^{2-}$ and $F^-$. The blue spheres represent the cations $Na^+$ and $Mg^{2+}$. With each ion, moving from left to right, a proton is added but no electron is added. With more protons pulling on the same number of electrons, the ions in an isoelectronic series become increasingly smaller. Figure 1.4 shows an isoelectronic series (a group of ions with the same number of electrons) consisting of oxygen, fluorine, sodium, and magnesium ions. (The size of the neon atom is provided for comparison). Each ion has a total of 10 electrons. The ions tend to get smaller with increasing atom number because more protons pull inward on the same number of electrons.

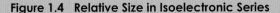
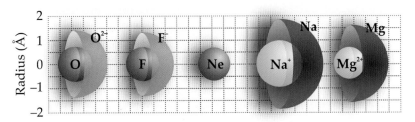

**Figure 1.4 Relative Size in Isoelectronic Series**

## 1.6 Periodic Trends

Coulomb's law, $F = kq_1q_2/r^2$, describes the electrostatic forces holding an electron to its nucleus. The distance between the electron and the nucleus is $r$. For $q_1$ we might plug in the positive charge of the nucleus, $Z$, and for $q_2$, the charge on an electron, $e$. This would work fine for hydrogen, where the lone electron feels 100% of the positive charge on the nucleus. However, in helium the first electron **shields** some of the nuclear charge from the second electron, so that the second electron doesn't *feel* the entire nuclear charge, $Z$. The amount of charge felt by the second electron is called the **effective nuclear charge ($Z_{eff}$)**. In complete or perfect shielding, each electron added to an atom would be completely shielded from the attractive force of all the protons except for the last proton added, and the $Z_{eff}$ would be 1 eV for each electron. Without shielding, each electron added would feel the full attractive force of all the protons in the nucleus, and the $Z_{eff}$ would simply be equal to $Z$ for each electron.

Figure 1.5 shows $Z_{eff}$ values (given in electron volts) for the highest energy electron in each element through sodium. Notice the drop in $Z_{eff}$ going from helium to lithium. This is because the last electron added to make lithium is added to an outer shell making the shielding effect strong. To form beryllium, an electron is added to the same shell and the shielding effect is not as great. To form boron, an electron is added to the 2$p$-subshell, a higher energy subshell, and shielding is stronger again. (We'll discuss subshells later in this lecture.) Going from nitrogen to oxygen, the next electron must share an orbital with one of the three $p$ orbitals resulting in some shielding and a reduction in $Z_{eff}$. Moving from neon to sodium, the next electron is added to an entirely new shell, the 3$s$-subshell. This causes a strong reduction in $Z_{eff}$, but notice that the outermost electron in sodium still experiences a higher $Z_{eff}$ than the outermost electron of the element immediately above it on the periodic table, lithium. $Z_{eff}$ generally increases going left to right across the periodic table and going top to bottom down the periodic table.

You can see in Figure 1.5 that $Z_{eff}$ for the outermost electron of helium is not 2, even though there are two protons in the helium nucleus. The $Z_{eff}$ is the nuclear charge $Z$ minus the average number of electrons between the nucleus and the electron in question. The $Z_{eff}$, and not $Z$, should be plugged in for q in Coulomb's law to find the force on the outermost electron. Note that the force is a function of both $q$ ($Z_{eff}$) and $r$ (the distance from the nucleus).

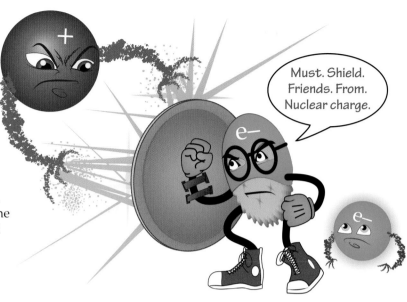

Must. Shield. Friends. From. Nuclear charge.

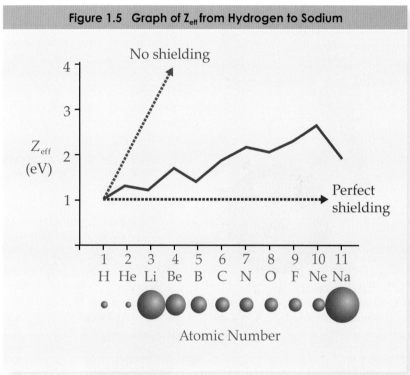

**Figure 1.5 Graph of $Z_{eff}$ from Hydrogen to Sodium**

No shielding

Perfect shielding

Atomic Number

When considering the effect of $Z_{eff}$, consider the strength of $Z_{eff}$ and the distance from the nucleus. The force pulling the electron inward goes up with $Z_{eff}$ but goes down with distance according to Coulomb's law: $F = kq_1q_2/r^2$.

With $Z_{eff}$ in mind, we can make general predictions about the elements based upon their positions in the periodic table. These predictions can be summarized as five **periodic trends** concerning:

1. Atomic Radius
2. Ionization Energy
3. Electronegativity
4. Electron Affinity
5. Metallic Character

The **atomic radius** is the distance from the center of the nucleus to the outermost electron. Atomic radius corresponds to the size of the atom. Since the effective nuclear charge increases when moving from left to right on the periodic table, each additional electron is pulled more strongly toward the nucleus. The result is that atoms tend to get smaller when adding electrons across the periodic table. However, when dropping down from atom to atom within a group, each drop represents the addition of a new electron shell, and thus atoms tend to grow as we move down a group.

When an electron is more strongly attached to a nucleus, more energy is required to detach it. The energy necessary to detach an electron from a nucleus is called the **ionization energy**. The energy necessary to detach an electron from a neutral atom and form a +1 cation is called the first ionization energy. (By definition, the atom being ionized is gaseous.) The energy for the removal of a second electron from the same atom to form a +2 cation is called the **second ionization energy**. Third, fourth, fifth, and other ionization energies are named in the same manner. The second ionization energy is always much greater than the first because when one electron is removed, the effective nuclear charge on the other electrons increases. Ionization energy generally increases along the periodic table from left to right and from bottom to top. This trend is related to $Z_{eff}$. Moving across a period to the right, higher $Z_{eff}$ values hold electrons more tightly to the nucleus requiring more energy to rip them off. Although $Z_{eff}$ also increases when moving down the periodic table, the distance of the electron from the nucleus increases as well. From Coulomb's law, $F = kqq/r^2$, we see that though the electric force, $F$, holding the electron onto the nucleus goes up proportionally with $q$ (recall that q in this case is $Z_{eff}$), the same force drops with the square of the distance from the nucleus, $r$. Less force means less energy required to remove the electron. The distance plays a more important role than the increased $Z_{eff}$ and ionization energy increases moving up a group.

Recall from Organic Chemistry Lecture 1.6, that electrons are shared in a covalent bond. Recall also that these electrons may be shared unequally. **Electronegativity** is the tendency of an atom to attract these shared electrons. The most commonly used measurement of electronegativity is the *Pauling scale*, which ranges from a value of 0.79 for cesium to a value of 4.0 for fluorine. Like ionization energy, electronegativity tends to increase across a period from left to right and up the group. The reasoning for this is similar to the reasoning for the trend of ionization energy. Since noble gases tend not to make bonds, electronegativity values are undefined for the noble gases.

Electronegativity allows us to predict what type of bond will form between two atoms. Atoms with large electronegativity differences (1.4 on the Pauling scale as a rule of thumb) will form ionic bonds with each other. For example, metals and non-metals usually exhibit large electronegativity differences and form ionic bonds to each other. Atoms with more moderate differences in electronegativities will generally form polar covalent bonds. Atoms with very minor electronegativity differences will form nonpolar covalent bonds.

Some atoms are better at sharing electrons than others.

**Electron affinity** is the willingness of an atom to accept an additional electron. More precisely, it is the energy released when an electron is added to an isolated atom. The sign of electron affinity changes for different atoms because some atoms release energy when accepting an electron and some atoms require energy to force the electron to add. Just like electronegativity (and for the same reasons), electron affinity tends to increase on the periodic table from left to right and from bottom to top. (**Warning:** Many books use the exothermic value for electron affinity, which is the negative of the energy released. We can state this as follows: electron affinity is more exothermic to the right and up on the periodic table.) The noble gases do not follow this trend. Electron affinity values for the noble gases are endothermic.

Some atoms have a very high affinity for electrons.

The final important periodic trend, **metallic character**, tends to increase from right to left and top to bottom.

| | | | | | | | | | | | | | H | | | | | He |
|---|---|---|---|---|---|---|---|---|---|---|---|---|---|---|---|---|---|---|
| Li | Be | | | | | | | | | | | | B | C | N | O | F | Ne |
| Na | Mg | | | | | | | | | | | | Al | Si | P | S | Cl | Ar |
| K | Ca | Sc | Ti | V | Cr | Mn | Fe | Co | Ni | Cu | Zn | Ga | Ge | As | Se | Br | Kr |
| Rb | Sr | Y | Zr | Nb | Mo | Tc | Ru | Rh | Pd | Ag | Cd | In | Sn | Sb | Te | I | Xe |
| Cs | Ba | La | Hf | Ta | W | Re | Os | Ir | Pt | Au | Hg | Tl | Pb | Bi | Po | At | Rn |
| Fr | Ra | Ac | Unq | Unp | Unh | Uns | Uno | Une | | | | | | | | | |

Energy of Ionization
Electron Affinity
Electronegativity

Atomic Radius
Metallic Character

E

An easy way to remember the 5 periodic trends is as follows: if it begins with an 'E', as shown here, then it increases going to the right and up; if it doesn't begin with an 'E', then it increases in the opposite direction. Be careful! This mnemonic requires that you think of 'ionization energy' as 'energy of ionization' so that it begins with an 'E'. $Z_{eff}$ is not considered a periodic trend for this mnemonic. Keep in mind that the trends are just trends, and are violated frequently.

The noble gases do not follow the trends for electronegativity or for electron affinity.

Notice that hydrogen has moved to a more appropriate position.

1. Which of the following increases with increasing atomic number within a family on the periodic table?

   A. electronegativity
   B. electron affinity
   C. atomic radius
   D. ionization energy

2. Which of the following molecules has the greatest dipole moment?

   A. $H_2$
   B. $O_2$
   C. HF
   D. HBr

3. How many carbon atoms exist in 12 amu of $^{12}C$?

   A. 1
   B. 12
   C. $6.02 \times 10^{23}$
   D. $7.22 \times 10^{24}$

4. Silicon has a silvery luster at room temperature. Silicon is brittle, and does not conduct heat or electricity well. Based on its position in the periodic table, silicon is most likely a:

   A. nonmetal
   B. metalloid
   C. metal
   D. chalcogen

5. Which of the following most likely represents the correct order of ion size from greatest to smallest?

   A. $O^{2-}$, $F^-$, $Na^+$, $Mg^{2+}$
   B. $Mg^{2+}$, $Na^+$, $F^-$, $O^{2-}$
   C. $Na^+$, $Mg^{2+}$, $O^{2-}$, $F^-$
   D. $Mg^{2+}$, $Na^+$, $O^{2-}$, $F^-$

6. A natural sample of carbon contains 99% of $^{12}C$. How many moles of $^{12}C$ are likely to be found in a 48.5 gram sample of carbon obtained from nature?

   A. 1
   B. 4
   C. 12
   D. 49.5

7. In 1869 both Mendeleev and Meyer, working separately, published nearly identical classification schemes for the elements that were the forerunners of the modern periodic table. Although scientists of that time had no knowledge of atomic numbers, both schemes ordered the elements in nearly correct order from lowest to highest atomic number. Which of the following is the most likely explanation?

   A. Both scientists noticed similar patterns in chemical and physical behaviors among the elements.
   B. Atomic number generally increases with atomic weight and the scientist knew the atomic weights of the elements.
   C. The chemical identity was predictable from the number of valence electrons which was known at the time.
   D. Although the number of protons for each element was not known, the number of neutrons was.

8. Which of the following could be a stable molecular structure?

A.

B.

C.

Se $=$ Se

D.

```
        Cl
        |
Cl ─── F ─── Cl
        |
        Cl
```

By international agreement, SI units are used for scientific measurements. "SI Units" stands for *Systeme International d'Unites*. SI units predominate on the MCAT.

There are seven base units in the SI system. The seven are listed in the table below:

| Table 1.2 SI Base Units | | |
|---|---|---|
| *Physical Quantity* | *Name of Unit* | *Abbreviation* |
| Mass | Kilogram | kg |
| Length | Meter | m |
| Time | Second | s |
| Electric current | Ampere | A |
| Temperature | Kelvin | K |
| Luminous intensity | Candela | cd |
| Amount of substance | Mole | mol |

Other SI units can be derived from these seven, such as a newton: $1 \text{ N} = 1 \text{ kg m s}^{-2}$. There are other units still commonly in use that you may also see on the MCAT, such as atm or torr for pressure. All such units will have an SI counterpart that you should know. We will point this out as we come across new units.

The SI system also employs standard prefixes for each unit. These prefixes are commonly seen on the MCAT. Table 1.3 lists these standard prefixes:

| Table 1.3 Prefixes for SI Units | | |
|---|---|---|
| *Prefix* | *Abbreviation* | *Meaning* |
| Mega- | M | $10^6$ |
| Kilo- | k | $10^3$ |
| Deci- | d | $10^{-1}$ |
| Centi- | c | $10^{-2}$ |
| Milli- | m | $10^{-3}$ |
| Micro- | μ | $10^{-6}$ |
| Nano- | n | $10^{-9}$ |
| Pico- | p | $10^{-12}$ |
| Femto- | f | $10^{-15}$ |

STOP! You were going to skip this page; weren't you? Memorize the SI units and the prefixes. They will help you in all the sciences.

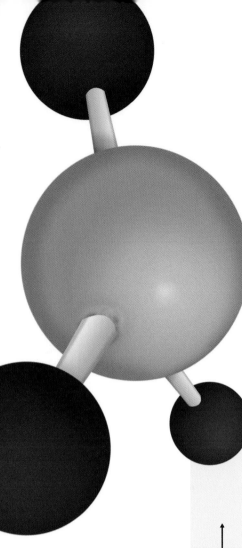

Boron Hydride (BH$_3$)

## 1.8 Molecules

Atoms can be held together by **bonds**. In one type of bond, two electrons are shared by two nuclei. This is called a **covalent bond**. The negatively charged electrons are pulled toward both positively charged nuclei by electrostatic forces. This 'tug of war' between the nuclei for the electrons holds the atoms together. If the nuclei come too close to each other, the positively charged nuclei repel each other. These repulsive and attractive forces achieve a balance to create a bond. Figure 1.6 compares the internuclear distance between two hydrogen atoms to their electrostatic potential energy level as a system. The **bond length** is defined as the point where the energy level is the lowest. Two atoms will only form a bond if they can lower their overall energy level by doing so. Nature tends to seek the lowest energy state.

If we separate the atoms by an infinite distance, the forces between them, and thus the energy, go to zero. The energy necessary to achieve a complete separation is given by the vertical distance on the graph between the energy at the bond length and zero. This is called the **bond dissociation energy** or **bond energy**. (Bond dissociation energy and bond energy are very closely related.)

**Figure 1.6   Bond Length in Relation to Potential Energy for H₂**

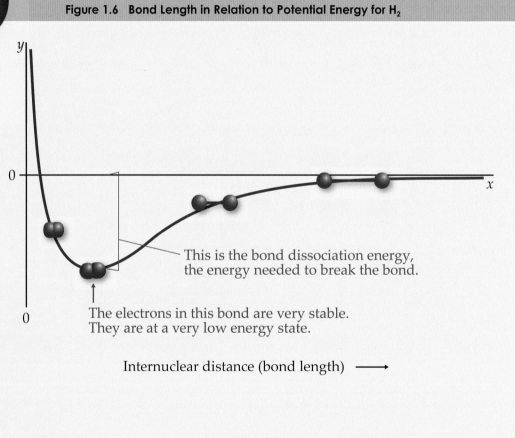

This is the bond dissociation energy, the energy needed to break the bond.

The electrons in this bond are very stable. They are at a very low energy state.

Internuclear distance (bond length) ⟶

Notice from Figure 1.6 that energy is always required to break a bond. Conversely, no energy is ever released by breaking a bond. (Energy from ATP is released when the new bonds of ADP and iP are formed, and not when the ATP bonds are broken.)

A substance made from two or more elements in definite proportions is called a **compound**. In all pure compounds, the relative number of atoms of one element to another can be represented by a ratio of whole numbers. This ratio is called the **empirical formula**. In molecular compounds, groups of atoms form repeated, separate, and distinct units called **molecules**. In molecular compounds, the exact number of elemental atoms in each molecule can be represented by a **molecular formula**. The empirical formula for glucose is CH$_2$O. The molecular formula is C$_6$H$_{12}$O$_6$.

From the empirical formula and the atomic weight of each atom, we can find the percent composition of a compound by mass. To do this, multiply an atom's atomic weight by the number of atoms it contributes to the empirical formula. Divide your result by the weight of all the atoms in the empirical formula. This gives you the mass fraction of the compound represented by the atom. Now multiply this fraction by 100, and you have the percent composition by mass.

---

**Figure 1.7   Percent by Mass of Carbon in Alanine**

The percent mass of carbon in glucose (empirical formula = $CH_2O$) is found as follows:

$$\frac{\text{molecular weight of carbon}}{\text{molecular weight of } CH_2O} = \frac{12}{30} = 0.4$$

$$0.4 \times 100 = 40$$

Glucose is 40% carbon by mass.

---

To find the empirical formula from the percent mass composition, you assume that you have a 100 gram sample. Now the percent translates directly to grams. When you divide the grams by atomic weight, you get moles. Now divide by the greatest common factor. This is the number of atoms represented by each element in the empirical formula. In order to find the molecular formula, we would need more information.

Don't use a calculator here! Get used to doing MCAT math.

---

**Figure 1.8   Determining an Empirical Formula**

If we are asked to find the empirical formula of a compound that is 6% hydrogen and 94% oxygen by mass, we do the following:

From a 100 gram sample:

$$\frac{6 \text{ g hydrogen}}{1 \text{ g/mol}} = 6 \text{ moles}$$

These must be whole numbers

$\dfrac{6}{6}$ is a one to one ratio

$$\frac{94 \text{ g oxygen}}{16 \text{ g/mol}} = 5.9 \text{ moles}$$

The empirical formula is HO

---

This stuff should be easy for you. You have to know it backwards and forwards. It will definitely be on the MCAT, and it should be a couple of fast and easy points. Practice this until you know it well.

---

The MCAT does not ask many questions that directly test your ability to name inorganic compounds. However, it is a good idea to be able to identify compounds when they are referred to.

**Ionic compounds** are named after their cation and anion. If the cation is metal and capable of having different charges (for example, copper can take on a charge of 1+ or 2+), then its name is followed by a Roman numeral in parentheses, as in copper(I) ion or copper(II) ion. An older method for naming cations that can take on different charges is to add –ic to the ending of the cation with the greater positive charge and –ous to the cation with the smaller charge, as in cupric ($Cu^{2+}$) and cuprous ($Cu^{+}$) ions. If the cation is made from a nonmetal, the cation name ends in –ium, such as ammonium ($NH_4^{+}$). A list of the names of important ions for the MCAT is provided in section 4.3 of this book.

Monatomic anions and simple polyatomic anions are given the suffix –ide, such as hydride ion ($H^{-}$) or hydroxide ion ($OH^{-}$). Polyatomic anions with multiple oxygens end with the suffix –ite or –ate depending upon the relative number of oxygens. The more oxygenated species will use the –ate suffix, such as nitrite ion ($NO_2^{-}$) versus nitrate ion ($NO_3^{-}$). If there are more possibilities, the prefixes hypo- and per- are used to indicate fewest and most oxygens respectively, such as the hypochlorite ($ClO^{-}$), chlorite ($ClO_2^{-}$), chlorate ($ClO_3^{-}$), and perchlorate ($ClO_4^{-}$) ions. If an oxyanion has a hydrogen, the word hydrogen is added as in hydrogen carbonate ion ($HCO_3^{-}$). The old name would have been bicarbonate ion.

To name an ionic compound, just put the cation name in front of the anion name as in barium sulfate ($BaSO_4$) or sodium hydride ($NaH$).

For **binary molecular compounds** (compounds with only two elements), the name begins with the name of the element that is farthest to the left and lowest in the periodic table. The name of the second element is given the suffix –ide and a Greek number prefix is used on the each element if necessary (e.g., dinitrogen tetroxide, $N_2O_4$).

**Acids** are named based on their anions. If the name of the anion ends in –ide, the acid name starts with hydro- and ends in –ic, as in hydrosulfuric acid ($H_2S$). If the acid is an oxyacid, the ending –ic is used for the species with more oxygens and –ous for the species with fewer oxygens, as in sulfuric acid ($H_2SO_4$) and sulfurous acid ($H_2SO_3$).

This nomenclature stuff is boring. Just memorize this stuff once and for all and get it over with. Don't get too involved in the myriad little rules in nomenclature. Keep it simple because the MCAT sure will.

*Notes:*

## 1.10 Chemical Reactions and Equations

When a compound undergoes a reaction and maintains its molecular structure and thus its identity, the reaction is called a physical reaction. Melting, evaporation, dissolution, and rotation of polarized light are some examples of physical reactions. When a compound undergoes a reaction and changes its molecular structure to form a new compound, the reaction is called a chemical reaction. Combustion, metathesis, and redox are examples of chemical reactions. Chemical reactions can be represented by a chemical equation with the molecular formulae of the reactants on the left and the products on the right.

$$CH_4 + 2O_2 \rightarrow CO_2 + 2H_2O$$

Notice that there is a conservation of atoms from the left to the right side of the equation. In other words, there is the same number of oxygen, hydrogen, and carbon atoms on the right as on the left. This means the equation is balanced. On the MCAT, if the answer is given in equation form, the correct answer will be a balanced equation unless specifically indicated to the contrary.

In the previous equation, $O_2$ is preceded by a coefficient of two. A coefficient of one is assumed for all molecules not preceded by a coefficient. Methane, then, has a coefficient of one. These coefficients indicate the relative number of molecules. They represent the number of single molecules, moles of molecules, dozens of molecules or any other quantity. They do not represent the mass, the number of grams, or kilograms.

To say that a reaction **runs to completion** means that it moves to the right until the supply of at least one of the reactants is depleted. (Reactions often don't run to completion because they reach equilibrium first.) As indicated by the equation above, two moles of oxygen ($O_2$) are needed to burn one mole of methane ($CH_4$). If we were to react four moles of methane with six moles of oxygen, and the reaction ran to completion, we would be left with 1 mole of methane. This is because, from the two to one ratio in the equation, six moles of oxygen are only enough to burn three moles of methane. Since we would run out of oxygen first, oxygen is our **limiting reagent**. Notice that the limiting reagent is not necessarily the reactant of which there is the least; it is the reactant that would be completely used up if the reaction were to run to completion. Also from the balanced equation, the one to one ratio of methane to carbon dioxide and the two to one ratio of methane to water, tells us that burning three moles of methane produces three moles of carbon dioxide and six moles of water.

Potassium reacting with water. Potassium (K) is a highly reactive metallic element of group one of the periodic table. It reacts with water to produce soluble potassium hydroxide (KOH) and hydrogen gas ($H_2$). The reaction produces enough heat to ignite.

> An unbalanced equation is a wrong answer unless specifically asked for. By the way, know the difference between a physical and chemical reaction.

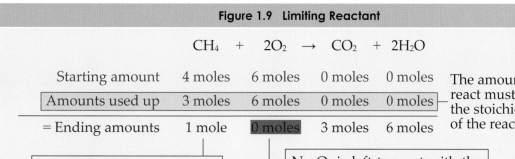

**Figure 1.9 Limiting Reactant**

| | CH₄ | 2O₂ | → | CO₂ | 2H₂O |
|---|---|---|---|---|---|
| Starting amount | 4 moles | 6 moles | | 0 moles | 0 moles |
| Amounts used up | 3 moles | 6 moles | | 0 moles | 0 moles |
| = Ending amounts | 1 mole | 0 moles | | 3 moles | 6 moles |

The amounts that react must follow the stoichiometry of the reaction.

1 mole remains since all 6 moles of $O_2$ are used to react the first 3 moles of $CH_4$.

No $O_2$ is left to react with the last mole of $CH_4$. $O_2$ is the limiting reactant.

> If you don't understand where the numbers came from in the table, take another look. You should understand this for the MCAT.

## 1.11 Chemical Yield

MCAT would probably give you the equation for the percent yield. Just understand the concept.

The amount of product produced when a reaction runs to completion is called the **theoretical yield**. The amount of actual product after a real experiment is the actual yield. As mentioned above, reactions often don't run to completion, and sometimes there are competing reactions that reduce the actual yield. Actual yield divided by the theoretical yield, times 100, gives the **percent yield**.

$$\frac{\text{Actual yield}}{\text{Theoretical yield}} \times 100 = \text{Percent yield}$$

## 1.12 Fundamental Reaction Types

Reactions can be categorized into types. The following lists four reaction types using hypothetical elements or molecules A, B, C, and D.

Nothing to do here but memorize these reaction types in case MCAT asks one question requiring you to identify which type. It won't be worth more than one question on an MCAT.

Combination: $A + B \rightarrow C$

Decomposition: $C \rightarrow A + B$

Single Displacement: $A + BC \rightarrow B + AC$     (also called single replacement)

Double Displacement: $AB + CD \rightarrow AD + CB$  (also called double replacement or metathesis)

Some other important reaction types shown in Table 1.4 are redox, combustion, Brønsted-Lowry acid-base, and Lewis acid-base. We will cover these types later in this book. Reaction types are not mutually exclusive, so one reaction can fall into more than one type.

| Table 1.4   Other Reaction Types | |
| --- | --- |
| *Reaction Type* | *Example* |
| Redox | $2Au^{3+} + 3Zn \rightarrow 2Au + 3Zn^{2+}$ |
| Combustion | $C_6H_{12} + 9O_2 \rightarrow 6CO_2 + 6H_2O$ |
| Brønsted-Lowry acid-base | $HI + ROH \rightarrow I^- + ROH_2^+$ |
| Lewis acid-base | $Ni^2 + 6NH_3 \rightarrow Ni(NH_3)_6^{2+}$ |

The decomposition reaction taking place is: $2Ag_2O \rightarrow 4Ag + O_2$. The oxides of unreactive metals, such as silver, are capable of being reduced to their metals by heat alone because less reactive metals do not tend to form stable compounds.

## 1.13 Reaction Symbols

The symbol '$\Delta$' usually means "change in" but '$\Delta$' above or below a reaction arrow indicates that heat is added. When a chemical is written above the reaction arrow, it is often a catalyst. Two arrows pointing in opposite directions (like this '$\rightleftharpoons$') indicate a reaction that can reach equilibrium. If one arrow is longer than the other, the equilibrium favors the side to which the long arrow points. A single arrow pointing in both directions (like this '$\leftrightarrow$') indicates resonance structures. Square brackets [ ] around an atom, molecule, or ion indicate concentration. The naught symbol '$^{\circ}$' indicates standard state conditions.

## 1.14 Bonding in Solids

Solids can be *crystalline* or *amorphous*. A crystal has a sharp melting point and a characteristic shape with a well ordered structure of repeating units which can be atoms, molecules or ions. A crystal is classified as *ionic, network covalent, metallic,* or *molecular* depending upon the nature of the chemical bonding and the intermolecular forces in the crystal. Ionic crystals consist of oppositely charged ions held together by electrostatic forces. Salts are ionic crystals. Metallic crystals are single metal atoms bonded together by delocalized electrons. These delocalized electrons allow metallic crystals to efficiently conduct heat and electricity. They also make metallic crystals malleable and ductile. Network covalent crystals consist of an infinite network of atoms held together by polar and nonpolar bonds. Diamond and crystal $SiO_2$ are common examples of network covalent crystals. It is not possible to identify individual molecules in ionic, metallic, and network covalent crystals. Molecular crystals are composed of individual molecules held together by intermolecular bonds. Ice is an example of a molecular crystal.

An amorphous solid has no characteristic shape and melts over a temperature range. Glass ($SiO_2$) is an amorphous solid usually with some impurities added to lower the melting point. Some substances are capable of forming both crystalline and amorphous solids.

*Polymers* are solids with repeated structural units. They consist of individual molecules, but each molecule may be very large. They can be crystalline or amorphous. Generally, rapid cooling of liquid polymers results in amorphous solids and slow cooling results in crystalline solids. There are many polymers found in living systems. Examples of biopolymers are DNA, glycogen, and protein.

Candle wax is an amorphous solid.

Amethyst is a crystalline solid.

The MCAT does not directly test your knowledge of the structure of solids beyond ionic and molecular solids; however, it is good to at least be aware that atoms can form substances in many ways. Molecular solids are actually less common than other types of solids. There has been an MCAT passage on this topic.

Questions 9 through 16 are **NOT** based on a descriptive passage.

**9.** What is the empirical formula of a neutral compound containing 58.6% oxygen, 39% sulfur, 2.4% hydrogen by mass?

**A.** $HSO_3^-$
**B.** $HSO_4^-$
**C.** $H_2SO_3$
**D.** $H_2SO_4$

**10.** Silica is a network solid of silicon and oxygen atoms. The empirical formula for silica is $SiO_2$. In silica, to how many oxygen atoms is each silicon bonded?

**A.** 1
**B.** 2
**C.** 3
**D.** 4

**11.** What is the percent by mass of carbon in $CO_2$?

**A.** 12%
**B.** 27%
**C.** 33%
**D.** 44%

**12.** Sulfur dioxide oxidizes in the presence of $O_2$ gas as per the reaction:

$$2SO_2(g) + O_2(g) \rightarrow 2SO_3(g)$$

Approximately how many grams of sulfur trioxide are produced by the complete oxidation of 1 mole of sulfur dioxide?

**A.** 1 g
**B.** 2 g
**C.** 80 g
**D.** 160 g

**13.** When gaseous ammonia is passed over solid copper(II) oxide at high temperatures, nitrogen gas is formed.

$$2NH_3(g) + 3CuO(s) \rightarrow N_2(g) + 3Cu(s) + 3H_2O(g)$$

What is the limiting reagent when 34 grams of ammonia form 26 grams of nitrogen in a reaction that runs to completion?

**A.** $NH_3$
**B.** $CuO$
**C.** $N_2$
**D.** $Cu$

**14.** Name the following compound: $Cu(ClO_4)_2$.

**A.** copper(I) chlorate
**B.** copper(II) perchlorite
**C.** copper(II) chlorate
**D.** copper(II) perchlorate

**15.** Polyethylene is a flexible plastic with many industrial uses. The synthesis of polyethylene is a radical reaction that follows the equation:

$$nCH_2 = CH_2 \rightarrow (CH_2CH_2)_n$$

Polyethylene is a(n):

**A.** molecular solid.
**B.** polymer.
**C.** ionic solid.
**D.** network solid.

**16.** What type of reaction is shown below?

$$2Mg(s) + O_2 \rightarrow 2MgO(s)$$

**A.** combination
**B.** single replacement
**C.** metathesis
**D.** decomposition



**STOP.**

## 1.15 Quantum Mechanics

The MCAT requires a small amount of knowledge concerning quantum mechanics. Everything that you'll need to know is in this Lecture. Quantum mechanics basically says that elementary particles can only gain or lose energy and certain other quantities in discrete units. This is analogous to walking up stairs as opposed to walking up a ramp. If each stairstep is one foot, you can only raise or lower yourself by increments of one foot on the stairs, while on the ramp you can move along until you are raised one half foot or any other fraction of a foot. In quantum mechanics these 'steps' are discrete units of energy. Each 'step' or energy unit is so small that the overall change in energy is insignificant when working in classical physics. Thus quantum mechanic effects are generally only important when dealing with elementary particles.

You can only move in discrete units.

## 1.16 Quantum Numbers

A set of four quantum numbers is the address or ID number for an electron in a given atom. The **Pauli Exclusion Principle** states that no two electrons in the same atom can have the same four quantum numbers.

The first quantum number is the **principle quantum number,** $n$. It designates the shell level for the electron.

The second quantum number is the **azimuthal quantum number,** $\ell$. It designates the **subshell.** $\ell = 0$ is the $s$-subshell, $\ell = 1$ is the $p$-subshell, $\ell = 2$ is the $d$-subshell, and $\ell = 3$ is the $f$-subshell.

The third quantum number is the **magnetic quantum number,** $m_\ell$. The magnetic quantum number designates the precise orbital of a given subshell. Each subshell will have orbitals with magnetic quantum numbers from $-\ell$ **to** $+\ell$. For instance, within the $p$-subshell ($\ell = 1$), there are three magnetic quantum numbers: -1, 0, and 1. Of these, one designates the $p_x$-orbital, one the $p_y$-orbital, and one the $p_z$-orbital.

The fourth quantum number is the **electron spin quantum number,** $m_s$. The electron spin quantum number can have values of $-\frac{1}{2}$ or $+\frac{1}{2}$. This final quantum number is used to distinguish the two electrons that may occupy the same orbital, since those electrons will have the same first three quantum numbers.

The number of total orbitals within a shell is equal to $n^2$. Solving for the number of orbitals for each shell gives 1, 4, 9, 16... Since there are two electrons in each orbital, the number of elements in the periods of the periodic table is 2, 8, 18, and 32.

> Let's summarize: The first quantum number is the shell. It corresponds roughly to the energy level of the electrons within that shell. The second quantum number is the subshell. It gives the shape. You need to recognize the shape of $s$- and $p$-orbitals. The third quantum number is the specific orbital within a subshell. The fourth quantum number distinguishes between two electrons in the same orbital; one is spin $+1/2$ and the other is spin $-1/2$.

| | | Table 1.5 Quantum Numbers | | |
|---|---|---|---|---|
| *Number* | *Name* | *Symbol* | *Value* | *Character* |
| 1st | principle | $n$ | $n$ | shell (energy level) |
| 2nd | azimuthal | $\ell$ | from zero to n-1 | subshell (shape: $s$, $p$, $d$, or $f$) |
| 3rd | magnetic | $m_\ell$ | between $\ell$ and $-\ell$ | orbital (3D orientation: $p_x$, $p_y$, $p_z$) |
| 4th | spin | $m_s$ | $\frac{1}{2}$ or $-\frac{1}{2}$ | spin ($\uparrow\downarrow$) |

## 1.17 The Heisenberg Uncertainty Principle

The **Heisenberg Uncertainty Principle** arises from the dual nature (wave-particle) of matter. It states that there exists an inherent uncertainty in the product of the position of a particle and its momentum, and that this uncertainty is on the order of Planck's constant.

$$\Delta x \Delta p \approx h$$

Here's the story with the Heisenberg uncertainty principle: the more we know about the momentum of any particle, the less we can know about the position. The amount of uncertainty is very small; on the order of Planck's constant ($6.63 \times 10^{-34}$ J s). There are other quantities besides position and momentum to which the uncertainty principle applies, but position and momentum is the pair that you are likely to need to know for the MCAT.

## 1.18 Energy Level of Electrons

**Figure 1.10 S and P Orbitals**

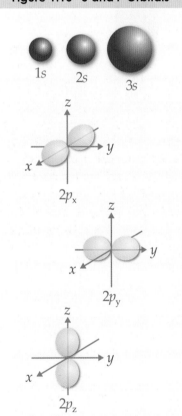

$1s$   $2s$   $3s$

$2p_x$

$2p_y$

$2p_z$

The **Aufbau principle** states that with each new proton added to create a new element, the new electron that is also added will occupy the lowest energy level that is available to it. Nature typically prefers a lower energy state. All other things being equal, the lower the energy state of a system, the more stable the system. Thus, electrons look for an available orbital in the lowest energy level whenever they add to an atom. The orbital with the lowest energy will be contained in the subshell with the lowest energy.

For the representative elements the **shell** level of the most recently added electrons is given by period in the periodic table. For instance, the most recently added electron of F is in shell 2 and the most recently added electron for Sr is in shell 5. For transition metals the shell of the most recently added electron lags one behind the period, and for the lanthanides and actinides lags two behind the period. For example, the most recently added electron of Os is in shell 5 and the most recently added electron for Ce is in shell 4.

The **subshells** are the orbital shapes with which we are familiar such as *s*, *p*, *d*, and *f*. Each subshell has a peculiar shape to its orbitals. The shapes are based on probability functions of the position of the electron. There is a 90% chance of finding the electron somewhere inside the given shape. You should recognize the shapes of the orbitals in the *s*- and *p*-subshells (Figure 1.10). By looking at the periodic table, we can tell when each type of subshell is filling. The *s*-subshells are filling in groups 1 and 2, the *p*-subshells are filling in groups 13–18, the *d*-subshells are filling in groups 3–12, and the *f*-subshells are filling in the lanthanide and actinide series.

We can, therefore, assign a shell and subshell to the most recently added electron for any element simply by looking at the periodic table. For example, the most recently added electron in *P* is in the 3*p* energy level; for Ru it is in the 4*d* energy level; for K it is in the 4*s* energy level.

**Valence electrons**, the electrons which contribute most to an element's chemical properties, are located in the outermost shell of an atom. Typically, but not always, only electrons from the *s*- and *p*-subshells are considered valence electrons.

The energy level rises as the electrons move further from the nucleus. To see why, we must consider the attractive force between the negatively charged electrons and the positively charged nucleus. Because the force is attractive, we must do work to separate them; we apply a force over a distance. Work is the transfer of energy into or out of a system. In this case, our system is the electron and the nucleus. We are doing work on the system, so we are transferring energy into the system. This energy shows up as increased electrostatic potential energy. Like the energy between bonding atoms, the energy between the electron and the nucleus increases from a negative number to zero as the electron moves to an infinite distance away from the nucleus.

If, for a given atom, we list the shells and the subshells in order from lowest to highest energy level, and we add a superscript to show the number of electrons in each subshell, we have the **electron configuration** of that atom. (Electron configurations do not have to be from lowest to highest energy subshells, but they usually are.) Electron configurations for several atoms are given below:

$$Na \Rightarrow 1s^2\, 2s^2\, 2p^6\, 3s^1$$
$$Ar \Rightarrow 1s^2\, 2s^2\, 2p^6\, 3s^2\, 3p^6$$
$$Fe \Rightarrow 1s^2\, 2s^2\, 2p^6\, 3s^2\, 3p^6\, 4s^2\, 3d^6$$
$$Br \Rightarrow 1s^2\, 2s^2\, 2p^6\, 3s^2\, 3p^6\, 4s^2\, 3d^{10}\, 4p^5$$

An abbreviated electron configuration can be written by using the configuration of the next smallest noble gas as follows:

$$Na \Rightarrow [Ne]\, 3s^1$$
$$Ar \Rightarrow [Ar]$$
$$Fe \Rightarrow [Ar]\, 4s^2\, 3d^6 \text{ (sometimes written } [Ar]\, 3d^6\, 4s^2)$$
$$Br \Rightarrow [Ar]\, 4s^2\, 3d^{10}\, 4p^5$$

Above are the electron configurations for atoms whose electrons are all at their lowest energy levels. This is called the **ground state**. Electron configurations can also be given for ions and atoms with excited electrons:

$$Na^+ \Rightarrow 1s^2\, 2s^2\, 2p^6 \text{ or } [Ne]$$
$$Fe^{3+} \Rightarrow [Ar]\, 3d^5$$
$$Br^- \Rightarrow [Ar]\, 4s^2\, 3d^{10}\, 4p^6 \text{ or } [Kr]$$
$$Be_{\text{with an excited electron}} \Rightarrow 1s^2\, 2s^1\, 2p^1$$

A simple trick to find the relative energies of the subshells is to use this table. The chart grows like stair-steps. An arrow is drawn down each diagonal as shown. If we follow the arrows as they go down the steps, they show us the order of increasing energy for the subshells. Notice that the energy levels are not exactly in numerical order. For example, the 4s-subshell is at a lower energy level than the 3d.

Be certain that the total number of electrons in your electron configuration equals the total number of electrons in the atom. Notice that for the ions of the representative elements, electron configuration resembles that of a noble gas. The electron configurations of the transition metal ions are not the same as the nearest noble gas. As noted before, for transition metals, ions are formed by losing electrons from the subshell with the highest principle quantum number first. Something else to know about transition metals is that their electron configurations aren't always that easy to predict. For instance, in the fourth period, the electron configurations of Cr and Cu have only one electron in the 4s orbital:

$$Cu => [Ar] \, 4s^1 \, 3d^{10}$$

This is because the 4s- and 3d- orbitals of these atoms are degenerate (at the same energy level). You don't have to memorize the electron configuration of each transition metal. Just be aware that they don't always follow the table given above, due to degenerate orbitals.

Also, notice that an electron can momentarily (for a matter of microseconds) absorb energy and jump to a higher energy level creating an atom in an excited state.

## Figure 1.11  Orbital Diagrams

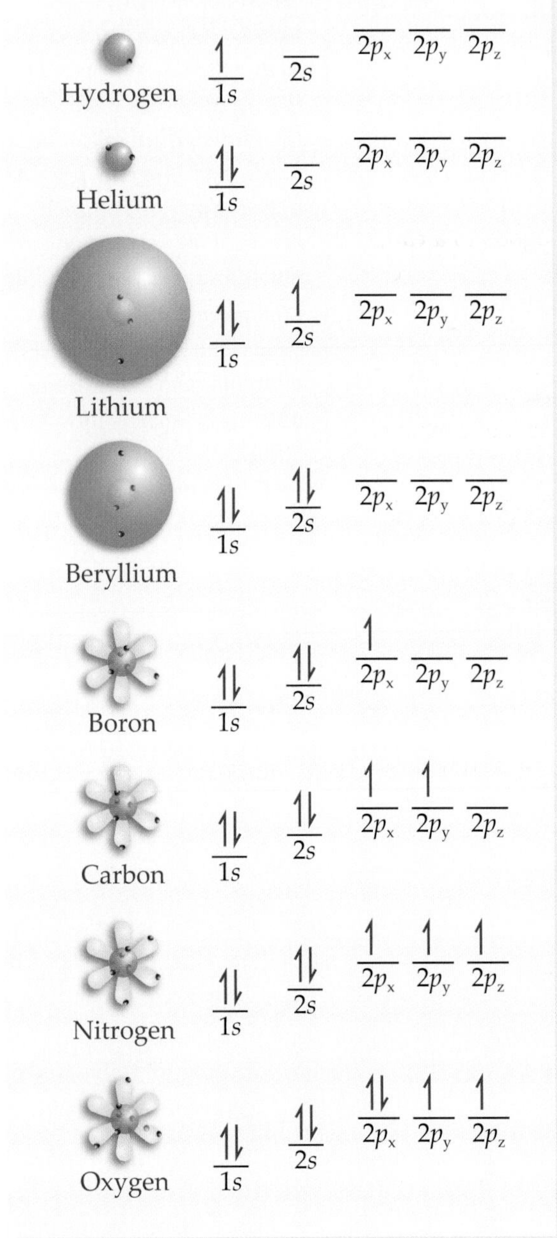

Like charges repel each other. If we considered the energy of two particles with like charges, we would find that as the particles near each other, the mutual repulsion creates an increase in potential energy. This is the case when electrons approach each other. It explains why only two electrons can fit into one orbital. It also helps explain Hund's rule: electrons will not fill any orbital in the same subshell until all orbitals in that subshell contain at least one electron, and the unpaired electrons will have parallel spins. Hund's rule can be represented graphically as shown in Figure 1.11. Electrons are represented by vertical arrows. Upward arrows represent electrons with positive spin, and downward arrows represent electrons with negative spin. When going from boron to carbon, the added electron has a choice of sharing the $2p_x$ orbital or taking the $2p_y$ orbital for itself. **Hund's rule** says that the electron prefers to have its own orbital when such an orbital is available at the same energy level.

*Notes:*

Max Planck is considered the father of quantum mechanics. Planck's quantum theory demonstrates that electromagnetic energy is quantized (i.e. it comes only in discrete units related to the wave frequency). In other words, if we transfer energy from one point to another via an electromagnetic wave, and we wish to increase the amount of energy that we are transferring without changing the frequency, we can only change the energy in discrete increments given by:

Max Planck (1858-1947), proposed that radiation must be emitted or received in energy packets (quanta), rather than continuously. Quantum theory was fully accepted after its successful prediction of the photoelectric effect (Einstein, 1905) and of the electronic structure of atoms (Bohr, 1913).

$$\Delta E = hf$$

where $h$ is Planck's constant ($6.6 \times 10^{-34}$ J s).

Einstein showed that if we considered light as a particle phenomenon with each particle as a photon, the energy of a single photon is given by the same equation: $E_{photon} = hf$. Neils Bohr applied the quantized energy theory to create an electron ladder model for hydrogen with each rung representing an allowed energy level for the electron. His model explained the line spectra for hydrogen but failed for atoms with more than one electron. *Louis de Broglie* then showed that electrons and other moving masses exhibit wave characteristics

$$\lambda = \frac{h}{mv}$$

that follow the equation:
The energy levels of electrons are quantized as well. The possible energy levels of an electron can be represented as an energy ladder. Each energy level is analogous to a rung on a ladder or the spheres shown in Figure 1.12. The electrons may occupy any rung, but do not occupy the space between rungs because this space represents forbidden energy levels.

When an electron falls from a higher energy rung to a lower energy rung, energy is released from the atom in the form of a photon. The photon must have a frequency which corresponds to the change in energy of the electron as per $\Delta E = hf$. Of course the reverse is also true. If a photon collides with an electron, it can only bump that electron to another energy level rung and not between energy level rungs. If the photon doesn't have enough energy to bump the electron to the next rung, the electron will not move from its present

*Notes:*

**Figure 1.12 Photoelectric Effect**

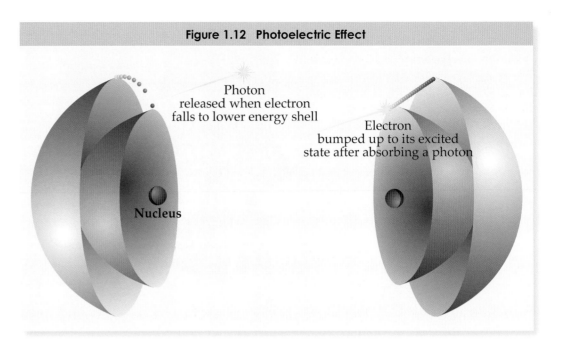

Photon
released when electron
falls to lower energy shell

Electron
bumped up to its excited
state after absorbing a photon

Nucleus

rung and the photon will be reflected away.

With the **photoelectric effect** Einstein demonstrated this one-to-one, photon to electron collision. He showed that the one-to-one collision proved that light was made up of particles. Einstein's reasoning went as follows: Light shining on a metal may cause the emission of electrons (sometimes called *photoelectrons* in the photoelectric effect). Since the energy of a wave is proportional to its intensity, we would expect that when the intensity of light shining on a metal is increased by increasing the number of photons, the kinetic energy of an emitted electron would increase accordingly. This is not the case. Instead, the kinetic energy of the electrons increases only when intensity is increased by increasing the frequency of each photon. If the frequency is low enough, no electrons at all will be emitted regardless of the number of photons. This demonstrates that the electrons must be ejected by one-to-one photon-electron collisions and not by the combined energies of two or more photons. It also shows that if a single photon does not have sufficient energy, no electron will be emitted. The minimum amount of energy required to eject an electron is called the *work function*, $\Phi$, of the metal. The kinetic energy of the ejected electron is given by the energy of the photon minus the work function ($K.E. = hf - \Phi$).

> Note that for the photoelectric effect, the kinetic energy of the electrons inceases only when the frequency is increased.

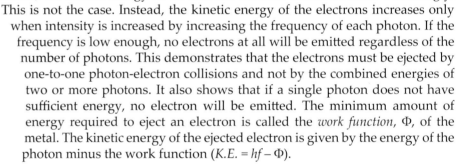

Early photoelectric cell. Photoelectric cells make use of an effect whereby metals emit electrons when exposed to light (photo-emissivity). A metal plate of either rubidium, potassium or sodium (the cathode) is enclosed in a vacuum and connected to the negative pole of a battery. A loop of wire (the anode) faces the plate. When exposed to light, electricity crosses the gap between the cathode and anode more easily, enabling the cell to produce impulses of electricity dependent on the intensity of the light falling on it.

## 1.19 Equation Summary

| Equations | |
|---|---|
| Moles | $$\text{moles} = \frac{\text{grams}}{\text{atomic or molecular weight}}$$ |
| Percent Yield | $$\frac{\text{Actual yield}}{\text{Theoretical yield}} \times 100 = \text{Percent yield}$$ |
| Planck's Quantum Theory | $$\Delta E = hf$$ |

## 1.20 Terms You Need To Know

| Terms | | |
|---|---|---|
| $6.022 \times 10^{23}$ | Electronegativity | Mole (mol) |
| amu | Electron Configuration | Molecular Formula |
| Avogadro's Number | Electrons | Molecules |
| Atomic Number | Elements | Nonmetals |
| Atomic Radius | Empirical Formula | Nucleus |
| Atomic Weight | First Ionization Energy | Period |
| Atoms | Ground State | Periodic Table |
| Bond Dissociation Energy | Groups or Families | Periodic Trends |
| Bond Energy | Hund's Rule | Photoelectric Effect |
| Bond Length | Inert Gases | Protons |
| Bonds | Ionization Energy | Second Ionization Energy |
| Compound | Isotopes | Shell |
| Covalent Bond | Mass Number | Shielding |
| Effective Nuclear Charge ($Z_{eff}$) | Metallic Character | Subshells |
| Electron Affinity | Metalloids | Transition Metals |
| | Metals | Valence Electrons |
| | Molar Mass (MM or M) | |

17. Which of the following species has an unpaired electron in its ground-state electronic configuration?

    A. Ne
    B. $Ca^+$
    C. $Na^+$
    D. $O^{2-}$

18. What is the electron configuration of chromium?

    A. $[Ar]\, 3d^6$
    B. $[Ar]\, 4s^1\, 3d^5$
    C. $[Ar]\, 4s^2\, 3d^3$
    D. $[Ar]\, 4s^2\, 4p^4$

19. In reference to the photoelectric effect, which of the following will increase the kinetic energy of a photoelectron?

    A. Increasing the work function
    B. Increasing the frequency of the incident light
    C. Increasing the number of photons in the incident light
    D. Increasing the mass of photons in the incident light

20. When an electron moves from a $2p$ to a $3s$ orbital, the atom containing that electron:

    A. becomes a new isotope.
    B. becomes a new element.
    C. absorbs energy.
    D. releases energy.

21. Compared to an electron with a principal quantum number of 1, an electron with a principal quantum number of 2 will have:

    A. a lower energy.
    B. a higher energy.
    C. a negative spin.
    D. a positive spin.

22. Which of the following best explains why sulfur can make more bonds than oxygen?

    A. Sulfur is more electronegative than oxygen.
    B. Oxygen is more electronegative than sulfur.
    C. Sulfur has $3d$ orbitals not available to oxygen.
    D. Sulfur has fewer valence electrons.

23. Hund's rule says that unpaired electrons in the same subshell:

    A. have opposite spins.
    B. have parallel spins.
    C. occupy the same orbital.
    D. cannot exist.

24. Aluminum has only one oxidation state, while chromium has several. Which of the following is the best explanation for this difference?

    A. Electrons in the $d$ orbitals of Cr may or may not be used to form bonds.
    B. Electrons in the $p$ orbitals of Cr may or may not be used to form bonds.
    C. Electrons in the $d$ orbitals of Al may or may not be used to form bonds.
    D. Electrons in the $p$ orbitals of Al may or may not be used to form bonds.

# Gases, Kinetics and Chemical Equilibrium

## 2.1   Gases

A typical real gas is a loose collection of weakly attracted atoms or molecules moving rapidly in random directions. In a gas, the volume of the molecules accounts for about 0.1 percent of the total volume occupied by the gas. By comparison, molecules in a liquid account for about 70 percent of the total volume occupied by the liquid. 0°C and 1 atm is called **standard temperature and pressure (STP)**. At STP, the average distance between gas molecules is about 35 Å. This is small on a macroscopic scale, but typically amounts to over a dozen molecular diameters on the microscopic scale. For instance, an oxygen molecule is about 2.5 Å from end to end. Gas molecules move at tremendous speeds. At STP, the average speed of oxygen molecules is about 1,078 mph (481 m/s). The **mean free path** is the distance traveled by a gas molecule between collisions. The mean free path of oxygen at STP is about 1600 Å, about 1 ten thousandth of a millimeter. Moving such small distances at such high speed results in one oxygen molecule making about 2,500,000,000 collisions with other molecules each second. This explains why some chemical reactions can appear to occur instantaneously.

This is an optical image of the Crab Nebula, also known as Messier 1, which consists mainly of hydrogen gas ($H_2$).

Gases will mix

If a gas is a mixture of compounds, then unlike liquids, the mixture will be homogeneous regardless of polarity differences. For instance, liquid gasoline and liquid water don't mix because gasoline is nonpolar while water is polar; however, water and gasoline vapors form a homogeneous mixture.

Liquids will separate

Although polarity differences do not cause gases to separate, when temperatures are low enough gravity causes denser gases to settle beneath less dense gases. Cold $CO_2$ gas from a fire extinguisher is heavier than air and smothers a fire by settling over the fire and displacing the air upward. Hot air rises because it is less dense than cold air.

> Unlike liquids, all gases are miscible with each other; they mix regardless of polarity differences. However, given time and low temperatures, heavier gases tend to settle below lighter gases.

Oil (nonpolar) and water (polar) mixture.

## 2.2 Kinetic Molecular Theory

To better understand the complex behavior of gases, scientists have theorized a model of an **ideal gas**. This model is called the **kinetic molecular theory**. In the kinetic molecular theory, an ideal gas lacks certain real gas characteristics. Ideal gas has the following four characteristics not shared by a real gas:

1. Gas molecules have zero volume;
2. Gas molecules exert no forces other than repulsive forces due to collisions;
3. Gas molecules make completely elastic collisions;
4. The average kinetic energy of gas molecules is directly proportional to the temperature of the gas.

Ideal gas obeys the **ideal gas law**:

$$PV = nRT$$

where $P$ is the pressure in atmospheres, $V$ is the volume in liters, $n$ is the number of moles of gas, $T$ is the temperature in Kelvin, and $R$ is the universal gas constant (0.08206 L atm $K^{-1}$ $mol^{-1}$ or 8.314 J $K^{-1}$ $mol^{-1}$). Special cases of the ideal gas law include: *Charles' law*: The volume of a gas is proportional to temperature at constant pressure; *Boyle's law*: The volume of a gas is inversely proportional to pressure at constant temperature; and *Avogadro's law*: The volume of a gas is proportional to the number of moles at constant temperature and pressure.

This balloon has been cooled from 300 Kelvin to 75 Kelvin using liquid nitrogen. The pressure remains approximately constant at 1 atm. According to Charles' law how many times smaller is the cold balloon?

Rather than memorizing Charles', Boyle's, and Avogadro's laws, you should have a good understanding of the ideal gas law. The equations associated with these laws have been left out purposely, so that you won't waste time memorizing them. The equations create confusion in the sense that they are true only within certain limitations. For instance, Charles' law requires constant pressure.

$PV = nRT$ will solve any problem that the other three laws might solve. By the way, you won't need to memorize the name of each law either.

Notice that there are four variables needed to define the state of a gas: $P$, $V$, $n$, and $T$. $R$ is a constant, not a variable. Four variables in one equation can be confusing. For instance, it is possible to cool a gas by increasing the volume, even though the equation $PV = nRT$ indicates that temperature is directly proportional to volume. When a gas expands in a container, the gas does work on its surrounding by pushing outward on the walls of the container. The force on the walls times the distance that the walls expand is the work done by the gas. This work represents a transfer of energy from the gas to the surroundings. The energy comes from the kinetic energy of the gas molecules. Both the temperature and the pressure are related to the kinetic energy of the molecules. The pressure is related to the kinetic energy per volume, and the temperature is related to the average kinetic energy per mole. When the gas expands, the pressure decreases due to both the loss in kinetic energy and the increase in volume. The temperature decreases due to the loss in kinetic energy via work done. So, if the volume of a gas were doubled, and the kinetic energy remained the same, the pressure would be reduced by a factor of two. But if no heat were added, the kinetic energy would be reduced. If the kinetic energy were reduced as the volume doubles, the pressure would be reduced by more than a factor of two. Thus the temperature would also decrease to preserve the equality in $PV = nRT$.

Notice that the ideal gas law does not change for different gases behaving ideally. (Of course not, it's written for an ideal gas.) This means that all gases (behaving ideally) will have the same volume, if they have the same temperature, pressure, and number of molecules. At STP one mole of any gas (behaving ideally) will occupy the **standard molar volume of 22.4 liters.**

## Thought Provoker

*Roger is filling balloons with helium gas for a birthday party. He knows that the volume of his helium tank is 2L. How many moles of helium are in the tank if the pressure is 730 torr and the temperature is 25 degrees Celsius? (Assume all the helium is in a gaseous state)*

*Answer: See page 55*

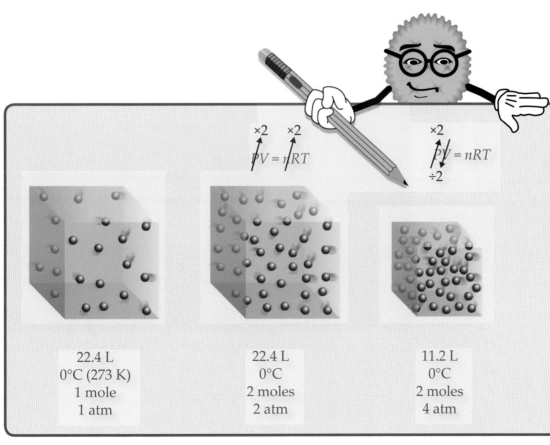

|  |  |  |
|---|---|---|
| 22.4 L | 22.4 L | 11.2 L |
| 0°C (273 K) | 0°C | 0°C |
| 1 mole | 2 moles | 2 moles |
| 1 atm | 2 atm | 4 atm |

You must recognize the standard molar volume and understand what it means. Learn to use this volume with the ideal gas law. For instance, 2 moles of gas at 0°C occupying 11.2 liters will have a pressure of 4 atm. To get this result, we start with the standard molar volume, 22.4 L, at STP. First, we double the number of moles, so, according to the ideal gas law, the pressure doubles. Second, we halve the volume, so pressure doubles again.

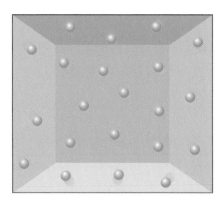

22.4 L
0°C
1 mole
1 atm

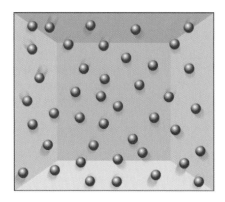

22.4 L
0°C
2 moles
2 atm

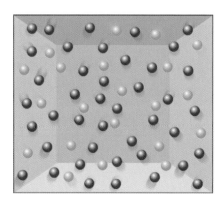

22.4 L
0°C
3 moles

$\chi_{green} = \frac{1}{3}$, $\chi_{blue} = \frac{2}{3}$
$P_{green} = 1$ atm
$P_{blue} = 2$ atm
$P_{total} = 3$ atm

As well as pure gases, we can apply the kinetic molecular theory to mixtures of gases. In a mixture of gases, each gas contributes to the pressure in the same proportion as it contributes to the number of molecules of the gas. This makes sense, given the kinetic molecular theory, because molecules have no volume, no interactive forces other than collisions, and kinetic energy is conserved when they collide. Thus, each gas in a mixture essentially behaves as if it were in its container alone.

The amount of pressure contributed by any gas in a gaseous mixture is called the partial pressure of that gas. The **partial pressure** of a particular gas is the total pressure of the gaseous mixture times the mole fraction of the particular gas. The equation for the partial pressure is:

$$P_a = \chi_a P_{total}$$

where $P_a$ is the partial pressure of gas 'a', and $\chi_a$ is the mole fraction of gas 'a'. (The mole fraction is the number of moles of gas 'a' divided by the total number of moles of gas in the sample.)

**Dalton's law** states that the total pressure exerted by a gaseous mixture is the sum of the partial pressures of each of its gases.

$$P_{total} = P_1 + P_2 + P_{3...}$$

Dalton's law is a good way to understand an ideal gas. Each gas behaves like it is in the container by itself so all the partial pressures added together equal the total pressure.

Scuba divers during the last minutes of their decompression time after a deep dive.

From the ideal gas law, we can derive the following equation relating average translational kinetic energy and the temperature of a gas:

$$K.E._{avg} = \frac{3}{2}RT$$

where the average translational kinetic energy is found from the root-mean-square (rms) velocity. (rms velocity is the square root of the average of the squares of the molecular velocities. rms velocity is slightly greater than the average speed.) $K.E. = 3/2\,RT$ is valid for any fluid system, including liquids. Notice that the kinetic energy derived from this equation is the average kinetic energy for <u>one mole</u> of gas molecules at a given moment. It does not represent the energy of every gas molecule or perhaps even any single gas molecule at any given moment. A gas molecule chosen at random may have almost any kinetic energy associated with it.

Since the temperature dictates the average kinetic energy of the molecules in a gas, the gas molecules of each gas in any gaseous mixture must have the same average kinetic energy. For instance, the air we breathe is made up of approximately 21% $O_2$ and 79% $N_2$ by number. The molecules of $O_2$ and $N_2$ in a sample of air have the same average kinetic energy. However, since $O_2$ and $N_2$ have different masses, their molecules have different rms velocities. By setting their kinetic energies equal to each other, we can derive a relationship between their rms velocities. This relationship, which gives the ratio of the rms velocities of two gases in a homogeneous mixture, is called **Graham's law**:

$$\frac{v_1}{v_2} = \frac{\sqrt{m_2}}{\sqrt{m_1}}$$

Where $v_1$ and $v_2$ are the rms velocities of the molecules of the respective gases and $m_1$ and $m_2$ are the masses of the molecules of the respective gases. Notice that the subscripts are inverted from one side of the equation to the other (i.e. the left side is 1 over 2, and the right side is 2 over 1).

Graham's law also tells us that the average speed of the molecules of a pure gas is inversely proportional to the square root of the mass of the gas molecules.

> When you imagine a fluid warming up, you should visualize the fluid molecules moving faster.

> In a sample of gas, the kinetic energy of the molecules will vary from molecule to molecule, but there will be an average kinetic energy of the molecules that is proportional to the temperature and independent of the type of gas.

Interestingly, Graham's law gives information about the rates of two types of gaseous spreading: effusion and diffusion. **Effusion** is the spreading of a gas from high pressure to very low pressure through a 'pinhole'. (A 'pinhole' is defined as an opening much smaller than the average distance between the gas molecules.) Because molecules of a gas with higher rms velocity will experience more collisions with the walls of a container, the rate at which molecules from such a gas find the pinhole and go through is likely to be greater. In fact, Graham's law predicts the comparative rates of effusion for two gases at the same temperature. The ratio of the rates of effusion of two gases is equal to the inverse of the ratio of the square roots of their molecular weights and equal to the ratio of their rms velocities.

$$\frac{\text{effusion rate}_1}{\text{effusion rate}_2} = \frac{\sqrt{M_2}}{\sqrt{M_1}}$$

where $M_1$ and $M_2$ are the molecular weights of the respective gases.

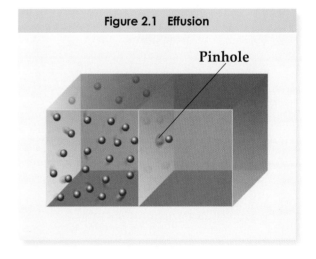

**Figure 2.1 Effusion**

Pinhole

Diffusion is the spreading of one gas into another gas or into empty space. The ratio of the diffusion rates of two gases (acting ideally) is approximated by Graham's law. The diffusion rate is much slower than the rms velocity of the molecules because gas molecules collide with each other and with molecules of other gases as they diffuse. For example, if we wet two cotton balls, one with aqueous $NH_3$ and the other with aqueous HCl, and place them into opposite ends of a glass tube, gaseous $NH_3$ and HCl will diffuse toward each other through the air inside the tube. Where they meet, they will react to form $NH_4Cl$, which will precipitate as a white solid. Graham's law accurately predicts that $NH_3$ will travel 1.5 times further than HCl. However, any particular molecule is far more crooked than even those shown in the diagram. Recall that the mean free path of a gas molecule is on the order of a few hundred nanometers.

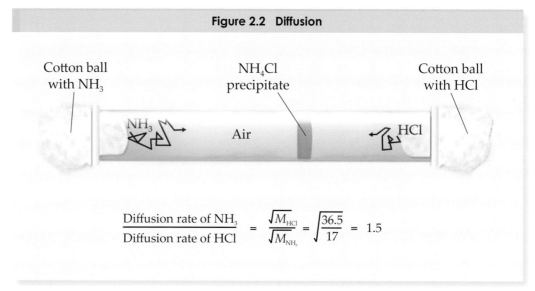

**Figure 2.2   Diffusion**

$$\frac{\text{Diffusion rate of } NH_3}{\text{Diffusion rate of HCl}} = \frac{\sqrt{M_{HCl}}}{\sqrt{M_{NH_3}}} = \sqrt{\frac{36.5}{17}} = 1.5$$

Ammonia ($NH_3$), left, reacting with hydrochloric acid (HCl), right. $NH_3$ diffuses at a faster rate than HCl.

## 2.3  Real Gases

Real gases deviate from ideal behavior when their molecules are close together. When this happens, the volume of the molecules become significant compared to the volume around the molecules. Also, as can be seen by Coulomb's law ($F = kqq/r^2$), when molecules are close together, the electrostatic forces increase and become significant. High pressure pushes gas molecules together causing deviations from ideal behavior. Low temperatures cause gas molecules to settle close together also resulting in deviations from ideal behavior. Gases generally deviate from ideal behavior at pressures above ten atmospheres and temperatures near their boiling points. Substances that we typically think of as gases closely approximate ideal behavior.

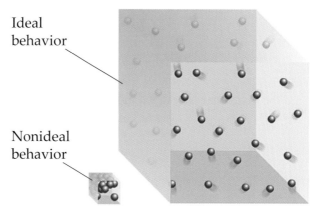

Ideal behavior

Nonideal behavior

**Figure 2.3   Real gases**

You should be aware of how real gases deviate from ideal behavior. Van der Waals equation:

$$\left[P+\left(\frac{n^2 a}{V^2}\right)\right](V-nb)=nRT$$

approximates the real pressure and real volume of a gas, where $a$ and $b$ are constants for specific gases. The variable $b$ is a measure of the actual volume occupied by a mole of gas. The variable $a$ reflects the strength of intermolecular attractions. The values of $a$ and $b$ generally increase with the molecular mass and molecular complexity of a gas.

You do not need to know van der Waals equation for the MCAT. It is more important that you have a qualitative understanding of real gas deviations from ideal behavior. First, since molecules of a real gas do have volume, their volume must be added to the ideal volume. Thus:

Nonideal behavior

$$V_{\text{real}} > V_{\text{ideal}}$$

where $V_{\text{ideal}}$ is calculated from $PV = nRT$.

> Once again, be careful about the confusion with $PV = nRT$. It seems like increasing pressure also increases temperature, so how can ideal behavior deviations occur with either an increase in pressure or a decrease in temperature? The answer is that to create deviations in ideal behavior, we just want to move the molecules closer together; in other words, decrease the volume. We can decrease the volume by squeezing the molecules together with high pressure, or by lowering the temperature and letting the molecules settle close together. From $PV = nRT$, we see that volume decreases with either increasing pressure or decreasing temperature.

Second, molecules in a real gas do exhibit forces on each other, and those forces are attractive when the molecules are far apart. In a gas, repulsive forces are only significant during molecular collisions or near collisions. Since the predominant intermolecular forces in a gas are attractive, gas molecules are pulled inward toward the center of the gas, and slow before colliding with container walls. Having been slightly slowed, they strike the container wall with less force than predicted by the kinetic molecular theory. Thus a real gas exerts less pressure than predicted by the ideal gas law:

$$P_{\text{real}} < P_{\text{ideal}}$$

where $P_{\text{ideal}}$ is calculated from $PV = nRT$.

### Figure 2.4   Deviations from Ideal Gas Law

Positive deviation due mainly to molecular volume.

$\frac{PV}{RT}$

$N_2$  $CH_4$

$H_2$

1.0

$P$

Negative deviation due mainly to attractive intermolecular forces.

From $PV = nRT$, we expect $PV/RT$ to equal one for one mole of ideal gas at any temperature and pressure. Since volume deviates positively from ideal behavior and pressure deviates negatively, if $PV/RT$ is greater than one for one mole of gas, then the deviation due to molecular volume must be greater than the deviation due to the intermolecular forces. If $PV/RT$ is less than one for one mole of gas, then the deviation due to intermolecular forces must be greater than the deviation due to molecular volume.

**25.** A 13 gram gaseous sample of an unknown hydrocarbon occupies a volume of 11.2 L at STP. What is the hydrocarbon?

    **A.** CH
    **B.** $C_2H_4$
    **C.** $C_2H_2$
    **D.** $C_3H_3$

**26.** If the density of a gas is given as ρ which of the following expressions represents the molecular weight of the gas?

    **A.** $P\rho/RT$
    **B.** $\rho RT/P$
    **C.** $nRT/P\rho$
    **D.** $P\rho/RT$

**27.** Ammonia burns in air to form nitrogen dioxide and water.

$$4NH_3(g) + 7O_2(g) \rightarrow 4NO_2(g) + 6H_2O(l)$$

If 8 moles of $NH_3$ are reacted with 14 moles of $O_2$ in a rigid container with an initial pressure of 11 atm, what is the partial pressure of $NO_2$ in the container when the reaction runs to completion? (Assume constant temperature.)

    **A.** 4 atm
    **B.** 6 atm
    **C.** 11 atm
    **D.** 12 atm

**28.** At moderately high pressures, the $PV/RT$ ratio for one mole of methane gas is less than one. The most likely reason for this is:

    **A.** Methane gas behaves ideally at moderate pressures.
    **B.** The temperature must be very low.
    **C.** At such pressures, molecular volume causes a greater deviation to ideal behavior than intermolecular forces for methane.
    **D.** At such pressures, intermolecular forces cause a greater deviation to ideal behavior than molecular volume for methane.

**29.** A force is applied to a container of gas reducing its volume by half. The temperature of the gas:

    **A.** decreases.
    **B.** increases.
    **C.** remains constant.
    **D.** The temperature change depends upon the amount of force used.

**30.** Equal molar quantities of oxygen and hydrogen gas were placed in container $A$ under high pressure. A small portion of the mixture was allowed to effuse for a very short time into the vacuum in container $B$. Which of the following is true concerning partial pressures of the gases at the end of the experiment?

    **A.** The partial pressure of hydrogen in container $A$ is approximately four times as great as the partial pressure of oxygen in container $A$.
    **B.** The partial pressure of oxygen in container $A$ is approximately four times as great as the partial pressure of hydrogen in container $A$.
    **C.** The partial pressure of hydrogen in container $B$ is approximately four times as great as the partial pressure of oxygen in container $B$.
    **D.** The partial pressure of oxygen in container $B$ is approximately four times as great as the partial pressure of hydrogen in container $B$.

**31.** HCl gas and $NH_3$ gas form $NH_4Cl$ precipitate according to the following equation:

$$HCl(g) + NH_3(g) \rightarrow NH_4Cl(s)$$

When cotton balls are moistened with the aqueous solutions of the respective gases and inserted into either end of a glass tube, the gases diffuse toward the middle of the glass tube to form the precipitate. If a 10 cm glass tube is used, at what distance $x$ will the precipitate form?

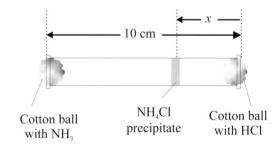

Cotton ball with $NH_3$      $NH_4Cl$ precipitate      Cotton ball with HCl

    **A.** 1.5 cm
    **B.** 2.5 cm
    **C.** 3.0 cm
    **D.** 4.0 cm

**32.** At STP, one liter of which of the following gases contains the most molecules?

    **A.** $H_2$
    **B.** He
    **C.** $N_2$
    **D.** Each gas contains the same number of molecules at STP.

## 2.4 Chemical Kinetics

Chemical kinetics is the study of reaction mechanisms and rates. As of yet, there are no unifying principles of kinetics, which means kinetics is a complicated field with many opposing theories as to how reactions proceed. Additionally, the mathematics of kinetics is complicated and well beyond the scope of MCAT. MCAT will address kinetics only in its simplest form. Keep in mind that kinetics deals with the rate of a reaction typically as it moves toward equilibrium, while thermodynamics deals with the balance of reactants and products after they have achieved equilibrium. Kinetics tells us how fast equilibrium is achieved, while thermodynamics tells us what equilibrium looks like. The two disciplines are intricately related, but they should not be confused.

## 2.5 The Collision Theory

The **collision model** of reactions provides an enlightening method for visualizing chemical reactions. In order for a chemical reaction to occur, the reacting molecules must collide. However, for most reactions, the rate of a given reaction is found to be much lower than the frequency of collisions. This indicates that most collisions do not result in a reaction.

There are two requirements for a given collision to create new molecules in a reaction. First, the relative kinetic energies of the colliding molecules must reach a threshold energy called the **activation energy**. The relative kinetic energy refers to the kinetic energy due to relative velocity only. In other words, velocity in a direction away from another molecule decreases the relative kinetic energy of a collision. Second, the colliding molecules must have the proper spatial orientation.

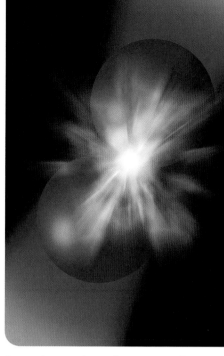

Artwork made of a particle collision. Collisions like this take place in particle accelerators at high energies near the speed of light. The new particles produced in such collisions allow particles physicists to test their theories on the fundamental nature of matter.

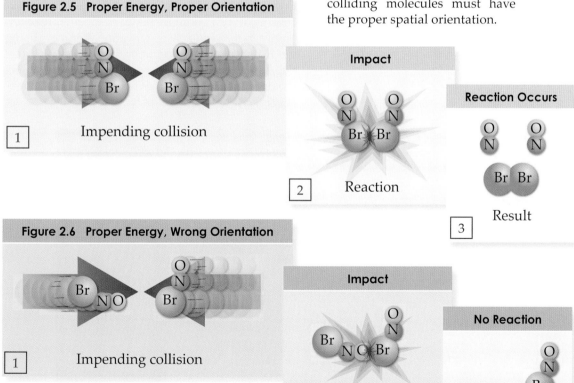

**Figure 2.5  Proper Energy, Proper Orientation**

1  Impending collision

**Impact**

2  Reaction

**Reaction Occurs**

3  Result

**Figure 2.6  Proper Energy, Wrong Orientation**

1  Impending collision

**Impact**

2  No reaction

**No Reaction**

3  Result

The product of the collision frequency $z$, the fraction of collisions having the effective spatial orientations $p$ (called the *steric factor*), and the fraction of collisions having sufficient relative energy $e^{-E_a/RT}$ (where $E_a$ is the activation energy) gives the rate constant $k$ of a reaction. This relationship is called the *Arrhenius equation*:

$$k = zpe^{-E_a/RT}$$

(often written as $k = Ae^{-E_a/RT}$). The value of the rate constant depends upon pressure, catalysts, and temperature. Pressure dependence is typically negligible. Catalysts will be discussed later in this Lecture. The temperature dependence is seen in the Arrhenius equation. The rate constant generally doubles to triples with each increase of 10°C. Since the effect of temperature on $E_a$ is negligible for most reactions, the fraction of collisions that have at least the activation energy ($e^{-E_a/RT}$) increases with the temperature. This, in turn, indicates that the rate constant $k$ increases with increasing temperature for nearly all reactions. As demonstrated by the rate law (discussed later in this lecture), the rate constant is directly proportional to the rate of a reaction. **The rate of a reaction increases with temperature** mainly because more collisions with sufficient relative kinetic energy occur each second.

The temperature dependence of rate is demonstrated by the graph in Figure 2.6, which compares two samples of identical gaseous mixtures reacting at different temperatures. The area under any section of the curve represents the relative number of collisions in that energy range. Notice the area to the right of the activation energy is greater at higher temperature. (i.e. The blue area for the higher temperature reaction is much larger and even includes the striped area of the lower temperature reaction.) At higher temperature there are more collisions with enough energy to create a reaction. Notice that the energy of activation does not change with temperature. (Actually, $E_a$ is temperature dependent, but for most reactions the dependence is extremely small, and, for the MCAT, $E_a$ should be considered independent of temperature.)

**Figure 2.7 Temperature Dependence in Relation to Rate**

Reaction at lower temperature

Reaction at higher temperature

Relative number of collisions

Energy of collisions $E_a$

---

### Thought Provoker

*Hank is doing a chemistry experiment in his university lab. He puts a 3.0 g strip of magnesium in a 0.5 M solution of HCl:*

$$Mg\,(s) + 2HCl\,(aq) \rightarrow MgCl_2\,(aq) + H_2\,(g)$$

*The lab manual instructs him to perform the reaction many times, increasing the rate of reaction each time. What are some ways that Hank can increase his rate of reaction for his experiment?*

*Hint: (Use collision theory to explain why there would be a rate increase.)*

*Answer: See page 55.*

## 2.6 Equations for Reaction Rates

Potassium Chlorate and Phosphorous mix to ignite a match.

For MCAT purposes we will consider only reactions occurring in gases and ideally dilute liquids at constant temperature. The rate of a reaction tells us how quickly the concentration of a reactant or product is changing. Rates are most often given in terms of molarity per second (mol $L^{-1}$ $s^{-1}$). Factors affecting the rate of a reaction are temperature, pressure, and concentration of certain substances in the reacting system; however, pressure effects on reaction rates are usually small enough to be ignored.

The rate of a reaction can be viewed in terms of the change in concentration of any one of the reacting participants. Consider the following elementary reaction where the lower case letters are the stoichiometric coefficients of the balanced equation:

$$a\mathbf{A} + b\mathbf{B} \rightarrow c\mathbf{C} + d\mathbf{D}$$

An *elementary reaction* is a reaction that occurs in a single step. The stoichiometric coefficients of an elementary equation give the *molecularity* of the reaction. The molecularity is the number of molecules colliding at one time to make a reaction. There are three possible molecularities: *unimolecular, bimolecular,* and *termolecular.* Since the reaction above is elementary, its molecularity is given by $a + b$. Chemical equations often represent multistep reactions called complex or composite reactions. There is no way to distinguish an elementary reaction from a complex reaction by inspection of the chemical equation. On the MCAT, the only way to know if a reaction is elementary is if you are told that it is elementary.

> In an elementary reaction, the coefficient tells you how many molecules participate in a reaction producing collision.

The average reaction rate for any brief time interval $t$ during the above reaction is:

$$rate = -\frac{1}{a}\frac{\Delta[\mathrm{A}]}{t} = -\frac{1}{b}\frac{\Delta[\mathrm{B}]}{t} = \frac{1}{c}\frac{\Delta[\mathrm{C}]}{t} = \frac{1}{d}\frac{\Delta[\mathrm{D}]}{t}$$

'$\Delta$' means "change in". The negative signs indicate that the reactant concentrations are decreasing as the reaction moves forward. Although the rate equation above is strictly correct only for an elementary reaction, it is a good approximation for a multistep reaction if the concentration of any intermediates is kept low. **Intermediates** are species that are products of one reaction and reactants of a later reaction in a reaction chain. The concentration of intermediates is often very low because they are often unstable and react as quickly as they are formed.

> Don't confuse the rate constant with the rate of the reaction. They are proportional, but they are NOT identical.

Chemical reactions are reversible; as the products are formed, products begin to react to form the reactants. This reverse reaction complicates the study of kinetics. For the time being, we will consider only the forward reactions. If we consider only the forward reaction, we can write a **rate law** for the reaction $a\mathrm{A} + b\mathrm{B} \rightarrow c\mathrm{C} + d\mathrm{D}$ as:

$$rate_{\mathrm{forward}} = k_f[\mathbf{A}]^\alpha[\mathbf{B}]^\beta$$

where $k_f$ is the rate constant for the forward reaction. $\alpha$ and $\beta$ are the **order of each respective reactant** and the sum $\alpha + \beta$ is the **overall order** of the reaction. If the reaction is elementary, $\alpha = a$ and $\beta = b$.

> **Warning:** Never assume that you can use the coefficients of the balanced equation in a rate law unless you know that the reaction is elementary.
>
> Also, since the rate law shown here is for a particular reaction, you should not memorize it. Instead, you should recognize its form and its relationship to an elementary reaction.

## 2.7 Determining the Rate Law by Experiment

Both the order of the reactants and the value of the rate constant must be determined through experiment. Finding the rate law on the MCAT is a relatively simple matter. Consider the hypothetical reaction:

$$2A + B + C \rightarrow 2D$$

In this case, we will assume that no reverse reaction occurs. We are given the following table with experimental data:

**Table 2.1  Experimental Data**

| Trial | Initial Concentration of A (mol L$^{-1}$) | Initial Concentration of B (mol L$^{-1}$) | Initial Concentration of C (mol L$^{-1}$) | Measured Initial Rate (mol L$^{-1}$) |
|---|---|---|---|---|
| 1 | 0.1 | 0.1 | 0.1 | $8.0 \times 10^{-4}$ |
| 2 | 0.2 | 0.1 | 0.1 | $1.6 \times 10^{-3}$ |
| 3 | 0.2 | 0.2 | 0.1 | $6.4 \times 10^{-3}$ |
| 4 | 0.1 | 0.1 | 0.4 | $8.0 \times 10^{-4}$ |

For MCAT, you must be able to derive the rate law from a table of trials as done in this section. When given a rate law, you must be able to predict what changing the concentration of a reactant will do to the rate.

We can find the order of each reactant by comparing the rates between two trials in which only the concentration of one of the reactants is changed. For instance, comparing Trial 1 to Trial 2, the initial concentration of A is doubled and the concentrations of B and C remain the same. The reaction rate also doubles. Thus the rate of this reaction is directly proportional to the concentration of A. In the rate law, [A] receives an exponent of 1, and the reaction is considered first order with respect to reactant A.

**Table 2.2  Comparison of Trial 1 and 2**

| Trial | Initial Concentration of A (mol L$^{-1}$) | Initial Concentration of B (mol L$^{-1}$) | Initial Concentration of C (mol L$^{-1}$) | Measured Initial Rate (mol L$^{-1}$) |
|---|---|---|---|---|
| 1 | 0.1 | 0.1 Same | 0.1 Same | $8.0 \times 10^{-4}$ |
| 2 | 2× 0.2 | 0.1 | 0.1 | $1.6 \times 10^{-3}$ |

Increase
$2\text{x} = 2^1$

Comparing Trials 2 and 3 we find that when only the concentration of B is doubled, the reaction rate is quadrupled. This indicates that the rate is proportional to the square of the concentration of B. [B] receives a 2 for its exponent in the rate law and the reaction is second order with respect to B.

| Table 2.3 Comparison of Trial 2 and 3 | | | | |
|---|---|---|---|---|
| Trial | Initial Concentration of A (mol L⁻¹) | Initial Concentration of B (mol L⁻¹) | Initial Concentration of C (mol L⁻¹) | Measured Initial Rate (mol L⁻¹) |
| 2 | 0.2  Same | 0.1 | 0.1  Same | $1.6 \times 10^{-3}$ |
| 3 | 0.2 | 0.2  2× | 0.1 | $6.4 \times 10^{-3}$ |

Increase
$4\times = 2^2$

Comparing Trials 1 and 4, the concentration of C is quadrupled, but there is no resulting change in the rate. The rate is independent of the concentration of C, so [C] receives an exponent of zero in the rate law. The reaction is zero order with respect to C.

| Table 2.4 Comparison of Trial 1 and 4 | | | | |
|---|---|---|---|---|
| Trial | Initial Concentration of A (mol L⁻¹) | Initial Concentration of B (mol L⁻¹) | Initial Concentration of C (mol L⁻¹) | Measured Initial Rate (mol L⁻¹) |
| 1 | 0.1  Same | 0.1  Same | 0.1 | $8.0 \times 10^{-4}$ |
| 4 | 0.1 | 0.1 | 0.4  4× | $8.0 \times 10^{-4}$ |

No change.

The complete rate law for our hypothetical reaction is:

$$rate_{forward} = k_f[\text{A}]^1[\text{B}]^2[\text{C}]^0$$

also written:

$$rate_{forward} = k_f[\text{A}][\text{B}]^2$$

By adding the exponents we find that the reaction overall is third order (1 + 2 + 0 = 3). Notice that the coefficients in the balanced chemical equation were not used to figure out the order.

Once we have derived the rate law from the experimental data, we can plug in the rate and concentrations from <u>any</u> of the experiments into the rate law, and solve for the rate constant $k$.

Notice that the rate may be increased by increasing the concentration of the reactants. If we consider the collision model, this makes sense. The greater the concentration of a species, the more likely are collisions.

The Rate Law WILL be determined by experiment!

The different orders of reactions have recognizably different characteristics. Keeping in mind that we are assuming that there is no reverse reaction taking place, we can compare graphs of the different orders of reaction for a single reactant. Plotting [A] with respect to time t for a zeroth order reaction results in a straight line with a slope $-k_f$.

In a first order reaction of the form:

$$A \rightarrow products \qquad rate = k_f[A]$$

where there is no reverse reaction, [A] decreases exponentially. A graph of a first order reaction comparing ln[A] with time $t$ gives a straight line with a slope of $-k_f$. The same first order reaction has a constant half life that is independent of the concentration of A. The molecularity of a first order reaction implies that no collision takes place since there is only one molecule reacting. However, current theory requires a collision with any other molecule, boosting the reactant to a higher energy state resulting in a reaction. Although this is a two step process, it exhibits first order kinetics (except under low pressure). This is referred to as *pseudo-first order kinetics*.

For a graph of an irreversible second order reaction with a single reactant of the form:

$$2A \rightarrow products \qquad rate = k_f[A]^2$$

plotting 1/[A] gives a straight line with a slope of $k_f$. The half life of this type of second order reaction is dependent upon the concentration of A. It has the interesting characteristic that each consecutive half-life is twice as long as the last. For instance, the time required to reduce the concentration of A from 100% to 50% is half as long as the time required to reduce the concentration from 50% to 25%.

The second order reaction of the form:

$$A + B \rightarrow products \qquad rate = k_f[A][B]$$

does not reveal the same graph, and does not have an easily predictable half life.
For a graph of an irreversible third order reaction with a single reactant of the form:

$$3A \rightarrow products \qquad rate = k_f[A]^3$$

plotting $1/(2[A]^2)$ gives a straight line with a slope of $k_f$.

To avoid the complications of reverse reactions, the technique of initial rates is often employed. In the initial moments of a reaction starting with all reactants and no products, the rate of the reverse reaction is zero. The rate law in section 2.7 was determined with initial rates.

**Figure 2.8  Reaction Orders**

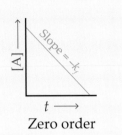

Zero order

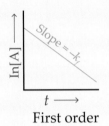

First order

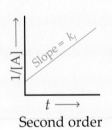

Second order

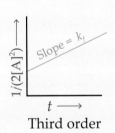

Third order

For the MCAT, just be concerned with the graphs for the zero order and first order rate laws. Note that, like a rate constant, the slope is a straight line and remains constant throughout the reaction. A typical MCAT question might draw your attention to the descending green line and ask you if the value of the rate constant decreases over time. Of course, it does not. It remains constant.

## 2.9 Rates of Multiple Step Reactions

Any complex reaction can be separated into elementary steps. The rate of the slowest elementary step determines the rate of the overall reaction and is called the **rate determining step**. If the slow step is the first step, the rate law can be derived directly from this step and no other. If the slow step is other than the first step, the slow step is still the rate determining step, but steps prior to the slow step will contribute to the rate law. Steps after the slow step will make no contribution to the rate law.

Consider the following reaction:

$$NO_2(g) + CO(g) \rightarrow NO(g) + CO_2(g)$$

This reaction has two elementary steps:

1. $NO_2(g) + NO_2(g) \rightarrow NO_3(g) + NO(g)$     *slow step*

2. $NO_3(g) + CO(g) \rightarrow NO_2(g) + CO_2(g)$     *fast step*

Notice that if we add these two equations together, we arrive at the original equation. Elementary steps must add to give the complex reaction. Since the first step is the slow step, the rate law for the overall reaction is given by this step and is:

$$rate = k_1[NO_2]^2$$

We know that the exponent for $[NO_2]$ is 2 because we derived the rate law from an elementary equation, and in the elementary equation two $NO_2$ molecules collide to create a reaction. Automatically using the coefficient of the balanced equation for the exponent in the rate law works only if the equation is elementary. Don't forget, the rate law above assumes negligible contribution from the reverse reaction, and it also assumes a sufficient concentration of CO for the fast step to occur.

When the first step of a reaction series is the fast step, things can be a little tricky. If the first reaction is the fast reaction, the rate of the overall reaction is still equal to the rate of the slowest step. However, now one of the products of the fast step is a reactant in the slow step. Such a species is called an intermediate. The concentration of the intermediate is tricky to predict. An intermediate is usually not stable. If we assume that the fast reaction reaches equilibrium very quickly, the concentration of the intermediate remains at its equilibrium concentration. We can use the equilibrium concentration of the intermediate in predicting the slow step. For instance:

$$2NO(g) + Br_2(g) \rightarrow 2NOBr(g)$$

This reaction has two elementary steps:

1. $NO(g) + Br_2(g) \rightarrow NOBr_2(g)$     *fast step*

2. $NOBr_2(g) + NO(g) \rightarrow 2NOBr(g)$     *slow step*

The rate law for this reaction is:

$$rate = k_2[NOBr_2][NO]$$

To better understand a rate determining step, let's consider a bridge with two consecutive tolls A and B. Imagine toll A has only one open lane and toll B has many open lanes. Traffic backs up at toll A. Once through toll A, there is no waiting at toll B. The rate at which cars cross the bridge is limited only by the rate at which cars pass toll A. If instead, toll A had many open lanes and toll B had only one open lane, toll B would limit the rate at which cars crossed the bridge. The slowest step in a multistep reaction limits the overall rate of the reaction.

Remember that the slow step determines the rate.

However, the concentration of $NOBr_2$ depends upon the first step. If we assume that the first step reaches equilibrium very quickly, the concentration of $NOBr_2$ can be written in terms of the equilibrium constant $K_c$ for step 1, $[NOBr_2] = K_c[NO][Br_2]$. Alternatively, since the first step is considered to be in equilibrium, we can set the forward reaction rate, $k_1[NO][Br_2]$, equal to the reverse rate, $k_{-1}[NOBr_2]$, and solve for $[NOBr_2]$. $[NOBr_2] = k_1/k_{-1} [NO][Br_2]$. The resulting rate law is:

$$rate = \frac{k_2 k_1}{k_{-1}} [NO]^2 [Br_2]$$

This method is called the *equilibrium approximation*, which assumes that all steps prior to the rate limiting step are in equilibrium. The equilibrium approximation requires that the slow step be significantly slower than the fast steps. Since $k_2 k_1/k_{-1}$ is a constant, it is usually replaced by a single constant, $k_{observed}$.

If there is not a step that is significantly slower than the others, we can use the steady state approximation. In the *steady state approximation*, the concentration of the intermediate is considered to be small and hardly changing. This leads to the same result as the equilibrium approximation.

## 2.10 Catalysis

A **catalyst** is a substance that increases the rate of a reaction without being consumed or permanently altered. Catalysts increase the rate of both the forward and the reverse reactions and are capable of enhancing product selectivities and reducing energy consumption. A catalyst may lower the activation energy, $E_a$, or increase the steric factor ($p$ from the Arrhenius equation) or both. Increasing the steric factor increases the number of favorable collisions. Most catalysts work by lowering the activation energy. The reaction rate depends exponentially on the activation energy. When the activation energy is lowered, more collisions have sufficient relative kinetic energy to create a reaction. This leads to more reactions and an increase in the overall reaction rate. This effect is shown in the energy vs. reaction coordinate diagram in Figure 2.8.

A catalyst works by providing an alternative reaction mechanism that competes with the uncatalyzed mechanism. **A catalyst cannot alter the equilibrium constant** of a reaction, so it must increase the rate of both the forward and the reverse reaction. Although a catalyst cannot change the equilibrium constant, it can, in some cases, change the composition of the mixture at equilibrium; however, the effect is usually very small and should be ignored for the MCAT. For the MCAT, catalysts do not change the equilibrium composition.

A catalyst can be either heterogeneous or homogeneous. A **heterogeneous catalyst** is in a different phase than the reactants and products. Heterogeneous catalysts are usually solids while the reactants and products are liquids or gases. A reactant may physically adsorb (via van der Waals forces) or, more often, chemically adsorb (usually via covalent bonds) to the surface of a solid catalyst. (Adsorption is the binding of molecules to a surface as opposed to absorption which refers to the uptake of molecules into an interior.) Molecules bind to a metal surface because, unlike metal atoms in the interior, metal atoms at the surface have unfulfilled valence requirements. The binding is almost always exothermic and the rate of catalysis depends upon the strength of the bond between the reactant and the catalyst. If bonds are too weak, not enough adsorption occurs; if bonds are too strong, too much energy is required to remove the reactant. Depending on the reaction, reactant molecules may bind to any of the atoms at the surface, or they may bind only to surface imperfections. Once adsorbed, molecules migrate from one adsorption site to the next. The more binding that occurs, the greater the reaction rate. Thus, reaction rates can be enhanced by increasing the surface area of a catalyst. Often this

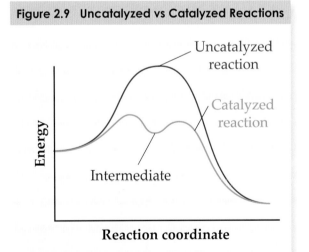

**Figure 2.9  Uncatalyzed vs Catalyzed Reactions**

Uncatalyzed reaction

Catalyzed reaction

Energy

Intermediate

**Reaction coordinate**

is done by grinding the solid into a powder. However, the concentration of a solid catalyst does not change so the concentration of a solid catalyst won't appear in the rate law.

A **homogeneous catalyst** is in the same phase as the reactants and products, usually in the gas or liquid phase. Aqueous acid or base solutions often act as homogeneous catalysts. Some reactions exhibit autocatalysis by generating the catalyst as a product. The acid catalyzed hydrolysis of an ester is an example of autocatalysis, where the carboxylic acid product acts as a catalyst to the reaction.

In the lab, concentrations of catalysts are usually small compared to the concentration of the reactants and products. In such cases, increasing the concentration of the catalyst increases the rate of the reaction. When this happens, the concentration of the catalyst will be found in the rate law. If the concentration of the catalyst is large compared to the reactants and products, the rate changes little or not at all with the catalyst concentration. In this case, the concentration of the catalyst may not be included in the rate law. Since catalysts alter reaction mechanisms, reactions with catalysts require separate rate constants. Remember, a catalyst doesn't prevent the original reaction from proceeding, so the total rate is given by the sum of the rates for both reactions. For instance, a first order uncatalyzed reaction may follow the rate law:

$$rate = k_0[A]$$

When the same reaction is catalyzed by acid, the new rate law would be:

$$rate = k_0[A] + k_{H+}[H^+][A]$$

Typically, the rate of the original reaction is negligible compared to the catalyzed rate.

Almost every chemical reaction in the human body is quickened by a protein catalyst called an enzyme. Enzymes are far more effective than inorganic catalysts. The number of reactions occurring at one active site on one enzyme is typically 1,000 per second and can be tens of thousands of times greater for the fastest enzymatic reactions. This number is called the *turnover number*.

> Remember that a catalyst increases the rate of a reaction by lowering the activation energy of that reaction. A catalyst doesn't change equilibrium and is not used up.

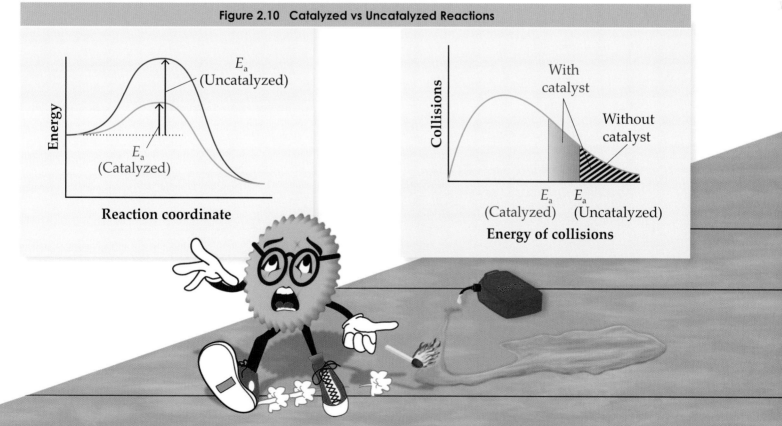

**Figure 2.10 Catalyzed vs Uncatalyzed Reactions**

Indigestion tablets react in water producing carbon dioxide gas.

## 2.11 Effects of Solvent on Rate

Roughly speaking, liquid molecules make around 100 times more collisions per second than gas molecules because liquid molecules are much closer to each other. However, most of the collisions in a liquid are with the solvent resulting in no reaction.

The rate constant in a liquid is a function of the solvent as well as the temperature. The reactant in a liquid is solvated. These solvent-reactant bonds must be broken before a reaction can take place. In addition, the bonds may stabilize an intermediate. The degree of solvation affects $k$. Solvents can electrically insulate reactants reducing the electrostatic forces between them. The dielectric of the solvent affects $k$. Solvent viscosity can affect $k$ as per the 'cage effect' described below.

Reactants in a liquid can be trapped in a cage of solvent molecules. They rattle around in such a cage at tremendous rates making hundreds of collisions before squeezing between solvent molecules and into a new solvent cage. If they are trapped in the cage with another reactant, many of their collisions are with the other reactant and a reaction is likely to occur, but if there is not another reactant in the solvent cage, they cannot react until they escape the cage. The net result is that reactants in a liquid make an approximately equal number of collisions with other reactants as they would in a gas with equal concentrations; collisions in a liquid occur at about the same rate as in a gas.

For liquids, stirring or shaking may greatly increase the reaction rate.

*Notes:*

33. Which of the following changes to a reaction will always increase the rate constant for that reaction?

    A. decreasing the temperature
    B. increasing the temperature
    C. increasing the concentration of the reactants
    D. increasing the concentration of the catalyst

34. All of the following may be true concerning catalysts and the reaction which they catalyze EXCEPT:

    A. Catalysts are not used up by the reaction.
    B. Catalysts lower the energy of activation.
    C. Catalysts increase the rate of the reverse reaction.
    D. Catalysts shift the reaction equilibrium to the right.

35. The table below shows 3 trials where the initial rate was measured for the reaction:

    $$2A + B \rightarrow C$$

    Which of the following expressions is the correct rate law for the reaction?

    | T | Molarity of A | Molarity of B | Initial Rate |
    |---|---------------|---------------|--------------|
    | 1 | 0.05 | 0.05 | $5 \times 10^{-3}$ |
    | 2 | 0.05 | 0.1 | $5 \times 10^{-3}$ |
    | 3 | 0.1 | 0.05 | $1 \times 10^{-2}$ |

    A. rate = 0.1[A]
    B. rate = [A]
    C. rate = [A][B]
    D. rate = [A]²[B]

36. The reaction below proceeds via the two step mechanism as shown.

    Overall Reaction: $2NO_2 + F_2 \rightarrow 2NO_2F$
    Step 1: $NO_2 + F_2 \rightarrow NO_2F + F$
    Step 2: $NO_2 + F \rightarrow NO_2F$

    $X$ is the rate of step 1, and $Y$ is the rate of step 2. If step 1 is much slower than step 2, then the rate of the overall reaction can be represented by:

    A. $X$
    B. $Y$
    C. $X + Y$
    D. $X - Y$

37. As temperature is increased in an exothermic gaseous reaction, all of the following increase EXCEPT:

    A. reaction rate.
    B. rate constant.
    C. activation energy.
    D. rms molecular velocity.

38. A container holds a pure sample of compound $X$ shown at $t = 0$ min. Compound $X$ undergoes a first order reaction to form compound $Y$. The same container is shown at $t = 15$ min. (Compound $X$ is shown as white circles and compound $Y$ is shown as black circles.)

    If the rate of the reverse reaction is negligible, which of the following might represent the container at t = 30 min?

    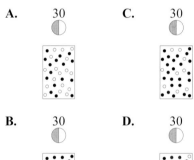

    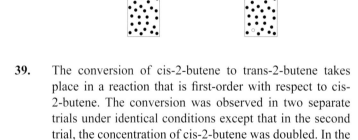

39. The conversion of cis-2-butene to trans-2-butene takes place in a reaction that is first-order with respect to cis-2-butene. The conversion was observed in two separate trials under identical conditions except that in the second trial, the concentration of cis-2-butene was doubled. In the second trial:

    A. the reaction rate will be halved.
    B. the reaction rate will be doubled.
    C. the rate constant will be halved.
    D. the rate constant will be doubled.

40. When a radioactive isotope undergoes nuclear decay, the concentration of the isotope decreases exponentially with a constant half-life. It can be determined from this that radioactive decay is a:

    A. zeroth order reaction.
    B. first order reaction.
    C. second order reaction.
    D. third order reaction.

*Equilibrium*

Chemical reactions are reversible. As reactants are converted to products, the concentration of the reactants decreases, and the concentration of the products increases. Since rates are related to concentrations, the rate of the forward reaction begins to slow, and the rate of the reverse reaction quickens as a reaction proceeds. Eventually, the two rates become equal. This condition, where the forward reaction rate equals the reverse reaction rate, is called **chemical equilibrium**. At chemical equilibrium, there is no change in the concentration of the products or reactants. Equilibrium will be reached from either direction, beginning with predominantly reactants or predominantly products.

If the two faucets flow at different rates, the bucket will empty or overflow. However, if the faucets flow at the same rate, an equilibrium will be reached and the water level will remain constant.

The object of this game is to get all the balls to the opponent's side. However, no one can win because inevitably an equilbrium will be reached. Although there are more players on one side, as fewer balls become available, more time is required to find a ball to throw. Thus, the rate at which balls are thrown from that side slows. On the other hand, as my side fills with balls, I am able to grab and throw balls more quickly, and the rate at which I throw increases. Eventually these rates equalize. The game has reached an equilibrium with no winner. Reactions work in a similar fashion.

Equilibrium is the point of greatest entropy. From the second law of thermodynamics we know that nature wants to increase entropy. This is why a reaction moves toward and then stays at equilibrium.

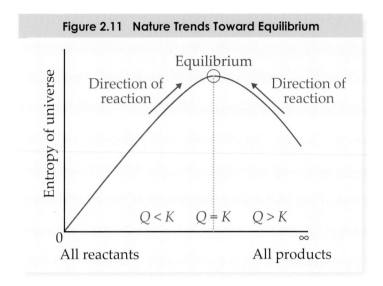

**Figure 2.11 Nature Trends Toward Equilibrium**

When concentrated nitric acid and copper react the system moves toward equilibrium and greatest entropy.

Consider the hypothetical first order elementary reaction:

$$A \rightarrow B$$

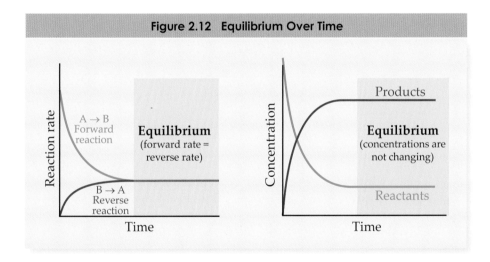

**Figure 2.12 Equilibrium Over Time**

Notice that by the rate definition:

$$rate = -\frac{1}{a}\frac{\Delta[A]}{t}$$

the rate at equilibrium is zero. Understand that zero is the net reaction rate, but there is a forward and a reverse reaction rate at equilibrium. Equilibrium is a dynamic process.

Notice from Figure 2.11 that the forward rate changes faster than the reverse rate as the reaction proceeds. This indicates that the forward rate constant is greater than the reverse rate constant. The rate law for the forward and reverse reactions are rate = $k_f$[A] and rate = $k_r$[B] respectively. The rate of the forward reaction is directly proportional to [A]. From the diagram, the rate of the forward reaction is reduced by more than half, so [A] is also reduced by more than half. For every molecule of A lost, a molecule of B is created, so at equilibrium [B] must be greater than [A]. Setting the rates equal, $k_f$[A] = $k_r$[B], we see that $k_f$ must be greater than $k_r$ if [B] is greater than [A] at equilibrium.

This is elementary!

For a homogeneous reaction, where all species are in the same phase, there will always be some of each species present at equilibrium; however, in some cases, the rate constant for the forward reaction is so much greater than the rate constant for the reverse reaction that, for all practical purposes, the reaction runs to completion. Alternatively, if a product is continually removed as the reaction proceeds (perhaps in the form of a gas leaving an aqueous solution), the reaction can run to completion.

Consider the hypothetical elementary reaction: $aA + bB \rightarrow cC + dD$. Since the reaction is elementary, we can use the stoichiometric coefficients for the forward and reverse rate laws:

$$rate_{forward} = k_f[A]^a[B]^b$$

$$rate_{reverse} = k_r[C]^c[D]^d$$

(**WARNING:** For the MCAT, never use the coefficients as the exponents in the rate law. We do it here because we are told that the reaction is elementary.) Since equilibrium occurs when these two rates are equal, then, for equilibrium conditions only, we set them equal to each other as shown below:

$$k_f[A]^a[B]^b = k_r[C]^c[D]^d$$

With a little algebraic manipulation we have:

$$\frac{k_f}{k_r} = \frac{[C]^c[D]^d}{[A]^a[B]^b}$$

In the equilibrium expression we use the coefficients as exponents; in the rate law we **cannot** use the coefficients as exponents unless we know the reaction is elementary

Since both $k$'s are constants, we can replace them with a new constant called the **equilibrium constant $K$**. (**2nd WARNING:** This simple relationship between $K$ equilibrium and $k$ rate is only true for elementary equations.) The relationship between a chemical equation and the equilibrium constant is called the **Law of Mass Action** and is written as an equilibrium expression as follows:

$$K = \frac{[C]^c[D]^d}{[A]^a[B]^b} = \frac{\text{Products}^{\text{cofficients}}}{\text{Reactants}^{\text{cofficients}}}$$

The equilibrium constant depends upon temperature only. Don't confuse the equilibrium constant with equilibrium.

The value of $K$ has no dimensions because the concentrations are actually approximations for a dimensionless quantity called an *activity*. The law of mass action is good for all chemical equations, including non-elementary equations. In other words, for equilibrium constants, use the chemical equation coefficients as the exponents of the concentrations regardless of molecularity. Notice that the equilibrium constant is a capital $K$ and the rate constant is represented by lowercase $k$. Also notice that the equilibrium constant for the reverse reaction is the reciprocal of the equilibrium constant of the forward reaction. This is true regardless of whether or not the reaction is elementary. Following this same line of reasoning will demonstrate that the equilibrium constant for a series of reactions is equal to the product of the equilibrium constants for each of its elementary steps. Since the rate constant depends upon temperature, the equilibrium constant must also depend upon temperature.

The concentration of a pure liquid or a pure solid is usually given a value of one for the equilibrium expression. Concentrations are only approximations for activities. Activities for pure solids and pure liquids are like 'effective' mole fractions. The mole fraction of a pure solid or liquid is one. Although solvents are not actually pure, they are usually considered ideally dilute on the MCAT, which means that their mole fraction is one. The activity of a pure solid or liquid is approximately one. Be aware that pure solids or liquids can still participate in the equilibrium. When they do, they must be present in order for equilibrium to exist.

> Don't use solids or pure liquids such as water in the law of mass action.

## Thought Provoker

The manufacturing of cement involves the decomposition of limestone. The reaction is as follows:

$$CaCO_3(s) \rightarrow CaO(s) + CO_2(g)$$

What is the equilibrium constant for this process?

Answer: See page 55.

*Notes:*

## 2.13 The Partial Pressure Equilibrium Constant

For reactions with more than one pathway, and for reactions with more than one step, *the principle for detailed balance* states that, at equilibrium, the forward and reverse reaction rates for each step must be equal, and any two or more single reactions or series of reactions resulting in the same products from identical reactants must have the same equilibrium constant for a given temperature. The equilibrium constant does not depend upon whether or not other substances are present.

For reactions involving gases, the equilibrium constant can be written in terms of partial pressures. For the all gas reaction $aA + bB \rightarrow cC + dD$, the partial pressure equilibrium expression is written as:

$$K_p = \frac{P_c P_d}{P_a P_b} = \frac{\text{products}^{\text{coefficients}}}{\text{reactants}^{\text{coefficients}}}$$

where $K_p$ is the partial pressure equilibrium constant and $P_a$, $P_b$, $P_c$, and $P_d$ are the partial pressures of the respective gases. The concentration equilibrium constant and the partial pressure equilibrium constant do not have the same value, but they are related by the equation:

$$K_p = K_c(RT)^{\Delta n}$$

where $K_p$ is the partial pressure equilibrium constant and n is the sum of the coefficients of the products minus the sum of the coefficients of the reactants. This equation is not required for the MCAT, but you must be able to work with partial pressure equilibrium constants.

### Figure 2.13  Air Composition

- Nitrogen  78%
- Oxygen  21%
- Other  1%

### Thought Provoker

An experiment is performed which requires a specific greenhouse air environment of 3.0 mol percent $CO_2$, 20.0 mol percent $O_2$, and 77.0 mol percent Ar.

1. What is the partial pressure of the $CO_2$ in the greenhouse if the total pressure is 750 torr?

2. If the greenhouse capacity is 145 L, how many moles of $CO_2$ are found in the greenhouse at 25 degrees Celsius?

Answer:  See page 55

## 2.14 The Reaction Quotient

The equilibrium constant describes only equilibrium conditions. If a reaction is at equilibrium, the concentrations of the products and reactants, when plugged into the equilibrium expression, must equal the equilibrium constant. However, it is possible to momentarily change those concentrations by adding a reactant or product. When we do so, for a moment the reaction is not at equilibrium, and, of course, when the concentrations of the products and reactants are plugged into the equilibrium expression, they will NOT equal the equilibrium constant. In such cases, we substitute a <u>variable</u> $Q$ for the equilibrium <u>constant</u> $K$. $Q$ is called the reaction quotient and is given by a formula identical to the equilibrium expression.

> Use the reaction quotient $Q$ to predict the direction in which a reaction will proceed.

$$Q = \frac{\text{Products}^{\text{coefficients}}}{\text{Reactants}^{\text{coefficients}}}$$

$Q$ may have any positive value.

Since reactions always move toward equilibrium, $Q$ will always change toward $K$. Thus we can compare $Q$ and $K$ for a reaction at any given moment, and learn in which direction the reaction will proceed.

- If $Q$ *is equal to* $K$, then the reaction is at equilibrium.

- If $Q$ *is greater than* $K$, then the ratio of the concentration of products to the concentration of reactants (as given by the reaction quotient equation above) is greater than when at equilibrium, and the reaction increases reactants and decreases products. In other words, the reverse reaction rate will be greater than the forward rate. This is sometimes called a leftward shift in the equilibrium. Of course, the equilibrium constant does not change during this type of equilibrium shift.

- If $Q$ *is less than* $K$, then the ratio of the concentration of products to the concentration of reactants (as given by the reaction quotient equation above) is less than when at equilibrium, and the reaction increases products and decreases reactants. In other words, the forward reaction rate will be greater than the reverse rate. This is sometimes called a rightward shift.

**Figure 2.14  K vs Q Relationship**

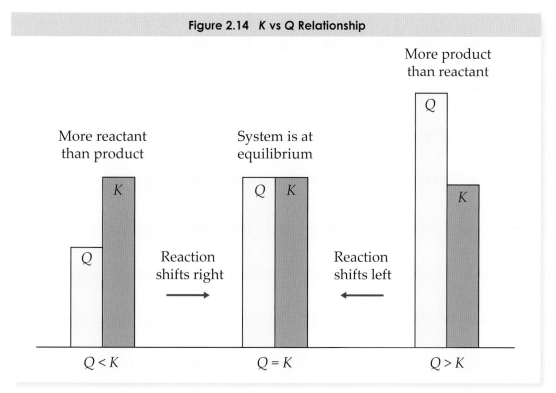

# 2.15 Le Châtelier's Principle

There is a general rule called Le Châtelier's principle that can often be applied to systems at equilibrium. **Le Châtelier's principle** states that when a system at equilibrium is stressed, the system will shift in a direction that will reduce that stress.

There are three types of stress that usually obey Le Châtelier's principle: 1) addition or removal of a product or reactant, 2) changing the pressure of the system, 3) heating or cooling the system.

The Haber process is important today because the fertilizer generated from ammonia is responsible for sustaining one-third of the Earth's population.

> Systems like equilibrium; so, when a system at equilibrium is stressed, the system will shift in a direction to reduce that stress.

The Haber Process is an all gas reaction commonly used on the MCAT to test Le Châtelier's principle. The Haber Process is an exothermic reaction, so it creates heat. For Le Châtelier purposes, we can think of heat as a product in the Haber Process:

$$N_2(g) + 3H_2(g) \rightarrow 2NH_3(g) + \text{Heat}$$

Imagine a rigid container with $N_2$, $H_2$, and $NH_3$ gas at equilibrium. If we add $N_2$ gas to our system, the system attempts to compensate for the increased concentration of nitrogen by reducing the partial pressure of $N_2$ with the forward reaction. The forward reaction uses up $H_2$ as well, reducing its partial pressure. $NH_3$ and heat are created by the forward reaction.

If we raise the temperature by adding heat, the reaction is pushed to the left. The concentrations of $N_2$ and $H_2$ are increased, while the concentration of $NH_3$ is decreased.

If the size of the container is reduced at constant temperature, total pressure increases. Since there are four gas molecules on the left side of the reaction and only 2 on the right, the equilibrium shifts to the right producing heat and raising the $NH_3$ concentration. Interestingly, a similar effect is found when a solution is concentrated or diluted. If one side contains more moles than the other, the equilibrium shifts to the side with fewer moles when the solution is concentrated.

**Warning:** Le Châtelier's principle does not always predict the correct shift. Notable exceptions are solvation reactions, and pressure increase due to the addition of a nonreactive gas. The solubility of salts generally increase with increasing temperature, even when the reaction is exothermic. This is largely due to the significant entropy increase that occurs with dissolution. The entropy factor becomes more important as the temperature increases. An example of a pressure increase where equilibrium is not affected is the addition of He to the Haber Process. If we add He gas to our container of $N_2$, $H_2$, and $NH_3$, the total pressure increases, but there is no shift in equilibrium. This can be seen by examining the partial pressure equilibrium constant. Adding He to a rigid container, does not change the partial pressures of the other gases, so the equilibrium does not shift.

The following reaction follows Le Châtlier's principle.

$$\text{Light} + 2Ag^+ + 2Cl^- \rightleftharpoons 2Ag + Cl_2$$

The compound silver chloride is found in adjustable shading sunglasses. When light strikes the sunglasses, this reaction shifts right producing metallic silver, Ag, and darkening the glasses. In the absence of light, the reaction shifts left and the glasses lighten.

## Examples of Le Châtelier's Principle

$$N_2(g) + 3H_2(g) \rightarrow 2NH_3(g) + \text{Heat}$$

**Figure 2.15  Normal Conditions**

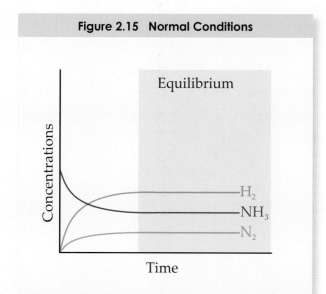

**Figure 2.16  Heat Added**

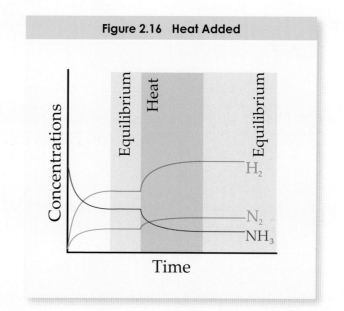

**Figure 2.17  N$_2$ Added**

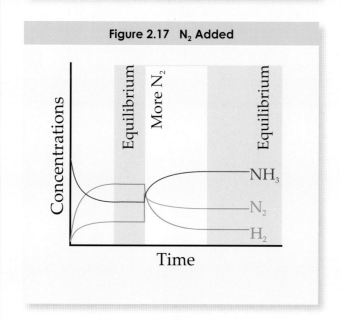

**Figure 2.18  Pressure Added**

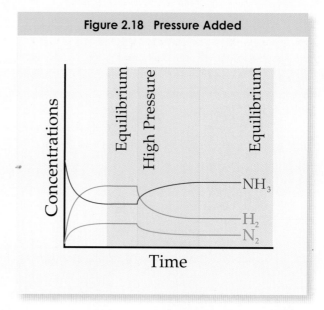

## 2.16 Equation Summary

| Equations | |
|---|---|
| **Ideal Gas Law** $$PV = nRT$$ | **Partial Pressure** $$P_a = \chi_a P_{total}$$ |

**Dalton's Law**

$$P_{total} = P_1 + P_2 + P_{3...}$$

**Average Translational Kinetic Energy and the Temperature of a Gas**

$$K.E._{avg} = \frac{3}{2}RT$$

**Graham's Law**

$$\frac{v_1}{v_2} = \frac{\sqrt{m_2}}{\sqrt{m_1}}$$

**Effusion**

$$\frac{\text{effusion rate}_1}{\text{effusion rate}_2} = \frac{\sqrt{M_2}}{\sqrt{M_1}}$$

**Deviations from Ideal Gas Law**

Volume of Gases

$$V_{real} > V_{ideal}$$

Pressure of Gases

$$P_{real} < P_{ideal}$$

**Rate Law**

$$rate_{forward} = k_f [A]^\alpha [B]^\beta$$

**The Law of Mass Action**

$$K = \frac{[C]^c [D]^d}{[A]^a [B]^b} = \frac{\text{Products}^{\text{cofficients}}}{\text{Reactants}^{\text{cofficients}}}$$

**The Reaction Quotient**

$$Q = \frac{\text{Products}^{\text{coefficients}}}{\text{Reactants}^{\text{coefficients}}}$$

| Terms | |
|---|---|
| Activation Energy | Kinetic Molecular Theory |
| Catalyst | Le Châtelier's Principle |
| Chemical Equilibrium | Mean Free Path |
| Collision Model | Order Of Each Respective Reactant |
| Dalton's Law | Overall Order |
| Diffusion | Partial Pressure |
| Effusion | Rate Determining Step |
| Equilibrium Constant $K$ | Rate Law |
| Graham's Law | Reaction Quotient |
| Heterogeneous Catalyst | Standard Molar Volume |
| Homogeneous Catalyst | Standard Temperature And Pressure (STP) |
| Ideal Gas | |
| Ideal Gas Law | |
| Intermediates | |

## Thought Provoker Answers

**Answer from page 29:**

*This is a pretty straightforward PV=nRT question. P=730 torr (approx. 0.96 atm), V=2L, n=?, R=constant, and T= 25 °C (298 K). Solving for moles we get 0.078 moles.*

**Answer from page 36:**

1. *Heat the reaction, which would cause the molecules to move more at a higher energy, thereby increasing the collision rate.*

2. *Increase the concentration of HCl, increasing collisions between magnesium and H⁺ ions.*

3. *Increase the surface area of the magnesium, creating more locations for potential collisions.*

**Answer from page 49:**

*The equilibrium constant (K) for this process only includes the gas phases for this case, making it K= [$CO_2$].*

**Answer from page 50:**

1. *A mole percent is the mole fraction times 100. The mole fraction of $CO_2$ is 0.030. Therefore, using the partial pressure equation, (0.030)(750 torr)= 22.5 torr.*

2. *To determine moles needed of $CO_2$, we simply use the PV=nRT equation. P=partial pressure $CO_2$, 22.5 torr, converted to atm=0.029 atm V= 145 L, R=Constant (0.08206 L\*atm/mol\*K), T= 25+273= 298K, Ans= 0.17 mol $CO_2$*

**41.** As temperature is increased, the equilibrium of a gaseous reaction will always:

    **A.** shift to the right.
    **B.** shift to the left.
    **C.** remain constant.
    **D.** The answer cannot be determined from the information given.

**42.** All of the following are true concerning a reaction at equilibrium EXCEPT:

    **A.** The rate of the forward reaction equals the rate of the reverse reaction.
    **B.** There is no change in the concentrations of both the products and the reactants.
    **C.** The activation energy has reached zero.
    **D.** The Gibbs free energy has reached a minimum.

**43.** Nitric acid is produced commercially by oxidation in the Oswald process. The first step of this process is shown below.

$$4NH_3(g) + 5O_2(g) \rightleftharpoons 4NO(g) + 6H_2O(g)$$

A container holds 4 moles of gaseous ammonia, 5 moles of gaseous oxygen, 4 moles of gaseous nitric oxide, and 6 moles of water vapor at equilibrium. Which of the following would be true if the container were allowed to expand at constant temperature?

    **A.** Initially during the expansion the forward reaction rate would be greater than the reverse reaction rate.
    **B.** The equilibrium would shift to the left.
    **C.** The partial pressure of oxygen would increase.
    **D.** The pressure inside the container would increase.

**44.** Nitrous oxide is prepared by the thermal decomposition of ammonium nitrate.

$$NH_4NO_3(s) \rightarrow N_2O(g) + 2H_2O(g)$$

The equilibrium constant for this reaction is:

    **A.** $[NH_4NO_3]/[N_2O][H_2O]^2$
    **B.** $[N_2O][H_2O]^2/[NH_4NO_3]$
    **C.** $[N_2O][H_2O]^2$
    **D.** $[N_2O][H_2O]$

**45.** Which of the following is true concerning a reaction that begins with only reactants and moves to equilibrium?

    **A.** The rate of the forward and reverse reactions decreases until equilibrium is reached.
    **B.** The rate of the forward and reverse reactions increases until equilibrium is reached.
    **C.** The rate of the forward reaction decreases, and the rate of the reverse reaction increases until equilibrium is reached.
    **D.** The rate of the forward reaction increases, and the rate of the reverse reaction decreases until equilibrium is reached.

Calcium carbonate decomposes to calcium oxide and carbon dioxide gas via the following reversible reaction:

$$CaCO_3(s) \leftrightarrows CaO(s) + CO_2(g)$$

Beaker I contains pure $CaCO_3$ and Beaker II contains pure CaO. The container is sealed.

**46.** Which of the following statements could be true about the system upon achieving equilibrium?

A. Beaker I is empty.
B. The number of calcium atoms in Beaker II has decreased.
C. The number of calcium atoms in Beaker II has increased.
D. Beaker II contains a mixture of $CaCO_3$ and CaO.

**47.** What is the equilibrium expression for the reaction?

A. $K = [CO_2]$

B. $K = [CaO][CO_2]$

C. $K = \dfrac{[CaO][CO_2]}{[CaCO_3]}$

D. $K = \dfrac{[CO_2]}{[CaCO_3]}$

**48.** The partial pressure equilibrium constant for the decomposition of $CaCO_3$ is $K_p$. If Beaker II is removed, under which of the following conditions would equilibrium NOT be achieved?

A. $K_p$ is less than the partial pressure of $CO_2$.
B. $K_p$ is greater than the partial pressure of $CO_2$.
C. $K_p$ is equal to the partial pressure of $CO_2$.
D. Equilibrium could not be achieved under any conditions because solid CaO is required to achieve equilibrium.

*Notes:*

# THERMODYNAMICS

## 3.1 Systems and Surroundings

Thermodynamics is the study of energy and its relationship to macroscopic properties of chemical systems. Thermodynamic functions are based on probabilities, and are valid only for systems composed of a large number of molecules. In other words, with few exceptions, the rules of thermodynamics govern complex systems containing many parts, and they cannot be applied to specific microscopic phenomena such as a single collision between two molecules.

Thermodynamic problems divide the universe into a **system** and its **surroundings**. The system is the section of the universe under study. The remainder of the universe outside the system is the surroundings. There are three systems: *open, closed,* and *isolated*. System definitions are based upon mass and energy exchange with the surroundings. Open systems exchange both mass and energy with their surroundings; closed systems exchange energy but not mass; and isolated systems do not exchange energy or mass (see Figure 3.1).

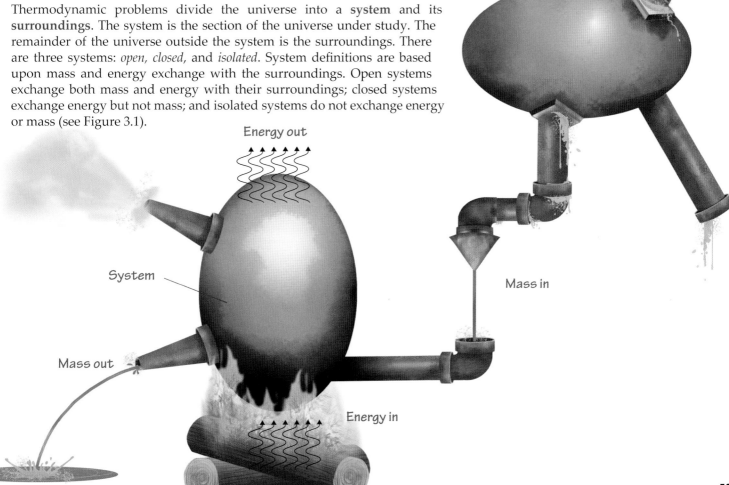

Energy out

System

Mass in

Mass out

Energy in

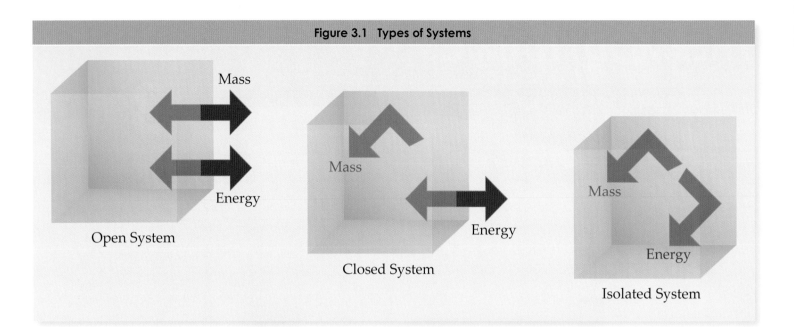

**Figure 3.1 Types of Systems**

Mass

Energy

Open System

Mass

Energy

Closed System

Mass

Energy

Isolated System

## 3.2 State Functions

A state is the physical condition of a system described by a specific set of thermodynamic property values. There are two types of properties that describe the macroscopic state of a system: 1) *extensive* and 2) *intensive*. Extensive properties are proportional to the size of the system; intensive properties are independent of the size of the system. If you combine two identical systems and a property is the same for both the single system and the combined system, that property is intensive. If a property doubles when the systems are combined, the property is extensive. If you divide one extensive property by another, the result is an intensive property. Volume $V$ and number of moles $n$ are examples of extensive properties. Pressure $P$ and temperature $T$ are examples of intensive properties.

The macroscopic state of any one-component fluid system in equilibrium can be described by just three properties, at least one of which is extensive. All other properties of the state of the same system can be derived from these three properties. For instance, if for a single component gas in equilibrium, pressure, temperature, and volume are known, all other properties which describe the state of that gas (such as number of moles, internal energy, enthalpy, entropy, and Gibbs energy) must have a specific single value. Since the state of a system can be described exactly by specific properties, it is not necessary to know how the state was formed or what reaction pathway brought a state into being. Such properties that describe the state of a system are called **state functions**. Properties that do not describe the state of a system, but depend upon the pathway used to achieve any state, are called *path functions*. Work and heat are examples of path functions.

> Extensive properties change with amount; intensive properties do not.
>
> You need to know what a state function is. State functions are pathway independent. They describe the state of a system. In other words, the change in a state property going from one state to another is the same regardless of the process used to change it.
>
> If you know three macroscopic properties of a one component system in equilibrium and at least one of which is extensive, then you know all the other properties.

## 3.3 Heat

There are only two ways to transfer energy between systems: **heat** ($q$) and **work** ($w$). Heat is the natural transfer of energy from a warmer body to a cooler body. Any energy transfer that is not heat is work.

Heat has three forms: conduction, convection, and radiation. **Conduction** is thermal energy transfer via molecular collisions. Conduction requires direct physical contact. In conduction, higher energy molecules of one system transfer some of their energy to the lower energy molecules of the other system via molecular collisions. Heat can also be conducted through a single object. An object's ability to conduct heat is called its thermal conductivity $k$. The thermal conductivity of an object depends upon its composition and, to a much lesser extent, its temperature. A slab of a given substance with face area $A$, length $L$, and thermal conductivity $k$ will conduct heat $Q$ from a hot body at temperature $T_h$ to a cold body at temperature $T_c$ in an amount of time $t$ (Figure 3.2).

> Heat is movement of energy via conduction, convection, or radiation always from hot to cold.

**Figure 3.2 Thermal Conductivity**

Slab     Hot reservoir     Cold reservoir

$$\frac{Q}{t} = kA\frac{T_h - T_c}{L}$$

> Given what we know about heat flow we can also understand Newton's Law of cooling, which states that the rate of cooling of a body is approximately proportional to the temperature difference between the body and its environment. A fresh cup of coffee initially cools quickly, since its temperature is much hotter than the surroundings, then cools more slowly as its temperature approaches room temperature.

$Q/t$ is the rate of heat flow or *heat current I*. The resistance to heat flow $R$ can be written as $L/(kA)$. A little algebra results in $\Delta T = IR$, an equation similar in form to Ohm's law in electricity. Like fluid flow in an ideal fluid (see Physics Lecture 6) or the flow of electric current through resistors in series (see Physics Lecture 7), in a steady state system the rate of heat flow is constant across any number of slabs between two heat reservoirs. In other words, if a series of slabs were lined up end to end between hot and cold reservoirs, the rate of heat flow, $Q/t$, would be the same in all slabs even if they each had different lengths, thicknesses, and different thermal conductivities (right side of Figure 3.2). Conservation of energy explains why. If the rate of energy transfer were not steady across all slabs, the slab that conducted heat the fastest would become cold. This is an impossibility. A cold slab could not conduct heat to warmer slabs because heat moves from hot to cold. It also follows that since the rate of energy transfer is the same for each slab, the order in which we place the slabs does not affect the overall conductivity. Finally, since the rate of heat flow is the same through each slab, a higher conductivity results in a lower temperature difference across any slab of a given length.

> The temperature difference in thermal conductivity is like the pressure difference in fluids or the potential difference in electricity. The rate of heat flow is like volume flow rate or current. Notice the similarity in these equations for the conduction of heat, fluids, and electricity.
>
> $$\Delta T = IR$$
> $$\Delta P = QR$$
> $$\Delta V = iR$$
>
> You can use this similarity to help you understand heat flow, fluid flow, and electron flow. For instance, in all cases, thicker conduits allow for greater flow, longer conduits impede flow, and flow rate depends upon the difference in a property of the reservoirs at either end of the conduit.

> Let's see how well you understand thermal conductivity. If I have a heavy blanket and a light blanket, which blanket should I place on top in order to stay warmer? The answer is: the order of the blankets will not make any difference since it will not change the rate of conduction.

### 3 Types of Heat

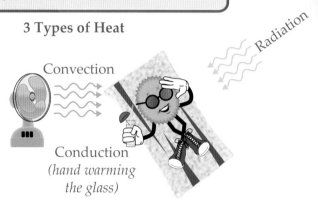

**Convection** is thermal energy transfer via fluid movements. In convection, differences in pressure or density drive warm fluid in the direction of cooler fluid. For instance, on a warm sunny day at the beach the air above the land heats up faster than the air above the water. As the air above the land warms, it becomes less dense and rises carrying its thermal energy with it. The cool air over the ocean moves in to fill the space over the land. The net result is circular current of air carrying the heat generated by the hot beach up and out to the cooler ocean. Ocean and air currents are common examples of convection (Figure 3.3).

**Radiation** is thermal energy transfer via electromagnetic waves. When metal is heated, it glows red, orange-yellow, white, and finally blue-white. The hot metal radiates visible electromagnetic waves. But even before the metal begins to glow, it radiates electromagnetic waves at a frequency too low to be visible to the human eye. In fact, all objects with a temperature above $0\,K$ radiate heat. The rate at which an object radiates electromagnetic radiation (its power $P$) depends upon its temperature and surface area, and is given by the *Stefan-Boltzman law*:

$$P = \sigma\varepsilon AT^4$$

where $A$ is the surface area of the object, $T$ is the temperature of the object in kelvins, $\sigma$ is the Stefan-Boltzman constant ($5.67 \times 10^{-8}$ W m$^{-2}$ K$^{-4}$), and $\varepsilon$ is the emissivity of the object's surface, which has a value between 0 and 1. If we substitute the temperature of the environment for the temperature of the object, we find the rate at which the object absorbs radiant heat from its environment. The net rate of heat transfer is the rate at which the body emits energy minus the rate at which it absorbs energy. The heat transfer will always be from hot to cold, and is given by:

$$P = \sigma\varepsilon A(T_e^4 - T_o^4)$$

where the $T_e$ is the temperature of the environment and $T_o$ is the temperature of the object

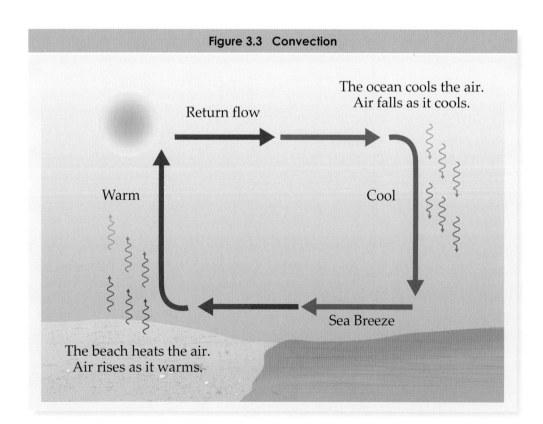

**Figure 3.3   Convection**

The ocean cools the air. Air falls as it cools.

Return flow

Warm

Cool

Sea Breeze

The beach heats the air. Air rises as it warms.

*Newton's law of cooling states* that the rate of cooling of a body is approximately proportional to the temperature difference between the body and its environment.

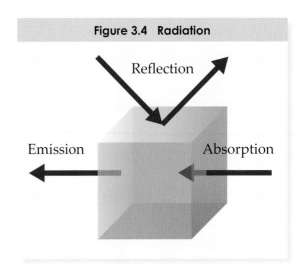

**Figure 3.4  Radiation**

Reflection

Emission

Absorption

> *P in the two equations is power, not pressure. Don't memorize these equations. Just recognize the relationships between power, temperature, and surface area.*

When radiation strikes an opaque surface, only a fraction is absorbed. The remainder is reflected. The fraction absorbed is indicated by the emissivity ε of the surface. The emissivity depends upon surface composition. As stated above, the emissivity of any surface is between 0 and 1. An object with an emissivity of 1 is called a blackbody radiator and is possible only in theory. All other objects reflect as well as absorb and radiate. Dark colors tend to radiate and absorb better than light colors, which tend to reflect.

Radiation is the only type of heat that transfers through a vacuum.

## Thought Provoker

*Notice that an object that radiates heat faster also absorbs heat faster. This means that an object that is a more efficient radiator comes to equilibrium with its environment more quickly. With this in mind, is it better to paint your house black or white?*

Answer:  See page 85

## 3.4  *Work*

From our discussion of heat, we know that work is any energy transfer that is not heat. In Physics Lecture 3 we defined work as an energy transfer due to a force. In physics problems, work typically changes the motion or position of a body. However, now we want to look at work as it applies to a chemical system at rest. A chemical system at rest can do two types of work, PV work and nonPV work. NonPV work done by a system at rest can take various forms, the most important of which for our purposes is electrical work. For now, we will examine PV work.

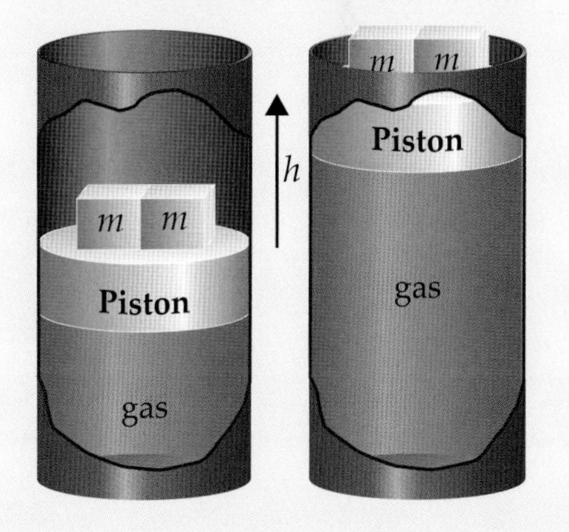

A system at rest may change its size or shape, but does not translate or change its position. A system at rest may still be able to do **PV work**. Imagine a cylinder full of gas compressed by a piston. If we place two blocks of mass *m* on the top of the piston and allow the gas pressure to lift the masses to a height *h*, the system has done work on the mass in the amount of the gravitational energy change 2*mgh*. Thus negative work has been done on the system. This work is called *PV* work because, at constant pressure, it is equal to the product of the pressure and the change in the volume (*P*Δ*V*).

**Figure 3.5  PV Work**

*m*  *m*

Piston

*h*

*m*  *m*

Piston

gas

gas

From Newton's second law *F=ma*, we know that if the masses are lifted at constant velocity, the force on the masses is constant and equal to 2*mg* (Figure 3.6, Case 1). From the definition of pressure *P* = *F/A*, we know that if the force remained constant, the pressure also remained constant. Constant pressure conditions allow us to calculate the work done using:

$$w = P\Delta V_{(\text{constant pressure})}$$

> This equation shows the work done by the gas. The work done on the gas is just the negative of the work done by the gas, so you might see this equation written with a negative sign as $w = -P\Delta V$.

The start point and end point of the expansion could also have been achieved by removing one mass, allowing the piston to rise, increasing the pressure to $2mg/A$ while holding the piston steady, and then replacing the second mass. This would have been a different pathway to achieve the same result. Since work is a path function, a different pathway results in a different amount of work; in this case the work would have been $mgh$ (Figure 3.6, Case 2).

Finally, the start and end point of the expansion could have been achieved by changing the pressure as the piston rose. In this case, $PV$ work is done, but it does not equal $P\Delta V$. To calculate the work in this case, you would need to use calculus (Figure 3.6, Case 3).

If we examine a pressure vs. volume graph for each case, the work done is given by the area under the curve. Notice that the area is different for each case.

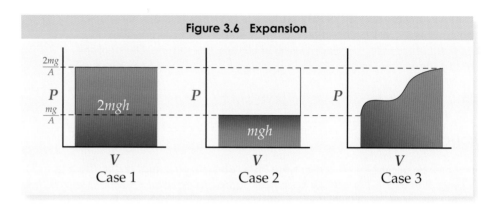

**Figure 3.6 Expansion**

### 3.5 The First Law of Thermodynamics

**The First Law of Thermodynamics** states that energy of the system and surroundings is always conserved. Thus any energy change to a system must equal the heat flow into the system plus the work done on the system.

$$\Delta E = q + w$$

**Warning:** We have chosen the convention where work on the system is positive. It is possible that an MCAT passage could define work done by the system as positive, in which case the formula would be $\Delta E = q - w$.

### 3.6 Heat Engines

Since all things contain internal energy, why not use that energy to do work? In other words, why not find hot objects, remove their internal energy as heat and do work with that internal energy? To do this, we need to design a heat engine. Let's start with our cylinder and piston system that we used to do *PV* work. First we turn the cylinder on its side. Now, instead of weights on the piston, we hold and move the piston with a force that we control. For simplicity we imagine a heat reservoir that has so much internal energy that the change in its temperature is negligible when it gives off heat to the gas in our piston. We adjust the force on our piston so that the external pressure is equal to the pressure of the gas, and we set the temperature of the gas equal to the temperature of our heat reservoir. Now our system, the gas, is in equilibrium with the surroundings. Without this equilibrium, we cannot proceed with a reversible process.

The cold reservoir shown in Figure 3.7 is not yet in contact with our system. Now we are ready to do work with internal energy from our heat reservoir.

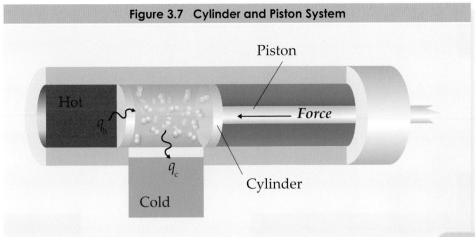

**Figure 3.7 Cylinder and Piston System**

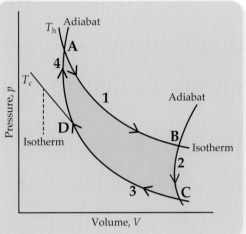

**Step 1:** Reversible isothermal expansion – from A to B. We decrease the force on our piston by an infinitesimal amount allowing the cylinder to expand infinitesimally slowly. Our system does PV work on the surroundings. Since energy leaves the gas as work, if this were the only energy transfer, the energy per mole of gas would be reduced, and the temperature of the gas would decrease; however, we have our system in thermal equilibrium with the heat reservoir, so the energy leaving the heat reservoir as work is replaced exactly by energy transferred as heat from the heat reservoir. Thus the temperature of the gas remains constant. The pressure of the gas, energy per volume, drops because the volume is expanding as energy remains constant. Since everything is done infinitely slowly, everything stays in equilibrium.

At first, it seems like we have solved the world's energy crisis! We are changing heat completely into work; we are able change the disordered energy of the random motion of molecules and completely into work. Since energy is never destroyed, if we could just continue this process indefinitely, we could do an endless amount of work continually recycling internal energy into useful work. But, of course, there are problems. The friction between the piston and the cylinder dissipates energy, but let's imagine that is negligible. Nevertheless, our cylinder doesn't go on forever; it has a finite length. Eventually, we have to push our piston back to the original starting point. If we just push the piston back to its starting point, we will have to do more work on the gas than the work that we got out of the gas because as the volume decreases the pressure will increase requiring a greater force over the same distance. Our work done will have been lost. This brings us to step 2.

**Step 2:** Reversible adiabatic expansion – from B to C. If we cool the gas before we push the piston back to its starting point, less work will be required to reset the piston, and our whole process will result in a net amount of work done on the surroundings. To cool the gas, we separate the heat reservoir from the gas, so no heat can be transferred to or from the gas. Now we continue to expand our gas infinitely slowly. This time, our gas must cool as we expand it because it is still transferring energy as work to the surroundings but no heat is replacing the transferred energy. Since the energy is decreasing and the volume is increasing, pressure, which is energy per volume, is also decreasing. At some point we stop the expansion and go to step 3.

## Figure 3.8   Net Work Completed

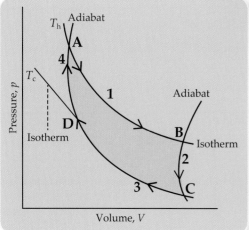

**Step 3.** Reversible isothermal compression – from C to D. Now our gas is at a lower pressure and temperature. We connect it to a cold reservoir at the same low temperature. We begin pushing the piston toward its original position by infinitesimally increasing the force. This force applied over a distance transfers energy to the gas via work; however, all the added energy transfers to cold reservoir as heat and the temperature, energy per mole, remains constant. The cold reservoir is so big that any change in its temperature is negligible. The pressure (energy per volume) rises because, although the energy remains constant, the volume is decreasing.

**Step 4.** Reversible adiabatic compression – from D to A. At a specific point before the piston reaches its original starting position, we will need to separate the cold reservoir from the gas. This is because we still need to increase the temperature of the gas back to its starting temperature. Once the cold reservoir is removed, the extra energy due to the work done on the gas has no place to go. As the energy per mole increases, the temperature increases. As the energy increases and the volume decreases, the pressure increases even faster. Finally, we arrive at the original starting point of the piston.

The four steps just described take the gas system through a complete cycle. By the end of each cycle the gas returns to its original volume, pressure, temperature, internal energy, and all other original state function values; there is no net change to the gas after one complete cycle. The result to the surroundings is that disordered random molecular energy has been ordered; <u>some</u> heat has been changed to work.

But there is another result. Some random molecular energy has also been transferred as heat from the hot reservoir to the cold reservoir. This energy is at a lower temperature. It is in the cold reservoir and, unless work is done, it can never be reused in the same heat reservoir from which it came. This energy has been 'downgraded'; it is less useful. Recall that this 'downgrading' occurred in Steps 3 and 4 of the cycle when we were returning the piston to its original condition. The 'downgrading' was the only way to complete the cycle and still get some net work done on the surroundings. So whenever we use energy, we 'downgrade energy'. Even though energy can never be destroyed, it cannot be endlessly reused. We haven't solved the world's energy crisis after all. This is the first of three ways to state the second law of thermodynamics: heat cannot be changed completely into work in a cyclical process.

Any machine that turns heat into work is called a heat engine. A heat engine can be diagrammed as shown in Figure 3.10. Notice that, via conservation of energy, the heat entering the engine $q_h$ must equal the net work done by the engine $w$ plus the heat leaving the engine $q_c$ ($q_h = w + q_c$).

We can reverse a heat engine to create a refrigerator. If we change the direction of the arrow in heat engine in Figure 3.10, the inside of the refrigerator is represented by the cold reservoir. Notice that the refrigerator requires work, and therefore the heat generated by the refrigerator is greater than the heat that it removes from the cold reservoir. This is the second of three ways to state **the second law of thermodynamics**: work is required to transfer energy from a cold reservoir to a hot reservoir.

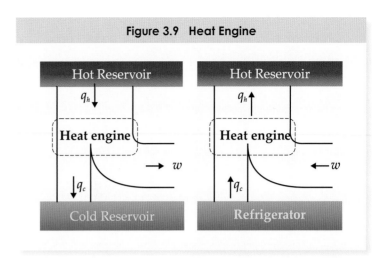

**Figure 3.9  Heat Engine**

The heat engine processes described earlier (isothermal expansion, adiabatic expansion, isothermal compression, and adiabatic compression) are all described as reversible. They are reversible because they are done in infinitesimal increments while the system is maintained in equilibrium. Such a process is called a Carnot cycle and such a heat engine is called a Carnot engine. The Carnot engine is an impossible ideal. It represents a maximum hypothetical efficiency for any heat engine. Because real processes are not infinitely slow, do not take place under perfect equilibrium conditions, and do have friction, no heat engine can be as efficient as a Carnot engine in converting heat to work. But even under the ideal conditions of the Carnot engine, heat cannot be completely converted to work.

The efficiency of a heat engine is the ratio of how much work it produces to how much heat input it requires to produce that work. The efficiency is given by:

$$e = \frac{w}{q_h} \qquad \text{or} \qquad e = 1 - \frac{T_c}{T_h}$$

(*Carnot* engine only)

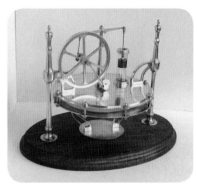

A Sterling engine converts heat energy to mechanical work.

where $e$ is the efficiency, $w$ is the work done by the engine, $q_h$ is the heat input into the system, and $T_h$ and $T_c$ are the temperatures of the hot and cold reservoirs respectively. The second equation applies only to a Carnot engine. From the equations, notice that the efficiency of any heat engine will be between 0 and 1 where 1 is perfect efficiency. Notice also from the second equation that the efficiency of an ideal heat engine gets closer to 1 as the $T_c$ becomes much colder than $T_h$, and could only reach 1 if $T_c$ is absolute zero or $T_h$ is infinitely large. Remember, the second equation applies only to an ideal engine, a Carnot Engine. All other heat engines will be less efficient. *Carnot's theorem* states that no engine operating between two heat reservoirs can be more efficient that a Carnot engine operating between the same two heat reservoirs.

By the way, as long as the processes are reversible, the engine is a Carnot engine regardless of how it is constructed or of what substance it is made or what kind of work it does; all Carnot engines are reversible engines with the same efficiency when placed between the same two heat reservoirs.

> Even under ideal conditions, heat cannot be completely converted to work. The second law of thermodynamics is not due to friction or man's inability to create a perfect machine. It is a result of the natural direction of energy flow.

**Thought Provoker**

*If we put a running refrigerator in a small closet, close the closet door and open the refrigerator door what will happen to the temperature of the closet?*

*Answer: See page 85*

> The heat engine stuff is given here in order to help you understand the relationship between heat and work. If it is on the MCAT, it will be explained in a passage. However, don't just ignore it. It is a possible passage topic and a good way to learn to understand heat and work. At the very least, know the second law of thermodynamics in terms of heat and work: heat cannot be completely converted to worked in a cyclical process.

**49.** Which of the following is true concerning an air conditioner that sits inside a thermally sealed room and draws energy from an outside power source?

  **A.** It requires more energy to cool the room than if part of the air conditioner were outside the room.
  **B.** It will require more time to cool the room than if part of the air conditioner were outside the room.
  **C.** It will require less energy to cool the room than if part of the air conditioner were outside the room.
  **D.** It cannot cool the room on a permanent basis.

**50.** Three blocks made from the same insulating material are placed between hot and cold reservoirs as shown below.

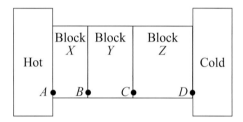

Which of the following must be true?

  **I.** The temperature difference between points *A* and *B* is less than the temperature difference between points *C* and *D*.
  **II.** The rate of heat flow through Block *X* is greater than the rate of heat flowing through Block *Z*.
  **III.** Switching the positions of Block *X* and Block *Z* would decrease the rate of heat flow.

  **A.** I only
  **B.** III only
  **C.** I and III only
  **D.** I, II, and III

**51.** Immediately upon bringing a hot piece of metal into a room, the heat is felt from 5 meters away. The type of heat transfer is probably:

  **A.** convection
  **B.** transduction
  **C.** radiation
  **D.** conduction

**52.** A box sliding down an incline increases in temperature due to friction. The name for this type of heat is:

  **A.** convection
  **B.** conduction
  **C.** radiation
  **D.** The energy transfer here is due to work and not to heat.

**53.** Which of the following gas properties is needed to calculate the work done by an expanding gas?

  **I.** The initial and final pressures
  **II.** The initial and final volumes
  **III.** The path followed during the expansion.

  **A.** I only
  **B.** II only
  **C.** I and II only
  **D.** I, II, and III

**54.** The heating bill for a homeowner is directly proportional to the rate at which heat is conducted out of the house and into the surroundings. The average temperature inside and outside of a house is measured on different months and recorded in Table 1.

| Month | Temperature outside (°C) | Temperature inside (°C) |
|-------|--------------------------|-------------------------|
| Nov | 8 | 22 |
| Dec | 5 | 25 |
| Jan | 3 | 20 |
| Feb | 13 | 26 |

For which month would the homeowner expect to have the largest heating bill?

  **A.** November
  **B.** December
  **C.** January
  **D.** February

**55.** A rigid container of constant volume is used to store compressed gas. When gas is pumped into the container, the pressure of the gas inside the container is increased and the temperature of the container also increases. Which statement is true of the work done on the container?

A. The work is equal to the increase in the pressure inside the container.
B. The work is equal to the increase in the temperature inside the container.
C. The work is equal to the sum of the pressure and temperature increases.
D. There is no work done on the container.

**56.** Under the best possible conditions, a steam engine will have an efficiency of slightly more than 20 percent. A normal steam engine has an efficiency of about 10 percent. This means that for a normal steam engine:

A. 10 percent of the input energy contributes to the work done by the engine.
B. 90 percent of the input energy contributes to the work done by the engine.
C. the internal temperature will increase by 10 percent during operation.
D. the internal temperature will increase by 90 percent during operation.

**STOP.**

## 3.7 Thermodynamic State Functions

To understand thermodynamics, you must be familiar with seven state functions:

**Table 3.1 Thermodynamic State Functions**

| Title | State Function | Prefix |
|-------|----------------|--------|
| 1 | Internal energy | $U$ |
| 2 | Temperature | $T$ |
| 3 | Pressure | $P$ |
| 4 | Volume | $V$ |
| 5 | Enthalpy | $H$ |
| 6 | Entropy | $S$ |
| 7 | Gibbs energy | $G$ |

Thermodynamic state functions are macroscopic properties of a system. Heat and work, which are also thermodynamic functions, are not state functions. Thermodynamic functions cannot be applied to systems on a molecular scale. The microscopic world (the motions of the individual molecules) is related to thermodynamic functions by statistics. Statistical predictions become more accurate as the number of subjects within a sample space increases. For instance, the more times you flip a coin, the more likely the total number heads will approach 50%. There are many millions of molecules within any macroscopic sample space making the statistically based thermodynamic functions highly useful for predictions on a macroscopic scale. However, if we try to apply thermodynamic functions to individual molecules, the sample space is far too small and our predictions will not be reliable.

## 3.8 Internal Energy

Internal energy is the collective energy of molecules measured on a microscopic scale. This energy includes vibrational energy, rotational energy, translational energy, electronic energy, intermolecular potential energy, and rest mass energy. Internal energy does not include macroscopic mechanical energies such as the kinetic energy of the entire system moving as one unit, or the gravitational energy of the entire system raised off the ground. In other words, internal energy is all the possible forms of energy imaginable on a molecular scale.

Perhaps because it is stationary, a glass of water sitting on a table appears to have no energy; however, it contains internal energy as well as gravitational potential energy.

**Figure 3.10  Internal Energy**

Temperature measures these parts of internal energy:

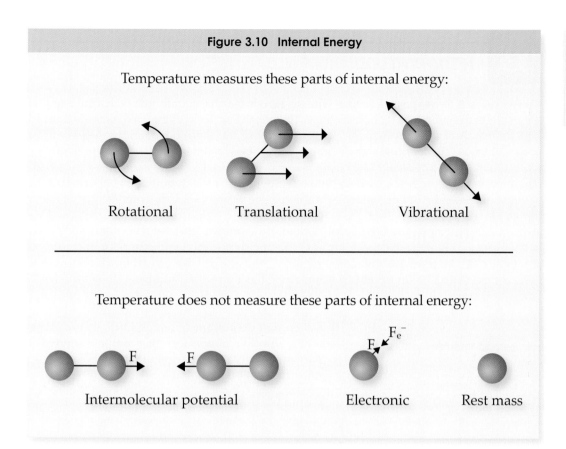

Rotational        Translational        Vibrational

Temperature does not measure these parts of internal energy:

Intermolecular potential        Electronic        Rest mass

*Vibrational energy* is created by the atoms vibrating within a molecule. Vibrational energy makes an insignificant contribution to internal energy for light diatomic molecules at temperatures below a few hundred Kelvin. Atoms in a monatomic gas have no vibrational energy.

*Rotational energy* is molecular movement where the spatial orientation of the body changes, while the center of mass remains fixed and each point within a molecule remains fixed relative to all other points. Atoms in a monatomic gas have no rotational energy.

*Translational energy* is the movement of the center of mass of a molecule.

*Electronic energy* is the potential electrical energy created by the attractions between the electrons and their respective nuclei. At temperatures below 5000 K, nearly all molecules are at their lowest electronic energy level. In a chemical reaction, the electronic energy accounts for the greatest change in internal energy. If no chemical reaction occurs, electronic energy remains nearly constant.

*Intermolecular potential energy* is the energy created by the intermolecular forces between molecular dipoles. For a gas at room temperature and pressure, intermolecular potential energy makes only a small contribution to internal energy, but at higher pressures, the contribution becomes significant. In liquids and solids, intermolecular potential energy is a substantial portion of internal energy.

*Rest mass energy* is the energy predicted by Einstein's famous equation $E = mc^2$. The sum of these energies for a very large group of molecules is called the internal energy.

If we have a closed system at rest with no electric or magnetic fields, the only energy change will be in internal energy, and the first law of thermodynamics can be rewritten as: $\Delta U = q + w$. For a reaction within such a system involving no change in volume, there is no work of any kind and the change in internal energy is equal to the heat: $\Delta U = q$ .

Internal energy is a state function. For an ideal gas, any state function can be expressed as a function of temperature and volume only. For an ideal gas, internal energy is independent of volume and is a function of temperature only.

The MCAT may refer to internal energy as 'heat energy', 'thermal energy', or even 'heat'. Heat energy and thermal energy are really the vibrational, rotational, and translational parts of internal energy. They are called thermal energy because they affect temperature. Heat is a transfer of energy, and using it as another name for internal energy can create confusion. Unfortunately, this is a common mistake.

## 3.9 Temperature

The *zeroth law of thermodynamics* states "Two systems in thermal equilibrium with a third system are in thermal equilibrium with each other." The zeroth law declares that two bodies in thermal equilibrium share a thermodynamic property, and that this thermodynamic property must be a state function. The thermodynamic property described by the zeroth law is **temperature**.

There are several methods used to define temperature. One definition is based upon the volume of an ideal gas. For an ideal gas the volume vs. temperature graph is exactly linear for any given pressure. Although all real gases become liquids at low temperatures, if we extrapolate back along the volume vs. temperature line, the lines for all pressures intersect at the same point on the temperature axis. We can define the temperature of this point as 0 K or –273°C. To establish the size of a unit of temperature, we can arbitrarily choose the freezing point and boiling point of water along the 1 atm line, and label those points 0°C and 100°C respectively.

> The zeroth law of thermodynamics just states that temperature exists. It's called the zeroth law because after the first, second, and third laws were already established it was realized that they depended upon a law that established the existence of temperature.

This and other definitions of temperature do not give a satisfying intuitive notion for what temperature really is. For an intuitive feel of temperature, we need to examine the motion of the molecules. When we look at internal energy, we see that the translational, rotational, and vibrational energies describe the energies of molecular motion. The sum of these energies is called *thermal energy*. Any increase in thermal energy increases temperature.

For a fluid, temperature is directly proportional to the translational kinetic energy of its molecules. Translational motion can be divided into three *degrees of freedom* or *modes*: 1) along the $x$ axis 2) along the $y$ axis and 3) along the $z$ axis. The *equipartition theory* states that for a normal system each mode of motion will have the same average energy and that the energy will be equal to $\frac{1}{2}kT$, where $T$ is the temperature, and $k$ is the Boltzmann constant ($1.38 \times 10^{-23}$ J K$^{-1}$). The Boltzmann constant k is related to the ideal gas constant R by Avagadro's number $N_A$: $R = N_A k$. Since there are three modes of kinetic energy each averaging $\frac{1}{2}kT$ joules, the average kinetic energy of a single molecule in any fluid (real or ideal) is given by: This is the same equation found in Lecture 2.

$$K.E._{\text{avg per mole}} = \frac{3}{2}RT$$

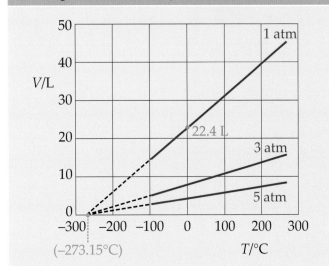

**Figure 3.11  Gas Temperature and Volume**

Volume vs. Temperature for one mole of N$_2$ gas extrapolated back to zero volume

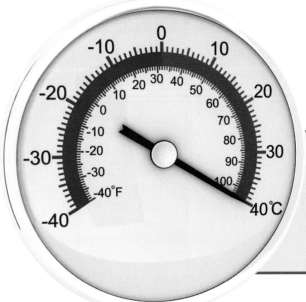

> Think of temperature as a measurement of how fast the molecules are moving or vibrating. When substances get hot, it is because their molecules move faster.
>
> MCAT won't test the equipartition theory. Just know the formula: $K.E. = \frac{3}{2}RT$

If we multiply this equation by Avogadro's number we arrive at the average translational kinetic energy for a mole of molecules in any fluid: The equipartition theorem is derived from classical physics and breaks down when quantum effects are significant. Quantum effects are greater for rotation than for translation, and greater still for vibration. The molecules of a solid do not translate or rotate; they vibrate. For solids at high temperatures where quantum effects are less important, temperature is proportional to the average kinetic energy of the vibration of molecules about their equilibrium position. For solids at low temperatures, there is deviation from this rule due to quantum effects.

The greater the random translational kinetic energy of gas molecules per mole, the greater the temperature. So loosely speaking, temperature can be thought of as the thermal energy per mole of molecules. Recall that when we divide one extensive property by another, we get an intensive property. Energy and number of moles are extensive properties. This makes temperature an intensive property, so when we connect two identical systems the temperature does not change; we double the thermal energy, but we also double the number of moles, so thermal energy per mole remains constant.

The MCAT will use two measurement systems for temperature: degrees Celsius and Kelvin. Celsius is just the centigrade system with a new name. At 1 atm, water freezes at 0°C and boils at 100°C. The lowest possible temperature is called absolute zero, and is approximately –273°C. To find approximate Kelvin from degrees Celsius, simply add 273. An increase of 1°C is equivalent to an increase of 1 K.

Virtually all physcial properties change with temperature.

> Molecules in a solid vibrate faster as temperature increases.

> When in doubt, use kelvin. In chemistry, you are always safe using the Kelvin scale because the Kelvin scale is absolute.
>
> Changing the temperature changes nearly everything.

> It is not completely accurate, but accurate enough for the MCAT to think of temperature as a measure of the thermal energy per mole of molecules. The greater the thermal energy per mole, the greater the temperature.

## 3.10 Pressure

Loosely speaking, pressure of an ideal gas is the random translational kinetic energy per volume. Pressure is an intensive state function. Pressure and volume are discussed in depth in Chemistry Lecture 2 and Physics Lecture 5.

> The greater the random translational kinetic energy of gas molecules per volume, the greater the pressure.

*Notes:*

**Enthalpy** is defined as an equation rather than as a description of a property. Enthalpy $H$ is defined as:

$$H \equiv U + PV$$

where $U$ represents internal energy. From our inexact but intuitive concept of pressure as the random translational kinetic energy per unit volume, we see that enthalpy actually counts random translational kinetic energy twice! Although enthalpy is measured in units of energy (joules), enthalpy itself is not conserved like energy. Enthalpy of the universe does not remain constant.

Since $U$, $P$, and $V$ are state functions, enthalpy is also a state function. Like internal energy, for an ideal gas enthalpy depends only on temperature. Enthalpy is an extensive property, so when we connect two identical systems the total enthalpy doubles.

As with many state functions, we are interested in the *change* in enthalpy and not its absolute value. For the MCAT, we will be interested in the change in enthalpy under constant pressure conditions only:

$$\Delta H = \Delta U + P\Delta V \quad (const.\ P)$$

For a system at rest recall that the first law of thermodynamics can be written as $\Delta U = w + q$. Work can be either non$PV$ work ($w_{nonPV}$) or $PV$ work ($w_{PV}$), so we have $\Delta U = w_{nonPV} + w_{PV} + P\Delta V + q$. At constant pressure in a reversible process, $PV$ work done by the system reduces energy in the system and is given by $w = -P\Delta V$. Substituting for $\Delta U$ in our equation for change in enthalpy gives:

$$\Delta H = [w_{nonPV} - P\Delta V + q] + P\Delta V$$

$$\Delta H = w_{nonPV} + q_{(const.\ P,\ closed\ system\ at\ rest,\ PV\ work\ only)}$$

So at constant pressure, enthalpy change of a system at rest is a measure of non$PV$ work and heat. These are the conditions inside a living cell. Non$PV$ work is mainly electrical work such as that done by contracting muscles, firing neurons, and batteries. If no non$PV$ work is performed, and only $PV$ work is performed, enthalpy change is the heat flow into the system at constant pressure.

$$\Delta H = q_{(constant\ pressure,\ closed\ system\ at\ rest)}$$

Many liquid and solid chemical reactions performed in the lab take place in systems at rest at constant pressure (1 atm). Remember that at constant volume $\Delta U = q$, which means that at constant volume and constant pressure $\Delta U \cong \Delta H$.

Heat of hydration of copper sulphate. Water being poured from a test tube onto anhydrous copper (II) sulphate (white). The copper (II) sulphate forms hydration bonds with the water in an exothermic reaction, resulting in hydrated copper (II) sulphate (blue). The heat of the reaction is enough to produce steam and disturb the powder.

> Enthalpy cannot be intuited. You must rely completely on the equation.

> For an ideal gas, enthalpy and internal energy depend ONLY on temperature. Enthalpy increases with temperature.

## Thought Provoker

*Galvanic cells (Chemistry Lecture 7) do nonPV work, so we cannot use $\Delta H = q$ for such reactions.*

*For reactions at constant volume, the internal energy change is equal to the heat, so for reactions that have both constant volume and constant pressure, enthalpy change approximately equals internal energy change.*

*What if we mix two chemicals and the reaction produces a gas to the open air? Can we still use $\Delta H = q$?*

*Answer: See page 85*

There are no absolute enthalpy values, so scientists have assigned enthalpy values to compounds based upon their standard state. **Standard state** should not be confused with STP. Standard state is a somewhat complicated concept that varies with phase and other factors and even has differnet values based upon which convention you choose to follow. As usual, we can simplify things greatly for the MCAT. Recall that a 'state' is described by a specific set of thermodynamic property values. For a pure solid or liquid, the standard state is the **reference form** of a substance at any chosen temperature $T$ and a pressure of 1 bar (about 750 torr or exactly 105 pascals). The reference form is usually the form that is most stable at 1 bar and $T$. For a pure gas there is an additional requirement that the gas behave like an ideal gas. An element in its standard state at 25°C is arbitrarily assigned an enthalpy value of 0 J/mol. From this value we can assign enthalpy values to compounds based upon the change in enthalpy when they are formed from raw elements in their standard states at 25°C. Such enthalpy values for compounds are called standard enthalpies of formation. The **standard enthalpy of formation** $\Delta H^\circ_f$ is the change in enthalpy for a reaction that creates one mole of that compound from its raw elements in their standard state. The symbol '$\circ$' (called naught) indicates standard state conditions. Standard enthalpies of formation can be found by experiment, and are available in books. An example of the enthalpy of formation of water is:

$$H_2(g) + \tfrac{1}{2}O_2(g) \rightarrow H_2O(l) \quad \Delta H^\circ_f = -285.8 \text{ kJ/mol}$$

$$\Delta H = q \quad \text{(const. } P \text{, closed system at rest, } PV \text{ work only)}$$

Since, in many reactions in the lab, enthalpy approximates heat, the change in enthalpy from reactants to products is often referred to as the heat of reaction.

$$\Delta H^\circ_{reaction} = \Delta H^\circ_{f\ products} - \Delta H^\circ_{f\ reactants}$$

Since enthalpy is a state function, the change in enthalpy when converting one group of compounds to another is not dependent upon what reaction or even series of reactions take place. The change in enthalpy depends only on the identities and thermodynamic states of the initial and final compounds. Thus, in any reaction, the steps taken to get from reactants to products do not affect the total change in enthalpy. **Hess' law** states "The sum of the enthalpy changes for each step is equal to the total enthalpy change regardless of the path chosen." For example:

| | | |
|---|---|---|
| $N_2 + O_2 \rightarrow 2NO$ | $\Delta H = 180 \text{ kJ}$ | step 1 |
| $2NO + O_2 \rightarrow 2NO_2$ | $\Delta H = -112 \text{ kJ}$ | + step 2 |
| $N_2 + 2O_2 \rightarrow 2NO_2$ | $\Delta H = 68 \text{ kJ}$ | = complete reaction |

Hess's law also indicates that a forward reaction has exactly the opposite change in enthalpy as the reverse. If the enthalpy change is positive, the reaction is said to be **endothermic**; if it is negative, it is said to be **exothermic**. If we consider a reaction where the change in enthalpy is equal to the heat (a constant pressure reaction), then an exothermic reaction produces heat flow to the surroundings, while an endothermic reaction produces heat flow to the system.

> Don't confuse standard state and STP.
>
> If MCAT says 'standard state', you assume 1 bar (about 1 atm). The temperature will probably be 25°C but it doesn't have to be. If it is a gas, adjust the volume for ideal behavior. Now just ask yourself, "Under these conditions is it a gas, liquid, or solid?" Your answer to this question is the reference form.

## Figure 3.12   A One Step Reaction

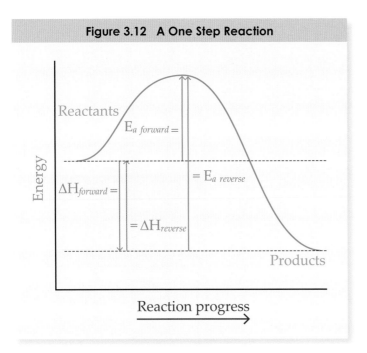

We can see this graphically if we compare the progress of a reaction with the energy of the molecules. (Due to the close relationship between internal energy and enthalpy, the term energy is used loosely for these types of graphs. You may see the y axis labeled as enthalpy, Gibbs free energy, or simply energy.) You can see from the graph that if the reaction progress is reversed, the enthalpy change is exactly reversed. Notice that there is an initial increase in energy regardless of which direction the reaction moves. This increase in energy is called the **activation energy** (the same activation energy as in Chemistry Lecture 2). The peak of this energy hill represents the molecules in a **transition state** where the old bonds are breaking and new bonds are forming. The transition state occurs during the reaction collision. Do not confuse the transition state with intermediates, which are the products of the first step in a two step reaction. A two step reaction has two humps as shown in Figure 2.8 in Chapter 2. The intermediates exist in the trough between the two humps.

Notice, on an energy diagram, how a catalyst lowers the activation energy. The activation energy for both the forward and the reverse reactions is lowered. Although the relative amount by which the activation energies are lowered is different, if we used the Arrhenius equation (Chemistry Lecture 2) to find the new rate constants, we would find that the rate constants are raised by the same relative amounts; thus, equilibrium is unaffected by a catalyst. For the MCAT you must remember that a catalyst affects the rate and not the equilibrium. Notice that a catalyst does not affect the enthalpy change either.

## Figure 3.13   Effect of Catalyst

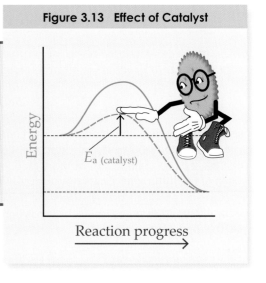

A computer interfaced sensor measuring the temperature change of an exothermic/exergonic reaction between aluminum foil and cupric chloride. The graph shows a steady increase in the temperature of the system after the aluminum foil was added. The reaction occurs spontaneously in water. The enthalpy change indicates that it is chemically an exothermic process. The release of free energy in the form of heat indicates that the reaction is exergonic.

How will you know what $\Delta H$ is for a reaction on the MCAT? There are five possible ways:

1. The problem or passage just tells you the $\Delta H$ for the reaction (Salty's favorite).

2. The heat can be measured with a calorimeter (see Lecture 5.3), and the heat is the $\Delta H$.

3. For some reactions, the sign of $\Delta H$ can be intuited, even if the MCAT doesn't expect you to know the magnitude. For example, we know combustion reactions release heat, so they have a negative $\Delta H$. We can also do this for phase changes (see Lecture 5.4). For example, we know that in order to melt something, you have to add heat to it. Melting, therefore, has a positive $\Delta H$.

4. If given a table of bond energies, you can keep track of how many of each type of bond is broken and formed during the course of a reaction. Since forming bonds releases energy and breaking bonds requires the input of energy, you can total up the net energy (heat) absorbed or released during the reaction.

5. You can calculate the $\Delta H$ for a reaction using standard enthalpies of formation ($\Delta H_f^\circ$).

*Notes:*

**57.** What is the enthalpy change in the following reaction?

| Compound | $\Delta H_f^\circ$ |
|----------|--------------------|
| $CH_4(g)$ | –75 kJ/mol |
| $CO_2(g)$ | –394 kJ/mol |
| $H_2O(l)$ | –286 kJ/mol |

$$CH_4(g) + 2O_2(g) \rightarrow CO_2(g) + 2H_2O(l)$$

- **A.** –755 kJ
- **B.** –891 kJ
- **C.** –1041 kJ
- **D.** 891 kJ

**58.** Which of the following properties of a gaseous system affect its enthalpy?

- **I.** pressure
- **II.** volume
- **III.** internal energy

- **A.** III only
- **B.** I and II only
- **C.** II and III only
- **D.** I, II, and III

**59.** A catalyst will change all of the following EXCEPT:

- **A.** enthalpy
- **B.** activation energy
- **C.** rate of the forward reaction
- **D.** rate of the reverse reaction

**60.** In an exothermic reaction, which of the following will most likely increase the ratio of the forward rate to the reverse rate?

- **A.** adding thermal energy to the system
- **B.** removing thermal energy from the system
- **C.** using a catalyst
- **D.** lowering the activation energy

**61.** The heats of combustion for graphite and diamond are as follows:

$$C_{graphite}(s) + O_2(g) \rightarrow CO_2(g) \quad \Delta H = -394 \text{ kJ}$$

$$C_{diamond}(s) + O_2(g) \rightarrow CO_2(g) \quad \Delta H = -396 \text{ kJ}$$

Diamond spontaneously changes to graphite. What is the change in enthalpy accompanying the conversion of two moles of diamond to graphite?

- **A.** –790 kJ
- **B.** –4 kJ
- **C.** 2 kJ
- **D.** 4 kJ

**62.** The standard enthalpy of formation for liquid water is:

$$H_2(g) + \tfrac{1}{2}O_2(g) \rightarrow H_2O(l) \quad \Delta H^\circ_f = -285.8 \text{ kJ/mol}$$

Which of the following could be the standard enthalpy of formation for water vapor?

- **A.** –480.7 kJ/mol
- **B.** –285.8 kJ/mol
- **C.** –241.8 kJ/mol
- **D.** +224.6 kJ/mol

**63.** For a particular reversible reaction, the forward process is exothermic and the reverse process is endothermic. Which of the following statements must be true about this reaction?

- **A.** The forward reaction will be spontaneous under standard conditions.
- **B.** The reverse reaction will be spontaneous under standard conditions.
- **C.** The activation energy will be greater for the forward reaction than for the reverse reaction.
- **D.** The activation energy will be greater for the reverse reaction than for the forward reaction.

**64.** Sulfur dioxide reacts with oxygen in a reversible reaction to form sulfur trioxide as shown.

$$2SO_2(g) + O_2(g) \rightleftharpoons 2SO_3(g) \quad \Delta H^\circ = -200 \text{ kJ}$$

If the temperature at which the reaction takes place is increased, which of the following will take place?

- **A.** The rates of both the forward and reverse reactions will increase.
- **B.** Only the rate of the forward reaction will increase.
- **C.** Only the rate of the reverse reaction will increase.
- **D.** The rates of neither the forward nor reverse reactions will increase.

## 3.12 Entropy

If you have studied entropy before, you have probably heard the following example: "Over time, a clean room will tend to get dirty. This is entropy at work." Entropy is nature's tendency toward disorder. A better definition of entropy incorporates the concept of probability. **Entropy (S)** is nature's tendency to create the most probable situation that can occur within a system. For instance, imagine four identical jumping beans that bounce randomly back and forth between two containers. If we label each bean A, B, C, and D respectively, we will find that the most likely situation is to have two beans in each container. The least likely situation is to have all four beans in either of the containers. For example, if we choose the left container, there is only one way for all four beans to be in the left container, but there are 6 possible ways that two beans can be in each container. Two beans in each container is six times more likely than four beans in the left container. Since the two-bean container situation is more likely, it has greater entropy.

If we replace the four jumping beans with millions of molecules moving randomly back and forth between two glass spheres connected by a glass tube, you should be able to see how the odds against having all the molecules in one sphere become astronomical. The odds are so poor, in fact, that the second law of thermodynamics states that it will never happen without some outside intervention, namely work. The third way to state **the second law of thermodynamics** is "The entropy of an isolated system will never decrease."

We can apply the second law of thermodynamics to any type of system if we recall that the surroundings of any system include everything that is not in the system. Thus, the system and the surroundings together make up the entire universe. The universe itself is an isolated system. Therefore, the sum of the entropy changes of any system and its surroundings equals the entropy change of the universe, which must be equal to or greater than zero.

$$\Delta S_{system} + \Delta S_{surroundings} = \Delta S_{universe} \geq 0$$

So the entropy of a system can decrease, only if, at the same time, the entropy of the surroundings increases by a greater or equal magnitude. Entropy is a state function and an extensive property.

> Entropy, and not energy, dictates the direction of a reaction.

### Figure 3.14 Probability in Relation to Entropy

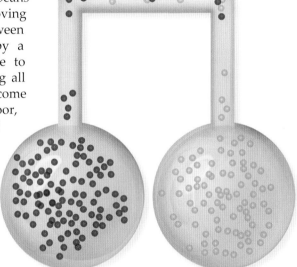

Six possible situations with two beans in one pan.

Only one possible situation with four beans in the left pan.

> The second law of thermodynamics is a funny law because it could be violated, but it is so unlikely to be violated that we say it won't be violated no matter what.

An intuitive way to view entropy is as nature's effort to spread energy evenly between systems. Nature likes to decrease the energy of a system when energy is high relative to the nearby surroundings and to increase energy of a system when energy is low relative to the energy of the nearby surroundings. A warm object will lose energy to its surroundings when placed in a cool room, but the same object will gain energy when placed in a hot room. If we consider the energy of the universe, no energy is gained or lost in either process. Instead, energy is just spread out. This means that it is entropy and not energy that drives reactions in a given direction. The second law of thermodynamics tells us that entropy of the universe is the driving force that dictates whether or not a reaction will proceed. A reaction can be unfavorable in terms of enthalpy, or even energy, and still proceed, but a reaction must increase the entropy of the universe in order to proceed.

Entropy is an extensive property; It increases with amount of substance. All other factors being equal, entropy increases with number, volume, and temperature. On the MCAT, if a reaction increases the number of gaseous molecules, then that reaction has positive entropy (for the reaction system, not necessarily for the surroundings or the universe). The greater the temperature of a substance the greater its entropy.

**The third law of thermodynamics** assigns by convention a zero entropy value to any pure substance (either an element or a compound) at absolute zero and in internal equilibrium. At absolute zero, atoms have very little motion. Absolute zero temperature is unattainable.

> Sometimes it's useful to think of entropy as nature trying to spread energy evenly throughout the universe.

A time lapse photo of the forces of nature working to increase entropy.

The units for entropy are J/K. Entropy change is defined mathematically by the infinitesimal change in heat $q_{rev}$ per kelvin in a reversible process. So at constant temperature, we have:

$$\Delta S = \frac{q_{rev}}{T}$$

Notice that change in entropy is defined for a reversible process. In an irreversible process between the same two states this equation will not apply. The heat $q$ will be different for an irreversible process because heat is pathway dependent. However, the entropy change $\Delta S$ will be the same for any process between the same two states, reversible or not. Thus $\Delta S$ for an irreversible process can be found by imagining a reversible process between the same two states and finding the heat transfer for that reversible process. Since entropy is a state function, the change in entropy for any process will be the same as the change in entropy for a reversible process between the same two states.

> Absolute entropy is undefined, however, by convention, pure substances in equilibrium are assigned an entropy approaching zero as they approach 0 Kelvin. These conventional entropy values are often mistakenly called absolute entropies.

Imagine what happens when you slide a box across the floor. The kinetic energy of the box is dissipated into internal energy of the box and floor via molecular collisions collectively called friction. Of course, energy is conserved; the increase in internal energy equals the initial kinetic energy. Now imagine the reverse reaction: the molecules of the floor and the box happen to be moving in a coordinated fashion so as to collide and make the stationary box suddenly start moving. The internal energy of the molecules becomes kinetic energy. Why doesn't this happen in real life? Energy is still conserved in the reverse reaction, so there is no violation of the first law of thermodynamics. The only reason boxes don't spontaneously start sliding across the floor is due to the decrease in entropy which would accompany such a reaction.

*Look out, Crouton! Reverse friction could start these boxes moving and crush you like a grape!*

*But there's no need to fear! Captain Entropy is here!*

## 3.13 *Reversibility*

From universal entropy change, we have a *thermodynamic definition of reversibility*. Imagine a reaction in an isolated system. Since the system is isolated, the forward reaction does not affect the surroundings and can change the entropy of only the system and not the surroundings. Entropy is a state function, so, if we run the reaction exactly in reverse, we bring the system back to its original state. Now the system must have the same entropy as when it started the forward reaction. However, the second law of thermodynamics says that the entropy of an isolated system cannot decrease for any reaction, so in order to be able to run the reaction both in the forward and the reverse direction, the entropy change must be zero in both directions. Thus, for any reversible reaction within an isolated system, the entropy change must be zero. The universe is an isolated system, so the entropy change of the universe must be zero for any reversible reaction.

In real life, reversible reactions do not happen; all known reactions and processes are accompanied by a positive change in the entropy of the universe. In the real world, all reactions are thermodynamically irreversible. However, hypothetically we can imagine a reversible reaction. A hypothetical reversible reaction will be a quasi-static process; one where the system is in equilibrium with the surroundings at all times. Any heat transfer must occur while the system and surroundings are at the same temperature. Pressure differences where PV work is done must be infinitesimal. All changes to the system will be infinitesimal and require an infinite amount of time.

Unfortunately, *alternative definitions of reversibility* are also used outside thermodynamics. Recall that thermodynamics deals with macroscopic properties, large numbers of molecules. If, instead, we examine a system microscopically, on the scale of two molecules reacting with each other, entropy is undefined. The second law of thermodynamics does not work on this scale and all reactions on a microscopic scale must be considered reversible from the stand point of classical mechanics. From the microscopic point of view, collisions

> If the entropy of an isolated system cannot decrease, the universal entropy change for any reversible reaction must be zero in both directions.

> The equilibrium point is the point of maximum universal entropy.

between individual molecules are exact opposites of their reverse collisions and there is no law in classical physics that favors one direction over another. All molecular collisions are reversible. On the microscopic scale, this definition of reversibility is contradictory to the thermodynamic definition. The macroscopic principles of thermodynamics should not be applied to the microscopic world. However, the reverse is not true; predictions about the macroscopic world can be made based upon microscopic conditions. Recall from Chemistry Lecture 2 that equilibrium is achieved when the rate of the forward reaction equals the rate of the reverse reaction. This is the point of greatest universal entropy. Reactions at equilibrium have achieved maximum universal entropy.

But there is still another *alternative to the meaning of reversibility*. Any chemical reaction has a threshold activation energy that must be reached before a reaction can take place. This threshold energy is related to the energy required to break chemical bonds before new bonds can be formed. Since products and reactants may be at different energy levels, more energy is required to reach the threshold energy from one side of the reaction than from the other. If the required energy is much greater, the reaction may be considered irreversible. This definition of irreversibility focuses on the system, and not on the universe. It is subjective and not directly related to the exact thermodynamic definition of reversibility as we have defined it.

## 3.14 Gibbs Free Energy

Just for a moment, let's define three types of equilibrium: mechanical, material, and thermal. A system is in mechanical equilibrium when it is not accelerating. A system is in material equilibrium when no net chemical reaction is occurring, and there is no matter transferring within the system. A system is in thermal equilibrium when its temperature is the same throughout. A system can also be in thermal equilibrium with its surroundings, which simply means that it is the same temperature as its surroundings. For a system to be in thermodynamic equilibrium it must be in mechanical, material, and thermal equilibrium.

> The different kinds of equilibrium will not be tested by the MCAT. It is given here only to help you understand Gibbs Energy.

The equilibrium achieved by maximizing the entropy of the universe, $\Delta S_{univ} = \Delta S_{surr} + \Delta S_{sys}$, is material equilibrium. A closed system undergoing an irreversible chemical reaction at constant pressure and temperature is in thermal and mechanical equilibrium, but not material equilibrium. The surroundings at the same temperature as the system are not undergoing an irreversible reaction and are in thermal, mechanical, and material equilibrium. If heat flows into the system, the heat flow is reversible from the standpoint of the surroundings, thus $\Delta S_{surr} = q_{surr}/T$. We also know that $q_{surr} = -q_{sys}$, so $\Delta S_{surr} = -q_{sys}/T$. Pressure is constant, so $\Delta H_{sys} = q_{sys}$. Substituting we have $\Delta S_{surr} = -\Delta H_{sys}/T$. Plugging the result into $\Delta S_{univ} = \Delta S_{surr} + \Delta S_{sys}$ gives:

> Do you remember that enthalpy is a man-made concept? Here's a reason why scientists made up enthalpy: It is easier to measure changes in your chosen system than in the entire universe of your surroundings. Measuring the enthalpy change of the system sometimes allows you to calculate the entropy change of the surroundings. Under certain conditions $\Delta S_{surr} = -\Delta H_{sys}/T$

$$\Delta S_{universe} = \frac{-\Delta H_{system}}{T} + \Delta S_{system}$$

If we multiply through by $-T$, and substitute $\Delta G$ for $-\Delta S_{universe}T$, we have the important MCAT equation for **Gibbs free energy (G)**:

$$\Delta G = \Delta H - T\Delta S \qquad \boxed{\text{Important MCAT equation!}}$$

> $\Delta G = 0$ means equilibrium. Negative $\Delta G$ indicates a spontaneous reaction.

All state functions in this equation refer to the system and not the surroundings. Notice that $\Delta G_{sys} = -T\Delta S_{universe}$. Since any real process moves in the direction of increasing $\Delta S_{universe}$, we say that a reaction that increases $\Delta S_{universe}$ is spontaneous. Since we require a positive $\Delta S_{universe}$ for a spontaneous reaction, it follows that a negative $\Delta G$ is required for a spontaneous reaction. Since $\Delta S_{universe} = 0$ indicates equilibrium, $\Delta G = 0$ is required for equilibrium. However, there are limitations attached to $\Delta G$ that were created when we derived our equation. At constant temperature and pressure, PV work only, for a closed system G decreases as the reaction approaches equilibrium. Nevertheless, for the MCAT, a negative $\Delta G$ will be good enough to indicate a spontaneous reaction.

Gibbs energy is an extensive property and a state function. It is not conserved in the sense of the conservation of energy law. An isolated system can change its Gibbs energy. The Gibbs energy represents the maximum non-*PV* work available from a reaction, hence the name 'free energy'. Again, contracting muscles, transmitting nerves, and batteries are some examples of things that do only non-*PV* work, making Gibbs energy a useful quantity when analyzing these systems.

You must know the Gibbs function, and, most importantly, that a negative $\Delta G$ indicates a spontaneous reaction. Realize that the terms $\Delta G$, $\Delta H$, and $\Delta S$ in the Gibbs function refer to changes in the system and not the surroundings. Also realize that since Gibbs energy is a function of enthalpy and entropy, like enthalpy and entropy, Gibbs energy of the universe is not conserved.

By the way, the negative of the Gibbs free energy is the amount of non*PV* work available in a completely reversible process, and we know that completely reversible processes are not quite possible in the real world. In other words, the actual amount of non*PV* work that we will get out of the system is always something less than $-\Delta G$.

If a reaction produces a positive change in enthalpy and a negative change in entropy, the reaction can never be spontaneous. Conversely, if a reaction produces a negative change in enthalpy and a positive change in entropy, it must be spontaneous. If the signs of both enthalpy and entropy are the same for a reaction, the spontaneity of the reaction will depend upon temperature. A higher temperature will favor the direction favored by entropy. Remember, these changes are changes in the system and not the surroundings.

To finish this lecture, let's summarize the laws of thermodynamics. It's not so important to memorize the laws, as it is to understand them and keep them in mind. The first and second laws are the important ones for the MCAT.

**0th Law:** Two bodies in thermal equilibrium with the same system are in thermal equilibrium with each other. (In other words, temperature exists and is a state function.)

**1st Law:** The energy of an isolated system is conserved for any reaction.

**2nd Law:** The entropy of the universe increases for any reaction.

**3rd Law:** A perfect crystal at zero kelvin is assigned an entropy value of zero. All other substances and all temperatures have a positive entropy value. (Zero kelvin is unattainable.)

**Summary:**
Think of heat and work as the only two ways to change the energy of a system. Together heat and work result in the change in internal energy of a system at rest. Think of temperature as thermal energy per mole. Think of pressure as thermal energy per volume. Think of enthalpy as $U + PV$, or think of change in enthalpy at constant pressure as the heat. Think of entropy as the spreading out of energy. Entropy increases with temperature, volume, and number. Think of Gibbs Energy change as the negative of the maximum amount of energy available to do non*PV* work such as electrical work in a cell.

## 3.15 Equation Summary

| Equations |
|---|

### Work

$$w = P\Delta V_{\text{(constant pressure)}}$$

### The First Law of Thermodynamics

$$\Delta E = q + w$$

### The Average Kinetic Energy of a Single Molecule

$$K.E._{\text{avg}} = \frac{3}{2}RT$$

### Enthalpy: Under Constant Conditions, No Change in Pressure

$$\Delta H = \Delta U + P\Delta V \quad (\text{const. } P)$$

### Enthalpy: No Change in Pressure, Closed System

$$\Delta H = q$$

### Heat of Reaction

$$\Delta H^\circ_{reaction} = \Delta H^\circ_{f\ products} - \Delta H^\circ_{f\ reactants}$$

### The Second Law of Thermodynamics, Entropy

$$\Delta S_{system} + \Delta S_{surroundings} = \Delta S_{universe} \geq 0$$

### Gibbs free energy, $G$

$$\Delta G = \Delta H - T\Delta S$$

| Terms | |
|---|---|
| Activation energy | *PV* work |
| Catalyst | Radiation |
| Conduction | Reference Form |
| Convection | Reversible |
| Endothermic | Standard Enthalpy of Formation |
| Enthalpy | Standard State |
| Entropy *S* | State Functions |
| Exothermic | Surroundings |
| Gibbs Free Energy *G* | System |
| Heat | Temperature |
| Heat of Reaction | The First Law of Thermodynamics |
| Hess' law | The Second Law of Thermodynamics |
| Internal Energy | The Third Law of Thermodynamics |
| Intermediates | Transition State |
| Irreversible | Work |

## Thought Provoker Answers

**Answer from page 63:**

*White is better. In summer, your house is cooler than the environment and white reflects away the heat. In winter, your house is warmer than the environment and white radiates away less heat.*

**Answer from page 67:**

*The closet will warm up because $q_h$ is greater than $q_c$.*

**Answer from page 70:**

*The potential and kinetic energies of the ball are transferred to the internal energy of the ball and the pavement as the molecules of both collide with each other causing the molecules of both to vibrate faster and slightly separate.*

**Answer from page 71:**

*An ideal gas is like a bunch of tiny, volumeless marbles bouncing off each other. There are no intermolecular attractions. The translational component of internal energy is the only part of internal energy that can change for an ideal gas. Therefore, any change in the internal energy of an ideal gas will result in a corresponding change in temperature. This is not necessarily true for real gasses, liquids, or solids because they can put energy into other parts of their internal energy.*

**Answer from page 74:**

*Yes, as long as no nonPV work is done, because the pressure is constant at about 1 atm.*

**65.** Which of the following describes a reaction that is always spontaneous?

    **A.** increasing enthalpy and increasing entropy
    **B.** decreasing enthalpy and decreasing entropy
    **C.** increasing enthalpy and decreasing entropy
    **D.** decreasing enthalpy and increasing entropy

**66.** Which of the following statements about entropy is false?

    **A.** The entropy of a system will always increase in a spontaneous reaction.
    **B.** Entropy is a measure of disorder.
    **C.** The entropy change of a forward reaction is exactly opposite to the entropy of the reverse reaction.
    **D.** Entropy increases with temperature.

**67.** Which of the following is a violation of the law of conservation of energy?

    **A.** Heat can be changed completely to work in cyclical process.
    **B.** A system undergoing a reaction with constant enthalpy experiences a temperature change.
    **C.** After sliding to a stop, a box with initial kinetic energy $K$ has only thermal energy in an amount less than $K$.
    **D.** A bond is broken and energy is released.

**68.** All of the following are examples of processes which increase system entropy EXCEPT:

    **A.** the expanding universe
    **B.** aerobic respiration
    **C.** melting ice
    **D.** building a bridge

**69.** Which of the following statements is most likely true concerning the reaction:

$$2A(g) + B(g) \rightarrow 2C(g) + D(s)$$

    **A.** System entropy is decreasing.
    **B.** System entropy is increasing.
    **C.** The reaction is spontaneous.
    **D.** The reaction is nonspontaneous.

**70.** The reaction below shows the condensation of water.

$$H_2O(g) \rightarrow H_2O(l)$$

Which of the following will be positive for the water at 25°C and 1 atm?

    **A.** $\Delta H$
    **B.** $\Delta S$
    **C.** $\Delta G$
    **D.** None of the above.

**71.**
$$AgCl(s) \rightarrow Ag^+(aq) + Cl^-(aq)$$

During the course of the reaction above, both entropy and enthalpy are increased. If the reaction is not spontaneous at a given temperature and pressure, what can be done to make the reaction occur spontaneously?

    **A.** Increase the temperature.
    **B.** Decrease the temperature.
    **C.** Increase the pressure.
    **D.** Decrease the pressure.

**72.** The normal boiling point of benzene ($C_6H_6$) is 80.1°C. If the partial pressure of benzene gas is 1 atm, which of the following is true of the reaction shown below at 80.1°C?

$$C_6H_6(l) \rightarrow C_6H_6(g)$$

    **A.** $\Delta S$ is negative
    **B.** $\Delta S$ is zero
    **C.** $\Delta G$ is negative
    **D.** $\Delta G$ is zero

# SOLUTIONS

## 4.1 Solutions

A **solution** is a homogeneous mixture of two or more compounds in a single phase, such as solid, liquid, or gas. The MCAT will probably test your knowledge of liquid solutions only. However, you should be aware that solutions are possible in other phases as well. Brass is an example of a solid solution of zinc and copper. Generally, in a solution with two compounds, the compound of which there is more is called the **solvent**, and the compound of which there is less is called the **solute**. Sometimes, when neither compound predominates, both compounds are referred to as solvents. Although a compound's behavior does depend upon the molecules around it, the label of 'solvent' or 'solute' does not indicate a particular behavior.

There are three types of solutions: *ideal solutions, ideally dilute solutions,* and *nonideal solutions*. Ideal solutions are solutions made from compounds that have similar properties. In other words, the compounds can be interchanged within the solution without changing the spatial arrangement of the molecules or the intermolecular attractions. Benzene in toluene is an example of a nearly ideal solution because both compounds have similar bonding properties and similar size. In an ideally dilute solution, the solute molecules are completely separated by solvent molecules so that they have no interaction with each other. Nonideal solutions violate both of these conditions. On the MCAT, you can assume that you are dealing with an ideally dilute solution unless otherwise indicated; however, you should not automatically assume that an MCAT solution is ideal.

> Solvent usually indicates the compound that predominates in a solution.

> The concepts of an ideal and an ideally dilute solution are not tested directly on the MCAT. They are mentioned here in order to deepen your understanding of solutions and to help explain some apparent paradoxes which result when they are not considered.
>
> In ideally dilute solutions, the mole fraction of the solvent is approximately equal to one.

A colloid is like a solution, only the solute particles are larger. The colloid particles are usually too small to be extracted by filtration but usually large enough or charged enough to be separated by a semipermeable membrane.

## 4.2 Colloids

Particles larger than small molecules may form mixtures with solvents. If gravity does not cause these particles to settle out of the mixture over time, the mixture is called a *colloidal system*, or *colloid*. (The term 'colloid' can also refer to the colloidal particles.) Colloidal particles are larger than solute particles, and can even be single large molecules such as hemoglobin. A colloidal system can be any combination of phases (except gas in gas). Some examples of colloidal systems are an *aerosol* (liquid or solid particles in a gas like fog or smoke), a *foam* (gas particles in a liquid like whipped cream), an *emulsion* (liquid particles in a liquid or solid like milk or butter), or a *sol* (solid particles in a liquid like paint).

Unlike a true solution, colloidal suspensions will scatter light, a phenomenon known as the *Tyndall effect*. A beam of light in a smoke filled theatre is visible due to the Tyndall effect.

Colloidal particles may be attracted (*lyophilic*) or repelled (*lyophobic*) by their *dispersion medium*. (The dispersion medium in a colloid is analagous to the solvent in a solution.) Lyophobic colloids form when amphipathic or charged particles adsorb to the surface of the colloidal particles stabilizing them in the dispersion medium. Protein in water is an example of a lyophilic colloid; emulsified fat in water is an example of a lyophobic colloid.

Colloidal particles are usually too small to be extracted by filtration; however, heating a colloid or adding an electrolyte may cause the particles to *coagulate*. The larger particles produced by coagulation will settle out or can be extracted by filtration. Colloidal systems can also be separated by a semipermeable membrane, a process called *dialysis*.

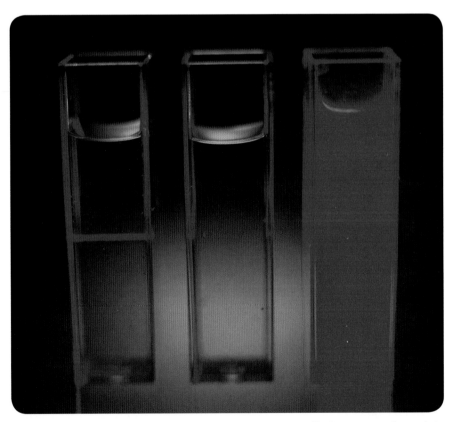

A characteristic of a colloid is that it illuminates a beam of light passing through it. Here, laser light passing first through tap water (at left) is revealed as a single beam due to the impurities in the water. On passing through the cuvette of distilled water (middle), so little dispersion of light occurs that the beam can hardly be seen at all. At right the colloidal suspension of gelatin has caused total dispersion of the light, illuminating the cuvette.

When a solute is mixed with a solvent, it is said to dissolve. The general rule for dissolution is **'like dissolves like'**. This rule refers to the polarity of the solute and solvent. Highly polar molecules are held together by strong intermolecular bonds formed by the attraction between their partially charged ends. Nonpolar molecules are held together by weak intermolecular bonds resulting from instantaneous dipole moments. These forces are called **London dispersion forces**. A polar solute interacts strongly with a polar solvent by tearing the solvent-solvent bonds apart and forming solvent-solute bonds. A nonpolar solute does not have enough charge separation to interact effectively with a polar solvent, and thus cannot intersperse itself within the solvent. A nonpolar solute can, however, tear apart the weak bonds of a nonpolar solvent. The bonds of a polar solute are too strong to be broken by the weak forces of a nonpolar solvent.

Water is a poor conductor of electricity unless it contains electrolytes. Electrolytes are compounds that form ions in aqueous solution.

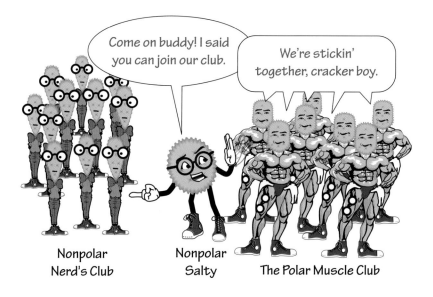

Come on buddy! I said you can join our club.

We're stickin' together, cracker boy.

Nonpolar Nerd's Club

Nonpolar Salty

The Polar Muscle Club

Like dissolves like; polar solvents dissolve polar solutes; nonpolar solvents dissolve nonpolar solutes.

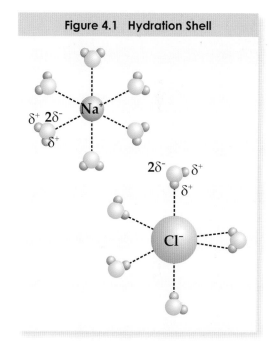

**Figure 4.1 Hydration Shell**

Ionic compounds are dissolved by polar substances. When ionic compounds dissolve, they break apart into their respective cations and anions and are surrounded by the oppositely charged ends of the polar solvent. This process is called **solvation**. Water acts as a good solvent for ionic substances. The water molecules surround the individual ions pointing their positive hydrogens at the anions and their negative oxygens toward the cations. When several water molecules attach to one side of an ionic compound, they are able to overcome the strong ionic bond, and break apart the compound. The molecules then surround the ion. In water this process is called **hydration**. Something that is hydrated is said to be in an **aqueous phase**. The number of water molecules needed to surround an ion varies according to the size and charge of the ion. This number is called the *hydration number*. The hydration number is commonly 4 or 6.

When ions form in aqueous solution, the solution is able to conduct electricity. A compound which forms ions in aqueous solution is called an **electrolyte**. Strong electrolytes create solutions which conduct electricity well and contain many ions. Weak electrolytes are compounds which form few ions in solution.

For the MCAT you should be aware of common names, formulae, and charges for the polyatomic ions listed in Table 4.1.

| Table 4.1 Polyatomic Ions | |
|---|---|
| *Name* | *Formula* |
| Nitrite | $NO_2^-$ |
| Nitrate | $NO_3^-$ |
| Sulfite | $SO_3^{2-}$ |
| Sulfate | $SO_4^{2-}$ |
| Hypochlorite | $ClO^-$ |
| Chlorite | $ClO_2^-$ |
| Chlorate | $ClO_3^-$ |
| Perchlorate | $ClO_4^-$ |
| Carbonate | $CO_3^{2-}$ |
| Bicarbonate | $HCO_3^-$ |
| Phosphate | $PO_4^{3-}$ |

While it is important to drink water, drinking too much water can result in reduced sodium levels, a condition known as hyponatremia. In hyponatremia, normal sodium levels of 135 to 145 m$M$, are reduced to 125m$M$ or below by drinking too much water. A sodium level below 120m$M$ can be critical, and even result in death.

## 4.4 Units of Concentration

There are several ways to measure the concentration of a solution, five of which you should know for the MCAT: molarity ($M$), molality ($m$), mole fraction ($\chi$), mass percentage, and parts per million (ppm). **Molarity** is the moles of the compound divided by the volume of the solution. Molarity generally has units of mol/L. **Molality** is moles of solute divided by kilograms of solvent. Molality generally has units of mol/kg and is usually used in formulae for colligative properties. The **mole fraction** is the moles of a compound divided by the total moles of all species in solution. Since it is a ratio, mole fraction has no units. **Mass percentage** is 100 times the ratio of the mass of the solute to the total mass of the solution. **Parts per million** is $10^6$ times the ratio of the mass of the solute to the total mass of the solution.

$$M = \frac{\text{moles of solute}}{\text{volume of solution}}$$

$$m = \frac{\text{moles of solute}}{\text{kilograms of solvent}}$$

$$\chi = \frac{\text{moles of solute}}{\text{total moles of all solutes and solvent}}$$

$$\text{mass \%} = \frac{\text{mass of solute}}{\text{total mass of solution}} \times 100$$

$$\text{ppm} = \frac{\text{mass of solute}}{\text{total mass of solution}} \times 10^6$$

> Notice that parts per million is NOT the number of solute molecules per million molecules. It is the mass of the solute per mass of solution times one million.

Remember that solution concentrations are always given in terms of the form of the solute before dissolution. For instance, when 1 mole of NaCl is added to 1 liter of water, it is approximately a 1 molar solution and NOT a 2 molar solution even though each NaCl dissociates into two ions.

*Normality* measures the number of *equivalents* per liter of solution. The definition of an equivalent will depend upon the type of reaction taking place in the solution. The only time normality is likely to appear on the MCAT is with an acid-base reaction. In an acid-base reaction an equivalent is defined as the mass of acid or base that can furnish or accept one mole of protons. For instance, a 1 molar solution of $H_2SO_4$ would be called a 2 normal solution because it can donate 2 protons for each $H_2SO_4$.

**73.** What is the approximate molarity of a NaCl solution with a specific gravity of 1.006?

A. 0.05 $M$
B. 0.06 $M$
C. 0.1 $M$
D. 0.2 $M$

**74.** Which of the following substances is least soluble in water?

A. $NH_3$
B. NaCl
C. $HSO_4^-$
D. $CCl_4$

**75.** Which of the following solutions is the most concentrated? (Assume 1 L of water has a mass of 1 kg.)

A. 1 $M$ NaCl
B. 1 $m$ NaCl
C. A aqueous solution with a NaCl mole fraction of 0.01
D. 55 grams of NaCl mixed with one liter of water

**76.** The air we breathe is approximately 21% $O_2$ and 79% $N_2$. If the partial pressure of nitrogen in air is 600 torr, then all of the following are true EXCEPT:

A. The mole fraction of nitrogen in air is 0.79.
B. The mass of nitrogen in a 22.4 L sample of air is 22.1 grams at $0°C$.
C. The partial pressure of oxygen is approximately 160 torr.
D. For every 21 grams of oxygen in an air sample, there are 79 grams of nitrogen.

**77.** A polar solute is poured into a container with a nonpolar solvent. Which of the following statements best explains the reaction?

A. The strong dipoles of the polar molecules separate the weak bonds between the nonpolar molecules.
B. The dipoles of the polar molecules are too weak to break the bonds between the nonpolar molecules.
C. The instantaneous dipoles of the nonpolar molecules are too weak to separate the bonds between the polar molecules.
D. The instantaneous dipoles of the nonpolar molecules separate the bonds between the polar molecules.

**78.** A solution contains 19 grams of $MgCl_2$ in 0.5 liters of distilled water. If $MgCl_2$ totally dissociates, what is the concentration of chloride ions in the solution?

A. 0.1 $M$
B. 0.2 $M$
C. 0.4 $M$
D. 0.8 $M$

**79.** A student has 0.8 liters of a 3 molar HCl solution. How many liters of distilled water must she mix with the 3 molar solution in order to create a 1 molar HCl solution?

A 0.8 L
B. 1.6 L
C. 2.4 L
D. 3.2 L

**80.** All of the following substances are strong electrolytes EXCEPT:

A $HNO_3$
B. $CO_2$
C. NaCl
D. KOH

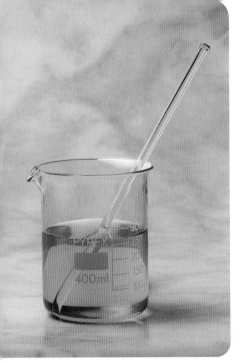

Iron (II) sulphate solution

## 4.5 Solution Formation for Condensed Phases

The formation of a solution is a physical reaction. It involves three steps:

**Step 1:** the breaking of the intermolecular bonds between solute molecules;

**Step 2:** the breaking of the intermolecular bonds between solvent molecules;

**Step 3:** the formation of intermolecular bonds between the solvent and the solute molecules.

Energy is required in order to break a bond. Recall from Chemistry Lecture 3 that a closed system at constant pressure the enthalpy change of a reaction equals the heat: $\Delta H = q$, and that for condensed phases not at high pressure (for instance the formation of most solutions that will be on the MCAT) enthalpy change approximately equals internal energy change: $\Delta H \approx \Delta U$. For solution chemistry of condensed phases we shall use these approximations. Thus the **heat of solution ($\Delta H_{sol}$)** is given by:

$$\Delta H_{sol} = \Delta H_1 + \Delta H_2 + \Delta H_3$$

Since energy is required to break a bond, the first two steps in dissolution are endothermic while the third step is exothermic.

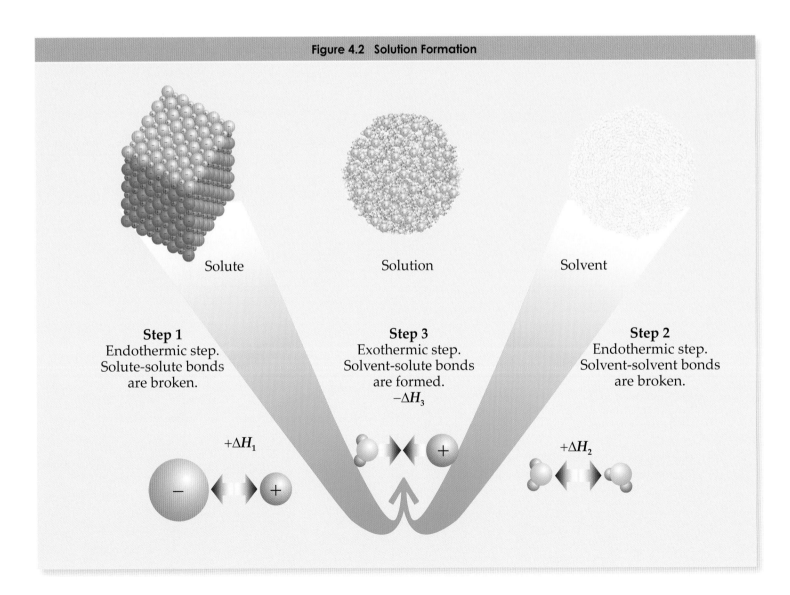

**Figure 4.2  Solution Formation**

Solute

Solution

Solvent

**Step 1**
Endothermic step.
Solute-solute bonds
are broken.

**Step 3**
Exothermic step.
Solvent-solute bonds
are formed.
$-\Delta H_3$

**Step 2**
Endothermic step.
Solvent-solvent bonds
are broken.

$+\Delta H_1$

$+\Delta H_2$

Instant cold pack placed on an injured ankle to reduce swelling. The cold pack contains ammonium nitrate and water, which when mixed together produce an endothermic reaction that feels cold.

Entropy usually increases for solid and liquids dissolving in liquids. Entropy usually decreases for gases dissolving in liquids.

If the overall reaction releases energy (is exothermic), the new intermolecular bonds are more stable than the old and, in general, the intermolecular attractions within the solution are stronger than the intermolecular attractions within the pure substances. Remember, less energy in the system usually means a more stable system. If the overall reaction absorbs energy (is endothermic), the reverse is true. Using the approximations mentioned above, the overall change in energy of the reaction is equal to the change in enthalpy and is called the heat of solution $\Delta H_{sol}$. A negative heat of solution results in stronger intermolecular bonds, while a positive heat of solution results in weaker intermolecular bonds. Some books combine steps 2 and 3 of solution formation for aqueous solutions calling the sum of their enthalpy changes the *heat of hydration*.

Since the combined mixture is more disordered than the separated pure substances, the formation of a solution usually involves an increase in entropy. One exception to this rule is when a gas dissolves in a liquid or solid. When a gas dissolves in a liquid or solid, entropy change is usually negative. On the MCAT, for one condensed phase (liquid or solid) dissolving into another it is safe to assume an increase in entropy.

Breaking a bond always requires energy input. Since enthalpy and heat are equal at constant pressure, a solution with a negative enthalpy will give off heat when it forms. Thus, a solution that gives off heat when it forms is creating stronger bonds within the solution.

Recall that $\Delta G = \Delta H - T\Delta S$ and that a negative $\Delta G$ indicates a spontaneous reaction. When a liquid or solid dissolves in a liquid, $\Delta S$ is usually positive, therefore $\Delta S$ usually favors spontaneous solution formation for condensed phases. $\Delta H_{sol}$ can be negative or positive. If $\Delta H$ is negative, then, according to $\Delta G = \Delta H - T\Delta S$, $\Delta G$ must also be negative, and solution formation is spontaneous. Nearly all condensed phases with negative heats of solution will dissolve spontaneously. If $\Delta H_{sol}$ is positive (and $\Delta S$ is positive), temperature determines whether $\Delta G$ is positive or negative and whether a solution will form. Only some of the solutes with positive heats of solution will dissolve spontaneously.

## 4.6 Vapor Pressure

Imagine a pure liquid in a vacuum-sealed container. If we were to examine the space inside the container above the liquid, we would find that it is not really a vacuum. Instead it would contain vapor molecules from the liquid that have escaped. The liquid molecules are held in the liquid by intermolecular bonds. However, they contain a certain amount of kinetic energy, which depends upon the temperature. Some of the liquid molecules at the surface contain enough kinetic energy to break the intermolecular bonds that hold them in the liquid. These molecules launch themselves into the open space above the liquid. As the space above the liquid fills with molecules, some of the molecules crash back into the liquid. When the rate of molecules leaving the liquid equals the rate of molecules entering the liquid, equilibrium has been established. At this point, the pressure created by the molecules in the open space is called the **vapor pressure** of the liquid.

**Figure 4.3  Vapor Pressure**

Vapor Pressure

Pure liquid

> Equilibrium between the liquid and gas phases of a compound occurs when the molecules move from the liquid to the gas as quickly as they move from the gas to the liquid. The partial pressure of the compound necessary to create this equilibrium is called the vapor pressure of the compound.

> This equation is not important for MCAT, but it can help you remember that vapor pressure always increases as temperature increases.

Since vapor pressure is related to the kinetic energy of the molecules, vapor pressure is a function of temperature. A derivation of the Clausius-Clapeyron equation relates vapor pressure and temperature to the heat of vaporization:

$$\ln(P_v) = -\frac{\Delta H_{vap}}{R}\left(\frac{1}{T}\right) + C$$

where $\Delta H_{vap}$ is the heat of vaporization (always positive), and $C$ is a constant specific to the compound. Vaporization is an endothermic process, so the equation indicates that vapor pressure increases with temperature.

> A compound evaporates when the vapor pressure of its liquid phase is greater than the partial pressure of its gaseous phase. It condenses when these conditions are reversed.

Imagine a puddle of water in the street on a still day. The puddle is exposed to the open air, so the gas above the puddle is made up of mostly oxygen and nitrogen. However, there is nearly always some moisture in the air. In other words, the air also contains water molecules. Recall from Chemistry Lecture 2.2 that there must be a partial pressure associated with these water molecules in the air. Imagine further that the temperature of the day is such that this partial pressure of water above the puddle happens to be equal to the vapor

pressure of water. This means that water molecules are entering and leaving the puddle at the same rate. Now along comes a wind. Recall from Bernoulli's equation in Physics Lecture 5.8 that when a fluid moves, its pressure decreases, so the partial pressure of the water vapor decreases when the wind blows. Since the vapor pressure is a function of temperature, the vapor pressure doesn't change. (It is a number that we looked up in a reference book.) As a result, the partial pressure of the water vapor is lower than the vapor pressure of water at that temperature, and the number of water molecules leaving the

**94**   EXAMKRACKERS MCAT® – Chemistry

puddle is greater than the number of water molecules entering the puddle; the water is **evaporating** from the puddle. If the reverse were true, and conditions made the air more moist so that the partial pressure of the water vapor were greater than the vapor pressure, then water would **condense** into the puddle. Of course the puddle doesn't have to be water. The same is true for any liquid.

When vapor pressure equals local atmospheric pressure, a compound boils. In our puddle example we compared vapor pressure and partial pressure. We can also compare vapor pressure and atmospheric pressure (in this case the total pressure applied to the liquid). Atmospheric pressure is the sum of all the partial pressures in the air above the puddle. A liquid boils when its vapor pressure equals the pressure applied to it. This can be done by raising the temperature, and thus raising the vapor pressure until it reaches the atmospheric pressure, or by lowering the atmospheric pressure until it equals the vapor pressure. Solids also have a vapor pressure. The melting point is the temperature at which the vapor pressures of the solid is equal to the vapor pressure of the liquid. Above the melting point the liquid vapor pressure is greater than that of the solid; below the melting point the liquid vapor pressure is less than that of the solid.

Boiling occurs when the vapor pressure of a liquid equals the atmospheric pressure. Melting occurs when the vapor pressure of the solid phase equals the vapor pressure of the liquid phase.

When a **nonvolatile solute** (a solute with no vapor pressure) is added to a liquid, some of those solute molecules will reach the surface of the solution, and reduce the amount of surface area available for the liquid molecules. Since the solute molecules don't break free of the solution but do take up surface area, the number of molecules breaking free from the liquid is decreased while the surface area of the solution and the volume of open space above the solution remain the same. From the ideal gas law, $PV = nRT$, we know that a decrease in $n$ at constant volume and temperature is proportional to a decrease in $P$. The vapor pressure of the solution $P_v$ is given by **Raoult's law**, and is proportional to the mole fraction of the liquid $\chi_a$ and the vapor pressure of the pure liquid $P_a$.

$$P_v = \chi_a P_a$$

If the solute is a **volatile solute** (a solute with a vapor pressure), the situation is a little more complicated. A volatile solute will also compete for the surface area of a liquid. However, some of the molecules of a volatile solute will escape from solution and contribute to the vapor pressure. If the solution is an ideal solution (solute and solvent have similar properties), the partial pressures contributed by the solvent and solute can be found by applying Raoult's law separately. The sum of the partial vapor pressures give the total vapor pressure of the solution, and we arrive at a modified form of Raoult's law:

$$P_v = \chi_a P_a + \chi_b P_b$$

where each $\chi P$ term represents the partial vapor pressure contributed by the respective solvent, and $P_v$ represents the total vapor pressure.

**Figure 4.4  Nonvolitile Solute**

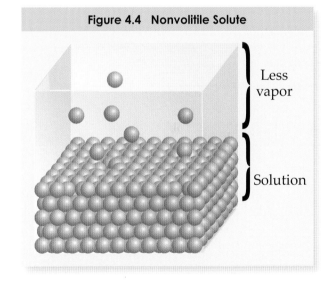

Less vapor

Solution

**Figure 4.5  Volatile Solute**

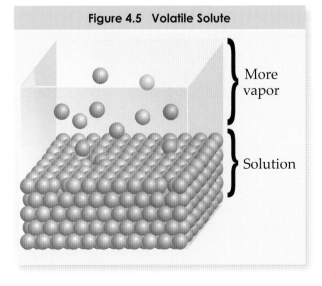

More vapor

Solution

> Raoult's law for nonvolatile solutes: If 97% of the solution is solvent, then the vapor pressure will be 97% of the vapor pressure of the pure solvent.
>
> Raoult's law for volatile solutes: If 97% of the solution is solvent, then the vapor pressure will be 97% of the vapor pressure of the pure solvent PLUS 3% of the vapor pressure of the pure solute.

> Negative heats of solution form stronger bonds and lower vapor pressure; positive heats of solution form weaker bonds and raise vapor pressure.

But this is not the entire story. As we saw with heats of solution, if the solution is not ideal, the intermolecular forces between molecules will be changed. Either less energy or more energy will be required for molecules to break the intermolecular bonds and leave the surface of the solution. This means that the vapor pressure of a nonideal solution will deviate from the predictions made by Raoult's law. We can make a general prediction of the direction of the deviation based upon heats of solution. If the heat of solution is negative, stronger bonds are formed, fewer molecules are able to break free from the surface and there will be a negative deviation of the vapor pressure from Raoult's law. The opposite will occur for a positive heat of solution.

> In order to really understand this section you must have a thorough understanding of many of the physics and chemistry concepts that we've studied so far (i.e. bond energy, thermodynamics, pressure, and solutions). I suggest that you re-read this section and be sure that you thoroughly understand the concepts.

The deviation of vapor pressure from Raoult's law can be represented graphically by comparing the mole fractions of solvents with their vapor pressures. Graph 1 below shows only the partial pressure of the solvent as its mole fraction increases. As predicted by Raoult's law, the relationship is linear. Graph 2 shows the vapor pressure of an ideal solution and the individual partial pressures of each solvent. Notice that the partial pressures add at every point to equal the total pressure. This must be true for any solution. Graph 3 and 4 show the deviations of nonideal solutions. The straight lines are the Raoult's law predictions and the curved lines are the actual pressures. Notice that the partial pressures still add at every point to equal the total pressure. Notice also that a positive heat of solution leads to an increase in vapor pressure, and a negative heat of solution, to a decrease in vapor pressure.

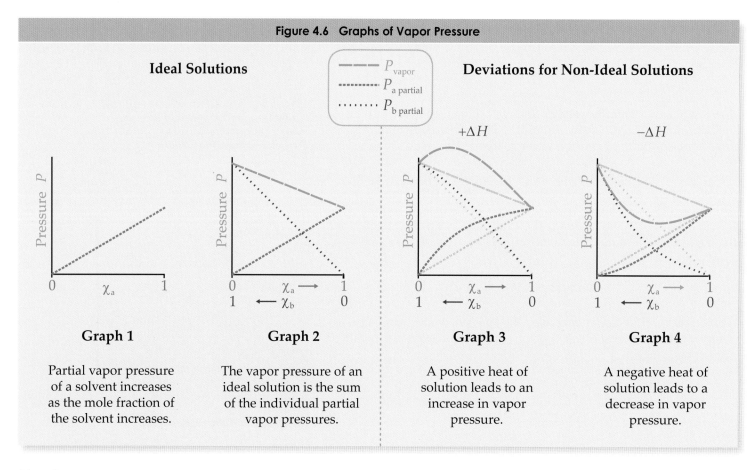

**Figure 4.6  Graphs of Vapor Pressure**

| | | | |
|---|---|---|---|
| Graph 1 | Graph 2 | Graph 3 | Graph 4 |
| Partial vapor pressure of a solvent increases as the mole fraction of the solvent increases. | The vapor pressure of an ideal solution is the sum of the individual partial vapor pressures. | A positive heat of solution leads to an increase in vapor pressure. | A negative heat of solution leads to a decrease in vapor pressure. |

Questions 81 through 88 are **NOT** based on a descriptive passage.

81. NaCl dissolves spontaneously in water. Based upon the following reaction:

$$NaCl(s) \rightarrow Na^+(g) + Cl^-(g) \quad \Delta H = 786 \text{ kJ/mol}$$

the heat of hydration for NaCl must be:

   A. negative with a magnitude less than 786.
   B. negative with a magnitude greater than 786.
   C. positive with a magnitude greater than 786.
   D. Nothing can be determined about the heat of hydration without more information.

82. Which of the following indicates an exothermic heat of solution?

   A. Heat is evolved.
   B. The final solution is acidic.
   C. A precipitate is formed.
   D. The reaction is spontaneous.

83. When two pure liquids, *A* and *B*, are mixed, the temperature of the solution increases. All of the following must be true EXCEPT:

   A. The intermolecular bond strength in at least one of the liquids is less than the intermolecular bond strength between *A* and *B* in solution.
   B. The reaction is exothermic.
   C. The vapor pressure of the solution is less than both the vapor pressure of pure *A* and pure *B*.
   D. The rms velocity of the molecules increases when the solution is formed.

84. Which of the following will increase the vapor pressure of a liquid?

   A. increasing the surface area of the liquid by pouring it into a wider container
   B. increasing the kinetic energy of the molecules of the liquid
   C. decreasing the temperature of the liquid
   D. adding a nonvolatile solute

85. When two volatile solvents are mixed, the vapor pressure drops below the vapor pressure of either solvent in its pure form. What else can be predicted about the solution of these solvents?

   A. The solution is ideal.
   B. The mole fraction of the more volatile solvent is greater than the mole fraction of the less volatile solvent.
   C. The heat of solution is exothermic.
   D. The heat of solution is endothermic.

86. A solution composed of ethanol and methanol can be thought of as ideal. At room temperature, the vapor pressure of ethanol is 45 mmHg and the vapor pressure of methanol is 95 mmHg. Which of the following will be true regarding the vapor pressure of a solution containing only ethanol and methanol?

   A. It will be less than 45 mmHg.
   B. It will be greater than 45 mmHg and less than 95 mmHg.
   C. It will be greater than 95 mmHg and less than 140 mmHg.
   D. It will be greater than 140 mmHg.

87. Benzene and toluene combine to form an ideal solution. At 80°C, vapor pressure of pure benzene is 800 mmHg and the vapor pressure of pure toluene is 300 mmHg. If the vapor pressure of the solution is 400 mmHg, what are the mole fractions of benzene and toluene?

   A. 60% benzene and 40% toluene
   B. 50% benzene and 50% toluene
   C. 40% benzene and 60% toluene
   D. 20% benzene and 80% toluene

88. When solute *A* is added to solvent *B*, heat is released. Which of the following must be true of the solvation process?

   A. The bonds broken in solute *A* must be stronger than the bonds broken in solvent *B*.
   B. The bonds broken in solute A must be weaker than the bonds broken in solvent *B*.
   C. The bonds formed in the solution must be stronger than the bonds broken in solute *A* and solvent *B*.
   D. The bonds formed in the solution must be weaker than the bonds broken in solute *A* and solvent *B*.

# 4.7 Solubility

**Solubility** is a solute's tendency to dissolve in a solvent. On the MCAT, the solute will usually be a salt, and the solvent will most often be water. Dissolution of a salt is reversible on a molecular scale; dissolved molecules of the salt reattach to the surface of the salt crystal. For a dissolving salt, the reverse reaction, called **precipitation**, takes place initially at a slower rate than dissolution. As the salt dissolves and the concentration of dissolved salt builds, the rate of dissolution and precipitation equilibrate. When the rate of dissolution and precipitation are equal, the solution is said to be **saturated**; the concentration of dissolved salt has reached a maximum in a saturated solution. Just like any other reaction, the equilibrium established at the saturation point is dynamic; the concentrations of products and reactants remain constant, but the forward and reverse reactions continue at the same rate.

Salt cave formation along the coast of the Dead Sea in Jordan.

The equilibrium of a solvation reaction has its own equilibrium constant called the **solubility product** $K_{sp}$. Use $K_{sp}$ the same way you would use any other equilibrium constant. Remember that solids and pure liquids have an approximate mole fraction of one and can be excluded from the equilibrium expression. Thus, solids are left out of the solubility product expression as in the example of the $K_{sp}$ for barium hydroxide shown below.

$$Ba(OH)_2(s) \rightleftharpoons Ba^{2+}(aq) + 2OH^-(aq)$$

$$K_{sp} = [Ba^{2+}][OH^-]^2$$

> For most salts, crystallization is exothermic.

> Use $K_{sp}$ like any other equilibrium constant to create an equilibrium expression. Set the $K_{sp}$ equal to products over reactants raised to the power of their coefficients in the balanced equation. As always, leave out pure solids and liquids.

Solubility and the solubility product ($K_{sp}$) are not the same thing. The solubility of a substance in a given solvent is found from the solubility product. The solubility is the number of moles of solute per liter of a solution that can be dissolved in a given solvent. Solubility depends upon the common ions in the solution. The solubility product is independent of the common ions, and can be found in a reference book.

> Solubility and the solubility product are not the same thing. Solubility product or $K_{sp}$ is a constant found in a book. Solubility is the maximum number of moles of the solute that can dissolve in solution.
>
> The solubility product changes only with temperature. The solubility depends upon the temperature and the ions in solution.

We can write an equation for the solvation of $BaF_2$ in water as follows:

$$BaF_2(s) \rightleftharpoons Ba^{2+}(aq) + 2F^-(aq)$$

The solubility product for $BaF_2$ is:

$$K_{sp} = [Ba^{2+}][F^-]^2$$

If we look in a book, we find that the $K_{sp}$ for $BaF_2$ has a value of $2.4 \times 10^{-5}$ at 25°C. Like any equilibrium constant, the $K_{sp}$ is unitless. From the $K_{sp}$ we can find the solubility of $BaF_2$ in any solution at 25°C. For instance, to find the solubility of $BaF_2$ in one liter of water, we simply saturate one liter of water with $BaF_2$. The solubility is the maximum number of moles per liter that can dissolve in the solution. We call the solubility '$x$', since it is unknown. If $x$ moles per liter of $BaF_2$ dissolve, then there will be $x$ moles per liter of $Ba^{2+}$ in solution and twice as many, or $2x$ moles per liter, of $F^-$. We plug these values into the $K_{sp}$ equation and solve for $x$.

$$2.4 \times 10^{-5} = (x)(2x)^2$$

$$x \approx 1.8 \times 10^{-2}$$

$1.8 \times 10^{-2}$ mol/L is the solubility of $BaF_2$ in one liter of water at 25°C.

What would happen if we added 1 mole of $F^-$ to our solution in the form of NaF? The solubility of $BaF_2$ would change. The NaF would completely dissociate forming 1 mole of $F^-$ and 1 mole of $Na^+$. The $Na^+$ ions are not in the equilibrium expression and (ideally) would have no effect on the equilibrium. Because they have no effect, the $Na^+$ ions are called **spectator ions**. The $F^-$ ions, however, do affect the equilibrium. Their disturbance of the equilibrium is called the **common ion effect** because it involves an ion common to an ion in the equilibrium expression. By Le Chatâlier's principle, the addition of a common ion will push the equilibrium in a direction which tends to reduce the concentration of that ion. In this case, the equilibrium will move to the left, and the solubility of $BaF_2$ will be reduced.

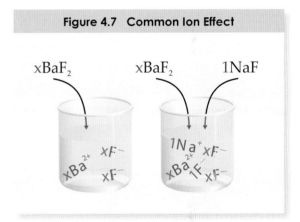

**Figure 4.7 Common Ion Effect**

To find out by exactly how much the solubility will be reduced, we go back to the equilibrium expression. One key to solving solubility problems is realizing that the order in which you mix the solution is irrelevant, so you should mix them in the order that is most convenient to you. In this case it is easiest to add the NaF first, since it completely dissociates. Now we add $BaF_2$ to a solution of 1 liter of water and 1 mole of $F^-$. Again, $x$ moles will dissolve leaving $x$ moles of $Ba^{2+}$. But this time, since there is already 1 mole of $F^-$, $2x + 1$ moles of $F^-$ will be in solution at equilibrium.

$$2.4 \times 10^{-5} = (x)(2x + 1)^2$$

Now here's a trick to simplify the math. We know that the equilibrium is shifting to the left, so $x$ will be smaller than our earlier calculations of $1.8 \times 10^{-2}$. Even $2x$ will be much smaller than 1. Thus, $2x + 1$ is going to be very close to 1. Therefore, we drop the $2x$ and solve:

$$2.4 \times 10^{-5} \approx (x)(1)^2$$

$$x \approx 2.4 \times 10^{-5}$$

Just to be sure that we were correct in our estimation of $2x$, we plug our estimated value of $x$ into the term that we deleted ($2x$), and we see if it is truly much smaller than the term to which we added it (in this case 1).

$$2x = 4.8 \times 10^{-5} \ll 1$$

Our assumption was valid. Thus our new solubility of $BaF_2$ is $2.4 \times 10^{-5}$ mol/L.

> A common ion added to a saturated solution will shift the equilibrium increasing precipitate. It does NOT affect the $K_{sp}$.
>
> A common ion added to a solution that is not saturated will NOT shift the equilibrium, because in an unsaturated solution, there is no equilibrium to shift.

Oil and water don't mix.

## 4.8 Solubility Guidelines

Compounds with water solubilities of less than $0.01 \text{ mol L}^{-1}$ are generally considered insoluble. MCAT will not require you to memorize the solubilities of different compounds. Nevertheless, here are a few solubility guidelines for compounds in water:

Nearly all ionic compounds containing nitrate ($NO_3^-$), ammonium ($NH_4^+$), and alkali metals ($Li^+$, $Na^+$, $K^+$...) are *soluble*.

Ionic compounds containing halogens ($Cl^-$, $Br^-$, $I^-$) are *soluble*, EXCEPT for silver, mercury, and lead compounds ($Ag^+$, $Hg_2^{2+}$, $Pb^{2+}$).

Sulfate compounds ($SO_4^{2-}$) are *soluble*, EXCEPT for mercury, lead, and the heavier alkaline metals ($Hg_2^{2+}$, $Pb^{2+}$, $Ca^{2+}$, $Sr^{2+}$, $Ba^{2+}$).

Compounds containing the heavier alkaline metals ($Ca^{2+}$, $Sr^{2+}$, $Ba^{2+}$) are *soluble* when paired with sulfides ($S^{2-}$) and hydroxides ($OH^-$).

Carbonates, phosphates, sulfides, and hydroxides ($CO_3^{2-}$, $PO_4^{3-}$, $S^{2-}$, $OH^-$) are generally *insoluble* other than in the cases mentioned above.

> It is very unlikely that an MCAT question would require that you know these solubilities. However, knowing them will make solution chemistry easier.

*Notes:*

## 4.9 Solubility Factors

Pressure and temperature affect solubilities. Pressure on liquids and solids has little effect, but pressure on a gas increases its solubility. For an ideally dilute solution, the increase in pressure of gas $a$ over a solution is directly proportional to the solubility of gas $a$, if the gas does not react with, or dissociate in, the solvent. This relationship is given by *Henry's law:*

$$C = k_{a1}P_v$$

where $C$ is the solubility of the gas $a$ (typically in moles per liter), $k_{a1}$ is Henry's law constant, which varies with each solute-solvent pair, and $P_v$ is the vapor partial pressure of gas $a$ above the solution. Strangely, Henry's law can also be written as:

$$P_v = \chi_a k_{a2}$$

where $\chi_a$ is the mole fraction of $a$ in solution, $P_v$ is the vapor partial pressure of gas $a$, and $k_{a2}$ is Henry's law constant. Although both equations show that the concentration of a gas in solution is proportional to the vapor partial pressure of the gas above the solution, the Henry's law constant in the second equation has a different value than the Henry's law constant in the first equation. If we compare the second equation with Raoult's law ($P_v = \chi_a P_a$), they appear to conflict unless $P_a$ has the same value as $k_{a2}$. In fact, they do NOT agree. Both are approximations. Raoult's law is most accurate when looking at the vapor partial pressure of a solvent with high concentration. Henry's law is more accurate when looking at the vapor partial pressure of a volatile solute where the solute has a low concentration. *In other words, in an ideally dilute solution, the solvent obeys Raoult's law and the solute obeys Henry's law.* One way to remember this is when the solvent concentration is high, each solvent molecule is surrounded by other solvent molecules, so it behaves more like a pure solvent. Thus the solvent vapor partial pressure is proportional to its vapor pressure as a pure liquid; Raoult's law. When the volatile solute concentration is low, each molecule is surrounded by solvent molecules creating a deviation from the behavior of the pure volatile solute. Thus its vapor partial pressure is not proportional to its pressure as a pure substance (Raoult's law doesn't work in this case), but is proportional to some constant; Henry's law.

> The most important thing to remember about Henry's law is that it demonstrates that the solubility of a gas is proportional to its vapor partial pressure. We can remember this by thinking of a can of soda. When we open the can and release the pressure, the solubility of the gas decreases causing some gas to rise out of the solution and create the familiar hiss and foam.

---

As shown by Raoult's law and Henry's law, the partial vapor pressure of a solution component is always proportional to its mole fraction. If the component predominates as the solvent, Raoult's law says that the partial vapor pressure is proportional to the pure vapor pressure. If the component represents a tiny amount of solution, Henry's law says that the vapor partial pressure is proportional to Henry's law constant.

| Raoult's law | Henry's law |
|---|---|
| ● Volatile solvent particles | Pressure on gas increases its solubility. |
| ○ Nonvolatile solute particles | |

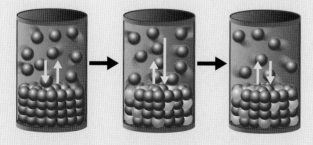

The addition of a nonvolatile solute in a liquid solvent results in a decrease in vapor pressure.

Equilibrium

Increased pressure causes more molecules to dissolve

Equilibrium

As the temperature increases, the solubility of salts generally increases.

Gases behave in the opposite fashion. As temperature increases, the solubililty of gases decreases. The can of soda is useful here as well. If we place a can of soda on the stove, the gas escapes the solution and expands in the can causing it to explode. (This is not the only reason that the can explodes, but it is a good memory aid.)

Le Chatâlier's principle, when applied to solutions, should be used with caution. Because heat energy is a product of a reaction with a negative heat of solution, Le Chatâlier's principle predicts that a temperature increase will push such a reaction to the left decreasing the solubility of the solute. However, entropy increase can be large in solution formation. From the equation $\Delta G = \Delta H - T\Delta S$, we see that a temperature increase emphasizes the $\Delta S$ term tending to result in a more negative $\Delta G$ and thus a more spontaneous reaction. Due to the large increase in entropy, the water solubility of many solids increases with increasing temperature regardless of the enthalpy change. To be absolutely certain, the change in solubility due to temperature must be found by experiment, but the solubility of most salts increases with temperature.

On the other hand, the entropy change when a gas dissolves into a liquid is usually negative. Thus the solubility of gases usually decreases with increasing temperature. You can remember this by understanding why hot waste water from factories that is dumped into streams is hazardous to aquatic life. The hot water has a double effect. First, it holds less oxygen than cold water. Second, it floats on the cold water and seals it off from the oxygen in the air above.

Other factors that affect the solubility of a gas are its size, and reactivity with the solvent. Heavier, larger gases experience greater van der Waals forces and tend to be more soluble. Gases that chemically react with a solvent have greater solubility.

West Indian Manatees attracted to the warm water effluent of power plants.

## 4.10 Equation Summary

### Equations

**Units of Concentration**

$$M = \frac{\text{moles of solute}}{\text{volume of solution}} \qquad m = \frac{\text{moles of solute}}{\text{kilograms of solvent}}$$

$$\chi = \frac{\text{moles of solute}}{\text{total moles of all solutes and solvent}}$$

$$\text{mass \%} = \frac{\text{mass of solute}}{\text{total mass of solution}} \times 100$$

$$\text{ppm} = \frac{\text{mass of solute}}{\text{total mass of solution}} \times 10^6$$

**Raoult's Law**

$$P_v = \chi_a + P_a \qquad P_v = \chi_a P_a + \chi_b P_b$$

## 4.11 Terms You Need To Know

### Terms

'Like Dissolves Like'

Aqueous Phase

Common Ion Effect

Electrolyte

Heat Of Solution ($\Delta H_{sol}$)

Hydration

London Dispersion Forces

Mass Percentage

Molality

Molarity

Mole

Mole Fraction

Nonvolatile Solute

Parts Per Million

Precipitation

Raoult's Law

Saturated

Solubility

Solubility Product ($K_{sp}$)

Solute

Solution

Solvation

Solvent

Spectator Ions

Vapor Pressure

Volatile Solute

89. When a solution is saturated:

    A. the solvent changes to solute, and the solute changes to solvent at an equal rate.
    B. the vapor pressure of the solution is equal to atmospheric pressure.
    C. the concentration of solvent is at a maximum.
    D. the concentration of solvent is at a minimum.

90. The addition of a strong base to a saturated solution of $Ca(OH)_2$ would:

    A. decrease the number of $OH^-$ ions in solution.
    B. increase the number of $Ca^{2+}$ ions in solution.
    C. cause $Ca(OH)_2$ to precipitate.
    D. decrease the pH.

91. $Na_2SO_4$ dissociates completely in water. From the information given in the table below, if $Na_2SO_4$ were added to a solution containing equal concentrations of aqueous $Ca^{2+}$, $Ag^+$, $Pb^{2+}$, and $Ba^{2+}$ ions, which of the following solids would precipitate first?

    | Compound | $K_{sp}$ |
    |----------|----------|
    | $CaSO_4$ | $6.1 \times 10^{-5}$ |
    | $Ag_2SO_4$ | $1.2 \times 10^{-5}$ |
    | $PbSO_4$ | $1.3 \times 10^{-8}$ |
    | $BaSO_4$ | $1.5 \times 10^{-9}$ |

    A. $CaSO_4$
    B. $Ag_2SO_4$
    C. $PbSO_4$
    D. $BaSO_4$

92. A sealed container holds gaseous oxygen and liquid water. Which of the following would increase the amount of oxygen dissolved in the water?

    A. expanding the size of the container
    B. adding an inert gas to the container
    C. decreasing the temperature of the container
    D. shaking the container

93. The $K_{sp}$ of $BaCO_3$ is $1.6 \times 10^{-9}$. How many moles of barium carbonate can be dissolved in 3 liters of water?

    A. $4 \times 10^{-5}$ moles
    B. $6.9 \times 10^{-5}$ moles
    C. $1.2 \times 10^{-4}$ moles
    D. $2.1 \times 10^{-4}$ moles

94. Which of the following expressions represents the solubility product for $Cu(OH)_2$?

    A. $K_{sp} = [Cu^{2+}][OH^-]^2$
    B. $K_{sp} = [Cu^{2+}]2[OH^-]$
    C. $K_{sp} = [Cu^{2+}]2[OH^-]^2$
    D. $K_{sp} = [Cu^{2+}][OH^-]$

95. If the solubility of $PbCl_2$ is equal to $x$, which of the following expressions will be equal to the solubility product for $PbCl_2$?

    A. $4x^3$
    B. $2x^3$
    C. $x^3$
    D. $x^2$

96. A beaker contains a saturated solution of $CaF_2$ ($K_{sp} = 4 \times 10^{-11}$). There are some $Na^+$ ions in the solution. If NaF is added to the beaker, which of the following will occur?

    A. The concentration of $Na^+$ will decrease.
    B. The concentration of $Ca^{2+}$ will decrease.
    C. The concentration of $F^-$ will decrease.
    D. All concentrations will remain constant.

# HEAT CAPACITY, PHASE CHANGE AND COLLIGATIVE PROPERTIES

## 5.1 Phases

If all the intensive macroscopic properties of a system are constant, that system is said to be *homogeneous*. Any part of a system that is homogeneous is called a **phase**. A phase is uniform throughout with respect to chemical composition and physical state. Some examples of different phases are crystalline solid, amorphous solid, aqueous solution, pure liquid, and gas. A system may have a number of solid and liquid phases, but it will usually have only one gaseous phase. Pure substances have only one gaseous phase and usually have only one liquid phase.

> Most of the time, you can think of phases as solid, liquid, and gas. Just be aware that this is not the technical definition. And when we discuss things like solutions, remember that pure water is a different phase than an aqueous solution containing Na⁺ ions. Another common example is rhombic sulfur and monoclinic sulfur; these are two different solid phases of the same element.

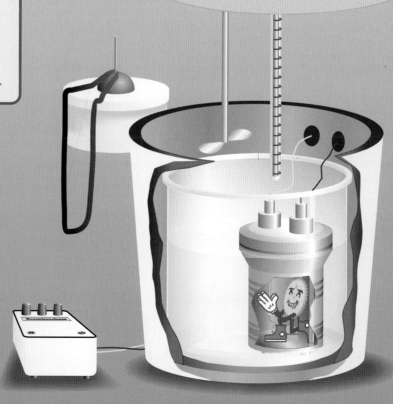

Phase changes arise through changes in the manner in which internal energy is distributed over molecules and space. In other words, a phase change may result when the energy of each molecule is decreased or increased, or when the space around each molecule is reduced or enlarged. Such changes are accomplished via heat or work. In order to understand phase changes then, we must understand how substances react to heat and *PV* work.

The **heat capacity** of a substance is the added energy required to increase the temperature of that substance by one degree. The heat capacity (*C*) is defined as:

$$C = \frac{q}{\Delta T}$$

Don't let the name 'heat capacity' fool you. Recall that heat is a process of energy transfer, and cannot be stored. Heat capacity was given its name before heat was fully understood. 'Internal energy capacity' would be a better, but not perfect, name. Not perfect because we can change the temperature of a substance at constant internal energy by changing only the volume. Likewise, in an isothermal expansion of a gas, we can expand a gas at constant temperature by adding heat during the expansion.

> If, while being heated, no PV work is done by a system at rest, nearly all the heat energy goes into increasing the temperature. When the system is allowed to expand at constant pressure, some energy leaves the system as work and the temperature increase is diminished. Thus constant pressure heat capacities are greater than constant volume heat capacities.

This Vickers Gun is a water cooled machine gun that saw service from 1912 right up until the 1960's. Water has a higher specific heat capacity than air, and as a result is more effective at cooling the gun. Therefore, the gun does not overheat as easily.

There are two heat capacities for any substance: a constant volume heat capacity $C_V$ and a constant pressure heat capacity $C_P$. If we recall the first law of thermodynamics for a system at rest, $\Delta U = q + w$, and remember the relationship between temperature and internal energy, we can understand why the same substance can have different responses to the same amount of energy change. For instance, if the volume of a system is held constant, then the system can do no $PV$ work; all energy change must be in the form of heat. This means that none of the energy going into the system can escape as work done by the system. Most of the energy must contribute to a temperature change. On the other hand, when pressure is held constant and the substance is allowed to expand, some of the energy can leave the system as $PV$ work done on the surroundings as the volume changes. Thus, at constant pressure, a substance can absorb energy with less change in temperature by expelling some of the energy to the surroundings as work. $C_P$ is greater than $C_V$.

$$C_V = \frac{q}{\Delta T_{\text{constant volume}}}$$

$$C_P = \frac{q}{\Delta T_{\text{constant pressure}}}$$

Notes:

Just think about the heat capacity of a substance as the amount of energy a substance can absorb per unit of temperature change. Don't worry too much about the difference between constant pressure and constant volume heat capacities. The MCAT might even ignore this fact completely.

A large amount of energy is required to change the state of water. For the sweat to evaporate, a large amount of heat energy is required, some of which is taken from our bodies. Because some heat is taken from our bodies, we begin to feel cooler when sweat evaporates

Finally, a compound can also absorb energy at either constant pressure or constant volume by stretching its bonds. This means that the more bonds a molecule has the more energy it can channel into bond stretching rather than into raising its temperature. Bond stretching, where possible, can account for a large amount of energy absorption, so, for a compound with lots of bonds, the value of $C_p$ approaches the value of $C_v$. The ratio of the heat capacities $C_p/C_v$ is called either the *isentropic expansion factor* or the *adiabatic index*, and is represented by $\gamma$ (or mechanical engineers use the symbol $\kappa$). This is the same gamma that appears in equations for sound waves (See Physics Lecture 6.1). When we examine $\gamma$ for various gases, we see that there is a general trend for $\gamma$ to approach 1 as the number of molecular bonds increases (See Table 5.1).

| Table 5.1 | Adiabatic Index in Relation to Bonds | |
|---|---|---|
| Gas | Number of β bonds per molecule | Adiabatic Index $\gamma = C_P/C_V$ |
| Helium | 0 | 1.67 |
| Argon | 0 | 1.67 |
| Hydrogen | 1 | 1.40 |
| Nitrogen | 1 | 1.40 |
| Water vapor | 2 | 1.33 |
| Methane | 4 | 1.30 |
| Ethylene | 5 | 1.24 |
| Ethane | 7 | 1.19 |

For a solid or a liquid, both of which experience very little change in volume, there is a more important reason why constant volume and pressure heat capacities differ. The intermolecular forces of a solid or liquid are much stronger than those of a gas. Small changes in the intermolecular distances of noncompressible phases result in large changes in intermolecular potential energy. Intermolecular potential energy does not affect temperature, and thus heat is absorbed at constant pressure with less change in temperature than when heat is absorbed at constant volume. Again: $C_P$ is greater than $C_V$.

Notice that something with a greater heat capacity can absorb more heat with less temperature change.

Although a negative heat capacity is theoretically possible under extremely unusual circumstances and has even been demonstrated by experiment, heat capacity on the MCAT will always be positive; the temperature will always increase when energy is added to a substance at constant volume or pressure. In the real world, heat capacity also changes with temperature; the amount of energy that a substance can absorb per change in temperature varies with the temperature. However, unless otherwise indicated, for the MCAT, assume that heat capacity does not change with temperature.

## Thought Provoker

On a hot summer day, a bucket of sand will be hotter than a bucket of water. If they both absorbed the same amount of heat, how can this be?

Answer: See page 120

Sometimes the MCAT will give you the heat capacity of an entire system. For instance, a thermometer may be made from several substances each with its own heat capacity. The thermometer may be immersed in a bath of oil. The oil has its own heat capacity. On the MCAT, the heat capacity of the thermometer-oil system may be precalculated and given in units of energy divided by units of temperature: i.e. J/K or cal/°C. For such a situation, we would use the following equation:

$$q = C\Delta T$$

Sometimes the MCAT will give a specific heat capacity c. *Specific* means divided by mass, so the **specific heat capacity** is simply the heat capacity per unit mass. A specific heat usually has units of J kg$^{-1}$ K$^{-1}$ or cal g$^{-1}$ °C$^{-1}$. When a specific heat is given, use the following equation:

The specific heat of cooking oil is about half the specific heat of water. About half as much energy is required to raise the temperature of an equal amount of oil.

$$q = mc\Delta T$$

The '*m*' in this equation is for mass, not molality. This equation is easy to remember because it looks like $q$ = MCAT. Notice that the symbol for specific heat is usually a lower case '*c*' while the symbol for heat capacity is usually an upper case '*C*'.

> Use units to help you solve heat capacity problems. For instance, if a heat capacity is given in cal g$^{-1}$ °$C^{-1}$, then you know that to find the heat (measured in calories) you simply multiply by grams and degrees Celsius. This gives you the equation $q = mc\Delta T$. Most of the time you don't have to know the formula, if you look at the units. Also with heat capacity problems, follow the energy flow, remembering that energy is always conserved: $\Delta E = q + w$.

> By the way, don't be surprised if you see molar heat capacity or something similar. Heat capacities can be given per mole, per volume, per gram, or per whatever. Just use the equation $q = mc\Delta T$ and rely on the units of c to find the units of m. For instance, if c is given as the molar heat capacity, m would be in moles.

For the MCAT you must know that water has a specific heat of 1 cal g$^{-1}$ °C$^{-1}$. This was once the definition of a calorie.

$$c_{water} = 1 \; cal \; g^{-1} \; °C^{-1}$$

## Thought Provoker

*When eating a piece of pizza it can be either a pleasant or painful experience. No, we're not talking about the quality of pizza, but rather where you bite. If you eat the crust right out of the oven, there usually isn't a problem. But if you bite into the hot cheese from right out of the oven, you could burn your mouth. Why does where you bite make such a difference?*

*Answer: See page 112*

# 5.3 Calorimeters

A calorimeter is a device which measures energy change. There are both constant pressure and constant volume calorimeters. A **coffee cup calorimeter** is an example of a constant pressure calorimeter because it measures energy change at atmospheric pressure. In a coffee cup calorimeter, two coffee cups are used to insulate the solution. A stirrer maintains equal distribution of energy throughout, and a thermometer measures the change in temperature. Obviously, a coffee cup calorimeter cannot contain expanding gases. Reactions that take place inside a coffee cup calorimeter occur at the constant pressure of the local atmosphere. A coffee cup calorimeter is used to measure **heats of reaction**. (Recall that at constant pressure $q = \Delta H$.) For instance, if we mix HCl and NaOH in a coffee cup calorimeter, the net ionic reaction is:

$$H^+ + OH^- \rightarrow H_2O$$

Using the specific heat of water, the mass of water, and the measured change in temperature, we can solve for $q$ in the equation: $q = mc\Delta T$. Since $q = \Delta H$ at constant pressure, we have the heat of reaction.

A **bomb calorimeter** measures energy change at constant volume. A bomb calorimeter tells us the internal energy change in a reaction. (Recall that at constant volume $q = \Delta U$.) In a bomb calorimeter, a steel container full of reactants is placed inside another rigid, thermally insulated container. When the reaction occurs, heat is transferred to the surrounding water (shown in the diagram). Using the known heat capacity of the container and the equation: $q = C\Delta T$, we can deduce the heat of the reaction, and thus the internal energy change in the reaction.

A bomb calorimeter

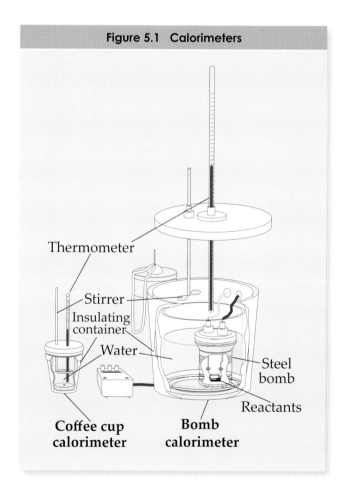

## Figure 5.1 Calorimeters

Thermometer
Stirrer
Insulating container
Water
Steel bomb
Reactants
**Coffee cup calorimeter**
**Bomb calorimeter**

**97.** 20 grams of NaCl is poured into a coffee cup calorimeter containing 250 ml of water. If the temperature inside the calorimeter drops 1°C by the time the NaCl is totally dissolved, what is the heat of solution for NaCl and water? (specific heat of water is 4.18 J/g °C.)

   **A.** –3 kJ/mol
   **B.** –1 kJ/mol
   **C.** 1 kJ/mol
   **D.** 3 kJ/mol

**98.** Using a bomb calorimeter, the change in energy for the combustion of one mole of octane is calculated to be $-5.5 \times 10^3$ kJ. Which of the following is true concerning this process?

   **A.** Since no work is done, the change in energy is equal to the heat.
   **B.** Since there is no work, the change in energy is equal to the enthalpy.
   **C.** Since work is done, the change in energy is equal to the heat.
   **D.** The work done can be added to the change in energy to find the enthalpy.

**99.** Which of the following are true statements?

   **I.** The heat capacity of a substance is the amount of heat that substance can hold per unit of temperature.
   **II.** The specific heat for a single substance is the same for all phases of that substance.
   **III.** When heat is added to a fluid, its temperature will change less if it is allowed to expand.

   **A.** I only
   **B.** III only
   **C.** I and III only
   **D.** I, II, and III

**100.** Substance $A$ has a greater heat capacity than substance $B$. Which of the following is most likely true concerning substances $A$ and $B$?

   **A.** Substance $A$ has larger molecules than substance $B$.
   **B.** Substance $B$ has a lower boiling point than substance $A$.
   **C.** At the same temperature, the molecules of substance $B$ move faster than those of substance $A$.
   **D.** Substance $A$ has more methods of absorbing energy than substance $B$.

**101.** In a free adiabatic expansion, a real gas is allowed to spread to twice its original volume with no energy transfer from the surroundings. All of the following are true concerning this process EXCEPT:

   **A.** No work is done.
   **B.** Increased potential energy between molecules results in decreased kinetic energy and the gas cools.
   **C.** Entropy increases.
   **D.** The gas loses heat.

Questions 102 through 104 refer to the table below, which lists several common metals and their specific heats.

| Metal | Specific Heat $c$ (J/g-°C) |
|-------|---------------------------|
| Fe | 0.44 |
| Au | 0.13 |
| Al | 0.90 |
| Cu | 0.39 |

**102.** If samples of equal mass of all of the metals listed are subjected to the same heat source, which metal would be expected to show the LEAST change in temperature?

   **A.** Iron
   **B.** Gold
   **C.** Aluminum
   **D.** Copper

**103.** In an experiment, it was found that 6 kJ of heat were required to raise the temperature of a sample of copper by 15°C. If the experiment was repeated with a gold sample of the same mass, how much heat would be required achieve the same temperature change?

   **A.** 2 kJ
   **B.** 4 kJ
   **C.** 12 kJ
   **D.** 18 kJ

**104.** When a sample of aluminum of unknown mass was subjected to 1.8 kJ of heat, the temperature of the aluminum sample increased from 26°C to 31°C. What was the mass of the sample?

   **A.** 200 g
   **B.** 400 g
   **C.** 600 g
   **D.** 800 g

**Phase Changes**

Notice that ice does not necessarily have a temperature of 0°C. At 1 atm, ice can be any temperature 0°C and below.

Recall from Chemistry Lecture 5.1 that a phase is any part of a system that is homogeneous. For MCAT purposes, we will consider only a pure substance changing from solid to liquid to gas. We shall examine $H_2O$ at constant pressure of 1 atm. If we start with ice at –10°C and begin heating uniformly at a constant rate, initially, the energy going into the ice increases the vibration of its molecules and raises its temperature. When the ice reaches 0°C, the temperature stops increasing. Energy now goes into breaking and weakening hydrogen bonds. This results in a phase change; the ice becomes liquid water. When all of the ice has changed to water, the temperature begins to rise again; the heat goes into increased movement of the molecules. When the water reaches 100°C, the temperature stops rising. The energy once again goes into breaking hydrogen bonds. This process results in a second phase change: liquid water to steam. Once all the hydrogen bonds are broken, the heat increases the speed of the molecules and the temperature rises again. This simplified explanation of phase change is diagrammed below in a heating curve.

**Figure 5.2   Phase Changes**

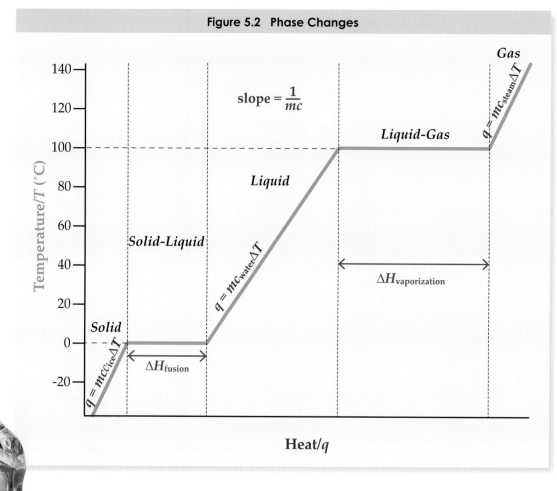

Notice that at 0°C and 100°C the heat stops changing the temperature until the phase change is complete. At these temperatures, the heat capacity is infinite. These points are called the **normal melting point** and **normal boiling point** for water. The word 'normal' indicates a constant pressure of 1 atm. Since the pressure is constant, heat equals the enthalpy change ($q = \Delta H$). The enthalpy change associated with melting is called the **heat of fusion**; the enthalpy change associated with boiling, the **heat of vaporization**. Since enthalpy change is a state function, exactly the same amount of heat absorbed during melting is released during freezing. This is also true for vaporization and condensation, and sublimation and deposition.

The slope of the heating curve, where not zero, is proportional to the inverse of the specific heat. Since the mass of a substance does not change with phase change, the slope is dependent on the specific heat. Notice that each phase of a substance has a unique slope, and therefore a unique specific heat.

Each phase of a substance has its own specific heat.

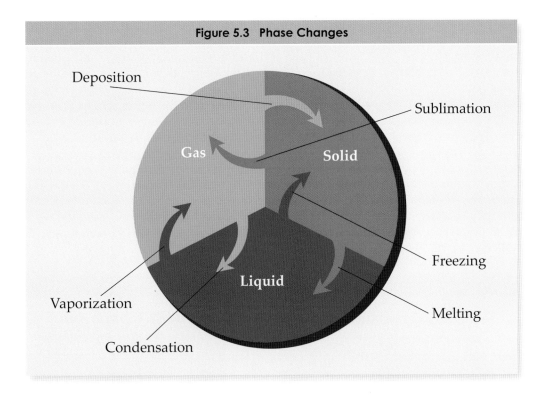

**Figure 5.3   Phase Changes**

You need to know the names of the types of phase changes:

solid to liquid = melting
liquid to solid = freezing

liquid to gas = vaporization
gas to liquid = condensation

solid to gas = sublimation
gas to solid = deposition

The heating curve shows that melting and boiling are endothermic processes; heat is added. This is also true for sublimation. You should also know that melting, boiling, and sublimation normally increase volume and molecular motion and therefore result in increased system entropy. This means that entropy and enthalpy have the same sign for a phase change; both entropy and enthalpy are positive for melting, vaporization, and sublimation. Thus entropy and enthalpy must be negative for freezing, condensation, and deposition. From the equation $\Delta G = \Delta H - T\Delta S$, recall from Chemistry Lecture 3.14 when enthalpy and entropy have the same sign for a process, temperature dictates the direction of that process. Higher temperatures push such a process toward an increase in entropy and a decrease in enthalpy, and lower temperatures push the same process towards a decrease in entropy and an increase in enthalpy. So phase changes at constant pressure are governed by temperature.

Evaporation occurs when the partial pressure above a liquid is less than the liquid's vapor pressure, but the atmospheric pressure is greater than the vapor pressure. Under these conditions, the liquid evaporates rather than boils. So ice, water, and steam all have different specific heats.

Sublimation of dry ice

Lecture **5** : Heat Capacity, Phase Change, and Colligative Properties **113**

Pressure and temperature are two important intensive properties that help determine the phase of a substance. A **phase diagram** indicates the phases of a substance at different pressures and temperatures. Each section of a phase diagram represents a different phase. The lines marking the boundaries of each section represent temperatures and pressures where the corresponding phases are in equilibrium with each other. Like other equilibriums in chemistry, this equilibrium is a dynamic equilibrium. For instance, when water and steam are in equilibrium, water molecules are escaping from the liquid phase at the same rate that they are returning. Notice that there is only one point where a substance can exist in equilibrium as a solid, liquid, and gas. This point is called the **triple point**.

There is also a temperature above which a substance cannot be liquefied regardless of the pressure applied. This temperature is called the **critical temperature**. The pressure required to produce liquefaction while the substance is at the critical temperature is called the **critical pressure**. Together, the critical temperature and critical pressure define the **critical point**. Fluid beyond the critical point has characteristics of both gas and liquid, and is called *supercritical fluid*.

Most solids are more dense than their liquid counterparts, but ice is less dense than water. The glass on the right shows ice floating on water. In the glass on the left is ice made from deuterium. Deuterium is a heavier than normal hydrogen isotope.

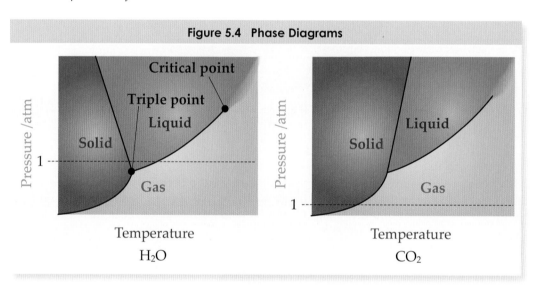

**Figure 5.4 Phase Diagrams**

$H_2O$

$CO_2$

For phase changes you must know where the energy goes. It enters the substance as heat or *PV* work, but what then? During a phase change, it breaks bonds and doesn't change the temperature. When the phase is NOT changing, energy increases molecular movement, which increases the temperature.

Think about this: for a single sample of a substance, *P*, *V*, *n*, and *T* are interrelated in such a way that if you know three of them, you can derive the other. This means that a phase diagram can also be given as a comparison between volume and pressure, or volume and temperature. What would that look like? See question 109 on the next page for the answer.

Comparing the phase diagrams for water and carbon dioxide, we notice some interesting things. Even if it were not labeled, we could approximate the location of the 1 atm mark for either diagram. We know that at atmospheric pressure, water exists in all three phases at different temperatures. Thus, we know that the 1 atmosphere mark must be above the triple point. Since carbon dioxide (dry ice) sublimes (changes from solid to gas) at one atmosphere, we know that the triple point must be above the 1 atm mark.

Compare the equilibrium line separating the liquid and solid phases on each diagram shown. For water, the line has a negative slope; for carbon dioxide, a positive slope. Most phase diagrams resemble carbon dioxide in this respect. The negative slope of water explains why ice floats. Since volume decreases with increasing pressure, as we move upward on the phase diagram from ice to liquid water, the volume occupied by $H_2O$ must be decreasing and thus the water must be increasing in density. Therefore, water must be denser than ice. The reason for this is that the crystal structure formed by ice requires more space than the random arrangement of water molecules.

**105.** What is the total heat needed to change 1 gram of water from −10°C to 110°C at 1 atm? ($\Delta H_{\text{fusion}}$ = 80 cal/g, $\Delta H_{\text{vaporization}}$ = 540 cal/g, specific heat of ice and steam are 0.5 cal/g °C)

   **A.** −730 cal
   **B.** −630 cal
   **C.** 630 cal
   **D.** 730 cal

**106.** When heat energy is added evenly throughout a block of ice at 0°C and 1 atm, all of the following are true EXCEPT:

   **A.** The temperature remains constant until all the ice is melted.
   **B.** The added energy increases the kinetic energy of the molecules.
   **C.** Entropy increases.
   **D.** Hydrogen bonds are broken.

**107.** Below is a phase diagram for carbon dioxide.

What is the critical temperature for carbon dioxide?

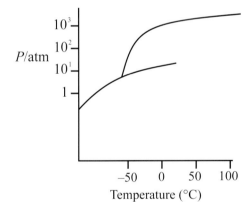

   **A.** −57°C
   **B.** 0°C
   **C.** 31°C
   **D.** 103°C

**108.** The diagram below compares the density of water in the liquid phase with its vapor phase.

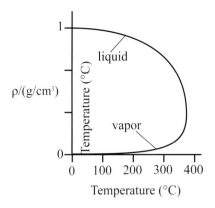

What is the critical temperature of water?

   **A.** 0°C
   **B.** 135°C
   **C.** 374°C
   **D.** 506°C

**109.** In graph (*a*) below, isotherms for water are plotted against pressure and volume. Graph (*b*) is a phase diagram of water with pressure vs. temperature.

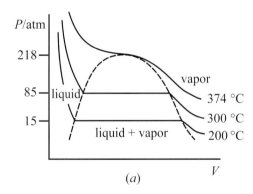

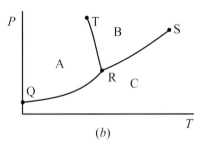

The area inside the dashed line on graph (*a*) is represented on graph (*b*) by:

   **A.** the line between points R and S.
   **B.** the area B.
   **C.** the area C.
   **D.** parts of both area B and C.

**110.** A solid 78 gram sample of benzene ($C_6H_6$) was gradually heated until it was melted completely. The heating curve for the sample is shown below.

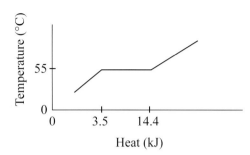

What is the heat of fusion of benzene?

A. 3.5 kJ/mole
B. 10.9 kJ/mole
C. 14.4 kJ/mole
D. 17.9 kJ/mole

**111.** At atmospheric pressure, the temperature of a pot of boiling water remains at 100°C, when heat is added. The best explanation as to why the added energy does not raise the temperature is that:

A. at the boiling point, the large heat capacity of water allows water to absorb the added energy.
B. the hydrogen bonds of water are strong enough to absorb the added energy without breaking.
C. as the water becomes steam, the added energy becomes kinetic energy of the gas molecules.
D. the added energy is used to break bonds between water molecules.

**112.** A student has a block of an unknown solid in the laboratory. Which of the following will most likely melt the block?

I. Heating the solid at constant pressure
II. Compressing the solid at constant temperature
III. Accelerating the solid to high speeds to increase its kinetic energy.

A. I only
B. I and II only
C. I and III only
D. I, II, and III

## 5.6 Colligative Properties

Some properties in chemistry depend solely on the number of particles, irrespective of the type of particle. Such properties are called **colligative**. There are four colligative properties of solutions: vapor pressure, boiling point, freezing point, and osmotic pressure.

Colligative properties depend upon number, not kind.

In Chemistry Lecture 4.6, we saw that the addition of a nonvolatile solute will lower the vapor pressure of the solution in direct proportion to the number of particles added, as per Raoult's law. The vapor pressure has an important relationship to the normal boiling point. When the vapor pressure of a solution rises to equal the pressure applied to the solution (typically local atmospheric pressure), the solution begins to boil. Thus, the boiling point of a substance is also changed by the addition of a solute. The addition of a nonvolatile solute lowers the the vapor pressure and elevates the boiling point. The equation for the **boiling point elevation** of an ideally dilute solution due to the addition of a nonvolatile solute is:

A substance boils when its vapor pressure equals the local atmospheric pressure.

$$\Delta T = k_b m i$$

where $k_b$ is a specific constant of the substance being boiled, $m$ is the molality of the solution, and $i$, called the **van't Hoff factor**, is the number of particles into which a single solute particle will dissociate when added to solution.

When using the nonvolatile solute equations, be sure to consider the number of particles after dissociation.

The van't Hoff factor has two possible values: the expected value and the observed value. For an ionic compound, the *expected value* of the van't Hoff factor is the number of ions created upon complete dissociation. For instance, the expected value of $i$ for NaCl is 2, and for $MgCl_2$ is 3. These values are for an ideally dilute solution. It turns out that, in a nonideal solution consisting of ions, there is *ion pairing*. Ion pairing is the momentary aggregation of two or more ions into a single particle. Ion pairing is not the solute incompletely dissolving; ion pairs are still in the aqueous phase. Ion pairs occur due to the strong attraction between positive and negative ions. The *observed value* of the van't Hoff factor will take into account ion pairing. Ion pairing increases with solution concentration, and decreases with increasing temperature. In a dilute solution, the observed value will be only slightly less than the expected value. On the MCAT, use the expected value unless otherwise instructed.

For boiling point and freezing point calculations molality is used instead of molarity because molality doesn't change with temperature while molarity does.

You cannot apply the boiling point elevation equation to volatile solutes. As shown in Chemistry Lecture 4.6, a volatile solute can actually decrease the boiling point by increasing the vapor pressure. If you know the heat of solution, you can make qualitative predictions about the boiling point change when a volatile solute is added. For instance, since you know that an endothermic heat of solution indicates weaker bonds, which lead to higher vapor pressure, you can predict that the boiling point will go down.

Melting point also changes when a solute is added, but it is not related to the vapor pressure. Instead, it is a factor of crystallization. Impurities (the solute) interrupt the crystal lattice and lower the freezing point. **Freezing point depression** for an ideally dilute solution is given by the equation:

$$\Delta T = k_f m i$$

Again, the constant $k_f$ is specific for the substance being frozen.

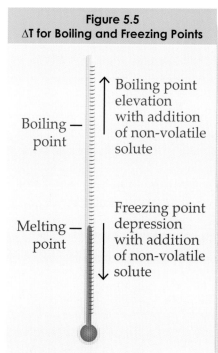

**Figure 5.5**
**ΔT for Boiling and Freezing Points**

Boiling point — | Boiling point elevation with addition of non-volatile solute

Melting point — | Freezing point depression with addition of non-volatile solute

In other words, if you add water to milk, at first you get watery milk. However, if you continue to add water you have something that looks more like milky water than watery milk. If you add enough water, you no longer even realize there is any milk. So when you add pure liquid B to pure liquid A, at first you are polluting liquid A and your freezing point drops below that of pure liquid A. At some point, however, if you continue to add pure liquid B, the freezing point of your solution begins to rise toward the freezing point of pure liquid B.

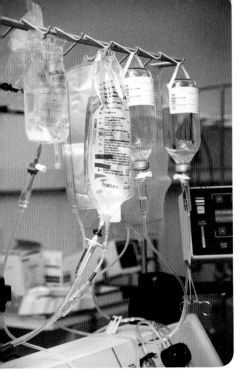

Albumin (shown here in solution in yellow) is a blood protein. Albumin plays a vital role in osmotic pressure regulation.

Be careful with freezing point depression. If you add a liquid solute, the impurities will initially lower the melting point; however, as the mole fraction of the solute increases, you will come to a point where the solvent becomes the impurity preventing the solute from freezing. At this point, additional solute acts to reduce the impurities creating a more pure solute, and the freezing point of the solution will rise as solute is added.

The fourth colligative property is **osmotic pressure**. Osmotic pressure is a measure of the tendency of water (or some other solvent) to move into a solution via osmosis. To demonstrate osmotic pressure, we divide a pure liquid by a membrane that is permeable to the liquid but not to the solute. We then add solute to one side. Due to entropy, nature wants to make both sides equally dilute. Since the solute cannot pass through the barrier to equalize the concentrations, the pure liquid begins to move to the solution side. As it does so, the solution level rises and the pressure increases. Eventually a balance between the forces of entropy and pressure is achieved. The extra pressure on the solution side is called osmotic pressure. Osmotic pressure $\Pi$ is given by:

$$\Pi = iMRT$$

where $M$ is the molarity of the solution.

Related to osmotic pressure is *osmotic potential*. Osmotic potential is a partial measure of a system's free energy. Pure water is arbitrarily assigned an osmotic potential of zero. When a solute is added, the osmotic potential becomes negative. At constant temperature and pressure, water flows from higher osmotic potential to lower osmotic potential. *Water potential*, another related term, is similar to osmotic potential but takes into account temperature and pressure. Water potential is essentially the same as free energy. When water and the solution in the diagram below have come to equilibrium, points $A$ and $B$ have the same water potential, but the osmotic potential of point $B$ is less than that of point $A$.

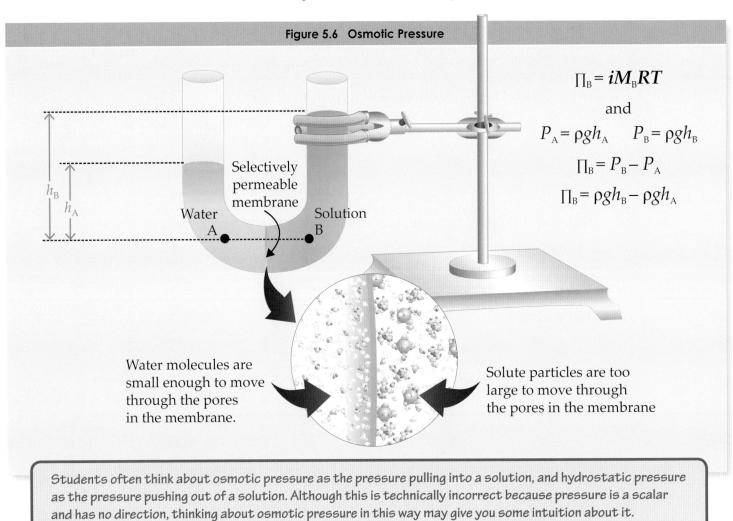

**Figure 5.6   Osmotic Pressure**

$$\Pi_B = iM_B RT$$

and

$$P_A = \rho g h_A \qquad P_B = \rho g h_B$$

$$\Pi_B = P_B - P_A$$

$$\Pi_B = \rho g h_B - \rho g h_A$$

Selectively permeable membrane

Water
A

Solution
B

Water molecules are small enough to move through the pores in the membrane.

Solute particles are too large to move through the pores in the membrane

Students often think about osmotic pressure as the pressure pulling into a solution, and hydrostatic pressure as the pressure pushing out of a solution. Although this is technically incorrect because pressure is a scalar and has no direction, thinking about osmotic pressure in this way may give you some intuition about it.

## 5.7 Equation Summary

| Equations |
|---|

**Heat Capacity**

$$q = C\Delta T$$

**Specific Heat Capacity**

$$q = mc\Delta T$$

**Calorie/ Specific Heat of Water**

$$c_{water} = 1 \; cal \; g^{-1} \; °C^{-1}$$

**Boiling Point Elevation**

$$\Delta T = k_b mi$$

**Freezing point depression**

$$\Delta T = k_f mi$$

**Osmotic Pressure**

$$\Pi = iMRT$$

| Terms | |
|---|---|
| Boiling Point Elevation | Heats of reaction |
| Bomb calorimeter | Heats of vaporization |
| Coffee cup calorimeter | Normal boiling point |
| Colligative Properties | Normal melting point |
| Critical point | Osmotic pressure |
| Critical pressure | Phase |
| Critical temperature | Phase diagram |
| Freezing point depression | Point elevation |
| Heat capacity $C$ | Triple point |
| Heats of fusion | Van't Hoff factor |

## Thought Provoker

*Answer from page 108:*

*The answer lies in the differences in specific heat. Sand has a very low specific heat of 0.48 J/(g·K). This means that it takes 0.48 J of energy to raise 1 gram of sand by 1 degree Celsius. Water, on the other hand, has a very high heat capacity at 4.18 J/(g·K). This means that it must absorb much more energy in order to raise 1g of water by 1 degree Celsius.*

*Answer from page 109:*

*Be careful here, the key in this question is to realize that both the cheese and the crust are at the same temperature. Looking at our equation, if ΔT is the same, the heat (q) is going to be the only difference. A higher specific heat will result in a greater q, thereby burning your mouth. Cheese must have a higher specific heat. Also, cheese conducts heat and transfers heat better than the crust.*

Questions 113 through 120 are **NOT** based on a descriptive passage.

113. Which of the following aqueous solutions will have the lowest boiling point?

    A. 0.5 $M$ glucose
    B. 1 $M$ glucose
    C. 0.5 $M$ NaCl
    D. 0.6 $M$ NaCl

114. An object experiences a greater buoyant force in seawater than in fresh water. The most likely reason for this is:

    A. Seawater has greater osmotic pressure making the pressure difference greater at different depths.
    B. Fresh water has greater osmotic pressure making the pressure difference greater at different depths.
    C. Seawater has greater density.
    D. Fresh water has greater density.

115. Glycol ($C_2H_6O_2$) is the main component in antifreeze. What mass of glycol must be added to 10 liters of water to prevent freezing down to –18.6°C? (The molal freezing point depression constant for water is 1.86°C kg/mol.)

    A. 3.1 kg
    B. 6.2 kg
    C. 10 kg
    D. 12.4 kg

116. A student holds a beaker of pure liquid $A$ in one hand and pure liquid $B$ in the other. Liquid $A$ has a higher boiling point than liquid $B$. When the student pours a small amount of liquid $B$ into liquid $A$, the temperature of the solution increases. Which of the following statements is true?

    A. The boiling point of the solution is lower than either pure liquid $A$ or $B$.
    B. The boiling point of the solution is higher than either pure liquid $A$ or $B$.
    C. The freezing point of the solution is higher than either pure liquid $A$ or $B$.
    D. The vapor pressure of the solution is higher than pure liquid $B$.

117. 500 ml of an aqueous solution having a mass of 503 grams and containing 20 grams of an unknown protein was placed into a bulb and lowered into pure water as shown. A membrane permeable to water but not to the solute separated the solution from the water.

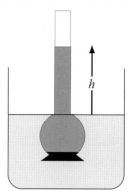

The height of the column of solution was found to be '$h$'. Which of the following statements is true concerning this procedure?

    A. A large value for $h$ indicates a low osmotic pressure in the solution.
    B. A large value for $h$ indicates a high osmotic pressure in the pure water.
    C. A large value for $h$ indicates that the protein has a low molecular weight.
    D. A large value for $h$ indicates that the protein has a high molecular weight.

118. Calcium chloride is sometimes sprinkled on winter sidewalks to melt snow and ice. If 333 grams of calcium chloride is dissolved completely in 1.00 kg of water, what will be the freezing point of the solution? (The molal freezing point depression constant for water is 1.86°C kg/mol.)

    A. –5.58°C
    B. –9.30°C
    C. –11.7°C
    D. –16.7°C

**119.** A popular experiment uses freezing point depression to find the molar mass of an unknown solute. If a known mass of an unknown non-polar solute is placed into a known mass of a known non-polar solvent and the freezing point depression is measured, which of the following expressions will be equal to the molar mass of the unknown solute?

A. $\dfrac{(k_f)(\text{grams of solute})}{(\Delta T)(\text{kg of solvent})}$

B. $\dfrac{(k_f)(\text{kg of solvent})}{(\Delta T)(\text{grams of solute})}$

C. $\dfrac{(\Delta T)(\text{grams of solute})}{(k_f)(\text{kg of solvent})}$

D. $\dfrac{(\Delta T)(\text{kg of solvent})}{(k_f)(\text{grams of solute})}$

**120.** A student prepared two solutions in separate flasks. Solution $A$ consisted of 0.1 mole of sodium fluoride in 1 liter of water. Solution $B$ consisted of 0.1 mole of potassium chloride in 1 liter of water. The student then heated both flasks and measured the boiling point of each solution. Which of the solutions would be expected to have the higher boiling point?

A. Solution $A$, because sodium fluoride has a lower molar mass than potassium chloride.
B. Solution $B$, because potassium chloride is less volatile than sodium fluoride.
C. Solution $A$, because potassium chloride will not dissociate completely in water.
D. Both solutions will have the same boiling point.

# ACIDS AND BASES

## 6.1 Definitions

There are three definitions of an acid that you must know for the MCAT: Arrhenius, Brønsted-Lowry, and Lewis. These definitions are given here in the order in which they were created. An **Arrhenius acid** is anything that produces hydrogen ions in aqueous solution, and an Arrhenius base is anything that produces hydroxide ions in aqueous solution. This definition covers only aqueous solutions. **Brønsted and Lowry** redefined acids as anything that donates a proton, and bases as anything that accepts a proton. Finally, the **Lewis** definition is the most general, defining an acid as anything that accepts a pair of electrons, and a base as anything that donates a pair of electrons. The Lewis definition includes all the acids and bases in the Brønsted-Lowry and more. Lewis acids include molecules that have an incomplete octet of electrons around the central atom, like $AlCl_3$ and $BF_3$. They also include all simple cations except the alkali and the heavier alkaline earth metal cations. The smaller the cation and the higher the charge, the stronger the acid strength. $Fe^{3+}$ is a common example of a Lewis acid. Molecules that are acidic only in the Lewis sense are not generally called acids unless they are referred to explicitly as Lewis acids.

Lewis
Acids

Brønsted-Lowry
Acids

Arrhenius
Acids

Notice that in the Bronsted definition, the acid 'donates', and in the Lewis definition the acid 'accepts'.

Acids taste sour or tart; bases taste bitter. Bases are slippery when wet.

Beware of Acid Rain

Relief work on the facade of St. Bartholomews Church in midtown Manhattan damaged from years of acid rain.

Although you must memorize the definitions, it is usually convenient to think of an acid as $H^+$ and a base as $OH^-$. In fact, aqueous solutions always contain both $H^+$ and $OH^-$. An aqueous solution containing a greater concentration of $H^+$ than $OH^-$ is acidic, while an aqueous solution containing a greater concentration of $OH^-$ than $H^+$ is basic. An aqueous solution with equal amounts of $H^+$ and $OH^-$ is neutral.

$$H^+ \qquad\qquad OH^-$$
$$\text{acid} \qquad\qquad \text{base}$$

> Many reactions in living cells involve the transfer of a proton. The rate of such reactions depends upon the concentration of $H^+$ ions or the pH.

One measure of the hydrogen ion concentration is called the pH, where $p(x)$ is a function in which, given any $x$, $p(x) = -\log(x)$. If we measure the hydrogen ion concentration in moles per liter ($[H+]$ the brackets always indicate concentration), pH is given by:

$$pH = -\log[H^+]$$

The scale for pH generally runs from 0 to 14, but since any $H^+$ concentration is possible, any pH value is possible. At 25°C, a pH of 7 is neutral; a lower pH is acidic and a higher pH is basic. Each point on the pH scale corresponds to a tenfold difference in hydrogen ion concentration. An acid with a pH of 2 produces 10 times as many hydrogen ions as an acid with a pH of 3, and 100 times as many hydrogen ions as an acid with a pH of 4.

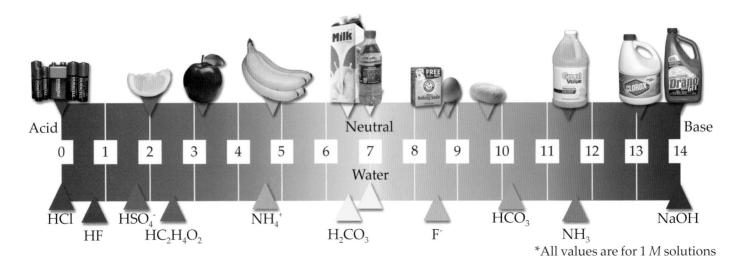

*All values are for 1 $M$ solutions

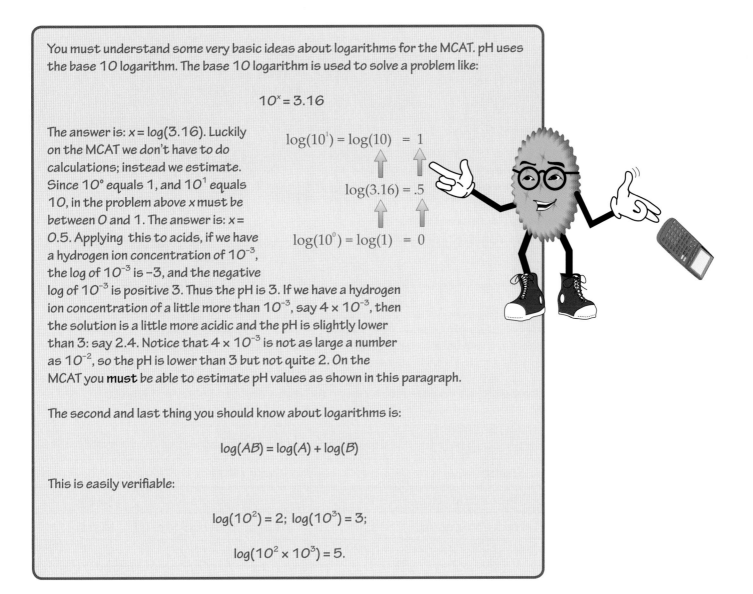

You must understand some very basic ideas about logarithms for the MCAT. pH uses the base 10 logarithm. The base 10 logarithm is used to solve a problem like:

$$10^x = 3.16$$

The answer is: $x = \log(3.16)$. Luckily on the MCAT we don't have to do calculations; instead we estimate. Since $10^0$ equals 1, and $10^1$ equals 10, in the problem above $x$ must be between 0 and 1. The answer is: $x = 0.5$. Applying this to acids, if we have a hydrogen ion concentration of $10^{-3}$, the log of $10^{-3}$ is $-3$, and the negative log of $10^{-3}$ is positive 3. Thus the pH is 3. If we have a hydrogen ion concentration of a little more than $10^{-3}$, say $4 \times 10^{-3}$, then the solution is a little more acidic and the pH is slightly lower than 3: say 2.4. Notice that $4 \times 10^{-3}$ is not as large a number as $10^{-2}$, so the pH is lower than 3 but not quite 2. On the MCAT you **must** be able to estimate pH values as shown in this paragraph.

$$\log(10^1) = \log(10) = 1$$
$$\log(3.16) = .5$$
$$\log(10^0) = \log(1) = 0$$

The second and last thing you should know about logarithms is:

$$\log(AB) = \log(A) + \log(B)$$

This is easily verifiable:

$$\log(10^2) = 2; \ \log(10^3) = 3;$$
$$\log(10^2 \times 10^3) = 5.$$

From the definitions of an acid, it must be clear that, if there is an acid in a reaction, there must also be a base; you can't have a proton donated without something to accept it. We can write a hypothetical acid-base reaction in aqueous solution as follows:

$$\textbf{HA} + \textbf{H}_2\textbf{O} \rightleftharpoons \textbf{H}_3\textbf{O}^+ + \textbf{A}^-$$

Here, HA is the acid, and, since water accepts the proton, water is the base. If we look at the reverse reaction, the hydronium ion donates a proton to $A^-$, making the hydronium ion the acid and $A^-$ the base. To avoid confusion, we refer to the reactants as the acid and base, and the products as the **conjugate acid** and **conjugate base**. Thus, in every reaction the acid has its conjugate base, and the base has its conjugate acid. Deciding which form is the conjugate simply depends upon in which direction you happen to be viewing the reaction.

You should recognize a hydronium ion $H_3O^+$. The hydronium ion is simply a hydrated proton. For MCAT acid and base reactions, a hydronium ion and a proton are the same thing.

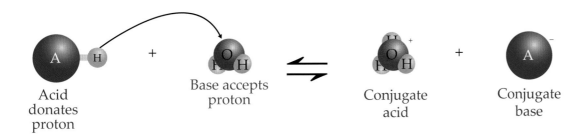

Acid donates proton

Base accepts proton

Conjugate acid

Conjugate base

In other words, it is correct to say either: "HA is the conjugate acid of base A⁻"; or "A⁻ is the conjugate base of acid HA." You must be able to identify conjugates on the MCAT.

You should also know that the stronger the acid, the weaker its conjugate base, and the stronger the base, the weaker its conjugate acid. **Warning:** Many students and even some prep books translate this into "Strong acids have weak conjugate bases, and weak acids have strong conjugate bases." The second part of this statement is incorrect! Acid strength is on the logarithmic scale and a weak acid may have a strong or weak conjugate base.

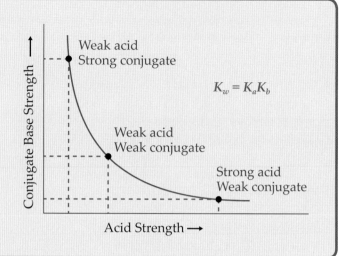

$$K_w = K_a K_b$$

Conjugate Base Strength ↑

Weak acid
Strong conjugate

Weak acid
Weak conjugate

Strong acid
Weak conjugate

Acid Strength →

Some substances act as either an acid or a base, depending upon their environment. They are called **amphoteric**. Water is a good example. In the reaction $HA + H_2O \rightarrow A^- + H_3O^+$, water acts as a base accepting a proton. Water can also act like an acid by donating a proton $A^- + H_2O \rightarrow HA + OH^-$.

For the MCAT, you need to recognize the strong acids and bases in Table 6.1.

By the way, when we say "strong acid" in inorganic chemistry, we mean an acid that is stronger than $H_3O^+$. A strong base is stronger than $OH^-$. With bases, we often call something as strong as $OH^-$, like NaOH, a strong base. For MCAT purposes, we assume that a strong acid or base completely dissociates in water.

| Table 6.1 Strong Acids and Bases | | | |
|---|---|---|---|
| *Strong Acids* | | *Strong Bases* | |
| Hydroiodic acid | HI | Sodium hydroxide | NaOH |
| Hydrobromic acid | HBr | Potassuim hydroxide | KOH |
| Hydrochloric acid | HCl | Amide ion | $NH_2^-$ |
| Nitric acid | $HNO_3$ | Hydride ion | $H^-$ |
| Perchloric acid | $HClO_4$ | Calcium hydroxide | $Ca(OH)_2$ |
| Chloric acid | $HClO_3$ | Sodium oxide | $Na_2O$ |
| Sulfuric acid | $H_2SO_4$ | Calcium oxide | CaO |

**Figure 6.1 Common Household Acids and Bases**

Acids

Bases

Some acids can donate more than one proton. These acids are called **polyprotic acids**. An acid that can donate just two protons can be called a **diprotic acid** as well as a polyprotic acid. The second proton donated by a polyprotic acid is usually so weak that its effect on the pH is negligible. On the MCAT the second proton can almost always be ignored. (The rule of thumb is that if the $K_a$ values differ by more than $10^3$, the second proton can be ignored.) For instance, the second proton from $H_2SO_4$ is a strong acid; yet, except with dilute concentrations (concentrations less than $1\ M$), it has a negligible effect on the pH of $H_2SO_4$ solution. This is because $H_2SO_4$ is so much stronger than $HSO_4^-$. Notice here that the percent dissociation of an acid decreases with acidity. This means that acids dissociate less in more concentrated solutions. It does not mean that concentrated solutions are less acidic.

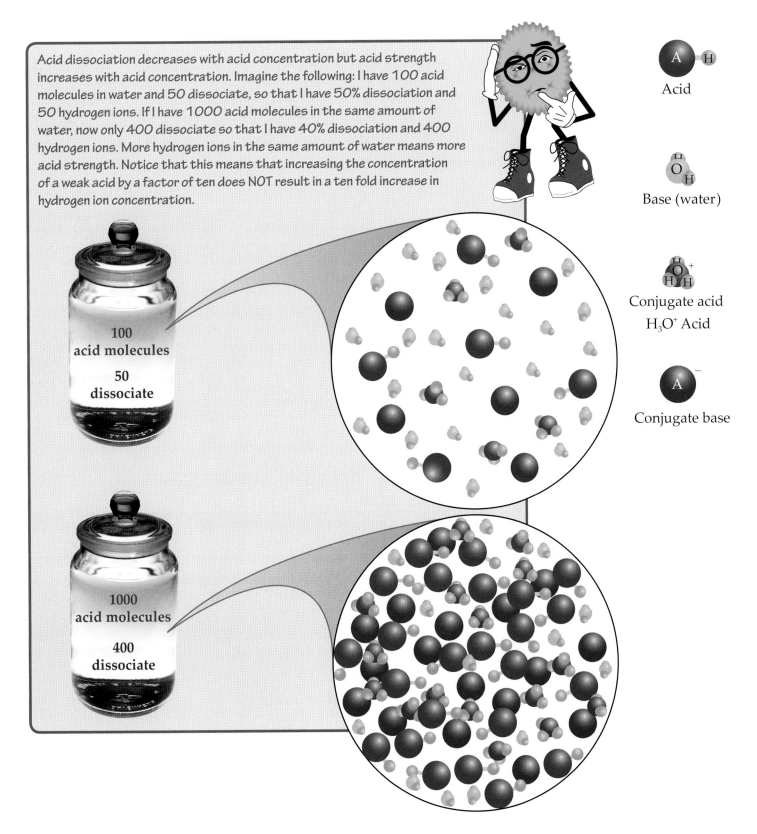

Acid dissociation decreases with acid concentration but acid strength increases with acid concentration. Imagine the following: I have 100 acid molecules in water and 50 dissociate, so that I have 50% dissociation and 50 hydrogen ions. If I have 1000 acid molecules in the same amount of water, now only 400 dissociate so that I have 40% dissociation and 400 hydrogen ions. More hydrogen ions in the same amount of water means more acid strength. Notice that this means that increasing the concentration of a weak acid by a factor of ten does NOT result in a ten fold increase in hydrogen ion concentration.

Acid

Base (water)

Conjugate acid
$H_3O^+$ Acid

Conjugate base

100
**acid molecules**

50
**dissociate**

1000
**acid molecules**

400
**dissociate**

## 6.2 How Molecular Structure Affects Acid Strength

There are three factors in molecular structure that determine whether or not a molecule containing a hydrogen will release its hydrogen into solution, and thus act as an acid:

1) The strength of the bond holding the hydrogen to the molecule;

2) The polarity of the bond; and

3) The stability of the conjugate base

If we examine the C–H bond in methane, which has extremely low acidity, it is nearly the same strength as the H–Cl bond in hydrochloric acid. However, the H–Cl bond is much more polar, and therefore the proton is more easily removed in aqueous solution. HCl is more acidic than methane. On the other hand, a comparison of the bond strengths and polarities of the hydrogen halides shows that, although the H–F bond is the most polar, it is also the strongest bond. In addition, the small size of the fluorine ion concentrates the negative charge and adds to its instability. In this case, the bond strength and conjugate instability outweigh the polarity, and HF is the weakest of the hydrogen halide acids.

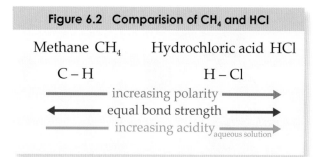

**Figure 6.2  Comparision of CH₄ and HCl**

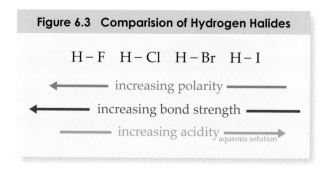

**Figure 6.3  Comparision of Hydrogen Halides**

> In a series of oxyacids, more oxygens means a stronger acid.

Keeping conjugate stability in mind, if we examine the oxyacids, we see that the electronegative oxygens draw electrons to one side of the bond, increasing polarity. The oxygens in the conjugate of an oxyacid can share the negative charge spreading it over a larger area and stabilizing the conjugate base. In similar oxyacids, the molecule with the most oxygens makes the strongest acid. Another way to look at this phenomenon is that the acidity increases with the oxidation number of the central atom.

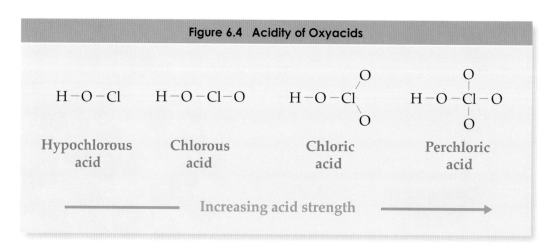

**Figure 6.4  Acidity of Oxyacids**

## 6.3 Hydrides

Binary compounds (compounds with only two elements) containing hydrogen are called hydrides. Hydrides can be basic, acidic, or neutral. On the periodic table, the basic hydrides are to the left, and the acidic hydrides are to the right. For instance, NaH is basic; $H_2S$ is acidic. Following this trend, metal hydrides are either basic or neutral, while nonmetal hydrides are acidic or neutral. (Ammonia, $NH_3$, is an exception to this rule.) The acidity of nonmetal hydrides tends to increase going down the periodic table. $H_2O < H_2S < H_2Se < H_2Te$

Calcium hydride ($CaH_2$) reacting with water, releasing hydrogen gas ($H_2$).

| Table 6.2  Non-metal Hydrides | | | | |
|---|---|---|---|---|
| | Group | | | |
| | 4A | 5A | 6A | 6A |
| Period 2 | $CH_4$ Neither acidic nor basic | $NH_3$ Weakly basic | $H_2O$ -------- | HF Weakly acidic |
| Period 3 | $SiH_4$ Neither acidic nor basic | $PH_3$ Weakly basic | $H_2S$ Weakly acidic | HCl Strongly acidic |

Increasing Acidity →

↓ Increasing Acidity

Increasing Acidity

Notes:

Questions 121 through 128 are **NOT** based on a descriptive passage.

**121.** Ammonia reacts with water to form the ammonium ion and hydroxide ion.

$$\mathbf{NH_3 + H_2O \rightarrow NH_4^+ + OH^-}$$

According to the Brønsted-Lowry definition of acids and bases, what is the conjugate acid of ammonia?

**A.** $NH_3$
**B.** $NH_4^+$
**C.** $OH^-$
**D.** $H^+$

**122.** By definition, a Lewis base:

**A.** donates a proton.
**B.** accepts a proton.
**C.** donates a pair of electrons.
**D.** accepts a pair of electrons.

**123.** Which of the following is the strongest base in aqueous solution?

**A.** $Cl^-$
**B.** $NH_4^+$
**C.** $F^-$
**D.** $Br^-$

**124.** Which of the following is amphoteric?

**A.** an amino acid
**B.** $H_2SO_4$
**C.** NaOH
**D.** HF

**125.** The addition of an electron withdrawing group to the alpha carbon of a carboxylic acid will:

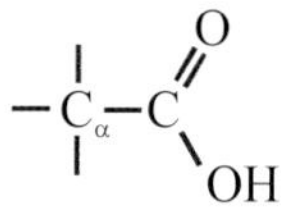

**A.** increase the acidity of the proton by making the O–H bond more polar.
**B.** increase the acidity of the proton by making the O–H bond stronger.
**C.** decrease the acidity of the proton by making the O–H bond more polar.
**D.** decrease the acidity of the proton by stabilizing the conjugate base.

**126.** A student prepared two acid solutions. Solution *A* has a hydrogen ion concentration of $6.0 \times 10^{-5}$ mole $L^{-1}$. Solution *B* has a hydrogen ion concentration of $1 \times 10^{-7}$ mole $L^{-1}$. The pH of solution *A* differs from that of solution *B* by:

**A.** 1.3
**B.** 2.8
**C.** 3.7
**D.** 5.0

**127.** In the reaction below, ammonia and boron trifluoride combine when a coordinate covalent bond is formed between nitrogen and boron. In this reaction, ammonia acts as a:

$$\mathbf{NH_3 + BF_3 \rightarrow H_3NBF_3}$$

**A.** Lewis acid
**B.** Lewis base
**C.** Brønsted-Lowry acid
**D.** Brøndted-Lowry base

**128.** Two chemical reactions involving water are shown below.

$$\mathbf{NH_4^+ + H_2O \rightarrow NH_3 + H_3O^+}$$
**Reaction 1**

$$\mathbf{NaH + H_2O \rightarrow Na^+ + OH^- + H_2}$$
**Reaction 2**

Which of the following is true?

**A.** Water acts as a base in Reaction 1 and an acid in Reaction 2.
**B.** Water acts as an acid in Reaction 1 and a base in Reaction 2.
**C.** Water acts as a base in both reactions.
**D.** Water acts as neither an acid nor a base.



**STOP.**

## 6.4 Equilibrium Constants for Acid-Base Reactions

Pure water reacts with itself to form hydronium and hydroxide ions as follows:

$$H_2O + H_2O \rightarrow H_3O^+ + OH^-$$

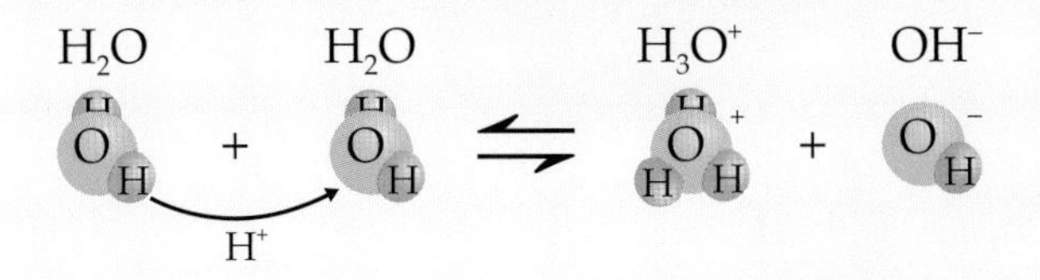

This is called the **autoionization of water**. $K_w$ is the equilibrium constant for this reaction.

$$K_w = [H^+][OH^-]$$

(For convenience, we have substituted $H^+$ for $H_3O^+$.) At 25°C the equilibrium of this reaction lies far to the left:

$$K_w = 10^{-14}$$

In a neutral aqueous solutions at 25°C, the $H^+$ concentration and the $OH^-$ concentration are equal at $10^{-7}$ mol $L^{-1}$. The pH of the solution is found by taking the negative log of the hydrogen ion concentration, which is: $-\log[10^{-7}] = 7$. An acid or base added to an aqueous solution will change the concentrations of both $H^+$ and $OH^-$, but $K_w$ will remain $10^{-14}$ at 25°C. For example, in a solution with a pH of 2, the ion concentrations will be: $[H^+] = 10^{-2}$ mol $L^{-1}$ and $[OH^-] = 10^{-12}$ mol $L^{-1}$. Using the p(x) function and the rule: $\log(AB) = \log(A) + \log(B)$, we can put this relationship into a simple equation:

$$pH + pOH = pK_w \qquad\qquad pH + pOH = 14$$

(For an aqueous solution at 25°C)

An acid will have its own equilibrium constant in water, called the **acid dissociation constant** $K_a$. If we use our hypothetical acid-base reaction: $HA + H_2O \rightarrow H_3O^+ + A^-$, then the acid dissociation constant for the acid HA is:

$$K_a = \frac{[H^+][A^-]}{[HA]}$$

Corresponding to every $K_a$, there is a $K_b$. The $K_b$ is the equilibrium constant for the reaction of the conjugate base with water. For the conjugate base $A^-$, the reaction is:

$$A^- + H_2O \rightarrow OH^- + HA$$

and the $K_b$ is:

$$K_b = \frac{[OH^-][HA]}{[A^-]}$$

Notice that the reaction for $K_b$ is the reaction of the conjugate base and water, and it is not the reverse of the reaction for $K_a$. Notice also that the product of the two constants is $K_w$.

$$K_a K_b = \frac{[H^+][A^-]}{[HA]} \times \frac{[OH^-][HA]}{[A^-]} = [H^+][OH^-] = K_w$$

$$K_a K_b = K_w$$

Using the p(x) function and the rule: $\log(AB) = \log(A) + \log(B)$, this formula can also be written as:

$$pK_a + pK_b = pK_w \qquad\qquad pK_a + pK_b = 14$$

(At 25°C)

### Figure 6.5  Autoionization of Water

It may seem like there are a lot of equations to memorize here, but it is really very simple.

**First**, all equilibrium constants are derived from the law of mass action. They are all products over reactants, where pure solids and liquids are given a concentration of one. Once you know how to find one $K$, you should know how to find any $K$. The subscript on the constant is supposed to make things less complicated, not more complicated.

**Second**, memorize that: $K_w = 10^{-14}$ at 25°C.

**Third**, remember the log rule, $\log(AB) = \log(A) + \log(B)$, and you can derive any of the equations.

Notice that the larger the $K_a$ and the smaller the $pK_a$, the stronger the acid. A $K_a$ greater than 1 or a $pK_a$ less than zero indicates a strong acid. The same is true of the $K_b$ and $pK_b$ of a base.

The pH of urine is affected by various chemicals in the blood.

Very strong acids and bases will dissociate almost completely. This means that the HA or BOH concentration (for the acid and base respectively) will be nearly zero. Since division by zero is impossible, for such acids and bases, there is no $K_a$ or $K_b$. Surprisingly, this fact makes it easier to find the pH of strong acid and strong base solutions. Since the entire concentration of acid or base is assumed to dissociate, the concentration of $H^+$ or $OH^-$ is the same as the original concentration of acid or base. For instance, a 0.01 molar solution of HCl will have 0.01 mol $L^{-1}$ of $H^+$ ions. Since $0.01 = 10^{-2}$, and $-\log(10^{-2}) = 2$, the pH of the solution will be 2. Likewise, in a 0.01 molar solution of NaOH, we will have 0.01 mol $L^{-1}$ of $OH^-$ ions. (Be careful here!) The pOH will equal 2 so the pH will equal 12. You can avoid a mistake here by remembering that an acid has a pH below 7 and a base has a pH above 7.

Weak acids and bases can be a little trickier. Doing a sample problem is the best way to learn. For example, in order to find the pH of a 0.01 molar solution of HCN, we do the following:

1.  Set up the equilibrium equation:

$$K_a = \frac{[H^+][CN^-]}{[HCN]} = 6.2 \times 10^{-10}$$

2.  If we add 0.01 moles of HCN to one liter of pure water, then '$x$' amount of that HCN will dissociate. Thus, we will have '$x$' mol $L^{-1}$ of $H^+$ ions and '$x$' mol $L^{-1}$ of $CN^-$ ions. The concentration of undissociated HCN will be whatever is left, or '$0.01 - x$'. Plugging these values into the equation above, we have:

$$\frac{[x][x]}{[0.01 - x]} = 6.2 \times 10^{-10}$$

3.  If we solve for $x$, we have a quadratic equation. Forget it! You don't need this for the MCAT. We make an assumption that $x$ is less than 5% of 0.01, and we will check it when we are done. Throwing out the $x$ in the denominator, we have:

$$\frac{[x][x]}{[0.01]} \approx 6.2 \times 10^{-10}$$

Thus, $x$ is approximately $2.5 \times 10^{-6}$. This is much smaller than 0.01, so our assumption was valid. '$x$' is the concentration of $H^+$ ions. The pH of the solution is between 5 and 6. This is close enough for the MCAT. Calculating the actual number gives us $-\log(2.5 \times 10^{-6}) = 5.6$. Just to make sure, we ask ourselves, "Is 5.6 a reasonable pH for a dilute weak acid?" The answer is yes.

For a weak base, the process is the same, except that we use $K_b$, and we arrive at the pOH. Subtract the pOH from 14 to find the pH. This step is often forgotten. If we ask ourselves, "Is this pH reasonable for a weak base?", we won't forget this step.

So notice that 0.01 M of weak acid yielded significantly less than 0.01 M H+ in solution, since weak acids do not dissociate completely. You should also appreciate that if we increase the concentration of the weak acid by a factor of 10, the pH will drop, but it will not drop down by a whole pH point. Again, this is because the extra added acid does not dissociate completely.

## 6.6 Salts

**Salts** are ionic compounds that dissociate in water. Often, when salts dissociate, they create acidic or basic conditions. The pH of a salt solution can be predicted qualitatively by comparing the conjugates of the respective ions. Find the conjugate of the salt cation by removing a proton from it. If the salt cation has no protons, then add OH to it to find the conjugate. Find the conjugate of the salt anion by adding a proton to it. Then compare the strength of the conjugates you've made. If the conjugates are both strong, then the salt solution is neutral. If one of the conjugates is strong and the other is weak, then the pH of the salt solution favors the strong conjugate. Here are some examples:

$Na^+$ and $Cl^-$ are the conjugates of NaOH and HCl respectively, so, as a salt, NaCl produces a neutral solution. $NH_4NO_3$ is composed of the conjugates of the base $NH_3$ and the strong acid $HNO_3$ respectively. Thus, $NH_4^+$ is acidic and $NO_3^-$ is neutral. As a salt, $NH_4NO_3$ is weakly acidic.

> When considering salts, remember, all cations, except those of the alkali metals and the heavier alkaline Earth metals ($Ca^{2+}$, $Sr^{2+}$, and $Ba^{2+}$), act as weak Lewis acids in aqueous solutions.

Himalayan rock salt
(sodium chloride)

Kala Namak (India)
(sodium chloride)

Alaea red salt (Hawaii)
(sodium chloride)

Black pearl salt (Hawaii)
(sodium chloride)

Maldon salt
(sodium chloride)

Himalayan salt
(sodium chloride)

Common salt
(sodium chloride)

Gerand salt
(sodium chloride)

Herb salt
(sodium chloride & herbs)

Atlantic sea salt
(sodium chloride)

Various types of salts are shown above. Salts vary in transparency, opacity, and color. The size of the individual crystals is a major determinant in the transparency of a salt.

**129.** Which of the following is the $K_b$ for the conjugate base of carbonic acid?

A. $\dfrac{[H_2CO_3]}{[H^+][HCO_3^-]}$

B. $\dfrac{[OH^-][HCO_3^-]}{[H_2CO_3]}$

C. $\dfrac{[H^+][H_2CO_3]}{[HCO_3^-]}$

D. $\dfrac{[OH^-][H_2CO_3]}{[HCO_3^-]}$

**130.** An aqueous solution of 0.1 $M$ HBr has a pH of:

A. 0
B. 1
C. 2
D. 14

**131.** Carbonic acid has a $K_a$ of $4.3 \times 10^{-7}$. What is the pH when 1 mole of $NaHCO_3$ is dissolved in 1 liter of water?

A. 3.2
B. 3.8
C. 10.2
D. 12.5

**132.** Stomach acid has a pH of approximately 2. Sour milk has a pH of 6. Stomach acid is:

A. 3 times as acidic as sour milk.
B. 4 times as acidic as sour milk.
C. 100 times as acidic as sour milk.
D. 10,000 times as acidic as sour milk.

**133.** Which of the following salts is the most basic?

A. $NaClO_3$
B. $NH_4Cl$
C. KBr
D. NaCN

**134.** The acid dissociation constant for HBrO is $2 \times 10^{-9}$. What is the base dissociation constant for $BrO^-$?

A. $5 \times 10^{-5}$
B. $5 \times 10^{-6}$
C. $5 \times 10^{-7}$
D. $5 \times 10^{-8}$

**135.** A solution of soapy water has a pH of 10. What is the hydroxide ion concentration?

A. $10^{-10}\ M$
B. $10^{-7}\ M$
C. $10^{-4}\ M$
D. $10^{-1}\ M$

**136.** When solid sodium acetate, $NaC_2H_3O_2$ is added to pure water, the pH of the solution will:

A. decrease because $Na^+$ acts as an acid.
B. increase because $Na^+$ acts as a base.
C. decrease because $C_2H_3O_2^-$ acts as an acid.
D. increase because $C_2H_3O_2^-$ acts as a base.

## 6.7 Titrations

A **titration** is the drop-by-drop mixing of an acid and a base. Titrations are performed in order to find the concentration of some unknown by comparing it with the concentration of the **titrant**. The changing pH of the unknown as the acidic or basic titrant is added is represented graphically as a sigmoidal curve. Figure 6.6 is the **titration curve** of a strong acid titrated by a strong base.

Notice the portion of the graph that most nearly approximates a vertical line. The midpoint of this line is called the **equivalence point** or the **stoichiometric point**. The equivalence point for a monoprotic acid is the point in the titration when there are equal equivalents of acid and base in solution. (An *equivalent* is the mass of acid or base necessary to produce or consume one mole of protons.) For instance, since there is a one to one correspondence between HCl with NaOH, the equivalence point for a titration of HCl with NaOH will be reached when the same number of moles of HCl and NaOH exist in solution. This is not necessarily when they are at equal volumes. If the concentrations differ (and they probably will) the equivalence point will not be where the volumes are equal.

For equally strong acid-base titrations, the equivalence point will usually be at pH 7. (**Warning!** For a diprotic acid whose conjugate base is a strong acid, like $H_2SO_4$, this is not the case.)

The graph to the right is for the titration of a strong acid with a strong base. In other words, we are slowly adding base to an acid. This is clear because we start with a very low pH and finish with a very high pH. For a titration of a strong base with a strong acid, we would simply invert the graph.

A titration of an acid in aqueous solution with a base.

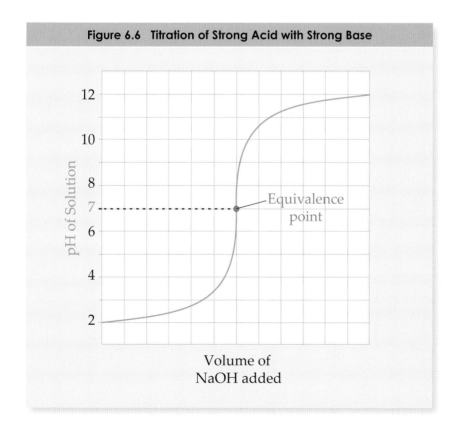

Figure 6.6  Titration of Strong Acid with Strong Base

*More Titrations and Buffered Solutions*

The titration of a weak acid with a strong base looks slightly different than the curve in Figure 6.6, and is shown below. The equivalence point is also not as predictable. Of course, if the base is stronger than the acid, the equivalence point will be above 7, and if the acid is stronger than the base, the equivalence point will be below 7.

Before a titration of a weak acid with a strong base begins you have 100% HA. At the half equivalence point the base has stripped the protons off of exactly half the molecules of acid, so at the half equivalence point HA = A⁻. At the equivalence point the base has stripped all the protons from all the acid molecules, and you have 100% A⁻.

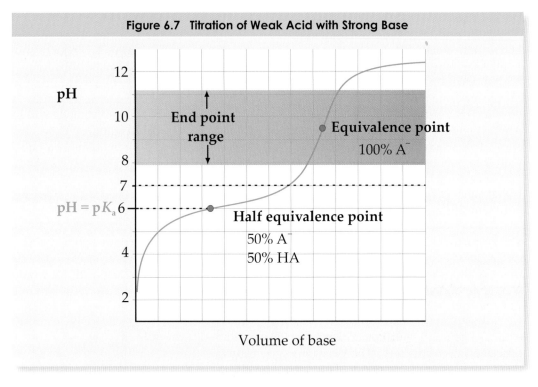

**Figure 6.7   Titration of Weak Acid with Strong Base**

Notice the half equivalence point. This is probably more likely be tested by the MCAT than the equivalence point. The **half equivalence point** is the point where exactly one half of the acid has been neutralized by the base. In other words, the concentration of the acid is equal to the concentration of its conjugate base. Notice that the half equivalence point occurs at the midpoint of the section of the graph that most represents a horizontal line. This is the spot where we could add the largest amount of base or acid with the least amount of change in pH. Such a solution is considered to be **buffered**. The half equivalence point shows the point in the titration where the solution is the most well buffered.

The Henderson-Hasselbalch equation is simply a form of the equilibrium expression for $K_a$:

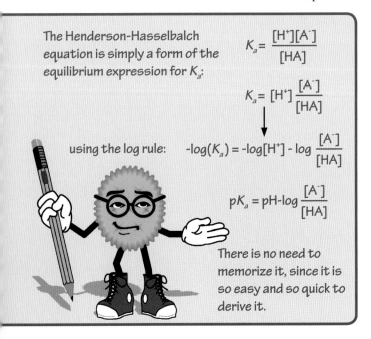

$$K_a = \frac{[H^+][A^-]}{[HA]}$$

$$K_a = [H^+]\frac{[A^-]}{[HA]}$$

using the log rule:  $-\log(K_a) = -\log[H^+] - \log\frac{[A^-]}{[HA]}$

$$pK_a = pH - \log\frac{[A^-]}{[HA]}$$

There is no need to memorize it, since it is so easy and so quick to derive it.

Notice also that, at the half equivalence point, the pH of the solution is equal to the $pK_a$ of the acid. This is predicted by the **Henderson-Hasselbalch equation**:

$$pH = pK_a + \log\frac{[A^-]}{[HA]}$$

Recall that $\log(1) = 0$; thus when $[A^-] = [HA]$, $pH = pK_a$.

If we were to make a buffer solution, we would start with an acid whose $pK_a$ is closest to the pH at which we want to buffer our solution. Next we would mix equal amounts of that acid with its conjugate base. We would want the concentration of our buffer solution to greatly exceed the concentration of outside acid or base affecting our solution. So, a buffer solution is made from equal and copious amounts of a weak acid and its conjugate base.

It appears from the Henderson-Hasselbalch equation that we could add an infinite amount of water to a buffered solution with no change in pH. Of course, this is ridiculous. Will adding Lake Tahoe to a beaker of buffered solution change the pH of that solution? The Henderson-Hasselbalch equation in the form above does not allow for *ion pairing*. (Ion pairing is when oppositely charged ions in solution bond momentarily to form a single particle.) Water will generally act like a base in acidic solution and an acid in basic solution. If you add a base or water to an acidic, buffered solution, it is clear from the titration curve that the pH will increase. It just won't increase as rapidly as other solutions less well buffered. However, a question on the MCAT is more likely to consider the ideal circumstance where adding a *small* amount of water to an ideally dilute, buffered solution will have no effect on the pH.

**Warning!** You cannot typically use the Henderson-Hasselbalch equation to find the pH at the equivalence point. Instead, you must use the $pK_b$ of the conjugate base. You can find the $K_b$ from the $pK_a$ and the $K_w$. The concentration of the conjugate base at the equivalence point is equal to the number of moles of acid divided by the volume of acid plus the volume of base used to titrate. Don't forget to consider the volume of base used to titrate. Unless the base has no volume, the concentration of the conjugate at the equivalence point will not be equal to the original concentration of the acid. The pH at the equivalence point involves much more calculation than the pH at the half equivalence point. For this reason, it is more likely that the MCAT will ask about the pH at the half equivalence point.

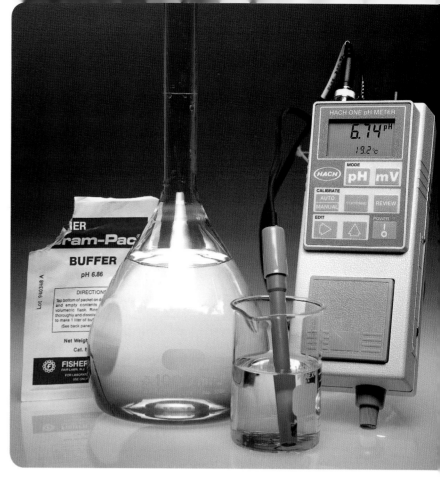

The pH of a buffer remains constant regardless of the volume of the solution.

Finding the pH at the equivalence point is a good exercise, but you won't have to do it on the MCAT. Here are the steps:

Use $K_a$ and $K_w$ to find the $K_b$

$$K_b = \frac{K_w}{K_a}$$

Set up the $K_b$ equilibrium expression.

$$K_b = \frac{[OH^-][HA]}{[A^-]}$$

Solve for the OH⁻ concentration, and find the pOH.

Subtract the pOH from 14 to find the pH.

$$14 - pOH = pH$$

Acid-base reaction with indicator. A reaction of lemon juice, baking powder, and a universal indicator.

## 6.9 Indicators and the End Point

To find the equivalence point, a chemical called an **indicator** is used. (A pH meter can also be used.) The indicator is usually a weak acid whose conjugate base is a different color. We can designate an indicator as HIn, where In⁻ represents the conjugate base. In order for the human eye to detect a color change, the new form of the indicator must reach ¹⁄₁₀ the concentration of the original form. For example, if we titrate an acid with a base, we add a small amount of indicator to our acid. (We add only a small amount because we don't want the indicator to affect the pH.) At the initial low pH, the HIn form of the indicator predominates. As we titrate, and the pH increases, the In⁻ form of the indicator also increases. When the In⁻ concentration reaches ¹⁄₁₀ of the HIn concentration, a color change can be detected by the human eye. If we titrate a base with an acid, the process works in reverse. Thus, the pH of the color change depends upon the direction of the titration. The pH values of the two points of color change give the **range** of an indicator. An indicator's range can be predicted by using the Henderson-Hasselbalch equation as follows:

$$ pH = pK_a + \log \frac{[In^-]}{[HIn]} $$

lower range of color change $\Rightarrow$ $pH = pK_a + \log \frac{1}{10} \Rightarrow pH = pK_a - 1$

upper range of color change $\Rightarrow$ $pH = pK_a + \log \frac{10}{1} \Rightarrow pH = pK_a + 1$

The point where the indicator changes color is called the **endpoint**. Do not confuse the equivalence point with the end point. We usually choose an indicator whose range will cover the equivalence point.

You can also monitor the pH with a pH meter. A pH meter is a concentration cell comparing the voltage difference between different concentrations of H⁺. (See Chemistry Lecture 7 for concentration cells.)

Since we established that the Henderson-Hasselbalch equation is not useful to find the pH of the equivalence point, how can it be useful to find an indicator range that will include the equivalence point?

The answer is that we are using the indicator concentrations in the Henderson-Hasselbalch equation, and the indicator never reaches its equivalence point in the titration. The indicator ions do not approach zero concentration near the color change range.

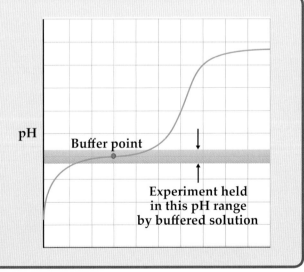

## 6.10 Polyprotic Titrations

Titrations of polyprotic acids will have more than one equivalence point and more than one half equivalence point. For the MCAT, assume that the first proton completely dissociates before the second proton begins to dissociate. (This assumption is only acceptable if the second proton is a much weaker acid than the first, which is usually the case.) Thus we have a titration curve like the one shown below.

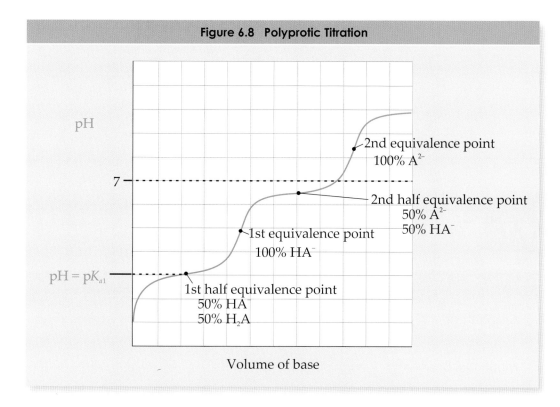

**Figure 6.8 Polyprotic Titration**

A digital pH meter measures the pH of a solution by comparing the electrical potential of the solution to the electrical potential of a standard solution inside the meter.

Notes:

## 6.11 Equation Summary

| Equations | | |
|---|---|---|
| **Acid** | **Base** | **pH** |
| $H^+$ | $OH^-$ | $pH = -\log[H^+]$ |

**Henderson-Hasselbalch equation**

$$pH = pK_a + \log\frac{[A^-]}{[HA]}$$

## 6.12 Terms You Need to Know

| Terms | |
|---|---|
| Amphoteric | Hydronium Ion $H_3O^+$ |
| Arrhenius Acid | Indicator |
| Arrhenius Base | $K_a$ |
| Autoionization of Water | $K_b$ |
| Brønsted-Lowry Acid | Lewis Acid |
| Brønsted-Lowry Base | Lewis Base |
| Buffered | Polyprotic |
| Conjugate Acid | Range |
| Conjugate Base | Salts |
| Diprotic | Stoichiometric Point |
| Endpoint | Titrant |
| Equivalence Point | Titration |
| Half Equivalence Point | Titration Curve |
| Henderson-Hasselbalch Equation | |

**137.** The titration curve below represents the titration of:

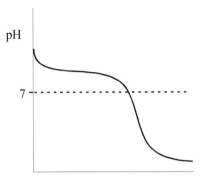

A. a strong acid with a weak base.
B. a strong base with a weak acid.
C. a weak acid with a strong base.
D. a weak base with a strong acid.

**138.** The following is a list of acid dissociation constants for 4 acids.

|  | $K_a$ |
| --- | --- |
| Acid 1 | $1.2 \times 10^{-7}$ |
| Acid 2 | $8.3 \times 10^{-7}$ |
| Acid 3 | $3.3 \times 10^{-6}$ |
| Acid 4 | $6.1 \times 10^{-5}$ |

Which acid should be used to manufacture a buffer at a pH of 6.1?

A. Acid 1
B. Acid 2
C. Acid 3
D. Acid 4

**139.** If the expected equivalence point for a titration is at a pH of 8.2, which of the following would be the best indicator for the titration?

| Indicator | $K_a$ |
| --- | --- |
| phenolphthalein | $1.0 \times 10^{-8}$ |
| bromthymol blue | $7.9 \times 10^{-8}$ |
| methyl orange | $3.2 \times 10^{-4}$ |
| methyl violet | $1.4 \times 10^{-3}$ |

A. phenolphthalein
B. bromthymol blue
C. methyl orange
D. methyl violet

**140.** On the titration curve of the $H_2CO_3$ pictured below, at which of the following points is the concentration of $HCO_3^-$ the greatest?

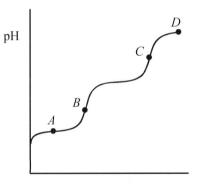

A. point $A$
B. point $B$
C. point $C$
D. point $D$

**141.** Which of the following is the equivalence point when the weak acid, acetic acid, is titrated with NaOH?

A. 4.3
B. 7
C. 8.7
D. 14

142. A buffered solution has a pH that cannot readily be changed. A buffered solution will be produced by mixing equal volumes of:

A. 1 $M$ HCl and 1 $M$ NaC$_2$H$_3$O$_2$
B. 1 $M$ HCl and 1 $M$ NaOH
C. 1 $M$ HC$_2$H$_3$O$_2$ and 1 $M$ NaC$_2$H$_3$O$_2$
D. 1 $M$ HC$_2$H$_3$O$_2$ and 1 $M$ NaOH

143. All of the following statements regarding HCO$_3^-$ are true EXCEPT:

A. HCO$_3^-$ can act as a Brønsted Lowry acid.
B. HCO$_3^-$ can act as a Lewis base.
C. HCO$_3^-$ is amphoteric.
D. HCO$_3^-$ is a polyprotic acid.

144. The acid dissociation constant for HC$_6$H$_7$O$_6$ is $8.0 \times 10^{-5}$. If a solution contains equal concentrations of HC$_6$H$_7$O$_6$ and C$_6$H$_7$O$_6^-$, what will be the pH of the solution?

A. 3.0
B. 4.1
C. 5.3
D. 9.0

# ELECTROCHEMISTRY

## 7.1 Oxidation-Reduction

In an oxidation-reduction reaction (called a **redox reaction** for short), electrons are transferred from one atom to another. The atom that loses electrons is **oxidized**; the atom that gains electrons is **reduced**.

## 7.2 Oxidation States

In order to keep track of the electrons in a redox reaction, you must memorize the **oxidation states** of certain atoms. Oxidation states are the possible charge values that an atom may hold within a molecule. In many cases, these charges don't truly exist; it is simply a system to follow the electrons of a redox reaction. Even though they do not represent actual charges, the oxidation states must add up to the charge on the molecule or ion. For instance, the sum of the oxidation states of the atoms in a neutral molecule must equal zero. The oxidation states that you must memorize for the MCAT are given in Table 7.1. When a conflict arises, the rule occupying the higher position on the table is given priority.

**Table 7.1 General Oxidation State Rules**

| Oxidation State | Atom |
|---|---|
| 0 | Atoms in their elemental form |
| -1 | Fluorine |
| +1 | Hydrogen (except when bonded to a metal, like NaH: then -1.) |
| -2 | Oxygen (except when it is in a peroxide, like $H_2O_2$: then -1.) |

In general, when in a compound, elements in the following groups have the oxidation states listed in the table below. It is helpful to know Table 7.2 but not crucial for the MCAT.

**Table 7.2  Group Oxidation States**

| Oxidation State | Group on Periodic Table |
|---|---|
| +1 | Group 1 elements (alkali metals) |
| +2 | Group 2 elements (alkaline earth metals) |
| -3 | Group 15 elements (nitrogen family) |
| -2 | Group 16 elements (oxygen family) |
| -1 | Group 17 elements (halogens) |

The idea is simple; a general guideline for oxidation states is the atom's variance from a noble gas configuration. However, if all atoms had permanent oxidation states, no redox reactions could take place. The oxidation states in Table 7.2 are to be used only as a general guideline. When the two tables conflict, the first table is given priority. For example, the oxidation state of nitrogen in $NO_3^-$ is +5 because the –2 on the oxygens have priority and dictate the oxidation state on nitrogen. (Don't forget that the oxidation states for $NO_3^-$ must add up to the 1– charge on the molecule.) The transition metals change oxidation states according to the atoms with which they are bonded. Although each transition metal has only certain oxidation states that it can attain, the MCAT will not require that you memorize these.

The following is an example of a redox reaction:

$$2H_2 + O_2 \rightarrow 2H_2O$$

Here oxygen and hydrogen begin in their elemental form, and thus have an oxidation state of zero. Once the water molecule is formed, hydrogen's oxidation state is +1, and oxygen's is –2. In this case, we say that hydrogen has been **oxidized**; hydrogen has lost electrons; its oxidation state has increased from 0 to +1. Oxygen, on the other hand, has been reduced; it has gained electrons; its oxidation state has been reduced from 0 to –2. Whenever there is oxidation, there must also be reduction.

Since in any redox reaction one atom is oxidized and another atom is reduced, there is a **reducing agent** (also called the **reductant**) and an **oxidizing agent** (also called the **oxidant**). Because the reducing agent is giving electrons to an atom, an atom in the reducing agent must be giving up some of its own electrons. Since an atom in the reducing agent gives up electrons, an atom in the reducing agent is oxidized. The reverse is true for the oxidizing agent. Thus, the reducing agent is the compound containing the atom being oxidized, and the oxidizing agent is the compound containing the atom being reduced. For example, in the following reaction, methane is the reducing agent and dioxygen is the oxidizing agent.

Carbon goes from –4 to +4.

$$CH_4 + 2O_2 \rightarrow CO_2 + 2H_2O$$

Oxygen goes from 0 to –2.

To help keep oxidation and reduction straight, just remember:

**L**ose **E**lectrons **O**xidation    **the Lion says...**    **G**ain **E**lectrons **R**eduction

Notice that the reducing agents and oxidizing agents are compounds, not atoms. In a redox reaction, the atom is oxidized or reduced; the compound is the oxidant or reductant. In the reaction:

$$Cd(s) + NiO_2(s) + 2H_2O(l) \rightarrow Cd(OH)_2(s) + Ni(OH)_2(s)$$

Ni is reduced. $NiO_2$ is the oxidizing agent.

> The oxidizing agent gets reduced;
> the reducing agent gets oxidized.

Psst! Take these electrons and get outta the country fast.

Reducing Agent Salty

## 7.3 Oxidation-Reduction Titrations

In a redox titration we want to find the molarity of a reducing agent. To do this, we titrate with a strong oxidizing agent. Instead of pH on the $y$-axis of our graph, we will have a voltage. Recall from Physics Lecture 7.1 that voltage is a potential <u>difference</u>, so, in order to even have a voltage, our solution must be <u>different</u> from another solution. We call that other solution a *standard solution*. When *referenced* to a standard solution, our solution with the reducing agent has a potential difference or voltage. As we add strong oxidizing agent to our solution, the voltage increases, at first gradually and then quite suddenly. Just like in an acid/base titration there is a half equivalence point near the middle of the gradual increase and an equivalence point when the voltage suddenly shoots up. Like an acid/base titration, we choose an indicator that changes color as close as possible to the expected equivalence point, or we simply monitor the voltage with a voltmeter.

> Knowledge of oxidation-reduction titrations is not required for the MCAT. However, it is possible that there will be a passage which explains them. They are included here just so you won't be shocked if you see one in a passage.

The equivalence point occurs when all the moles of reducing agent in our solution have been completely oxidized. Unlike an acid/base titration where the number of moles of base required to reach the equivalence points is equal to the number of moles of acid in the solution being titrated, in a redox titration the number of moles of oxidizing agent required to reach the equivalence point will be <u>either</u> equal <u>or</u> some multiple of the number of moles of the reducing agent in the solution being titrated. This is because one molecule of the oxidizing agent may accept a different number of electrons than one molecule of the reducing agent gives up.

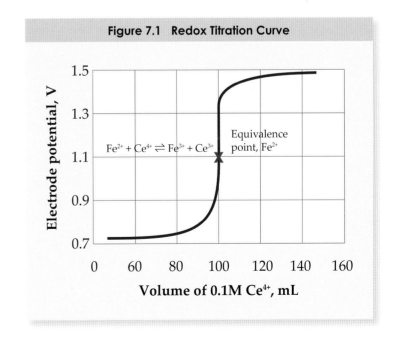

**Figure 7.1  Redox Titration Curve**

$Fe^{2+} + Ce^{4+} \rightleftharpoons Fe^{3+} + Ce^{3+}$

Equivalence point, $Fe^{2+}$

Electrode potential, V

Volume of 0.1M $Ce^{4+}$, mL

For example, imagine we have 100 mL of a solution with an unknown concentration of $Sn^{2+}$ ions. To discover the concentration, we titrate with a 5 mM solution of the strong oxidizing agent $Ce^{4+}$. In this reaction, $Sn^{2+}$ will be oxidized to $Sn^{4+}$, while $Ce^{4+}$ will be reduced to $Ce^{3+}$.

$$Sn^{2+} \rightarrow Sn^{4+} + 2e^-$$
$$Ce^{4+} + e^- \rightarrow Ce^{3+}$$

Since each atom of $Sn^{2+}$ is giving up two electrons, and each atom of $Ce^{4+}$ is accepting only one electron, two $Ce^{4+}$ atoms will be required for each $Sn^{2+}$ atom. If 2 mL of $Ce^{4+}$ solution are required to reach the equivalence point, we find the molarity of the original $Sn^{2+}$ solution as follows:

$$2 \text{ mL}_{Ce^{4+} \text{ solution}} \times \frac{5 \text{ mmol}}{L} \times \frac{1L}{1000 \text{ mL}} = 0.01 \text{ mmoles of } Ce^{4+}$$

Since we need two atoms of $Ce^{4+}$ to oxidize only one atom of $Sn^{2+}$, 0.01 mmoles of $Ce^{4+}$ are required to oxidize 0.005 mmoles of $Sn^{2+}$.

$$\frac{0.005 \text{ mmoles of } Sn^{2+}}{100 \text{ mL}_{\text{Unknown}Sn^{2+} \text{ solution}}} \times \frac{1000 \text{ mL}}{L} = 0.05 \text{ mM}_{Sn^{2+} \text{ solution}}$$

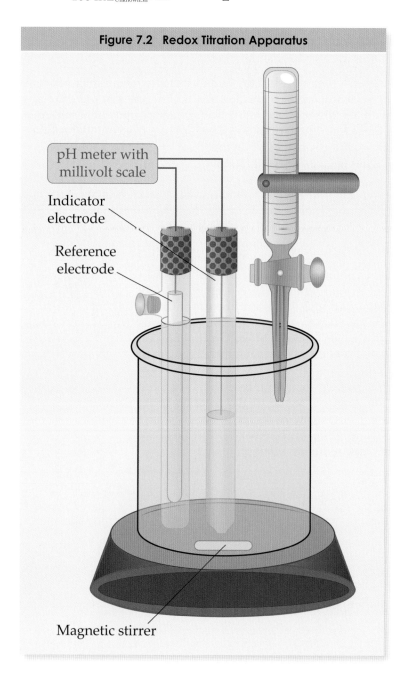

**Figure 7.2   Redox Titration Apparatus**

pH meter with millivolt scale

Indicator electrode

Reference electrode

Magnetic stirrer

**145.** What is the oxidation state of sulfur in $HSO_4^-$?

   **A.** $-2$
   **B.** $+3$
   **C.** $+6$
   **D.** $+7$

**146.** Which of the following statements is true concerning the reaction:

$$2Al_2O_3 + 3C \rightarrow 4Al + 3CO_2$$

   **A.** Both aluminum and carbon are reduced.
   **B.** Both aluminum and carbon are oxidized.
   **C.** Aluminum is reduced and carbon is oxidized.
   **D.** Carbon is reduced and aluminum is oxidized.

**147.** What is the reducing agent in the following reaction:

$$2HCl + Zn \rightarrow ZnCl_2 + H_2$$

   **A.** $Zn$
   **B.** $Zn^{2+}$
   **C.** $H^+$
   **D.** $Cl^-$

**148.** The first step in producing pure lead from galena (PbS) is as follows:

$$2PbS(s) + 3O_2(g) \rightarrow 2PbO(s) + 2SO_2(g)$$

All of the following are true concerning this reaction EXCEPT:

   **A.** Both lead and sulfur are oxidized.
   **B.** Oxygen is the oxidizing agent.
   **C.** Lead sulfide is the reducing agent.
   **D.** Lead is neither oxidized nor reduced.

**149.** All of the following are always true concerning oxidation-reduction reactions EXCEPT:

   **A.** An atom in the reducing agent is always oxidized.
   **B.** If reduction takes place, so must oxidation.
   **C.** An atom in the oxidizing agent gains electrons.
   **D.** If an atom of the reductant loses two electrons, an atom of the oxidant gains two electrons.

**150.** The process below takes place in acidic solution.

$$NO_2^-(aq) \rightarrow NO_3^-(aq)$$

In this process, the oxidation state of nitrogen is:

   **A.** reduced from +2 to +3.
   **B.** oxidized from +2 to +3.
   **C.** reduced from +3 to +5.
   **D.** oxidized from +3 to +5.

**151.** Which of the following statements is true about the reaction below?

$$HNO_3 + NaHCO_3 \rightarrow NaNO_3 + H_2CO_3$$

   **A.** Nitrogen is reduced and oxygen is oxidized.
   **B.** Oxygen is reduced and carbon is oxidized.
   **C.** Hydrogen is reduced and sodium is oxidized.
   **D.** No oxidation or reduction takes place.

**152.**
$$Cl_2 + 2Br^- \rightarrow Br_2 + 2Cl^-$$

In the reaction shown above,

   **A.** $Cl_2$ is the oxidizing agent and $Br^-$ is oxidized.
   **B.** $Cl_2$ is the oxidizing agent and $Br^-$ is reduced.
   **C.** $Cl_2$ is the reducing agent and $Br^-$ is oxidized.
   **D.** $Cl_2$ is the reducing agent and $Br^-$ is reduced.

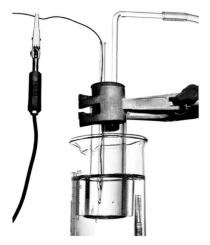

Standard hydrogen electrodes are devices constructed to provide a standard baseline against which to measure oxidation-reduction potentials.

Notice that, except for nickel, the metals used to make coins have negative oxidation potentials. In other words, unlike most metals, platinum, gold, silver, mercury, and copper do not oxidize (or dissolve) spontaneously under standard conditions in the presence of aqueous H⁺.

Also notice that Table 7.3 gives us the reduction potential for $Ag^{2+}(aq)$ and the oxidation potential for $Ag(s)$. (Warning: The table does not give us the oxidation potential for $Ag^{2+}$.) The strongest oxidizing agent is shown on the upper left hand side of a reduction table. The strongest reducing agent is shown on the lower right hand side of a reduction table. Notice that water is both a poor oxidizing agent and a poor reducing agent.

Finally, notice that the second half reaction in Table 7.3 is part of the final reaction in aerobic respiration where oxygen accepts electrons to form water. Predictably, this reaction has a high positive potential.

## 7.4 Potentials

Since in a redox reaction electrons are transferred, and since electrons have charge, there is an **electric potential (E)** associated with any redox reaction. The potentials for the oxidation component and reduction component of a reaction can be approximated separately based upon a *standard hydrogen electrode* (SHE) discussed later in this lecture. Each component is called a **half reaction**. Of course, no half reaction will occur by itself; any reduction half reaction must be accompanied by an oxidation half reaction. There is only one possible potential for any given half reaction. Since the reverse of a reduction half reaction is an oxidation half reaction, it would be redundant to list potentials for both the oxidation and reduction half reactions. Therefore, half reaction potentials are usually listed as **reduction potentials**. To find the oxidation potential for the reverse half reaction, the sign of the reduction potential is reversed. Table 7.3 is a list of some common reduction potentials.

| Table 7.3 Standard Reduction Potentials at 25° C | |
|---|---|
| *Half Reaction* | *Potential E°* |
| $Au^{3+}(aq) + 3e^- \rightarrow Au(s)$ | 1.50 |
| $O_2(g) + 4H^+(aq) + 4e^- \rightarrow H_2O(l)$ | 1.23 |
| $Pt^{2+}(aq) + 2e^- \rightarrow Pt(s)$ | 1.2 |
| $Ag^{2+}(aq) + 2e^- \rightarrow Ag(s)$ | 0.80 |
| $Hg^{2+}(aq) + 2e^- \rightarrow Hg(l)$ | 0.80 |
| $Cu^+(aq) + e^- \rightarrow Cu(s)$ | 0.52 |
| $Cu^{2+}(aq) + 2e^- \rightarrow Cu(s)$ | 0.34 |
| $2H^+(aq) + 2e^- \rightarrow H_2(g)$ | 0.00 |
| $Fe^{3+}(aq) + 3e^- \rightarrow Fe(s)$ | -0.036 |
| $Ni^{2+}(aq) + 2e^- \rightarrow Ni(s)$ | -0.23 |
| $Fe^{2+}(aq) + 2e^- \rightarrow Fe(s)$ | -0.44 |
| $Zn^{2+}(aq) + 2e^- \rightarrow Zn(s)$ | -0.76 |
| $H_2O(l) + 2e^- \rightarrow H_2(g) + 2OH^-(aq)$ | -0.83 |

Reactants in this direction are stronger oxidizing agents and more easily reduced.

Products in this direction are stronger reducing agents and more easily oxidized.

Recall from physics that electric potential has no absolute value. Thus the values in the table above are assigned based upon the arbitrary assignment of a zero value to the half reaction that occurs at a standard hydrogen electrode:

$$2H^+ + 2e^- \rightarrow H_2 \qquad E° = 0.00 \text{ V}$$

This is the only reduction potential that you need to memorize.

An example of an oxidation potential taken from the table above would be:

$$Ag(s) \rightarrow Ag^{2+}(aq) + 2e^- \qquad E° = -0.80 \text{ V}$$

If we wish to find the potential of the following ionic reaction:

$$2Au^{3+} + 3Cu \rightarrow 3Cu^{2+} + 2Au$$

we can separate the reaction into its two half reactions and add the half reaction potentials:

$$2(Au^{3+} + 3e^- \rightarrow Au) \qquad E° = \ 1.50 \ V$$
$$3(Cu \rightarrow Cu^{2+} + 2e^-) \qquad \underline{E° = -0.34 \ V}$$
$$= \ 1.16 \ V$$

**Warning:** Since reduction potentials are intensive properties, we do not multiply the half reaction potential by the number of times it occurs.

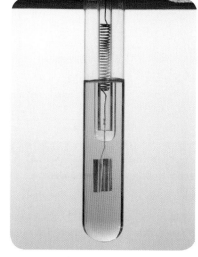

A platinum-hydrogen electrode is the standard used to measure redox (reduction-oxidation) potentials of ions. In this case the iron (III) to iron (II) redox potential is +0.77 volts.

## 7.5 Balancing Redox Reactions

Balancing redox reactions can be tricky. When you have trouble, follow the steps below to balance a redox reaction that occurs in acidic solution.

1.  Divide the reaction into its corresponding half reactions.

2.  Balance the elements other than H and O.

3.  Add $H_2O$ to one side until the O atoms are balanced.

4.  Add $H^+$ to one side until the H atoms are balanced.

5.  Add $e^-$ to one side until the charge is balanced.

6.  Multiply each half reaction by an integer so that an equal number of electrons are transferred in each reaction.

7.  Add the two half reactions and simplify.

For redox reactions occurring in basic solution, follow the same steps, then neutralize the $H^+$ ions by adding the same number of $OH^-$ ions to both sides of the reaction.

> All this effort to balance a redox reaction will get you, at most, one point on the MCAT. MCAT just doesn't require the balancing of redox reactions very often, so spend your time accordingly.

*Notes:*

> A galvanic cell turns chemical energy into electrical energy. It's a battery, like the one that starts your car, powers your cell phone, or energizes your toy rabbit.

If two distinct electrically conducting chemical phases are placed in contact, and one charged species from one phase cannot freely flow to the other phase, a tiny amount of charge difference may result. This tiny charge difference creates an electric potential between the phases (typically one or two volts). By offering an alternative path for electron flow, a **galvanic cell** (also called a **voltaic cell**) uses the electric potential between such phases to generate a current of electrons from one phase to another in a conversion of chemical energy to electrical energy.

A galvanic cell is made of a multiphase series of components with no component occurring in more than one phase. All phases must conduct electricity, but at least one phase must be impermeable to electrons. Otherwise, electrons would move freely throughout the circuit and come to a quick equilibrium. The phase that is impermeable to electrons is an ionic conductor carrying the current in the form of ions. The ionic conducting phase is usually an electrolyte solution in the form of a **salt bridge**. The components of a simple galvanic cell can be symbolized by the letters T-E-I-E'-T', where T represents the **terminals** (electronic conductors such as metal wires), E represents the electrodes (also electronic conductors), and I the ionic conductor (often the salt bridge). When the cell is formed, the emf is the electric potential difference between T and T'.

> Remember: RED CAT; AN OX: reduction cathode; anode oxidation.

A simple galvanic cell has two **electrodes**: the **anode** and the **cathode**. The anode is marked with a negative sign and the cathode is marked with a positive sign. The oxidation half reaction takes place at the anode, and the reduction half reaction takes place at the cathode. Depending upon the text, electrodes may refer to only a strip of metal or both a strip of metal and the electrolyte solution in which it is submerged. The strip of metal and solution together may also be called a *half cell*.

A voltaic cell may be made by inserting zinc and copper electrodes into a watermelon. In this example a potential of over 0.9 V is obtained.

Only potential differences between chemically identical forms of matter are easily measurable, so the two terminals of a galvanic cell must be made of the same material. The **cell potential ($E$)**, also called the **electromotive force (emf)**, is the potential difference between the terminals when they are not connected. Connecting the terminals reduces the potential difference due to internal resistance within the galvanic cell. The drop in the emf increases as the current increases. The current from one terminal to the other through the *load* (or resistance) flows in the direction opposite the electron flow. Since electrons in the anode have higher potential energy than those in the cathode, electrons flow through the load from the anode to the cathode.

Alternatively, you can remember that reduction occurs at the cathode, and reduction is the adding of electrons, so electrons flow to the cathode. Or else, since the anode is negative and the cathode is positive, you can think of this as electrons being repelled by the negative charge on the anode and attracted to the positive charge on the cathode. Recall that electron flow is in the opposite direction of current flow, so current flows from the cathode to the anode.

The standard state cell potential is simply the sum of the standard state potentials of the corresponding half reactions. The cell potential for a galvanic cell is always positive; a galvanic cell always has chemical energy that can be converted to work. The real cell potential depends upon the half reactions, the concentrations of the reactants and products, and the temperature.

Below is an example of a simple galvanic cell with the standard hydrogen electrode (SHE). Hydrogen gas is bubbled over the platinum plate. The platinum acts as a catalyst in the production of $H^+$ ions. The half reaction is shown. The platinum plate carries an electron through the wire to the silver strip. $Ag^+$ accepts the electron converting the $Ag^+$ ion to solid silver and allowing a chloride ion to solvate into the aqueous solution.

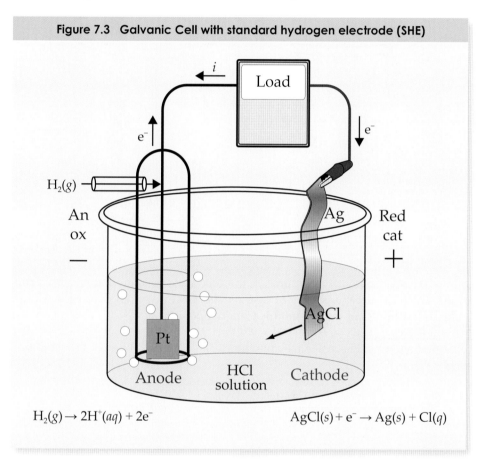

**Figure 7.3 Galvanic Cell with standard hydrogen electrode (SHE)**

$$H_2(g) \rightarrow 2H^+(aq) + 2e^-$$

$$AgCl(s) + e^- \rightarrow Ag(s) + Cl(q)$$

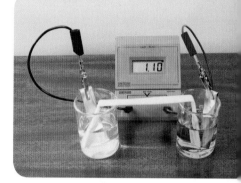

A voltmeter (orange) measures a voltage (potential difference) of 1.1 volts for a zinc-copper battery cell.

Since, by convention, the oxidation potential of hydrogen is zero, the cell potential of any electrode used in conjunction with the SHE will be exactly equal to the reduction potential of the half reaction occurring at the other electrode. Thus, some half reaction reduction potentials can be measured using the SHE.

Notice that there is no salt bridge in the SHE Galvanic Cell. Both electrodes are in contact with the same solution so no salt bridge is necessary. When a cell contains two different solutions, a liquid junction is required to separate the solutions. Because ions can move across a liquid junction, any liquid junction creates an additional small potential difference that affects the potential of the galvanic cell. A **salt bridge** is a type of liquid junction that minimizes this potential difference. Typically a salt bridge is made from an aqueous solution of KCl. The salt bridge allows ionic conduction between solutions without creating a strong extra potential within the galvanic cell. It is able to minimize the potential because the $K^+$ ions move toward the cathode at about the same rate that the $Cl^-$ move toward the anode. Below is an example of a simple galvanic cell that requires a salt bridge. Without the salt bridge, the solutions in the cell below would mix providing a low resistance path for electrons to move from $Zn(s)$ to $Cu^{2+}(aq)$ effectively short circuiting the cell, and leaving it with a cell potential of zero.

You should sketch a couple of your own galvanic cells so that you know how they are made. Notice that the concentrations are 1 M. This represents standard conditions and allows the use of the values from the reduction half reaction table to calculate the cell potential.

To find the cell potential when the concentrations are not 1 M, see Chemistry Lecture 7.9 The Nernst Equation.

Figure 7.4 Galvanic Cell

Here is exactly what's going on in the galvanic cell diagram in Figure 7.5. The solid zinc atoms would like to get rid of their electrons, but they need a place to put them. The $Cu^{2+}$ ions in solution are happy to take them. This creates a potential difference. The question is how to transfer electrons without building up a charge difference. Remember that separating charges is energy expensive. The "sea of electrons" in the copper wire allow the electrons a path of low resistance, but the electrons won't flow if they are building up a charge difference. The salt bridge allows ions to move (negative ions toward the anode and positive ions toward the cathode), and carry away any charge build up. As electrons leave the solid zinc strip, $Zn^{2+}$ ions are formed dissolving into solution. At the cathode $Cu^{2+}$ ions catch the electrons coming through the wire and form solid Cu.

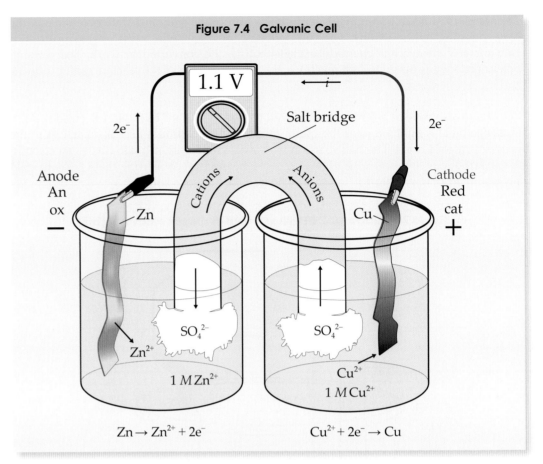

Even in a galvanic cell with a salt bridge, there is some leakage of ions across the liquid junction, which causes the battery to lose its chemical potential over time. Commercial cells use an insoluble salt to prevent this from happening.

For the cell diagram in Figure 7.5 we can refer to Table 7.3 and solve for the standard emf as follows:

$$Cu^{2+}(aq) + 2e^- \rightarrow Cu(s) \qquad E° = 0.34 \text{ V}$$
$$Zn^{2+}(aq) + 2e^- \rightarrow Zn(s) \qquad -[E° = -0.76 \text{ V}]$$
$$\overline{\qquad\qquad\qquad\qquad\qquad\qquad emf = 1.1 \text{ V}}$$

Again, remember that this is the potential when the concentrations are at standard state and 25° C; this means 1 molar concentrations.

## 7.7 IUPAC Conventions

Galvanic cells can be represented by a *cell diagram*. Each phase is listed from left to right beginning with the terminal attached to the anode and ending with the terminal attached to the cathode. The terminals are often omitted because they are always the same material and do not take part in the reaction. A vertical line is placed between phases. A double vertical line is used to indicate a salt bridge. A dotted vertical line indicates a boundary between two miscible liquids, and species in the same phase are separated by a comma.

$$\textbf{Pt}'(s) \,|\, \textbf{Zn}(s) \,|\, \textbf{Zn}^{2+}(aq) \,\|\, \textbf{Cu}^{2+}(aq) \,|\, \textbf{Cu}(s) \,|\, \textbf{Pt}(s)$$

**Cell Diagram**

The standard state emf can be found from the cell diagram by subtracting the potential of the reduction half reaction on the left (the reaction at the anode) from the potential of the reduction half reaction on the right (the reaction at the cathode).

It is unlikely that MCAT will require that you know the IUPAC conventions for a galvanic cell diagram. You can remember that the cathode is on the right because reduction and right both begin with an 'r'. Don't spend too much time here.

# Free Energy and Chemical Energy

A positive cell potential indicates a spontaneous reaction as shown by the following equation:

$$\Delta G = -nFE_{max}$$

where $n$ is the number of moles of electrons that are transferred in the balanced redox reaction, and $F$ is Faraday's constant, which is the charge on one mole of electrons (96,486 $C\ mol^{-1}$). This equation says that the free energy represents the product of the total charge $nF$ times the voltage E. Recall from Physics Lecture 7 that the product of charge and voltage equals work ($w = qV$). Since this is electrical work, it is not the result of a change in pressure or volume, so it represents non$PV$ work. Recall from Chemistry Lecture 3 that the change in Gibbs free energy represents the maximum amount of non$PV$ work available from a reaction at constant temperature and pressure. A negative $\Delta G$ indicates that the work is being done <u>by</u> the system and not <u>on</u> the system.

Since $F$ is a positive constant and $n$ can only be positive, $E_{max}$ must be positive when $\Delta G$ is negative. Thus a positive $E_{max}$ indicates a spontaneous reaction in a galvanic cell.

When all the conditions are standard, we can write the equation above using the '°' symbol as follows (the 'max' is part of the definition of $\Delta G$ and is assumed):

$$\Delta G^{\circ} = -nFE^{\circ}$$

$\Delta G^{\circ}$ can be found in books, but what about $\Delta G$ for non-standard state conditions? There are an infinite number of possible combinations of concentrations of reactants and products and temperatures with which we could start a reaction. How can we predict the maximum available work from these combinations? In order to make predictions about reactions that do not occur at standard state, we must use the following equation, which relates $\Delta G$ with $\Delta G^{\circ}$:

$$\Delta G = \Delta G^{\circ} + RT\ln(Q)$$

where $Q$ is the reaction quotient discussed in Chemistry Lecture 2, and 'ln( )' is the natural logarithm. You may see this equation written using a base 10 logarithm as:

$$\Delta G = \Delta G^{\circ} + 2.3RT\log(Q)$$

This is based upon the crude approximation: $2.3\log(x) \approx \ln(x)$.

There is no need to confuse $\Delta G$ and $\Delta G^{\circ}$. $\Delta G^{\circ}$ is a specific $\Delta G$ only one molar concentrations for $Q$, then $Q = 1$, and $RT\ln(Q) = 0$, leaving us with $\Delta G = \Delta G^{\circ}$. This is what we would expect for a reaction at standard conditions. (Remember, standard conditions don't actually indicate a particular temperature; you can have standard conditions at any temperature. Standard conditions are usually assumed to be 298 K.)

Recall from Chemistry Lecture 3 that at equilibrium, there is no available free energy with which to do work; $\Delta G = 0$ by definition. Thus, if we have equilibrium conditions, we can plug in a value of 0 for $\Delta G$, and rewrite "$\Delta G = \Delta G^{\circ} + RT\ln(Q)$" as:

$$\Delta G^{\circ} = -RT\ln(K)$$

Michael Faraday (1791-1867), British chemist and physicist, suggested the concepts of electric and magnetic fields.

> Memorizing this equation isn't nearly as important as understanding what it says about the relationship between $\Delta G$, $\Delta G^{\circ}$, $Q$ and $K$.

> Remember that $\ln(1) = 0$.

In this equation, both $K$ and $\Delta G°$ vary with temperature. Whenever you specify a new temperature, you must look up a new $\Delta G°$ for that temperature. Notice that since this equation uses the natural log of the equilibrium constant, a value of 1 for $K$ will result in a value of 0 for $\Delta G°$. For the MCAT you should understand the relationship between $K$ and $\Delta G°$.

$$\text{if } K = 1 \quad \text{then} \quad \Delta G° = 0$$
$$\text{if } K > 1 \quad \text{then} \quad \Delta G° < 0$$
$$\text{if } K < 1 \quad \text{then} \quad \Delta G° > 0$$

**Warning:** This relationship does NOT say that if a reaction has an equilibrium constant that is greater than one, then the reaction is always spontaneous. That doesn't make any sense, since the spontaneity of a reaction depends upon starting concentrations of products and reactants. It does say that if a reaction has an equilibrium constant that is greater than one, the reaction is spontaneous at standard state (starting molar concentrations of exactly 1 $M$) and the particular temperature used to derive that particular equilibrium constant.

## 7.9 The Nernst Equation

The galvanic cell pictured below is drawn with standard conditions of 1 $M$ concentrations. That's great for the instant that the concentrations are all one molar, but what about for the rest of the time? How can we find the potential when the concentrations aren't one molar? If we take the equation:

$$\Delta G = \Delta G° + RT \ln(Q)$$

and substitute $-nFE$ for $\Delta G$, and $-nFE°$ for $\Delta G°$, and then divide by $-nF$, we get:

$$E = E° - \frac{RT}{nF} \ln(Q)$$

This is the *Nernst equation*. At 298 K, and in base 10 logarithm form, the Nernst equation is:

$$E = E° - \frac{0.06}{n} \log(Q)$$

The Nernst equation allows us to plug in nonstandard concentrations to create $Q$ and find the cell potential.

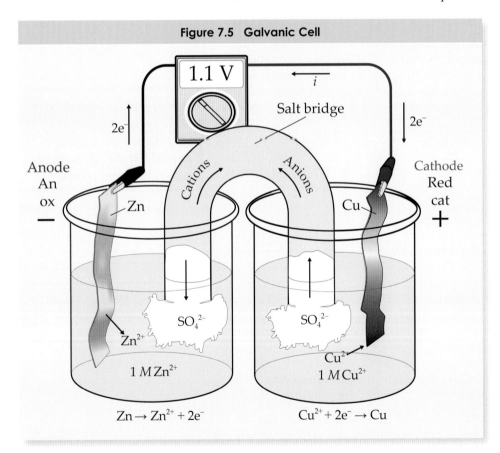

**Figure 7.5  Galvanic Cell**

1.1 V

Salt bridge

$i$

2e⁻

2e⁻

Cations

Anions

Anode
An
ox
−

Zn

Cathode
Red
cat
+

Cu

$SO_4^{2-}$

$SO_4^{2-}$

$Zn^{2+}$

$Cu^{2+}$

1 $M$ $Zn^{2+}$

1 $M$ $Cu^{2+}$

$Zn \rightarrow Zn^{2+} + 2e^-$

$Cu^{2+} + 2e^- \rightarrow Cu$

**153.** Which of the following statements about a galvanic cell is false?

**A.** If $E° = 0$, a reaction may still be spontaneous depending upon the chemical concentrations.
**B.** A galvanic cell with a positive potential can perform work.
**C.** Reduction takes place at the cathode.
**D.** A salt bridge balances the charge by allowing positive ions to move to the anode.

**154.** The values of all of the following are reversed when a reaction is reversed EXCEPT:

**A.** enthalpy
**B.** Gibbs energy
**C.** the rate constant
**D.** reaction potential

**155.** Which of the following is true for a reaction, if $\Delta G°_{298} = 0$? (The 298 subscript indicates a temperature of 298 $K$.)

**A.** The reaction is at equilibrium.
**B.** At 298 $K$ and 1 $M$ concentrations of products and reactants the equilibrium constant equals one.
**C.** $\Delta G$ is also zero.
**D.** The reaction is spontaneous at temperatures greater than 298 $K$.

**156.** The following is a table of half reactions:

| Half Reaction | $E°$ (V) |
|---|---|
| $Ag^{2+} + e^- \rightarrow Ag^+$ | 1.99 |
| $Fe^{3+} + e^- \rightarrow Fe^{2+}$ | 0.77 |
| $Cu^{2+} + 2e^- \rightarrow Cu$ | 0.34 |
| $2H^+ + 2e^- \rightarrow H_2$ | 0.00 |
| $Fe^{2+} + 2e^- \rightarrow Fe$ | −0.44 |
| $Zn^{2+} + 2e^- \rightarrow Zn$ | −0.76 |

The strongest reducing agent shown in the table is:

**A.** Zn
**B.** $Zn^{2+}$
**C.** $Ag^+$
**D.** $Ag^{2+}$

**157.** A negative cell potential indicates which of the following:

**A.** Both half reactions are nonspontaneous.
**B.** The reduction half reaction potential is greater than the oxidation half reaction potential.
**C.** The oxidation half reaction potential is greater than the reduction half reaction potential.
**D.** The cell is electrolytic.

Questions 158 through 160 are based on the information below.

A galvanic cell uses the reaction between solid tin and aqueous copper ions to produce electrical power.

$$Sn(s) + 2Cu^{2+}(aq) \rightarrow Sn^{2+}(aq) + 2Cu(s)$$

$Sn^{2+}(aq) + 2e^- \rightarrow Sn(s)$      $E° = -0.14$ V
$2Cu^{2+}(aq) + 2e^- \rightarrow Cu(s)$      $E° = 0.15$ V

**158.** The standard state cell potential for this reaction is:

**A.** 0.01 V
**B.** 0.16 V
**C.** 0.29 V
**D.** 0.44 V

**159.** The reaction in the cell is allowed to proceed. As the reaction in the cell progresses, the cell potential will:

**A.** decrease as the concentration of $Sn^{2+}$ increases.
**B.** decrease as the concentration of $Sn^{2+}$ decreases.
**C.** increase as the concentration of $Sn^{2+}$ increases.
**D.** increase as the concentration of $Sn^{2+}$ decreases.

**160.** Which of the following is true of the tin/copper cell reaction?

**A.** $K > 1$ and $\Delta G° > 0$
**B.** $K > 1$ and $\Delta G° < 0$
**C.** $K < 1$ and $\Delta G° > 0$
**D.** $K < 1$ and $\Delta G° < 0$

A **concentration cell** is a limited form of a galvanic cell with a reduction half reaction taking place in one half cell and the exact reverse of that half reaction taking place in the other half cell.

> The concentration cell is just a type of galvanic cell. It is never at standard conditions, so the Nernst equation is required to solve for the cell potential.

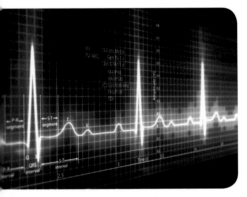

Contractions of the heart are controlled by a combination of electrochemistry and semipermeable membranes. Cell membranes have variable permeability with respect to ions $Na^+$, $K^+$, and $Ca^{2+}$. The difference in concentrations of $K^+$ ions between the intracellular fluid, or ICF and extracellular fluid, or ECF generates a concentration cell. Changes in the relative concentrations in the ICF and ECF lead to changes in the emf of the voltaic cell.

**Figure 7.6   Concentration Cell**

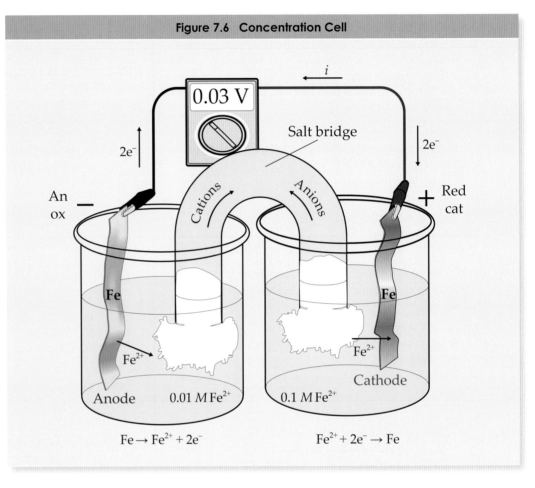

$$Fe \rightarrow Fe^{2+} + 2e^- \qquad Fe^{2+} + 2e^- \rightarrow Fe$$

Of course, when we add the two half reactions we get: $E° = 0$. If the concentrations were equal on both sides, the concentration cell potential would be zero. You can use the Nernst equation to find the potential for a concentration cell. (If you need the Nernst equation, the MCAT will give it to you.) It is much more likely that the MCAT will ask you a qualitative question like "In which direction will current flow in the concentration cell?" In this case, we must think about nature's tendency for balance; nature wants to create the greatest entropy. The more concentrated side will try to become less concentrated, and electrons will flow accordingly.

To use the Nernst equation to find the potential of a concentration cell at 25°C, we must realize that $Fe^{2+}$ is both a product and a reactant. Thus, we simply substitute for $Q$ the ratio of the $Fe^{2+}$ concentrations on either side. For the case above we have:

$$E = E° - \frac{0.06}{2} \log\left(\frac{0.01}{0.1}\right)$$

$n = 2$ because 2 electrons are used each time the reaction occurs, and $E°$ equals zero. Concentration cells tend to have small potentials.

If we hook up a power source across the resistance of a galvanic cell, and force the cell to run backwards, we have created another type of cell, the **electrolytic cell**. Any electrolytic cell on the MCAT will have a negative emf. In the electrolytic cell, the cathode is marked negative and the anode is marked positive. Reduction still takes place at the cathode and oxidation at the anode.

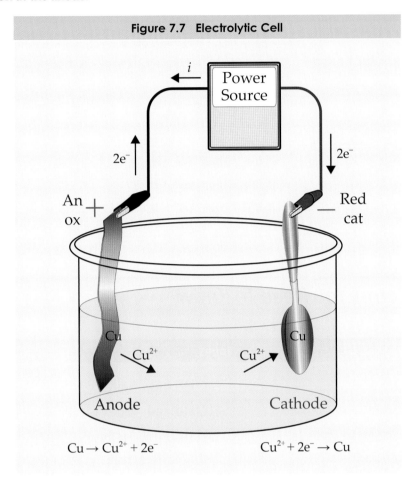

**Figure 7.7 Electrolytic Cell**

$$Cu \rightarrow Cu^{2+} + 2e^-$$ $$Cu^{2+} + 2e^- \rightarrow Cu$$

In a copper refinery plant large electrolytic cells (brown) are used to purify impure copper by passing an electric current through it while it is molten. The impurities collect at one electrode, and the pure copper can be run off to be collected for processing.

Electrolytic cells are used in industry for metal plating, and for purifying metals. For instance, pure sodium can be collected through electrolysis of sodium chloride solution in a *Downs cell*. The half reactions are as follows:

$$Na^+ + e^- \rightarrow Na \qquad E° = -2.71 \text{ V}$$
$$2Cl^- \rightarrow 2e^- + Cl_2 \qquad E° = -1.36 \text{ V}$$

Notice that this reaction will not run in aqueous solution because, from Table 7.3, we see that water has a less negative reduction potential than sodium. In fact, this indicates that solid sodium will oxidize spontaneously in water.

> For cells, you should learn to diagram a galvanic cell by yourself. Once you can do that, the other cells can be created from the galvanic cell. Remember that galvanic cells have a positive cell potential; electrolytic cells have a negative potential. Galvanic cells are spontaneous; electrolytic are forced by an outside power source.
>
> 'Electrochemical' cell can mean either 'galvanic' or 'electrolytic' cell.
>
> For any and all cells, remember 'Red Cat, An Ox'. This translates to Reduction at the Cathode, and Oxidation at the Anode.

The assignment of positive and negative to electrodes in galvanic and electrolytic cells is based upon perspective. Galvanic cells are used to provide energy to an external load, so the electrodes are labeled so that negative electrons will flow toward the positive electrode. Electrons flow from the load to the cathode, so the cathode is labeled positive in the galvanic cell. The focus of electrolytic cells is within the cell itself. For instance, electrophoresis uses an electrolytic cell. It is important that negatively charged amino acids within the electrolytic cell flow toward the positive electrode, so the anode is labeled positive in the electrolytic cell.

## 7.11 Equation Summary

| Equations |
|---|
| $2H^+ + 2e^- \rightarrow H_2 \qquad E° = 0.00 \text{ V}$ |
| $\Delta G = -nFE_{max}$ <br> $\Delta G = \Delta G° + RT\ln(Q)$ <br> $\Delta G° = -RT\ln(K)$ |
| if $K = 1$ then $\Delta G° = 0$ <br> if $K > 1$ then $\Delta G° < 0$ <br> if $K < 1$ then $\Delta G° > 0$ |

## 7.12 Terms You Need To Know

| Terms | |
|---|---|
| Anode | Oxidation States |
| Cathode | Oxidized |
| Cell Potential (E) | Oxidizing Agent |
| Concentration Cell | Redox Reaction |
| Electric Potential (*E*) | Reduced |
| Electrodes | Reducing Agent |
| Electrolytic Cell | Reductant |
| Electromotive Force (Emf) | Reduction Potentials |
| Galvanic Cell | Salt Bridge |
| Half Reaction | Terminals |
| Oxidant | Voltaic Cell |

161. A galvanic cell is prepared with solutions of $Mg^{2+}$ and $Al^{3+}$ ions separated by a salt bridge. A potentiometer reads the difference across the electrodes to be 1.05 Volts. The following standard reduction potentials at 25°C apply:

| Half Reaction | $E°$ (V) |
|---|---|
| $Al^{3+} + 3e^- \rightarrow Al$ | −1.66 |
| $Mg^{2+} + 2e^- \rightarrow Mg$ | −2.37 |

Which of the following statements is true concerning the galvanic cell at 25°C?

A. Magnesium is reduced at the cathode.
B. The concentrations of ions are 1 $M$.
C. The reaction is spontaneous.
D. For every aluminum atom reduced, an equal number of magnesium atoms are oxidized.

162. Which of the following is true for an electrolytic cell?

A. Reduction takes place at the anode.
B. The reaction is spontaneous.
C. electrons flow to the cathode.
D. An electrolytic cell requires a salt bridge.

163. A concentration cell contains 0.5 $M$ aqueous $Ag^+$ on one side and 0.1 $M$ aqueous $Ag^+$ on the other. All of the following are true EXCEPT:

A. Electrons will move from the less concentrated side to the more concentrated side.
B. Electrons will move from the anode to the cathode.
C. As the cell potential moves toward zero, the concentrations of both sides will tend to even out.
D. $\Delta G > 0$

164. According to the Nernst equation:

$$E = E° - \frac{0.06}{n} \log\left(\frac{x}{y}\right)$$

if a concentration cell has a potential of 0.12 V, and a concentration of 0.1 $M$ $Ag^+$ at the anode, what is the concentration of $Ag^+$ at the cathode?

A. $10^{-3}$ $M$
B. $10^{-1}$ $M$
C. 1 $M$
D. 10 $M$

165. A spoon is plated with silver in an electrolytic process where the half reaction at the cathode is:

$$Ag^+(aq) + e^- \rightarrow Ag(s) \quad E° = 0.8 \text{ V}$$

If the current $i$ is held constant for $t$ seconds, which of the following expressions gives the mass of silver deposited on the spoon? ($F$ is Faraday's constant.)

A. 107.8 $itF$

B. 107.8 $\dfrac{it}{F}$

C. 107.8 $\dfrac{i}{tF}$

D. 107.8 $\dfrac{iF}{t}$

166. The charge on 1 mole of electrons is given by Faraday's constant, 96,500 C/mol. A galvanic cell was operated continuously for 5 minutes and 0.01 moles of electrons were passed through the wire. If the voltage remained constant for the entire time, what is the current generated by the cell?

A. 3 A
B. 5 A
C. 6 A
D. 9 A

167. The reduction potential for two half reactions are given below.

$$2H_2O(l) + 2e^- \rightarrow H_2(g) + 2OH^-(aq) \quad E° = -0.8 \text{ V}$$

$$Na^+(aq) + e^- \rightarrow Na(s) \quad E° = -2.7 \text{ V}$$

Aqueous sodium cannot be reduced to solid sodium in an electrolytic cell because:

A. aqueous sodium will combine with aqueous hydroxide to form solid sodium hydroxide.
B. liquid water is more easily reduced than aqueous sodium.
C. aqueous sodium must be oxidized to form solid sodium.
D. hydrogen gas is more easily oxidized than solid sodium.

168. The reaction above takes place in a galvanic cell. Which of the following is true?

$$2Ag^{2+} + Fe \rightarrow 2Ag^+ + Fe^{2+} \quad E° = 2.4 \text{ V}$$

A. $Ag^{2+}$ is reduced at the anode.
B. $Ag^{2+}$ is oxidized at the anode.
C. $Ag^{2+}$ is reduced at the cathode.
D. $Ag^{2+}$ is oxidized at the cathode.

# STOP!

DO NOT LOOK AT THESE EXAMS UNTIL CLASS.

**30-MINUTE IN-CLASS EXAM FOR LECTURE 1**

## Passage I (Questions 1-7)

There are five types of interactions within and between molecules. Intramolecular interactions include covalent and ionic bonds. Intermolecular interactions include van der Waals's forces, dipole-dipole, and hydrogen bonds. Table 1 lists the typical energies for these interactions.

| Interaction | Typical Energy kJ mol$^{-1}$ |
|---|---|
| Van der Waals's | 0.1 – 5 |
| Dipole-dipole | 5 – 20 |
| Hydrogen bond | 5 – 50 |
| Ionic bond | 400 – 500 |
| Covalent bond | 150 – 900 |

**Table 1** Energies of interactions

The boiling point of a substance increases with the strength of its intermolecular bonds. Figure 1 shows the boiling points of hydrides for some main-group elements and of the noble gases.

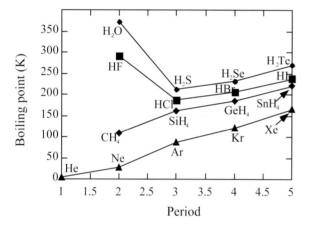

**Figure 1** Boiling points of some main-group hydrides and the noble gases.

1. Why does the boiling point of $H_2O$ and HF deviate from the trend in Figure 1?

   A. F and O both occur in the second period.
   B. The size of $H_2O$ and HF are small relative to the other molecules
   C. $H_2O$ and HF are less polarizable.
   D. $H_2O$ and HF can hydrogen bond.

2. What type of bonding holds together the compound $MgCl_2$?

   A. covalent
   B. ionic
   C. hydrogen
   D. van der Waals's

3. Why do the boiling points of the noble gases increase as the period increases?

   A. The bonds are stronger because larger atoms are more polarizable as period increases.
   B. The bonds are weaker because larger atoms are more polarizable as period increases.
   C. The bonds are stronger because larger atoms are less polarizable as period increases.
   D. The bonds are weaker because larger atoms are less polarizable as period increases.

4. The atomic radius of Ne is:

   A. greater than Ar
   B. less than Ar
   C. the same as Ar
   D. cannot be determined

5. Why are boiling points a better indication of intermolecular bonding than melting points?

   A. Vaporization requires more energy than melting.
   B. Vaporization requires less energy than melting.
   C. Transition from solid to liquid involves other factors such as crystalline lattice structures.
   D. Vaporization is easier to measure.

6. What type of intermolecular bonding occurs in gaseous $CH_4$?

   A. covalent
   B. ionic
   C. hydrogen
   D. van der Waals's

7. Why is a dipole-dipole interaction stronger than a van der Waals's interaction?

   A. Dipole-dipole is an electrostatic interaction.
   B. Van der Waals's interactions rely on temporarily induced dipoles.
   C. Van der Waals's interactions require a large surface area.
   D. Dipole-dipole interactions only occur with ionically bonded compounds.

Figure 1 shows atomic radius as a function of atomic number for the first three periods of the periodic table. Within a period the atomic radius decreases as the atomic number increases, but the atomic radius increases as the period increases.

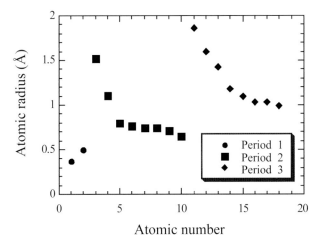

**Figure 1** Atomic radius as a function of atomic number

Electronegativity of an atom also follows a trend in the periodic table. Electronegativity for any element (X) is based upon the difference ($\Delta$) between the actual bond energy of a bond between element X and hydrogen and the expected bond energy of the same bond:

$$\Delta = (H\text{—}X)_{\text{actual bond energy}} - (H\text{—}X)_{\text{expected bond energy}}$$

where the expected bond energy is given by:

$$H\text{—}X_{\text{exp bond energy}} = \frac{H\text{—}H_{\text{bond energy}} + X\text{—}X_{\text{bond energy}}}{2}$$

Pauling electronegativity values are assigned to each element based upon its $\Delta$ value with respect to fluorine. Flourine is arbitrarily given a value of 4.0. The electronegativity of elements may be used to predict the type of bonding found in a molecule. Large differences in electronegativities of atoms in a bond result in an ionic bond.

8. If Se has an atomic radius of 1.16 Å, what is the predicted atomic radius of As?

    A. 1.05 Å
    B. 1.15 Å
    C. 1.25 Å
    D. 1.97 Å

9. Which of the following elements is the most chemically similar to Na?

    A. H
    B. Mg
    C. C
    D. Cs

10. Which element has the largest atomic radius?

    A. Li
    B. Ne
    C. Rb
    D. Br

11. Why is the electronegativity scale adjusted to fluorine?

    A. The researcher who discovered electronegativity was working with fluorine.
    B. Fluorine has the smallest atomic radius.
    C. Fluorine has the smallest electronegativity.
    D. Fluorine has the greatest electronegativity.

12. How does electron affinity change with atomic number?

    A. Electron affinity becomes more exothermic as atomic number increases in a period and a group.
    B. Electron affinity becomes less exothermic as atomic number increases in a period and a group.
    C. Electron affinity becomes more exothermic as atomic number increases in a period and less exothermic as atomic number increases in a group.
    D. Electron affinity becomes less exothermic as atomic number increases in a period and more exothermic as atomic number increases in a group.

13. Why does the atomic radius follow the trends observed in Figure 1?

    A. As the atomic number increases, the nuclear charge increases.
    B. As the atomic number increases, the nuclear charge decreases.
    C. As the atomic number increases, the nuclear charge increases and as the period increases the number of electron shells increases.
    D. As the atomic number increases, the nuclear charge increases and as the period increases the number of electron shells decreases.

14. Hydrogen has a Pauling electronegativity of 2.1. What is the value of Δ for hydrogen?

    **A.**    0
    **B.**    1.0
    **C.**    2.1
    **D.**    4.0

15. What type of intramolecular bonding is found in a CO molecule?

    **A.**    covalent
    **B.**    ionic
    **C.**    hydrogen
    **D.**    van der Waals's

**Passage III (Questions 16-21 )**

The empirical formula of a hydrocarbon can be determined using an instrument similar to the one shown in Figure 1. A sample hydrocarbon is combusted. The absorption chambers absorb all the water and carbon dioxide from the reaction. $CaCl_2$ can absorb both water and $CO_2$. The masses of the chambers before and after the reaction are compared to find the moles of carbon and hydrogen in the sample.

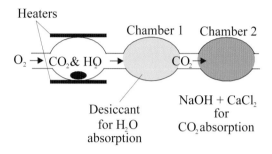

**Figure 1** A combustion train

For example: propane can be combusted in the apparatus as follows:

$$C_3H_8 + 5O_2 \rightarrow 4H_2O + 3CO_2$$

In an experiment using the combustion train, a gaseous fuel used in welding (containing only C and H) is reacted with $O_2$. The mass of the absorbers in Chamber 1 increases by 0.9 grams and the mass of the absorbers in Chamber 2 increases by 4.4 grams.

The density of the welding gas is 1.1 g $L^{-1}$ at 25°C and atmospheric pressure. At the same conditions, $O_2$ has a density of 1.3 g $L^{-1}$.

16. What is the empirical formula of the welding gas?

    **A.**    CHO
    **B.**    CH
    **C.**    $C_2H_2$
    **D.**    $C_3H_8$

17. What is the molecular weight of the gas?

    **A.**    13 g/mol
    **B.**    26 g/mol
    **C.**    32 g/mol
    **D.**    60 g/mol

18. A compound has an empirical formula of $CH_2O$. Using osmotic pressure, the molecular weight is determined to be 120 g/mol. What is the molecular formula for this compound?

    A.    $CH_2O$
    B.    $C_4H_4O_3$
    C.    $C_3H_6O_3$
    D.    $C_4H_8O_4$

19. If 1 mole of $C_3H_8$ is reacted with 2.5 moles of $O_2$, how many moles of $H_2O$ will be produced?

    A.    1 mole of $H_2O$
    B.    2 moles of $H_2O$
    C.    3 moles of $H_2O$
    D.    4 moles of $H_2O$

20. What would happen if the order of the chambers in the combustion train were reversed?

    A.    The amount of $CO_2$ calculated would be higher than the actual amount produced.
    B.    The amount of $CO_2$ calculated would be lower than the actual amount produced.
    C.    The amount of $H_2O$ calculated would be higher than the actual amount produced.
    D.    Nothing, the experiment would still give the same results.

21. Why is it necessary to react the $O_2$ in excess when using a combustion train?

    A.    In addition to the combustion reaction, the $O_2$ is used as a carrier gas.
    B.    In addition to the combustion reaction, the $O_2$ is used as a source of energy to propel the non-spontaneous reaction.
    C.    $O_2$ needs to be the limiting reagent in order for the calculations to be correct.
    D.    The sample needs to be the limiting reagent in order for the calculations to be correct.

---

Questions 22 through 23 are **NOT** based on a descriptive passage.

22. What is the electron configuration of a chloride ion?

    A.    [Ne] $3s^2\ 3p^5$
    B.    [Ne] $3s^2\ 3p^6$
    C.    [Ne] $3s^2\ 3d^{10}\ 3p^5$
    D.    [Ar] $3s^2\ 3p^6$

23. According to the Heisenberg uncertainty principle, which of the following pairs of properties of an electron cannot be known with certainty at the same time?

    A.    charge and velocity
    B.    spin and subshell
    C.    average radius and energy
    D.    momentum and position

---

**STOP.** IF YOU FINISH BEFORE TIME IS CALLED, CHECK YOUR WORK. YOU MAY GO BACK TO ANY QUESTION IN THIS TEST BOOKLET.

---

STOP.

# 30-MINUTE IN-CLASS EXAM FOR LECTURE 2

Over the years, many attempts have been made to find an equation which represents the behavior of non-ideal gases. Although none of the equations are completely accurate, they do allow an investigation of some of the macroscopic properties of real gases. The most commonly used of these is the *Van der Waals equation:*

$$\left(P + a\frac{n^2}{v^2}\right)(V - nb) = nRT$$

where $P$ is the absolute pressure, $n$ is the number of moles, $V$ is the volume, $T$ is the absolute temperature, $R$ is the gas constant (0.08206 L atm/mol K), and $a$ and $b$ are constants determined experimentally for each gas studied. Table 1 gives the values of $a$ and $b$ for some common gases:

| Gas | $a$ (atm L$^2$/mol) | $b$ (L/mol) |
|-----|------|--------|
| Ar | 1.4 | 0.032 |
| HCl | 3.7 | 0.041 |
| Cl$_2$ | 6.4 | 0.054 |
| H$_2$ | 0.25 | 0.027 |
| NH$_3$ | 4.3 | 0.037 |
| O$_2$ | 4.3 | 0.032 |

**Table 1** Van der Waals constants for various gases

To help quantify the deviation of a real gas from ideality, a *compression factor* $Z$ has been defined by $Z = PV/nRT$. Figure 1 shows how the compression factor for ammonia depends on pressure at several different temperatures.

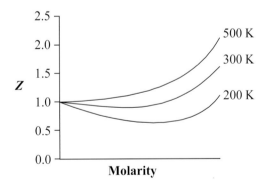

**Figure 1** Compression factors for ammonia

**24.** For an ideal gas, which of the following is most likely the correct graph?

**A.**

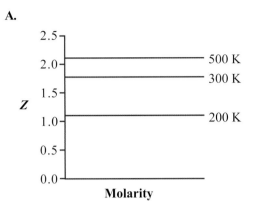

**B.**

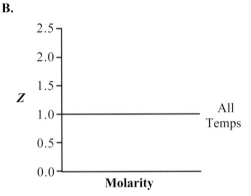

**C.**

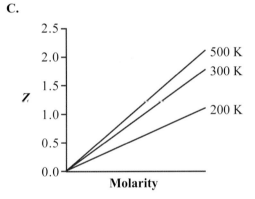

**D.**

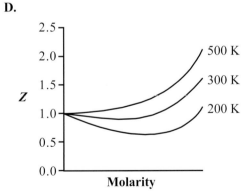

**25.** For an ideal gas, what can be said about the constants *a* and *b*?

- **A.** They are both zero.
- **B.** They are both positive and equal to each other.
- **C.** They depend on the temperature of the gas.
- **D.** They must be determined experimentally.

**26.** Based on the information in the passage, under which of the following conditions does ammonia behave most ideally?

- **A.** Low temperatures and low pressures
- **B.** Low temperatures and high pressures
- **C.** High temperatures and low pressures
- **D.** High temperatures and high pressures

**27.** Which of the following statements is NOT true for an ideal gas?

- **A.** The average kinetic energy of the molecules depends only on the temperature of the gas.
- **B.** At constant volume in a sealed container, the pressure of the gas is directly proportional to its temperature.
- **C.** At constant temperature in a sealed container, the volume of the gas is directly proportional to its pressure.
- **D.** The intermolecular attractions between the gas molecules are negligible.

**28.** Which of the following demonstrates nonideal behavior of a gas?

- **A.** Some of the molecules move more rapidly than others.
- **B.** Condensation occurs at low temperatures.
- **C.** The gas exerts a force on the walls of its container.
- **D.** The average speed of the molecules in the gas is proportional to the square root of the absolute temperature.

**29.** Why must absolute temperature be used in the Van der Waals equation?

- **A.** Because the Van der Waals equation is a nonrelativistic equation.
- **B.** Because it is impossible to have a negative absolute temperature.
- **C.** Because ratios of temperatures on other scales, such as the Celsius scale, are meaningless.
- **D.** Because international convention requires it.

**Passage II (Questions 30-37)**

In 1889, Svante Arrhenius proposed that the rate constant for a given reaction is given by the formula:

$$k = Ae^{-\frac{E_a}{RT}}$$

where $E_a$ is the *activation energy* for the reaction, $R$ is the gas constant (8.314 J/mol K), $T$ is the absolute temperature, and $A$ is a factor, which depends on factors such as molecular size. *Catalysts* change the reaction pathway, which may result in a change in $E_a$, $A$, or both.

In *heterogeneous catalysis*, the catalyst is in a different phase from the reactants and products. For example, a solid may catalyze a fluid-phase reaction. Such a catalysis involves the following steps:

1. A reactant molecule diffuses through the liquid to the surface of the catalyst.

2. The reactant molecule bonds to the catalyst (*adsorption*).

3. Adsorbed molecules bond with each other or with a molecule which collides with the adsorbed molecules.

4. The product leaves the catalyst.

In *homogeneous catalysis*, the catalyst is in the same phase as the reactants and products. Acids often act by this mechanism.

**30.** Which of the following is true of a catalyzed reaction?

- **A.** A catalyst may be the limiting reagent.
- **B.** At equilibrium, more products are produced when a catalyst is present.
- **C.** The catalyzed reaction pathway has a lower energy of activation than the uncatalyzed reacton pathway.
- **D.** The rate of the reverse reacton will be slower for the catalyzed reaction.

**31.** Consider the following mechanism:

$$Cl + O_3 \rightarrow ClO + O_2$$
$$ClO + O \rightarrow Cl + O_2$$

In this mechanism, what is the catalyst?

- **A.** Cl
- **B.** $O_3$
- **C.** ClO
- **D.** $O_2$

**GO ON TO THE NEXT PAGE.**

**32.** As the temperature of a reaction increases, which of the following always occurs?

**A.** The rate constant increases.
**B.** The rate constant decreases.
**C.** The activation energy increases.
**D.** The activation energy decreases.

**33.** Consider a reversible reaction. If the activation energy for the forward reaction is lowered by a catalyst, what can be said about the activation energy for the reverse reaction?

**A.** It is also lowered.
**B.** It is raised.
**C.** It is unaffected by the catalyst.
**D.** The effect of the catalyst on the reverse reaction cannot be predicted without more information.

**34.** Suppose a reaction is acid-catalyzed by a solution of pH 3.0. What can be said about the pH of the resulting solution?

**A.** It will be greater than 3.0 because the acid is consumed.
**B.** It will be equal to 3.0 because the acid is regenerated.
**C.** It will be equal to 3.0 because catalysts have no effect on equilibrium.
**D.** It cannot be predicted without information on the acidity of the reactants and products.

**35.** The rate of a reaction may depend on which of the following?

**I.** Concentrations of the reactants
**II.** Concentration of a catalyst
**III.** Surface area of a heterogeneous catalyst
**IV.** Temperature

**A.** I only
**B.** IV only
**C.** I and IV only
**D.** I, II, III, and IV

**36.** $H_2$ can be added to ethylene in the presence of a heterogeneous catalyst such as solid platinum. What might account for the initial attraction between the hydrogen molecules and the solid platinum?

**A.** hydrogen bonding
**B.** metallic bonding
**C.** van der Waals attraction
**D.** the plasma continuum effect

**37.** If the solid line in the graph below represents the reaction profile for an uncatalyzed reaction, which line might represent the reaction profile for the catalyzed reaction?

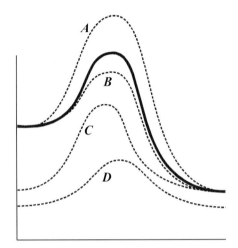

**A.** A
**B.** B
**C.** C
**D.** D

     **GO ON TO THE NEXT PAGE.**

Peroxydisulfate (persulfate) ion reacts with the iodide anion according to Reaction 1.

$$S_2O_8^{2-} (aq) + 3I^- (aq) \rightleftharpoons 2SO_4^{2-} (aq) + I_3^- (aq)$$

**Reaction 1**

The amount of $I_3^-$ formed can be determined by adding a known amount of $S_2O_3^{2-}$ and allowing it to react according to Reaction 2.

$$2S_2O_3^{2-} (aq) + I_3^- (aq) \rightleftharpoons S_4O_6^{2-} (aq) + 3I^- (aq)$$

**Reaction 2**

If starch is also added, any excess $I_3^-$ will react to form a blue-black $I_2$ complex. The formation of this complex indicates the completion of Reaction 2. The rate of Reaction 1 can be determined by the following equation where $t$ is the elapsed time from the addition of the last component to the formation of the blue-black starch, $I_2$ complex.

$$rate = \frac{\frac{1}{2}[S_2O_3^{2-}]}{t}$$

**Equation 1**

**38.** Why can Equation 1 be used to measure the rate of Reaction 1?

  **A.** Reaction 2 must be much faster than Reaction 1, thus the rate in Equation 1 is the rate of formation of $I_3^-$.

  **B.** Reaction 2 must be much slower than Reaction 1, thus the rate in Equation 1 is the rate of formation of $I_3^-$.

  **C.** Reactions 1 and 2 must occur at the same rate, thus the rate in Equation 1 is the rate of formation of $I_3^-$.

  **D.** Equation 1 can be derived directly from the rate laws of Reactions 1 and 2.

**39.** What would happen to the time and the rate in Equation 1, if the temperature were reduced?

  **A.** Time would increase and rate would decrease.

  **B.** Time would decrease and rate would increase.

  **C.** Time would increase and rate would remain unchanged.

  **D.** Time would remain the same and rate would increase.

**40.** The following table gives the relative concentrations and rates found using the method described in the passage. What is the rate law for Reaction 1?

| | 1 | 2 | 3 |
|---|---|---|---|
| $[I^-]$,(M) | 0.060 | 0.030 | 0.030 |
| $[S_2O_8^{2-}]$,(M) | 0.030 | 0.030 | 0.015 |
| Rate,(M/sec) | $6.0 \times 10^{-6}$ | $3.0 \times 10^{-6}$ | $1.5 \times 10^{-6}$ |

  **A.** $k[I^-]^2[S_2O_8^{2-}]^2$

  **B.** $k[I^-]fi[S_2O_8^{2-}]^2$

  **C.** $k[I^-]^3[S_2O_8^{2-}]$

  **D.** $k[I^-][S_2O_8^{2-}]$

**41.** The rate expression for the reaction of $H_2$ with $Br_2$ is:

$$rate = k[H_2][Br_2].$$

  **A.** The rate is first order with respect to $H_2$, and first order overall.

  **B.** The rate is first order with respect to $H_2$, and second order overall.

  **C.** The rate is second order with respect to $H_2$, and first order overall.

  **D.** The rate is second order with respect to $H_2$, and second order overall.

**42.** A student is performing the kinetic study described in the passage and forgets to add starch. What will be the result of the experiment?

  **A.** The rates of both reactions as measured by the student will increase because the starch slows the reactions.

  **B.** The rate of Reaction 1 as measured by the student will decrease because starch speeds up the reaction.

  **C.** The rate of Reaction 1 as measured by the student will stay the same because starch has no effect on the rate.

  **D.** The rate of Reaction 1 as measured by the student will not be able to be determined by the method described in the passage.

43. What would happen to the time and the rate in Equation 1, if more $S_2O_3^{2-}$ were added, and all other conditions remained the same?

    A.    Time would increase and rate would decrease.
    B.    Time would decrease and rate would increase.
    C.    Time would increase and rate would remain unchanged.
    D.    Time would remain the same and rate would increase.

44. What would happen to the time and the rate in Equation 1, if a catalyst is added to Reaction 1, and all other conditions remain the same?

    A.    Time would increase and rate would decrease.
    B.    Time would decrease and rate would increase.
    C.    Time would increase and rate would remain unchanged.
    D.    Time would remain the same and rate would increase.

Questions 45 through 46 are **NOT** based on a descriptive passage.

45. Which of the following are true concerning any reaction at equilibrium?

    I.    The concentration of products is equal to the concentration of reactants.
    II.   The rate of change in the concentration of the products is equal to the rate of change in the concentration of reactants.
    III.  The rate constant of the forward reaction is equal to the rate constant of the reverse reaction.

    A.    II only
    B.    I and II only
    C.    II and III only
    D.    I, II, and III

46. Equal concentrations of hydrogen and oxygen gas are placed on side 1 of the container shown below. Side 2 contains a vacuum. A small pin hole exists in the barrier separating side 1 and side 2. Which of the following statements is true?

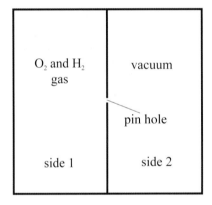

O₂ and H₂ gas    vacuum

pin hole

side 1    side 2

    A.    The partial pressure of oxygen on side 1 will increase.
    B.    The partial pressure of hydrogen on side 1 will increase.
    C.    The mole fraction of oxygen on side 1 will increase.
    D.    The mole fraction of hydrogen on side 1 will increase.

**STOP.** IF YOU FINISH BEFORE TIME IS CALLED, CHECK YOUR WORK. YOU MAY GO BACK TO ANY QUESTION IN THIS TEST BOOKLET.

# 30-MINUTE IN-CLASS EXAM FOR LECTURE 3

## Passage I (Questions 47-52)

Nickel is purified by the Mond process, which relies on the equilibrium:

$$Ni(s) + 4CO(g) \rightleftharpoons Ni(CO)_4(g)$$

$$\Delta H^\circ = -160.8 \text{ kJ}, \Delta S^\circ = -409.5 \text{ JK}^{-1} \text{ at } 25°C$$

**Reaction 1** The Mond process

Two chemists analyze the equilibrium.

*Chemist A*

Chemist A argues that Reaction 1 will be spontaneous in the forward direction because the product is more stable than the reactants. Furthermore, if the temperature is raised, the reaction will run in reverse because it is an exothermic reaction.

*Chemist B*

Chemist B argues that Reaction 1 will be spontaneous in the reverse direction because the entropy is higher for the reactants than for the products. Furthermore, if the temperature is raised, the spontaneity of the reverse reaction will increase.

**47.** The $\Delta H^\circ_f$ for $Ni(s)$ is:

  A.   0 kJ/mol
  B.   −160.8 kJ/mol
  C.   160.8 kJ/mol
  D.   409.5 kJ/mol

**48.** Which of the following is a logical conclusion of Chemist *A*'s argument?

  A.   The enthalpy change of a reaction is an indicator of the relative stability of the reactants and products.
  B.   The entropy change of a reaction is an indicator of the relative stability of the reactants and products.
  C.   At higher temperatures, the reactants of Reaction 1 will be more stable than the products.
  D.   Reactions do not necessarily need to increase the entropy of the universe in order to be spontaneous.

**49.** What are the most efficient conditions for purifying nickel when using the Mond process?

  A.   low pressure and low temperature
  B.   low pressure and high temperature
  C.   high pressure and low temperature
  D.   high pressure and high temperature

**50.** Which of the following explains the error in Chemist *B*'s argument?

  A.   Higher temperatures favor a reaction that decreases entropy.
  B.   The entropy change of a reaction is the entropy change of the universe.
  C.   A positive entropy of reaction does not necessarily indicate an entropy increase for the universe.
  D.   The reaction will only run in the reverse direction until entropy is maximized for the reaction system.

**51.** What is the change in Gibbs free energy for Reaction 1 at standard state and 25°C?

  A.   −38 kJ
  B.   38 kJ
  C.   −150.5 kJ
  D.   150.5 kJ

**52.** Consider the reaction below:

$$C(s) + O_2 (g) \rightarrow CO_2 (g)$$

$$\Delta H^\circ \text{ is } -393.51 \text{ kJ and } \Delta S^\circ \text{ is } 2.86 \text{ JK}^{-1} \text{ at } 25°C$$

If solid carbon is exposed to 1atm of oxygen and 1 atm of carbon dioxide gas at room temperature, will carbon dioxide gas form spontaneously?

  A.   No, because the enthalpy of formation for $CO_2$ is negative.
  B.   No, because the change in Gibbs energy is negative.
  C.   Yes, because the enthalpy of formation for $CO_2$ is negative.
  D.   Yes, because the change in Gibbs energy is negative.

## Passage II (Questions 53-58)

A heat engine converts heat energy to work via a cyclical process which necessarily results in some of the heat energy being transferred from a higher temperature heat reservoir to a lower temperature heat reservoir. A heat engine obeys the *First Law of Thermodynamics*. The efficiency $e$ of a heat engine is the fraction of heat energy input converted to useful work and is given by:

$$e = \frac{W}{Q_h}$$

where $W$ is the work done by the heat engine on the surroundings and $Q_h$ is the heat removed from the higher temperature reservoir. Work on the surroundings can also be represented by:

$$W = Q_h - Q_c$$

where $Q_c$ is the heat energy expelled into the cold reservoir.

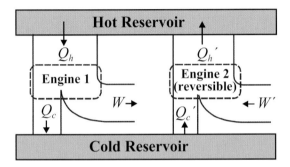

**Figure 1** A schematic diagram of two heat engines operating between the same two heat reservoirs. (Not drawn to scale.)

The *Carnot theorem* states: no engine working between two heat reservoirs can be more efficient than a reversible engine working between those same reservoirs. Such a reversible engine is called a Carnot engine. This theorem can be proven with the *Second Law of Thermodynamics*, which states that for any process other than a reversible process the entropy change of the universe is greater than zero, and for a reversible process the entropy change of the universe is zero. Thus a Carnot engine obeys the following equation:

$$\Delta S = \frac{Q_c}{T_c} - \frac{Q_h}{T_h} = 0$$

Figure 1 shows a schematic representation of two heat engines working between the same two reservoirs. Engine 1 is absorbing heat energy from the hot reservoir and doing work while emitting heat energy into the cold reservoir. Engine 2 is a Carnot engine and is being run backwards removing heat energy from the cold reservoir and rejecting heat energy into the hot reservoir.

53. If both Engines 1 and 2 are operating at the same time as shown in Figure 1, and the rate of heat energy being removed from each reservoir is equal to the rate of heat energy being added then:

A. $W' > W$.
B. $W' < W$.
C. Engine 1 is a Carnot engine.
D. The efficiency of Engine 2 is greater than the efficiency of Engine 1.

54. Which of the following is true of the engines in Figure 1 if Engine 1 is not a Carnot engine and the work from Engine 1 is used to run Engine 2?

A. $Q_c < Q_c{}'$ and $Q_h < Q_h{}'$.
B. $Q_c > Q_c{}'$ and $Q_h < Q_h{}'$.
C. $Q_c > Q_c{}'$ and $Q_h > Q_h{}'$.
D. The work from Engine 1 cannot be used to run Engine 2.

55. Assume Engine 2 is running in the opposite direction as shown in Figure 1. Which of the following changes to Engine 2 will increase its efficiency as a heat engine?

A. increasing $Q_h{}'$
B. decreasing $Q_c{}'$
C. decreasing the temperature difference between the reservoirs
D. increasing the temperature difference between the reservoirs

56. Which of the following would allow a Carnot engine to operate at 100% efficiency where $e = 1$.

A. The work on the surroundings must be very large.
B. The engine must be reversible.
C. The hot reservoir must be at the same temperature as the cold reservoir.
D. The cold reservoir must be at a temperature of absolute zero.

57. What is the minimum power required for a heat engine to lift a 80 kg mass 5 m in 20 s if it releases 1000 J of heat energy from its exhaust each second?

A. 200 W
B. 500 W
C. 1200 W
D. 3000 W

GO ON TO THE NEXT PAGE.

**58.** A certain Carnot engine requires 18 kg of water in the form of steam as its working substance. When $5 \times 10^5$ J of heat energy are added at a constant temperature of $400\ K$ the gas expands to 4 m$^3$. What is the approximate pressure of the gas after the initial expansion? (The ideal gas constant is $R = 8.314$ J/K mol)

A. $8.3 \times 10^5$ Pa
B. $8.3 \times 10^7$ Pa
C. $1.3 \times 10^6$ Pa
D. $1.3 \times 10^8$ Pa

## Passage III (Questions 59-65)

As shown in Figure 1, Reaction 1 is thermodynamically favored because the products are at a lower energy state than the reactants. However, at low temperatures this reaction will be too slow to be observed because the reactant molecules do not have enough energy to form the activated complex.

$$NO_2 + CO \rightleftharpoons NO + CO_2$$

**Reaction 1**

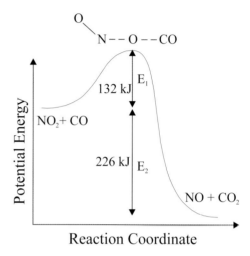

**Figure 1** Energy diagram for Reaction 1.

As shown in Figure 2, Reaction 2 is not thermo-dynamically favored, but it has a smaller reaction barrier. The reactants require less energy to form the activated complex.

$$H_2 + Br \rightleftharpoons H + HBr$$

**Reaction 2**

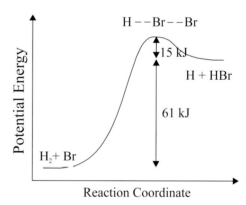

**Figure 2** Energy diagram for Reaction 2

**59.** What does the symbol H--Br--Br represent in Figure 2?

  **A.** an intermediate
  **B.** a transition state
  **C.** a reactant of the second step of the reaction
  **D.** a product of the first step of the reaction

**60.** What is $E_a$ for Reaction 2 as written?

  **A.** 15 kJ/mole
  **B.** 61 kJ/mole
  **C.** 76 kJ/mole
  **D.** 132 kJ/mole

**61.** Which reaction is most kinetically favored?

  **A.** $NO_2 + CO \rightarrow NO + CO_2$
  **B.** $NO + CO_2 \rightarrow NO_2 + CO$
  **C.** $H_2 + Br \rightarrow H + HBr$
  **D.** $H + HBr \rightarrow H_2 + Br$

**62.** Which reaction is most thermodynamically favored?

  **A.** $NO_2 + CO \rightarrow NO + CO_2$
  **B.** $NO + CO_2 \rightarrow NO_2 + CO$
  **C.** $H_2 + Br \rightarrow H + HBr$
  **D.** $H + HBr \rightarrow H_2 + Br$

**63.** If a catalyst were added to Reaction 1, what would happen?

  **A.** $E_1$ would be less than 132 kJ but $E_2$ would remain unchanged.
  **B.** $E_1$ would be less than 132 kJ and $E_2$ would be less than 226 kJ.
  **C.** $E_2$ would be less than 226 but $E_1$ would remain unchanged.
  **D.** A catalyst doesn't affect the thermodynamic properties of the reactants and products. $E_1$ and $E_2$ would remain unchanged but the reaction rate would increase.

**64.** What is $\Delta E$ for Reaction 2 as written?

  **A.** 15 kJ/mole
  **B.** 61 kJ/mole
  **C.** 76 kJ/mole
  **D.** −76 kJ/mole

**65.** For the reaction,

the ratio of products changes with temperature. At −80°C, 80% of 1 and 20% of 2 form. At 40°C, 15% of 1 and 85% of 2 form. Assuming the relative stability of products vs. reactants does not change significantly with the change in temperature, which product is the kinetically favored one?

  **A.** 1
  **B.** 2
  **C.** both 1 and 2
  **D.** neither 1 nor 2

**GO ON TO THE NEXT PAGE.**

Questions 66 through 69 are **NOT** based on a descriptive passage.

**66.** An iron skillet is laid on a hot stove. After a few minutes the handle gets hot. The method of heat transfer described is:

- **A.** convection.
- **B.** conduction.
- **C.** radiation.
- **D.** translation.

**67.** A man straightens up his room. His action does not violate the second law of thermodynamics because:

- **A.** the entropy of his room increased.
- **B.** energy of the universe was conserved.
- **C.** the entropy increase by the breakdown of nutrients in his body is greater than the entropy decrease by the straightening of his room.
- **D.** his action does violate the second law of thermodynamics.

**68.** A metal rod is in thermal contact with two heat reservoirs both at constant temperature, one at 100 K and the other at 200 K. The rod conducts 1000 J of heat from the warmer to the colder reservoir. If no energy is exchanged with the surrounws, what is the total change of entropy?

- **A.** −5 J/K
- **B.** 0 J/K
- **C.** 5 J/K
- **D.** 10 J/K

**69.** Two ideal gases, $A$ and $B$, are at the same temperature, volume and pressure. Gas $A$ is reversibly expanded at constant temperature to a volume $V$. Gas $B$ is allowed to expand into an evacuated chamber until it also has a total volume $V$, but without exchanging heat with its surroundings. Which of the following most accurately describes the two gases?

- **A.** Gas $A$ has a higher temperature and enthalpy than gas $B$.
- **B.** Gas $A$ has a higher temperature but a lower enthalpy than gas $B$.
- **C.** Gas $B$ has a higher temperature and enthalpy than gas $A$.
- **D.** Gas $A$ and $B$ have equal temperatures and enthalpies.

---

**STOP.** IF YOU FINISH BEFORE TIME IS CALLED, CHECK YOUR WORK. YOU MAY GO BACK TO ANY QUESTION IN THIS TEST BOOKLET.

---

# 30-MINUTE IN-CLASS EXAM FOR LECTURE 4

## Passage I (Questions 70-75)

The following tests were carried out on samples of an unknown solution in order to identify any presence of nitrate and nitrite ions.

*Experiment 1*

In acidic solution nitrites react with sulfamic acid ($HNH_2SO_3$) according to the following reaction:

$$NO_2^- + NH_2SO_3^- \rightarrow N_2(g) + SO_4^{2-} + H_2O$$

Barium sulfate is insoluble while barium sulfamate is soluble.

In a test tube, $BaCl_2$ is added to a few drops of a sample of the unknown solution. No precipitate is formed. A few crystals of sulfamic acid are then mixed into the sample.

No visible reaction occurs.

*Experiment 2*

Active metals such as aluminum and zinc in alkaline solution reduce nitrate to ammonia. Nitrite ion will also form ammonia under these conditions. Devarda's alloy (50% Cu, 45% Al, 5% Zn) gives the following reaction with nitrate ion:

$$Al + NO_3^- \rightarrow Al(OH)_4^- + NH_3(g)$$

Several drops of the unknown solution are mixed with an equal amount of 6 *M* NaOH and placed into a dry test tube. Care is taken not to wet the walls of the tube. Devarda's alloy is then added and a loose cotton plug pushed one third of the way down the tube. The tube is warmed briefly in a water bath and removed. A bent strip of red litmus with a moistened fold is then placed at the top of the tube as shown in Figure 1. The moistened section of the litmus turns blue.

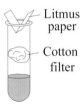
Litmus paper

Cotton filter

**Figure 1**

70. The unknown solution contains which of the following ions:

   A.  nitrite but not nitrate
   B.  both nitrite and nitrate
   C.  nitrate but not nitrite
   D.  neither nitrite nor nitrate

71. In Experiment 1, why is $BaCl_2$ added before the sulfamic acid crystals?

   A.  to acidify the solution
   B.  to remove any sulfate ions existing prior to the reaction with nitrite
   C.  to prevent sulfamic acid from reacting with $BaCl_2$
   D.  $BaCl_2$ is needed to react with nitrite and form the precipitate.

72. If the unknown solution contained nitrite what would be the expected result of Experiment 1?

   A.  A precipitate would be formed before the addition of sulfamic acid.
   B.  Bubbles and precipitate would be observed after the addition of sulfamic acid.
   C.  Bubbles but no precipitate would be observed after the addition of sulfamic acid.
   D.  No visible reaction would be observed after the addition of sulfamic acid.

73. If carbonate ion is present in the unknown, which of the following reactions might interfere with Experiment 1?

   A.  $2H^+ + CO_3^{2-} \rightarrow CO_2(g) + H_2O$
   B.  $Ba^{2+} + 2OH^- + CO_2 \rightarrow BaCO(s) + H_2O$
   C.  $NH_4^+ + CO_3^{2-} \rightarrow NH_3 + HCO_3^-$
   D.  $H_2CO_3 \rightarrow CO(g) + O_2(g) + H_2(g)$

74. When the solution in Experiment 2 is warmed in the water bath, all of the following may be true EXCEPT:

   A.  The equilibrium constant $K$ of the reaction changes.
   B.  The rate constant $k$ of the reaction changes.
   C.  The rate of the reaction decreases.
   D.  The rate of the reaction increases.

75. Which of the following represents the reaction taking place in the litmus paper in Experiment 2?

   A.  $NO_3^- + H_2O \rightarrow OH^- + HNO_3$
   B.  $HNO_3 + H_2O \rightarrow H_3O^+ + NO_3^-$
   C.  $NH_4^+ + H_2O \rightarrow H_3O^+ + NH_3$
   D.  $NH_3 + H_2O \rightarrow NH_4^+ + OH^-$

## Passage II (Questions 76-82)

When $Ca(IO_3)_2$ dissolves in a solution containing H+ the following two reactions occur.

$$Ca(IO_3)_2 \rightleftharpoons Ca^{2+} + 2IO_3^-$$

**Reaction 1**

$$H^+ + IO_3^- \rightleftharpoons HIO_3$$

**Reaction 2**

$HIO_3$ is a weak acid. The $K_{sp}$ for $Ca(IO_3)_2$ and the $K_a$ for $HIO_3$ can be determined from the solubility ($S$) of $Ca(IO_3)_2$ for solutions of varying $[H^+]$. The solubility is related to the initial hydrogen ion concentration $[H^+]$ by the following equation:

$$2(S)^{\frac{1}{2}} = K_{sp}^{\frac{1}{2}} + \left[\frac{K_{sp}^{\frac{1}{2}}}{K_a}\right][H^+]$$

A student prepared four saturated solutions by mixing $Ca(IO_3)_2$ with a strong acid. Excess solid was filtered off. The student found the $S$ for each solution with constant ionic strength, using iodometric titrations. The resulting data are shown in Table 1.

| Solution | $[H^+]$ (*mol/l*) | S (*mol/l*) |
|----------|-------------------|-------------|
| 1 | $1.0 \times 10^{-7}$ | $5.4 \times 10^{-3}$ |
| 2 | $2.5 \times 10^{-1}$ | $9.9 \times 10^{-3}$ |
| 3 | $5.0 \times 10^{-1}$ | $1.4 \times 10^{-2}$ |
| 4 | 1 | $2.0 \times 10^{-2}$ |

**Table 1** Solubility data for $Ca(IO_3)_2$

76. The $K_{sp}$ for $Ca(IO_3)_2$ and the $K_a$ for $HIO_3$, respectively are:

   **A.** $[Ca^{2+}][IO_3^-]^2$ and $\dfrac{[H^+][IO_3^-]}{[HIO_3]}$

   **B.** $\dfrac{[Ca^{2+}][IO_3^-]^2}{[Ca(IO_3)_2]}$ and $\dfrac{[H^+][IO_3^-]}{[HIO_3]}$

   **C.** $[Ca^{2+}][IO_3^-]^2$ and $[H^+][IO_3^-]$

   **D.** $[Ca^{2+}][IO_3^-]^2$ and $\dfrac{[HIO_3]}{[H^+][IO_3^-]}$

77. As $[H^+]$ increases, the solubility of $Ca(IO_3)_2$:

   **A.** increases and $K_{sp}$ increases.
   **B.** decreases and $K_{sp}$ decreases.
   **C.** increases and $K_{sp}$ does not change.
   **D.** does not change and $K_{sp}$ increases.

78. The graph of $2(\underline{S})^{3/2}$ versus $[H^+]$ for the data shown in Table 1 would most closely resemble which of the following?

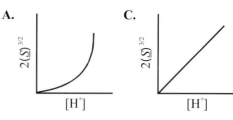

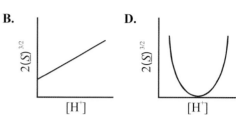

79. After filtering out excess solid, a student adds HCl to Solution 1 in Table 1. He then adds a small amount of $CaSO_4$, which dissolves completely. Which of the following also occurs in the new solution?

   **A.** Some $Ca(IO_3)_2$ precipitates when the $CaSO_4$ is added.
   **B.** Undissociated $HIO_3$ increases when the HCl is added.
   **C.** Aqueous $IO_3^-$ decreases when $CaSO_4$ is added.
   **D.** Aqueous $Ca^{2+}$ decreases when $CaSO_4$ is added.

80. According to Table 1, what is the value of $K_{sp}$ for $Ca(IO_3)_2$?

   **A.** $1.0 \times 10^{-14}$
   **B.** $6.4 \times 10^{-7}$
   **C.** $5.4 \times 10^{-3}$
   **D.** $1.1 \times 10^{-1}$

81. If $Ca(OH)_2$ is added to the Solution 3 in Table 1:

   **A.** the concentration of $H^+$ will increase.
   **B.** the concentration of $HIO_3$ will increase.
   **C.** the concentration of $IO_3^-$ will increase
   **D.** $Ca(IO_3)_2$ will precipitate.

82. How will the addition of $HIO_3$ affect Solution 2 from Table 1?

   **A.** The lower pH will shift Reaction 2 to the right.
   **B.** The increased hydrogen ion concentration will dissolve more $Ca(IO_3)_2$.
   **C.** The common ion effect will shift Reaction 1 to the left.
   **D.** The lower pH will balance out the common ion effect and the equilibrium will not change.

## Passage III (Questions 83-89)

Many carbonate minerals are found in the earth's crust. As a result, the waters of several lakes, rivers, and even oceans are in contact with these minerals. $CaCO_3$ is the primary component of limestone and marble, while dolomite $(CaMg(CO_3)_2)$ and magnesite $(MgCO_3)$ are minerals found in other rock formations.

Limestone lines many of the river and lake beds resulting in contamination of the fresh water supply with $Ca^{2+}$ and $Mg^{2+}$. The amount of these minerals present in water can be measured in parts per million (ppm). The "hardness" of water is determined by the ppm of $Ca^{2+}$ and $Mg^{2+}$ present. Hard water is the cause of many problems in the home. Scale buildup in pipes, on pots and pans, and in washing machines are just a few of the problems.

The hardness of water can be measured by titrating a sample of water with the ligand ethylenediamine tetraacetic acid (EDTA) and the indicator eriochrome black T. This ligand forms a coordination complex with metal cations (M) in a one-to-one stochiometry in the following association reaction:

$$EDTA + M \rightarrow EDTA-M$$

The structure of EDTA is shown in Figure 1. It has six binding sites to form a very stable complex ion with most metal ions.

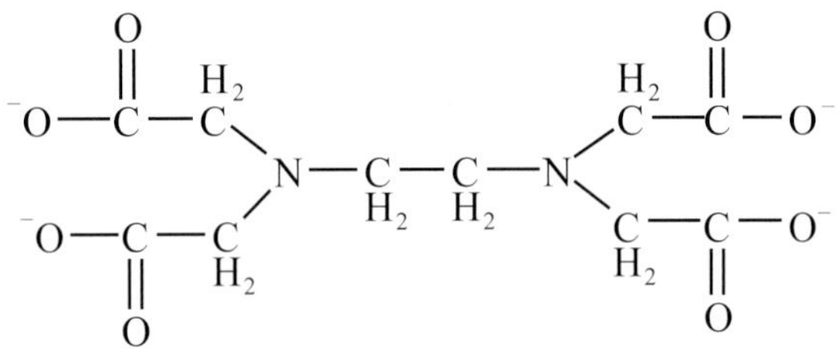

**Figure 1** The structure of EDTA

The association constants for EDTA with several metal ions are listed in Table 1.

| Metal | $K_{assoc}$ |
|-------|-------------|
| $Hg^{2+}$ | $6 \times 10^{21}$ |
| $Mg^{2+}$ | $5 \times 10^{8}$ |
| $Ca^{2+}$ | $5 \times 10^{10}$ |
| $Al^{3+}$ | $1 \times 10^{16}$ |
| $Fe^{2+}$ | $2 \times 10^{14}$ |
| $Fe^{3+}$ | $1 \times 10^{25}$ |
| $Cu^{2+}$ | $6 \times 10^{18}$ |

**Table 1** Association constants for EDTA with metal ions

Many households soften hard water using ion exchange resins. These resins replace the $Ca^{2+}$ and $Mg^{2+}$ ions with smaller cations such as $Na^+$ and $H^+$.

83. A scientist determines how hard the tap water is in the laboratory, using an EDTA titration. If the pipes in the building are old and some rust dissolves into the tap water, how will the results of the test change?

   A. The results will not change because the EDTA titration only works with $Ca^{2+}$ and $Mg^{2+}$.
   B. The titration will not be able to be carried out because the tap water will be colored.
   C. The tap water will appear to have less $Ca^{2+}$ and $Mg^{2+}$ present.
   D. The tap water will appear to have more $Ca^{2+}$ and $Mg^{2+}$ present.

84. When EDTA reacts with a metal ion to form a complex ion, EDTA is acting as a(n):

   A. oxidizing agent.
   B. reducing agent.
   C. Lewis base.
   D. Lewis acid.

85. Salt water contains a high concentration of $Cl^-$ ions. These ions form complexes ($CaCl^+$) with $Ca^{2+}$. How will the solubility of limestone change in ocean water compared to fresh water?

   A. It will increase.
   B. It will decrease.
   C. It will remain the same.
   D. The change in solubility cannot be determined.

86. A 25 mL sample of hard water is titrated with a 0.001 solution of EDTA, and the endpoint of the titration is reached at 50 mL of EDTA added. What is the concentration of $Ca^{2+}$ and $Mg^{2+}$ ions in solution?

   A. 0.0005 $M$
   B. 0.001 $M$
   C. 0.002 $M$
   D. 0.006 $M$

**87.** The EDTA titrations are carried out at a pH of 10. Why is it necessary to buffer the pH at 10?

    **A.**    A low pH will cause metal hydroxides to form.

    **B.**    $CaCO_3$ requires a high pH in order to dissolve.

    **C.**    The indicator requires pH 10 to change color.

    **D.**    The coordinating atoms must be deprotonated in order to bond with the metal ion.

**88.** Why does replacing the cations found in hard water with $Na^+$ or $H^+$ soften the water (i.e. reduce the unwanted residue produced by hard water)?

    **A.**    The smaller cations do not form insoluble mineral deposits.

    **B.**    Twice as many smaller ions are necessary to react with soaps and other ligands.

    **C.**    No minerals contain Na and H.

    **D.**    H is found in water so there is no addition of new atoms.

**89.** 9 ppm is equivalent to an aqueous concentration of approximately $5 \times 10^{-4}$ mol/L. If a water sample were reduced from 18 ppm $Mg^{2+}$ to 9 ppm $Mg^{2+}$ by the addition of EDTA, according to Table 1 what would be the concentration of the remaining unbound EDTA?

    **A.**    $2 \times 10^{-9}$ mol/L

    **B.**    $5 \times 10^{-4}$ mol/L

    **C.**    $1 \times 10^{-3}$ mol/L

    **D.**    $5 \times 10^{-3}$ mol/L

---

Questions 90 through 92 are **NOT** based on a descriptive passage.

---

**90.** The vapor pressure of pure water at 25°C is approximately 23.8 torr. Which of the following is the vapor pressure of pure water at 95°C?

    **A.**    10 torr

    **B.**    23.8 torr

    **C.**    633.9 torr

    **D.**    800 torr

**91.** Benzene and toluene form a nearly ideal solution. If the vapor pressure for benzene and toluene at 25°C is 94 mm Hg and 29 mm Hg respectively, what is the approximate vapor pressure of a solution made from 25% benzene and 75% toluene at the same temperature?

    **A.**    29 mm Hg

    **B.**    45 mm Hg

    **C.**    94 mm Hg

    **D.**    123 mm Hg

**92.** When volatile solvents $A$ and $B$ are mixed in equal proportions heat is given off to the surroundings. If pure $A$ has a higher boiling point than pure $B$, which of the following could NOT be true?

    **A.**    The boiling point of the mixture is less than pure $A$.

    **B.**    The boiling point of the mixture is less than pure $B$.

    **C.**    The vapor pressure of the mixture is less than pure $A$.

    **D.**    The vapor pressure of the mixture is less than pure $B$.

---

**STOP.** IF YOU FINISH BEFORE TIME IS CALLED, CHECK YOUR WORK. YOU MAY GO BACK TO ANY QUESTION IN THIS TEST BOOKLET.

---

**STOP.**

# 30-MINUTE IN-CLASS EXAM FOR LECTURE 5

## Passage I (Questions 93-100)

Two students performed the following experiment to calculate the molecular weight of an unknown substance. The apparatus shown in Figure 1 was used.

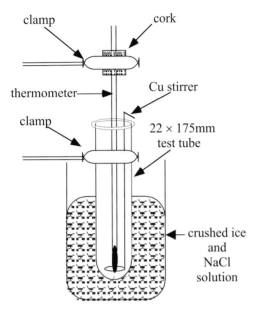

**Figure 1** Freezing point apparatus

Both students placed 10.00 mL of cyclohexane into the test tube at room temperature. Next 0.500 gram of an unknown solid was dissolved in the cyclohexane. The test tube and contents were lowered into the ice bath, which was maintained at a temperature of −5.0°C by adjusting the relative amounts of NaCl, ice, and water. The students monitored the temperature of the cyclohexane mixtures by taking readings from the thermometer at 30 seconds intervals. The freezing point of the solution for a given trial is the temperature maintained for four consecutive readings. The experiment was repeated two more times by warming the cyclohexane to room temperature then freezing it again.

The results obtained by the students are recorded in Table 1.

| Time, seconds | 30 | 60 | 90 | 120 | 150 | 180 | 210 | 240 |
|---|---|---|---|---|---|---|---|---|
| Student 1 | 22.0 | 6.0 | 4.0 | -3.5 | -3.5 | -3.5 | -3.5 | -3.5 |
| Student 2 | 22.0 | 12.0 | 6.0 | 0.6 | 0.6 | 0.6 | 0.6 | 0.4 |

**Table 1** Solution temperature (°C) with time

(The $K_f$ for cyclohexane is 20.2°C kg/mol, the freezing point is 6.6°C, and the density is 0.78 g/mL. The $K_f$ for water is 1.86°C kg/mol.)

93. Why was NaCl added to the ice bath?

   A. To lower the freezing point of the water and cool the cyclohexane solution more quickly.
   B. To lower the freezing point of the cyclohexane solution below the freezing point of the water.
   C. To lower the freezing point of the water below the freezing point of the cyclohexane solution.
   D. To raise the freezing point of the water.

94. Which salt is the most efficient per gram at lowering the freezing point of water?

   A. $Ba(OH)_2$
   B. $MgSO_4$
   C. NaCl
   D. $CaCl_2$

95. The purpose of the copper stirrer is:

   A. to ensure that the solid stays in solution.
   B. to create heat to offset the chilling effect of the ice bath.
   C. to ensure that the solution temperature remains homogenous.
   D. to allow the student to see when crystals begin to form.

96. According to the results in Table 1, which student had the unknown with the greatest molecular weight? (Assume no dissociation of the unknown solids occurs.)

   A. Student 1
   B. Student 2
   C. The molecular weights were the same.
   D. It cannot be determined based on the given information.

97. Student 1 recorded a lower freezing point for the experiment because:

   A. the concentration of particles in Student 1's crushed ice solution was lower than in Student 2's crushed ice solution.
   B. the concentration of particles in Student 1's crushed ice solution was greater than in Student 2's crushed ice solution.
   C. the concentration of particles in Student 1's cyclohexane solution was lower than in Student 2's cyclohexane solution.
   D. the concentration of particles in Student 1's cyclohexane solution was greater than in Student 2's cyclohexane solution.

**98.** In order to calculate the molecular weight of their unknown solid the students probably used all of the following data EXCEPT:

    **A.** the mass of the unknown solid added to the solution.
    **B.** the time required for the cyclhexane solution to freeze.
    **C.** the temperature at the freezing point of the cycloexane solution.
    **D.** the volume of the cyclohexane solution.

**99.** A professor must choose the unknown from the following solutes. Which of the following would be the most appropriate for the experiment in the passage?

    **A.** NaCl
    **B.** $Mg(OH)_2$
    **C.** $CH_3OH$
    **D.** $C_{10}H_8$

**100.** Why does the temperature in Student 2's experiment begin to drop after 210 seconds?

    **A.** Student 2 used too much ice in the ice bath.
    **B.** Student 2's cyclohexane solution was completely frozen at 210 seconds.
    **C.** Student 2 stopped stirring the solution at 180 seconds.
    **D.** Student 2 stopped dissolving the unknown solid.

## Passage II (Questions 101-106)

A series of experiments are performed using the calorimeter shown in Figure 1.

**Figure 1** Coffee Cup Calorimeter

A volume of 0.5 $M$ NaOH is placed near the calorimeter, which contains an equal volume of 0.5 $M$ HCl. The temperatures of both solutions are monitored until they equilibrate to room temperature.

The NaOH solution is added to the HCl solution through the funnel. The temperature is recorded every 30 seconds for 5 minutes. The experiment is repeated three times with three different volumes of HCl and NaOH. The results of one of these experiments are shown in the graph in Figure 2. The data for all experiments are recorded in Table 1.

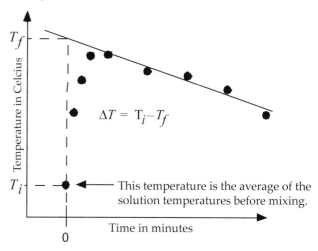

**Figure 2** Temperature change of solution over time

| Trial | Volume of HCL and NaOH (ml) | Initial Temperature °C | Initial Temperature °C |
|-------|------------------------------|-------------------------|-------------------------|
| 1 | 30 | 22.0 | 25.3 |
| 2 | 40 | 20.0 | 23.3 |
| 3 | 50 | 21.0 | 24.3 |

**Table 1**

101. What reaction is taking place in the calorimeter to cause the temperature change?

    **A.**   $H^+ + OH^- \rightarrow H_2O$
    **B.**   $Na^+ + Cl^- \rightarrow NaCl$
    **C.**   $NaCl \rightarrow Na^+ + Cl^-$
    **D.**   $Na^+ + 1e^- \rightarrow Na$

102. The reaction in the calorimeter is an:

    **A.**   endothermic reaction.
    **B.**   exothermic reaction.
    **C.**   oxidation reaction.
    **D.**   isothermic reaction.

103. Assuming that the heat capacity of the solution is the same as the heat capacity of water, what is the enthalpy change for the reaction in Trial 2 as recorded in Table 1? (The heat capacity for water is $1.0$ cal $°C^{-1}$ mL$^{-1}$)

    **A.**   −132 cal
    **B.**   132 cal
    **C.**   −330 cal
    **D.**   330 cal

104. If 0.5 $M$ $NH_4OH$ (a weaker base) were used instead of NaOH, how would this affect the results of the experiment?

    **A.**   The temperature change would be greater because more energy is required to dissociate $NH_4OH$.
    **B.**   The temperature change would be less because more energy is required to dissociate $NH_4OH$.
    **C.**   The temperature change would be greater because less energy is required to dissociate $NH_4OH$.
    **D.**   It would not change the results because both bases are ionic compounds and the energy required to separate equal charges is always the same.

105. Which trial would be expected to result in the greatest heat of solution per mole of reactants?

    **A.**   1
    **B.**   2
    **C.**   3
    **D.**   They should all be the same.

106. If the solutions in the experiment began at room temperature, which of the following explains the heat transfer between the calorimeter and its surroundings for the experiment shown in Figure 2?

    **A.**   Initially heat is transferred from the surroundings to the calorimeter, and then heat is transferred from the calorimeter to the surroundings.
    **B.**   Initially heat is transferred from the calorimeter to the surroundings, and then heat is transferred from the surroundings to the calorimeter.
    **C.**   Heat is transferred from the surroundings to the calorimeter throughout the experiment.
    **D.**   Heat is transferred from the calorimeter to the surroundings throughout the experiment.

Phase diagrams show the changes in phase of a material as a function of temperature and pressure. Student A prepared a phase diagram for $CO_2$. After observing the phase diagram, he concluded that raising the pressure isothermally promotes a substance to change from a gas to a liquid to a solid as demonstrated by the dashed line in Figure 1.

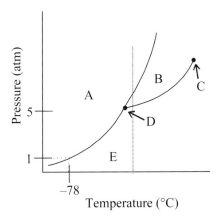

**Figure 1** Phase diagram of $CO_2$

Student B chose to make a phase diagram of $H_2O$. She observed that raising the pressure isothermally promotes a substance to convert from vapor to solid then to liquid as indicated by the dashed line in Figure 2.

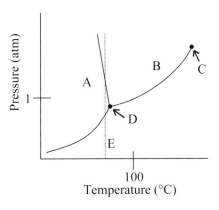

**Figure 2** Phase diagram of $H_2O$

**107.** Which of the following explains the discrepancy between the observation the two students?

- **A.** Water expands when going from liquid to solid, whereas $CO_2$ contracts.
- **B.** $CO_2$ expands when going from liquid to solid, whereas water contracts.
- **C.** The two chemists observed the phase changes at different temperatures.
- **D.** $CO_2$ is a gas at room temperature, while $H_2O$ is a liquid.

**108.** According to Figure 1, at $-78°C$ and 1 atm $CO_2$ will:

- **A.** exist as a liquid.
- **B.** exist in equilibrium as a gas and liquid.
- **C.** exist in equilibrium as a gas and solid.
- **D.** exist in equilibrium as a liquid and solid.

**109.** The temperature and pressure above which the gas and liquid phases of a substance can not be distinguished is called the:

- **A.** critical point
- **B.** triple point
- **C.** boiling point
- **D.** super point

**110.** At temperatures and pressures greater than point C in Figure 1:

- **A.** $CO_2$ is a vapor.
- **B.** $CO_2$ is a liquid.
- **C.** $CO_2$ is in both liquid and vapor phase.
- **D.** the vapor and liquid phases of $CO_2$ cannot be distinguished.

**111.** According to Figure 2, as the pressure increases the melting point of $H_2O$:

- **A.** increases.
- **B.** decreases.
- **C.** does not change.
- **D.** increases than decreases.

**112.** The normal boiling point for $O_2$ is 90.2 K. Which of the following could be the triple point for $O_2$?

- **A.** 1.14 mmHg and 54.4 K
- **B.** 1.14 mmHg and 154.6 K
- **C.** 800 mmHg and 54.4 K
- **D.** 37,800 mmHg and 154.6 K

**113.** Describe the phase change for $H_2O$ as the pressure is raised at 100°C.

- **A.** sublimation
- **B.** vaporization
- **C.** condensation
- **D.** melting

114. During a solid to liquid phase change, energy is:

    **A.** absorbed by bond breakage.
    **B.** released by bond breakage.
    **C.** absorbed by increased kinetic energy of the liquid molecules.
    **D.** released by increased kinetic energy of the liquid molecules.

115. On his honeymoon the chemist, Joule, took with him a long thermometer with which to measure the temperature difference between the waters at the top and the bottom of Niagra Falls. If the height of the falls is 60 meters and the specific heat of water is approximately 4200 J kg$^{-1}$ K$^{-1}$, what is the expected temperature difference?

    **A.** 1/7 K
    **B.** 7 K
    **C.** 70 K
    **D.** 700 K

**STOP.** IF YOU FINISH BEFORE TIME IS CALLED, CHECK YOUR WORK. YOU MAY GO BACK TO ANY QUESTION IN THIS TEST BOOKLET.

# 30-MINUTE IN-CLASS EXAM FOR LECTURE 6

The solubility of $Ca(OH)_2$ (Reaction 1) can be determined by titrating the saturated solution containing no precipitate against a standardized HCl solution and determining [OH$^-$].

$$Ca(OH)_2 \rightleftharpoons Ca^{2+} + 2OH^-$$

**Reaction 1**

Once [OH$^-$] is determined, the solubility ($S$) of $Ca(OH)_2$ is calculated using the following equation:

$$S = \frac{1}{2}[OH^-]_{Ca(OH)_2}$$

**Equation 1**

where [OH$-]_{Ca(OH)_2}$ is the concentration of hydroxide ion due only to $Ca(OH)_2$. The solubilities of $Ca(OH)_2$ in a variety of solutions of varying [OH$^-$] concentrations were determined by the above method, but the calculation of $S$ had to be altered slightly due to the presence of additional hydroxide ions.

$$S = \frac{1}{2}\{[OH^-]_{total} - [OH^-]_{solvent}\}$$

**Equation 2**

The results of the experiment are summarized in Table 1.

| Trial | Solution | Solubility |
|-------|----------|------------|
| 1 | $H_2O$ | 0.0199 $M$ |
| 2 | 0.01793 $M$ NaOH | 0.0100 $M$ |
| 3 | 0.03614 $M$ NaOH | 0.0047 $M$ |
| 4 | 0.07119 $M$ NaOH | 0.0015 $M$ |

**Table 1** Solubility data for $Ca(OH)_2$

**116.** How does the solubility of $Ca(OH)_2$ change as the [OH$^-$] in the solvent increases?

 A. It decreases because the increase in OH$^-$ shifts Reaction 1 toward the left.
 B. It decreases because the increase in OH$^-$ interferes with the acid titration.
 C. It increases because the increase in OH$^-$ shifts Reaction 1 toward the left.
 D. It increases because the increase in OH$^-$ interferes with the acid titration.

**117.** How do the titrations in Trials 1 and 3 compare?

 A. The pH of the equivalence points are the same, but more HCl is required to reach the equivalence point in Trial 3.
 B. The pH of the equivalence point in Trial 1 is higher, and less HCl is required to reach it.
 C. The pH of the equivalence point in Trial 3 is higher, and less HCl is required to reach it.
 D. The pH of the equivalence point in Trial 3 is higher, and more HCl is required to reach it.

**118.** The $K_{sp}$ for Reaction 1 in the presence of NaOH is:

 A. $[Ca^{2+}][OH^-]^2_{Ca(OH)_2}$
 B. $[Ca^{2+}][OH^-]^2_{Total}$
 C. $[Ca^{2+}][2OH^-]^2_{Ca(OH)_2}$
 D. $[Ca^{2+}][2OH^-]^2_{Total}$

**119.** What is the pH of the solution in Trial 3 before the titration?

 A. 1.1
 B. 7.0
 C. 9.3
 D. 12.7

**120.** Which indicator would be best for the titration in this experiment?

 A. Phenolphthalein: (acid color is colorless, base is red, and the transition pH is $8.0 - 9.6$).
 B. Thymolphthalein: (acid color is colorless, base is blue, and the transition pH is $8.3 - 10.5$).
 C. Bromocresol purple: (acid color is yellow, base is purple, and the transition pH is $5.2 - 6.8$).
 D. Neutral red: (acid color is red, base color is yellow, and the transition pH is $6.8 - 8.0$).

**121.** If a pH meter were placed into the titration beaker, what would be the resulting curve for Trial 1?

**A.**

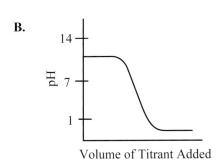

Volume of Titrant Added

**B.**

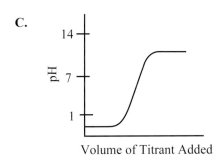

Volume of Titrant Added

**C.**

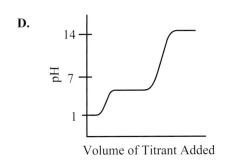

Volume of Titrant Added

**D.**

Volume of Titrant Added

**Passage II (Questions 122-127)**

The reaction for the autoionization of water is shown below:

$$2H_2O \rightarrow H_3O^+ + OH^-$$

The equilibrium constant ($K_w$) is temperature dependent. Table 1 lists the value of $K_w$ at several temperatures.

| Temperature (°C) | $K_w$ |
|---|---|
| 0 | $0.114 \times 10^{-14}$ |
| 10 | $0.292 \times 10^{-14}$ |
| 20 | $0.681 \times 10^{-14}$ |
| 25 | $1.01 \times 10^{-14}$ |
| 30 | $1.47 \times 10^{-14}$ |
| 40 | $2.92 \times 10^{-14}$ |
| 50 | $5.47 \times 10^{-14}$ |
| 60 | $9.61 \times 10^{-14}$ |

**Table 1** Equilibrium constants for water at different temperatures

Water has a leveling effect on acids. Any acid stronger than $H_3O^+$ appears to have the same behavior in aqueous solution. For example, 1 $M$ HCl and 1 $M$ HClO$_4$ have the same concentration of $H_3O^+$ even though in anhydrous acetic acid, HClO$_4$ is a stronger acid.

**122.** What is the pH of $H_2O$ at 40°C?

    **A.** 7.5
    **B.** 7.0
    **C.** 6.7
    **D.** 6.0

**123.** At 10°C, the concentration of OH$^-$ in 1 $M$ HCl is approximately:

    **A.** $1 \times 10^{-7}\ M$
    **B.** $1 \times 10^{-14}\ M$
    **C.** $3 \times 10^{-15}\ M$
    **D.** $1 \times 10^{-15}\ M$

**124.** As temperature increases, the pH of pure water:

    **A.** increases.
    **B.** decreases.
    **C.** becomes less than the pOH.
    **D.** becomes greater than the pOH.

**GO ON TO THE NEXT PAGE.**

**125.** What is the conjugate base of $H_2SO_4$?

    **A.**   $H_2O$

    **B.**   $OH^-$

    **C.**   $HSO_4^-$

    **D.**   $SO_4^{2-}$

**126.** Why can the relative strength of HCl and $HClO_4$ be determined in acetic acid but not in water?

    **A.**   because acetic acid is a weaker acid than $H_3O^+$

    **B.**   because acetic acid is a stronger acid than $H_3O^+$

    **C.**   because acetic acid is a weaker Bronsted-Lowry base than $H_2O$

    **D.**   because acetic acid is a stronger Bronsted-Lowry base than $H_2O$

**127.** The equation for $K_w$ at 50°C is:

    **A.**   $[OH^-][H_3O^+]$

    **B.**   $\dfrac{[OH^-][H_3O^+]}{[H_2O]^2}$

    **C.**   $\dfrac{[OH^-][H_3O^+]}{[H_2O]}$

    **D.**   $[H_3O^+]$

## Passage III (Questions 128-134)

Acid rain results when $SO_3(g)$, produced by the industrial burning of fuel, dissolves in the moist atmosphere.

$$SO_3(g) + H_2O(l) \rightarrow H2SO_4(aq)$$

The rain formed from the condensation of this acidic water is an environmental hazard destroying trees and killing the fish in some lakes. (The pH of the water varies depending upon the level of pollution in the area. The $pK_a$ values are about −2 for $H_2SO_4$ and 1.92 for $HSO_4^-$.)

Another pollutant which dissolves in water vapor and reacts to form acid rain is $SO_2(g)$. This gas forms $H_2SO_3(aq)$ which can be oxidized to $H_2SO_4$. (The $pK_a$ values are 1.81 for $H_2SO_3$ and 6.91 for $HSO_3^-$.)

The table below gives the color changes of many acid base indicators used to test the pH of water.

| Indicator | Color Change | pH of Color Change |
|---|---|---|
| Malachite green | yellow to green | 0.2 – 1.8 |
| Thymol blue | red to yellow | 1.2 – 2.8 |
| Methyl orange | red to yellow | 3.2 – 4.4 |
| Methyl red | red to yellow | 4.8 – 6.0 |
| Phenolphthalein | clear to red | 8.2 – 10.0 |
| Alizarin yellow | yellow to red | 10.1 – 12.0 |

**Table 1**

**128.** A sample of rainwater tested with methyl orange results in a yellow color, and the addition of methyl red to a fresh sample of the same water results in a red color. What is the pH of the sample?

    **A.**   between 1.2 and 1.8

    **B.**   between 3.2 and 4.4

    **C.**   between 4.4 and 4.8

    **D.**   between 4.8 and 6.0

**129.** If there is no oxidant present in the air and the same number of moles of $SO_2$ and $SO_3$ are dissolved, which gas would produce acid rain with a lower pH?

    **A.**   $SO_2$ because $H_2SO_3$ has a higher $pK_a$ than $H_2SO_4$.
    **B.**   $SO_2$ because $HSO_3^-$ has a higher $pK_a$ than $HSO_4^-$.
    **C.**   $SO_3$ because $H_2SO_4$ has a lower $pK_a$ than $H_2SO_3$.
    **D.**   $SO_3$ because $HSO_4^-$ has a lower $pK_a$ than $HSO_3^-$.

**130.** What is the $pK_b$ for $HSO_3^-$?

    **A.**   0
    **B.**   6.91
    **C.**   7.09
    **D.**   12.19

**131.** $H_2SO_4$ is a stronger acid than:

    **I.**   $H_2O$
    **II.**   $H_3O^+$
    **III.**   $H_2SO_3$

    **A.**   III only
    **B.**   I and II only
    **C.**   I and III only
    **D.**   I, II, and III

**132.** What is the oxidation state of sulfur in $H_2SO_4$ and $H_2SO_3$ respectively?

    **A.**   +6, +4
    **B.**   +4, +6
    **C.**   −6, −4
    **D.**   −4, −6

**133.** What is the pH of a $5.0 \times 10^{-8}$ $M$ aqueous solution of $H_2SO_4$ at room temperature?

    **A.**   8.3
    **B.**   7.3
    **C.**   6.8
    **D.**   6.0

**134.** A sample of rainwater polluted with $SO_3$ is titrated with NaOH. Which of the following most resembles the shape of titration curve.

**A.**

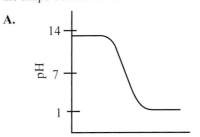

Volume of Titrant Added

**B.**

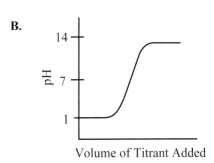

Volume of Titrant Added

**C.**

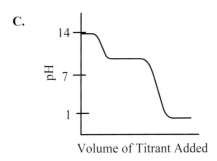

Volume of Titrant Added

**D.**

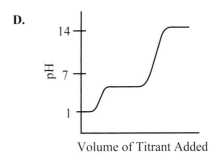

Volume of Titrant Added

**GO ON TO THE NEXT PAGE.**

135. Which of the following is the strongest base?

    A.  $ClO^-$
    B.  $ClO_2^-$
    C.  $ClO_3^-$
    D.  $ClO_4^-$

136. A weak acid is titrated with a strong base. When the concentration of the conjugate base is equal to the concentration of the acid, the titration is at the:

    A.  stoichiometric point.
    B.  equivalence point.
    C.  half equivalence point.
    D.  end point.

137. A buffer solution is created using acetic acid and its conjugate base. If the ratio of acetic acid to its conjugate base is 10 to 1, what is the approximate pH of the solution? (The $K_a$ of acetic acid is $1.8 \times 10^{-5}$)

    A.  3.7
    B.  4.7
    C.  5.7
    D.  7.0

138. $NH_3$ has a $K_b$ of $1.8 \times 10^{-5}$. Which of the following has a $K_a$ of $5.6 \times 10^{-10}$?

    A.  $NH_3$
    B.  $NH_4^+$
    C.  $NH_2^-$
    D.  $H^+$

**STOP.** IF YOU FINISH BEFORE TIME IS CALLED, CHECK YOUR WORK. YOU MAY GO BACK TO ANY QUESTION IN THIS TEST BOOKLET.

# 30-MINUTE IN-CLASS EXAM FOR LECTURE 7

## Passage I (Questions 139-144)

When $Fe^{2+}$ is titrated with dichromate ($Cr_2O_7^{2-}$) according to Reaction 1, the titration curve similar to the one shown in Figure 1 results. The curve was generated by measuring the potential difference between the reaction solution and a standard solution after each addition of a known volume and concentration of dichromate. The potential is measured using a voltmeter attached to an *orp* electrode.

$$6Fe^{2+} + Cr_2O_7^{2-} + 14H^+ \rightleftharpoons 2Cr^{3+} + 7H_2O + 6Fe^{3+}$$

$$E° = 1.33 \text{ V}$$

**Reaction 1**

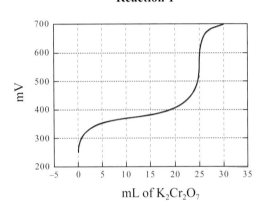

**Figure 1.** Titration curve for Reaction 1

Chromium (III) is green in color, and dichromate solution is orange. The orange is not intense enough to be used as an indicator. Instead, the endpoint of the titration can be indicated by the redox indicator diphenylamine sulfonic acid (DAS), which changes from colorless to violet when oxidized. The color change observed during the titration is from green to violet. After all the $Fe^{2+}$ ions have been oxidized, the dichromate ion oxidizes DAS. However, the formal potential of the $Fe^{2+}$ solution must be lowered in order to match the endpoint with the equivalence point of the titration. This is accomplished by the addition of $H_2SO_4$ and $H_3PO_4$ immediately before titration.

**139.** Which of the following is true concerning Reaction 1?

  A. Cr is oxidized and $Cr_2O_7^{2-}$ is the oxidizing agent.
  B. Cr is reduced and $Cr_2O_7^{2-}$ is the reducing agent.
  C. Cr is reduced and $Cr_2O_7^{2-}$ is the oxidizing agent.
  D. Cr is oxidized and $Cr_2O_7^{2-}$ is the reducing agent.

**140.** What is the oxidation state of Cr in $Cr_2O_7^{2-}$ ?

  A. +12
  B. +7
  C. +6
  D. +3

**141.** What is the volume of dichromate added to the titration at the equivalence point?

  A. 13 mL
  B. 15 mL
  C. 25 mL
  D. 30 mL

**142.** Which of the following expressions gives the concentration of $Fe^{2+}$ in the unknown solution in terms of the volume of dichromate added $V_{Cr_2O_7^{2-}}$, the molarity of dichromate $M_{Cr_2O_7^{2-}}$, and the original volume of $Fe^{2+}$ solution $V_{Fe}$?

  A. $\dfrac{\left(V_{Cr_2O_7^{2-}}\right)\left(M_{Cr_2O_7^{2-}}\right)}{V_{Fe}}$

  B. $\dfrac{\left(6V_{Cr_2O_7^{2-}}\right)\left(M_{Cr_2O_7^{2-}}\right)}{V_{Fe}}$

  C. $\dfrac{\left(V_{Cr_2O_7^{2-}}\right)\left(M_{Cr_2O_7^{2-}}\right)}{6V_{Fe}}$

  D. $\dfrac{\left(2V_{Cr_2O_7^{2-}}\right)\left(M_{Cr_2O_7^{2-}}\right)}{V_{Fe}}$

**143.** If the formal potential of the solution is not lowered, which of the following will be the result of the titration when DAS is used as the indicator?

  A. The solution will turn violet before the equivalence point is reached.
  B. The solution will turn violet after the equivalence point is reached.
  C. Dichromate ion will not be able to oxidize DAS.
  D. Dichromate ion will reduce DAS to its colorless form.

**144.** Which of the following statements is true at the equivalence point of the titration in the passage?

  A. Each iron ion has lost one electron and each chromium ion has gained three electrons.
  B. Each iron ion has lost one electron and each chromium ion has gained six electrons.
  C. Each iron ion has gained one electron and each chromium ion has lost three electrons.
  D. Each iron ion has gained one electron and each chromium ion has lost six electrons.

Rechargeable batteries have become an essential part of our environmentally conscientious society. The nickel-cadmium cell battery is a rechargeable battery used in small electronic devices. The half reactions that take place in the nickel-cadmium battery during discharge are:

$$Cd(OH)_2(s) + 2e^- \rightarrow Cd(s) + 2OH^-$$

$$E° = -0.4 \text{ V}$$

**Half Reaction 1**

$$2NiO_2(s) + H_2O + 2e^- \rightarrow 2Ni(OH)_2(s) + 2OH^-$$

$$E° = 0.5 \text{ V}$$

**Half Reaction 2**

Other types of rechargeable batteries currently being developed are those using sodium or lithium metal as the anode and sulfur as the cathode. These batteries must operate at high temperatures because the metals must be in the liquid state, but they provide a high energy density, which means the batteries will be very light weight.

**145.** The reaction taking place at the anode when the nickel-cadmium batteries are discharging is:

- A. $Cd(s) + 2OH^- \rightarrow Cd(OH)_2(s) + 2e^-$
- B. $2NiO_2(s) + H_2O + 2e^- \rightarrow 2Ni(OH)_2(s) + 2OH^-$
- C. $Cd(OH)_2(s) + 2e^- \rightarrow Cd(s) + 2OH^-$
- D. $2Ni(OH)_2(s) + 2OH^- \rightarrow 2NiO_2(s) + H_2O + 2e^-$

**146.** When the nickel-cadmium battery is recharging, what is the reaction at the anode?

- A. $Cd(s) + 2OH^- \rightarrow Cd(OH)_2(s) + 2e^-$
- B. $2NiO_2(s) + H_2O + 2e^- \rightarrow 2Ni(OH)_2(s) + 2OH^-$
- C. $Cd(OH)_2(s) + 2e^- \rightarrow Cd(s) + 2OH^-$
- D. $2Ni(OH)_2(s) + 2OH^- \rightarrow 2NiO_2(s) + H_2O + 2e^-$

**147.** What is the oxidizing agent in the nickel cadmium battery during discharge?

- A. Cd
- B. $Cd(OH)_2$
- C. $NiO_2$
- D. $2Ni(OH)_2$

**148.** Which of the following is true concerning the nickel-cadmium battery when it is recharging?

- A. The cell is a nonspontaneous electrolytic cell.
- B. The cell is a nonspontaneous galvanic cell.
- C. The cell is a spontaneous electrolytic cell.
- D. The cell is a spontaneous galvanic cell.

**149.** In order to recharge the nickel-cadmium battery back to standard conditions, what is the minimum voltage that must be applied across its electrodes?

- A. 0.1 V
- B. 0.2 V
- C. 0.9 V
- D. 1.8 V

**150.** In a sodium-sulfur battery, what is the half reaction for sodium in the spontaneous direction?

- A. $Na^+ + e^- \rightarrow Na$
- B. $Na \rightarrow Na^+ + e^-$
- C. $Na \rightarrow Na^{2+} + 2e^-$
- D. $Na^+ + OH^- \rightarrow NaOH$

**151.** The nickel-cadmium battery is used to power a light bulb. The current in the light bulb flows:

- A. in the same direction as the flow of electrons, from the side with Half Reaction 1 to the side with Half Reaction 2.
- B. in the same direction as the flow of electrons, from the side with Half Reaction 2 to the side with Half Reaction 1.
- C. in the opposite direction to the flow of electrons, from the side with Half Reaction 1 to the side with Half Reaction 2.
- D. in the opposite direction to the flow of electrons, from the side with Half Reaction 2 to the side with Half Reaction 1

**GO ON TO THE NEXT PAGE.**

A pH meter is a concentration cell which measures the potential difference between a reference solution and a test solution and reports the difference in terms of pH. In a simplified version of a pH meter the half reactions are:

$$H_2 + 2H_2O \rightarrow 2H_3O^+ + 2e^-$$

$$2H_3O^+ + 2e^- \rightarrow H_2 + 2H_2O$$

The potential difference between the two solutions is derived from the Nernst equation as follows:

$$E = -\frac{0.0592}{2} \log\left(\frac{[H_3O^+]_{\text{test solution}}}{[H_3O^+]_{\text{reference solution}}}\right)^2$$

where $E$ is given in volts. This equation can be rewritten in terms of the pH of the solutions as follows:

$$E = 0.059(pH_{\text{test}} - pH_{\text{reference}})$$

Because it is inconvenient to bubble $H_2$ gas through a solution, a more sophisticated pH meter is used in standard laboratory practice. Dilute hydrochloric acid is used as the reference solution. The test solution is in contact with a thin glass membrane in which a silver wire coated with silver chloride is imbedded. This glass membrane is dipped into the test solution and the potential difference between the solutions is measured and interpreted by a computer, which displays the pH of the test solution. The same equation holds for both pH meters.

**152.** What is the reaction quotient ($Q$) in the Nernst equation for the simple pH meter?

A. $\dfrac{\left[H_3O^+\right]^2_{\text{test solution}}}{\left[H_2\right]}$

B. $\dfrac{\left[H_2\right]}{\left[H_3O^+\right]^2_{\text{test solution}}}$

C. $\dfrac{\left[H_3O^+\right]^2_{\text{test solution}}\left[H_2\right]_{\text{reference solution}}}{\left[H_3O^+\right]^2_{\text{reference solution}}\left[H_2\right]_{\text{test solution}}}$

D. $\dfrac{\left[H_3O^+\right]^2_{\text{test solution}}}{\left[H_3O^+\right]^2_{\text{reference solution}}}$

**153.** What would be the approximate potential difference measured by a pH meter if the test solution had a pH of 2 and the reference solution had a pH of 4?

A. −118 mV
B. −59 mV
C. 59 mV
D. 118 mV

**154.** The potential difference measured by a pH meter is directly proportional to:

A. the difference in the hydrogen ion concentrations of the test and reference solution.
B. the difference in the pH of the test and reference solution.
C. the pH of the test solution.
D. the hydrogen ion concentration of the test solution.

**155.** If the reference solution of a pH meter were 1 $M$ HCl, and the potential difference measured by the meter were 59 mV, what would be the pH of the test solution?

A. 0
B. 1
C. 2
D. 8

**156.** How would the potential difference registered by a pH meter change for a given test solution if the hydrogen ion concentration of the reference solution were increased by a factor of 10?

A. The potential difference would increase by 59 mV.
B. The potential difference would decrease by 59 mV.
C. The potential difference would increase by a factor of 10.
D. The potential difference would decrease by a factor of 10.

157. A galvanic cell is prepared by connecting two half cells with a salt bridge and a wire. One cell has a Cu electrode and 1 $M$ CuSO$_4$, and the other has a Cu electrode and 2 $M$ CuSO$_4$. Which direction will the current flow through the wire?

A. toward the 1$M$ CuSO$_4$ solution.
B. toward the 2$M$ CuSO$_4$ solution.
C. current will not flow because the half reactions are the same for both sides.
D. current will not flow because both half cells have Cu electrodes.

158. Which of the following is true for an acid-base concentration cell such as the one used by the pH meter?

A. Current always flows toward the more acidic solution.
B. Current always flows toward the more basic solution.
C. Current always flows toward the more neutral solution.
D. Current always flows away from the more neutral solution.

---

Questions 159 through 161 are **NOT** based on a descriptive passage.

159. Consider the reduction potential:

$$Zn^{2+} + 2e^- \rightarrow Zn(s) \qquad E° = -0.76 \text{ V}.$$

When solid Zinc is added to aqueous HCl, under standard conditions, does a reaction take place?

A. No, because the oxidation potential for Cl$^-$ is positive.
B. No, because the reduction potential for Cl$^-$ is negative.
C. Yes, because the reduction potential for H$^+$ is positive.
D. Yes, because the reduction potential for H$^+$ is zero.

160. Chemicals are mixed in a redox reaction and allowed to come to equilibrium. Which of the following must be true concerning the solution at equilibrium?

A. $K = 1$
B. $\Delta G° = 0$
C. $E = 0$
D. $\Delta G° = \Delta G$

161. At 298 K all reactants and products in a certain oxidation-reduction reaction are in aqueous phase at initial concentrations of 1 $M$. If the total potential for the reaction is E = 20 mV, which of the following must be true?

A. $K = 1$
B. $E°_{298} = 20 \text{ mV}$
C. $\Delta G$ is positive
D. $K < 1$

---

**STOP.** IF YOU FINISH BEFORE TIME IS CALLED, CHECK YOUR WORK. YOU MAY GO BACK TO ANY QUESTION IN THIS TEST BOOKLET.

# ANSWERS & EXPLANATIONS

## FOR

## 30-MINUTE IN-CLASS EXAMINATIONS

# ANSWERS FOR THE 30-MINUTE IN-CLASS EXAMS

| Lecture 1 | Lecture 2 | Lecture 3 | Lecture 4 | Lecture 5 | Lecture 6 | Lecture 7 |
|---|---|---|---|---|---|---|
| 1. D | 24. B | 47. A | 70. C | 93. C | 116. A | 139. C |
| 2. B | 25. A | 48. C | 71. B | 94. C | 117. A | 140. C |
| 3. A | 26. C | 49. B | 72. B | 95. C | 118. B | 141. C |
| 4. B | 27. C | 50. C | 73. A | 96. B | 119. D | 142. B |
| 5. C | 28. B | 51. A | 74. C | 97. D | 120. D | 143. A |
| 6. D | 29. C | 52. D | 75. D | 98. B | 121. A | 144. A |
| 7. B | 30. C | 53. C | 76. A | 99. D | 122. C | 145. A |
| 8. C | 31. A | 54. C | 77. C | 100. B | 123. C | 146. D |
| 9. D | 32. A | 55. D | 78. B | 101. A | 124. B | 147. C |
| 10. C | 33. A | 56. D | 79. B | 102. B | 125. C | 148. A |
| 11. D | 34. D | 57. C | 80. B | 103. A | 126. C | 149. C |
| 12. C | 35. D | 58. A | 81. D | 104. B | 127. A | 150. B |
| 13. C | 36. C | 59. B | 82. C | 105. D | 128. C | 151. D |
| 14. A | 37. B | 60. C | 83. D | 106. D | 129. C | 152. D |
| 15. A | 38. A | 61. D | 84. C | 107. A | 130. D | 153. A |
| 16. B | 39. A | 62. A | 85. A | 108. C | 131. D | 154. B |
| 17. B | 40. D | 63. A | 86. C | 109. A | 132. A | 155. B |
| 18. D | 41. B | 64. B | 87. D | 110. D | 133. C | 156. A |
| 19. B | 42. D | 65. A | 88. A | 111. B | 134. D | 157. A |
| 20. A | 43. C | 66. B | 89. A | 112. A | 135. A | 158. B |
| 21. D | 44. B | 67. C | 90. C | 113. C | 136. C | 159. D |
| 22. B | 45. A | 68. C | 91. B | 114. A | 137. A | 160. C |
| 23. D | 46. C | 69. D | 92. B | 115. A | 138. B | 161. B |

## MCAT CHEMISTRY

| Raw Score | Estimated Scaled Score |
|---|---|
| 21 | 15 |
| 20 | 14 |
| 19 | 13 |
| 18 | 12 |
| 17 | 11 |
| 15-16 | 10 |
| 14 | 9 |
| 12-13 | 8 |

## MCAT CHEMISTRY

| Raw Score | Estimated Scaled Score |
|---|---|
| 11 | 7 |
| 9-10 | 6 |
| 8 | 5 |
| 6-7 | 4 |
| 5 | 3 |
| 3-4 | 2 |
| 1-2 | 1 |

# EXPLANATIONS TO IN-CLASS EXAM FOR LECTURE 1

## Passage I

1. **D is correct.** If you get a boiling point question on the MCAT, look for hydrogen bonding. It increases the strength of intermolecular attractions. Stronger intermolecular attractions leads to higher boiling point.

2. **B is correct.** You should recognize this compound as ionic because alkaline earth metals like to form ionic compounds with halogens.

3. **A is correct.** In order to explain an increase in boiling point, we have to look for a reason that intermolecular bond strength would increase. The intermolecular bonds in noble gases are totally due to van der Waals forces. If the atoms are more polarizable, instantaneous dipoles can have greater strength. Larger atoms are more polarizable because the electrons can get farther from the nucleus and create a larger dipole moment.

4. **B is correct.** This is a periodic trend. Radius increases going down and to the left on the periodic table.

5. **C is correct.** Crystallization depends upon molecular symmetry as well as intermolecular bonding. Boiling point is strongly dependent upon intermolecular bond strength.

6. **D is correct.** Methane is nonpolar, so its only intermolecular bonding is through van der Waals forces.

7. **B is correct.** All intermolecular bonding is via electrostatic forces. The dipoles in van der Waals forces are temporary whereas dipole-dipole interactions may be due to permanent dipoles.

## Passage II

8. **C is correct.** 'As' is just to the left of 'Se' on the periodic table. Therefore, its radius should be slightly larger than Se.

9. **D is correct.** Elements in the same family tend to be chemically similar. Hydrogen is an exception.

10. **C is correct.** Atomic radius is a periodic trend increasing down and to the left.

11. **D is correct.** Only D is a true statement. A is knowledge that would not be required by the MCAT.

12. **C is correct.** Electron affinity is a periodic trend increasing (becoming more exothermic) to the right and up.

13. **C is correct.** The answer we are looking for must explain shielding. With each new period, a new shell is added which shields the new electrons from the greater nuclear charge.

14. **A is correct.** If you substitute H for X in the equation for $\Delta$ in the passage, you can only arrive at zero.

15. **A is correct.** C and O are close together in electronegativity and will form a covalent bond.

## Passage III

16. **B is correct.** Only water is caught in Chamber 1. The change in mass of chamber 1, 0.9 grams, is all water. 0.9 grams of water divided by 18 g/mol gives 0.05 mole of water. All the hydrogen came from the sample, and all the oxygen came from the excess oxygen. For every mole of water, there are 2 moles of hydrogens, so there is $0.05 \times 2 = 0.1$ mole of hydrogen in the sample. Doing the same with the carbon dioxide caught in Chamber 2 we have: $4.4/44.2 = 0.1$ of $CO_2$, or 0.1 mole of carbon from the sample. This is a 1:1 ratio. The empirical formula is CH.

17. **B is correct.** The molarity of $O_2$ is equal to the molarity of the welding gas or any other ideal gas at the same temperature and pressure. Density divided by molecular weight is molarity. Therefore, we can set the ratios of density to molecular weight for oxygen and the welding gas equal to each other. We get: $1.3/32 = 1.1/M.W.$

18. **D is correct.** $CH_2O$ has a molecular weight of 30 g/mol. Thus, we must multiply this by 4 to get 120. So, for the molecular formula we need four times as many atoms of each element from the empirical formula.

19. **B is correct.** $O_2$ is the limiting reagent. Only 0.5 mole of propane can react, producing 2 moles of water.

20. **A is correct.** The passage says that $CaCl_2$ absorbs water. Thus if Chamber 2 were in front of Chamber 1, it would weigh more because it would absorb both water and carbon dioxide. The amount of carbon dioxide is calculated from the weight of Chamber 2, so the calculated value would be too high.

21. **D is correct.** All of the welding gas must be reacted because the mass of the original sample is divided by the moles of carbon and hydrogen to find the molecular weight. If all the gas were not reacted, the calculated molecular weight would be too large. Adding excess oxygen ensures that all of the welding gas reacts.

**Stand Alones**

22. **B is correct.** Chlorine takes on an additional electron to become an ion.

23. **D is correct.** This is the Heisenberg uncertainty principle.

# EXPLANATIONS TO IN-CLASS EXAM FOR LECTURE 2

**Passage I**

24. **B is correct.** The definition of $Z = PV/(nRT)$ is always 1 for an ideal gas.

25. **A is correct.** If a and b are both zero, the van der Waals equation becomes $PV = nRT$, the ideal gas law.

26. **C is correct.** You can figure this out from the passage, but it's a lot easier to fall back on your previous knowledge: gases behave most ideally at high temperature and low pressures.

27. **C is correct.** Volume is inversely proportional to pressure. A: $K.E. = 3/2\ kT$. B: $PV = nRT$, D: This is one of the assumptions underlying the derivation of the ideal gas law.

28. **B is correct.** Condensation is due to intermolecular attractions, which are neglected for ideal gases. For D, start with $K.E. = 3/2\ kT$. Then $1/2\ mv^2 = 3/2\ kT$, so v is proportional to the square root of T.

29. **C is correct.** Equations involving products or ratios of temperature are meaningless if the zero of the temperature scale is not absolute zero. A and B are true statements, but they don't explain why absolute temperature must be used.

**Passage II**

30. **C is correct.** A catalyst acts to lower the activation energy of a reaction, so the catalyzed reaction will have a lower activation energy than the uncatalyzed reaction.

31. **A is correct.** A catalyst is neither produced nor consumed in a reaction and does not appear in the net reaction. The net reaction for the mechanism shown is:

$$O_3 + O \rightarrow 2O_2$$

The catalyst, Cl, does not appear. ClO also does not appear, but it is produced and consumed in the reaction making it an intermediate.

32. **A is correct.** See the Arrhenius equation:

$$k = zpe^{-Ea/RT}$$

You should also memorize the fact that temperature always increases the rate of a reaction. Even in the case of biologically catalyzed reactions, heat increases the reaction rate until the enzyme is denatured. Once the enzyme is denatured, although the reaction rate slows, the reaction takes a new pathway, and is no longer the same reaction.

33. **A is correct.** If a catalyst only affected the rate in one direction, the equilibrium would be affected. A catalyst doesn't change the equilibrium. This can also be seen from a reaction profile diagram as shown in question 37.

34. **D is correct.** The catalyst is not necessarily the only factor influencing pH.

**35.** **D is correct.** Choice I is seen from the standard form of the rate law: rate = $k$[A][B]. For choice II, imagine the saturation kinetics exhibited by enzyme catalysts:

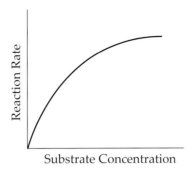

This should make it clear that the ratio of concentrations of the catalyst and the substrates affects the rate of a reaction. This ratio can be changed by changing the concentration of the catalyst. Thus the concentration of a catalyst can affect the rate of a reaction. For choice III, a heterogeneous catalyst is one that is not in the same phase as the reactants. Increasing the surface area of a heterogeneous catalyst is like increasing the concentration. The reaction is affected for the same reasons as in choice II. The reason that a heterogeneous catalyst is typically in the form of metal shavings as opposed to a solid metal bar is to increase surface area. Choice IV you should know from the Arrhenius equation: $k = zpe^{-Ea/RT}$

**36.** **C is correct.** The MCAT sometimes uses the phrase "van der Waals" forces as a synonym for London Dispersion Forces. A more modern meaning is as a synonym for intermolecular forces. In either case, this is a correct answer. Hydrogen bonding requires a hydrogen atom bonded to a nitrogen, fluorine, or oxygen. D is from an episode of Star Trek.

**37.** **B is correct.** Only the activation energy is changed by a catalyst. The initial and final states are not affected!

## Passage III

In this experiment, Reaction 2 uses up $I_3^-$ as it is formed. When all the $S_2O_3^{2-}$ is used up in Reaction 2, the $I_3^-$ reacts with the starch to turn black. The black color signals the experimenter that all the $S_2O_3^{2-}$ is used up. The experimenter now knows that half as much $I_3^-$ was used up in the same time, and can calculate the rate for Reaction 1. This depends upon Reaction 2 being the fastest reaction.

**38.** **A is correct.** If we look at Reactions 1 and 2 as two steps of a single reaction, we know that the rate of the slow step is equal to the rate of the overall reaction. Equation 1 measures the time necessary for a specific number of moles of $I_3^-$ to be used by Reaction 2. (Notice that the rate of change of $1/2[S_2O_3^{2-}]$ will be equal to the rate of change of $[I_3^-]$) If Reaction 2 were not the fast step, then Equation 1 would not measure the rate of Reaction 1 accurately. Since Reaction 2 is the fast step, the time $t$ required to use up $1/2[S_2O_3^{2-}]$ is equal to the time needed to produce $[I_3^-]$. The $[I_3^-]$ concentration produced divided by the time necessary to produce it is the rate of Reaction 1. Equation 1 is not derivable from the rate laws of Reactions 1 and 2.

**39.** **A is correct.** A temperature decrease reduces rate and makes the reaction take longer.

**40.** **D is correct.** The rate law is found by comparing the rate change from one trial to the next when the concentration of only one reaction is changed. Comparing trials 1 and 2, when the concentration of $I^-$ is reduced by a factor of two, the rate is also reduced by a factor of two. This indicates a first order reaction with respect to $I^-$. D is the only possible answer.

**41.** **B is correct.** The exponents in the rate law indicate the order of the reaction with respect to each concentration.

**42.** **D is correct.** The starch is used to measure the rate of Reaction 1, and does not affect the rate. Although C is true, it does not answer the question as well as D.

**43.** **C is correct.** Equation 1 gives the rate of Reaction 1. $S_2O_3^{2-}$ is not part of Reaction 1 and its concentration does not change the rate. If rate doesn't change, then, according to Equation 1, t must increase with $S_2O_3^{2-}$.

**44.** **B is correct.** A catalyst increases the rate of a reaction.

45.    **A is correct.** In a reaction at equilibrium, the rate of change in the concentrations of both products and reactants is zero. This does not mean that the concentrations of reactants and products are equal, nor that the rate constants are equal.

46.    **C is correct.** Some of both gases will effuse from side 1 to side 2. This means that the partial pressures of both gases will decrease. (Remember, partial pressure is the pressure of the gas as if it were alone in the container. Thus if we reduce the number of moles of a gas at constant volume and temperature, we reduce its partial pressure.)  Since hydrogen will diffuse more rapidly than oxygen, the mole fraction of oxygen will increase.

## EXPLANATIONS TO IN-CLASS EXAM FOR LECTURE 3

### Passage I

47.    **A is correct.** Nickel is an element and is a solid in its natural state at 298 K. Thus, the enthalpy of formation of solid nickel at 298 K is zero.

48.    **C is correct.** Chemist A chooses the direction of the reaction based upon chemical stability, and then says that the direction will change at higher temperatures. This is tantamount to saying that the stability will switch at higher temperatures, which, by the way, is also correct. D is, of course, a false statement. The entropy shown for Reaction 1 is the entropy of the reaction. In other words, it is the entropy of the system, and not the entropy of the universe. Chemist A's statement is correct, and does not contradict the second law of thermodynamics. A and B are contradicted because Chemist A says the direction is temperature dependent.

49.    **B is correct.** Use Le Chatelier's principle. Read the first sentence of the passage carefully, and notice that to purify nickel, the reaction must move to the left. There are four gas molecules on the left side of the reaction and only one on the right. Pressure pushes the reaction to the right. The reaction is exothermic when moving to the right, so high temperature pushes the reaction to the left.

50.    **C is correct.** The reaction is the system, and everything outside the reaction makes up the surroundings. The entropy change given in the passage refers to the system not the universe. The second law of thermodynamics says that a reaction is spontaneous when the entropy of the universe is positive. The entropy of the system may be positive or negative. A and B are false statements. D is a false statement as well. The reaction runs until the entropy of the universe is maximized.

51.    **A is correct.** Use $\Delta G = \Delta H - T\Delta S$. Don't forget to convert J/K to kJ/K.

52.    **D is correct.** Spontaneity is dictated by Gibbs energy. 1 atm. is standard state for a gas, so $\Delta G = \Delta G°$. When Gibbs energy is negative, a reaction is spontaneous. if enthalpy change is negative and entropy change is positive, then Gibbs energy change must be negative. You can use $\Delta G° = \Delta H° - T\Delta S°$. Check this as follows: If the partial pressures are 1, then the reaction quotient Q is 1, and the log of the reaction quotient is zero. From the equation $\Delta G = \Delta G° + RT\ln Q$ we see that $\Delta G = \Delta G°$. The reaction is spontaneous.

### Passage II

Note: A heat engine obeys the first law of thermodynamics. It must expel the same amount of energy as it takes in.

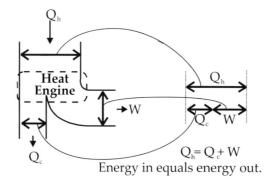

Energy in equals energy out.

53. **C is correct.** If $Q_h' = Q_h$ and $Q_c' = Q_c$ then $W' = W$. Thus the efficiencies of the engines must be equal. Since only a Carnot engine can be as efficient as another Carnot engine, Engine 1 must be a Carnot engine.

54. **C is correct.** If the all the work done by Engine 1 is done on Engine 2, the net work is zero. Since Engine 1 is not a Carnot engine, the entire process is not reversible. The result of any nonreversible process where no work is done must be that heat energy is transferred from the hot reservoir to the cold reservoir. Engine 1 has a lower $e$ than Engine 2 and thus requires more heat energy to create as much work. According to conservation of energy, this extra heat energy input must be matched by extra heat energy output.

55. **D is correct.** Engine 2 is a Carnot engine, and, as the passage states, it has the highest possible efficiency of any engine working between the existing heat reservoirs. Thus only a change in the heat reservoirs will increase its efficiency. **The answer must therefore be C or D.** For greatest efficiency we want to remove the most heat energy possible from the hot reservoir and expel the least amount possible to the cold reservoir thus getting the most work with the least amount of wasted energy. Removing heat energy from the hot reservoir decreases its entropy, while adding heat energy to the cold reservoir increases its entropy. As the temperature of the hot reservoir increases, removing heat energy has less effect on the change in entropy, so more heat energy can be removed. The reverse is true for the cold reservoir. Since, in a Carnot engine, the change in entropy must be zero, the extra heat energy removed from the hot reservoir must be added to work. The engine becomes more efficient. Thus maximizing the temperature difference increases efficiency. This can be derived from the equation in the passage (the long method) as follows. Considering magnitudes only we have:

$$\frac{Q_h}{T_h} = \frac{Q_c}{T_c} \qquad\qquad \frac{Q_c}{Q_h} = \frac{T_c}{T_h}$$

$$e = \frac{W}{Q_h} \qquad e = \frac{(Q_h - Q_c)}{Q_h} \qquad e = 1 - \frac{Q_c}{Q_h}$$

substituting $\dfrac{T_c}{T_h}$ for $\dfrac{Q_c}{Q_h}$ we have:

$$e = 1 - \frac{T_c}{T_h}$$

56. **D is correct.** From the derivation for efficiency in the previous explanation, if $T_c$ is zero, $e = 1$. However, it is probably easier to eliminate the other answer choices insead. Choice A is wrong because by the equation for efficiency given in the passage, $e = W/Q_h$, a large $W$ by itself won't give $e = 1$. Choice B is wrong because as per the passage all Carnot engines are reversible, but all Carnot engines are not 100% efficient. Choice C is wrong because from the entropy formula, if $T_c$ and $T_h$ were at the same temperature, $Q_h$ and $Q_c$ would also have to be at the same temperature, which gives $W = Q_h - Q_c = O$, and an efficiency of zero. 100% efficiency is an impossibility.

57. **C is correct.** The exhaust is wasted energy. $Q_h = W + Q_c$. $P = Q_h/t = W/t + Q_c/t = (mgh)/ 20 \text{ s} + 1000 \text{ J/s} = 4000/20 + 1000 = 1200 \text{ J}$.

58. **A is correct.** $PV = nRT = (m/M.W.)RT$. $P = 1000 \times 8.314 \times 400/4 = 8.314 \times 10^5$ Pa. By the way, if the gas did not behave ideally, the real pressure would be lower. There is no answer lower than A, and the gas does behave very nearly ideally because it is at high temperature.

## Passage III

59. **B is correct.** The transition state corresponds to the top of the energy curve.

60. **C is correct.** The energy of activation is given by the vertical displacement from the reactants to the top of the energy curve.

61. **D is correct.** The smallest energy of activation is the most kinetically favored.

62. **A is correct.** The largest drop in energy is the most thermodynamically favored.

63. **A is correct.** A catalyst lowers the energy of activation but does not change the energy difference between the reactants and products.

64. **B is correct.** The change in energy is energy of products minus reactants.

65. **A is correct.** The kinetically favored product is the one with a lower energy of activation. The difference in their equilibrium is due to conflicting thermodynamics and kinetics. At a low temperature ($T_2$), the thermodynamically favored product does not have enough energy to reach the activated complex, so no reaction occurs. The kinetically favored reaction does reach the activated state and a reaction can occur. At the high temperature ($T_1$) both reactions occur but the reverse of the thermodynamically favored occurs only with a relatively lower probability. Thus the thermodynamically favored reaction predominates. This is not always true but is a concept of which you must be aware.

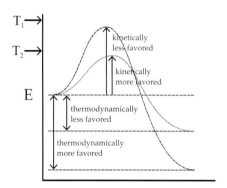

## Stand Alones

66. **B is correct.** Transfer by contact is conduction.

67. **C is correct.** The second law of thermodynamics says that entropy of the universe increases for any process. By straightening up his room, the man increased the order in his room, and thus decreased its entropy. In order for the entropy of the universe to have increased, there must be a larger increase in entropy of the surroundings. Only C provides an explanation for this.

68. **C is correct.** The entropy of the system is equal to change in entropy of the two reservoirs. $\Delta S = Q/T$ for each reservoir. The change in entropy of the first reservoir is negative because heat energy is leaving the system ($-1000/200 = -5$), and the change in entropy of the second reservoir is positive because heat energy is entering the system ($1000/100 = 10$). The sum of the two entropy changes is +5. You should have at least narrowed down the possibilities to C and D because the change in entropy for any isolated system must be positive for any irreversible process.

69. **D is correct.** The temperature of Gas A remains constant because the question says so. Temperature is kinetic energy (due to random motion) per mole. Gas B does no work and doesn't exchange heat so its energy doesn't change; it has the same kinetic energy (due to random motion) per mole as when it began. Thus, its temperature doesn't change either.

    Enthalpy is $PV + U$. $P$ and $V$ are the same for both gases because they are at the same temp, volume and therefore pressure ($PV = nRT$). $U$ doesn't change for Gas A because any energy removed is replaced to keep the temperature the same. $U$ doesn't change for Gas B because no energy is exchanged with the surroundings for Gas B.

## EXPLANATIONS TO IN-CLASS EXAM FOR LECTURE 4

### Passage I

70. **C is correct.** The first experiment shows that no nitrite was in the solution. Had there been nitrite, nitrogen bubbles would have formed as per the reaction, and then barium sulfate would have precipitated upon the addition of barium chloride. The second experiment demonstrates that nitrates exist. The water in the moistened litmus paper reacted with ammonia gas to make $OH^-$ ions turning the paper blue. Ammonia gas resulted from the reaction of nitrate with Devarda's alloy.

71. **B is correct.** Any sulfate ions that exist in solution before sulfamic acid is added must be removed. They are removed by the addition of $BaCl_2$. Choice A is incorrect because $BaCl_2$ does not acidify the solution. Choice C is incorrect because $BaCl_2$ doesn't react with sulfamic acid, it reacts with sulfate. Choice D is incorrect because nitrite doesn't form a precipitate with $BaCl_2$, sulfate does.

72. **B is correct.** The precipitate would result when the sulfate ion from the reaction reacts with the barium ion to form barium sulfate. The bubbles would be created by the formation of nitrogen gas.

73.     **A is correct.** Choice A produces gas bubbles which could be confused with nitrogen gas bubbles. The $BaCl_2$ actually prevents this from happening by forming a precipitate with carbonate before the sulfamic acid-nitrite reaction. Choice B is incorrect because the solution in Experiment 1 is acidic not basic, and because the precipitate would come out before the sulfamic acid-nitrite reaction. Choice C is incorrect because there is no ammonium in solution. Choice D is not carbonate ion, and although carbonic acid is formed by carbonate ion in aqueous solution, you should know that it breaks down to water and carbon dioxide, not carbon monoxide, hydrogen, and oxygen. A reaction you should know: $H_2CO_3 \rightarrow CO_2(g) + H_2O$

74.     **C is correct.** Change in temperature can change the rate constant and the equilibrium constant but it can only increase the rate of the reaction.

75.     **D is correct.** The litmus paper is turned blue when the basic ammonia gas from the reaction in the experiment reacts with the water in the paper.

## Passage II

76.     **A is correct.** This is definitional: products over reactants excluding pure liquids and solids.

77.     **C is correct.** $K_{sp}$ is a constant; solubility of $Ca(IO_3)_2$ is not. By Reaction 2, as acidity increases, $IO_3^-$ ions are used up, pulling Reaction 1 to the right. Or just look at Table 1. If you want to see why you can't just use Le Chatelier's principle on Reaction 2, simply add the two equations together to get:

$$Ca(IO_3)_2 + H^+ \rightarrow Ca^{2+} + IO_3^- + HIO_3$$

Now when you add $H^+$ to this equation, it moves to the right, dissolving $Ca(IO_3)_2$.

78.     **B is correct.** You should recognize the $y = mx + b$ form of the equation. This is the equation of a line. The $b$ in this case is not zero, but is ($K_{sp}$).

79.     **B is correct.** You must realize that the new solution is no longer saturated. These means that Reaction 1 is not in equilibrium. No precipitate exists. New $Ca^{2+}$ ions do not immediately create precipitate because the solution is not saturated. There is no leftward shift because there is no equilibrium. Thus A, C and D are wrong. Iodic acid is in equilibrium however. Increasing $H^+$ ions shifts Reaction 2 to the right, creating more $HIO_3$. This is, of course, why Solution 1 is no longer saturated after adding the acid.

80.     **B is correct.** The easiest way to find the $K_{sp}$ is to plug the value of $S$ for Solution 1 into the equation. Notice that the $[H^+]$ value in Solution 1 is for neutral water. It is so small that the second term in the solubility equation becomes negligible. The equation becomes

$$2S^{3/2} = K_{sp}^{1/2}.$$

Squaring both sides gives: $4S^3 = K_{sp}$

$$\Rightarrow 4 \times (5.4 \times 10^{-3})^3 = K_{sp}.$$

The only answer that is even close is choice B at $10^{-7}$.

81.     **D is correct.** The net equation is $Ca(IO_3)_2(s) + H^+(aq) \rightarrow Ca^{2+}(aq) + IO_3^-(aq) + HIO_3(aq)$. $CaOH_2$ in aqueous solution will produce both $OH^-$ and $Ca^{2+}$. The $OH^-$ will reduce the $H^+$ in solution. Since the solution is saturated (in equilibrium), Le Chatelier's principle predicts that both of these changes will shift the reaction to the left producing $Ca(IO_3)_2(s)$.

82.     **C is correct.** Reaction 2 will shift left via Le Chatelier's principle. The resulting increase in $IO_3^-$ will shift Reaction 1 to the left due to the common ion effect, creating precipitate in the already saturated solution. The $H^+$ ion concentration in the formula for solubility is from hydrogen ions in solution before iodic acid is added. If a different acid were added (like HCl), the $H^+$ ion concentration would move Reaction 2 to the right and thus Reaction 1 to the right.

## Passage III

A ligand is an ion or neutral molecule that can donate a pair of electrons to form a coordinate covalent bond with a metal ion. EDTA is a chelating agent (a ligand that makes more than one bond to a <u>single</u> metal ion). It wraps around its metal ion like a claw. Chele (χηλη) means claw in Greek.

83.     **D is correct.** The passage states that EDTA reacts with other metal ions. If more EDTA is used up, the scientist will assume that it is being used up by calcium and magnesium ions. This will result in an over-estimation of these ions.

84.     **C is correct.** EDTA is donating a pair of electrons in a coordinate covalent bond, so it is a Lewis Base.

85. **A is correct.** This is LeChatelier's Principle. The chlorine ion will remove some of the $Ca^{2+}$ pulling the reaction to the right.

86. **C is correct.** The passage states that there is a one-to-one stoichiometry between EDTA and its metal ion. (50 mL)(0.001 mol/L) = (25 mL)$x$. $x$ = 0.002 mol/L

87. **D is correct.** D is the best explanation. Under high pH conditions, protons are stripped from the carboxylic acids allowing the ligand to bond to the cation. Indicators change color over a range so C is wrong. Calcium carbonate dissolves in an acid solution so B is wrong. A is irrelevant.

88. **A is correct.** You should know that $Na^+$ is very soluble, and $H^+$ does not form mineral deposits.

89. **A is correct.** The association constant from Table 1 is $5 \times 108$. The association reaction is:

$$Mg^{2+} + EDTA \rightarrow EDTA - Mg.$$

$$\text{The } K_{assoc} = 5 \times 10^8 = [EDTA - Mg]/[EDTA][Mg^{2+}]$$

Since half the magnesium is bound, [EDTA-Mg] is 9 ppm, which is $5 \times 10^{-4}$. The remaining half of $[Mg^{2+}]$ is 9 ppm, which is also $5 \times 10^{-4}$. Plugging these into the equilibrium expression leaves the remaining concentration [EDTA] = $1/(5 \times 10^8)$ or $2 \times 10^{-9}$.

## Stand Alones

90. **C is correct.** Water boils at 100°C and atmospheric pressure, 760 torr. Boiling point is where vapor pressure meets atmospheric pressure. Thus water vapor pressure must be below 760 at 95°C. But it must also rise with increasing temperature, so it must be above 23.8 torr.

91. **B is correct.** No calculations are required since the vapor pressure would be somewhere between the vapor pressures of the pure liquids. The solution follows Raoult's law.

92. **B is correct.** Since the reaction was exothermic, the vapor pressure deviated negatively from Raoult's law. Depending upon the ratios of the liquids in solution, the vapor pressure could be lower than either or just lower than B. (A has a higher boiling point thus a lower vapor pressure.) The boiling point must have gone up from B because the vapor pressure went down from B.

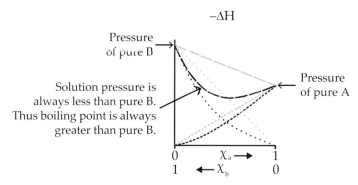

## EXPLANATIONS TO IN-CLASS EXAM FOR LECTURE 5

### Passage I

93. **C is correct.** The salt lowers the freezing point of water. This is necessary in order to insure that the water can bring the unknown solution to its freezing point.

94. **C is correct.** Even if the others completely dissociate, NaCl still releases more particles per gram than the others. (2 particles/58 grams) (A = 3/172, B = 2/120, and D = 3/115)

95. **C is correct.** The copper stirrer acts to evenly distribute the heat throughout the solution by convection.

96. **B is correct.** Since the freezing point depression was lower for Student 1, there must have been more particles for the same amount of mass. Thus Student 1 had an unknown with lower molecular weight.

97. **D is correct.** A greater concentration of particles lowers freezing point more. The freezing point data was collected and recorded for the cyclohexane solution, not the crushed ice solution.

98.    **B is correct.** Time is not a factor in the calculation of the molecuar weight of the unknown solid. The molecular weight of the unknown solid can be calculated as follows:

$$\Delta T = K_f m:$$

$$m = (\text{grams}_{\text{solute}}/\text{M.W.})/(\text{volume}_{\text{solvent}} \times \text{density}_{\text{solvent}} \times \text{kg/gram})$$

plugging into $\Delta T = K_f m$ and rearranging we have:

$$\text{M.W.} = (K_f)(\text{grams}_{\text{solute}}) / \{(\Delta T)(\text{volume}_{\text{solvent}} \times \text{density}_{\text{solvent}} \times \text{kg/gram})\}$$

$$K_f = 20.2, (\text{grams}_{\text{solute}}) = 0.5, \Delta T = (6.6 - -3.5) = 10.1,$$

$$\text{volume}_{\text{solvent}} = 10.0, \text{density}_{\text{solvent}} = 0.78, \text{kg/gram} = 1/1000$$

Thus

$$\text{M.W.} = (K_f)(\text{grams}_{\text{solute}}) / \{(\Delta T)(\text{volume}_{\text{solvent}} \times \text{density}_{\text{solvent}} \times \text{kg/gram})\}$$

99.    **D is correct.** D is the only nonvolatile, nonpolar solute that is soluble in cyclohexane.

100.   **B is correct.** The only explanation is B. As long as some solution remains liquid, the energy removed by the ice bath creates bonds forming a solid. As soon as the entire solution is frozen, the energy removed from solution lowers the temperature.

## Passage II

101.   **A is correct.** The acid and base are totally dissociated to begin with. This reaction takes high energy molecules and makes a low energy molecule, releasing heat.

102.   **B is correct.** Heat is released.

103.   **A is correct.** 40 mL × 1 cal/°C mL × –3.3°C = –132 cal. Since heat is released, we already know the answer is negative.

104.   **B is correct.** The ammonium nitrate would require energy to dissociate before releasing energy to form water.

105.   **D is correct.** Heat per mole is an intensive property.

106.   **D is correct.** The temperature of the calorimeter is higher than the surroundings throughout the experiment. Heat always moves from hot to cold.

## Passage III

107.   **A is correct.** The negative slope on the phase diagram demonstrates that water expands when freezing.

108.   **C is correct.** The line between A and E represents equilibrium of gas and solid.

109.   **A is correct.** Point C in Figure 1 is the critical point, which is the temperature and pressure above which the gas and liquid phases cannot be distinguished.

110.   **D is correct.** Point C in Figure 1 is the critical point, which is the temperature and pressure above which the gas and liquid phases cannot be distinguished.

111.   **B is correct.** The negative slope between the solid and liquid phases of water in Figure 2 represents melting point at different temperatures and pressures. As pressure increases, the temperature decreases moving along the line.

112.   **A is correct.** The normal boiling point is the boiling point at local atmospheric conditions (1 atm). To have a normal boiling point, the triple point must be at a pressure below 1 atm. In that case, the temperature of the triple point will be below the temperature of the normal boiling point.

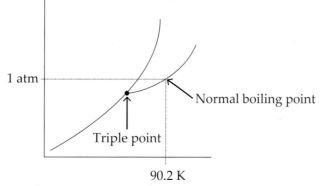

113.   **C is correct.** See the graph.

114.    **A is correct.** During a phase change, temperature, and thus molecular kinetic energy, is constant. Breaking bonds always absorbs energy. Ice cools things when it melts.

115.    **A is correct.** The potential energy of the water at the top of the falls becomes kinetic energy as it drops, and then thermal energy at the bottom of the falls. Thus mgh = $Q$ = $mc\Delta T$, or $\Delta T$ = $gh/c$.

# EXPLANATIONS TO IN-CLASS EXAM FOR LECTURE 6

## Passage I

116.    **A is correct.** This is the common ion effect in Reaction 1.

117.    **A is correct.** For all trials, at the equivalence point there are $Ca^{2+}$ ions, $Na^+$ and $Cl^-$ ions. (Trial 1 has no $Na^+$ ions, but these don't affect pH anyway.) The $Ca^{2+}$ started as a saturated solution. As $OH^-$ ions are removed from solution by the acid, there is no precipitation of $Ca(OH)_2$. When all the $OH^-$ ions are neutralized by the acid, the pH is 7 for all trials. The equivalence point is 7 for all trials. For trials with NaOH, the pH begins higher. More HCl is required to neutralize this extra base. The curves are exactly the same, but the trial one curve starts at a lower pH and requires less HCl.

118.    **B is correct.** This is just the normal $K_{sp}$.

119.    **D is correct.** pOH = $-\log[OH^-]$ In this case, the significant $OH^-$ ion contribution comes completely from NaOH which dissociates completely. 1 > pOH > 2 The pH is 14 – pOH = between 12 and 13.

120.    **D is correct.** The $Ca(OH)_2$ solution begins as basic, and when the $Ca(OH)_2$ is totally dissolved, it should be neutral. See answer to question #117.

121.    **A is correct.** This is the titration of a strong base with a strong acid. See question #117.

## Passage II

122.    **C is correct.** Since the $K_w$ is higher at 40°C, the hydrogen ion concentration will also be higher. Thus the pH will decrease. Note that the hydrogen ion concentration would have to be 10 times higher in order for the pH to be higher.

123.    **C is correct.** Set $K_w$ equal to 1 mole of hydrogen ions times the OH concentration.

124.    **B is correct.** As $T$ increases, the hydrogen ion concentration increases.

125.    **C is correct.** A proton is lost to form the conjugate base of a Bronsted acid.

126.    **C is correct.** The leveling effect in water occurs because water readily accepts all protons from both acids. The equilibrium in water is so far to the right for both reactions that no comparison can be made. Although acetic acid accepts protons from both HCl and $HClO_4$, it does not do so as readily as water (it is a weaker proton acceptor or Bronsted-Lowry base). Thus, an equilibrium is established for both reactions, and the equilibriums can be compared.

127.    **A is correct.** Definitional.

## Passage III

128.    **C is correct.** The pH must be where both indicators can have the proper color.

129.    **C is correct.** The lower $pK_a$ of sulfuric acid demonstrates that it is a stronger acid than sulfurous acid. The second proton is not the major contributor to the acid strength, so D is wrong.

130.    **D is correct.** The $K_b$ is found by adding the base to water. If the $pK_a$ is known, the $pK_b$ of the conjugate base can be found by subtracting the $pK_a$ from 14. $HSO_3^-$ is the conjugate base of $H_2SO_3$. The $pK_a$ of $H_2SO_3$ is given as 1.81. 14 – 1.81 = 12.19.

131.    **D is correct.** The lowest $pK_a$ is the strongest acid. You should know that sulfuric acid is stronger than the other acids.

132.    **A is correct.** Minus eight for the oxygens, plus two for the hydrogens leaves minus six which must be counter balanced. Minus six for the oxygens, plus two for the hydrogens leaves minus four which must be counter balanced.

133.    **C is correct.** We could never raise the pH by adding an acid. Water is the main contributor of $H^+$. To find the pH, we add the $5 \times 10^{-8}$ ions contributed by $H_2SO_4$ to the $1 \times 10^{-7}$ ions contributed by water. This leaves $1.5 \times 10^{-7}$ $H^+$.

134. **D is correct.** This is the titration of a diprotic acid with a strong base.

## Stand Alones

135. **A is correct.** Perchloric acid is the strongest acid, thus it has the weakest conjugate base. In oxy acids, the more oxygens, the greater the acid strength.

136. **C is correct.** This is the definition of the half equivalence point.

137. **A is correct.** Use the Henderson-Hasselbalch equation. $pH = pK_a + \log(A^-/HA) \Rightarrow pH = -\log(1.8 \times 10^{-5}) + \log(1/10) \Rightarrow pH = 4.7 - 1 = 3.7$

138. **B is correct.** The conjugate acid has the $K_a$ that equals $K_w/K_b$.

# EXPLANATIONS TO IN-CLASS EXAM FOR LECTURE 7

## Passage I

139. **C is correct.** $Cr_2O_7^{2-}$ is reduced to $Cr^{3+}$. Although this doesn't look like reduction from the charges, Cr in the dichromate has an original oxidation state of +6.

140. **C is correct.** Oxygen is –2. There are 7 oxygens which make –14. The 2– charge on the ion takes care of 2 of the 14 negatives. The 2 chromiums must take care of the other 12. That's +6 for each chromium.

141. **C is correct.** This is simply reading the graph.

142. **B is correct.** For each mole of dichromate that is reduced, 6 moles of Fe are oxidized. The top portion of B gives the number of moles of dichromate reduced times six, which is the number of moles of Fe oxidized. (The equivalence point is where all the iron has been oxidized.) We divide this by the original volume of Fe solution and get the molarity.

143. **A is correct.** The equivalence point is defined as the point when the $Fe^{2+}$ is completely oxidized. Changing the formal potential won't change that definition. The endpoint is when the indicator changes color. This should be at the equivalence point, but it doesn't have to be. The passage says that the formal potential is *lowered* so that the equivalence point and endpoint will coincide. This indicates that the indicator will change color at a low potential. If the formal potential isn't lowered, the indicator will change color early (still at the low potential) before the equivalence point is reached. The passage states that the indicator changes from colorless to violet; choice A. Dichromate ion will still oxidize DAS, but it will do so before oxidizing $Fe^{2+}$, so choice C is incorrect. Dichromate ion is an oxidizing agent and will not reduce anything, so choice D is incorrect.

144. **A is correct.** Each iron goes from a +2 to a +3 oxidation state by losing one electron. Each chromium goes from a +6 to a +3 oxidation state by gaining 3 electrons.

## Passage II

145. **A is correct.** The half reactions must be rearranged in such a fashion that the total voltage is positive (meaning the battery is discharging). This requires reversing the top half reaction. When reversed, this reaction becomes oxidation, which takes place at the anode.

146. **D is correct.** When we recharge the battery, the reactions are both reversed from the positions in question one.

147. **C is correct.** Ni is being reduced, so $NiO_2$ is the oxidizing agent. The compound with many oxygens is often the oxidizing agent.

148. **A is correct.** The cell has a negative potential and is forced to run in the nonspontaneous direction.

149. **C is correct.** The two half reaction potentials must be added after they have been rearranged to represent the galvanic cell. This means that the first half reaction is reversed. If this potential is applied, the cell can be recharged back to this potential which is the standard potential.

150. **B is correct.** The passage tells us that sodium is at the anode so it is oxidized. Sodium is not normally oxidized to a +2.

151. **D is correct.** Current moves opposite to electrons. Since electrons flow from Half Reaction 1 to 2, current flows from Half Reaction 2 to 1.

## Passage III

152. **D is correct.** The reaction quotient is in the same form as the equilibrium constant. Pure solids and liquids should not be used in the law of mass action to solve for the equilibrium constant.

153. **A is correct.** Plug the numbers into the Nernst equation. $(10^2)^2$ is $10^4$. The log of $10^4$ is 4. Thus the potential is negative and the voltage is twice 0.0592 V.

154. **B is correct.** See the last equation in the passage.

155. **B is correct.** See the last equation in the passage. A 1 $M$ solution of HCl has a pH of 0.

156. **A is correct.** An increase of $H^+$ by a factor of 10 is a decrease in pH of 1. $E = 0.059$ ($pH_{test} - pH_{reference}$) Each decrease in $pH_{reference}$ of 1 amounts to an increase in $E$ of 0.059 V or 59 mV.

157. **A is correct.** The current will try to equalize the charges in the solutions. Since we have more positive charge on the concentrated side, the current moves to the less concentrated side.

158. **B is correct.** Again, current flows toward the less positive side, which is the basic side, which has less H+ ions.

## Stand Alones

159. **D is correct.** You should know this one reduction potential: $2H^+ + 2e^- \rightarrow H_2$   $E = 0$. When this is added to the oxidation of solid zinc, the potential is positive, which means spontaneous.

160. **C is correct.** At equilibrium, there can be no potential; neither direction of the reaction is favored.

161. **B is correct.** The products and reactants are at standard state, and therefore their potential defines the standard potential $E°$. A is wrong because they are not at equilibrium when $Q = 1$. C is wrong because the potential is positive. D is wrong because $Q$ is at 1 and $Q$ will move toward $K$. The reaction is spontaneous from here so products will increase, and $Q$ will increase. Therefore, $K$ must be greater than 1.

# ANSWERS & EXPLANATIONS

## FOR

## QUESTIONS IN THE LECTURES

# ANSWERS TO THE LECTURE QUESTIONS

| Lecture 1 | Lecture 2 | Lecture 3 | Lecture 4 | Lecture 5 | Lecture 6 | Lecture 7 |
|-----------|-----------|-----------|-----------|-----------|-----------|-----------|
| 1.  C | 25.  C | 49.  D | 73.  C | 97.  D | 121.  B | 145.  C |
| 2.  C | 26.  B | 50.  A | 74.  D | 98.  A | 122.  C | 146.  C |
| 3.  A | 27.  A | 51.  C | 75.  A | 99.  B | 123.  C | 147.  A |
| 4.  B | 28.  D | 52.  D | 76.  D | 100.  D | 124.  A | 148.  A |
| 5.  A | 29.  B | 53.  D | 77.  C | 101.  D | 125.  A | 149.  D |
| 6.  B | 30.  C | 54.  B | 78.  D | 102.  C | 126.  B | 150.  D |
| 7.  B | 31.  D | 55.  D | 79.  B | 103.  A | 127.  B | 151.  D |
| 8.  B | 32.  D | 56.  A | 80.  B | 104.  B | 128.  A | 152.  A |
| 9.  C | 33.  B | 57.  B | 81.  D | 105.  D | 129.  D | 153.  D |
| 10.  D | 34.  D | 58.  D | 82.  A | 106.  B | 130.  B | 154.  C |
| 11.  B | 35.  A | 59.  A | 83.  C | 107.  C | 131.  C | 155.  B |
| 12.  C | 36.  A | 60.  B | 84.  B | 108.  C | 132.  D | 156.  A |
| 13.  B | 37.  C | 61.  B | 85.  C | 109.  A | 133.  D | 157.  D |
| 14.  D | 38.  C | 62.  C | 86.  B | 110.  B | 134.  B | 158.  C |
| 15.  B | 39.  B | 63.  D | 87.  D | 111.  D | 135.  C | 159.  A |
| 16.  A | 40.  B | 64.  A | 88.  C | 112.  A | 136.  D | 160.  B |
| 17.  B | 41.  D | 65.  D | 89.  D | 113.  A | 137.  D | 161.  C |
| 18.  B | 42.  C | 66.  A | 90.  C | 114.  C | 138.  B | 162.  C |
| 19.  B | 43.  A | 67.  D | 91.  D | 115.  B | 139.  A | 163.  D |
| 20.  C | 44.  C | 68.  D | 92.  C | 116.  B | 140.  B | 164.  D |
| 21.  B | 45.  C | 69.  A | 93.  C | 117.  C | 141.  C | 165.  B |
| 22.  C | 46.  D | 70.  D | 94.  A | 118.  D | 142.  C | 166.  A |
| 23.  B | 47.  A | 71.  A | 95.  A | 119.  A | 143.  D | 167.  B |
| 24.  A | 48.  A | 72.  D | 96.  B | 120.  D | 144.  B | 168.  C |

# ANSWERS & EXPLANATIONS FOR LECTURE QUESTIONS

1. **C is correct.** A family or group is the name for any vertical column on the periodic table. Of the choices given, only atomic radius increases going down a column. Although electron affinity is a possible choice depending upon the definition used, atomic radius is an unambiguous choice.

2. **C is correct.** The dipole moment will be greatest for the atoms with greatest difference in electronegativity. Based upon periodic trends, H and F will have the greatest dipole moment.

3. **A is correct.** By definition there are 12 amu in one atom of $^{12}C$.

4. **B is correct.** Metals are lustrous, but they are also malleable and good conductors of electricity and heat. Silicon is positioned along the diagonal of elements in the periodic table sometimes referred to as metalloids.

5. **A is correct.** This is an isoelectronic series, which means that the number of electrons on each ion is the same. In an isoelectronic series of ions, the nuclear charge increases with increasing atomic number and draws the electrons inward with greater force. The ion with fewest protons produces the weakest attractive force on the electrons and thus has the largest size.

6. **B is correct.** Don't do any complicated calculations. This is the type of problem that everyone will get right, but many will spend too much time trying to be exact. First assume that 100% of the sample is $^{12}C$. Now use the formula: moles = grams/molecular weight. This is very close to 4. The 1% that is not $^{12}C$ is insignificant.

7. **B is correct.** We are looking for an answer that would allow for the prediction of the order of atomic number. If atomic number increases with atomic weight, the scientists could have made accurate predictions.

8. **B is correct.** Sulfur can form four bonds. In choice A, Cl has the wrong number of electrons. In choice C, Se is too large to form stable pi bonds, so it can't double bond. In choice D, fluorine cannot make more than one bond. This question may require a little too much detailed knowledge to be on the MCAT.

___

9. **C is correct.** We start by assuming a 100 gram sample. By dividing grams by molecular weight, we obtain moles. $58.6/16 \approx 3.6$, $2.4/1 = 2.4$, $39/32 = 1.2$. Now we divide through by the lowest number of moles:

   $3.6/1.2 = 3$; $2.4/1.2 = 2$; $1.2/1.2 = 1$. This gives you the molar ratio of each element. Just to reduce the necessary calculations, the question tells you that it is a <u>neutral</u> compound. Nevertheless, MCAT questions with this much calculation occasionally come up, but they are few and far between. Maybe three on one entire exam.

10. **D is correct.** Silicon is too large to form pi bonds like carbon does. In order to complete its octet, it must make four bonds. It makes one bond with each of four oxygens. Each oxygen bonds with two silicon atoms.

11. **B is correct.** C has 12 g/mol and O has 16 g/mol. The total weight of $CO_2$ is 44 g/mol. Carbon's weight divided by the total weight is $12/44 = 0.27$. We multiply by 100 to get 27%.

12. **C is correct.** When one mole of sulfur dioxide is oxidized, one mole of sulfur trioxide is produced. One mole of sulfur trioxide has a mass of 80 g.

13. **B is correct.** Normally, 34 grams of ammonia (2 moles) could make 28 grams of nitrogen (1 mole), but here, only 26 grams were made. In a reaction that runs to completion, this must be due to lack of CuO.

14. **D is correct.** Each perchlorate ion has a 1– charge giving the copper ion a 2+ charge.

15. **B is correct.** This is an unusual looking reaction because it is a polymerization. Here it is drawn in a more representative form showing the repeated unit of the polymer as the product:

$$n\text{CH}_2{=}\text{CH}_2 \longrightarrow \left(\begin{array}{cc} \text{H} & \text{H} \\ | & | \\ -\text{C}-\text{C}- \\ | & | \\ \text{H} & \text{H} \end{array}\right)_n$$

16. **A is correct.** This reaction has the form A + B → C. This is the form of a combination reaction.

17. **B is correct.** The quickest way to see this is by realizing that atoms like to form ions with electron configurations similar to the nearest noble gas. Of course a noble gas does not have any unpaired electrons. You should recognize that Ca likes to form a 2+ ion not a 1+ ion.

18. **B is correct.** This question borders on requiring too much specific knowledge for the MCAT. The knowledge that the $4s$ and $3d$ orbitals are at the same energy level for the first row transition metals is probably beyond the MCAT. Rather than memorize specific exceptions to the Aufbau principle, answer this question by eliminating that A, C, and D must be wrong. A is wrong because there is no reason to skip the s subshell entirely. C is wrong because it contains the wrong number of electrons. D is wrong because we should be in the $3d$ subshell, not the $4d$ subshell. You may be able to see that, by Hund's rule, each electron would rather take its own orbital than share an orbital at the same energy level with another electron. Thus for Chromium, electrons fill the orbitals like this:

Chromium looks like this: $\quad$ [Ar] $\underset{4s}{\uparrow}$ $\quad$ $\underset{3d}{\uparrow}$ $\underset{3d}{\uparrow}$ $\underset{3d}{\uparrow}$ $\underset{3d}{\uparrow}$ $\underset{3d}{\uparrow}$

not like this: $\quad$ [Ar] $\underset{4s}{\uparrow\downarrow}$ $\quad$ $\underset{3d}{\uparrow}$ $\underset{3d}{\uparrow}$ $\underset{3d}{\uparrow}$ $\underset{3d}{\uparrow}$ $\underset{3d}{}$

Copper is the only other first row transition metal that breaks the Aufbau principle. Its electron configuration is [Ar] $4s^1\,3d^{10}$.

19. **B is correct.** According to the Heisenberg uncertainty principle, the kinetic energy of the electrons increases only when intensity is increased by increasing the frequency. Increasing the work function (a) would actually decrease the kinetic energy (see formula). A single photon must have enough energy, or else no electron will be emitted.

20. **C is correct.** The atom must absorb energy in order for one of its electrons to move to a higher energy level orbital.

21. **B is correct.** The principle quantum number ($n$) represents the energy level of the electron. The lowest energy shell is $n = 1$. As n increases, the shells move farther from the nucleus and energy increases.

22. **C is correct.** Because sulfur is larger than oxygen, sulfur has $3d$ subshells available that allow electrons to form bonds and break the octet rule of the Lewis structure.

23. **B is correct.** Hund's rule says that electrons added to the same subshell will occupy empty orbitals first and the unpaired electrons will have parallel spins.

24. **A is correct.** Since chromium forms more than one oxidation state and aluminum forms only one, chromium requires the variability in number of bonds formed. This means choices C and D are out. Chromium has electrons in the orbitals of the $2p$ subshell, but these are core electrons and not used for making bonds. Chromium has 6 valence electrons, 5 of which are in the orbitals of the $3d$ subshell.

---

## LECTURE 2

25. **C is correct.** You should recognize that 1 mole of gas occupies 22.4 liters at STP, so there is 0.5 moles of gas in the sample. 13 g/0.5 mol = 26 g/mol.

26. **B is correct.** Since density ($\rho$) is mass ($m$) divided by volume ($V$), and mass is moles ($n$) times molecular weight (MW), we have ($n$MW)/$V$ = $\rho$. After some algebra we have: MW = ($\rho V$)/$n$. From the ideal gas law we know that $V/n = RT/P$. Substituting we have answer B.

27. **A is correct.** The number of moles of gas is extra information. If the container began at 11 atm then each gas is contributing a pressure in accordance with its stoichiometric coefficient. When the reaction runs to completion, the only gas in the container is nitrogen dioxide, so the partial pressure of nitrogen dioxide is the total pressure. The volume of the container remains constant, so the pressure is in accordance with the stoichiometric coefficient of nitrogen dioxide.

28. **D is correct.** An ideal gas has a $PV/RT$ equal to one. Real volume is greater than predicted by the ideal gas law, and real pressure is less than predicted by the ideal gas law. Volume deviations are due to the volume of the molecules, and pressure deviations are due to the intermolecular forces. Thus, a negative deviation in this ratio would indicate that the intermolecular forces are having a greater affect on the nonideal behavior than the volume of the molecules. (see the graph on page 27)

29. **B is correct.** The force does work on the gas, which means that the internal energy of the gas is increased. Since the internal energy of the gas is increased, and the number of moles remains the same, the temperature, which is average kinetic energy per mole, also increases.

30. **C is correct.** From Graham's law we know that the effusion rate for hydrogen is four times that of oxygen.

$$\frac{H_{2\ \text{effusion rate}}}{O_{2\ \text{effusion rate}}} = \sqrt{\frac{M.W._{\text{oxygen}}}{M.W._{\text{hydrogen}}}} = \sqrt{\frac{32}{2}} = 4$$

Since we don't know how many moles of gas were initially in container A, nor how many moles effused out, we don't know the ratio of hydrogen to oxygen. However, since we know that four times as many moles of hydrogen effused from container A into B, we know that container B contains four times as many moles of hydrogen. We can neglect any effusion in the reverse direction since the question says a "very short time".

31. **D is correct.** The diffusion rate for $NH_3$ is 1.5 times that of HCl. If HCl diffuses 4 cm, $NH_3$ will diffuse 6 cm. 4 cm + 6 cm = 10 cm.

$$\frac{\text{diffusion rate of } NH_3}{\text{diffusion rate of HCl}} = \frac{\sqrt{M_{\text{HCl}}}}{\sqrt{M_{NH_3}}} = \sqrt{\frac{36.5}{17}} = 1.5$$

32. **D is correct.** At STP, equal volumes of any gas behaving ideally contain the same number or moles.

---

33. **B is correct.** Changing the concentration of the reactants will not change the rate constant. Increasing the concentration of a catalyst will only increase the rate of the reaction if the supply of catalyst is so small that the reactants are waiting for a catalyst. Most of the time on the MCAT, you can assume that the supply of catalyst is large enough so that a change in concentration will not change the reaction rate. (See Biology Lecture 2 for the graph relating reaction rate to enzyme catalysts.) Increasing the amount of catalyst never increases the rate constant. Increasing the temperature will always increase the rate constant, and the rate of the reaction. If the reaction is catalyzed by an enzyme, the enzyme may denature, slowing the reaction; however, the reaction without the enzyme is considered a different reaction.

34. **D is correct.** Catalysts do not directly affect the equilibrium of a reaction. Catalysts do increase the rate of the reverse reaction as well as the forward reaction.

35. **A is correct.** When the concentration of B is doubled, the rate doesn't change. When the concentration of A is doubled, the rate doubles. The reaction is first order overall, and first order with respect to A. By choosing a trial and plugging the values into the rate law, we find that the rate constant has a value of 0.1.

36. **A is correct.** The slow step determines the rate of a reaction.

37. **C is correct.** Exothermicity concerns the thermodynamics of the reaction, and not the rate. You can ignore it. The energy of activation is the energy required for a collision of properly oriented molecules to produce a reaction. This does not change with temperature.

38. **C is correct.** A first order reaction has a constant half life. In the first 15 minutes, 16 out of 33 white dots (compound $X$) turned black, so 15 minutes represents approximately one half life. In the next 15 minutes, the second half life, half of the remaining 17 white dots should turn black. This represents choice C where there are 9 white dots left. Once you identify that 15 minutes is the half life, you should be able to eliminate answer A because there is no change and answer choice B and D because there are very few dots left. Even if you didn't know that a first order reaction has a constant half life, you should know that the reaction will be proportional to the concentration of white dots. In choice B and D, the rate of the reaction hasn't changed in the second 15 minutes even though the concentration of white dots has been reduced after the first 15 minutes, so this can't be right.

39. **B is correct.** For a first order reaction the reaction rate is directly proportional to the concentration of reactant, according to the equation, rate = $k$[A]. So if the concentration of *cis*-2-butene is doubled, the reaction rate will also double. The rate constant is not affected by changes in the concentrations of reactants.

40. **B is correct.** The concentration of reactants decreases exponentially in a first order reaction. Another way of saying that is that the graph of ln[reactants] will be linear.

---

41. **D is correct.** Equilibrium will probably shift with temperature. The direction is dictated by thermodynamics. We need more information.

42. **C is correct.** The activation energy is dictated by the reaction itself and doesn't change during the reaction. We will see later that the Gibbs free energy is at a minimum when a reaction is at equilibrium.

43. **A is correct.** By Le Chatelier's principle the equilibrium would shift to the right causing an increase in the forward reaction.

44. **C is correct.** The equilibrium constant is products over reactants with the coefficients as exponents. However, reactants and products in pure liquid and solid phases generally have an exponent of zero, so they are not included in the equilibrium expression.

45. **C is correct.** Initially there are no products, so the reverse reaction begins at zero. As the reactants are used up, the forward reaction slows down. Equilibrium is the point where the rates equalize.

46. **D is correct.** A must be false because some of both solids must be present in order for equilibrium to exist. B and C are false because, as part of a solid molecule, calcium atoms have no way of leaving their respective beakers (other than a negligible amount of vapor pressure from their respective solids). D is true because when CaO in Beaker II combines with $CO_2$ gas in the container, $CaCO_3$ is formed in Beaker II. An equilibrium is achieved in both beakers.

47. **A is correct.** Pure solids are not included in the equilibrium expression.

48. **A is correct.** "$K_p$ is equal to the partial pressure of $CO_2$" is the equilibrium expression for this reaction. If $K_p$ were less than the partial pressure of $CO_2$, the reaction would want to go to the left, but there would be no CaO to react to form $CaCO_3$. Regarding choice D, although solid CaO is required to achieve equilibrium, solid CaO could be formed with the decomposition of $CaCO_3$.

---

# LECTURE 3

49. **D is correct.** The second law of thermodynamics states that a heat engine cannot have 100% efficiency in converting heat to work in a cyclical process. An air conditioner is a heat engine running backwards. Thus an air conditioner must expel more heat than it takes in when it runs perpetually. A specially made air conditioner could initially cool the room, but to cool the room permanently, it must expel the heat to a heat reservoir.

50. **A is correct.** I. The temperature difference is directly proportional to the distance between two points of the same material.

$$\frac{Q}{t} = kA\frac{T_h - T_c}{L}$$

II. The rate of heat flow is constant throughout the blocks, or else heat would build up at the point of slowest flow. III. Since heat flow rate is constant, changing the order of the blocks won't change the rate of heat flow.

51. **C is correct.** There is no type of heat transfer called transduction. Conduction through the air would take a very long time and be very inefficient. Convection would require some type of air current or breeze. Radiation is as fast as light, and is the correct explanation.

52. **D is correct.** Unless the box and the incline are at different temperatures, there can be no heat. Energy transfer due to friction is work.

53. **D is correct.** Work is not a state function, thus we must know the path in order to calculate it.

54.    **B is correct.** The rate at which heat is conducted is directly proportional to the difference in temperatures between the hot and cold reservoirs. In December, the difference is 25 – 5 = 20 degrees. That's the largest difference on the table.

55.    **D is correct.** Since the container is at rest and has constant volume, no work is done.

56.    **A is correct.** The efficiency of a thermodynamic process describes what percent of the input energy is converted into work. No thermodynamic process can be 100 percent efficient.

---

57.    **B is correct.** To find the enthalpy of the reaction we use the following formula:

$$\Delta H^\circ_{\text{reaction}} = \Delta H^\circ_{f\,\text{products}} - \Delta H^\circ_{f\,\text{reactants}}$$

The table gives these enthalpies. Don't forget that enthalpy is an extensive process, so quantity matters. We must multiply the enthalpies by the number of moles formed for each molecule. The enthalpy of formation of $O_2$ is zero, like that of any other molecule in its elemental form at 298 K.

58.    **D is correct.** The definition of enthalpy is: $H \equiv U + PV$

59.    **A is correct.** A catalyst affects the kinetics of a reaction and not the thermodynamics.

60.    **B is correct.** Altering the ratio of the rates of a reaction will change the equilibrium. Removing thermal energy from an exothermic reaction will <u>probably</u> push it forward according to Le Chatelier's principle, since heat is a product. Answer C and D concern catalysts and will not change the ratio of the forward and reverse reaction.

61.    **B is correct.** This is Hess's law. We reverse the equation for graphite, so that graphite is a product. In doing so, we must also reverse the sign of the enthalpy. Now we add the two equations and their enthalpies. Don't forget that we must multiply by two for the two moles. Enthalpy is an extensive property.

62.    **C is correct.** Condensation must occur to form liquid water. Condensation is an exothermic process, so the formation of liquid water should be more exothermic than the formation of water vapor. The standard enthalpy of formation of water vapor will not be an endothermic process, so D is wrong.

63.    **D is correct.** The reaction coordinate diagram below shows the energy of activation for an endothermic reaction is greater than for an exothermic reaction.

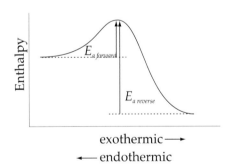

64.    **A is correct.** Increasing the temperature increases the energy available to both the forward and the reverse reactions, enabling both to more easily overcome the activation energy. Just so you know, because the reverse reaction is endothermic, its rate will increase more. That's what causes the increase in the concentration of reactants predicted by LeChatelier's law.

---

65.    **D is correct.** According to the equation $\Delta G = \Delta H - T\Delta S$, to guarantee that a reaction is spontaneous, enthalpy of the system must decrease and entropy of the system must increase.

66.    **A is correct.** The entropy of the universe will increase in a spontaneous reaction. The entropy of a system may or may not increase.

67.    **D is correct.** Energy is always required to break a bond.

68.    **D is correct.** The process of building a bridge is an ordering process.

**69.** **A is correct.** Since the number of moles of gas is decreasing with the forward reaction, positional entropy is decreasing. This almost always means that overall system entropy is decreasing. Since the MCAT doesn't distinguish between positional entropy and any other kind of entropy, you can always view a reaction with decreasing number of gas particles as decreasing in entropy and vice versa.

**70.** **D is correct.** Bonds are formed when water condenses, so energy is released and $\Delta H$ is negative. The water molecules become less random, so $\Delta S$ is negative. Condensation occurs spontaneously at 25°C (room temperature), so $\Delta G$ is negative. Notice that you can answer this question without being given any numbers.

**71.** **A is correct.** $\Delta G = \Delta H - T\Delta S$. For a spontaneous reaction, $\Delta G$ must be negative. As $T$ is increased, the negative part of the equation increases in magnitude. If $T$ is increased enough, eventually $\Delta G$ will switch from positive to negative. Changing the pressure will have no effect on a nongaseous reaction that takes place in a solution.

**72.** **D is correct.** At the boiling point, benzene is in equilibrium between the liquid and gas phases. At equilibrium, $\Delta G$ for a reaction is equal to zero. $S$ is positive for the reaction shown because gases are more random than liquids.

# LECTURE 4

**73.** **C is correct.** One liter of water weighs 1 kg; one liter of this solution weighs 1.006 kilograms. If we assume that the volume of water changes very little when NaCl is added, then about 0.006 kg, or 6 g, of NaCl are in each liter of solution. The molecular weight of NaCl is 58.6. 6 grams is about 0.1 moles. (By the way, even if the salt increased the volume of 1 liter of solution by 10 cubic centimeters, the molarity would still be slightly greater than 0.099 $M$. So this is a good approximation. Remember, for dilute solutions, the volume of the solute is negligible.)

**74.** **D is correct.** Remember that like dissolves like. Water is polar, and will dissolve polar and ionic substances. A, B, C are ions, ionic compounds, or capable of hydrogen bonding. Carbon tetrachloride is a nonpolar molecule.

**75.** **A is correct.** For all practical purposes, choices A and B are the same. However, since the question asks you to compare them, a one molar solution is 1 mole of NaCl in slightly less than a liter of water. This is because the NaCl requires some volume. A one molal solution is one mole in one full liter of water. (This question assumes that a liter of water has a mass of 1 kg. This is true at 1 atm and approximately 3°C. Water at 1 atm is at its most dense state at a temperature of slightly over 3°C.) There are 55.5 moles of water in a liter (grams/molecular weight = moles). 1/100 = 0.01 and 1/50 = 0.02. Thus a solution with a mole fraction of 0.01 is closer to a 0.5 molar solution than a 1 molar solution. The last answer choice is less than one mole of NaCl in one liter of water.

**76.** **D is correct.** You should know that 1 atm is equal to 760 torr. Since the partial pressure of nitrogen is 600, the mole fraction of nitrogen is 0.79. This means that the percentages given are by particle and not by mass. D would be true if the percentages were based on mass. If you chose B, you need to go back to Lecture 3 and review standard molar volume.

**77.** **C is correct.** No solution is formed, so either B or C must be correct. B is not true.

**78.** **D is correct.** First calculate the number of moles of $MgCl_2$

$$\text{moles} = \text{grams/MW} = 19 \text{ g/95 g/mol} = 0.2 \text{ mol}$$

0.2 moles of $MgCl_2$ will dissociate to produce 0.4 moles of $Cl^-$ ions.

$$[Cl^-] = \text{moles/liters} = 0.4 \text{ mol/0.5 L} = 0.8 \ M$$

**79.** **B is correct.** First find the number of moles of HCl.

$$\text{moles} = (\text{mol/L})(\text{L}) = (3 \text{ mol/L})(0.8 \ L) = 2.4 \text{ moles}$$

Now find the number of liters needed to make the solution 1 molar

$$L = \text{mol/mol/L} = 2.4 \text{ mol/1} \ M = 2.4 \text{ L}$$

Now be careful. You already have 0.8 liters of solution, so in order to get 2.4 L, you have to add 1.6 L of water.

80. **B is correct.** A strong electrolyte is a substance that dissociates completely in water to form ions, which can then conduct electricity. Carbon dioxide does not dissociate to form ions so it is not an electrolyte.

---

81. **D is correct.** The change in entropy is positive in solution formation and Gibbs free energy is negative in a spontaneous reaction. From $\Delta G = \Delta H_{sol} - T\Delta S$ we see that the heat of solution may be either positive or negative in this case. The heat of hydration is the separation of water molecules (which requires energy) and the formation of bonds between the ions and water molecules (which releases energy). Thus, the value of the heat of hydration could be either positive or negative. The actual heat of hydration is –783 kJ/mol making the heat of solution +3 kJ/mol.

82. **A is correct.** At constant pressure, change in enthalpy is equal to heat.

83. **C is correct.** The vapor pressure of solution might be lower than just one of the pure substances but not the other. You can see this from the graph below.

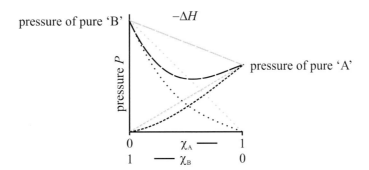

84. **B is correct.** You should notice that B and C are opposites, so one of them must be the answer. Molecules break free of the surface of a liquid and add to the vapor pressure when they have sufficient kinetic energy to break the intermolecular bonds.

85. **C is correct.** The solution had to deviate from Raoult's law and therefore could not be ideal. Since it deviated negatively from Raoult's law, the heat of solution is exothermic.

86. **B is correct.** In an ideal solution, the vapor pressure will be somewhere in between the vapor pressures of the solute and the solvent, depending on their relative mole fractions.

87. **D is correct.** Try testing the answer choices to see which one is right.

    (0.2)(800 mmHg) + (0.8)(300 mmHg) = 400 mmHg.

88. **C is correct.** If heat is released, the solvation process must be exothermic. The breaking of bonds is an endothermic process and the forming of bonds is an exothermic process, so in order for the process to be exothermic overall, the bonds formed must be stronger than the bonds that were broken.

---

89. **D is correct.** Think in terms of mole fraction. The concentration of solvent is at a minimum when the concentration of solute is at a maximum.

90. **C is correct.** This is the common ion effect (very important for the MCAT).

91. **D is correct.** We can compare the solubilities in one liter of water. For the compounds that dissociate into two parts, the smallest $K_{sp}$ will be the least soluble and first to precipitate. This is $BaSO_4$. We don't have to compare $BaSO_4$ with $Ag_2SO_4$ because $Ag_2SO_4$ dissociates into three particles. This means that if their $K_{sp}$s were equal, then $Ag_2SO_4$ would be more soluble than $BaSO_4$. However, the $K_{sp}$ for $BaSO_4$ is much lower, so we know for sure that it is less soluble.

92. **C is correct.** Gases become more soluble under greater pressure and lower temperatures. The pressure must be the partial pressure of the soluble gas. Adding an inert gas would not change the partial pressure of oxygen in this example. Shaking the can is adding energy, and is similar to heating the can. Think about shaking a can of soda.

93. **C is correct.** The solubility of $BaCO_3$ in 3 liters of water is found from the equilibrium expression:

$$K_{sp} = [Ba^{2+}][CO_3^{2-}]$$
$$1.6 \times 10^{-9} = [x][x]$$
$$x = 4 \times 10^{-5}$$

This is the saturated concentration in mol/L. We multiply this by 3 liters to get the total number of moles.

94. **A is correct.** The solubility product is created by multiplying the concentrations of the products of the solvation while turning the coefficients into exponents.

95. **A is correct.** The $K_{sp}$ expression is as follows.

$$K_{sp} = [Pb^{2+}][Cl^-]^2$$

For every $PbCl_2$ in solution, there is 1 $Pb^{2+}$ and 2 $Cl^-$. So $[Pb^{2+}] = x$ and $[Cl^-] = 2x$.

$$K_{sp} = (x)(2x)^2 = (x)(4x^2) = 4x^3$$

96. **B is correct.** NaF is very soluble, so when it is added to the solution, it will introduce more $Na^+$ and $F^-$ ions. The introduction of extra $F^-$ ions will shift the $CaF_2$ equilibrium toward solid $CaF_2$, which removes $Ca^{2+}$ ions from the solution.

---

# LECTURE 5

97. **D is correct.** First figure out the heat evolved by the reaction using $q = mc\Delta T$ =>

$$q = 250 \text{ grams} \times 4.18 \text{ J/g } ^\circ C \times 1 \,^\circ C \approx 1050 \text{ joules}$$

Next divide by moles of NaCl (20 grams is about ⅓ of a mole). This gives you 3150 joules, which is equal to 3 kJ. Since the temperature went down, the reaction is endothermic with positive enthalpy. Notice all the rounding. This problem should have been done with very little math.

98. **A is correct.** Remember, $\Delta E = w + q$. There is no work done because there is no change in volume in a bomb calorimeter. Thus, the total change in energy is heat. Heat is not enthalpy. Heat equals enthalpy at constant pressure. The pressure is not constant in a bomb calorimeter.

99. **B is correct.** I is false because objects cannot contain heat, and because the same amount of the same substance can have the same amount of energy and be at different temperatures. Nevertheless, this is treading the MCAT edge of required knowledge. Don't feel too bad if you chose C. II is false. Different phases will have different specific heats. III is true.

100. **D is correct.** A, B, and C are false. Temperature is proportional to kinetic energy not just velocity, so more mass per molecule does not make a difference. Boiling point does not make sense; substance A might be water and substance B ice. Answer C mistakenly relies upon speed and not kinetic energy for temperature. D is the correct choice by process of elimination. The more ways that a substance has to absorb energy, the more heat it can absorb with the least change in temperature.

101. **D is correct.** No energy transfer takes place, so there is no heat or work.

102. **C is correct.** Aluminum has the largest value for specific heat, which means that it can absorb the most energy while showing the smallest temperature change.

103. **A is correct.** Since the specific heat for Au is one-third as large as the specific heat for Cu, one-third as much heat will be required to get the same temperature change.

104. **B is correct.** Use the equation $q = mc\Delta T$. The change in temperature is $31 - 26 = 5$. Don't forget to convert 1.8 kJ into 1800 J.

$$m = q/c\Delta T = (1800)/(0.90)(5) = 400 \text{ g.}$$

---

**105.** **D is correct.** We can solve this problem by summing the $q$'s on the heat curve. The heat is positive because heat is added to the system.

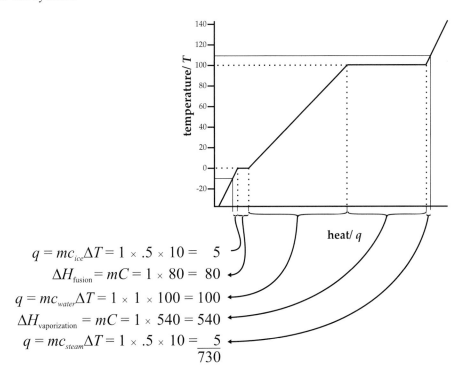

$$q = mc_{ice}\Delta T = 1 \times .5 \times 10 = \quad 5$$
$$\Delta H_{fusion} = mC = 1 \times 80 = \quad 80$$
$$q = mc_{water}\Delta T = 1 \times 1 \times 100 = 100$$
$$\Delta H_{vaporization} = mC = 1 \times 540 = 540$$
$$q = mc_{steam}\Delta T = 1 \times .5 \times 10 = \underline{\quad 5\quad}$$
$$730$$

**106.** **B is correct.** The added energy goes into breaking bonds, and as is demonstrated by the heat curve above, the temperature remains constant until all the ice is melted. Entropy increases moving to the right on the heat curve.

**107.** **C is correct.** This is just a phase diagram with pressure on a log scale. There are many ways to manipulate the phase diagram. Don't be intimidated. Try to compare it to what you know.

**108.** **C is correct.** Above the critical point, liquid and vapor water have the same density. The critical temperature will be the highest temperature on the graph where the two lines meet.

**109.** **A is correct.** The area in the dashed line is the point where water is changing phase. Like along line RS, in the dashed line area water and steam exist in equilibrium.

**110.** **B is correct.** The heat of fusion is the amount of heat that must be added to convert one mole of a substance completely from solid to liquid. Benzene has a molecular mass of 78, so the sample contains 1 mole. The flat line on the heating curve represents the heat being added while the phase changes from solid to liquid, so the heat of fusion can be found by measuring the length of the flat line. So 14.4 kJ – 3.5 kJ = 10.9 kJ.

**111.** **D is correct.** At the boiling point, any added energy is used to break intermolecular bonds and not to increase kinetic energy, so while the water is boiling, there is no temperature increase.

**112.** **A is correct.** Heating the solid will raise its temperature which will eventually melt it. Compressing the solid will raise the pressure on the solid which will most likely keep it a solid. A few substances like water will melt under pressure, but for most solids, pressure changes a liquid to a solid. It is the random kinetic energy of the molecules of a solid and not the uniform translational motion kinetic energy of the solid that increases its temperature and would make it melt.

---

**113.** **A is correct.** Boiling point elevation is a colligative property. The more particles the higher the boiling point. NaCl dissociates so that the normality is twice the molarity. Thus, the least number of particles will be in 0.5 $M$ glucose solution.

**114.** **C is correct.** The osmotic pressure will not create a difference in the buoyant force. The equation for buoyant force ($F_b = \rho Vg$) does not include osmotic pressure. Seawater has greater density because salts are heavier than water, and the salt added does not create an appreciable difference in volume.

Lecture Question Expls.

115. **B is correct.** You must recognize from the formula that glycerol does not dissociate; it is not ionic. Then use $\Delta T = K_f m$, which gives you a molality of 10. Molality is moles of solute divided by kg of solvent. Assume that 1 liter of water has a mass of 1 kg. Thus 100 moles of glycerol are required. Glycerol has a molecular weight of 62 g/mol. 6200 g = 6.2 kg.

116. **B is correct.** The reaction is exothermic because the temperature increased. An exothermic reaction makes stronger bonds. Stronger bonds lower vapor pressure. A lower vapor pressure means more energy is needed to raise the vapor pressure to equal atmospheric pressure. Thus, a lower vapor pressure means a higher boiling point.

117. **C is correct.** The question has a lot of extra information to mislead you. A high value for $h$ indicates a high osmotic pressure in the solution. From the formula for osmotic pressure, $\Pi = iMRT$, we know that a high osmotic pressure corresponds to a high molarity. A high molarity means many particles per gram of protein placed into the solution. Thus a high osmotic pressure means a low molecular weight.

118. **D is correct.** The freezing point depression formula is $\Delta T = kmi$. We know that $k$ is 1.86. The molar mass of $CaCl_2$ is 111, so there are 3 moles of salt in 1 kg of water and $m$ is 3. $CaCl_2$ dissociates into 3 particles, so $i$ is 3.

$$\Delta T = (1.86)(3)(3) = 16.7°C$$

119. **A is correct.** The freezing point expression is $\Delta T = kmi$. The solute is non-polar, so $i$ is 1 and we can leave it out. Now let's remember the definition of molality.

$$m = (\text{moles of solute})/(\text{kg of solvent})$$

$$\text{but (moles of solute)} = (\text{grams of solute})/(\text{molar mass of solute})$$

Substituting, we get $\Delta T = (k)(\text{grams of solute})/(\text{molar mass of solute})(\text{kg of solvent})$

If you solve for the molar mass, you get choice A.

120. **D is correct.** Boiling point is a colligative property, which means that it depends only on the number of particles in solution, not on their specific properties. Both NaF and KCl dissociate completely into 2 particles each, so they will have the same effect on the boiling point of water.

# LECTURE 6

121. **B is correct.** The conjugate acid is the molecule after it accepts a proton.

122. **C is correct.** By definition, a Lewis base donates a pair of electrons.

123. **C is correct.** $NH_4^+$ is an acid. The strongest base is the conjugate of the weakest acid.

124. **A is correct.** An amino acid can act as an acid or a base depending upon the pH. Although the conjugate base of sulfuric acid is amphoteric, sulfuric acid cannot accept a proton and is not amphoteric.

125. **A is correct.** The electron withdrawing group will further polarize the O-H bond, and polarization increases acidity in aqueous solution.

126. **B is correct.** The pH of solution B is 7. The pH of solution A is between 4 and 5. The difference in pH must be between $7 - 5 = 2$ and $7 - 4 = 3$. Choice B is the only one in that range.

127. **B is correct.** In a coordinate covalent bond, one atom donates an electron pair to share with another atom. In this case, ammonia has the unbonded pair to donate to boron, so ammonia is the Lewis base and boron is the Lewis acid.

128. **A is correct.** In Reaction 1, water accepts a proton to become $H_3O^+$, so it is acting as a Bronsted-Lowry base. In Reaction 2, water gives up a proton to become $OH^-$, so it acts as a Bronsted-Lowry acid.

129. **D is correct.** $K_b$ is the reaction of the conjugate base with water.

130. **B is correct.** HBr dissociates completely, so the concentration of $H^+$ ions will be equal to the concentration of solution. The $-\log(0.1) = 1$.

**131.** **C is correct.** The $K_b$ for $NaHCO_3$ is $K_w/K_a = K_b \approx 0.25 \times 10^{-7}$. We can set up the equilibrium expression:

$$K_b = \frac{[OH^-][H_2CO_3]}{[HCO_3^-]}$$

$$0.25 \times 10^{-7} = \frac{[x][x]}{[1 \,\cancel{-x}]} \quad \text{This } x \text{ is insignificant.}$$

$$2.5 \times 10^{-8} = x^2$$

$$1.5 \times 10^{-4} = x$$

Thus, the pOH = between 3 and 4. Subtracting from 14, the pH = between 10 and 11.

**132.** **D is correct.** Each unit of pH is a tenfold increase of acidity.

**133.** **D is correct.** You should recognize $CN^-$ as the conjugate base of a weak acid. Choices A, B, and C are conjugates of strong acids, and thus weaker bases.

**134.** **B is correct.** $BrO^-$ is the conjugate base of $HBrO$, so you can find the base dissociation constant $K_b$ by dividing. $1 \times 10^{-14}/2 \times 10^{-9}$. You get $0.5 \times 10^{-5}$, which is the same as $5 \times 10^{-6}$.

**135.** **C is correct.** If the pH is 10, the pOH must be 4. If the pOH is 4, then the hydroxide ion concentration must be $10^{-4}\ M$.

**136.** **D is correct.** Acetate ion, $C_2H_3O_2^-$, is the conjugate base of a weak acid, so it will act as a base in solution. Sodium ion, $Na^+$, is the conjugate acid of a strong base, so it is neutral in solution.

---

**137.** **D is correct.** The pH starts basic so a base is being titrated. It ends very acidic so a strong acid is titrating.

**138.** **B is correct.** A buffer is made from equal amounts of an acid and its conjugate. The buffer works best when the pH = $pK_a$. $-\log(8.3 \times 10^{-7})$ = between 6 and 7. 8.3 is close to ten, making the $pK_a$ closer to 6.

**139.** **A is correct.** An indicator generally changes color within plus or minus one pH point of its $pK_a$.

**140.** **B is correct.** The concentration of the conjugate base of the first acid is the greatest at the first equivalence point.

**141.** **C is correct.** The equivalence point of a titration of a weak acid with a strong base will always be greater than 7. It is the same as adding the conjugate base of the acid to pure water. 14 is way too basic. Pure 1 $M$ NaOH has a pH of 14.

**142.** **C is correct.** A buffered solution is formed when equal amounts of a weak acid and its conjugate base are present in a solution. Acetic acid is a weak acid and the acetate ion is its conjugate.

**143.** **D is correct.** $HCO_3^-$ can act as a Bronsted Lowry acid and give up a hydrogen ion to become $CO_3^{2-}$. It can also act as a Lewis base and donate an electron pair to a hydrogen ion to become $H_2CO_3$. It is amphoteric because it can act as an acid or base. It is not polyprotic because it has only one hydrogen.

**144.** **B is correct.** From the Henderson-Hasselbalch equation, you can see that when a weak acid and its conjugate base are present in a solution in equal amounts, the pH will be equal to the $pK_a$. If you take the negative logarithm of $8.0 \times 10^{-5}$, it will be between 4 and 5. That's choice B.

---

# LECTURE 7

**145.** **C is correct.** Each oxygen has an oxidation state of –2, and hydrogen has an oxidation state of +1. In order for the ion to have a 1– charge, the sulfur must have a +6 oxidation state. (Notice that oxidation states are given as $+n$, and actual charges are given as $n+$.)

**146.** **C is correct.** Aluminum begins as +3 and ends as 0, while carbon begins as 0 and ends as +4.

147. **A is correct.** The Zn is oxidized from an oxidation state of 0 to +2. Thus, it is the reducing agent.

148. **A is correct.** Both A and D cannot be true, so the answer must be A or D. The trickiest part of this problem is to know that lead is comfortable at +2 and sulfur, being in the oxygen family, is comfortable at –2; thus these are their oxidation states when they are together. But when they are with oxygen, the –2 of the oxygen rules.

149. **D is correct.** An example of where this is false is:

$$2HCl + Zn \rightarrow ZnCl_2 + H_2$$

Here each atom of the reducing agent, zinc, loses two electrons, and the hydrogen atom of the oxidizing agent, HCl, gains one electron. Of course, there must be two hydrogens for each zinc.

150. **D is correct.** The two oxygens in $NO_2^-$ have a total oxidation number of –4, so nitrogen must have an oxidation number of +3 to get a total of –1 on the polyatomic ion. The three oxygens in $NO_3^-$ have a total oxidation number of –6, so nitrogen must have an oxidation number of +5 to get a total of –1 on the polyatomic ion. Since the oxidation state is increasing from +3 to +5, electrons are being lost and oxidation is taking place.

151. **D is correct.** None of the oxidation states are changed during the course of this acid-base neutralization reaction, so no redox takes place.

152. **A is correct.** Don't forget, the oxidation states for Cl and Br in $Cl_2$ and $Br_2$ are zero by definition because the two elements are in their uncombined states. Chlorine gains electrons, so it is reduced. Since it is reduced, it is the oxidizing agent. Bromine loses electrons, so it is oxidized.

---

153. **D is correct.** Positive ions move across the salt bridge to the cathode. You can remember this because the salt bridge is used to balance the charges. Since negative electrons move to the cathode, positive ions must balance the charge by moving to the cathode.

154. **C is correct.** The forward and reverse reaction rates are only equal at equilibrium, and their rate constants are rarely equal.

155. **B is correct.** This question requires knowledge of the equation: $\Delta G^\circ = -RT \ln(K)$. This equation is a statement about the relationship between $\Delta G^\circ$ and $K$ at a specific temperature. If $\Delta G^\circ = 0$, then $K = 1$. The standard state for an aqueous solution is $1\ M$ concentrations.

156. **A is correct.** The strongest reducing agent is the one most easily oxidized; thus we must reverse the equations and the signs of the potentials.

157. **D is correct.** Although a both a Galvanic cell and an electrolytic cell can have a positive potential, only an electrolytic cell can have a negative potential.

158. **C is correct.** The potential given are reduction potentials. Since copper is reduced, we can use its potential (0.15 V) as written. Tin is oxidized, so we have to change the sign before we calculate. The total potential is 0.15 V + 0.14 V = 0.29 V. Notice that we ignore the coefficients when we do cell potential calculations.

159. **A is correct.** You can use the Nernst equation here, or you can just think about LeChatelier's law. As the concentration of products increases, the reaction will become less spontaneous. The less spontaneous the reaction, the lower the reaction potential.

160. **B is correct.** A galvanic cell generates power via a spontaneous reaction, so $\Delta G^\circ$ must be less than zero. From the expression $\Delta G^\circ = -RT \ln(K)$, you can figure out that if $\Delta G^\circ$ is negative, then $K$ must be greater than 1.

161. **C is correct.** Reactions in galvanic cells are always spontaneous. To find the reaction for this cell we must flip the more negative half reaction. Now we have a spontaneous cell.

$$Al^{3+} + 3e^- \rightarrow Al \qquad -1.66$$
$$Mg \rightarrow Mg^{2+} + 2e^- \qquad \underline{2.37}$$
$$0.71$$

We also have to multiply the aluminum reaction by 2 and the magnesium reaction by 3. Notice, however, that we do not multiply their potentials.

$$2Al^{3+} + 3Mg \rightarrow 3Mg^{2+} + 2Al \qquad E^\circ = 0.71 \text{ V}$$

Since the potential for this cell does not equal this, the conditions must not be standard.

162. **C is correct.** Reduction always takes place at the cathode in any cell. This means that the cathode gains electrons.

163. **D is correct.** A concentration cell is a special type of galvanic cell. It is always spontaneous. The concentrations in the cell even out at equilibrium.

164. **D is correct.** In this cell the cathode has the greater concentration because electrons flow toward it to reduce the number of cations. Also in a concentration cell $E^\circ = 0$, since the reduction half reaction is simply the reverse of the oxidation half reaction. $n = 1$ because only one electron is transferred in each reaction. $x/y$ must be a fraction so that the log will be negative and $E$ will be positive. Thus we have:

$$E = -(0.06/1)\log(0.1/y) = 0.12$$

$$y = 10 \text{ so that } x/y = 10^{-2}.$$

165. **B is correct.** Use units to solve the problem. We want to go from current to grams. Current is C/s. $F$ is coulombs per mole of electrons. For every mole of electrons there is one mole of silver. The molecular weight of silver is 107.8 g/mol

$$C/s \times s = C \quad \Rightarrow \quad C \times mol/C = mol \quad \Rightarrow \quad mol \times grams/mol = grams$$

so:

$$i \times t \times (1/F) \times 107.8 = grams$$

166. **A is correct.** Remember, $I = Q/t$. The charge $Q$ is $(96,500)(0.01) = 965$ C. The time $t$ in seconds is $(5)(60) = 300$. So $Q/t = 965/300 = 3$. The answer is rounded to 3 because there is only 1 significant digit in some of the numbers used in the calculation.

167. **B is correct.** If a voltage is applied to a solution containing $Na^+$ and $H_2O$, the $H_2O$ will take the electrons first because it has a larger reduction potential. As long as there is $H_2O$ present, the aqueous sodium will not react.

168. **C is correct.** $Ag^{2+}$ gains an electron to become $Ag^+$, so it is reduced (LEO the lion says GER). Reduction takes place at the cathode (ANOX/REDCAT).

# Photo Credits

## Covers

Front cover, hydrogen fuel cell, Electrolysis concept: © TiaClara/iStockphoto.com

Back cover, Chemical reaction: © E. R. Degginger/Science Source

## Chapter 1

Pg. 2, Mole of carbon: © Andrew Lambert Photography/Photo Researchers, Inc

Pg. 3, Metals malleability: © Alexey Tkachenko/iStockphoto.com

Pg. 3, Calcium: © Charles D. Winters/Photo Researchers, Inc

Pg. 3, Magnesium: © Charles D. Winters/Photo Researchers, Inc

Pg. 3, Lithium: © Charles D. Winters/Photo Researchers, Inc

Pg. 4, Phosphorus: © Charles D. Winters/Photo Researchers, Inc

Pg. 4, Granulated mineral sulfur: © Dean Turner/iStockphoto.com

Pg. 5, Flasks containing bromine and iodine: © Charles D. Winters/Photo Researchers, Inc

Pg. 15, Potassium with water: © Charles D. Winters/Photo Researchers, Inc

Pg. 16, A decomposition reaction: © Andrew Lambert Photography/Photo Researchers, Inc

Pg. 17, Candle wax: © Krystian Kaczmarski/iStockphoto.com

Pg. 17, Amethyst: © Besedin/iStockphoto.com

Pg. 23, Max Planck: © Science Source/Photo Researchers, Inc

Pg. 24, Early photoelectric cell: © Sheila Terry/Photo Researchers, Inc

## Chapter 2

Pg. 27, Crab Nebula: © European Southern Observatory/Photo Researchers, Inc.

Pg. 28, Orange balloons: © David Taylor/Photo Researchers, Inc

Pg. 30, Scuba divers: © Miguel Angelo Silva/iStockphoto.com

Pg. 32, Ammonia reacting with hydrochloric acid: © Charles D. Winters/Photo Researchers, Inc

Pg. 33, Bad dog: © Diane Diederich/iStockphoto.com

Pg. 35, Particle collision: © Victor de Schwanberg/Photo Researchers, Inc

Pg. 36, Magnesium reacting with Hydrochloric Acid: © Charles D. Winters/Photo Researchers, Inc.

Pg. 37, Ignite a match: © Sunnybeach/iStockphoto.com

Pg. 41, The Dartford Crossing: © Ian Hamilton/Istockphoto.com

Pg. 44, Indigestion tablets: © Gusto Productions/Photo Researchers, Inc.

Pg. 47, Nitric acid and copper react: © E. R. Degginger/Photo Researchers, Inc.

Pg. 49, Pouring cement: © DeepDesertPhoto/Veer.com

Pg. 52, Haber process: © Federico Rostagno/Istockphoto.com

Pg. 53, Sunglasses: © Krzysztof Gawor/Istockphoto.com

## Chapter 3

Pg. 61, Hot cup of coffee: © Studiocasper/iStockphoto.com

Pg. 67, Sterling engine: © Used by permission of www.stirlingengine.com

Pg. 70, Glass of water: © Robert Payne/iStockphoto.com

Pg. 72, Thermometer: © alxpin/iStockphoto.com

Pg. 74, Heat of hydration of copper sulphate: © Martyn F. Chillmaid / Photo Researchers, Inc.

Pg. 76, Computer interface measuring temperature: © Martin Shields/Photo Researchers, Inc.

Pg. 80, Coffee cup and saucer falling to floor (multiple exposure): © Ryan McVay/Gettyimages.com

## Chapter 4

Pg. 87, Solutions: © ElementalImaging/iStockphoto.com

Pg. 88, Aerosol spray: © Dorling Kindersley/Gettyimages.com

Pg. 88, Illuminating the cuvette: © Charles D. Winters/Photo Researchers, Inc

Pg. 89, Lightening: © Salih Külcü/iStockphoto.com

Pg. 90, Drinking too much water: © Jacom Stephens/iStockphoto.com

Pg. 92, Iron (II) sulphate solution: © Martyn F. Chillmaid/Photo Researchers, Inc.

Pg. 93, Cold pack: © Dana Kelley

Pg. 94, Puddle: © Patricia Hogan/iStockphoto.com

Pg. 95, Boiling water: © Dorling Kindersley/Gettyimages.com

Pg. 98, Salt cave: © MickyWiswedel/iStockphoto.com

Pg. 98, Chemical powder to a blue solution in a beaker: © ElementalImaging/iStockphoto.com

Pg. 100, Oil and water: © Charles D. Winters/Photo Researchers, Inc

Pg. 101, Soda pouring: © Arthur Carlo Franco/iStockphoto.com

Pg. 102, Manatees and power plants: © Mark Conlin/Gettyimages.com

## Chapter 5

Pg. 106, Vickers Machine Gun: © Olga Milkina/iStockphoto.com

Pg. 107, Low-key eye: © Knape/iStockphoto.com

Pg. 108, Beach buckets: © Daniela Andreea Spyropoulos/iStockphoto.com

Pg. 109, Turkey frying in an outdoor deep fryer: © Thomas Shortell/iStockphoto.com

Pg. 110, Bomb calorimeter: © Charles D. Winters/Photo Researchers, Inc
Pg. 112, Three ice cubes: © Okea/iStockphoto.com
Pg. 113, Dry ice: © Charles D. Winters/Photo Researchers, Inc
Pg. 114, Heavy water: © Charles D. Winters/Photo Researchers, Inc
Pg. 118, Albumin: © Antonia Reeve/Photo Researchers, Inc

## Chapter 6

Pg. 123, Acid rain: © David Woodfall/Gettyimages.com
Pg. 124, Facade of St. Bartholomews Church: © John Kaprielian/Photo Researchers, Inc.
Pg. 124, Batteries: © Dana Kelley
Pg. 124, Lemon: © Dana Kelley
Pg. 124, Apple: © Marek Mnich/iStockphoto.com
Pg. 124, Bananas: © Dana Kelley
Pg. 124, Milk: © craftvision/iStockphoto.com
Pg. 124, Water: © Dana Kelley
Pg. 124, Baking soda: © Dana Kelley
Pg. 124, Egg: © Anthia Cumming/iStockphoto.com
Pg. 124, Soap: © DNY59/iStockphoto.com
Pg. 124, Ammonia: © Dana Kelley
Pg. 124, Bleach: © Dana Kelley
Pg. 124, Drain cleaner: © Dana Kelley
Pg. 126, Common household acids and bases: © Dana Kelley
Pg. 127, Glass specimen jar: © Victor de Schwanberg/Photo Researchers, Inc.
Pg. 129, Calcium Hydride Reaction: © Charles D. Winters/ Photo Researchers, Inc.
Pg. 132, Urine analysis: © Faye Norman/Photo Researchers, Inc.
Pg. 133, Various types of salts: © lunanaranja/iStockphoto.com
Pg. 135, Titration: © Charles D. Winters/Photo Researchers, Inc.
Pg. 137, Buffer Solution: © Charles D. Winters/Photo Researchers, Inc.
Pg. 138, Acid-base reaction with indicator: © Martyn F. Chillmaid/Photo Researchers, Inc
Pg. 139, Student using a digital pH meter: © SPL/Photo Researchers, Inc

## Chapter 7

Pg. 148, Hydrogen electrode apparatus: © Martyn F. Chillmaid/Photo Researchers, Inc
Pg. 149, Iron-platinum electrochemistry: © Andrew Lambert Photography/Photo Researchers, Inc
Pg. 150, Voltaic cell: © Andrew Lambert Photography/ Photo Researchers, Inc
Pg. 151, Voltmeter and Zinc-copper battery: © Andrew Lambert Photography/Photo Researchers, Inc
Pg. 153, Michael Faraday: © Sheila Terry/Photo Researchers, Inc
Pg. 156, Contractions of the heart: © Andrey Prokhorov/ iStockphoto.com
Pg. 157, Copper refinery plant: © Maximilian Stock Ltd/ Photo Researchers, Inc.

# INDEX

## Symbols

π-bonds  4, 5

## A

acid dissociation constant  131, 134, 142
acids  5, 123-141
actinides  20
activation energy  35, 36, 42, 43
activity  48, 49
actual yield  16
aerosol  88
alkali metals  4, 100, 133, 144
alkaline earth metals  4, 5, 144
ammonium  14, 93, 100
amorphous  17, 105
amphipathic  88
amphoteric  5, 126
angstrom  1
anions  6, 14, 89
anode  150-160
aqueous phase  89, 117
Arrhenius  36, 42, 76, 123, 140
Arrhenius acid  123
Arrhenius equation  36, 42, 76
atmospheric pressure  95, 110, 113, 114, 117
atoms  1-10, 13, 17, 19-23
atomic mass units  2
atomic number  2, 6
atomic radius  8
atomic weight  2
ATP  12
Aufbau principle  20
autocatalysis  43
autoionization of water  131
Avogadro's law  28
Avogadro's number  2, 25, 73
azimuthal quantum number  19

## B

Balancing Redox Reactions  143, 149
bases  4, 123, 126, 132
bimolecular  37
binary molecular compounds  14
blackbody radiator  63
Bohr, Neils  23
boiling point  72, 112, 117, 120-122,
boiling point elevation  117
bomb calorimeter  110
bond dissociation energy  12
bond energy  12, 96
bond length  12
bonds  4, 5, 8, 12, 17, 42, 44, 76, 77, 89, 92-94, 96, 108, 112, 114, 117

Boron  12
Boyle's law  28
Broglie, Louis de  23
bromine  5
Brønsted and Lowry  123
Brønsted-Lowry  16, 123, 140
buffered  136, 137
buffer solution  136

## C

cage effect  44
calorimeter  110
carbon  2, 4, 5, 22, 44, 114
carbonates  100
carbon dioxide  15, 44
Carnot engine  67
catalyst  17, 42, 43, 76, 151
cathode  24, 150-152, 157
cations  4, 6, 14, 89, 123, 133
cell diagram  152
cell potential  150-157
celsius  73
centigrade  73
cesium  8
chalcogens  4
Charles' law  28, 29
chemical equilibrium  46
chlorine  5, 212
coagulate  88
coffee cup calorimeter  110, 111
cold reservoir  64, 66, 67
colligative  90, 117, 118
collision model  35, 39
colloid  88, 118
combination reaction  16
combustion reaction  15-16
common ion effect  99
compound  2, 12-15, 18, 53, 75, 87, 89, 94, 95, 117, 144, 145
concentration cell  156
condensation  112, 113
condense  95
conduction  61, 62, 151
conduction  61, 85
conjugate acid  125, 126, 215
conjugate base  125, 126, 128, 131, 134-138
conservation of energy  67, 70, 83
convection  62, 85
copper  14, 47, 74, 87, 149-152, 157
Coulomb's law  7, 8, 32
covalent bond  4, 5, 8, 12
critical point  114
critical pressure  114
critical temperature  114, 115
crystal  17, 98, 117

crystallization 98, 117

# D

Dalton's law 30
decomposition 16
degenerate orbitals 22
degrees of freedom 72
delocalized electrons 17
deposition 112, 113
deuterium 2, 114
deviations from ideal behavior 32, 33
dialysis 88
diatomic 4, 5, 71
diffusion 31-32, 55
diprotic acid 127, 135
dispersion medium 88
dissolution 89, 90, 92, 98
DNA 17
d orbitals 4, 5
double bonds 4
double displacement 4
double replacement 16
Downs cell 157

# E

Ea 36, 42
effective nuclear charge 7, 8
efficiency 67
effusion 31, 54, 55
Einstein 23, 24, 71
electrical work 63, 74, 83
electric potential 148, 150
electrochemical cell 157
electrodes 148, 150, 151, 157
electrolysis 157
electrolyte 150, 225
electrolytic cell 157
electromagnetic waves 62
electromotive force 150
electromotive force 158
electron affinity 8, 9, 25
electron configuration 25
electronegative 4, 5, 128
electronic charge 1
electronic energy 70, 71
electrons 1-9, 12, 17, 19-24, 143-153, 157
electron spin quantum number 19
electron units 1
electrostatic forces 7, 12, 17, 32, 44
elementary reaction 37, 47, 48
elements 2-6, 14, 19-22, 129, 144
Emf 158
emissivity 24, 62, 63
empirical formula 12, 13, 18
emulsion 88
endothermic 9, 75, 92-94, 113, 117
endpoint 138, 140
energy ladder 23
enthalpy 59, 70, 74, 84, 85

entropy 47, 52, 79-83, 93, 113
equilibrium 46-53, 60, 63-65, 67, 80-83, 94, 98, 99, 114, 118, 150, 153, 154
equilibrium approximation 42
equilibrium constant 42, 48, 50-52, 98, 99, 131, 154
equipartition theory 72
equivalence point 135-141, 145, 146
equivalents 90, 135
evaporation 15
exothermic 92, 93, 98
extensive properties 60

# F

families 3
First Law of Thermodynamics 59, 64, 84, 85
fluorine 5, 6, 8, 128
foam 88, 101
free energy 76, 82-85, 118, 153
freezing 72, 112, 113
freezing point 72
freezing point depression 117, 119, 120

# G

galvanic cell 150-154, 156, 157,
Gibbs Free Energy 59-60, 70, 82-83
glucose 12, 132
glycogen 17
Graham's law 31, 32
ground state 21, 25
groups 3, 4, 12, 20, 144

# H

Haber Process 52
half cell 150, 156
half equivalence point 136, 137, 139, 145
half life 40
half reaction 148-152, 156
halides 5, 128
halogens 4, 5, 100, 144
HCl 124, 126
heat 60-67, 70, 71, 74, 75, 77, 80-85, 92-94, 96, 106-114
heat capacity 106-112, 120
heat engine 67
heating curve 112, 113
heat of fusion 112
heat of hydration 93, 97, 225
heat of solution 92, 93, 96, 102, 117
heat of vaporization 94, 112
heats of hydration 5
heats of reaction 110, 120
Heisenberg Uncertainty Principle 1, 20
helium 7, 29
Henderson-Hasselbalch equation 136-138, 140
Henry's law 101
Hess' law 75
heterogeneous catalyst 42, 170
hot reservoir 66, 67
Hund's rule 22
hydration 5, 74, 89, 93

hydration number 89
hydrides 4, 129
hydrogen 2, 4, 5, 7, 108, 128, 143, 148, 151
hydrogen halide acids 128
hydroxide 4, 14, 15, 98, 100, 123, 126, 130, 131, 134, 135

# I

ideal gas 28-31, 33, 71-75, 85, 95
ideal gas 33, 54, 55
Ideal Gas Law 33, 54, 55
ideally dilute solution 87, 101, 117
ideal solutions 87
indicator 135, 138, 145
inert gases 5
intensive properties 60, 114, 149
intermediates 37, 42, 76
intermediates 37, 55, 76, 85
intermolecular potential energy 70, 71, 108
internal energy 70, 71, 106
iodine 5
ionic compounds 4, 6, 14, 89, 100, 133
ionic oxides 3, 5
ionization energy 8, 9, 25
ion pairing 117
ions 6, 14, 17, 89-91, 98, 99, 124, 131-133, 137, 150-152, 156
irreversible 40, 64, 80-82
isotopes 2

# K

kinetic molecular theory 28, 30, 33

# L

lanthanides 20
law of mass action 48, 49, 54, 131, 215
lead 100, 117, 156
Le Châtelier's Principle 27, 52
Lewis 4, 16, 123, 130
Lewis acids 133
Lewis bases 4
like dissolves like 89
limiting reagent 15, 18
liquid junction 151, 152
lithium 3
london dispersion forces 89
lyophilic 88
lyophobic 88

# M

magnesium 3, 159
magnetic quantum number 19
main-group elements 4, 162
mass 1, 2, 13, 15, 25, 31, 33, 48, 49, 59, 63, 64, 70, 71, 90, 109, 110, 113, 131, 135
mass number 2
mass percentage 90
mean free path 27, 32, 55
melting 15, 77, 95, 117

melting point 95, 112, 118
mercury 3, 100
metal 3, 4, 25
metallic character 3, 9
metalloids 4, 25
metal plating 157
metathesis 15, 16
methane 15, 108
modes 72
molarity 90, 117, 118, 145, 146
molar mass 2, 122, 228
mole 2, 15, 29-31, 33, 87, 90, 95, 96, 98, 99, 101, 109, 135, 153
molecular formula 12, 13
molecularity 37, 40, 48
molecular weight 2
molecules 5, 12, 15-17, 28-33, 35, 37
mole fraction 30, 87, 90, 95, 96, 98, 101, 118

# N

neon 6, 7
Nernst equation 154, 156
network 17
neutrons 1, 2, 10
Newton's Law of cooling 61
Newton's second law 63
nitrate 14, 93, 100
nitrite 89
nitrogen 4, 5, 7, 28, 52, 94, 144
noble gases 5, 6, 8, 9, 162, 205
nonideal solutions 87, 96
nonmetals 4, 25
nonvolatile solute 95, 101, 117
normal boiling point 112, 117
normality 90
normal melting point 112
nuclear charge 7, 8
nucleon 1
nucleus 1, 2, 7, 8, 21
nuclide 2

# O

orbital 6, 7, 19, 20, 22, 26
order 37-40, 43, 47, 80, 81, 87
osmosis 118
osmotic potential 118
osmotic pressure 117, 118, 121
overall order 37
oxidant 144, 145, 147, 195
oxidation 143-145, 148-150
oxidation half reaction 148, 150
oxidation potential 148, 149, 151
oxidation-reduction reaction 143
oxidation State 143, 144
oxides 3-5, 16
oxidized 143-145, 146
oxidizing agent 144-146, 149
oxyacid 14, 128
oxygen 4-7, 15, 27, 94, 102, 144, 149
ozone 4

## P

partial pressure  30, 50, 52, 55, 94-96, 101, 113
parts per million  90, 103
path functions  60
Pauli Exclusion Principle  19
Pauling scale  8
percent yield  16
period  3, 5, 8, 20, 22
periodic table  2-9, 14, 15, 19, 20
periodic trends  8, 9
peroxides  4
phase  94, 95, 105, 106, 112-114, 117, 150, 152
phase changes  77, 106, 113, 114
phase diagram  114
pH meter  138, 139
phosphates  100
Phosphorous  4, 37
photoelectric effect  23, 24
photoelectrons  24
photon  23, 24
Planck, Max  23
Planck's constant  20, 23
Planck's quantum theory  23
platinum  149, 151
polymers  17
polyprotic acids  127, 139
p orbitals  5, 7
precipitation  98
principle for detailed balance  50
principle quantum number  19, 22
protein  17, 43, 118, 132
protium  2
proton  1, 2, 6, 7, 20, 123-128, 133, 139
protons  1, 2, 6, 7, 10, 90, 127, 133, 135, 136
purifying metals  157
PV work  63-65, 74, 75, 81-83, 85, 106, 107, 114

## Q

quadratic equation  132
quantum mechanics  19, 23

## R

radiation  62, 63, 85
range of an indicator  138
Raoult's law  95, 96, 101, 117
rate constant  36-40, 44, 47, 48, 222
rate determining step  41
rate law  36-43, 47, 48, 171
reaction coordinate  42
reaction quotient  51, 153
redox  143, 145, 146, 149
redox reaction  143-145, 148, 149, 153
reduced  143-147
reducing agent  144, 145, 149
reductant  144, 145
reduction  143-145, 148-152, 156, 157
reduction half reaction  148, 150-152, 156
reduction potentials  148, 149, 151, 159
reference form  75

## S

representative elements  6
resonance  17
rest mass energy  71
reversible  37, 46, 57, 64, 67, 74, 80-83, 98, 170
root-mean-square (rms)  31
rotational energy  71
rotation of polarized light  15
runs to completion  15, 16, 18, 48

salt bridge  150-152, 159
salts  133, 140
saturated solution  98, 99
second ionization energy  8
second law of thermodynamics  66, 67, 79-81
SHE  148, 151
shell  6-8, 19, 20, 21, 106
shielding  7
silver  16, 53, 100, 149, 151
single Displacement  16
single replacement  16, 18
SI units  11
sodium  6, 7, 14, 24, 90, 134, 135, 157
solubility  87, 98, 100, 101, 103
solubility Guidelines  87, 100
solubility product  98, 99, 104
solute  87-90, 92, 95, 96, 98, 101, 102, 117, 118
solution  110, 117, 118
solvation  52, 89, 98, 99
solvent  87-98, 101, 102, 104, 118
specific heat capacity  109
spectator ions  99
spontaneous reaction  82, 83, 93, 102, 153, 165
standard enthalpy of formation  75
standard hydrogen electrode  148, 151
standard molar volume  29
standard solution  145, 198
standard state  17, 75, 151-154
standard state cell potential  151
standard temperature and pressure  27
standard Temperature And Pressure  55
state  20-22, 60, 61, 66, 67, 70-76, 79-83, 105, 107, 112, 144
state Functions  59, 60, 70, 85
steady state  42, 61
steady state approximation  42
Stefan-Boltzman law  62
steric factor  36, 42
sterling engine  67
stoichiometric point  135
STP  27, 29, 55, 75
strong nuclear force  1
sublimation  112, 113
subshell  6, 7, 19-22
sulfate  14
sulfides  4, 100
sulfur  4, 5, 18, 105
sulfuric acid  14
supercritical fluid  114
surroundings  59, 61, 64-66, 79-83
system  59-61, 63-67, 70-75, 78, 79-83

# T

temperature  28, 29, 31, 33, 36, 37, 61-67, 71-75, 80-85, 93-95, 101, 102, 106-110, 112-114, 117, 118
terminals  150, 152
termolecular  37
theoretical yield  16
thermal conductivity  61, 62
thermodynamic functions  70
third law of thermodynamics  80
titration  135-139, 145
titration curve  135, 137, 139
transition metals  4, 6, 20, 22, 144
transition state  76
translational energy  71
triple bonds  4
triple point  114,
tritium  2
turnover number  43
Tyndall effect  88

# U

unimolecular  37
universal gas constant  28

# V

valence electrons  21
Van der Waals equation  33
Van der Waals forces  42, 102
Van't Hoff factor  117
vaporization  94, 112, 113, 120
vapor pressure  94-96, 101, 104, 113, 117
vibrational energy  70, 71
volatile solute  95, 101, 117
voltaic cell  150, 156
volume  54, 55, 60, 70, 72

# W

water  15
water potential  118
work  63-67, 79, 81-83, 85, 101
work function  24

# Z

z  36, 72
$Z_{eff}$  7, 8, 9
zeroth law of thermodynamics  72

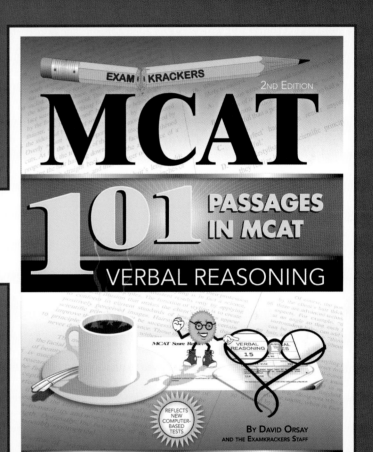

# An Unedited Student Review of This Book

The following review of this book was written by Teri R—. from New York. Teri scored a 43 out of 45 possible points on the MCAT. She is currently attending UCSF medical school, one of the most selective medical schools in the country.

*"The Examkrackers MCAT books are the best MCAT prep materials I've seen-and I looked at many before deciding. The worst part about studying for the MCAT is figuring out what you need to cover and getting the material organized. These books do all that for you so that you can spend your time learning. The books are well and carefully written, with great diagrams and really useful mnemonic tricks, so you don't waste time trying to figure out what the book is saying. They are concise enough that you can get through all of the subjects without cramming unnecessary details, and they really give you a strategy for the exam. The study questions in each section cover all the important concepts, and let you check your learning after each section. Alternating between reading and answering questions in MCAT format really helps make the material stick, and means there are no surprises on the day of the exam-the exam format seems really familiar and this helps enormously with the anxiety. Basically, these books make it clear what you need to do to be completely prepared for the MCAT and deliver it to you in a straightforward and easy-to-follow form. The mass of material you could study is overwhelming, so I decided to trust these books—I used nothing but the Examkrackers books in all subjects and got a 13-15 on Verbal, a 14 on Physical Sciences, and a 14 on Biological Sciences. Thanks to Jonathan Orsay and Examkrackers, I was admitted to all of my top-choice schools (Columbia, Cornell, Stanford, and UCSF). I will always be grateful. I could not recommend the Examkrackers books more strongly. Please contact me if you have any questions."*

*Sincerely,*
*Teri R—*

# About the Author

Jonathan Orsay is uniquely qualified to write an MCAT preparation book. He graduated on the Dean's list with a B.A. in History from Columbia University. While considering medical school, he sat for the real MCAT three times from 1989 to 1996. He scored in the 90 percentiles on all sections before becoming an MCAT instructor. He has lectured in MCAT test preparation for thousands of hours and across the country. He has taught premeds from such prestigious Universities as Harvard and Columbia. He was the editor of one of the best selling MCAT prep books in 1996 and again in 1997. He has written and published the following books and audio products in MCAT preparation: "Examkrackers MCAT Physics"; "Examkrackers MCAT Chemistry"; "Examkrackers MCAT Organic Chemistry"; "Examkrackers MCAT Biology"; "Examkrackers MCAT Verbal Reasoning & Math"; "Examkrackers 1001 questions in MCAT Physics", "Examkrackers MCAT Audio Osmosis with Jordan and Jon".

*Notes:*

EXAMKRACKERS MCAT®

# ORGANIC CHEMISTRY

8TH EDITION

OSOTE PUBLISHING

ISBN 10: 1-893858-64-2 (Volume 3)
ISBN 13: 978-1-893858-64-0 (5 Volume Set)

8th Edition

To purchase additional copies of this book or the rest of the 5 volume set,
call 1-888-572-2536 or fax orders to 1-859-255-0109.

Examkrackers.com

Osote.com

Audioosmosis.com

Cover/inside layout design/illustrations: Examkrackers' staff

Printed and bound in the United States of America.

# Acknowledgements

Although I am the author, the hard work and expertise of many individuals contributed to this book. The idea of writing in two voices, a science voice and an MCAT voice, was the creative brainchild of my imaginative friend Jordan Zaretsky. I would like to thank Scott Calvin for lending his exceptional science talent and pedagogic skills to this project. I also must thank thirteen years worth of ExamKrackers students for doggedly questioning every explanation, every sentence, every diagram, and every punctuation mark in the book, and for providing the creative inspiration that helped me find new ways to approach and teach organic chemistry. Finally, I wish to thank my wife, Silvia, for her support during the difficult times in the past and those that lie ahead.

I also wish to thank the following individuals:

## Contributors

Jennifer Birk-Goldschmidt
Dr. Jerry Johnson
Timothy Peck
Kathy Shaganaw
Gibran Shaikh
Vani Takiar
Steven Tersigni
Sara Thorp
Dale Wilson

# Read This Section First!

This manual contains all the organic chemistry tested on the MCAT® and more. It contains more organic chemistry than is tested on the MCAT® because a deeper understanding of basic scientific principles is often gained through more advanced study. In addition, the MCAT® often presents passages with imposing topics that may intimidate the test-taker. Although the questions don't require knowledge of these topics, some familiarity will increase the confidence of the test-taker.

In order to answer questions quickly and efficiently, it is vital that the test-taker understand what is, and is not, tested directly by the MCAT®. To assist the test-taker in gaining this knowledge, this manual will use the following conventions. Any term or concept which is tested directly by the MCAT® will be written in **red, bold type**. To ensure a perfect score on the MCAT®, you should thoroughly understand all terms and concepts that are in **red, bold type** in this manual. Sometimes it is not necessary to memorize the name of a concept, but it is necessary to understand the concept itself. These concepts will also be in **bold and red**. It is important to note that the converse of the above is not true: just because a topic is not in **bold and red**, does not mean that it is not important.

Any formula that must be memorized will also be written in **red, bold type.**

If a topic is discussed purely as background knowledge, it will be written in *italics*. If a topic is written in italics, it is not likely to be required knowledge for the MCAT® but may be discussed in an MCAT® passage. Do not ignore items in italics, but recognize them as less important than other items. Answers to questions that directly test knowledge of italicized topics are likely to be found in an MCAT® passage.

Text written in orange is me, Salty the Kracker. I will remind you what is and is not an absolute must for MCAT. I will help you develop your MCAT intuition. In addition, I will offer mnemonics, simple methods of viewing a complex concept, and occasionally some comic relief. Don't ignore me, even if you think I am not funny, because my comedy is designed to help you understand and remember. If you think I am funny, tell the boss. I could use a raise.

Each chapter in this manual should be read three times: twice before the class lecture, and once immediately following the lecture. During the first reading, you should not write in the book. Instead, read purely for enjoyment. During the second reading, you should both highlight and take notes in the margins. The third reading should be slow and thorough.

The 24 questions in each lecture should be worked during the second reading before coming to class. The in-class exams in the back of the book are to be done in class after the lecture. Do not look at them before class.

**Warning:** Just attending the class will not raise your score. You must do the work. Not attending class will obstruct dramatic score increases. If you have Audio Osmosis, then listen to the appropriate lecture before and after you read a lecture.

If you are studying independently, read the lecture twice before doing the in-class exam and then once after doing the in-class exam. If you have Examkrackers *MCAT® Audio Osmosis With Jordan and Jon*, listen to that before taking the in-class exam and then as many times as necessary after taking the exam.

A scaled score conversion chart is provided on the answer page. This is not meant to be an accurate representation of your MCAT score. Do not become demoralized by a poor performance on these exams; they are not accurate reflections of your performance on the real MCAT®. The thirty minute exams have been designed to educate. They are similar to an MCAT® but with most of the easy questions removed. We believe that you can answer most of the easy questions without too much help from us, so the best way to raise your score is to focus on the more difficult questions. This method is one of the reasons for the rapid and celebrated success of the Examkrackers prep course and products.

If you find yourself struggling with the science or just needing more practice materials, use the Examkrackers 1001 Questions series. These books are designed specifically to teach the science. If you are already scoring 10s or better, these books are not for you.

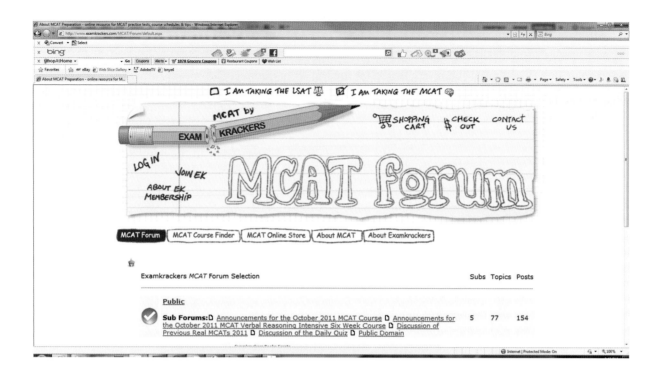

You should take advantage of the forums at www.examkrackers.com. The forum allows you to discuss any question in the book with an MCAT® expert at Examkrackers. All discussions are kept on file so you have a bank of discussions to which you can refer to any question in this book.

Although we are very careful to be accurate, errata is an occupational hazard of any science book, especially those that are updated regularly as is this one. We maintain that our books have fewer errata than any other prep book. Most of the time what students are certain are errata is the student's error and not an error in the book. So that you can be certain, any errata in this book will be listed as it is discovered at www.examkrackers.com on the bulletin board. Check this site initially and periodically. If you discover what you believe to be errata, please post it on this board and we will verify it promptly. We understand that this system calls attention to the very few errata that may be in our books, but we feel that this is the best system to ensure that you have accurate information for your exam. Again, we stress that we have fewer errata than any other prep book on the market. The difference is that we provide a public list of our errata for your benefit.

Study diligently, trust this book to guide you, and you will reach your MCAT® goals.

# Table of Contents

# BIOLOGICAL SCIENCES

**DIRECTIONS.** Most questions in the Biological Sciences test are organized into groups, each preceded by a descriptive passage. After studying the passage, select the one best answer to each question in the group. Some questions are not based on a descriptive passage and are also independent of each other. You must also select the one best answer to these questions. If you are not certain of an answer, eliminate the alternatives that you know to be incorrect and then select an answer from the remaining alternatives. A periodic table is provided for your use. You may consult it whenever you wish.

## PERIODIC TABLE OF THE ELEMENTS

| 1 H 1.0 | | | | | | | | | | | | | | | | | | 2 He 4.0 |
|---|---|---|---|---|---|---|---|---|---|---|---|---|---|---|---|---|---|---|
| 3 Li 6.9 | 4 Be 9.0 | | | | | | | | | | | 5 B 10.8 | 6 C 12.0 | 7 N 14.0 | 8 O 16.0 | 9 F 19.0 | 10 Ne 20.2 |
| 11 Na 23.0 | 12 Mg 24.3 | | | | | | | | | | | 13 Al 27.0 | 14 Si 28.1 | 15 P 31.0 | 16 S 32.1 | 17 Cl 35.5 | 18 Ar 39.9 |
| 19 K 39.1 | 20 Ca 40.1 | 21 Sc 45.0 | 22 Ti 47.9 | 23 V 50.9 | 24 Cr 52.0 | 25 Mn 54.9 | 26 Fe 55.8 | 27 Co 58.9 | 28 Ni 58.7 | 29 Cu 63.5 | 30 Zn 65.4 | 31 Ga 69.7 | 32 Ge 72.6 | 33 As 74.9 | 34 Se 79.0 | 35 Br 79.9 | 36 Kr 83.8 |
| 37 Rb 85.5 | 38 Sr 87.6 | 39 Y 88.9 | 40 Zr 91.2 | 41 Nb 92.9 | 42 Mo 95.9 | 43 Tc (98) | 44 Ru 101.1 | 45 Rh 102.9 | 46 Pd 106.4 | 47 Ag 107.9 | 48 Cd 112.4 | 49 In 114.8 | 50 Sn 118.7 | 51 Sb 121.8 | 52 Te 127.6 | 53 I 126.9 | 54 Xe 131.3 |
| 55 Cs 132.9 | 56 Ba 137.3 | 57 La* 138.9 | 72 Hf 178.5 | 73 Ta 180.9 | 74 W 183.9 | 75 Re 186.2 | 76 Os 190.2 | 77 Ir 192.2 | 78 Pt 195.1 | 79 Au 197.0 | 80 Hg 200.6 | 81 Tl 204.4 | 82 Pb 207.2 | 83 Bi 209.0 | 84 Po (209) | 85 At (210) | 86 Rn (222) |
| 87 Fr (223) | 88 Ra 226.0 | 89 Ac= (227) | 104 Rf (267) | 105 Db (268) | 106 Sg (271) | 107 Bh (272) | 108 Hs (270) | 109 Mt (276) | 110 Ds (281) | 111 Rg (280) | 112 Cn (285) | 113 Uut (284) | 114 Fl (289) | 115 Uup (288) | 116 Lv (293) | 117 Uus (294) | 118 Uuo (294) |

| | 58 Ce 140.1 | 59 Pr 140.9 | 60 Nd 144.2 | 61 Pm (145) | 62 Sm 150.4 | 63 Eu 152.0 | 64 Gd 157.3 | 65 Tb 158.9 | 66 Dy 162.5 | 67 Ho 164.9 | 68 Er 167.3 | 69 Tm 168.9 | 70 Yb 173.0 | 71 Lu 175.0 |
|---|---|---|---|---|---|---|---|---|---|---|---|---|---|---|
| = | 90 Th 232.0 | 91 Pa (231) | 92 U 238.0 | 93 Np (237) | 94 Pu (244) | 95 Am (243) | 96 Cm (247) | 97 Bk (247) | 98 Cf (251) | 99 Es (252) | 100 Fm (257) | 101 Md (258) | 102 No (259) | 103 Lr (260) |

# MOLECULAR STRUCTURE

## 1.1  Introduction

Organic chemistry is probably the most feared topic on the MCAT. Few MCAT test-takers feel confident about their organic chemistry skills. If you feel confident about organic chemistry, it is probably either because you have a PhD, or because you have only taken first-year organic chemistry and haven't yet learned that organic chemistry is far more complex than your first-year textbook led you to believe.

Attempting to master advanced organic chemistry concepts in order to improve your MCAT score is not *just* a futile waste of time; it is likely to lower your MCAT score. The writers of the MCAT neither test nor claim to test any organic chemistry beyond "content typically covered in undergraduate introductory science courses". In fact, they go to great lengths to ensure that the test does not require knowledge beyond "content typically covered in undergraduate introductory science courses". If you *think* that MCAT might test more, and you look for more in an MCAT organic chemistry question, you are likely to overlook the obvious answer, which is based upon "content typically covered in undergraduate introductory science courses". You are also likely to spend more time on each question because you are choosing the answer from a larger pool of knowledge; more answer choices will *seem* possible within your larger, but inaccurate, context.

Any and all organic chemistry required to answer any question on the MCAT will be covered in this book. For the reasons stated in the preceding paragraph, it is possible that using other organic chemistry MCAT prep books to supplement this book could alter your perception of what is tested by the MCAT thereby lowering your score. We suggest against it.

You should expect questions to look complex and to *appear* that they require in-depth knowledge of organic chemistry. When answering such questions, consider only the simplest organic chemistry concepts and answer the questions accordingly.

There are three rules for forming **Lewis dot structures**.

1.  Find the total number of valence electrons for all atoms in the molecule.

2.  Use one pair of electrons to form one bond between each atom.

3.  Arrange the remaining electrons around the atoms to satisfy the duet rule for hydrogen and the octet rule for other atoms.

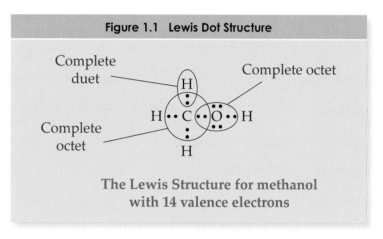

**Figure 1.1  Lewis Dot Structure**

The Lewis Structure for methanol
with 14 valence electrons

Gilbert Lewis (1875-1946), devised a theory of molecular bonds in which atoms were bound together by sharing pairs of electrons.

**Exceptions:** Sometimes atoms within a molecule break the octet rule. The atoms may have less than an octet or more than an octet. Boron and Beryllium do not contain a full octet. Atoms from the third period or higher in the periodic table may have an expanded octet due to vacant d orbitals available for hybridization

When writing Lewis structures, don't worry about which electrons come from which atoms. Simply count the number of total electrons and distribute them to complete the valence shells. It is useful to know the atom's **valence** (the number of bonds it usually forms). Some important valences for common atoms in organic chemistry are as follows: carbon is tetravalent; nitrogen is trivalent; oxygen is divalent; hydrogens and halogens are monovalent. (Halogens other than fluorine are capable of making more than one bond.)

Know how many bonds these elements like to make.

Carbon (4)
Hydrogen (1)
Nitrogen (3)
Oxygen (2)
Phosphorous (3)
Sulfur (2)

CHNOPS

It is also useful to know the **formal charge** of an atom. The formal charge is the number of electrons in the isolated atom, minus the number of electrons assigned to the atom in the Lewis structure. For instance, in the cyanide ion carbon has a pair of nonbonding electrons and one electron from each bond in the triple bond for a total of five electrons.

$$[\text{:}C \equiv N\text{:}]^-$$

### Cyanide ion

A neutral carbon atom has only four valance electrons, so the formal charge on carbon in the cyanide ion is minus one. It is important to know that, although the sum of the formal charges for each atom in a molecule or ion represents the total charge on that molecule or ion, the formal charge on a given atom does not represent a real charge on that atom. The actual charge distribution requires consideration of electronegativity differences among all the atoms in the molecule.

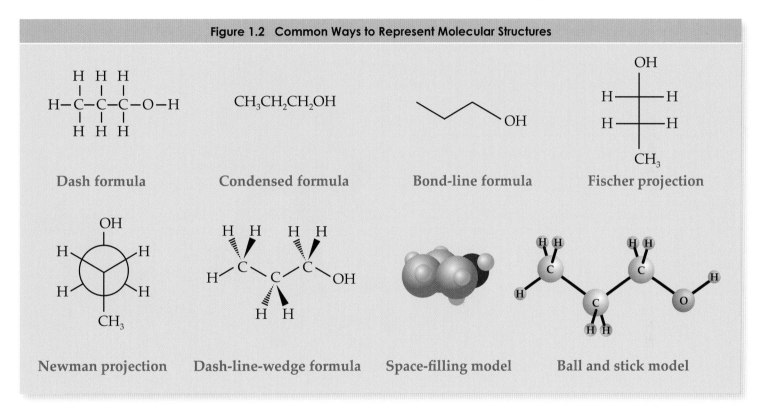

### Figure 1.2 Common Ways to Represent Molecular Structures

| Dash formula | Condensed formula | Bond-line formula | Fischer projection |

| Newman projection | Dash-line-wedge formula | Space-filling model | Ball and stick model |

There are multiple ways to represent molecules on a two-dimensional page.

The **dash formula** shows the bonds between atoms, but does not show the three-dimensional structure of the molecule.

The **condensed formula** does not show bonds. Central atoms are usually followed by the atoms that bond to them even though this is not the bonding order. For instance, the three hydrogens following the carbon in $CH_3NH_2$ do not bond to the nitrogen.

The **bond-line formula** is likely to be the most prevalent on the MCAT. In the bond-line formula, line intersections, corners, and endings represent a carbon atom unless some other atom is drawn in. The hydrogen atoms that are attached to the carbons are not usually drawn but are assumed to be present.

The **Fischer projection** is also important on the MCAT. In Fischer projections the vertical lines are assumed to be oriented into the page. The horizontal lines are assumed to be oriented out of the page.

The **Newman projection** is a view straight down the axis of one of the σ-bonds. Both the intersecting lines and the large circle are assumed to be carbon atoms.

In the **dash-line-wedge formula** the black wedge is assumed to be coming out of the page, the dashed wedge is assumed to be going into the page, and the lines are assumed to be in the plane of the page.

The **space-filling model** is a three dimensional, scale representation of a molecule with spheres of different colors representing the different elements

Unless otherwise indicated, atomic radius for atoms part of **ball and stick models** in this manual will be drawn to scale. However, bond lengths are drawn to approximately twice their length so that the atoms are clearly visible.

These are all just different ways of representing the same molecule; each conveys different information about the molecule. For example, Newman projections give information about steric hindrance with respect to a particular σ bond. Fischer projections are an easy way to represent carbohydrates and give information about stereochemistry. Ball and stick representations give information of the relative size of atoms. Bond-line diagrams are a way of representing bigger molecules easily; watch out for the hydrogens that are not shown! Finally, condensed formulas are often used to show portions of the molecule that are not immediately relevant to the reaction chemistry; for example, the inert hydrocarbon portion of fatty acids.

**Thought Provoker**

*Given the following molecule, indicate the formal charges of each of the atoms.*

*Answer:  See page 29*

## 1.3 Degrees of Unsaturation

The **index of deficiency** indicates the number of pairs of hydrogens a compound requires in order to become a saturated alkane. Since a saturated alkane contains $2n + 2$ hydrogens (where $n$ is the number of carbons), in order to find the index of deficiency of any compound, subtract the compound's total number of hydrogens from the number of hydrogens on a corresponding saturated alkane and divide by two. For this procedure count halogens as hydrogens, ignore oxygen atoms, and count nitrogen atoms as one half of a hydrogen atom. Of course, the index of hydrogen deficiency for any saturated alkane will be zero. As a rule of thumb, remember that a double bond is one **degree of unsaturation** as is a cylic structure, and a triple bond is two degrees of unsaturation. So, for example, all of the following have the same number of degrees of unsaturation: 1.

| Figure 1.3  Degrees of Unsaturation |
| :---: |
| C = number of carbons |
| H = number of hydrogens |
| N = number of nitrogens |
| X = number of halogens |

$$\text{Degree of unsaturation} = \frac{(2C + 2 + N - X - H)}{2}$$

> Degrees of unsaturation is primarily used as a tool to determine constitutional isomers for a given molecular formula (see section 1.12).

## 1.4 Functional Groups

The first step in solving any organic chemistry problem on the MCAT is to recognize which functional groups are involved in the reaction. The MCAT tests only reactions involving the basic functional groups. Many of the molecules on the MCAT are likely to be large and unfamiliar; however, in order to solve an MCAT problem, it is only important to be familiar with the attached functional groups and how they react. A molecule may have a complicated structure, but its chemistry is governed by its functional groups. For example:

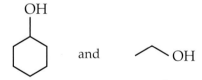

phenol and enthanol undergo many of the same reactions even though they have different structures. This is becuase they share the same functional group, an alcohol.

Most MCAT organic chemistry problems involve recognizing the basic functional groups as part of a more complicated molecule. First learn the names fo these functional groups. As you study the reactions in this book familiarize yourself with the "personality" of each group. How does it behave? Where do its electrons like to be and like to go? Is it hungry for positive or negative charge? How stable is it as a leaving group? Focus on the behavior of the functional group, rather than the details of each reaction. You will begin to gain an intuition of organic chemistry and that will allow you to make predictions about the outcome of unfamiliar reactions.

Functional groups are reactive, non-alkane portions of molecules. The following two lists display functional groups. Memorization of List #1 (Figure 1.4) is absolutely vital to success on the MCAT. List #2 (Figure 1.5) is less important, but should still be memorized.

**Figure 1.4   List #1**

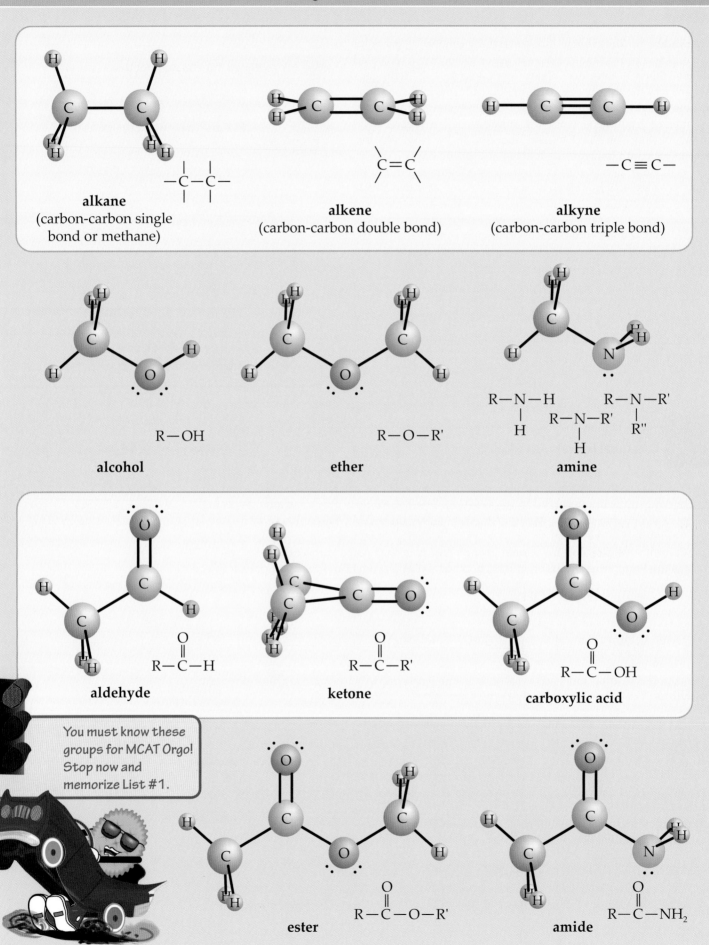

**alkane**
(carbon-carbon single
bond or methane)

**alkene**
(carbon-carbon double bond)

**alkyne**
(carbon-carbon triple bond)

R—OH

**alcohol**

R—O—R'

**ether**

R—N—H          R—N—R'
     |                   |
     H    R—N—R'        R"
               |
               H

**amine**

O
‖
R—C—H

**aldehyde**

O
‖
R—C—R'

**ketone**

O
‖
R—C—OH

**carboxylic acid**

You must know these
groups for MCAT Orgo!
Stop now and
memorize List #1.

O
‖
R—C—O—R'

**ester**

O
‖
R—C—NH₂

**amide**

Figure 1.5 List #2 - Additional Functional Groups

**alkyl**
(one hydrogen substituted
from an alkane)

halogen
(halo-)

**gem-dihalide**

**vic-dihalide**

—OH
**hydroxyl**

—OR
**alkoxy**

**hemiacetal**

**hemiketal**

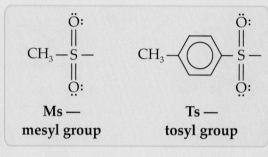

Ms—
**mesyl group**

Ts—
**tosyl group**

**carbonyl**

**acetyl**

**acyl**

**anhydride**

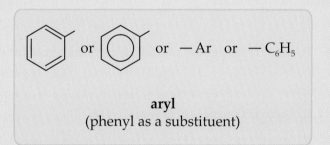

or or —Ar or —C₆H₅

**aryl**
(phenyl as a substituent)

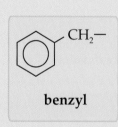

**benzyl**

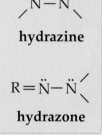

**hydrazine**

**hydrazone**

**vinyl**

**vinylic**

**allyl**

—C≡N̈

**nitrile**

**epoxide**

**enamine**

**imine**

**tautomer**

**oxime**

**nitro**

**nitroso**

The MCAT requires knowledge of basic organic chemistry nomenclature. For alkanes you must memorize the following:

I met Ethyl and proposed, but pensive Hector Helped Oct-Non Decide.

Look, I don't know who Oct-Non is either, I am just trying to help you remember the list!

**Table 1.1   Prefixes for Organic Nomenclature**

| Prefix | Number of Carbons |
|--------|-------------------|
| Meth-  | 1  |
| Eth-   | 2  |
| Prop-  | 3  |
| But-   | 4  |
| Pent-  | 5  |
| Hex-   | 6  |
| Hept-  | 7  |
| Oct-   | 8  |
| Non-   | 9  |
| Dec-   | 10 |

In addition you should be able to recognize the following structures drawn in any orientation:

**Figure 1.6   Common Substituent Groups**

$CH_3 - CH_2 - CH_2 -$

*n*-propyl

$CH_3 - CH_2 - CH_2 - CH_2 -$

*n*-butyl

$$CH_3 - CH_2 - \overset{\displaystyle CH_3}{\underset{\displaystyle |}{CH}} -$$

*sec*-butyl

$$CH_3 - \underset{\displaystyle |}{CH} - CH_3$$

isopropyl

$$CH_3 - \underset{\displaystyle \underset{\displaystyle |}{CH_2}}{\overset{\displaystyle |}{CH}} - CH_3$$

isobutyl

$$CH_3 - \overset{\displaystyle CH_3}{\underset{\displaystyle \underset{\displaystyle CH_3}{|}}{\overset{\displaystyle |}{C}}} - CH_3$$

*tert*-butyl

**The following are the IUPAC rules for nomenclature:**

- The longest carbon chain with the most substituents determines the base name.

- The end carbon closest to a carbon with a substituent is always the first carbon. In the case of a tie, look to the next substituent.

- Any substituent is given the same number as its carbon.

- If the same substituent is used more than once, use the prefixes di-, tri-, tetra, and so on.

- Order the substituents alphabetically.

- The ending of the molecules name is based on the most important functional group in the molecule based on IUPAC priority:

  - Carboxylic acids
  - Aldehydes
  - Ketones
  - Alcohols
  - Amines
  - Alkynes
  - Alkenes
  - Alkanes

Alkane nomenclature is likely to be on the MCAT.

---

**Figure 1.7    Nomenclature**

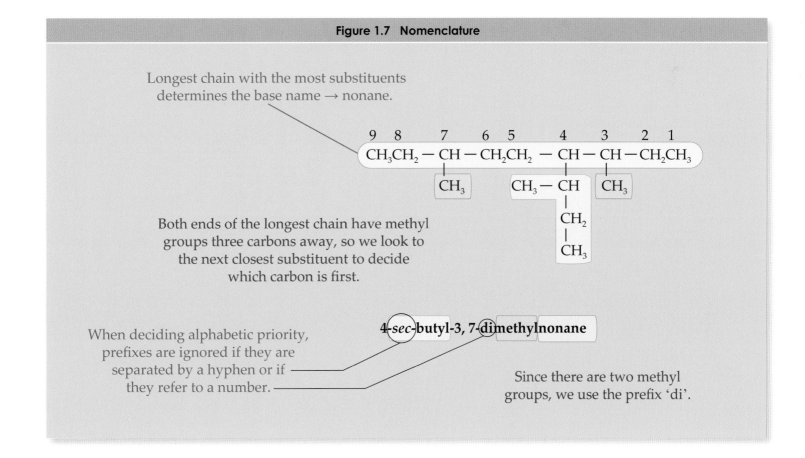

Longest chain with the most substituents determines the base name → nonane.

Both ends of the longest chain have methyl groups three carbons away, so we look to the next closest substituent to decide which carbon is first.

When deciding alphabetic priority, prefixes are ignored if they are separated by a hyphen or if they refer to a number.

4-sec-butyl-3, 7-dimethylnonane

Since there are two methyl groups, we use the prefix 'di'.

Questions 1 through 8 are **NOT** based on a descriptive passage.

**1.** β-D-(+)-glucose is reacted with methanol and dry hydrogen chloride. The product of this reaction is then treated with methyl sulfate and sodium hydroxide yielding methyl β-2,3,4,6-tetra-O-methyl-D-glucoside. Which of the following molecules is this product?

**A.**

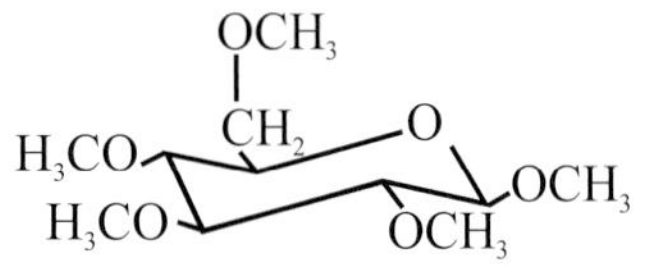

**B.**

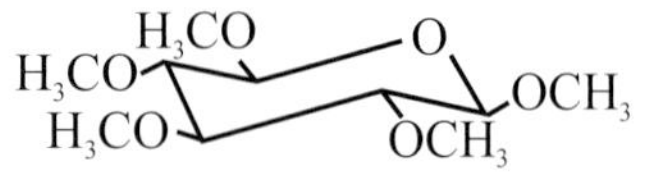

**C.**

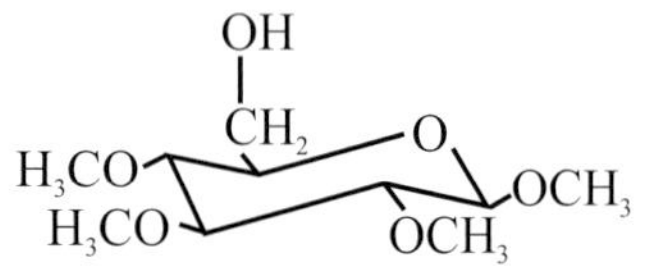

**D.**

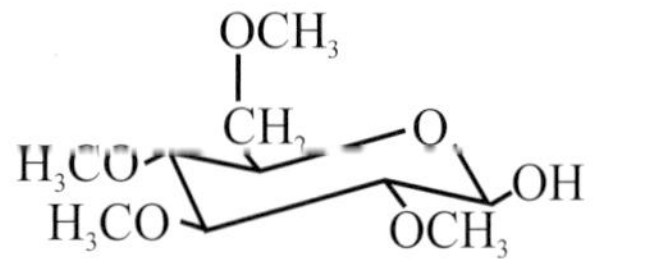

**2.** Benzoyl chloride reacts with ammonia to form benzamide. Which of the following molecules is the correct structure for benzamide?

**A.**

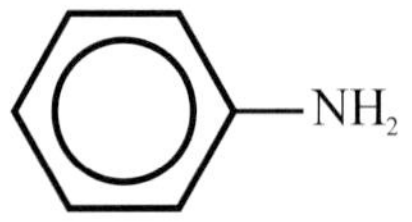

**C.**

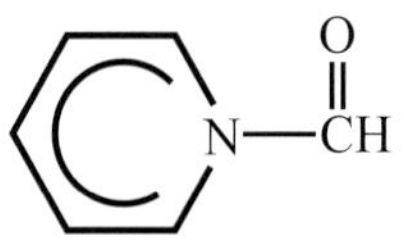

**B.**

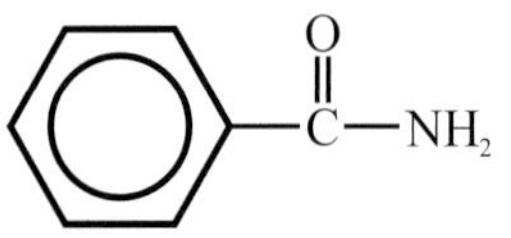

**D.**

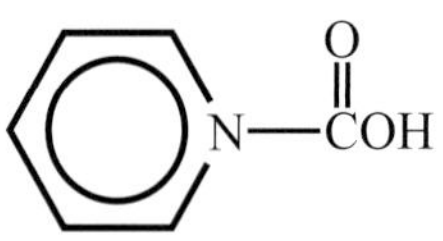

**3.** Of the bonds listed in the table below, the most stable bond is between:

| **Bond** | **Energy** |
|---|---|
| $C_2H_5 - Cl$ | 339 |
| $C_2H_5 - CH_3$ | 356 |
| $H_2C = CH - Cl$ | 352 |
| $H_2C = CH - CH_3$ | 385 |
| $C_6H_5 - Cl$ | 360 |
| $C_6H_5 - CH_3$ | 389 |

*bond energies given in kJ/mol

**A.** a saturated alkyl group and a halogen.
**B.** a saturated alkyl group and a methyl group.
**C.** an unsaturated alkyl group and a halogen.
**D.** an unsaturated alkyl group and a methyl group.

**4.** An α-hydroxy acid is heated to form the compound shown below. What functional group is created in this reaction?

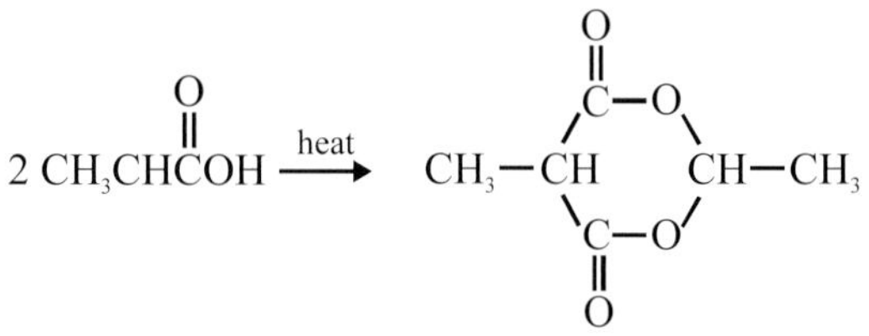

**A.** ether
**B.** aldehyde
**C.** ester
**D.** ketone

**5.** How many amide groups are there in the molecule of guanosine shown below?

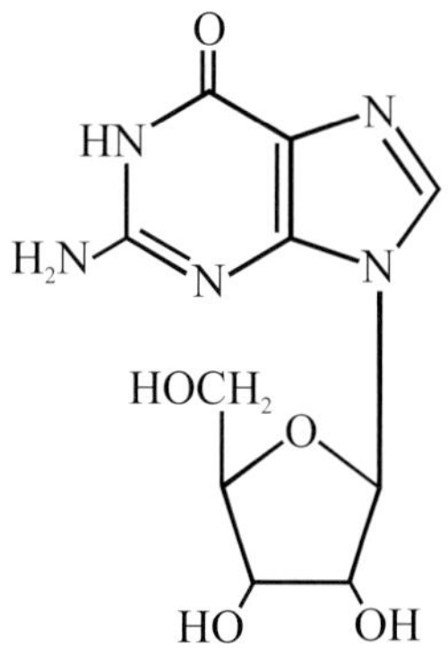

**A.** 0
**B.** 1
**C.** 3
**D.** 5



**GO ON TO THE NEXT PAGE.**

**6.** Just as ammonia, $NH_3$, is a weak Lewis base, there is a large group of nitrogen-containing organic compounds that behave like weak bases and are known as:

A. amides
B. amines
C. ethanol alcohols
D. ethers

**7.** Which of the following functional groups are found in phenylalanine?

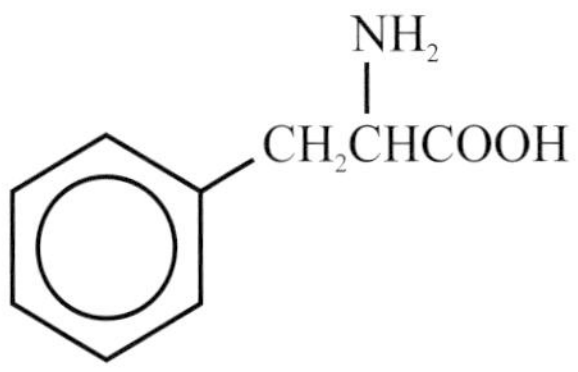

$$NH_2$$
$$CH_2CHCOOH$$

Phenylalanine

A. alkyl, double bond and aromatic ring
B. amine, carboxylic acid and aromatic ring
C. double bond, amide, and alcohol
D. aromatic ring, halide and ketone

**8.** Which of the following is the IUPAC name for this non-polar alkane?

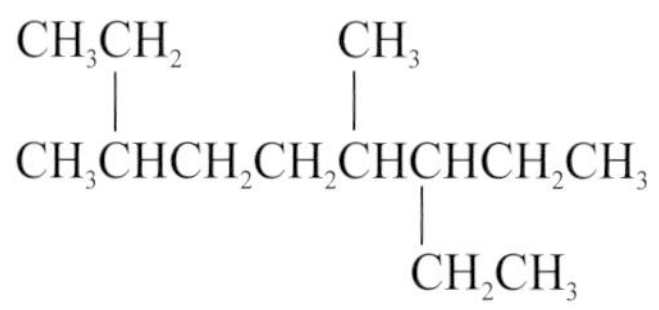

$$CH_3CH_2 \qquad CH_3$$
$$CH_3CHCH_2CH_2CHCHCH_2CH_3$$
$$CH_2CH_3$$

A. 3-Ethyl-4-methylheptane
B. 3-Ethyl-4, 7-dimethylnonane
C. 3-Methyl-7-ethyldecane
D. 3,4-Diethyl-5, 7-dimethylnonane

The paper is held to the comb by electrostatic forces.

You should know that it takes two electrons to form a bond. When the force between two objects is attractive and decreases with distance, the lowest potential energy level for those objects is when they are the closest to each other. Electrons are at their lowest energy level when they form a bond because they have minimized their distance from both nuclei.

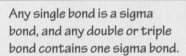

Any single bond is a sigma bond, and any double or triple bond contains one sigma bond.

Double and triple bonds are made by adding π-bonds to a sigma bond. Each additional bond shortens the distance between the bonding atoms.

## 1.6 Bonding

MCAT organic chemistry is about tracking electrons through reactions of carbon compounds. If we can keep track of the electrons we can understand the reactions and we can master MCAT organic chemistry.

Electrons are negatively charged. They are attracted to positively charged nuclei. It is the **electrostatic force** between the electrons and the nuclei that creates all molecular bonds. Both nuclei tug on both electrons, and the result is a bond between the two nuclei.

Electrons are transitory passengers on their respective nuclei. They are in constant search of ways to unload some of their energy and will do so whenever possible. They are at their lowest energy state when they are nearest to a positive charge and farthest from a negative charge. Because negative charge in proximity to electrons raises their energy level, electrons will share an orbital with, at most, only one other electron. The only thing which prevents an electron from releasing all its energy and crashing into the positively charged nucleus is the quantization of energy. The electron must give up a minimum quantum of energy. This minimum amount is greater than the amount that would be released if the electron collided with the nucleus.

A bond is formed when a pair of electrons can lower their energy level by positioning themselves between two nuclei in such a way as to take advantage of the positive charge of both nuclei.

Two electrons are required to form a bond. Each of the bonded nuclei can donate a single electron to the bond, or, in a **coordinate covalent bond**, one nucleus can donate both electrons.

## 1.7 σ and π Bonds

A **σ-bond** (sigma-bond) forms when the bonding pair of electrons are *localized* directly between the two bonding atoms. Since the electrons in a σ-bond are as close as possible to the two sources of positive charge (the two nuclei), a σ-bond has the lowest energy and is the most stable form of covalent bond. Thus σ-bonds are strong. A σ-bond is always the first type of covalent bond to be formed between any two atoms; a single bond must be a σ-bond.

If additional bonds form between two σ-bonded atoms, the new bonds are called **π-bonds**. Because the σ-bond leaves no room for other electron orbitals directly between the atoms, the orbital of the first π-bond forms above and below the σ-bonding electrons. A double bond now exists between the two atoms. If still another π-bond is formed, the new orbital is formed on either side of the σ-bond. A triple bond now exists between the two atoms. Double and triple bonds are always made of one σ-bond and one or two π-bonds.

Although a π-bond is weaker than a σ-bond (less energy is required to break the bond), π-bonds are always added to an existing σ-bond, and thus strengthen the overall bond between the atoms. Since bond strength is inversely correlated to bond length, the additional π-bonds shorten the overall bond. The bond energy of a double bond is greater than that of a single bond. Bond energy can be thought of as the energy necessary to break a bond.

The electrons in a π-bond are further from the nuclei than the electrons of a σ-bond, and therefore at a higher energy level, less stable, and form a weaker bond. This is important because less stability means π-bonds are more reactive. Third row elements form weaker π-bonds than second row elements. Double and triple bonds are rare for all atoms except carbon, nitrogen, oxygen, and sulfur.

π-bonds are more reactive than sigma bonds. Carbon, nitrogen, oxygen and sulfur are the only atoms that commonly form π-bonds. Phosphorous forms π-bonds with oxygen in nucleotide phosphates such as ATP.

## 1.8 Hybridization

If we examine the electrons of a lone carbon atom in its ground state we would see that its four valence electrons are in their expected atomic orbitals, two in the orbital of the s subshell and two in orbitals of the *p* subshell. The *p* electrons are at a higher energy state than the s electrons.

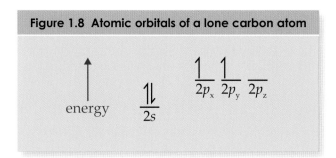

**Figure 1.8 Atomic orbitals of a lone carbon atom**

However, if we examine a carbon with four σ-bonds, we find that the four bonds are typically indistinguishable. Since the bonds are indistinguishable, the orbitals which form them must be equivalent. In order to form four σ-bonds, the electrons form four new orbitals. The new orbitals are hybrids of the old *s* and *p* orbitals and are equivalent to each other in shape and energy.

**Figure 1.9 Atomic orbitals of a carbon atom with four σ-bonds**

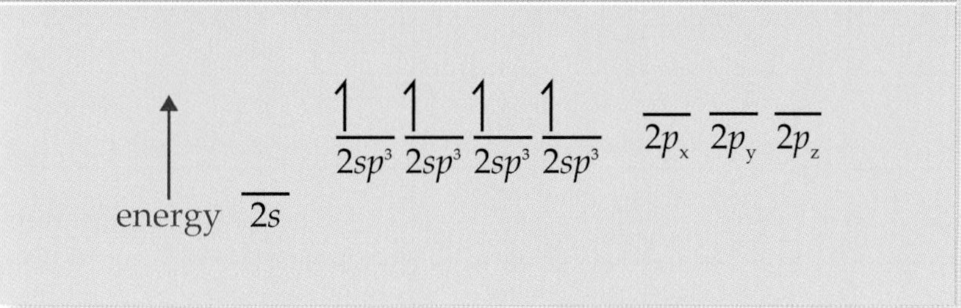

When one of these **hybrid orbitals** overlaps an orbital of another atom, a σ-bond is formed in the area where the orbitals coincide. π-bonds are formed by the overlap of pure *p* orbitals.

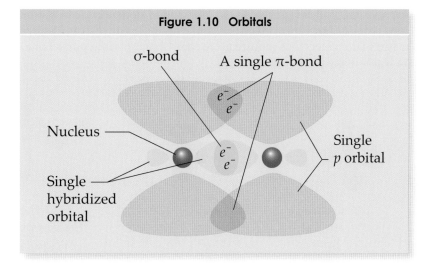

**Figure 1.10 Orbitals**

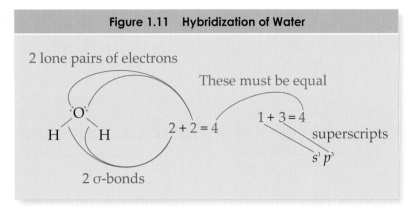

**Figure 1.11   Hybridization of Water**

2 lone pairs of electrons

These must be equal

2 + 2 = 4

1 + 3 = 4

superscripts

$s^1 p^3$

2 σ-bonds

There are several types of hybrid orbitals: $sp$, $sp^2$, $sp^3$, $dsp^3$, $d^2sp^3$, etc. In order to figure out the type of hybrid orbital formed by an atom on the MCAT, simply count the number of sigma bonds and lone pairs of electrons on that atom. Match this number to the sum of the superscripts in a hybrid name (letters without superscripts are assumed to have the superscript '1'). Remember, there are one orbital in the $s$ subshell, which must be formed first, three orbitals in the $p$ subshell, which must be formed next, and five orbitals in the $d$ subshell, to be formed only after the $s$ and $p$ orbitals are formed. For example, water makes two sigma bonds and has two lone pairs of electrons. Thus the sum of the superscripts in the name of the hybrid must add up to four. The oxygen in water must be $sp^3$ hybridized.

> When molecules are formed, $s$ and $p$ atomic orbitals hybridize to form new shapes and energy levels.

A hybrid orbital resembles in shape and energy the $s$ and $p$ orbitals from which it is formed to the same extent that $s$ or $p$ orbitals are used to form it. This extent is referred to as **character**. The superscripts indicate the character as follows: an $sp^2$ orbital is formed from one $s$ and two $p$ orbitals and thus has 33.3% $s$ character and 66.7% $p$ character; an $sp$ orbital is formed from one $s$ and one $p$ orbital and has a 50% $s$ character and 50% $p$ character; and so on. The more $s$ character a bond has, the more stable, the stronger, and the shorter it becomes.

The electrons in an orbital seek to minimize their energy by moving as far away from other electron pairs as possible, thus lessening repulsive forces. This leads to specific bond angles and molecular shape for different numbers and combinations of σ-bonds and lone pair electrons.

**Table 1.2   Hybridization and Molecular Shape**

| Hybridization | Bond angles | Shape | Example |
|---|---|---|---|
| $sp$ | 180° | Linear | Ethyne $C_2H_2$ |
| $sp^2$ | 120° | Trigonal planar | The carboxylic acid part of acetic acid $CH_3COOH$ |
| $sp^3$ | 109.5° | Tetrahedral, Pyramidal, or Bent | Methane $CH_4$, Ammonia $NH_3$, Water $H_2O$ |
| $sp^3d$ | 90°, 120° | Trigonal-bipyramidal, seesaw, t-shaped or linear | Phosphorus pentachloride |
| $sp^3d^2$ | 90°, 90° | Octahedral, square pyramidal, or square planar | Sulfur hexaflouride |

Where more than one possible shape exists, the shape depends upon the number and position of lone pairs. Lone pairs, π electrons, and ring strain can distort the predicted bond angles. Lone pairs and π electrons require more room than bonding pairs. For example, the lone pairs on water make the bond angle 104.5°.

Linear

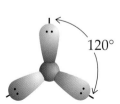

Trigonal planar, or Bent

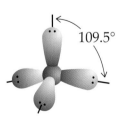

Tetrahedral, Pyramidal or Bent

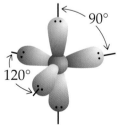

Trigonal-bipyramidal, Seesaw, T-shaped, or Linear

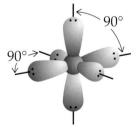

Octhedral, Square pyramidal, or Square planar

## 1.9 Electron Delocalization

Sometimes bonding electrons are spread out over three or more atoms. These electrons are called *delocalized electrons*. For MCAT purposes delocalized electrons only result from π-bonds. Molecules containing delocalized electrons can be represented by a combination of two or more Lewis structures called **resonance structures**. The weighted average of these Lewis structures most accurately represents the real molecule. The real molecule must be at a lower energy than any single Lewis structure representing it since otherwise it would simply retain that structure. The difference between the energy of the real molecule and the energy of the most stable Lewis structure is called the *resonance energy*. Remember, the real molecule does not alternate between these structures but is a stable weighted average of all contributing structures.

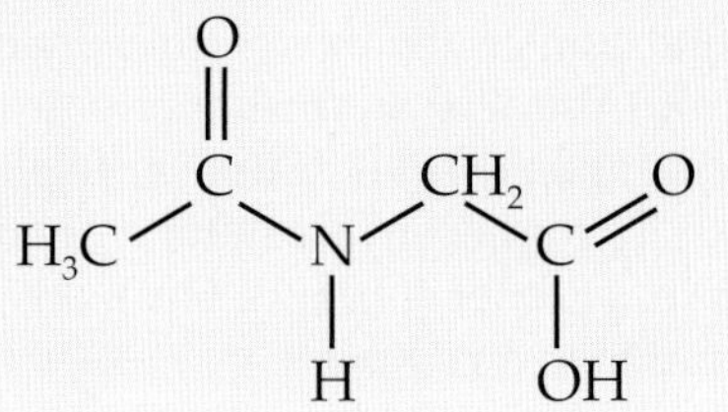

> Electron delocalization results from the shifting of π bonds

**Figure 1.12   Benzene Resonance Structures and their Weighted Averages**

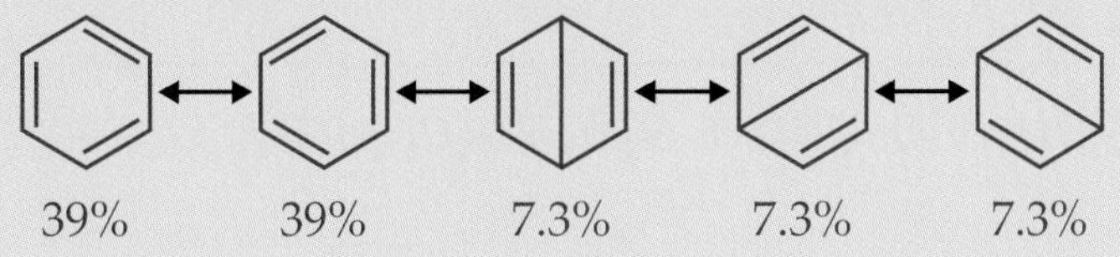

39%       39%       7.3%       7.3%       7.3%

The following are **four rules for writing resonance structures**:

**For all resonance structures:**

- **Atoms must not be moved.** Move electrons, not atoms.
- **Number of unpaired electrons must remain constant.**
- **Resonance atoms must lie in the same plane.**
- **Only proper Lewis structures allowed.**

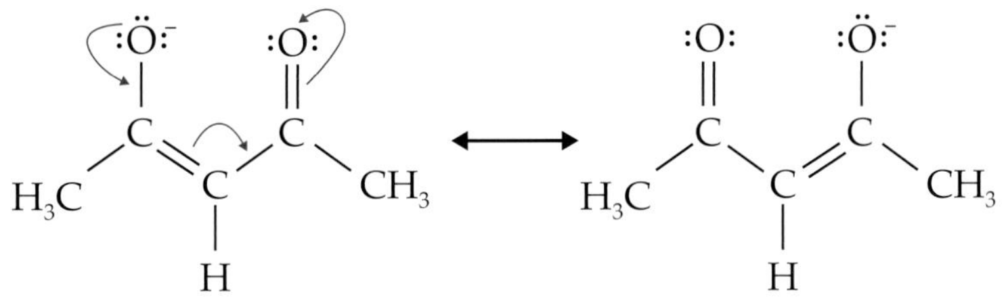

**Figure 1.13   Resonance Structures**

The contribution made to the actual molecule by any given structure is roughly proportional to that structure's stability; the most stable structures make the greatest contribution and equivalent structures make equal contributions. In general, the more covalent the bonds, the more stable the structure. Separation of charges within a molecule decreases stability.

For MCAT purposes, two conditions must exist for resonance to occur: 1) a species must contain an atom either with a $p$ orbital or an unshared pair of electrons; 2) that atom must be single bonded to an atom that possesses a double or triple bond. Such species are called *conjugated unsaturated systems*. The adjacent $p$ orbital in a conjugated system may contain zero, one, or two electrons (as in another $\pi$-bond). The $p$ orbital allows the adjacent $\pi$-bond to extend and encompass more than two nuclei.

The above two conditions are required but not always sufficient for resonance. Ring structures must also satisfy *Huckel's rule*, which states: planar monocyclic rings with $4n + 2$ $\pi$-electrons (where $n$ is any integer, including zero) should be **aromatic** (display resonance).

### Thought Provoker

Draw at least three resonance forms of the following molecule:

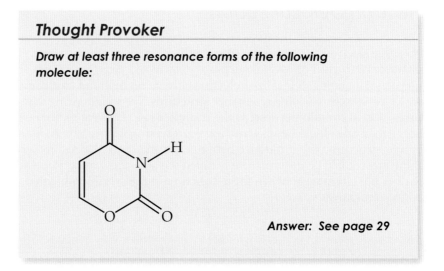

Answer: See page 29

## 1.10 Dipole Moments and Intermolecular Bonding

A **dipole moment** occurs when the center of positive charge on a molecule or bond does not coincide with the center of negative charge. A dipole moment can occur in a bond or a molecule. The concept of center of charge is analogous to the concept of the center of mass. All the positive charge in a molecule comes from the protons of the nuclei. All the negative charge comes from the electrons. In chemistry the dipole moment is represented by an arrow pointing from the center of positive charge to the center of negative charge. The arrow is crossed at the center of positive charge. The dipole moment is measured in units of the *debye*, D, and given by the equation:

$$\mu = qd$$

where $q$ is the magnitude of charge of either end of the dipole, and $d$ is the distance between the centers of charge.

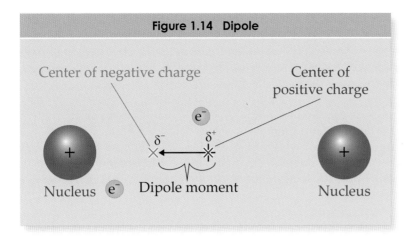

**Figure 1.14 Dipole**

Center of negative charge

Center of positive charge

Nucleus    Dipole moment    Nucleus

A molecule or bond which has a dipole moment is referred to as polar; a molecule or bond without a dipole moment is referred to as nonpolar.

A polar bond results from the difference in electronegativity of its atoms. Atoms with greater electronegativities attract the electrons in a bond more strongly, pulling the center of negative charge toward themselves, and thus creating a dipole moment.

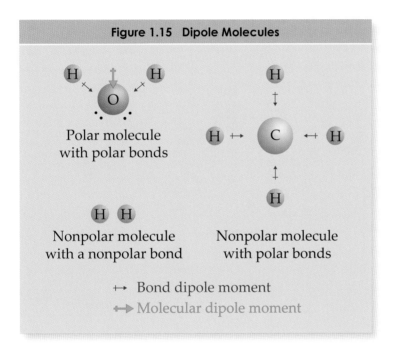

**Figure 1.15 Dipole Molecules**

Polar molecule with polar bonds

Nonpolar molecule with a nonpolar bond

Nonpolar molecule with polar bonds

↔ Bond dipole moment
↔ Molecular dipole moment

A molecule with polar bonds may or may not have a net dipole moment. Since a dipole moment is a vector, it is possible for the sum of the dipole moments in the polar bonds of a molecule to equal zero, leaving the molecule without a dipole moment.

A dipole moment can be momentarily induced in an otherwise nonpolar molecule or bond by a polar molecule, ion, or electric field. The polar molecule or ion creates an electric field, which pushes the electrons and nuclei in opposite directions, separating the centers of positive and negative charge. Such dipole moments are called **induced dipoles**. Induced dipoles are common in nature and are generally weaker than permanent dipoles.

An **instantaneous dipole moment** can exist in an otherwise nonpolar molecule. Instantaneous dipoles arise because the electrons in a bond move about the orbital, and at any given moment may not be distributed exactly between the two bonding atoms even when the atoms are identical. Although instantaneous dipoles are generally very short lived and weaker than induced dipoles, they can act to induce a dipole in a neighboring atom.

**Intermolecular attractions** (attractions between separate molecules) occur solely due to dipole moments. The partial negatively charged side of one molecule is attracted to the partial positively charged side of another molecule. Dipole forces are much weaker than covalent forces; generally about 1% as strong. The attraction between two molecules is roughly proportional to their dipole moments.

When hydrogen is attached to a highly electronegative atom, such as nitrogen, oxygen, or fluorine, a large dipole moment is formed leaving hydrogen with a strong partial positive charge. When the hydrogen approaches a nitrogen, oxygen, or fluorine on another molecule, the intermolecular bond formed is called a **hydrogen bond**. This is the strongest type of dipole-dipole interaction. It is hydrogen bonding that is responsible for the high boiling point of water.

The weakest dipole-dipole force is between two instantaneous dipoles. These dipole-dipole bonds are called **London Dispersion Forces**. Although London Dispersion Forces are very weak, they are responsible for the phase changes of nonpolar molecules. All molecules exhibit London Dispersions Forces, even when they are capable of stronger intermolecular interactions.

I can't talk right now. I'm bonding with my FON.

Fluorine

Oxygen

Nitrogen

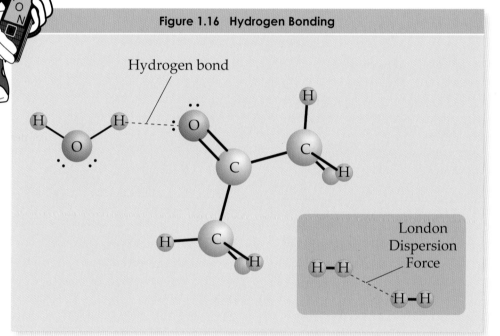

**Figure 1.16 Hydrogen Bonding**

Hydrogen bond

London Dispersion Force

---

For this section, you should understand what hybridization is, and be able to identify $sp$, $sp^2$, and $sp^3$ orbitals. Also, you must be able to recognize resonance structures. Learn the rules for resonance. Most of the bonding stuff is review from inorganic chemistry, but it is important. Understand that intermolecular and intramolecular forces are electrostatic. Make the connection between energy level of electrons and position relative to positive charge. In other words, as electrons move closer to positive charge they lower their energy level. Remember this by realizing that it would require energy input to separate opposite charges. Nature likes to spread the energy around. A system with low energy is a stable system. Thus, a bond is formed when electron energy level is the lowest.

Just a reminder: bond energy is closely related to bond dissociation energy and in many cases, it is the same thing. Bond energy is the average energy required to break a bond. Thus, high bond energy indicates a bond with electrons at very low energy, and is a stable bond. Recall from inorganic chemistry that this is because the high energy bond is really a high negative energy bond.

**9.** Pyrrole, shown below, exhibits resonance stabilization.

pyrrole

Which of the following is a valid resonance structure of pyrrole?

**A.**  **C.**

**B.**  **D.**

**10.** In the Wittig reaction a phosphorous ylide reacts with a ketone to yield an alkene.

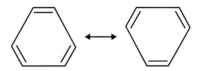

betaine
intermediate

What is the hybridization of carbon 2 in the ketone, the betaine, and the alkene, respectively?

**A.** $sp^3$; $sp^2$; $sp^3$
**B.** $sp^2$; $sp^2$; $sp^3$
**C.** $sp^2$; $sp^3$; $sp^2$
**D.** $sp^3$; $sp^4$; $sp^3$

**11.** Benzene exhibits resonance. The carbon-carbon bonds of benzene are:

**A.** shorter and stronger than the double bond of an alkene.
**B.** longer and weaker than the double bond of an alkene.
**C.** longer and stronger than the carbon-carbon bond of an alkane.
**D.** longer and weaker than the carbon-carbon bond of an alkane.

**12.** The electron pair in the π-bond of an alkene have:

**A.** 33% *p* character and are at a lower energy level than the electron pair in the σ-bond.
**B.** 50% *p* character and are at a higher energy level than the electron pair in the σ-bond.
**C.** 100% *p* character and are at a lower energy level than the electron pair in the σ-bond.
**D.** 100% *p* character and are at a higher energy level than the electron pair in the σ-bond.

**13.** The structures below are 1,3,5-cyclohexatriene. Although double bonds are shorter than single bonds, the structures below could not qualify as proper resonance contributors for benzene because:

**A.** 1,3,5-cyclohexatriene is a higher energy molecule than benzene.
**B.** benzene is more stable than 1,3,5-cyclohexatriene.
**C.** benzene actually resonates between these two structures.
**D.** the positions of the atoms are different in the two structures.

**14.** When dealing with organic compound hybridization, which angle is associated with the strongest bond formation?

**A.** 109°
**B.** 120°
**C.** 180°
**D.** 360°

**15.** All of the following compounds have a dipole moment EXCEPT:

**A.** $CH_3Cl$
**B.** $H_2O$
**C.** Benzene
**D.** $H_2C=N=N$

**16.** Natural gas consists of chiefly methane, but also contains ethane, propane, butane and isobutene. Which of the following compounds is NOT found in natural gas?

**A.** sec-butane
**B.** 2-methylbutane
**C.** olefin ($CH_2CH_2$)
**D.** cyclopropane

## 1.11 Stereochemistry

There is relatively little to know about stereochemistry on the MCAT. The concepts are not difficult to understand and can be easily memorized. The difficult aspect of stereochemistry on the MCAT is mentally manipulating three-dimensional molecular structures. The only way to become better at manipulating molecular structures is to practice. It is best to acquire a molecular model set and actually build some of the replica molecules with your own hands.

## 1.12 Isomerism

Isomers are unique molecules with the same molecular formula. "Iso" is a Greek prefix meaning "the same" or "equal". A lone molecule cannot be an isomer by itself. It must be an isomer to another molecule. Two molecules are isomers if they have the same molecular formula but are different compounds.

**Conformational isomers** or **conformers** are not true isomers. Conformers are different spatial orientations of the same molecule. At room temperature, atoms rotate rapidly about their σ-bonds resulting in a mix of conformers at any given moment. Because of the difference in energy levels between eclipsed and staggered conformers, staggered conformers can sometimes be isolated at low temperatures. The difference in energy levels is due in large part to steric strain. The simplest way to distinguish between conformers is with **Newman projections**. Figure 1.17 shows the Newman projections of the conformers of butane and their relative energy levels.

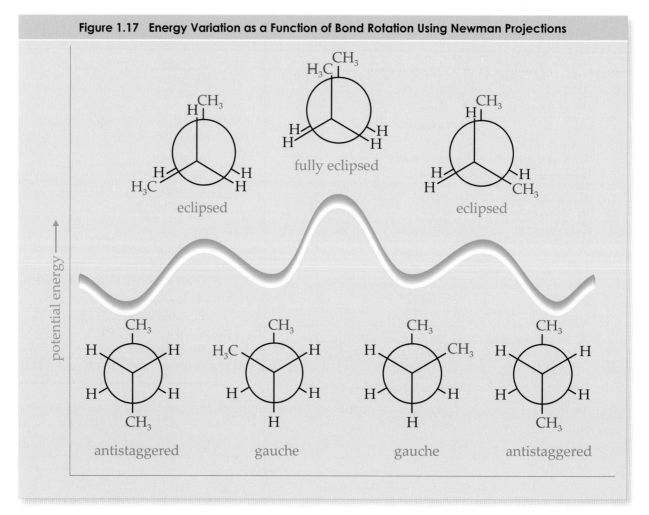

**Figure 1.17 Energy Variation as a Function of Bond Rotation Using Newman Projections**

The simplest form of isomer is a **structural isomer**. Structural isomers have the same molecular formula but different bond-to-bond connectivity. If two unique molecules have the same molecular formula and the same bond-to-bond connectivity, they are stereoisomers. In order to distinguish stereoisomers we must first understand chirality.

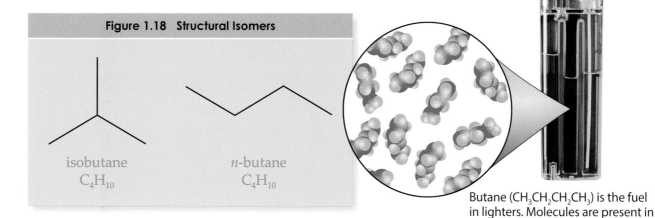

**Figure 1.18   Structural Isomers**

isobutane
$C_4H_{10}$

*n*-butane
$C_4H_{10}$

Butane ($CH_3CH_2CH_2CH_3$) is the fuel in lighters. Molecules are present in both the liquid and gaseous states inside the lighter.

## 1.13 *Chirality*

Try to describe a left hand by its physical characteristics alone, and distinguish it from a right hand without using the words "right" or "left". It can't be done. The only physical difference between a right hand and a left hand is their "handedness". Yet, the physical difference is very important. Something designed to be used with the right hand is very difficult to use with the left hand. Notice that the mirror image of a right hand is a left hand. In chemistry, this "handedness" is called chirality. The Greek word "chiros" means hand.

Some molecules also have "handedness". Such molecules are called **chiral molecules**. Chiral molecules differ from their reflections, while achiral molecules are exactly the same as their reflections.

Chirality has important ramifications in biology. Many nutrients are chiral, and the human body might not assimilate the mirror image of such a nutrient.

Chirality on the MCAT will mainly be concerned with carbon. Any carbon is chiral when it is bonded to **four different substituents**.

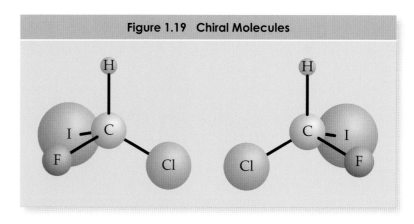

**Figure 1.19   Chiral Molecules**

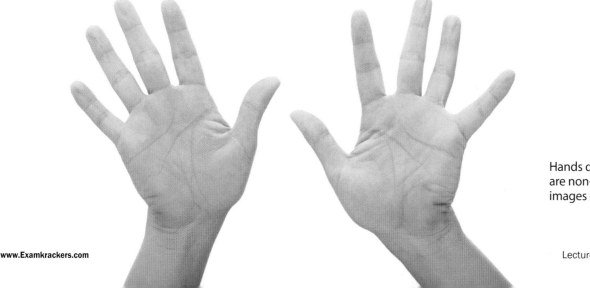

Hands display chirality. They are non-superimposable mirror images of each other.

## 1.14 Absolute Configuration

There is only one way to physically describe the orientation of atoms about a chiral center such as a chiral carbon. That is by **absolute configuration**. Since there are two possible configurations, the molecule and its mirror image, absolute configuration is given as **R** (*rectus*: the Latin word for *right*) or **S** (*sinister*: the Latin word for *left*). In order to determine the configuration of a given molecule, the atoms attached to the chiral center are numbered from highest to lowest *priority*. The largest atomic weights are given the highest priority. If two of the atoms are the same element, then their substituents are sequentially compared in order of decreasing priority until one of the substituents is found to have a greater priority than the corresponding substituent on the other atom. Substituents on double and triple bonds are counted two and three times respectively. In the molecule shown in Figure 1.20, the carbon marked 2 has a higher priority than the carbon marked 3 because bromine has a higher priority than oxygen. The carbon marked 3 is considered to have two oxygens for priority purposes. Once priorities have been assigned, the chiral molecule is rotated about one of the σ-bonds as shown in Figure 1.21 so that the lowest priority group faces away. In this orientation a circle is drawn in the direction from highest to lowest priority for the remaining three substituents. The circle will point clockwise or counterclockwise. A clockwise circle indicates an absolute configuration of R and a counterclockwise circle indicates an absolute configuration of S. The mirror image of a chiral molecule always has the opposite absolute configuration.

**Figure 1.20  Atom Priority**

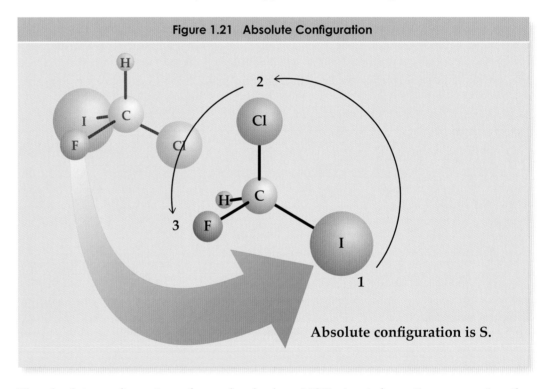

**Figure 1.21  Absolute Configuration**

Absolute configuration is S.

The absolute configuration of a molecule does NOT give information concerning the direction in which a compound rotates plane-polarized light.

## 1.15 Relative Configuration

**Relative configuration** is not related to absolute configuration. Two molecules have the same relative configuration about a carbon if they differ by only one substituent and the other substituents are oriented identically about the carbon. In an $S_N2$ reaction, it is the relative configuration that is inverted.

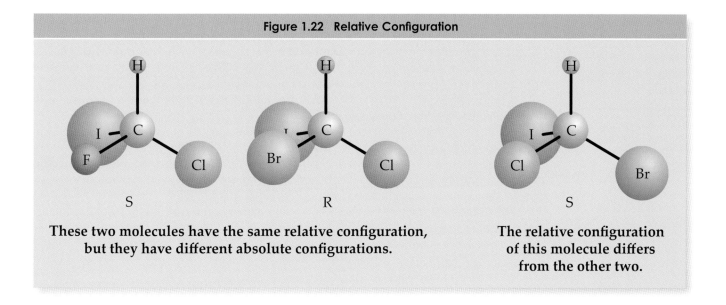

**Figure 1.22  Relative Configuration**

S       R       S

**These two molecules have the same relative configuration, but they have different absolute configurations.**

**The relative configuration of this molecule differs from the other two.**

## 1.16  *Observed Rotation*

The direction and the degree to which a compound rotates plane-polarized light is given by its **observed rotation**.

Light is made up of electromagnetic waves. A single photon can be described by a changing electric field and its corresponding changing magnetic field, both fields being perpendicular to each other and to the direction of propagation. For simplicity, the magnetic field is often ignored and only the direction of the electric field is considered. A typical light source releases millions of photons whose fields are oriented in random directions. A **polarimeter** screens out photons with all but one orientation of electric field. The resulting light consists of photons with their electric fields oriented in the same direction. This light is called **plane-polarized light**.

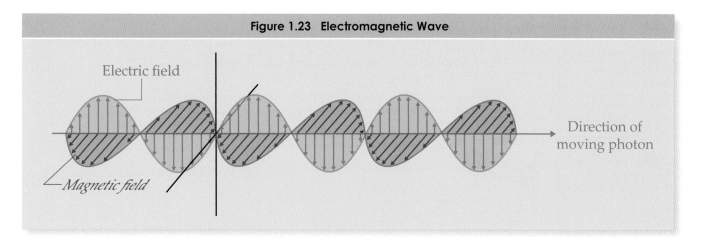

**Figure 1.23  Electromagnetic Wave**

Electric field

Magnetic field

Direction of moving photon

When a photon reflects off any molecule, the orientation of the electric field produced by that photon is rotated. The mirror image of that molecule will rotate the electric field to the same degree but in the opposite direction. In a typical compound where a photon is just as likely to collide with either mirror image, there are so many millions of molecules producing so many collisions that the photon is most likely to leave the compound with the same electric field orientation with which it entered the compound. No single molecular orientation is favored and so the net result is no rotation of the plane of the electric field. Such compounds are **optically inactive**. Optically inactive compounds may be compounds with no chiral centers or molecules with internal mirror planes (meso compounds).

If you understand observed rotation, you won't have any trouble with specific rotation should it come up in a passage on the MCAT.

Chiral molecules can be separated from their mirror images by chemical, and in rare cases physical, means. The result of such a separation is a compound containing molecules with no mirror image existing in the compound. When plane-polarized light is projected through such a chiral compound, the orientation of its electric field is rotated. Such a compound is **optically active**. If the compound rotates plane-polarized light clockwise it is designated with a '+' or '*d*' for *dextrotorary*. If it rotates plane-polarized light counterclockwise it is designated with a '−' or '*l*' for *levorotary* (Latin: *dexter*; right: *laevus*; left).

The direction and number of degrees that the electric field in plane-polarized light rotates when it passes through a compound is called the compound's observed rotation. **Specific rotation** is simply a standardized form of observed rotation that is arrived at through calculations using observed rotation and experimental parameters. For instance, the degree of rotation to which polarized light is rotated depends upon the length of the polarimeter, the concentration of the solution, the temperature, and the type of wavelength of light used. Specific rotation is equal to the observed rotation after these adjustments have been made.

## 1.17 Stereoisomers

Two molecules with the same molecular formula and the same bond-to-bond connectivity that are not the same compound are called **stereoisomers**. Unless they are geometric isomers, stereoisomers must each contain at least one chiral center in the same location. There are two types of stereoisomers: enantiomers and diastereomers.

## 1.18 Enantiomers

Enantiomers must have opposite absolute configurations at each and every chiral carbon.

**Enantiomers** have the same molecular formula, have the same bond-to-bond connectivity, are mirror images of each other, but are not the same molecule. Enantiomers must have opposite absolute configurations at each chiral carbon.

When placed separately into a polarimeter, enantiomers rotate plane-polarized light in opposite directions to an equal degree. For example, the specific rotation of (*R*)-2-Butanol is −13.52° while its enantiomer, (*S*)-2-Butanol, has a specific rotation of +13.52°.

Except for interactions with plane-polarized light and reactions with other chiral compounds, enantiomers have the same physical and chemical properties.

What's this? An-ant-in-a-mirror!

Enantiomers are mirror images of each other.

When enantiomers are mixed together in equal concentrations, the resulting mixture is called a **racemic mixture**. Since the mirror image of all orientations of each molecule exist in a racemic mixture with equal probability, racemic mixtures do not rotate plane-polarized light. Unequal concentrations of enantiomers rotate plane-polarized light. In unequal concentrations, the light is rotated in the same direction as a pure sample of the excess enantiomer would rotate it but only to a fraction of the degree, the same fraction that exists as excess enantiomer. The ratio of actual rotation to the rotation of pure sample is called *optical purity*; the ratio of pure enantiomer to racemic mixture is called *enantiomeric purity*. Optical purity equals enantiomeric purity for any mixture of enantiomers. The separation of enantiomers is called **resolution**.

Pictured to the side are molecular models of the *S*- (left) and *R*- (right) forms of the drug thalidomide. Thalidomide was used as a sedative for pregnant women during the 1950s, but it was found to cause deformities in fetuses. Further research discovered that only *S*-thalidomide caused the deformities. The *S*- and *R*- forms are enantiomers with a chiral center out the yellow atom.

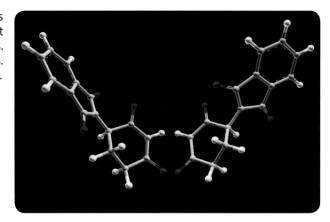

> For enantiomers, you must know that they have the same chemical and physical characteristics except for two cases:
>
> 1. interactions with other chiral compounds;
> 2. interactions with polarized light.

## 1.19  Diastereomers

**Diastereomers** have the same molecular formula, have the same bond-to-bond connectivity, are NOT mirror images to each other, and are NOT the same compound. One special type of diastereomer is called a **geometric isomer**. Geometric isomers exist due to hindered rotation around a double bond. Rotation may be hindered due to a ring structure or a double or triple bond. Since rotation is hindered, similar substituents on opposing carbons may exist on the same-side or opposite sides of the hindered bond. Molecules with same side substituents are called *cis*-**isomers**; those with opposite-side substituents are called *trans*-**isomers** (Latin: *cis*: on the same side; *trans*: on the other side).

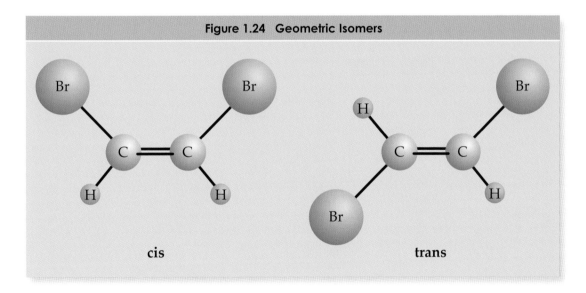

**Figure 1.24  Geometric Isomers**

cis                    trans

Geometric isomers have **different physical properties**. For the MCAT, it is important to know that *cis* molecules have a dipole moment while *trans* molecules do not. As a rule of thumb, the following predictions can be made concerning the melting and boiling points of geometric isomers: due to their dipole moment, *cis* molecules have stronger intermolecular forces leading to higher boiling points; due to their lower symmetry, however, *cis* molecules do not form crystals as readily, and thus have lower melting points.

The substituent groups in the *cis* position may crowd each other; a condition known as **steric hindrance**. Steric hindrance in *cis* molecules produces higher energy levels resulting in higher heats of combustion.

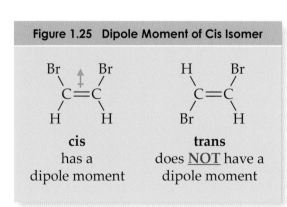

**Figure 1.25  Dipole Moment of Cis Isomer**

cis
has a
dipole moment

trans
does **NOT** have a
dipole moment

**Figure 1.26  Tri- and Tetra-substituted Diastereomers**

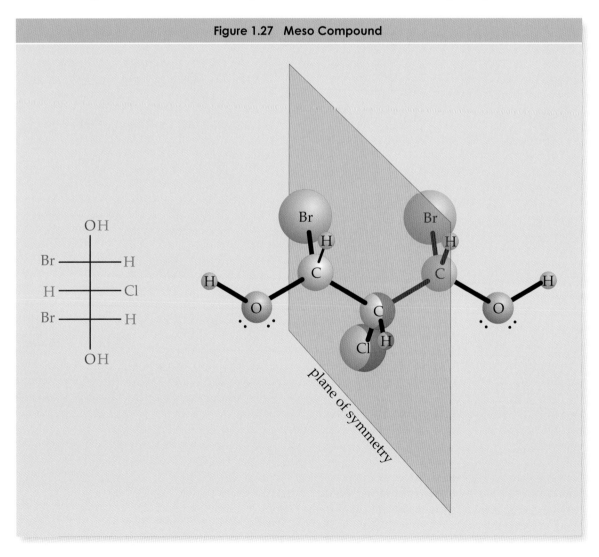

For tri and tetrasubstituted alkenes or ring structures, the terms *cis* and *trans* may be ambiguous or simply meaningless. The following system may be used to describe all geometric isomers unambiguously. First, the two substituents on each carbon are prioritized using atomic weight, similar to the system in absolute configuration. If the higher priority substituent for each carbon exists on the opposite sides, the molecule is labeled **E** for *entgegen*; if on the same side, then **Z** for *zusammen* (German: entgegen: opposite; zusammen: together).

Diastereomers have different physical properties (i.e. rotation of plane-polarized light, melting points, boiling points, solubilities, etc...). Their chemical properties also differ.

The maximum number of optically active isomers that a single compound can have is related to the number of its chiral centers by the following formula:

**maximum number of optically active isomers = $2^n$**

where $n$ is the number of chiral centers.

Two chiral centers in a single molecule may offset each other creating an optically inactive molecule. Such compounds are called **meso compounds**. Meso compounds have a plane of symmetry through their centers which divides them into two halves that are mirror images to each other. Meso compounds are achiral and therefore optically inactive.

**Figure 1.27  Meso Compound**

Diasteromers that differ at only one chiral carbon are called **epimers**. If a ring closure occurs at the epimeric carbon, two possible diastereomers may be formed. These new diastereomers are called **anomers**. The chiral carbon of an anomer is called the **anomeric carbon**. Anomers are distinguished by the orientation of their substituents. Glucose forms anomers. When the hydroxyl group on the anomeric carbon on glucose is oriented "down" with respect to its hydrogen, it is labeled $\alpha$; when it is oriented "up" with respect to its hydrogen, the anomer is $\beta$.

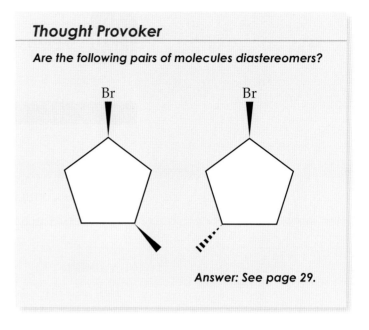

**Thought Provoker**

*Are the following pairs of molecules diastereomers?*

Answer: See page 29.

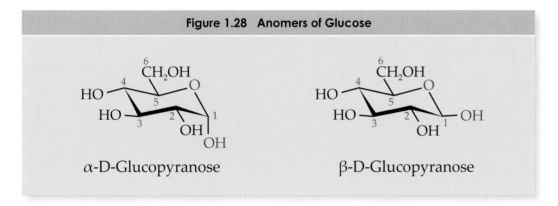

**Figure 1.28  Anomers of Glucose**

$\alpha$-D-Glucopyranose

$\beta$-D-Glucopyranose

Keeping track of all the different kinds of isomers can be confusing. Use the chart in Figure 1.29 to keep things straight.

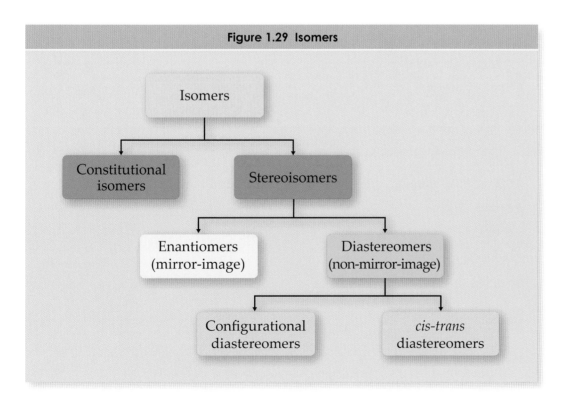

**Figure 1.29  Isomers**

Isomers

Constitutional isomers

Stereoisomers

Enantiomers (mirror-image)

Diastereomers (non-mirror-image)

Configurational diastereomers

*cis-trans* diastereomers

| Terms | |
|---|---|
| σ-Bond | Hydrogen Bond |
| π-Bond | Index of Deficiency |
| Absolute Configuration | Induced Dipoles |
| Anomeric Carbon | Instantaneous Dipole Moment |
| Anomers | Intermolecular Attractions |
| Aromatic | Isomers |
| Ball and Stick Models | Lewis Dot Structure |
| Bond-Line Formula | London Dispersion Forces |
| Character | Meso Compounds |
| Chiral Character | Newman Projection |
| *Cis*-isomers | Observed Rotation |
| Condensed Formula | Optically Active |
| Configuration | Optically Inactive |
| Conformational Isomers | Plane-Polarized Light |
| Conformers | Polarimeter |
| Coordinate Covalent Bond | Properties |
| Dash Formula | Racemic Mixture |
| Dash-Line-Wedge Formula | Relative Configuration |
| Deficiency | Resolution |
| Degree Of Unsaturation | Resonance Structures |
| Diastereomers | *sp* |
| Different Physical | $sp^2$ |
| Dipole Moment | $sp^3$ |
| Electrostatic Force | Specific Rotation |
| Enantiomers | Stereoisomers |
| Epimers | Steric Hindrance |
| Fischer Projection | Structural Isomer |
| Formal Charge | *Trans*-isomers |
| Formula | Valence |
| Geometric Isomer | |

## Thought Provoker Answers

**Answer from page 4:**

N (+), F (+), O (single bonded to carbon) (-), all other atoms have a formal charge of 0

**Answer from page 15:**

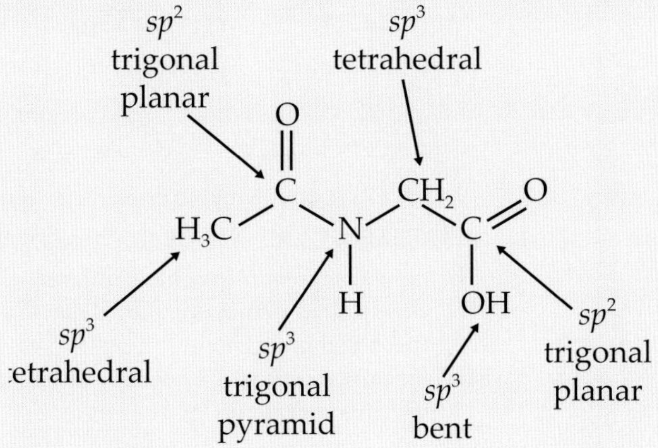

**Answer from page 16:**

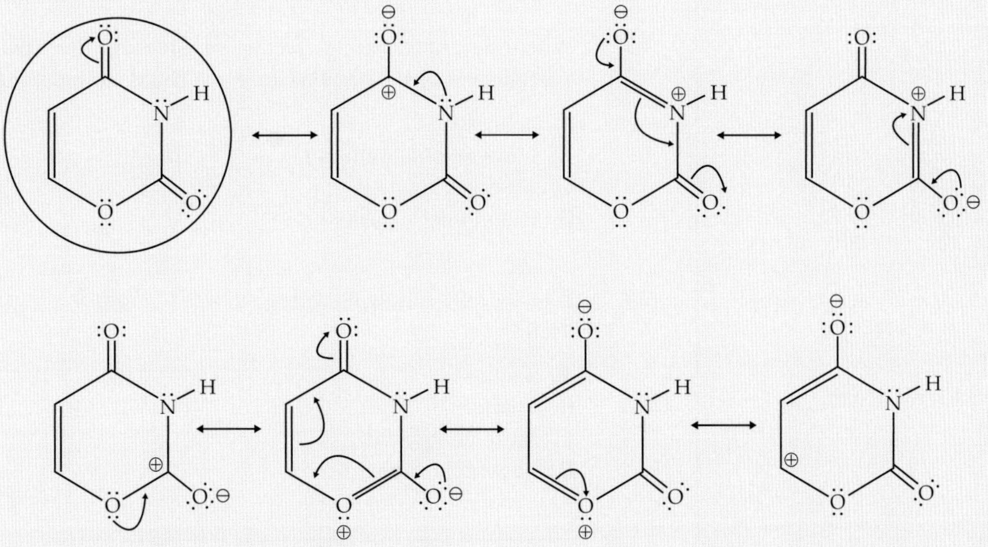

**Answer from page 27:**

These molecules are diastereomers. These molecules are not mirror images of one another, and they are non-superimposable, which can be seen by flipping one of the molecules 180 degrees, as shown below. The stereochemistry is the same in one place (the methyls) and is different in another place (the bromines).

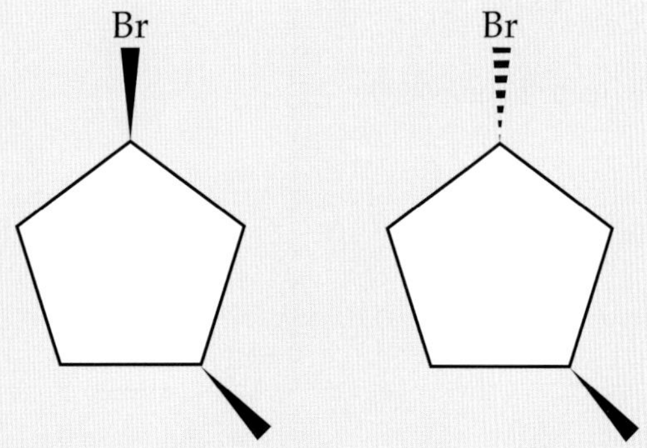

**17.** Which of the following compounds can exist as either a *cis* or *trans* isomer?

A. $CH_3CH_2CCl = CClH$

B. 2-methyl-2-butene

C.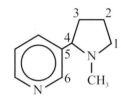

D.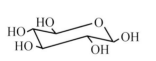

**18.** (−)-nicotine shown below is an alkaloid found in tobacco.

nicotine

At which of the following carbons does the structure of (+)-nicotine differ from (−)-nicotine?

A. carbons 1,4, and 6 only
B. carbons 4 and 5 only
C. carbon 4 only
D. carbon 5 only

**19.** All of the following compounds are optically active EXCEPT:

A.

C. $CH_3CHClCH_2OH$

B.

D.

**20.** Which one of the following properly named compounds could exist in enantiomeric form?

A. 3-chloro-1-propene
B. 3-chloro-1,4-dichlorocyclohexane
C. *trans*-1,4-dichlorocyclohexane
D. 4-chloro-1-cyclohexene

**21.** Which of the following compounds is not optically active?

A.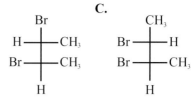

C.

B.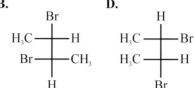

D.

**22.** Which of the following characteristics correctly describe differences between structural (constitutional) isomers?

I. these compounds may have different carbon skeletons
II. chemical properties are altered due to differences in functional groups
III. functional groups may occupy different positions on the carbon skeleton

A. I only
B. II and III only
C. I and III only
D. I, II and III

**23.** When described using rectus or sinister, the spatial arrangement of substituents around a chiral atom is called:

A. achirality
B. absolute configuration
C. observed rotation
D. enantiomeric purity

**24.** Which of the following stereoisomers is a mirror image of itself?

A. anomer
B. epimer
C. meso compound
D. geometric isomer

# HYDROCARBONS, ALCOHOLS, AND SUBSTITUTIONS

## 2.1   Alkanes

Methane and compounds whose major functional group contains only carbon-carbon single bonds are **alkanes**. Carbons in alkanes are referred to as **primary**, **secondary**, **tertiary**, or **quaternary** depending upon how many carbons are bonded to them (Figure 2.1). Primary carbons have no attached carbons, secondary have two, tertiary have three, and quaternary have four.

Alkanes can branch. The carbons attaching an alkyl branch to a main alkane chain is called either **methyl**, **primary**, **secondary**, or **tertiary** depending upon the number of other alkyl groups attached to it (Figure 2.2). The difference is a matter of perspective.

### Figure 2.1   Carbon Types I

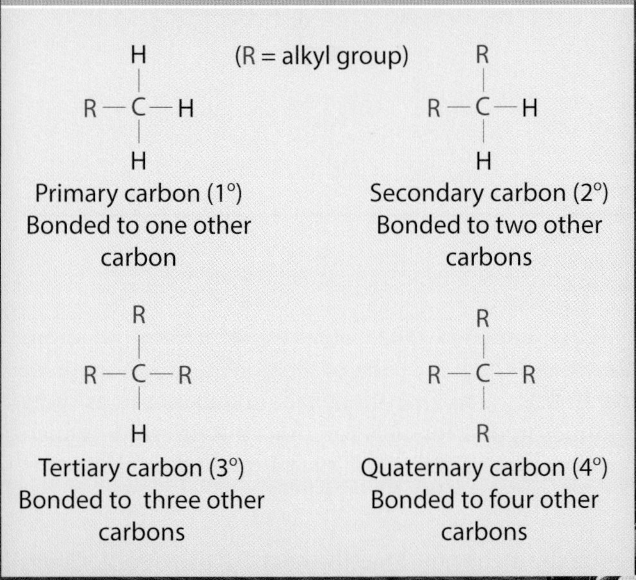

(R = alkyl group)

Primary carbon (1°)
Bonded to one other carbon

Secondary carbon (2°)
Bonded to two other carbons

Tertiary carbon (3°)
Bonded to three other carbons

Quaternary carbon (4°)
Bonded to four other carbons

Crude oil is a mixture of hydrocarbons.

### Figure 2.2   Carbon Types II

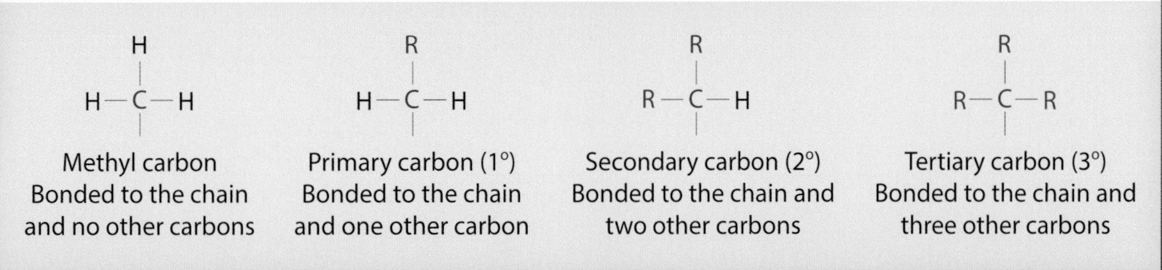

Methyl carbon
Bonded to the chain and no other carbons

Primary carbon (1°)
Bonded to the chain and one other carbon

Secondary carbon (2°)
Bonded to the chain and two other carbons

Tertiary carbon (3°)
Bonded to the chain and three other carbons

## 2.2 Physical Properties

The **physical properties** of alkanes follow certain general trends. Boiling point is governed by intermolecular forces. As carbons are added in a single chain and molecular weight increases, the intermolecular forces increase and, thus, the boiling point of the alkane increases. Branching, however, significantly lowers the boiling point. Melting points of unbranched alkanes also tend to increase with increasing molecular weight, though not as smoothly. This is because intermolecular forces within a crystal depend upon shape as well as size.

Alkanes have the lowest density of all groups of organic compounds. Density increases with molecular weight.

Alkanes are almost totally insoluble in water. They are soluble in benzene, carbon tetrachloride, chloroform, and other hydrocarbons. If an alkane contains a polar functional group, the polarity of the entire molecule, and thus its solubility, decreases as the carbon chain is lengthened.

There is a lot to memorize with physical properties of alkanes. The most important things to remember are that molecular weight increases boiling point and melting point, and branching decreases boiling point but increases melting point.

Alkanes of four carbons or less are gases at room temperature.

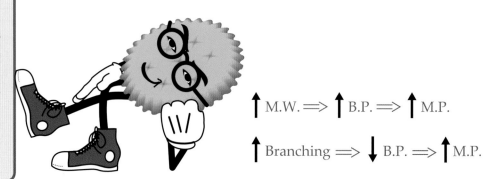

$$\uparrow \text{M.W.} \Longrightarrow \uparrow \text{B.P.} \Longrightarrow \uparrow \text{M.P.}$$

$$\uparrow \text{Branching} \Longrightarrow \downarrow \text{B.P.} \Longrightarrow \uparrow \text{M.P.}$$

## 2.3 Cycloalkanes

Cycloalkanes are alkane rings. For the MCAT, remember that some ring structures put strain on the carbon-carbon bonds because they bend them away from the normal 109.5° angle of the $sp^3$ carbon and cause crowding. **Ring strain** is zero for cyclohexane and increases as rings become larger or smaller. The trend continues up to a nine-carbon ring structure, after which ring strain decreases to zero as more carbons are added to the ring. Less ring strain means lower energy and more stability.

Cyclohexane exists as three conformers: the **chair**; the *twist*; and the **boat**. All three conformers exist at room temperature; however, the chair predominates almost completely because it is at the lowest energy. Although the boat configuration is often discussed, the twist-boat is usually intended.

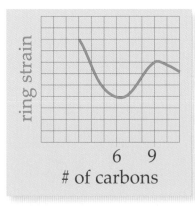

ring strain

6    9

# of carbons

**Figure 2.3 Relative Energy of Different Conformations of Cyclohexane**

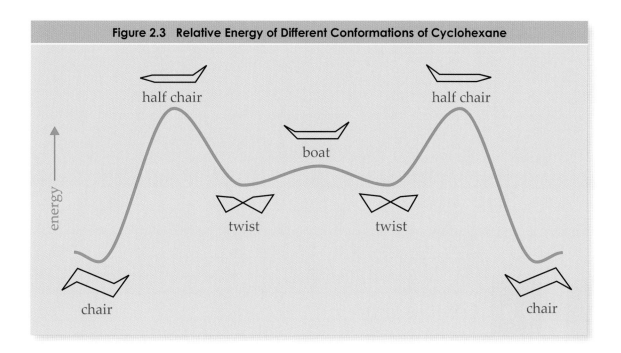

Each carbon on cyclohexane has two hydrogens. In the chair conformation, the two hydrogens are oriented in different directions. The hydrogens projecting outward from the center of the ring are called **equatorial hydrogens**; the hydrogens projecting upward or downward are called **axial hydrogens**. When the ring reverses its conformation, all the hydrogens reverse their conformation. Neither axial nor equatorial hydrogens are energetically favored. However, when the ring has substituent groups attached, crowding occurs most often between groups in the axial position. Crowding causes instability and raises the energy level of the ring. Thus most substituent groups are favored in the equatorial position.

**Figure 2.4   Equatorial and Axial Hydrogens**

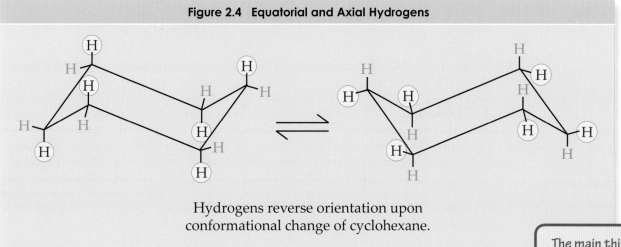

Hydrogens reverse orientation upon
conformational change of cyclohexane.

Since the carbons in a ring cannot rotate about the σ-bonds, *cis* and *trans* isomerism is possible in a ring structure without a double bond. Ring structure *cis* and *trans* isomers have different physical properties, but the trends are not as predictable as alkene *cis* and *trans* isomers. However, like other *cis* molecules, ring structures with *cis* groups on adjacent carbons may experience steric hindrance resulting in a higher energy level for the entire molecule. Notice that for five-carbon rings and less, the *cis* isomers are meso compounds. Each chair conformation of *cis*-1,2-dimethylhexane (also for 1,3 and 1,4 isomers and higher carbon rings) exists in equilibrium with its own mirror image and thus is optically inactive as well.

> The main things to know about ring structures are in terms of energy. For instance, for small rings, ring strain is lowest in cyclohexane, so it is the most stable ring structure. Also, large substituents in the axial position require more energy and create less stability.

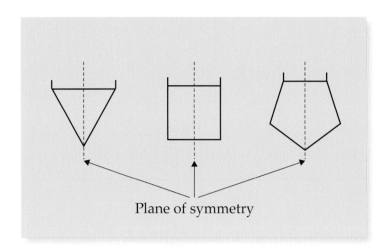

Plane of symmetry

*Combustion*

Alkanes were originally called paraffins (Latin: *parum affinis*: low inclination) because they are not inclined to react with other molecules. They do not react with strong acids or bases or with most other reagents. However, with a sufficiently large energy of activation, they are capable of violent reactions with oxygen. This reaction is called **combustion**. Combustion takes place when alkanes are mixed with oxygen and energy is added. Combustion of alkanes only takes place at high temperatures, such as inside the flame of a match. Once begun, however, combustion generates its own heat and can be self-perpetuating.

For the MCAT you should know that combustion takes place when oxygen is added to an alkane at high temperatures. You should know that the products are $CO_2$, $H_2O$, and, especially, heat.

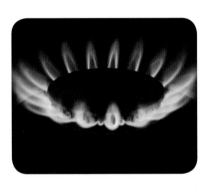

Combustion occurs as a rapid exothermic chemical reaction between oxygen and the combustible elements of a fuel which, for natural gas, are carbon and hydrogen.

$$CH_4 + 2O_2 \xrightarrow{\text{flame}} CO_2 + 2H_2O + \text{Heat}$$

Combustion is a **radical reaction**. (Radical reactions are discussed in the halogenation section later.)

**Heat of Combustion** is the change in enthalpy of a combustion reaction. Combustion of isomeric hydrocarbons requires equal amounts of $O_2$ and produces equal amounts of $CO_2$ and $H_2O$. Therefore heats of combustion can be used to compare relative stabilities of isomers. The higher the heat of combustion, the higher the energy level of the molecule, the less stable the molecule. For cycloalkanes, comparisons can be made of different size rings on a "per $CH_2$" basis to reveal relative stabilities. Although the molar heat of combustion for cyclohexane is nearly twice that of cyclopropane, the "per $CH_2$" group heat of combustion is greater for cyclopropane due to ring strain.

*Halogenation*

Alkanes will react with halogens (F, Cl, and Br, but not I) in the presence of heat or light to form a **free radical**. Energy from light or heat homolytically cleaves the diatomic halogen. In homolytic cleavage each atom in the bond retains one electron from the broken bond. The result is two highly reactive species each with an unpaired electron and each called a free radical. The free radicals are the active, reacting species in the halogenation of the alkane.

Halogenation is a chain reaction with at least three steps. You must know all three steps for the MCAT. They are demonstrated in Figure 2.5.

1. **Initiation**: The halogen starts as a diatomic molecule. The molecule is homolytically cleaved by heat or by UV light, resulting in two free radicals.

2. **Propagation**: The halogen radical removes a hydrogen from the alkane resulting in an alkyl radical. The alkyl radical may now react with a diatomic halogen molecule creating an alkyl halide and a new halogen radical. Propagation can continue indefinitely.

3. **Termination**: Either two radicals bond or a radical bonds to the wall of the container to end the chain reaction or propagation.

In halogenation, most of the product is formed during propagation, NOT during termination.

Halogenation is an exothermic process.

The stability of the alkyl radical follows the same order as carbocation stability:

$$3° > 2° > 1° > \text{methyl}$$

Alkyl radicals exhibit trigonal planar geometry.

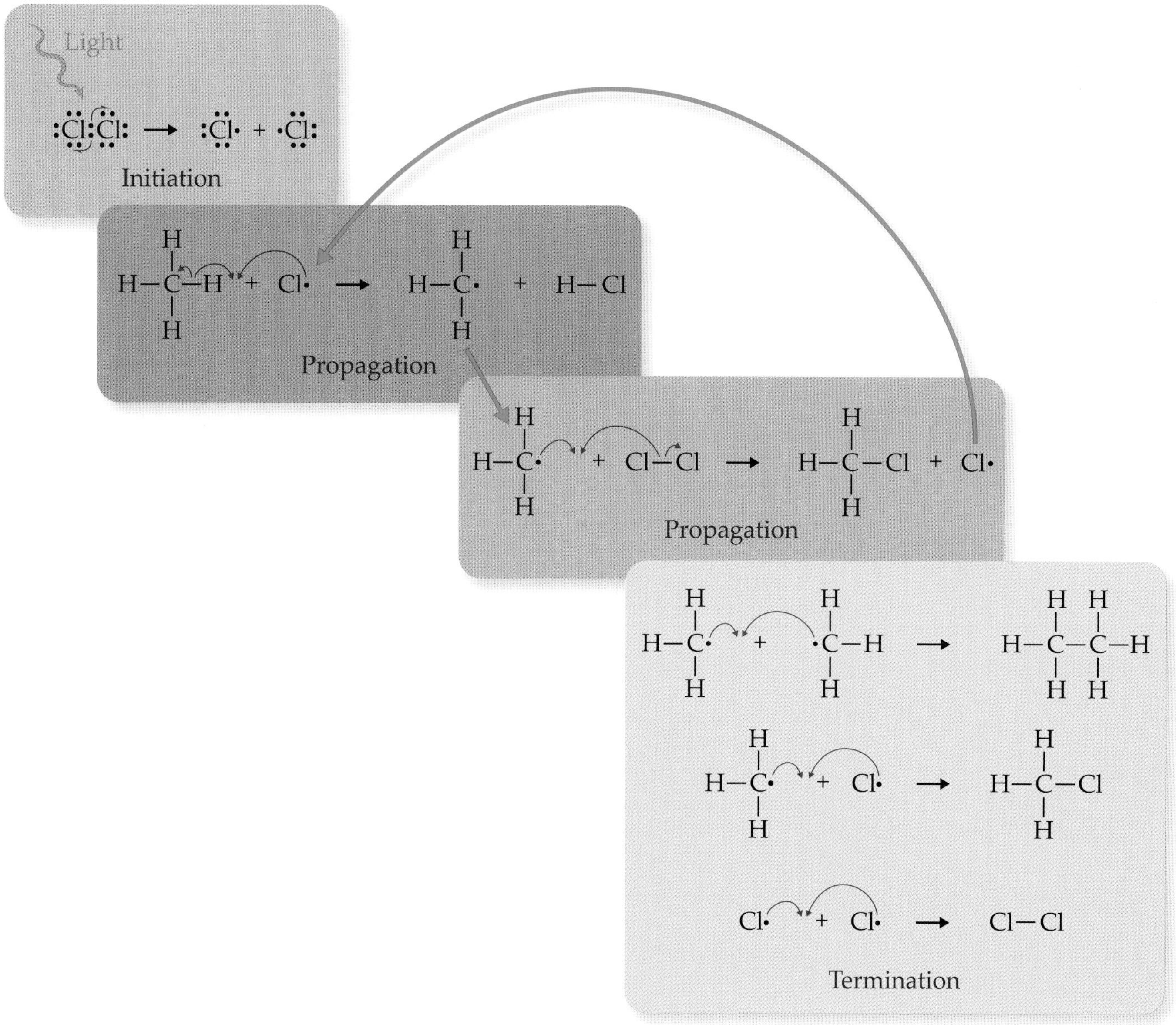

**Figure 2.5  Halogenation**

The reactivity of halogens from most reactive to least is as follows: F, Cl, Br, I. Fluorine is so reactive that it can be explosive, whereas bromine requires heat to react and iodine won't react at all. *Selectivity* of the halogens follows exactly the opposite order. (Selectivity is how selective a halogen radical is when choosing a position on an alkane.) Even though we know the order of selectivity, we must be careful when predicting products. For instance, since chlorine is somewhat selective, we might suppose that the primary product of 2-methylbutane and chlorine reacting at 300°C would be 2-chloro-2-methyl butane, the tertiary alkyl halide. This would be wrong. Although chlorine is five times more likely to react with the single hydrogen on the tertiary carbon to produce the more stable tertiary radical, there are nine hydrogens attached to primary carbons and two hydrogens attached to the secondary carbon which can also react. Thus, on 2-methylbutane, a chlorine free radical will collide with a primary hydrogen nine times as often as it will collide with the tertiary. As a rough rule of thumb, assume the order of reactivity for chlorine with tertiary, secondary, and primary hydrogens will follow a 5:4:1 ratio. In other words, a primary hydrogen will require five times as many collisions to react as a tertiary and so on.

## Figure 2.6 Halogenation Product Distribution

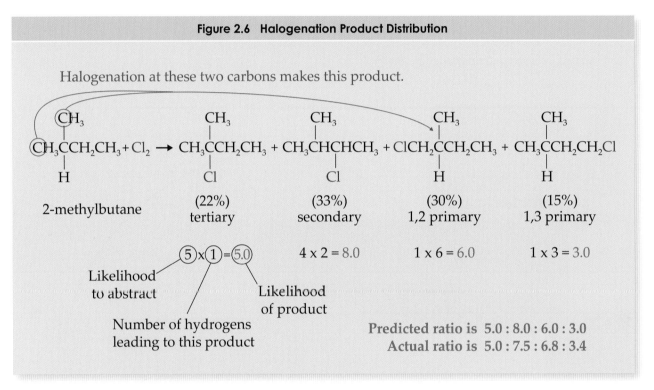

This example demonstrates that the rule of thumb is an estimate at best. Most importantly, it is a reminder that the tertiary product will not necessarily be the primary product. Bromine is more selective than chlorine and substituting bromine for chlorine in the same reaction will result in predominately 2-bromo-2-methylbutane. Fluorine, on the other hand, is so reactive that the primary product would predominate.

Another concern in halogenation is multi-halogenated products. Increased concentration of the halogen will result in the di-, tri-, and tetra-halogenated products, while dilute solutions will yield only monohalogenated products. This is because in a dilute solution the halogen radical is more likely to collide with an alkane than an alkyl halide.

**25.** Which of the following compounds contains the fewest tertiary carbons?

   **A.** $(CH_3)_3C(CH_2)_2CH_3$

   **B.** 4-isobutylheptane

   **C.**

   **D.**

**26.** Which of the following halogens will give the greatest percent yield of tertiary alkyl halide when reacted with isobutane in the presence of heat and light?

   **A.** $F_2$

   **B.** $Cl_2$

   **C.** $Br_2$

   **D.** Isobutane will not yield a tertiary product.

**27.** Which of the following compounds produces the most heat per mole of compound when reacted with oxygen?

   **A.** $CH_4$

   **B.** $C_2H_6$

   **C.** cyclohexane

   **D.** cycloheptane

**28.** In a sample of *cis*-1,2-dichlorocyclohexane at room temperature, the chlorines will:

   **A.** both be equatorial whenever the molecule is in the chair conformation.

   **B.** both be axial whenever the molecule is in the chair conformation.

   **C.** alternate between both equatorial and both axial whenever the molecule is in the chair conformation.

   **D.** both alternate between equatorial and axial but will never exist both axial or both equatorial at the same time.

**29.** In an alkane halogenation reaction, which of the following steps will never produce a radical?

   **A.** initiation

   **B.** propagation

   **C.** conjugation

   **D.** termination

**30.** Cycloalkanes are a group of cyclic saturated hydrocarbons with a general formula of $C_nH_{2n}$. Which of the following compounds will display the LEAST amount of free rotation around a C—C single bond?

   **A.** alkanes, which are relatively inert chemically

   **B.** alkanes, which are able to form numerous types of isomers

   **C.** cycloalkanes, which are limited by geometric constraints

   **D.** cycloalkanes, which are polar and water soluble

**31.**

In the above compound, how many hydrogen atoms can be identified as primary?

   **A.** 3

   **B.** 15

   **C.** 17

   **D.** 18

**32.** General reaction mechanism:

$$A—B + C—D \rightarrow A—C + B—D$$

What reaction type is being demonstrated by the equation above?

   **A.** addition

   **B.** elimination

   **C.** substitution

   **D.** rearrangement

## 2.6 | Alkenes

If a carbon chain contains a carbon-carbon double bond, it is an **alkene**. Alkenes have π-bonds. π-bonds are less stable than σ-bonds; thus, alkenes are more reactive than alkanes. When dealing with alkenes, remember that π-bonds are electron-hungry. This explains why alkenes are more acidic than alkanes. When a proton is removed, the π-bond of the alkene absorbs some of the negative charge stabilizing the conjugate base. However, at the same time remember that the π-bond is a large area of negative charge and is thus attractive to electrophiles.

The more highly substituted the alkene, the more thermodynamically stable.

**Figure 2.7   Relative Stability of Alkenes**

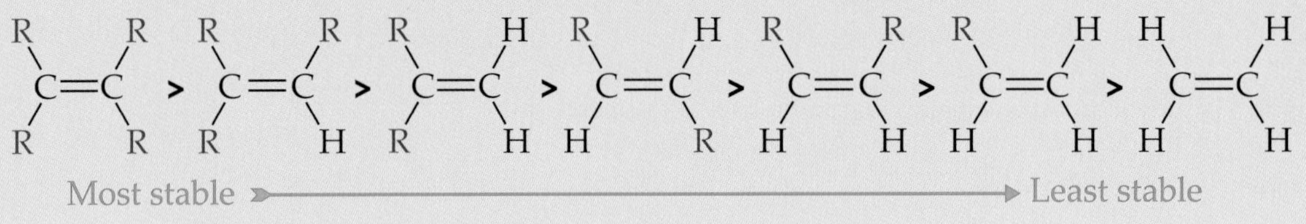

Most stable ━━━━━━━━━━━━━━━━━━━━━━━━━━━━━━━━━━━━━▶ Least stable

Figure 2.7 refers to thermodynamic stability. When we discuss addition reactions you will see that the most stable alkene when mixed with an electrophile is the most reactive according to this diagram. This paradox is due to the intermediate, usually a carbocation. Since a tertiary carbocation is more stable, the energy of activation is lower and a reaction with a tertiary intermediate proceeds more quickly. In general, to predict the alkene product, use the above diagram as a reference, but to predict the most reactive alkene to an electrophile, the order is based on cation formation and is nearly reversed.

## 2.7 | Physical Properties

Alkenes follow the same trends as alkanes. An increase in molecular weight leads to an increase in boiling point. Branching decreases boiling point. Alkenes are very slightly soluble in water and have a lower density than water. They are more acidic than alkanes.

Alkynes, carbon chains containing a carbon-carbon triple bond, have similar physical property trends to alkanes and alkenes. They are only slightly more polar than alkenes and only slightly more soluble in water.

## 2.8 | Synthesis of Alkenes

Synthesis of an alkene occurs via an **elimination reaction**. One or two functional groups are eliminated or removed to form a double bond. **Dehydration of an alcohol** is an E1 reaction where an alcohol forms an alkene in the presence of hot concentrated acid. E1 means that the rate depends upon the concentration of only one species. In this case, the rate depends upon the concentration of the alcohol. In the first step, the acid protonates the hydroxyl group producing the good leaving group, water. In the next and slowest step (the rate-determining step), the water drops off, forming a carbocation. As always, when a carbocation is formed, rearrangement may occur. **Carbocation stability** follows the same trend as radical stability. From most stable to least stable the order is: **3°, 2°, 1°, methane**. Rearrangement will only occur if a more stable carbocation can be formed. In the final step, a water molecule deprotonates the carbocation and an alkene is formed. Notice that the major product is the most stable,

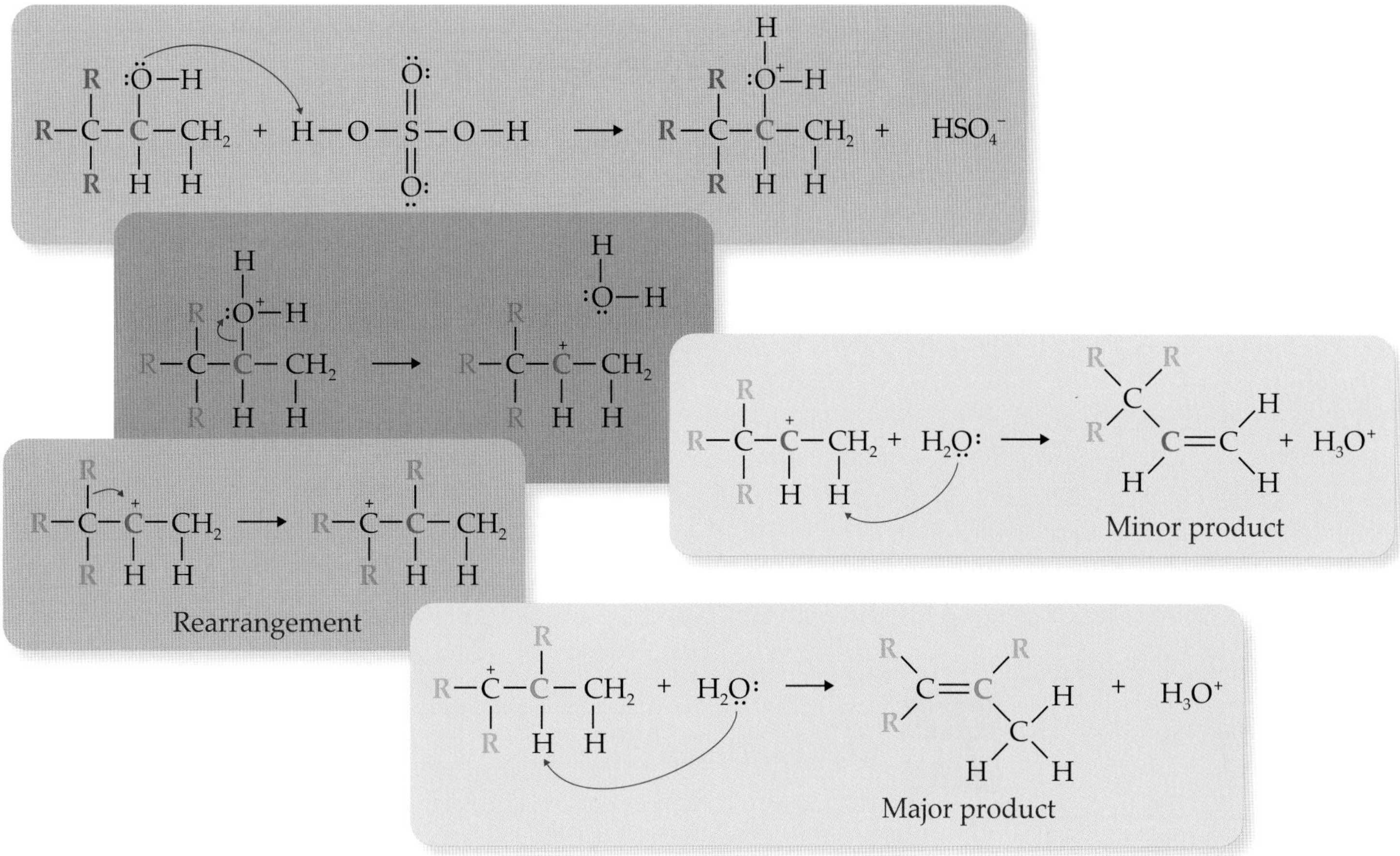

**Figure 2.8   Dehydration of an Alcohol**

most substituted alkene. The **Saytzeff rule** states that the major product of elimination will be the most substituted alkene.

**Dehydrohalogenation** may proceed either by an E1 mechanism (absence of a strong base) or by an E2 mechanism (a high concentration of a strong, bulky base). In the E1 reaction, the halogen drops off in the first step and a hydrogen is removed in the second step. In the E2 reaction, the base removes a proton from the carbon next to the halogen-containing carbon, and the halogen drops off, leaving an alkene. The E2 reaction is one step. The bulky base prevents an $S_N2$ reaction, but, if the base is too bulky, the Saytzeff rule is violated, leaving the least substituted alkene.

> A nucleophile is an electron-rich compound, typically symbolized as Nu or :Nu⁻. Nucleophiles donate an electron pair to form a covalent bond.

**Figure 2.9A   Dehydrohalogenation-E1**

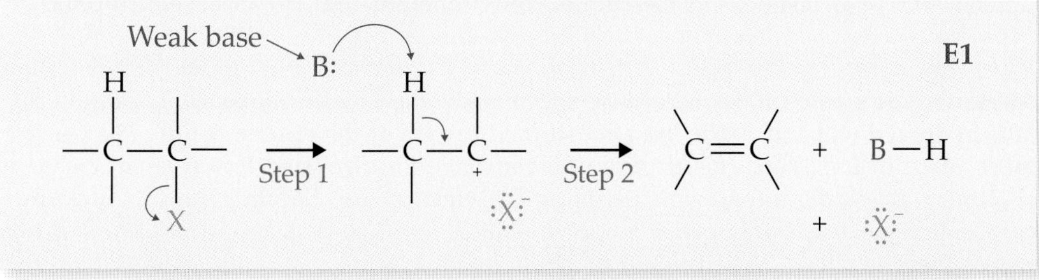

**Figure 2.9B   Dehydrohalogenation-E2**

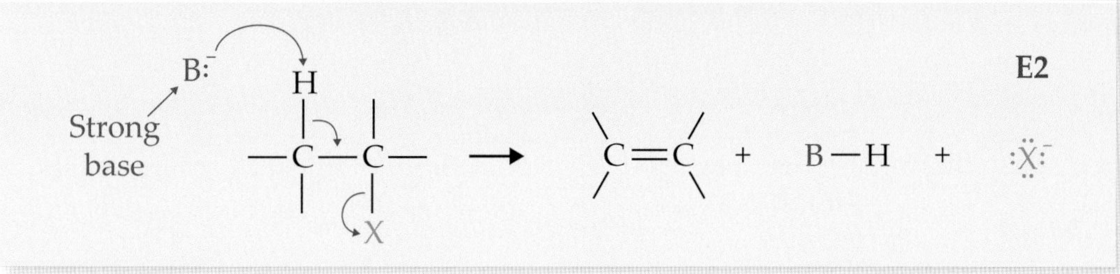

> Notice that in elimination, the base abstracts a hydrogen. This is a different behavior than that of a nucleophile in a substitution reaction. In a substitution reaction, the nucleophile attacks the carbon.

## 2.9 Catalytic Hydrogenation

Hydrogenation is an example of an addition reaction. In order for hydrogenation to occur at an appreciable rate, a *heterogeneous* catalyst is employed. Catalytic hydrogenation can be used to convert unsaturated fats to saturated fats (see Lecture 4). A heterogeneous catalyst is a catalyst that exists in a different phase (i.e. gas, liquid, solid, aqueous, etc.) than the reactants or products. Normally tiny shavings of metal act as the catalyst to promote **syn addition** (same side addition).

Hydrogenation is an exothermic reaction with a high energy of activation. Heats of hydrogenation can be used to measure relative stabilities of alkenes. The lower the heat of hydrogenation, the more stable the alkene.

Syn addition of alkynes creates a *cis* alkene.

**Figure 2.10   Syn Addition in Catalytic Hydrogenation**

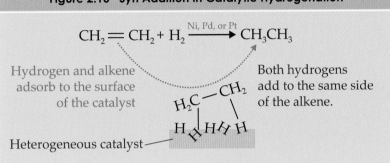

Hydrogen and alkene adsorb to the surface of the catalyst

Both hydrogens add to the same side of the alkene.

Heterogeneous catalyst

## 2.10 Oxidation of Alkenes

*Oxidation* of alkenes may produce glycols (hydroxyl groups on adjacent carbons) or oxidation may cleave the alkene at the double bond as in *ozonolysis*.

Alkynes produce carboxylic acids when undergoing ozonolysis.

> Ozone contains reactive electron pairs with a high charge density, so it is very reactive; it breaks right through alkenes and alkynes.

**Figure 2.11   Ozonolysis of an Alkene**

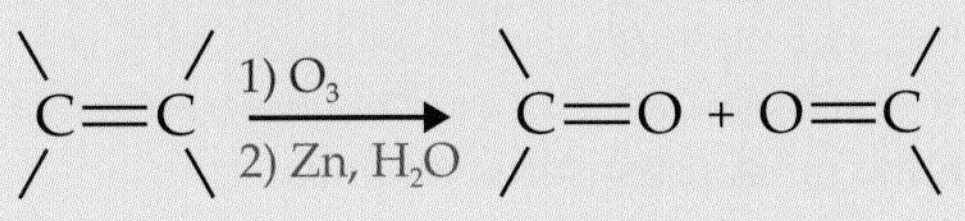

$$\diagdown C = C \diagup \xrightarrow[\text{2) Zn, H}_2\text{O}]{\text{1) O}_3} \diagdown C = O + O = C \diagup$$

## 2.11 Electrophilic Addition

**Electrophilic addition** is an important reaction for alkenes. When you see an alkene on the MCAT, check for electrophilic addition. An **electrophile** is an electron-loving species, so it will have at least a partially positive charge, even if it is only from a momentary dipole. The double bond of an alkene is an electron-rich environment and will attract electrophiles.

When hydrogen halides (HF, HCl, HBr, and HI) are added to alkenes, they follow **Markovnikov's rule** unless otherwise specified on the MCAT. Markovnikov's rule says "the hydrogen will add to the least substituted carbon of the double bond". The reaction takes place in two steps. First, the hydrogen halide, a Brønsted-Lowry acid, creates a positively charged proton, which acts as the electrophile. Second, the newly formed carbocation picks up the negatively charged halide ion. The first step is the slow step and determines the rate.

**Figure 2.12   Electrophilic Addition**
via Markovnikov's rule forming the most stable carbocation

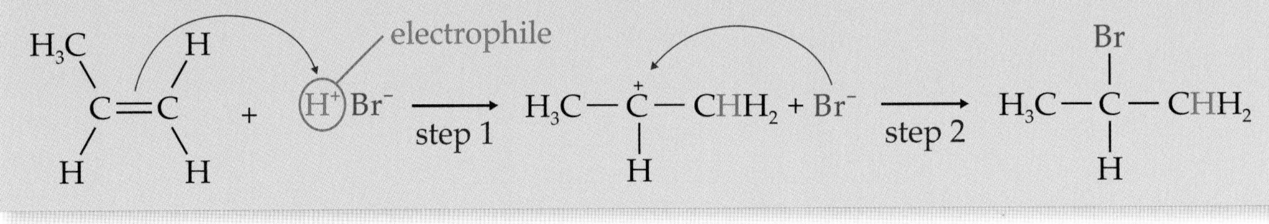

$$H_3C \diagdown C = C \diagup H \quad + \quad (H^+)Br^- \quad \xrightarrow{\text{step 1}} \quad H_3C - \overset{+}{\underset{H}{C}} - CHH_2 + Br^- \quad \xrightarrow{\text{step 2}} \quad H_3C - \underset{H}{\overset{Br}{C}} - CHH_2$$

electrophile

The reaction follows Markovnikov's rule because the rule dictates the formation of the more stable carbocation. You should be aware that if peroxides (ROOR) are present, the *bromine*, not the hydrogen, will add to the least substituted carbon. This is called an **anti-Markovnikov addition**. The other halogens will still follow Markovnikov's rule even in the presence of peroxides.

The most reactive alkenes in electrophilic addition are the most thermodynamically stable. This is because they also have the lowest activation energy when forming carbocations. Hydrogen halides add to alkynes in nearly the same way they add to alkenes.

In the flask at left is bromine water, with a characteristic orange color. When added to cyclohexene, the bromine water loses its color. This is because the bromine attacks and breaks the double bond of cyclohexene, bonding with it and forming the colorless 1, 2- dibromocyclohexane. This is an addition reaction.

---

### Figure 2.13  Hydraton and Dehydration

$$\text{Alkene} + \text{H}_2\text{O} \rightleftharpoons \text{Alcohol}$$

⟵——— Concentrated acid and heat

Dilute acid and cold ———⟶

---

**Hydration of an alkene** also follows Markovnikov's rule. Hydration takes place when water is added to an alkene in the presence of an acid. This reaction is the reverse of dehydration of an alcohol. Low temperatures and dilute acid drive this reaction toward alcohol formation; high temperatures and concentrated acid drive the reaction toward alkene formation.

Another reaction which creates an alcohol from an alkene is *oxymercuration/demercuration* (Figure 2.14). This is a two-step process which also follows Markovnikov's rule but rarely results in rearrangement of the carbocation. A two-step theory has the mercury-containing reagent partially dissociate to $^+$Hg(OAc). The $^+$Hg(OAc) acts as an electrophile creating a *mercurinium ion*. Water attacks the mercurinium ion to form the *organomercurial alcohol* in an **anti-addition** (addition from opposite sides of the double bond). The second step is demercuration to form the alcohol by addition of a reducing agent and base.

> What's important here is not to memorize the mechanism, but to realize that in organometallic compounds the metal likes to lose electrons and take on a full or partial positive charge.

---

### Figure 2.14  Oxymercuration/Demercuration

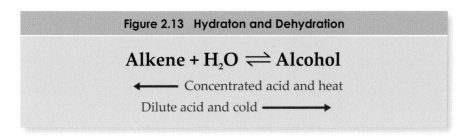

If an alcohol is used instead of water, the corresponding ether is produced. This is called an *alkoxymercuration/demercuration* reaction.

*Hydroboration* provides yet another mechanism to produce an alcohol from an alkene. This is an anti-Markovnikov and a syn addition.

Notice that this reaction is in the presence of peroxide. This should help you remember that it is anti-Markovnikov. You may see hydroboration on the MCAT, but you probably won't have to know anything about it to answer the questions.

**Figure 2.15 Hydroboration**

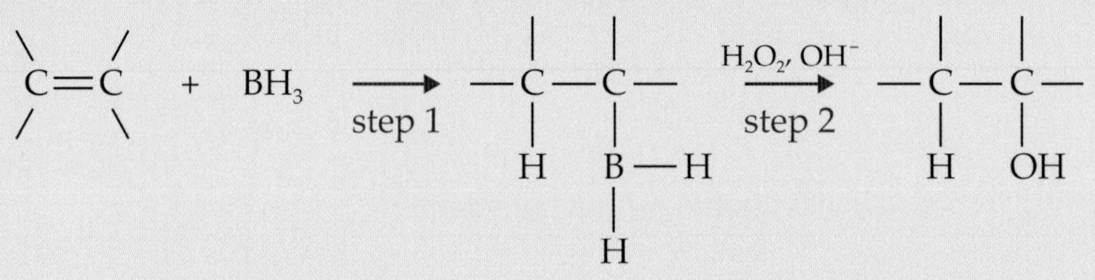


Halogens are much more reactive toward alkenes than toward alkanes. $Br_2$ and $Cl_2$ add to alkenes readily via anti-addition to form *vic-dihalides* (two halogens connected to adjacent carbons).

You should know halogenation of an alkene for the MCAT. Notice that alkanes will not react with halogens without light or heat, but alkenes will. Alkynes behave just like alkenes when exposed to halogens.

**Figure 2.16 Halogenation of an Alkene**

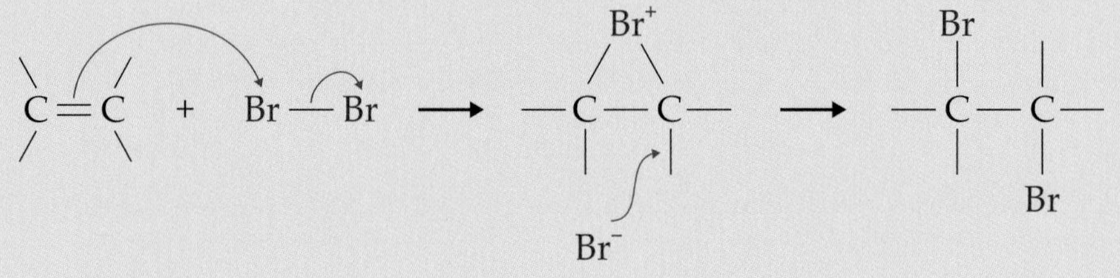


When this reaction takes place with water, a *halohydrin* is formed and Markovnikov's rule is followed where the electrophile adds to the least substituted carbon. Water acts as the nucleophile in the second step instead of the bromide ion. (A halohydrin is a hydroxyl group and a halogen attached to adjacent carbons.)

## 2.12 Benzene

**Benzene** undergoes **substitution NOT addition**. From stereochemistry, we know that resonance atoms must be in the same plane, so benzene is a **flat molecule**. Benzene is stabilized by **resonance** and its carbon-carbon bonds have partial double bond character. Although benzene is normally drawn without its six hydrogens, don't forget that they exist. If a benzene ring contains one substituent, the remaining 5 positions are labeled **ortho, meta,** or **para** (Figure 2.17).

## Figure 2.17  Benzene

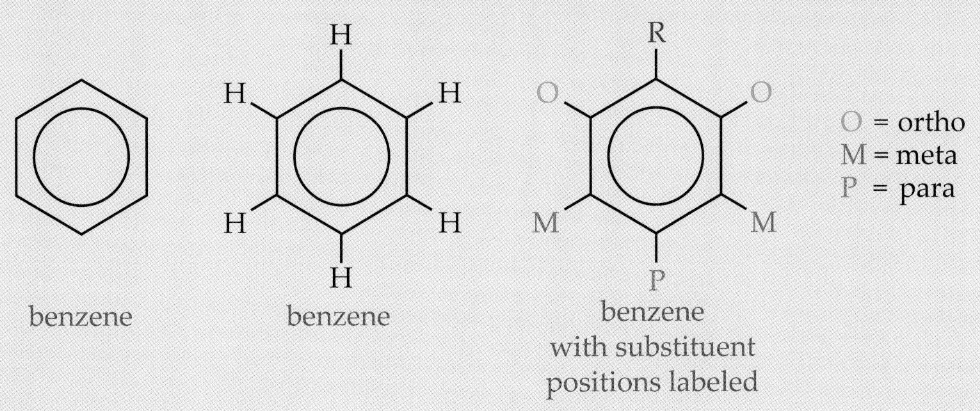

benzene        benzene        benzene
                               with substituent
                               positions labeled

O = ortho
M = meta
P = para

Don't let ring structures intimidate you. Since benzene only undergoes substitution, benzene presents little challenge on the MCAT. AAMC claims that they stopped asking questions on benzene a decade ago. Nevertheless, we still think it is useful to learn the names of the substituted positions: ortho, meta, para.

When an **electron withdrawing group** is in the R position, it deactivates the ring and directs any new substituents to the meta position. **Electron donating groups** activate the ring and direct any new substituents to ortho and para positions. **Halogens are an exception** to the rule. They are electron withdrawing and deactivate the ring as expected. However, they are ortho-para directors. (To deactivate the ring simply means to make it less reactive.) Knowing whether a functional group is electron withdrawing or donating can be very helpful in all of organic chemistry.

## Figure 2.18  Electron Donating and Withdrawing Properties of Functional Groups

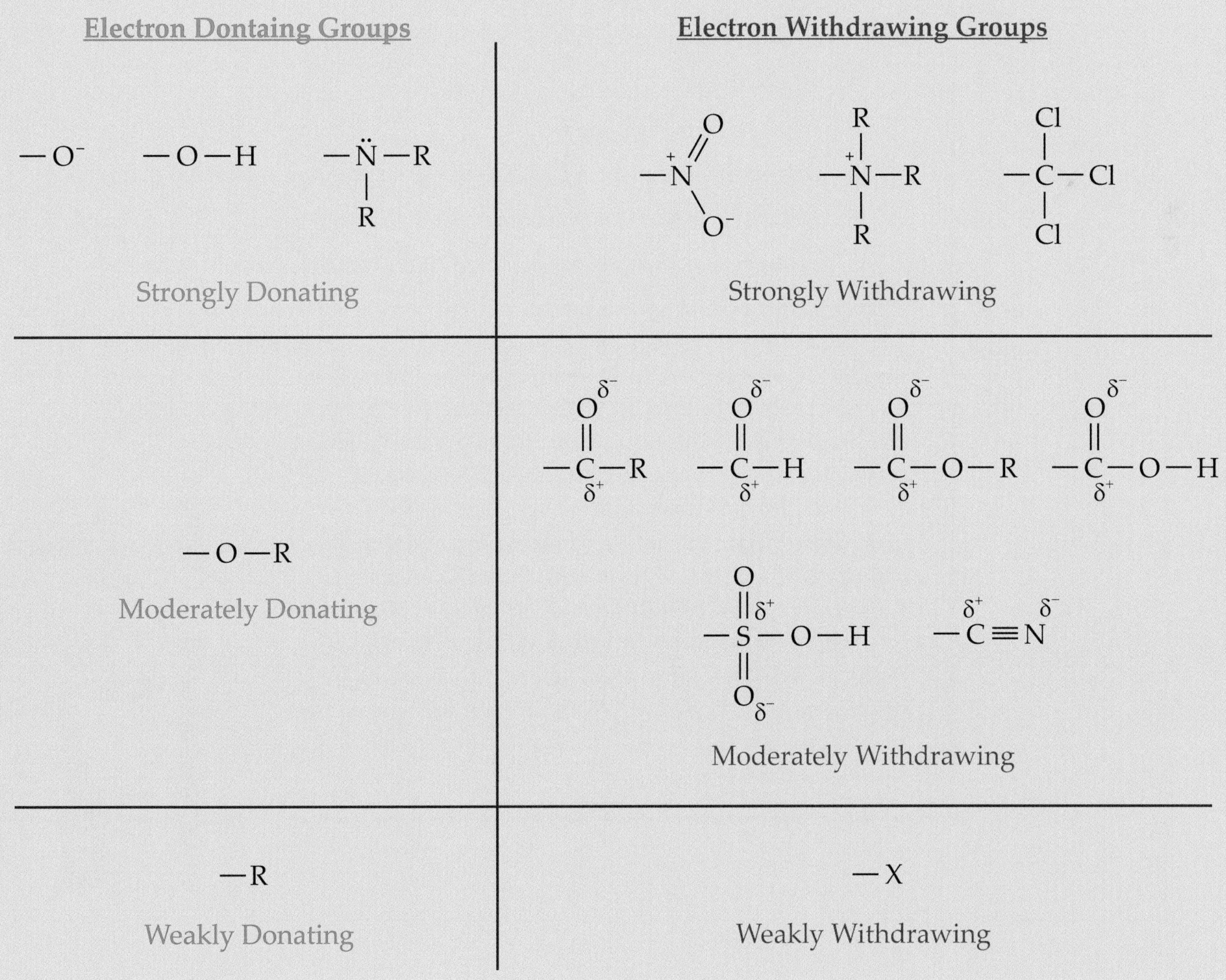

**Electron Dontaing Groups**

Strongly Donating

Moderately Donating

Weakly Donating

**Electron Withdrawing Groups**

Strongly Withdrawing

Moderately Withdrawing

Weakly Withdrawing

The groups are labeled in relation to the electron withdrawing-donating tendencies of a lone hydrogen atom. Hydrogen is considered neither electron withdrawing nor electron donating. Benzene, itself, is an ortho-para director and ring activator; however, for reasons that are well beyond the MCAT, it is best to consider benzene as electron withdrawing in most other situations.

It may help to familiarize yourself with the names of the following benzene compounds, but it is unlikely that a correct MCAT answer will require this knowledge.

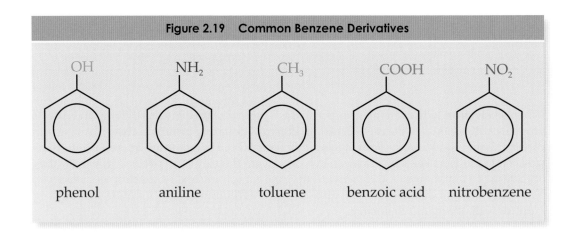

**Figure 2.19    Common Benzene Derivatives**

phenol        aniline        toluene        benzoic acid        nitrobenzene

Don't memorize too many reactions. So far, you should thoroughly understand:

1. combustion;

2. halogenation of an alkane;

3. dehydration of an alcohol and the reverse reaction, hydration of an alkene;

4. electrophilic addition (via Comrade Markovnikov); and

5. halogenation of an alkene. Assume that alkynes behave like alkenes.

Rather than memorizing other reactions, be familiar with the behavior of functional groups. For instance, the double bond of alkenes makes a large electron cloud that is attractive to an electrophile, but alkenes withdraw electrons through their bonds, making them stabilized by electron donating groups, and making them more acidic than alkanes; benzene hates addition; etc. A strong start toward understanding functional groups is memorizing their electron withdrawing and donating natures. We will come back to electron withdrawing and donating properties time and again. Remember, the MCAT is not going to require that you have an obscure reaction committed to memory; much more likely, the MCAT will show you a reaction that you have never seen and ask you "why?" The answer will be because the functional group involved normally behaves that way. Know your functional groups.

**33.** Which of the following compounds is the most thermodynamically stable?

   **A.** $CH_3CH_2CH{=}CH_2$

   **B.** $CH_3CH{=}CH_2$

   **C.**

   **D.**

**34.** Which of the following compounds will be the most reactive with HBr?

   **A.** $CH_3CH_2CH{=}CH_2$

   **B.** $CH_3CH{=}CH_2$

   **C.**

   **D.**

**35.** What is the product of the following oxidation reaction?

   **A.**

   **B.**

   **C.**

   **D.**

**36.** What is the major product of the following reaction?

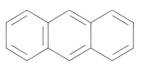

   **A.**

   **B.**

   **C.**

   **D.**

**37.** When 2,4-dimethyl-2-pentene is hydrated with cold dilute acid, the major product is:

   **A.**

   **B.**

   **C.**

   **D.**

**38.** Anthracene is an aromatic compound described by which of the following characteristics?

Anthracene

   **I.** cyclic
   **II.** planar
   **III.** satisfies Huckel's rule
   **IV.** has an even number of π electrons

   **A.** I and II only
   **B.** II, III, and IV only
   **C.** I, III, and IV only
   **D.** I, II, III, and IV

**39.** Which of the following statements is true regarding the two reaction mechanisms and the deuterium (D) effect?

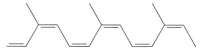

[1-Bromo-2-phenylethane]

[1-Bromo-2,2-dideuterio
-2-phenylethane]

A. Deuterium (D) isotope is identical to hydrogen in every way.
B. C—H or C—D bond is broken in the reaction rate limiting step.
C. 1-Bromo-2-phenylethane reactant undergoes a one step substitution reaction.
D. Carbon hydrogen bond is stronger than the corresponding carbon deuterium bond.

**40.** Natural rubber is a diene polymer known as isoprene. What is the most likely explanation for isoprene's ability to stretch?

Isoprene (2 methyl-1,3-butadiene)

A. Isoprene undergoes vulcanization, which induces cross-linking between carbon atoms in nearby rubber chains.
B. Double bonds induce shape irregularities, which prevent neighboring chains from nestling together.
C. Alkane polymer chains orient along the direction of pull by sliding over each other.
D. Isoprene is able to undergo rapid hydration/dehydration reaction.

Substitution reactions occur when one functional group replaces another. Two important types of substitution reactions are $S_N1$ and $S_N2$. These are substitution, nucleophilic, unimolecular and bimolecular. The numbers represent the order of the rate law and NOT the number of steps.

**2.14** $S_N1$

An $S_N1$ reaction has 2 steps and has a rate that is dependent on only one of the reactants. The first step is the formation of the carbocation. This is the slow step and thus the **rate-determining step**. Since this step has nothing to do with the nucleophile, the rate is independent of the concentration of the nucleophile and is directly proportional to the concentration of the **substrate** (the substrate is the electrophile or the molecule being attacked by the nucleophile.) In an $S_N1$ reaction the **leaving group** (the group being replaced) simply breaks away on its own to leave a carbocation behind. The second step happens very quickly. The nucleophile attacks the carbocation.

**Figure 2.20  Mechanism of $S_N1$ Reaction**

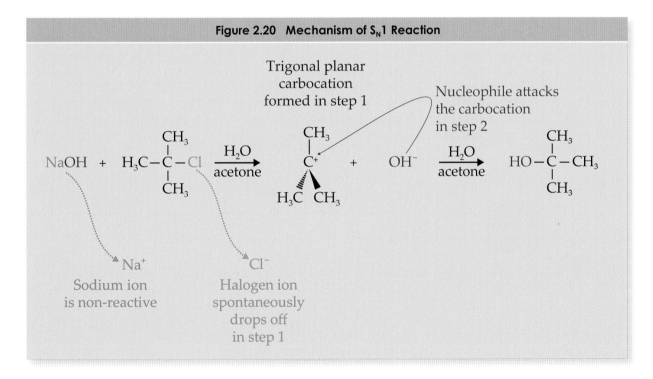

Notice that if the carbocation carbon began and ended an $S_N1$ reaction as a chiral carbon, both enantiomers would be produced. The intermediate carbocation is planar and the nucleophile is able to attack it from either side. Carbon skeleton rearrangement may occur if the carbocation can rearrange to a more stable form. Elimination (E1) often accompanies $S_N1$ reactions because the nucleophile may act as a base to abstract a proton from the carbocation, forming a carbon-carbon double bond.

> Since the carbocation must be formed spontaneously in an $S_N1$ reaction, a tertiary substrate is more likely to undergo an $S_N1$ reaction than is a primary or secondary substrate. On the MCAT, probably only tertiary substrates will undergo $S_N1$. The rate of an $S_N1$ reaction is determined solely by the concentration of the substrate.

## 2.15 $S_N2$

$S_N2$ reactions occur in a single step. The rate is dependent on the concentration of the nucleophile and the substrate. In an $S_N2$ reaction a nucleophile attacks the intact substrate from behind the leaving group and knocks the leaving group free while bonding to the substrate.

**Figure 2.21 Substitution, Nucleophilic, Bimolecular**

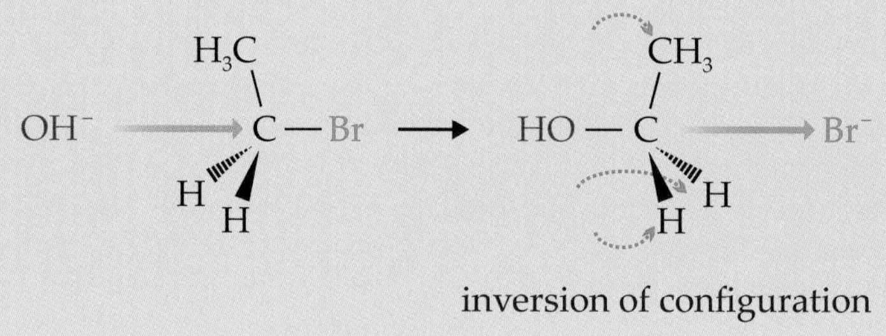

inversion of configuration

Notice the **inversion of configuration** on the carbon being attacked by the nucleophile. If the carbon were chiral, the relative configuration would be changed but the absolute configuration might or might not be changed. Notice also that a tertiary carbon would **sterically hinder** the nucleophile in this reaction. The rate of $S_N2$ reactions decreases from primary to secondary substrates. $S_N2$ reactions don't typically occur with tertiary substrates. If the nucleophile is a strong base and the substrate is too hindered, an elimination (E2) reaction may occur. In an E2 reaction, the nucleophile acts as a base abstracting a proton and, in the same step, the halogen leaves the substrate forming a carbon-carbon double bond. Bulky nucleophiles also hinder $S_N2$ reactions.

## 2.16 Nucleophilicity

The strength of the nucleophile is unimportant for an $S_N1$ reaction but important for an $S_N2$ reaction. A base is always a stronger nucleophile than its conjugate acid, but basicity is not the same thing as nucleophilicity. If a nucleophile behaves as a base, elimination results. To avoid this, we use a less bulky nucleophile. A negative charge and polarizability add to nucleophilicity. Electronegativity reduces nucleophilicity. In general, nucleophilicity decreases going up and to the right on the periodic table.

## 2.17 Solvents

*Polar protic solvents* (polar solvents that can hydrogen bond) stabilize the nucleophile and any carbocation that may form. A stable nucleophile slows $S_N2$ reactions, while a stable carbocation increases the rate of $S_N1$ reactions. Thus polar protic solvents increase the rate of $S_N1$ and decrease the rate of $S_N2$. *Polar aprotic solvents* (polar solvents that can't form hydrogen bonds) do not form strong bonds with ions and thus increase the rate of $S_N2$ reactions while inhibiting $S_N1$ reactions. In $S_N1$ reactions, the solvent is often heated to reflux (boiled) in order to provide energy for the formation of the carbocation.

In *solvolysis* the solvent acts as the nucleophile.

| Figure 2.22 Solvation of the Nucleophile | Figure 2.23 Stabilization of the Carbocation Intermediate |

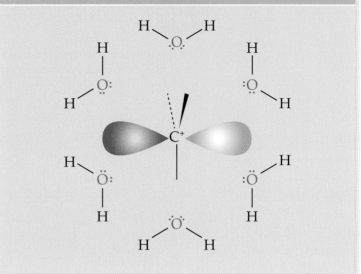

A solvated anion
(reduced nucleophilicity due to
enhanced ground-state stability)

## 2.18 Leaving Groups

The best leaving groups are those that are stable when they leave. Generally speaking, the weaker the base, the better the leaving group. Electron withdrawing effects and polarizability also make for a good leaving group. The leaving group will always be more stable than the nucleophile.

## 2.19 $S_N1$ vs. $S_N2$

There are six things to remember about $S_N1$ vs. $S_N2$. Remember the six things as "The nucleophile and the five Ss": 1) **Substrate**; 2) **Solvent**; 3) **Speed**; 4) **Stereochemistry**; and 5) **Skeleton** rearrangement.

**The nucleophile**: $S_N2$ requires a strong nucleophile, while nucleophilic strength doesn't affect $S_N1$.

    **1st S**: $S_N2$ reactions don't occur with a sterically hindered **Substrate**. $S_N2$ requires a methyl, primary, or secondary substrate, while $S_N1$ requires a secondary or tertiary substrate.

    **2nd S**: A highly polar **Solvent** increases the reaction rate of $S_N1$ by stabilizing the carbocation, but slows down $S_N2$ reactions by stabilizing the nucleophile.

    **3rd S**: The **Speed** of an $S_N2$ reaction depends upon the concentration of the substrate and the nucleophile, while the speed of an $S_N1$ depends only on the substrate.

    **4th S**: $S_N2$ inverts **Stereochemistry** about the chiral center, while $S_N1$ creates a racemic mixture.

    **5th S**: $S_N1$ may be accompanied by carbon **Skeleton** rearrangement, but $S_N2$ never rearranges the carbon skeleton.

Also remember that elimination reactions can accompany both $S_N1$ and $S_N2$ reactions. Elimination occurs when the nucleophile behaves as a base rather than a nucleophile; it abstracts a proton rather than attacking a carbon. Elimination reactions always result in a carbon-carbon double bond. E1 and E2 kinetics are similar to $S_N1$ and $S_N2$ respectively.

## 2.20 Physical Properties of Alcohols

**Alcohols** follow the same general trends as alkanes. The boiling point goes up with molecular weight and down with branching. The melting point trend is not as reliable but still exists. Melting point also goes up with molecular weight. Branching generally lowers boiling point and has a less clear effect on melting. Although alcohols follow the same trend as alkanes, their boiling and melting points are much higher than alkanes due to **hydrogen bonding**. The hydrogen bonding increases the intermolecular forces, which must be overcome to change phase.

Alcohols follow trends similar to hydrocarbons, but alcohols hydrogen bond, giving them considerably higher boiling points and water solubilities than similar-weight hydrocarbons.

Alcohols are more soluble in water than alkanes and alkenes. The hydroxyl group increases polarity and allows for hydrogen bonding with water. The longer the carbon chain, the less soluble the alcohol.

**Figure 2.24  Geometery of Alcohol vs. Water**

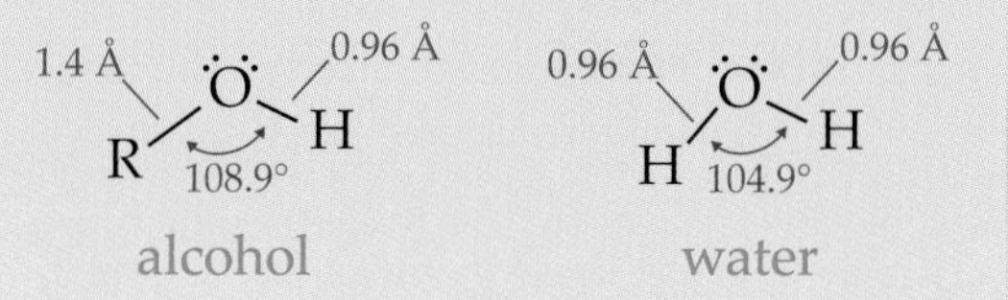

## 2.21 Alcohols as Acids

| Acid | $pK_a$ |
|------|--------|
| hydrochloric acid | −2.2 |
| acetic acid | 4.8 |
| phenol | 10 |
| water | 15.7 |
| ethanol | 15.9 |
| t-butyl alcohol | 18 |

Since an alcohol can lose a proton, it can act like an acid. However, alcohols are less acidic than water. The order of acidity for alcohols from strongest to weakest is: methyl; 1°; 2°; 3°. If we examine the conjugate base of each alcohol, the most stable conjugate base will be the conjugate of the strongest acid. Since excess charge is an instability, the most stable conjugate base will have the weakest negative charge. Methyl groups are electron donating compared to hydrogens, thus they act to prevent the carbon from absorbing some of the excess negative charge of the conjugate. For example since a tertiary alcohol has more methyl groups than a primary alcohol, a tertiary carbon can absorb less negative charge; the conjugate base of a tertiary alcohol is less stable; and a tertiary alcohol is less acidic than a primary alcohol.

Electron donation and withdrawal helps to explain many of the reactions in MCAT organic chemistry. For instance, placing an electron withdrawing group on the alcohol increases its acidity by reducing the negative charge on the conjugate base.

**Figure 2.25  Comparison of Acidic Properties of Alcohols**

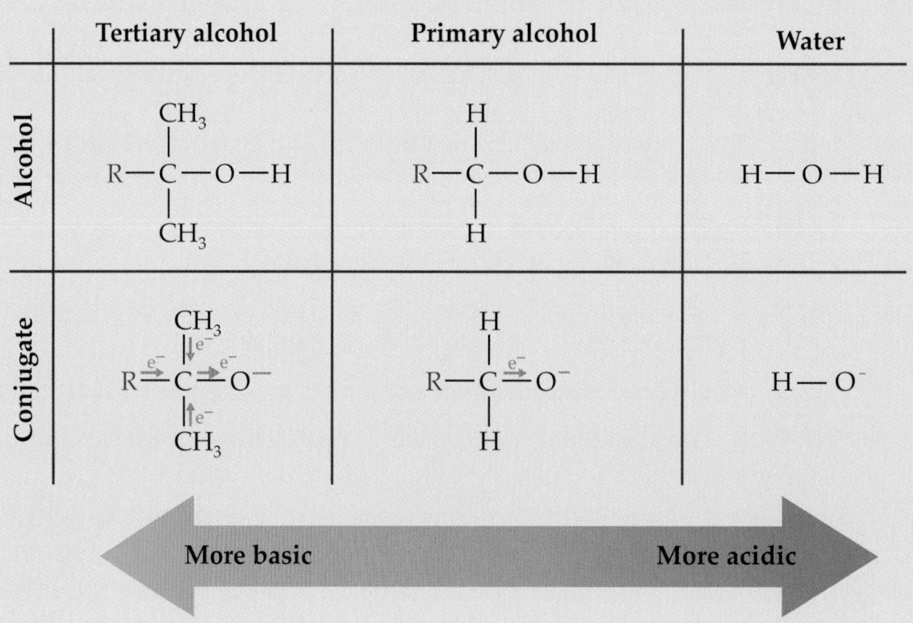

# 2.22 Synthesis of Alcohols

We've already looked at several alcohol synthesis reactions: hydration of an alkene, oxymercuration/demercuration, hydroboration, and nucleophilic substitution. Another method of synthesizing an alcohol is with an organometallic compound. Organometallic reagents possess a highly polarized carbon-metal bond. The carbon is more electronegative than the metal, so the carbon takes on a strong partial negative charge. The polarized carbon-metal bond and the partial negative charge on the carbon atom makes this carbon a strong nucleophile and base. The most common reaction for organometallic compounds is nucleophilic attack on a carbonyl carbon, which, after an acid bath, produces an alcohol.

### Figure 2.26   Grignard Synthesis of an Alcohol

$$\overset{\delta^-}{R_c}-\overset{\delta^+}{MgX} \;+\; \overset{\delta^+}{\underset{R_b}{\overset{R_a}{\diagdown}}}C=\overset{\delta^-}{O} \longrightarrow R_c-\underset{R_b}{\overset{R_a}{\underset{|}{\overset{|}{C}}}}-O^-\;{}^+MgX \xrightarrow{H_3O^+} R_c-\underset{R_b}{\overset{R_a}{\underset{|}{\overset{|}{C}}}}-O-H \;+\; XMgOH$$

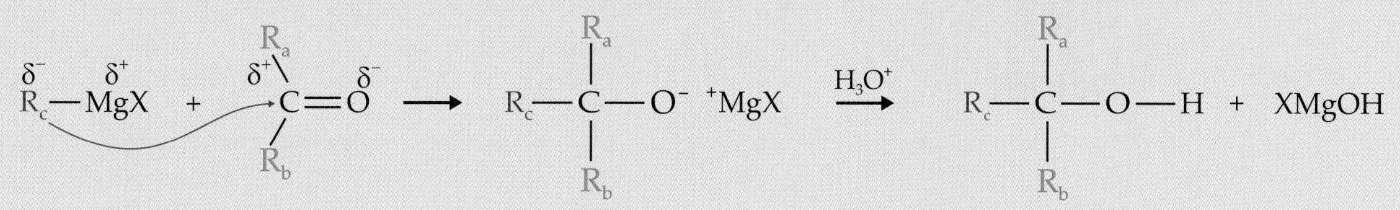

Grignard reagents will react in a similar fashion with C=N, C≡N, S=O, N=O. The Grignard is a strong enough base to deprotonate the following species: O—H, N—H, S—H, —C≡C–H. Grignard reagents are made in ether, and are incompatible with water and acids stronger than water.

In a nucleophilic attack mechanism similar to Grignard synthesis of an alcohol, hydrides (H–) will react with carbonyls to form alcohols. Unlike Grignard synthesis of an alcohol, the use of hydrides does not extend the carbon skeleton.

### Figure 2.27   Reduction Synthesis of an Alcohol

From NaBH$_4$ or LiAlH$_4$

$$H^- \;+\; \overset{\delta^+}{\underset{R_b}{\overset{R_a}{\diagdown}}}C=\overset{\delta^-}{O} \longrightarrow H-\underset{R_b}{\overset{R_a}{\underset{|}{\overset{|}{C}}}}-O^- \xrightarrow{H_3O^+} H-\underset{R_b}{\overset{R_a}{\underset{|}{\overset{|}{C}}}}-O-H$$

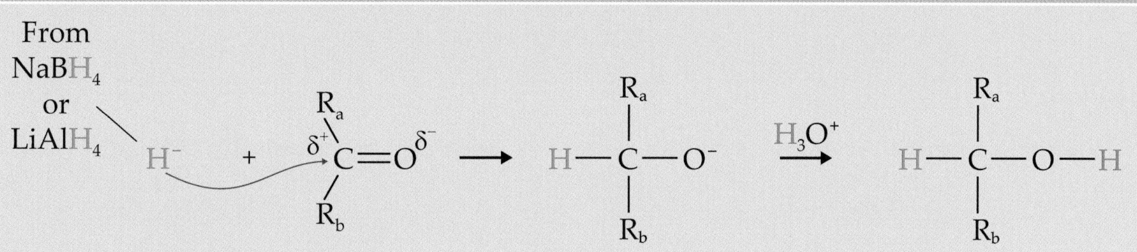

In reduction synthesis, both NaBH$_4$ and LiAlH$_4$ will reduce aldehydes and ketones, but only LiAlH$_4$ is strong enough to reduce esters and acetates.

### Figure 2.28   Reactivity of Various Carbonyl Compounds with Hydride

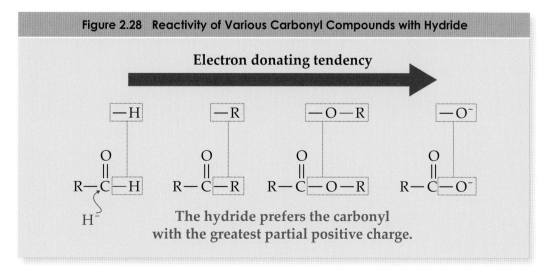

**Electron donating tendency**

The hydride prefers the carbonyl with the greatest partial positive charge.

Lecture **2** : *Hydrocarbons, Alcohols, and Substitutions*  **51**

**Question:** Why is it more difficult to reduce esters and acetates than ketones and aldehydes?

**Answer:** Because the group attached to the carbonyl of the ester or acetate is a stronger electron donor than an alkyl group or hydrogen. By donating electrons more strongly, it reduces the positive charge on the carbonyl carbon making it less attractive to the nucleophile.

## 2.23 Reactions with Alcohols

We've already seen dehydration of an alcohol. Most of the time on the MCAT, if an alcohol is a reactant, it will be acting as a nucleophile. The two lone pairs of electrons on the oxygen are pushed out by the bent shape, and they search for a positive charge. The oxygen will find and connect to the substrate and the positively charged proton will drop off into solution.

Figure 2.29    Alcohols as Nucleophiles

Either...

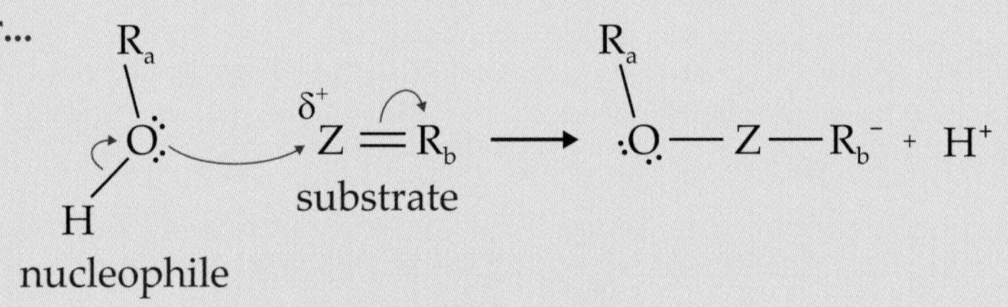

Nucleophilic addition

Or...

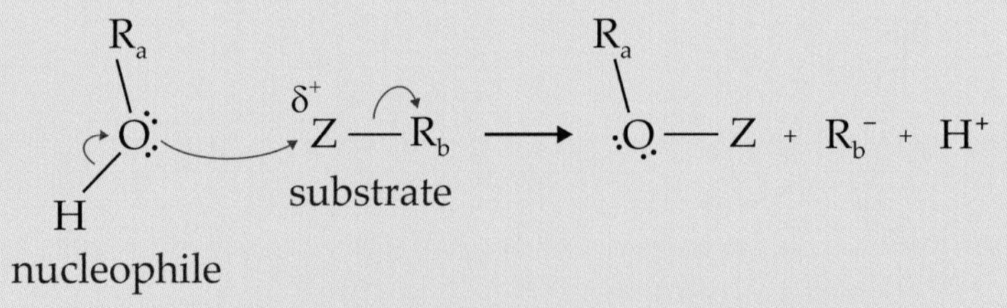

Nucleophilic substitution

Alcohols like to be nucleophiles

Primary and secondary alcohols can be oxidized. For MCAT purposes, assume tertiary alcohols cannot be oxidized. In organic chemistry, you can use the following rule to determine if a compound has been oxidized or reduced:

> **Oxidation**: loss of $H_2$; addition of O or $O_2$; addition of $X_2$ ( X = halogens)
>
> **Reduction**: addition of $H_2$ (or $H^-$); loss of O or $O_2$; loss of $X_2$
>
> **Neither Oxidation nor reduction**: addition or loss of $H^+$, $H_2O$, HX, etc.

Primary alcohols oxidize to aldehydes, which, in turn, oxidize to carboxylic acids. Secondary alcohols oxidize to ketones. In each case, the reverse process is called **reduction**.

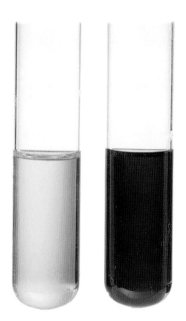

In oxidation of a primary alcohol (propan-1-ol) by potassium dichromate solution (K2Cr2O7, yellow, left), the dichromate is a strong oxidizing agent that is reduced when it reacts, forming a green solution (right). This primary alcohol (propan-1-ol) turns into a carboxylic acid (propanoic acid).

**Figure 2.30   Oxidation and Reduction**

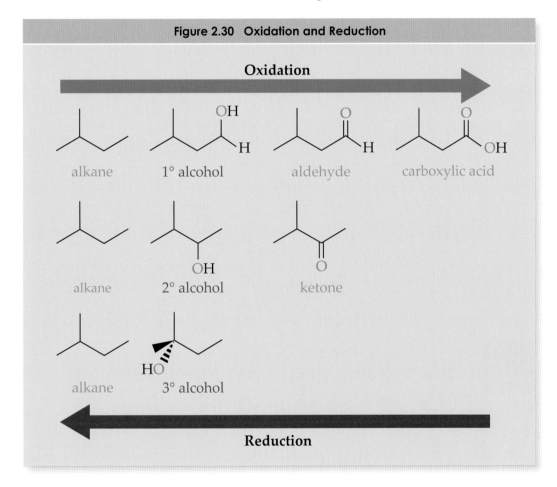

Generally speaking, *oxidizing agents* will have lots of oxygen and *reducing agents* will have lots of hydrogen. Table 2.3 shows common oxidizing and reducing agents.

| Table 2.1   Oxidizing and Reducing Agents | |
| :---: | :---: |
| *Oxidizing Agents* | *Reducing Agents* |
| $K_2C_2O_7$ | $LiAlH_4$ |
| $K_2MnO_4$ | $NaBH_4$ |
| $H_2CrO_4$ | $H_2$ + pressure |
| $O_2$ | |
| $Br_2$ | |

## 2.25 Alkyl Halides from Alcohols

We saw in the $S_N2$ reaction that the halogen ion, as a weak base, is a good leaving group, and the hydroxyl group, as a strong base, is a good nucleophile. However, if the hydroxyl group is protonated by an acid, it becomes water, an excellent leaving group. The halide ion is an unusual nucleophile in that it is a very weak base and does not become protonated in acidic solution.

### Figure 2.31 Formation of an Alkyl Halide from an Alcohol

This reaction can occur as $S_N1$ with a tertiary alcohol or $S_N2$ with other alcohols.

Notice that this reaction breaks the C—O bond rather than the O—H bond. When the C—O bond is broken, alcohol is behaving as an electrophile. When the O—H bond is broken, it is a nucleophile. Alcohols are very weak electrophiles because the hydroxyl group is such a weak leaving group. Protonating the hydroxyl group makes the good leaving group water. However, protonating an alcohol requires a strong acid. Strong acids react with most good nucleophiles, destroying their nucleophilicity.

Alcohols can also be converted to alkyl halides by phosphorus halides such as $PCl_3$, $PBr_3$, and $PI_3$, via an $S_N2$ reaction with tertiary alcohols. This, however, results in poor yields. Another reagent for producing alkyl halides from alcohols is thionyl chloride, $SOCl_2$, resulting in sulfur dioxide and hydrochloric acid.

## 2.26 Preparation of Mesylates and Tosylates

Alcohols form esters called sulfonates. The **formation of the sulfonates** (Figure 2.32) is a nucleophilic substitution, where alcohol acts as the nucleohile. The reaction proceeds with retention of configuration, so if the carbon atom bearing the hydroxyl group is stereogenic, it is NOT inverted as it would be in an $S_N2$ reaction.

**Tosylates** and **mesylates** are commonly used sulfonates that you need to know for the MCAT. The sulfonate ions are very weak bases and excellent leaving groups. When tosylates and mesylates are leaving groups, the reaction may proceed via an $S_N1$ or $S_N2$ mechanism. Alcohols can be converted to tosylates or mesylates so they do not react. They can then be converted back to alcohols. By this method, tosylates and mesylates can be used to protect alcohol moeties from unintended reactions.

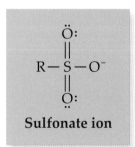

**Sulfonate ion**

Figure 2.32 Synthesis of a tosylate and Mesylate

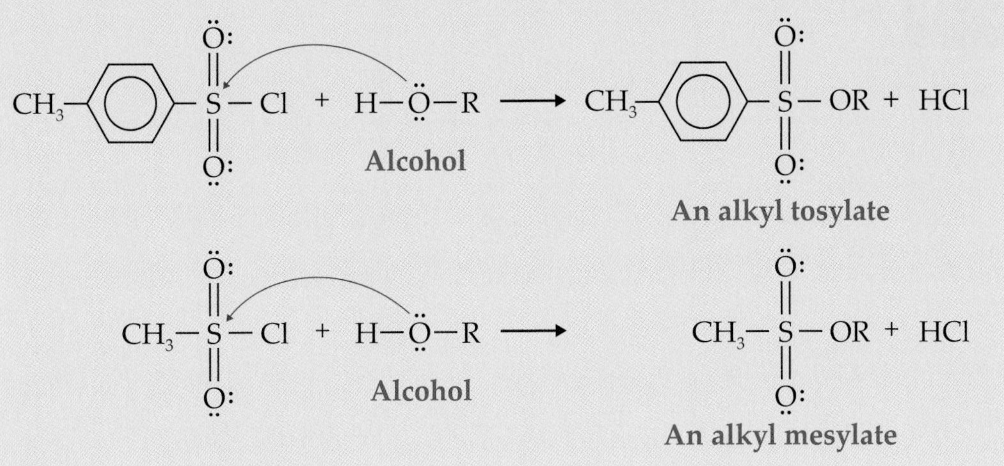

An alkyl tosylate

An alkyl mesylate

Tosylates and mesylates can be used to protect alcohols.

## 2.27 The Pinacol Rearrangement

The **pinacol rearrangement** is a dehydration of an alcohol that results in an unexpected product. When hot sulfuric acid is added to an alcohol, the expected product of dehydration is an alkene. However, if the alcohol is a vicinal diol, the product will be a ketone or aldehyde. The reaction follows the mechanism shown in Figure 2.33. The first hydroxyl group is protonated and removed by the acid to form a carbocation in an expected dehydration step. Now, a methyl group may move to form an even more stable carbocation. This new carbocation exhibits resonance as shown. Resonance Structure 2 is favored because all the atoms have an octet of electrons. The water deprotonates Resonance Structure 2, forming pinacolone and regenerating the acid catalyst.

### Figure 2.33 The Pinacol Rearrangement

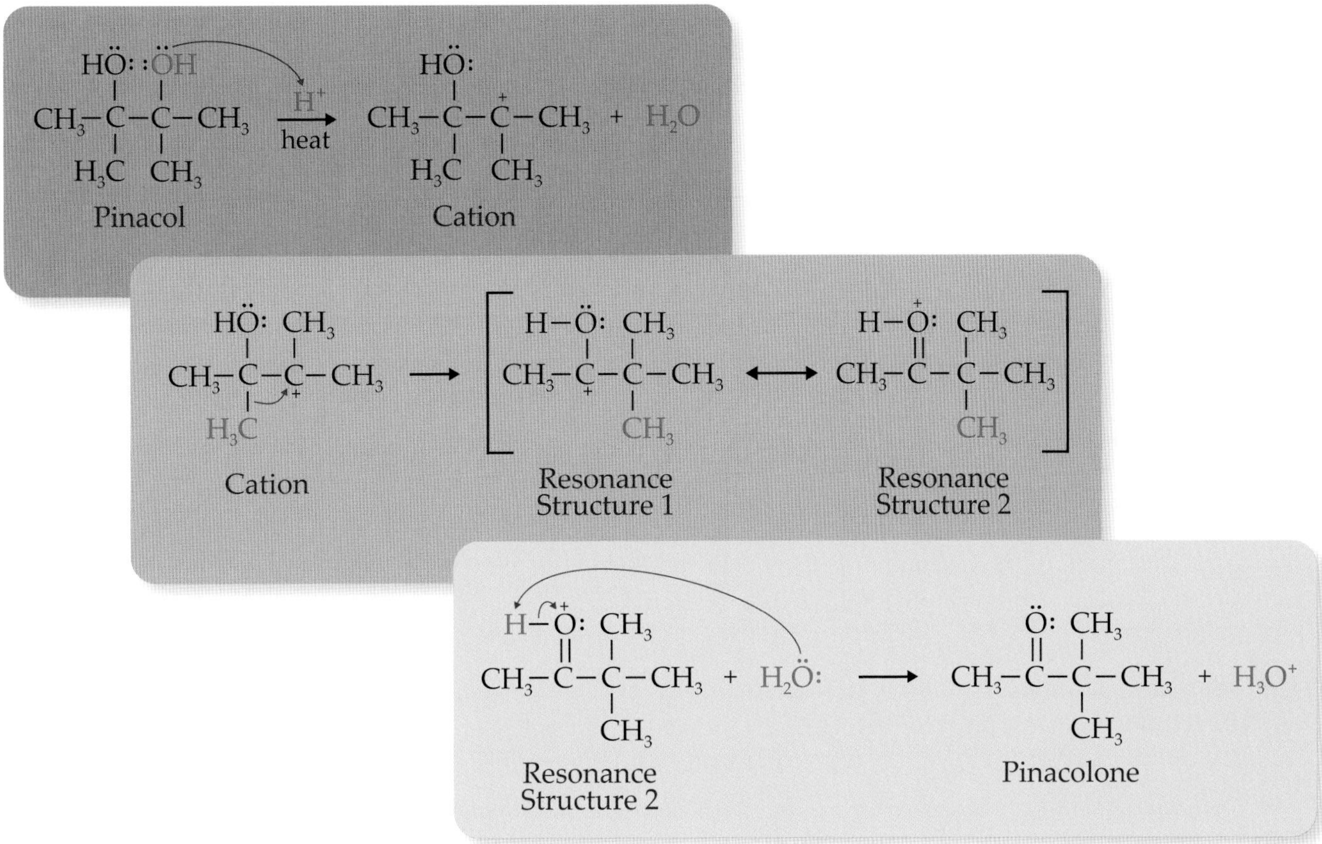

## 2.28 Ethers

Ethers (other than epoxides) are relatively non-reactive. They are polar. Although they cannot hydrogen bond with themselves, they can hydrogen bond with compounds that contain a hydrogen attached to a N, O, or F atom. Ethers are roughly as soluble in water as alcohols of similar molecular weight, yet organic compounds tend to be much more soluble in ethers than alcohols because no hydrogen bonds need to be broken. These properties make ethers useful solvents.

Since an ether cannot hydrogen bond with itself, it will have a boiling point roughly comparable to that of an alkane with a similar molecular weight. Their relatively low boiling points increase their usefulness as solvents.

For the MCAT, ethers (other than epoxides) undergo one reaction. Ethers are cleaved by the halo-acids HI and HBr to form the corresponding alcohol and alkyl halide. If a large concentration of acid is used, the excess acid will react with the alcohol, as described above, to form another alkyl halide.

### Figure 2.34  Cleavage of an Ether with Strong Acid

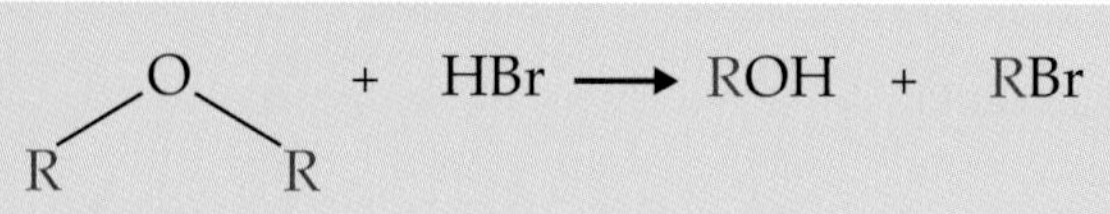

$$R{-}O{-}R \quad + \quad HBr \longrightarrow ROH \quad + \quad RBr$$

Ethers can also be oxidized to peroxides, but this is unlikely to be on the MCAT.

## 2.29 Epoxides

*Epoxides* (also called *oxiranes*) are three-membered cyclic ethers. They are more reactive than typical ethers due to the strain created by the small ring. Epoxides react with water in the presence of an acid catalyst to form diols, commonly called glycols. This is an anti-addition.

### Figure 2.35  Opening of an epoxide

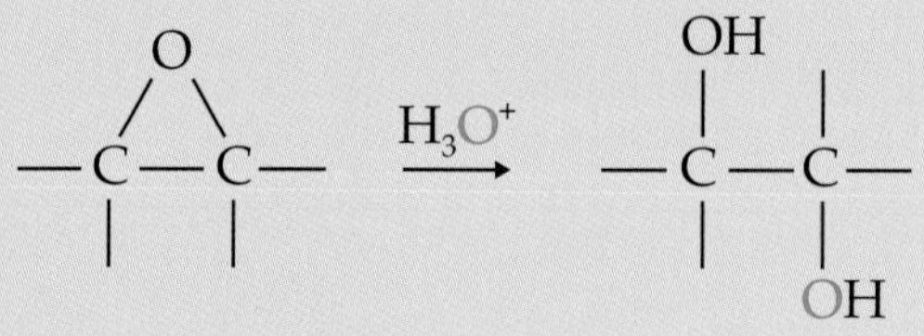

$$\xrightarrow{H_3O^+}$$

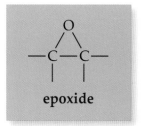

epoxide

The epoxide oxygen is often protonated to form an alcohol when one of the carbons is attacked by a nucleophile.

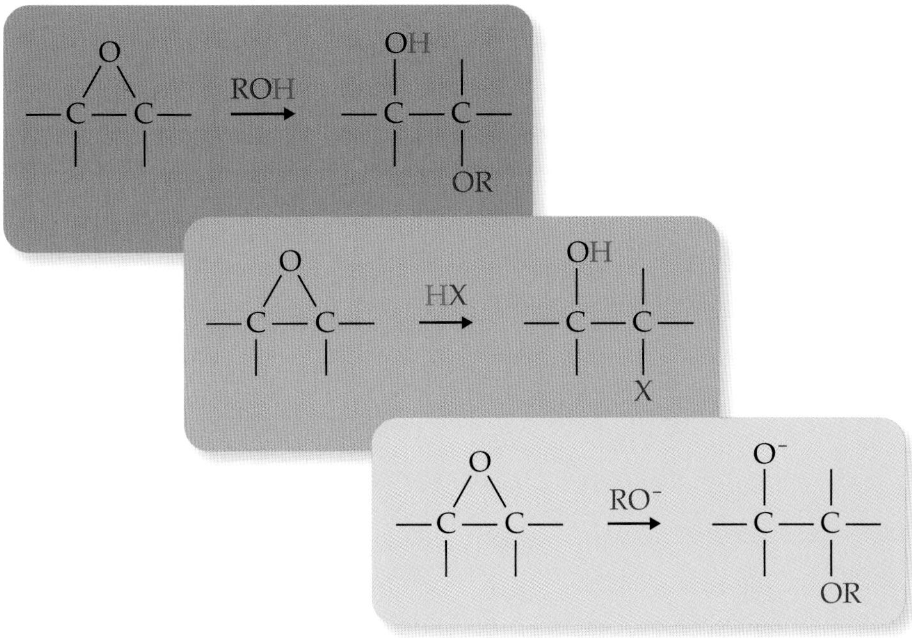

An epoxide is an ether but is far more reactive. You don't have to memorize the reactions of epoxides for the MCAT.

**Figure 2.36   Example Reactions of Expoxides**

## 2.30 | Acidities of the Functional Groups

Now that you know all about the important functional groups, it is a good idea to know their acidities. From weakest to strongest acids, they are as follows:

**Figure 2.37   Relative Acidity of the Fuctional Groups**

$$H_3C-CH_3 \; < \; H_2C=CH_2 \; < \; H_2 \; < \; NH_3 \; < \; HC\equiv CH \; < \; H_3C-\overset{\overset{\displaystyle O}{\|}}{C}-H$$

$$< \; H_3C-CH_2-OH \; < \; H_2O \; < \; H_3C-\overset{\overset{\displaystyle O}{\|}}{C}-OH$$

Acid Strength

| Terms |
|---|

| | |
|---|---|
| Alcohols | Markovnikov's Rule |
| Alkanes | Mesylates |
| Alkene | Meta |
| Anti-addition | Nucleophile |
| Anti-Markovnikov Addition | Ortho |
| Axial Hydrogens | Oxidation |
| Benzene | Para |
| Boat | Pinacol Rearrangement |
| Carbocation Stability | Primary Carbon |
| Combustion | Propogation Step |
| Chair | Quaternary Carbon |
| Dehydration Of An Alcohol | Radical Reaction |
| Dehydrohalogenation | Rate Determining Step |
| Electron Donating Group | Reduction |
| Electron Withdrawing group | Resonance |
| Electrophile | Ring Strain |
| Electrophilic Addition | Saytzeff Rule |
| Elimination | Secondary Carbon |
| Equatorial Hydrogens | $S_N1$ |
| Ethers | $S_N2$ |
| Free Radical | Substitution |
| Grignard Reagents | Substrate |
| Grignard Synthesis | Syn Addition |
| Heat of Combustion | Termination Step |
| Hydration Of An Alkene | Tertiary Carbon |
| Initiation Step | Tosylates |
| Leaving Group | |

**41.** A student added NaCl to ethanol in the polar aprotic solvent DMF, and no reaction took place. To the same solution, he then added HCl. A reaction took place resulting in chloroethane. Which of the following best explains the student's results?

A.  The addition of HCl increased the chloride ion concentration which increased the rate of the reaction and pushed the equilibrium to the right.
B.  The chloride ion is a better nucleophile in a polar protic solvent and the HCl protonated the solvent.
C.  The HCl protonated the hydroxyl group on the alcohol making it a better leaving group.
D.  The HCl destabilized the chloride ion complex between the chloride ion and the solvent.

**42.** All of the following will increase the rate of the reaction shown below EXCEPT:

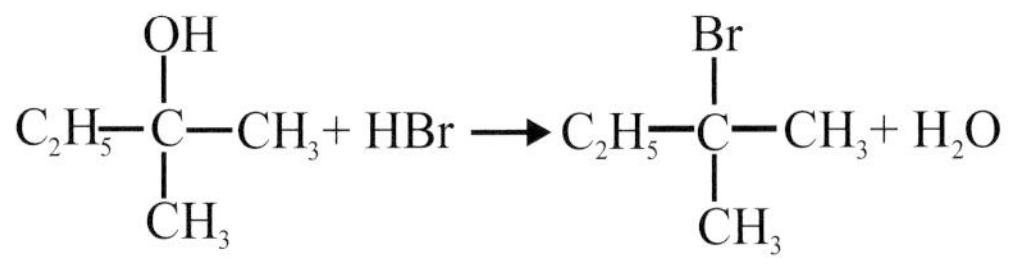

$$C_2H_5{-}\underset{\underset{CH_3}{|}}{\overset{\overset{OH}{|}}{C}}{-}CH_3 + HBr \longrightarrow C_2H_5{-}\underset{\underset{CH_3}{|}}{\overset{\overset{Br}{|}}{C}}{-}CH_3 + H_2O$$

I.   increasing the concentration of *tert*-butyl alcohol
II.  increasing the concentration of hydrobromic acid
III. increasing the temperature

A.  I only
B.  II only
C.  III only
D.  II and III only

**43.** The following reaction is one of many steps in the laboratory synthesis of cholesterol. What type of reaction is it?

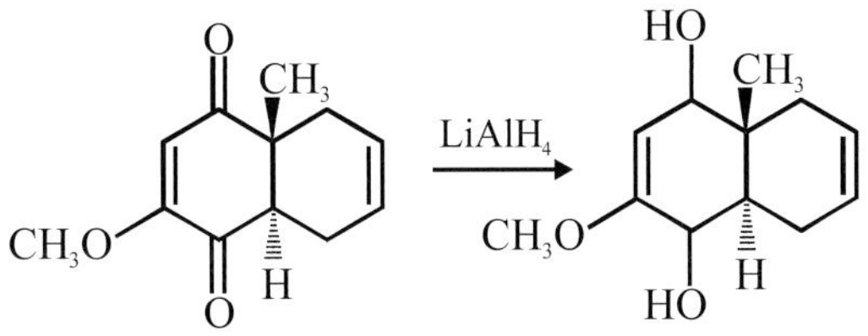

A.  reduction reaction
B.  oxidation reaction
C.  catalytic hydrogenation
D.  electrophilic substitution

**44.** Labetalol is a β-adrenergic antagonist which reduces blood pressure by blocking reflex sympathetic stimulation of the heart.

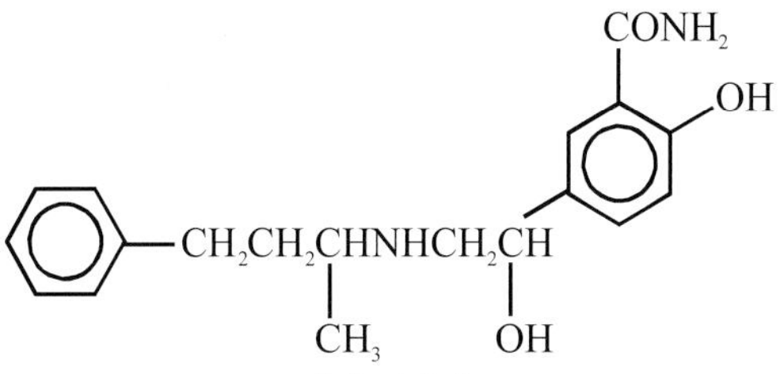

**labetalol**

Which of the following intermolecular bonds contributes least to the water solubility of labetalol?

A.

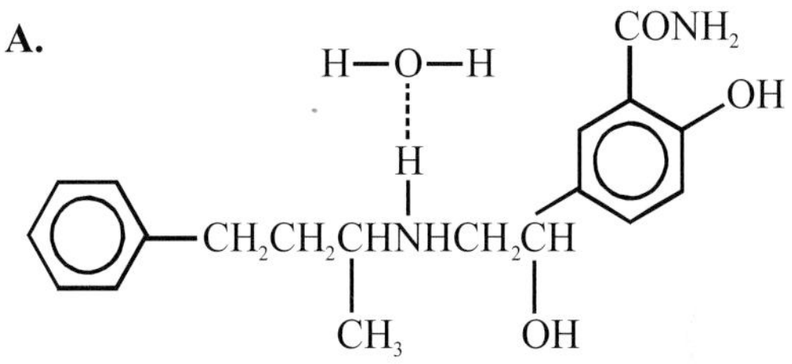

B.

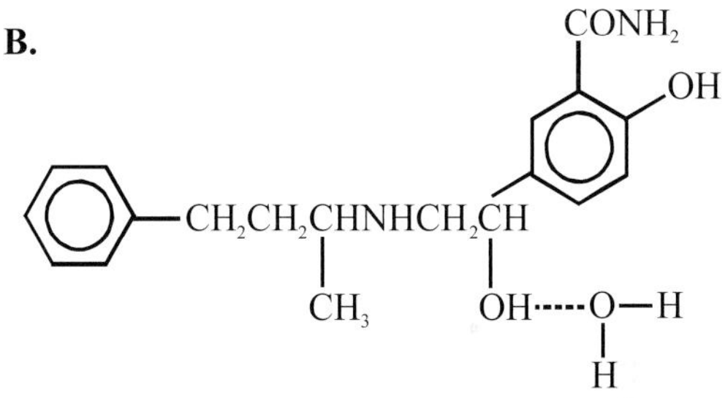

C.

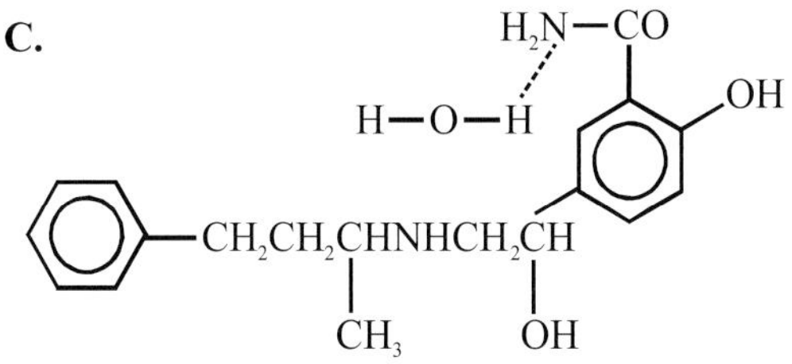

D.

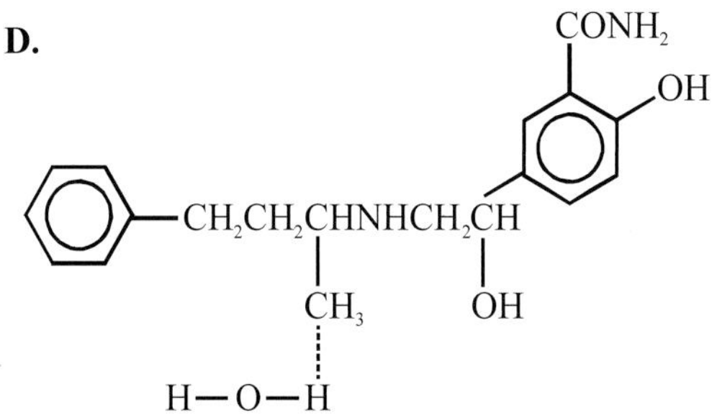

**45.** The Lucas test distinguishes between the presence of primary, secondary, and tertiary alcohols based upon reactivity with a hydrogen halide. The corresponding alkyl chlorides are insoluble in Lucas reagent and turn the solution cloudy at the same rate that they react with the reagent. The alcohols, A, B, and C, are solvated separately in Lucas reagent made of hydrochloric acid and zinc chloride. If the alcohols are primary, secondary, and tertiary respectively, what is the order of their rates of reaction from fastest to slowest?

A. A, B, C
B. B, A, C
C. C, B, A
D. B, C, A

**46.** Reactions 1 and 2 were carried out in the presence of peroxides. Which of the following is the most likely explanation for why Product B fails to form?

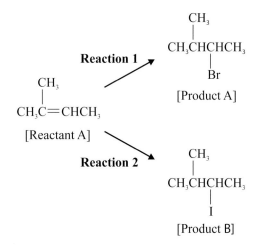

A. Hydrogen halides always yield products of Markovnikov's addition.
B. Reactions 1 and 2 show Markovnikov and anti-Markovnikov addition, respectively.
C. Peroxide dependent anti-Markovnikov addition succeeds only with bromine.
D. Markovnikov addition reactions 1 and 2 are driven by reagent concentrations.

**47.** The most common reaction of alcohols is nucleophilic substitution. All of the following correctly describe $S_N2$ reactions, EXCEPT:

I. reaction rate = $k$ [S][Nucleophile]
II. racemic mixture of products results
III. inversion of configuration occurs

A. I and II only
B. II only
C. III only
D. I, II and III

**48.** Which statement is the most likely explanation for why 1-chloro-1,2-diphenylethane proceeds via $S_N1$ at a constant rate independent of nucleophilic quality or concentration?

A. 1-chloro-1,2-diphenylethane prefers $S_N2$ mechanism for rapid substitution
B. $S_N1$ rate-limiting step determines the overall reaction rate
C. 1-chloro-1,2-diphenylethane concentration increase will not cause an increase in product synthesis
D. reaction product accumulation has a direct effect on the rate-limiting step

# CARBONYLS AND AMINES

## 3.1 The Carbonyl

A **carbonyl** is a carbon double bonded to an oxygen. The double bond is shorter and stronger than the double bond of an alkene. Aldehydes, ketones, carboxylic acids, amides, and esters all contain carbonyls. Whenever you see a carbonyl on the MCAT think about two things:

1) **planar stereochemistry** and;

2) partial negative charge on the oxygen, **partial positive charge on the carbon**.

The planar stereochemistry of a carbonyl leaves open space above and below, making it susceptible to chemical attack. The partial positive charge on the carbon means that any attack on the carbonyl carbon will be from a nucleophile. Aldehydes and ketones typically undergo nucleophilic addition, while other carbonyl compounds prefer nucleophilic substitution. The partial negative charge on the oxygen means that it is easily protonated.

**Figure 3.1   Carbonyl**

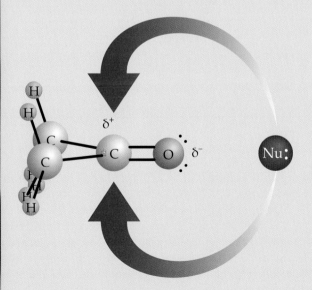

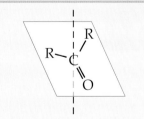

Planar stereochemistry of a carbonyl carbon

Carbonyl carbons readily undergo nucleophilic attack.

## 3.2 Aldehydes and Ketones

You should be able to recognize and give the common name for the simple **aldehydes** and **ketones** shown below.

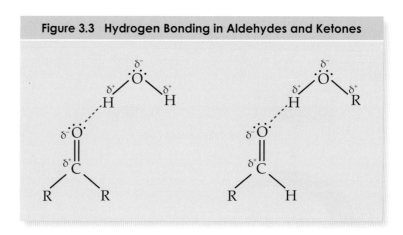

**Figure 3.2   Aldehydes and Ketones**

aldehyde  •  formaldehyde (methanal)  •  ketone  •  acetone (2-propanone)

## 3.3 Physical Properties

Aldehydes and ketones are more polar and have higher boiling points than alkanes and alkenes of similar molecular weight. However, they cannot hydrogen bond with each other, so they have lower boiling points than corresponding alcohols. Aldehydes and ketones do accept hydrogen bonds with water and other compounds that can hydrogen bond. This makes them excellent solvents for these substances. Aldehydes and ketones with up to four carbons are soluble in water.

**Figure 3.3   Hydrogen Bonding in Aldehydes and Ketones**

## 3.4 Chemical Properties

Most of the time on the MCAT an **aldehyde** or **ketone** will be acting either as the **substrate in nucleophilic addition** or as a Brønsted-Lowry acid by donating one of its α-hydrogens. A carbon that is attached to a carbonyl carbon is in the **alpha position** and is called an **α-carbon**. The next carbon is called a β-*carbon*; the next is the γ-*carbon* and so on down the Greek alphabet. An α-hydrogen is any hydrogen attached to an α-carbon. Normally hydrogens are not easily removed from carbons because carbon anions are very strong bases and unstable. However, α-carbon anions are stabilized by resonance. This anion is called an *enolate ion* (en from alkene and ol from alcohol).

Tollens reagent is used to distinguish between aldehydes and ketones. The Tollen's reagent and an aldehyde are reacted in a test tube (left). The aldehyde reduces the complex silver ions to metallic silver, which deposit on the inside of the reaction vessel (right).

**Figure 3.4   Enolate Ion**

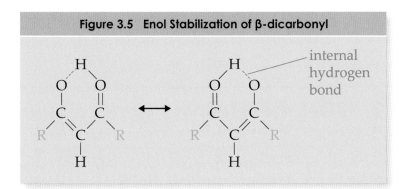

**An enolate ion is stabilized by resonance.**

When the β-carbon is also a carbonyl (called a β-dicarbonyl), the enol form becomes far more stable due to internal hydrogen bonding and resonance.

**Figure 3.5   Enol Stabilization of β-dicarbonyl**

internal hydrogen bond

> The dicarbonyl increases the acidity of the α-hydrogen between the carbonyls, making it more acidic than water or alcohol.

Because alkyl groups are electron donating and a ketone has two alkyl groups attached to the carbonyl, the carbonyl carbon of the conjugate base of the ketone is less able to distribute negative charge and is slightly less stable than that of an aldehyde. Thus, aldehydes are slightly more acidic than ketones. This same property makes aldehydes more reactive than ketones. Both aldehydes and ketones are less acidic than alcohols. Any electron withdrawing groups attached to the α-carbon or the carbonyl tend to stabilitze the conjugate base and thus increase the acidity.

**Figure 3.6   Keto-enol Tautomerization**

Keto-enol tautomerization is a reaction at equilibrium and NOT a resonance.

As with other equilibrium processes, the rate of reaction may be increased by adding a catalyst. Keto-enol tautomerization may be either acid or base catalyzed. Any electron withdrawing groups attached to the α-carbon or the carbonyl tend to stabilize the conjugate base and thus increase acidity. Due to the properties of the α-hydrogen and carbonyl, ketones and aldehydes exist at room temperature as enol **tautomers**. Tautomerization involves a proton shift, in this case from the α-carbon position to the carbonyl oxygen position. Both tautomers exist at room temperature, but the ketone or aldehyde tautomer is usually favored. Tautomerization is a reaction at equilibrium, not a resonance. (Remember, in resonance structures atoms don't move and neither resonance structure actually exists.)

> There are other forms of tautomerization but keto-enol tautomerization is the most likely form to be tested on the MCAT. In order to recognize other forms, simply watch for the proton shift in equilibrium.

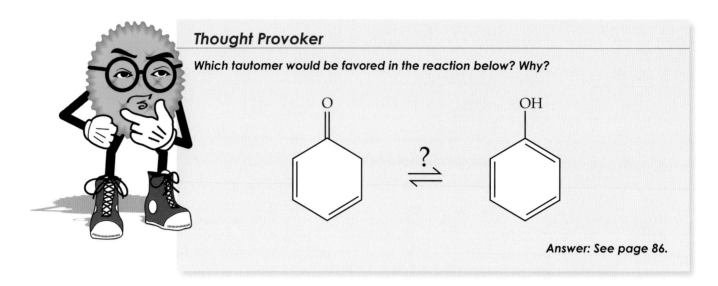

Artisanal distillery is shown above. Acetaldehyde diethyl acetal is an important flavouring compound in distilled beverages.

## 3.5 Formation of Acetals

Aldehydes and ketones react with alcohols to form *hemiacetals* and *hemiketals*, respectively. In this reaction the alcohols react in typical fashion as the nucleophile. When aldehydes and ketones are attacked by a nucleophile, they undergo addition. Aldehydes and hemiacetals, and ketones and hemiketals, exist in equilibrium when an aldehyde or ketone is dissolved in an alcohol; however, usually the hemiacetal or hemiketal is too unstable to be isolated unless it exists as a ring structure. If a second molar equivalent of alcohol is added, an *acetal* is formed from a hemiacetal, or a *ketal* is formed from a hemiketal.

### Figure 3.7 Nucleophilic Addition of Alcohol to Aldehydes and Ketones

aldehyde          hemiacetal          acetal

ketone          hemiketal          ketal

The aldehyde products can be easily distinguished from the ketone products by the lone hydrogen. The hemi products can be distinguished from the acetals and ketals because the hemi products both have alcohol functional groups while the full acetals and ketals don't. Hemi formation is catalyzed by acid or base. In formation of acetal and ketal from the hemi forms the hydroxyl group must be protonated to make a good leaving group, thus this part of the reaction is catalyzed by acid only.

Because acetals and ketals are unreactive toward bases, they are often used *as blocking groups*. In other words, a base would typically act as a nucleophile to attack an aldehyde or ketone at the carbonyl carbon, but the aldehyde or ketone can be temporarily changed to an acetal or ketal to prevent it from reacting with a base.

### Figure 3.8   A Protection Reaction

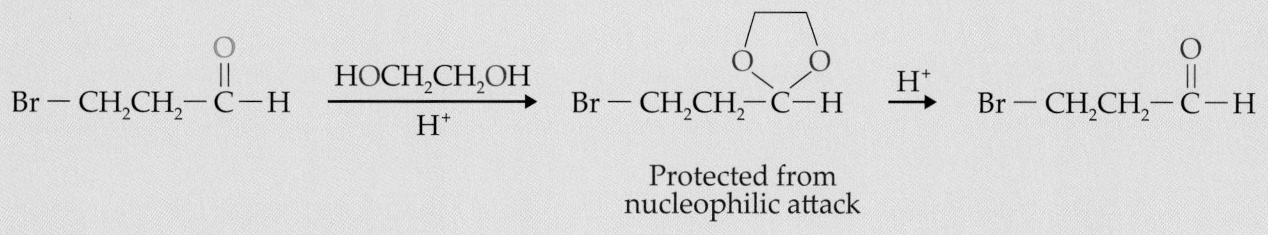

$$Br - CH_2CH_2 - \overset{\overset{\displaystyle O}{||}}{C} - H \quad \xrightarrow[\text{H}^+]{\text{HOCH}_2\text{CH}_2\text{OH}} \quad Br - CH_2CH_2 - C - H \quad \xrightarrow{\text{H}^+} \quad Br - CH_2CH_2 - \overset{\overset{\displaystyle O}{||}}{C} - H$$

Protected from
nucleophilic attack

In a similar reaction, when aldehydes or ketones are dissolved in aqueous solution, they establish an equilibrium with their hydrate, a geminal diol.

### Figure 3.9   Hydration of an Aldehyde and  Ketone

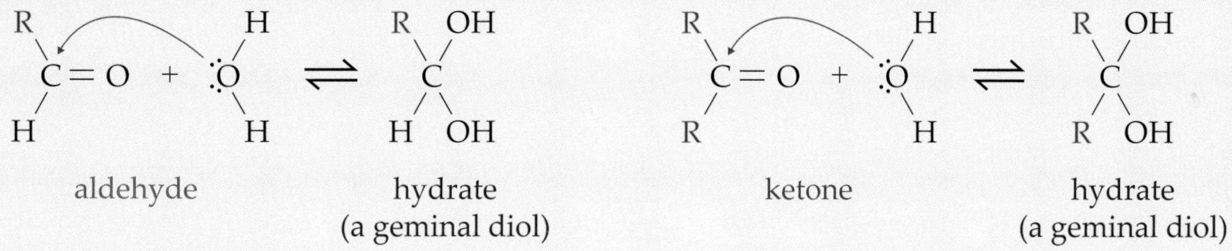

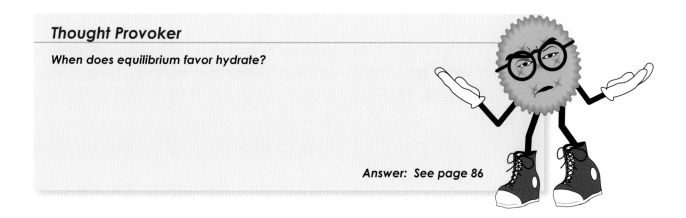

aldehyde     hydrate (a geminal diol)     ketone     hydrate (a geminal diol)

## Thought Provoker

**When does equilibrium favor hydrate?**

Answer:  See page 86

# Aldol Condensation

**Aldol condensation** is a favorite on the MCAT because it demonstrates both $\alpha$-hydrogen activity and the susceptibility of carbonyl carbons to a nucleophile. *Aldol* (<u>ald</u> from aldehyde and <u>ol</u> from alcohol) condensation occurs when one aldehyde reacts with another, when one ketone reacts with another, or when an aldehyde reacts with a ketone. The reaction is catalyzed by an acid or base. In the first step of the base-catalyzed reaction, the base abstracts an $\alpha$-hydrogen leaving an enolate ion. In the second step, the enolate ion acts as a nucleophile and attacks the carbonyl carbon to form an *alkoxide* ion. The alkoxide ion is a stronger base than a hydroxide ion and thus removes a proton from water to complete the aldol. (Notice that the alkoxide ion is stronger because it has an electron donating alkyl group attached to the oxygen, thus increasing its negative charge.) The aldol is unstable and is easily dehydrated by heat or a base to become an *enal*. The enal is stabilized by its conjugated double bonds.

**Figure 3.10   Aldol Condensation**

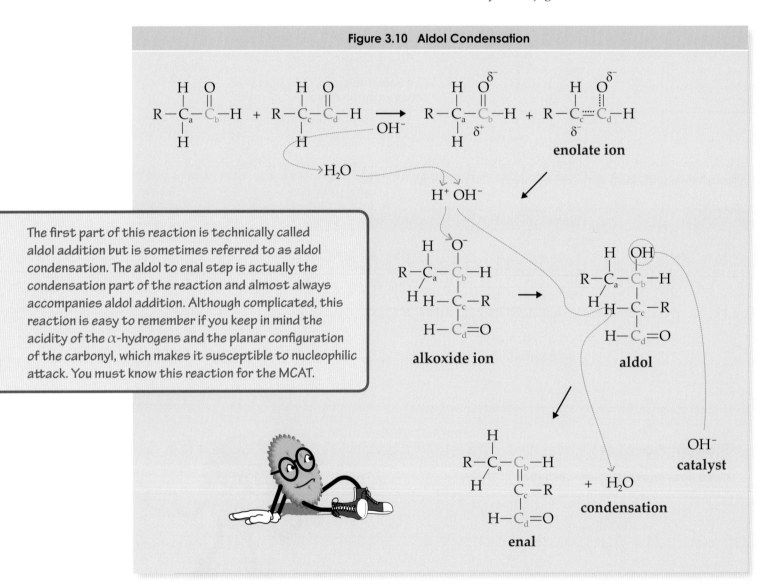

The first part of this reaction is technically called aldol addition but is sometimes referred to as aldol condensation. The aldol to enal step is actually the condensation part of the reaction and almost always accompanies aldol addition. Although complicated, this reaction is easy to remember if you keep in mind the acidity of the $\alpha$-hydrogens and the planar configuration of the carbonyl, which makes it susceptible to nucleophilic attack. You must know this reaction for the MCAT.

## 3.7 Halogenation and the Haloform reaction

Halogens add to ketones at the alpha carbon in the presence of a base or an acid. When a base is used, it is difficult to prevent halogenation at more than one of the alpha positions. The base is also consumed by the reaction with water as a by-product, whereas the acid acts as a true catalyst and is not consumed.

**Figure 3.11 Halogenation of a Ketone**

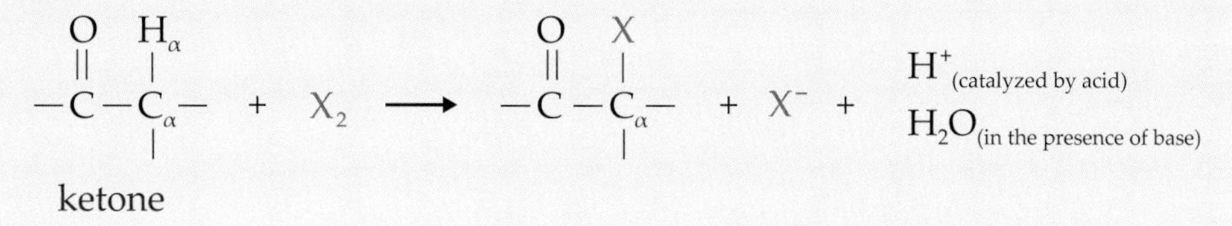

When a base is used with a methyl ketone, the alpha carbon will become completely halogenated. This trihalo product reacts further with the base to produce a carboxylic acid and a haloform (chloroform, $CHCl_3$; bromoform, $CHBr_3$; or iodoform, $CHI_3$). This is called the "Haloform Reaction".

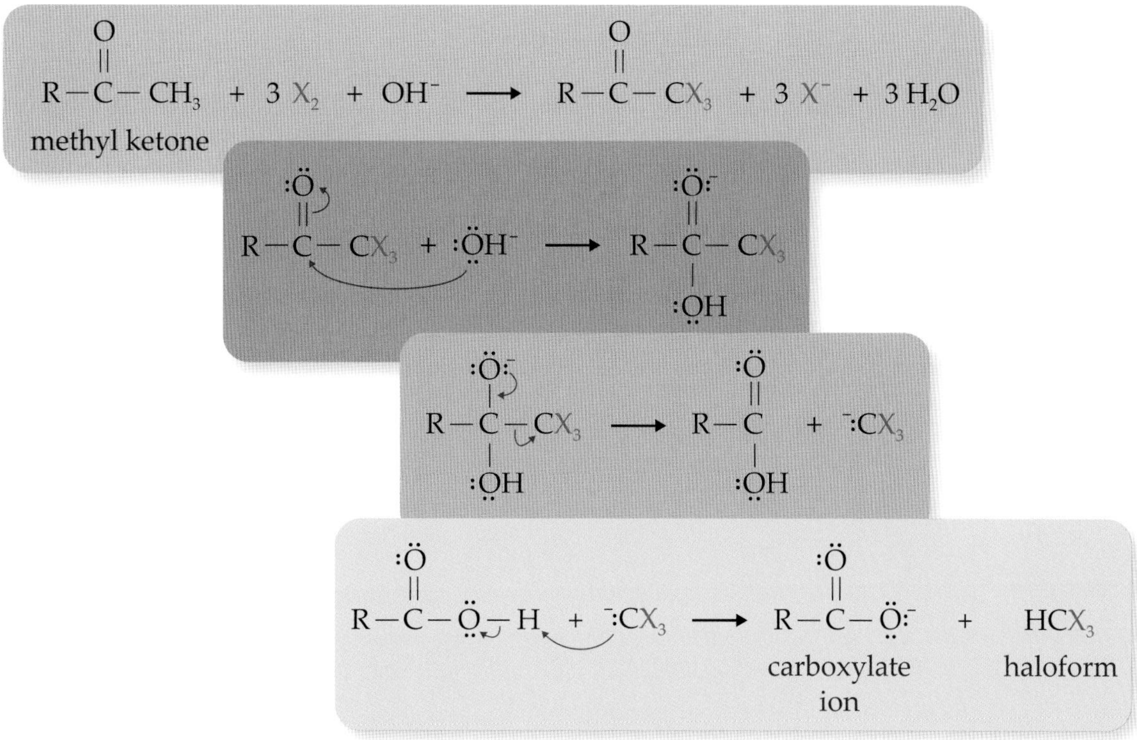

**Figure 3.12 Haloform Reaction**

## 3.8 The Wittig Reaction

**The Wittig reaction** converts a ketone to an alkene. A phosphorous ylide (pronounced "ill'-id") is used. An ylide is a neutral molecule with a negatively charged carbanion.

The ketone behaves in its normal fashion, first undergoing nucleophilic addition from the ylide to form a betaine (pronounced "bay'-tuh-ene"). However, the betaine is unstable and quickly breaks down to a triphenylphosphine oxide and the alkene. When possible, a mixture of both *cis* and *trans* isomers are formed by the Wittig reaction.

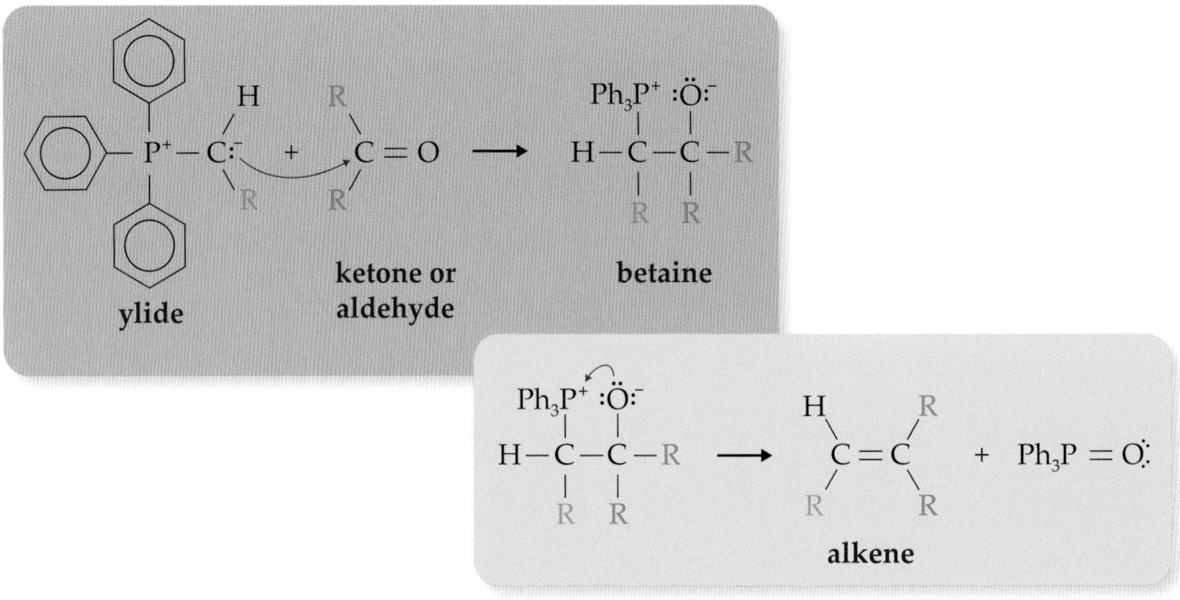

**Figure 3.13 Wittig Reaction**

*Notes:*

## 3.9 α–β Unsaturated Carbonyls

A carbonyl compound with a double bond between the α and β carbon has some special properties. The carbocation that is produced at the carbonyl carbon when the electrons in the carbonyl double bond shift to the oxygen atom (giving the oxygen a negative charge) is stabilized by resonance. Additionally, the electron withdrawing carbonyl group pulls electrons from the carbon-carbon double bond and makes it less susceptible to attack by an electrophile (electrophile addition). Thus, rather than the nucleophile adding to the β-carbon, it may sometime add to the oxygen atom, forming the enol-keto tautomers.

Even more strange is the ability of the β-carbon to undergo nucleophilic addition directly. This is sometimes called *conjugate addition*.

**Figure 3.14  Conjugate Addition**

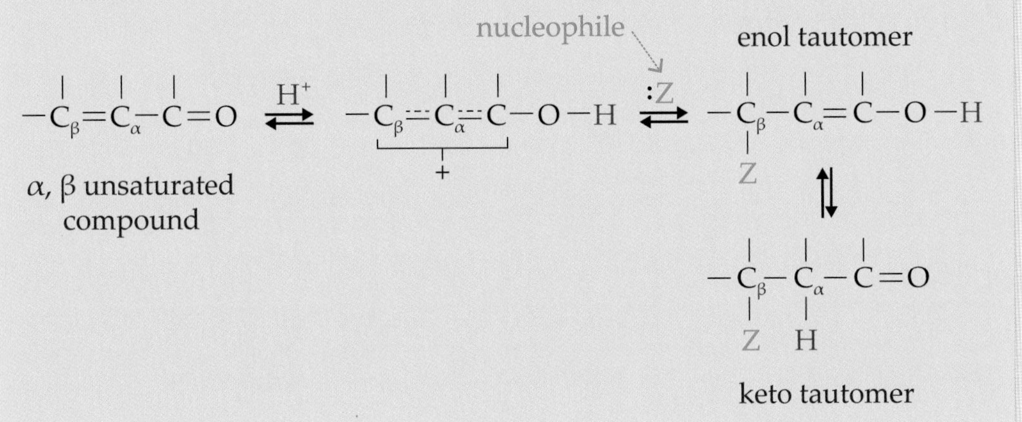

Of course, we know that aldehydes and ketones undergo nucleophilic addition at the carbonyl, and for many nucleophiles this carbonyl addition is still the major product in the above reaction.

**Figure 3.15  Nucleophilic Addition**

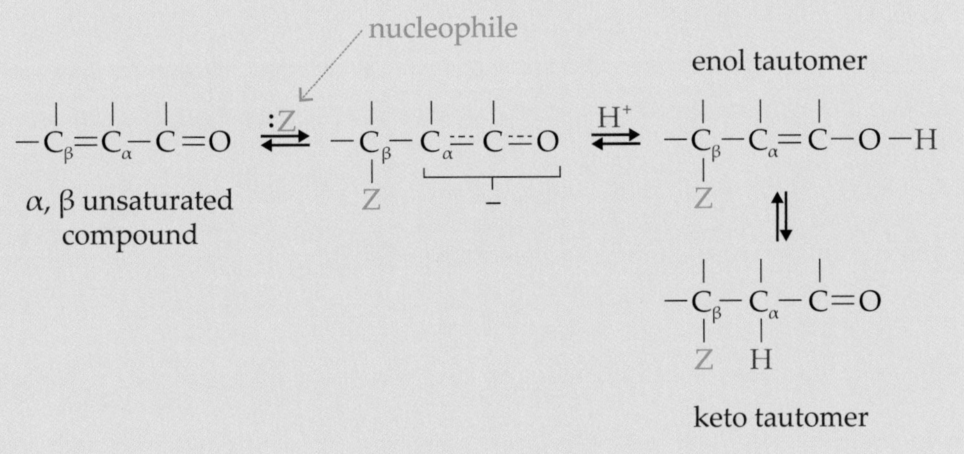

Questions 49 through 56 are **NOT** based on a descriptive passage.

**49.** What is the major product of the crossed aldol reaction shown below?

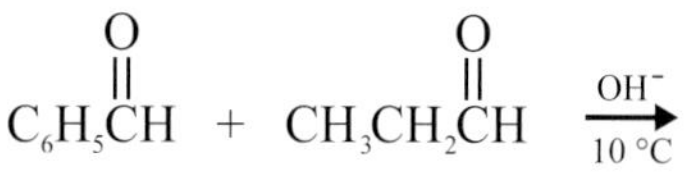

**A.**

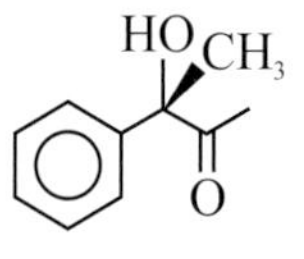

**B.**

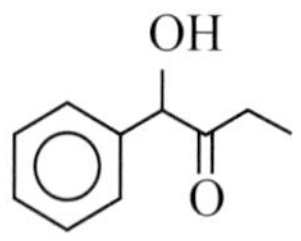

**C.**

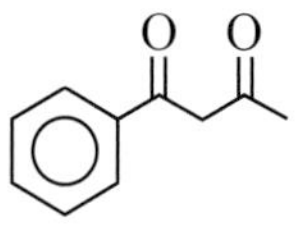

**D.**

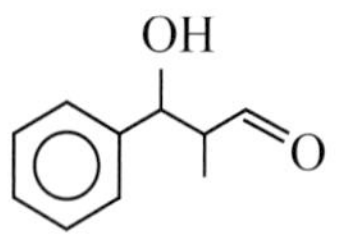

**50.** Which of the following statements are true concerning the molecule shown below?

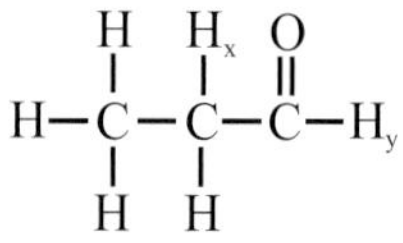

**I.** $H_x$ is more acidic than $H_y$.
**II.** $H_y$ is more acidic than $H_x$.
**III.** This molecule typically undergoes nucleophilic substitution.

**A.** I only
**B.** II only
**C.** I and III only
**D.** II and III only

**51.** Which of the following is the product of an aldehyde reduction reaction?

**A.**

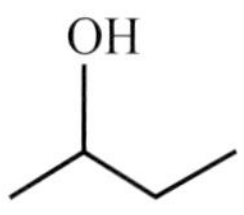

**B.**

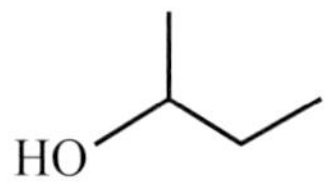

**C.**

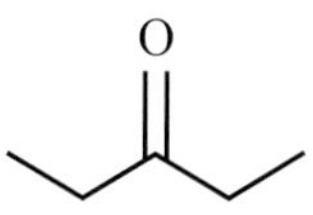

**D.**

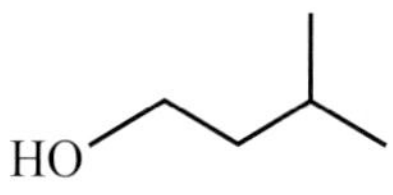

**52.** If the first step were omitted in the following set of reactions, what would be the final product?

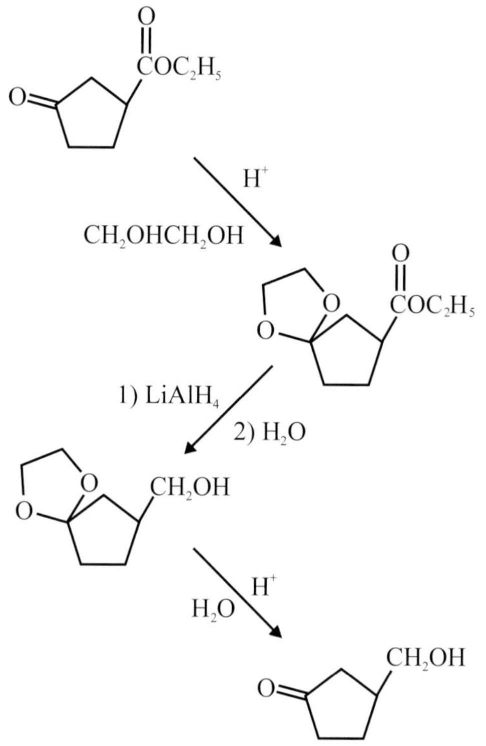

**A.**

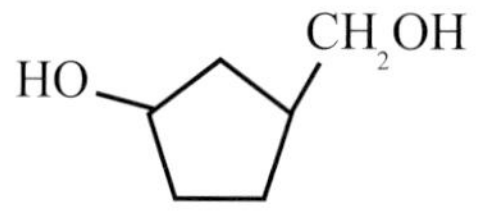

**B.**

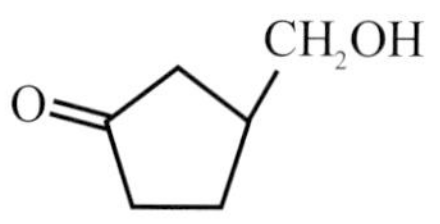

**C.**

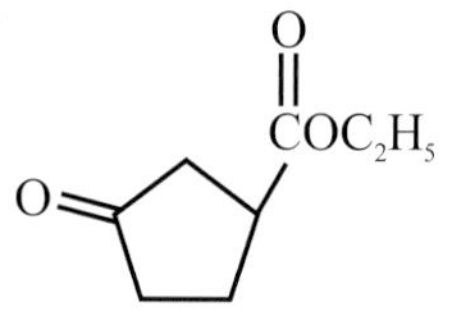

**D.**

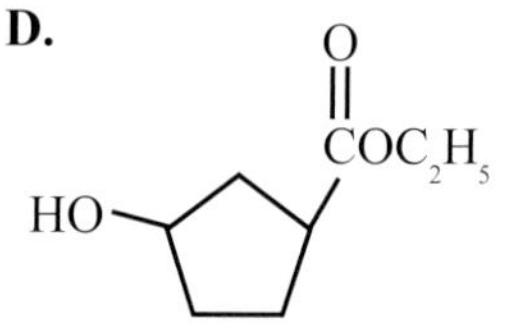

**53.** Which of the following is the strongest acid?

**A.**

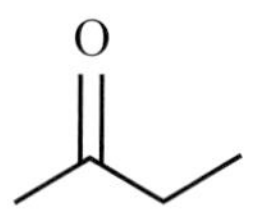

**B.**

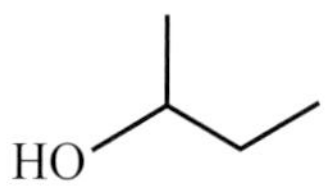

**C.**

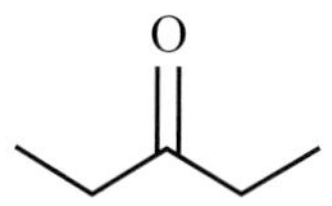

**D.**

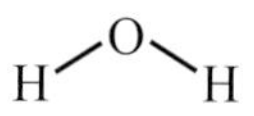



**GO ON TO THE NEXT PAGE.**

**54.** Aldehydes are readily oxidized to yield carboxylic acids, but ketones are inert to oxidation. Which is the most likely explanation regarding this difference in reactivity?

**A.** Aldehydes have a proton attached to the carbonyl that is abstracted during oxidation. Ketones lack this proton and so cannot be oxidized.
**B.** Reducing agents like $HNO_3$ are sterically hindered by ketone's carbonyl carbon.
**C.** Aldehydes and ketones are of similar hybridization.
**D.** The rate of the forward oxidation reaction is equal to the rate of the reverse reduction reaction in ketones.

**55.** 1,3-cyclohexane dione is shown below.

[1,3 cyclohexane dione]

Which of the following is not a tautomer of 1,3-cyclohexane done?

**A.**

**C.**

**B.**

**D.**

**56.** Glucose reduces Tollens reagent to give an aldonic acid, ammonia, water, and a silver mirror. Methyl β-glucoside does not reduce Tollens reagent. Based on the structures shown below, which of the following best explains why methyl β-glucoside gives a negative Tollens test?

Glucose                    methyl b-glucoside

**A.** Aldehydes are not oxidized by Tollens reagent.
**B.** Ketones are not oxidized by Tollens reagent.
**C.** Hemiacetal rings are stable and do not easily open to form straight chain aldehydes.
**D.** Acetal rings are stable and do not easily open to form straight chain aldehydes.

_____

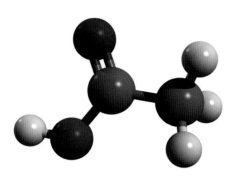

Acetic acid, also called ethanoic acid, is the component of vinegar that gives it its sour taste and pungent smell. It is used as a preservative and in the production of plastics.

## 3.10 Carboxylic Acids

You should be able to recognize and give the common name for the simplest **carboxylic acids** shown below.

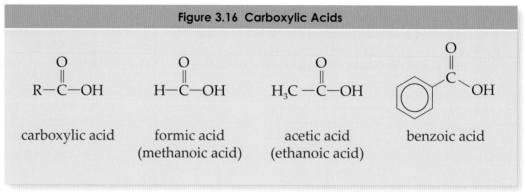

**Figure 3.16 Carboxylic Acids**

carboxylic acid | formic acid (methanoic acid) | acetic acid (ethanoic acid) | benzoic acid

sodium acetate
(sodium ethanoate)
A salt of acetic acid.

Carboxylic acids where the R group is an alkyl group are called *aliphatic acids*. The salts of carboxylic acids are named with the suffix *-ate*. The *-ate* replaces the *-ic* (or *-oic* in IUPAC names), so that "acetic" becomes "acetate". (Acetate is sometimes abbreviated –OAc.) In IUPAC rules, the carbonyl carbon of a carboxylic acid takes priority over all groups discussed so far.

On the MCAT, look for carboxylic acid to behave as an acid or as the substrate in a **nucleophilic substitution reaction**. Like any carbonyl compound, its stereochemistry makes it susceptible to nucleophiles. When the hydroxyl group is protonated, the good leaving group, water, is formed and substitution results.

As far as organic acids go, carboxylic acids are very strong. When the proton is removed, the conjugate base is stabilized by resonance.

Electron withdrawing groups on the α-carbon help to further stabilize the conjugate base and thus increase the acidity of the corresponding carboxylic acid.

Resonance stabilization of a carboxylate ion

## 3.11 Physical Properties

Carboxylic acids are able to make strong double **hydrogen bonds** to form a dimer. The dimer significantly increases the boiling point of carboxylic acids by effectively doubling the molecular weight of the molecules leaving the liquid phase. Saturated carboxylic acids with more than 8 carbons are generally solids. The double bonds in unsaturated carboxylic acids impede the crystal lattice and lower melting point.

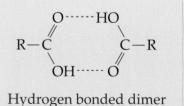

Hydrogen bonded dimer

Citric acid ($C_6H_8O_7$) is a tricarboxylic acid found in citrus fruit, such as lemons.

Carboxylic acids with four carbons or less are miscible with water. Carboxylic acids with five or more carbons become increasingly less soluble in water. Carboxylic acids with more than 10 carbons are insoluble in water. Carboxylic acids are soluble in most nonpolar solvents because the dimer form allows the carboxylic acid to solvate without disrupting the hydrogen bonds of the dimer.

# 3.12 Decarboxylation

When a carboxylic acid loses $CO_2$ the reaction is called **decarboxylation**. Although the reaction is usually exothermic, the energy of activation is usually high, making the reaction difficult to carry out. The energy of activation is lowered when the β-carbon is a carbonyl because either the anion intermediate is stabilized by resonance or the acid forms a more stable cyclic intermediate. (A carboxylic acid with a carbonyl β-carbon is called a β-*keto acid*.)

**Figure 3.17  Decarboxylation**

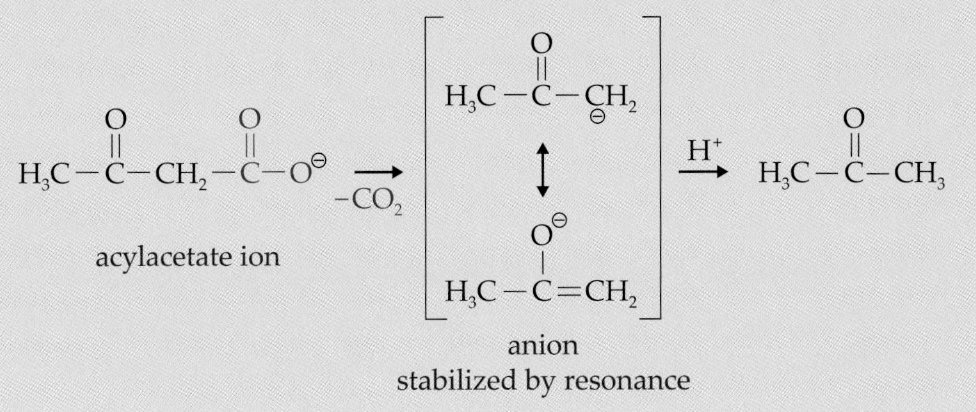

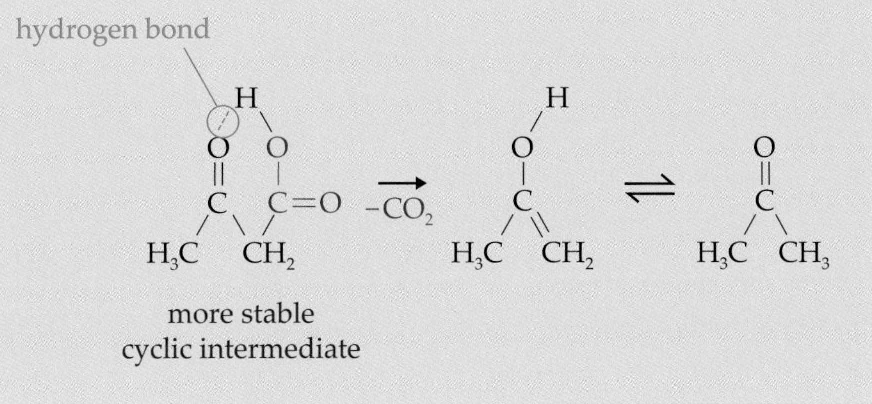

Notice that the first reaction starts with the anion and the second reaction starts with the acid. Notice also that the final products of both reactions are tautomers.

O
‖
R—C—

**acyl group**

## 3.13 Carboxylic Acid Derivatives

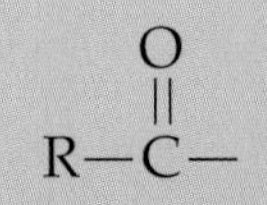

Derivatives of carboxylic acids contain the *acyl* group. As a rule, less reactive acyl derivatives can be synthesized from more reactive ones.

Inorganic acid chlorides like $SOCl_2$, $PCl_3$, and $PCl_5$ each react with carboxylic acids by nucleophilic substitution to form *acyl chlorides* (also called acid chlorides).

**Figure 3.18   Acyl Chloride Synthesis**

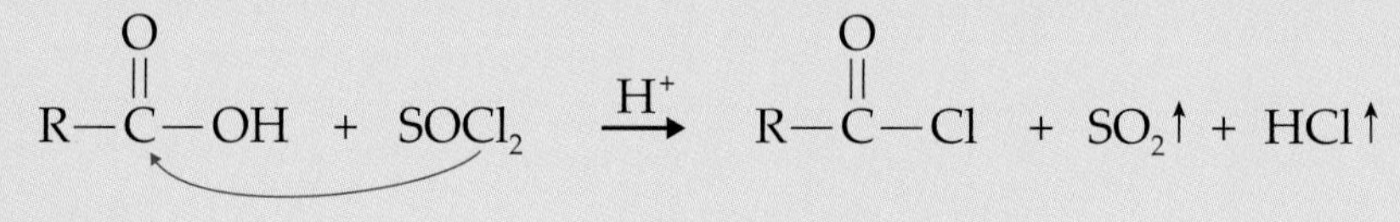

$$R-\overset{\overset{\displaystyle O}{\|}}{C}-OH \ + \ SOCl_2 \ \xrightarrow{H^+} \ R-\overset{\overset{\displaystyle O}{\|}}{C}-Cl \ + \ SO_2\uparrow \ + \ HCl\uparrow$$

Acyl chlorides are Brønsted-Lowry acids, and, just like aldehydes, they donate an α-hydrogen. The electron withdrawing chlorine stabilizes the conjugate base more than the lone hydrogen of an aldehyde, making acyl chlorides significantly stronger acids than aldehydes.

Acid chlorides are the most reactive of the carboxylic acid derivatives because of the stability of the Cl⁻ leaving group.

**Figure 3.19   Relative Reactivity of the Acyl Derivatives**

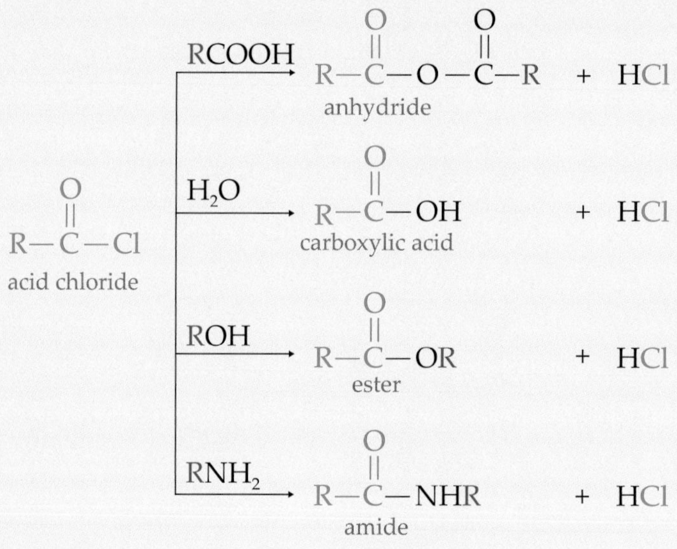

$$
\begin{array}{lll}
RCOOH & R-\overset{\overset{\displaystyle O}{\|}}{C}-O-\overset{\overset{\displaystyle O}{\|}}{C}-R & + \ HCl \\
& \text{anhydride} & \\
H_2O & R-\overset{\overset{\displaystyle O}{\|}}{C}-OH & + \ HCl \\
& \text{carboxylic acid} & \\
ROH & R-\overset{\overset{\displaystyle O}{\|}}{C}-OR & + \ HCl \\
& \text{ester} & \\
RNH_2 & R-\overset{\overset{\displaystyle O}{\|}}{C}-NHR & + \ HCl \\
& \text{amide} &
\end{array}
$$

$$R-\overset{\overset{\displaystyle O}{\|}}{C}-Cl$$
acid chloride

Acid chlorides are the most reactive of the carboxylic acid derivatives. Acid chlorides love nucleophiles.

All carboxylic acid derivatives hydrolyze to give the carboxylic acid. Typically, hydrolysis can occur under either acidic or basic conditions.

## Figure 3.20  Hydrolysis of Carboxylic Acids Derivatives

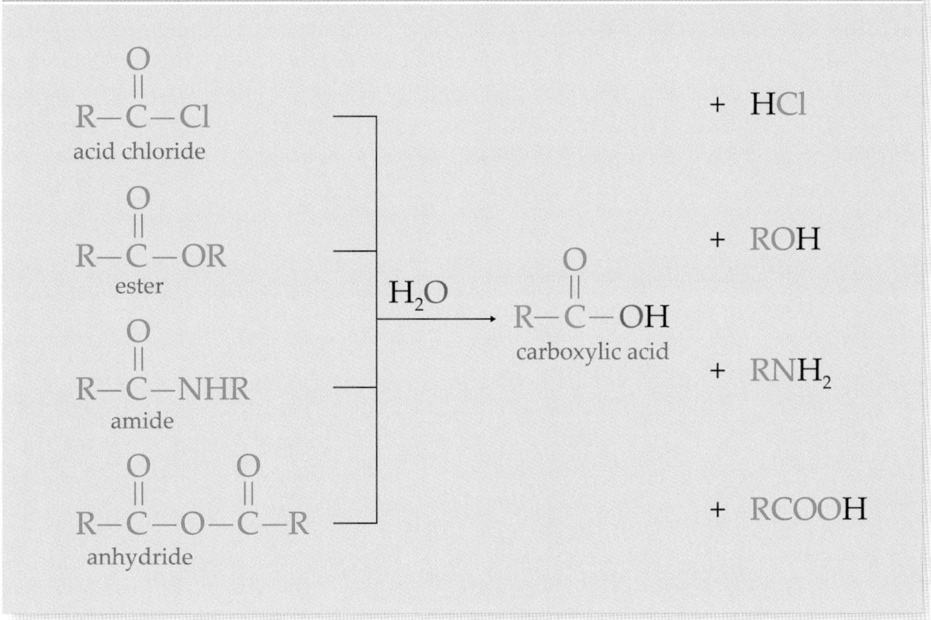

$$
\begin{array}{l}
\underset{\text{acid chloride}}{R-\overset{\overset{\displaystyle O}{\|}}{C}-Cl} \\[2em]
\underset{\text{ester}}{R-\overset{\overset{\displaystyle O}{\|}}{C}-OR} \\[2em]
\underset{\text{amide}}{R-\overset{\overset{\displaystyle O}{\|}}{C}-NHR} \\[2em]
\underset{\text{anhydride}}{R-\overset{\overset{\displaystyle O}{\|}}{C}-O-\overset{\overset{\displaystyle O}{\|}}{C}-R}
\end{array}
\quad\xrightarrow{H_2O}\quad
\underset{\text{carboxylic acid}}{R-\overset{\overset{\displaystyle O}{\|}}{C}-OH}
\quad
\begin{array}{l}
+ \ HCl \\[2em]
+ \ ROH \\[2em]
+ \ RNH_2 \\[2em]
+ \ RCOOH
\end{array}
$$

Nylon is a generic term for various synthetic fibers having a protein-like structure. They are formed by the condensation between an amino group of one molecule and a carboxylic acid group of another.

Alcohols react with carboxylic acids through nucleophilic substitution to form **esters**. A strong acid catalyzes the reaction by protonating the hydroxyl group on the carboxylic acid.

## Figure 3.21  Esterification

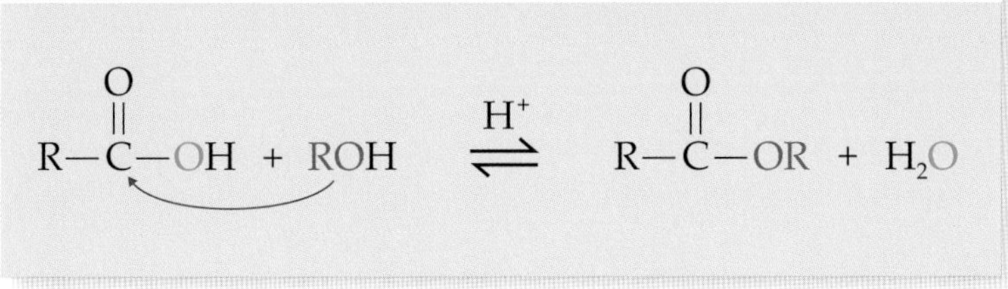

$$
R-\overset{\overset{\displaystyle O}{\|}}{C}-OH + ROH \ \underset{}{\overset{H^+}{\rightleftharpoons}} \ R-\overset{\overset{\displaystyle O}{\|}}{C}-OR + H_2O
$$

The yield in this reaction can be adjusted in accordance with LeChatlier's principle by adding water or alcohol. A more effective method for preparing esters is to use an anhydride instead of a carboxylic acid in the above reaction.

Alcohols react in a similar way with esters in a reaction called **transesterification**, where one alkoxy group is substituted for another. An equilibrium results in this reaction as well, where the result can be controlled by adding an excess of the alcohol in the product or the reactant.

Transesterification is just trading alkoxy groups on an ester.

## Figure 3.22  Transesterification

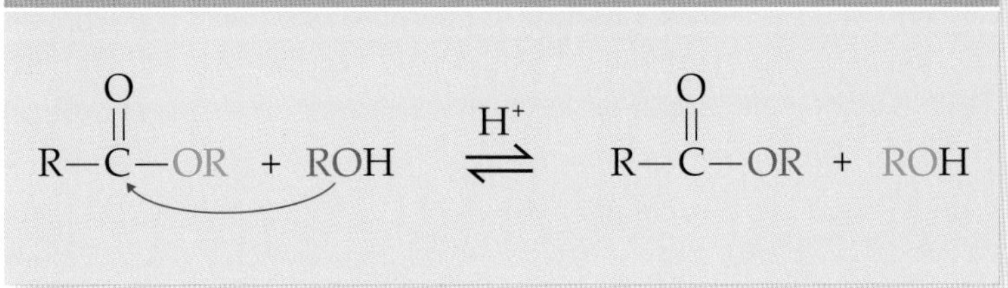

$$
R-\overset{\overset{\displaystyle O}{\|}}{C}-OR + ROH \ \underset{}{\overset{H^+}{\rightleftharpoons}} \ R-\overset{\overset{\displaystyle O}{\|}}{C}-OR + ROH
$$

Once again, you should watch for the β-dicarbonyl compounds, which increase the acidity of the alpha hydrogens between the carbonyls. Specifically, with esters you have acetoacetic ester. **Acetoacetic ester synthesis** is the production of a ketone from acetoacetic ester due to the strongly acidic properties of the alpha hydrogen. A base is added to remove the alpha hydrogens. The resulting enolate ion is alkylated by an alkyl halide or tosylate leaving the alkylacetoacetic ester. Alkylacetoacetic ester is a β-keto ester that can be decarboxylated by the addition of acid. The acetoacetic ester synthesis is finished with the decarboxylation leaving the ketone.

**Figure 3.23  Acetoacetic ester synthesis**

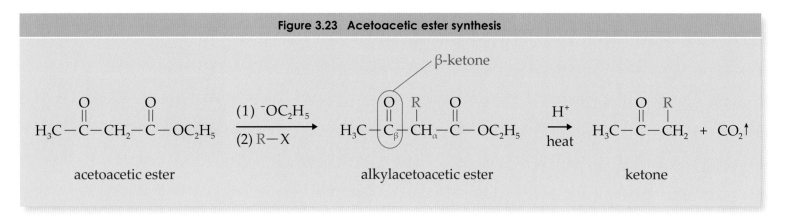

acetoacetic ester                    alkylacetoacetic ester                    ketone

> In all of the reactions with carboxylic acid derivatives, the carbonyl carbon is acting as the substrate in acyl substitution. Rather than memorize all these reactions, you should remember that carboxylic acids and their derivatives undergo acyl substitution; aldehydes and ketones prefer nucleophilic addition.

**Amides** are formed when an **amine**, acting as a nucleophile, substitutes at the carbonyl of a carboxylic acid or one of its derivatives. (Amines are discussed in the next section of this lecture.)

> Many of these reactions are reversible, but equilibrium will prefer the more stable products. In other words, since a strong base makes a poor leaving group, the equilibrium will favor the formation of the compound whose leaving group is a stronger base. This explains the order of reactivity of carboxylic acid derivatives.

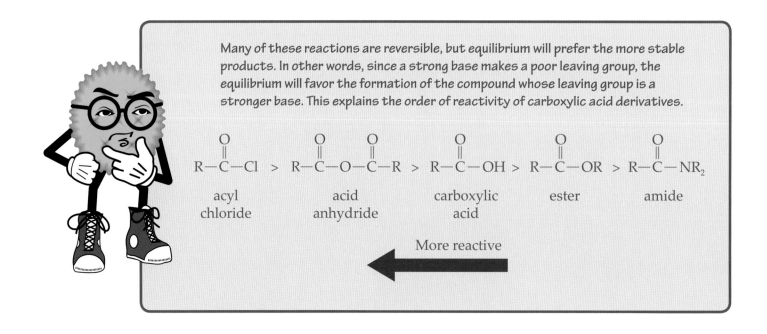

57. All of the following can form hydrogen bonds with water EXCEPT:

    **A.** aldehydes
    **B.** carboxylic acids
    **C.** ethers
    **D.** alkenes

58. Which of the following are products when an alcohol is added to a carboxylic acid in the presence of a strong acid?

    I.    water
    II.   ester
    III.  aldehyde

    **A.** I only
    **B.** II only
    **C.** I and II only
    **D.** I and III only

59. Carboxylic acids typically undergo all of the following reactions EXCEPT:

    **A.** nucleophilic addition
    **B.** nucleophilic substitution
    **C.** decarboxylation
    **D.** esterification

60. Which of the following will most easily react with an amine to form an amide?

    **A.** acyl chloride
    **B.** ester
    **C.** carboxylic acid
    **D.** acid anhydride

61. Which of the following compounds will result in a positive haloform reaction, which only occurs with methyl ketones?

    **A.** $CH_3C{\equiv}N$
    **B.** $C_6H_5COCH_3$
    **C.** $CH_3CH_2CHO$
    **D.** $CH_3CH_2COOH$

62. Phthalic anhydride reacts with two equivalents of ammonia to form ammonium phthalamate. One equivalent is washed away in an acid bath to form phthalamic acid.

    Phthalic anhydride

    What two functional groups are created in phthalamic acid?

    **A.** a carboxylic acid and an amide
    **B.** a carboxylic acid and a ketone
    **C.** a carboxylic acid and an aldehyde
    **D.** an aldehyde and an amide

63. The normal reactivity of methyl benzoate is affected by the presence of certain substituents. Which of the following substituents will decrease methyl benzoate reactivity making it safer for transport?

    $CO_2CH_3$

    Methyl benzoate

    **A.** $NO_2$
    **B.** hydrogen
    **C.** Br
    **D.** $CH_3$

64. When mildly heated with aqueous base or acid, nitriles are hydrolyzed to amides. What may be the product of hydrolysis under stronger conditions?

    **A.** aldehyde
    **B.** ketone
    **C.** ester
    **D.** carboxylic acid

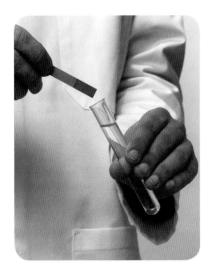

Amines form alkaline solutions in water. Litmus paper turns blue in alkaline solutions, and red in acidic solutions.

## 3.14  Amines

**Amines** are derivatives of **ammonia**. You should be able to identify ammonia and all types of amines.

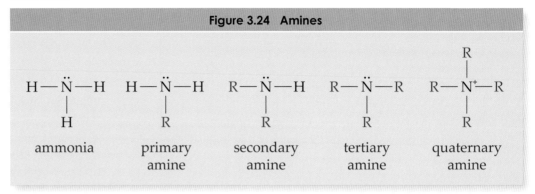

**Figure 3.24  Amines**

ammonia       primary amine       secondary amine       tertiary amine       quaternary amine

Notice that **nitrogen can take three or four bonds**. When nitrogen takes four bonds it has a positive charge. Also notice the lone pair of electrons on an uncharged nitrogen. When you see nitrogen on the MCAT and it has only three bonds, you should draw in the lone pair of electrons immediately. On the MCAT, there are three important considerations when dealing with nitrogen containing compounds:

1. they may act as a Lewis base donating their lone pair of electrons;

2. they may act as a nucleophile where the lone pair of electrons attacks a positive charge; and

3. nitrogen can take on a fourth bond (becoming positively charged).

**Ammonia and amines act as weak bases** by donating their lone pair of electrons. Electron withdrawing substituents decrease the basicity of an amine whereas electron donating substituents increase the basicity of an amine. However, steric hindrance created by bulky functional groups tends to hinder the ability of an amine to donate its lone pair, thus decreasing its basicity. For the MCAT you should know this general trend of amine basicity from highest to lowest when the functional groups are electron donating: 2°, 1°, ammonia.

Aromatic amines (amines attached directly to a benzene ring) are much weaker bases than nonaromatic amines because the electron pair can delocalize around the benzene ring. Substituents that withdraw electrons from the benzene ring will further weaken the aromatic amine.

Since amines like to donate their negative electrons, they tend to stabilize carbocations when they are part of the same molecule.

### Table 3.1  Basicity of Various Amines

| Name | Structure | $pK_a$ of Ammonium ion |
|---|---|---|
| Ammonia | $NH_3$ | 9.26 |
| **Primary alkylamine** | | |
| Methylamine | $CH_3NH_2$ | 10.64 |
| Ethylamine | $CH_3CH_2NH_2$ | 10.75 |
| **Secondary alkylamine** | | |
| Diethylamine | $(CH_3CH_2)_2NH$ | 10.98 |
| Pyrrolidine | ⬠NH | 11.27 |
| **Tertiary alkylamine** | | |
| Triethylamine | $(CH_3CH_2)_2NH$ | 10.76 |
| **Arylamine** | | |
| Aniline | ⬡—$NH_2$ | 4.63 |

> Note that electron-donating groups bonded to the nitrogen tend to increase basicity. Electron withdrawing groups like aromatic group make the amine substantially less basic.

## 3.15 Physical Properties

Given the shape of amines we might expect some secondary and tertiary amines to be optically active. However, at room temperature the lone pair of electrons moves very rapidly (as many as $2 \times 10^{11}$ times per second in ammonia) from one side of the molecule to the other, inverting the configuration. Thus each chiral molecule spends equal time as both its enantiomers. If we imagine that the tertiary amine in Figure 3.24 is rapidly inverting, it becomes easier to appreciate the manner in which the large substituents sterically hinder the electrons.

Ammonia, primary amines, and secondary amines can **hydrogen bond** with each other. All amines can hydrogen bond with water. This makes the lower molecular weight amines very soluble in water. Amines with comparable molecular weights have higher boiling points than alkanes but lower boiling points than alcohols.

> Don't become confused by memorizing too much detail about the physical properties of ammonia and amines. For the MCAT, just keep in mind that ammonia and amines hydrogen bond, which raises boiling point and increases solubility.

## 3.16 Condensation with Ketones

Amines react with aldehydes and ketones losing water to produce **imines** and **enamines**. (Substituted imines are sometimes called *Schiff bases*.) In this reaction the amine acts as a nucleophile, attacking the electron deficient carbonyl carbon of the ketones. As expected, the ketone undergoes nucleophilic addition. An acid catalyst protonates the product to form an unstable intermediate. The intermediate loses water and a proton to produce either an enamine or an imine. If the original amine is secondary (2°), it has no proton to give up, so the ketone must give up its alpha proton. As a result, an enamine is produced. If the original amine is primary (1°), it gives up its proton to form an imine.

### Figure 3.25 Formation of Imines and Enamines

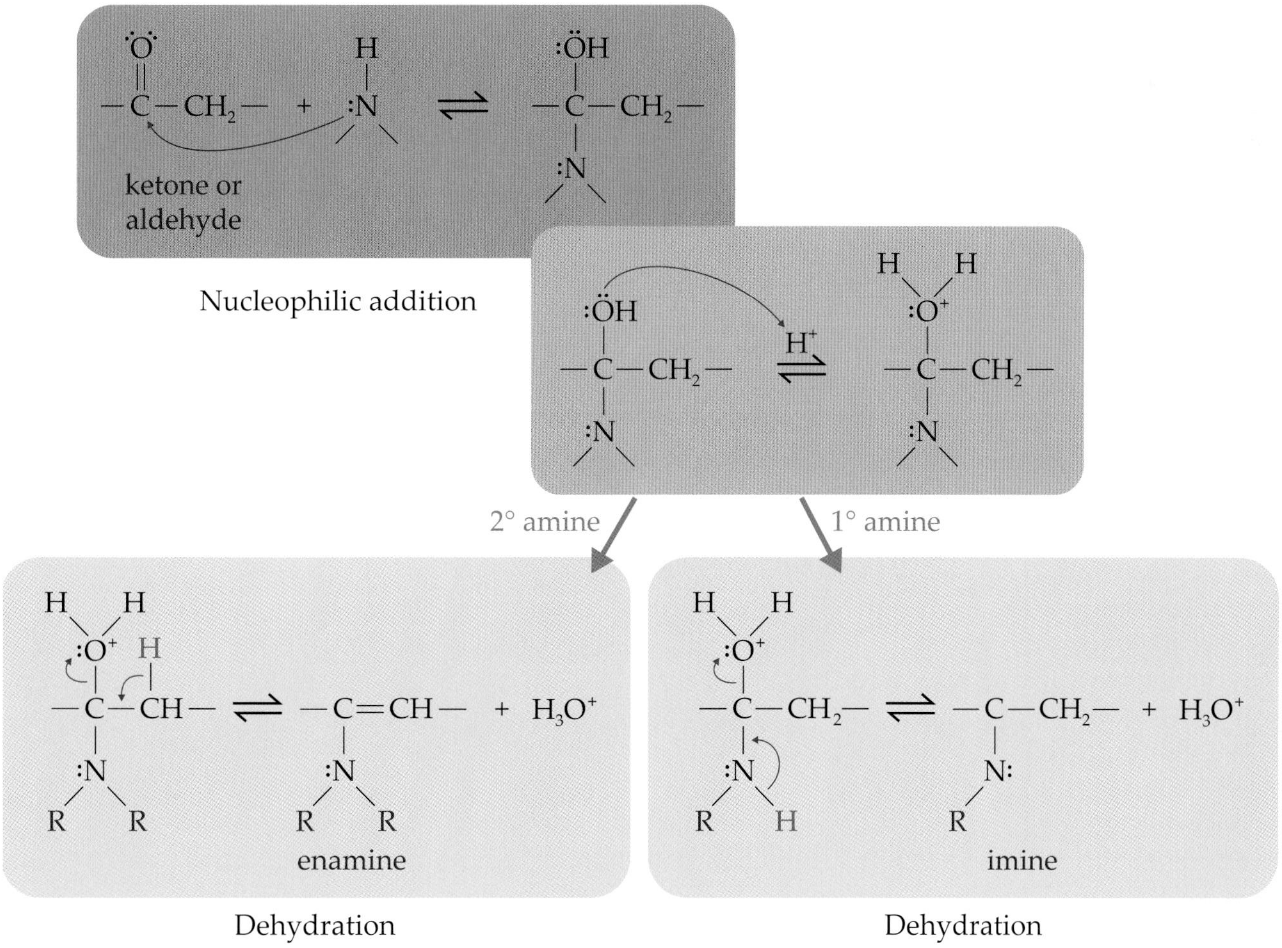

Nucleophilic addition

2° amine      1° amine

enamine        imine

Dehydration          Dehydration

**Figure 3.26 Tautomerization**

Note that if too much acid is used in this reaction, the amine will become protonated before the first step. The protonated amine will have a positive charge and become a poor nucleophile, preventing the first step of the reaction from going forward.

The imine product shown exists as a tautomer with its corresponding enamine.

imine          enamine

## 3.17  Wolff-Kishner Reduction

It is possible to replace the oxygen of a ketone or aldehyde with two hydrogens by adding hot acid in the presence of amalgamated zinc (zinc treated with mercury); however, some ketones and aldehydes may not be able to survive such a treatment. For these ketones and aldehydes, the **Wolff-Kishner Reduction** may be used. The first step of the Wolff-Kishner Reduction follows the same mechanism as imine formation shown on the previous page only a hydrazine is used rather than an amine. The addition of hydrazine to the ketone or aldehyde produces a hydrozone by nucleophilic addition. A hot strong base is added to the hydrazone to deprotanate the nitrogen and produce the desired product with water and nitrogen gas as by-products. A high-boiling solvent is usually used to facilitate the high temperature.

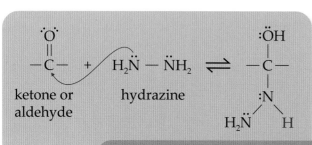

ketone or aldehyde     hydrazine

**Figure 3.27  The Wolff-Kishner Reduction**

hydrazone

The Wolff-Kishner Reduction does nothing more than reduce a ketone or aldehyde by removing the oxygen and replacing it with two hydrogens. You can do the same thing by adding hot acid to a ketone or aldehyde, but some ketones and aldehydes can't survive the hot acid. That's where the Wolff-Kishner Reduction comes in.

$$-\overset{\|}{\underset{\underset{H_2\ddot{N}}{\overset{|}{N}:}}{C}} - \quad \xrightarrow[\text{heat}]{\text{KOH}} \quad \overset{H \quad H}{\underset{/ \ \backslash}{C}} \quad + \ H_2O \ + \ N_2$$

Desired product

## 3.18 Alkylation and the Hofmann Elimination

Amines can be alkylated with alkylhalides.

**Figure 3.28 Amine Alkylation**

$$NH_3 \ + \ R-X \ \longrightarrow \ RNH_2 \ + \ HX$$

$$NRH_2 \ + \ R-X \ \longrightarrow \ R_2NH \ + \ HX$$

$$NR_2H \ + \ R-X \ \longrightarrow \ R_3N \ + \ HX$$

$$NR_3 \ + \ R-X \ \longrightarrow \ R_4N^+ \ + \ X^-$$

This is a nucleophilic substitution reaction with the amine acting as a nucleophile.

As a leaving group, an amino group would be $^-NH_2$, so amino groups are very poor leaving groups. However, an amino group can be converted to a quaternary ammonium salt by repeated alkylations. The quaternary ammonium salt is an excellent leaving group.

The elimination of a quarternary ammonium salt usually follows an E2 mechanism requiring a strong base. The quarternary alkyl halide, typically an ammonium iodide, is converted to a quarternary ammonium hydroxide using silver oxide.

**Figure 3.29 Conversion to a Hydroxide Salt**

$$2\,R-\overset{+}{N}(CH_3)_3\,^-I \ + \ Ag_2O + H_2O \ \longrightarrow \ 2\,R-\overset{+}{N}(CH_3)_3\,^-OH \ + \ 2\,AgI \downarrow$$

Heating the quarternary ammonium hydroxide results in the **Hofmann elimination** to form an alkene.

**Figure 3.30 Hofmann Elimination**

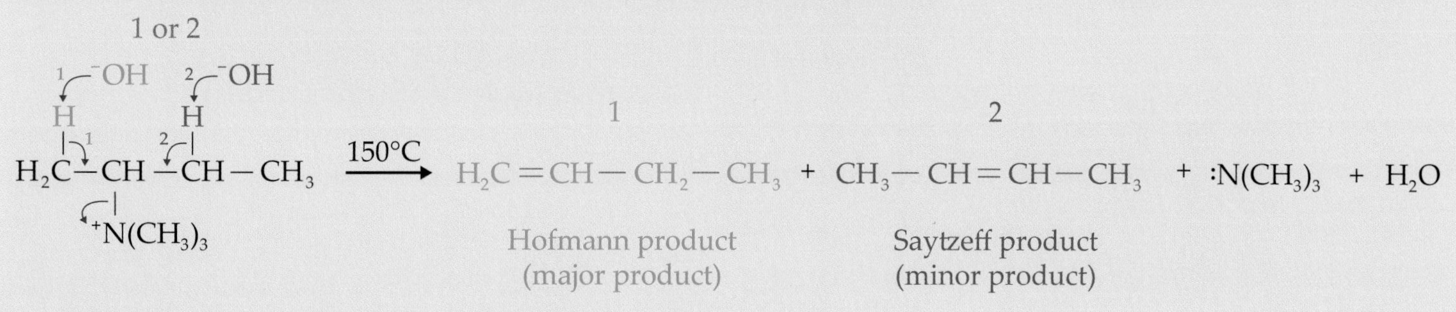

Notice that the LEAST stable alkene is the major product in the Hofmann elimination, called the Hofmann product.

## 3.19 Amines and Nitrous Acid

Nitrous acid is a weak acid. A strong acid can dehydrate nitrous acid to produce nitrosonium ion and water.

**Figure 3.31 Reactions of the Diazonium Group**

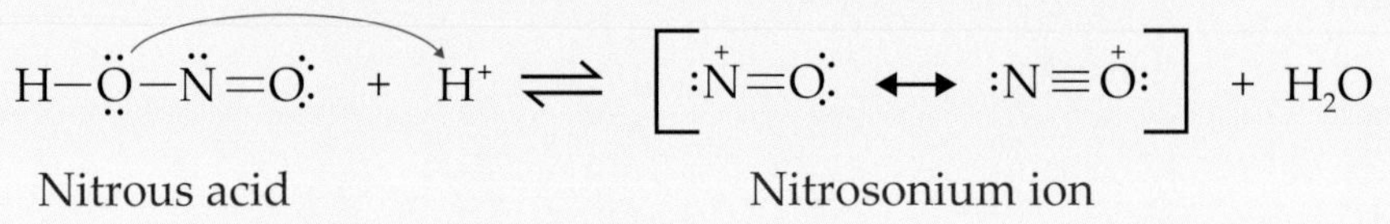

$$H-\ddot{O}-\ddot{N}=\ddot{O}: \ + \ H^+ \ \rightleftharpoons \ \left[ :\overset{+}{\ddot{N}}=\ddot{O}: \ \longleftrightarrow \ :N \equiv \overset{+}{O}: \right] \ + \ H_2O$$

Nitrous acid          Nitrosonium ion

Most reactions with amines and nitrous acid involve the nitrosonium ion.

Primary amines react with nitrous acid to form *diazonium salts*. Aliphatic (nonaromatic) amines form extremely unstable salts that decompose spontaneously to form nitrogen gas. Aromatic amines also form unstable diazonium salts, but at temperatures below 5°C they decompose very slowly.

> This reaction is pretty long. When thinking about nitrous acid and primary amines, just think diazonium ion, and remember that only aromatic amines work.

The reaction, called **diazotization of an amine** goes as follows. Nitrous acid is protonated by a strong acid to form the nitrosonium ion. Nitrosonium ion reacts with the primary amine to form *N*-nitrosoammonium, an unstable compound. *N*-nitrosoammonium deprotonates to form *N*-nitrosoamine. *N*-nitrosoamine tautomerizes to diazenol. In the presence of acid, diazenol dehydrates to diazonium ion.

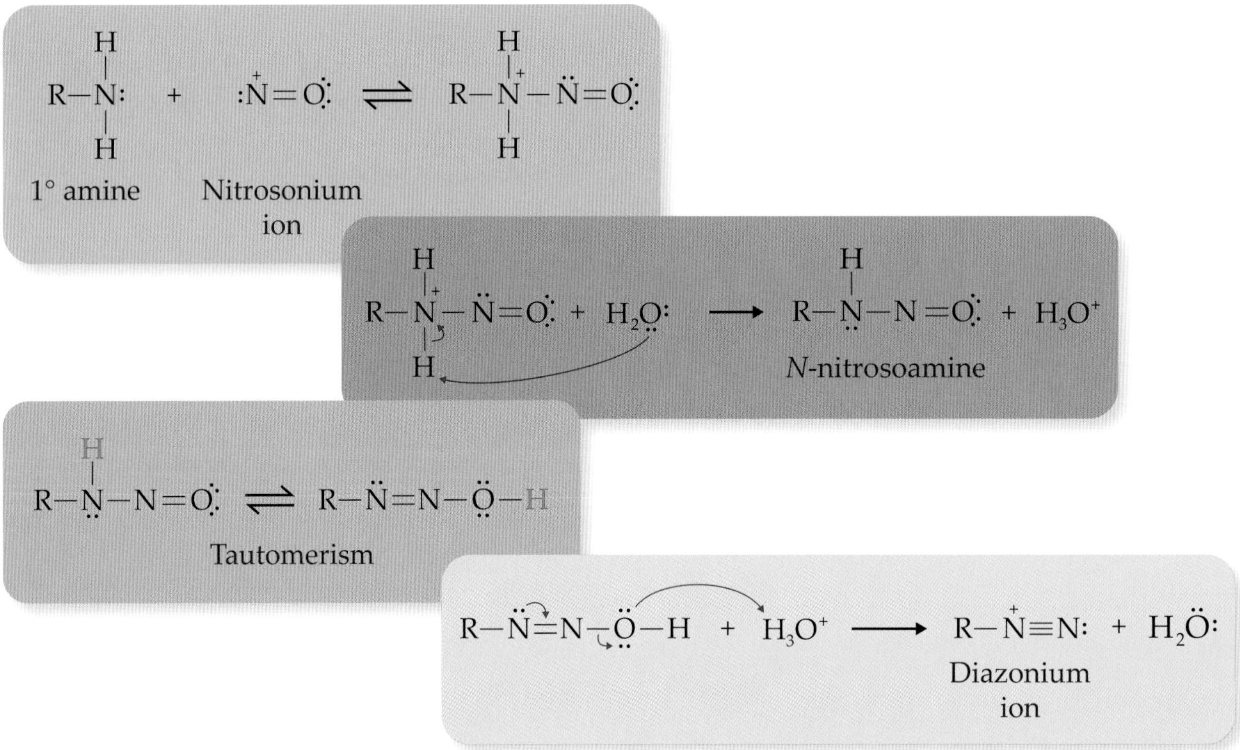

Figure 3.32 Diazotization of an Amine

The diazonium group can be easily replaced by a variety of other groups, making the diazotization of an amine a useful reaction.

**Figure 3.33  Aromatic Diazonium Reactions**

$$Ar-\overset{+}{N}\equiv N: \longrightarrow \begin{cases} Ar-OH \\ Ar-X \\ Ar-H \\ Ar-N=N-Ar \end{cases}$$

$$-\overset{+}{N}\equiv N:$$
**diazonium group**

Phenyldiazonium chloride ($C_6H_5N_2Cl$) reacts with phenol (or carbolic acid, $C_6H_5OH$) to produce a diazonium dye (orange).

Unlike primary amines, secondary amines have an extra R group instead of the tautomeric proton. No tautomer can form. Notice from the diazotization reaction above that, if the *N*-nitrosoamine can't make a tautomer, the reaction will be stopped at the *N*-nitrosoamine. When nitrous acid is added to a secondary amine, the product is an *N*-nitrosoamine.

# 3.20  Amides

Amides that have no substituent on the nitrogen are called primary amides. Primary amides are named by replacing the *-ic* in the corresponding acid with *-amide*. For instance, acetamide is formed when the –OH group of acetic acid is replaced by –NH$_2$. Substituents on the nitrogen are prefaced by *N-*. For instance, if one hydrogen on acetamide is replaced by an ethyl group, the result is *N*-ethylacetamide.

Amides can behave as a weak acid or a weak base. They are less basic than amines due to the electron withdrawing properties of the carbonyl. Amides are hydrolyzed by either strong acids or strong bases.

Amides with a hydrogen attached to the nitrogen are able to hydrogen bond to each other.

$$H_3C-\overset{\overset{\displaystyle O}{\|}}{C}-NH_2$$
**acetamide**

$$H_3C-\overset{\overset{\displaystyle O}{\|}}{C}-NHC_2H_5$$
**N-ethylacetamide**

**Figure 3.34  Hydrogen Bonding**

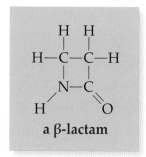

# 3.21  β-Lactams

Cyclic amides are called lactams. A Greek letter is assigned to the lactam to denote size. β-lactams are 4-membered rings, γ-lactams have 5 members, δ-lactams have 6 members, and so on. Although amides are the most stable of the carboxylic acid derivatives, β-lactams are highly reactive due to large ring strain. Nucleophiles easily react with β-lactams. β-lactams are found in several types of antibiotics.

**a β-lactam**

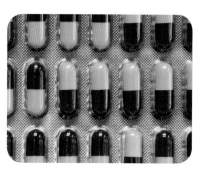

Amoxicillin is a penicillin antibiotic classed as a β-lactam antibiotic. It works by attacking the cell walls of bacteria.

## 3.22 The Hofmann Degradation

Primary amides react with strongly basic solutions of chlorine or bromine to form primary amines with carbon dioxide as a by-product. This reaction is called the **Hofmann degradation**. The amide is deprotoned by the strong base. The deprotonated amide picks up a halogen atom leaving a halide ion. The product is an *N*-haloamide. The *N*-haloamide is more acidic than the original primary amide and is deprotonated as well. Now a tricky rearrangement occurs. The R group of the amide migrates to the nitrogen to form an isocyanate. Isocyanate reacts with water to form a carbamic acid. The carbamic acid is decarboxylated, giving off carbondioxide and leaving the amine.

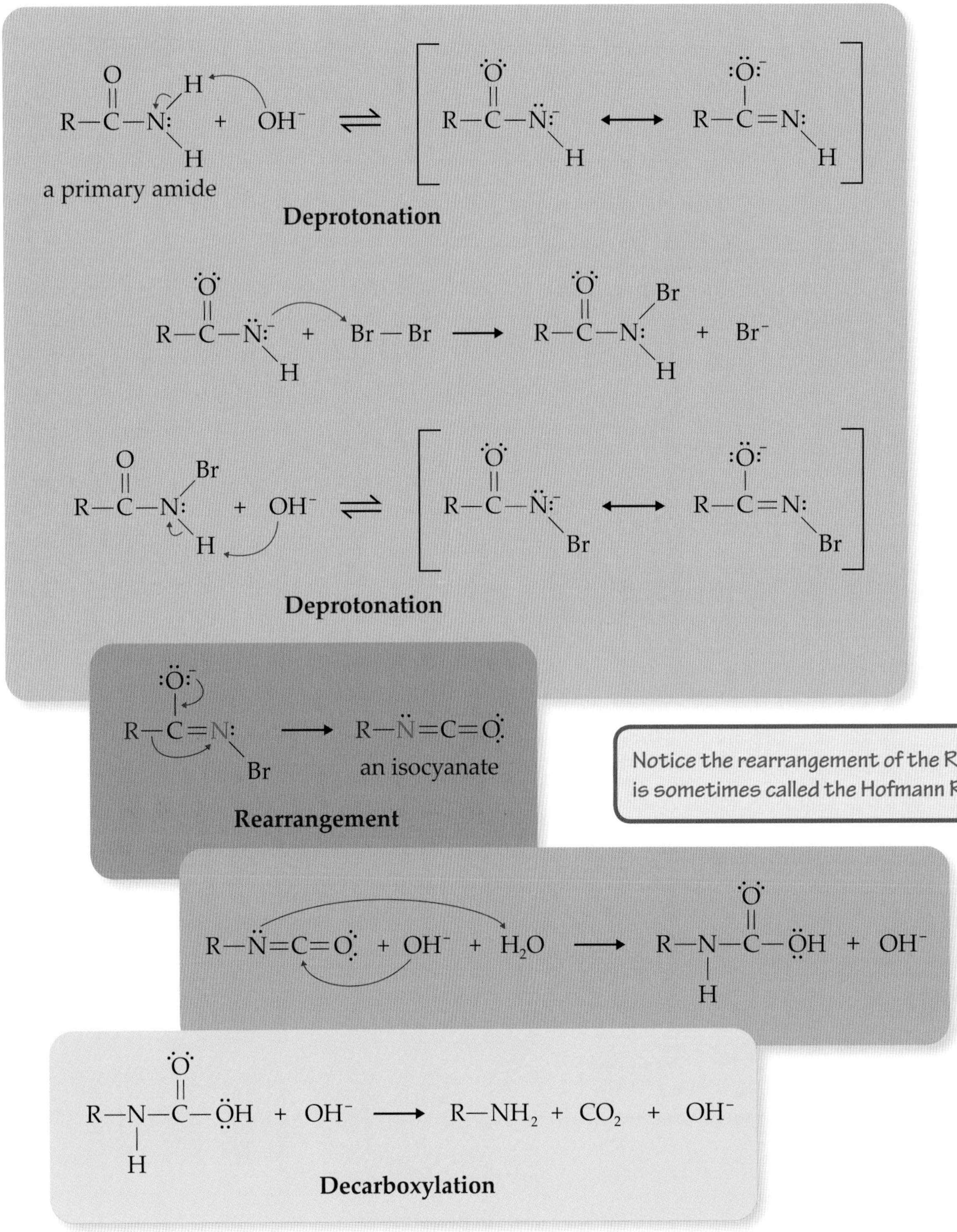

Notice the rearrangement of the R group. This reaction is sometimes called the Hofmann Rearrangement.

**Figure 3.35 The Hofmann Degradation**

The advantage of the Hofmann degradation over other methods of producing amines is that other methods rely upon an $S_N2$ mechanism. This prevents the production of amines on a tertiary carbon. The Hofmann degradation can produce amines with a primary, secondary, or tertiary alkyl position.

## 3.23 Phosphoric Acid

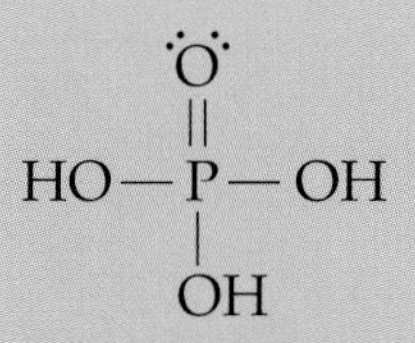

You need to know the structure of **phosphoric acids** for the MCAT. When heated, phosphoric acid forms **phosphoric anhydrides**. Phosphoric acids react with alcohols to form esters.

**Figure 3.36  Phosphoric Adhydride**

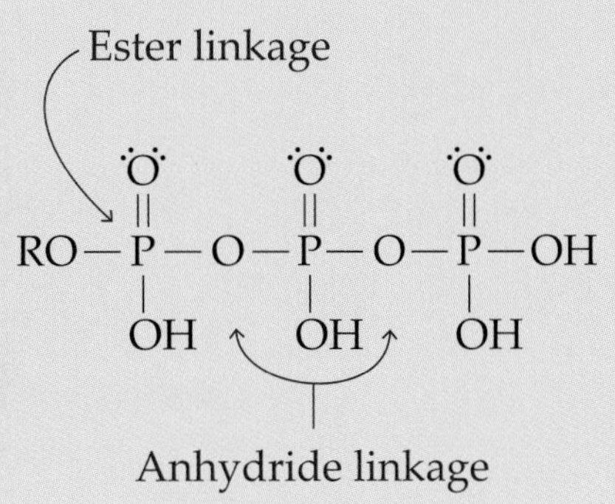

Ester linkage

Anhydride linkage

phosphoric
acid

In a living cell at a pH of about 7, triphosphates exist as negatively charged ions, making them less susceptible to nucleophilic attack and relatively stable. ATP is an example of an important triphosphate.

## 3.24 *Terms You Need to Know*

| Terms | |
|---|---|
| α-Hydrogen | Enamines |
| α-Carbon | Esters |
| Acetoacetic Ester Synthesis | Hofmann Degradation |
| Acyl Substitution Reaction | Hofmann Elimination |
| Aldehyde | Imines |
| Aldol Condensation | Ketone |
| Amides | Phosphoric Acids |
| Amine | Phosphoric Anhydrides |
| β-carbon | Tautomers |
| Carbonyl | Transesterification |
| Carboxylic Acids | Wittig Reaction |
| Decarboxylation | Wolff-Kishner Reduction |
| Diazotization of an Amine | |

### *Thought Provoker*

*From page 64.*

*Answer:*

*The enol would predominate in solution because it allows for the formation of a benzene ring. Benzene is highly stabilized due to the phenomenon of aromaticity.*

*From page 65.*

*Answer:*

*when carbonyl group is destabilized*

- *alkyl groups stabilize C=O*
- *electron-withdrawing groups destabilize C=O*

**65.** If all substituents are alkyl groups, which of the following is the least basic amine?

   **A.** primary
   **B.** secondary
   **C.** tertiary
   **D.** quaternary

**66.** Ammonia is best described as:

   **A.** a Lewis acid
   **B.** a Lewis base
   **C.** an electrophile
   **D.** an aromatic compound

**67.** Which of the following would have the lowest solubility in water?

   **A.**
$$H-\underset{\underset{CH_3}{|}}{N}-H$$

   **C.**
$$H_3C-\underset{\underset{CH_3}{|}}{N}-CH_3$$

   **B.**
$$H-\underset{\underset{CH_3}{|}}{N}-COOH$$

   **D.**
$$H_3C-\underset{\underset{CH_3}{|}}{N}-COOH$$

**68.** Which of the following is a possible product of the reaction shown below?

**A.**

**C.**

**B.**

**D.**

**69.** Ethylamine can be alkylated with iodomethane in the presence of a strong base. The strong base is needed:

   **A.** to neutralize the strong acid ethyl-methylamine that is formed during the reaction.
   **B.** to neutralize the strong acid HI that is formed during the reaction.
   **C.** to protonate the methyl group.
   **D.** to deprotonate the methyl group.

**70.** In the prepolymer shown below, which of the following moities contains the most reactive bond?

Prepolymer

   **A.**

   **C.**
$$-O-CH_2-$$

   **B.**
$$\underset{CH_2-}{\overset{Cl}{|}}$$

   **D.**

**71.** In a coordinate covalent bond, the shared electrons are furnished by only one species. Which of the following molecules is LEAST likely to be involved in a coordinate covalent bond?

   **A.** sodium chloride (NaCl)
   **B.** chlorate ion ($ClO_3^-$)
   **C.** ammonia ($NH_3$)
   **D.** water ($H_2O$)

**72.** When $D_2O$ is added to cyclohexanone, all acidic hydrogens (atomic weight = 1) are replaced with deuterons (atomic weight = 2). What is the new atomic weight of cyclohexanone following $D_2O$ treatment?

Cyclohexanone
(Atomic weight = 98 g/mol)

   **A.** 98
   **B.** 100
   **C.** 102
   **D.** 108

*Notes:*

# BIOCHEMISTRY AND LAB TECHNIQUES

## 4.1 Fatty Acids

**Fatty acids** are long carbon chains with a carboxylic acid end. They serve three basic functions in the human body: 1. they serve as hormones and intracellular messengers (i.e. *eicosanoids* such as *prostaglandins*); 2. they are components of the phospholipids and glycolipids of cell membranes; and 3. they act as fuel for the body. The first of these functions will not be tested on the MCAT unless it is explained in a passage. For the second function of fatty acids you should be able to recognize the structure of a phospholipid as shown in Lecture 3 of the biology manual.

As fuel for the body, fatty acids are stored in the form of *triacylglycerols*. Triacylglycerols can be hydrolyzed to form glycerol and the corresponding fatty acids in a process called **lipolysis**. Notice that this process is simply the reverse of esterification. In the lab triacylglycerols can be cleaved by the addition of NaOH, a process called **saponification**. Saponification is a key reaction in the production of soap (Figure 4.2).

Notice that melting point tends to increase with molecular weight and that unsaturated fatty acids have lower melting points than saturated fatty acids.

### Figure 4.1 Common Fatty Acids

| Name | No. of carbons | Melting point (°C) | Structure |
|------|----------------|--------------------|-----------| 
| **Saturated** | | | |
| Lauric | 12 | 44 | $CH_3(CH_2)_{10}CO_2H$ |
| Myristic | 14 | 58 | $CH_3(CH_2)_{12}CO_2H$ |
| Palmitic | 16 | 63 | $CH_3(CH_2)_{14}CO_2H$ |
| Stearic | 18 | 71 | $CH_3(CH_2)_{16}CO_2H$ |
| Arachidic | 20 | 77 | $CH_3(CH_2)_{18}CO_2H$ |
| | | | |
| **Unsaturated** | | | |
| Palmitoleic | 16 | 1 | $(Z)\text{-}CH_3(CH_2)_5CH = CH(CH_2)_7CO_2H$ |
| Oleic | 18 | 16 | $(Z)\text{-}CH_3(CH_2)_7CH = CH(CH_2)_7CO_2H$ |
| Linoleic | 18 | 5 | $(Z,Z)\text{-}CH_3(CH_2)_4(CH = CHCH_2)_2(CH_2)_6CO_2H$ |
| Linolenic | 18 | −11 | $(all\ Z)\text{-}CH_3CH_2(CH = CHCH_2)_3(CH_2)_6CO_2H$ |
| Arachidonic | 20 | −49 | $(all\ Z)\text{-}CH_3(CH_2)_4(CH = CHCH_2)_4CH_2CH_2CO_2H$ |

**Figure 4.2  Hydrolytic Cleavage of a Saturated Triacylglycerides**

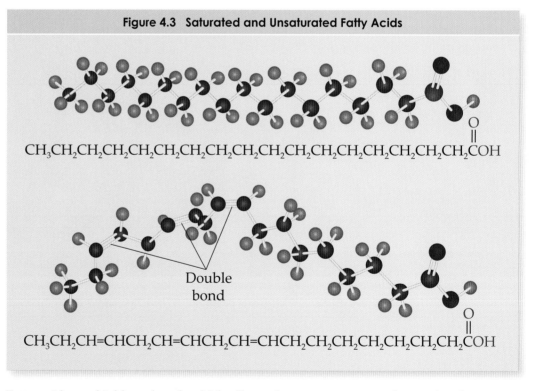

For nomenclature purposes, the carbonyl carbon of a fatty acid is assigned the number 1. The carbon next to the carbonyl is called the $\alpha$-carbon (alpha carbon) and the carbon at the opposite end of the chain is called the $\omega$-carbon (omega carbon). The $pK_a$ of most fatty acids is around 4.5, so most fatty acids exist in their anion form in the cellular environment.

The carbon chains on fatty acids may be **saturated** or **unsaturated**. Fatty acids are **amphipathic**, meaning they contain a hydrophobic and a hydrophilic end. Since the hydrophobic carbon chain predominates, fatty acids are **nonpolar**.

**Figure 4.3  Saturated and Unsaturated Fatty Acids**

> Saturated fatty acids are straight, while unsaturated fatty acids have 'kinks'.

$$CH_3CH_2CH_2CH_2CH_2CH_2CH_2CH_2CH_2CH_2CH_2CH_2CH_2CH_2CH_2CH_2CH_2COH$$

Double bond

$$CH_3CH_2CH=CHCH_2CH=CHCH_2CH=CHCH_2CH_2CH_2CH_2CH_2CH_2CH_2COH$$

> The important things to remember about fatty acids are molecular structure, lipolysis, energy storage, and that they enter into the Krebs cycle two carbons at a time.

Fatty acids are highly reduced, which allows them to store more than twice the energy (about 9 kcal/gram) of carbohydrates or proteins (about 4 kcal/gram). Fatty acids are stored as triacylglycerols in adipose cells. Lipolysis of triacylglycerols takes place inside the adipose cells when blood levels of epinephrine, norepinephrine, glucagon, or ACTH are elevated. The resulting fatty acid products are then exported to different cells for the utilization of their energy. Once inside a cell, the fatty acid is linked to Coenzyme A and carried into the mitochondrial matrix by the $\gamma$-amino acid L-carnitine. The fatty acid is then oxidized two carbons at a time with each oxidation yielding an NADH, FADH$_2$, and an acetyl CoA. Each acetyl CoA enters the Krebs cycle for further oxidation by condensation with oxaloacetate.

**Amino acids** are the building blocks of proteins. A single protein consists of one or more chains of amino acids strung end to end by **peptide bonds**. Hence the name **polypeptide**. You must be able recognize the structure of an amino acid and a polypeptide. A peptide bond creates the functional group known as an **amide** (an amine connected to a carbonyl carbon). It is formed via condensation of two amino acids. The reverse reaction is the hydrolysis of a peptide bond.

**Figure 4.4   Hydrolysis of a Peptide Bond**

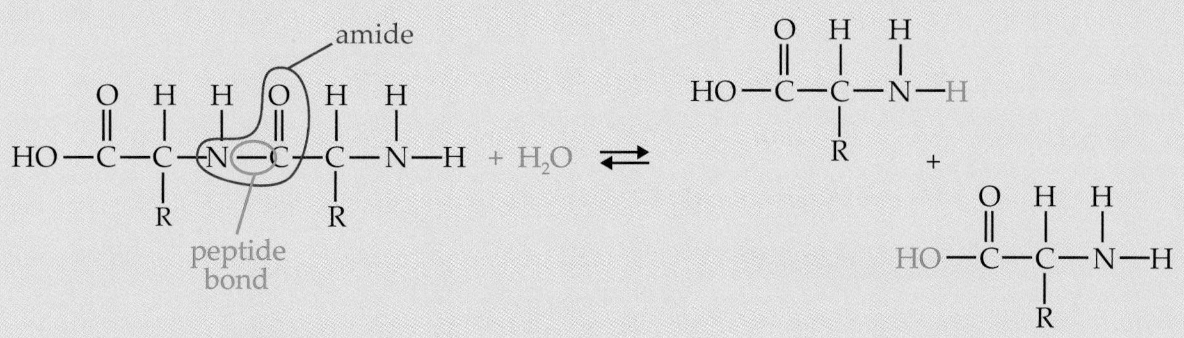

dipeptide                                    amino acids

Amino acids used by the human body are α-amino acids. They are called alpha-amino acids because the amine group is attached to the carbon which is alpha to the carbonyl carbon, similar to α-hydrogens of ketones and aldehydes.

Since nitrogen is comfortable taking on four bonds and oxygen is comfortable with a partial negative charge, electrons delocalize creating a resonance that gives the peptide bond a partial double bond character. The double bond character prevents the bond from rotating freely and affects the secondary and to some extent the tertiary structure of the polypeptide.

Notice the R group on each amino acid. The R group is called the **side chain** of the amino acid. Nearly all organisms use the same **20 α-amino acids** to synthesize proteins. Many amino acids and amino acid derivatives, such as *hydroxyproline* and *cystine*, can be created by post-translational modifications after the polypeptide is formed. **Ten** amino acids are **essential**. ("Essential" means that they cannot be synthesized by the body, so they must be ingested. Some books list 8 or 9 amino acids as essential. The discrepancy involves whether or not to list as essential those amino acids that are derivatives of other essential

**Table 4.1   Amino Acid Types**

| Nonpolar | Polar | Acidic | Basic |
|---|---|---|---|
| valine | serine | aspartic acid | histidine |
| isoleucine | threonine | glutamic acid | arginine |
| proline | cysteine | | lysine |
| methionine | tyrosine | | |
| alanine | glutamine | | |
| leucine | asparagine | | |
| tryptophan | | | |
| phenylalanine | | | |
| glycine | | | |

It is unlikely that the MCAT would require you to know the chemical category that an amino acid will fall; however, here are the amino acids listed under their specific categories, just in case.

amino acids.) Each amino acid differs only in its R group. The R groups have different chemical properties. These properties are divided into four categories: 1. acidic, 2. basic, 3. polar, and 4. nonpolar. All acidic and basic R groups are also polar. Generally, if the side chain contains carboxylic acids, then it is acidic; if it contains amines, then it is basic. Only the three basic amino acids have an **isoelectric point** (discussed below) above a pH of 7; all other amino acids have an isoelectric point below 7.

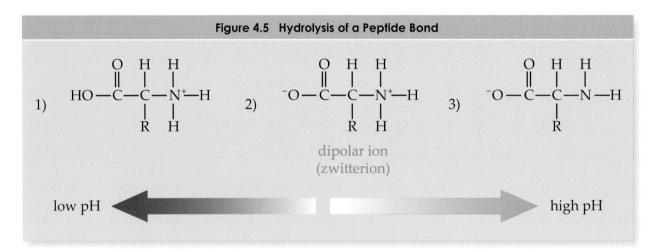

**amino acid**

Polar side groups are **hydrophilic** and will turn to face an aqueous solution such as cytosol. Nonpolar side groups are **hydrophobic** and will turn away from an aqueous solution. These characteristics affect a protein's tertiary structure.

Although we often draw an amino acid as shown to the left it actually never exists as such. In the cytosol, amino acids exist in one of the three forms drawn below:

**Figure 4.5   Hydrolysis of a Peptide Bond**

Close examination of species 1 reveals it to be a diprotic acid. If we choose an amino acid with no ionizable substituents on its R group, and we titrate it with a strong base, we observe the following: as the pH increases, the stronger acid, the carboxylic acid, is first to lose its proton, creating species 2, its conjugate base. When species 1 and 2 exist in equal proportions, we have reached the half-equivalence point. As we continue the titration, we remove the proton from all of the carboxylic acids until we have 100% of species 2. The pH at this point is called the **isoelectric point, p$I$.** (Technically, the p$I$ for any amino acid is the pH where the population has no net charge and the maximum number of species are zwitterions.) Continuing the titration, the base begins to remove a proton from the amine. When we have equal amounts of 2 and 3, we are at the second half-equivalence point of our titration. Once we have removed the acidic proton from each amine group leaving 100% of species 3, we have reached the second equivalence point. The isoelectric point is dictated by the side group of an amino acid. The more acidic the side group, the lower the p$I$; the more basic the side group, the greater the p$I$.

**Figure 4.6   Hydrolysis of a Peptide Bond**

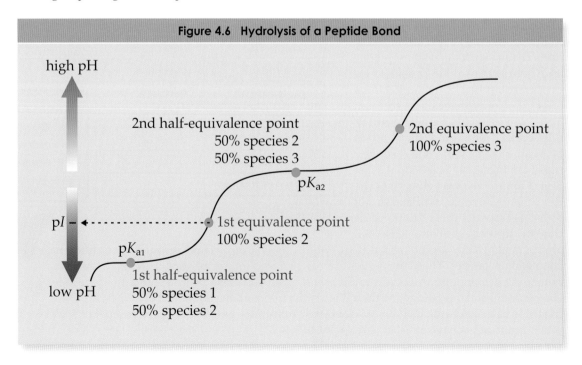

Questions 73 through 80 are **NOT** based on a descriptive passage.

**73.** Electrophoresis can separate amino acids by subjecting them to an electric field. The electric field applies a force whose strength and direction is dependent upon the net charge of the amino acid. If a solution of amino acids at a pH of 8 underwent electrophoresis, which of the following would most likely move the furthest toward the anode?

**A.** lysine
**B.** arginine
**C.** glutamic acid
**D.** histidine

**74.** Fatty acids and glycerol react within the body to form triacylglycerides. Which of the following functional groups are contained in any triacylglyceride?

**A.** aldehyde
**B.** carboxylic acid
**C.** ester
**D.** amine

**75.** The partial double bond character of a peptide bond has its greatest effect in which structure of an enzyme?

**A.** primary
**B.** secondary
**C.** tertiary
**D.** quaternary

**76.** Which of the following nutrients has the greatest heat of combustion?

**A.** carbohydrate
**B.** protein
**C.** saturated fat
**D.** unsaturated fat

**77.** A student conducted the titration of an amino acid with a strong base. The point in the titration when 50% of the amino acid exists as a zwitterion is called:

**A.** the isoelectric point.
**B.** the equivalence point.
**C.** the half-equivalence point.
**D.** the end point.

**78.** Which of the following amino acids has the lowest solubility in aqueous solution?

**A.**

(Asp)

**B.**

(Arg)

**C.**

(Phe)

**D.**

(His) (Asp)

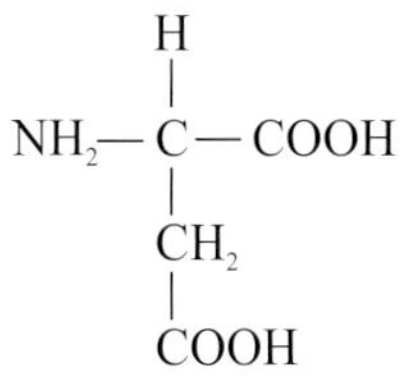

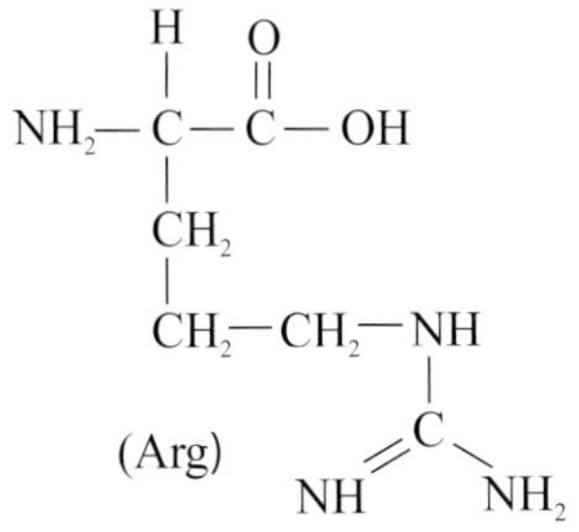

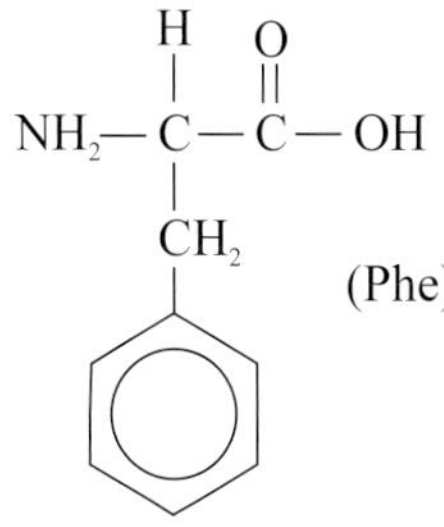

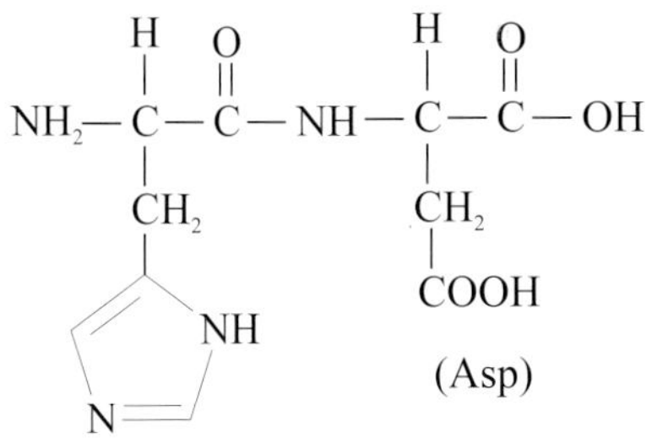

**79.** How many complete monomers can be extracted from the compound below and utilized for analysis?

O    H  O        H  O        H
‖         ‖            ‖
— C — NH — C — C — NH — C — C — NH — C —
            |                |                |
            CH₂              CHCH₃            H
            |                |
            ⬡                CH₂
                             |
                             CH₃

A.  2
B.  3
C.  4
D.  8

**80.** Based on structural properties alone, which of the following compounds is most likely to interrupt alpha-helix structures found in myoglobin?

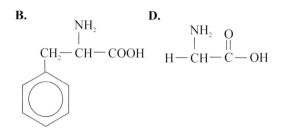

A.
NH₂
|
CH₃CH — CH — COOH
|
CH₃

B.
NH₂
|
CH₂— CH — COOH
|
⬡

C.
NH
CH — COOH

D.
NH₂  O
|        ‖
H — CH — C — OH

## 4.3 Carbohydrates

**Carbohydrates** can be thought of as carbon and water. For each carbon atom there exists one oxygen and two hydrogens. The formula for any carbohydrate is:

$$C_n(H_2O)_n$$

The carbohydrates most likely to appear on the MCAT are fructose and glucose. Both are six carbon carbohydrates called **hexoses**. These may appear as Fischer projections or ring structures. The Fischer projections are shown below:

Notice that glucose is an aldehyde and fructose is a ketone. Polyhydroxyaldehydes like glucose are called **aldoses**. Polyhydroxyketones like fructose are called **ketoses**. Carbohydrates are also named for the number of carbons they possess: triose, tetrose, pentose, hexose, heptose, and so on. The names are commonly combined making glucose an **aldohexose**.

Notice also that several of the carbons are chiral. Carbohydrates are labeled D or L as follows: When in a Fischer projection as shown, if the hydroxyl group on the highest numbered chiral carbon points to the right, the carbohydrate is labeled D; if to the left, then L.

In a carbohydrate the alcohol group on the chiral carbon farthest from the carbonyl may act as a nucleophile and attack the carbonyl. When this happens, nucleophilic addition to an aldehyde or ketone results and the corresponding hemiacetal is formed, creating a ring structure. Carbon 1 in Figure 4.7 is now called the anomeric carbon. The **anomeric carbon** can be identified as the only carbon attached to two oxygens and because its alcohol group may point upwards or downwards on the ring structure resulting in either the α or β anomer.

The cyclic structures are named according to the number of ring members (including oxygen): a five-membered ring is called a **furanose**; a six-membered ring is called a **pyranose**. So the glucose ring becomes **glucopyranose**.

The human body can assimilate only D-fructose and D-glucose and cannot assimilate L-fructose and L-glucose. D is for delicious.

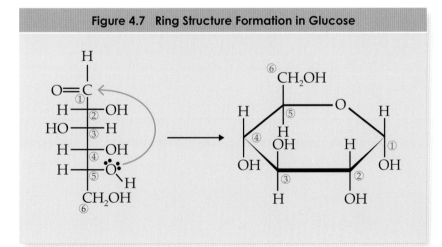

**Figure 4.7  Ring Structure Formation in Glucose**

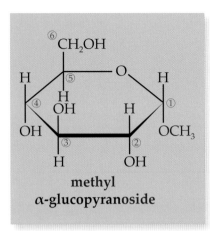

**methyl α-glucopyranoside**

Names of reducing sugars end in -ose; names of nonreducing sugars end in -oside. This detailed nomenclature of carbohydrates is unlikely to be tested directly on the MCAT, but it doesn't hurt to know it.

Sugars that are acetals (not hemiacetals) are called glycosides. The names of such sugars end in -oside. For instance, if the hydroxyl group on the anomeric carbon of glucose were replaced with an O-methyl group, it would form methyl glucopyranoside. The group attached to the anomeric carbon of a glycoside is called an *aglycone*.

*Tollens reagent* is a basic reagent that detects aldehydes. Aldoses have an aldehyde on their open-chain form and reduce Tollens reagent. Tollens reagent promotes enediol rearrangement of ketoses so that ketoses also reduce Tollens reagent. Recall from Lecture 3 that acetals are used as blocking groups because they do not react with basic reducing agents. Since Tollens reagent must react with the open-chain form of a sugar, glycosides (which are closed ring acetals) do NOT reduce Tollens reagent, while nonglycosides do.

Disaccharides and polysaccharides are glycosides where the aglycone is another sugar. The anomeric carbon of a sugar can react with any of the hydroxyl groups of another sugar, but there are only three bonding arrangements that are common: a 1,4' link, a 1,6' link, and a 1,1' link. The numbers refer to the carbon numbers on the sugars. The linkages are called glycosidic linkages. A disaccharide or polysaccharide will only react with Tollens reagent if there is an anomeric carbon that is not involved in a glycosidic bond and is free to react.

There are several disaccharides and polysaccharides for which you should know the common name.

**Sucrose:** 1,1' glycosidic linkage: glucose and fructose (This linkage is alpha with respect to glucose and beta with respect to fructose. It is more accurately called a 1,2' linkage because the anomeric carbon on fructose is numbered 2, not 1 like glucose.)

**Maltose:** α-1,4' glucosidic linkage: two glucose molecules

**Lactose:** β-1,4' galactosidic linkage: galactose and glucose

**Cellulose:** β-1,4' glucosidic linkage: a chain of glucose molecules

**Amylose (Starch):** α-1,4' glucosidic linkage: a chain of glucose molecules

**Amylopectin:** α-1,4' glucosidic linkage: a branched chain of glucose molecules with α-1,6' glucosidic linkages forming the branches

**Glycogen:** α-1,4' glucosidic linkage: a branched chain of glucose molecules with α-1,6' glucosidic linkages forming the branches

Glycosidic linkages are broken via hydrolysis. Without an enzyme, they are broken down only slowly by water. Animals do not possess the enzyme to break the β-1,4' glucosidic linkage in cellulose. Some adult humans lack the enzyme to break the β-1,4' galactosidic linkage in lactose.

**81.** How many stereoisomers exist of D-altrose, shown below?

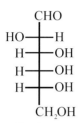

**D-altrose**

A.   2
B.   8
C.   16
D.   32

**82.** Which of the following types of reactions describes ring formation in glucose when the alcohol group nucleophilically attacks the carbonyl carbon atom?

A.   hemiacetal formation
B.   hemiketal formation
C.   acetal formation
D.   ketal formation

**83.** Which of the following is the ketose most abundant in fruits?

A.   fructose
B.   glucose
C.   proline
D.   glycerol

**84.** From only the drawing shown below, which of the following statements can be discerned as true?

```
        CHO
   H ───┼─── OH
       CH₂OH
```

I.    The molecule is a carbohydrate.
II.   The stereochemical designation of the molecule is D.
III.  The molecule rotates polarized light clockwise.

A.   I only
B.   II only
C.   I and II only
D.   I, II, and III

**85.** Which of the following statements are true concerning carbohydrates?

I.    Carbohydrates can exist as meso compounds.
II.   The human body is capable of digesting all isomers of glucose.
III.  Glucose is an aldehyde.

A.   III only
B.   I and II only
C.   I and III only
D.   I, II, and III

**86.** Aspartame, saccharine, and sodium cyclamate are all synthetic sweeteners used to replace glucose.

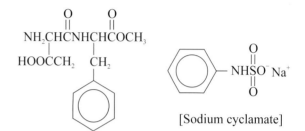

[Sodium cyclamate]

[Aspartame]

[Saccharin]

Which of the following properties are shared by both glucose and the synthetic sweeteners?

I.    All activate gustatory receptors at the tip of the human tongue.
II.   All can hydrogen bond.
III.  All are carbohydrates.

A.   I only
B.   III only
C.   I and II only
D.   I, II, and III

**87.** Fructose can cyclize into a five-membered ring known as a furanose. The hydroxyl group on which carbon of fructose behaves as a nucleophile during the formation of a furan?

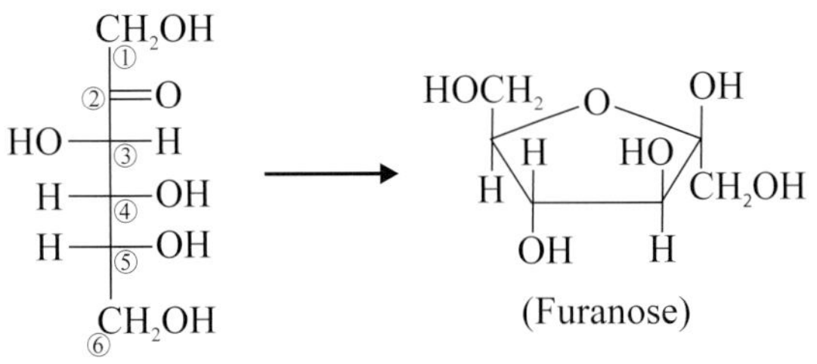

(Furanose)

A. carbon 1
B. carbon 3
C. carbon 5
D. carbon 6

**88.** Sugar A and B are what type of carbohydrates, respectively?

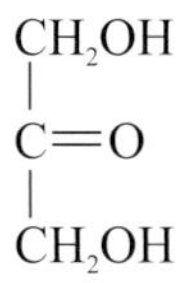

[Sugar A]

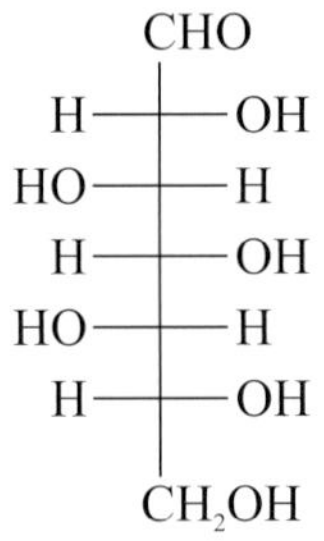

[Sugar B]

A. ketotriose and ketohexose
B. aldotriose and aldohexose
C. aldotriose and ketoheptose
D. ketotriose and aldoheptose

## 4.4 Lab Techniques

There are three types of lab techniques that you must know for the MCAT: spectroscopy, spectrometry, and separations. Spectroscopy will be either **nuclear magnetic resonance (nmr)**, **infrared spectroscopy (IR)**, or **ultraviolet spectroscopy (UV)**. You will need to understand how **mass spectrometry** works. Separation techniques will include **chromatography**, **distillation**, **crystallization**, and **extraction**.

## 4.5 NMR

NMR refers to **nuclear magnetic resonance** spectroscopy. The nucleus most commonly studied with nmr is the hydrogen nucleus, but it is possible to study the nucleus of carbon-13 and other atoms as well.

Nuclei with an odd atomic number or odd mass number exhibit *nuclear spin* that can be observed by an nmr spectrometer. The spin creates a magnetic field around the nucleus similar to the field created by a small magnet. When placed in an external magnetic field, the nucleus aligns its own field with or against the external field. Nuclei aligned with the magnetic field have a lower energy state than those aligned against the field. The stronger the magnetic field, the greater the difference between these energy states.

This is a nuclear magnetic resonance (NMR) laboratory.

When photons (electromagnetic radiation) of just the right frequency (energy state) are shone on the nuclei, those nuclei whose magnetic fields are oriented with the external magnetic field can absorb the energy of the photon and flip to face against the external field. A nucleus that is subjected to this perfect combination of magnetic field strength and electromagnetic radiation frequency is said to be in resonance. An nmr spectrometer can detect the energy absorption of a nucleus in resonance.

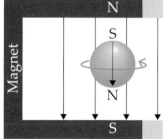
low energy state

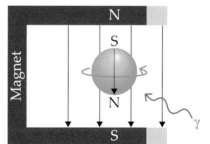

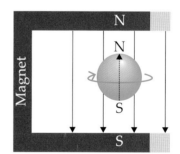
high energy state

In nmr, the frequency of the electromagnetic radiation is held constant while the magnetic field strength is varied.

Absent any electrons, all protons absorb electromagnetic energy from a constant-strength magnetic field at the same frequency (about 60 MHz in a magnetic field of 14,092 gauss). However, hydrogen atoms within different compounds experience unique surrounding-electron densities and are also uniquely affected by the magnetic fields of other nearby protons. The electrons *shield* the protons from the magnetic field. As a result, the external field must be strengthened for a shielded proton to achieve resonance. Thus protons within a compound absorb electromagnetic energy of the *same frequency at different magnetic field strengths*.

An nmr spectrum (shown in Figure 4.8) is a graph of the magnetic field strengths absorbed by the hydrogens of a specific compound at a single frequency. The field strength is measured in *parts per million, ppm,* and, despite the *decreasing* numbers, *increases* from left to right. The leftward direction is called *downfield* and the rightward is called *upfield*. All the way to the right is a peak at 0 ppm. This peak is due to a reference compound (tetramethylsilane, discussed below) used to calibrate the instrument.

### Figure 4.8 NMR Spectum

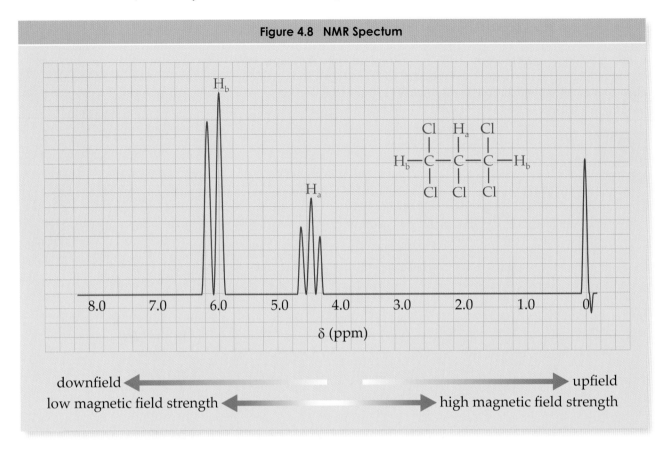

δ (ppm)

downfield ← → upfield
low magnetic field strength ← → high magnetic field strength

Although nmr is based on quantum mechanics and can be a very complex subject, there is actually very little to understand about nmr for the MCAT. First and most importantly, remember that, **unless otherwise indicated, nmr is concerned with hydrogens**. Given an nmr spectrum, you should be able to identify which peaks belong to which hydrogens on a given compound, or which of four compounds might create the given spectrum. To do this you must understand the following:

- **Each peak** represents **chemically equivalent hydrogens**;
- **Splitting** of peaks is created by "neighboring hydrogens".

Each peak indicates one or a group of chemically equivalent hydrogens (in other words, hydrogens indistinguishable from each other by way of their positions on the compound). Such hydrogens are said to be *enantiotropic*. Enantiotropic hydrogens are represented by the same peak in an nmr spectrum. They have the same **chemical shift**. Chemical shift is the difference between the resonance frequency of the chemically shifted hydrogens and the resonance frequency of hydrogens on a reference compound such as tetramethylsilane. Tetramethylsilane is the most common nmr reference compound because it contains many hydrogens that are all enantiotropic and are very well shielded. In the graph above, although not all of the $H_b$ are attached to the same carbon, they are stereochemically similar, and thus represented by the same group of peaks. Their chemical shift is approximately 6.0 ppm.

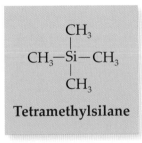

**Tetramethylsilane**

The area under a peak is proportional to the number of hydrogens represented by that peak. The more chemically equivalent hydrogens, the greater the area. The tallest peak does not necessarily correspond to the greatest area. The **integral trace** is a line drawn above the peaks that rises each time it goes over a peak. The rise of the integral trace is in proportion to the number of chemically equivalent hydrogens in the peak beneath it. A newer instrument, called a *digital trace*, records numbers which correspond to the rise in the line. The exact number of hydrogens cannot be determined from the integral trace or the digital trace; only the ratio of hydrogens from one peak to another can be determined.

Lateral position on a spectrum is dictated by *electron shielding*, thus limited predictions can be made based upon electron-withdrawing and electron-donating groups. Electron-withdrawing groups tend to lower shielding and thus decrease the magnetic field strength at which resonance takes place. This means that hydrogens with less shielding tend to have peaks downfield or to the left. Likewise, electron-donating groups tend to increase shielding and increase the required field strength for resonance.

**Splitting** (also called **spin-spin splitting**) results from neighboring hydrogens that are not chemically equivalent. (*Spin-spin coupling* is the same thing except that it also includes hydrogens that are chemically equivalent. The MCAT will not test this distinction.) The number of peaks due to splitting for a group of chemically equivalent hydrogens is given by the simple formula, $n + 1$, where $n$ is the number of **neighboring hydrogens** that are not chemically equivalent. A neighboring hydrogen is one that is on an atom adjacent to the atom to which the hydrogen is connected.

For proton nmr spectroscopy, follow these steps:

- Identify chemically equivalent hydrogens.

- Identify and count neighboring hydrogens that are not chemically equivalent. Use $n + 1$ to figure the number of peaks created by splitting for the chemically equivalent hydrogens.

- If necessary, identify electron withdrawing/donating groups near the chemically equivalent hydrogens. Withdrawing groups will move their signal to the left.

Something else you should know:
Aldehyde protons have a very distinctive shift at 9.5 ppm. Watch for it.

In a rare situation, carbon nmr may also appear on the MCAT. Remember, the nucleus must have an odd atomic or mass number to register on nmr, so carbon-13 is the only carbon isotope to register. Treat carbon nmr the same way as proton nmr, except ignore splitting.

Of course, nmr can be more complicated than is described here. However, like everything else on the MCAT, any complications tested will be explained and answerable from this small body of knowledge just presented. We have provided one more spectrum on the next page in order for you to test your understanding. Before reading further, turn the page and see if you can predict which hydrogens belong to which group of peaks.

## Figure 4.9 NMR Spectrum with Intergral Trace

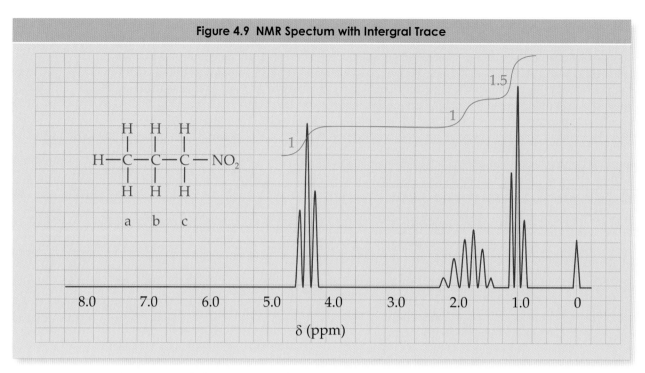

**Answer:** Each letter, *a*, *b*, and *c*, represents a group of chemically equivalent hydrogens. The groups of peaks from left to right correspond to the *c*, *b*, and *a* hydrogens respectively. Since $NO_2$ is electron-withdrawing, the *c* hydrogens are further downfield. The *b* hydrogens have 5 neighbors, so their peak has 6 peaks. The digital trace shows the peak furthest upfield as having 1.5 times as many hydrogens as the other peaks. The ratio of *a* hydrogens to *b* or *c* hydrogens is 3 to 2, so this must be the peak representing the *a* hydrogens.

## Thought Provoker

*Match the following compounds with their NMR specra:*

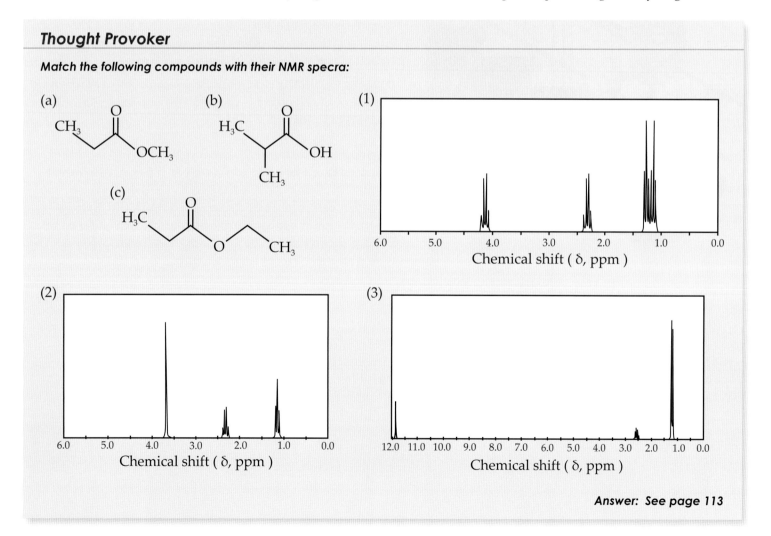

*Answer: See page 113*

## 4.6 | IR Spectroscopy

A dipole exists when the centers of positive and negative charge do not coincide. When exposed to an electric field, these oppositely charged centers will move in opposite directions; either toward each other or away from each other. In infrared radiation, the direction of the electric field oscillates, causing the positive and negative centers within polar bonds to move toward each other and then away from each other. Thus, when exposed to **infrared radiation**, the polar bonds within a compound stretch and contract in a vibrating motion.

**Figure 4.10   Vibration of a Dipole**

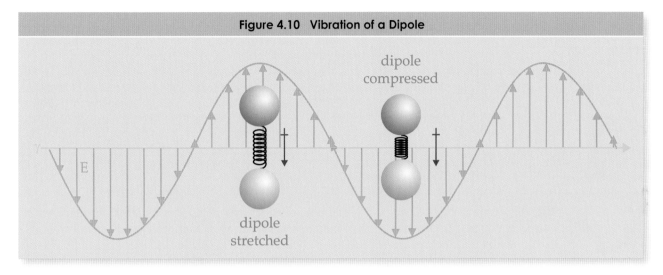

Different bonds vibrate at different frequencies. When the resonance frequency of the oscillating bond is matched by the frequency of infrared radiation, the IR energy is absorbed. In **IR Spectroscopy**, an infrared spectrometer slowly changes the frequency of infrared light shining upon a compound and records the frequencies of absorption in reciprocal centimeters, $cm^{-1}$ (number of cycles per cm).

If a bond has no dipole moment, then the infrared radiation does not cause it to vibrate and no energy is absorbed. However, energy can also be absorbed due to other types of stretching and scissoring motions of the molecules in a compound.

The most predictable section of the IR spectrum is in the 1600 to 3500 $cm^{-1}$ region. In Figure 4.11 are some distinguishing characteristics of this range of the IR spectrum for the functional groups MCAT may test. You should be familiar with these shapes and frequencies.

IR questions on the MCAT used to be as easy as reading a chart. Now, the MCAT sometimes requires limited memorization of the IR spectra of certain functional groups. The most likely spectra that would be asked by MCAT are the C=O, a sharp dip around 1700 cm$^{-1}$; and the O-H, a broad dip around 3200-3600.

**Figure 4.11 IR Absorption of Common Function Groups**

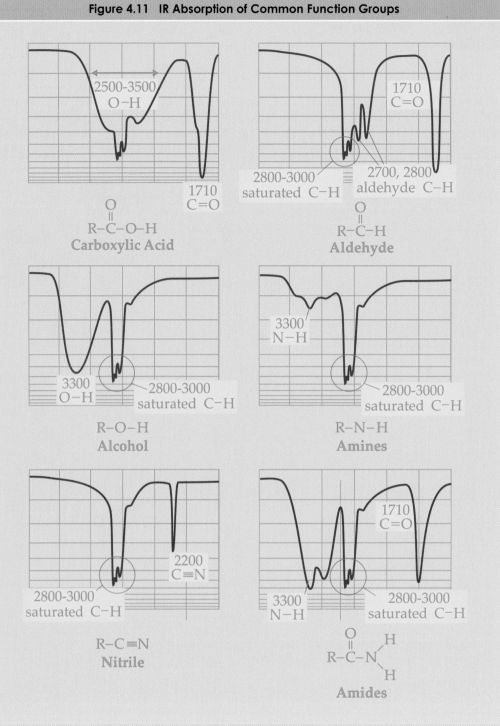

Limited predictions about vibration can be made based upon the *mass of the atoms involved* and the *stiffness of the bond* between them. Atoms with greater mass resonate at lower frequencies; stiffer bonds, such as double and triple bonds, resonate at higher frequencies. Bond strength and bond stiffness follow the same order: $sp > sp^2 > sp^3$.

An IR spectrum can help identify which functional groups are in a compound, but it does not readily reveal the shape or size of the carbon skeleton. However, two compounds are very unlikely to have exactly the same IR spectrum. This makes an IR spectrum like a fingerprint for each compound. Many of the complex vibrations that distinguish one compound from a similar compound are found in the 600 to 1400 cm$^{-1}$ region, called the **fingerprint region**. In Figure 4.12 are three sample spectra that include the fingerprint region. Know where the fingerprint region is, and know why it is called the fingerprint region, but use the higher frequency range to identify functional groups.

> The fingerprint region of the IR spectrum is unique to nearly all compounds, but it is very difficult to read it. You should know about the fingerprint region, but you should use IR to identify functional groups based upon the region from 1600 to 3500 cm$^{-1}$.

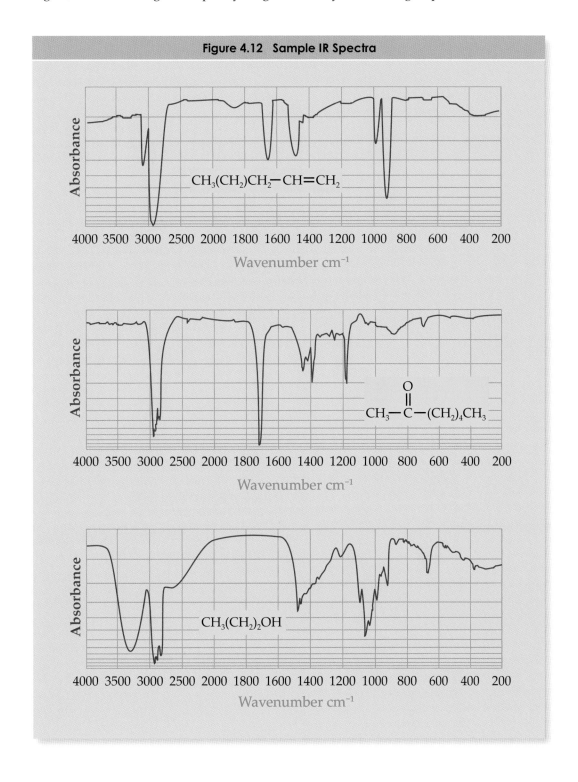

**Figure 4.12  Sample IR Spectra**

## Thought Provoker

*Using the Figure 4.12 on page 104 if necessary, match the following compounds with their IR spectrum below*

(a)

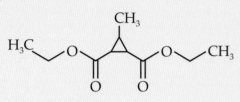

(b)

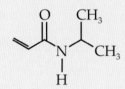

(c)

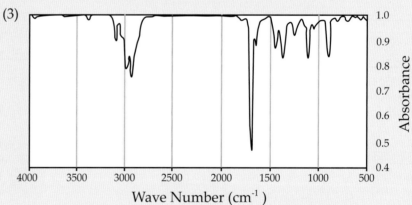

(1)

(2)

(3)

**Answer: See page 114**

Notes:

The wavelength of ultraviolet light is between 200 and 400 nm, much shorter than infrared light and at a much higher energy level. Ultraviolet (UV) spectroscopy detects conjugated double bonds (double bonds separated by one single bond) by comparing the intensities of two beams of light from the same monochromatic light source. One beam is shone through a sample cell and the other is shone through a reference cell. The sample cell contains the sample compound to be analyzed dissolved in a solvent. The reference cell contains only the solvent. The sample cell will absorb more energy from the light beam than the reference cell. The difference in the radiant energy is recorded as a UV spectrum of the sample compound.

The UV spectrum provides limited information about the length and structure of the conjugated portion of the molecule. When a photon collides with an electron in a molecule in the sample, the electron may be bumped up to a vacant molecular orbital and the photon absorbed. These are typically $\pi$-electron movements from bonding to nonbonding orbitals ($\pi \rightarrow \pi^*$). Electrons in $\sigma$-bonds usually require more energy to reach the next highest orbital, and thus they are typically unaffected by wavelengths of greater than 200 nm. Conjugated systems with $\pi$-bonds, on the other hand, have vacant orbitals at energy levels close to their highest occupied molecular orbital (HOMO) energy levels. The vacant orbitals are called LUMO (lowest unoccupied molecular orbital). UV photons are able to momentarily displace electrons to the LUMO, and the energy is absorbed. If a conjugated system is present in the sample, the sample beam intensity $I_s$ will be lower than the reference beam intensity $I_r$. The absorbance $A$ is given by $A_l = \log(I_s/I_r)$. The absorbance is plotted on the UV spectra. Absorbance also equals the product of concentration of the sample ($c$), the length of the path of light through the cell ($l$), and the molar absorptivity ($\varepsilon$)(or *molar extinction coefficient*).

$$A = \varepsilon c l$$

> UV starts at around 217 nm with butadiene.

> The rule of thumb for UV is 30 to 40 nm increase for each additional conjugated double bond, and a 5 nm increase for each additional alkyl group.

The molar absorptivity is a measure of how strongly the sample absorbs light at a particular wavelength. It is probably easiest to think of it mathematically as $\varepsilon = A/cl$.

Ethylene, though not conjugated, absorbs wavelengths at 171 nm. Absorption at this wavelength is obscured by oxygen in the air. Butadiene has a higher HOMO and lower LUMO than ethylene, allowing for an absorption at 217 nm. Conjugated trienes absorb at even longer wavelengths. The longer the chain of conjugated double bonds, the greater the wavelength of absorption. The rule of thumb is that each additional **conjugated** double bond increases the wavelength by about 30 to 40 nm. An additional alkyl group attached to any one of the atoms involved in the conjugated system increases the spectrum wavelength by about 5 nm. **Isolated** double bonds do not increase the absorption wavelength.

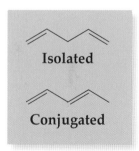

**Isolated**

**Conjugated**

UV spectra lack detail. Samples must be extremely pure or the spectrum is obscured. Figure 4.13 is a UV spectrum of 2-methyl-1,3-butadiene dissolved in methanol. The methyl group increases the absorption wavelength slightly. The methanol solvent makes no contribution to the spectrum. Spcetra are typically not printed, but instead given as lists. The spectrum in Figure 4.13 would be listed as:

$$\lambda_{max} = 222 \text{ nm} \qquad \varepsilon = 20,000$$

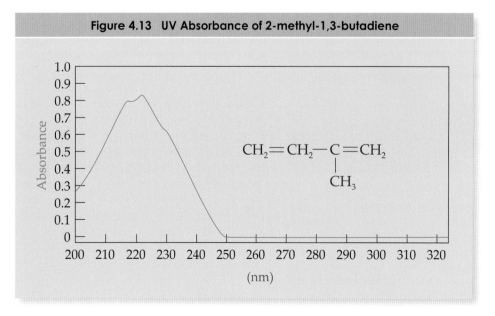

**Figure 4.13   UV Absorbance of 2-methyl-1,3-butadiene**

Carbonyls, compounds with carbon-oxygen double bonds, also absorb light in the UV region. For instance, acetone has a broad absorption peak at 280 nm. In this example, the electron can be excited from an unshared pair into a nonbonding $\pi$-orbital. ($\pi \rightarrow \pi^*$)

$\overset{\diagdown}{\underset{\diagup}{C}} = \ddot{O}: \longrightarrow \overset{\diagdown}{\underset{\diagup}{C}} \dot{=} \dot{O}:$

$n \longrightarrow \pi^*$

$\overset{\diagdown}{\underset{\diagup}{C}} = \ddot{O}: \longrightarrow \overset{\diagdown}{\underset{\diagup}{C}} \overset{\cdot}{\underset{\cdot}{=}} \ddot{O}:$

$\pi \longrightarrow \pi^*$

**Thought Provoker**

**Which of the following would show absorbance in the UV spectrum (200-400 nm)?**

(a)  (b)  (c) CN

(d) Aspirin  (e) $CH_3$  (f) Indole

**Answer: See page 114**

---

## 4.8 Visible Spectrum

If a compound has eight or more double bonds, its absorbance moves into the visible spectrum. **β-carotene**, a precursor of vitamin A, has 11 conjugated double bonds. β-carotene has a maximum absorbance at 497 nm. Electromagnetic radiaton of 497 nm has a blue-green color. Carrots, having β-carotene, absorb blue-green light, giving them the **complementary color** of red-orange.

---

## 4.9 Mass Spectrometry

Mass spectrometry gives the molecular weight, and, in the case of high resolution mass spectrometry, the molecular formula. In mass spectrometry, the molecules of a sample are bombarded with electrons, causing them to break apart and to ionize. The largest ion is the size of the original molecule but short one electron. This cation is called the *molecular ion*. For instance, if methane were the sample, the molecular ion would be $CH_4^+$. The ions are accelerated through a magnetic field. The resulting force deflects the ions around a curved path. The radius of curvature of their path depends upon the **mass to charge ratio** of the ion ($m/z$). Most of the ions have a charge of 1+. The magnetic field strength is altered to allow the passage of different size ions through the flight tube (shown in Figure 4.14). A computer records the amount of ions at different magnetic field strengths as peaks on a chart. The largest peak is called the base peak. The peak made by the molecular ions is called the **parent peak**. Notice that the parent peak is made by molecules that did not fragment. Look for the parent peak all the way to the right of the spectrum. Only heavy isotopes will be further right. All peaks are assigned *abundances* as percentages of the base peak. In Figure 4.14, the parent peak has an abundance of 10 because it is 10% as high as the base peak.

A mass spectrometer ionizes and fragments molecules in a sample, and fires the fragments through a magnetic field. The amount the fragments deviate is indicative of their mass and charge. This can provide detailed information about the sample's composition.

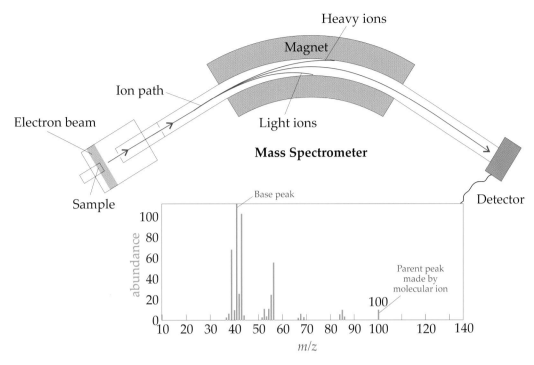

**Figure 4.14 Mass Spectrometer**

Labels in figure: Heavy ions; Magnet; Ion path; Light ions; Electron beam; Sample; Mass Spectrometer; Base peak; abundance; Parent peak made by molecular ion; Detector; 100; m/z

# 4.10 *Chromatography*

**Chromatography** is the resolution (separation) of a mixture by passing it over or through a matrix that adsorbs different compounds with different affinities, ultimately altering the rate at which they lose contact with the resolving matrix. The mixture is usually dissolved into a solution to serve as the mobile phase, while the resolving matrix is often a solid surface. The surface adsorbs compounds from the mixture, establishing the stationary phase. The compounds in the mixture that have a greater affinity for the surface move more slowly. Typically, the more polar compounds elute more slowly because they have a greater affinity for the stationary phase. The result of chromatography is the establishment of separate and distinct layers, one pertaining to each component of the mixture. Different types of chromatography include:

## Solid to Liquid

*Column chromatography* is where a solution containing the mixture is dripped down a column containing the solid phase (usually glass beads). The more polar compounds in the mixture travel more slowly down the column, creating separate layers for each compound. Each compound can subsequently be collected as it elutes with the solvent and drips out of the bottom of the column.

Gas chromatography is carried out to separate complex mixtures of compounds into individual components, allowing the composition to be analysed and particular fractions isolated.

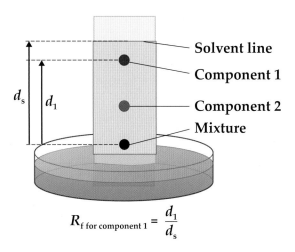

$$R_{\text{f for component 1}} = \frac{d_1}{d_s}$$

**Figure 4.15  Paper Chromatography**

In *paper chromatography* (Figure 4.15) a small portion of the sample to be separated is spotted onto paper. One end of the paper is then placed into a solvent. The solvent moves up the paper via capillary action and dissolves the sample as it passes over it. As the solvent continues to move up the paper, the more polar components of the sample move more slowly because they are attracted to the polar paper. The less polar components are not attracted to the paper and move more quickly. The result is a series of colored dots representing the different components of the sample with the most polar near the bottom and the least polar near the top. An $R_f$ *factor* can be determined for each component of the separation by dividing the distance traveled by the component by the distance traveled by the solvent. Nonpolar components have an $R_f$ factor close to one; polar components have a lower $R_f$ factor. The $R_f$ factor is always between 0 and 1.

*Thin layer chromatography* is similar to paper chromatography except that a coated glass or plastic plate is used instead of paper, and the results are visualized via an iodine vapor chamber.

## Gas to Liquid

In *gas chromatography* the liquid phase is the stationary phase. The mixture is dissolved into a heated carrier gas (usually helium or nitrogen) and passed over a liquid phase bound to a column. Compounds in the mixture equilibrate with the liquid phase at different rates and elute as individual components at an exit port.

## 4.11  Distillation

**Distillation** is separation based upon vapor pressure. A solution of two volatile liquids with boiling point differences of approximately 20°C or more may be separated by slow boiling. The **compound with the lower boiling point (higher vapor pressure) will boil off and can be captured** and condensed in a cool tube. Be careful. If a solution of two volatile liquids exhibits a positive deviation to Rault's law, the solution will boil at a lower temperature than either pure compound. The result will be a solution with an exact ratio of the two liquids called an *azeotrope*. An azeotrope cannot be separated by distillation. 5% water and 95% ethanol make an azeotrope that has a lower boiling point than pure water or pure ethanol. An azeotrope can also form when the solution has a higher boiling point than either pure substance. *Fractional distillation* is simply a more precise method of distillation. In fractional distillation, the vapor is run through glass beads allowing the compound with the higher boiling point to condense and fall back into the solution.

## 4.12 Crystallization

Crystallization is based upon the principle that **pure substances form crystals** more easily than impure substances. The classic example is an iceberg. An iceberg is formed from the ocean but is made of pure water, not salt water. This is because pure water forms crystals more easily. You should know that crystallization is a very inefficient method of separation; it is very difficult to arrive at a pure substance through crystallization. Crystallization of most salts is an exothermic process.

During the process of freezing most of the salty impurities are frozen out of the iceberg. This is an example of crystallization.

## 4.13 Extraction

**Extraction** is based upon **solubility due to similar polarities**. Like dissolves like. We start with an organic mixture on top of an aqueous layer. They have different polarities and don't mix. There are three steps:

1. add a strong acid and shake. The acid protonates bases like amines in the organic layer, making them polar. The polar amines dissolve in the aqueous layer and are drained off.

2. add a weak base. The base deprotonates only the stronger acids like carboxylic acids, making them more polar. The polar carboxylic acids dissolve in the aqueous layer and are drained off.

3. add a strong base. The strong base reacts with the rest of the acids (hopefully all weak acids like phenol). These acids dissolve in the aqueous layer and are drained off.

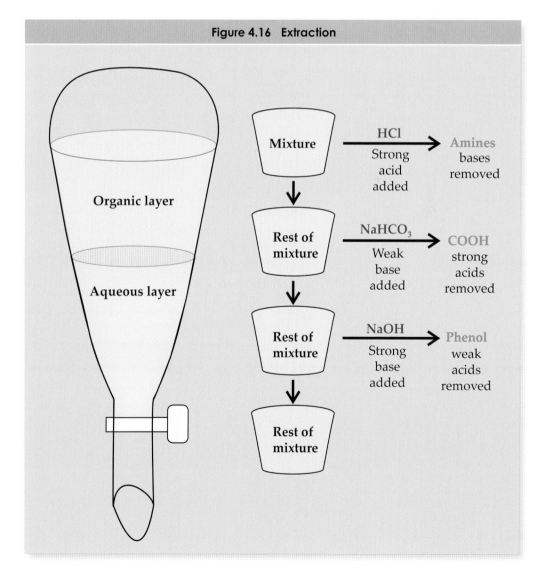

**Figure 4.16  Extraction**

## 4.14 Terms You Need To Know

| Terms | |
|---|---|
| $\alpha$-Amino Acids | Hydrophilic |
| Amide | Hydrophobic |
| Amino Acid | Infrared Spectroscopy (IR) |
| Aldose | Integral Trace |
| Amphipathic | Isoelectric Point, p$I$ |
| Amylopectin | Isolated |
| Amylose | Ketoses |
| Anomeric Carbon | Lactose |
| Carbohydrates | Lipolysis |
| Cellulose | Maltose |
| Chemical Shift | Mass To Charge Ratio |
| Chemically Equivalent Hydrogens | Neighboring Hydrogens |
| Chromatography | Nonpolar |
| Conjugated | Nuclear Magnetic Resonance (nmr) |
| Crystallization | Parent Peak |
| Distillation | Peptide Bonds |
| Essential Amino Acid | Polypeptide |
| Extraction | Pyranose |
| Fatty Acids | Saponification |
| Fingerprint Region | Saturated |
| Furanose | Splitting (Spin-Spin Splitting) |
| Glucopyranose | Sucrose |
| Glycogen | Ultraviolet Spectroscopy (UV) |
| Hexose | Unsaturated |

# Thought Provoker Answers

Answer from page 102:

*In spectrum (2) there is a single peak at ~3.6 ppm, which indicates that there are no Hs on the adjacent atoms, so this must be structure (a). In spectrum (3) the single peak at ~11.8 ppm is from a carboxylic acid, so this must be structure (b). In spectrum (1) the 6 peaks ~1.3 ppm indicates Hs is two slightly different environments on Cs next to a C with 2 Hs, so this must be structure (c).*

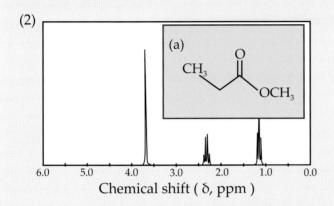

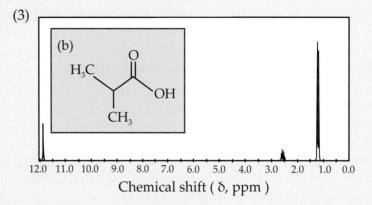

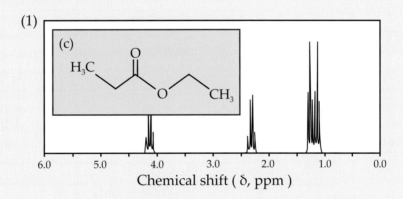

Notes:

## Thought Provoker Answers

*Answer from page 106:*

*All of the spectra have carbonyl groups, which have a peak at ~1700 cm⁻¹. In spectrum (1) the peak at ~ 3300 cm⁻¹ is indicative of N-H, so this is structure (c). Spectra (2) and (3) are similar. In spectrum (3) there is a small peak ~1650 cm⁻¹ which indicates a C=C, so this is structure (a).*

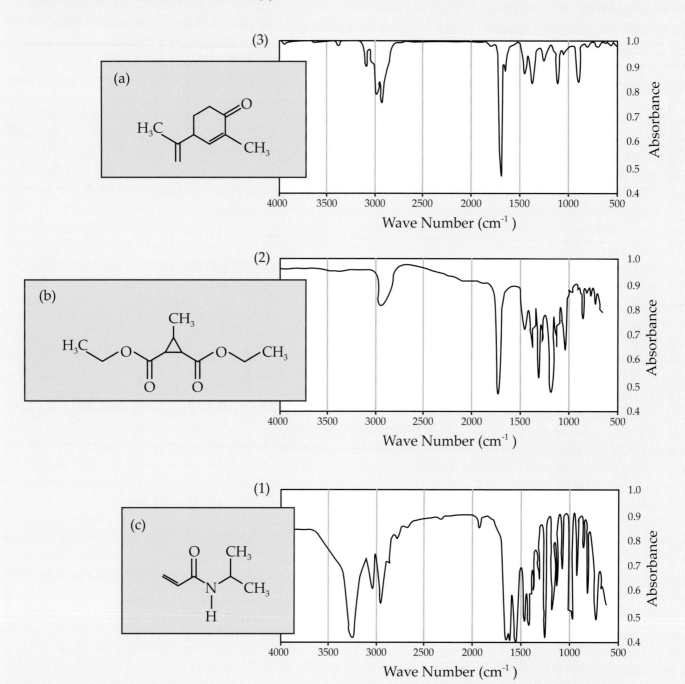

*Answer from page 108:*

*Structures (b), (d), and (f) have conjugated double bonds, so they will have absorbance in the UV spectrum between 200 and 400 cm⁻¹.*

**89.** All of the following are true concerning nmr spectroscopy EXCEPT:

A. Protons are distinguished when they absorb magnetic energy at different field strengths.

B. Downfield is to the left on an nmr spectrum.

C. Functional groups are distinguished when they absorb magnetic energy at different field strengths.

D. Delocalized electrons generate magnetic fields that can either shield or deshield nearby protons.

**90.** Extraction is an effective method for separating compounds which can be treated with an acid or base and made to differ in:

A. boiling point.

B. molecular weight.

C. water solubility.

D. optical activity.

**91.** A carbonyl will absorb infrared radiation at a frequency of approximately:

A. 700 – 900 Hz

B. 1630 – 1700 Hz

C. 2220 – 2260 Hz

D. 3300 – 3500 Hz

**92.** In thin layer chromatography polar compounds will:

A. rise more slowly through the silica gel than nonpolar compounds.

B. rise more quickly through the silica gel than nonpolar compounds.

C. move to the left through the silica gel.

D. move to the right through the silica gel.

**93.** Which of the following statements are true concerning separations?

I. Any two compounds with sufficiently different boiling points can be separated completely by distillation.

II. Crystallization is an efficient method of compound purification for most compounds.

III. Distillation is more effective when done slowly.

A. I only

B. III only

C. I and III only

D. II and III only

**94.** *Refining* is the separation of crude oil into four primary products:

| Petroleum Product | Boiling Point (°C) |
|---|---|
| Straight-run gasoline | 30-180 |
| Kerosene | 175-300 |
| Gas oil | 295-400 |
| Lubricating wax | 425-700 |

Petroleum product refining can also be described as:

A. high pressure distillation

B. nuclear magnetic resonance separation

C. liquid chromatography extraction

D. organic phase purification

**95.** Which statement accounts for the fact that dimethyl sulfoxide is miscible in water, whereas dimethyl sulfide is not?

$$CH_3-\overset{\overset{\displaystyle O}{\|}}{S}-CH_3 \qquad CH_3-S-CH_3$$

Dimethyl sulfoxide      Dimethyl sulfide
(bp 187°C)          (bp 37°C)

A. Dimethyl sulfoxide is a non-polar compound that rapidly penetrates the skin.

B. Dimethyl sulfide is symmetrical, which causes it to develop a dipole moment.

C. Dimethyl sulfide has a low boiling point and density issues prevent it from being water soluble.

D. Dimethyl sulfoxide is a polar compound.

**96.** What is the predicted number of $^{13}C$ nmr peaks for methylcyclopentane and 1,2-dimethylbenzene, respectively?

Methylcyclopentane   1,2-Dimethylbenzene

A. 2,3

B. 3,4

C. 4,4

D. 5,3

Notes:

# STOP!

DO NOT LOOK AT THESE EXAMS UNTIL CLASS.

**30-MINUTE IN-CLASS EXAM FOR LECTURE 1**

With few exceptions, enantiomers cannot be separated through physical means. When in racemic mixtures, they have the same physical properties. Enantiomers have similar chemical properties as well. The only chemical difference between a pair of enantiomers occurs in reactions with other chiral compounds. Thus resolution of a racemic mixture typically takes place through a reaction with another optically active reagent. Since living organisms usually produce only one of two possible enantiomers, many optically active reagents can be obtained from natural sources. For instance, (S)-(+)-lactic acid can be obtained from animal muscle tissue and (S)-(-)-2-methyl-1-butanol, from yeast fermentation.

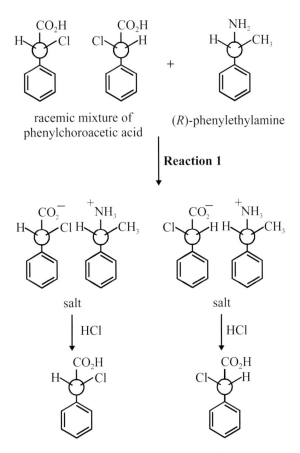

racemic mixture of phenylchloroacetic acid

(R)-phenylethylamine

**Reaction 1**

salt          salt

HCl          HCl

**Figure 1** Separation of enantiomers

In the resolution of a racemic acid, a solution of (R)-phenylethylamine is reacted with a racemic mixture of phenylchloroacetic acid to form the corresponding salts. The salts are then separated by careful fractional crystallization. Hydrochloric acid is added to the separated salts, and the respective acids are precipitated from their solutions.

Resolution of a racemic base can be accomplished in the same manner with tartaric acid.

1. Quinine, a natural anti-malarial, is commonly used as an optically active reagent to resolve acidic enantiomers. How many chiral carbons exist in the quinine molecule drawn below?

Quinine

A. 1
B. 2
C. 3
D. 4

2. Which of the following alcohols is a natural product of anaerobic respiration?

A.
$CH_3$
HO——$CH_3$
H——H
$CH_3$

B.
$CH_2OH$
$H_3C$——H
H——H
$CH_3$

C.
$CH_2OH$
H——H
H——$CH_3$
$CH_3$

D.
$CH_2OH$
H——$CH_3$
H——H
$CH_3$

3. The salts created in Reaction 1 are:

A. diastereomers
B. enantiomers
C. structural isomers
D. meso compounds

**4.** The following reaction proceeds with retention of configuration:

$$CH_2BrCHOHCO_2H \xrightarrow{\text{Zn, H}^+} CH_3CHOHCO_2H$$

If the product is the naturally occurring lactic acid, which of the compounds below could be a reactant?

**A.**

COOH
Br►C◄OH
CH₃

**C.**

COOH
HO►C◄Br
CH₃

**B.**

COOH
H►C◄OH
CH₂Br

**D.**

COOH
HO►C◄H
CH₂Br

**5.** D-(+)-glyceraldehyde undergoes the series of reactions below to yield two isomers of tartaric acid. What type of isomers are they?

```
      CHO
  H ──┼── OH        HCN
     CH₂OH     ───────────►

D-(+)-glyceraldehyde
                    Ba(OH)₂
                      │
                      ▼
  COOH       COOH
H─┼─OH   HO─┼─H        HNO₃
H─┼─OH    H─┼─OH   ◄───────
  COOH       COOH

     tartaric acid
        isomers
```

**A.** enantiomers
**B.** diastereomers
**C.** structural isomers
**D.** conformational isomers

**6.** Which of the following compounds might be used to resolve a racemic mixture of acidic enantiomers?

**A.**

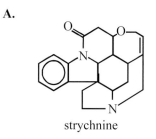

strychnine

**B.**

CH₂CH₂NH₂ on imidazole ring (HN, N)

histamine

**C.**

CH₃O, CH₃O─, CH₃O benzene ring — CH₂CH₂NH₂

mescaline

**D.**

HO─ indole ring with CH₂CH₂NH₂

serotonin

**GO ON TO THE NEXT PAGE.**

A chemical reaction is *stereoselective* when a certain stereoisomer or set of stereoisomers predominate as products. A reaction is *stereospecific* if different isomers lead to isomerically opposite products.

Bromine adds to 2-butene to form the *vic*-dihalide, 2,3-dibromobutane. A student proposed the following two mechanisms for the addition of bromine to alkenes. In order to test each mechanism the student designed two experiments.

*Mechanism A*

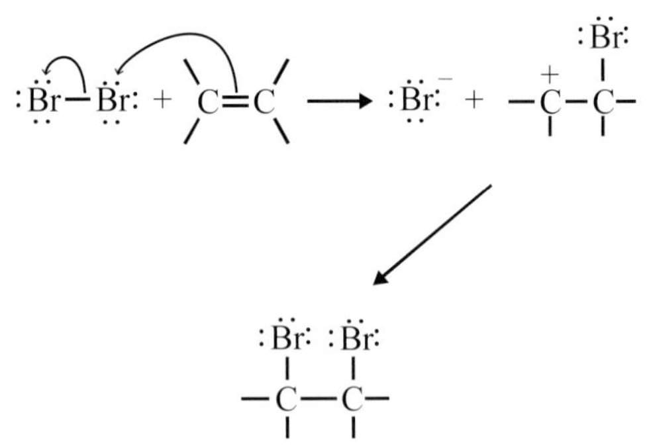

*vic*-dihalide

*Mechanism B*

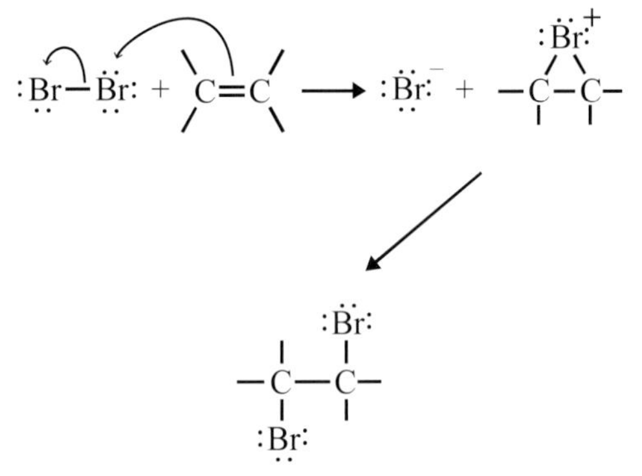

*vic*-dihalide

*Experiment 1*

Cyclopentene was dissolved in $CCl_4$. Bromine was added to the solution at low temperatures and low light. The product tested negative for optical activity. An optically active reagent was then added and, upon fractional distillation, two fractions were obtained. Each fraction was then precipitated and rinsed in an acid bath. The final products were found to have opposite observed rotations.

*Experiment 2*

The same procedure as in Experiment 1 was followed for both the *cis* and *trans* isomers of 2-butene. The results depended upon which isomer was used.

7.  In the second step of *Mechanism B*, the bromine ion acts as:

    A.  a halophile.
    B.  a catalyst.
    C.  an electrophile.
    D.  a nucleophile.

8.  If *Mechanism B* is correct, how many fractions should the student obtain from the distillation in Experiment 2 when the *trans* isomer is used?

    A.  1
    B.  2
    C.  3
    D.  4

9.  What is the expected angle between the bonds of the carbocation in *Mechanism A*?

    A.  90°
    B.  109°
    C.  120°
    D.  180°

10. The results of the experiments demonstrate that *Mechanism B* is correct. The addition of bromine to alkenes is:

    A.  stereoselective but not stereospecific.
    B.  stereospecific but not stereoselective.
    C.  both stereoselective and stereospecific.
    D.  neither stereoselective nor stereospecific.

**11.** If, instead of CCl$_4$, water is used as the solvent in a halogen addition reaction, a halohydrin is formed. The student proposed that such a reaction would follow *Mechanism A* with water replacing bromine as the nucleophile. If this hypothesis is correct, which of the following is the most likely product for the addition of bromine to propene in water?

**A.** 1,2-dibromopropane
**B.** 1,3-dibromo-2-propanol
**C.** 1-bromo-2-propanol
**D.** 2-bromo-1-propanol

**12.** If *Mechanism B* is correct, the *trans* isomer in Experiment 2 will produce:

**A.** a meso compound.
**B.** a pair of enantiomers.
**C.** only one optically active compound.
**D.** a pair of structural isomers.

**13.** In *Experiment 1*, why did the student use low light and low temperature?
**A.** to decrease the rate of the reaction
**B.** to prevent combustion of the alkene
**C.** to avoid contamination of the product via a radical reaction
**D.** to increase the yield of the endothermic reaction

## Passage III (Questions 14-19)

It is possible for asymmetrical molecules, such as enzymes, to distinguish between identical substituents on some symmetrical molecules. Such symmetrical molecules are called *prochiral*. A prochiral molecule is an achiral molecule with three different substituents. If one of the two identical substituents on a prochiral molecule is substituted for a different substituent not already present on the molecule, then the molecule would become chiral. The amino acid glycine is a prochiral molecule.

The molecule in Figure 1 is an example of a prochiral molecule. The asymmetrical enzyme binds only to hydrogen 'a' and not to hydrogen 'b' due to the spatial arrangement of its active site with respect to the other substituents on the prochiral carbon. All known dehydrogenases are stereospecific in this manner.

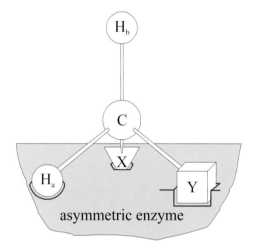

**Figure 1** An asymmetrical enzyme distinguishing between identical substituents on a symmetrical molecule.

*Experiment 1*

An experimenter labeled oxaloacetate with $^{14}$C at the carboxyl carbon farthest from the keto group. The oxaloacetate was allowed to undergo the portion of the Kreb's cycle depicted in Figure 2. The acetyl group donated by acetyl CoA is not removed during the Kreb's cycle. The experimenter found that all of the label emerged in the CO$_2$ of the second decarboxylation.

**GO ON TO THE NEXT PAGE.**

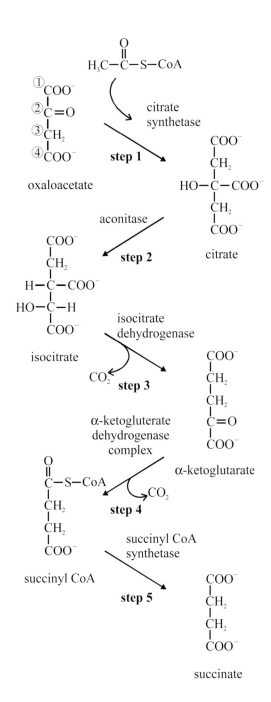

**Figure 2** A portion of the Kreb's cycle

**14.** Which of the following reactants in step 1 of Figure 2 contains a water soluble vitamin as a component part?

A. citrate
B. oxaloacetate
C. acetyl CoA
D. citrate synthetase

**15.** All of the following molecules are prochiral at the third carbon EXCEPT:

A. succinate
B. citrate
C. α-ketoglutarate
D. isocitrate

**16.** Which one of the carbons numbered in oxaloacetate is removed from isocitrate by the decarboxylation in step 3 of Figure 2?

A. 1
B. 2
C. 3
D. 4

**17.** The hybridization of the labeled carbon in oxaloacetate, citrate, and α-ketogluterate, respectively, is:

A. $sp^2$; $sp^2$; $sp^2$
B. $sp^2$; $sp^2$; $sp^3$
C. $sp^2$; $sp^3$; $sp^2$
D. $sp^3$; $sp^3$; $sp^3$

**18.** Which of the following structures is the enol form of α-ketogluteric acid?

A.

C.

B.

D.

**19.** What are the products when deuterium labeled alcohol is reacted with NAD$^+$ in the presence of alcohol dehydrogenase as shown below?

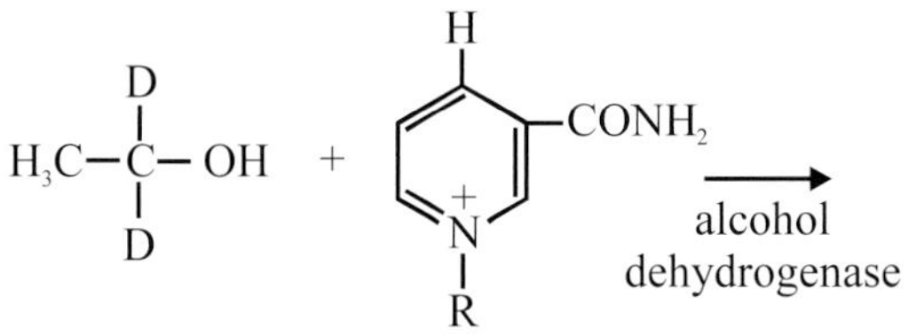

**A.**

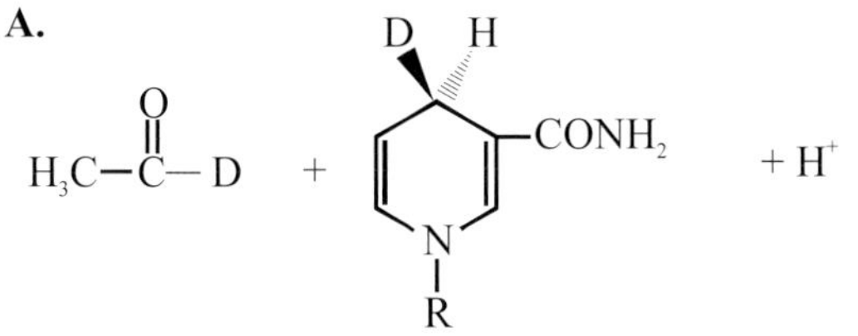

**B.**

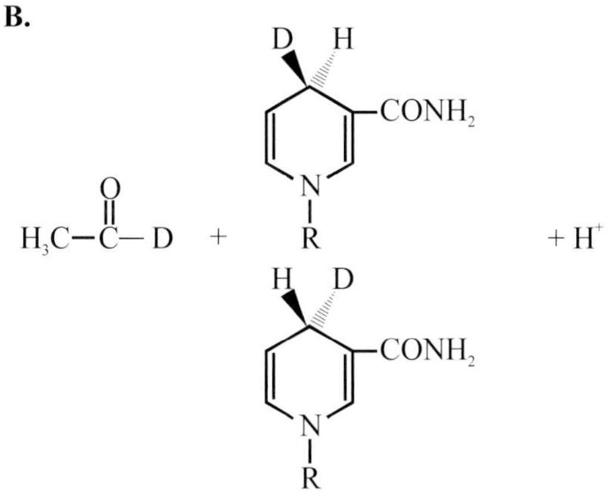

**C.**

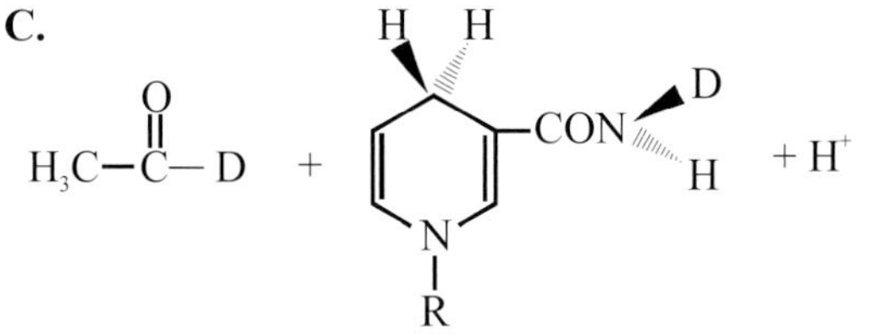

**D.**

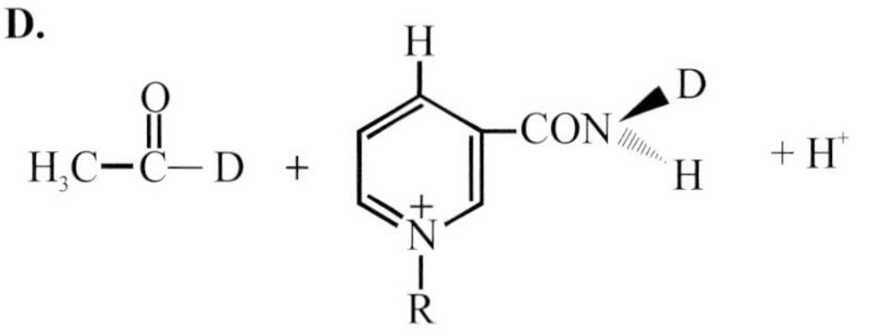

Questions 20 through 23 are **NOT** based on a descriptive passage.

**20.** Which of the following is true concerning meso compounds?

   **I.** They are achiral.
   **II.** They rotate plane polarized light.
   **III.** They contain a chiral carbon.

   **A.** I only
   **B.** I and II only
   **C.** I and III only
   **D.** II and III only

**21.** Which of the following is true concerning chirality?

   **I.** Chiral molecules are never the same as their mirror images.
   **II.** All chiral molecules have a mirror image which is their enantiomer.
   **III.** If a molecule is not the same as its mirror image, then it is chiral.

   **A.** I only
   **B.** II only
   **C.** III only
   **D.** I, II, and III

**22.** The name of the compound shown below is:

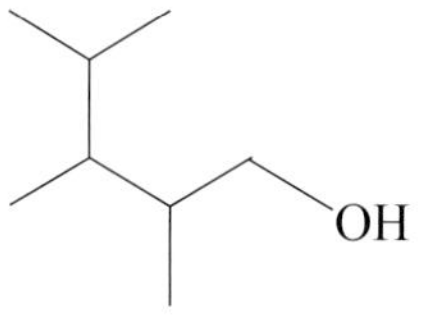

   **A.** 2-isopropyl-3-methyl-5-pentanol
   **B.** 3-isopropyl-2-methyl-1-butanol
   **C.** 2,3,4-trimethyl-1-pentanol
   **D.** 3,4,5-trimethyl-1-hexanol

**23.** Which of the following is true concerning conformational isomers?

   **A.** No conformer can be isolated.
   **B.** They only exist at high energy levels.
   **C.** The anti-conformation has the highest energy level.
   **D.** At low temperatures the anti-conformation is the most common.

**STOP.** IF YOU FINISH BEFORE TIME IS CALLED, CHECK YOUR WORK. YOU MAY GO BACK TO ANY QUESTION IN THIS TEST BOOKLET.

**STOP.**

# 30-MINUTE IN-CLASS EXAM FOR LECTURE 2

## Passage I (Questions 24-29)

A chemist performs the following experiment.

*Step 1*

Chlorine is added to (*S*)-*sec*-butyl chloride at 300°C. The reaction proceeds with retention of configuration. The products are carefully separated by fractional distillation. The chemist identifies five fractions as isomers of dichlorobutane and labels them: Compounds A, B, C, D, and E. Compounds C and D are formed in a 7 to 3 ratio. The boiling points of all five compounds are listed in Table 1.

| Compound | Boiling Point (°C) |
|----------|--------------------|
| A | 134° |
| B | 124° |
| C | 118° |
| D | 115° |
| E | 104° |

**Table 1** Boiling points of selected fractions from Step 1

*Step 2*

The labeled compounds are each checked with a polarimeter for the rotation of plane-polarized light. Only Compounds A, B, and C are optically active.

*Step 3*

Upon nmr spectroscopy, Compounds C and D were revealed to be stereoisomers.

**24.** After the distillation in Step 1, which of the following properties, if known for each fraction, would identify a fraction as a dichlorobutane?

- **A.** boiling point
- **B.** melting point
- **C.** molecular weight
- **D.** observed rotation

**25.** Compounds A and E are:

- **A.** diastereomers.
- **B.** enantiomers.
- **C.** conformational isomers.
- **D.** constitutional isomers.

**26.** If (*R*,*R*)-2,3-dichlorobutane is found to have a specific rotation of $[\alpha]_D^{20}$ -25.66, then which compound has a specific rotation of $[\alpha]_D^{20}$ +25.66?

- **A.** Compound A
- **B.** Compound B
- **C.** Compound C
- **D.** Compound D

**27.** Which of the following is NOT true concerning the compounds listed in Table 1?

- **A.** Although the relative configuration about the original chiral center is retained, the absolute configuration may have changed.
- **B.** Both configurations about any new chiral center appeared in equal proportions.
- **C.** One of the compounds is a meso compound.
- **D.** Although the relative configuration about the original chiral center is retained, the direction of observed rotation may change.

**28.** Compound E is most likely which of the following?

**A.**

CH₃
H——Cl
H——Cl
CH₃

**C.**

CH₃
H——H
Cl——Cl
CH₃

**B.**

CH₃      CH₃
H——Cl  Cl——H
Cl——H  H——Cl
CH₃      CH₃

**D.**

CH₃
H——H
Cl——H
CH₃

**29.** If NaOH is added to (*S*)-*sec*-butyl chloride, what is the most likely product?

- **A.** (*R*)-*sec*-butyl alcohol
- **B.** (*S*)-*sec*-butyl alcohol
- **C.** (*S*)-2-chloro-2-butanol
- **D.** (*R*)- 2-chloro-2-butanol

---

The *neighboring mechanism* occurs when a neighboring atom or functional group otherwise not involved in a reaction, affects the reaction by carrying electrons close to the reacting group. If the neighboring group helps to expel the leaving group, it is said to *give anchimeric assistance*.

The halohydrin 3-bromo-2-butanol undergoes the following reactions with hydrobromic acid.

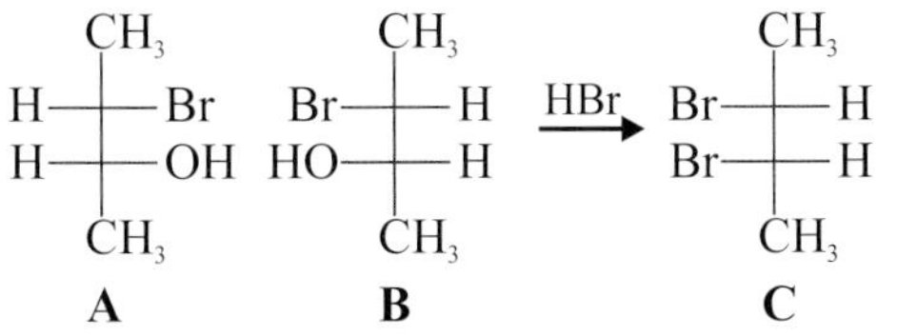

**A**          **B**          **C**

**Reaction 1**

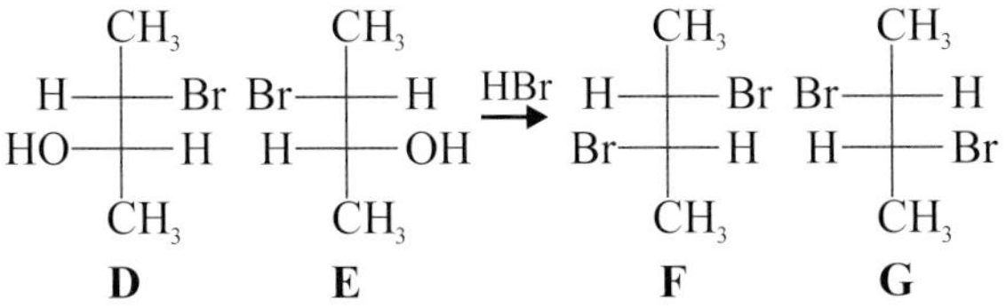

**D**       **E**       **F**       **G**

**Reaction 2**

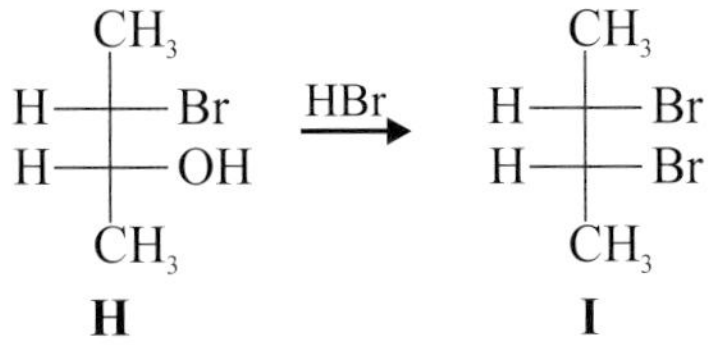

**H**          **I**

**Reaction 3**

**J**       **K**       **L**

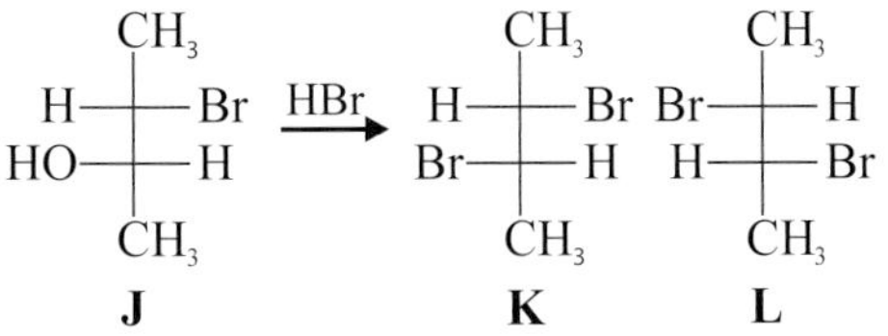

**Reaction 4**

A chemist proposed the following *neighboring mechanism* to explain the results of the above reactions:

*Mechanism I*

When the alcohol is protonated by the hydrobromic acid, the attached bromine attacks the adjacent carbon, ejecting the leaving group to form a bromonium ion. The bromine ion is then equally likely to attach via pathway a or b in Figure 1. Both the formation of the bromonium ion and attachment of the bromine ion are similar to an $S_N2$ mechanism where attachment of the nucleophile and detachment of the leaving group occur in a single step.

The process of bromonium ion formation is related to rearrangement of the carbon skeleton of carbocations. A nearby atom or group may relieve the electron deficiency of another atom through induction, resonance, or, as in bromonium ion formation, by actually carrying the electrons to where they are needed.

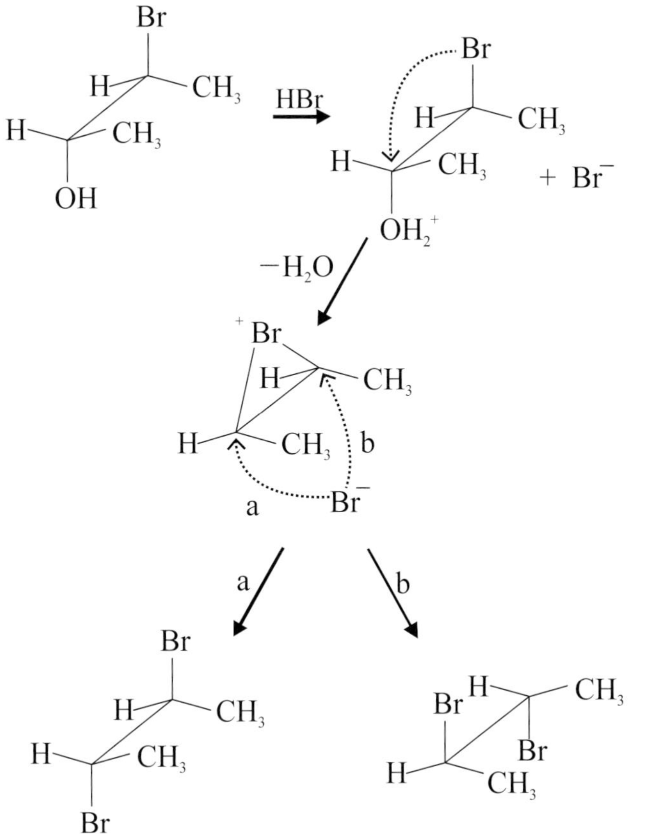

**Compound 1**          **Compound 2**

**Figure 1** Diagram of Mechanism 1

30. How many stereoisomers exist of 2,3-dibromobutane?

   A. 1
   B. 2
   C. 3
   D. 4

**31.** Which of the following statements is true concerning Reaction 4?

    **A.** Product K shows retention of configuration at both chiral centers and product L shows inversion of configuration at both chiral centers.

    **B.** Both products K and L show inversion of configuration at one chiral center and retention of configuration at the other chiral center.

    **C.** Only product K shows retention of configuration at one chiral center and inversion of configuration at the other chiral center.

    **D.** Only product L shows retention of configuration at one chiral center and inversion of configuration at the other chiral center.

**32.** An even mixture of which of the following compounds from the reactions in the passage will rotate plane-polarized light?

    **I.** A and B
    **II.** C and I
    **III.** H and J

    **A.** I only
    **B.** II only
    **C.** III only
    **D.** I and II only

**33.** Which of the following techniques could be used to distinguish the products of Reaction 1 from the mixture of products of Reaction 2?

    **A.** mass spectroscopy
    **B.** distillation
    **C.** rotation of polarized light
    **D.** infrared spectroscopy

**34.** If no neighboring mechanism occurred in Reaction 4, the expected products would be:

    **A.** compounds K and L only.
    **B.** compound K only.
    **C.** compound L only.
    **D.** compound C only.

**35.** Assuming HCl reacts similarly to HBr. which of the following would be the expected product of pathway b of Mechanism 1 for the reaction given below?

$$
\begin{array}{c}
CH_3 \\
HO \!-\!\!-\! H \\
H \!-\!\!-\! Br \\
CH_3
\end{array}
\quad \xrightarrow{\ HCl\ }
$$

**A.**
$$
\begin{array}{c}
CH_3 \\
Br \!-\!\!-\! H \\
Cl \!-\!\!-\! H \\
CH_3
\end{array}
$$

**C.**
$$
\begin{array}{c}
CH_3 \\
H \!-\!\!-\! Br \\
Cl \!-\!\!-\! H \\
CH_3
\end{array}
$$

**B.**
$$
\begin{array}{c}
CH_3 \\
H \!-\!\!-\! Br \\
H \!-\!\!-\! Cl \\
CH_3
\end{array}
$$

**D.**
$$
\begin{array}{c}
CH_3 \\
Cl \!-\!\!-\! H \\
H \!-\!\!-\! Br \\
CH_3
\end{array}
$$

**36.** According to Mechanism 1, which of the following most likely affects the initial rate of Reaction 3?

    **I.** the concentration of reactant H
    **II.** the concentration of HBr
    **III.** the concentration of product I

    **A.** I only
    **B.** II only
    **C.** I and II only
    **D.** I, II, and III

## Passage III (Questions 37-42)

Complicated alcohols that cannot be obtained on the market are often synthesized in the lab with a Grignard reagent. The Grignard reagent is made by reacting metallic magnesium with an organic halide. Many types of organic halides may be used, including primary, secondary. and tertiary alkylhalides and aromatic halides. However, the reagent is a very powerful base and it is impossible to prepare it from a compound having a hydrogen more acidic than an alkene. The halide may be a chloride, bromide, or iodide but chlorine based reagents require a special solvent.

The basic formula of a Grignard reagent is RMgX. The magnesium-carbon bond is covalent but extremely polar making the Grignard reagent a strong nucleophile. It is this characteristic of the reagent that is used in the synthesis of alcohols.

$$RMgX + O{=}C\!\!\begin{smallmatrix}R'\\\\H\end{smallmatrix} \longrightarrow R{-}\underset{H}{\overset{R'}{C}}{-}OMgX \overset{H^+}{\longrightarrow} R{-}\underset{H}{\overset{R'}{C}}{-}OH + MgX$$

**Reaction 1** Alcohol synthesis from a Grignard reagent

In alcohol synthesis, the reagent reacts with a carbonyl compound to make the magnesium salt of the corresponding alcohol. The product is then bathed in dilute mineral acid forming an alcohol and a water soluble magnesium halide salt.

37. Which of the following compounds would make the best solvent in a Grignard synthesis with an alkyl bromide?

   A.  $H_2O$
   B.  $(C_2H_5)_2O$
   C.  $C_2H_3O_2Na$
   D.  $C_2H_5OH$

38. What type of reaction takes place between the Grignard reagent and the carbonyl compound?

   A.  $S_N1$
   B.  $S_N2$
   C.  nucleophilic addition
   D.  bimolecular elimination

39. Which of the following alcohols would react the most strongly with a Grignard reagent?

   A.  $CH_3OH$
   B.  $(CH_3)_3OH$
   C.  $CH_3CHOHCH_3$
   D.  $CH_3(CH_2)_{11}CH_2OH$

40. Which of the following compounds could be reacted with the Grignard reagent shown below to create a tertiary alcohol?

   A.

   B.

   C.

   D.

41. Which of the following most accurately represents the charge distribution in the magnesium-carbon bond of the Grignard reagent?

   A.  $^{\delta+}CMg^{\delta-}$
   B.  $^{\delta-}CMg^{\delta+}$
   C.  $^{\delta+}CMg^{\delta+}$
   D.  $^{\delta-}CMg^{\delta-}$

42. If the alcoholic product of Reaction 1 were oxidized by $H_2CrO_4$ and acid, what would be the major product?

   A.  an aldehyde
   B.  a carboxylic acid
   C.  a ketone
   D.  an alkene

**GO ON TO THE NEXT PAGE.**

**43.** The dehydration of 2-pentanol in the presence of a strong acid and heat results in a(n):

    **A.** alkane
    **B.** alkene
    **C.** aldehyde
    **D.** carboxylic acid

**44.** Which of the following has the greatest boiling point?

    **A.** methane
    **B.** methanol
    **C.** chloromethane
    **D.** ammonia

**45.** NaCl will not react with ethanol via an $S_N2$ reaction because:

    **A.** an hydroxide ion is less stable than the chlorine ion.
    **B.** an hydroxide ion is more stable than the chlorine ion.
    **C.** steric hindrance prevents the reaction.
    **D.** the chloride ion is a better nucleophile than the hydroxyl group.

**46.** Which of the following is the most soluble in water?

    **A.** 1-butanol
    **B.** butane
    **C.** 1-butene
    **D.** propane

**STOP.** IF YOU FINISH BEFORE TIME IS CALLED, CHECK YOUR WORK. YOU MAY GO BACK TO ANY QUESTION IN THIS TEST BOOKLET.

# 30-MINUTE IN-CLASS EXAM FOR LECTURE 3

In 1877 two chemists working together developed a new method for the preparation of alkylbenzenes and acylbenzenes. In the Friedel-Crafts acylation, named after these two chemists, an acyl group is added to benzene in the presence of a Lewis acid. The Lewis acid usually reacts with the acyl group to form an acylium ion. The acylium ion is stabilized by resonance. Next, the acylium ion acts as an electrophile attacking the benzene ring

to form an arenium ion. The arenium ion then loses a proton to generate the final product. Powerful electron-withdrawing groups on the benzene ring such as another acyl group will block this reaction.

Naphthalene is the simplest and most important of the fused ring hydrocarbons. Five percent of all constituents of coal tar are naphthalene. Naphthalene can be manufactured using the Friedel-Crafts reaction via the reaction pathway shown in Scheme 1.

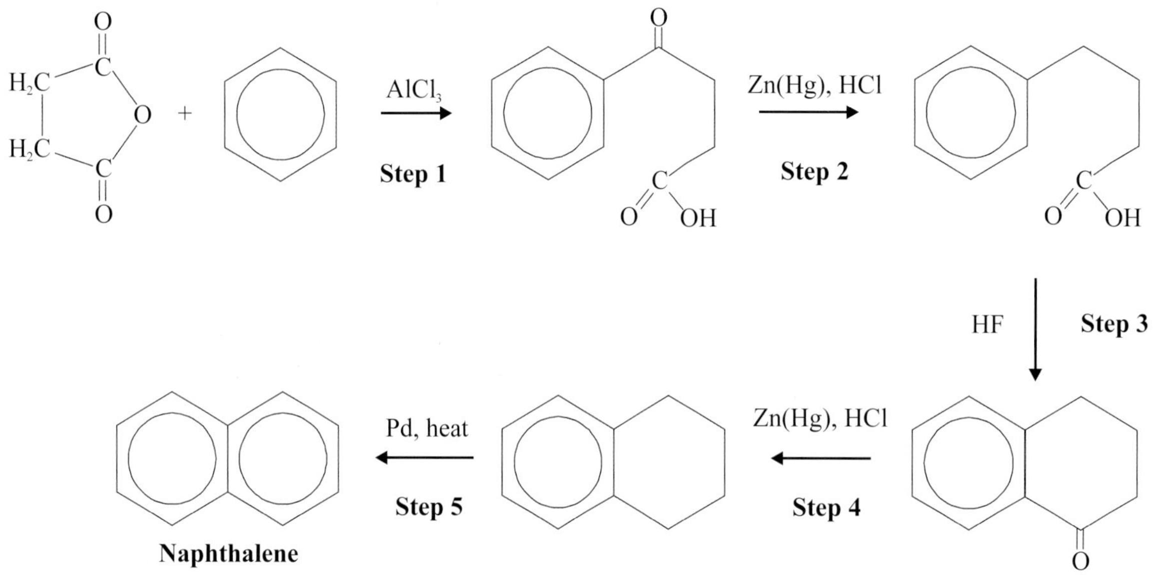

Scheme 1

47. The Friedel-Crafts reaction occurs twice in Scheme 1. Which two steps represent Friedel-Crafts reactions?

   A. steps 1 and 3
   B. steps 1 and 5
   C. steps 2 and 4
   D. steps 3 and 5

48. Step 2 is which of the following types of reactions?

   A. an oxidation reaction
   B. a reduction reaction
   C. an elimination reaction
   D. a Friedel-Crafts reaction

49. Why is step 2 necessary in order for ring closure to take place in step 3?

   A. Step 2 activates the ring by changing the electron releasing alkyl group to an electron withdrawing acyl group.
   B. Step 2 deactivates the ring by changing the electron releasing acyl group to an electron withdrawing alkyl group.
   C. Step 2 activates the ring by changing the electron withdrawing acyl group to an electron releasing alkyl group.
   D. Step 2 deactivates the ring by changing the electron withdrawing alkyl group to an electron releasing acyl group.

**50.** What are the most likely products of the following reaction?

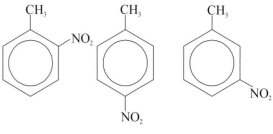

(reaction scheme: acetic anhydride (H₃CC(=O)–O–CC(=O)H₃) + naphthalene, with AlCl₃ →)

**A.**

$C_2H_8$ +

(structure: benzophenone-2-carboxylic acid, two benzene rings joined by C=O, one ring bearing COOH)

**B.**

$CH_3COH$ +

(structure: naphthalene with CCH₃ (=O) acetyl group)

O
‖
CH₃COH

**C.**

O
‖
CH₃CH +

(structure: naphthalene with COCH₃ group)

**D.**

O
‖
CH₃CH +

(structure: naphthalene with OCCH₃ group)

**51.** Toluene reacts with nitric acid to form the following products:

$o$-Nitrotoluene (59%)    $p$-Nitrotoluene (37%)    $m$-Nitrotoluene (4%)

If the position of substitution were chosen at random, what would be the expected percentage of $m$-nitrotoluene from the reaction?

A. 0%
B. 4%
C. 33%
D. 40%

**52.** Which of the following is an acylium ion?

A.                                C.

AlCl₄                             O
                                 ‖
                                 CH₃CO⁻

B.                                D.

(structure: cyclohexadienyl cation with +)          O
                                                    ‖
                                                    CH₃C⁺

In-Class Exams

When unknown compounds are identified without the aid of spectroscopy, classification tests are used. Reacting the carbonyl in a ketone or aldehyde with an amine (2,4 dinitrophenylhydrazine) to form an imine is the easiest way to detect a ketone or aldehyde (Reaction 1). The imine that forms is a highly colored solid. The color of the solid also helps to indicate structural characteristics. Ketones and aldehydes with no conjugation tend to form imines with yellow to orange colors, while highly conjugated ketones or aldehydes form imines with red color.

2, 4-nitrophenylhydrazine        dinitrophenylhydrazone

**Reaction 1**

The presence of a colored solid confirms the presence of a ketone or aldehyde, but the imine formation does not indicate whether the unknown is a ketone or aldehyde. A second classification test is used to distinguish the two functionalities. This test is called the Tollens' test, and the significant reaction is shown in Reaction 2.

**Reaction 2**

Aldehydes will form a silver mirror or a black precipitate if the test tube is dirty, while ketones will not.

Once the unknown is determined to be a ketone or an aldehyde, the melting point of the imine derivative is determined. The melting point and other physical characteristics (i.e., solubility of unknown and boiling point or melting point of the unknown) are used to determine the unknown's identity. The information is compared to tables in books which contain the melting points of derivatives and other physical data for organic compounds.

**53.** Why does the Tollens' test produce solid silver with aldehydes and not with ketones?

  **A.** Ketones are more sterically hindered than aldehydes.
  **B.** Aldehydes can be oxidized to the carboxylic acid, while ketone cannot.
  **C.** Ketones do not have an acidic proton while aldehydes do have one.
  **D.** Aldehydes are more sterically hindered than ketones.

**54.** A red 2,4 dinitrophenylhydrazone is obtained from the reaction of an unknown with an amine. Of the following four structures, which ketone or aldehyde could have formed this imine?

  **A.**

  **B.**

  **C.**

  **D.**

**55.** What type of reaction is Reaction 1?

  **A.** bimolecular elimination
  **B.** dehydration
  **C.** hydrolysis
  **D.** saponification

**56.** In Reaction 1, the nitrogen of the amine is

  **A.** a nucleophile
  **B.** an electrophile
  **C.** an acid
  **D.** an oxidant

**57.** The structures shown below are:

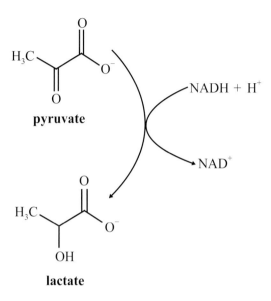

and

A. enantiomers
B. diastereomers
C. epimers
D. tautomers

**58.** The hemiketal of acetone can be formed by adding:

A. HCl
B. $CH_3OH$
C. NaOH
D. formaldehyde

**59.** Instead of using the Tollens' test, a student uses nmr spectroscopy to distinguish an aldehyde from a ketone. What should the student expect to find?

A. More splitting in the nmr peaks of ketones than of aldehydes.
B. Less splitting in the nmr peaks of ketones than of aldehydes.
C. One peak downfield in the aldehyde but not in the ketone.
D. Two peaks upfield in the aldehyde but not the ketone.

## Passage III (Questions 60-66)

During high-frequency stimulation of muscles, an anaerobic condition is created. As a result, the pyruvate produced from glycolysis (the breakdown of glucose to produce ATP) is converted to lactate by single enzyme mediation (Figure 1) rather than the pyruvate entering the Krebs cycle. The lactate formation maintains $NAD^+$ for glycolsis, but produces less ATP than the completion of the Krebs cycle.

**pyruvate**

**lactate**

**Figure 1** Conversion of pyruvate to lactate

The lactate produced by this cycle is passed into the blood and is transported to the liver. In the liver, the lactate is converted back to glucose. This cycle is called the Cori cycle.

The increase in the lactic acid produced from glycolysis causes metabolic acidosis and muscle fatigue.

**60.** Which of the following is true concerning the acidity of pyruvic acid and lactic acid?

A. Pyruvic acid is more acidic.
B. Lactic acid is more acidic.
C. Both acids have the same acidity.
D. Relative acidity cannot be determined based on structures alone.

**61.** The transformation of pyruvate to lactate is:

A. a decarboxylation
B. an oxidation
C. a reduction
D. hydration

**GO ON TO THE NEXT PAGE.**

**62.** The product of the reaction below is:

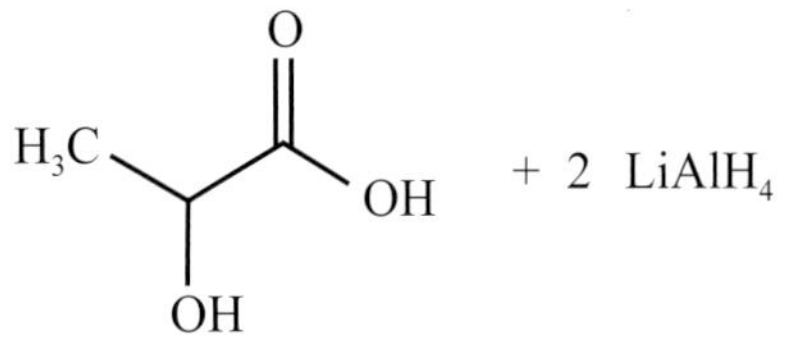

lactic acid

**A.**

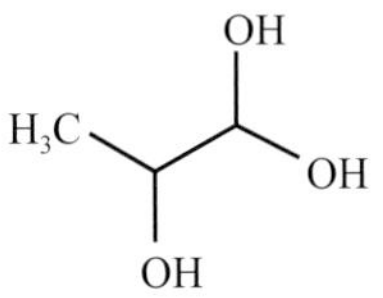

**B.**

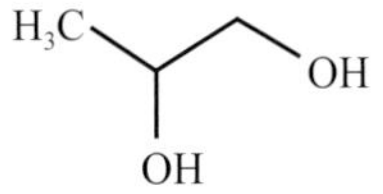

**C.**

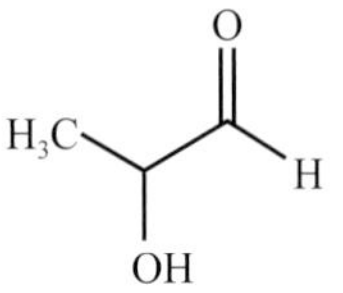

**D.**

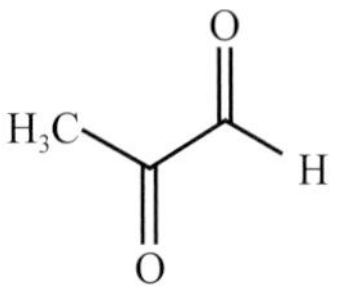

**63.** Why does weightlifting produce lactic acid buildup in muscle tissue?

  **A.** Some highly active muscle tissue uses ATP faster than can be supplied by aerobic respiration.
  **B.** Some highly active muscle tissue uses ATP faster than can be supplied by anaerobic respiration.
  **C.** Lactic acid is always a byproduct of ATP production.
  **D.** The Krebs cycle produces lactic acid.

**64.** Under aerobic conditions additional ATP is produced, following glycolysis, when

  **A.** pyruvate enters the Krebs cycle.
  **B.** pyruvate is converted to lactate.
  **C.** lactate is converted back to glucose in the liver completing the Cori cycle.
  **D.** muscles become fatigued.

**65.** What is the product of the following reaction?

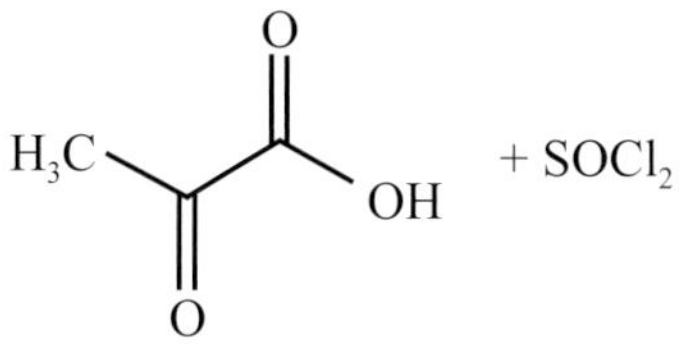

**A.**

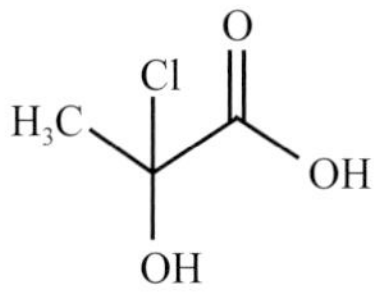

**B.**

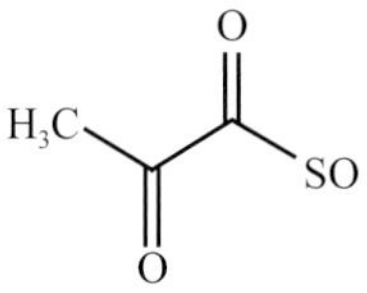

**C.**

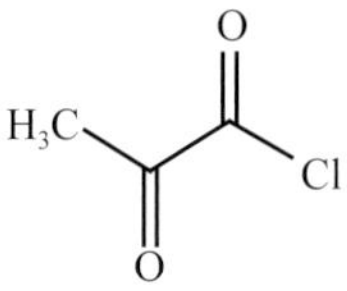

**D.**

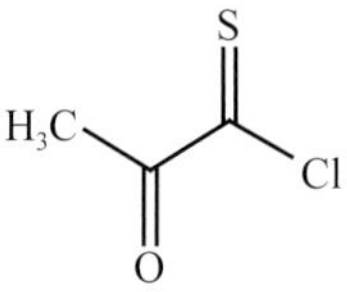

**66.** How do the water solubility and boiling point of pyruvic acid and lactic acid compare?

  **A.** Pyruvic acid has a higher boiling point and is more water soluble.
  **B.** Lactic acid has a higher boiling point and is more water soluble.
  **C.** Pyruvic acid has a higher boiling point but lactate is more water soluble.
  **D.** Lactic acid has a higher boiling point but pyruvate is more water soluble.

Questions 67 through 69 are **NOT** based on a descriptive passage.

67. When nucleophilic substitution occurs at a carbonyl, the weakest base is usually the best leaving group. What is the order of reactivity in a nucleophilic substitution reaction from most reactive to least reactive for the following compounds?

   **I.** acid chloride
   **II.** ester
   **III.** amide

   **A.** I, II, III
   **B.** I, III, II
   **C.** III, I, II
   **D.** III, II, I

68. All of the following reactions may result in a ketone EXCEPT:

   **A.** ozonolysis of an alkene.
   **B.** aldol condensation.
   **C.** oxidation of a primary alcohol
   **D.** Friedel-Crafts acylation

69. All of the following qualities of a carbonyl carbon make it a good electrophile EXCEPT:

   **A.** its stereochemistry
   **B.** its partial positive charge
   **C.** its planar shape
   **D.** its lone pair of electrons

**STOP.** IF YOU FINISH BEFORE TIME IS CALLED, CHECK YOUR WORK. YOU MAY GO BACK TO ANY QUESTION IN THIS TEST BOOKLET.

**STOP.**

# 30-MINUTE IN-CLASS EXAM FOR LECTURE 4

## Passage I (Questions 70-76)

In 1888 Emil Fishcer set out to discover the structure of (+)-glucose. Methods for determining absolute configuration had not yet been developed so Fischer arbitrarily limited his attention to the eight D configurations shown in Figure 1. Starting with a sample of glucose and these eight possible structures, Fischer deduced the correct structure of glucose by following a process of elimination similar to the four steps described below.

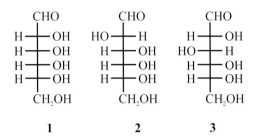

**1**      **2**      **3**

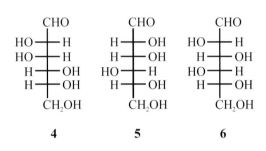

**4**      **5**      **6**

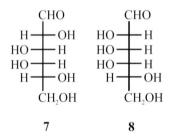

**7**      **8**

**Figure 1**

Steps used by Fischer to determine the structure of glucose:

1.  Aldoses react with dilute nitric acid at both the CHO group and the terminal $CH_2OH$ group to produce a $CO_2H$ group at either end. Glucose produces an optically active compound in this reaction.

2.  Aldoses can be degraded by the following two reactions. First the aldehyde is oxidized with bromine water to form a carboxylic acid. Next the carboxylic acid is decarboxylated with hydrogen peroxide and ferric sulfate leaving an aldehyde. The new aldose is one carbon shorter. When glucose is degraded in this manner, and the product is oxidized by dilute nitric acid, an optically active compound is formed.

3.  The Kiliani-Fischer synthesis lengthens the carbon chain of an aldose by one carbon at the aldehyde end and forms a new aldose with its corresponding epimers. When glucose and its epimer are produced from the corresponding pentose via the Kiliani-Fischer synthesis, and then both epimers are reacted with dilute nitric acid, both form optically active compounds.

4.  The two remaining possible structures for glucose were now examined. The end groups (CHO and $CH_2OH$) were exchanged on each. When the end groups were exchanged on one of the sugars it remained as the same compound. However, when the end groups of glucose were exchanged, a new sugar was created.

70. How many stereoisomers are possible for glucose?
    - **A.** 2
    - **B.** 8
    - **C.** 16
    - **D.** 32

71. The reactions between an aldose and dilute nitric acid as described in step 1 are which of the following types of reactions?
    - **A.** reduction
    - **B.** oxidation
    - **C.** hydrolysis
    - **D.** elimination

72. If only step 2 is performed, which of the structures in Figure 1 are eliminated as possible structures of glucose?
    - **A.** 1 and 2 only
    - **B.** 1, 4, and 7 only
    - **C.** 1, 2, 5, and 6 only
    - **D.** 3, 4, 7, and 8 only

**73.** Which of the following pentoses, when undergoing the Kiliani-Fischer synthesis, will yield D-glucose and D-mannose?

**A.**

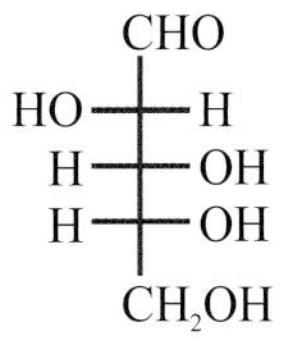

CHO
HO——H
H——OH
H——OH
CH₂OH

**C.**

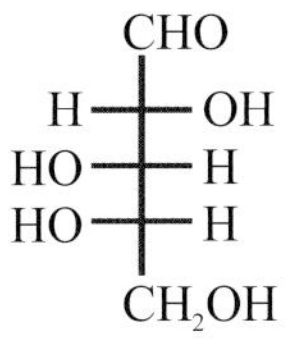

CHO
H——OH
HO——H
HO——H
CH₂OH

**B.**

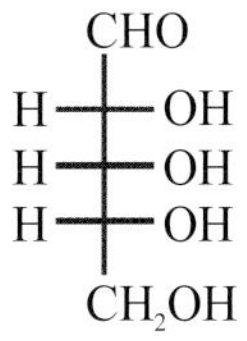

CHO
H——OH
H——OH
H——OH
CH₂OH

**D.**

CHO
H——OH
H——OH
HO——H
CH₂OH

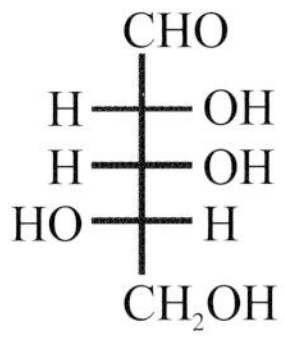

**74.** D-(+)-glyceraldehyde was allowed to undergo the Kiliani-Fischer synthesis, and the reaction ran to completion. After separation of any isomers, how many optically active products were formed?

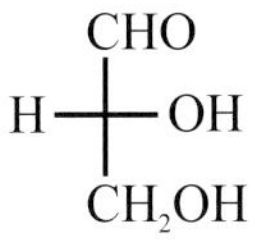

CHO
H——OH
CH₂OH

D-(+)-glyceraldehyde

 **A.** 0
 **B.** 1
 **C.** 2
 **D.** 4

**75.** Which structures can be eliminated by step 1?

 **A.** 1 and 7 only
 **B.** 4 and 6 only
 **C.** 1, 4, 6, and 7 only
 **D.** 2, 3, 5, and 8 only

**76.** Before carrying out step 4, Fischer had eliminated all but two possible structures for glucose. Which of the following was the structure that step 4 proved NOT to be glucose?

 **A.** 2
 **B.** 4
 **C.** 5
 **D.** 8

**Passage II (Questions 77-82)**

In 1951 a chemist made $C_{10}H_{10}Fe$ by reacting two moles of cyclopentadienylmagnesium bromide (a Grignard reagent) with anhydrous ferrous chloride. The structure of the resulting stable solid was uncertain and became an area of great interest in the following years. The structure proposed by the original chemist is shown in Figure 1.

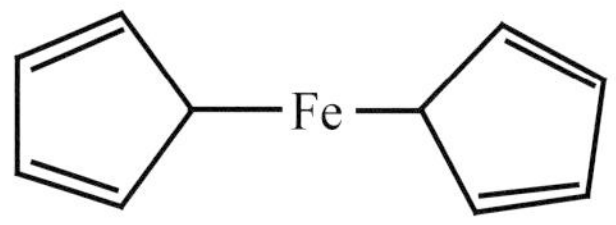

**Figure 1.** Proposed structure 1

Chemists later proposed a new structure called a "sandwich" complex which is shown in Figure 2.

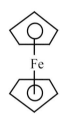

**Figure 2.** Proposed structure 2

The spectroscopy for $C_{10}H_{10}Fe$ is shown in Tables 1 and 2.

| Chemical Shift | Coupling Pattern | Integral Value |
|---|---|---|
| 4.12 ppm | singlet | 10 |

**Table 1** Proton NMR data

| Frequency | Description of Peak |
|---|---|
| 2900 cm⁻¹ | very strong |

**Table 2** IR peaks
at frequencies greater than 1500 cm⁻¹

**GO ON TO THE NEXT PAGE.**

When $C_{10}H_{10}Fe$ is reacted with acetic anhydride in the presence of an acid as shown in Reaction 1, a dark orange solid is formed with the molecular formula $C_{12}H_{12}OFe$. The reaction of $C_{10}H_{10}Fe$ with the anhydride helped scientists to confirm which structure was valid.

**Reaction 1**

A summary of the spectroscopy for the product shown in Reaction 1 is given in Tables 3 and 4.

| Chemical Shift | Coupling Pattern | Integral Value |
|---|---|---|
| 2.30 ppm | singlet | 3 |
| 4.20 ppm | singlet | 5 |
| 4.50 ppm | doublet | 2 |
| 4.80 ppm | doublet | 2 |

**Table 3** Proton NMR data

| Frequency | Description of Peak |
|---|---|
| 2900 $cm^{-1}$ | very strong |
| 1700 $cm^{-1}$ | very strong |

**Table 4** IR peaks at frequencies greater than 1500 $cm^{-1}$

77. What is the other product that is produced in Reaction 1 but not shown?

    A. a carboxylic acid
    B. a ketone
    C. an aldehyde
    D. an ester

78. The source of the new peak in the IR data after the reaction with acetic anhydride comes from:

    A. a carbonyl stretch.
    B. a C-H stretch.
    C. the coupling of two protons.
    D. a C-C-H bend.

79. The NMR peak at 2.30 ppm in Table 3 is from protons:

    A. on the carbon of the double bonds in the cyclopentadiene ring.
    B. on the carbon of the methyl group attached to the cyclopentadiene ring.
    C. on the carbon of the methyl group attached to a carbonyl carbon.
    D. on the carbon of the cyclopentadiene ring, not in a double bond.

80. Why is it important that the ferrous chloride be anhydrous in the reaction to form $C_{10}H_{10}Fe$?

    A. The cyclopentadienylmagnesium bromide will react with water.
    B. The ferrous chloride will turn to ferric chloride.
    C. Ferrous chloride will not dissolve in water.
    D. The water would catalyze the reaction and it would erupt.

81. In Figure 2, the five-membered rings are:

    A. aromatic
    B. antiaromatic
    C. nonaromatic
    D. aromaticity can not be determined for any structures that do not contain benzene

82. How does the spectroscopy done before the reaction indicate that structure 1 is not the true structure?

    A. If structure 1 were the true structure, there would be 3 chemical shifts in Table 1.
    B. If structure 1 were the true structure, there would be 4 chemical shifts in Table 1.
    C. If structure 1 were the true structure, there would be a frequency of 1700 $cm^{-1}$ and not a frequency at 2900 $cm^{-1}$ in Table 2.
    D. If structure 1 were the true structure, there would be a frequency of 1700 $cm^{-1}$ as well as the frequency at 2900 $cm^{-1}$ in Table 2.

In a student experiment designed to demonstrate microscale extraction techniques, the three compounds shown in Figure 1 are dissolved in diethyl ether and separated. Their physical properties are shown in Table 1.

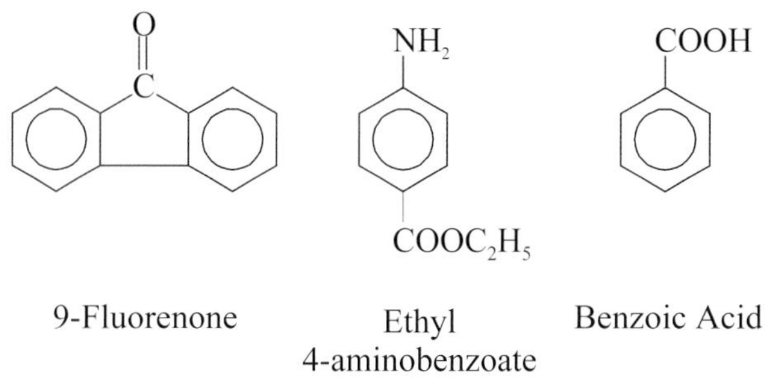

**Figure 1** Compounds to be separated by extraction

The mixture is created by dissolving 50 mg of each compound in 4 mL of diethyl ether. 2 mL of 3 $M$ HCl is added creating a two phase system. The system is mixed thoroughly and then allowed to separate. The aqueous layer is removed and the step is repeated with the remainder of the mixture.

6 $M$ NaOH is added to the extracted aqueous solution. The solution is cooled in an ice bath and precipitate is collected and washed with distilled water. The precipitate is then weighed and the melting point is determined.

The remaining mixture is now separated by extraction with two 2 mL portions of 3 $M$ NaOH. 6 $M$ HCl is added to the alkaline solution, which is then cooled to form a precipitate. The precipitate is then weighed and the melting point is determined.

The remaining component is washed with distilled water. Next, 250 mg of $Na_2SO_4$ are added. The $Na_2SO_4$ is then filtered off using a filter pipet and the remaining solution is transferred to an Erlenmeyer flask. The Erlenmeyer flask is placed in a warm sand bath. A precipitate forms and is weighed and the melting point determined.

| Compound | mp(°C) | bp(°C) | Specific gravity |
|---|---|---|---|
| 9-Fluorenone | 122 | | |
| Ethyl 4-aminobenzoate | 89 | | |
| Benzoic acid | 154 | | |
| Diethyl ether | | 40 | 0.713 |

**Table 1** Physical properties

83. What is the function of the $Na_2SO_4$ when added to the ether solution?

   A. $Na_2SO_4$ catalyzes the separation of the 9-fluorenone and ether.
   B. $Na_2SO_4$ catalyzes the separation of the benzoic acid and ether.
   C. $Na_2SO_4$ removes the remaining impurities of the solution.
   D. $Na_2SO_4$ acts as a drying agent.

84. Which of the following comes out in the aqueous layer of the first extraction with 3 $M$ HCl?

   A. 9-fluorenone
   B. ethyl 4-aminobenzoate
   C. benzoic acid
   D. diethyl ether

85. What is the expected molecular weight of the compound extracted by NaOH?

   A. 46 g/mol
   B. 122 g/mol
   C. 165 g/mol
   D. 180 g/mol

86. In the first extraction, the aqueous layer will be:

   A. below the organic layer because it has a lower density than the organic layer.
   B. below the organic layer because it has a greater density than the organic layer.
   C. above the organic layer because it has a lower density than the organic layer.
   D. above the organic layer because it has a greater density than the organic layer.

87. What is the purpose of the warm sand bath?

   A. Heat evaporates the ether concentrating the 9-fluorenone.
   B. Heat evaporates the ether concentrating benzoic acid.
   C. Heat accelerates the endothermic precipitation reaction.
   D. Heat accelerates the exothermic precipitation reaction.

GO ON TO THE NEXT PAGE.

88. IR spectroscopy is normally used to distinguish between:

    A. neighboring protons on different compounds.
    B. neighboring protons on the same compound.
    C. different functional groups on the same compound.
    D. acids and bases.

89. Which of the following is true concerning amino acids?

    A. Amino acids are monoprotic.
    B. Amino acids have peptide bonds.
    C. The side chain on an α-amino acid determines its acidity relative to other α-amino acids.
    D. All amino acids have water soluble side groups.

90. Peptide bond formation is an example of:

    A. saponification.
    B. electrophilic addition.
    C. bimolecular elimination.
    D. dehydration.

91. Triglycerides are composed from which of the following?

    A. esters, alcohols, and phospholipids
    B. fatty acids, alcohol, and esters
    C. fatty acids and glycerol
    D. glycerol and fatty esters

92. Which of the following is water soluble?

    A. a saturated fatty acid
    B. an unsaturated fatty acid
    C. the side chain on valine
    D. glucose

---

**STOP.** IF YOU FINISH BEFORE TIME IS CALLED, CHECK YOUR WORK. YOU MAY GO BACK TO ANY QUESTION IN THIS TEST BOOKLET.

---

# ANSWERS & EXPLANATIONS

## FOR

## 30-MINUTE IN-CLASS EXAMINATIONS

# ANSWERS FOR THE 30-MINUTE IN-CLASS EXAMS

| Lecture 1 | Lecture 2 | Lecture 3 | Lecture 4 |
|-----------|-----------|-----------|-----------|
| 1. D | 24. C | 47. A | 70. C |
| 2. B | 25. D | 48. B | 71. B |
| 3. A | 26. C | 49. C | 72. C |
| 4. D | 27. B | 50. B | 73. A |
| 5. B | 28. C | 51. D | 74. C |
| 6. A | 29. A | 52. D | 75. A |
| 7. D | 30. C | 53. B | 76. B |
| 8. A | 31. A | 54. D | 77. A |
| 9. C | 32. C | 55. B | 78. A |
| 10. C | 33. B | 56. A | 79. C |
| 11. C | 34. D | 57. D | 80. A |
| 12. A | 35. C | 58. B | 81. A |
| 13. C | 36. C | 59. C | 82. A |
| 14. C | 37. B | 60. A | 83. D |
| 15. D | 38. C | 61. C | 84. B |
| 16. A | 39. A | 62. B | 85. B |
| 17. A | 40. D | 63. A | 86. B |
| 18. C | 41. B | 64. A | 87. A |
| 19. A | 42. C | 65. C | 88. C |
| 20. C | 43. B | 66. B | 89. C |
| 21. D | 44. B | 67. A | 90. D |
| 22. C | 45. A | 68. C | 91. C |
| 23. D | 46. A | 69. D | 92. D |

## MCAT ORGANIC CHEMISTRY

| Raw Score | Estimated Scaled Score |
|-----------|------------------------|
| 11 | 7 |
| 9-10 | 6 |
| 8 | 5 |
| 6-7 | 4 |
| 5 | 3 |
| 3-4 | 2 |
| 1-2 | 1 |

## MCAT ORGANIC CHEMISTRY

| Raw Score | Estimated Scaled Score |
|-----------|------------------------|
| 21 | 15 |
| 20 | 14 |
| 19 | 13 |
| 18 | 12 |
| 17 | 11 |
| 15-16 | 10 |
| 14 | 9 |
| 12-13 | 8 |

# EXPLANATIONS TO IN-CLASS EXAM FOR LECTURE 1

## Passage I

**1.** **D is correct.**

Quinine

**2.** **B is correct.** Fermentation is anaerobic respiration. The passage states that (S)-2-methyl-1-butanol is the product of the fermentation of yeast. Looking at this molecule (above right), we prioritize the groups around the chiral carbon. Since the lowest priority group (the proton) is projected sideways, we must reverse the direction of our prioritization circle. This gives us the S configuration.

**3.** **A is correct.** The salts are stereoisomers because they have the same bond-to-bond connectivity, and they must be diastereomers because they can be separated by physical means (crystallization). Notice from the diagram that they are NOT mirror images of each other, and therefore cannot be enantiomers.

**4.** **D is correct.** Both A and C are wrong because they have the bromine attached to the wrong carbon to be the reactant. Since we know that configuration is retained, we simply substitute a hydrogen atom for the bromine and look for the molecule with the S configuration. (Remember, we are looking for the configuration of the product, not the reactant, so we must substitute the hydrogen for the bromine.) Retention of configuration does not mean that absolute configuration is retained; it means that there is no inversion. Because the lowest priority group is to the side in a Fischer projection, we reverse the direction of the circle shown below.

**5.** **B is correct.** The isomer on the left is a meso compound and has no enantiomer. Both isomers have the same bond-to-bond connectivity and are therefore diastereomers.

**6.** **A is correct.** Strychnine is the only chiral molecule and thus the only possibility. The passage states that the only chemical difference between enantiomers is their reactions with chiral compounds. Strychnine is often employed as a resolving agent for racemic acids.

## Passage II

**7.** **D is correct.** The bromide ion is a negatively charged intermediate looking for a positive charge. Question: What's a halophile? Answer: Who cares? No one taking the MCAT. Answer choice A is a trap.

**8.** **A is correct.** The *trans* isomer will produce only a meso compound. If you're confused by this question, see the explanation to question 12 below.

**9.** **C is correct.** Carbocations are $sp^2$ hybridized and should be planar with bond angles of 120°.

**10.** **C is correct.** The reaction produces only certain stereoisomeric products so it is stereoselective. Experiment 2 says that the products depend upon the isomeric formation of the reactants, so it is stereospecific. Any reaction that is stereospecific is also stereoselective, but the converse is not true.

**11.** **C is correct.** The key is that the secondary carbocation is more stable than the primary (and most likely to form). You don't need to know what a halohydrin is to answer this question. Just look at Mechanism A, and substitute water for bromine as the nucleophile (the negatively charged species).

12. **A is correct.** Since the addition is always anti (attachment on opposite sides), only the meso compound will be formed. This is a very difficult question to visualize. Draw it out.

These are the same compound.
It is a meso compound.

13. **C is correct.** Bromine will add to the alkane section of the ring when exposed to light via a radical reaction.

## Passage III

14. **C is correct.** Acetyl CoA is a coenzyme. Vitamins are components of coenzymes.

15. **D is correct.** Isocitrate's third carbon is chiral. All of the other compounds' third carbons are attached to two distinct substituents and two identical substituents.

16. **A is correct.** The removal of either carbon 2 or 3 would break the chain, so the answer must be either carbon 1 or 4. The radio labeled carbon is carbon 4. Since this is removed in step 4 (as per the passage), the answer must be carbon 1.

17. **A is correct.** The labeled carbon is carbon 4, a carbonyl carbon throughout.

18. **C is correct.** An enol is both an alkene and an alcohol at the same carbon. The question refers to the tautomeric pairing of an alkene and enol. In that pairing, a proton shifts to the carbonyl oxygen and the oxygens' electrons form a carbon-carbon double bond. D is wrong because it does not have a carboxyl at both ends. A is wrong because it is a ketone – not an enol (A is $\alpha$-ketogluterate). The carbon attached to the alcohol in B does not have a double bond, so it is wrong.

19. **A is correct.** The passage states that all known dehydrogenases are stereospecific in reactions with prochiral molecules. NADH is prochiral at the deuterium labeled carbon in answer choice A. B does not show a stereospecific reaction. In answer choice C a substitution reaction occurred at the amine, and an addition reaction occurred on the ring. This can't be correct. More importantly, in answer choice C the deuterium is not distinguishable from the hydrogen. This is not stereospecific. Answer choice D has too few hydrogens.

## Stand Alones

20. **C is correct.** Meso compounds are (by definition) achiral although they do contain chiral carbons. They are not optically active (do not rotate plane-polarized light).

21. **D is correct.** All are true.

22. **C is correct.** If you missed this, try drawing the dash formula representation of this molecule and/or go back and study nomenclature.

23. **D is correct.** Conformational isomers, or conformers, are not true isomers. Conformers are different spatial orientations of the same molecule. Answer choices D and C are opposites, so one is likely to be true. At low temperatures, some conformers can be isolated.

# EXPLANATIONS TO IN-CLASS EXAM FOR LECTURE 2

## Passage I

Step one produces five dichlorobutanes among other products. These are separated by distillation to give:

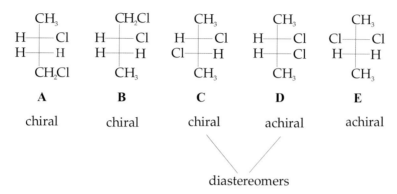

(S)-sec-butylchloride

| A | B | C | D | E |
|---|---|---|---|---|
| chiral | chiral | chiral | achiral | achiral |

diastereomers

**24.** **C is correct.** The molecular weight of all the dichloro products would be 127 g/mol and differ from all other possible products in this regard.

**25.** **D is correct.** As per the passage, only compounds C and D are stereoisomers (thus answers A and B are wrong). But all the compounds are dichlorobutane, so any two must be structural isomers. Structural isomerism is the same as constitutional isomerism.

**26.** **C is correct.** This question simply asks, "Which compound is the enantiomer to (R,R)-2,3-dichlorobutane?" Since we have retention of configuration, only one enantiomer of 2,3-dichlorobutane is made. The one that is made will be a stereoisomer to the meso compound and will rotate plane-polarized light in the opposite direction of (R,R) enantiomer. Enantiomers rotate polarized light, so compound A, B, or C must be this enantiomer. And since C and D are stereoisomers, one must be the meso compound of 2,3-dichlorobutane and one must be the (S,S) enantiomer of (R,R)-2,3-dichlorobutane.

**27.** **B is correct.** From the passage, the configurations of C and D appeared in a 7:3 ratio. As per question 26, C and D are the (S,S) and (S,R) configurations of 2,3-dichlorobutane.

**28.** **C is correct.** Compound E is achiral, and is not the meso compound because D is (see question 26). Answer A is meso. Answer choice B could not have been formed because there is a change in relative configuration about the original chiral compound. Answer D is chiral. Only answer choice C is left.

**29.** **A is correct.** A reaction will most likely occur via an $S_N2$ mechanism with $Cl^-$ as the leaving group. The reaction would then proceed with inversion of configuration (and stereochemistry). Since the priority of OH and Cl are both first, the configuration of the product is R.

## Passage II

**30.** **C is correct.** 2,3-dibromobutane has two enantiomers and a meso compound. Four stereoisomers are possible according to the $2^n$ formula, but since there is a meso, only 3 exist.

**31.** **A is correct.** In product K the relative configurations are the same as the reactant. In product L, the relative configurations are reversed.

**32.** **C is correct.** A & B is a racemic mixture. C & I are the same meso compound. H & J are diastereomers, which rotate plane-polarized light to different degrees.

**33.** **B is correct.** The compounds are diastereomers, so they have different physical properties (like boiling points) and could thus be separated by distillation. A and D are wrong because both compounds have the same mass and the same functional groups. Neither group rotates polarized light, since Reaction 1 produces a meso compound and Reaction 2 produces a racemic mixture.

34. **D is correct.** The reaction would be a simple S$_N$2 reaction at the hydroxyl carbon proceeding with inversion of configuration to produce the meso compound.

35. **C is correct.** In pathway b, both configurations are inverted, and the halogen already attached to the molecule replaces the OH group.

36. **C is correct.** Although there are two steps, both reactants are required for the first step. The acid is needed to protonate the hydroxyl group. Products do not affect the initial rate.

## Passage III

37. **B is correct.** Ether is the best choice for any solvent question on the MCAT. The passage states that the reagent will react with any hydrogen more acidic than an alkene hydrogen. A and D are more acidic than an alkene. C is a salt, not a solvent. In most cases, but not all, a solvent should not react with the reactants.

38. **C is correct.** The partially negative charged carbon on the Grignard reagent acts as a nucleophile and adds to the carbonyl carbon.

39. **A is correct.** Methyl alcohol is the strongest acid and will thus react the most vigorously with a Grignard reagent. The strongest acid is the primary alcohol with the shortest carbon chain.

40. **D is correct.** From the passage we know that the carbon attached to the Mg will act as a nucleophile on the carbonyl carbon. Only D will result in a tertiary alcohol.

41. **B is correct.** The passage states that the bond is covalent and polar and that the carbon is a good nucleophile. Thus the carbon would have a partial negative charge.

42. **C is correct.** Oxidation of a secondary alcohol always produces a ketone.

## Stand Alones

43. **B is correct.** The dehydration of an alcohol forms a double bond.

44. **B is correct.** In this case, the differences in molecular weights ((g/mol); methane: 16; methanol: 32; chloromethane: 50.5; ammonia: 17) is outweighed by the extreme bond strength differences. Stronger intermolecular bonds increase boiling point. Hydrogen bonds are the strongest intermolecular bonds. Oxygen is more electronegative than nitrogen and so makes stronger hydrogen bonds. The boiling points (°C) are methane: -164; methanol: 65; chloromethane: -24.2; ammonia: -33. Notice that, although ammonia is one-third the weight of chloromethane, its hydrogen bonding gives it a boiling point nearly as high. By comparing the boiling points of ammonia and methanol (or even water), you should notice also how much stronger the hydrogen bonds of oxygen are than those of nitrogen.

45. **A is correct.** The hydroxyl group must be protonated in order for the alcohol to react with the chloride ion in an S$_N$2 reaction; there is no acid present to protonate the alcohol.

46. **A is correct.** The alcohol can form hydrogen bonds with water.

# EXPLANATIONS TO IN-CLASS EXAM FOR LECTURE 3

## Passage I

47. **A is correct.** According to the passage, a Friedel-Crafts reaction substitutes *something* (an acyl group) onto a benzene ring in the presence of an acid. Steps 1 and 3 are the only steps that involve substituting onto a benzene ring.

48. **B is correct.** Step 2 must be a reduction reaction because we lose oxygen and gain two hydrogens.

49. **C is correct.** Benzene rings are activated by electron releasing groups and deactivated by electron withdrawing groups, so A and D must be wrong. The passage states that acyl groups are electron withdrawing, so B must be wrong. The passage also states that acyl groups block the Friedel-Crafts reaction. Step 2 removes the ketone, which is an acyl group.

50. **B is correct.** Scheme 1, step 1 shows an anhydride reacting with an aromatic ring in the presence of AlCl$_3$ to form a carboxylic acid and a ketone. This reaction has the same form. This is a Friedel-Crafts reaction.

51. **D is correct.** There are two meta positions out of five possible positions. 2/5 = 0.4 or 40%.

52. **D is correct.** According to the passage, the acylium ion must be positively charged because it acts as an electrophile, so A and C are out. B is no good because the acylium ion attacks the benzene ring so it must be producible from the anhydride in step 1. That leaves only D.

## Passage II

53. **B is correct.** Reaction 2 shows an aldehyde being oxidized to a carboxylate ion to form the precipitate. Answer A is true, but does not answer the question. C and D are false.

54. **D is correct.** According to the passage, red coloring indicates a highly conjugated product. Only choice D has alternating double and single bonds.

55. **B is correct.** Water is lost.

56. **A is correct.** Nitrogen often acts as a nucleophile.

57. **D is correct.** Tautomerization involves a proton shift where the double bond of the carbonyl shifts to the carbonyl/$\alpha$-carbon bond when the carbonyl oxygen is protonated. You should memorize tautomer formation and structure.

58. **B is correct.** Alcohols add to aldehydes and ketones to form hemiacetals and hemiketals, respectively. You should be able to recognize this reaction for the MCAT.

59. **C is correct.** You should know that an aldehyde will demonstrate a peak (downfield) when compared to a ketone.

## Passage III

60. **A is correct.** The carbonyl group withdraws negative charge, stabilizing the conjugate base of pyruvate.

61. **C is correct.** Ketones can be reduced to yield secondary alcohols.

62. **B is correct.** The first equivalent of lithium aluminum hydride reduces the carboxylic acid to the primary alcohol, which is then completely reduced by the second equivalent of the hydride. The secondary alcohol does not reduce easily with lithium aluminum hydride.

63. **A is correct.** Lactic acid is a by-product of anaerobic respiration. Under active use conditions, some muscle tissues switch completely to anaerobic respiration.

64. **A is correct.** Aerobic means $O_2$ is present.

65. **C is correct.** Inorganic acid chlorides react with carboxylic acids by nucleophilic substitution to form acyl chlorides; you should memorize this reaction.

66. **B is correct.** Lactate can form hydrogen bonds, which increase its water solubility and boiling point.

## Stand Alones

67. **A is correct.** The chlorine ion is the weakest base, then the alkoxide ion, then the $NH_2^-$. Note that you don't need to know what an acid chloride is to answer the question.

68. **C is correct.** Oxidation of a primary alcohol produces an aldehyde, not a ketone; note that you don't need to know the Friedel-Crafts reaction to answer this question.

69. **D is correct.** Carbonyl carbons don't have a lone pair of electrons.

# EXPLANATIONS TO IN-CLASS EXAM FOR LECTURE 4

## Passage I

**See page 202 for a complete diagram of Passage I**. Structure 1 is eliminated by steps 1, 2, and 3; structure 2 is eliminated by steps 2 and 3; structure 4 is not eliminated except by step 4; structures 5 and 6 are eliminated by step 2; structure 7 is eliminated by steps 1 and 3; and structure 8 is eliminated by step 3.

70. **C is correct.** Glucose has four chiral carbons so there are $2^4$ possible stereoisomers for glucose. The passage shows half of them.

71. **B is correct.** Converting an aldehyde or a primary alcohol into a carboxylic acid is done via oxidation. If you didn't remember this, you are reminded in step 2 of the passage.

72. **C is correct.** Step 2 removes the top carbon from each structure and places a $CH_2OH$ group group at both ends of the new, 5-carbon structures. When looking at the original 8 aldohexose structures, you should notice that molecules 1 & 2 are epimers with respect to carbon #2; 3 & 4 are epimers with respect to carbon #2; 5 & 6 are epimers with respect to carbon #2, and 7 & 8 are epimers with respect to carbon #2. Since the treatment of step 2 is removing carbon #1 from all 8 aldohexoses and replacing carbon #2 with a non-chiral center, then performing step 2 will convert compounds 1 & 2 to the same compound after treatment; the same is true for structures 3 & 4, 5 & 6, and 7 & 8. Thus, If you can eliminate compound 1, then you can eliminate compound 2, and vice versa; the same can be applied to 3 & 4, 5 & 6, and 7 & 8. It should be obvious that structures 1 & 2 give optically inactive molecules with a plane of symmetry; thus answer choices B and D can be eliminated because they do not contain both compounds 1 & 2. Molecules 3 and 4 and 7 & 8 give optically active compounds. Molecules 5 and 6 generate a plane of symmetry through the new carbon #3 (previously carbon #4); eliminating answer choice A.

73. **A is correct.** C and D are wrong because for a D-isomer, the hydroxyl group on the second carbon from the bottom must be on the right. Furthermore, if the hexoses that are created by the Kiliani-Fischer synthesis from B, C, and D were degraded and oxidized by nitric acid, all would result in meso compounds (optically inactive). To see this, add one chiral carbon just below the aldehyde (making both epimers). Now replace the end groups with carboxylic acids. All now form (at least one) meso compound. You don't need to know the structure of mannose for the MCAT and it is not given in the passage, so you know that this is extra information. Ignore it. As for answer A, the passage explains that the Kiliani-Fischer synthesis adds one more chiral carbon above the other chiral carbons of an aldose as viewed in a Fischer projection. Answer A must be correct because structure 3 in Figure 1 is glucose. If you recognized the structure of glucose, you could have made this question easier, but the passage also states (in step 2) that, when degraded and oxidized by nitric acid, glucose leaves an optically active compound.

74. **C is correct.** A pair of enantiomers would be formed by the addition of one chiral carbon. Only one configuration of glyceraldehyde is used, so that chiral carbon does not increase the number of enantiomers.

75. **A is correct.** 1 and 7 produce meso compounds, which are optically inactive.

76. **B is correct.** This question is answerable from the information in step 4 alone. If you do step 4 on all the answer choices, only structure 4 produces the same sugar.

## Passage II

77. **A is correct.** Anhydrides can participate in an acylation reaction in which half of the anhydride adds to another molecule and the other half yields a carboxylic acid. Simply counting the total atoms in the reactants and subtracting the total atoms of the products shown for reaction 1 can give you a clue to answer this question.

78. **A is correct.** You should probably memorize that a carbonyl stretch is 1700 $cm^{-1}$. Remember that IR measures the existence of functional groups.

79. **C is correct.** The integral value is three. This is the only place where there are three protons.

80. **A is correct.** A Grignard is a strong base and will react with water.

81. **A is correct.** This should be an easy question. Each ring in isolation (cyclopentadienyl anion; not bonding to the metal atom) has a negative charge giving it 6 pi electrons, which equals $4n + 2$ where $n = 1$.

82. **A is correct.** The protons close to the iron would have a different chemical shift than the protons farther from the iron. There are three different carbons with hydrogens attached: the ones attached to the iron, the ones attached to those, and the ones attached to those.

## Passage III

83. **D is correct.** Water has some slight solubility in organic extracts. Inorganic anhydrous salts such as magnesium, sodium, and calcium sulfate readily form insoluble hydrates, removing the water from wet organic phases. Answers A and B must be wrong because the ether is distilled from the last fraction in the sand bath. There is no basis for thinking sodium sulfate could remove impurities.

84. **B is correct.** The acid protonates the basic amino group on ethyl 4-aminobenzoate, making it soluble in the aqueous solution. The other compounds are not basic and would not be made soluble by the acid.

85. **B is correct.** The benzoic acid will be deprotonated by NaOH, making it soluble in the aqueous layer. The MW of benzoic acid = 122 g/mol.

86. **B is correct.** From the table, we see that diethyl ether has a lower density than water, which will make it float on top of the aqueous layer. However, this is NOT always true for extractions; sometimes the aqueous layer is less dense than the organic layer and will therefore float on top of the organic layer. Refer to the specific gravities of the given compounds to determine which will be on top and which will be below.

87. **A is correct.** From Table 1 we see that ether has a low boiling point. As the ether evaporates, the neutral compound, 9-fluorenone, is concentrated.

## Stand Alones

88. **C is correct**. IR distinguishes functional groups.

89. **C is correct.** All amino acids are at least diprotic compounds; under appropriate conditions, both the carboxyl and amino groups can act as acids (some side chains can also act as acids, making some amino acids triprotic), so A is wrong. Proteins have peptide bonds, not amino acids, so B is wrong. D is wrong because some amino acids (like leucine) have nonpolar side groups.

90. **D is correct.** Water is removed to form peptide bonds.

91. **C is correct.** Fatty acids and the three-carbon backbone of glycerol form triglycerides.

92. **D is correct.** Valine's side chain is hydrophobic. Fats are hydrophobic, and glucose is soluble in water.

# Steps used by Fischer to determine glucose

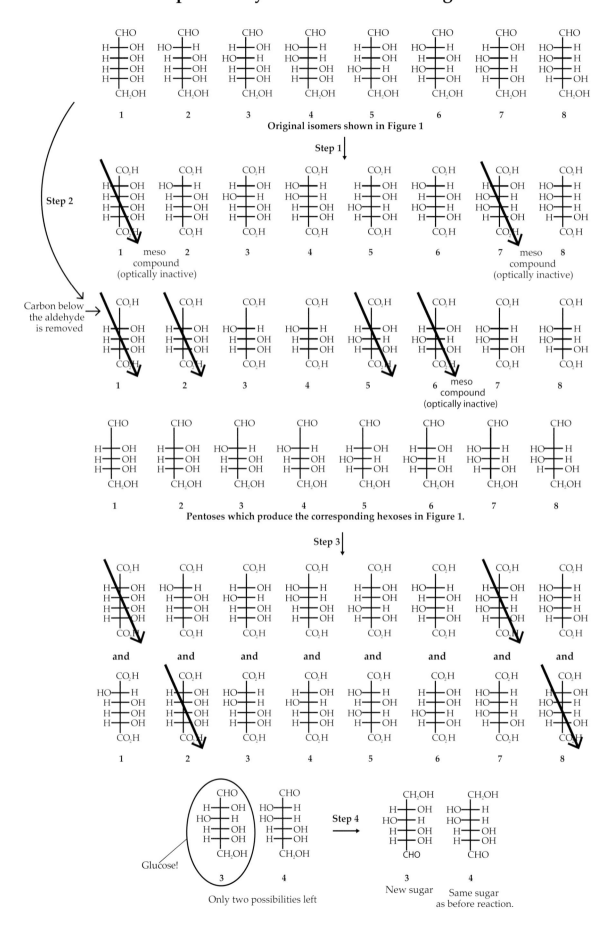

# ANSWERS & EXPLANATIONS

## FOR

## QUESTIONS IN THE LECTURES

# ANSWERS TO THE LECTURE QUESTIONS

| Lecture 1 | Lecture 2 | Lecture 3 | Lecture 4 |
|---|---|---|---|
| 1. A | 25. A | 49. D | 73. C |
| 2. B | 26. C | 50. A | 74. C |
| 3. D | 27. D | 51. D | 75. B |
| 4. C | 28. D | 52. A | 76. C |
| 5. B | 29. D | 53. D | 77. C |
| 6. B | 30. C | 54. A | 78. C |
| 7. B | 31. B | 55. C | 79. A |
| 8. B | 32. C | 56. D | 80. C |
| 9. A | 33. C | 57. D | 81. C |
| 10. C | 34. D | 58. C | 82. A |
| 11. B | 35. A | 59. A | 83. A |
| 12. D | 36. D | 60. A | 84. C |
| 13. D | 37. B | 61. B | 85. A |
| 14. C | 38. D | 62. A | 86. C |
| 15. C | 39. B | 63. A | 87. C |
| 16. B | 40. B | 64. D | 88. D |
| 17. A | 41. C | 65. D | 89. C |
| 18. C | 42. B | 66. B | 90. C |
| 19. B | 43. A | 67. C | 91. B |
| 20. D | 44. D | 68. A | 92. A |
| 21. B | 45. C | 69. B | 93. B |
| 22. D | 46. C | 70. D | 94. A |
| 23. B | 47. B | 71. A | 95. D |
| 24. C | 48. B | 72. C | 96. C |

# EXPLANATIONS TO QUESTIONS IN LECTURE 1

1. **A is correct.** Of course no MCAT test-taker would be expected to know this reaction. The entire first half of this question is misdirection. The clue is that there must be six carbons because there is a substituent on the sixth carbon. Next, the carbons must be numbered starting from one end of the chain. Carbon one is the anomeric carbon (the one attached to the oxygen in the ring and an O-methyl group). The O-methyl group on this carbon is represented by the first methyl in the name *methyl* β-2,3,4,6-tetra-O-methyl-D-glucoside. There are four more O-methyl groups attached to their respective numbered carbons. Answer B doesn't have a sixth carbon if we account for five methyl groups. Answers C and D don't have enough methyl groups.

2. **B is correct.** Of course you don't need to know the structure of benzamide. But you should know that it's an amide derivative of benzene. B is the only amine with benzene. Also, you will see in Organic Chemistry Lecture 2 that benzene undergoes substitution, so answers C and D imply that a nitrogen has replaced a carbon atom in the benzene ring; these structures cannot be correct. Answer choice A is the amine derivative of benzene, aniline, not the amide derivative. And finally, D requires a positive charge on the nitrogen atom.

3. **D is correct.** The most stable bond is the bond with the highest bond energy. Remember, bond energy is the average energy needed to break a bond (closely related to bond dissociation energy). Bond energy is actually negative potential energy, so the higher the magnitude, the lower the energy level, the more energy necessary to break the bond, and the more stable the bond. The highest bond energy is between the methyl group bonded to a ring structure. All ring structures are unsaturated.

4. **C is correct.** You must be able to recognize the basic functional groups.

5. **B is correct.**

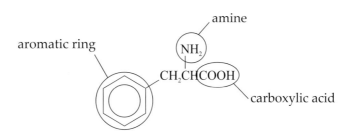

guanosine

6. **B is correct.** Amines ($-NH_2$) behave as weak Lewis bases and are most similar to ammonia ($NH_3$). A Lewis base is any species that can donate a pair of electrons and form a coordinate covalent bond. Amides contain a carbonyl carbon and therefore are not similar to ammonia. Ether and ethanol are not nitrogen-containing compounds.

7. **B is correct.**

8.  **B is correct.** The following IUPAC rules of nomenclature must be used to name an alkane:

    •   Find the longest continuous carbon chain to serve as parent name – in this case, nonane.

    •   Number the carbons of the parent chain, beginning at the end nearest to the most branch points.

    •   Identify and number the parent chain substituents – in this case, two methyl (on carbons 4,7) and one ethyl (on carbon 3) groups.

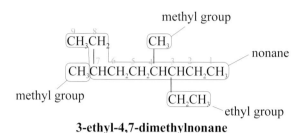

**3-ethyl-4,7-dimethylnonane**

---

9.  **A is correct.** B is missing a hydrogen. C has the charges reversed. In D, nitrogen has five bonds.

10. **C is correct.** The number of σ-bonds on the three species respectively is 3, 4, 3.

11. **B is correct.** The bonds are stabilized by resonance and are shorter and stronger than carbon-carbon alkane bonds but longer and weaker than carbon-carbon alkene bonds.

12. **D is correct.** A π-bond has 100% *p* character and is at a higher energy level than a σ-bond.

13. **D is correct.** Moving atoms is a violation of the rules of resonance. The actual molecule is always at a lower energy level than any of its resonance structures. Although A and B are true, they don't answer the question. Notice that A and B say the same thing. This is a good indicator that they are both wrong.

14. **C is correct.** *sp* hybridization allows the formation of a triple bond, which consists of one σ-bond and two π-bonds. Triple bonds display 180° bond angle linear geometry and are stronger than double or single bonds. Double bonds are $sp^2$ hybridized with 120° trigonal planar geometry. $sp^3$ hybridization, such as seen in the single bonds of tetrahedral compounds (i.e., methane), have 109.5° angles.

15. **C is correct.** NaCl and $CCl_4$ are provided as reference compounds.

| Compound | Dipole moment (D) |
|----------|-------------------|
| NaCl | 8.75 |
| $CH_3Cl$ | 1.95 |
| $H_2O$ | 1.85 |
| $H_2C=N=N$ | 1.50 |
| Benzene | 0 |
| $CCl_4$ | 0 |

16. **B is correct.** The rule of thumb is that any carbon chain with four or fewer carbons is usually a gas. 2-methylbutane is a five-carbon compound and is therefore a liquid. A skeletal backbone of 16 carbons or more is usually seen in lipids and waxes.

---

17. **A is correct.** At least one of the double-bonded carbons in every other answer choice has two substituents exactly the same.

18. **C is correct.** C is the only carbon attached to four different substituents so is therefore the only chiral carbon.

19. **B is correct.** B is a meso compound with a plane of symmetry through the middle of the oxygen atom and the third carbon. All three other molecules are chiral.

20. **D is correct.** A has no chiral carbon. B is named improperly. It is a trichloro compound. C is a meso compound. In D, the number 4 carbon is chiral. Any chiral molecule has an enantiomer.

21.     **B is correct.** Both carbons are chiral in each compound, but B is a meso compound.

22.     **D is correct.** All isomers are made up of the same set of elements and have identical molecular weights. Structural isomers are further subdivided by carbon chain differences, functional group position, and type variations. For instance, ethyl alcohol and dimethyl ether are structural isomers.

$$CH_3CH_2OH \qquad CH_3OCH_3$$

Ethyl alcohol      Dimethyl ether

23.     **B is correct.** Absolute configuration describes the R or S configuration around a chiral atom. Observed rotation describes the direction of rotation of plane-polarized light. The direction of rotation cannot be predicted by the absolute configuration alone.

24.     **C is correct.** Diastereomers – epimers, anomers, and geometric isomers – are stereoisomers that are not mirror images of each other. A meso compound is an achiral molecule, which is identical to its mirror image.

---

# EXPLANATIONS TO THE QUESTIONS IN LECTURE 2

25.     **A is correct.** A contains no tertiary carbons.

26.     **C is correct.** Bromine is the most selective.

27.     **D is correct.** Cycloheptane has the most ring strain and is at the greatest energy level. It will produce more heat per mole than methane or ethane because it is a larger molecule.

28.     **D is correct.** *Cis* groups on cyclohexane will never be both equatorial or both axial while in the chair configuration.

29.     **D is correct.** Only termination does not produce a radical. Conjugation is not a step in halogenation.

30.     **C is correct.** Alkanes (i.e., *n*-butane) are a class of saturated hydrocarbons containing only carbon-carbon single bonds. They are unreactive and are either straight-chained or branched. Cycloalkanes (i.e., cyclobutane), on the other hand, contain rings of carbon atoms. Although free rotation is possible around carbon-carbon single bonds in alkanes, geometric hindrance greatly reduces the possibility of rotation in cycloalkanes. For this reason, cycloalkanes are "stuck" as *cis* or *trans* isomers. The *cis* isomer has both substituents on the same side of the ring, while the *trans* form has substituents on opposite sides of the cycloalkane ring.

31.     **B is correct.** Primary hydrogen atoms are attached to primary carbons. Primary carbons are bound to only one other carbon. This parent compound houses five primary carbons with three hydrogens on each one.

32.     **C is correct.** There are four main reaction types seen in organic chemistry: addition, elimination, substitution and rearrangement. In an *addition reaction* (A + B → C), two reactants add together to form a single product. One reactant splitting into two products is known as an *elimination reaction* (A → B + C). *Substitutions* (A—B + C—D → A—C + B—D) occur when two reactants exchange parts to yield two new products. *Rearrangement reaction* (A → B) is defined by a reactant undergoing bond reorganization to give an entirely new product.

---

33. **C is correct.** The most stable alkene is the most substituted. *Trans* is more stable than *cis*.

34. **D is correct.** The most reactive will be the one with the lowest energy of activation. Since D makes the most stable carbocation (a tertiary carbocation), it is the most reactive in an electrophilic addition reaction.

35. **A is correct.** Don't let the ring structure intimidate you. Look for the functional groups and ask yourself "How do they react?" The only functional group that we know here is alkene. It's not electrophilic addition; it must be ozonolysis of an alkene. Ozone is highly reactive. It rips right through the double bond of an alkene. The result is a cleavage of the alkene at the double bond to form two aldehydes.

36. **D is correct.** This reaction is dehydration of an alcohol and proceeds with rearrangement of the carbocation intermediate from secondary to tertiary. (See page 53.)

37. **B is correct.** This is hydration of an alkene and follows Markovnikov's rule.

38. **D is correct.** Anthracene is a larger version of benzene, a prototypic aromatic compound. It satisfies Huckel's rule, which states that if a compound has *planar, monocyclic rings* with *(4n + 2) π electrons* (*n* being any integer, including zero), it is by definition an aromatic compound. Benzene houses six π electrons, a pair for each double bond (while anthracene has 14 π electrons).

39. **B is correct.** The question stem presents a mechanism for an elimination reaction (the product gains a double bond) that relies on a rapid C—H bond dissociation as the rate-limiting step. When the heavier deuterium (D) is used instead of a pure hydrogen atom, the reaction rate decreases because of a stronger carbon—deuterium bond.

40. **B is correct.** Isoprene is a diene (alkene), which occupies an irregular shape as a result of all those double bonds. When stretched, disorganized chains straighten out but can always revert back to their original random state. Isoprene *vulcanization* (cross-link induction) serves to prevent stretching.

---

41. **C is correct.** The hydroxide ion is more basic than the chloride ion and substitution will not result unless the hydroxide is protonated to make water, which is less basic than the chloride ion. The answer choices requiring knowledge of solvents should be immediately dismissed as being too difficult for the MCAT.

42. **B is correct.** This is an $S_N1$ reaction and increasing the concentration of the nucleophile will not affect the rate of the reaction because the slow step is the formation of a carbocation. Adding heat always increases the rate of the reaction.

43. **A is correct.** Reduction of a ketone produces a secondary alcohol. In this case two ketones were reduced. You might recognize $LiAlH_4$ as a reducing agent but you don't need to.

44. **D is correct.** D is not a hydrogen bond. For a hydrogen bond to occur, a N, O, or F must be intermolecularly bonded (the hydrogen bond itself) to a H that is covalently bonded to another N, O, or F.

45. **C is correct.** Regardless of whether or not the mechanism is $S_N1$ or $S_N2$, the hydroxyl group will not leave until it has been protonated. For $S_N1$, the formation of the cation, although rate determining, is very fast after protonation. For $S_N2$, the chloride ion must collide with the opposite side of a protonated molecule, so many collisions do not result in a reaction. Thus, $S_N1$ is faster. Tertiaries are the fastest to react in $S_N1$, then secondaries. Primaries react only through $S_N2$. Tertiaries react in less than a minute; secondaries in 1 to 5 minutes; while primaries may take days. This is a very tough MCAT question. You may have two of these per MCAT at the most. The important thing on a question like this is not to spend too much time. Narrow it down to A or C and take your best guess.

46. **C is correct.** Anti-Markovnikov alkene free radical addition is demonstrated by reaction mechanisms 1 and 2, both of which rely on peroxides as reagents. Based on the experimental results provided by the question stem, anti-Markovnikov addition only succeeds using HBr.

47.     **B is correct.**

*S$_N$1 substitution reaction:*

- two-step reaction
- follows first order reaction kinetics (rate = $k$[S])
- proceeds through a carbocation intermediate
- prefers tertiary carbons to increase carbocation stability
- prefers protic solvent
- produces a racemic mixture of products

*S$_N$2 substitution reaction:*

- one-step reaction
- follows second-order reaction kinetics (rate = $k$[S][Nucleophile])
- proceeds through a transition state
- prefers primary carbons
- prefers aprotic solvent
- produces optically active product
- causes an inversion of stereochemistry

48.     **B is correct.** S$_N$1 mechanism depends on the rate-limiting step, which is the carbocation formation and is nucleophile independent; all subsequent steps occur at a much faster rate and do not affect the rate of the reaction.

## EXPLANATIONS TO THE QUESTIONS IN LECTURE 3

49.     **D is correct.** Even if you don't recognize the reaction, the name aldol means that the product must be an alcohol. This eliminates C. You should recognize that the alpha hydrogen is the most reactive hydrogen on an aldehyde or ketone. For A or B to be correct, the carbonyl hydrogen must be removed while the alpha hydrogen remains intact. Not likely. Notice also that since in an aldol reaction between two aldehydes the product must be an aldehyde, A, B, and C are eliminated; they are ketones.

50.     **A is correct.** Only H$_x$ is an alpha hydrogen. Aldehydes and ketones typically undergo nucleophilic addition, not substitution.

51.     **D is correct.** The reduction of an aldehyde results in a primary alcohol. A and B are the same molecule; both secondary alcohols.

52.     **A is correct.** Ketones reduce more easily than esters. The first step is ketal formation to form blocking groups so that the ketone is not reduced. If the first step were omitted, the ketone would be reduced to a secondary alcohol.

53.     **D is correct.** Water is a stronger acid than alcohol, which is stronger than aldehyde, which is stronger than ketone.

54.     **A is correct.** When aldehydes are oxidized, they lose the hydrogen attached to the carbonyl carbon. Ketones have no such hydrogen to lose.

55.     **C is correct.** Tautomerization is an equilibrium represented by a proton shift. Ketones tautomerize to form enols where the carbonyl carbon from the ketone becoms part of an alkene by forming a double bond with a neighboring carbon. In choice C, the carbonyl carbon does not form part of the alkene.

56.     **D is correct.** The Tollens test gives a silver mirror for reducing sugars. Reducing sugars are hemiacetals in their ring form and either aldehydes or ketones in their straight-chain form. Acetals do not open easily because they contain the blocking groups discussed under "Formation of Acetals". However, to answer this question you just need to see that methyl β-glucoside is an acetal. Choice A is incorrect because glucose is an aldehyde and reduces Tollens reagent. Choice B is irrelevant because neither sugar is a ketone. Additionally, Tollens reagent promotes enediol rearrangement of ketones to aldehydes. Choice C is incorrect because glucose is a hemiacetal that opens to an aldehyde and reacts with Tollens reagent.

57.     **D is correct.** Alkenes have no N, O, or F with which to hydrogen bond.

58. **C is correct.** This is an esterification reaction. (See Figure 3.36 on page 107.)

59. **A is correct.** Carboxylic acids typically undergo nucleophilic substitution, not addition.

60. **A is correct.** This question may require a little too much knowledge for the MCAT. It is more likely that a question like this will be associated with a passage that explains reactivity of carboxylic acid derivatives. To find the answer, we look at the strengths of the leaving groups:

$$R-\overset{\overset{\displaystyle O}{\|}}{C}-LG \quad + \quad NR_2H \quad \longrightarrow \quad R-\overset{\overset{\displaystyle O}{\|}}{C}-NR_2 \quad + LG-H$$

LG = leaving group

| Derivative | leaving group | conjugate acid of leaving group |
|---|---|---|
| $R-\overset{\overset{\displaystyle O}{\|}}{C}-Cl$ | $Cl^-$ | $HCl$ |
| $R-\overset{\overset{\displaystyle O}{\|}}{C}-O-\overset{\overset{\displaystyle O}{\|}}{C}-R$ | $^-O-\overset{\overset{\displaystyle O}{\|}}{C}-R$ | $RCOOH$ |
| $R-\overset{\overset{\displaystyle O}{\|}}{C}-OH$ | $^-OH$ | $H_2O$ |
| $R-\overset{\overset{\displaystyle O}{\|}}{C}-OR$ | $^-OR$ | $HOR$ |
| $R-\overset{\overset{\displaystyle O}{\|}}{C}-NH_2$ | $^-NH_2$ | $NH_3$ |

increasing base strength (downward)

increasing acid strength (upward)

The weakest leaving group is the most stable and the most likely to be formed.

61. **B is correct.** This is the only methyl ketone listed.

62. **A is correct.** The anhydride reacts with ammonia to form an amide and a carboxylate ion. The addition of acid to the carboxylate creates carboxylic acid.

63. **A is correct.** $NO_2$ is an electron withdrawing substituent (deactivating) that stabilizes the methyl benzoate, decreasing reactivity. This will make the compound safer for transport and storage.

64. **D is correct.** Stronger conditions take the reaction further. Under acidic and basic conditions, an amide hydrolyzes to a carboxylic acid.

---

65. **D is correct.** The quaternary amine with all alkyl groups is not basic at all since its electrons have already been donated.

66. **B is correct.** Ammonia can donate a pair of electrons to act as a Lewis base.

67. **C is correct.** This molecule cannot hydrogen bond as easily as the others.

68. **A is correct.** The amine acts as a nucleophile and adds to the ketone. You should be able to predict this based upon your knowledge of amines and/or ketones.

69. **B is correct.** This is a simple alkylation of an amine. You should have this reaction memorized. Even if you don't, only B and D are possibilities for a base. Ethyl-methylamine is not an acid.

**70.** **D is correct.** Epoxides, oxygen-containing cyclic compounds, have much higher reactivity levels than other ethers. This is due to a highly strained three-member ring that can be opened by nucleophilic attack. Benzene is stabilized by electron delocalization, which is possible in aromatic compounds.

**71.** **A is correct.** Sodium chloride is a prototypic example of an ionic bond. In a coordinate covalent bond, both shared electrons come from the same atom; for instance, a Lewis base (i.e., ammonia) or oxygen-containing compound (i.e., water). Although both shared electrons come from the same atom, a coordinate covalent bond is a single bond similar in chemical properties to a covalent bond.

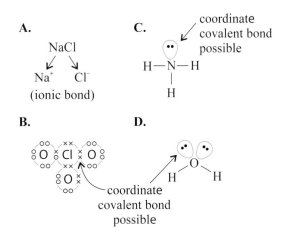

**72.** **C is correct.** Cyclohexanone ketone is flanked by four acidic alpha hydrogens, which will be replaced by deuterium. Since each deuterium is twice as heavy as hydrogen, the atomic weight is expected to increase by four (from 98 g/mol to 102 g/mol).

## EXPLANATIONS TO THE QUESTIONS IN LECTURE 4

**73.** **C is correct.** By definition, in electrophoresis negatively charged amino acids will move toward the anode. Only amino acids with an acidic isoelectric point will be negatively charged at a pH of 8. All amino acids except histidine, arginine, and lysine have acidic isoelectric points. Most likely on the MCAT, a question like this one would be accompanied with isoelectric points given in a passage. However, it is possible that a rare question would require you to memorize the three basic amino acids: histidine, arginine, and lysine.

**74.** **C is correct.** This reaction is between a carboxylic acid and an alcohol to form an ester. See page 107.

**75.** **B is correct.** The amino acid bias and shapes of the secondary structures (α-helix and β-pleated sheets) is partially explained by the rigid structure of the peptide bond, whose double bond character prevents rotation. This rigidity provides steric constraints on hydrogen bond formation for some amino acids that precludes them from participating, or even breaking secondary structure.

**76.** **C is correct.** Saturated fats have the greatest energy storage potential, about twice that of carbohydrates and proteins.

**77.** **C is correct.** The isoelectric point is where 100% of the amino acid exists as a zwitterion. The isoelectric point occurs at the first equivalence point.

**78.** **C is correct.** The solubilities of amino acids differ based upon the R group. Phenylalanine has a benzene R group and is the least polar amino acid listed. The carboxylic acids and amines on the other R groups increase solubility. You may have also memorized the four groups of amino acid side chains as either nonpolar, polar, acidic, or basic. Acidic, basic, and polar amino acids have greater water solubility than nonpolar amino acids.

79. **A is correct.** You may read this question and be uncertain of what it means by "monomer". Such an experience is not uncommon on the MCAT. The minimum that you need to understand for this question is that a monomer is some type of "equivalent unit". Since it is an MCAT question, you should assume that monomer refers to something that you already know. You make this assumption because MCAT doesn't test science that is not covered in these books. Next you need to recognize the chemical shown as a polypeptide. You need to know that polypeptides are divided into amino acid residues, and you must be able to recognize where these residues begin and end.

80. **C is correct.** A proline residue interrupts alpha-helix formation (and beta-pleated sheets) because the amide nitrogen has no hydrogen to contribute to the hydrogen bonding that drives and stabilizes the alpha-helix structure. Also, proline induces a kink, or turn in the polypeptide chain that further disrupts hydrogen bonding between neighboring amino acids in secondary structure.

---

81. **C is correct.** The formula for the number of isomers of a carbohydrate is $2^n$, where n is the number of chiral carbons.

82. **A is correct.** In this question you must know that glucose is an aldehyde and that an aldehyde and alcohol react to form, first, a hemiacetal. If a second equivalent of alcohol is added, an acetal will form.

83. **A is correct.** Of the choices, only fructose is a ketose. Notice that you did not have to know anything about fruit in this question. This question could have been rephrased as, "Which of the following is a ketose?"

84. **C is correct.** The general formula for a carbohydrate is $C_n(H_2O)_n$. Since this carbohydrate is in the Fischer projection with the aldehyde or ketone at the top, and the bottom chiral carbon is positioned to the right, it is of the D configuration. The only way to know about polarized light is to use a polarimeter.

85. **A is correct.** Carbohydrates have different functional groups on either end and cannot exist as a meso compound. Humans cannot digest all isomers of carbohydrates. Humans cannot digest L-glucose for example. You must know that glucose is an aldehyde.

86. **C is correct.** You may not remember that the gustatory receptors at the tip of the tongue stimulate a sweet taste. You don't need to because you should recognize that glucose and the artificial sweeteners can all hydrogen bond. You should also know that glucose ($C_{12}O_6H_{12}$) is a carbohydrate (is made from carbon and water alone), but the synthetic sweeteners are not. They contain nitrogen and other elements not contained in carbohydrates.

[Glucose]

87. **C is correct.** Carbon 5 hydroxyl group acts as a nucleophile by attacking the number 2 carbonyl carbon, leading to α or β furanose ring formation.

88. **D is correct.** Sugar A is a ketotriose and Sugar B is an aldoheptose.

---

89. **C is correct.** nmr deals with protons, not functional groups. D is true but is far more information about nmr than you are required to know.

90. **C is correct.** Extraction is separation based upon solubilitiy differences between molecules in a mixture.

91. **B is correct.** It is possible that one question on the MCAT may require specific knowledge of the IR table of frequencies for groups as basic as the carbonyl.

92. **A is correct.** The silica gel in TLC is polar and adsobs polar compounds stronger than nonpolar compounds; this results in polar compounds rising (migrating) more slowly.

93. **B is correct.** Distillation will not completely separate two compounds which form an azeotrope. Crystallization is a very inefficient method of purification. Distillation is more effective when done slowly.

94. **A is correct.** The *distillation process*, a workhorse of the chemical industry, relies on extreme varying of boiling points to separate complex chemical mixtures like petroleum. The tall towers seen at oil refineries are in fact distillation columns. *Liquid chromatography* is column chromatography, which separates compounds based on polarity, size, charge, and/or liquid or gas phase differences. *Nuclear magnetic resonance* (nmr) spectroscopy induces energy absorption to determine different types of carbon and/or hydrogen present in a compound.

95. **D is correct.** Dimethyl sulfoxide is a dipolar compound with a high boiling point as a result. It is miscible in water because it can hydrogen bond.

96. **C is correct.**

4 peaks on $C^{13}$ nmr

---

# Photo Credits

## Covers

Front cover, Digital illustration of a dna: © cosmin4000/
iStockphoto.com

Back cover, Close up of mass spectrometer: © sidsnapper/
iStockphoto.com

## Chapter 1

Pg. 1, Nanotube structure, artwork: © animate4.com ltd./
Photo Researchers, Inc.

Pg. 2, Gilbert Lewis: © Science Source/Photo Researchers,
Inc

Pg. 12, Comb with static electricity: © GIPhotoStock/Photo
Researchers, Inc.

Pg. 21, Lighter: © kolosigor/iStockphoto.com

Pg. 21, Hands display chirality: © Eva Serrabassa/
iStockphoto.com

Pg. 25, Thalidomide: © Alfred Pasieka/Photo Researchers,
Inc.

## Chapter 2

Pg. 31, Oil slick: © Michael Watkins/Istockphoto.com

Pg. 34, Natural gas burner: © John Kaprielian/Photo
Researchers, Inc.

Pg. 41, Addition reaction,: © Jerry Mason/Photo
Researchers, Inc.

Pg. 53, Alcohol oxidation: © Andrew Lambert Photography/
Photo Researchers, Inc.

## Chapter 3

Pg. 61, Carbonyl Iron Powder (SEM): © Eye of Science/
Photo Researchers, Inc.

Pg. 62, Brady's reagent: © Andrew Lambert Photography/
Photo Researchers, Inc.

Pg. 64, artisnal distillery: © John Burke/Gettyimages.com

Pg. 72, Acetic acid: © Friedrich Saurer/Photo Researchers,
Inc.

Pg. 72, Lemons: © Anna Liebiedieva/iStockphoto.com

Pg. 75, Nylon making: © Charles D. Winters/Photo
Researchers, Inc.

Pg. 78, Litmus test for amine solution: © Martyn F.
Chillmaid/Photo Researchers, Inc.

Pg. 83, Azo dye formation: © Andrew Lambert
Photography/Photo Researchers, Inc.

Pg. 83, Blisterpack of the antibiotic drug Amoxicillin:
© Dr. P. Marazzi/Photo Researchers, Inc.

## Chapter 4

Pg. 89, Omega-3 fatty acid pills: © Dana Kelley

Pg. 99, Nuclear magnetic resonance (NMR) laboratory:
© Hank Morgan/Photo Researchers, Inc.

Pg. 108, Close up of mass spectrometer: © Sidsnapper/
iStockphoto.com

Pg. 109, GCMS sample: © Tek Image/Photo Researchers,
Inc.

Pg. 111, Iceburg: © Paul Souders/The Image Bank/
Gettyimages.com

# INDEX

## Symbols

3°, 2°, 1°, methane 38
20 α-amino acids 91
α-amino acids 91, 144
α-carbon 62, 63, 72, 90, 151
α-hydrogens 62, 66
β-carotene 108
π-bond 12, 13, 16, 19, 38, 158
σ-bond 12, 13, 19, 158
Ω-carbon 90

## A

absolute configuration 22, 26, 30, 126, 140, 147, 159
abundances 108
acetal 64, 65, 97, 161, 164
Acetoacetic ester synthesis 76
Acidities 31
Acyl chlorides 74
acyl substitution reaction 72
adipose cells 90
Alcohols 9, 31, 58, 75, 151
aldehyde 10, 62-66, 70, 74, 77, 80, 93, 95-97, 129, 130, 134, 135, 140, 142, 151, 152, 161, 164
aldehydes 62-65, 69, 71, 74, 76, 77, 79, 80, 91, 96, 134, 135, 151, 160, 161
Aldehydes 9, 61, 62, 64, 71, 134, 161
aldohexose 95, 98, 152
Aldol condensation 66
aldoses 95
aliphatic acids 72
alkanes 8, 31, 32, 34, 37, 38, 42, 44, 62, 79, 159
alkene 19, 33, 38-42, 44, 61, 62, 68, 81, 121, 129, 130, 137, 148, 150, 158, 160, 161
Alkene 40, 42, 58
alkoxide 66, 151
alkoxymercuration 42
alkyl groups 63, 87, 162
alpha position 62
amide 10, 11, 77, 83, 84, 91, 137, 157, 162, 164
Amides 61, 76, 83, 86, 157
amine 11, 76-84, 87, 91-93, 134, 148, 157, 162
Amine 81, 82, 86
amines 11, 78, 79, 82-85, 91, 111, 162, 163
Amino acids 91, 144
ammonia 10, 11, 71, 77-79, 87, 130, 150, 157, 162, 163
Ammonia 14, 78, 79, 87, 162
amphipathic 90
Amylopectin 96, 112
Amylose (Starch) 96
anhydrides 85
anomeric carbon 27, 95, 96, 157
anomers 27, 159

## B

ball and stick models 4
Benzene 19, 31, 42-44, 58, 150, 158, 160, 163
Beryllium 2
blocking groups 65, 96, 161
boat 32
bond dissociation 18, 157, 160
Bond energy 12, 18, 157
bond-line formula 3
Boron 2

anti-addition 41, 42
anti-Markovnikov addition 41, 60, 160
aromatic 11, 16, 45, 78, 82, 87, 129, 142, 150, 160, 163
atomic orbitals 13, 14
axial hydrogens 33
azeotrope 110, 165

## C

Carbocation stability 38
Carbohydrates 89, 95, 97, 112, 164
carbon 2, 3, 9, 12, 13, 19, 21, 22, 24, 26, 27, 29-34, 36, 38-42, 46, 47, 61-63, 65-67, 69, 71-73, 76, 79, 84-86, 89-91, 95-101, 105, 108, 121-123, 127, 129, 137, 140, 142, 147, 148, 150-153, 157-161, 164, 165
carbonyl 61-63, 65, 66, 69, 71- 73, 76, 79, 83, 90, 91, 95, 97, 114, 115, 129, 134, 137, 142, 148, 150-152, 157, 161, 165
carboxylic acids 40, 61, 71, 72, 74-77, 91, 92, 111, 151, 152, 163
Carboxylic acids 9, 72, 73, 77, 162
Cellulose 96, 112
chair 32, 33, 37, 159
character 14, 19, 42, 91, 93, 158, 163
chemically equivalent hydrogens 100-102
chemical shift 100, 152
chiral center 22, 24, 126, 128, 152
chirality 21, 123
chiral molecules 21, 123
chromatography 99, 109, 110, 115, 165
Chromatography 89, 109, 110, 112
cis 25, 26, 30, 33, 37, 40, 68, 120, 159, 160
cis-isomers 25
Column chromatography 109
combustion 25, 34, 36, 44, 93, 121
complementary color 108
condensed formula 3
Conformational isomers 20, 148
conformers 20, 32, 148
conjugate addition 69
conjugated 16, 66, 107, 108, 114, 134, 151
conjugated unsaturated systems 16
coordinate covalent bond 12, 87, 157, 163
crystallization 99, 111, 118, 147

Cyanide ion  3
cyclohexane  32-34, 37, 71, 159
cystine  91

## D

dash formula  3, 148
dash-line-wedge formula  4
debye  16
decarboxylation  73, 76, 77, 121, 122, 135
degree of unsaturation  5
Dehydration  38, 58
Dehydration of an alcohol  38
Dehydrohalogenation  39, 58
delocalized electrons  15
demercuration  41, 42
Diastereomers  1, 25-28, 159
diazonium salts  82
diazotization of an amine  82, 83
different physical properties  25, 26, 33, 149
digital trace  101, 102
dimer  72, 73
dipole moment  16-19, 25, 103, 115
distillation  99, 110, 115, 120, 126, 128, 149, 165
Distillation  89, 110, 112, 115, 165
$d$ orbitals  2
downfield  100-102, 135, 151

## E

eclipsed  20
eicosanoids  89
electromagnetic waves  23
Electron donating groups  43
electronegativity  3, 17
electron shielding  101
electron withdrawing group  43
electrophile  38, 40-42, 44, 47, 69, 87, 120, 132, 134, 137, 150
Electrophilic addition  40
electrostatic force  12
elimination  37-39, 81, 129, 132, 134, 140, 144, 159, 160
elimination reaction  38, 132, 159, 160
enamines  79
enantiomeric purity  24, 30
Enantiomers  1, 24, 27, 28, 118, 149
enantiotropic  100
Enantiotropic hydrogens  100
enolate ion  62, 66, 76
entgegen  26
epimers  27, 135, 140, 152, 159
Epoxides  31, 163
equatorial hydrogens  33
essential  91
esters  61, 75, 76, 85, 144, 161
ether  10, 42, 143, 152, 153, 159
Ethers  31, 58
extraction  99, 115, 143
Extraction  89, 111, 112, 115, 165

## F

factor  110

Fatty acids  89, 90, 93, 153
fingerprint region  105
Fischer projection  3, 95, 147, 152, 164
flat molecule  42
formal charge  3, 29
four different substituents  21, 158
four rules for writing resonance structures  15
Fractional distillation  110
free radical  34, 36, 160
furanose  95, 98, 165

## G

gas chromatography  110
geminal diol  65
geometric isomer  25, 30
glucopyranose  95
Glycogen  96, 112
Grignard  58, 129, 141, 150, 152
Grignard synthesis  129

## H

Halogens  2, 42, 43, 67
Halogens are an exception  43
halohydrin  42, 121, 127, 147
Heat of Combustion  34, 58
hemiacetals  64, 96, 151, 161
hemiketals  64, 151
heterogeneous catalyst  40
hexoses  95, 152
Hofmann degradation  84, 85
Hofmann elimination  81
HOMO  107
Huckel's rule  16
Hybridization  1, 13, 14
hybrid orbitals  13, 14
Hydration of an alkene  41
Hydroboration  42
hydrogen bond  18, 46, 62, 79, 83, 97, 160-165
hydrogen bonds  62, 72, 73, 77, 150, 151
hydrogens  2, 3, 5, 33, 36, 42, 62, 66, 76, 80, 87, 91, 95, 99, 100, 101, 102, 148, 150, 152, 159, 163
hydrophilic  90, 92
hydrophobic  90, 92, 153
hydroxyproline  91

## I

imines  79
increases  32, 63, 72, 79, 92, 99, 107, 160
index of deficiency  5
index of hydrogen deficiency  5
induced dipoles  17
infrared radiation  103, 115
infrared spectroscopy (IR)  99
initiation  35, 37
instantaneous dipole moment  17
integral trace  101
Intermolecular attractions  18
inversion  60, 128, 147, 149, 150, 161
inversion of configuration  60, 128, 149, 150

## S

saponification 89, 134, 144
saturated 90
Saytzeff rule 39
Schiff bases 79
secondary 31, 36, 47, 60, 79, 83, 85, 87, 91, 93, 129, 147, 150, 151, 160, 161, 163, 164
Selectivity 36
shield 99, 115
side chain 91, 144, 153
sigma-bond 12
$S_N1$ 31, 47, 58, 60, 129, 160, 161
$S_N2$ 22, 31, 39, 47, 58, 60, 85, 127, 129, 130, 149, 150, 160, 161
solubility due to similar polarities 111
solvolysis 48
*sp* 14, 18, 28, 105, 158
*sp*$^2$ 14, 18, 19, 28, 105, 122, 147, 158
*sp*$^3$ 14, 18, 19, 28, 32, 105, 122, 158
Space-filling model 4
Specific rotation 24
Spin-spin coupling 101
spin-spin splitting 101
Splitting 100, 101, 112
staggered 20
stereochemistry 4, 20, 29, 42, 61, 72, 137, 149, 161
stereoisomers 21, 24, 30, 97, 120, 126, 127, 140, 147, 149, 151, 159
sterically hinder 48, 79
steric hindrance 4, 25, 33, 78, 130
stiffness of the bond 105
structural isomer 21
substitution 37, 39, 42, 43, 46, 47, 59-61, 70, 72, 74-77, 81, 133, 137, 148, 151, 157, 159, 160, 161, 162
Substitution 47, 58, 86
substitution NOT addition 42
substrate 47, 62, 72, 76
Sucrose 96, 112
syn addition 40, 42

## T

tautomers 63, 69, 73, 135
Ten 91
termination 35, 37, 159
tertiary 31, 36-38, 47, 60, 79, 85, 87, 91-93, 129, 150, 159, 160, 161
Tetramethylsilane 100
Thin layer chromatography 110
Tosylates 31, 58

## trans

trans 25-27, 30, 33, 68, 120, 121, 147, 159
transesterification 75
trans-isomers 25
triacylglycerols 89, 90
twist 32

## U

ultraviolet spectroscopy (UV) 99
unsaturated 10, 16, 40, 72, 89, 90, 93, 144, 157
upfield 100, 102, 135

## V

valence 2, 13
vic-dihalides 42

## W

water 14, 18, 32, 37, 38, 41, 42, 59, 62, 63, 66, 67, 71-73, 75, 77-80, 82, 84, 87, 95, 96, 110, 111, 115, 121, 122, 129, 130, 136, 140, 142-144, 147, 150-153, 160, 163-165
Wittig reaction 19, 68
Wolff-Kishner Reduction 61, 80, 86

## Z

zusammen 26

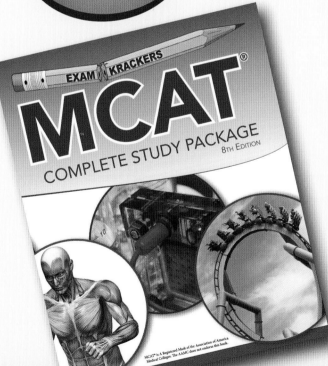

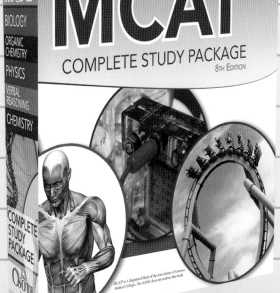

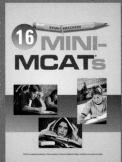
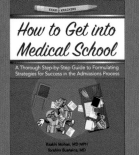

# An Unedited Student Review of This Book

The following review of this book was written by Teri R—. from New York. Teri scored a 43 out of 45 possible points on the MCAT. She is currently attending UCSF medical school, one of the most selective medical schools in the country.

*"The Examkrackers MCAT books are the best MCAT prep materials I've seen-and I looked at many before deciding. The worst part about studying for the MCAT is figuring out what you need to cover and getting the material organized. These books do all that for you so that you can spend your time learning. The books are well and carefully written, with great diagrams and really useful mnemonic tricks, so you don't waste time trying to figure out what the book is saying. They are concise enough that you can get through all of the subjects without cramming unnecessary details, and they really give you a strategy for the exam. The study questions in each section cover all the important concepts, and let you check your learning after each section. Alternating between reading and answering questions in MCAT format really helps make the material stick, and means there are no surprises on the day of the exam-the exam format seems really familiar and this helps enormously with the anxiety. Basically, these books make it clear what you need to do to be completely prepared for the MCAT and deliver it to you in a straightforward and easy-to-follow form. The mass of material you could study is overwhelming, so I decided to trust these books—I used nothing but the Examkrackers books in all subjects and got a 13-15 on Verbal, a 14 on Physical Sciences, and a 14 on Biological Sciences. Thanks to Jonathan Orsay and Examkrackers, I was admitted to all of my top-choice schools (Columbia, Cornell, Stanford, and UCSF). I will always be grateful. I could not recommend the Examkrackers books more strongly. Please contact me if you have any questions."*

*Sincerely,*
*Teri R—*

# About the Author

Jonathan Orsay is uniquely qualified to write an MCAT preparation book. He graduated on the Dean's list with a B.A. in History from Columbia University. While considering medical school, he sat for the real MCAT three times from 1989 to 1996. He scored in the 90 percentiles on all sections before becoming an MCAT instructor. He has lectured in MCAT test preparation for thousands of hours and across the country. He has taught premeds from such prestigious Universities as Harvard and Columbia. He was the editor of one of the best selling MCAT prep books in 1996 and again in 1997. He has written and published the following books and audio products in MCAT preparation: "Examkrackers MCAT Physics"; "Examkrackers MCAT Chemistry"; "Examkrackers MCAT Organic Chemistry"; "Examkrackers MCAT Biology"; "Examkrackers MCAT Verbal Reasoning & Math"; "Examkrackers 1001 questions in MCAT Physics", "Examkrackers MCAT Audio Osmosis with Jordan and Jon".

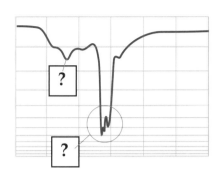

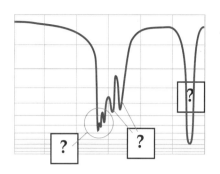

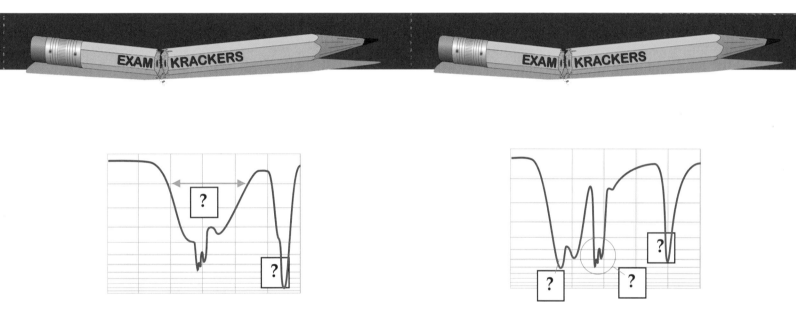

**Name the derivatives.**

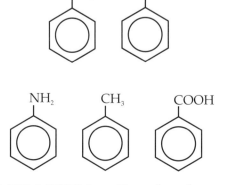

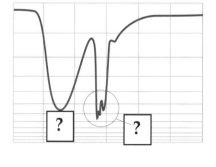

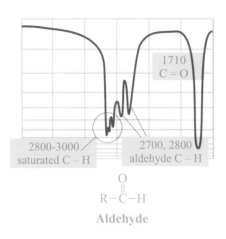

O
‖
R−C−H
**Aldehyde**

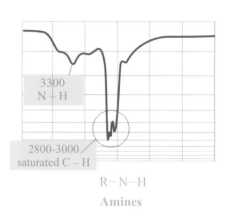

R−N−H
**Amines**

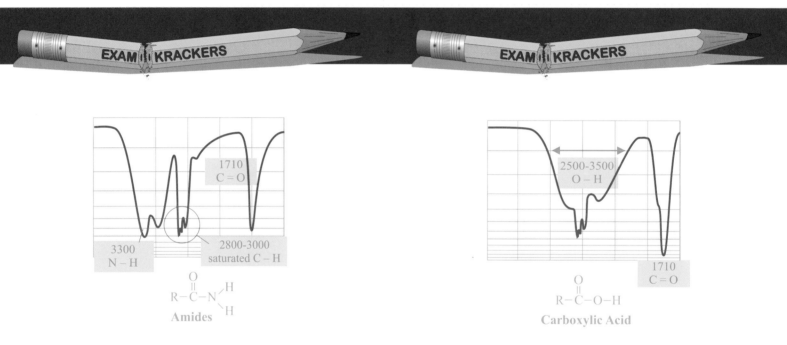

O
‖
R−C−N−H
|
H
**Amides**

O
‖
R−C−O−H
**Carboxylic Acid**

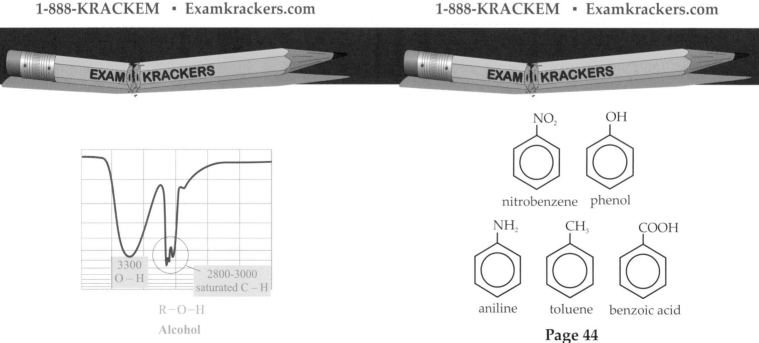

R−O−H
**Alcohol**

nitrobenzene    phenol

aniline    toluene    benzoic acid

**Page 44**

**Find the electron donating groups.**

—O⁻

—X

—R

—O—R

—O—H

$\ddot{N}$—R with R below

$-\overset{+}{N}(=O)(O^-)$

$-\overset{+}{N}(R)(R)$—R

$-\overset{|}{C}(Cl)(Cl)$—Cl

$-\overset{O^{\delta-}}{\underset{\delta+}{C}}$—R

$-\overset{O^{\delta-}}{\underset{\delta+}{C}}$—H

$-\overset{O^{\delta-}}{\underset{\delta+}{C}}$—O—R

$-\overset{O^{\delta-}}{\underset{\delta+}{C}}$—O—H

$-\overset{O^{\delta-}}{\underset{O^{\delta}}{S}}{}_{\delta+}$—O—H

$-\overset{\delta+}{C}\equiv N^{\delta-}$

---

**What are the six ways
that $S_N1$ differs from $S_N2$?**

---

$Cl_2$ + $CH_4$ $\xrightarrow{\text{light}}$

---

**Arrange green protons
in order of acid strength.**

$H_3C-\overset{O}{\overset{\|}{C}}-OH$  **A**

$H_3C-\overset{O}{\overset{\|}{C}}-CH_2-H$  **B**

$H-\overset{H}{\underset{H}{C}}-H$  **C**

$H-\overset{}{\underset{H}{N}}-H$  **D**

$CH_3-\overset{CH_3}{\underset{H}{C}}-OH$  **E**

$H-O-H$  **F**

$\overset{H}{\underset{H}{C}}=\overset{H}{\underset{H}{C}}$  **G**

---

$-\overset{H}{\underset{}{C}}-\overset{}{\underset{Br}{C}}-$ $\xrightarrow{OH^-}$

---

$CH_4$ + $2O_2$ $\xrightarrow{\text{flame}}$

**The nucleophile:** $S_N2$ requires a strong nucleophile, while nucleophilic strength doesn't affect $S_N1$.

<u>1st S:</u> $S_N2$ reactions don't occur with a sterically hindered Substrate. $S_N2$ requires a methyl, primary, or secondary substrate, while $S_N1$ requires a secondary or tertiary substrate.

<u>2nd S:</u> A highly polar **Solvent** slows down $S_N2$ reactions by stabilizing the nucleophile.

<u>3rd S:</u> The **Speed** of an $S_N2$ reaction depends upon the concentration of the substrate and the nucleophile, while the speed of an $S_N1$ depends only on the substrate.

<u>4th S:</u> $S_N2$ inverts **Stereochemistry** about the chiral center, while $S_N1$ creates a racemic mixture.

<u>5th S:</u> $S_N1$ may be accompanied by carbon **Skeleton** rearrangement, but $S_N2$ never rearranges the carbon skeleton.

**Page 49**

---

$$-O^- \qquad -O-H \qquad -\overset{\cdot\cdot}{N}-R$$
$$\qquad\qquad\qquad\qquad\qquad\quad |$$
$$\qquad\qquad\qquad\qquad\qquad\quad R$$

$$-R \qquad -O-R$$

**Electron donating groups.**
**Page 43**

---

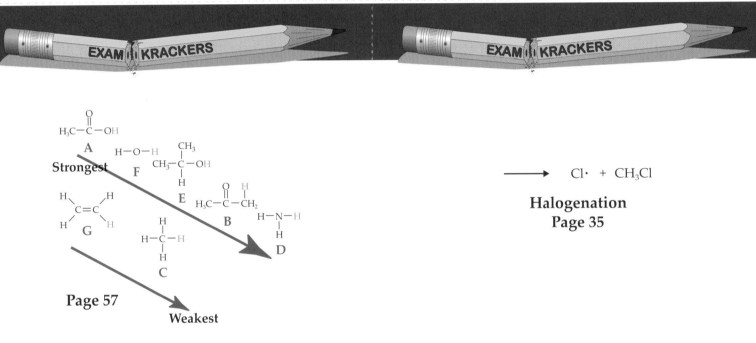

**Page 57**

---

$$\longrightarrow \quad Cl\cdot \; + \; CH_3Cl$$

**Halogenation**
**Page 35**

---

$$\longrightarrow \quad CO_2 \; + \; 2H_2O \; + \; Heat$$

**Combustion**
**Page 34**

---

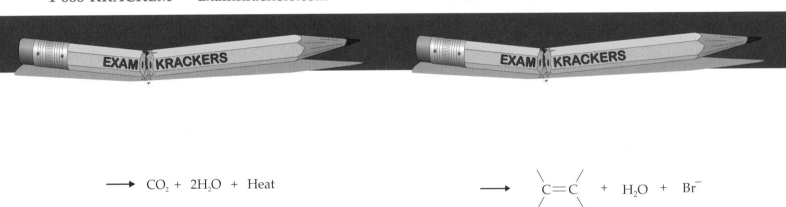

$$\longrightarrow \quad C=C \quad + \; H_2O \; + \; Br^-$$

**Dehydrohalogenation**
**Page 39**

$$CH_2 = CH_2 + H_2 \xrightarrow{\text{Ni, Pd, or Pt}}$$

$$\text{R} - \overset{\overset{\displaystyle R}{|}}{\underset{\underset{\displaystyle R}{|}}{C}} - \overset{\overset{\displaystyle OH}{|}}{\underset{\underset{\displaystyle H}{|}}{C}} - CH_3 \xrightarrow{\text{H}^+}$$

$$\overset{\diagup}{\underset{\diagdown}{C}} = \overset{\diagup}{\underset{\diagdown}{C}} \quad + \quad BH_3 \longrightarrow \xrightarrow{\text{H}_2\text{O}_2, \text{ OH}^-}$$

$$\overset{\diagup}{\underset{\diagdown}{C}} = \overset{\diagup}{\underset{\diagdown}{C}} \quad + \quad Br - Br \longrightarrow$$

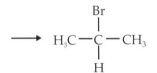

major product          minor product          + H₂O

**Dehydration of an Alcohol**
**Page 39**

⟶ CH₃CH₃

**Hydrogenation**
**with a heterogeneous catalyst**
**Page 40**

$$H_3C - \underset{\underset{H}{|}}{\overset{\overset{Br}{|}}{C}} - CH_3$$

**Electrophilic addition**
**Page 40**

⟶ C=O + O=C

**Ozonolysis**
**Page 40**

$$-\underset{\underset{Br}{|}}{\overset{\overset{Br}{|}}{C}} - \overset{|}{\underset{|}{C}} -$$

**Halogenation of an Alkene**
**Page 42**

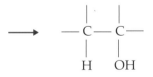

**Hydroboration**
**Page 42**

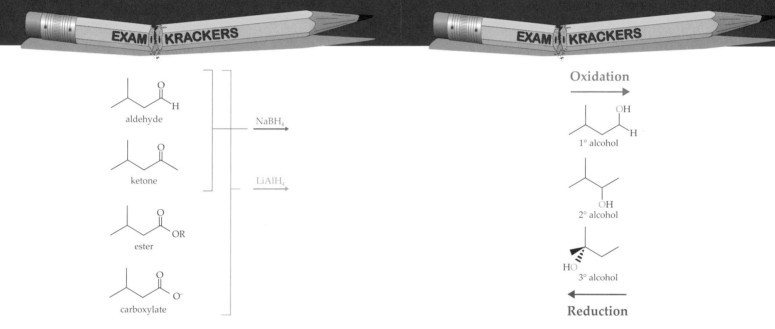

$$\text{CH}_3\text{CH}_2\text{OH} + \text{HCl} \longrightarrow$$

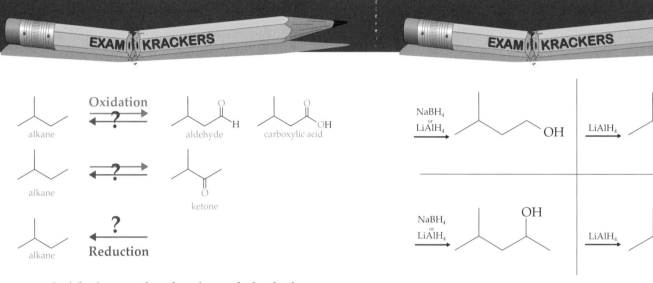

Grignard synthesis of an alcohol
Page 51

Oxymercuration/Demercuration
Page 41

Oxidation and reduction of alcohols
Page 53

Reduction
Page 51

An alkyl tosylate

Formation of a sulfonate
Page 55

$CH_3CH_2Cl + H_2O$

Substitution
Page 54

ROR + HBr $\longrightarrow$

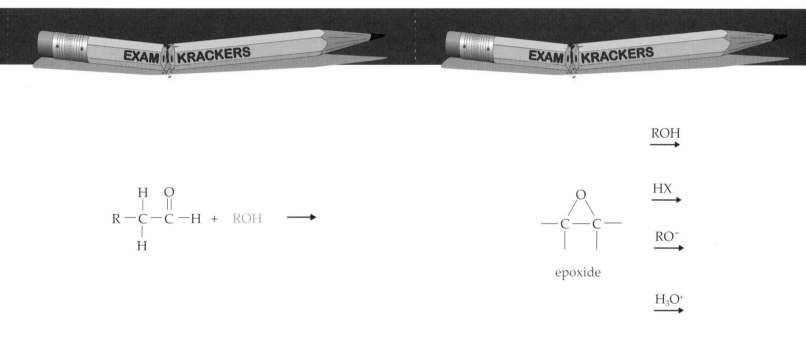

vic diol

$$\underset{\substack{H_3C \quad CH_3}}{\overset{\substack{HO \quad OH}}{CH_3-\overset{|}{\underset{|}{C}}-\overset{|}{\underset{|}{C}}-CH_3}} \xrightarrow[\text{heat}]{H^+}$$

$$R-\overset{\overset{\displaystyle H}{|}}{\underset{\underset{\displaystyle H}{|}}{C}}-\overset{\overset{\displaystyle O}{\|}}{C}-H + ROH \longrightarrow$$

epoxide

$$\xrightarrow{ROH}$$

$$\xrightarrow{HX}$$

$$\xrightarrow{RO^-}$$

$$\xrightarrow{H_3O^+}$$

$$R-\overset{\overset{\displaystyle O}{\|}}{C}-H \xrightarrow[H^+]{HOCH_2CH_2OH}$$

aldehyde

$$R-\overset{\overset{\displaystyle O}{\|}}{C}-H + H_2O \xrightarrow{OH^-}$$

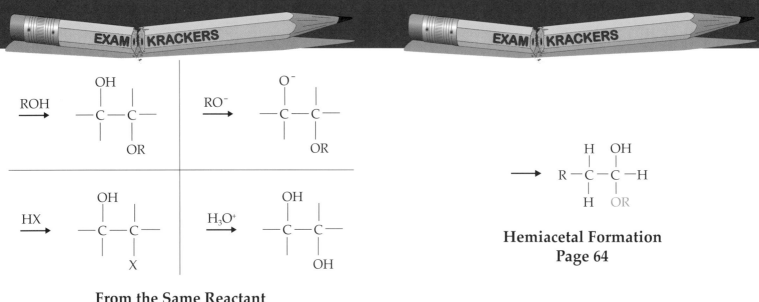

$\longrightarrow$   CH₃—C(=O)—C(CH₃)₂—CH₃   +   H₂O

**Pinacol Rearrangement**
**Page 55**

$\longrightarrow$   ROH   +   RBr

**Acid Cleavage**
**Page 56**

ROH $\longrightarrow$ 

RO⁻ $\longrightarrow$ 

HX $\longrightarrow$ 

H₃O⁺ $\longrightarrow$ 

**From the Same Reactant**
**Pages 56-57**

$\longrightarrow$   R—CH₂—CH(OH)(OR)

**Hemiacetal Formation**
**Page 64**

$\longrightarrow$   R—C(OH)₂—H

hydrate

**Gem Diol Formation**
**Page 65**

$\longrightarrow$ 

**Acetal formation**
**Blocking Groups**
**Page 65**

ylide     ketone
or
aldehyde

methyl ketone

$$R-\overset{O}{\underset{}{C}}-OH \;+\; SOCl_2 \;\xrightarrow{H^+}$$

thionyl
chloride

$$H_3C-\overset{O}{\underset{}{C}}-CH_2-\overset{O}{\underset{}{C}}-O^{\ominus} \;\xrightarrow[-CO_2]{}\; \xrightarrow{H^+}$$

acylacetate ion

alkene

**The Wittig reaction**
**Page 68**

**Aldol addition**
**Page 66**

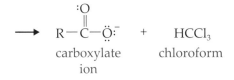

carboxylate    chloroform
ion

**Haloform reaction**
**Page 67**

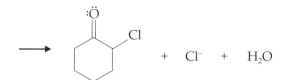

**Base promoted halogenation**
**Page 67**

**Decarboxylation**
**Page 73**

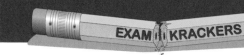

**Acid chloride synthesis**
**Page 74**

$$\text{R}-\overset{\overset{\displaystyle O}{\|}}{\text{C}}-\text{Cl}$$
acid chloride

$$\xrightarrow{\text{H}_2\text{O}}$$

$$\xrightarrow{\text{ROH}}$$

$$\xrightarrow{\text{RNH}_2}$$

$$\xrightarrow{\text{RCOOH}}$$

$$\text{R}-\overset{\overset{\displaystyle O}{\|}}{\text{C}}-\text{Cl}$$
acid chloride $$\xrightarrow{\text{H}_2\text{O}}$$

$$\text{R}-\overset{\overset{\displaystyle O}{\|}}{\text{C}}-\text{OR}$$
ester $$\xrightarrow{\text{H}_2\text{O}}$$

$$\text{R}-\overset{\overset{\displaystyle O}{\|}}{\text{C}}-\text{NHR}$$
amide $$\xrightarrow{\text{H}_2\text{O}}$$

$$\text{R}-\overset{\overset{\displaystyle O}{\|}}{\text{C}}-\text{O}-\overset{\overset{\displaystyle O}{\|}}{\text{C}}-\text{R}$$
anhydride $$\xrightarrow{\text{H}_2\text{O}}$$

$$\text{R}-\overset{\overset{\displaystyle O}{\|}}{\text{C}}-\text{OH} \;+\; \text{ROH} \;\xrightarrow{\text{H}^+}\;$$

$$\text{R}-\overset{\overset{\displaystyle O}{\|}}{\text{C}}-\text{OR} \;+\; \text{ROH} \;\xrightarrow{\text{H}^+}\;$$

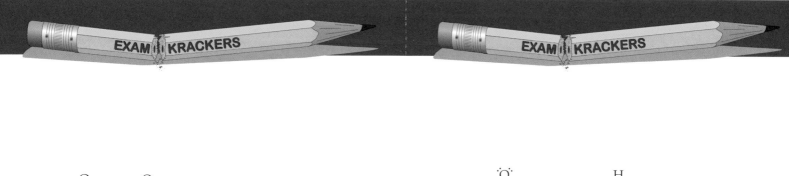

$$\text{H}_3\text{C}-\overset{\overset{\displaystyle O}{\|}}{\text{C}}-\text{CH}_2-\overset{\overset{\displaystyle O}{\|}}{\text{C}}-\text{OC}_2\text{H}_5$$
acetoacetic ester

$$\xrightarrow[\text{(2) R}-\text{X}]{\text{(1) }^-\text{OC}_2\text{H}_5} \xrightarrow[\text{heat}]{\text{H}^+}$$

$$-\overset{\overset{\displaystyle \overset{..}{\text{O}}{\cdot}}{\|}}{\text{C}}-\text{CH}_2- \;+\; \overset{\text{H}}{\underset{\text{R}\,\,\,\,\text{R}}{\overset{|}{\text{:N}}}} \;\xrightarrow{\text{H}_3\text{O}^+}\;$$
ketone
or aldehyde

→    +   HCl

→

O
‖
R—C—OH    +   ROH

carboxylic acid

→    +   RNH₂

→    +   RCOOH

**Hydrolysis**
**Page 75**

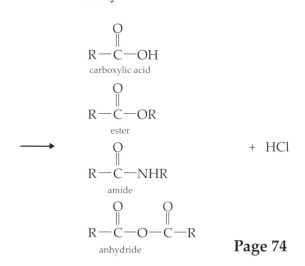

O
‖
R—C—OH
carboxylic acid

O
‖
R—C—OR
ester

→    +   HCl

O
‖
R—C—NHR
amide

O    O
‖     ‖
R—C—O—C—R
anhydride

**Page 74**

O
‖
→   R—C—OR + ROH

**Transesterification**
**Page 75**

O
‖
→   R—C—OR + H₂O

**Esterification**
**Page 75**

→ —C=CH—   +   H₂O
    |
    :N
   / \
  R    R

enamine

**Nucleophilic addition**
**Page 79**

O    R
‖     |
→   H₃C—C—CH₂ + CO₂↑

ketone

**Acetoacetic ester synthesis**
**Page 76**

$$\overset{\overset{\ddot{O}}{\|}}{-C}-CH_2- \quad + \quad \overset{H}{\underset{R\qquad R}{:N}} \quad \xrightarrow{H_3O^+}$$

ketone
or aldehyde

$$\overset{\overset{\ddot{O}}{\|}}{-C}- \quad + \quad H_2\ddot{N}-\ddot{N}H_2 \quad \xrightarrow{H^+} \quad \xrightarrow[\text{heat}]{KOH}$$

**ketone
or aldehyde** **hydrazine**

$$NH_3 \quad + \quad R-X \quad \longrightarrow$$

$$H_3C-\underset{\underset{^+N(CH_3)_3}{|}}{CH}-CH_2-CH_3 \quad \xrightarrow[150°C]{\text{base}}$$

$$H-\ddot{O}-\ddot{N}=\ddot{O} \quad + \quad R-\overset{H}{\underset{H}{N}}: \quad \xrightarrow{\text{acid}}$$

**Nitrous acid**

**1° amine**

$$\overset{\overset{O}{\|}}{R-C}-\overset{H}{\underset{H}{N:}} \quad + \text{ Base} + Br_2 \quad \longrightarrow$$

a primary amide

$$\longrightarrow \quad \underset{\substack{| \\ C \\ |}}{\overset{H \qquad H}{}} \quad + \quad H_2O \quad + \quad N_2$$

Desired
Product

**The Wolff-Kishner
Reduction
Page 80**

$$\longrightarrow \quad \underset{\substack{\| \\ N: \\ | \\ R}}{-C-CH_2-} \quad + \quad H_2O$$

imine

**Nucleophilic addition
Page 79**

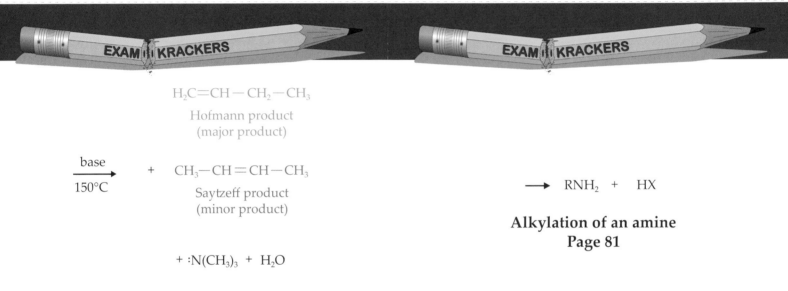

$$H_2C{=}CH-CH_2-CH_3$$

Hofmann product
(major product)

$$\xrightarrow[150°C]{base} \quad + \quad CH_3-CH{=}CH-CH_3$$

Saytzeff product
(minor product)

$$+ \; :N(CH_3)_3 \; + \; H_2O$$

**The Hofmann Elimination
Page 81**

$$\longrightarrow \quad RNH_2 \quad + \quad HX$$

**Alkylation of an amine
Page 81**

$$\longrightarrow \quad R-NH_2 \; + \; CO_2 \; + \; OH^-$$

a primary amine

**The Hofmann Degradation
Page 84**

$$\longrightarrow \quad R-\overset{+}{N}{\equiv}N: \; + \; H_2\ddot{O}:$$

Diazonium
ion

**Diazotization of an Amine
Page 82**

EXAMKRACKERS MCAT®

# BIOLOGY

## 8TH EDITION

OSOTE
PUBLISHING

ISBN 10: 1-893858-62-6 (Volume 1)
ISBN 13: 978-1-893858-62-6 (5 Volume Set)

8th Edition

To purchase additional copies of this book or the rest of the 5 volume set, call 1-888-572-2536 or fax orders to 1-859-255-0109.

Examkrackers.com

Osote.com

Audioosmosis.com

Cover/inside layout design/illustrations: Examkrackers' staff

Printed and bound in the United States of America.

# Acknowledgements

Although I am the author, the hard work and expertise of many individuals contributed to this book. The idea of writing in two voices, a science voice and an MCAT voice, was the creative brainchild of my imaginative friend Jordan Zaretsky. I would like to thank Scott Calvin for lending his exceptional science talent and pedagogic skills to this project. I also must thank thirteen years worth of ExamKrackers students for doggedly questioning every explanation, every sentence, every diagram, and every punctuation mark in the book, and for providing the creative inspiration that helped me find new ways to approach and teach biology. Finally, I wish to thank my wife, Silvia, for her support during the difficult times in the past and those that lie ahead.

I also wish to thank the following individuals:

## Contributors

Jennifer Birk-Goldschmidt
Patrick Butler
Dr. Jerry Johnson
Jordie Mann
Graeme McHenry
Timothy Peck
Gibran Shaikh
Vinita Takiar
Sara Thorp
Ruopeng Zhu

# Read This Section First!

This manual contains all the biology tested on the MCAT® and more. It contains more biology than is tested on the MCAT® because a deeper understanding of basic scientific principles is often gained through more advanced study. In addition, the MCAT® often presents passages with imposing topics that may intimidate the test-taker. Although the questions don't require knowledge of these topics, some familiarity will increase the confidence of the test-taker.

In order to answer questions quickly and efficiently, it is vital that the test-taker understand what is, and is not, tested directly by the MCAT®. To assist the test-taker in gaining this knowledge, this manual will use the following conventions. Any term or concept which is tested directly by the MCAT® will be written in **red, bold type**. To ensure a perfect score on the MCAT®, you should thoroughly understand all terms and concepts that are in **red, bold type** in this manual. Sometimes it is not necessary to memorize the name of a concept, but it is necessary to understand the concept itself. These concepts will also be in **bold and red**. It is important to note that the converse of the above is not true: just because a topic is not in **bold and red**, does not mean that it is not important.

Any formula that must be memorized will also be written in **red, bold type.**

If a topic is discussed purely as background knowledge, it will be written in *italics*. If a topic is written in italics, it is not likely to be required knowledge for the MCAT® but may be discussed in an MCAT® passage. Do not ignore items in italics, but recognize them as less important than other items. Answers to questions that directly test knowledge of italicized topics are likely to be found in an MCAT® passage.

Text written in orange is me, Salty the Kracker. I will remind you what is and is not an absolute must for MCAT. I will help you develop your MCAT intuition. In addition, I will offer mnemonics, simple methods of viewing a complex concept, and occasionally some comic relief. Don't ignore me, even if you think I am not funny, because my comedy is designed to help you understand and remember. If you think I am funny, tell the boss. I could use a raise.

Each chapter in this manual should be read three times: twice before the class lecture, and once immediately following the lecture. During the first reading, you should not write in the book. Instead, read purely for enjoyment. During the second reading, you should both highlight and take notes in the margins. The third reading should be slow and thorough.

The 24 questions in each lecture should be worked during the second reading before coming to class. The in-class exams in the back of the book are to be done in class after the lecture. Do not look at them before class.

**Warning:** Just attending the class will not raise your score. You must do the work. Not attending class will obstruct dramatic score increases. If you have Audio Osmosis, then listen to the appropriate lecture before and after you read a lecture.

If you are studying independently, read the lecture twice before doing the in-class exam and then once after doing the in-class exam. If you have Examkrackers *MCAT® Audio Osmosis With Jordan and Jon*, listen to that before taking the in-class exam and then as many times as necessary after taking the exam.

A scaled score conversion chart is provided on the answer page. This is not meant to be an accurate representation of your MCAT score. Do not become demoralized by a poor performance on these exams; they are not accurate reflections of your performance on the real MCAT®. The thirty minute exams have been designed to educate. They are similar to an MCAT® but with most of the easy questions removed. We believe that you can answer most of the easy questions without too much help from us, so the best way to raise your score is to focus on the more difficult questions. This method is one of the reasons for the rapid and celebrated success of the Examkrackers prep course and products.

If you find yourself struggling with the science or just needing more practice materials, use the Examkrackers 1001 Questions series. These books are designed specifically to teach the science. If you are already scoring 10s or better, these books are not for you.

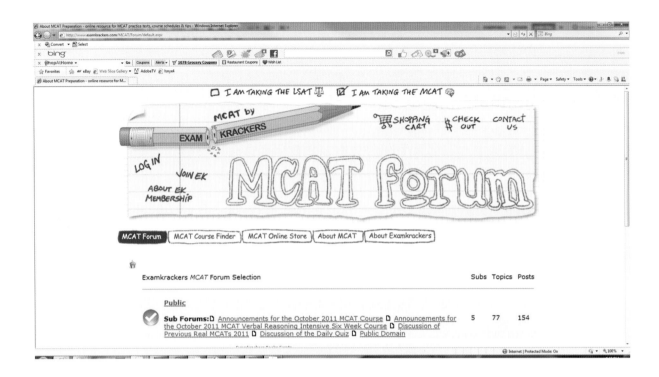

You should take advantage of the forums at www.examkrackers.com. The bulletin board allows you to discuss any question in the book with an MCAT® expert at Examkrackers. All discussions are kept on file so you have a bank of discussions to which you can refer to any question in this book.

Although we are very careful to be accurate, errata is an occupational hazard of any science book, especially those that are updated regularly as is this one. We maintain that our books have fewer errata than any other prep book. Most of the time what students are certain are errata is the student's error and not an error in the book. So that you can be certain, any errata in this book will be listed as it is discovered at www.examkrackers.com on the bulletin board. Check this site initially and periodically. If you discover what you believe to be errata, please post it on this board and we will verify it promptly. We understand that this system calls attention to the very few errata that may be in our books, but we feel that this is the best system to ensure that you have accurate information for your exam. Again, we stress that we have fewer errata than any other prep book on the market. The difference is that we provide a public list of our errata for your benefit.

Study diligently, trust this book to guide you, and you will reach your MCAT® goals.

# Table of Contents

# BIOLOGICAL SCIENCES

**DIRECTIONS.** Most questions in the Biological Sciences test are organized into groups, each preceded by a descriptive passage. After studying the passage, select the one best answer to each question in the group. Some questions are not based on a descriptive passage and are also independent of each other. You must also select the one best answer to these questions. If you are not certain of an answer, eliminate the alternatives that you know to be incorrect and then select an answer from the remaining alternatives. A periodic table is provided for your use. You may consult it whenever you wish.

## PERIODIC TABLE OF THE ELEMENTS

| 1 H 1.0 | | | | | | | | | | | | | | | | | 2 He 4.0 |
|---|---|---|---|---|---|---|---|---|---|---|---|---|---|---|---|---|---|
| 3 Li 6.9 | 4 Be 9.0 | | | | | | | | | | | 5 B 10.8 | 6 C 12.0 | 7 N 14.0 | 8 O 16.0 | 9 F 19.0 | 10 Ne 20.2 |
| 11 Na 23.0 | 12 Mg 24.3 | | | | | | | | | | | 13 Al 27.0 | 14 Si 28.1 | 15 P 31.0 | 16 S 32.1 | 17 Cl 35.5 | 18 Ar 39.9 |
| 19 K 39.1 | 20 Ca 40.1 | 21 Sc 45.0 | 22 Ti 47.9 | 23 V 50.9 | 24 Cr 52.0 | 25 Mn 54.9 | 26 Fe 55.8 | 27 Co 58.9 | 28 Ni 58.7 | 29 Cu 63.5 | 30 Zn 65.4 | 31 Ga 69.7 | 32 Ge 72.6 | 33 As 74.9 | 34 Se 79.0 | 35 Br 79.9 | 36 Kr 83.8 |
| 37 Rb 85.5 | 38 Sr 87.6 | 39 Y 88.9 | 40 Zr 91.2 | 41 Nb 92.9 | 42 Mo 95.9 | 43 Tc (98) | 44 Ru 101.1 | 45 Rh 102.9 | 46 Pd 106.4 | 47 Ag 107.9 | 48 Cd 112.4 | 49 In 114.8 | 50 Sn 118.7 | 51 Sb 121.8 | 52 Te 127.6 | 53 I 126.9 | 54 Xe 131.3 |
| 55 Cs 132.9 | 56 Ba 137.3 | 57 La* 138.9 | 72 Hf 178.5 | 73 Ta 180.9 | 74 W 183.9 | 75 Re 186.2 | 76 Os 190.2 | 77 Ir 192.2 | 78 Pt 195.1 | 79 Au 197.0 | 80 Hg 200.6 | 81 Tl 204.4 | 82 Pb 207.2 | 83 Bi 209.0 | 84 Po (209) | 85 At (210) | 86 Rn (222) |
| 87 Fr (223) | 88 Ra 226.0 | 89 Ac⁼ 227.0 | 104 Unq (261) | 105 Unp (262) | 106 Unh (263) | 107 Uns (262) | 108 Uno (265) | 109 Une (267) | | | | | | | | | |

| | 58 Ce 140.1 | 59 Pr 140.9 | 60 Nd 144.2 | 61 Pm (145) | 62 Sm 150.4 | 63 Eu 152.0 | 64 Gd 157.3 | 65 Tb 158.9 | 66 Dy 162.5 | 67 Ho 164.9 | 68 Er 167.3 | 69 Tm 168.9 | 70 Yb 173.0 | 71 Lu 175.0 |
|---|---|---|---|---|---|---|---|---|---|---|---|---|---|---|
| * | | | | | | | | | | | | | | |
| = | 90 Th 232.0 | 91 Pa (231) | 92 U 238.0 | 93 Np (237) | 94 Pu (244) | 95 Am (243) | 96 Cm (247) | 97 Bk (247) | 98 Cf (251) | 99 Es (252) | 100 Fm (257) | 101 Md (258) | 102 No (259) | 103 Lr (260) |

# MOLECULAR BIOLOGY; CELLULAR RESPIRATION

## 1.1 Introduction

This lecture discusses the structure and basic functions of the major chemical components of living cells and their surroundings. Although most of the details of this biochemistry are not required on the MCAT, this knowledge does create a strong base from which to understand the rest of the manual.

Most biological molecules can be classified as lipids, proteins, carbohydrates or nucleotide derivatives. Each of these types of molecules possesses a carbon skeleton. Together with water and minerals, they form living cells and their environment.

Cellular respiration provides the energy needed for muscles to do work.

## 1.2 Water

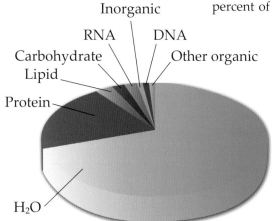

Inorganic
RNA    DNA
Carbohydrate    Other organic
Lipid
Protein
H₂O

Water is the solvent in which the chemical reactions of living cells take place. 70 to 80 percent of a cell's mass is due to water (chart on left). Water is a small polar molecule that can **hydrogen bond**. Most compounds as light as water would exist as a gas at typical cell temperatures. The ability of water to hydrogen bond allows it to maintain its liquid state in the cellular environment. Hydrogen bonding also provides strong cohesive forces between water molecules. These cohesive forces "squeeze" **hydrophobic** (Greek: hydros → water, phobos → fear) molecules away from water, and cause them to aggregate. **Hydrophilic** (Greek: philos → love) molecules dissolve easily in water because their negatively charged ends attract the positively charged hydrogens of water, and their positively charged ends attract the negatively charged oxygen of water (Figure 1.1). Thus, water molecules surround (solvate) a hydrophilic molecule separating it from the group.

Hydrogen bonding between individual water molecules creates cohesive forces that are strong enough to support this Raft Spider.

**Figure 1.1  The Solvent Properties of Water**

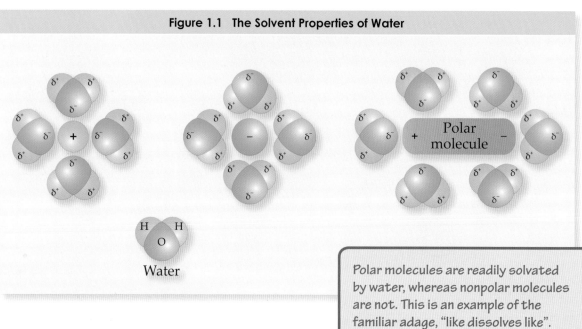

Water

Polar molecules are readily solvated by water, whereas nonpolar molecules are not. This is an example of the familiar adage, "like dissolves like".

Besides acting as a solvent, water often acts as a reactant or product. Most macromolecules of living cells are broken apart via **hydrolysis** (Greek: lysis → separation), and are formed via **dehydration** synthesis. (Hydrolysis and dehydration are discussed in Biology Lecture 7, and in the Organic Chemistry manual.)

A **lipid** is any biological molecule that has low solubility in water and high solubility in nonpolar organic solvents. Because they are hydrophobic, they make excellent barriers separating aqueous environments. Six major groups of lipids are: fatty acids, triacylglycerols, phospholipids, glycolipids, steroids, and terpenes (Figure 1.2).

Besides being lipids themselves, **fatty acids** are the building blocks for most, but not all, complex lipids. They are long chains of carbons truncated at one end by a carboxylic acid. There is usually an even number of carbons, with the maximum number of carbons in humans being 24. Fatty acids can be saturated or unsaturated. **Saturated fatty acids** possess only single carbon-carbon bonds. **Unsaturated fatty acids** contain one or more carbon-carbon double bonds. Oxidation of fatty acids liberates large amounts of chemical energy for a cell. Most fats reach the cell in the form of fatty acids, and not as triacylglycerols.

Triacylglycerols, phospholipids, and glycolipids are sometimes referred to as fatty acids. **Triacylglycerols** (Latin: tri → three), commonly called **triglycerides** or simply **fats** and **oils**, are constructed from a three carbon backbone called **glycerol**, which is attached to three fatty acids (Figure 1.2). Their function in a cell is to store energy. They may also function to provide thermal insulation and padding to an organism. **Adipocytes** (Latin: adips → fat, Greek: kytos → cell), also called fat cells, are specialized cells whose cytoplasm contains almost nothing but triglycerides.

Omega-3 fatty acids are lipids. Omega-3 fatty acids are found in fish and other seafood including algae and krill, some plants, and nut oils.

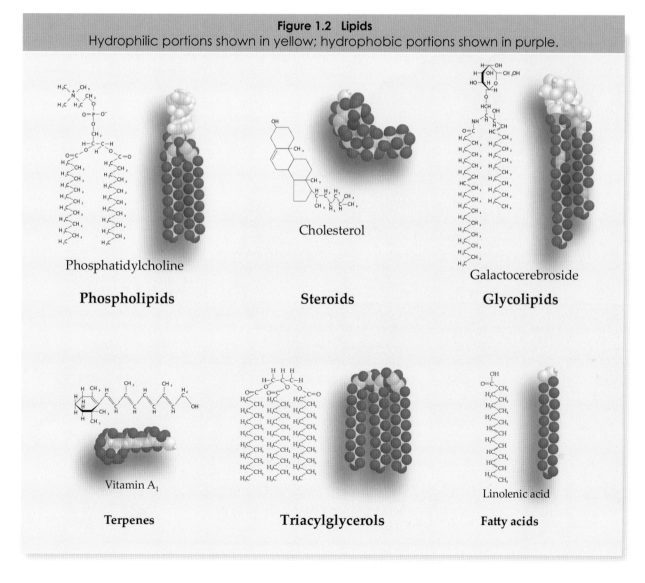

**Figure 1.2  Lipids**
Hydrophilic portions shown in yellow; hydrophobic portions shown in purple.

Phosphatidylcholine

**Phospholipids**

Cholesterol

**Steroids**

Galactocerebroside

**Glycolipids**

Vitamin A₁

**Terpenes**

**Triacylglycerols**

Linolenic acid

**Fatty acids**

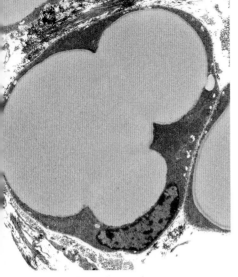

Each fat cell or adipocyte consists of a large central lipid droplet (yellow) surrounded by a thin layer of cytoplasm (red) containing the nucleus (blue). Fat cells store energy as an insulating layer of fat under the skin.

**Phospholipids** are built from a glycerol backbone as well, but a polar phosphate group replaces one of the fatty acids. The phosphate group lies on the opposite side of the glycerol from the fatty acids making the phospholipid polar at the phosphate end and nonpolar at the fatty acid end. This condition is called **amphipathic** (Latin: ambo → both) and makes phospholipids especially well suited as the major component of membranes. The polar end of the phospholipid to the right is in pink.

*Glycolipids* (Greek: glucus → sweet) are similar to phospholipids, except that glycolipids have one or more carbohydrates attached to the three-carbon glycerol backbone instead of the phosphate group. Glycolipids are also amphipathic. They are found in abundance in the membranes of myelinated cells composing the human nervous system.

**Steroids** are four ringed structures. They include some hormones, *vitamin D*, and cholesterol, an important membrane component.

*Terpenes* are a sixth class of lipids which include *vitamin A*, a vitamin important for vision.

Another class of lipids (not shown in Figure 1.2 but often listed as a fatty acid) is the 20 carbon *eicosanoids* (Greek: eikosi → twenty). Eicosanoids include prostaglandins, thromboxanes, and leukotrienes. Eicosanoids are released from cell membranes as local hormones that regulate, among other things, blood pressure, body temperature, and smooth muscle contraction. (See Paracrine System in Lecture 4 for more on local hormones.) Aspirin is a commonly used inhibitor of the synthesis of prostaglandins.

Since lipids are insoluble in aqueous solution, they are transported in the blood via *lipoproteins*. A lipoprotein contains a lipid core surrounded by phospholipids and *apoproteins* (apoproteins are discussed below). Thus the lipoprotein is able to dissolve lipids in its hydrophobic core, and then move freely through the aqueous solution due to its hydrophilic shell. Lipoproteins are classified by their density. The greater the ratio of lipid to protein, the lower the density. The major classes of lipoproteins in humans are chylomicrons, *very low density lipoproteins (VLDL)*, *low density lipoproteins (LDL)*, and *high density lipoproteins (HDL)*. (For more on lipoproteins, see Biology Lecture 6.11 – Fats.)

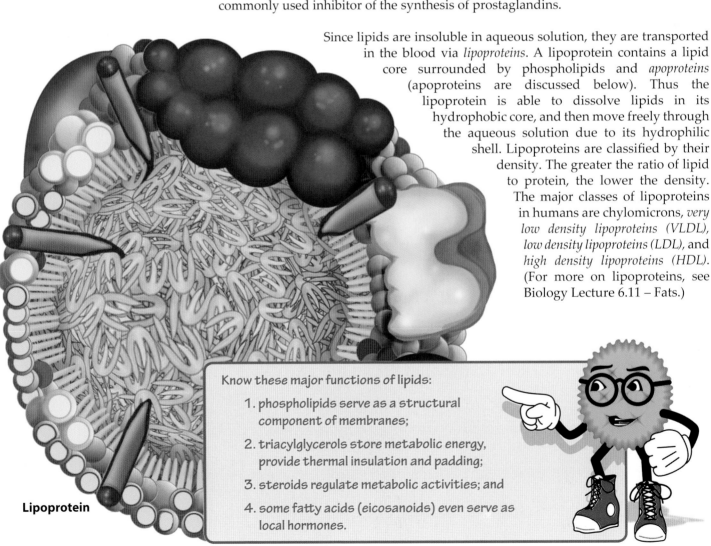

**Lipoprotein**

Know these major functions of lipids:

1. phospholipids serve as a structural component of membranes;

2. triacylglycerols store metabolic energy, provide thermal insulation and padding;

3. steroids regulate metabolic activities; and

4. some fatty acids (eicosanoids) even serve as local hormones.

## 1.4 Proteins

**Proteins** are built from a chain of **amino acids** linked together by **peptide bonds** (Peptide bonds are discussed in Organic Chemistry Lecture 4). Thus proteins are sometimes referred to as **polypeptides** (Greek: polys → many). Nearly all proteins in all species are built from the same 20 α-amino acids. They are called alpha amino acids because the amine is attached to the carbon in the alpha position to the carbonyl. In humans, ten of the amino acids are **essential**. In other words the body cannot manufacture these 10, so they must be ingested directly. Each amino acid in a polypeptide chain is referred to as a *residue*; very small polypeptides are sometimes referred to as peptides. The amino acids typically differ from each other only in their **side chains**, often designated as the R group. The side chain is also attached to the α-carbon. Digested proteins reach the cells of the human body as single amino acids. The 20 amino acids are shown in Figure 1.3.

Peanuts are a source of protein.

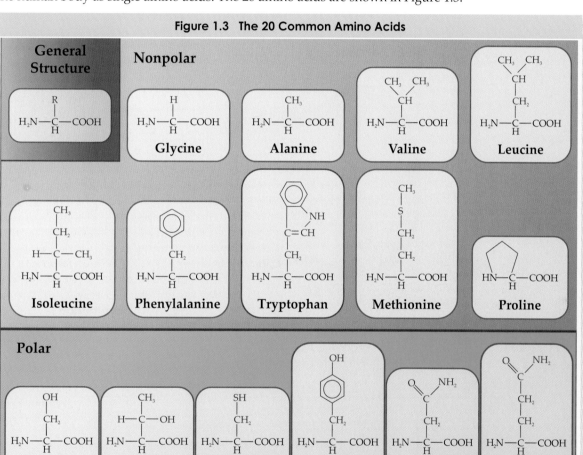

**Figure 1.3 The 20 Common Amino Acids**

The amino acid stuctures shown in Figure 1.3 are artificial. Amino acids in solution will always carry one or more charges. The position and nature of the charges will depend upon the pH of the solution.

Protein is found in nearly all unprocessed foods.

The number and sequence of amino acids in a polypeptide is called the **primary structure**. Once the primary structure is formed, the single chain can twist into an α-helix, or lie along side itself and form a **β-pleated sheet**. With β-pleated sheets, the connecting segments of the two strands of the sheet can lie in the same direction (*parallel*) or in opposite directions (*antiparallel*). Both α-helices and β-pleated sheets are reinforced by hydrogen bonds between the carbonyl oxygen and the hydrogen on the amino group. A single protein usually contains both structures at various locations along its chain. The α-helix and the β-pleated sheets are the **secondary structure** and contribute to the *conformation* of the protein. All proteins have a primary structure and most have a secondary structure. Larger proteins (globular, fibrous/structural, etc...) can have a tertiary and quaternary structure. The **tertiary structure** refers to the three dimensional shape formed when the peptide chain curls and folds. Five forces create the tertiary structure: 1.) covalent **disulfide bonds** between two cysteine amino acids on different parts of the chain, 2.) electrostatic (ionic) interactions mostly between acidic and basic side chains 3.) hydrogen bonds, 4.) van der Waals forces, 5.) hydrophobic side chains pushed away from water toward the center of the protein (see Figure 1.4).

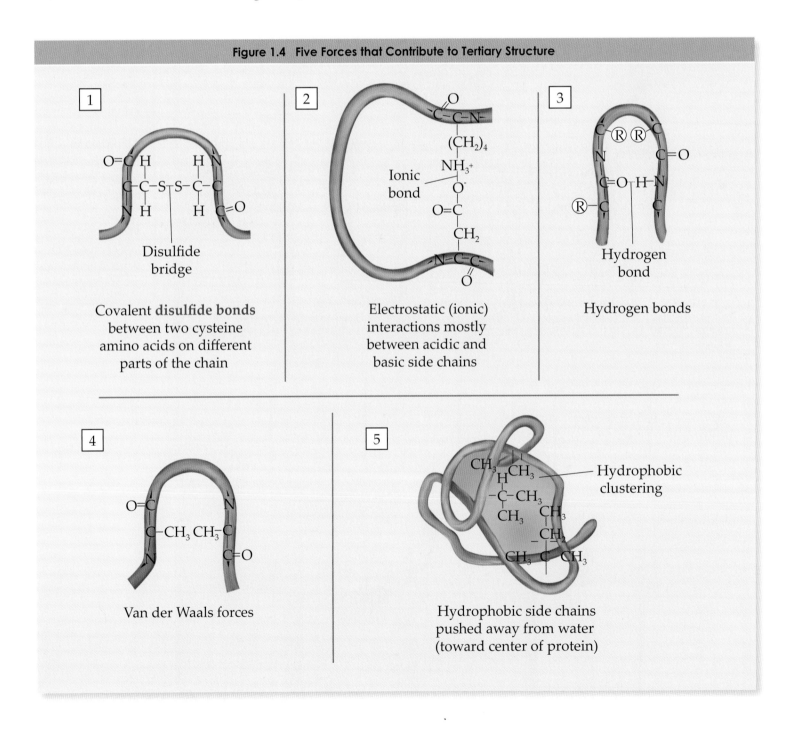

**Figure 1.4   Five Forces that Contribute to Tertiary Structure**

In addition to these forces, the amino acid proline induces turns in the polypeptide that will disrupt both α-helix and β-pleated sheet formation. When two or more polypeptide chains bind together, they form the **quaternary structure** of the protein. The same five forces at work in the tertiary structure can also act to form the quaternary structure.

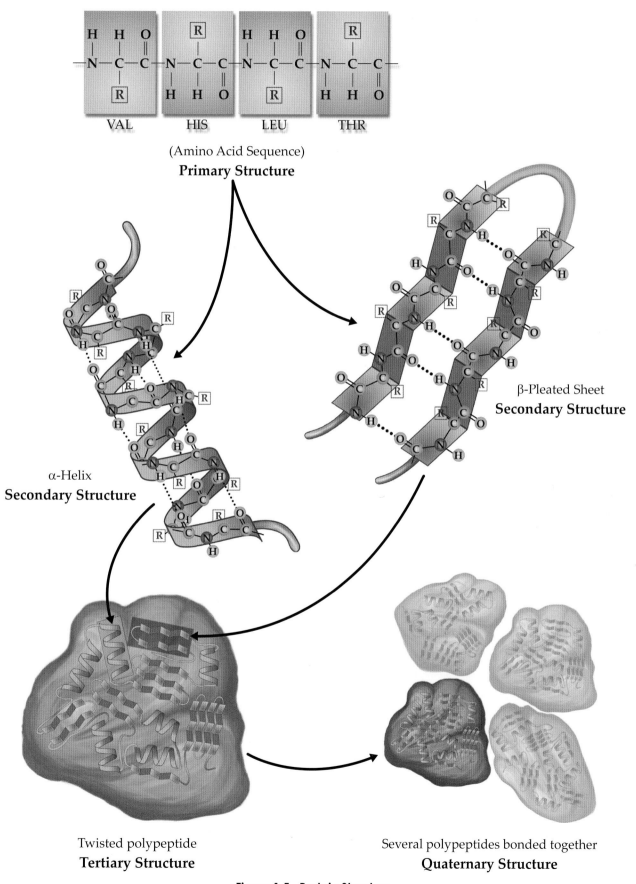

(Amino Acid Sequence)
**Primary Structure**

α-Helix
**Secondary Structure**

β-Pleated Sheet
**Secondary Structure**

Twisted polypeptide
**Tertiary Structure**

Several polypeptides bonded together
**Quaternary Structure**

**Figure 1.5 Protein Structure**

When the conformation is disrupted, the protein is said to be **denatured**. A denatured protein has lost most of its secondary, tertiary, and quaternary structure. Some denaturing agents and the forces that they disrupt are given in Table 1.1. Very often, once the denaturing agent is removed, the protein will spontaneously refold to its original conformation. This suggests that the amino acid sequence plays a key role in the conformation of a protein.

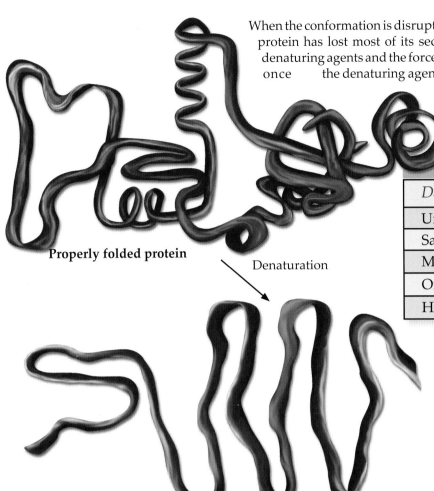

**Properly folded protein**

Denaturation

**Denatured protein**

| Table 1.1 Denaturing Agents | |
|---|---|
| *Denaturing Agents* | *Forces Disrupted* |
| Urea | Hydrogen bonds |
| Salt or Change in pH | Electrostatic bonds |
| Mercaptoethanol | Disulfide bonds |
| Organic solvents | Hydrophobic forces |
| Heat | All forces |

As alluded from the previous page, there are two types of proteins: *globular* and *structural*. There are more types of globular proteins than types of structural proteins. Globular proteins function as enzymes (i.e. pepsin), hormones (i.e. insulin), membrane pumps and channels (i.e. $Na^+/K^+$ pump and voltage gated sodium channels), membrane receptors (i.e. nicotinic receptors on a post-synaptic neuron), intercellular and intracellular transport and storage (i.e. hemoglobin and myoglobin), osmotic regulators (i.e. albumin), in the immune response (i.e. antibodies), and more.

Structural proteins are made from long polymers. They maintain and add strength to cellular and matrix structure. *Collagen* (Figure 1.6), a structural protein made from a unique type of helix, is the most abundant protein in the body. Collagen fibers add great strength to, among others, skin, tendons, ligaments, and bone. Microtubules, which make up eukaryotic flagella and cilia, are made from globular tubulin, which polymerizes under the right conditions to become a structural protein.

*Glycoproteins* are proteins with carbohydrate groups attached. These are a component of cellular plasma membranes. *Proteoglycans* are also a mixture of proteins and carbohydrates, but they generally consist of more than 50% carbohydrates. Proteoglycans are the major component of the extracellular matrix as discussed in Biology Lecture 4 – Cellular Matrix.

Heat, salt, and changes in pH can cause a protein to lose its higher-level conformations. Notice, for example, that the denatured form of the protein does not contain any of the α-helices that the properly folded protein has. Denaturing agents rarely affect the primary structure of a protein, which contains the essential information for conformation. Thus, mildly denatured proteins can often spontaneously return to their original conformation.

## Figure 1.6  Structure of Collagen

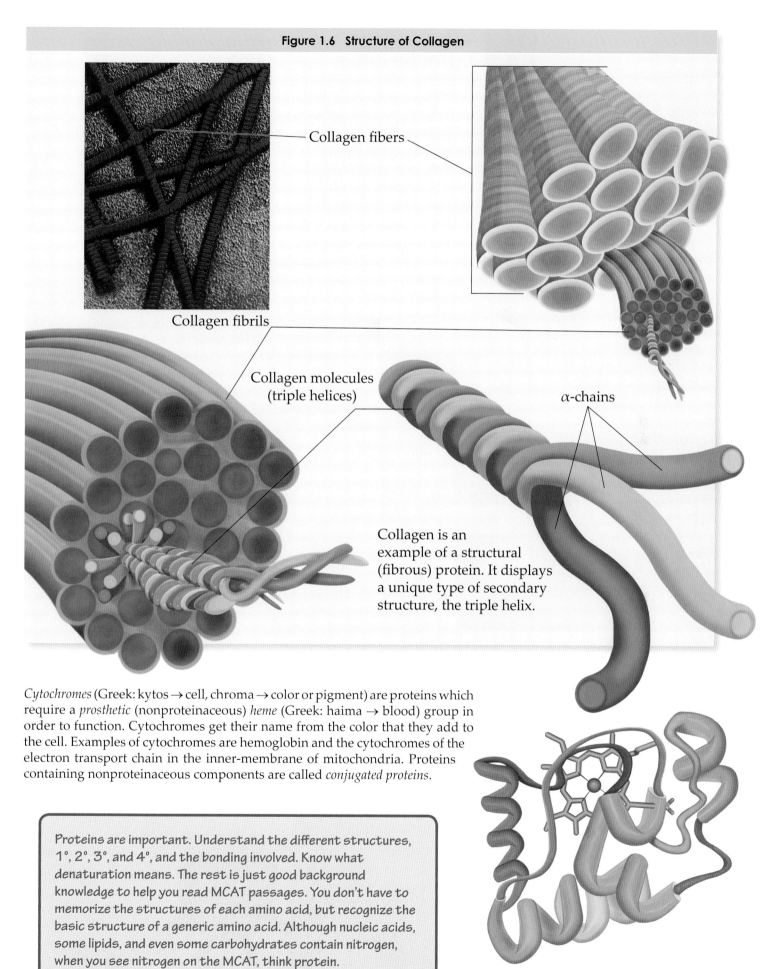

Collagen fibers

Collagen fibrils

Collagen molecules
(triple helices)

α-chains

Collagen is an example of a structural (fibrous) protein. It displays a unique type of secondary structure, the triple helix.

*Cytochromes* (Greek: kytos → cell, chroma → color or pigment) are proteins which require a *prosthetic* (nonproteinaceous) *heme* (Greek: haima → blood) group in order to function. Cytochromes get their name from the color that they add to the cell. Examples of cytochromes are hemoglobin and the cytochromes of the electron transport chain in the inner-membrane of mitochondria. Proteins containing nonproteinaceous components are called *conjugated proteins*.

Proteins are important. Understand the different structures, 1°, 2°, 3°, and 4°, and the bonding involved. Know what denaturation means. The rest is just good background knowledge to help you read MCAT passages. You don't have to memorize the structures of each amino acid, but recognize the basic structure of a generic amino acid. Although nucleic acids, some lipids, and even some carbohydrates contain nitrogen, when you see nitrogen on the MCAT, think protein.

Cytochrome proteins carry out electron transport via oxidation and reduction of the heme group.

## 1.5 *Carbohydrates*

As implied by the name, **carbohydrates** (also called sugars or saccharides) are made from carbon and water. They have the empirical formula $C(H_2O)$. Five and six carbon carbohydrates (pentoses and hexoses) are the most common in nature. The six carbon carbohydrate called **glucose** (Greek: glucus → sweet) is the most commonly occurring six carbon carbohydrate. Glucose normally accounts for 80% of the carbohydrates absorbed by humans. Essentially all digested carbohydrates reaching body cells have been converted to glucose by the liver or enterocytes. Glucose exists in aqueous solution in an unequal equilibrium heavily favoring the ring form over the chain form. The ring form has two **anomers**. In the first anomer, α-glucose, the hydroxyl group on the anomeric carbon (carbon number one) and the methoxy group (carbon number six) are on opposite sides of the carbon ring. In β-glucose the hydroxyl group and the methoxy group are on the same side of the carbon ring. The cell can oxidize glucose transferring its chemical energy to a more readily useable form, ATP. If the cell has sufficient ATP, glucose is polymerized to the polysaccharide, **glycogen** or converted to fat. As shown in Figure 1.7, glycogen is a branched glucose polymer with alpha linkages. Glycogen is found in all animal cells, but especially large amounts are found in muscle and liver cells. The liver regulates the blood glucose level, so liver cells are one of the few cell types capable of reforming glucose from glycogen and releasing it back into the blood stream. Only certain epithelial cells in the digestive tract and the proximal tubule of the kidney are capable of absorbing glucose against a concentration gradient. This is done via a secondary active transport mechanism down the concentration gradient of sodium. All other cells absorb glucose via facilitated diffusion. Insulin increases the rate of facilitated diffusion for glucose and other monosaccharides. In the absence of insulin, only neural and hepatic cells are capable of absorbing sufficient amounts of glucose via the facilitated transport system. Plants form **starch** and **cellulose** from glucose. Starch comes in two forms: *amylose* and *amylopectin*. Amylose is an isomer of cellulose that may be branched or unbranched and has the same alpha linkages as glycogen. Amylopectin resembles glycogen but has a different branching structure. Cellulose has beta linkages. Most animals have the enzymes to digest the alpha linkages of starch and glycogen but not the beta linkages of cellulose. Some animals such as cows have bacteria in their digestive systems that release an enzyme to digest the beta linkages in cellulose. Recent research suggests that certain insects do produce an enzyme to digest the beta linkages of cellulose.

Diabetics monitor how much glucose is in their blood.

In the absence of insulin, only the brain and the liver continue to absorb glucose.

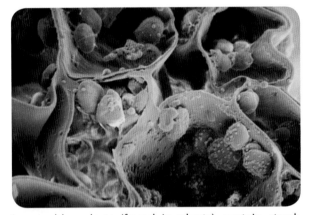

Large chloroplasts (found in plants) contain starch granules made by photosynthesis.

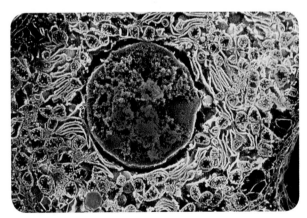

Liver cells contain large amounts of glycogen. This helps the liver regulate blood glucose levels.

Not bad, but I think I prefer alpha linkages in my salad.

Know the basic structure of a carbohydrate. You should also be familiar with the different polysaccharides and where they come from. For glucose, remember that animals eat the alpha linkages, but only bacteria break the beta linkages.

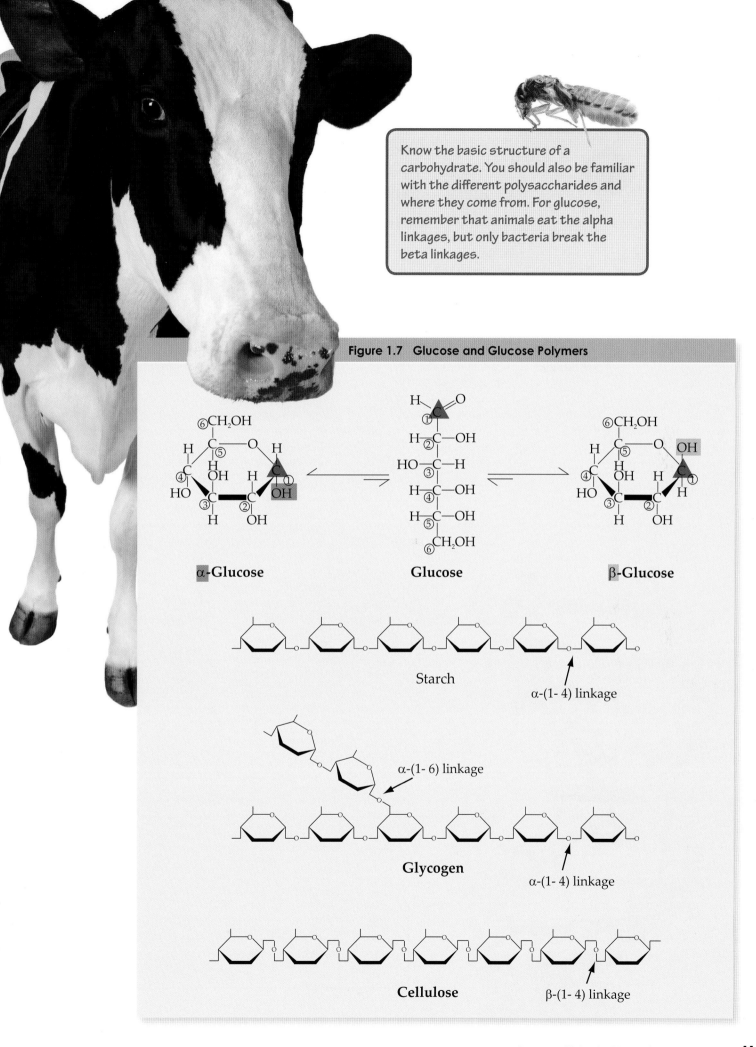

**Figure 1.7 Glucose and Glucose Polymers**

α-Glucose     Glucose     β-Glucose

Starch

α-(1- 4) linkage

α-(1- 6) linkage

**Glycogen**

α-(1- 4) linkage

**Cellulose**     β-(1- 4) linkage

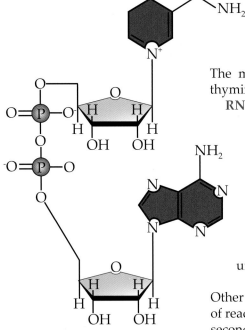

NADH is an example of a dinucleotide. Notice that phosphodiester linkages join the two nucleotides.

**Nucleotides** are composed of three components (Figure 1.8):

1. a five carbon sugar;
2. a nitrogenous base;
3. a phosphate group.

The most common nitrogenous bases in nucleotides are adenine, guanine, cytosine, thymine, and uracil. Nucleotides form polymers to create the **nucleic acids**, **DNA** and **RNA**. In nucleic acids, nucleotides are joined together by **phosphodiester bonds** between the phosphate group of one nucleotide and the 3$^{rd}$ carbon of the pentose of the other nucleotide forming long strands. By convention, a strand of nucleotides in a nucleic acid is written as a list of its nitrogenous bases. A nucleotide attached to the number 3 carbon (3') of its neighbor, follows that neighbor in the list. In other words, nucleotides are written 5'→ 3'. In typical DNA, two strands are joined by hydrogen bonds to make the structure called a **double helix**. Adenine and thymine form two hydrogen bonds, while cytosine and guanine form three. By convention, DNA is written so that the top strand runs 5'→ 3' and the bottom runs 3'→ 5'. In typical RNA there is only one strand and no helix is formed; also uracil replaces thymine. (More will be said about nucleic acids in Biology Lecture 2.)

Other important nucleotides include **ATP** (adenosine triphosphate: Figure 1.8), the source of readily available energy for the cell; also **cyclic AMP**, an important component in many second messenger systems; **NADH** and **FADH$_2$**, the coenzymes involved in the Krebs cycle.

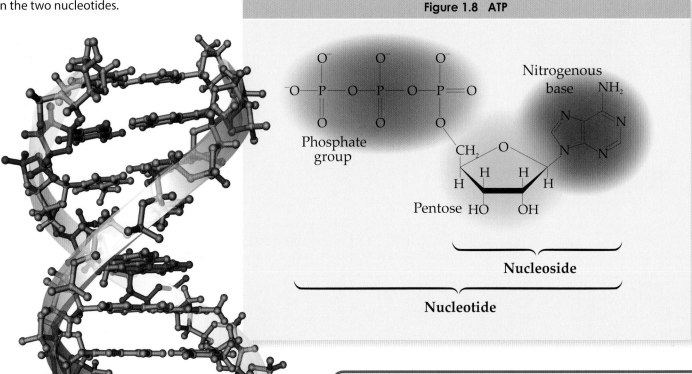

**Figure 1.8  ATP**

Nucleoside

Nucleotide

You should know that a nucleotide consists of three parts: the pentose sugar, the phosphate group, and the nitrogenous base. We'll hear more about nucleotides when we discuss genetics in the next lecture.

**DNA**

## 1.7 Minerals

**Minerals** are the dissolved inorganic ions inside and outside the cell. By creating electrochemical gradients across membranes, they assist in the transport of substances entering and exiting the cell. They can combine and solidify to give strength to a matrix, such as *hydroxyapatite* in bone. Minerals also act as cofactors (discussed later in this lecture) assisting enzyme or protein function. For instance, iron is a mineral found in *heme,* the prosthetic group of *cytochromes.*

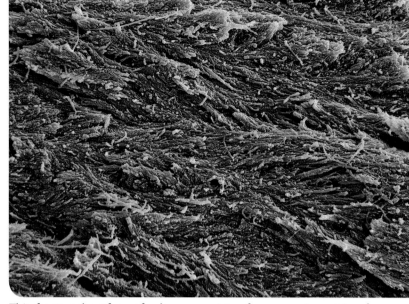

This fractured surface of a bone consists of an organic matrix of collagen fibers and mineral-based molecules such as hydroxyapatite and chondroitin sulfate.

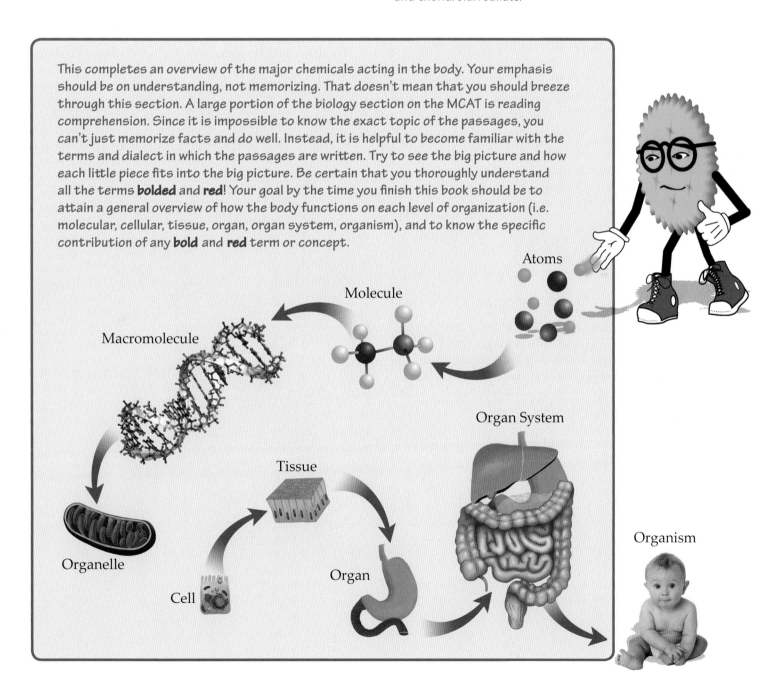

This completes an overview of the major chemicals acting in the body. Your emphasis should be on understanding, not memorizing. That doesn't mean that you should breeze through this section. A large portion of the biology section on the MCAT is reading comprehension. Since it is impossible to know the exact topic of the passages, you can't just memorize facts and do well. Instead, it is helpful to become familiar with the terms and dialect in which the passages are written. Try to see the big picture and how each little piece fits into the big picture. Be certain that you thoroughly understand all the terms **bolded** and **red**! Your goal by the time you finish this book should be to attain a general overview of how the body functions on each level of organization (i.e. molecular, cellular, tissue, organ, organ system, organism), and to know the specific contribution of any **bold** and **red** term or concept.

Atoms

Molecule

Macromolecule

Organ System

Tissue

Organelle

Organ

Organism

Cell

1. The most common catabolic reaction in the human body is:

    A. dehydration.
    B. hydrolysis.
    C. condensation.
    D. elimination.

2. A molecule of DNA contains all of the following EXCEPT:

    A. deoxyribose sugars.
    B. polypeptide bonds.
    C. phosphodiester bonds.
    D. nitrogenous bases.

3. Which of the following is a carbohydrate polymer that is stored in plants and digestible by animals?

    A. starch
    B. glycogen
    C. cellulose
    D. glucose

4. Excessive amounts of nitrogen are found in the urine of an individual who has experienced a period of extended fasting. This is most likely due to:

    A. glycogenolysis in the liver.
    B. the breakdown of body proteins.
    C. lipolysis in adipose tissue.
    D. a tumor on the posterior pituitary causing excessive ADH secretion.

5. Proline is not technically an α-amino acid. Due to the ring structure of proline, it cannot conform to the geometry of the α-helix and creates a bend in the polypeptide chain. This phenomenon assists in the creation of what level of protein structure?

    A. primary
    B. secondary
    C. tertiary
    D. quaternary

6. Metabolism of carbohydrate and fat spare protein tissue. All of the following are true of fats EXCEPT:

    A. Fats may be used in cell structure.
    B. Fats may be used as hormones.
    C. Fats are a more efficient form of energy storage than proteins.
    D. Fats are a less efficient form of energy storage than carbohydrates.

7. Which of the following is found in the RNA but not the DNA of a living cell?

    A. thymine
    B. a double helix
    C. an additional hydroxyl group
    D. hydrogen bonds

8. Like cellulose, chitin is a polysaccharide that cannot be digested by animals. Chitin differs from cellulose by possessing an acetyl-amino group at the second carbon. What molecule is a reactant in the breaking of the β-1,4-glycoside linkages of cellulose and chitin?

    A. water
    B. oxygen
    C. α-1,4-glucosidase
    D. β-1,4-glucosidase

_____

## 1.8 Enzymes

Virtually all biological reactions are governed by enzymes. Although there are a few nucleic acids that act as enzymes, typically **enzymes** are globular proteins. The function of any enzyme is to act as a **catalyst**, lowering the energy of activation for a biological reaction and increasing the rate of that reaction. Enzymes increase reaction rates by magnitudes of as much as thousands of trillions. This is a much greater increase than typical lab catalysts. Such extreme control over reaction rates gives enzymes the ability to pick and choose which reactions will or will not occur inside a cell. Enzymes, like any catalysts, are not consumed nor permanently altered by the reactions which they catalyze. Only a small amount of catalyst is required for any reaction. Like any catalyst, enzymes do not alter the **equilibrium** of a reaction. (See Chemistry Lecture 2 for more on equilibrium and catalysts.)

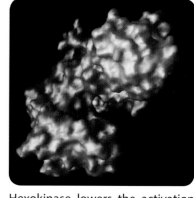

Hexokinase lowers the activation energy for the phosphorylation of glucose.

The reactant or reactants upon which an enzyme works are called the **substrates**. Substrates are generally smaller than the enzyme. The position on the enzyme to where the substrate binds, usually with numerous noncovalent bonds, is called the **active site**. The enzyme bound to the substrate is called the **enzyme-substrate complex**.

Normally, enzymes are designed to work only on a specific substrate or group of closely related substrates. This is called **enzyme specificity**. The **lock and key theory** is an example of enzyme specificity. In this theory, the active site of the enzyme has a specific shape like a lock that only fits a specific substrate, the key. The lock and key model explains some but not all enzymes. In a second theory called the **induced fit** model, the shape of both the enzyme and the substrate are altered upon binding. Besides increasing specificity, the alteration actually helps the reaction to proceed. In reactions with more than one substrate, the enzyme may also orient the substrates relative to each other, creating optimal conditions for a reaction to take place.

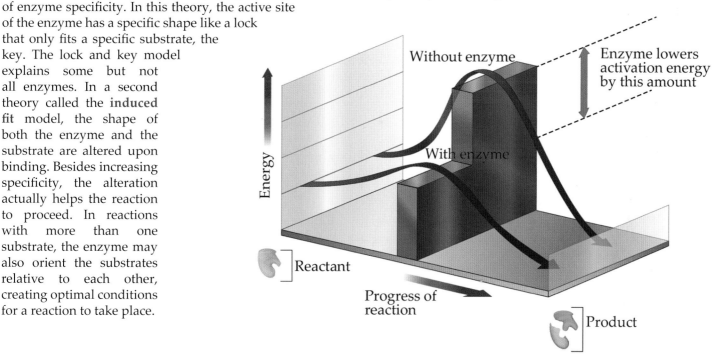

Without enzyme

Enzyme lowers activation energy by this amount

With enzyme

Energy

Reactant

Progress of reaction

Product

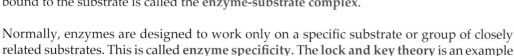

**Figure 1.9  Enzymatic Reaction**

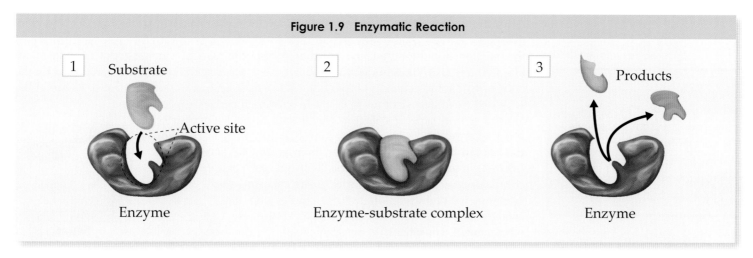

1  Substrate

Active site

Enzyme

2

Enzyme-substrate complex

3  Products

Enzyme

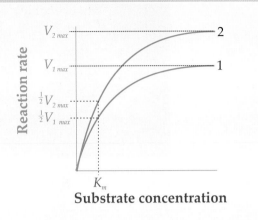

**Figure 1.10 Enzymatic Reactions Compared at Different Enzyme Concentrations**

Enzymes exhibit **saturation kinetics**; as the relative concentration of substrate increases, the rate of the reaction also increases, but to a lesser and lesser degree until a maximum rate ($V_{max}$) has been achieved (Figure 1.10). This occurs because as more substrate is added, individual substrates must begin to wait in line for an unoccupied enzyme. Thus, $V_{max}$ is proportional to enzyme concentration. *Turnover number* is the number of substrate molecules one enzyme active site can convert to product in a given unit of time when an enzyme solution is saturated with substrate. Related to $V_{max}$ is the *Michaelis constant* ($K_m$). $K_m$ is the substrate concentration at which the reaction rate is equal to $\frac{1}{2}V_{max}$. Unlike $V_{max}$, $K_m$ does not vary when the enzyme concentration is changed. Under certain conditions, $K_m$ is therefore a good indicator of an enzyme's affinity for its substrate.

> Don't fret over $V_{max}$ and $K_m$, they're not on the MCAT. If you are able to understand them, however, they provide a deeper understanding of enzyme kinetics, which <u>is</u> on the MCAT. We'll hear more about $V_{max}$ and $K_m$ later, but remember, the stuff in italics is not tested on the MCAT directly.

Temperature and pH also affect enzymatic reactions. At first, as the temperature increases, the reaction rate goes up, but at some point, the enzyme denatures and the rate of the reaction drops off precipitously. For enzymes in the human body, the optimal temperature is most often around 37° C. Enzymes also function within specific pH ranges. The optimal pH varies depending upon the enzyme. For instance, pepsin, active in the stomach, prefers a pH below 2, while trypsin, active in the small intestine, works best at a pH between 6 and 7.

> The important relationships between enzymes and their environment are represented by these three graphs. Memorize these three graphs and understand them.

In order to reach their optimal activity, many enzymes require a non-protein component called a **cofactor** (Latin: co- → with or together). Cofactors can be coenzymes or metal ions. **Coenzymes** are divided into two types: *cosubstrates* and *prosthetic groups*. Both types are organic molecules. Cosubstrates reversibly bind to a specific enzyme, and transfer some chemical group to another substrate. The cosubstrate is then reverted to its original form by another enzymatic reaction. This reversion to original form is what distinguishes a cosubstrate from normal substrates. **ATP** is an example of a cosubstrate type of coenzyme. Prosthetic groups, on the other hand, remain covalently bound to the enzyme throughout the reaction, and, like the enzyme, emerge from the reaction unchanged. Coenzymes are often **vitamins** or vitamin derivatives. (Vitamins are essential [cannot be produced by the body] organic molecules.) As mentioned before, *heme* is a prosthetic group. Heme binds with *catalase* in peroxisomes to degrade hydrogen peroxide. Metal ions are the second type of cofactor. Metal ions can act alone or with a prosthetic group. Typical metal ions that function as cofactors in the human body are iron, copper, manganese, magnesium, calcium, and zinc. An enzyme without its cofactor is called an *apoenzyme* (Greek: apo- → away from) and is completely nonfunctional. An enzyme with its cofactor is called a *holoenzyme* (Greek: holos → whole, entire, complete).

> Just know that some enzymes need cofactors to function, and that cofactors are either minerals or coenzymes. Also remember that many coenzymes are vitamins or their derivatives.

## 1.9 Enzyme Inhibition

Enzyme activity can be inhibited. Enzyme inhibitors can be classified according to three different mechanisms: irreversible inhibitors, competitive inhibitors, and noncompetitive inhibitors (Figure 1.11). Agents which bind covalently to enzymes and disrupt their function are **irreversible inhibitors**. A few irreversible inhibitors bind noncovalently. Irreversible inhibitors tend to be highly toxic. For example, *penicillin* is an irreversible inhibitor that binds to a bacterial enzyme that assists in the manufacturing of peptidoglycan cell walls.

> Irreversible inhibitors bond to enzymes and disrupt their function. Irreversible inhibitors tend to be highly toxic.

**Competitive inhibitors** compete with the substrate by binding reversibly with noncovalent bonds to the active site. Since, typically, they bind directly to the active site for only a fraction of a second, they block the substrate from binding during that time. Of course, the reverse is also true; if the substrate binds first, it blocks the inhibitor from binding. Thus, competitive inhibitors raise the apparent $K_m$ but do not change $V_{max}$. In other words, in the presence of a competitive inhibitor, the rate of the reaction can be increased to the original, uninhibited $V_{max}$ by increasing the concentration of the substrate. Overcoming inhibition by increasing substrate concentration is the classic indication of a competitive inhibitor. Competitive inhibitors often resemble the substrate. *Sulfanilamide* is an antibiotic which competitively inhibits a bacterial enzyme that manufactures folic acid leading to the death of bacterial cells. Although humans require folic acid, sulfanilamide does not harm humans because we use a different enzymatic pathway to manufacture folic acid.

**Noncompetitive inhibitors** bind noncovalently to an enzyme at a spot other than the active site and change the conformation of the enzyme. Noncompetitive inhibitors do not prevent the substrate from binding, and they bind just as readily to enzymes that have a substrate as to those that don't. Noncompetitive inhibitors do not resemble the substrate, so they commonly act on more than one enzyme. Unlike competitive inhibitors, they cannot be overcome by excess substrate, and they lower $V_{max}$. They do not, however, lower the enzyme affinity for the substrate, so $K_m$ remains the same.

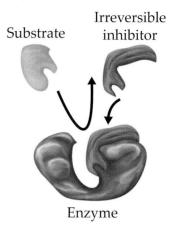

**Irreversible Inhibition**

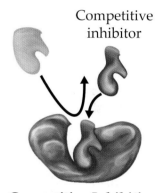

**Competitive Inhibition**

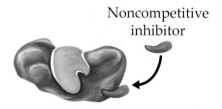

**Noncompetitive Inhibition**

**Figure 1.11  Enzyme Inhibitors**

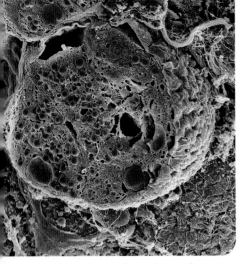

This acinar cell produces digestive enzymes in zymogen granules (purple). These enzymes are excreted into the pancreatic ducts and carried to the small intestine, where they are activated and aid in the breakdown of carbohydrates, fats, and proteins.

## 1.10 Enzyme Regulation

Enzymes select which reactions take place within a cell, so the cell must regulate enzyme activity. Enzymes are regulated by four primary means:

1.  *Proteolytic cleavage (irreversible covalent modification)*—Many enzymes are released into their environment in an inactive form called a **zymogen** or **proenzyme** (Greek: pro → before). When specific peptide bonds on zymogens are cleaved, the zymogens become irreversibly activated. Activation of zymogens may be instigated by other enzymes, or by a change in environment. For instance, pepsinogen (notice the "–ogen" at the end indicating zymogen status) is the zymogen of pepsin and is activated by low pH.

2.  *Reversible covalent modification*—Some enzymes are activated or deactivated by phosphorylation or the addition of some other modifier such as AMP. The removal of the modifier is almost always accomplished by hydrolysis. Phosphorylation typically occurs in the presence of a *protein kinase*.

3.  *Control proteins*—Control proteins are protein subunits that associate with certain enzymes to activate or inhibit their activity. *Calmodulin* or *G-proteins* are typical examples of control proteins.

4.  **Allosteric interactions**—Allosteric regulation is the modification of the enzyme configuration resulting from the binding of an activator or inhibitor at a specific binding site on the enzyme. (Allosteric regulation is discussed below.)

Normally, an enzyme governs just one reaction in a series of reactions. If one of the products downstream in a reaction series comes back and inhibits the enzymatic activity of an earlier reaction, this phenomenon is called **negative feedback** or **feedback inhibition**. Negative feedback provides a shut down mechanism for a series of enzymatic reactions when that series has produced a sufficient amount of product. Most enzymes work within some type of negative feedback cycle. **Positive feedback** also occurs, where the product returns to activate the enzyme. Positive feedback mechanisms occur less often than negative feedback.

Negative feedback inhibition is typical in many amino acid synthesis pathways. It is wasteful and unnecessary to synthesize amino acids that are readily available in the environment. Therefore, upstream enzymes involved in a particular synthetic metabolic pathway typically have allosteric inhibitory sites that bind the final amino acid product. If the final product is present in the environment, further synthesis will shut down.

**Figure 1.12 Enzyme Regulation**

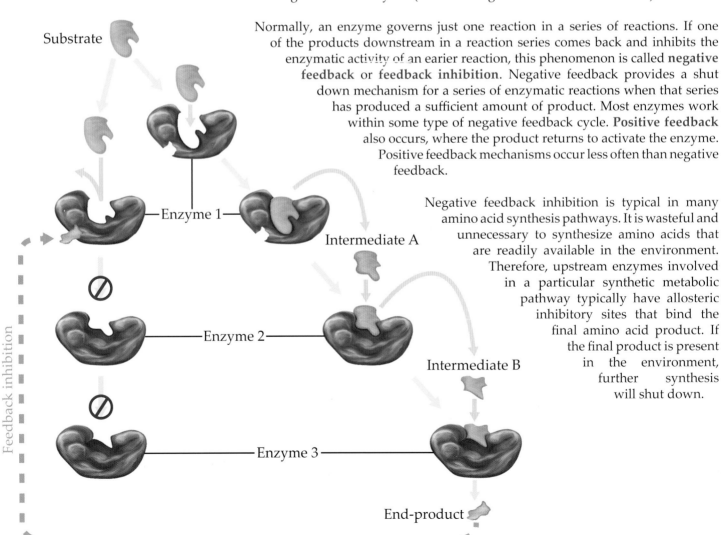

Feedback inhibitors do not resemble the substrates of the enzymes that they inhibit. Instead, they bind to the enzyme and cause a conformational change. This is called **allosteric regulation** (Greek: allos → different or other, stereos → solid). There exist both **allosteric inhibitors** and **allosteric activators**. All allosteric inhibitors and activators are not necessarily noncompetitive inhibitors, because many alter $K_m$ without affecting $V_{max}$. Allosteric enzymes do not exhibit typical kinetics because they normally have several binding sites for different inhibitors, activators, and even substrates. At low substrate concentrations, small increases in substrate concentration increase enzyme efficiency as well as reaction rate. The first substrate changes the shape of the enzyme allowing other substrates to bind more easily. This phenomenon is called **positive cooperativity**. **Negative cooperativity** occurs as well. It is cooperativity in the presence of the allosteric inhibitor *2,3BPG* that gives the oxygen dissociation curve of hemoglobin its sigmoidal shape.

## 1.11 Enzyme Classification

Enzymes are named according to the reactions that they catalyze. Very often, the suffix "-ase" is simply added to the end of the substrate upon which the enzyme acts. For instance, acetylcholinesterase acts upon the ester group in acetylcholine.

Enzymes are classified into six categories:

1. *oxidoreductases*
2. *transferases;*
3. *hydrolases;*
4. *lyases;*
5. *isomerases;*
6. *ligases.*

Negative Feedback

> Hold on! Don't go overboard here. You don't have to memorize the names of each type of inhibition. You just have to understand the concepts. Nor will you be asked to distinguish allosteric inhibition from noncompetitive inhibition. Many good bio texts don't distinguish them, and the MCAT certainly won't. However, you must understand negative feedback. Negative feedback will be tested on the MCAT.

> Look for the "-ase" ending. Often a seemingly complicated question about a complex chemical will depend upon the simple fact that the chemical is an enzyme, and the only clue is the "-ase" at the end of the name. Once you recognize that the chemical is an enzyme, you know that it contains nitrogen, and it is subject to denaturation. Similarly, many carbs are easy to recognize by their "-ose" ending.
>
> You don't have to memorize the six categories of enzymes.

The only distinction between classifications that might be of interest to an MCAT taker is between lyases and ligases. A lyase that catalyzes addition of one substrate to a double bond of a second substrate is sometimes called a *synthase*. ATP synthase is an example of a lyase. A ligase also governs an addition reaction, but requires energy from ATP or some other nucleotide. Ligases are sometimes called *synthetases*.

*Kinases* and *phosphatases* may also come up on the MCAT. A kinase is an enzyme which phosphorylates something, while a phosphatase is an enzyme which dephosphorylates something. Often times a kinase phosphorylates another enzyme in order to activate or deactivate it. *Hexokinase* is the enzyme which phosphorylates glucose as soon as it enters a cell.

> Something else: Some nonenzymatic proteins undergo regulation. Hemoglobin is an example of a protein that is not an enzyme, but exhibits several of the regulation characteristics described here.

9.    Enzymes are required by all living things because enzymes:

    A. raise the free energy of chemical reactions.
    B. properly orient reactants and lower activation energy.
    C. increase the temperature of reacting molecules.
    D. increase the number of reacting molecules.

10.    All of the following must change the rate of an enzyme-catalyzed reaction EXCEPT:

    A. changing the pH.
    B. lowering the temperature.
    C. decreasing the concentration of substrate.
    D. adding a noncompetitive inhibitor.

11.    Since an increase in temperature increases the reaction rate, why isn't the elevation of temperature a method normally used to accelerate enzyme-catalyzed reactions?

    A. Raising the temperature causes the reaction to occur too quickly.
    B. Raising the temperature does not sufficiently surmount the activation energy barrier.
    C. Heat changes the configuration of proteins.
    D. Heat does not increase the probability of molecular collision.

12.    Which of the following is (are) true concerning feedback inhibition?

    I. It often acts by inhibiting enzyme activity.
    II. It works to prevent a build up of excess nutrients.
    III. It only acts through enzymes.

    A. I only
    B. II only
    C. I and II only
    D. I, II, and III

13.    One mechanism of enzyme inhibition is to inhibit an enzyme without blocking the active site, but by altering the shape of the enzyme molecule. This mechanism is called:

    A. competitive inhibition.
    B. noncompetitive inhibition.
    C. feedback inhibition.
    D. positive inhibition.

14.    The continued production of progesterone caused by the release of HCG from the growing embryo is an example of:

    A. positive feedback.
    B. negative feedback.
    C. feedback inhibition.
    D. feedback enhancement.

15.    Peptidases that function in the stomach most likely:

    A. *increase* their function in the small intestine due to *increased* hydrogen ion concentration.
    B. *decrease* their function in the small intestine due to *increased* hydrogen ion concentration.
    C. *increase* their function in the small intestine due to *decreased* hydrogen ion concentration.
    D. *decrease* their function in the small intestine due to *decreased* hydrogen ion concentration.

16.    The rate of a reaction slows when the reaction is exposed to a competitive inhibitor. Which of the following might overcome the effects of the inhibitor?

    A. decreasing enzyme concentration
    B. increasing temperature
    C. increasing substrate concentration
    D. The effects of competitive inhibition cannot be overcome.

_____

## 1.12 Cellular Metabolism

**Metabolism** is all cellular chemical reactions. It consists of *anabolism* (Greek: ana → up, ballein → to throw), molecular synthesis, and *catabolism* (Greek: kata → down), molecular degradation. There are three basic stages of *catabolic* metabolism:

1) Macromolecules (polysaccharides, proteins, and lipids) are broken down into their constituent parts (monosaccharides, amino acids, and fatty acids and glycerol) releasing little or no energy.

2) Constituent parts are oxidized to acetyl CoA, pyruvate or other metabolites forming some ATP and reduced coenzymes (NADH and $FADH_2$) in a process that does not directly utilize oxygen.

3) If oxygen is available and the cell is capable of using oxygen, these metabolites go into the citric acid cycle to capture large amounts of energy (more NADH, $FADH_2$, or ATP); otherwise the coenzyme $NAD^+$ and other byproducts are either recycled or expelled as waste. The second and third stages, the energy acquiring stages, are called **respiration**. If oxygen is used, the respiration is aerobic; if oxygen is not used, the respiration is anaerobic.

> ### Thought Provoker
>
> *Which of the following are anabolic? Catabolic?*
>
> *1. Beta oxidation of fats*
>
> *2. Cholesterol synthesis*
>
> *3. Glucose synthesis (gluconeogenesis)*
>
> *4. Glycogen degregation (glycogenolysis)*
>
> *5. Photosynthesis*
>
> *Answer: See page 28*

*Notes:*

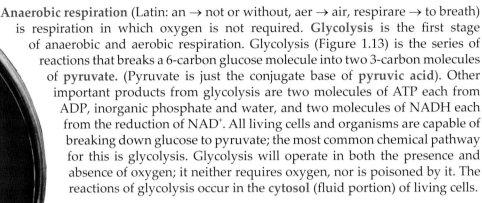

## 1.13 *Glycolysis*

**Anaerobic respiration** (Latin: an → not or without, aer → air, respirare → to breath) is respiration in which oxygen is not required. **Glycolysis** is the first stage of anaerobic and aerobic respiration. Glycolysis (Figure 1.13) is the series of reactions that breaks a 6-carbon glucose molecule into two 3-carbon molecules of **pyruvate.** (Pyruvate is just the conjugate base of **pyruvic acid**). Other important products from glycolysis are two molecules of ATP each from ADP, inorganic phosphate and water, and two molecules of NADH each from the reduction of NAD⁺. All living cells and organisms are capable of breaking down glucose to pyruvate; the most common chemical pathway for this is glycolysis. Glycolysis will operate in both the presence and absence of oxygen; it neither requires oxygen, nor is poisoned by it. The reactions of glycolysis occur in the **cytosol** (fluid portion) of living cells.

The first step of glycolysis occurs upon the entry of glucose into any human cell. *Hexokinase* phosphorylates glucose to *glucose 6-phosphate* with a phosphate group from ATP. (The liver and pancreas use an *isozyme* [an enzyme with the same function] of hexokinase called *glucokinase*.) Under normal cellular conditions the phosphorylation of glucose is irreversible, and assists the facilitated diffusion mechanism which transports glucose into the cell. (The liver, which must make glucose from glycogen and export it, possesses a special enzyme, *glucose 6-phosphatase*, which dephosphorylates glucose 6-phosphate to reform glucose. Glucose 6-phosphatase is also found in kidney cells.) Phosphorylated molecules cannot diffuse through the membrane. Although this is the first step in glycolysis, the process does not necessarily continue. Glucose 6-phosphate may be converted to *glucose 1-phosphate* and then to glycogen. If glucose 6-phosphate follows the glycolytic pathway, it goes to *fructose 6-phosphate* in the second step of glycolysis. In the third step of glycolysis, a second phosphate group is added at the expense of one more ATP. This step is irreversible and commits the molecule to the glycolytic pathway. Now, the six carbon *fructose 1,6-bisphosphate* is broken into Glyceraldehyde 3-phosphate (PGAL) and dihydroxyacetone phosphate. Dihydroxyacetone phosphate is subsequently converted to PGAL. Up to this point, no energy has been captured from the breakdown of glucose, but two ATPs have been spent.

Next, each 3-carbon molecule is phosphorylated while reducing one NAD⁺ to NADH. The resulting 3-carbon molecules each transfer one of their phosphate groups to an ADP to form one ATP each in **substrate level phosphorylation.** (Substrate level phosphorylation is the formation of ATP from ADP and inorganic phosphate using the energy released from the decay of high energy phosphorylated compounds as opposed to using the energy from diffusion of ions down their concentration gradient, as with oxidative phosphorylation.) The remaining 3-carbon molecules go through three more steps before donating their phosphate group to ADP to yield ATP and pyruvate. Altogether, 2 ATPs are spent and 4 ATPs are produced. The two pyruvate molecules and the two NADH molecules that are left are still relatively high energy molecules.

The products of carbohydrate digestion in the alimentary tract are approximately 80% glucose, and 20% fructose and galactose. *Fructose* and *galactose* are monosaccharides. Much of the fructose and galactose ingested by humans is converted into glucose in the liver enterocytes; however, fructose can enter glycolysis as fructose 6-phosphate or *glyceraldehyde 3-phosphate*, and galactose can be converted to glucose 6-phosphate to enter glycolysis. Simple table sugar is a disaccharide made from glucose and fructose. *Lactose* is a disaccharide found in milk, and is broken down into glucose and galactose in the small intestine. 95% of the monosaccharides in the blood are glucose.

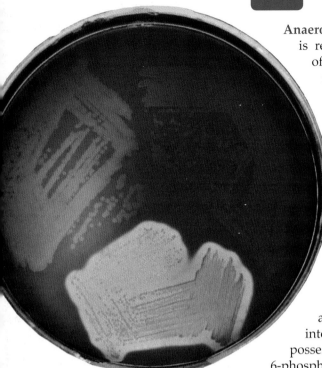

*Streptococcus spp.,* a bacterium taken from a human mouth, uses glycolysis to capture energy from glucose.

Notice that glycolysis has two stages: a six carbon stage and a three carbon stage. The six carbon stage expends two ATPs to phosphorylate the molecule; kind of like "priming a pump". The three carbon stage synthesizes two ATP with each three carbon molecule. Also recognize pyruvate and NADH (the names, not the structures), but don't worry too much about the names of the other chemicals. Just recognize them as part of glycolysis. Know the products of glycolysis, especially the net production of 2 ATPs.

# Figure 1.13

# Glycolysis

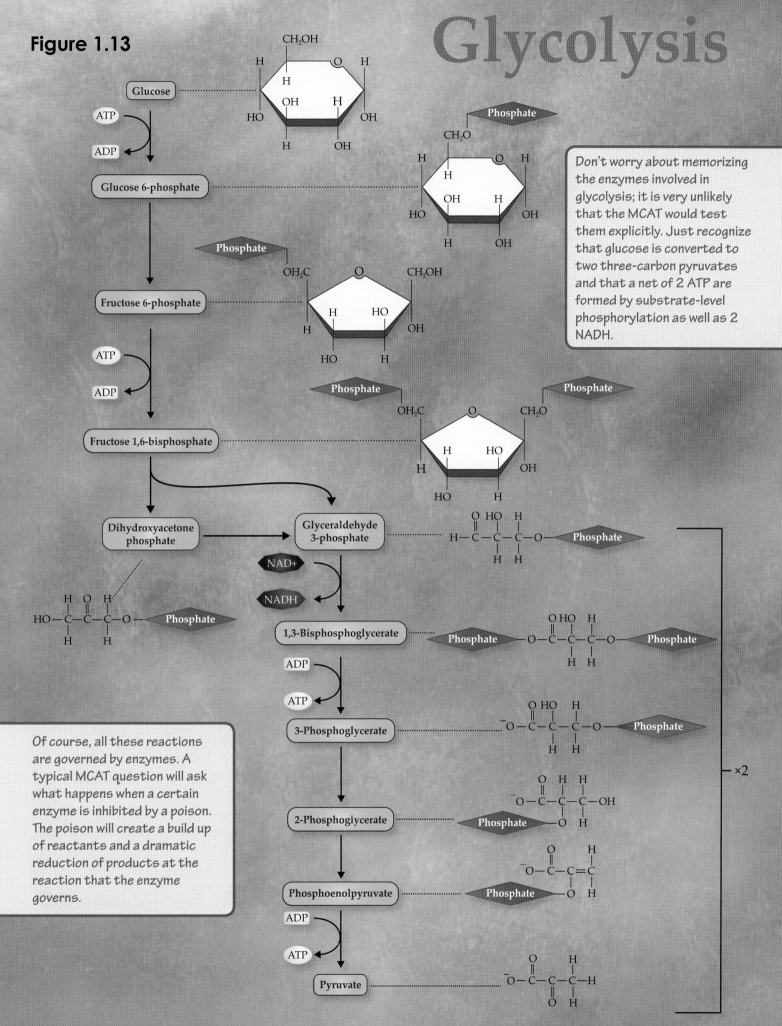

Don't worry about memorizing the enzymes involved in glycolysis; it is very unlikely that the MCAT would test them explicitly. Just recognize that glucose is converted to two three-carbon pyruvates and that a net of 2 ATP are formed by substrate-level phosphorylation as well as 2 NADH.

Of course, all these reactions are governed by enzymes. A typical MCAT question will ask what happens when a certain enzyme is inhibited by a poison. The poison will create a build up of reactants and a dramatic reduction of products at the reaction that the enzyme governs.

## 1.14 Fermentation

**Fermentation** is anaerobic respiration. It includes the process of glycolysis, the reduction of pyruvate to ethanol or lactic acid, and the oxidation of the NADH back to the NAD$^+$. Yeast and some microorganisms produce ethanol, while human muscle cells and other microorganisms produce lactic acid. Fermentation takes place when a cell or organism is either unable to assimilate the energy from NADH and pyruvate, or has no oxygen available to do so. In fermentation, the NAD$^+$ is restored for use in its role in glycolysis as a coenzyme, and the lactic acid or ethanol with carbon dioxide is expelled from the cell as a waste product.

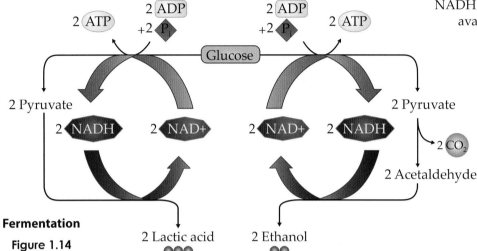

**Fermentation**

**Figure 1.14**

Understand that fermentation recycles NADH back to NAD$^+$. Yeast ferment pyruvate to the ethanol, a 2 carbon molecule, while animal muscle ferments pyruvate to lactic acid, a 3 carbon molecule.

When an animal muscle uses up oxygen faster than the blood can supply it, the muscles cells will switch to fermentation producing lactic acid.

## 1.15 Aerobic Respiration

**Aerobic respiration** requires oxygen (Figure 1.15). If oxygen is present in a cell that is capable of aerobic respiration, the products of glycolysis (pyruvate and NADH) will move into the **matrix of a mitochondrion**. The outer membrane of a mitochondrion is permeable to small molecules, and both pyruvate and NADH pass via facilitated diffusion through a large membrane protein called *porin*. The **inner mitochondrial membrane**, however, is less permeable. Although pyruvate moves into the matrix via facilitated diffusion, each NADH (depending upon the mechanism used for transport) may or may not require the hydrolysis of ATP. Once inside the matrix, pyruvate is converted to **acetyl CoA** in a reaction that produces NADH and $CO_2$.

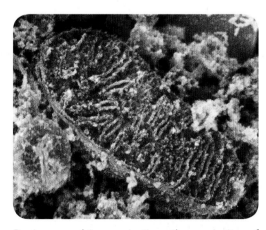

During aerobic respiration the majority of ATPs are produced inside the mitochondrion.

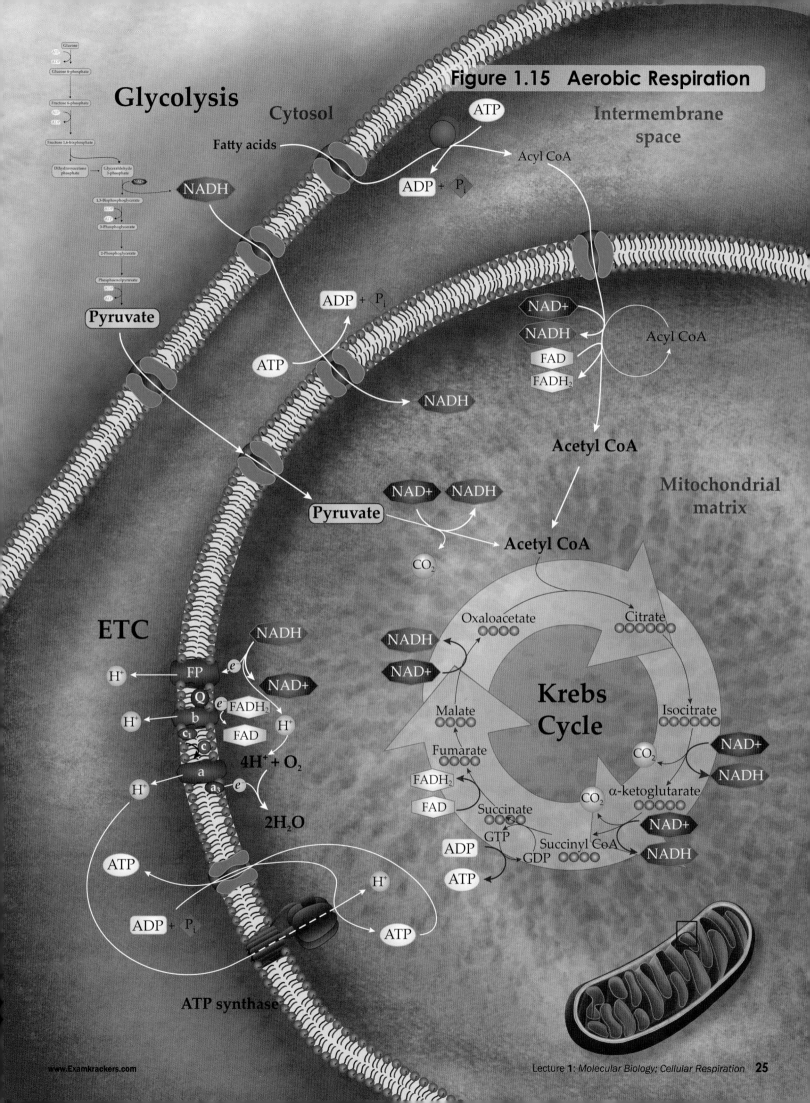

## Glycolysis

Cytosol

### Figure 1.15 Aerobic Respiration

Fatty acids

ATP

Intermembrane space

NADH

Acyl CoA

ADP + P$_i$

**Pyruvate**

ADP + P$_i$

NAD+

NADH

ATP

FAD

FADH$_2$

Acyl CoA

NADH

**Acetyl CoA**

Mitochondrial matrix

NAD+   NADH

**Pyruvate**

CO$_2$

**Acetyl CoA**

### ETC

NADH

Oxaloacetate

Citrate

H$^+$        FP   $e$

NADH

NAD+

Q   $e$   FADH$_2$

**Krebs Cycle**

H$^+$        b

c$_1$        FAD        H$^+$

Malate

Isocitrate

c

4H$^+$ + O$_2$

Fumarate

CO$_2$        NAD+

a

FADH$_2$

NADH

H$^+$        a$_3$   $e$

FAD

CO$_2$        α-ketoglutarate

2H$_2$O

Succinate

NAD+

ATP

GTP

Succinyl CoA

NADH

ADP        GDP

ADP + P$_i$

H$^+$

ATP

ATP

**ATP synthase**

## 1.16 Krebs Cycle

Acetyl CoA is a coenzyme which transfers two carbons (two carbons from pyruvate) to the 4-carbon oxaloacetic acid to begin the **Krebs cycle** (also called the **citric acid cycle**). Each turn of the Krebs cycle (Figure 1.16) produces 1 ATP, 3 NADH, and 1 $FADH_2$. The process of ATP production in the Krebs cycle is called **substrate-level phosphorylation**. During the cycle, two carbons are lost as $CO_2$, and oxaloacetic acid is reproduced to begin the cycle over again.

Sir Hans Krebs (1900-81), German-British biochemist and Nobel Laureate

Note that the Krebs Cycle turns twice; once for each pyruvate generated by glycolysis.

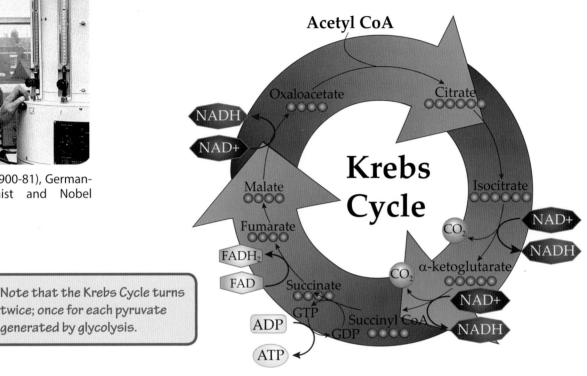

**Figure 1.16   Kreb's Cycle**

Triglycerides can also be catabolized for ATP. Fatty acids are converted into acyl CoA along the outer membrane of the mitochondrion and endoplasmic reticulum at the expense of 1 ATP. They are then brought into the matrix, and two carbons at a time are cleaved from the acyl CoA to make acetyl CoA. This reaction also produces $FADH_2$ and NADH for every two carbons taken from the original fatty acid. Acetyl CoA then enters into the Krebs cycle as usual. The glycerol backbone is converted to PGAL.

Amino acids are deaminated in the liver. The deaminated product is either chemically converted to pyruvic acid or acetyl CoA, or it may enter the Krebs cycle at various stages depending upon which amino acid was deaminated.

**Figure 1.17   Digestion Metabolism of Proteins and Fats**

Proteins → Amino acids → $NH_3$

Polysaccharides → Simple sugars → PGAL → Pyruvic acid → Acetyl CoA → Krebs cycle

Fats → glycerol, fatty acid / fatty acid / fatty acid → Acetyl CoA

Amino acids must first be deaminated, after which they can either enter the Krebs Cycle as pyruvate or as one of the Krebs Cycle intermediates. Nucleotides must also be deaminated before entering the Krebs Cycle as one of its intermediates. Fats are converted to Acetyl-CoA, which can then enter the Krebs Cycle.

The **electron transport chain (ETC)** (Figure 1.18) is a series of proteins, including cytochromes with heme, in the inner membrane of the mitochondrion. The first protein complex in the series oxidizes NADH by accepting its high energy electrons. Electrons are then passed down the protein series and ultimately accepted by oxygen to form water. As electrons are passed along, protons are pumped into the intermembrane space for each NADH. This establishes a proton gradient called the **proton-motive force** which propels protons through **ATP synthase** to manufacture ATP. Production of ATP in this fashion is called **oxidative phosphorylation**. From 2 to 3 ATPs are manufactured for each NADH. $FADH_2$ works in a similar fashion to NADH, except $FADH_2$ reduces a protein further along in the ETC series, and thus only produces about 2 ATPs.

> You should know that aerobic respiration produces about 36 net ATPs (includes glycolysis). You should also know that 1 NADH brings back 2 to 3 ATPs and that 1 $FADH_2$ brings back about 2 ATPs. Know how many NADHs, $FADH_2$s, and ATPs are produced in each turn of the Krebs cycle, and that one glucose produces two turns. Don't worry too much about the fatty acids and amino acids. Just realize that they can be catabolized for energy via the Krebs cycle.

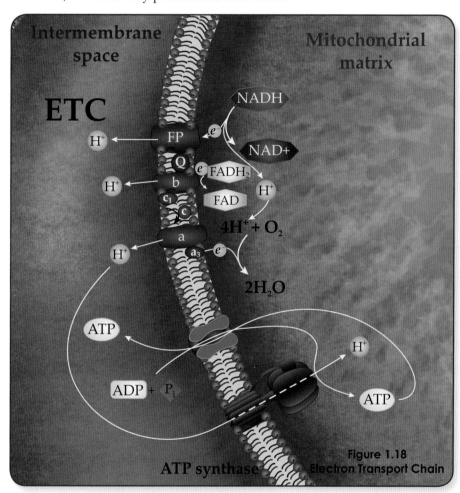

**Figure 1.18**
Electron Transport Chain

Notice that the environment in the intermembrane space has a lower pH than the matrix.

You don't have to memorize the names of all the chemicals; however, you should recognize them as being in the Krebs cycle. You should pay special attention to acetyl CoA and ATP synthase. Also know the difference between oxidative phosphorylation and substrate level phosphorylation. You should definitely know the products and reactants for respiration:

$$Glucose + O_2 \rightarrow CO_2 + H_2O$$
(This reaction is not balanced)

This is a combustion reaction. Finally, be sure that you remember that the final electron acceptor is oxygen. This is why oxygen is necessary for aerobic respiration.

## 1.18 Terms You Need To Know

| Terms | | |
|---|---|---|
| α-helix | FADH$_2$ | Phosphodiester Bonds |
| β-pleated Sheet | Fats | Phospholipids |
| Active Site | Fatty Acids | Polypeptides |
| Adipocytes | Feedback Inhibition | Positive Feedback |
| Aerobic Respiration | Fermentation | Primary Structure |
| Allosteric Regulation | Glucose | Proenzyme |
| Amino Acids | Glycerol | Proteins |
| Amphipathic | Glycogen | Proton-Motive Force |
| Anaerobic Respiration | Glycolysis | Pyruvate |
| ATP | Hydrogen Bond | Quaternary Structure |
| ATP Synthase | Hydrolysis | RNA |
| Carbohydrates | Hydrophilic | Saturation Kinetics |
| Catalyst | Hydrophobic | Saturated Fatty Acids |
| Cellular Respiration | Induced-Fit Model | Secondary Structure |
| Cellulose | Inner Mitochondrial | Side Chains |
| Citric Acid Cycle | Membrane | Starch |
| Coenzymes | Irreversible Inhibitors | Steroids |
| Cofactor | Krebs Cycle | Substrate-Level |
| Competitive Inhibitors | Lipid | Phosphorylation |
| Cooperativity | Lock and Key Model | Substrates |
| Cyclic AMP | Mitochondrial Matrix | Tertiary Structure |
| Disulfide Bonds | Metabolism | Triglycerides |
| Dehydration | Minerals | Unsaturated Fatty |
| Denatured | NADH | Acids |
| DNA | Negative Feedback | Vitamins |
| Double Helix | Noncompetitive | Water |
| Electron Transport | Inhibitors | Zymogen |
| Chain (ETC) | Nucleic Acids | |
| Enzymes | Nucleotides | |
| Enzyme Specificity | Oils | |
| Enzyme-Substrate | Oxidative | |
| Complex | Phosphorylation | |
| Essential Amino Acid | Peptide Bonds | |

17. As electrons are passed from one protein complex to another, the final electron acceptor of the electron-transport chain is:

    A. ATP.
    B. $H_2O$.
    C. NADH.
    D. $O_2$.

18. In a human renal cortical cell, the Krebs cycle occurs in the:

    A. cytosol.
    B. mitochondrial matrix.
    C. inner mitochondrial membrane.
    D. intermembrane space.

19. As electrons move within the electron transport chain, each intermediate carrier molecule is:

    A. oxidized by the preceding molecules and reduced by the following molecule.
    B. reduced by the preceding molecule and oxidized by the following molecule.
    C. reduced by both the preceding and the following molecules.
    D. oxidized by both the preceding and the following molecules.

20. In aerobic respiration, the energy from the oxidation of NADH:

    A. directly synthesizes ATP.
    B. passively diffuses protons from the intermembrane space into the matrix.
    C. establishes a proton gradient between the intermembrane space and the mitochondrial matrix.
    D. pumps protons through ATP synthase.

21. Which of the following processes occurs under both aerobic and anaerobic conditions?

    A. fermentation
    B. Krebs cycle
    C. glycolysis
    D. oxidative phosphorylation

22. Glycolysis takes place in the cytoplasm of an animal cell. Which of the following is NOT a product or reactant in glycolysis?

    A. glucose
    B. pyruvate
    C. ATP
    D. $O_2$

23. What is the net ATP production from fermentation?

    A. 0 ATP
    B. 2 ATP
    C. 4 ATP
    D. 8 ATP

24. Heart and liver cells can produce more ATP for each molecule of glucose than other cells in the body. This most likely results from:

    A. a more efficient ATP synthase on the outer mitochondrial membrane.
    B. an additional turn of the Kreb's cycle for each glucose molecule.
    C. a more efficient mechanism for moving NADH produced in glycolysis into the mitochondrial matrix.
    D. production of additional NADH by the citric acid cycle.

*Notes:*

# GENES

"I look good in genes..."

## 2.1 The Gene

A **gene** is a sequence of DNA nucleotides that codes for rRNA, tRNA, or a single polypeptide via an mRNA intermediate. (In the case of a virus, a gene may be an RNA sequence.) It is the gene (i.e. DNA sequence), and not the trait (i.e. eye color) that is inherited. Eukaryotes have more than one copy of some genes, while **prokaryotes** have only one copy of each gene. Genes are often referred to as *unique sequence DNA*, while regions of non-coding DNA (found only in eukaryotes) are called *repetitive sequence DNA*. In eukaryotes, unique sequence DNA dominates. Eukaryotic genes that are being actively transcribed by a cell are associated with regions of DNA called euchromatin, while genes not being actively transcribed are associated with tightly packed regions of DNA called heterochromatin.

> Generally speaking: one gene; one polypeptide. One exception is postranscriptional processing of RNA.

There are between 20,000 and 25,000 genes in the human genome. The entire DNA sequence of an organism is called the **genome**. Only a little over 1% of the human genome actually codes for protein. Variation of the nucleotide sequence among humans is small; human DNA differs from individual to individual at approximately 1 nucleotide out of every 1200 or about 0.08%. The variation between humans and chimpanzees is about 2%.

> A small variation in a genome can make a big difference.

**The Central Dogma** of gene expression is that DNA is transcribed to RNA, which is translated to amino acids forming a protein (Figure 2.1). All living organisms use this same method to express their genes. Retroviruses (not a living organism) store their information as RNA and must first convert their RNA to DNA in order to express their genes.

> DNA ⇨ RNA ⇨ Protein

**Figure 2.1  Central Dogma of Molecular Biology**

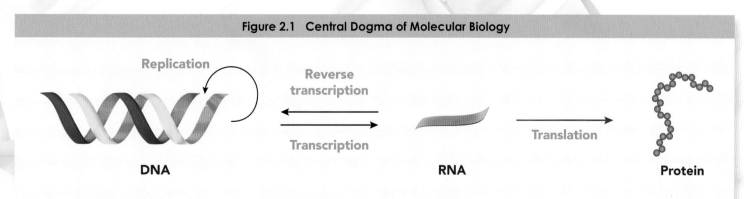

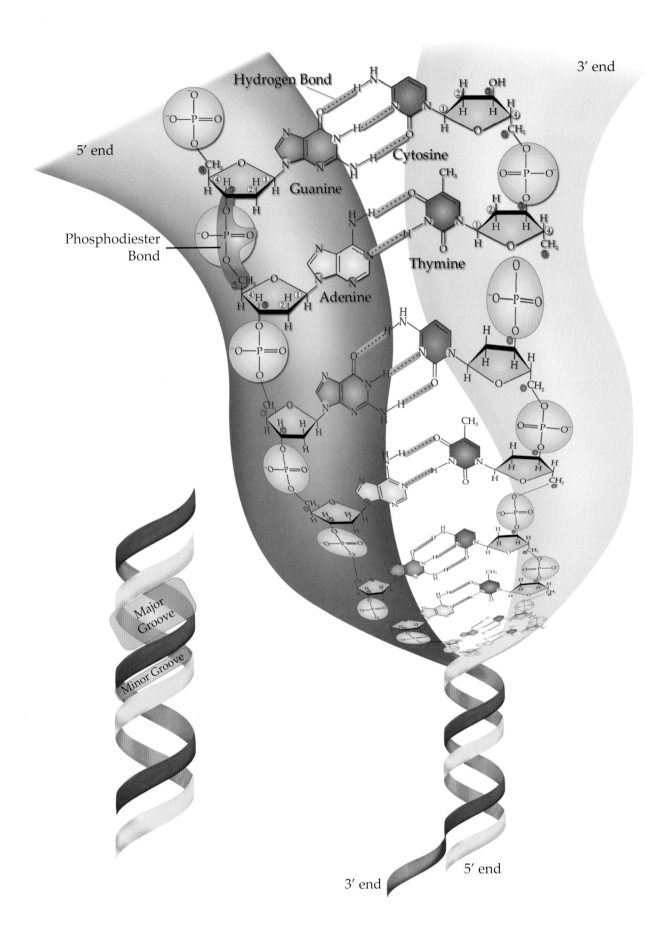

**Figure 2.2 DNA Double Helix**

## 2.2 DNA

DNA (*deoxyribonucleic acid*) is a polymer of nucleotides. DNA nucleotides differ from each other only in their nitrogenous base. Four nitrogenous bases exist in DNA: **adenine (A)**, **guanine (G)**, **cytosine (C)**, **thymine (T)**. Adenine and guanine are two ring structures called **purines**, while cytosine and thymine are single ring structures called **pyrimidines** (Figure 2.3). The DNA nucleotide with the base adenine is called *adenosine phosphate*; however, it is common to refer to the nucleotides by their base name only. Each nucleotide is bound to the next by a **phosphodiester bond** between the third carbon of one deoxyribose and the fifth carbon of the other creating the sugar-phosphate backbone of a single strand of DNA with a 5′→ 3′ **directionality**. The 5′ and 3′ indicate the carbon numbers on the sugar (Figure 2.2). The end 3′ carbon is attached to an –OH group and the end 5′ arbon is attached to a phosphate group. In a living organism, two DNA strands lie side by side in opposite 3′ → 5′ directions (**antiparallel**) bound together by hydrogen bonds between nitrogenous bases to form a **double stranded** structure. This hydrogen bonding is commonly referred to as **base-pairing**. The length of a DNA strand is measured in base-pairs **(bp)**. Under normal circumstances, the hydrogen bonds form only between specific purine-pyrimidine pairs; adenine forms 2 hydrogen bonds with thymine, and guanine forms 3 hydrogen bonds with cytosine. Therefore, in order for two strands to bind together, their bases must match up in the correct order. Two strands that match in such a fashion are called **complementary strands**. When complementary strands bind together, they curl into a **double helix** (Figure 2.2). The double helix contains two distinct grooves called the major groove and the minor groove. Each groove spirals once around the double helix for every ten base-pairs. The diameter of the double helix is about 2 nanometers or 13 times the diameter of a carbon atom.

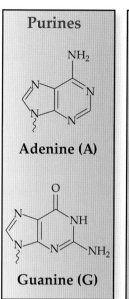
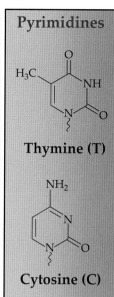

**Figure 2.3   Nucleotide Bases in DNA**

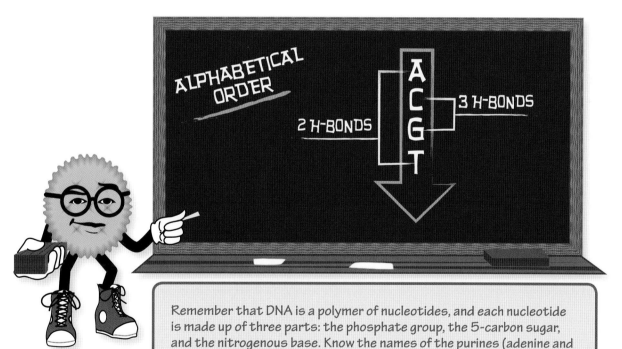

Remember that DNA is a polymer of nucleotides, and each nucleotide is made up of three parts: the phosphate group, the 5-carbon sugar, and the nitrogenous base. Know the names of the purines (adenine and guanine) and the pyrimidines (cytosine and thymine). A good way to remember this is: "pyrimidine" contains a "y," and so do "cytosine" and "thymine." Uracil, a nitrogenous base in RNA, is also a pyrimidine. This is easy to remember since it replaces the pyrimidine thymine. Know the pairings (AT, GC) and the number of H-bonds between each pair. Two hydrogen bonds hold together AT, while three hold together CG. This means that GC bonds require more energy to separate.

## 2.3 Replication

One time in each life cycle, a cell replicates its DNA. **DNA replication** is **semiconservative**. This means that when a new double strand is created, it contains one strand from the original DNA, and one newly synthesized strand.

The process of DNA replication (Figure 2.4) is governed by a group of proteins called a *replisome*. Replication does not begin at the end of a chromosome, but toward the middle at a site called the *origin of replication*. A single eukaryotic chromosome contains multiple origins on each chromosome, while replication in prokaryotes usually takes place from a single origin on the circular chromosome. From the origin, two replisomes proceed in opposite directions along the chromosome making replication a **bidirectional** process. The point where a replisome is attached to the chromosome is called the *replication fork*. Each chromosome of eukaryotic DNA is replicated in many discrete segments called *replication units* or *replicons*.

As part of the replisome, *DNA helicase* unwinds the double helix separating the two strands. **DNA polymerase**, the enzyme that builds the new DNA strand, cannot initiate a strand from two nucleotides; it can only add nucleotides to an existing strand. *Primase*, an RNA polymerase, creates an RNA **primer** approximately 10 ribonucleotides long to initiate the strand. DNA polymerase adds deoxynucleotides to the primer and moves along each DNA strand creating a new complementary strand. DNA polymerase reads the parental strand in the $3' \rightarrow 5'$ direction, creating the new complementary strand in the $5' \rightarrow 3'$ direction. (By convention, the nucleotide sequence in DNA is written $5' \rightarrow 3'$ as well. This direction is sometimes referred to as downstream and the $3' \rightarrow 5'$ direction as upstream.) Each nucleotide added to the new strand requires the removal of a *pyrophosphate group* (two phosphates bonded together) from a deoxynucleotide triphosphate. Some of the energy derived from the hydrolysis of the pyrophosphate is used to drive replication. For instance, the DNA nucleotide containing adenine is made by cleaving the second phosphate bond in the deoxy-version of ATP. (The 'deoxy-version of ATP' just means that the hydroxyl group on the 2' carbon has been replaced with a hydrogen.)

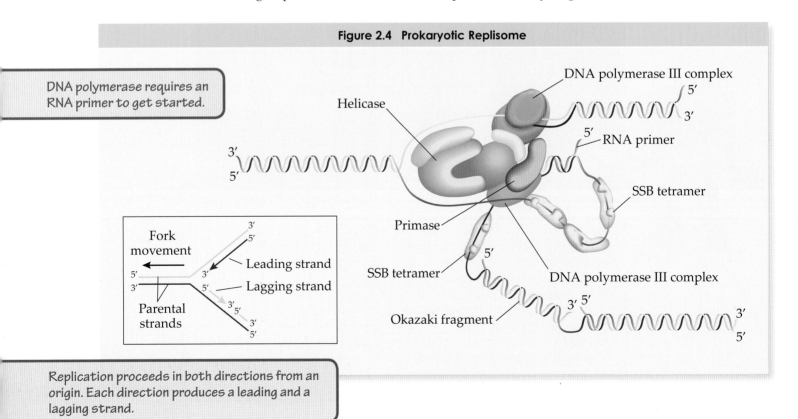

**Figure 2.4  Prokaryotic Replisome**

DNA polymerase requires an RNA primer to get started.

Helicase

DNA polymerase III complex

5'
3'

5' — RNA primer

SSB tetramer

Primase

SSB tetramer

DNA polymerase III complex

Okazaki fragment

Fork movement
Leading strand
Lagging strand
Parental strands

Replication proceeds in both directions from an origin. Each direction produces a leading and a lagging strand.

Since DNA polymerase reads in only one direction, one strand of DNA is looped around the replisome giving it the same orientation as the other. The single strand in the loop is prevented from folding back onto itself by the *SSB tetramer* proteins (also called *helix destabilizer proteins*). As is shown in Figure 2.4, the polymerization of the new strand is continuously interrupted and restarted with a new RNA primer. This interrupted strand is called the **lagging strand**; the continuous new strand is called the **leading strand**. The lagging strand is made from a series of disconnected strands called **Okazaki fragments**. Okazaki fragments are about 100 to 200 nucleotides long in eukaryotes and about 1000 to 2000 nucleotides long in prokaryotes. **DNA ligase** (Latin: ligare → to fasten or bind) moves along the lagging strand and ties the Okazaki fragments together to complete the polymer. Since the formation of one strand is continuous and the other fragmented, the process of replication is said to be **semidiscontinuous**.

Besides being a polymerase, one of the subunits in DNA polymerase is an exonuclease (it removes nucleotides from the strand). This enzyme automatically proofreads each new strand, and makes repairs when it discovers any mismatched nucleotides, such as thymine matched with guanine. DNA replication in eukaryotes is extremely accurate. Only one base in $10^9$–$10^{11}$ is incorrectly incorporated.

In order to complete the copy of an entire genome, replication must be fast. The DNA polymerase shown in Figure 2.4 moves at over 500 nucleotides per second. DNA polymerase in humans moves much more slowly at around 50 nucleotides per second. However, multiple origins of replication allow the over 6 billion base pairs that make up the 46 human chromosomes to be replicated quite quickly. Replication in a human cell requires about 8 hours.

The ends of eukaryotic chromosomal DNA possess telomeres. **Telomeres** are repeated six nucleotide units from 100 to 1,000 units long that protect the chromosomes from being eroded through repeated rounds of replication. *Telomerase* catalyzes the lengthening of telomeres.

Although there are some differences, replication in eukaryotes and prokaryotes is very similar. Except where specified, the process described above is accurate for both.

> Replication has five steps:
> 1. Helicase unzips the double helix;
> 2. RNA Polymerase builds a primer;
> 3. DNA Polymerase assembles the leading and lagging strands;
> 4. the primers are removed;
> 5. Okazaki fragments are joined.

> DNA replication is fast and accurate.

## 2.4 | RNA

**RNA (ribonucleic acid)** is identical to DNA in structure except that:

1) carbon number 2 on the pentose is not "deoxygenated" (it has a hydroxyl group attached);

2) RNA is **single stranded**; and

3) RNA contains the pyrimidine **uracil** (shown in Figure 2.5) instead of thymine.

Unlike DNA, RNA can move through the nuclear pores and is not confined to the nucleus. Three important types of RNA are mRNA, rRNA, and tRNA. **mRNA (messenger RNA)** delivers the DNA code for amino acids to the cytosol where the proteins are manufactured. **rRNA (ribosomal RNA)** combines with proteins to form **ribosomes**, the intracellular complexes that direct the synthesis of proteins. rRNA is synthesized in the **nucleolus**. **tRNA (transfer RNA)** collects amino acids in the cytosol, and transfers them to the ribosomes for incorporation into a protein. Notice the similarity between uracil and thymine. This is a common cause of mutations in DNA.

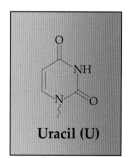

**Uracil (U)**

**Figure 2.5   Uracil**

> You should know these differences between DNA and RNA. DNA is made from deoxyribose; RNA is made from ribose. DNA is double stranded; RNA is single stranded. DNA has thymine; RNA has uracil. DNA is produced by replication; RNA is produced by transcription. In eukaryotes, DNA is only in the nucleus and mitochondrial matrix only, while RNA is also in the cytosol.

## 2.5 Transcription

All RNA is manufactured from a DNA template in a process called **transcription**. Since DNA cannot leave the nucleus or the mitochondrial matrix, eukaryotic transcription must take place only in these two places. The beginning of transcription is called **initiation**. In initiation, a group of proteins called *initiation factors* finds a promoter on the DNA strand, and assembles a *transcription initiation complex*, which includes **RNA polymerase**. Prokaryotes have one type of RNA polymerase, whereas eukaryotes (other than plants) have three: one for rRNA; one for mRNA and some snRNAs; and one for tRNA and other RNAs. A **promoter** is a sequence of DNA nucleotides that designates a beginning point for transcription. The promoter in prokaryotes is located at the beginning of the gene (said to be upstream). The transcription start point is part of the promoter. The first base-pair located at the transcription start point is designated +1; base-pairs located before the start point such as those in the promoter are designated by negative numbers. The most commonly found nucleotide sequence of a promoter recognized by the RNA polymerase of a given species is called the *consensus sequence*. Variation from the consensus sequence causes RNA polymerase to bond less tightly and less often to a given promoter, which leads to those genes being transcribed less frequently.

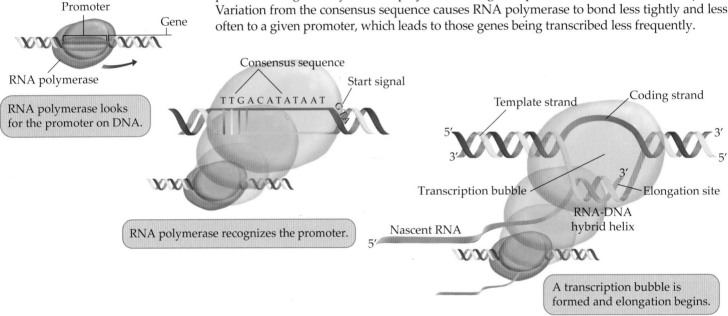

Figure 2.6 Transcription

After binding to the promoter, RNA polymerase unzips the DNA double helix creating a *transcription bubble*. Next the complex switches to **elongation** mode. In elongation, RNA polymerase transcribes only one strand of the DNA nucleotide sequence into a complementary RNA nucleotide sequence. Only one strand in a molecule of double stranded DNA is transcribed. This strand is called the *template strand* or (–) *antisense strand*. The other strand, called the *coding strand* or (+) *sense strand* protects its partner against degradation. Like DNA polymerase, RNA polymerase moves along the DNA strand in the 3′ → 5′ direction building the new RNA strand in the 5′ → 3′. Transcription proceeds ten times more slowly than DNA replication. In addition, RNA polymerase does not contain a proofreading mechanism, and the rate of errors for transcription is higher than for replication. (Errors in RNA are not called mutations.) Since the errors are created in RNA, they are not transmitted to progeny. Most genes are transcribed many times in a cell life cycle, so the problems arising from errors in transcription are not generally harmful.

The end of transcription is called **termination**, and requires a special *termination sequence* and special proteins to dissociate RNA polymerase from DNA.

Replication makes no distinction between genes. Instead, genes are activated or deactivated at the level of transcription. For all cells, most regulation of gene expression occurs at the level of transcription via proteins called **activators** and **repressors**. Activators and repressors bind to DNA close to the promoter, and either activate or repress the activity of RNA polymerase. Activators and repressors are often allosterically regulated by small molecules such as cAMP.

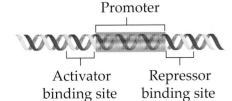

Figure 2.7 Prokaryotic Gene

The primary function of gene regulation in prokaryotes is to respond to the environmental changes. Changes in gene activity are a response to the concentration of specific nutrients in and around the cell. In contrast, lack of change or *homeostasis* of the intracellular and extracellular compartments is the hallmark of multicellular organisms. The primary function of gene regulation in multicellular organisms is to control the intra- and extracellular environments of the cell.

Prokaryotic mRNA typically includes several genes in a single transcript (*polycistronic*), whereas eukaryotic mRNA includes only one gene per transcript (*monocistronic*). The genetic unit usually consisting of the operator, promoter, and genes that contribute to a single prokaryotic mRNA is called the **operon**. A commonly used example of an operon is the *lac* operon. The lac operon codes for enzymes that allow *E. coli* to import and metabolize lactose when glucose is not present in sufficient quantities. Low glucose levels lead to high cAMP levels. cAMP binds to and activates a *catabolite activator protein (CAP)*. The activated CAP protein binds to a *CAP site* located adjacent and upstream to the promoter on the *lac* operon. The promoter is now activated allowing the formation of an initiation complex and the subsequent transcription and translation of three proteins. A second regulatory site on the *lac* operon, called the *operator*, is located adjacent and downstream to the promoter. The operator provides a binding site for a *lac* repressor protein. The *lac* repressor protein is inactivated by the presence of lactose in the cell. The *lac* repressor protein will bind to the operator unless lactose binds to the lac repressor protein.

The binding of the *lac* repressor to the operator in the absence of lactose prevents the transcription of the *lac* genes. Lactose, then, can *induce* the transcription of the *lac* operon only when glucose is not present. The promoter and gene for the *lac* repressor is located adjacent and upstream to the CAP binding site.

> Most genetic regulation occurs at transcription when regulatory proteins bind DNA and activate or inhibit its transcription. In other words, the amount of a given type of protein within a cell is likely to be related to how much of its mRNA is transcribed. One reason for this is that mRNA has a short half-life in the cytosol, so soon after transcription is completed, the mRNA is degraded and its protein is no longer translated. A second reason is that many proteins can be transcribed from a single mRNA, so there is an amplifying effect.

> An operon is a sequence of bacterial DNA containing an operator, a promoter, and related genes. The genes of an operon are transcribed on one mRNA. Genes outside the operon may code for activators and repressors.

**Figure 2.8 Structure of Lac Operon**

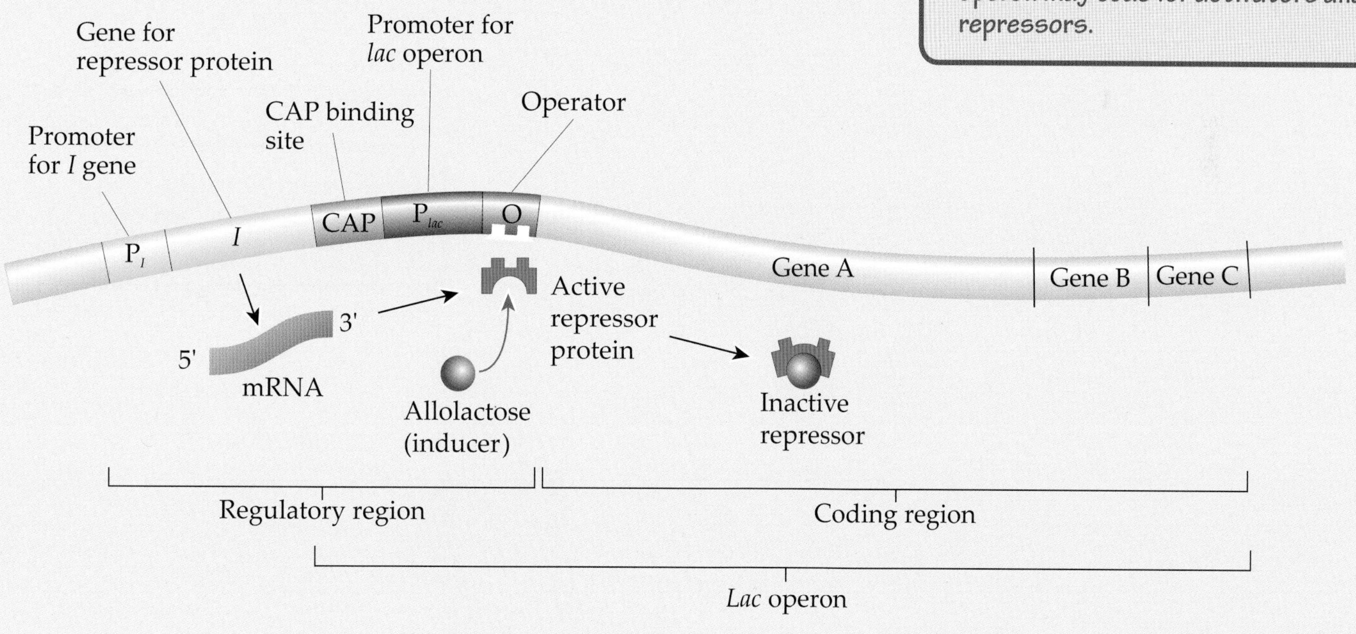

Gene regulation in eukaryotes is more complicated involving the interaction of many genes. Thus more room is required than is available near the promoter. *Enhancers* are short, non-coding regions of DNA found in eukaryotes. Their function is similar to activators and repressors but they act at a much greater distance from the promoter.

> You don't need to memorize anything about the lac operon.
> Just understand how it works.

## 2.6 Post-transcriptional Processing

Post-transcriptional processing of RNA occurs in both eukaryotic and prokaryotic cells. In prokaryotes, rRNA and tRNA go through posttranscriptional processing, but almost all mRNA is directly translated to protein. In eukaryotes, each type of RNA undergoes posttranscriptional processing and posttranscriptional processing allows for additional gene regulation.

The initial mRNA nucleotide sequence arrived at through transcription is called the **primary transcript** (also called *pre-mRNA*, or *heterogeneous nuclear RNA [hnRNA]*). The primary transcript is processed in three ways: 1) addition of nucleotides; 2) deletion of nucleotides; 3) modification of nitrogenous bases. Even before the eukaryotic mRNA is completely transcribed, its 5′ end is capped in a process using GTP. **The 5′ cap serves as an attachment site in protein synthesis and as a protection against degradation by *exonucleases*. The 3′ end is *polyadenylated* with a **poly A tail**, also to protect it from exonucleases.

The primary transcript is much longer than the mRNA that will be translated into a protein. Before leaving the nucleus, the primary transcript is cleaved into **introns** and **exons**. Enzyme-RNA complexes called small nuclear ribonucleoproteins (**snRNPs** "snurps") recognize nucleotides sequences at the ends of the introns. Several snRNPs associate with proteins to form a complex called a *spliceosome*. Inside the spliceosome, the introns are looped bringing the exons together. The introns are then excised by the spliceosomes and the exons are spliced together to form the single mRNA strand that ultimately codes for a polypeptide. Introns do not code for protein and are degraded within the nucleus. In certain cases, alternative splicing patterns can incorporate different exons into the mature mRNA. Although there are only an estimated 20,000-25,000 protein-coding genes in the human genome, there are about 120,000 proteins made possible by differential splicing of exons. Generally, intron sequences are much longer than exon sequences. Introns represent about 24 % of the genome, while exons represent about 1.1%. The average number of exons per gene is seven. The sequences of DNA that code for introns and exons are also called introns and exons.

> Post-transcriptional modification only occurs in the nucleus in eukaryotes.

> Remember that introns remain in the nucleus, and EXons EXit the nucleus to be translated.

> One reason there are more proteins than genes is that different splicing patterns of the same gene can create different polypeptides.

> Most of a typical gene consists of introns removed by snRNPs in the nucleus.

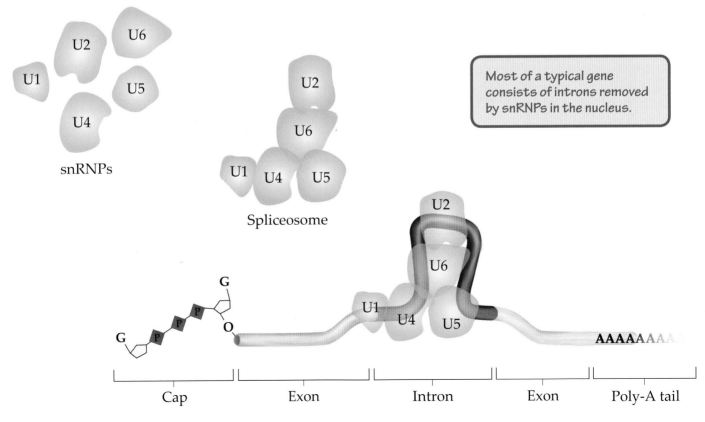

**Figure 2.9  Introns**

# DNA Technology

When heated or immersed in high concentration salt solution or high pH solution, the hydrogen bonds connecting the two strands in a double stranded DNA molecule are disrupted, and the strands separate; the DNA molecule is said to be **denatured** or *melted*. The temperature needed to separate DNA strands is called the *melting temperature* ($T_m$). Since guanine and cytosine make three hydrogen bonds while thymine and adenine make only two, DNA with more G-C base pairs has a greater $T_m$. Heating to 95°C (just below the boiling point of water) is generally sufficient to denature any DNA sequence. Denatured DNA is less viscous, denser, and more able to absorb UV light.

Separated strands will spontaneously associate with their original partner or any other complementary nucleotide sequence. Thus, the following double stranded combinations can be formed through **nucleic acid hybridization**: DNA-DNA, DNA-RNA, and RNA-RNA. Hybridization techniques enable scientists to identify nucleotide sequences by binding a known sequence with an unknown sequence.

One method bacteria use to defend themselves from viruses is to cut the viral DNA into fragments with restriction enzymes. The bacteria protect their own DNA from these enzymes by *methylation* (adding a –$CH_3$). Methylation is usually, but not always, associated with inactivated genes. **Restriction enzymes** (also called restriction endonucleases) *digest* (cut) nucleic acid only at certain nucleotide sequences along the chain (see Figure 2.10). Such a sequence is called a *restriction site* or *recognition sequence*. Typically, a restriction site will be a **palindromic** sequence four to six nucleotides long. (Palindromic means that it reads the same backwards as forwards.) Most restriction endonucleases cleave the DNA strand unevenly, leaving complementary single stranded ends. These ends can reconnect through hybridization and are termed *sticky ends*. Once paired, the phosphodiester bonds of the fragments can be joined by DNA ligase. There are hundreds of restriction endonucleases known, each attacking a different restriction site. A given sample of DNA of significant size (number of base=pairs) is likely to contain a recognition sequence for at least one restriction endonuclease. Two DNA fragments cleaved by the same endonuclease can be joined together regardless of the origin of the DNA. Such DNA is called **recombinant DNA**; it has been artificially recombined.

> To denature DNA means to separate the two strands of the double helix.

> DNA prefers to be double stranded and will look for a complementary partner.

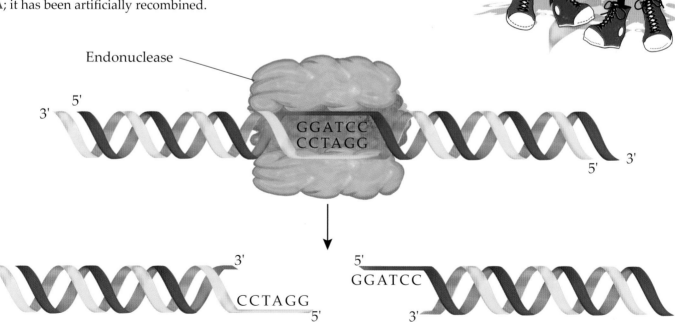

**Figure 2.10  Polypeptide Synthesis**

Recombinant DNA can be made long enough for bacteria to replicate and then placed within the bacteria using a **vector**, typically a **plasmid** or sometimes an infective virus. The bacteria can then be grown in large quantity forming a **clone** of cells containing the vector with the recombinant DNA fragment. The clones can be saved separately producing a **clone library**.

> To make a DNA library, take your DNA fragment, use a vector to insert it into a bacterium, and reproduce that bacterium like crazy. Now you have clones of bacteria with your DNA fragment.

Because not all bacteria take up the vector and not all vectors take up the DNA fragment, a library may contain some clones that do not contain vectors or contain vectors that do not contain the recombinant DNA fragment. By including in the original vector a gene for resistance to a certain antibiotic and the *lacZ* gene, which enables the bacteria to metabolize the sugar X-gal, libraries can later be screened for the appropriate clones. When an antibiotic is added to a library of clones, clones without resistance will be eliminated. Clones without resistance must not have taken up the vector.

In order to screen out clones that contain the original vector and not the DNA fragment, an endonuclease with a recognition site that cuts the *lacZ* gene in two should be used to place the DNA fragment into the vector. Since the endonuclease cleaves the *lacZ* gene, the *lacZ* gene will not work when the DNA fragment is placed in the vector. Clones with an active *lacZ* gene turn blue in the presence of X-gal. Clones with the cleaved form of the gene do not turn blue. Clones with the DNA fragment then will not turn blue when placed on a medium with X-gal.

Part of the screening process involves actually finding the desired DNA sequence from a library. One technique to find a particular gene in a library is hybridization. The radioactively labeled complementary sequence of the desired DNA fragment (called a **probe**) is used to search the library. The radiolabeled clones are identified by laying them over photographic film which they expose and non-radiolabeled clones do not.

Eukaryotic DNA contains introns. Since bacteria have no mechanism for removing introns, it is useful to clone DNA with no introns. In order to do this, the mRNA produced by the DNA is reverse transcribed using reverse transcriptase. The DNA product is called **complementary DNA** or **cDNA**. Adding DNA polymerase to cDNA produces a double strand of the desired DNA fragment.

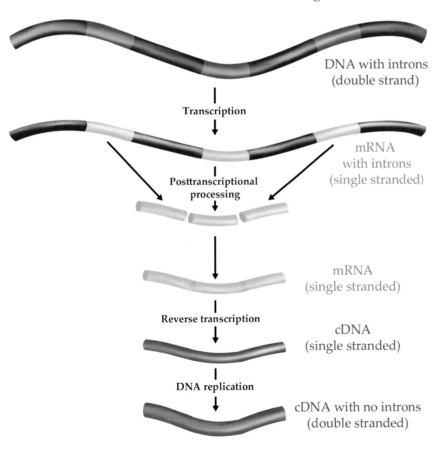

DNA with introns
(double strand)

Transcription

mRNA
with introns
(single stranded)

Posttranscriptional
processing

mRNA
(single stranded)

Reverse transcription

cDNA
(single stranded)

DNA replication

cDNA with no introns
(double stranded)

**Figure 2.11 cDNA Synthesis**

> cDNA is just DNA reverse transcribed from mRNA. The great thing about cDNA is that it lacks the introns that would normally be found in eukaryotic DNA.

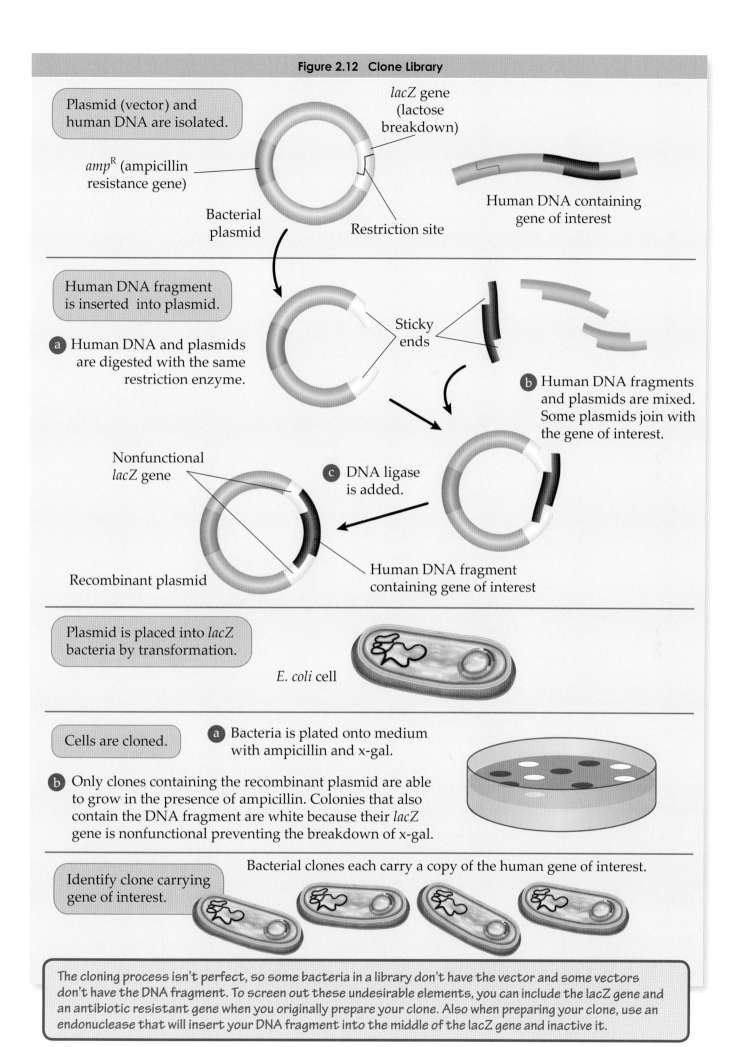

**Figure 2.12   Clone Library**

Plasmid (vector) and human DNA are isolated.

*lacZ* gene (lactose breakdown)

*amp*^R (ampicillin resistance gene)

Bacterial plasmid

Restriction site

Human DNA containing gene of interest

Human DNA fragment is inserted into plasmid.

**a** Human DNA and plasmids are digested with the same restriction enzyme.

Sticky ends

**b** Human DNA fragments and plasmids are mixed. Some plasmids join with the gene of interest.

Nonfunctional *lacZ* gene

**c** DNA ligase is added.

Recombinant plasmid

Human DNA fragment containing gene of interest

Plasmid is placed into *lacZ* bacteria by transformation.

*E. coli* cell

Cells are cloned.

**a** Bacteria is plated onto medium with ampicillin and x-gal.

**b** Only clones containing the recombinant plasmid are able to grow in the presence of ampicillin. Colonies that also contain the DNA fragment are white because their *lacZ* gene is nonfunctional preventing the breakdown of x-gal.

Identify clone carrying gene of interest.

Bacterial clones each carry a copy of the human gene of interest.

The cloning process isn't perfect, so some bacteria in a library don't have the vector and some vectors don't have the DNA fragment. To screen out these undesirable elements, you can include the lacZ gene and an antibiotic resistant gene when you originally prepare your clone. Also when preparing your clone, use an endonuclease that will insert your DNA fragment into the middle of the lacZ gene and inactive it.

A much faster method of "cloning" called **polymerase chain reaction (PCR)** has been developed using a specialized polymerase enzyme found in a species of bacterium adapted to life in nearly boiling waters. In PCR, the double strand of DNA to be "cloned" or (speaking more precisely) *amplified* is placed in a mixture with many copies of two DNA primers, one for each strand. The mixture is heated to 95°C to denature the DNA. When the mixture is cooled to 60°C, the primers hybridize (or **anneal**) to their complementary ends of the DNA strands. Next, the heat resistant polymerase is added with a supply of nucleotides, and the mixture is heated to 72°C to activate the polymerase. The polymerase amplifies the complementary strands doubling the amount of DNA. The procedure can be repeated many times without adding more polymerase because it is heat resistant. The result is an exponential increase in the amount of DNA. Starting with a single fragment, 20 cycles produces over one million copies ($2^{20}$). What used to require days with recombinant DNA techniques, can now be done in hours with PCR. Another advantage of PCR is that minute DNA samples can be amplified. PCR requires that the base sequence flanking the ends of the DNA fragment be known, so that the complementary primers can be chosen.

### Figure 2.13   PCR

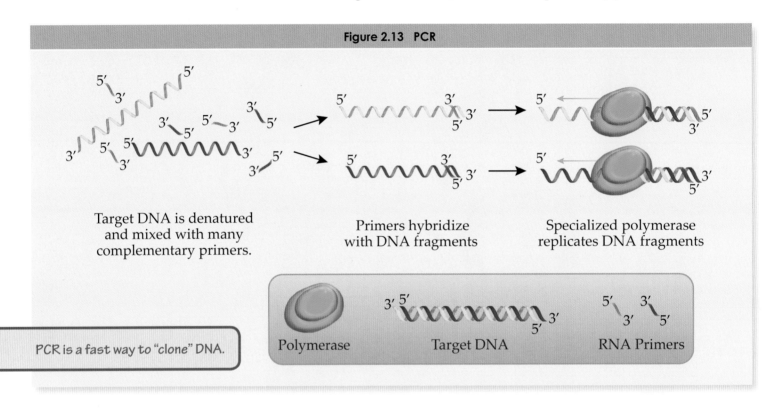

Target DNA is denatured and mixed with many complementary primers.

Primers hybridize with DNA fragments

Specialized polymerase replicates DNA fragments

Polymerase          Target DNA          RNA Primers

PCR is a fast way to "clone" DNA.

The recipe for a Southern blot is:

1. Chop up some DNA;

2. Use an electric field to spread out pieces according to size;

3. Blot it onto a membrane;

4. Add a radioactive probe made from DNA or RNA;

5. Visualize with radiographic film.

**Southern blotting** is a technique used to identify target fragments of known DNA sequence in a large population of DNA. In a southern blot, the DNA to be identified is cleaved into restriction fragments. The fragments are resolved (separated) according to size by gel electrophoresis. Large fragments move more slowly through the gel than small fragments. Next, the gel is made alkaline to denature the DNA fragments. A membrane, such as a sheet of *nitrocellulose*, is used to blot the gel which transfers the resolved single stranded DNA fragments onto the membrane. A radio-labeled probe with a nucleotide sequence complementary to the target fragment is added to the membrane. The probe hybridizes with and marks the target fragment. The membrane is exposed to radiographic film which reveals the location of the probe and the target fragment.

**Southern blotting**: A researcher transfers an electrophoresis gel containing DNA into a tray of salt solution prior to blotting the DNA onto nitrocellulose paper. The purple dye shows how far electrophoresis has progressed. Southern blotting is a technique to reveal specific fragments of DNA (deoxyribonucleic acid) in a complex mixture. The total DNA is cut into fragments and separated according to size by gel electrophoresis. The DNA is then blotted onto a sheet of nitrocellulose placed on top, and a radioactive DNA probe added to the nitrocellulose. The resulting banding pattern, revealed by autoradiography, can be used to map the structure of particular genes.

> A Southern blot identifies specific sequences of DNA by nucleic acid hybridization, and a Northern blot uses the same techniques to identify specific sequences of RNA.

A **Northern blot** is just like a Southern blot, but it identifies RNA fragments, not DNA fragments.

A **Western blot** can detect a particular protein in a mixture of proteins. First a mixture of proteins are resolved by size using electrophoresis. Next they are blotted onto a nitrocellulose membrane. An antibody (the *primary antibody*) specific to the protein in question is then added and binds to that protein. Next, a *secondary antibody-enzyme* conjugate is added. The secondary antibody recognizes and binds to the primary antibody and marks it with the enzyme for subsequent visualization. The reaction catalyzed by the enzyme attached to the secondary antibody can produce a colored, fluorescent or radioactive reaction product which can be visualized or detected with xray film.

> If Western blot shows up on the MCAT, it is likely to be described thoroughly in a passage. Just recognize that this is the one that detects a <u>protein</u> with <u>antibodies</u>.

*Restriction fragment length polymorphisms* (**RFLP**) analysis identifies individuals as opposed to identifying specific genes. The DNA of different individuals possesses different restriction sites and varying distances between restriction sites. The population of humans is *polymorphic* for their restriction sites. After fragmenting the DNA sample with endonucleases, a band pattern unique to an individual is revealed on radiographic film via Southern blotting techniques. RFLPs (pronounced "riflips") are the DNA fingerprints used to identify criminals in court cases.

The genome of one human differs from the genome of another at about one nucleotide in every 1000. These differences have been called *single nucleotide polymorphisms* (SNPs). Like RFLPs, SNPs can serve as a fingerprint to an individuals genome.

25. Which of the following is always true concerning the base composition of DNA?

    A. In each single strand, the number of adenine residues equals the number thymine residues.
    B. In each single strand, the number of adenine residues equals the number of guanine residues.
    C. In a molecule of double stranded DNA, the ratio of adenine residues to thymine residues equals the ratio of cytosine residues to guanine residues.
    D. In a molecule of double stranded DNA, the number of adenine residues plus thymine residues equals the number of cytosine residues plus guanine residues.

26. An mRNA molecule being translated at the rough endoplasmic reticulum is typically shorter than the gene from which it was transcribed because:

    A. the primary transcript was cut as it crossed the nuclear membrane.
    B. normally multiple copies of the mRNA are produced and spliced.
    C. introns in the primary transcript are excised.
    D. several expressed regions of the primary transcript have equal numbers of base pairs.

27. In PCR amplification, a primer is hybridized to the end of a DNA fragment and acts as the initiation site of replication for a specialized DNA polymerase. The DNA fragment to be amplified is shown below. Assuming that the primer attaches exactly to the end of the fragment, which of the following is most likely the primer? (Note: The N stands for any nucleotide.)

    5′-ATGNNNNNNNNNNNNNNNGCT-3′
    DNA fragment

    A. 5′-GCT-3′
    B. 5′-TAC-3′
    C. 5′-TCG-3′
    D. 5′-AGC-3′

28. Which of the following is NOT true concerning DNA replication?

    A. DNA ligase links the Okazaki fragments.
    B. Helicase unwinds the DNA double helix.
    C. Only the sense strand is replicated.
    D. DNA strands are synthesized in the 5′ to 3′ direction.

29. The gene for triose phosphate isomerase from maize (a corn plant) spans over 3400 base pairs of DNA and contains eight introns and nine exons. Which of the following would most likely represent the number of nucleotides found in the mature mRNA after posttranscriptional processing?

    A. 1050
    B. 3400
    C. 6800
    D. 13,600

30. Complementary strands of DNA are held together by:

    A. phosphodiester bonds.
    B. covalent bonds.
    C. hydrophobic interactions.
    D. hydrogen bonds.

31. Eukaryotic mRNA production occurs in the following sequence:

    A. transcription from DNA in the cytoplasm followed by post transcriptional processing on the ribosome.
    B. transcription from DNA in the nucleus followed by post transcriptional processing in the nucleus.
    C. translation from DNA in the nucleus followed by post-transcriptional processing in the nucleus.
    D. translation from DNA in the cytoplasm followed by post-transcriptional processing on the ribosome.

32. In Southern blotting, DNA fragments are separated based upon size during electrophoresis. Which of the following is true of this process?

    A. Positively charged DNA fragments move toward the cathode.
    B. Positively charged DNA fragments move toward the anode.
    C. Negatively charged DNA fragments move toward the cathode.
    D. Negatively charged DNA fragments move toward the anode.

mRNA nucleotides are strung together to form a **genetic code** which translates the DNA nucleotide sequence into an amino acid sequence and ultimately into a protein. There are four different nucleotides in RNA that together must form an unambiguous code for the 20 common amino acids. The number of possible combinations of a row of two nucleotides, where each nucleotide might contain any one of the four nitrogenous bases, is $4^2 = 16$, not enough to code for 20 amino acids (see Table 2.1). Therefore, the code must be a combination of three nucleotides. However, any three nucleotides gives $4^3 = 64$ possible combinations. These are more possibilities than there are amino acids. Thus more than one series of three nucleotides may code for any amino acid; the code is **degenerative**. But any single series of three nucleotides will code for one and only one amino acid; the code is **unambiguous**. In addition, the code is **almost universal**; nearly every living organism uses the same code.

**Table 2.1**

|   | A | C | G | T |
|---|---|---|---|---|
| **A** | AA | CA | GA | TA |
| **C** | AC | CC | GC | TC |
| **G** | AG | CG | GG | TG |
| **T** | AT | CT | GT | TT |

**Table 2.2**

| First position 5' end ↓ | Second position U C A G | | | | Third position 3' end ↓ |
|---|---|---|---|---|---|
| **U** | Phe | Ser | Tyr | Cys | U |
|  | Phe | Ser | Tyr | Cys | C |
|  | Leu | Ser | STOP | STOP | A |
|  | Leu | Ser | STOP | Trp | G |
| **C** | Leu | Pro | His | Arg | U |
|  | Leu | Pro | His | Arg | C |
|  | Leu | Pro | Gln | Arg | A |
|  | Leu | Pro | Gln | Arg | G |
| **A** | Ile | Thr | Asn | Ser | U |
|  | Ile | Thr | Asn | Ser | C |
|  | Ile | Thr | Lys | Arg | A |
|  | Met | Thr | Lys | Arg | G |
| **G** | Val | Ala | Asp | Gly | U |
|  | Val | Ala | Asp | Gly | C |
|  | Val | Ala | Glu | Gly | A |
|  | Val | Ala | Glu | Gly | G |

Memorize the start codon, AUG, and the stop codons UAA, UAG, and UGA. It is necessary to understand that a single codon (such as GUC) always codes for only one amino acid, in this case valine; but that there are other codons (GUU, GUA, GUG) that also code for valine. The first part of this means that the code is unambiguous, and the second part means that the code is degenerate. Finally, you must understand probabilities. For instance, you must be able to figure out how many possible codons exist. As discussed above, four possible nucleotides can be placed in each of 3 positions giving $4^3 = 64$.

**Try this:** A polypeptide contains 100 amino acids. How many possible amino acid sequences are there for this polypeptide?

Answer: See page 62

Three consecutive nucleotides on a strand of mRNA represent a **codon**. All but three possible codons code for amino acids. The remaining codons, UAA, UGA, and UAG, are **stop codons** (also called **termination codons**). Stop codons signal an end to protein synthesis. The start codon, AUG, also acts as a codon for the amino acid methionine.

The genetic code is given in Table 2.2. Be certain that you can read this table. For instance, the codons for lysine (Lys) are AAA and AAG. By convention, a sequence of RNA nucleotides is written 5′→ 3′.

## 2.9 Translation

Translation (Figure 2.14) is the process of protein synthesis directed by mRNA. Each of the three major types of RNA plays a unique role in translation. mRNA is the template which carries the genetic code from the nucleus to the cytosol in the form of codons. tRNA contains a set of nucleotides that is complementary to the codon, called the **anticodon**. tRNA sequesters the amino acid that corresponds to its anticodon. rRNA with protein makes up the **ribosome**, which provides the site for translation to take place. rRNA actively participates in the translation process.

The ribosome is composed of a **small subunit** and a **large subunit** made from rRNA and many separate proteins. The ribosome and its subunits are measured in terms of *sedimentation coefficients* given in *Svedberg units (S)*. The sedimentation coefficient gives the speed of a particle in a centrifuge, and is proportional to mass and related to shape and density. Prokaryotic ribosomes are smaller than eukaryotic ribosomes. Prokaryotic ribosomes are made from a 30S and a 50S subunit and have a combined sedimentary coefficient of 70S. Eukaryotic ribosomes are made of 40S and 60S subunits and have a combined sedimentary coefficient of 80S. The complex structure of ribosomes requires a special organelle called the **nucleolus** in which to manufacture them. (Prokaryotes do not possess a nucleolus, but synthesis of prokaryotic ribosomes is similar to that of eukaryotic ribosomes.) Although the ribosome is assembled in the nucleolus, the small and large subunits are exported separately to the cytoplasm.

> Notice that the sedimentation coefficients don't add up:
> 40 + 60 ≠ 80.

After posttranscriptional processing in a eukaryote, mRNA leaves the nucleus through the nuclear pores and enters the cytosol. With the help of *initiation factors* (proteins), The 5′ end attaches to the small subunit of a ribosome. A tRNA possessing the 5′-CAU-3′ anticodon sequesters the amino acid methionine and settles in at the **P site** (peptidyl site). This is the signal for the large subunit to join and form the **initiation complex**. This process is termed **initiation**.

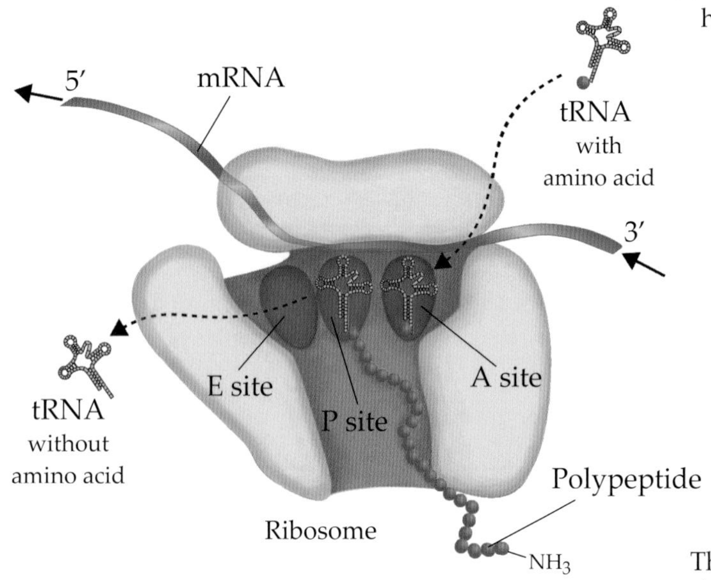

Now **elongation** of the polypeptide begins. A tRNA with its corresponding amino acid attaches to the **A site** (aminoacyl site) at the expense of two GTPs. The C-terminus (carboxyl end) of methionine attaches to the *N-terminus* (amine end) of the amino acid at the A site in a dehydration reaction catalyzed by *peptidyl transferase*, an enzyme possessed by the ribosome. In an elongation step called **translocation**, the ribosome shifts 3 nucleotides along the mRNA toward the 3′ end. The tRNA that carried methionine moves to the **E site** where it can exit the ribosome. The tRNA carrying the nascent (newly formed) dipeptide moves to the P site, clearing the A site for the next tRNA. Translocation requires the expenditure of another GTP. The elongation process is repeated until a stop codon reaches the P site.

**Figure 2.14   Translation**

Translation ends when a stop codon is reached in a step called **termination**. When a stop (or *nonsense*) codon reaches the A site, proteins known as *release factors* bind to the A site allowing a water molecule to add to the end of the polypeptide chain. The polypeptide is freed from the tRNA and ribosome, and the ribosome breaks up into its subunits to be used again for another round of protein synthesis later.

> Know the process of translation: initiation, elongation, and termination. Know the role of each type of RNA.

Even as the polypeptide is being translated, it begins folding. The amino acid sequence determines the folding conformation and the folding process is assisted by proteins called *chaperones*. In **post-translational modifications**, sugars, lipids, or phosphate groups may be added to amino acids. The polypeptide may be cleaved in one or more places. Separate polypeptides may join to form the quaternary structure of a protein.

Translation may take place on a free floating ribosome in the cytosol producing proteins that function in the cytosol, or a ribosome may attach itself to the rough ER during translation and inject proteins into the ER lumen. Proteins injected into the ER lumen are destined to become membrane bound proteins of the nuclear envelope, ER, Gogli, lysosomes, plasma membrane, or to be secreted from the cell. Free floating ribosomes are identical in structure to ribosomes that attach to the ER. The growing polypeptide itself may or may not cause the ribosome to attach to the ER depending upon the polypeptide. A 20 amino acid sequence called a **signal peptide** near the front of the polypeptide is recognized by protein-RNA **signal-recognition particle** (SRP) that carries the entire ribosome complex to a receptor protein on the ER. There the protein grows across the membrane where it is either released into the lumen or remains partially attached to the ER. The signal peptide is usually removed by an enzyme. Signal peptides may also be attached to polypeptides to target them to mitochondria, the nucleus, or other organelles.

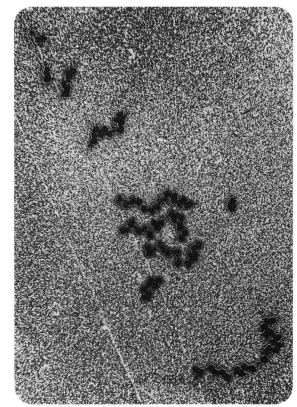

This false-color transmission electron micrograph (TEM) of a structural gene from the bacterium *Eschericia coli* shows the coupled transcription of DNA into mRNA and the simultaneous translation into protein molecules. The DNA fiber runs down the image (in yellow) from top left, with numerous ribosomes (in red) attached to each mRNA chain. The longer chains (called polysomes) are furthest from the point of gene origin.

> Translation begins on a free floating ribosome. A signal peptide at the beginning of the translated polypeptide may direct the ribosome to attach to the ER, in which case the polypeptide is injected into the lumen. Polypeptides injected into the lumen may be secreted from the cell via the Golgi or may remain partially attached to the membrane.

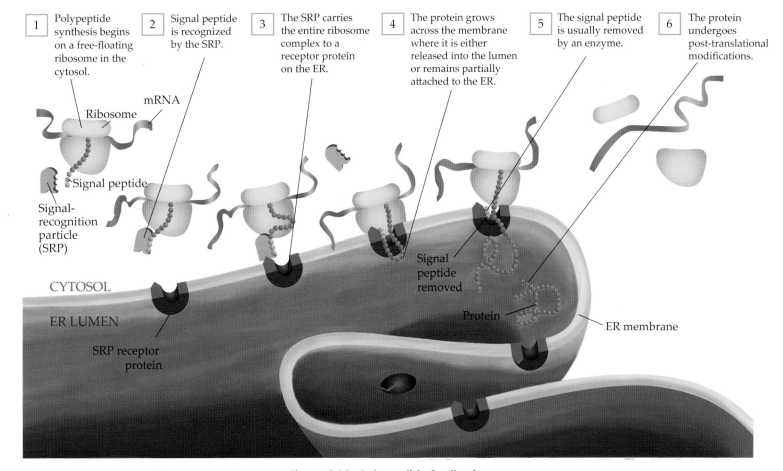

1 Polypeptide synthesis begins on a free-floating ribosome in the cytosol.

2 Signal peptide is recognized by the SRP.

3 The SRP carries the entire ribosome complex to a receptor protein on the ER.

4 The protein grows across the membrane where it is either released into the lumen or remains partially attached to the ER.

5 The signal peptide is usually removed by an enzyme.

6 The protein undergoes post-translational modifications.

mRNA

Ribosome

Signal peptide

Signal-recognition particle (SRP)

Signal peptide removed

Protein

ER membrane

CYTOSOL

ER LUMEN

SRP receptor protein

**Figure 2.15 Polypeptide Synthesis**

## 2.10 Mutations

Any alteration in the genome that is not genetic recombination is called a **mutation**. (The genome is the totality of DNA.) Mutations may occur at the chromosomal level, or the nucleotide level. A **gene mutation** is the alteration in the sequence of DNA nucleotides in a single gene. A **chromosomal mutation** occurs when the structure of a chromosome is changed. In multicellular organisms, a mutation in a somatic cell (Greek: soma → body) is called a *somatic mutation*. A somatic mutation of a single cell may have very little effect on an organism with millions of cells. A mutation in a germ cell, from which all other cells arise, can be very serious for the offspring. Only about one out of every million gametes will carry a mutation for a given gene.

Mutations can be *spontaneous* (occurring due to random errors in the natural process of replication and genetic recombination) or *induced* (occurring due to physical or chemical agents called **mutagens**). The effects on the cell are the same in either case. A mutagen is any physical or chemical agent that increases the frequency of mutation above the frequency of spontaneous mutations. If a mutation changes a single **base-pair** of nucleotides in a double strand of DNA, that mutation is called a **point mutation**. One type of point mutation called a **base-pair substitution mutation** results when one base-pair is replaced by another. A base pair substitution exchanging one purine for the other purine (A ↔ G) or one pyrimidine for the other pyrimidine (C ↔ T) is called a *transition mutation*. A base-pair substitution exchanging a purine for a pyrimidine or a pyrimidine for a purine is called a *transversion mutation*. A **missense mutation** is a base-pair mutation that occurs in the amino acid coding sequence of a gene. A missense mutation may or may not alter the amino acid sequence of a protein, and an alteration of a single amino acid may or may not have serious effects on the function of the protein. (Sickle cell anemia, for instance, is a disease caused by a single amino acid difference in hemoglobin.) If there is no change in protein function, the mutation is called a *neutral mutation*, and if the amino acid is not changed, it is called a *silent mutation*. Even a silent mutation may be significant because it may change the rate of transcription.

**Figure 2.16 Base-pair Substitutions**

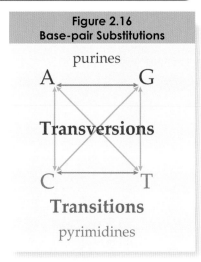

**Figure 2.17 Example of a Missense Mutation**

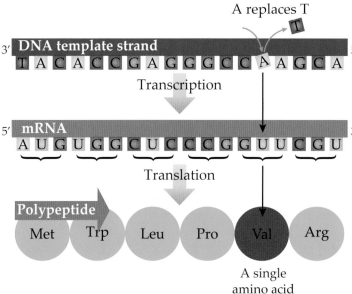

A single amino acid is changed.

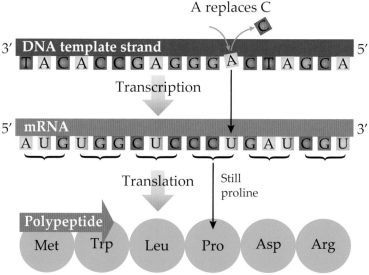

No change in amino acid sequence.

**Figure 2.18 Example of a Silent Mutation**

An **insertion or deletion** of a base-pair, may result in a **frameshift mutation**. A frameshift mutation results when the deletions or insertions occur in multiples other than three. This is because the genetic code is read in groups of three nucleotides, and the entire sequence after the mutation will be shifted so that the three base sequences will be grouped incorrectly. For instance, if a single T nucleotide were inserted into the series: AAA|GGG|CCC|AAA, so that it reads AAT|AGG|GCC|CAA|A, each 3-nucleotide sequence downstream from the mutation would be changed because the entire series would be shifted one to the right. On the other hand, if three T nucleotides were inserted randomly, the downstream sequence would not be shifted, and only one or a few 3-nucleotide sequences would be changed. AAT|TAG|GTG|CCC|AAA This is a nonframeshift mutation. Frameshift mutations often result in a completely nonfunctional protein, whereas nonframeshift mutations may still result in a partially or even completely active protein.

Male white lions are found only in wildlife reserves in South Africa, where they are selectively bred. It is not an albino, but a leucistic. Unlike albinism, which is a reduction in just melanin, leucism is caused by a mutation that reduces all types of skin or hair pigment.

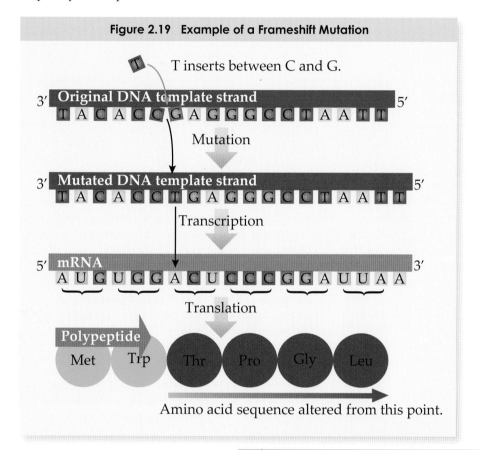

If a base-pair substitution or an insertion or deletion mutation creates a stop codon, a **nonsense mutation** results. Nonsense mutations are usually very serious for the cell because they prevent the translation of a functional protein entirely.

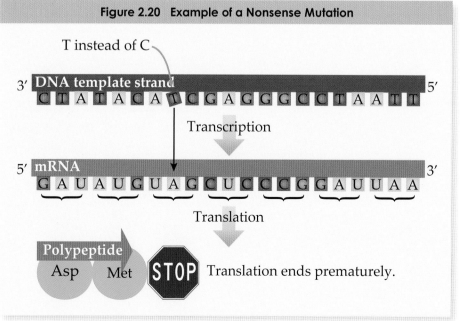

Structural changes may occur to a chromosome in the form of deletions, duplications, translocations, and inversions. Chromosomal **deletions** occur when a portion of the chromosome breaks off, or when a portion of the chromosome is lost during homologous recombination and/or crossing over events. **Duplications** occur when a DNA fragment breaks free of one chromosome and incorporates into a homologous chromosome. Deletion or duplication can occur with entire chromosomes *(aneuploidy)* or even entire sets of chromosomes *(polyploidy)*.

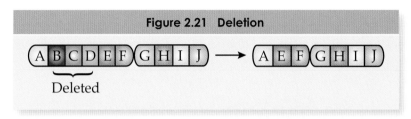

**Figure 2.21  Deletion**

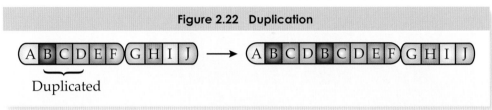

**Figure 2.22  Duplication**

When a segment of DNA from one chromosome is exchanged for a segment of DNA on another chromosome, the resulting mutation is called a reciprocal **translocation**. In **inversion** the orientation of a section of DNA is reversed on a chromosome. Translocation and inversion can be caused by transposition. Transposition takes place in both prokaryotic and eukaryotic cells. The DNA segments called **transposable elements** or **transposons** can excise themselves from a chromosome and reinsert themselves at another location. Transposons can contain one gene, several genes, or just a control element. A transposon within a chromosome will be flanked by identical nucleotide sequences. A portion of the flanking sequence is part of the transposon. When moving, the transposon may excise itself from the chromosome and move; it may copy itself and move, or copy itself and stay, moving the copy. Transposition is one mechanism by which a somatic cell of a multicellular organism can alter its genetic makeup without meiosis.

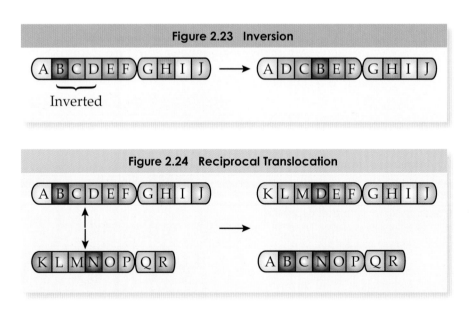

**Figure 2.23  Inversion**

**Figure 2.24  Reciprocal Translocation**

A mutation can be a **forward mutation** or a **backward mutation**. These terms refer to an already mutated organism that is mutated again. The mutation can be forward, tending to change the organism even more from its original state, or backward, tending to revert the organism back to its original state. The original state is called the **wild type**. For example, you may be working in the lab with bacteria that normally produce histidine, and you mutate a sample so that the bacteria in that sample no longer produce histidine. Now you have the wild type, his+, and the mutants, his-. If you back mutated the his-, you would produce the wild type, his+. If you forward mutated the his-, they may lose the ability to produce some other amino acid in addition to histidine.

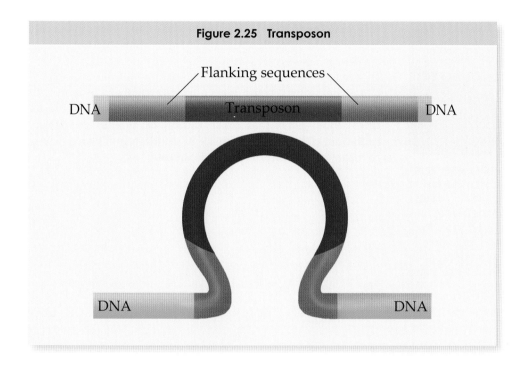

**Figure 2.25 Transposon**

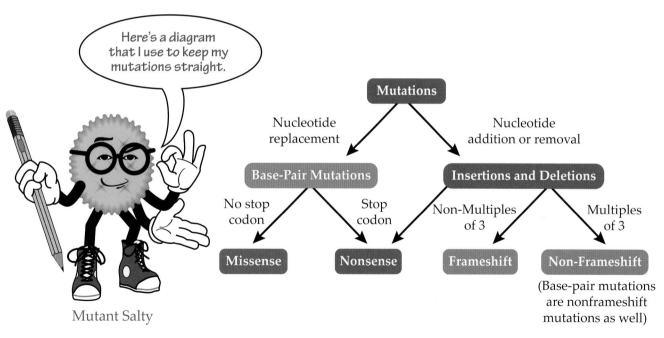

Mutant Salty

## 2.11 Cancer

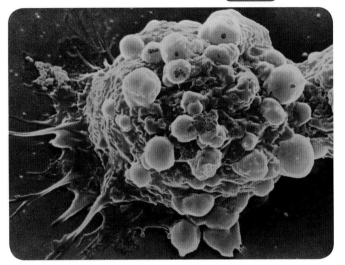

A single breast cancer cell has an uneven surface with blebs (blue) and cytoplasmic projections (red, at left). Clumps of cancerous (malignant) cells form tumors, which possess the ability to invade and destroy surrounding tissues and travel to distant parts of the body to seed secondary tumors. Malignant cells proliferate and grow in a chaotic manner, with defective cell division retained within each new generation of cells. Variations also occur in size and structure of the cancer cell from its original type.

Cancer is the unrestrained and uncontrolled growth of cells. Normal cells divide 20 to 50 times before they stop dividing and die, but cancer cells continue to grow and divide indefinitely. A mass of cancer cells is called a *tumor*. A tumor is benign if it is localized in a small lump. When an individual has a tumor invasive enough to impair function of an organ, the tumor is said to be *malignant* and the individual is said to have cancer. Cancer cells may separate from the tumor and enter the bodies circulatory systems and establish tumors in other parts of the body. This process is called metastasis.

Certain genes that stimulate normal growth in human cells are called *proto-oncogenes*. Proto-oncogenes can be converted to **oncogenes**, genes that cause cancer, by mutagens such as UV radiation, chemicals, or simply by random mutations. Mutagens that can cause cancer are called **carcinogens**.

*Notes:*

**33.** If each of the following mRNA nucleotide sequences contains three codons, which one contains a start codon?

    **A.** 3´-AGGCCGUAG-5´
    **B.** 3´-GUACCGAAC-5´
    **C.** 5´-AAUGCGGAC-3´
    **D.** 5´-UAGGAUCCC-3´

**34.** Translation in a eukaryotic cell is associated with each of the following organelles or locations EXCEPT:

    **A.** the mitochondrial matrix.
    **B.** the cytosol.
    **C.** the nucleus.
    **D.** the rough endoplasmic reticulum.

**35.** Which of the following is true concerning the genetic code?

    **A.** There are more amino acids than codons.
    **B.** Any change in the nucleotide sequence of a codon must result in a new amino acid.
    **C.** The genetic code varies from species to species.
    **D.** There are 64 codons.

**36.** The large subunit of an 80S ribosome is made from:

    **A.** rRNA only.
    **B.** protein only.
    **C.** rRNA and protein only.
    **D.** rRNA and protein bound by a phospholipid bilayer.

**37.** A tRNA molecule attaches to histidine. The anticodon on the tRNA is 5´-AUG-3´. Which of the following nucleotide sequences in an mRNA molecule might contain the codon for histidine?

    **A.** 3´-GCUAGGCCU-5´
    **B.** 3´-GGTACCTAC-5´
    **C.** 5´-CATTCTTAC-3´
    **D.** 5´-UCAUGGAUC-3´

**38.** One difference between prokaryotic and eukaryotic translation is:

    **A.** eukaryotic ribosomes are larger containing more subunits.
    **B.** prokaryotic translation may occur simultaneously with transcription while eukaryotic translation cannot.
    **C.** prokaryotes don't contain supra molecular complexes such as ribosomes.
    **D.** prokaryotic DNA is circular so does not require a termination sequence.

**39.** During translation the growing polypeptide can be found attached to a tRNA at which site on the ribosome?

    **A.** the E site
    **B.** the P site
    **C.** the A site
    **D.** the Z site

**40.** During translation, a signal peptide is synthesized and attaches to an SRP complex in order to:

    **A.** inactivate the new protein.
    **B.** activate the new protein.
    **C.** prevent the ribosome from attaching to the endoplasmic reticulum.
    **D.** direct the ribosome to attach to the endoplasmic reticulum.

## 2.12 Chromosomes

In animals, DNA is found only in the nucleus and the mitochondria.

If a double strand of all the DNA in a single human cell were stretched out straight, it would measure around 5 ft. Since the nucleus is much smaller than this, the sections of DNA that are not in use are wrapped tightly around globular proteins called **histones**. Eight histones wrapped in DNA form a **nucleosome**. Nucleosomes, in turn, wrap into coils called *solenoids*, which wrap into *supercoils*. The entire DNA/protein complex (including a very small amount of RNA) is called **chromatin** (Greek: chroma: color) (Figure 2.26). By mass, chromatin is about one third DNA, two thirds protein, and a small amount of RNA. Chromatin received its name because it absorbs basic dyes due to the large basic amino acid content in histones. The basicity of histones gives them a net positive charge at the normal pH of the cell.

The tricky thing about chromosomes is "How many are there?" In the nucleus of human cells, there are 46 chromosomes before replication, and 46 chromosomes after replication. The duplicates can be referred to separately as sister chromatids.

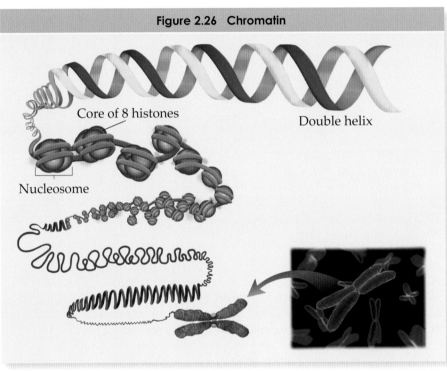

**Figure 2.26 Chromatin**

Core of 8 histones

Double helix

Nucleosome

Chromatin condensed in the manner described above is called *heterochromatin* (Greek: heteros → other). Some chromatin, called *constitutive heterochromatin*, is permanently coiled. When transcribed, chromatin must be uncoiled. Chromatin that can be uncoiled and transcribed is called euchromatin (Greek: eu → well or properly). Euchromatin is only coiled during nuclear division.

Inside the nucleus of a human somatic cell, there are 46 double stranded DNA molecules. The chromatin associated with each one of these molecules is called a **chromosome** (Greek: chroma → color, soma → body). Each chromosome contains hundreds or thousands of genes.

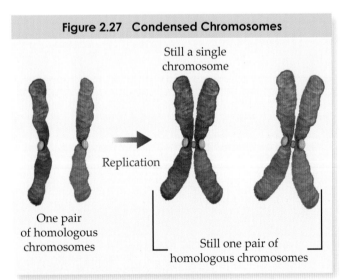

**Figure 2.27 Condensed Chromosomes**

Still a single chromosome

Replication

One pair of homologous chromosomes

Still one pair of homologous chromosomes

In human cells, each chromosome possesses a partner that codes for the same **traits** as itself. Two such chromosomes are called **homologues** (Greek: homologein → to agree with, homo → same, logia → collection). Humans possess 23 homologous pairs of chromosomes. Although the traits are the same, the actual genes may be different. Different forms of the same gene are called *alleles*. For instance, the trait may be eye color, but the eye color gene on one chromosome may code for blue eyes while the other codes for brown eyes. Any cell that contains homologous pairs is said to be **diploid** (Greek: di- → twice). Any cell that does not contain homologues is said to be **haploid** (Greek: haploos → single or simple).

Diploid means that the cell has homologous pairs. It's that simple. Diploid = homologues

## 2.13 | *Cell Life Cycle*

Every cell has a life cycle (Figure 2.38) that begins with the birth of the cell and ends with the death or division of the cell. The life cycle of a typical somatic cell of a multicellular organism can be divided into four stages: the first growth phase ($G_1$); synthesis (S); the second growth phase ($G_2$); mitosis or meiosis (M); and cytokinesis (C). $G_1$, S, and $G_2$ collectively are called **interphase**.

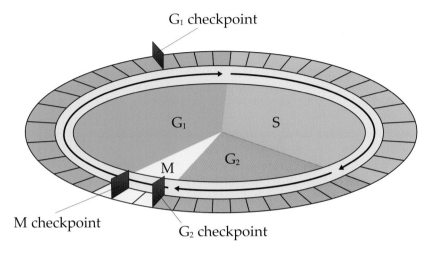

**Figure 2.28   The Cell Life Cycle**

In $G_1$, the cell has just split, and begins to grow in size producing new organelles and proteins. Regions of heterochromatin have been unwound and decondensed into euchromatin. RNA synthesis and protein synthesis are very active. The cell must reach a certain size, and synthesize sufficient protein in order to continue to the next stage. Cell growth is assessed at the $G_1$ checkpoint near the end of $G_1$. If conditions are favorable for division, the cell enters the S phase, otherwise the cell enters the $G_0$ phase. The main factor in triggering the beginning of S is cell size based upon the ratio of cytoplasm to DNA. $G_1$ is normally, but not always, the longest stage.

$G_0$ is a nongrowing state distinct from interphase. The $G_0$ phase allows for the differences in length of the cell cycle. In humans, enterocytes of the intestine divide more than twice per day, while liver cells spend a great deal of time in $G_0$ dividing less than once per year. Mature neurons and muscle cells remain in $G_0$ permanently.

In S, the cell devotes most of its energy to replicating DNA. Organelles and proteins are produced more slowly. In this stage, each chromosome is exactly duplicated, but, by convention, the cell is still considered to have the same number of chromosomes, only now, each chromosome is made of two identical sister **chromatids**.

In $G_2$, the cell prepares to divide. Cellular organelles continue to duplicate. RNA and protein (especially tubulin for microtubules) are actively synthesized. $G_2$ typically occupies 10-20% of the cell life cycle. Near the end of $G_2$ is the $G_2$ checkpoint. The $G_2$ checkpoint checks for mitosis promoting factor (MPF). When the level of MPF is high enough, mitosis is triggered.

There is an M checkpoint during mitosis that triggers the start of $G_1$.

## 2.14 Mitosis

Mitosis (Greek: mitos → cell) is nuclear division without genetic change. Mitosis has four stages: prophase, metaphase, anaphase, and telophase (Figure 2.30). These stages in turn are also divided, but this is beyond the MCAT. Mitosis varies among eukaryotes. (For instance, fungi don't have centrioles and never lose their nuclear membranes.) The following stages describe mitosis in a typical animal cell.

Prophase is characterized by the condensation of chromatin into chromosomes. **Centrioles** located in the **centrosomes** move to opposite ends of the cell. First the nucleolus and then the nucleus disappear. The **spindle apparatus** begins to form consisting of **aster** (microtubules radiating from the centrioles), *kinetochore microtubules* growing from the **centromeres** (a group of proteins located toward the center of the chromosome), and **spindle microtubules** connecting the two centrioles. (The **kinetochore** is a structure of protein and DNA located at the centromere of the joined chromtids of each chromosome.)

In **metaphase** (Greek: meta → between) chromosomes align along the equator of the cell.

**Anaphase** begins when sister chromatids split at their attaching centromeres, and move toward opposite ends of the cell. This split is termed *disjunction*. **Cytokinesis**, the actual separation of the cellular cytoplasm due to constriction of microfilaments about the center of the cell, may commence toward the end of this phase.

In **telophase** (Greek: teleios → complete) the nuclear membrane reforms followed by the reformation of the nucleolus. Chromosomes decondense and become difficult to see under the light microscope. Cytokinesis continues.

**Figure 2.29   Spindle Apparatus**

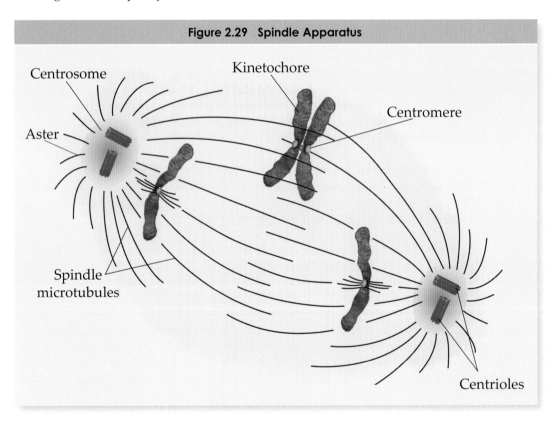

Centrosome

Kinetochore

Centromere

Aster

Spindle microtubules

Centrioles

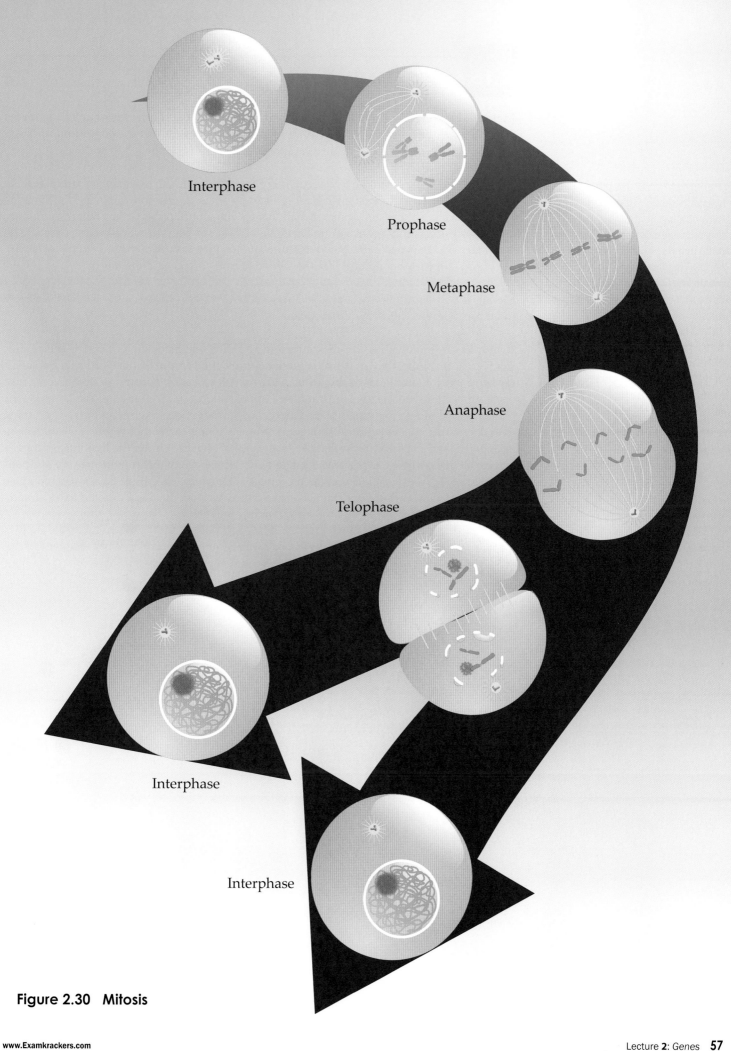

Interphase

Prophase

Metaphase

Anaphase

Telophase

Interphase

Interphase

**Figure 2.30  Mitosis**

## 2.15 Meiosis

**Meiosis** (Figure 2.32) is a double nuclear division which produces four haploid **gametes** (also called **germ cells**). In humans, only the **spermatogonium** and the **oogonium** undergo meiosis. All other cells are somatic cells and undergo mitosis only.

After replication occurs in the S phase of interphase, the cell is called a **primary spermatocyte** or **primary oocyte**. In the human female, replication takes place before birth, and the life cycle of all germ cells are arrested at the primary oocyte stage until puberty. Just before ovulation, a primary oocyte undergoes the first meiotic division to become a secondary oocyte. The secondary oocyte is released upon ovulation, and the penetration of the secondary oocyte by the sperm stimulates anaphase II of the second meiotic division in the oocyte.

Meiosis is two rounds of division called meiosis I and meiosis II. Meiosis I proceeds similarly to mitosis with the following differences.

In **prophase I** homologous chromosomes line up along side each other, matching their genes exactly. At this time, they may exchange sequences of DNA nucleotides in a process called **crossing over**. **Genetic recombination** in eukaryotes occurs during crossing over. Since each duplicated chromosome in prophase I appears as an 'x', the side by side homologues exhibit a total of four **chromatids**, and are called **tetrads** (Greek: tetras → four). If crossing over does occur, the two chromosomes are "zipped" along each other where nucleotides are exchanged, and form what is called the *synaptonemal complex*. Under the light microscope, a synaptonemal complex appears as a single point where the two chromosomes are attached creating an 'x' shape called a **chiasma** (Greek: chiasmata → cross). Genes located close together on a chromosome are more likely to cross over together, and are said to be linked.

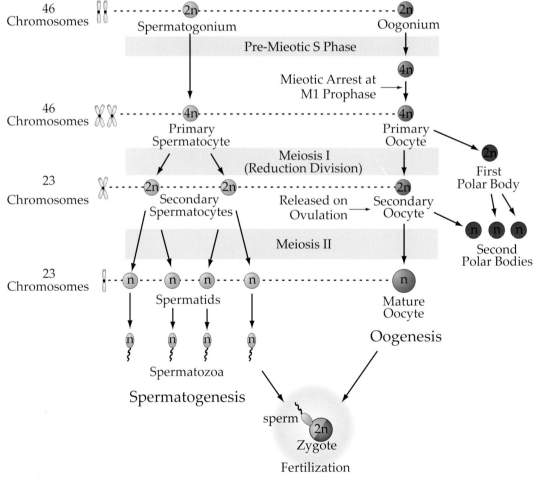

**Figure 2.31  Gamete Formation**

Prophase

Metaphase

Anaphase

*Meiosis I*

Interphase

Telophase

Prophase II

Metaphase II

*Meiosis II*

Anaphase II

Interphase

Telophase II

**Figure 2.32  Meiosis**

In **metaphase I** the homologues remain attached, and move to the metaphase plate. Rather than single chromosomes aligned along the plate as in mitosis, tetrads align in meiosis.

**Anaphase I** separates the homologues from their partners.

In **telophase I**, a nuclear membrane may or may not reform, and cytokinesis may or may not occur. In humans the nuclear membrane does reform and cytokinesis does occur. If cytokinesis occurs, the new cells are haploid with 23 replicated chromosomes, and are called **secondary spermatocytes** or **secondary oocytes**. In the case of the female, one of the oocytes, called the first **polar body**, is much smaller, and degenerates. This occurs in order to conserve cytoplasm, which is contributed only by the ovum. The first polar body may or may not go through meiosis II producing two polar bodies. These four phases together are called **meiosis I**. Meiosis I is **reduction division**.

**Meiosis II** proceeds with **prophase II**, **metaphase II**, **anaphase II**, and **telophase II** appearing under the light microscope much like normal mitosis. The final products are haploid gametes each with 23 chromosomes. In the case of the spermatocyte, four sperm cells are formed. In the case of the oocyte, a single ovum is formed. In the female, telophase II produces one gamete and a second polar body.

If during anaphase I or II the centromere of any chromosome does not split, this is called **nondisjunction**. As a result of primary nondisjunction (nondisjunction in anaphase I), one of the cells will have two extra chromatids (a complete extra chromosome) and the other will be missing a chromosome. The extra chromosome will typically line up along the metaphase plate and behave normally in meiosis II. Nondisjunction in anaphase II will result in one cell having one extra chromatid and one cell lacking one chromatid. Nondisjunction can also occur in mitosis but the ramifications are less severe since the genetic information in the new cells is not passed on to every cell in the body. Down syndrome may be caused by non disjunction of chromosome 21. An abnormal gamete with two chromosome 21s may combine with a normal gamete and the resulting zygote will have three copies of chromosome 21. This is sometimes referred to as trisomy 21.

*Notes:*

| Terms | |
|---|---|
| Adenine (A) | Gametes (Germ Cells) |
| Anaphase I | Gene |
| Anaphase II | Genetic Code |
| Anneal | Genetic Recombination |
| Anticodon | Genome |
| Antiparallel | Guanine (G) |
| Base-Pairing (BP) | Haploid |
| Base-Pair Substitution Mutation | Histones |
| Carcinogens | Homologues |
| Centromeres | Insertion |
| Chiasma | Initiation |
| Chromatids | Initiation Complex |
| Chromatin | Interphase |
| Chromosome | Introns |
| Chromosomal Mutation | Inversion |
| Clone | Kinetochore |
| Clone Library | Lagging Strand |
| Codon | Large Subunit |
| Complementary DNA (cDNA) | Leading Strand |
| Complementary Strands | Meiosis I |
| Crossing Over | Meiosis II |
| Cytokinesis | Metaphase |
| Cytosine (C) | Missense Mutation |
| Denatured | Mitosis |
| Degenerative | Mutagens |
| Deletion | Mutation |
| Diploid | Nondisjunction |
| DNA | Nonsense Mutation |
| DNA Ligase | Northern Blot |
| DNA Polymerase | Nucleic Acid Hybridization |
| Double Helix | Nucleolus |
| Elongation | Nucleosome |
| Exons | Okazaki Fragments |
| Forward Mutation | Oncogenes |
| Frameshift Mutation | Oogonium |

| Terms |
|-------|

| | |
|---|---|
| Operon | snRNPS |
| Palindromic | Southern Blotting |
| Phosphodiester Bond | Spermatogonium |
| Poly-A Tail | Spindle Apparatus |
| Plasmid | Spindle Microtubules |
| Point Mutation | Stop Codons |
| Polar Body | Telomeres |
| Polymerase Chain Reaction (PCR) | Telophase |
| Post-Translational Modifications | Termination |
| Primary Oocyte | Tetrads |
| Primary Spermatocyte | Thymine (T) |
| Primary Transcript | Traits |
| Primer | Transcription |
| Probe | Transcription Activators |
| Prokaryote | Translation |
| Promoter | Translocation |
| Prophase | Transposons |
| Recombinant DNA | Vector |
| Reduction Division | Western Blot |
| Restriction Enzymes | Wild Type |
| RFLP | |
| Ribosome | |
| RNA Polymerase | |
| Secondary Oocyte | |
| Secondary Spermatocytes | |
| Semiconservative DNA Replication | |
| Semidiscontinuous Replication | |
| Signal Peptide | |
| Small Subunit | |

Answer from page 45:

20 possible amino acids (you should know that) and 100 positions gives $20^{100}$ possible sequences.

Questions 41 through 48 are **NOT** based on a descriptive passage.

**41.** How many chromosomes does a human primary spermatocyte contain?

A. 23
B. 46
C. 92
D. 184

**42.** In which of the following life cycle phases does translation, transcription, and replication take place?

A. G1
B. S
C. G2
D. M

**43.** A scientist monitors the nucleotide sequence of the third chromosome as a cell undergoes normal meiosis. What is the earliest point in meiosis at which the scientist can deduce with certainty the nucleotide sequence of the third chromosome of each gamete?

A. prophase I
B. metaphase I
C. prophase II
D. telophase II

**44.** Which of the following is a process undergone by germ cells only?

A. meiosis
B. mitosis
C. interphase
D. cytokinesis

**45.** Which of the following represents a germ cell in metaphase I?

A.

C.

B.

D.

**46.** Which of the following characterizes mitotic prophase?

A. chromosomal alignment along the equator of the cell
B. separation of sister chromatids
C. centriole migration to the cell poles
D. cytokinesis

**47.** All of the following might describe events occurring in prophase I of meiosis EXCEPT:

A. tetrad formation.
B. spindle apparatus formation.
C. chromosomal migration.
D. genetic recombination.

**48.** When a human female is born, the development of her oocytes is arrested in:

A. prophase of mitosis.
B. prophase I of meiosis.
C. prophase II of meiosis.
D. interphase.

Notes:

# MICROBIOLOGY

## 3.1 Viruses

Viruses are tiny infectious agents, much smaller than bacteria. They are comparable in size to large proteins (Some viruses are larger and some are much smaller.) In its most basic form, a virus consists of a protein coat, called a **capsid**, and from one to several hundred genes in the form of DNA or RNA inside the capsid. No virus contains both DNA and RNA. Most animal viruses, some plant viruses, and very few bacterial viruses surround themselves with a lipid-rich **envelope** either borrowed from the membrane of their host cell or synthesized in the host cell cytoplasm. The envelope typically contains some virus-specific proteins. A mature virus outside the host cell is called a *virion*. All organisms experience viral infections.

Although there is debate as to the vitality of viruses, viruses are not currently classified as living organisms; they do not belong to any of the taxonomical kingdoms of organisms. Viruses differ from living organisms in the following ways. Although viruses can reproduce through a process involving the transfer of genetic information, they always require the host cell's reproductive machinery in order to do so. Viruses do not metabolize organic nutrients. Instead they use the ATP made available by the host cell. Unlike living organisms, viruses in their active form are not separated from their external environment by some type of barrier such as a cell wall or membrane. All living organisms possess both DNA and RNA; viruses possess either DNA or RNA, but never both. Viruses can be crystallized without losing their ability to infect.

A viral infection begins when a virus adsorbs to a specific chemical receptor site on the **host**. The host is the cell that is being infected. The chemical **receptor** is usually a specific glycoprotein on the host cell membrane. The virus cannot infect the cell if the specific receptor is not available. Next, the nucleic acid of the virus penetrates into the cell. In a **bacteriophage** (Greek: phagein: to eat), a virus that infects bacteria (Figure 3.1), the nucleic acid is normally injected through the **tail** after viral enzymes have digested a hole in the cell wall (Figure 3.2). (Notice that this indicates that some viruses also include enzymes within their capsids.) Most viruses that

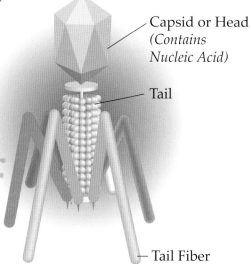

Capsid or Head
*(Contains Nucleic Acid)*

Tail

Tail Fiber

**Figure 3.1 Bacteriophage**

| Landing | Attachment | Tail contraction | Penetration and Injection |

**Figure 3.2 Adsorption and Injection**

A bacteriophage lands on the surface of a bacterium and injects its DNA into the cell.

infect eukaryotes are engulfed by an **endocytotic** process. Once inside the cell, there are two possible paths: a lysogenic infection, or a lytic infection (Figure 3.3).

In a **lytic** (Greek: lysis → separation) infection, the virus commandeers the cell's reproductive machinery and begins reproducing new viruses. There is a brief period before the first fully formed virion appears. This period is called the *eclipse period*. The cell may fill with new viruses until it lyses or bursts, or it may release the new viruses one at a time in a reverse endocytotic process. The period from infection to lysis is called the latent period. The **latent period** encompasses the eclipse period. A virus following a lytic cycle is called a **virulent virus**.

In a **lysogenic** infection, the viral DNA is incorporated into the host genome, or, if the virus is an RNA virus and it possesses the enzyme **reverse transcriptase**, DNA is actually reverse-transcribed from RNA and then incorporated into the host cell genome. When the host cell replicates its DNA, the viral DNA is replicated as well. A virus in a lysogenic cycle is called a **temperate virus**. A host cell infected with a temperate virus may show no symptoms of infection. While the viral DNA remains incorporated in the host DNA, the virus is said to be **dormant** or **latent**, and is called a **provirus** (a **prophage** [Greek: pro → before, phagein → eat] if the host cell is a bacterium). The dormant virus may become active when the host cell is under some type of stress. Ultraviolet light or carcinogens also may activate the virus. When the virus becomes active, it becomes virulent.

Be sure to know the differences between the two cycles. Pay particularly close attention to how the viral genetic material is converted to proteins and also how it is incorporated into the host cell genome, since the MCAT seems to enjoy testing this. Feel free to look back to genetics for information about transcription and translation.

Most animal viruses do not leave capsids outside the cell, but enter the cell through receptor-mediated endocytosis.

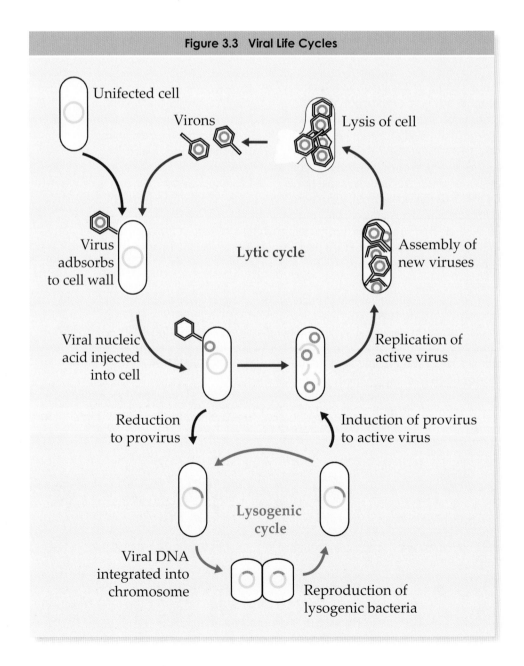

**Figure 3.3   Viral Life Cycles**

Unifected cell

Virons

Lysis of cell

Virus adbsorbs to cell wall

Lytic cycle

Assembly of new viruses

Viral nucleic acid injected into cell

Replication of active virus

Reduction to provirus

Induction of provirus to active virus

Lysogeinc cycle

Viral DNA integrated into chromosome

Reproduction of lysogenic bacteria

There are many of types of viruses. One way to classify them is by the type of nucleic acid that they possess. A virus with *unenveloped* **plus-strand RNA** is responsible for the common cold. (Therefore, not all animal viruses are enveloped.) The "plus-strand" indicates that proteins can be directly translated from the RNA. Enveloped plus-strand RNA viruses include **retroviruses** such as the virus that causes AIDS. A retrovirus carries the enzyme **reverse transcriptase** in order to create DNA from its RNA. The DNA is then incorporated into the genome of the host cell. **Minus-strand RNA** viruses include measles, rabies, and the flu. Minus-strand RNA is the complement to mRNA and must be transcribed to plus-RNA before being translated. There are even **double stranded RNA viruses**, and **single and double stranded DNA viruses**.

*Viroids* are a related form of infectious agent. Viroids are small rings of naked RNA without capsids. Viroids only infect plants. There also exists naked proteins called *prions* that cause infections in animals. Prions are capable of reproducing themselves, apparently without DNA or RNA.

UAGGCAUCUUUCGCA
⇓ (translation)
protein
**mRNA**

UAGGCAUCUUUCGCA
⇓ (translation)
protein
**Plus-strand RNA**

AUCCGUAGAAAGCGU
⇓ (transcription)
UAGGCAUCUUUCGCA
⇓ (translation)
protein
**Minus-strand RNA**

**Figure 3.4  A virus may have plus-strand or minus-strand RNA.**

| Table 3.1   Some Types of Viruses | | |
|---|---|---|
| *Disease* | *Pathogen* | *Genome* |
| A.I.D.S. | 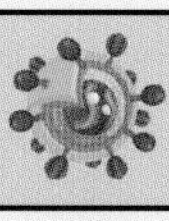 HIV | (+) Single-stranded RNA (two copies) |
| Chicken Pox, Shingles |  Varicella-zoster virus | Double-stranded DNA |
| Ebola |  Filoviruses | (-) Single-stranded RNA |
| Hepatitis B (viral) | 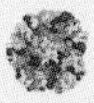 Hepadnavirus | Double-stranded DNA |
| Herpes | 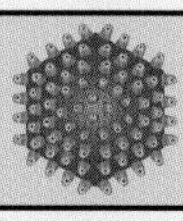 Herpes simplex virus | Double-stranded DNA |
| Influenza | 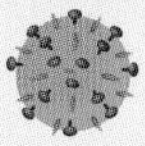 Influenza virus | (-) Single-stranded RNA (two copies) |
| Measles | 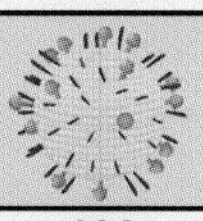 Paramyxoviruses | (-) Single-stranded RNA |
| Mononucleosis | 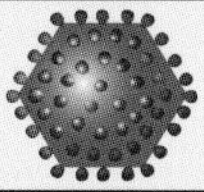 Epstein-Barr virus | Double-stranded DNA |
| Polio |  Enterovirus | (+) Single-stranded RNA |
| Rabies | 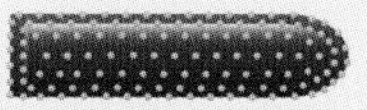 Rhabdovirus | (-) Single-stranded RNA |
| SARS | 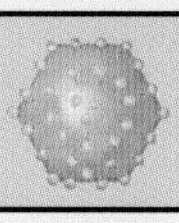 Coronavirus | (-) Single-stranded RNA |
| Small Pox | 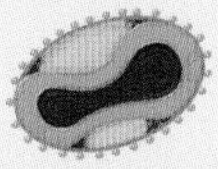 Variola virus | Double-stranded DNA |
| Yellow Fever |  Flavivirus | (+) Single-stranded RNA |

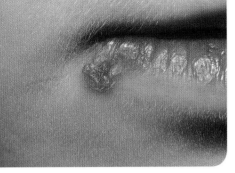

Herpes is a viral infection of the epidermal cells.

## 3.2 Defense Against Viral Infection

The human body fights viral infections with antibodies, which bind to a viral protein, and with cytotoxic T cells, which destroy infected cells. Although the envelope is borrowed from the host cell, *spike proteins* encoded from the viral nucleic acids protrude from the envelope. These proteins bind to receptors on a new host cell causing the virus to be infectious. However, it is also the spike proteins that human antibodies recognize when fighting the infection. Since RNA polymerase does not contain a proofreading mechanism, changes in the spike proteins are common in RNA viruses. When the spike proteins change, the antibodies fail to recognize them, and the virus may avoid detection until new antibodies are formed. A **vaccine** can be either an injection of antibodies or an injection of a nonpathogenic virus with the same capsid or envelope. The later allows the host immune system to create its own antibodies. Vaccines against rapidly mutating viruses are generally not very effective.

Another difficulty of fighting viral infections is that more than one animal may act as a **carrier population**. Even if all viral infections of a certain type were eliminated in humans, the virus may continue to thrive in another animal, thus maintaining the ability to reinfect the human population. For instance, ducks carry the flu virus, apparently without any adverse symptoms. One of the reasons that the fight against small pox was so successful was because the virus can only infect humans.

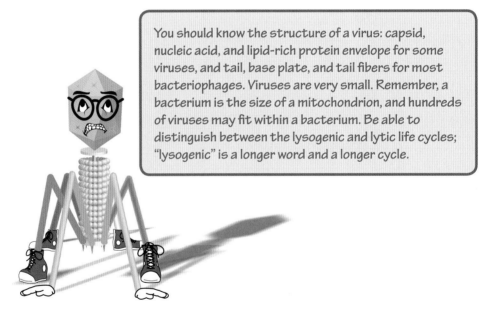

You should know the structure of a virus: capsid, nucleic acid, and lipid-rich protein envelope for some viruses, and tail, base plate, and tail fibers for most bacteriophages. Viruses are very small. Remember, a bacterium is the size of a mitochondrion, and hundreds of viruses may fit within a bacterium. Be able to distinguish between the lysogenic and lytic life cycles; "lysogenic" is a longer word and a longer cycle.

Viral Salty

49. Which of the following events does NOT play a role in the life cycle of a typical retrovirus?

    A. Viral DNA is injected into the host cell.
    B. Viral DNA is integrated into the host genome.
    C. The gene for reverse transcriptase is transcribed and the mRNA is translated inside the host cell.
    D. Viral DNA incorporated into the host genome may be replicated along with the host DNA.

50. A mature virus outside the host cell is called a virion. A virion may contain all of the following EXCEPT:

    A. a capsid.
    B. an envelope made from a phospholipid bilayer.
    C. core proteins.
    D. both RNA and DNA.

51. Prior to infecting a bacterium, a bacteriophage must:

    A. reproduce, making copies of the phage chromosome.
    B. integrate its genome into the bacterial chromosome.
    C. penetrate the bacterial cell wall completely.
    D. attach to a receptor on the bacterial cell membrane.

52. Most viruses that infect animals:

    A. enter the host cell via endocytosis.
    B. do not require a receptor protein to recognize the host cell.
    C. leave their capsid outside the host cell.
    D. can reproduce independently of a host cell.

53. Viruses most closely resemble:

    A. facultative anaerobes.
    B. aerobes.
    C. saprophytes.
    D. parasites.

54. Which of the following describes a lysogenic cell?

    A. a cell that harbors an inactive virus in its genome
    B. a cell that has developed immunity from viral infection
    C. any cell infected with a virus
    D. a cell that is about to lyse as a result of viral infection

55. A bacteriophage is easily recognizable due to:

    A. a lysogenic life cycle.
    B. a protein capsid.
    C. circular nucleic acids.
    D. a tail and fibers.

56. Which of the following would never be found in the capsid of a virion?

    A. single stranded DNA
    B. double stranded RNA
    C. ribosomes
    D. reverse transcriptase

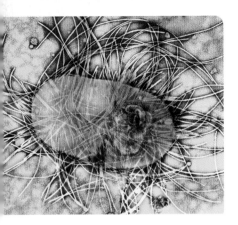

Most Gram-negative rod-shaped bacteria have flagellae. Many are a normal part of the gut flora found in the intestines, but some are pathogenic, such as Salmonella enterica and certain strains of Escherichia coli, and can cause foodborne illnesses.

Don't get caught up in all the minute differences between Archaea and Bacteria. Just know that there is a distinction and that, although both Archaea and Bacteria are prokaryotes, Archaea have similarities to eukaryotes.

MCAT expects you to know two aspects of the classification system:

1) energy source and

2) carbon source.

Autotrophs and heterotrophs differ in their source of carbon: autotrophs use $CO_2$ and heterotrophs use organic matter. 'Photo' and 'chemo' refer to where the organism derives its energy; 'photo' from light and 'chemo' from chemicals. Only prokaryotes can acquire energy from an inorganic source other than light.

**Prokaryotes** do not have a membrane bound nucleus. They are split into two domains called Bacteria and Archaea. **Archaea** have as much in common with eukaryotes as they do with bacteria. They are typically found in the extreme environments such as salty lakes and boiling hot springs. Unlike bacteria, the cell walls of archaea are not made from peptidoglycan. Most known prokaryotes are members of the domain **Bacteria** (Greek: bakterion: small rod). The introduction of the two domains makes the kingdom Monera obsolete. The kingdom monera was the kingdom containing all prokaryotes.

In order to grow, all organisms require the ability to acquire carbon, energy, and electrons (usually from hydrogen). Organisms can be classified according to the sources from which they gather these commodities.

A carbon source can be organic or inorganic. Most carbon sources also contribute oxygen and hydrogen. $CO_2$ is a unique inorganic carbon source because it has no hydrogens. To some degree, all microorganisms are capable of **fixing $CO_2$** (reducing it and using the carbon to create organic molecules usually through a process called the *Calvin cycle*). However, the reduction of $CO_2$ is energy expensive and most microorganisms cannot use it exclusively as their carbon source. **Autotrophs** (Greek: autotrophos: supplying one's own food, aut-:self, trephein:to nourish) are organisms that are capable of using $CO_2$ as their sole source of carbon. **Heterotrophs** (Greek: heteros: different or other) use preformed organic molecules as their source of carbon. Typically these organic molecules come from other organisms both living and dead, but it is believed that at the dawn of life they formed spontaneously in the environment of primitive Earth.

All organisms acquire energy from one of two sources:

1. light; or

2. oxidation of organic or inorganic matter.

Organisms that use light as their energy source are called **phototrophs**; those that use oxidation of organic or inorganic matter are called **chemotrophs**.

Electrons or hydrogens can be acquired from inorganic matter by *lithotrophs*, or organic matter by *organotrophs*.

All organisms can be classified as one of each of the three types. For instance, a flesh eating bacterium is a chemoorganotrophic heterotroph. Most heterotrophs also use organic matter as their energy source, making them some type of chemotrophic heterotrophs. Bacteria are found in all classifications.

Some bacteria are capable of *fixing nitrogen*. Atmospheric nitrogen is abundant, but in a strongly bound form that is useless to plants. Nitrogen fixation is the process by which $N_2$ is converted to ammonia. Most plants are unable to use ammonia, and must wait for other bacteria to further process the nitrogen in a process called *nitrification*. Nitrification is a two step process that creates nitrates, which are useful to plants, from ammonia. Nitrification requires two genera of chemoautotrophic prokaryotes. The relevant reactions are shown below.

$$NH_4^+ + 1\tfrac{1}{2}O_2 \rightarrow NO_2^- + H_2O + 2H^+$$
$$NO_2^- + \tfrac{1}{2}O_2 \rightarrow NO_3^-$$

Chemoautotrophy is an inefficient mechanism for acquiring energy, so chemoautotrophs require large amounts of substrate. This means that chemoautotrophs have a large environmental impact, which is reflected in processes like nitrification. All known chemoautotrophs are prokaryotes.

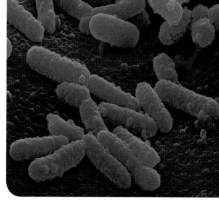

## 3.4 Structure of Prokaryotes

The typical structure of prokaryotes (Figure 3.5) is simpler than that of eukaryotes. The most basic distinction between eukaryotes and prokaryotes is that prokaryotes don't have a nucleus, and eukaryotes always have at least one nucleus. Instead of a nucleus, prokaryotes usually have a single, circular double stranded molecule of DNA. This molecule is twisted into *supercoils* and is associated with histones in Archaea and with proteins that are different from histones in Bacteria. The DNA, RNA and protein complex in prokaryotes forms a structure visible under the light microscope called a **nucleoid** (also called the chromatin body, nuclear region, or nuclear body). The nucleoid is not enclosed by a membrane.

E. coli bacteria, Gram-negative bacilli (rod-shaped) bacteria, are normal inhabitants of the human intestine, and are usually harmless. However, under certain conditions their numbers may increase to such an extent that they cause infection. They cause 80% of all urinary tract infections, travellers' diarrhea, particularly in tropical countries & gastroenteritis in children. They are also widely used in genetic research.

There are two major shapes of bacteria: **cocci** (round) and **bacilli** (rod shaped). There are many other shapes, including helical. Helically shaped bacteria are called **spirilla** if they are rigid. Otherwise they are called **spirochetes**. Certain species of spirochetes may have given rise to eukaryotic flagella through a symbiotic relationship.

Prokaryotes have no complex, membrane-bound organelles. All living organisms contain both DNA and RNA, so prokaryotes have RNA. Since they translate proteins, prokaryotes have **ribosomes**. Prokaryotic ribosomes are smaller than eukaryotic ribosomes. They are made from a 50S and a 30S subunit to form a 70S ribosome.

A prokaryote may or may not contain a *mesosome*. Mesosomes are invaginations of the plasma membrane. They may be in the shape of tubules, lamellae, or vesicles. Under the light microscope mesosomes may appear as bubbles inside the bacterium. They may be involved in cell wall formation during cellular division.

Prokaryotes also have *inclusion bodies*. Inclusion bodies are granules of organic or inorganic matter that may be visible under a light microscope. Inclusion bodies may or may not be bound by a single layer membrane.

> Recognize that the name of the bacteria often reveals the shape, like: <u>spiro</u>plasma, staphylo<u>coccus</u>, or pneumo<u>coccus</u>.

MRSA (Methicillin-resistant *Staphylococcus aureus*) is a Gram-positive spherical (coccus) bacteria. Some strains are resistant to most antibiotic drug agents. MRSA is common in hospitals infecting wounds of patients.

> Prokaryotes lack a nucleus. In fact, they have no complex, membrane-bound organelles at all. The key words are 'complex' and 'membrane-bound'. They have organelles: ribosomes, nucleoid, mesosomes etc...; just not complex, membrane-bound organelles.

The thick capsule or slime layer (glycocalyx) is a slimy or gummy material secreted by many bacteria onto their surfaces. The capsule can aid in attaching to host cells and may also protect the bacterium from immune cells such as phagocytes.

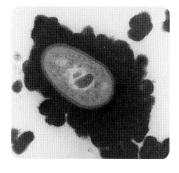

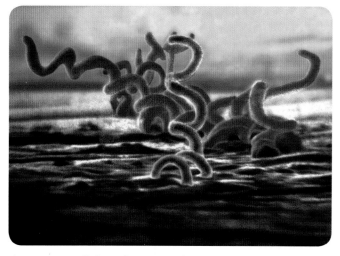

*Treponema pallidum*, the cause of syphilis, is a spirochete that wiggles vigorously when viewed under a microscope.

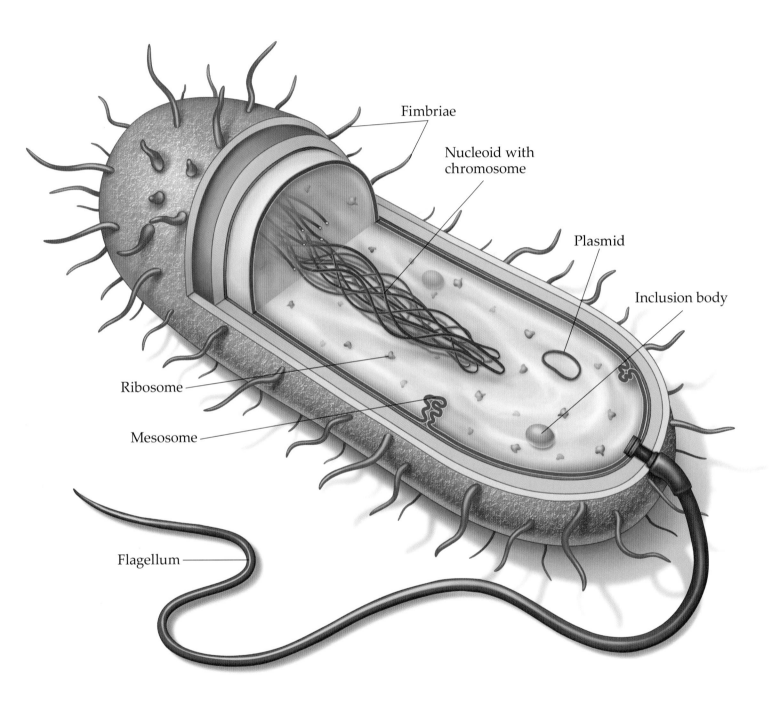

**Figure 3.5 Bacterium**

## 3.5 Membranes

The cytosol of nearly all prokaryotes is surrounded by a phospholipid bilayer called the **plasma membrane**. (The membranes of archaea differ in their lipid structure. This is unlikely to be on the MCAT.) The **phospholipid** (Figure 3.8) is composed of a **phosphate group**, **two fatty acid chains**, and a **glycerol** backbone. The phospholipid is often drawn as a balloon with two strings. The balloon portion represents the phosphate group, and the strings represent the fatty acids. The phosphate group is polar, while the fatty acid chains are nonpolar, making the molecule **amphipathic** (having both a polar and a nonpolar portion). When placed in aqueous solution, amphipathic molecules spontaneously aggregate, turning their polar ends toward the solution, and their nonpolar ends toward each other. The resulting spherical structure is called a **micelle** (Figure 3.7). If enough phospholipids exist, and the solution is subjected to ultrasonic vibrations, *liposomes* may form. A liposome is a vesicle surrounded and filled by aqueous solution. It contains a lipid bilayer like that of a plasma membrane. The inner and outer layers of a membrane are referred to as *leaflets*. As well as phospholipids, the plasma membrane contains other types of lipids such as glycolipids. Unlike eukaryotic membranes, prokaryotic plasma membranes usually do not contain steroids such as cholesterol. Instead, some bacterial membranes contain steroid-like molecules called hopanoids (see Figure 3.6.) Different lipid types are arranged asymmetrically between the leaflets. For instance, glycolipids are found on the outer leaflet only.

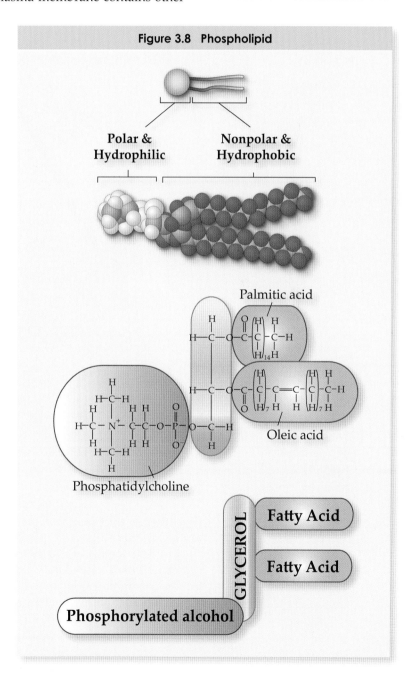

**Figure 3.6  Generalized Structure of Steroid and Hopanoid**

Steroid

Hopanoid

**Figure 3.8  Phospholipid**

Polar & Hydrophilic

Nonpolar & Hydrophobic

Palmitic acid

Phosphatidylcholine

Oleic acid

GLYCEROL

**Fatty Acid**

**Fatty Acid**

**Phosphorylated alcohol**

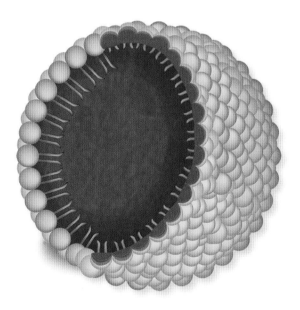

**Figure 3.7  Micelle**

> Micelles form spontaneously whereas membranes must be actively assembled. So, if you dump some phospholipids into an aqueous solution, expect that a micelle will form because it is the most thermodynamically stable conformation.

Figure 3.9 Functions of Membrane Proteins

Outside of cell    Inside of cell

Transporter

Receptor

Attachment

Idenifier

Adhesion

Enzyme

Also embedded within the plasma membrane are proteins. Most of the functional aspects of membranes are due to their proteins. Membrane proteins act as transporters, receptors, attachment sites, identifiers, adhesive proteins, and enzymes (Figure 3.9). As transporters, membrane proteins select which solutes enter and leave the cell. Other membrane proteins act as receptors by receiving chemical signals from the cellular environment. Some membrane proteins are attachment sites that anchor to the cytoskeleton. Membrane proteins can act as identifiers which other cells recognize. Adhesion by one cell to another is accomplished by membrane proteins. Many of the chemical reactions that occur within a cell are governed by membrane proteins on the inner surface. Amphipathic proteins that traverse the membrane from the inside of the cell to the outside are called **integral** or **intrinsic proteins**. **Peripheral** or **extrinsic proteins** are situated entirely on the surfaces of the membrane. They are ionically bonded to integral proteins or the polar group of a lipid. Both integral and peripheral proteins may contain carbohydrate chains making them glycoproteins. The carbohydrate portion of membrane *glycoproteins* always protrudes toward the outside of the cell. *Lipoproteins* (sometimes called *lipid anchored proteins*) also exist in some plasma membranes with their lipid portions embedded in the membrane and their protein portions at the surfaces. Membrane proteins are distributed asymmetrically throughout the membrane and between the leaflets. Neither proteins nor lipids flip easily from one leaflet to the other.

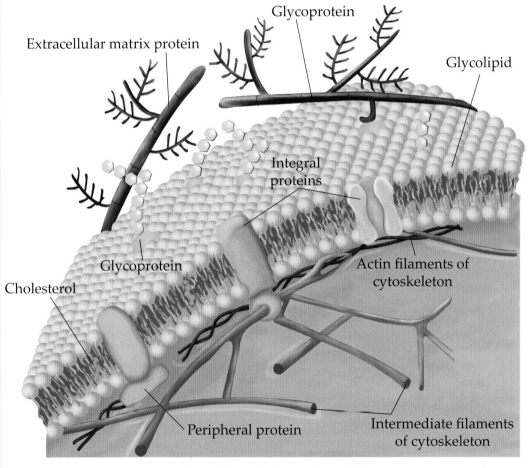

Figure 3.10 Fluid Mosaic Model

Since the forces holding the entire membrane together are intermolecular, the membrane is fluid; its parts can move laterally but cannot separate. The model of the membrane as just described is known as the **fluid mosaic model**. A mosaic is a picture made by placing many small, colored pieces side by side. The mosaic aspect of the membrane is reflected in the asymmetrical layout of its proteins. In eukaryotic membranes, cholesterol moderates membrane fluidity. In the prokaryotic plasma membrane, hopanoids probably reduce the fluidity of the membrane.

> You should be familiar with the fluid mosaic model of a membrane. Most prokaryotic membranes differ only slightly from eukaryotic membranes.

## 3.6 | Membrane Transport

A membrane is not only a barrier between two aqueous solutions of different composition; it actually creates the difference in the compositions of the solutions. At normal temperatures for living organisms, all molecules move rapidly in random directions frequently colliding with one another. This random movement is called *Brownian motion*. Brownian motion creates the tendency of compounds to mix completely with each other over time. If two compounds, X and Y, are placed on opposite sides of the same container, the net movement of X will be toward Y. This movement is called **diffusion**. For molecules without an electric charge, diffusion occurs in the direction of lower concentration. In Figure 3.11, X diffuses in the direction of lower concentration of X, and Y toward lower concentration of Y. A gradual change in concentration of a compound over a distance is called a chemical concentration gradient. The **chemical concentration gradient** is a series of vectors pointing in the direction of lower concentration. For molecules with a charge, there is also an **electrical gradient** pointing in the direction that a positively charged particle will tend to move. The two gradients can be added to form a single **electrochemical gradient** for a specific compound. The electrochemical gradient for compound X points in the direction that particle X will tend to move. (Note: There are other factors affecting the direction of diffusion, including heat and pressure. In this text, we shall assume these factors to be included in the electrochemical gradient. In strict terms, diffusion occurs in the direction of decreasing free energy, or in the strictest terms, in the direction of increasing universal entropy.)

If compounds X and Y are separated by an impermeable membrane, diffusion is stopped. However, if the molecules of X can wiggle their way across the membrane, then diffusion is only slowed. Since the membrane slows the diffusion of X, but does not stop it, the membrane is **semipermeable** to compound X.

Blue food coloring begins to diffuse in a beaker of water. Diffusion is caused by the tiny, random movements of molecules in a solution. Over a period of time these movements cause the dissolved substance to become evenly dispersed throughout the solvent.

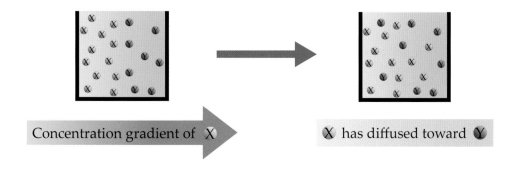

Concentration gradient of X

X has diffused toward Y

**Figure 3.11  Diffusion**

Figure 3.12 shows examples of membrane transport. Natural membranes are semipermeable to most compounds, but there are degrees of semipermeability. There are two aspects of a compound that affect its semipermeability: **size** and **polarity**. The larger the molecule, the less permeable the membrane to that molecule. A natural membrane is generally impermeable to polar molecules with a molecular weight greater than 100 without some type of assistance. The greater the polarity of a molecule (or if the molecule has a charge), the less permeable the membrane to that molecule. Very large lipid soluble (nonpolar) molecules like steroid hormones can move right through the membrane. When considering permeability, it is important to consider both size and polarity. For example, water is larger than a sodium ion, but water is polar, while the sodium ion possesses a complete charge. Therefore, a natural membrane is more permeable to water than to sodium; in this case, the charge difference outweighs the size difference. A natural membrane is, in fact, highly permeable to water. However, if the membrane were made only of a phospholipid bilayer, and did not contain proteins, the rate of diffusion for water would be very slow. Most of

Figure 3.12   Membrane Transport

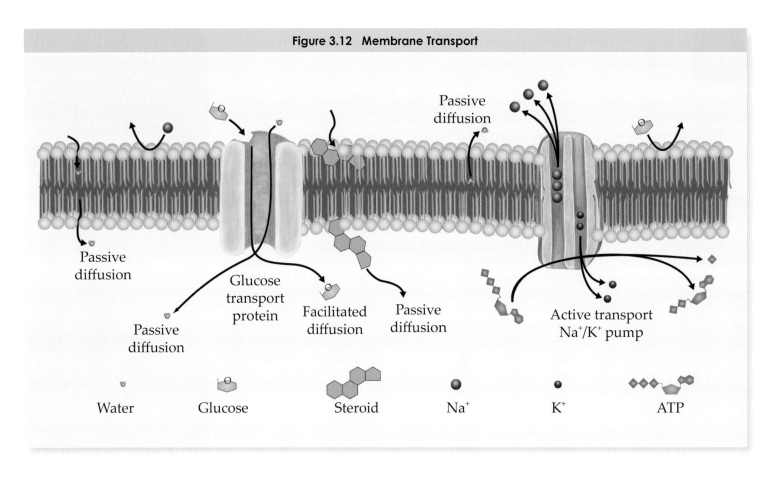

Figure 3.12   Membrane Transport

There are some important concepts here that require understanding as well as memorization. The membrane stuff is worth a second read through. Basically, passive diffusion through the membrane depends on lipid solubility (Are you nonpolar enough to slide right through the phospholipid bilayer?) and size (Can you fit through the cracks around the integral proteins?). If you're big and polar, you must rely upon facilitated diffusion, a helper protein to open up a space designed just for you. To move against your electrochemical gradient, it doesn't matter if you are large or small, polar or nonpolar, you need active transport. Only active transport can move something against its concentration gradient.

the diffusion of polar or charged molecules across a natural membrane takes place through incidental holes (sometimes called *leakage channels*) created by the irregular shapes of integral proteins. The function of these proteins is not to aid in diffusion. This is merely an incidental contribution.

The diffusion just described, where molecules move through leakage channels across the membrane due to random motion, is called **passive diffusion**. As mentioned previously, some molecules are too large or too charged to passively diffuse, yet they are needed for the survival of the cell. To assist these molecules in moving across the membrane, specific proteins are embedded into the membrane. These proteins, called **transport** or **carrier proteins**, are designed to facilitate the diffusion of specific molecules across the membrane. There are several mechanisms used by transport proteins in facilitated diffusion, but, in order for the passage to be called **facilitated diffusion**, diffusion must occur down the electro-chemical gradient of all species involved. Most, but not all, human cells rely on facilitated diffusion for their glucose supply. Facilitated diffusion is said to make the membrane **selectively permeable** because it is able to select between molecules of similar size and charge.

A living organism must be able to concentrate some nutrients against their electrochemical gradients. Of course, diffusion will not do this. Movement of a compound against its electrochemical gradient requires **active transport**. Active transport requires expenditure of energy. Active transport can be accomplished by the direct expenditure of ATP to acquire or expel a molecule against its electrochemical gradient. It can also be accomplished indirectly by using ATP to create an electrochemical gradient, and then using the energy of the electrochemical gradient to acquire or expel a molecule. The latter method is called *secondary active transport*.

## 3.7 Bacterial Envelope

The bacterial plasma membrane and everything inside it is called the *protoplast*. A protoplast is not a complete bacterium. Surrounding the protoplast is the **bacterial envelope** (Figure 3.13). The component of the envelope adjacent to the plasma membrane is the cell wall. (*Archaea* possess cell walls with a different chemical composition than will be described here. This will not be on the MCAT unless it is explained in a passage.) One of the functions of the cell wall is to prevent the protoplast from bursting. Most bacteria are **hypertonic** (Greek: hyper: above) to their environment. This means that the aqueous solution of their cytosol contains more particles than the aqueous solution surrounding them. This is compared to **isotonic** (Greek: iso: same) where the cytosol contains the same amount of particles and **hypotonic** (Greek: hypo: below) where the cytosol contains less particles. When there are more particles on one side of a barrier than the other, the particles want to move down their concentration gradient to the other side of the barrier. If the particles are prevented from crossing the barrier, water will try to cross in the opposite direction. (This is actually water moving down its electrochemical gradient.) The cell wall is strong and able to withstand high pressure. As the cell fills with water and the **hydrostatic pressure** builds, it eventually equals the **osmotic pressure**, and the filling stops (see Physics Lecture 5 for more on hydrostatic and osmotic pressure). Water continues to move in and out of the cell very rapidly, but an equilibrium is reached. If the cell wall is removed, the plasma membrane cannot withstand the pressure, and the bacterium will burst.

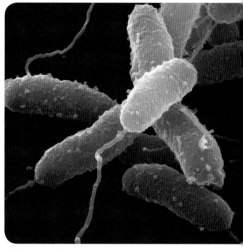

*Vibrio cholerae*, Gram-negative rod-shaped bacteria, have a single polar flagellum (long, thin), which they use to propel themselves through water. They are the cause of cholera, an infection of the small intestine that is transmitted to humans via contaminated food or water.

The cell wall is made of **peptidoglycan** (also called *murein*). (Archaea do not have peptidoglycan cell walls.) Peptidoglycan is a series of disaccharide polymer chains with amino acids, three of which are not found in proteins. These chains are connected by their amino acids, or crosslinked by an *interbridge* of more amino acids. The chains are continuous, forming a single molecular sac around the bacterium. Peptidoglycan is more elastic than cellulose. (Cellulose is the component of plant cell walls. [see Biology Lecture 1] ). It is also porous, so it allows large molecules to pass through. Many antibiotics such as *penicillin* attack the amino acid crosslinks of peptidoglycan. Lysozyme, an enzyme produced naturally by humans, attacks the disaccharide linkage in peptidoglycan. In both cases the cell wall is disrupted and the cell lyses, killing the bacterium.

One method of classification of bacteria is according to the type of cell wall that they possess. **Gram staining** is a staining technique used to prepare bacteria for viewing under the light microscope which stains two major cell wall types differently. The first type is called **gram-positive bacteria** because its thick peptidoglycan cell wall prevents the gram stain from leaking out. These cells show up as purple when stained with this process. Gram-positive bacteria have a cell wall that is approximately four times thicker than the plasma membrane. The space between the plasma membrane and the cell wall is called the *periplasmic space*. The periplasmic space contains many proteins that help the bacteria acquire nutrition, such as hydrolytic enzymes.

**Gram-negative bacteria** appear pink when gram stained. Their thin peptidoglycan cell wall allows most of the gram stain to be washed off. The peptidoglycan of gram-negative bacteria is slightly different from that of gram-positive. Outside the cell wall, gram-negative bacteria have a phospholipid bilayer. This second membrane is more permeable than the first, even allowing molecules the size of glucose to pass right through. It is similar in structure to the plasma membrane, but also possesses *lipopolysaccharides*. The polysaccharide is a long chain of carbohydrates which protrudes outward from the cell. These polysaccharide chains can form a protective barrier from antibodies and many antibiotics. A lipoprotein in the outer membrane called *Braun's lipoprotein* points inward toward the cell wall and attaches covalently to the peptidoglycan. In gram-negative bacteria the *periplasmic space* is the space between the two membranes. (Different species of Archaea may stain positive or negative.)

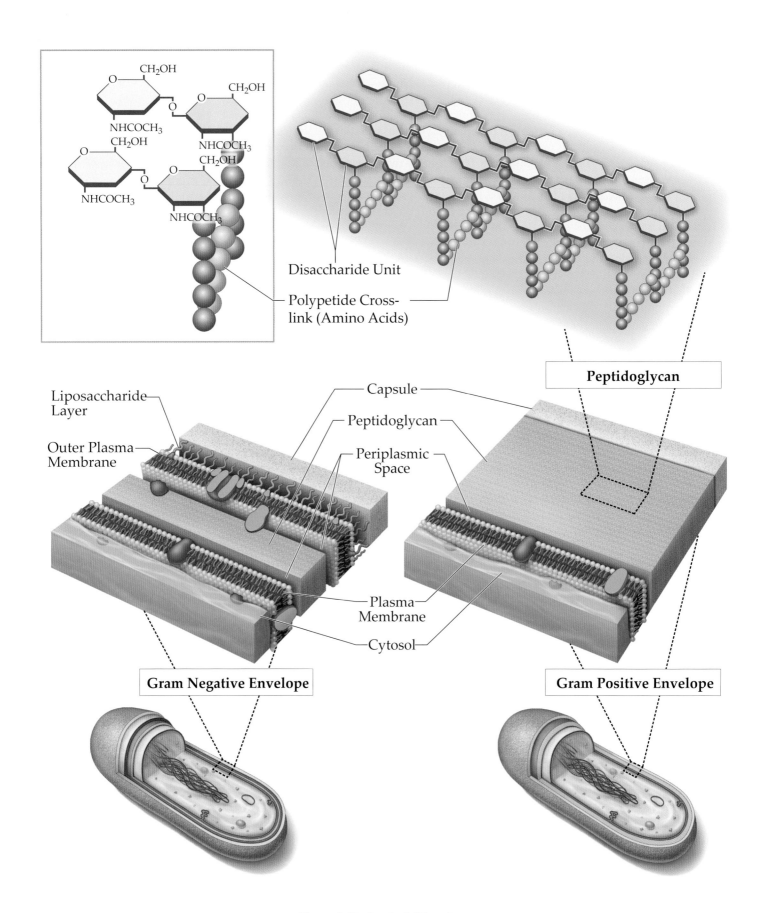

CH₂OH

NHCOCH₃

CH₂OH

NHCOCH₃

CH₂OH

NHCOCH₃

CH₂OH

NHCOCH₃

Disaccharide Unit

Polypetide Cross-
link (Amino Acids)

Peptidoglycan

Liposaccharide
Layer

Outer Plasma
Membrane

Capsule

Peptidoglycan

Periplasmic
Space

Plasma
Membrane

Cytosol

**Gram Negative Envelope**

**Gram Positive Envelope**

Figure 3.13   Bacterial Envelope

Many bacteria are wrapped in either a *capsule* or a *slime layer*. Both capsules and slime layers are usually made of polysaccharide. Slime layers are easily washed off, while capsules are not. A capsule can protect the bacterium from phagocytosis, desiccation, some viruses, and some components of the immune response of an infected host.

Some gram-negative bacteria possess *fimbriae* or *pili* (not to be confused with the sex pilus discussed below). Fimbriae are short tentacles, usually numbering in the thousands, that can attach a bacterium to a solid surface. They are not involved in cell motility.

Bacterial **flagella** are long, hollow, rigid, helical cylinders made from a globular protein called **flagellin**; these should not be confused with eukaryotic flagella, which composed of microtubules. They rotate counterclockwise (from the point of view of looking at the cell from the outside) to propel the bacterium in a single direction. When they are rotated clockwise, the bacterium *tumbles*. The tumbling acts to change the orientation of the bacterium allowing it to move forward in a new direction. The flagellum is propelled using the energy from a proton gradient rather than by ATP. Some bacteria can move via a gliding motion that has not yet been explained. Spirochetes, the flexible, helical shaped bacteria, can move through viscous fluids by flexing and spinning.

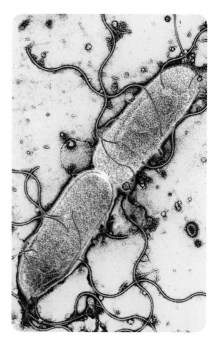

You should have some idea about the differences between gram positive and gram negative bacteria, but most of the details on the structure of bacteria are just good background information.

## 3.8 *Bacterial Reproduction*

Sexual reproduction is one method of recombining the genetic information between individuals of the same species to produce a genetically different individual. Sexual reproduction requires meiosis. Bacteria do not undergo meiosis or mitosis, and cannot reproduce sexually. However, they have three alternative forms of **genetic recombination**: conjugation, transformation, and transduction. They are also capable of undergoing a type of cell division called **binary fission** (Latin: fissus:split). Binary fission is a type of asexual reproduction (Figure 3.14).

In binary fission, the circular DNA is replicated in a process similar to replication in eukaryotes. (See Biology Lecture 2 for the replication process.) Two DNA polymerases begin at the same point on the circle (**origin of replication**) and move in opposite directions making complementary single strands that combine with their template strands to form two complete DNA double stranded circles. The cell then divides, leaving one circular chromosome in each daughter cell. The two daughter cells are genetically identical.

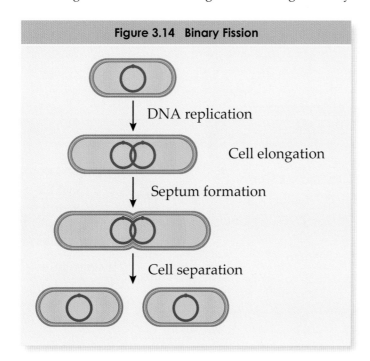

**Figure 3.14  Binary Fission**

DNA replication

Cell elongation

Septum formation

Cell separation

A single bacterium divides into identical daughter bacteria. Under optimal conditions, some bacteria can grow and divide extremely rapidly, and bacterial populations can double as quickly as every 10 minutes.

Binary fission results in two genetically identical daughter cells.

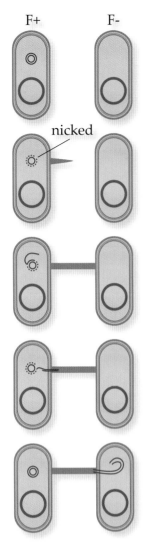

F+    F-

nicked

**Figure 3.15  Conjugation**

The first method of genetic recombination, **conjugation** (Figure 3.15), requires that one of the bacterium have a **plasmid** with the gene that codes for the **sex pilus**. Plasmids are small circles of DNA that exist and replicate independently of the bacterial chromosome. If the plasmid can integrate into the chromosome it is also called an *episome*. Plasmids are not essential to a bacterium which carries them. Not all bacteria with plasmids can conjugate. In order for a bacterium to initiate conjugation, it must contain a *conjugative plasmid*. Conjugative plasmids possess the gene for the sex pilus. The sex pilus is a hollow, protein tube that connects two bacteria to allow the passage of DNA. The passage of DNA is always from the cell containing the conjugative plasmid to the cell that does not. The plasmid replicates differently than the circular chromosome. One strand is *nicked*, and one end of this strand begins to separate from its complement as its replacement is replicated. The loose strand is then replicated and fed through the pilus.

There are two important plasmids that may be mentioned on the MCAT: the **F plasmid** and the *R plasmid*. The F plasmid is called the **fertility factor** or **F factor**. It was the first plasmid to be described. A bacterium with the F factor is called F+, one without the F factor is called F–. The F plasmid can be in the form of an episome, and if the pilus is made while the F factor is integrated into the chromosome, some or all of the rest of the chromosome may be replicated and transferred. The R plasmid donates resistance to certain antibiotics. It is also a conjugative plasmid. It was once common practice to prescribe multiple antibiotics for patients to take at one time. Such conditions promote conjugation of different R plasmids providing different resistances to antibiotics to produce a super-bacterium that contains many antibiotic resistances on one or more R plasmids. Some R plasmids are readily transferred between species further promoting resistance and causing serious health problems for humans.

**Transformation** is the process by which bacteria may incorporate DNA from their external environment into their genome. DNA may be added to the external environment in the lab, or it may occur due to lyses of other bacteria. The typical experimental procedure which demonstrates transformation is when heat-killed virulent bacteria are mixed with harmless living bacteria. The living bacteria receive the genes of the heat-killed bacteria through transformation, and become virulent.

**Figure 3.16  Bacterial Transformation**

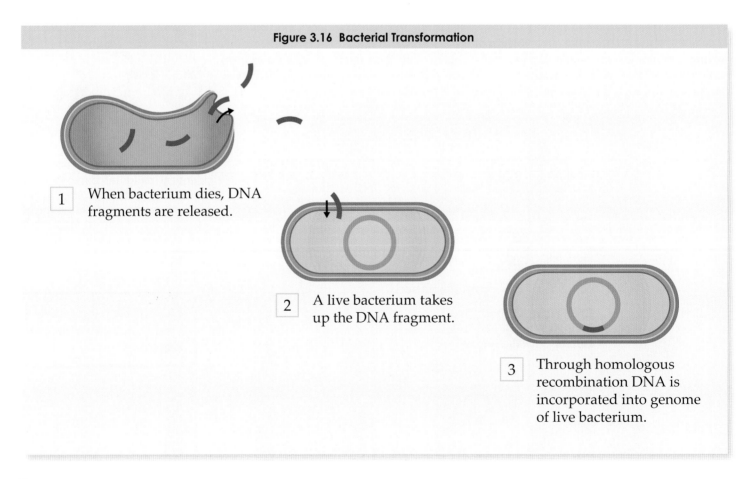

1   When bacterium dies, DNA fragments are released.

2   A live bacterium takes up the DNA fragment.

3   Through homologous recombination DNA is incorporated into genome of live bacterium.

Sometimes, the capsid of a bacteriophage will mistakenly encapsulate a DNA fragment of the host cell. When these virions infect a new bacterium, they inject harmless bacterial DNA fragments instead of virulent viral DNA fragments. This type of genetic recombination is called **transduction**. The virus that mediates transduction is called the **vector**. Transduction can be mediated artificially in the lab.

**Figure 3.17  Transduction**

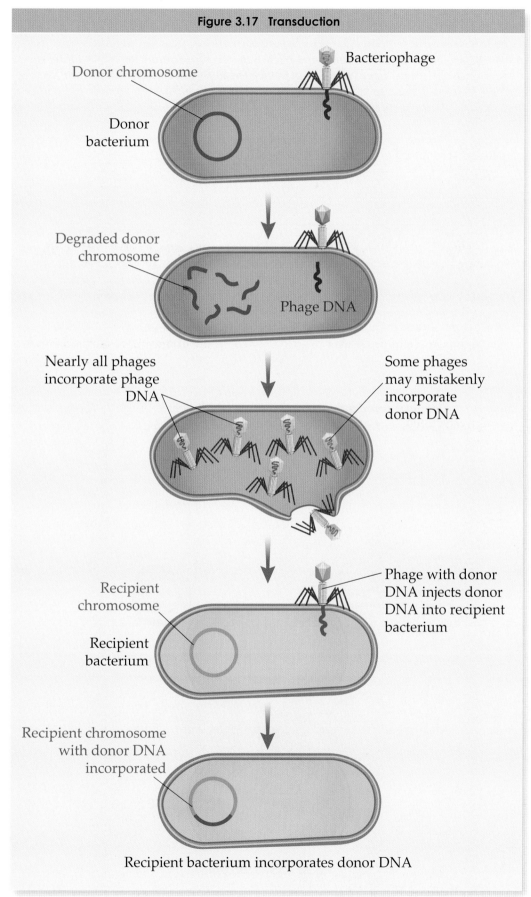

Donor chromosome

Bacteriophage

Donor bacterium

Degraded donor chromosome

Phage DNA

Nearly all phages incorporate phage DNA

Some phages may mistakenly incorporate donor DNA

Recipient chromosome

Recipient bacterium

Phage with donor DNA injects donor DNA into recipient bacterium

Recipient chromosome with donor DNA incorporated

Recipient bacterium incorporates donor DNA

## 3.9 Endospores

Some gram-positive bacteria can form *endospores* (Greek: endon: within, speirein:to seed or sow) that can lie dormant for hundreds of years. Endospores are resistant to heat, ultraviolet radiation, chemical disinfectants, and desiccation. Endospores can survive in boiling water for over an hour. Endospore formation is usually triggered by a lack of nutrients. In endospore formation, the bacterium divides within its cell wall. One side then engulfs the other. The chemistry of the cell wall of the engulfed bacterium changes slightly to form the cortex of the endospore. Several protein layers lie over the cortex to form the resistant structure called the *spore coat*. A delicate covering, called the *exosporium*, sometimes surrounds the spore coat. The outer cell then lyses, releasing the dormant endospore. The endospore must be *activated* before it can *germinate* and grow. Activation usually involves heating. Germination is triggered by nutrients.

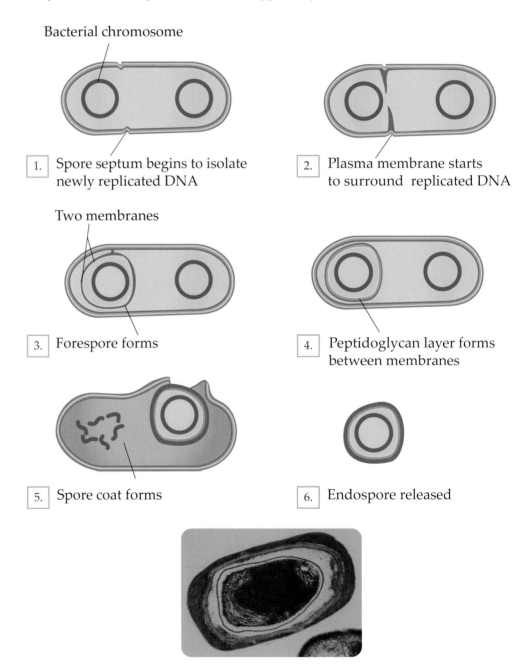

Bacterial chromosome

1. Spore septum begins to isolate newly replicated DNA

2. Plasma membrane starts to surround replicated DNA

Two membranes

3. Forespore forms

4. Peptidoglycan layer forms between membranes

5. Spore coat forms

6. Endospore released

Endospore of Bacillus subtilis

**Figure 3.18  Endospore**

**57.** Which of the following structures are found in prokaryotes?

    **I.** A cell wall containing peptidoglycan.
    **II.** A plasma membrane lacking cholesterol.
    **III.** Ribosomes

    **A.** I only
    **B.** II only
    **C.** I and II only
    **D.** I, II, and III

**58.** DNA from phage resistant bacteria is extracted and placed on agar with phage-sensitive E. coli. After incubation it is determined that these E. coli are now also resistant to phage attack. The most likely mechanism for their acquisition of resistance is:

    **A.** transduction.
    **B.** sexual reproduction.
    **C.** transformation.
    **D.** conjugation.

**59.** Bacteriophages are parasites that infect bacterial cells in order to carry on their life function. When a phage transfers bacterial DNA from one host to another this process is called:

    **A.** transformation.
    **B.** transduction.
    **C.** conjugation.
    **D.** transmission.

**60.** The lipopolysaccharide layer outside the peptidoglycan cell wall of a gram negative bacterium:

    **A.** absorbs and holds gram stain.
    **B.** protects the bacterium against certain antibiotics.
    **C.** does not contain phospholipids.
    **D.** allows the bacterium to attach to solid objects.

**61.** The exponential growth that occurs in *E. coli* at 37°C following inoculation of a sterile, nutrient-rich solution results from:

    **A.** conjugation.
    **B.** transformation.
    **C.** sporulation.
    **D.** binary fission.

**62.** A staphylococcus infection is most likely caused by an organism that is:

    **A.** rod-shaped.
    **B.** spherical.
    **C.** a rigid helix.
    **D.** a non-rigid helix.

**63.** Which of the following is a mechanism for reproduction in Bacteria?

    **A.** transduction
    **B.** conjugation
    **C.** binary fission
    **D.** transformation

**64.** Penicillin interferes with peptidoglycan formation. Penicillin most likely inhibits bacterial growth by disrupting the production of:

    **A.** bacterial plasma membranes.
    **B.** prokaryotic cell walls.
    **C.** the bacterial nucleus.
    **D.** bacterial ribosomes.

**Fungi** represent a distinct kingdom of organisms with tremendous diversity. Three divisions exist within this kingdom: *Zygomycota, Ascomycota,* and *Basidiomycota* (Greek: mykes: mushroom). (*Oomycota*, which are slime molds and water molds, are not true fungi, and are in the protista kingdom.) Like plants, fungi are separated into divisions not phyla. All fungi are eukaryotic heterotrophs that obtain their food by absorption rather than by ingestion: they secrete their digestive enzymes outside their bodies and then absorb the products of digestion. Although most fungi are considered **saprophytic** (Greek: sapros: rotten or decayed), many fungi do not distinguish between living and dead matter, and thus can be potent pathogens (disease causing). (Saprophytic means to live off dead organic matter.) Most fungi possess cell walls, called **septa** (Latin: saeptum:fence or wall), made of the polysaccharide, **chitin**. Chitin is more resistant to microbial attack than is cellulose. It is the same substance of which the exoskeleton of *arthropods* is made. (Arthropods are insects and crustaceans.) Septa are usually perforated to allow exchange of cytoplasm between cells, called cytoplasmic streaming. *Cytoplasmic streaming* allows for very rapid growth. One division of fungi, zygomycota, possesses no cell walls at all, except in their sexual structures. With the exception of yeasts, fungi are multicellular. (Yeasts are unicellular fungi.) A fungal cell may contain one or more nuclei. The nuclei in a single cell may or may not be identical. Fungi lack centrioles, and mitosis in fungi takes place entirely within the nucleus; the nuclear envelope never breaks down. In their growth state, fungi consist of a tangled mass (called a **mycelium**) of multiply branched thread-like structures, called **hyphae**.

The white areas on this mold fungus are mycellium, a mass of thread-like structures (hyphae) that absorb nutrients.

The fungi are far too diverse and complex to justify memorizing a lot of specifics. The MCAT will not require knowledge of specifics beyond what is in bold and red. Just remember the basics about fungi. Fungi are eukaryotic heterotrophs and spend most of their lives in the haploid state. They can reproduce sexually or asexually; remember when and why.

Fungus can grow on living things.

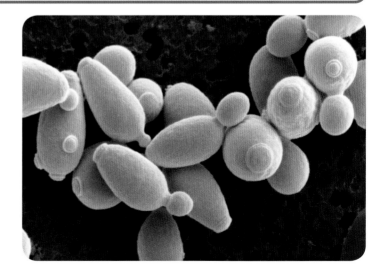

Yeast ferments sugar and produces ethanol and carbon dioxide. Yeast is essential to the making of wine, beer, and bread.

## 3.11 Fungal Reproduction and Life Cycle

Like most organisms, fungi alternate between haploid and diploid stages in their life cycle; however, the **haploid** stage predominates and is their growth stage. Hyphae are haploid. Some hyphae may form reproductive structures called *sporangiophores* in *Zygomycota*, *condiophores* in *Ascomycota*. These structures release haploid **spores** that give rise to new mycelia in asexual reproduction. *Basidiomycota*, which rarely reproduce asexually, produce *basidiospores* via sexual reproduction. (Note that spore formation is not always via asexual reproduction.) Spores are borne by air currents, water, or animals to locations suitable for new mycelial growth. Yeasts rarely produce sexually by producing spores. More often in yeasts, asexual reproduction occurs by **budding** (also called **cell fission**), in which a smaller cell pinches off from the single parent cell.

When sexual reproduction occurs (Figure 3.20), it is between hyphae from two mycelia of different mating types + and –. These two hyphae grow towards one another, eventually touching and forming a conjugation bridge. The tip of each hypha forms a complete septum in all divisions of fungi, and becomes a gamete-producing cell, called a *gametangium*. In Zygomycota, the gametangia remain attached to the parent hyphae and the nuclei fuse with one another to produce a diploid zygote, called a *zygospore*. The zygospore separates from the parent hyphae and usually enters a dormant phase. When activated by the appropriate environmental conditions, the zygospore undergoes meiosis to produce haploid cells, one of which immediately grows a short sporangiophore to asexually reproduce many spores. Except for the zygospore, all cells of Zygomycota are haploid.

Sexual reproduction in Ascomycota and Basidiomycota is similar, but slightly more complicated. The important thing to understand about fungal reproduction is that asexual reproduction normally occurs when conditions are good; sexual reproduction normally occurs when conditions are tough. This is because if conditions are good for the parent, they will be good for asexually reproduced offspring that are exactly like the parent, but if conditions are bad for the parent, they may not be bad for sexually reproduced offspring that are different from the parent.

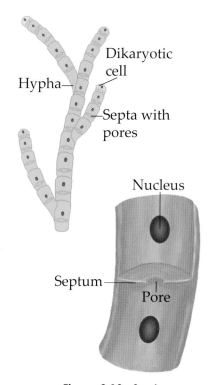

**Figure 3.19   Septum**

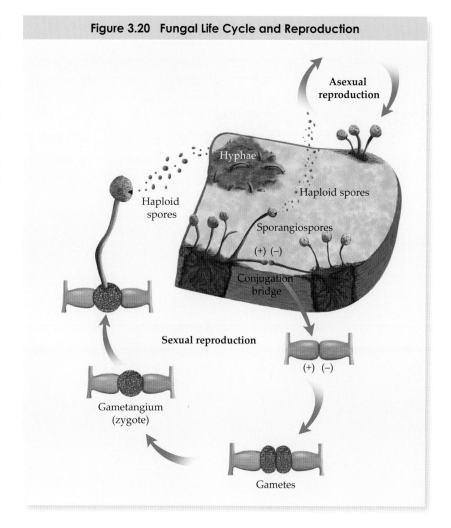

**Figure 3.20   Fungal Life Cycle and Reproduction**

## 3.12 Terms You Need To Know

| Terms | | |
|---|---|---|
| Active Transport | Extrinsic Proteins | Nucleoid |
| Amphipathic | F Plasmid | Origin of Replication |
| Archaea | Facilitated Diffusion | Osmotic Pressure |
| Autotrophs | Fertility Factor | Passive Diffusion |
| Bacilli | Flagella | Peptidoglycan |
| Bacteria | Flagellin | Phospholipid |
| Bacterial Envelope | Fluid Mosaic Model | Phototrophs |
| Bacteriophage | Fungi | Plasma Membrane |
| Binary Fission | Glycerol | Plasmid |
| Budding | Gram-negative | Plus-strand RNA |
| Capsid | Bacteria | Polarity |
| Carrier Population | Gram-positive Bacteria | Prokaryotes |
| Carrier Proteins | Gram Staining | Prophage |
| Chitin | Haploid | Provirus |
| Chemical | Heterotrophs | Retroviruses |
| Concentration | Host | Reverse Transcriptase |
| Gradient | Hydrostatic Pressure | Saprophytic |
| Chemotrophs | Hypertonic | Selectively Permeable |
| Cocci | Hyphae | Septa |
| Conjugation | Hypotonic | Sex Pilus |
| Diffusion | Intrinsic Proteins | Spirilla |
| DNA Viruses | Isotonic | Spirochetes |
| Dormant Viruses | Lysogenic | Spores |
| Electrical Gradient | Lytic | Transduction |
| Electrochemical | Membrane Transport | Transformation |
| Gradient | Micelle | Vaccine |
| Endocytotic | Minus-strand RNA | Vector |
| Envelope | Mycelium | Virus |

**65.** Fungi are classified as a distinct kingdom because:

  **A.** they don't undergo mitosis.
  **B.** they reproduce asexually.
  **C.** sexual reproduction involves the union of different mating types, plus and minus strains.
  **D.** they have characteristics that are both plant-like and animal-like.

**66.** Which of the following is not a result of sexual reproduction in fungi?

  **A.** hyphae of + and – mycelia meet and fuse
  **B.** fertilization produces a diploid state
  **C.** diploid cell undergoes meiosis
  **D.** cell division lengthens mycelia

**67.** Fungi are considered saprophytic because:

  **A.** they reproduce by budding.
  **B.** they reproduce by sporulation.
  **C.** they absorb chemicals through a mass of tiny threads.
  **D.** they acquire energy from the break down of the dead remains of living organisms.

**68.** All of the following statements are true concerning most fungi EXCEPT:

  **A.** They have cell walls made of chitin.
  **B.** They are autotrophs.
  **C.** Their growth stage is composed of filaments containing many nuclei.
  **D.** Their life cycle alternates between a haploid and diploid stage.

**69.** What selective advantage is offered by the haploid state of fungi?

  **A.** The haploid state can reproduce more quickly than the diploid state under favorable conditions.
  **B.** The haploid state is more genetically diverse.
  **C.** The haploid state produces a large number of cells.
  **D.** The haploid state requires less energy to sustain itself.

**70.** Which of the following is the best explanation for why fungicides tend to cause more side effects in humans than do bacterial antibiotics?

  **A.** Chitin is more difficult to break down than peptidoglycan.
  **B.** Fungus doesn't respond to penicillin.
  **C.** Fungal cells are more similar to human cells than are bacterial cells.
  **D.** Fungus is a topical infection.

**71.** The Kingdom of Fungi is divided into:

  **A.** phyla.
  **B.** divisions.
  **C.** orders.
  **D.** species.

**72.** Which of the following is true of Fungi?

  **A.** Fungi prey upon only dead organic matter.
  **B.** Fungi digest their food outside their bodies.
  **C.** Fungi undergo meiosis during asexual reproduction.
  **D.** All fungi are obligate aerobes.

*Notes:*

# THE EUKARYOTIC CELL; THE NERVOUS SYSTEM

## 4.1 The Nucleus

The major feature distinguishing eukaryotic (Greek: eu → well, karyos → kernel) cells from prokaryotic cells is the **nucleus** of the eukaryote (Figure 4.1). The nucleus contains all of the DNA in an animal cell (except for a small amount in the mitochondria). The aqueous 'soup' inside the nucleus is called the nucleoplasm. The nucleus is wrapped in a double phospholipid bilayer called the **nuclear envelope** or **membrane**. The nuclear envelope is perforated with large holes called nuclear pores. RNA can exit the nucleus through the **nuclear pores**, but DNA cannot. Within the nucleus is an area called the **nucleolus** where rRNA is transcribed and the subunits of the ribosomes are assembled. The nucleolus is not separated from the nucleus by a membrane.

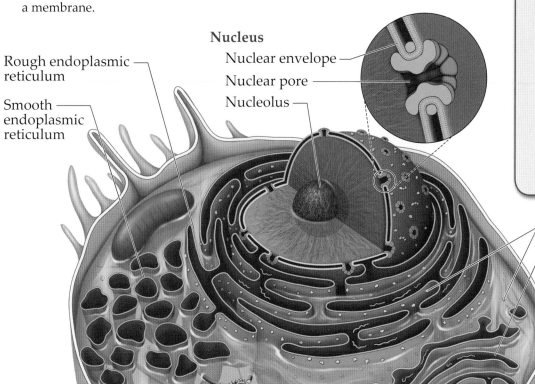

**Nucleus**
Nuclear envelope
Nuclear pore
Nucleolus

Rough endoplasmic reticulum

Smooth endoplasmic reticulum

Ribosomes

Golgi complex

Peroxisome

Centriole

Microtubule

Lysosome

Vesicle

Mitochondria

**Figure 4.1 Eukaryotic Cell**

Only eukaryotes have nuclei. If you remember that DNA cannot leave the nucleus, then you will remember that transcription must take place in the nucleus. RNA leaves the nucleus through nuclear pores.

## *The Membrane*

Besides transport across the membrane (discussed in Biology Lecture 3), cells can acquire substances from the extracellular environment through **endocytosis** (Figure 4.2). There are several types of endocytosis: **phagocytosis** (Greek: phagein: to eat), pinocytosis (Greek: pinein: to drink), and *receptor mediated endocytosis*. In phagocytosis, the cell membrane protrudes outward to envelope and engulf particulate matter. Only a few specialized cells are capable of phagocytosis. The impetus for phagocytosis is the binding of proteins on the particulate matter to protein receptors on the phagocytotic cell. In humans, *antibodies* or *complement proteins* (discussed in Biology Lecture 8) bind to particles and stimulate receptor proteins on *macrophages* and *neutrophils* to initiate phagocytosis. Once the particulate matter is engulfed, the membrane bound body is called a *phagosome*.

**Figure 4.2  Types of Endocytosis**

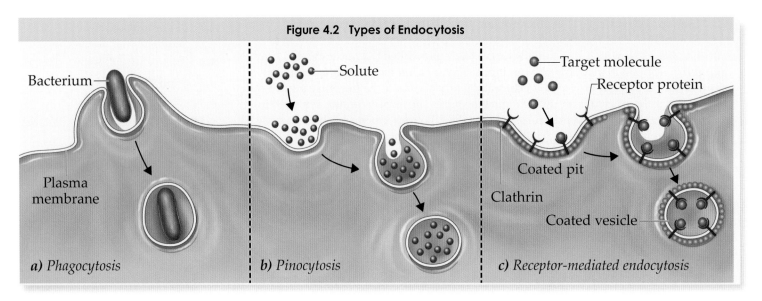

*a) Phagocytosis*  *b) Pinocytosis*  *c) Receptor-mediated endocytosis*

> On the MCAT, you will probably not have to distinguish between the different types of endocytosis, but you should understand the basic concept, and be aware that multiple methods for particles to gain access to the interior of a cell.

In pinocytosis, extracellular fluid is engulfed by small invaginations of the cell membrane. This process is performed by most cells, and in a random fashion; it is nonselective.

Receptor mediated endocytosis refers to specific uptake of macromolecules such as hormones and nutrients. In this process, the ligand binds to a receptor protein on the cell membrane, and is then moved to a *clathrin coated pit*. Clathrin is a protein that forms a polymer adding structure to the underside of the coated pit. The coated pit invaginates to form a *coated vesicle*. One way that this process differs from phagocytosis is that its purpose is to absorb the ligands, whereas the ligands in phagocytosis exist only to act as signals to initiate phagocytosis of other particles.

**Exocytosis** is simply the reverse of endocytosis.

**Figure 4.3  Exocytosis**

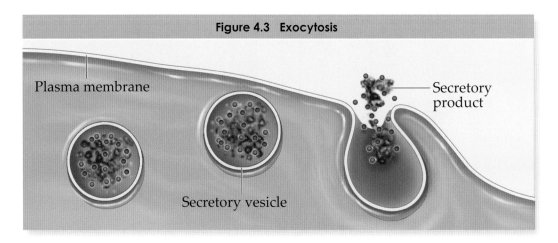

The structure of the phospolipid bilayer of the eukaryotic membrane is similar to the prokaryotic plasma membrane discussed in Biology Lecture 3. However, in the eukaryotic cell, the membrane invaginates and separates to form individual, membrane bound compartments and organelles. The eukaryotic cell contains a thick maze of membranous walls called the **endoplasmic reticulum (ER)** separating the **cytosol** (the aqueous solution inside the cell) from the **ER lumen** or **cisternal space** (the "extracellular fluid" side of the ER). In many places the ER is contiguous with the cell membrane and the nuclear membrane. The ER lumen is contiguous in places with the space between the double bilayer of the nuclear envelope.

ER near the nucleus has many ribosomes attached to it on the cytosolic side, giving it a granular appearance, hence the name **granular** or **rough ER**. Translation on the rough ER propels proteins into the ER lumen as they are created. These proteins are tagged with a *signal sequence* of amino acids and sometimes *glycosylated* (carbohydrate chains are added). The newly synthesized proteins are moved through the lumen toward the **Golgi apparatus** or **Golgi complex**. The Golgi apparatus is a series of flattened, membrane bound sacs. Small *transport vesicles* bud off from the ER and carry the proteins across the cytosol to the Golgi. The Golgi organizes and concentrates the proteins as they are shuttled by transport vesicles progressively outward from one compartment or *cisterna* of the Golgi to the next. Proteins are distinguished based upon their signal sequence and carbohydrate chains. Those proteins not possessing a signal sequence are packaged into secretory vesicles and expelled from the cell in a process called *bulk flow*. The Golgi may change proteins chemically by *glycosylation* or by removing amino acids. Some polysaccharide formation also takes place within the Golgi. The end-product of the Golgi is a vesicle full of proteins. These protein filled vesicles may either be expelled from the cell as **secretory vesicles**, released from the Golgi to mature into **lysosomes**, or transported to other parts of the cell such as the mitochondria or even back to the ER (Figure 4.4 and 4.5).

**Secretory vesicles** (sometimes called *zymogen granules*) may contain enzymes, growth factors, or extracellular matrix components. Secretory vesicles release their contents through exocytosis. Since exocytosis incorporates vesicle membranes into the cell membrane, secretory vesicles also act as the vehicle with which to supply the cell membrane with its integral proteins and lipids, and as the mechanism for membrane expansion. In the reverse process, endocytotic vesicles made at the cell membrane are shuttled back to the Golgi for recycling of the cell membrane. Secretory vesicles are continuously released by most cells in a process called *constitutive secretion*. Some specialized cells can release secretory vesicles in response to a certain chemical or electrical stimulus. This is called *regulated secretion*. Some proteins are activated within the secretory vesicles. For instance, proinsulin is cleaved to insulin only after the secretory vesicle buds off the Golgi.

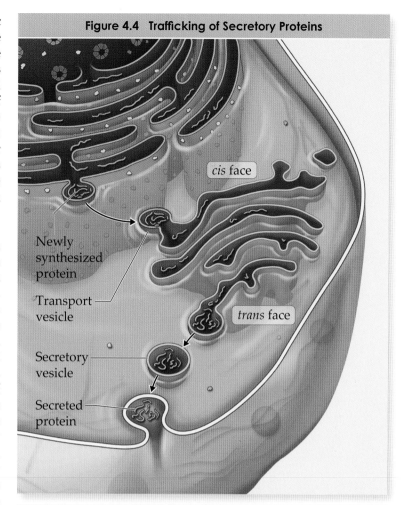

**Figure 4.4  Trafficking of Secretory Proteins**

*cis* face

Newly synthesized protein

Transport vesicle

*trans* face

Secretory vesicle

Secreted protein

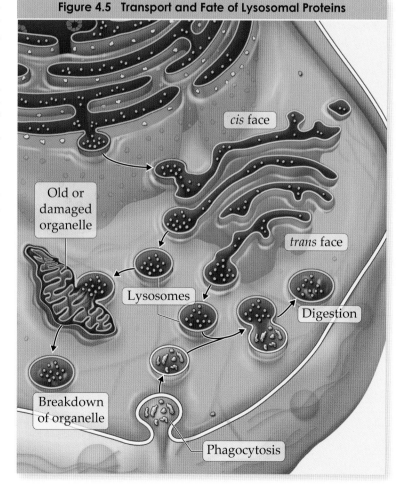

**Figure 4.5  Transport and Fate of Lysosomal Proteins**

*cis* face

Old or damaged organelle

*trans* face

Lysosomes

Digestion

Breakdown of organelle

Phagocytosis

**Lysosomes** contain *acid hydrolases* (hydrolytic enzymes that function best in an acid environment) such as *proteases*, *lipases*, *nucleases* and *glycosidases*. Together, these enzymes are capable of breaking down every major type of macromolecule within the cell. Lysosomes generally have an interior pH of 5. They fuse with endocytotic vesicles (the vesicles formed by phagocytosis and pinocytosis), and digest their contents. Any material not degraded by the lysosome is ejected from the cell through exocytosis. Lysosomes also take up and degrade cytosolic proteins in an endocytotic process. Under certain conditions lysosomes will rupture and release their contents into the cytosol killing the cell in a process called *autolysis*. Autolysis is useful in the formation of certain organs and tissues, like in the destruction of the tissue between the digits of a human fetus in order to form fingers.

Endoplasmic reticulum, which lacks ribosomes, is called **agranular** or **smooth endoplasmic reticulum**. Rough ER tends to resemble flattened sacs, whereas smooth ER tends to be tubular. Smooth ER plays several important roles in the cell. Smooth ER contains *glucose 6-phosphatase*, the enzyme used in the liver, the intestinal epithelial cells, and renal tubule epithelial cells, to hydrolyze glucose 6-phosphate to glucose, an important step in the production of glucose from glycogen. Triglycerides are produced in the smooth ER and stored in fat droplets. **Adipocytes** are cells containing predominately fat droplets. Such cells are important in energy storage and body temperature regulation. The smooth ER and the cytosol share in the role of cholesterol formation and its subsequent conversion to various steroids. Most of the phospholipids in the cell membrane are originally synthesized in the smooth ER. The phospholipids are all synthesized on the cytosol side of the membrane and then some are flipped to the other side by proteins called phospholipid translocators located exclusively in the smooth ER. Finally, smooth ER oxidizes foreign substances, detoxifying drugs, pesticides, toxins, and pollutants.

**Peroxisomes** are vesicles in the cytosol. They grow by incorporating lipids and proteins from the cytosol. Rather than budding off membranes like lysosomes from the golgi, peroxisomes self-replicate. They are involved in the production and breakdown of hydrogen peroxide. Peroxisomes inactivate toxic substances such as alcohol, regulate oxygen concentration, play a role in the synthesis and the breakdown of lipids, and in the metabolism of nitrogenous bases and carbohydrates.

Delivery for Mr. Membrane.

*Golgi Salty*

There is a lot of background information here that is not required by the MCAT. For the MCAT you should know the following:

1. There are many internal compartments in a cell (organelles) separated from the cytosol by membranes. In order to enter into a cell, a substance must be transported via passive transport, active transport, or facilitated diffusion or it can be bulk transported via endocytosis.

2. Rough ER has ribosomes attached to its cytosol side, and it synthesizes virtually all proteins not used in the cytosol. Proteins synthesized on the rough ER are pushed into the ER lumen and sent to the Golgi.

3. The Golgi modifies and packages proteins for use in other parts of the cell and outside the cell.

4. Lysosomes contain hydrolytic enzymes that digest substances taken in by endocytosis. Lysosomes come from the Golgi.

5. Smooth ER is the site of lipid synthesis including steroids. The smooth ER also helps to detoxify some drugs.

## 4.3 Cellular Filaments

The structure and motility of a cell is determined by a network of filaments known as the **cytoskeleton**. The cytoskeleton anchors some membrane proteins and other cellular components, moves components within the cell, and moves the cell itself. Two major types of filaments in the cytoskeleton are **microtubules** (Figure 4.6) and microfilaments. Microtubules are larger than **microfilaments**. They are rigid hollow tubes made from a protein called **tubulin**. Although tubulin is a globular protein, under certain cellular conditions it polymerizes into long straight filaments. Thirteen of these filaments lie alongside each other to form the tube. The spiral appearance is due to the two types of tubulin, α and β, used in the synthesis. The **mitotic spindle** (see Biology Lecture 2) is made from microtubules.

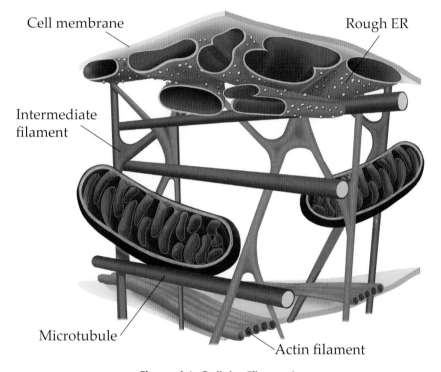

**Figure 4.6 Cellular Filaments**

Cell membrane
Rough ER
Intermediate filament
Microtubule
Actin filament

> You must know the difference between microtubules and microfilaments. Microtubules are larger and are involved in flagella and cilia construction, and the spindle apparatus. In humans, cilia are found only in the fallopian tubes and the respiratory tract. Microfilaments squeeze the membrane together in phagocytosis and cytokinesis. They are also the contractile force in microvilli and muscle.

**Flagella** and **cilia** are specialized structures also made from microtubules. The major portion of each flagellum and cilium, called the **axoneme**, contains nine pairs of microtubules forming a circle around two lone microtubules in an arrangement known as **9+2**. Cross bridges made from a protein called **dynein** connect each of the outer pairs of microtubules to their neighbor. The cross bridges cause the microtubule pairs to slide along their neighbors creating a whip action in cilia causing fluid to move laterally, or a wiggle action in flagella causing fluid to move directly away from the cell.

Microtubules have a + and − end. The − end attaches to a *microtubule-organizing center (MTOC)* in the cell. A microtubule grows away from an MTOC at its + end. The major MTOC in animal cells is the **centrosome**. The **centrioles** function in the production of flagella and cilia, but are not necessary for microtubule production.

Microfilaments are smaller than microtubules. The polymerized protein **actin** forms a major component of microfilaments. Microfilaments produce the contracting force in muscle (discussed in Biology Lecture 8) as well as being active in **cytoplasmic streaming** (responsible for amoeba-like movement), phagocytosis, and microvilli movement.

There is also a third class of cellular filaments that you should be aware of: intermediate filaments. When fully formed, they have a diameter that is smaller than microtubules but larger than microfilaments. Intermediate filaments are not nearly as dynamic as microtubules or microfilaments and primarily serve to impart structural rigidity to the cell. Keratin, a type of intermediate filament found in epithelial cells, is associated with hair and skin.

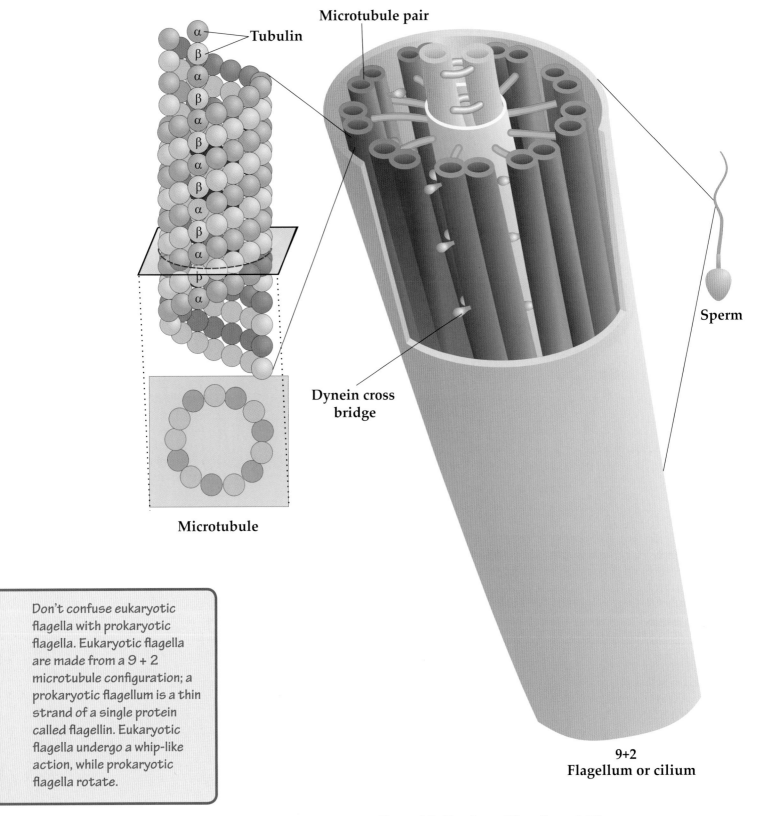

Don't confuse eukaryotic flagella with prokaryotic flagella. Eukaryotic flagella are made from a 9 + 2 microtubule configuration; a prokaryotic flagellum is a thin strand of a single protein called flagellin. Eukaryotic flagella undergo a whip-like action, while prokaryotic flagella rotate.

**Figure 4.7  Structure of Flagella and Cilia**

## 4.4 Cellular Junctions

There are three types of junctions or attachments that connect animal cells: tight junctions, desmosomes, and gap junctions (Figure 4.8). Each junction performs a different function. **Tight junctions** form a watertight seal from cell to cell that can block water, ions, and other molecules from moving around and past cells. Tissue held together by tight junctions may act as a complete fluid barrier. Epithelial tissue in organs like the bladder, the intestines, and the kidney are held together by tight junctions in order to prevent waste materials from seeping around the cells and into the body. Since proteins have some freedom to move laterally about the cell membrane, tight junctions also act as a barrier to protein movement between the *apical* and the *basolateral* surface of a cell. (The part of a cell facing the lumen of a cavity is called the apical surface. The opposite side of a cell is called the basolateral surface.)

**Desmosomes** join two cells at a single point. They attach directly to the cytoskeleton of each cell. Desmosomes do not prevent fluid from circulating around all sides of a cell. Desmosomes are found in tissues that normally experience a lot of stress, like skin or intestinal epithelium. Desmosomes often accompany tight junctions.

**Gap junctions** are small tunnels connecting cells. They allow small molecules and ions to move between cells. Gap junctions in cardiac muscle provide for the spread of the action potential from cell to cell.

You can think of tight junctions like the plastic rings around a six pack of beer. The beer cans are the cells. The plastic rings hold the cans together and provide a water tight barrier around them. Although the beer cans are impermeable to water, real cells may or may not be impermeable.

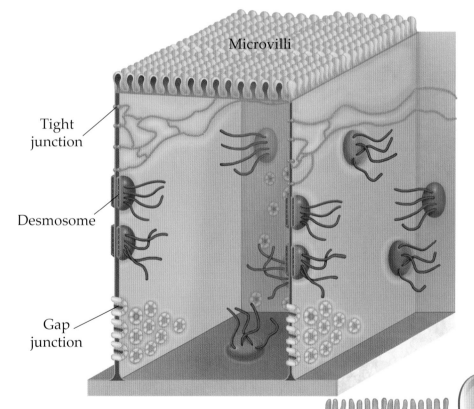

Microvilli

Tight junction

Desmosome

Gap junction

**Figure 4.8   Cellular Junctions**

Remember the three types of cellular junctions. Tight junctions act as a fluid barrier around cells. Demosomes are like spot-welds holding cells together. Gap junctions are tunnels between cells allowing for the exchange of small molecules.

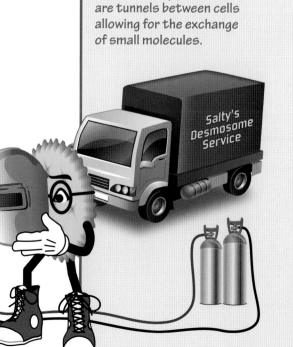

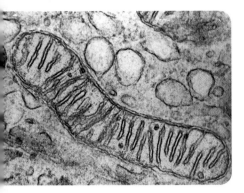

The inner membrane on mitochondria folds inward to form cristae.

## 4.5 Mitochondria

**Mitochondria** (Figure 4.9) are the powerhouses of the eukaryotic cell. We have already seen that the Krebs cycle takes place inside the mitochondria. According to the **endosymbiont theory**, mitochondria may have evolved from a symbiotic relationship between ancient prokaryotes and eukaryotes. Like prokaryotes, mitochondria have their own circular DNA that replicates independently from the eukaryotic cell. This DNA contains no histones or nucleosomes. Most animals have a few dozen to several hundred molecules of circular DNA in each mitochondrion. The genes in the mitochondrial DNA code for mitochondrial RNA that is distinct from the RNA in the rest of the cell. Thus mitochondria have their own ribosomes with a sediment coefficient of 55-60S in humans. However, most proteins used by mitochondria are coded for by nuclear DNA, not mitochondrial DNA. Antibiotics that block translation by prokaryotic ribosomes but not eukaryotic ribosomes, also block translation by mitochondrial ribosomes. Interestingly, some of the codons in mitochondria differ from the codons in the rest of the cell, presenting an exception to the universal genetic code! Mitochondrial DNA is passed maternally (from the mother) even in organisms whose male gamete contributes to the cytoplasm.

Mitochondria are surrounded by two phospholipid bilayers. The **inner membrane** invaginates to form **cristae**. It is the inner membrane that holds the electron transport chain. Between the inner and **outer membrane** is the **intermembrane space**.

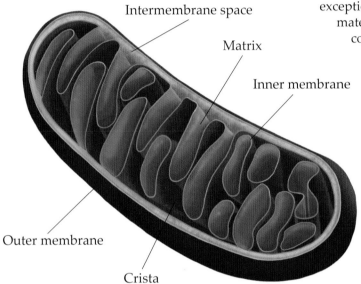

Intermembrane space

Matrix

Inner membrane

Outer membrane

Crista

**Figure 4.9   Mitochondrion**

> Memorize the parts of the mitochondrion and its purpose. Relate the parts to respiration discussed in Biology Lecture 1.

## 4.6 The Extracellular Matrix

Most cells in multicellular organisms form groups of similar cells, or cells that work together for a common purpose, called *tissue*. In some tissues, cells called fibroblasts secrete fibrous proteins such as elastin and collagen that form a molecular network that holds tissue cells in place called an *extracellular matrix*. Different tissues form dramatically different matrices. The matrix can constitute most of the tissue as in bone, where a few cells are interspersed in a large matrix, or the matrix may be only a small part of the tissue. The consistency of the matrix may be liquid as in blood, or solid as in bone.

An extracellular matrix may provide structural support, help to determine the cell shape and motility, and affect cell growth.

Three classes of molecules make up animal cell matrices:

1. *glycosaminoglycans* and *proteoglycans*;
2. structural proteins;
3. adhesive proteins.

Glycosaminoglycans are polysaccharides that typically have proteoglycans attached. They make up over 90% of the matrix by mass. This first class of molecules provides pliability to the matrix. Structural proteins provide the matrix with strength. The most common extracellular matrix structural protein in the body is collagen. Collagen is the structural protein that gives cartilage and bone their tensile strength. Adhesive proteins help individual cells within a tissue to stick together.

You may see basal lamina (which along with the reticular lamina forms the basement membrane) in an MCAT passage. The basal lamina is a thin sheet of matrix material that separates epithelial cells from *support tissue*. (Epithelial cells separate the outside environment from the inside of the body. Support tissue is composed of the cells adjacent to the epithelial cells on the inside of the body.) Basal lamina is also found around nerves, and muscle and fat cells. Basal lamina typically acts as a sieve type barrier, selectively allowing the passage of some molecules but not others.

Many animal cells contain a carbohydrate region analogous to the plant cell wall or bacterial cell wall, called the *glycocalyx*. The glycocalyx separates the cell membrane from the extracellular matrix; however, a part of the glycocalyx is made from the same material as the matrix. Thus, the glycocalyx is often difficult to identify. The glycocalyx may be involved in cell-cell recognition, adhesion, cell surface protection, and permeability.

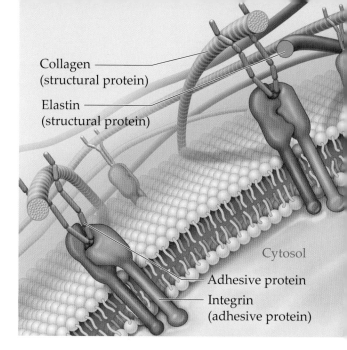

**Figure 4.10 The Extracellular Matrix**

Don't worry about memorizing anything about the extracellular matrix. Just know that it's the stuff that surrounds the cell and that it is formed by the cell itself.

## 4.7 Organization in Multicellular Eukaryotes

In multicellular eukaryotes, groups of cells work together, each type of cell performing a unique function that contributes to the specialized function of the group. These groups of cells are called *tissues*. Cells in the same tissue usually have similar embryology; they arise from the same embryonic germ layer. There are four basic types of tissue in animals: *epithelial tissue, muscle tissue, connective tissue*, and *nervous tissue*. Epithelial tissue separates free body surfaces from their surroundings. *Simple epithelium* is one layer thick, while *stratified epithelium* is two or more layers thick. Simple epithelium includes *endothelium* lining the various vessels of the body including the heart. Connective tissue is characterized by an extensive matrix. Examples include: blood, lymph, bone, cartilage, and connective tissue proper making up tendons and ligaments. Muscle and nervous tissue will be discussed later.

Different tissue types work together to form *organs*. For example, the stomach is an organ with an outer layer made from epithelial tissue and connective tissue, a second layer of muscle tissue, and an innermost layer of epithelial tissue.

Organs that work together to perform a common function are called *systems*. The remainder of this manual (except for Lecture 9) is devoted to the study of biological systems in the human body. Many of the details are not required knowledge for the MCAT. However, if you keep in mind the holistic concept (the body is not simply many disconnected parts but an entire organism with systems that work in conjunction with each other), you will attain a stronger recall of the details and a greater understanding of material.

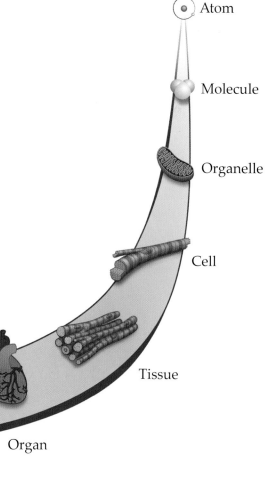

73. All of the following are composed of microtubules EXCEPT:

    A. the tail of a sperm cell.
    B. the spindle apparatus.
    C. the cilia of the fallopian tubes.
    D. the flagella of bacteria.

74. Which of the following is true concerning the nucleolus?

    A. It is bound by a phospholipid membrane.
    B. It disappears during prophase.
    C. It is the site of translation of ribosomal RNA.
    D. It is found in most bacteria.

75. In some specialized cells, glucose is transported against its concentration gradient via an integral protein using the energy of the sodium ion electrochemical gradient. If no ATP is used for this transport, it is most likely:

    A. active transport.
    B. facilitated transport.
    C. passive transport.
    D. osmosis.

76. Which of the following cells would be expected to contain the most smooth endoplasmic reticulum?

    A. a liver cell
    B. an islet cell from the pancreas
    C. a mature sperm
    D. a zygote

77. Which of the following statements is true concerning tight junctions?

    I. They connect adjacent cells.
    II. They may form a barrier to extracellular fluids.
    III. They have the greatest strength of all cellular adhesions.

    A. I only
    B. I and II only
    C. II and III only
    D. I, II, and III

78. Which of the following is not a membrane bound organelle?

    A. the golgi body
    B. the nucleus
    C. the smooth endoplasmic reticulum
    D. the ribosome

79. One function of the liver is to detoxify alcohol taken into the body. The organelle within the liver cell that most directly affects this process is:

    A. the smooth endoplasmic reticulum
    B. the nucleus
    C. the Golgi apparatus
    D. the rough endoplasmic reticulum

80. When a primary lysosome fuses with a food vesicle to become a secondary lysosome:

    A. its pH drops via active pumping of protons into its interior.
    B. its pH drops via active pumping of protons out of its interior.
    C. its pH rises via active pumping of protons into its interior.
    D. its pH rises via active pumping of protons out of its interior.

## 4.8 Intercellular Communication

In multicellular organisms, cells must be able to communicate with each other so that the organism can function as a single unit. Communication is accomplished chemically via three types of molecules: 1) neurotransmitters; 2) local mediators; 3) hormones. These methods of communication are governed by the nervous system, the paracrine system, and the endocrine system respectively.

There are several distinctions between the methods of communication, the major distinction being the distance traveled by the mediator. Neurotransmitters travel over very short intercellular gaps; local mediators function in the immediate area around the cell from which they were released; hormones travel throughout the organism via the blood stream.

For the MCAT, you should focus on the distinctions between neurotransmitter and hormonal mediated communication. Neurotransmitters are released by neurons. **Neuronal communication** tends to be **rapid**, direct, and **specific**. **Hormonal communication**, on the other hand, tends to be **slower, spread throughout the body, and affect many cells and tissues in many different ways.**

## 4.9 Paracrine System

Local mediators are released by a variety of cells into the **interstitial fluid** (fluid between the cells) and act on neighboring cells a few millimeters away. Local mediators may be proteins, other amino acid derivatives, or even fatty acids. *Prostaglandins* are fatty acid derivative local mediators. Prostaglandins affect smooth muscle contraction, platelet aggregation, inflammation and other reactions. Aspirin inhibits prostaglandin synthesis and thus is an anti-inflammatory. Growth factors and lymphokines, discussed later, are other examples of local mediators.

> Specific knowledge of the paracrine system will not be tested by the MCAT. However, you should be aware of the existence of this intermediate communication system.

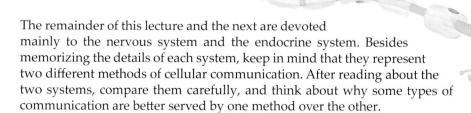

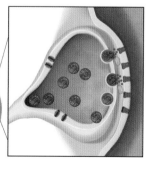

The remainder of this lecture and the next are devoted mainly to the nervous system and the endocrine system. Besides memorizing the details of each system, keep in mind that they represent two different methods of cellular communication. After reading about the two systems, compare them carefully, and think about why some types of communication are better served by one method over the other.

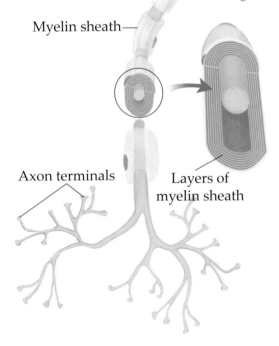

Dendrites

Mitochondrion

Nucleus

Axon hillock

Node of Ranvier

Myelin sheath

Axon terminals

Layers of myelin sheath

**Figure 4.11 Myelinated Neuron**

> You must know the basic anatomy of a neuron. Remember that a signal travels from the dendrites to the axon hillock, where an action potential is generated and moves down the axon to the synapse. Neurons do not depend upon insulin to obtain glucose.

# 4.10 Nervous System

The nervous system allows for rapid and direct communication between specific parts of the body resulting in changes in muscular contractions or glandular secretions. Included within the nervous system are the brain, spinal cord, nerves and neural support cells, and certain sense organs such as the eye, and the ear.

The functional unit of the nervous system is the **neuron** (Figure 4.12). A neuron is a highly specialized cell capable of transmitting an electrical signal from one cell to another via electrical or chemical means. The neuron is so highly specialized that it has lost the capacity to divide. In addition, it depends almost entirely upon glucose for its chemical energy. Although the neuron uses facilitated transport to move glucose from the blood into its cytosol, unlike most other cells, the neuron is not dependent upon insulin for this transport. The neuron depends heavily on the efficiency of aerobic respiration. However, it has low stores of glycogen and oxygen, and must rely on blood to supply sufficient levels of these nutrients. Neurons in different parts of the body have a different appearance, but all neurons have a basic anatomy consisting of many dendrites, a single cell body, and usually one axon with many small branches.

The **dendrites** receive a signal to be transmitted. Typically, the cytosol of the cell body is highly conductive and any electrical stimulus creates a disturbance in the electric field that is transferred immediately to the axon hillock. If the stimulus is great enough, the **axon hillock** generates an action potential in all directions, including down the **axon**. The membrane of the cell body usually does not contain enough ion channels to sustain an action potential. The axon, however, carries the action potential to a synapse, which passes the signal to another cell.

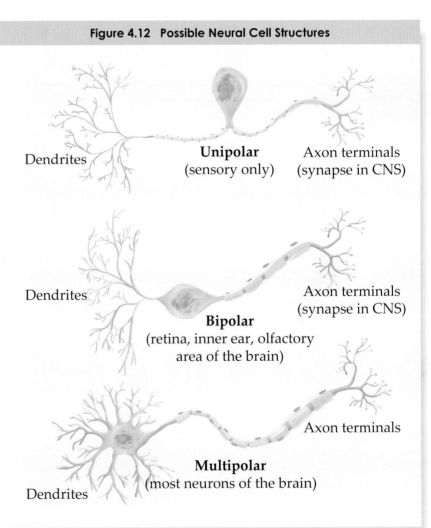

**Figure 4.12  Possible Neural Cell Structures**

Dendrites

**Unipolar**
(sensory only)

Axon terminals
(synapse in CNS)

Dendrites

**Bipolar**
(retina, inner ear, olfactory area of the brain)

Axon terminals
(synapse in CNS)

Axon terminals

**Multipolar**
(most neurons of the brain)

Dendrites

## 4.11 The Action Potential

The **action potential** is a disturbance in the electric field across the membrane of a neuron. To understand the action potential, we first must understand the **resting potential**. The resting potential is established mainly by an equilibrium between passive diffusion of ions across the membrane and the Na⁺/K⁺ pump. The Na⁺/K⁺ pump moves three positively charged sodium ions out of the cell while bringing two positively charged potassium ions into the cell. This action increases the positive charge along the membrane just outside the cell relative to the charge along the membrane on the inside of the cell. As the electrochemical gradient of Na⁺ increases, the force pushing the Na⁺ back into the cell also increases. The rate at which Na⁺ passively diffuses back into the cell increases until it equals the rate at which it is being pumped out of the cell. The same thing happens for potassium. When all rates reach equilibrium, the inside of the membrane has a negative potential difference (voltage) compared to the outside. This potential difference is called the resting potential. Although other ions are involved, Na⁺ and K⁺ are the major players in establishing the resting potential.

The membrane of a neuron also contains integral membrane proteins called **voltage gated sodium channels**. These proteins change configuration when the voltage across the membrane is disturbed. Specifically, they allow Na⁺ to flow through the membrane for a fraction of a second as they change configuration. As Na⁺ flows into the cell, the voltage changes still further, causing more sodium channels to change configuration, allowing still more sodium to flow into the cell in a positive feedback mechanism. Since the Na⁺ concentration moves toward equilibrium, and the K⁺ concentration remains higher inside the cell, the membrane potential actually reverses polarity so that it is positive on the inside and negative on the outside. This process is called **depolarization**. The neuronal membrane also contains **voltage gated potassium channels**. The potassium channels are less sensitive to voltage change so they take longer to open. By the time they begin to open, most of the sodium channels are closing. Now K⁺ flows out of the cell, making the inside more negative in a process called **repolarization**. The potassium channels are so slow to close that, for a fraction of a second, the inside membrane becomes even more negative than the resting potential. This portion of the process is called **hyperpolarization**. Passive diffusion returns the membrane to its resting potential. The entire process just described is called the action potential (Figure 4.14). Throughout the action potential, the Na⁺/K⁺ pump keeps working.

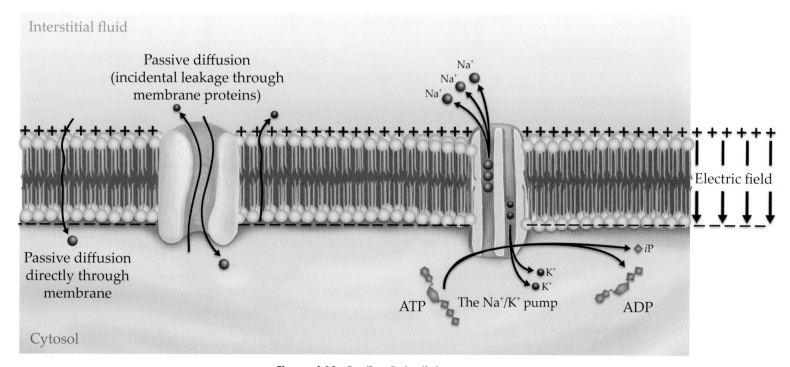

**Figure 4.13  Resting Potential**

The action potential occurs at a point on a membrane and propagates along that membrane by depolarizing the section of membrane immediately adjacent to it. In Figure 4.14, the protein channels marked 1 are about to recieve the action potential while the protein channels marked 5 have already received the action potential. Therefore, the action potential is traveling from right to left along the membrane (Figure 4.14 and 4.15); the synapse would be to the left of the portion of the membrane shown. The voltage as a function of time at any given point on the membrane is given by the wave shown. The entire action potential as measured at one point on the membrane of a neuron takes place in a fraction of a millisecond.

### Figure 4.14 Steps of the Action Potential

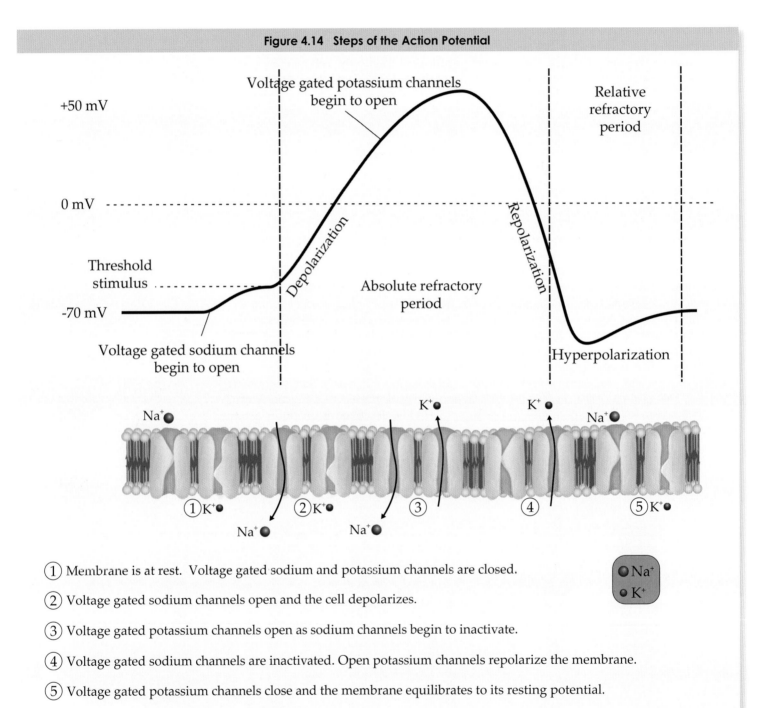

① Membrane is at rest. Voltage gated sodium and potassium channels are closed.

② Voltage gated sodium channels open and the cell depolarizes.

③ Voltage gated potassium channels open as sodium channels begin to inactivate.

④ Voltage gated sodium channels are inactivated. Open potassium channels repolarize the membrane.

⑤ Voltage gated potassium channels close and the membrane equilibrates to its resting potential.

> You must understand the dynamics of the membrane potential. Use the Na⁺/K⁺ pump to help you remember that the inside of the membrane is negative with respect to the outside. Different cells have different action potentials. If you understand the principle, you should be able to understand any action potential. Remember that an action potential originates at the axon hillock. This section is important for the MCAT. If you don't thoroughly understand it, then you should reread it.

An action potential is **all-or-nothing**; the membrane completely depolarizes or no action potential is generated. In order to create an action potential, the stimulus to the membrane must be greater than the **threshold stimulus**. Any stimulus greater than the threshold stimulus creates the same size action potential. If the threshold stimulus is reached, but is reached very slowly, an action potential still may not occur. This is called *accommodation*. Once an action potential has begun, there is a short period of time called the *absolute refractory period* in which no stimulus will create another action potential. The *relative refractory period* gives the time during which only an abnormally large stimulus will create an action potential.

Other cells, such as skeletal and cardiac muscle cells also conduct action potentials. Although these action potentials are slightly different in duration, shape, and even the types of ions, they work on the same principles.

The action potential in Figure 4.15 moves along the axon from right to left.

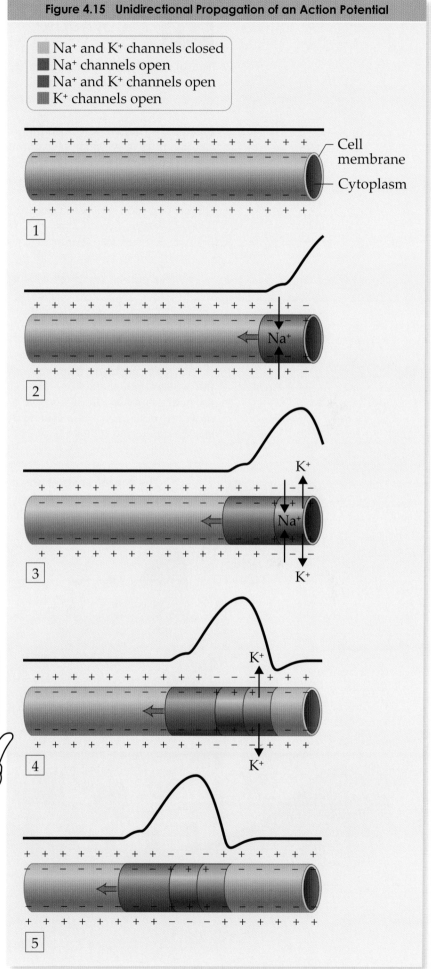

**Figure 4.15   Unidirectional Propagation of an Action Potential**

Na⁺ and K⁺ channels closed
Na⁺ channels open
Na⁺ and K⁺ channels open
K⁺ channels open

## 4.12 The Synapse

Neural impulses are transmitted from one cell to another chemically or electrically via a **synapse**. The transmission of the signal from one cell to another is the slowest part of the process of nervous system cellular communication, yet it occurs in a fraction of a second.

**Electrical synapses** are uncommon. They are composed of gap junctions between cells. Cardiac muscle, visceral smooth muscle, and a very few neurons in the central nervous system contain electrical synapses. Since they don't involve diffusion of chemicals, they transmit signals much faster than chemical synapses and in both directions.

A more common synapse, a **chemical synapse** (Figure 4.16) (called a motor end plate when connecting a neuron to a muscle), is **unidirectional**. In a chemical synapse, small vesicles filled with neurotransmitter rest just inside the presynaptic membrane. The membrane near the synapse contains an unusually large number of $Ca^{2+}$ voltage gated channels. When an action potential arrives at a synapse, these channels are activated allowing $Ca^{2+}$ to flow into the cell. In a mechanism not completely understood, the sudden influx of calcium ions causes some of the neurotransmitter vesicles to be released through an exocytotic process into the **synaptic cleft**. The neurotransmitter diffuses across the synaptic cleft via **Brownian motion** (the random motion of the molecules). The postsynaptic membrane contains neurotransmitter receptor proteins. When the neurotransmitter attaches to the receptor proteins, the postsynaptic membrane becomes more permeable to ions. Ions move across the postsynaptic membrane through proteins called *ionophores*, completing the transfer of the neural impulse. In this way, the impulse is not attenuated by electrical resistance as it moves from one cell to the next. If a cell is fired too often (hundreds of times per second for several minutes) it will not be able to replenish its supply of neurotransmitter vessicles, and the result is *fatigue* (the impulse will not pass to the postsynaptic neuron).

The **neurotransmitter** attaches to its receptor for only a fraction of a second, and is released back into the synaptic cleft. If the neurotransmitter remains in the synaptic cleft, the postsynaptic cell may be stimulated over and over. There are several mechanisms by which the cell deals with this problem. The neurotransmitter may be destroyed by an enzyme in the matrix of the synaptic cleft and its parts recycled by the presynaptic cell. It may be directly absorbed by the presynaptic cell via active transport. The neurotransmitter may also diffuse out of the synaptic cleft.

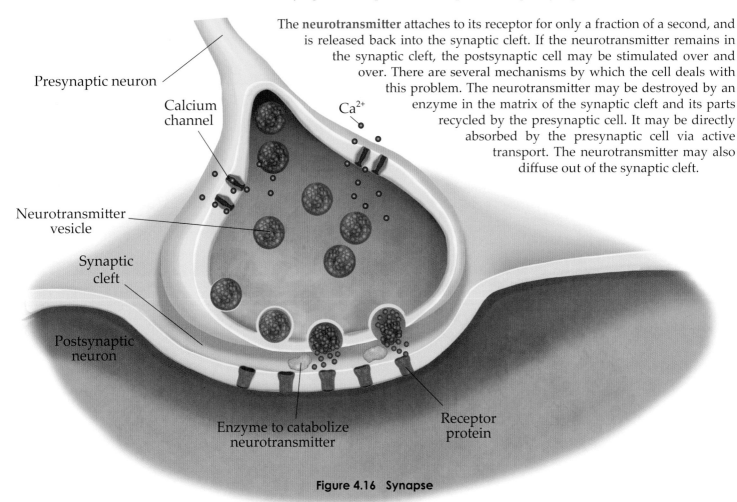

Presynaptic neuron

Calcium channel

$Ca^{2+}$

Neurotransmitter vesicle

Synaptic cleft

Postsynaptic neuron

Enzyme to catabolize neurotransmitter

Receptor protein

**Figure 4.16   Synapse**

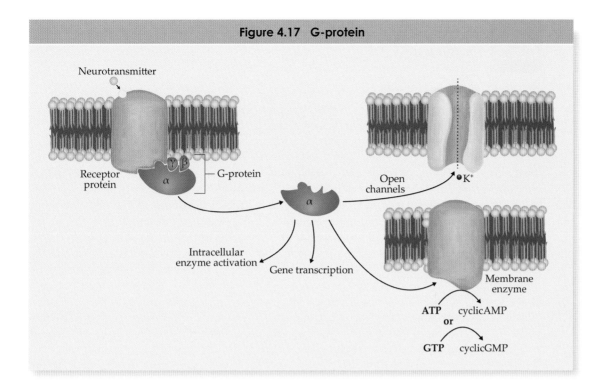

**Figure 4.17  G-protein**

Over 50 types of neurotransmitters have been identified. Different neurotransmitters are characteristic of different parts of the nervous system (i.e. certain neurotransmitters are found in certain areas of the nervous system). A single synapse usually releases only one type of neurotransmitter and is designed either to inhibit or to excite, but not both. A single synapse cannot change from inhibitory to excitatory, or vice versa. On the other hand, some neurotransmitters are capable of inhibition or excitation depending upon the type of receptor in the postsynaptic membrane. Acetylcholine, a common neurotransmitter, has an inhibitory effect on the heart, but an excitatory effect on the visceral smooth muscle of the intestines.

Receptors may be ion channels themselves, which are opened when their respective neurotransmitter attaches, or they may act via a **second messenger system** activating another molecule inside the cell to make changes. For prolonged change, such as that involved in memory, the second messenger system is preferred. *G-proteins* (Figure 4.17) commonly initiate second messenger systems. A G-protein is attached to the receptor protein along the inside of the postsynaptic membrane. When the receptor is stimulated by a neurotransmitter, part of the G-protein, called the *α-subunit*, breaks free. The *α*-subunit may:

1.  activate separate specific ion channels;
2.  activate a second messenger (i.e. cyclic AMP or cyclic GMP);
3.  activate intracellular enzymes;
4.  activate gene transcription.

A single neuron may make a few to as many as 200,000 synapses (Figure 4.18). Most synapses contact dendrites, but some may directly contact other cell bodies, other axons, or even other synapses. The firing of one or more of these synapses creates a change in the neuron cell potential. This change in the cell potential is called either the *excitatory postsynaptic potential (EPSP)* or the *inhibitory postsynaptic potential (IPSP)*. Normally, 40-80 synapses must fire simultaneously on the same neuron in order for an EPSP to create an action potential within that neuron.

> The chemical synapse is the important synapse for the MCAT. Understand that it is the slowest step in the transfer of a nervous signal, and that it can only transfer a signal in one direction. Also recognize what a second messenger system is.

**Figure 4.18  Motor Neuron with Synaptic Terminals**

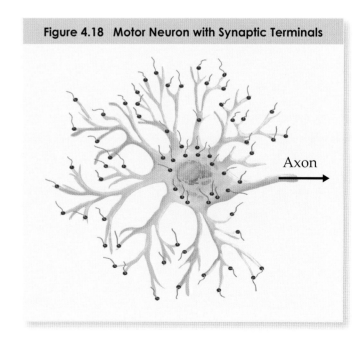

Axon

## 4.13 Support Cells

Besides neurons, nervous tissue contains many support cells called *glial cells* or *neuroglia*. In fact, in the human brain, glial cells typically outnumber neurons 10 to 1. Neuroglia are capable of cellular division, and, in the case of traumatic injury to the brain, it is the neuroglia that multiply to fill any space created in the central nervous system.

There are six types of glial cells: *microglia*; *ependymal cells*; *satellite cells*; *astrocytes*; *oligodendrocytes*; and *neurolemmocytes* or Schwann cells. Microglia arise from white blood cells called monocytes. They phagocytize microbes and cellular debris in the central nervous system. Ependymal cells are epithelial cells that line the space containing the cerebrospinal fluid. Ependymal cells use cilia to circulate the cerebrospinal fluid. Satellite cells support *ganglia* (groups of cell bodies in the peripheral nervous system). Astrocytes are star-shaped neuroglia in the central nervous system that give physical support to neurons, and help maintain the mineral and nutrient balance in the interstitial space. Oligodendrocytes wrap many times around axons in the central nervous system creating electrically insulating sheaths called **myelin**. In the peripheral nervous system, myelin is produced by **Schwann cells**. Myelin increases the rate at which an axon can transmit signals. To the naked eye, myelinated axons appear white while the neuronal cell bodies appear gray. Hence the name **white matter** and **gray matter**. Tiny gaps between myelin are called **nodes of Ranvier**. When an action potential is generated down a myelinated axon, the action potential jumps from one node of Ranvier to the next as quickly as the disturbance moves through the electric field between them. This is called **saltatory conduction** (Latin *saltus*: a jump).

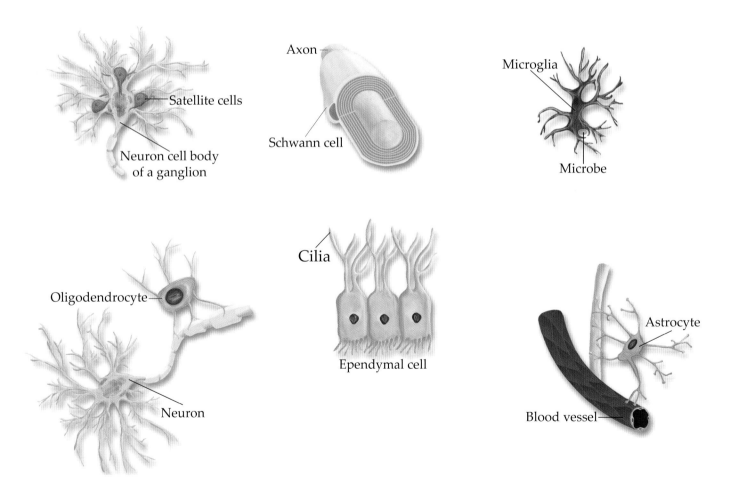

**Figure 4.19  Neuroglia**

81. Which of the following gives the normal direction of signal transmission in a neuron?

    A. from the axon to the cell body to the dendrites
    B. from the dendrites to the cell body to the axon
    C. from the cell body to the axon and dendrites
    D. from the dendrites to the axon to the cell body

82. Novocaine is a local anesthetic used by many dentists. Novocaine most likely inhibits the action potential of a neuron by:

    A. stimulating calcium voltage gated channels at the synapse.
    B. increasing chloride ion efflux during an action potential.
    C. uncoiling Schwann cells wrapped around an axon.
    D. blocking sodium voltage gated channels.

83. A cell membrane is normally slightly passively permeable to potassum ions. If a neuronal membrane were to become suddenly impermeable to potassium ions but retain an active $Na^+/K^+$-ATPase, the neurons resting potential would:

    A. become more positive because potassium ion concentration would increase inside the neuron.
    B. become more positive because potassium ion concentration would increase outside the neuron.
    C. become more negative because potassium ion concentration would increase inside the neuron.
    D. become more negative because potassium ion concentration would increase outside the neuron.

84. If an acetylcholinesterase inhibitor were administered into a cholinergic synapse, what would happen to the activity of the postsynaptic neuron?

    A. It would decrease, because acetylcholine would be degraded more rapidly than normal.
    B. It would decrease, because acetylcholinesterase would bind to postsynaptic membrane receptors less strongly.
    C. It would increase, because acetylcholine would be produced more rapidly than normal.
    D. It would increase, because acetylcholine would be degraded more slowly than normal.

85. White matter in the brain and spinal cord appears white because:

    A. it contains large amounts of myelinated axons.
    B. it does not contain any myelinated axons.
    C. it is composed primarily of cell bodies.
    D. it contains a high concentration of white blood cells to protect the central nervous system from infection.

86. The jumping of an action potential from one node of Ranvier to the next is known as:

    A. Brownian motion.
    B. saltatory conduction.
    C. a threshold stimulus.
    D. an all-or-nothing response.

87. What is the ratio of sodium ions to potassium ions transferred by the Na+/K+ pump out of and into the cell?

    A. 2 sodium ions in; 3 potassium ions out
    B. 3 sodium ions in; 2 potassium ions out
    C. 3 sodium ions out; 2 potassium ions in
    D. 2 sodium ions in; 3 potassium ions in

88. Which of the following is found in vertebrates but NOT in invertebrates?

    A. a dorsal, hollow nerve chord
    B. mylenation to increase the speed of nervous impulse transmission along the axon
    C. axons through which the nervous impulse is conducted
    D. $Na^+/K^+$-pump

---

## 4.14 The Structure of the Nervous System

Neurons may perform one of three functions.

1. **Sensory (afferent) neurons** receive signals from a receptor cell that interacts with its environment. The sensory neuron then transfers this signal to other neurons. 99% of sensory input is discarded by the brain.

2. **Interneurons** transfer signals from neuron to neuron. 90% of neurons in the human body are interneurons.

3. **Motor (efferent) neurons** carry signals to a muscle or gland called the **effector**. Sensory neurons are located dorsally (toward the back) from the spinal cord, while motor neurons are located ventrally (toward the front or abdomen).

Figure 4-20 shows a simple reflex arc using all three types of neurons. Some reflex arcs do not require an interneuron. Neuron processes (axons and dendrites) are typically bundled together to form **nerves** (called tracts in the CNS as discussed below).

**Figure 4.20   Simple Reflex Arc of the Somatic Nervous System**

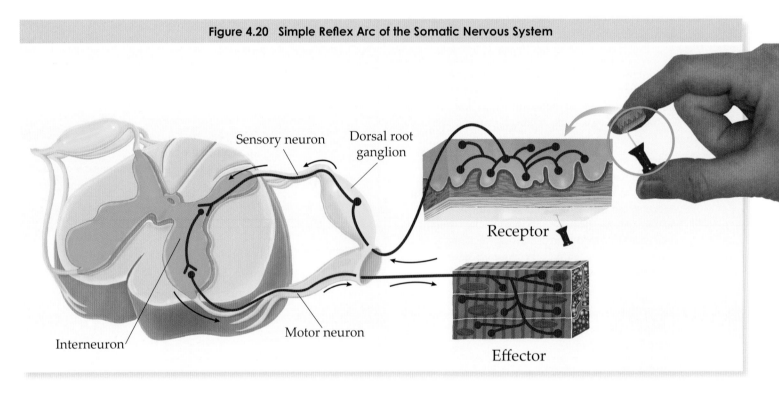

Sensory neuron

Dorsal root ganglion

Receptor

Interneuron

Motor neuron

Effector

> For the MCAT, think of the CNS as the brain and spinal cord, and the PNS as everything else.

The nervous system has two major divisions: the **central nervous system (CNS)** and the **peripheral nervous system (PNS)**. The CNS consists of the interneurons and support tissue within the brain and the spinal cord. The function of the CNS is to integrate nervous signals between sensory and motor neurons.

The CNS is connected to the peripheral parts of the body by the PNS. Parts of the PNS, such as the *cranial nerves* and the *spinal nerves*, project into the brain and spinal cord. The PNS handles the sensory and motor functions of the nervous system. The PNS can be further divided into the **somatic nervous system** and **autonomic nervous system (ANS)**. The somatic nervous system is designed primarily to respond to the external environment. It contains sensory and motor functions. Its motor neurons innervate only skeletal muscle. The cell bodies of somatic motor neurons are located in the ventral horns of the spinal cord. These neurons synapse directly on their effectors and use acetylcholine for their neurotransmitter. The motor functions of the somatic nervous system can be consciously controlled and are considered voluntary. The sensory neuron cell bodies are located in the *dorsal root ganglion*.

The sensory portion of the ANS receives signals primarily from the viscera (the organs inside the ventral body cavity). The motor portion of the ANS then conducts these signals to smooth muscle, cardiac muscle, and glands. The function of the ANS is generally involuntary. The motor portion of the ANS is divided into two systems: **sympathetic** and **parasympathetic** (Figure 4.21). Most internal organs ar innervated by both with the two systems working antagonistically. The sympathetic ANS deals with "fight or flight" responses. For instance, its action on the heart would be to increase beat rate and stroke volume; it works to constrict blood vessels around the digestive and excretory systems in order to increase blood flow around skeletal muscles. Parasympathetic action, on the other hand, generally works toward the opposite goal, to "rest and digest". Parasympathetic activity slows the heart rate and increases digestive and excretory activity.

Sympathetic                                    Parasympathetic

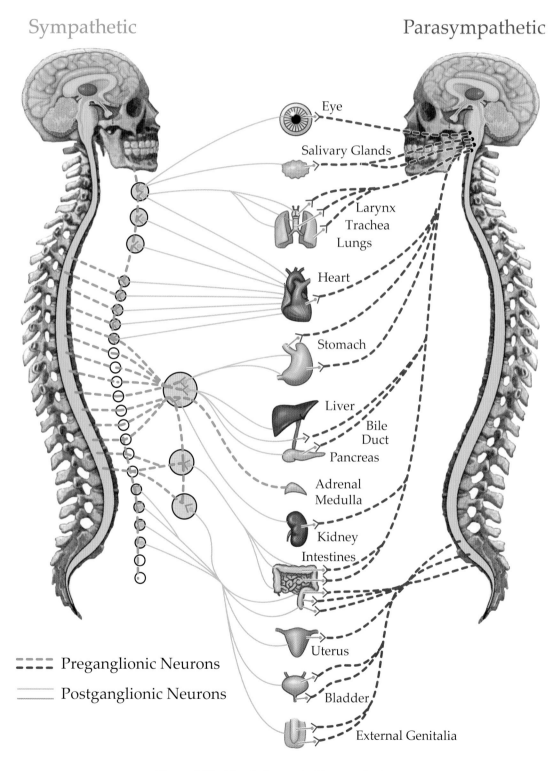

- - - - Preganglionic Neurons
———— Postganglionic Neurons

**Figure 4.21   The Autonomic Nervous System**

Sympathetic signals originate in neurons whose cell bodies are found in the spinal cord, while parasympathetic signals originate in neurons whose cell bodies can be found in both the brain and spinal cord. (A group of cell bodies located in the CNS is called a *nucleus*; if located outside the CNS, it is called a *ganglion*.) These neurons extend out from the spinal cord to synapse with neurons whose cell bodies are located outside the CNS. The former neurons are called preganglionic neurons; the later are called postganglionic neurons. The cell bodies of sympathetic postganglionic neurons lie far from their effectors generally within the paravertebral ganglion, which runs parallel to the spinal cord, or within the prevertebral ganglia in the abdomen. The cell bodies of the parasympathetic postganglionic neurons lie in ganglia inside or near their effectors.

With few exceptions, the neurotransmitter used by all preganglionic neurons in the ANS and by postganglionic neurons in the parasympathetic system is **acetylcholine**; the postganglionic neurons of the sympathetic nervous system use either **epinephrine** or **norepinephrine** (also called **adrenaline** and **noradrenaline**).

Receptors for acetylcholine are called *cholinergic receptors*. There are two types of cholinergic receptors: *nicotinic* and *muscarinic*. Generally, nicotinic receptors are found on the postsynaptic cells of the synapse between ANS preganglionic and postganglionic neurons and on skeletal muscle membranes at the neuromuscular junction. Muscarinic receptors are found on the effectors of the parasympathetic nervous system. The receptors for epinephrine and norepinephrine are called *adrenergic*.

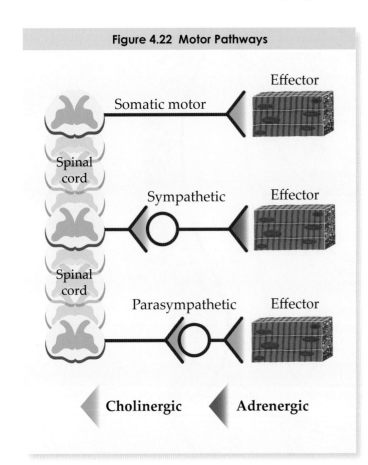

**Figure 4.22 Motor Pathways**

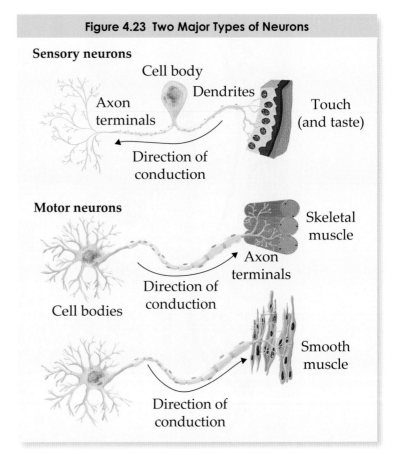

**Figure 4.23 Two Major Types of Neurons**

The autonomic nervous system is involuntary and innervates cardiac and smooth muscle, and some glands; the somatic nervous system innervates skeletal muscle. Autonomic pathways are controlled mainly by the hypothalamus.

You must be familiar with the neurotransmitters, acetylcholine, epinephrine, and norepinephrine. You should relate acetylcholine to the somatic and parasympathetic nervous systems and epinephrine and norepinephrine to the sympathetic nervous system only.

## 4.15 The Central Nervous System

The CNS consists of some of the spinal cord, the lower brain, and all of the higher brain. Although the spinal cord acts mainly as a conduit for nerves to reach the brain, it does possess limited integrating functions such as walking reflexes, leg stiffening, and limb withdrawal from pain. (See Figure 4.20 for the reflex arc.)

The lower brain consists of the **medulla**, *pons*, *mesencephalon*, **hypothalamus**, **thalamus**, **cerebellum**, and *basal ganglia*. It integrates subconscious activities such as the respiratory system, arterial pressure, salivation, emotions, and reaction to pain and pleasure.

The higher brain or cortical brain consists of the **cerebrum** or **cerebral cortex**. The cerebral cortex is incapable of functioning without the lower brain. It acts to store memories and process thoughts.

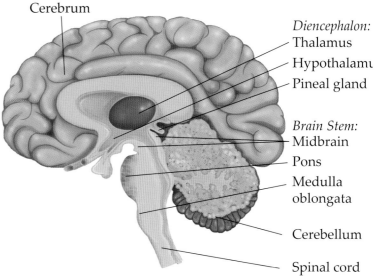

Cerebrum

*Diencephalon:*
Thalamus
Hypothalamus
Pineal gland

*Brain Stem:*
Midbrain
Pons
Medulla oblongata

Cerebellum

Spinal cord

Don't worry to much about memorizing the specific parts of the brain. Just realize that the brain is involved in the processing of sensory information, regulation of the body's internal enviroment, and responding to stimuli. You should also know that the forebrain (cerebrum) is resposible for higher level thoughts and consciousness.

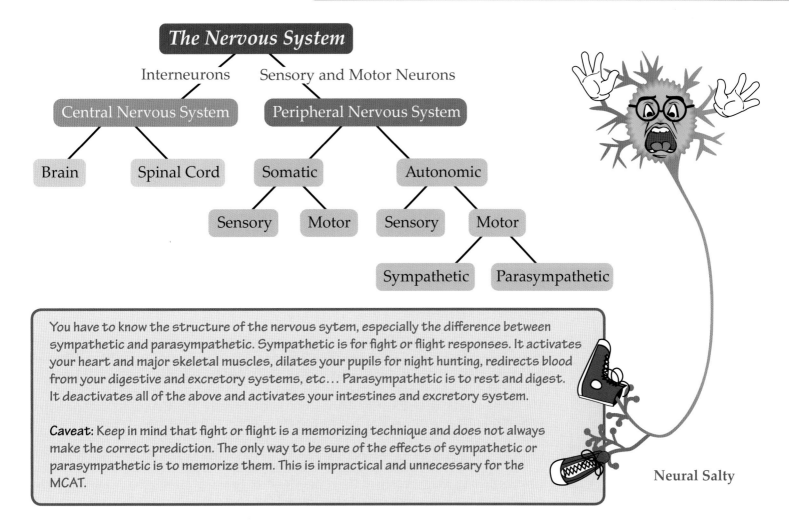

## The Nervous System

Interneurons — Sensory and Motor Neurons

Central Nervous System — Peripheral Nervous System

Brain — Spinal Cord

Somatic — Autonomic

Sensory — Motor (Somatic)

Sensory — Motor (Autonomic)

Sympathetic — Parasympathetic

You have to know the structure of the nervous sytem, especially the difference between sympathetic and parasympathetic. Sympathetic is for fight or flight responses. It activates your heart and major skeletal muscles, dilates your pupils for night hunting, redirects blood from your digestive and excretory systems, etc... Parasympathetic is to rest and digest. It deactivates all of the above and activates your intestines and excretory system.

**Caveat:** Keep in mind that fight or flight is a memorizing technique and does not always make the correct prediction. The only way to be sure of the effects of sympathetic or parasympathetic is to memorize them. This is impractical and unnecessary for the MCAT.

**Neural Salty**

## 4.16 Sensory Receptors

Although the somatic sensory neurons transfer signals from the external environment to the brain, they are incapable of distinguishing between different types of stimuli, and are not designed to be the initial receptors of such signals. Instead, the body contains *5 types of sensory receptors:*

1. *mechanoreceptors* for touch;
2. *thermoreceptors* for temperature change;
3. *nociceptors* for pain;
4. *electromagnetic receptors* for light; and
5. *chemoreceptors* for taste, smell and blood chemistry.

Each receptor responds strongly to its own type of stimulus and weakly or not at all to other types of stimuli. Each type of receptor has its own neural pathway and termination point in the central nervous system which results in the various sensations.

## 4.17 The Eye

For the MCAT®, you should know the basic anatomy of the eye (Figure 4.24), and understand the function of a few of its parts. A good way to remember this is to follow the path of light as it enters the eye.

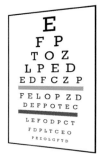

Light reflects off an object in the external environment and first strikes the eye on the **cornea**. (The light first strikes a very thin, protective layer known as the corneal epithelium.) The cornea is nonvascular and made largely from collagen. It is clear with a refractive index of about 1.4, which means that the most bending of light actually occurs at the interface of the air and the cornea and not at the lens.

From the cornea, the light enters the *anterior cavity*, which is filled with *aqueous humor*. Aqueous humor is formed by the *ciliary processes* and leaks out the *canal of Schlemm*. Blockage of the canal of Schlemm increases intraocular pressure resulting in one form of *glaucoma* and possibly blindness.

From the anterior cavity, light enters the **lens**. The lens would have a spherical shape, but stiff suspensory ligaments tug on it and tend to flatten it. These ligaments are connected to the **ciliary muscle**. The ciliary muscle circles the lens. When the ciliary muscle contracts, the opening of the circle decreases allowing the lens to become more like a sphere and bringing its focal point closer to the lens; when the muscle relaxes, the lens flattens increasing the focal distance. The elasticity of the lens declines with age making it difficult to focus on nearby objects as one gets older.

The eye system just described focuses light through the gel-like *vitreous humor* and onto the retina. Since the eye acts as a converging lens, and the object is outside the focal distance, the image on the retina is real and inverted. (See Physics Lecture 8 for more on lenses.)

The **retina** covers the inside of the back (distal portion) of the eye. It contains light sensitive cells called **rods** and **cones**. These cells are named for their characteristic shapes. The tips of these cells contain light sensitive photochemicals called *pigments* that go through a chemical change when one of their electrons is struck by a single photon. The pigment in rod cells is called *rhodopsin*. Rhodopsin is made of a protein bound to a prosthetic group called *retinal* which is derived from vitamin A. The photon isomerizes retinal causing the membrane of the rod cell to become less permeable to sodium ions and hyperpolarize. The hyperpolarization

Very little knowledge concerning the sensory receptors is required for the MCAT. However, you should know some very basic anatomy of the eye and ear. Also realize that sensory receptors transduce physical stimulus to neural signals.

is transduced into a neural action potential and the signal is sent to the brain.

Rods sense all photons with wavelengths in the visible spectrum (390 nm to 700 nm). Thus rods cannot distinguish colors. There are three types of cones, each with a different pigment that is stimulated by a slightly different spectrum of wavelengths. Thus cones distinguish colors. Vitamin A is a precursor to all the pigments in rods and cones.

The *fovea* is a small point on the retina containing mostly cones. The fovea marks the point on the retina where vision is most acute.

One other feature of the eye with which you should be familiar is the **iris** (Greek: irid:colored circle). The iris is the colored portion of the eye that creates the opening called the **pupil**. The iris is made from circular and radial muscles. In a dark environment, the sympathetic nervous system contracts the iris dilating the pupil and allowing more light to enter the eye. In a bright environment, the parasympathetic nervous system contracts the circular muscles of the iris constricting the pupil and screening out light.

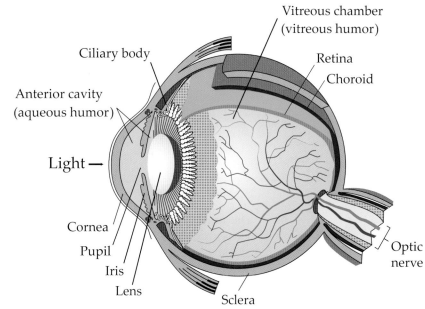

**Figure 4.24  The Eye**

Remember that cones distinguish colors and rods don't.

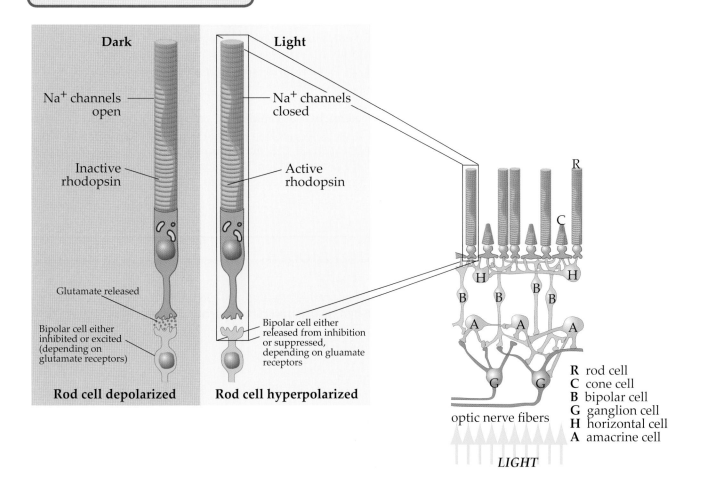

## 4.18 The Ear

Like the eye, you should know the basic parts of the ear (Figure 4.25) and the functions of these parts. The ear is divided into three parts:

1. the **outer ear**;

2. the **middle ear**; and

3. the **inner ear**.

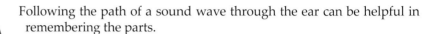

Following the path of a sound wave through the ear can be helpful in remembering the parts.

The *auricle* or *pinna* is the skin and cartilage flap that is commonly called the ear. The auricle functions to direct the sound wave into the *external auditory canal*. The external auditory canal carries the wave to the **tympanic membrane** or eardrum. The tympanic membrane begins the middle ear.

The middle ear contains the three small bones: the **malleus**, the **incus**, and the **stapes**. These three small bones act as a lever system translating the wave to the *oval window*. Like any lever system, these bones change the combination of force and displacement from the inforce to the outforce. The displacement is actually lessened, which creates an increase in force. In addition, the oval window is smaller than the tympanic membrane, acting to increase the pressure. (See Physics Lecture 4 for more on machines and mechanical advantage.) This increase in force is necessary because the wave is being transferred from the air in the outer ear to a more resistant fluid (the *perilymph*) within the inner ear.

The wave in the inner ear moves through the *scala vestibuli* of the **cochlea** to the center of the spiral, and then spirals back out along the *scala tympani* to the *round window*. As the wave moves through the cochlea, the alternating increase and decrease in pressure moves the *vestibular membrane* in and out. This movement is detected by the **hair cells** of the **organ of Corti** and transduced into neural signals, which are sent to the brain. The hair cells do not actually contain hair, but contain instead a specialized microvilli called *stereocilia*, which detect movement.

Also in the inner ear are the **semicircular canals**. The semicircular canals are responsible for balance. Each canal contains fluid and hair cells. When the body moves or the head position changes with respect to gravity, the momentum of the fluid is changed impacting on the hair cells, and the body senses motion. The canals are oriented at right angles to each other, in order to detect movement in all directions.

## 4.19 The Nose and Mouth

The senses of smell and taste are called *olfactory* and *gustatory*, respectively. These senses involve chemoreceptors. Different chemoreceptors sense different chemicals. There are only four primary taste sensations:

1. bitter

2. sour

3. salty and

4. sweet.

All taste sensations are combinations of these four.

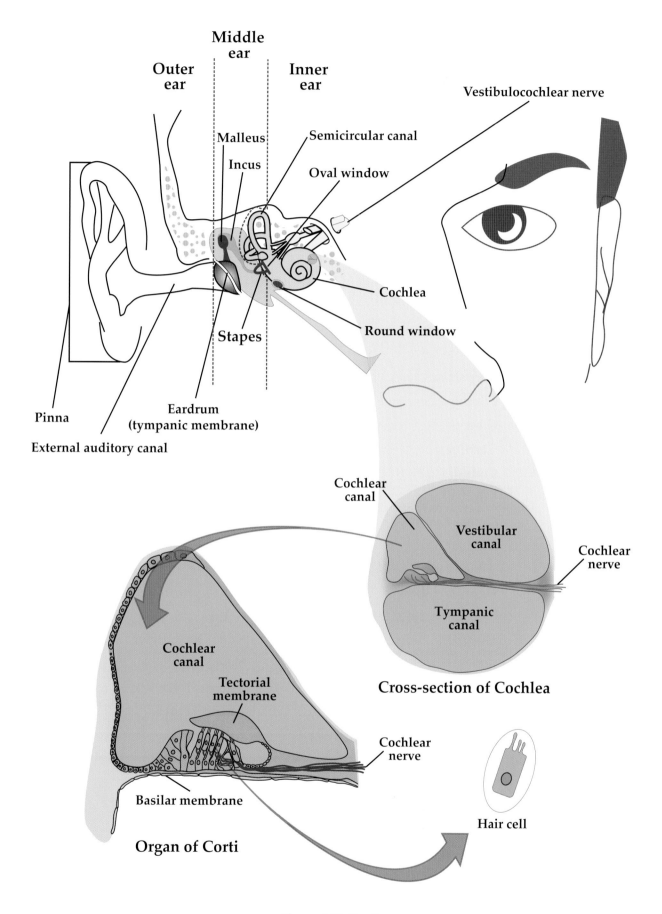

**Figure 4.25 The Ear**

## 4.20 Terms You Need To Know

| Terms | |
|---|---|
| Acetylcholine | Hyperpolarization |
| Actin | Hypothalamus |
| Action potential | Incus |
| Adipocytes | Inner Ear |
| Autonomic Nervous System (ANS) | Interneurons |
| Axon | Interstitial Fluid |
| Axon Hillock | Iris |
| Central Nervous System (CNS) | Lens |
| Centriole | Lysosomes |
| Cerebellum | Malleus |
| Cerebral Cortex | Medulla |
| Cerebrum | Microfilaments |
| Chemical Synapse | Microtubules |
| Cilia | Middle Ear |
| Cochlea | Mitochondria |
| Cones | Mitotic Spindle |
| Cornea | Motor (Efferent) Neurons |
| Cytoskeleton | Myelin |
| Cytosol | Neuron |
| Dendrites | Neuronal Communication |
| Depolarization | Neurotransmitter |
| Desmosomes | Nerves |
| Dynein | Nodes of Ranvier |
| Effector | Norepinephrine |
| Electrical Synapses | Nuclear Envelope |
| Endocytosis | Nuclear Pores |
| Endoplasmic Reticulum (ER) | Nucleus |
| Endosymbiont Theory | Nucleolus |
| Epinephrine | Organ of Corti |
| Exocytosis | Outer Ear |
| Flagella | Parasympathetic |
| Gap Junctions | Peripheral Nervous |
| Golgi Apparatus | System (PNS) |
| Grey Matter | Peroxisomes |
| Hair Cells | Phagocytosis |
| Hormonal Communication | Pupil |

# *Terms You Need To Know, Continued...*

| Terms | |
|---|---|
| Repolarization | Sympathetic |
| Resting Potential | Synapse |
| Retina | Synaptic Cleft |
| Rods | Thalamus |
| Saltatory Conduction | Threshold Stimulus |
| Schwann Cell | Tight Junctions |
| Second Messenger System | Tubulin |
| Secretory Vesicles | Tympanic Membrane |
| Semicircular Canal | Voltage Gated Potassium Channels |
| Sensory (afferent) Neurons | Voltage Gated Sodium Channels |
| Somatic Nervous System | White Matter |
| Stapes | |

*Notes:*

89. Which of the following activities is controlled by the cerebellum?

    A. Involuntary breathing movements
    B. Fine muscular movements during a dance routine
    C. Contraction of the thigh muscles during the knee-jerk reflex
    D. Absorption of nutrients across the microvilli of the small intestine

90. If an acetylcholine antagonist were administered generally into a person, all of the following would be affected EXCEPT:

    A. the neuroeffector synapse in the sympathetic nervous system.
    B. the neuroeffector synapse in the parasympathetic nervous system
    C. the neuromuscular junction in the somatic nervous system.
    D. the ganglionic synapse in the sympathetic nervous system.

91. Which of the following occurs as a result of parasympathetic stimulation?

    A. Vasodilation of the arteries leading to the kidneys
    B. Increased rate of heart contraction.
    C. Piloerection of the hair cells of the skin.
    D. Contraction of the abdominal muscles during exercise.

92. Pressure waves in the air are converted to neural signals at the:

    A. retina
    B. tympanic membrane
    C. cochlea
    D. semicircular canals

93. Reflex arcs:

    A. involve motor neurons exiting the spinal cord dorsally.
    B. require fine control by the cerebral cortex.
    C. always occur independently of the central nervous system.
    D. often involve inhibition as well as excitation of muscle groups.

94. Which of the following structures is NOT part of the central nervous system?

    A. a parasympathetic effector
    B. the medulla
    C. the hypothalamus
    D. the cerebral cortex

95. Which part of the brain controls higher-level thought processes?

    A. the thalamus
    B. the cerebellum
    C. the cerebrum
    D. the medulla

96. A cook touches a hot stove and involuntarily withdraws his hand before he feels pain. Which of the following would not be involved in the stimulus-response pathway described?

    A. a neuron in the cerebellum
    B. a neuron in the spinal cord
    C. a motor neuron
    D. a sensory neuron

# THE ENDOCRINE SYSTEM

## 5.1   Hormone Chemistry

The neurotransmitters and local mediators discussed in Biology Lecture 4 are often referred to as local hormones. General hormones are the hormones released by the endocrine system. They are referred to as 'general' because they are released into the body fluids, often the blood, and may affect many cell types in a tissue, and multiple tissues in the body. Although the following section concentrates on general hormones, the chemistry described is accurate for local hormones as well.

The endocrine glands differ from **exocrine glands** in the following manner. Exocrine glands release enzymes to the external environment through ducts. Exocrine glands include *sudoriferous* (sweat), *sebaceous* (oil), *mucous*, and digestive glands. **Endocrine glands** release hormones directly into body fluids. For instance, the pancreas acts as both an exocrine gland, releasing digestive enzymes through the pancreatic duct, and an endocrine gland releasing insulin and glucagon directly into the blood. (See Biology Lecture 6 for more on the pancreas.)

The effects of the endocrine system tend to be slower, less direct, and longer lasting than those of the nervous system. Endocrine hormones may take anywhere from seconds to days to produce their effects. They do not move directly to their target tissue, but are released into the general circulation. All hormones act by binding to proteins called **receptors**. Each receptor is highly specific for its hormone. One method of hormone regulation occurs by the reduction or increase of these receptors in the presence of high or low concentrations of the hormone. Some hormones have receptors on virtually all cells, while other hormones have receptors only on specific tissues. Very low concentrations of hormones in the blood have significant effects on the body.

In general, the effects of the endocrine system are to alter metabolic activities, regulate growth and development, and guide reproduction. The endocrine system works in conjunction with the nervous system. Many endocrine glands are stimulated by neurons to secrete their hormones.

Hormones exist in three basic chemistry types:

1. **peptide hormones;**
2. **steroid hormones;** and
3. **tyrosine derivatives.**

> Always remember that hormones need a receptor, either on the membrane or inside the cell. Also, when comparing the endocrine system with the nervous system remember that the endocrine system is slow, indirect, and long lasting.

**Figure 5.1   Endocrine and exocrine glands**

**Exocrine gland**
Releases enzymes to external environments through ducts

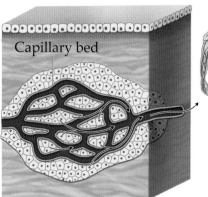

Capillary bed

**Endocrine gland**
Releases hormones into fluids that circulate throughout the body

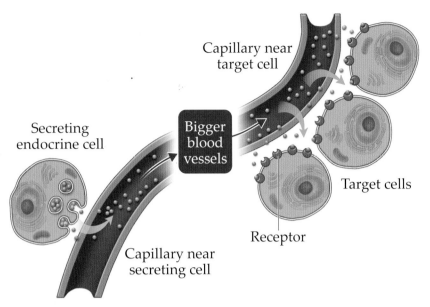

**Figure 5.2  Transport of Hormones in the Blood**

*Peptide hormones* are derived from peptides. They may be large or small, and often include carbohydrate portions. All peptide hormones are manufactured in the rough ER, typically as a *preprohormone* that is larger than the active hormone. The preprohormone is cleaved in the ER lumen to become a *prohormone*, and transported to the Golgi apparatus. In the Golgi, the prohormone is cleaved and sometimes modified with carbohydrates to its final form. The Golgi packages the hormone into secretory vesicles, and, upon stimulation by another hormone or a nervous signal, the cell releases the vesicles via exocytosis.

Since they are peptide derivatives, peptide hormones are water soluble, and thus move freely through the blood, but have difficulty diffusing through the cell membrane of the **effector**. (The effector is the **target cell** of the hormone, the cell that the hormone is meant to affect.) Instead of diffusing through the membrane, peptide hormones attach to a membrane-bound receptor. Once bound by a hormone, the receptor may act in several ways. The receptor may itself act as an ion channel increasing membrane permeability to a specific ion, or the receptor may activate or deactivate other intrinsic membrane proteins also acting as ion channels. Another effect of the hormone binding to the receptor may be to activate an **intracellular second messenger** such as cAMP, cGMP, or calmodulin. These chemicals are called second messengers because the hormone is the original, or first messenger, to the cell. The second messenger activates or deactivates enzymes and/or ion channels and often creates a 'cascade' of chemical reactions that amplifies the effect of the hormone. A cascade is one way that a small concentration of hormone can have a significant effect.

> The endocrine system delivers hormones to target cells throughout the body via the circulatory system.

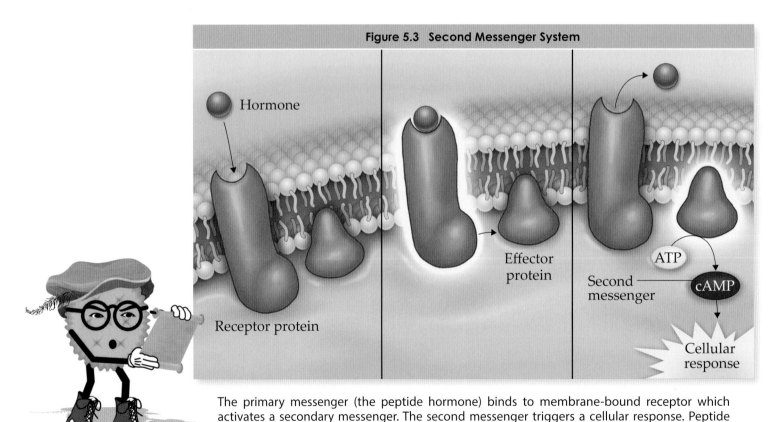

**Figure 5.3  Second Messenger System**

Hormone

Effector protein

ATP

Second messenger

cAMP

Receptor protein

Cellular response

The primary messenger (the peptide hormone) binds to membrane-bound receptor which activates a secondary messenger. The second messenger triggers a cellular response. Peptide hormones typically utilize a secondary messenger system.

*2nd messenger Salty*

The peptide hormones that you must know for the MCAT are:

1. the anterior pituitary hormones: FSH, LH, ACTH, hGH, TSH, Prolactin;

2. the posterior pituitary hormones: ADH and oxytocin;

3. the parathyroid hormone PTH;

4. the pancreatic hormones: glucagon and insulin.

The specifics of these hormones will be discussed later in this lecture.

**Steroid hormones** are derived from and are often chemically similar to cholesterol. They are formed in a series of steps taking place mainly in the smooth endoplasmic reticulum and the mitochondria. Since they are lipids, steroids typically require a protein transport molecule (carrier protein) in order to dissolve into the blood stream. (Usually, a fraction of the steroid concentration is bound to a transport molecule and a fraction is freeform in the blood.) Being lipid soluble, steroids diffuse through the cell membrane of their effector. Once inside the cell, they combine with a receptor in the cytosol. The receptor transports the steroid into the nucleus, and the steroid acts at the transcription level. Thus, the typical effect of a steroid hormone is to increase certain membrane or cellular proteins within the effector.

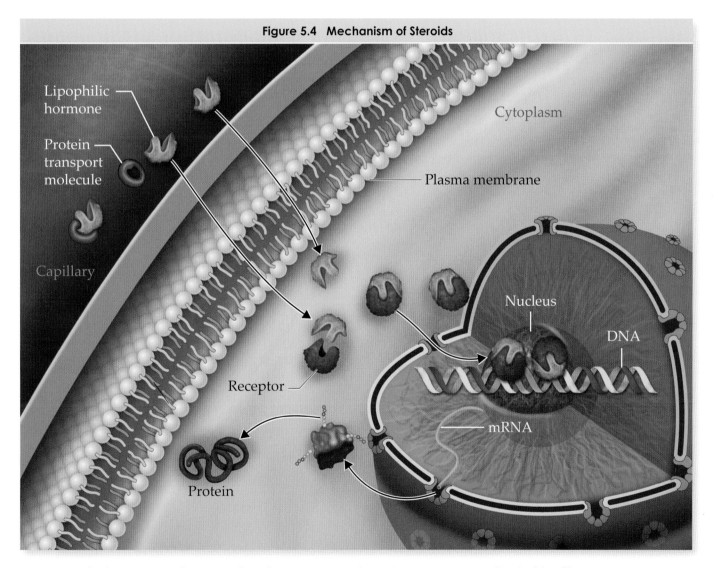

**Figure 5.4 Mechanism of Steroids**

Lipophilic hormone

Protein transport molecule

Cytoplasm

Plasma membrane

Capillary

Nucleus

DNA

Receptor

mRNA

Protein

Non-polar hormones such as steroids and some tyrosine-derivatives are transported in the blood by carrier proteins. Once they reach their target cell, they freely diffuse across the membrane and attach to receptors. The receptor-hormone complex then moves to the nucleus where it regulates transcription of certain genes or gene families.

The important steroid hormones for the MCAT are:

1.  the **glucocorticoids and mineral corticoids of the adrenal cortex: cortisol and aldosterone;**

2.  the **gonadal hormones: estrogen, progesterone, testosterone.** (Estrogen and progesterone are also produced by the placenta.) The specifics of these steroids will be discussed later in this lecture.

The **tyrosine derivatives are: the thyroid hormones T₃ (triiodothyronine contains 3 iodine atoms) and T₄ (thyroxine contains 4 iodine atoms), and the catecholamines formed in the adrenal medulla: epinephrine and norepinephrine.** All tyrosine derivative hormones are formed by enzymes in the cytosol or on the rough ER.

Thyroid hormones are lipid soluble and must be carried in the blood by plasma protein carriers. They are slowly released to their target tissues and bind to receptors inside the nucleus. Their high affinity to their binding proteins in the plasma and in the nucleus create a latent period in their response and increase the duration of the effect of thyroid hormones. Thyroid hormones increase the transcription of large numbers of genes in nearly all cells of the body.

Epinephrine and norepinephrine are water soluble and dissolve in the blood. They bind to receptors on the target tissue and act mainly through the second messenger cAMP.

The specifics of the tyrosine derivative hormones will be discussed later in this lecture.

You should know which hormones are steroids, which are tyrosines, and which are peptides. Then you should know where and how each of these types of hormones reacts. This isn't really so tough. First, steroid hormones come only from the adrenal cortex, the gonads, or the placenta. Second, tyrosines are the thyroid hormones and the catecholamines (the adrenal medulla hormones). The rest of the hormones discussed in this book are peptide hormones. Since steroids are lipids, they diffuse through the membrane and act in the nucleus. Since peptides are proteins, they can't diffuse through the membrane, so they bind to receptors on the membrane and act through a second messenger. The tyrosines are split: thyroid hormones diffuse into the nucleus and catecholamines act on receptors at the membrane.

Endocrine glands tend to over-secrete their hormones. Typically, some aspect of their effect on the target tissue will inhibit this secretion. This is an example of negative feedback (discussed in Biology Lecture 1). An important aspect to understand about negative feedback in endocrine glands is that the control point of the feedback is the conduct of the effector, not the concentration of hormone. In other words, the gland lags behind the effector. For instance, high insulin levels do not typically create low blood glucose. Instead, high insulin levels are caused by high blood glucose, and low blood glucose would cause high blood glucagon levels. So if an MCAT question indicates that a patient has high blood glucose and asks whether high levels or insulin or high levels of glucagon would be expected, the correct answer is the hormone that is responding to the condition, not creating it; in this case insulin.

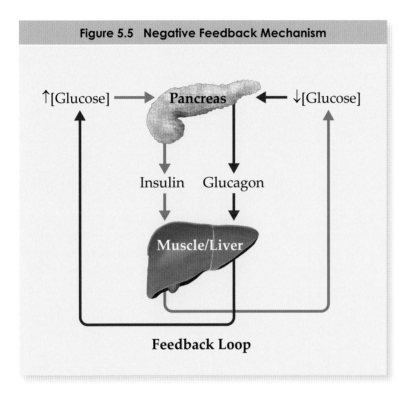

**Figure 5.5  Negative Feedback Mechanism**

↑[Glucose] → **Pancreas** ← ↓[Glucose]

Insulin    Glucagon

**Muscle/Liver**

**Feedback Loop**

There will be a negative feedback question on the MCAT. See if you get the idea. If ADH holds water in the body decreasing urine output and increasing blood pressure, does a person with high blood pressure (holding water) have a high ADH blood level or a low ADH blood level?

If you said high ADH, then you reasoned that the ADH created the high blood pressure. WRONG! If you said low ADH, then you reasoned that the ADH output responded to the body. CORRECT!

How about another? A secondary effect of aldosterone is to increase blood pressure. Would expected aldosterone levels be high or low in a person with low blood pressure?

The answer: since aldosterone increases blood pressure, and the body tries to bring blood pressure back to normal, the adrenal cortex should release more aldosterone into the blood. Expected aldosterone levels would be higher than normal.

97. Aldosterone exerts its effects on target cells by:

    A. binding to a receptor at the cell surface, setting off a second-messenger cascade.
    B. diffusing into adrenal cortical cells, where it influences transcription of certain DNA sequences.
    C. flowing across the synapse, where it binds and initiates an action potential.
    D. entering into target cells, where it increases the rate of production of sodium-potassium pump proteins.

98. A patient develops an abdominal tumor resulting in the secretion of large quantities of aldosterone into the bloodstream. Which of the following will most likely occur?

    A. Levels of renin secreted by the kidney will increase.
    B. Levels of oxytocin secreted by the pituitary will increase.
    C. Levels of aldosterone secreted by the adrenal cortex will decrease.
    D. Levels of aldosterone secreted by the tumor will decrease.

99. Which of the following is true for all endocrine hormones?

    A. They act through a second messenger system.
    B. They bind to a protein receptor.
    C. They dissolve in the blood.
    D. They are derived from a protein precursor.

100. All of the following act as second messengers for hormones EXCEPT:
    A. cyclic AMP.
    B. calmodulin.
    C. acetylcholine.
    D. cyclic GMP.

101. Which of the following is true of all steroids?

    A. The target cells of any steroid include every cell in the body.
    B. Steroids bind to receptor proteins on the membrane of their target cells.
    C. Steroids are synthesized on the rough endoplasmic reticulum.
    D. Steroids are lipid soluble.

102. The pancreas is a unique organ because it has both exocrine and endocrine function. The exocrine function of the pancreas releases:

    A. digestive enzymes straight into the blood.
    B. digestive enzymes through a duct.
    C. hormones straight into the blood.
    D. hormones through a duct.

103. Most steroid hormones regulate enzymatic activity at the level of:

    A. replication.
    B. transcription.
    C. translation.
    D. the reaction.

104. Which of the following side-effects might be experienced by a patient who is administered a dose of thyroxine?

    A. an increase in endogenous TSH production
    B. a decrease in endogenous TSH production
    C. an increase in endogenous thyroxine production
    D. a decrease in endogenous parathyroid hormone production

## 5.3 Specific Hormones and Their Function

Memorization of several major hormones, their glands, and their target tissues is required for the MCAT. As a memory aid, you should group hormones according to the gland that secretes them. A given gland produces steroids, peptides, or tyrosine derivatives, but not two categories of hormones. (The adrenal glands are really two glands. The cortex produces steroids; the medulla produces catecholamines. The thyroid is a true exception. The thyroid secretes $T_3$ and $T_4$, which are tyrosine derivatives, and calcitonin, which is a peptide.) We will start by discussing the hormones of the anterior pituitary.

| Table 5.1  Glands Producing Water-soluable Homones |
| --- |
| • anterior pituitary |
| • posterior pituitary |
| • parathyroid |
| • pancreas |
| • adrenal medulla |

## 5.4 Anterior Pituitary

The **anterior pituitary** (Figure 5.6) (also called the *adenohypophysis*) is located in the brain beneath the **hypothalamus**. The hypothalamus controls the release of the anterior pituitary hormones with *releasing and inhibitory hormones* of its own. These releasing and inhibitory hormones are carried to the capillary bed of the anterior pituitary by small blood vessels. The release of the releasing and inhibitory hormones is, in turn, controlled by nervous signals throughout the nervous system.

The anterior pituitary releases six major hormones and several minor hormones. All of these are peptide hormones. For the MCAT you should be familiar with the six major hormones, their target tissues, and their functions. The hormones are:

| Table 5.2  Glands Producing Lipid-soluable Homones |
| --- |
| • adrenal cortex |
| • ovaries |
| • testes |
| • placenta |

1. human growth hormone (hGH);
2. adrenocorticotropin (ACTH);
3. thyroid-stimulating hormone (TSH);
4. follicle-stimulating hormone (FSH);
5. luteinizing hormone (LH) and;
6. prolactin.

**Figure 5.6  Anterior pituitary**

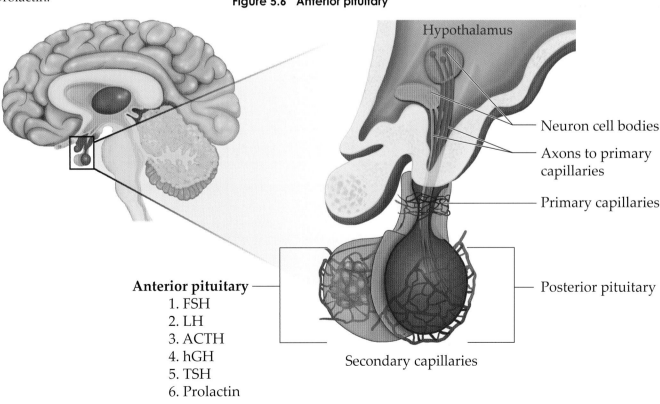

Hypothalamus

Neuron cell bodies

Axons to primary capillaries

Primary capillaries

Posterior pituitary

**Anterior pituitary**
1. FSH
2. LH
3. ACTH
4. hGH
5. TSH
6. Prolactin

Secondary capillaries

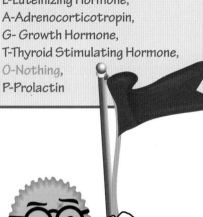

## hGH

**Human growth hormone (hGH)** (also called *somatotropin*), a peptide, stimulates growth in almost all cells of the body. All other hormones of the anterior pituitary have specific target tissues. hGH stimulates growth by increasing episodes of mitosis, increasing cell size, increasing the rate of protein synthesis, mobilizing fat stores, increasing the use of fatty acids for energy, and decreasing the use of glucose. The effect on proteins by hGH is accomplished by increasing amino acid transport across the cell membrane, increasing translation and transcription, and decreasing the breakdown of protein and amino acids.

## ACTH

**Adrenocorticotropic hormone (ACTH)**, a peptide, stimulates the adrenal cortex to release glucocorticoids via the second messenger system using cAMP. Release of ACTH is stimulated by many types of stress. Glucocorticoids are stress hormones. (See below for the effects of the adrenal cortical hormones.)

## TSH

**Thyroid-stimulating hormone (TSH)** (also called thyrotropin), a peptide, stimulates the thyroid to release $T_3$ and $T_4$ via the second messenger system using cAMP. Among other effects on the thyroid, TSH increases thyroid cell size, number, and the rate of secretion of $T_3$ and $T_4$. It is important to note that $T_3$ and $T_4$ concentrations have a negative feedback effect on TSH release, both at the anterior pituitary and the hypothalamus. (See below for effects of $T_3$ and $T_4$.)

## FSH and LH

(These peptides are discussed in this lecture under reproduction.)

## Prolactin

**Prolactin**, a peptide, promotes lactation (milk production) by the breasts. The reason that milk is not normally produced before birth is due to the inhibitory effects of milk production by progesterone and estrogen. Although the hypothalamus has a stimulatory effect on the release of all other anterior pituitary hormones, it mainly inhibits the release of prolactin. The act of suckling, which stimulates the hypothalamus to stimulate the anterior pituitary to release prolactin, inhibits the menstrual cycle. It is not known whether or not this is directly due to prolactin. The milk production effect of prolactin should be distinguished from the milk ejection effect of oxytocin.

## 5.5 Posterior Pituitary

The **posterior pituitary** is also called the *neurohypophysis* because it is composed mainly of support tissue for nerve endings extending from the hypothalamus. The hormones oxytocin and ADH are synthesized in the neural cell bodies of the hypothalamus, and transported down axons to the posterior pituitary where they are released into the blood. Both oxytocin and ADH are small polypeptides.

## Oxytocin

Oxytocin is a small peptide hormone that increases uterine contractions during pregnancy and causes milk to be ejected from the breasts.

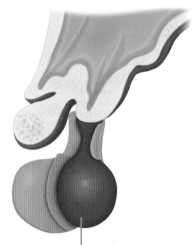

**Posterior pituitary**
1. Oxytocin
2. ADH

**Figure 5.7 Posterior pituitary**

## ADH

**Antidiuretic hormone (ADH)** (also called **vasopressin**) is a small peptide hormone which causes the collecting ducts of the kidney to become permeable to water reducing the amount of urine and concentrating the urine. Since fluid is reabsorbed, ADH also increases blood pressure. Coffee and beer are ADH blockers that increase urine volume.

## 5.6 | *Adrenal Cortex*

**Adrenal medulla**
1. Epinephrine
2. Norepinephrine

**Adrenal cortex**
1. Aldosterone
2. Cortisol

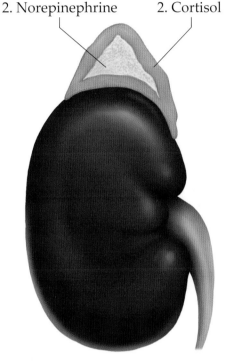

The **adrenal glands** (Figure 5.8) are located on top of the kidneys. They are generally separated into the adrenal cortex and the adrenal medulla. The **adrenal cortex** is the outside portion of the gland. The cortex secretes only steroid hormones. There are two types of steroids secreted by the cortex: **mineral corticoids** and **glucocorticoids**. (The cortex also secretes a small amount of sex hormones, significant in the female but not the male.) Mineral corticoids affect the electrolyte balance in the blood stream; glucocorticoids increase blood glucose concentration and have an even greater effect on fat and protein metabolism. About 30 corticoids have been isolated from the cortex, but the major mineral corticoid is aldosterone, and the major glucocorticoid is cortisol.

### Aldosterone

**Aldosterone**, a steroid, is a mineral corticoid that acts in the distal convoluted tubule and the collecting duct to increase $Na^+$ and $Cl^-$ reabsorption and $K^+$ and $H^+$ secretion. It creates a net gain in particles in the plasma, which results in an eventual increase in blood pressure. Aldosterone has the same effect, but to a lesser extent, on the sweat glands, salivary glands, and intestines.

For the MCAT, the main effect of aldosterone is the $Na^+$ reabsorption and $K^+$ secretion in the collecting tubule of the kidney. The increase in blood pressure is a secondary effect.

**Figure 5.8   Adrenal Gland**

### Cortisol

**Cortisol**, a steroid, is a glucocorticoid that increases blood glucose levels by stimulating **gluconeogenesis** in the liver. (Gluconeogenesis is the creation of glucose and glycogen, mainly in the liver, from amino acids, glycerol, and/or lactic acid.)  Cortisol also degrades adipose tissue to fatty acids to be used for cellular energy. In addition, cortisol causes a moderate decrease in the use of glucose by the cells. Cortisol causes the degradation of nonhepatic proteins, a decrease of nonhepatic amino acids and a corresponding increase in liver and plasma proteins and amino acids.

Cortisol is a stress hormone. The benefit of excess cortisol under stressful situations is not fully understood. One explanation may include anti-inflammatory properties possessed by cortisol. Cortisol also diminishes the capacity of the immune system to fight infection.

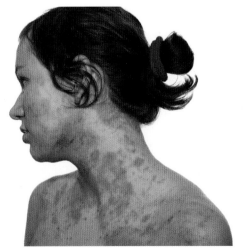

The anti-inflammatory properties of cortisal make it useful for treating eczema.

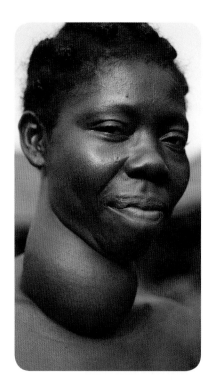

Goiter, which is caused by a dietary deficiency of iodine, results in decreased thyroxine production. Sensing low thyroxine levels, the anterior pituitary responds by releasing excess TSH, which stimulates abnormal growth of the thyroid gland.

Calcitonin works in opposition to PTH, just like insulin works in opposition to glucagon.

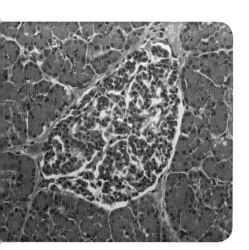

Pancreatic islets of Langerhans release hormones into the blood. They are composed of numerous beta cells, which secrete insulin, and the less numerous alpha cells, which secrete glucagon.

## Catecholamines

The *catecholamines* are the tyrosine derivatives synthesized in the adrenal medulla: **epinephrine** and **norepinephrine** (also called **adrenaline** and **noradrenaline**). The effects of epinephrine and norepinephrine on the target tissues are similar to their effects in the sympathetic nervous system but they last much longer. Epinephrine and norepinephrine are vasoconstrictors (they constrict blood vessels) of most internal organs and skin, but are vasodilators of skeletal muscle (they increase blood flow); this is consistent with the 'fight-or-flight' response of these hormones. Because of their 'fight or flight' response, the catecholamines are also considered stress hormones.

## 5.7 Thyroid

The thyroid hormones are *triiodothyronine* ($T_3$), thyroxine ($T_4$), and calcitonin. The thyroid (Figure 5.9) is located along the trachea just in front of the larynx.

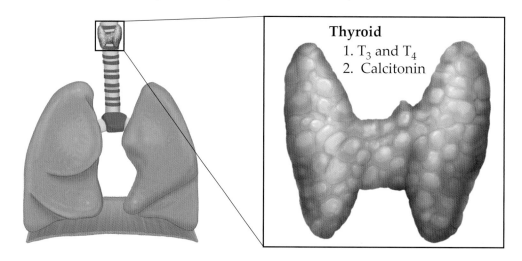

**Thyroid**
1. $T_3$ and $T_4$
2. Calcitonin

**Figure 5.9   Thyroid Hormones**

## $T_3$ and $T_4$

$T_3$ and $T_4$ are very similar in effect, and no distinction will be made on an MCAT question unless it is thoroughly explained in a passage. $T_3$ contains three iodine atoms, and $T_4$ contains four. Both hormones are lipid soluble tyrosine derivatives that diffuse through the lipid bilayer and act in the nucleus of the cells of their effector. Their general effect is to increase the **basal metabolic rate** (the resting metabolic rate). Thyroid hormone secretion is regulated by TSH.

## Calcitonin

**Calcitonin** is a large peptide hormone released by the thyroid gland. Calcitonin slightly decreases blood calcium by decreasing osteoclast activity and number. Calcium levels can be effectively controlled in humans in the absence of calcitonin.

## 5.8 Pancreas (Islets of Langerhans)

The pancreas (Figure 5.10) acts as both an endocrine and an exocrine gland. For the MCAT, the two important endocrine hormones released into the blood by the pancreas are the peptide hormones insulin and glucagon. *Somatostatin*, not likely to be seen on the MCAT, is released by the δ-cells of the pancreas. Somatostatin inhibits both insulin and glucagon. The role of somatostatin may be to extend the period of time over which nutrients are absorbed.

## Insulin

**Insulin**, a peptide hormone, is released by the *β-cells* of the pancreas. It is associated with energy abundance in the form of high energy nutrients in the blood. Insulin is released when blood levels of carbohydrates or proteins are high. It affects carbohydrate, fat, and protein metabolism. In the presence of insulin, carbohydrates are stored as glycogen in the liver and muscles, fat is stored in adipose tissue, and amino acids are taken up by the cells of the body and made into proteins. The net effect of insulin is to lower blood glucose levels.

Insulin binds to a membrane receptor beginning a cascade of reactions inside the cell. Except for neurons in the brain and a few other cells which are not affected by insulin, the cells of the body become highly permeable to glucose upon the binding of insulin. The insulin receptor itself is not a carrier for glucose. The permeability of the membrane to amino acids is also increased. In addition, intracellular metabolic enzymes are activated and, much more slowly, even translation and transcription rates are affected.

## Glucagon

**Glucagon**, a peptide hormone, is released by the *α-cells* of the pancreas. The effects of glucagon are nearly opposite to those of insulin. Glucagon stimulates glycogenolysis (the breakdown of glycogen), and gluconeogenesis in the liver. It acts via the second messenger system of cAMP. In higher concentrations, glucagon breaks down adipose tissue increasing the fatty acid level in the blood. The net effect of glucagon is to raise blood glucose levels.

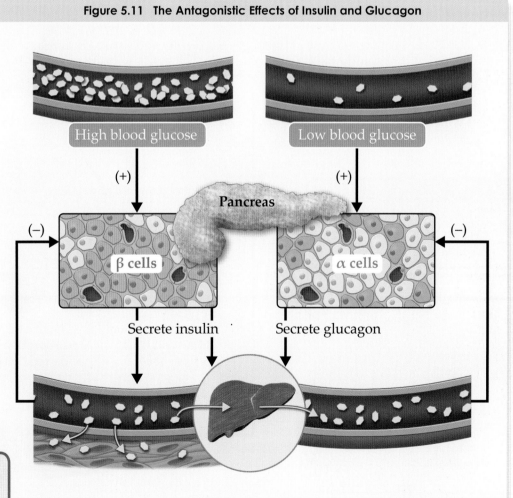

**Pancreas**
1. Insulin
2. Glucagon

**Figure 5.10   Pancreatic Hormones**

> Remember, only the pancreas acts as both an endocrine and an exocrine gland.

**Figure 5.11   The Antagonistic Effects of Insulin and Glucagon**

> In Type I diabetes the islets of Langerhans do not produce insulin.

> Insulin *decreases* blood glucose levels.
> Glucagon *increases* blood glucose.

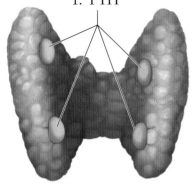

**Parathyroid**
*(behind Thyroid)*
1. PTH

**Figure 5.12 Parathyroid**

### 5.9 | *Parathyroid*

There are four small **parathyroid glands** (Figure 5.12) attached to the back of the thyroid. The parathyroid glands release **parathyroid hormone**.

## PTH

**Parathyroid hormone (PTH)**, a peptide, increases blood calcium. It increases osteocyte absorption of calcium and phosphate from the bone and stimulates proliferation of osteoclasts. PTH increases renal calcium reabsorption and renal phosphate excretion. It increases calcium and phosphate uptake from the gut by increasing renal production of the steroid, *1,25 dihydroxycholecalciferol (DOHCC)*, derived from vitamin D. PTH secretion is regulated by the calcium ion plasma concentration, and the parathyroid glands shrink or grow accordingly.

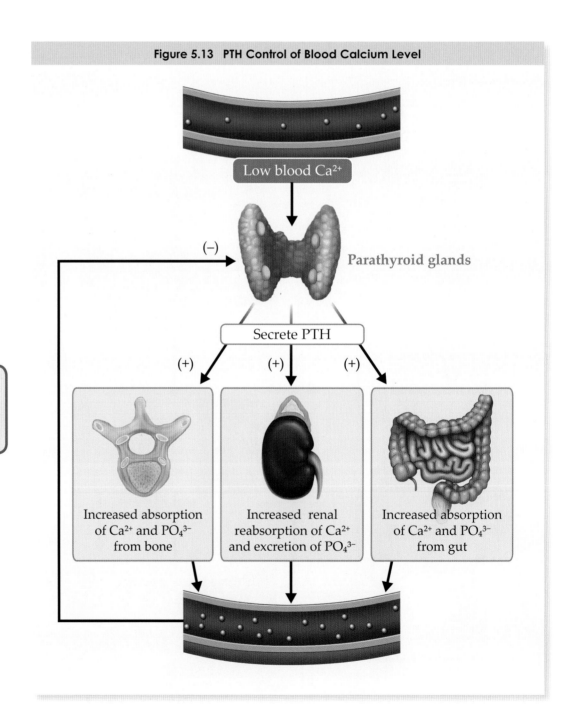

**Figure 5.13 PTH Control of Blood Calcium Level**

Low blood Ca²⁺

(−)

Parathyroid glands

Secrete PTH

(+)    (+)    (+)

Increased absorption of Ca²⁺ and PO₄³⁻ from bone

Increased renal reabsorption of Ca²⁺ and excretion of PO₄³⁻

Increased absorption of Ca²⁺ and PO₄³⁻ from gut

**105.** Sympathetic stimulation results in responses most similar to release of which of the following hormones?
   **A.** insulin
   **B.** acetylcholine
   **C.** epinephrine
   **D.** aldosterone

**106.** When compared with the actions of the nervous system, those of the endocrine system are:

   **A.** quicker in responding to changes, and longer-lasting.
   **B.** quicker in responding to changes, and shorter-lasting.
   **C.** slower in responding to changes, and longer-lasting.
   **D.** slower in responding to changes, and shorter-lasting.

**107.** Insulin shock occurs when a patient with diabetes self-administers too much insulin. Typical symptoms are extreme nervousness, trembling, sweating, and ultimately loss of consciousness. The physiological effects of insulin shock most likely include:

   **A.** a pronounced increase in gluconeogenesis by the liver.
   **B.** a rise in blood fatty acid levels leading to atherosclerosis.
   **C.** a dramatic rise in blood pressure.
   **D.** dangerously low blood glucose levels.

**108.** Vasopressin, a hormone involved in water balance, is produced in the:

   **A.** hypothalamus.
   **B.** posterior pituitary.
   **C.** anterior pituitary.
   **D.** kidney.

**109.** Osteoporosis is an absolute decrease in bone tissue mass, especially trabecular bone. All of the following might be contributory factors to the disease EXCEPT:

   **A.** increased sensitivity to endogenous parathyroid hormone.
   **B.** defective intestinal calcium absorption.
   **C.** menopause.
   **D.** abnormally high blood levels of calcitonin.

**110.** All of the following hormones are produced by the anterior pituitary EXCEPT:

   **A.** thyroxine.
   **B.** growth hormone.
   **C.** prolactin.
   **D.** leutinizing hormone.

**111.** Which of the following hormonal and physiologic effects of stress would NOT be expected in a marathoner in the last mile of a marathon?

   **A.** Increased glucagon secretion
   **B.** Increased heart rate
   **C.** Decreased ACTH secretion
   **D.** Decreased blood flow to the small intestine

**112.** Parathyroid hormone is an important hormone in the control of blood calcium ion levels. Parathyroid hormone directly impacts:

   **I.** bone density
   **II.** renal calcium reabsorption
   **III.** blood calcium concentration

   **A.** I only
   **B.** I and II only
   **C.** I and III only
   **D.** I, II and III

## 5.10 Reproduction

Except for **FSH**, **LH**, **HCG**, and *inhibin*, which are peptides, the reproductive hormones discussed below are steroids released from the testes, ovaries and placenta.

## 5.11 The Male Reproductive System

You should know the basic anatomy of the male and female reproductive systems (Figure 5.14 and 5.19). The male **gonads** are called the **testes**. Production of sperm (Figure 5.15 and 5.16) occurs in the **seminiferous tubules** of the testes. **Spermatogonia** located in the seminiferous tubules arise from epithelial tissue to become spermatocytes, spermatids, and then spermatozoa. *Sertoli cells* stimulated by FSH surround and nurture the spermatocyte and spermatids. *Leydig cells*, located in the interstitium between the tubules, release **testosterone** when stimulated by LH. Testosterone is the primary **androgen** (male sex hormone), and stimulates the germ cells to become sperm. Testosterone is also responsible for the development of secondary sex characteristics such as pubic hair, enlargement of the larynx, and growth of the penis and seminal vesicles. While testosterone helps to initiate the growth spurt at puberty, it also stimulates closure of the epiphyses of the long bones, ending growth in stature. Sertoli cells secrete *inhibin*, a peptide hormone (actually a glycoprotein) which acts on the pituitary gland to inhibit FSH secretion.

> Be aware of basic male anatomy but don't stress too much about it.

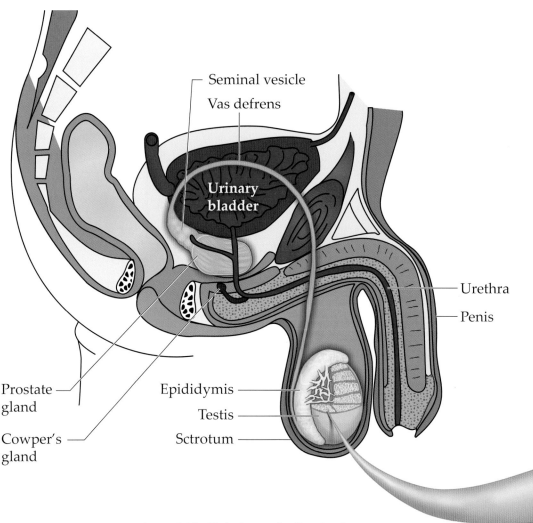

**Figure 5.14  Male Reproductive Anatomy**

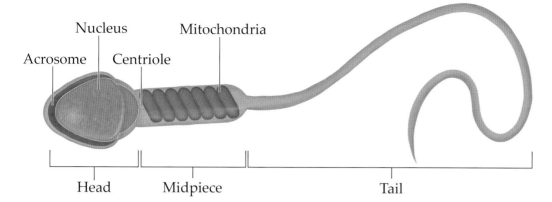

**Figure 5.15 Spermatozoan**

The spermatid has the characteristics of a typical cell. However, as it becomes a spermatozoon it loses its cytoplasm and forms the *head, midpiece,* and *tail* shown in Figure 5.15. The head is composed of the nuclear material and an *acrosome*. The acrosome contains lysosome-like enzymes for penetrating the egg during fertilization. The midpiece contains many mitochondria to provide energy for movement of the tail. Only the nuclear portion of the sperm enters the egg.

Once freed into the tubule lumen, the spermatozoon is carried to the **epididymis** to mature. Upon ejaculation, spermatozoa are propelled through the **vas deferens** into the **urethra** and out of the penis. **Semen** is the complete mixture of spermatozoa and fluid that leaves the penis upon ejaculation. Semen is composed of fluid from the **seminal vesicles**, the **prostate**, and the **bulbourethral glands** (also called **Cowper's glands**). Spermatozoa become activated for fertilization in a process called *capacitation*, which takes place in the vagina.

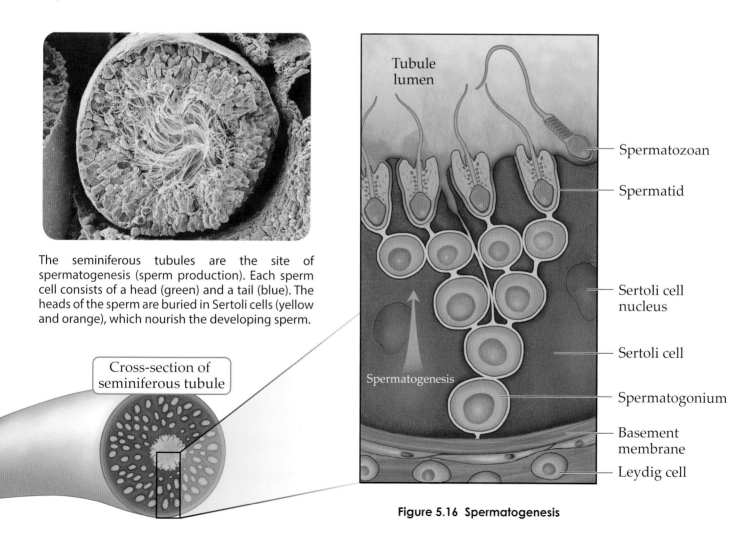

The seminiferous tubules are the site of spermatogenesis (sperm production). Each sperm cell consists of a head (green) and a tail (blue). The heads of the sperm are buried in Sertoli cells (yellow and orange), which nourish the developing sperm.

**Figure 5.16 Spermatogenesis**

## 5.12 The Female Reproductive System

Oogenesis begins in the ovaries of the fetus. All the eggs of the female are arrested as primary oocytes at birth. At puberty, FSH stimulates the growth of *granulosa cells* around the primary oocyte (Figure 5.17). The granulosa cells secrete a viscous substance around the egg called the **zona pellucida**. The structure at this stage is called a *primary follicle*. Next, theca cells differentiate from the interstitial tissue and grow around the follicle to form a *secondary follicle*. Upon stimulation by LH, theca cells secrete androgen, which is converted to **estradiol** (a type of **estrogen**) by the granulosa cells in the presence of FSH and secreted into the blood. The Estradiol is a steroid hormone that prepares the uterine wall for pregnancy. The follicle grows and bulges from the ovary. Typically, estradiol inhibits LH secretion by the anterior pituitary. However, just before **ovulation** (the bursting of the follicle), the estradiol level rises rapidly, actually causing a dramatic increase in LH secretion. This increase is called the luteal surge. The **luteal surge** results from a positive feedback loop of rising estrogen levels which increase LH levels, which increase estrogen. The luteal surge causes the follicle to burst, releasing the egg (now a secondary oocyte) into the body cavity. The egg is swept into the **Fallopian (uterine) tube** or **oviduct** by the *fimbriae*. The remaining portion of the follicle is left behind to become the **corpus luteum**. The corpus luteum secretes estradiol and progesterone throughout pregnancy, or, in the case of no pregnancy, for about 2 weeks until the corpus luteum degrades into the **corpus albicans**.

The cycle just described repeats itself approximately every 28 days after puberty unless pregnancy occurs. This cycle is called the **menstrual cycle** (Figure 5.18). With each menstrual cycle, several primordial oocytes may begin the process, but, normally, only one completes the development to ovulation. The cycle is divided into three phases:

1. the *follicular phase*, which begins with the development of the follicle and ends at ovulation;

2. the *luteal phase*, which begins with ovulation and ends with the degeneration of the corpus luteum into the corpus albicans;

3. *flow*, which is the shedding of the uterine lining lasting approximately 5 days.

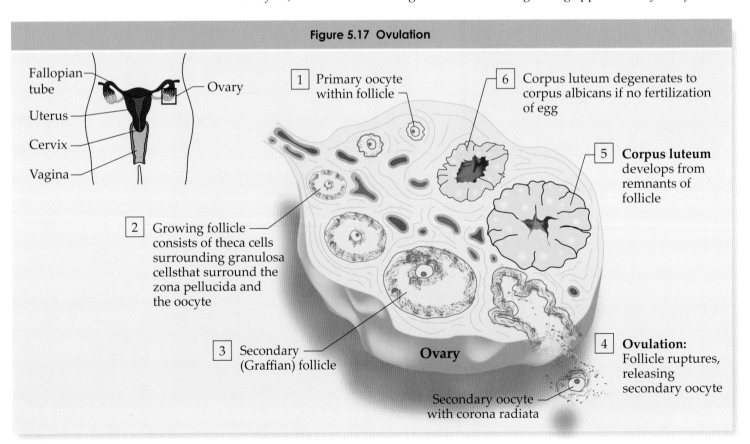

**Figure 5.17 Ovulation**

Fallopian tube
Ovary
Uterus
Cervix
Vagina

1 Primary oocyte within follicle

6 Corpus luteum degenerates to corpus albicans if no fertilization of egg

5 **Corpus luteum** develops from remnants of follicle

2 Growing follicle consists of theca cells surrounding granulosa cellsthat surround the zona pellucida and the oocyte

3 Secondary (Graffian) follicle

**Ovary**

4 **Ovulation:** Follicle ruptures, releasing secondary oocyte

Secondary oocyte with corona radiata

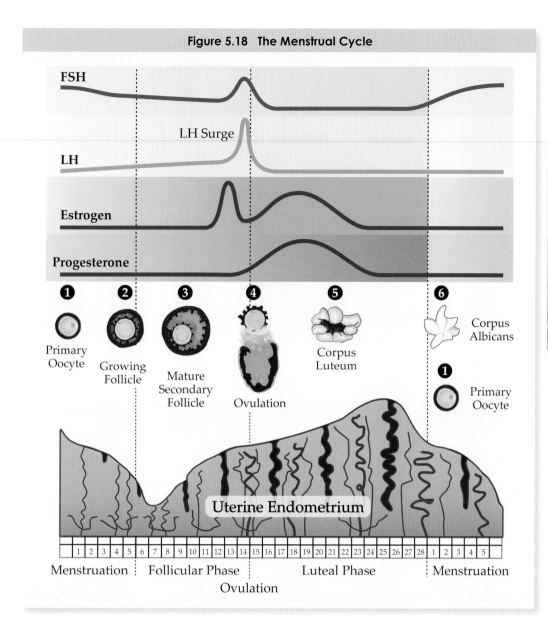

**Figure 5.18 The Menstrual Cycle**

FSH

LH Surge

LH

Estrogen

Progesterone

① Primary Oocyte

② Growing Follicle

③ Mature Secondary Follicle

④ Ovulation

⑤ Corpus Luteum

⑥ Corpus Albicans

① Primary Oocyte

Uterine Endometrium

| 1 | 2 | 3 | 4 | 5 | 6 | 7 | 8 | 9 | 10 | 11 | 12 | 13 | 14 | 15 | 16 | 17 | 18 | 19 | 20 | 21 | 22 | 23 | 24 | 25 | 26 | 27 | 28 | 1 | 2 | 3 | 4 | 5 |

Menstruation | Follicular Phase | Luteal Phase | Menstruation

Ovulation

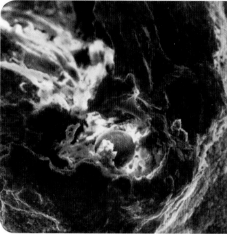

This is a mature ovum (Graafian follicle) at ovulation. The ovum (red) is surrounded by remnants of corona cells & liquid from the ruptured ovarian follicle.

## 5.13 *Fertilization and Embryology*

Once in the Fallopian tube, the egg is swept toward the uterus by cilia. Fertilization normally takes place in the Fallopian tubes. The enzymes of the acrosome in the sperm are released upon contact with the egg, and digest a path for the sperm through the granulosa cells and the zona pellucida. The cell membranes of the sperm head and the oocyte fuse upon contact, and the sperm nucleus enters the cytoplasm of the oocyte. The entry of the sperm causes the *cortical reaction*, which prevents other sperms from fertilizing the same egg. Now the oocyte goes through the second meiotic division to become an **ovum** and releases a second polar body. Fertilization occurs when the nuclei of the ovum and sperm fuse to form the **zygote**.

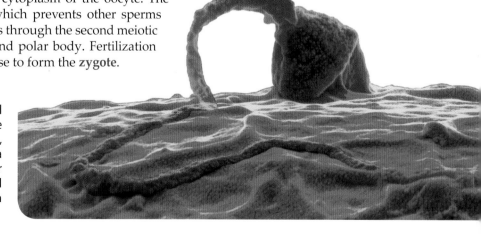

Sperm cell fertilizing an egg cell. The sperm cell (brown) is trying to penetrate the surface of the egg cell (blue). Once a sperm has fertilized the egg, rapid chemical changes make the outer layer (zona pellucida) of the egg cell thicken, preventing other sperm cells from entering. The head of the successful sperm cell releases genetic material that mixes with the genetic material in the egg cell.

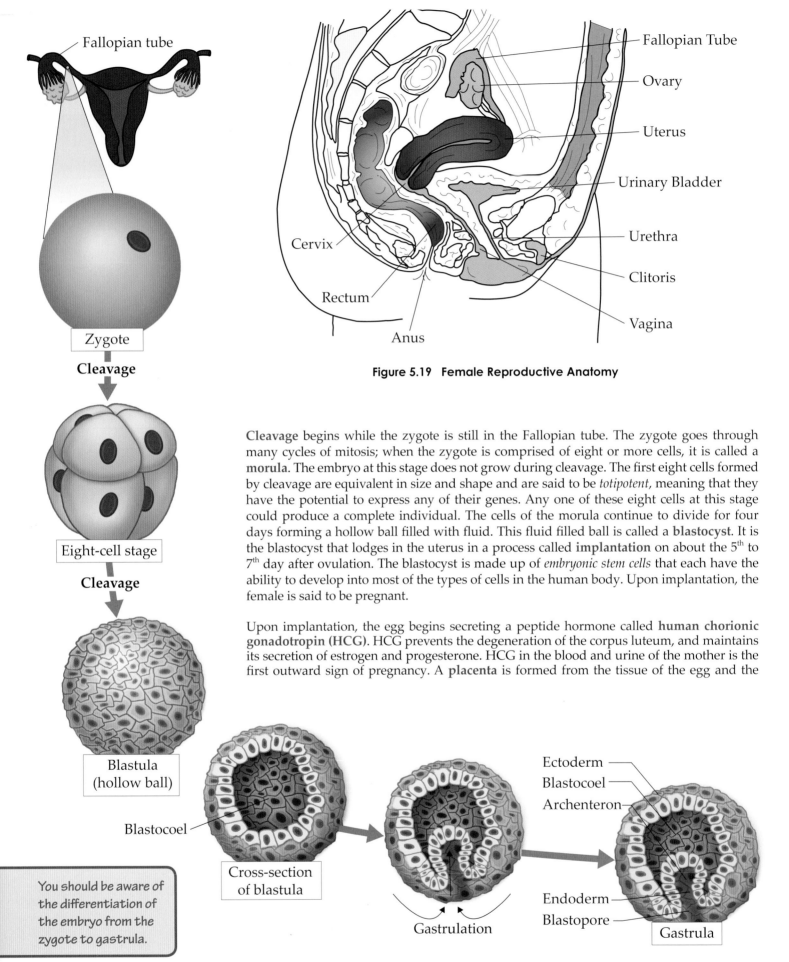

**Figure 5.19  Female Reproductive Anatomy**

**Cleavage** begins while the zygote is still in the Fallopian tube. The zygote goes through many cycles of mitosis; when the zygote is comprised of eight or more cells, it is called a **morula**. The embryo at this stage does not grow during cleavage. The first eight cells formed by cleavage are equivalent in size and shape and are said to be *totipotent*, meaning that they have the potential to express any of their genes. Any one of these eight cells at this stage could produce a complete individual. The cells of the morula continue to divide for four days forming a hollow ball filled with fluid. This fluid filled ball is called a **blastocyst**. It is the blastocyst that lodges in the uterus in a process called **implantation** on about the 5th to 7th day after ovulation. The blastocyst is made up of *embryonic stem cells* that each have the ability to develop into most of the types of cells in the human body. Upon implantation, the female is said to be pregnant.

Upon implantation, the egg begins secreting a peptide hormone called **human chorionic gonadotropin (HCG)**. HCG prevents the degeneration of the corpus luteum, and maintains its secretion of estrogen and progesterone. HCG in the blood and urine of the mother is the first outward sign of pregnancy. A **placenta** is formed from the tissue of the egg and the

You should be aware of the differentiation of the embryo from the zygote to gastrula.

**Figure 5.20  Early Cleavages in Animal Development**

mother, and takes over the job of hormone secretion. The placenta reaches full development by the end of the first trimester, and begins secreting its own estrogen and progesterone while lowering its secretion of HCG.

As the embryo develops past the eight cell stage, the cells become different from each other due to cell-cell interactions. This process where a cell becomes committed to a specialized developmental path is called **determination**. Cells become determined to give rise to a particular tissue early on. The specializaton that occurs at the end of the development forming a specialized tissue cell is called **differentiation**. The fate of a cell is typically determined early on, but that same cell usually doesn't differentiate into a specialized tissue cell until much later at the end of the developmental process. Recent research has shown that the fate of even a fully differentiated cell can be altered given the proper conditions.

The formation of the **gastrula** occurs in the second week after fertilization in a process called **gastrulation**. Cells begin to slowly move about the embryo for the first time. In mammals, a *primitive streak* is formed, which is analogous to the blastopore in aquatic vertebrates. Cells destined to become mesoderm migrate into the primitive streak. During gastrulation, the three primary germ layers are formed:

1.  the **ectoderm**;
2.  the **mesoderm**;
3.  the **endoderm**.

Although there is no absolute rule for memorizing which tissues arise from which germ layer, for the MCAT certain guidelines can be followed. The ectodermal cells develop into the outer coverings of the body, such as the outer layers of skin, nails, and tooth enamel, and into the cells of the nervous system and sense organs. The endodermal cells develop into the lining of the digestive tract, and into much of the liver and pancreas. The mesoderm is the stuff that lies between the inner and outer covering of the body, the muscle, bone, and the rest. (**WARNING:** These are just guidelines, not absolute rules.)

In the third week, the gastrula develops into a **neurula** in a process called **neurulation**. In neurulation, the **notochord** (made from mesoderm) **induces** the overlying ectoderm to thicken and form the *neural plate*. The notochord eventually degenerates, while a *neural tube* forms from the neural plate to become the spinal cord, brain, and most of the nervous system. For the MCAT you must know that induction occurs when one cell type affects the direction of differentiation of another cell type.

Part of normal cell development is programmed cell death or **apoptosis**. Apoptosis is essential for development of the nervous system, operation of the immune system, and destruction of tissue between fingers and toes to create normal hands and feet in humans. Damaged cells may undergo apoptosis as well. Failure to do so may result in cancer. Apoptosis is a complicated process in humans, but it is basically regulated by protein activity as opposed to regulation at the transcription or translation level. The proteins involved in apoptosis are present but inactive in a normal healthy cell. In mammals, mitochondria play an important role in apoptosis.

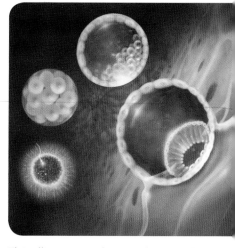

This illustration depicts the initial stages of fetal development, beginning at the lower left corner and moving clockwise. In the first stage, the spermatozoon penetrates the ovum. Their nuclei unite and the cells grow rapidly. At approximately day two, the cells form a solid cluster called a morula. As the number of cells increases, the mass descends down the uterine tube, forming a blastocyst, a hollow sphere of cells. In the last stage shown, the blastocyst implants itself in the uterine wall, approximately five days after fertilization.

| Table 5.3 | Fates of the Primary Germ Layers |
|---|---|
| **Ectoderm** | Epidermis of skin, nervous system, sense organs |
| **Mesoderm** | Skeleton, muscles, blood vessels, heart, blood, gonads, kidneys, dermis of skin |
| **Endoderm** | Lining of digestive and respiratory tracts, liver, pancreas, thymus, thyroid |

## Table 5.4 Major Hormones of the Endocrine System

| Gland | Hormone | Solubility | Effect |
|---|---|---|---|
| **Anterior pituitary** | hGH | Water soluble | Growth of nearly all cells |
| | ACTH | Water soluble | Stimulates adrenal cortex |
| | FSH | Water soluble | Growth of follicles in female; Sperm production in male |
| | LH | Water soluble | Causes ovulation; stimulates estrogen and testosterone secretion |
| | TSH | Water soluble | Stimulates release of $T_3$ and $T_4$ in the thyroid |
| | Prolactin | Water soluble | Promotes milk production |
| **Posterior pituitary** | Oxytocin | Water soluble | Milk ejection and uterine contraction |
| | ADH | Water soluble | Water absorption by the kidney; increase blood pressure |
| **Adrenal cortex** | Aldosterone | Lipid soluble | Reduces $Na^+$ excretion; increases $K^+$ excretion; raises blood pressure |
| | Cortisol | Lipid soluble | Increase blood levels of carbohydrates, proteins, and fats |
| **Adrenal medulla** | Epinephrine | Water soluble | Stimulates sympathetic actions |
| | Norepinephrine | Water soluble | Stimulates sympathetic actions |
| **Thyroid** | $T_3, T_4$ | Lipid soluble | Increases basal metabolic rate |
| | Calcitonin | Water soluble | Lowers blood calcium |
| **Parathyroid** | PH | Water soluble | Raises blood calcium |
| **Pancreas** | Insulin | Water soluble | Promotes entry of glucose into cells, decreasing glucose blood level |
| | Glucagon | Water soluble | Increases gluconeogenesis, increasing glucose blood levels |
| **Ovaries** | Estrogens | Lipid soluble | Growth of female sex organs; causes LH surge |
| | Progesterone | Lipid soluble | Prepares and maintains uterus for pregnancy |
| **Testes** | Testosterone | Lipid soluble | Secondary sex characteristics; closing of epiphyseal plate |
| **Placenta** | HCG | Water soluble | Stimulates corpus luteum to grow and release estrogen and progesterone |
| | Estrogens | Lipid soluble | Growth of mother sex organs; causes LH surge |
| | Progesterone | Lipid soluble | Prepares and maintains uterus for pregnancy |

You are expected to know these hormones and their functions.

| Terms | | |
|---|---|---|
| Adrenal Cortex | Exocrine Glands | Ovulation |
| Adrenal Glands | Fallopian (Uterine) | Ovum |
| Adrenaline | Tube | Parathyroid Glands |
| Adrenocorticotropic | FSH | Parathyroid Hormone |
| Hormone (ACTH) | Gastrula | (PTH) |
| Aldosterone | Gastrulation | Peptide Hormones |
| Androgen | Glucagon | Placenta |
| Anterior Pituitary | Glucocorticoids | Posterior Pituitary |
| Antidiuretic Hormone | Gluconeogenesis | Prolactin |
| (ADH) | Gonadotropin (HCG) | Prostrate |
| Apoptosis | Gonads | Semen |
| Basal Metabolic Rate | HCG | Seminal Vesicles |
| Blastocyst | Human Growth | Seminiferous Tubules |
| Calcitonin | Hormone | Spermatogonia |
| Cleavage | (hGH) | Steroid Hormones |
| Corpus Albicans | Hypothalamus | $T_3$ and $T_4$ |
| Corpus Luteum | Implantation | Testes |
| Cortisol | Insulin | Testosterone |
| Cowper's Glands | Intracellular Second | Thyroid-Stimulating |
| Determination | Messenger | Hormone (TSH) |
| Differentiation | LH | Tyrosine Derivatives |
| Ectoderm | Luteal Surge | Urethra |
| Effector | Mesoderm | Vas Deferens |
| Endocrine Glands | Mineral Corticoids | Vasopressin |
| Endoderm | Morula | Zona Pellucida |
| Epididymus | Neurula | Zygote |
| Epinephrine | Norepinephrine | |
| Estradiol | Notochord | |
| Estrogen | Oviduct | |

113. A drug that causes increased secretion of testosterone from the interstitial cells of a physically mature male would most likely:

    A. cause the testes to descend prematurely.
    B. delay the onset of puberty.
    C. cause enhanced secondary sex characteristics.
    D. decrease core body temperature.

114. During the female menstrual cycle, increasing levels of estrogen cause:

    A. a positive feedback response, stimulating LH secretion by the anterior pituitary.
    B. a positive feedback response, stimulating FSH secretion by the anterior pituitary.
    C. a negative feedback response, stimulating a sloughing-off of the uterine lining.
    D. a negative feedback response, stimulating decreased progesterone secretion by the anterior pituitary.

115. The function of the epididymis is to:

    A. store sperm until they are released during ejaculation.
    B. produce and secrete testosterone.
    C. conduct the ovum from the ovary into the uterus.
    D. secrete FSH and LH to begin the menstrual cycle.

116. Decreasing progesterone levels during the luteal phase of the menstrual cycle are associated with:

    A. thickening of the endometrial lining in preparation for implantation of the zygote.
    B. increased secretion of LH, leading to the luteal surge and ovulation.
    C. degeneration of the corpus luteum in the ovary.
    D. increased secretion of estrogen in the follicle, leading to the flow phase of the menstrual cycle.

117. The inner linings of the Fallopian tubes are covered with a layer of cilia. The purpose of this layer is to:

    A. remove particulate matter that becomes trapped in the mucus layer covering the Fallopian tubes.
    B. maintain a layer of warm air close to the inner lining, protecting the ovum from temperature changes occurring in the external environment.
    C. kill incoming sperm, thus preventing fertilization
    D. facilitate movement of the ovum towards the uterus.

118. Which of the following endocrine glands produce testosterone?

    A. The anterior pituitary
    B. The pancreas
    C. The adrenal cortex
    D. The adrenal medulla

119. Which of the following does NOT describe cleavage in human embryos?

    A. The solid ball of cells produced during cleavage is called a morula.
    B. The size of the embryo remains constant throughout the cell divisions of cleavage.
    C. Cell division occurs in one portion of the egg in meroblastic cleavage.
    D. Daughter cells are genetically identical to parent cells.

120. The heart, bone and skeletal muscle most likely arise from which of the following primary germ layers?

    A. The ectoderm
    B. The endoderm
    C. The gastrula
    D. The mesoderm

# THE DIGESTIVE SYSTEM; THE EXCRETORY SYSTEM

## 6.1    Anatomy

Digestion is the break down of ingested foods before they are absorbed into the body. The major reaction involved in the digestion of all macromolecules is hydrolysis.

You should know the basic anatomy of the digestive tract (Figure 6.1), which goes as follows: **mouth; esophagus; stomach; small intestine** (*duodenum, ileum, jejunum*); **large intestine** (*ascending colon, transverse colon, descending colon, sigmoid colon*); **rectum** and; **anus**.

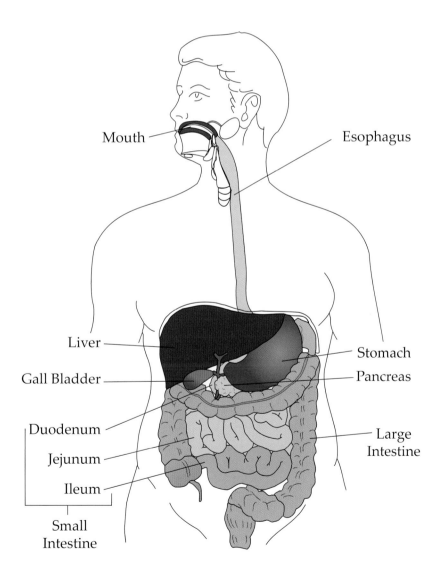

Mouth

Esophagus

Liver

Gall Bladder

Duodenum

Jejunum

Ileum

Small Intestine

Stomach

Pancreas

Large Intestine

**Figure 6.1   Anatomy of the Digestive System**

Know the basic anatomy of the digestive system.

## 6.2 The Mouth and Esophagus

Digestion begins in the mouth with α-**amylase** contained in saliva. Starch is the major carbohydrate in the human diet. α-amylase begins breaking down the long straight chains of starch into polysaccharides. Chewing also increases the surface area of food, which enables more enzymes to act on the food at any one time. Chewed food forms a clump in the mouth called a *bolus*. The bolus is pushed into the **esophagus** by swallowing, and then moved down the esophagus via **peristaltic action**. (Technically, swallowing includes the movement of the bolus from the esophagus into the stomach, and is composed of a voluntary and involuntary stage.) Peristaltic action is a wave motion, similar to squeezing a tube of toothpaste at the bottom and sliding your fingers toward the top to expel the toothpaste. The peristaltic movement is performed by smooth muscle. Saliva acts to lubricate the food helping it to move down the esophagus. No digestion occurs in the esophagus.

## 6.3 The Stomach

The bolus moves into the stomach through the *lower esophageal sphincter* (or *cardiac sphincter*). (A sphincter is a ring of muscle that is normally contracted so that there is no opening at its center.) The stomach is a very flexible pouch that both mixes and stores food, reducing it to a semifluid mass called **chyme**. The stomach contains **exocrine glands** (two types that are very similar) whose *gastric pits* are shown in Figure 6.2. Another important function of the stomach is to begin protein digestion with the enzyme pepsin. The low pH of the stomach assists this process by denaturing the proteins. A full stomach has a pH of 2. The low pH also helps to kill ingested bacteria.

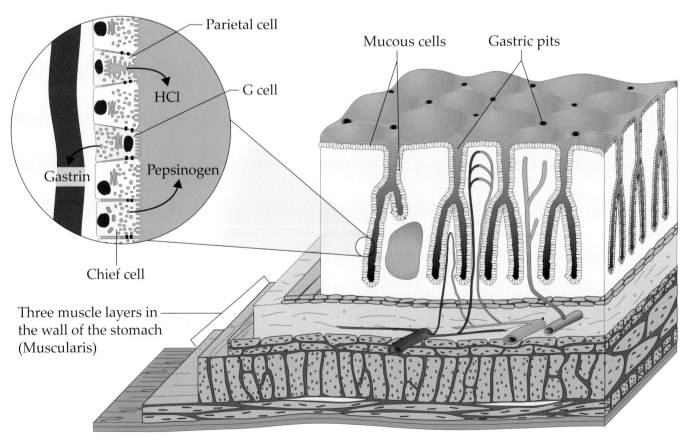

**Figure 6.2 A Sectional View of the Stomach**

There are four major cell types in the stomach (Figure 6.3):
1. **mucous cells**;
2. **chief (peptic) cells**;
3. **parietal (oxyntic) cells** and;
4. **G cells**.

There are different types of **mucous cells**, but all of them perform the same basic function, secreting mucus. The mucous cells line the stomach wall and the necks of the exocrine glands. Mucus, composed mainly of a sticky glycoprotein and electrolytes, lubricates the stomach wall so that food can slide along its surface without causing damage, and mucus protects the **epithelial lining** from the acidic environment of the stomach. Some mucous cells also secrete a small amount of pepsinogen.

**Chief cells** are found deep in the exocrine glands. They secrete **pepsinogen**, the zymogen precursor to **pepsin**. Pepsinogen is activated to pepsin by the low pH in the stomach. Once activated, pepsin begins protein digestion.

**Parietal cells** are also found in the exocrine glands of the stomach. Parietal cells secrete **hydrochloric acid (HCl)**, which diffuses to the lumen. The exact method used by the parietal cells to manufacture HCl has not been agreed upon, but the amount of energy necessary to produce the concentrated acid is great. Carbon dioxide is involved in the process, making carbonic acid inside the cell. The hydrogen from the carbonic acid is expelled to the lumen side of the cell, while the bicarbonate ion is expelled to the interstitial fluid side. The net result is to lower the pH of the stomach and raise the pH of the blood. Parietal cells also secrete *intrinsic factor*, which helps the ileum absorb $B_{12}$.

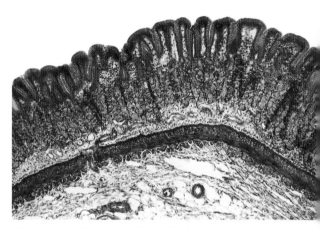

The lining of the stomach is called the mucosa.

**G cells** secrete **gastrin** into the interstitium. Gastrin, a large peptide hormone, is absorbed into the blood and stimulates parietal cells to secrete HCl.

The major hormones that affect the secretion of the stomach juices are acetylcholine, gastrin, and *histamine*. Acetylcholine increases the secretion of all cell types. Gastrin and histamine mainly increase HCl secretion.

## Figure 6.3  Gastric Gland Cell Types

**G cell**
secreting Gastrin

**Mucous cell**
containing rough ER and
Golgi to make mucous

Mucus

**Parietal cell**
with many mitochondria
needed to produce sufficient
energy to establish a
proton gradient

HCl

**Chief cell**
synthesizing pepsinogen
on rough ER

Pepsinogen

Gastrin

For the MCAT, be familiar with
the different cell types,.

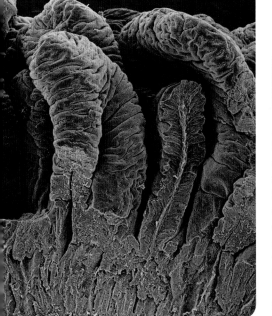

*The Small Intestine*

About 90% of digestion and absorption occurs in the small intestine. In a living human the small intestine is about 3 m in length. (In a cadaver the length increases to about 6 m due to loss of smooth muscle tone.) The small intestine is divided into three parts. From smallest to largest they are the *duodenum, jejunum,* and *ileum*. Most of digestion occurs in the duodenum, and most of the absorption occurs in the jejunum and ileum. The wall of the small intestine is similar to the wall of the stomach except that the outermost layer contains finger-like projections called villi (Figure 6.4). The villi increase the surface area of the intestinal wall allowing for greater digestion and absorption. Within each villus are a capillary network and a lymph vessel, called a **lacteal**. Nutrients absorbed through the wall of the small intestine pass into the capillary network and the lacteal.

On the apical (lumen side) surface of the cells of each villus (cells called *enterocytes*) are much smaller finger-like projections called **microvilli**. The microvilli increase the surface area of the intestinal wall still further. Under a light microscope the microvilli appear as a fuzzy covering. This fuzzy covering is called the **brush border**. The brush border contains membrane bound digestive enzymes, such as carbohydrate-digesting enzymes (*dextrinase, maltase, sucrase,* and *lactase*) protein-digesting enzymes called peptidases; and nucleotide-digesting enzymes called *nucleosidases*. Some of the epithelial cells are **goblet cells** that secrete mucus to lubricate the intestine and help protect the brush border from mechanical and chemical damage. Dead cells regularly slough off into the lumen of the intestine and are replaced by new cells.

Located deep between the villi are the intestinal exocrine glands, the crypts of *Lieberkuhn*. These glands secrete an intestinal juice with a pH of 7.6 and *lysozyme*. Lysozyme helps to regulate the bacteria within the intestine.

False-colour scanning electron micrograph of a section through the wall of the human duodenum, showing the villi, which project 0.5 to 1 mm out into the intestinal lumen. They greatly increase the effective absorptive and secretory surface of the mucosa (mucus membrane) which lines the small intestine. Each villus contains a central core of connective tissue (yellowish orange), known as the lamina propria. This contains large blood vessels, capillaries, some smooth muscle cells and a blind-ended lymph vessel known as a lacteal.

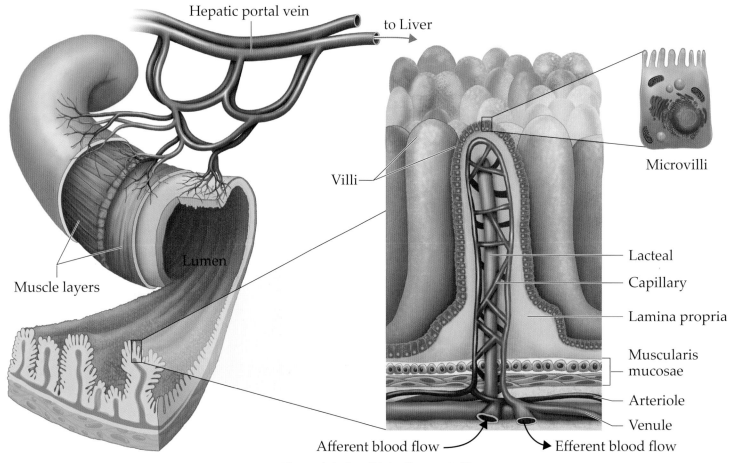

**Figure 6.4   Small Intestine and Villus**

## 6.5   The Pancreas

The semifluid **chyme** is squeezed out of the stomach through the *pyloric sphincter* and into the duodenum. The fluid inside the duodenum has a **pH of 6** due mainly to **bicarbonate ion** secreted by the pancreas. The pancreas also acts as an exocrine gland, releasing enzymes from the *acinar cells* through the *pancreatic duct* into the duodenum. The major enzymes released by the pancreas are **trypsin, chymotrypsin, pancreatic amylase, lipase, ribonuclease, and deoxyribonuclease**. All enzymes are released as zymogens. Trypsin is activated by the enzyme *enterokinase* located in the brush border. Activated trypsin then activates the other enzymes.

**Trypsin** and **chymotrypsin** degrade proteins into small polypeptides. Another pancreatic enzyme, *carboxypolypeptidase*, cleaves amino acids from the sides of these peptides. Most proteins reach the brush border as small polypeptides. Here they are reduced to amino acids, dipeptides, and tripeptides before they are absorbed into the enterocytes. Enzymes within the *enterocytes* (the cells of the brush border) reduce the dipeptides and tripeptides to amino acids.

Like salivary amylase, **pancreatic amylase** hydrolyzes polysaccharides to disaccharides and trisaccharides; however, pancreatic amylase is much more powerful. Pancreatic amylase degrades nearly all the carbohydrates from the chyme into oligosaccharides. The brush border enzymes finish degrading these polymers to their respective monosaccharides before they are absorbed.

**Lipase** degrades fat, specifically **triglycerides**. However, since the intestinal fluid is an aqueous solution, the fat clumps together, reducing its surface area. This problem is solved by the addition of bile. Bile is produced in the **liver** and stored in the **gall bladder**. The gall bladder releases bile through the *cystic duct*, which empties into the *common bile duct* shared with the liver. The common bile duct empties into the *pancreatic duct* before connecting to the duodenum at the *ampulla of Vater*. Bile emulsifies the fat, which means it breaks it up into small particles without changing it chemically. This increases the surface area of the fat, allowing the lipase to degrade it into mainly fatty acids and monoglycerides. These products are shuttled to the brush border in bile micelles, and then absorbed by the enterocytes. Bile also contains *bilirubin*, an end product of hemoglobin degradation. Much of the bile is reabsorbed by the small intestine and transported back to the liver.

Chyme is moved through the intestines by **peristalsis**. A second type of intestinal motion, *segmentation*, mixes the chyme with the digestive juices.

Several lobes of the pancreas are seen here, separated by fissures. The smaller sections seen on each lobe are clusters of acini cells. These are exocrine cells, secreting digestive enzymes. The enzymes drain into a highly branched system of ducts of increasing size, that terminates in the main pancreatic duct, which feeds into the duodenum (small intestine). The other function of the pancreas is the endocrinal secretion of hormones, in particular insulin. Fragments of connective tissue and blood vessels are also seen.

> You must know the pancreatic enzymes trypsin, chymotrypsin, amylase, and lipase, and know their functions in the small intestine.

> Understand that bile is necessary to increase the surface area of fat, but that it does not digest the fat. In other words, bile physically separates fat molecules, but does not break them down chemically.

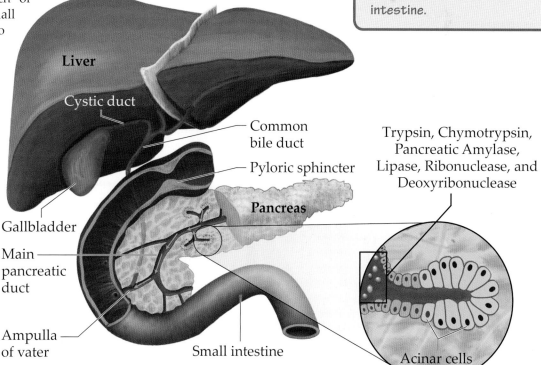

Trypsin, Chymotrypsin, Pancreatic Amylase, Lipase, Ribonuclease, and Deoxyribonuclease

**Figure 6.5   The Pancreas**

The large intestine, or colon, has four parts:

1. *ascending colon*;
2. *transverse colon*;
3. *descending colon* and;
4. *sigmoid colon*.

The major functions of the large intestine are **water absorption** and **electrolyte absorption**. When this function fails, diarrhea results. The large intestine also contains the bacteria *E. coli*. The bacteria produce vitamin K, $B_{12}$, thiamin, and riboflavin.

Healthy feces are composed of 75% water. The remaining solid mass is 30% dead bacteria, 10-20% fat (mainly from bacteria and sloughed enterocytes), 10-20% inorganic matter, 2-3% protein, and 30% roughage (i.e. cellulose) and undigested matter (i.e. sloughed cells).

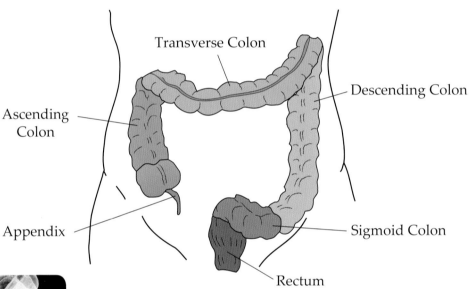

**Figure 6.6   Large Intestine**

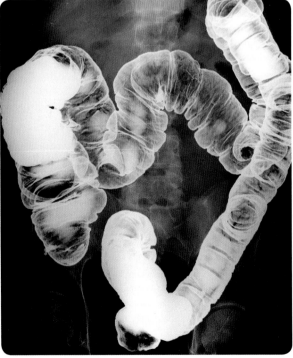

Whenever you get a large intestine question on the MCAT, think water reabsorption. Profuse water loss in the form of diarrhea often results when there is a problem with the large intestine. You should be aware that there is a mutualistic symbiosis between humans and bacteria in the large intestine. Bacteria get our leftovers; we get certain vitamins from them. We have more bacteria in our gut than we have cells. They are not good anywhere else, but in the large intestine are absolutely necessary for our survival. (See Biology 9.3, Symbiosis)

## 6.7 Gastrointestinal Hormones Involved in Digestion

*Secretin*, *cholecystokinin*, and *gastric inhibitory peptide* are local peptide hormones secreted by the small intestine after a meal. Each of these hormones increases blood insulin levels especially in the presence of glucose.

Gastric inhibitory peptide is released in response to fat and protein digestates in the duodenum, and to a lesser extent, in response to carbohydrates. It has a mild effect in decreasing the motor activity of the stomach.

Hydrochloric acid in the duodenum causes secretin release. Secretin stimulates sodium bicarbonate secretion by the pancreas.

Food in the upper duodenum, especially fat digestates, causes the release of cholecystokinin. Cholecystokinin causes gallbladder contraction and pancreatic enzyme secretion. It also decreases the motility of the stomach allowing the duodenum more time to digest fat.

You don't have to remember these gastrointestinal hormones, although they may appear in a passage. Instead, understand the ideas of digestion. The body eats to gain energy in the form of food. The digestive system breaks down the food so it can be absorbed into the body. One problem is that the food may move too fast through the digestive tract and come out undigested. The stomach stores food, and releases small amounts at a time to be digested and absorbed by the intestine. This way, the body can take in (eat) a large amount of food at a single time and take a long time to digest it. One of the jobs of the gastrointestinal hormones just described is to help regulate this process.

**Table 6.1 Major Digestive Enzymes of Humans**

| Source/Enzyme | Action |
|---|---|
| **SALIVARY GLANDS** | |
| Salivary amylase | Starch → Maltose |
| **STOMACH** | |
| Pepsin | Proteins → Peptides; autocatalysis |
| **PANCREAS** | |
| Pancreatic amylase | Starch → Maltose |
| Lipase | Fats → Fatty acid and glycerol |
| Nuclease | Nucleic acids → Nucleotides |
| Trypsin | Proteins →Peptides; Zymogen activation |
| Chymotrypsin | Proteins →Peptides |
| Carboxypeptidase | Peptides → Shorter peptides and amino acids |
| **SMALL INTESTINE** | |
| Aminopeptidase | Peptides → Shorter peptides and amino acids |
| Dipeptidase | Dipeptides → Amino acids |
| Enterokinase | Trypsinogen → Trypsin |
| Nuclease | Nucleic acids → Nucleotides |
| Maltase | Maltose → Glucose |
| Lactase | Lactose → Galactose and glucose |
| Sucrase | Sucrose → Fructose and glucose |

We have looked at digestion, the breakdown of food. Next, we will look at absorption, the assimilation of the by-products of digestion.

121. As chyme is passed from the stomach to the small intestine, the catalytic activity of pepsin:

   A. increases because pepsin works synergistically with trypsin.
   B. increases because pepsin is activated from its zymogen form.
   C. decreases in response to the change in pH.
   D. decreases because pepsin is digested by pancreatic amylase in the small intestine.

122. Which of the following is the best explanation for why pancreatic enzymes are secreted in zymogen form?

   A. A delay in digestion is required in order for bile to increase the surface area chyme.
   B. Enzymes are most active in zymogen form.
   C. Zymogens will not digest bile in the pancreatic duct.
   D. Pancreatic cells are not as easily replaced as intestinal epithelium.

123. Omeprazole is used to treat duodenal ulcers that result from gastric acid hypersecretion. Omeprazole blocks the secretion of HCl from the parietal cells of the stomach. Which of the following is LEAST likely to occur in a patient taking omeprazole?

   A. an increase in microbial activity in the stomach
   B. a decrease in the activity of pepsin
   C. an increase in stomach pH
   D. a decrease in carbohydrate digestion in the stomach

124. Which of the following reaction types is common to the digestion of all macronutrients?

   A. hydrolysis
   B. reduction
   C. glycolysis
   D. phosphorylation

125. One function of the large intestine is:

   A. to absorb water.
   B. to secrete excess water.
   C. to digest fat.
   D. to secrete urea.

126. Salivary α–amylase begins the digestion of:

   A. lipids.
   B. nucleic acids.
   C. proteins.
   D. carbohydrates.

127. All of the following enzymes are part of pancreatic exocrine function EXCEPT:

   A. bile
   B. chymotrypsin
   C. pancreatic amylase
   D. lipase

128. In humans, most chemical digestion of food occurs in the:

   A. mouth.
   B. stomach.
   C. duodenum.
   D. ileum.

## 6.8 Absorption and Storage

The function of the entire digestive tract described in the previous section is to convert ingested food into basic nutrients that the small intestine is able to absorb. Once absorbed into the enterocytes, nutrients are processed and carried to the individual cells for use. The following section describes the process of absorption and the post-absorptive fates of the major nutrients: carbohydrates, proteins, and fats. This section is provided mainly as background knowledge; very little of this information will be tested directly on the MCAT.

## 6.9 Carbohydrates

By far the major carbohydrates in a human diet are sucrose, lactose, and starch. Cellulose (the polysaccharide making up the cell wall of plants) cannot be digested by humans, and is considered *roughage*. Sucrose and lactose are disaccharides made from glucose and fructose, and from glucose and galactose, respectively. Starch is a straight chain of glucose molecules. Typically, 80% of the end product of carbohydrate digestion is glucose. 95% of the carbohydrates in the blood are glucose.

Carbohydrate absorption is shown in Figure 6.7. Glucose is absorbed by a secondary active transport mechanism down the concentration gradient of sodium. Sodium is actively pumped out of the enterocyte on the basolateral side. The resulting low sodium concentration inside the enterocyte drags sodium from the intestinal lumen into the cell through a transport protein, but only after glucose has also attached itself to the protein. Thus glucose is dragged into the enterocyte by sodium. As the concentration of glucose inside the cell builds, it moves out of the cell on the basolateral side via facilitated transport. At high concentrations of lumenal glucose, glucose builds up in the paracellular space and raises the osmotic pressure there. The aqueous solution of the lumen is dragged into the paracellular space pulling glucose along with it. Glucose is absorbed by this second method only when present in high concentrations.

Galactose follows a similar absorption path to glucose. Fructose is absorbed via facilitated diffusion, and much of it is converted to glucose while inside the enterocyte.

All carbohydrates are absorbed into the bloodstream and carried by the portal vein to the liver. One of the jobs of the liver is to maintain a fairly constant blood glucose level (90 mg/dl between meals to 140 mg/dl after a meal). The liver absorbs the carbohydrates and converts nearly all the galactose and fructose into glucose, and then into glycogen for storage. The formation of glycogen is called **glycogenesis**. When the blood glucose level decreases, **glycogenolysis** takes place in the liver, and glucose is returned to the blood.

In all cells except enterocytes and the cells of the renal tubule, glucose is transported from high concentration to low concentration via facilitated diffusion. Nearly all cells are capable of producing and storing some glycogen; however, only muscle cells and especially liver cells store large amounts. When the cells have reached their saturation point with glycogen, carbohydrates are converted to fatty acids and then triglycerides in a process requiring a small amount of energy.

> You can ignore most of the details here and concentrate on the big picture of carbohydrate digestion, absorption, and metabolism. Relate this information to glycolysis and the Krebs cycle in Biology Lecture 1 for a complete picture. Notice that most of the glucose is stored for later use. When the glycogen stores are full, the glucose is converted to fat, a long-term form of energy storage. The conversion of glucose to fat takes place in the liver and adipocytes and is stored in the adipocytes. Keep in mind the role of the liver in processing carbohydrates. We will talk more about this later.

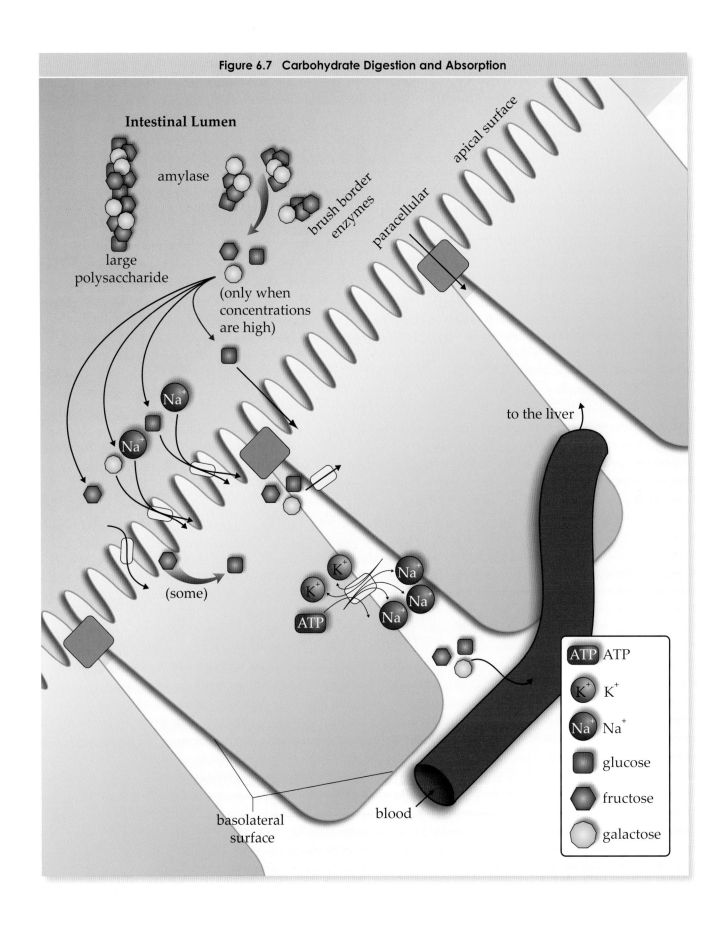

**Figure 6.7  Carbohydrate Digestion and Absorption**

Intestinal Lumen

amylase

brush border
enzymes

apical surface

paracellular

large
polysaccharide

(only when
concentrations
are high)

to the liver

Na⁺

Na⁺

K⁺

Na⁺

K⁺

Na⁺

(some)

ATP

Na⁺

ATP ATP

K⁺ K⁺

Na⁺ Na⁺

glucose

fructose

basolateral
surface

blood

galactose

## 6.10 Proteins

Protein digestion results in amino acids, dipeptides, and tripeptides. Absorption of many of these products occurs via a cotransport mechanism down the concentration gradient of sodium, similar to the mechanism used by glucose. A few amino acids are transported by facilitated diffusion. Because the chemistry of amino acids varies greatly, each transport mechanism is specific to a few amino acids or polypeptides.

Nearly all polypeptides absorbed into an enterocyte are hydrolyzed to their amino acid constituents by enzymes within the enterocytes. From the enterocytes, amino acids are absorbed directly into the blood and then quickly taken up by all cells of the body, especially the liver. Transport into the cells may be facilitated or active, but is never passive, since amino acids are too large and polar to diffuse through the membrane. The cells immediately create proteins from the amino acids so that the intracellular amino acid concentration remains low. However, most proteins are easily broken down and returned to the blood when needed. When the cells reach their upper limit for protein storage, amino acids can be burned for energy (see Biology Lecture 1) or converted to fat for storage. The energy that can be gained from burning protein is about 4 Calories per gram of protein. This can be compared to carbohydrates, which produce about 4.5 Calories per gram, and fat, which produces about 9 Calories per gram. Ammonia, a nitrogen containing compound, is a by-product of gluconeogenesis from proteins. Nearly all ammonia is converted to **urea** by the liver and then excreted in the urine by the kidney.

This is the normal surface pattern of the jejunal mucosa.

This is the jejunal mucosa of a person with Celiac Disease. Celiac Disease is an uncommon condition caused by hypersensitivity to a component of gluten, a protein in wheat flour.

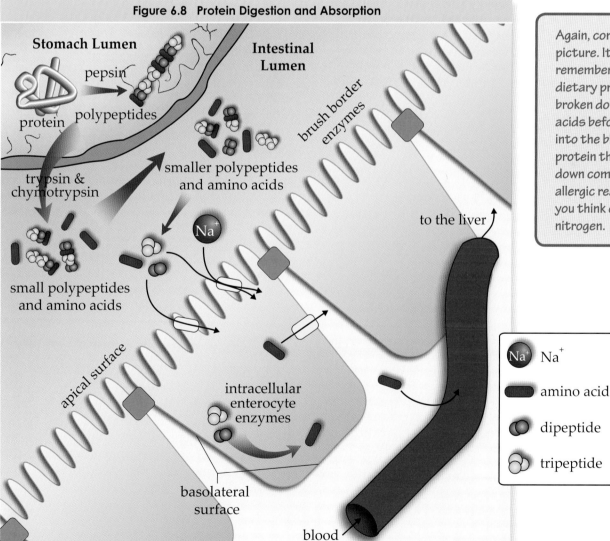

**Figure 6.8  Protein Digestion and Absorption**

Stomach Lumen

pepsin

protein  polypeptides

trypsin & chymotrypsin

Intestinal Lumen

brush border enzymes

smaller polypeptides and amino acids

Na⁺

to the liver

small polypeptides and amino acids

apical surface

intracellular enterocyte enzymes

basolateral surface

blood

Na⁺  Na⁺

amino acid

dipeptide

tripeptide

Again, concentrate on the big picture. It may be helpful to remember that virtually all dietary protein is completely broken down to its amino acids before being absorbed into the blood. In fact, any protein that is not broken down completely may cause allergic reactions. Also, when you think of proteins, think nitrogen.

## 6.11 Fats

Most of dietary fat consists of triglycerides, which are broken down to monoglycerides, and fatty acids, before they are shuttled to the brush border by bile micelles, and diffuse through the enterocyte membrane (Figure 6.9). After delivering their cargo, the micelles shuttle back to the chyme to pick up more fat digestates. Micelles also carry other fat digestates such as small amounts of hydrolyzed phospholipids and cholesterol, which also diffuse through the enterocyte membrane.

Once inside the enterocyte, monoglycerides, and fatty acids, are turned back into triglycerides at the smooth endoplasmic reticulum. The newly synthesized triglycerides aggregate within the smooth endoplasmic reticular lumen along with some cholesterol and phospholipids. These amphipathic molecules orient themselves like a micelle with their charged ends pointing outward toward the aqueous solution of the lumen. Apoproteins attach to the outside of these globules. (See Biology Lecture 1 for more on apoproteins.) The globules move to the Golgi apparatus and are released from the cell into the interstitial fluid via exocytosis. Most of these globules, now called *chylomicrons*, move into the lacteals of the lymph system. 80-90% of ingested fat that is absorbed by this process, moves through the lymph system, and is emptied into the large veins of the neck at the *thoracic duct*. Small amounts of more water soluble fatty acids (short chain fatty acids) are absorbed directly into the blood of the villi.

The chylomicron concentration in the blood peaks about 1-2 hours after a meal, but falls rapidly (chylomicrons have a half life of about 1 hour) as the fat digestates are absorbed into the cells of the body. The major absorption of fat occurs in the liver and adipose tissue. Chylomicrons stick to the side of capillary walls where *lipoprotein lipase* hydrolyzes the triglycerides, the products of which immediately diffuse into the fat and liver cells. Inside the fat and liver cells, the triglycerides are reconstituted at the smooth endoplasmic reticulum. Thus, the first stop for most of the digested fat is the liver.

From adipose tissue, most fatty acids are transported in the form of *free fatty acid*, which combines immediately in the blood with **albumin**. A single albumin molecule typically carries 3 fatty acid molecules, but is capable of carrying up to 30.

Between meals (called the *postabsorptive state*) 95% of lipids in the plasma are in the form of *lipoproteins*. Lipoproteins look like small chylomicrons, or, more precisely, chylomicrons are large lipoproteins. Besides chylomicrons, there are four different types of lipoproteins:

1. *very low-density lipoproteins*;
2. *intermediate-density lipoproteins*;
3. *low-density lipoproteins* and;
4. *high-density lipoproteins*.

All are made from triglycerides, cholesterol, phospholipids, and protein. As the density increases, first the amount of triglycerides decrease, and then the amount of cholesterol and phospholipids decrease. Thus, very low-density lipoproteins have a lot of triglycerides, and high-density lipoproteins have very few triglycerides. Most lipoproteins are made in the liver. Very-low density lipoproteins transport triglycerides from the liver to adipose tissue. Intermediate and low-density lipoproteins transport cholesterol and phospholipids to the cells of the body. The function of high-density lipoproteins is less well understood. Hardening of the arteries seems to be induced by the lower density lipoproteins, but impeded by high-density lipoproteins.

> Although lipoproteins are a hot topic, they are not a required topic for the MCAT. Once again, look at the big picture here. Keep in mind that fat is insoluble in water, so typically requires a carrier (i.e. a lipoprotein, or albumin). For the MCAT, you should associate fat with efficient long-term energy storage; lots of calories (energy) with little weight.

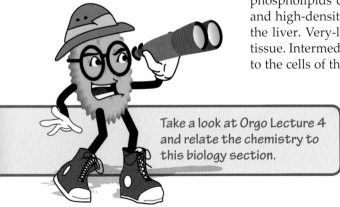

> Take a look at Orgo Lecture 4 and relate the chemistry to this biology section.

Figure 6.9 Fat Digestion and Absorption

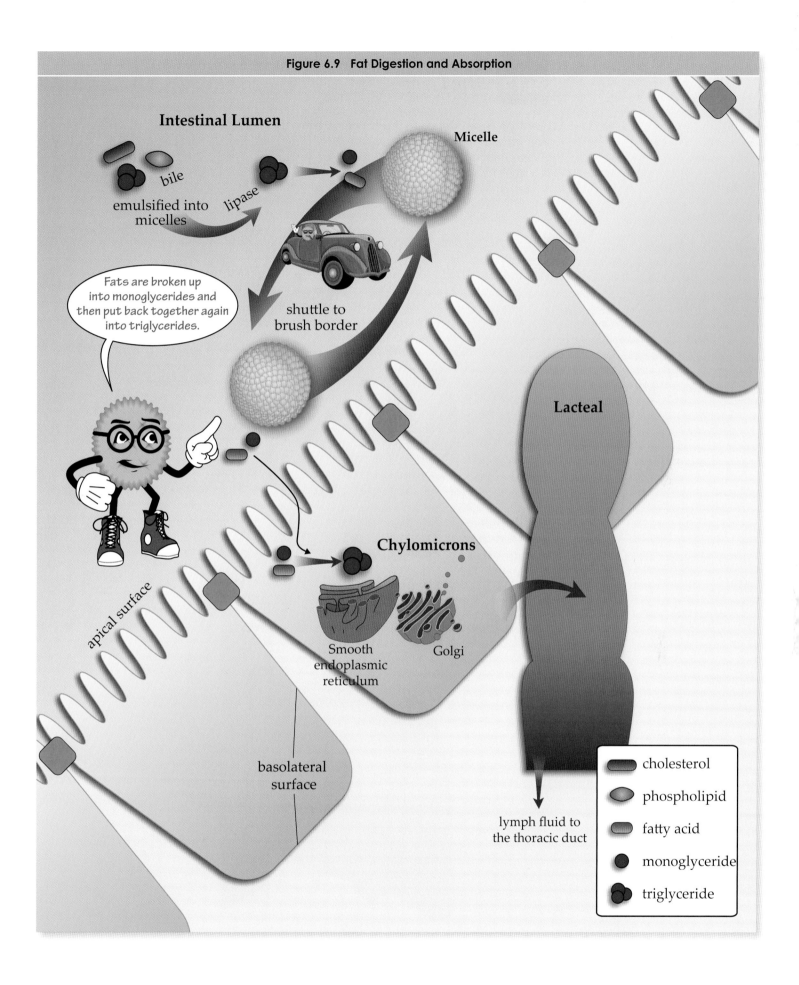

## 6.12 The Liver

The liver is positioned to receive blood from the capillary beds of the intestines, stomach, spleen, and pancreas via the *hepatic portal vein*. This blood is 'worked upon' by the liver. A second blood supply, used to oxygenate the liver, is received through the hepatic artery. All blood received by the liver moves through large flattened spaces called the *hepatic sinusoids* and collects in the *hepatic vein*, which leads to the **vena cava**.

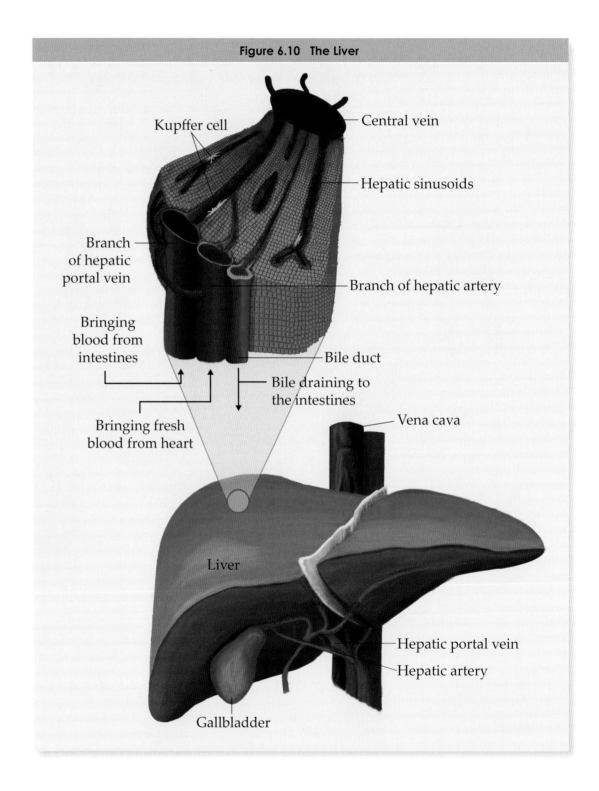

**Figure 6.10 The Liver**

The liver has the following interrelated functions (Figure 6.11).

- **Blood storage**: the liver can expand to act as a blood reservoir for the body.

- **Blood filtration**: *Kupffer cells* phagocytize bacteria picked up from the intestines.

- **Carbohydrate metabolism**: The liver maintains normal blood glucose levels through **gluconeogenesis** (the production of glycogen and glucose from noncarbohydrate precursors), glycogenesis, and storage of glycogen.

- **Fat metabolism**: The liver synthesizes bile from cholesterol and converts carbohydrates and proteins into fat. It oxidizes fatty acids for energy, and forms most lipoproteins.

- **Protein metabolism**: The liver deaminates amino acids, forms **urea** from ammonia in the blood, synthesizes plasma proteins such as fibrinogen, prothrombin, albumin, and most globulins, and synthesizes nonessential amino acids.

- **Detoxification**: Detoxified chemicals are excreted by the liver as part of bile or polarized so they may be excreted by the kidney.

- **Erythrocyte destruction**: *Kupffer cells* also destroy irregular erythrocytes, but most irregular erythrocytes are destroyed by the spleen.

- **Vitamin storage**: The liver stores vitamins such as vitamins A, D, and B12. The liver also stores iron combining it with the protein *apoferritin* to form of *ferritin*.

> Prothrombin and fibrinogen are two important clotting factors. Albumin is the major osmoregulatory protein in the blood. Globulins are a group of proteins that include antibodies. Antibodies, however, are not made in the liver. They are made by plasma cells.

When the liver mobilizes fat for energy, it produces acids called *ketone bodies*. This often results in a condition called *ketosis* or *acidosis*. For the MCAT, you should know that when the liver mobilizes fat or protein for energy, the blood acidity increases.

**Figure 6.11  Functions of the Liver**

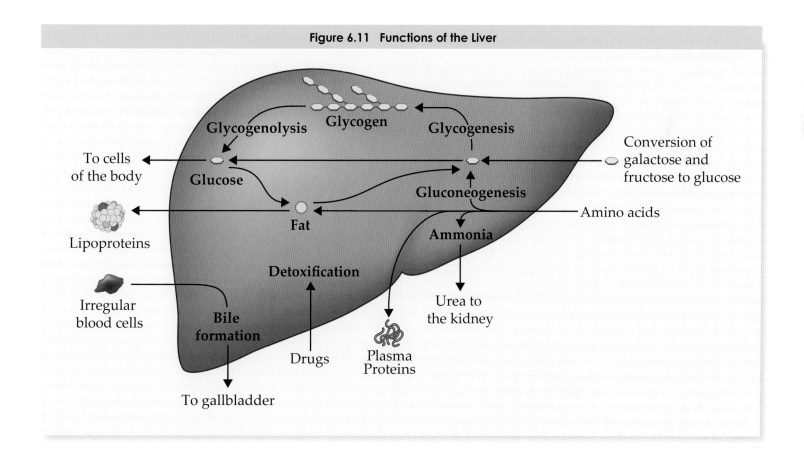

129. A stomach ulcer may increase the acidity of the stomach. The stomach cells most affected by a stomach ulcer are:

    A. goblet cells.
    B. parietal cells.
    C. chief cells.
    D. G cells.

130. Which of the following occurs mainly in the liver?

    A. fat storage
    B. protein degradation
    C. glycolysis
    D. gluconeogenesis

131. Dietary fat consists mostly of neutral fats called triglycerides. Most digestive products of fat:

    A. enter intestinal epithelial cells as chylomicrons.
    B. are absorbed directly into the capillaries of the intestines.
    C. are degraded to fatty acids by the smooth endoplasmic reticulum of enterocytes.
    D. enter the lymph system before entering the blood stream.

132. Which of the following is not true concerning the digestive products of dietary protein?

    A. They are used to synthesize essential amino acids in the liver.
    B. Some of the products are absorbed into the intestines by facilitated diffusion.
    C. Energy is required for the intestinal absorption of at least some of these products.
    D. Deamination of these products in the liver leads to urea in the blood.

133. Cholera is an intestinal infection that can lead to severe diarrhea causing profuse secretion of water and electrolytes. A glucose-electrolyte solution may be administered orally to patients suffering from cholera. What is the most likely reason for mixing glucose with the electrolyte solution?

    A. When digested, glucose increases the strength of the patient.
    B. The absorption of glucose increases the uptake of electrolytes.
    C. Glucose is an electrolyte.
    D. Glucose stimulates secretion of the pancreatic enzyme, amylase.

134. Most of the glycogen in the human body is stored in the liver and the skeletal muscles. Which of the following hormones inhibits glycogenolysis?

    A. Cortisol
    B. Insulin
    C. Glucagon
    D. Aldosterone

135. Free fatty acids do not dissolve in the blood, so they must be transported within the body bound to protein carriers. The most likely explanation for this is:

    A. Blood is an aqueous solution and only hydrophobic compounds are easily dissolved.
    B. Blood is an aqueous solution and only hydrophilic compounds are easily dissolved.
    C. Blood serum contains chylomicrons which do not bind to fatty acids.
    D. Blood serum is lipid based and the polar region of a fatty acid will not be dissolved.

136. Essential amino acids must be ingested because they cannot be synthesized by the body. In what form are these amino acids likely to enter the blood stream?

    A. single amino acids
    B. dipeptides
    C. polypeptides
    D. proteins

*The Kidney*

The function of the **kidney** is:

    1. to excrete waste products, such as urea, uric acid, ammonia, and phosphate;

    2. to maintain homeostasis of the body fluid volume and solute composition and;

    3. to help control plasma pH.

There are two kidneys. Each kidney is a fist-sized organ made up of an outer **cortex** and an inner **medulla**. Urine is created by the kidney and emptied into the **renal pelvis**. The renal pelvis is emptied by the **ureter**, which carries urine to the **bladder**. The bladder is drained by the **urethra**.

The functional unit of the kidney is the **nephron** (Figures 6.12, 6.13, and 6.14). Blood flows into the first capillary bed of the nephron called the **glomerulus**. Together, **Bowman's capsule** and the glomerulus make up the **renal corpuscle**. **Hydrostatic pressure** forces some plasma through **fenestrations** of the glomerular endothelium and into Bowman's capsule. Like a sieve, the fenestrations screen out blood cells and large proteins from entering Bowman's capsule. The fluid that finds its way into Bowman's capsule is called *filtrate* or *primary urine*. Filtrate moves from Bowman's capsule to the **proximal tubule**. The proximal tubule is where most **reabsorption** takes place. Secondary active transport proteins in the apical membranes of the proximal tubule cells are responsible for the reabsorption of nearly all glucose, most proteins, and other solutes. These transport proteins can become saturated. The concentration of a solute that saturates its transport proteins is called the *transport maximum*. Once a solute has reached its transport maximum, any more solute is washed into the urine. Some solutes that are not actively reabsorbed are reabsorbed by passive or facilitated diffusion. Water is reabsorbed into the renal interstitium of the proximal tubules across relatively permeable tight junctions due to the favorable osmotic gradient.

Drugs, toxins, and other solutes are **secreted** into the filtrate by the cells of the proximal tubule. Hydrogen ions are secreted through an **antiport** system with sodium, which is driven by the sodium concentration gradient. This antiport system is similar to the transport system of glucose with sodium, except the proton crosses the membrane in the opposite direction to sodium. Uric acid, bile pigments, antibiotics and other drugs are also secreted into the proximal tubule.

The net result of the proximal tubule is to reduce the amount of filtrate in the nephron while changing the solute composition without changing the osmolarity.

From the proximal tubule, the filtrate flows into the **loop of Henle**. The loop of Henle dips into the medulla. The function of the loop of Henle is to increase the solute concentration, and thus the osmotic pressure, of the medulla. As filtrate descends into the medulla, water passively diffuses out of the loop of Henle and into the medulla. The descending loop of Henle has low permeability to salt, so filtrate osmolarity goes up. As the filtrate rises out of the medulla, salt diffuses out of the ascending loop of Henle, passively at first, then actively. The

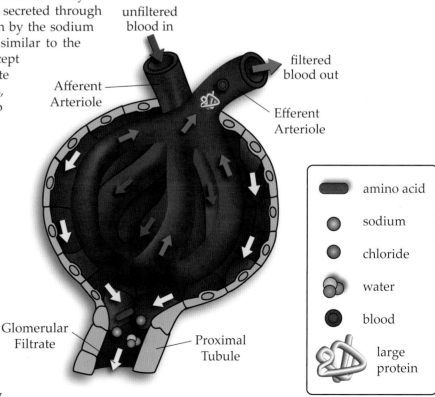

unfiltered
blood in

filtered
blood out

Afferent
Arteriole

Efferent
Arteriole

Glomerular
Filtrate

Proximal
Tubule

amino acid

sodium

chloride

water

blood

large
protein

**Figure 6.12 Glomerulus**

ascending loop of Henle is nearly impermeable to water. A second capillary bed, called the *vasa recta*, surrounds the loop of Henle and helps to maintain the concentration of the medulla.

The **distal tubule** reabsorbs $Na^+$, and $Ca^{2+}$ while secreting $K^+$, $H^+$, and $HCO_3^-$. Aldosterone acts on the distal tubule cells to increase sodium and potassium membrane transport proteins. The net effect of the distal tubule is to lower the filtrate osmolarity. At the end of the distal tubule, called the *collecting tubule* (The collecting tubule is a portion of the distal tubule, not to be confused with the collecting duct), ADH acts to increase the permeability of the cells to water. Therefore, in the presence of ADH, water flows from the tubule, concentrating the filtrate.

The distal tubule empties into the **collecting duct**. The collecting duct carries the filtrate into the highly osmotic medulla. The collecting duct is impermeable to water, but is also sensitive to ADH. In the presence of ADH, the collecting duct becomes permeable to water allowing it to passively diffuse into the medulla, concentrating the urine. Many collecting ducts line up side by side in the medulla to make the *renal pyramids*.

The collecting ducts lead to a *renal calyx*, which empties into the renal pelvis.

## 6.14 *The Juxtaglomerular Apparatus*

The **juxtaglomerular apparatus** monitors filtrate pressure in the distal tubule. Specialized cells, called *granular cells*, in the juxtaglomerular apparatus secrete the enzyme renin. Renin initiates a regulatory cascade producing angiotensin I, II, and III, which ultimately stimulates the adrenal cortex to secrete aldosterone. Aldosterone acts on the distal tubule, stimulating the formation of membrane proteins that absorb sodium and secrete potassium.

There are many details about the kidney that you must be able to recall for the MCAT. You should know the function of each section of the nephron: filtration occurs in the renal corpuscle; reabsorption and secretion mostly in the proximal tubule; the loop of Henle concentrates solute in the medulla; the distal tubule empties into the collecting duct; the collecting duct concentrates the urine. Understand that the amount of filtrate is related to the hydrostatic pressure of the glomerulus. You should know that the descending loop of Henle is permeable to water, and that the ascending loop of Henle is impermeable to water and actively transports sodium into the kidney.

Don't lose sight of the big picture; the function of the kidney is homeostasis.

**Figure 6.13 The Nephron**

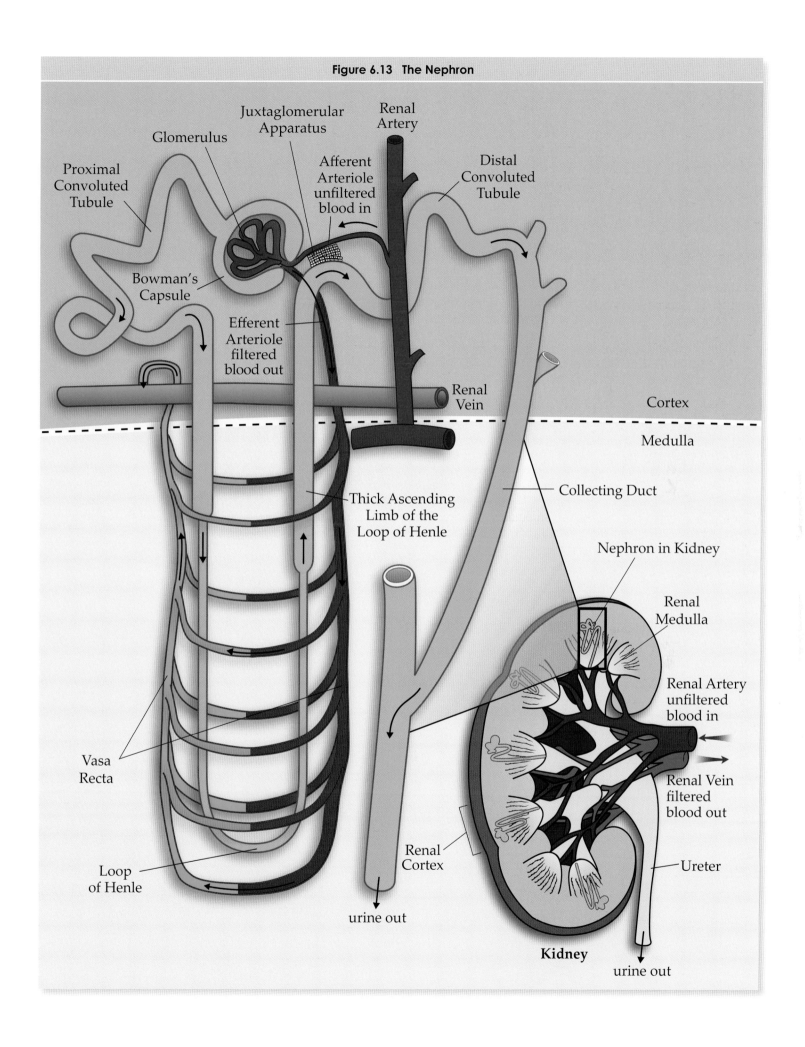

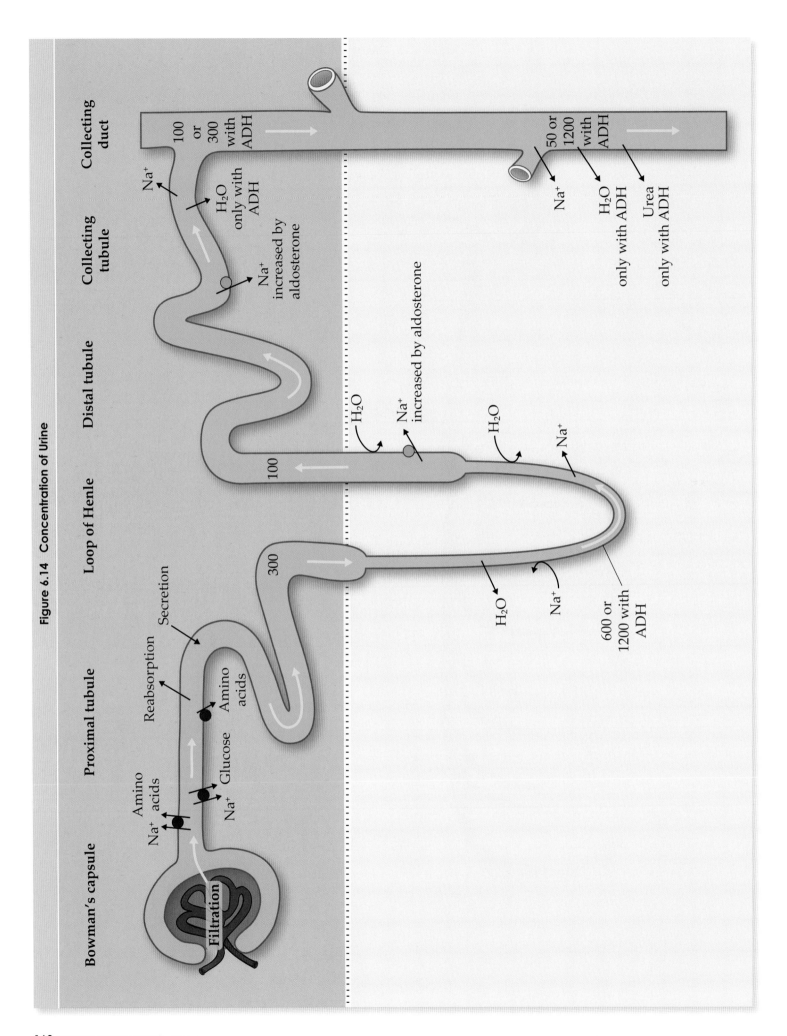

**Figure 6.14  Concentration of Urine**

| Terms | | |
|---|---|---|
| Antiport | Glycogenesis | Pancreatic Amylase |
| Bicarbonate Ion | Glycogenolysis | Parietal (Oxyntic) Cells |
| Bladder | Goblet Cells | Pepsinogen |
| Bowman's Capsule | Hydrochloric Acid | Peristalsis |
| Brush Border | (HCl) | Proximal Tubule |
| Chief (Peptic) Cells | Hydrostatic Pressure | Reabsorption |
| Chyme | Juxtaglomerular | Rectum |
| Chymotrypsin | Apparatus | Renal Corpuscle |
| Collecting Duct | Kidney | Renal Pelvis |
| Cortex | Lacteal | Ribonuclease |
| Deoxyribonuclease | Large Intestine | Salivary Amylase |
| Distal Tubule | Lipase | Small Intestine |
| Esophagus | Liver | Stomach |
| Exocrine Glands | Loop of Henle | Triglycerides |
| Fenestrations | Medulla | Trypsin |
| G Cells | Microvilli | Urea |
| Gallbladder | Mouth | Ureter |
| Gastrin | Mucous Cells | Urethra |
| Glomerulus | Nephron | |

*Notes:*

137. Bowman's capsule assists in clearing urea from the blood by:

   A. actively transporting urea into the filtrate using ATP-driven pumps.
   B. exchanging urea for glucose in an antiport mechanism.
   C. allowing urea to diffuse into the filtrate under filtration pressure.
   D. converting urea to amino acids.

138. Tests reveal the presence of glucose in a patient's urine. This is an indication that:

   A. glucose transporters in the loop of Henle are not functioning properly.
   B. the patient is healthy, as glucose normally appears in the urine.
   C. the proximal tubule is over-secreting glucose.
   D. glucose influx into the filtrate is occurring faster than it can be reabsorbed.

139. The epithelial cells of the proximal convoluted tubule contain a brush border similar to the brush border of the small intestine. The most likely function of the brush border in the proximal convoluted tubule is to:

   A. increase the amount of filtrate that reaches the loop of Henle.
   B. increase the surface area available for the absorption.
   C. slow the rate of at which the filtrate moves through the nephron.
   D. move the filtrate through the nephron with cilia like action.

140. If a patient were administered a drug that selectively bound and inactivated renin, which of the following would most likely result?

   A. The patient's blood pressure would increase.
   B. Platelets would be found in the urine.
   C. The amount of filtrate entering Bowman's capsule would increase.
   D. Sodium reabsorption by the distal tubule would decrease.

141. Which of the following correctly orders the structures through which urine flows as it leaves the body?

   A. urethra, urinary bladder, ureter, collecting duct
   B. collecting duct, urinary bladder, urethra, ureter
   C. collecting duct, ureter, urinary bladder, urethra
   D. ureter, collecting duct, urethra, urinary bladder

142. How are the blood levels of vasopressin and aldosterone in a dehydrated individual likely to compare with those of a healthy individual?

   A. Vasopressin and aldosterone levels are likely to be lower in a dehydrated individual.
   B. Vasopressin and aldosterone levels are likely to be higher in a dehydrated individual.
   C. Vasopressin levels are likely to be higher while aldosterone levels are likely to be lower in a dehydrated individual.
   D. Vasopressin levels are likely to be lower while aldosterone levels are likely to be higher in a dehydrated individual.

143. An afferent arteriole in a glomerular tuft contains microscopic fenestrations which increase fluid flow. In a hypertensive patient (a patient with high blood pressure):

   A. these fenestrations would constrict resulting in decreased urinary output.
   B. filtrate volume would be expected to be larger due to increased fluid pressure.
   C. filtrate volume would be expected to be smaller due to increased fluid pressure.
   D. urinary output will most likely be diminished due to increased solute concentration.

144. Long loops of Henle on juxtamedullary nephrons allow for greater concentration of urine. For an individual with highly concentrated urine, filtrate entering the loop of Henle is likely to be:

   A. more concentrated than filtrate exiting the loop Henle.
   B. less concentrated than filtrate exiting the loop of Henle.
   C. more voluminous than filtrate exiting the loop of Henle.
   D. less voluminous than filtrate exiting the loop of Henle.

# THE CARDIOVASCULAR SYSTEM; THE RESPIRATORY SYSTEM

## 7.1   Cardiovascular Anatomy

The cardiovascular system consists of the heart, blood, and blood vessels (Figure 7.1). For the MCAT, you must be able to trace the circulatory path of the blood. Beginning with the **left ventricle**, blood is pumped through the **aorta**. From the aorta, branch many smaller **arteries**, which themselves branch into still smaller **arterioles**, which branch into still smaller **capillaries**. Blood from the capillaries is collected into **venules**, which themselves collect into larger **veins**, which collect again into the **superior and inferior vena cava**. The vena cava empty into

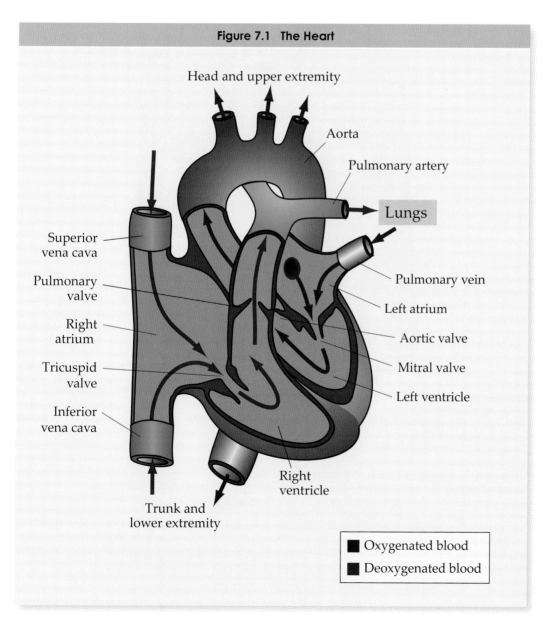

**Figure 7.1   The Heart**

Head and upper extremity

Aorta

Pulmonary artery

Lungs

Superior vena cava

Pulmonary valve

Right atrium

Tricuspid valve

Inferior vena cava

Pulmonary vein

Left atrium

Aortic valve

Mitral valve

Left ventricle

Right ventricle

Trunk and lower extremity

■ Oxygenated blood
■ Deoxygenated blood

the **right atrium** of the heart. This first half of the circulation as just described is called the **systemic circulation**. From the right atrium, blood is squeezed into the **right ventricle**. The right ventricle pumps blood through the **pulmonary arteries**, to arterioles, to the capillaries of the lungs. From the capillaries of the lungs, blood collects in venules, then in veins, and finally in the **pulmonary veins** leading to the heart. (True capillaries branch off arterioles, and do not represent the only route between an arteriole and venule.) The pulmonary veins empty into the **left atrium**, which fills the left ventricle. This second half of the circulation is called the **pulmonary circulation**. Since there are no openings for the blood to leave the vessels, the entire system is said to be a **closed circulatory system**.

The heart itself is a large muscle. Unlike skeletal muscle, it is not attached to bone. Instead, its fibers form a net and the net contracts upon itself squeezing blood into the arteries. Systole occurs when the ventricles contract; diastole occurs during relaxation of the entire heart and then contraction of the atria.

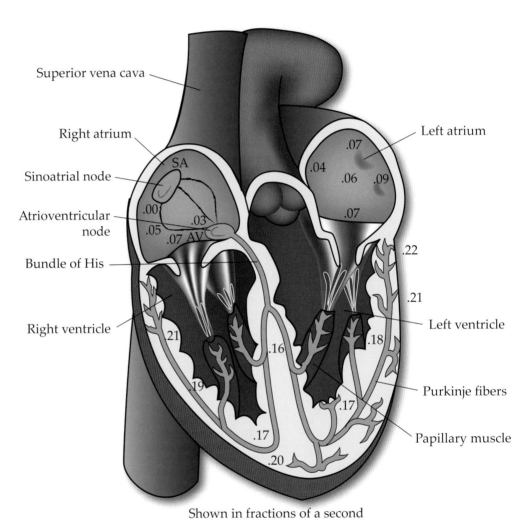

Shown in fractions of a second

**Figure 7.2  Transmission of the Cardiac Impulse**

The blood is propelled by the hydrostatic pressure created by the contraction of the heart. The rate of these contractions is controlled by the autonomic nervous system, but the autonomic nervous system does not initiate the contractions. The heart contracts automatically, paced by a group of specialized cardiac muscle cells called the **sinoatrial node (SA node)** located in the right atrium. The SA node is *autorhythmic* (contracts by itself at regular intervals), spreading its contractions to the surrounding cardiac muscles via **electrical synapses** made from **gap junctions**. The pace of the SA node is faster than normal heartbeats but the parasympathetic **vagus nerve** innervates the SA node, slowing the contractions. The action potential generated by the SA node spreads around both atria causing them to contract, and, at the same time, spreads to the **atrioventricular node (AV node)** located in the interatrial septa (the wall of cardiac muscle between the atria). The AV node is slower to contract, creating a delay which allows the atria to finish their contraction, and to squeeze their contents into the ventricles before the ventricles begin to contract. From the AV node, the action potential moves down conductive fibers called the **bundle of His**. The bundle of His is located in the wall separating the ventricles. The action potential branches out through the ventricular walls via conductive fibers called Purkinje fibers. From the **Purkinje fibers**, the action potential is spread through gap junctions from one cardiac muscle to the next. The Purkinje fibers in the ventricles allow for a more unified, and stronger, contraction.

**Arteries** are elastic, and stretch as they fill with blood. When the ventricles finish their contraction, the stretched arteries recoil, keeping the blood moving more smoothly. Arteries are wrapped in smooth muscle that is typically innervated by the sympathetic nervous system. Epinephrine is a powerful vasoconstrictor causing arteries to narrow. Larger arteries have less smooth muscle per volume than medium size arteries, and are less affected by sympathetic innervation. Medium sized arteries, on the other hand, constrict enough under sympathetic stimulation to reroute blood. **Arterioles** are very small. They are wrapped by smooth muscle. Constriction and dilation of arterioles can be used to regulate blood pressure as well as rerouting blood.

**Capillaries** are microscopic blood vessels (Figure 7.3). Capillary walls are only one cell thick, and the diameter of a capillary is roughly equal to that of a single red blood cell. Nutrient and gas exchange with any tissue other than vascular tissue takes place only across capillary walls, and not across arterioles or venules. There are four methods for materials to cross capillary walls:

1. pinocytosis;
2. diffusion or transport through capillary cell membranes;
3. movement through pores in the cells called fenestrations;
4. movement through the space between the cells.

**Figure 7.3 Capillary**

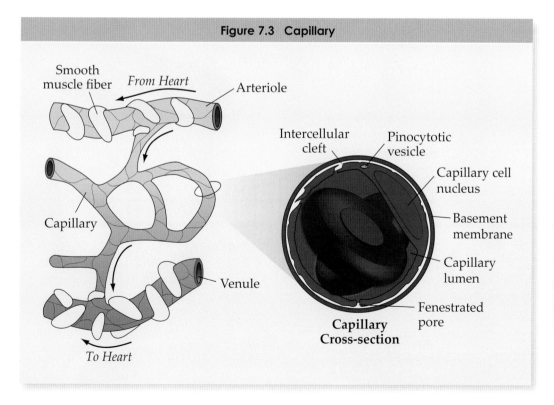

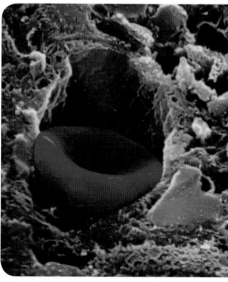

A red blood cell enters a capillary.

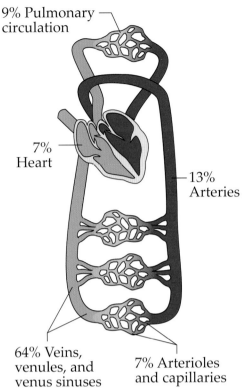

9% Pulmonary circulation

7% Heart

13% Arteries

64% Veins, venules, and venus sinuses

7% Arterioles and capillaries

**Figure 7.4  Blood Volume**

An artery carries blood away from the heart; a vein carries blood toward the heart. Don't confuse oxygenated blood with the definition for arteries. The pulmonary arteries contain the most deoxygenated blood in the body.

**Capillaries** are found close to all cells of the body. As blood flows into a capillary (Figure 7.5), hydrostatic pressure is greater than osmotic pressure, and net fluid flow is out of the capillary, and into the interstitium. Although osmotic pressure remains relatively constant throughout the capillary, hydrostatic pressure drops from the arteriole end to the venule end. Thus, osmotic pressure overcomes hydrostatic pressure near the venule end of a capillary, and net fluid flow is into the capillary and out of the interstitium. The net result of fluid exchange by the capillaries is a 10% loss of fluid to the interstitium.

**Venules** and **veins** are similar in structure to arterioles and arteries. The lumen is larger than the lumen of comparable arteries, and veins contain a far greater volume of blood. (Figure 7.4) Veins, venules, and venus sinuses in the systemic circulation hold about 64% of the blood in a body at rest, and act as a reservoir for blood. Arteries, arterioles, and capillaries in the systemic circulation contain about 20% of the blood.

The cross-sectional area of the veins is about four times that of the arteries. The total cross-sectional area of the capillaries is far greater than the cross-sectional area of the arteries or veins. Since the blood volume flow rate is approximately constant, the blood velocity is inversely proportional to the cross-sectional area. Therefore, the blood moves the slowest through the capillaries. Although Bernoulli's equation tells us that pressure is inversely related to cross-sectional area, it is evident from Figure 7.6 that this is not the case in the blood vessels. The blood is not an ideal flow, and you should memorize Figure 7.6 for the MCAT. The pumping force of the heart is the major contributor to pressure in the blood vessels. To compensate for the lower pressure, veins have a valve system that prevents back flow of blood. Contraction of skeletal muscle helps blood move through veins; however, the major propulsive force moving blood through the veins is the pumping of the heart.

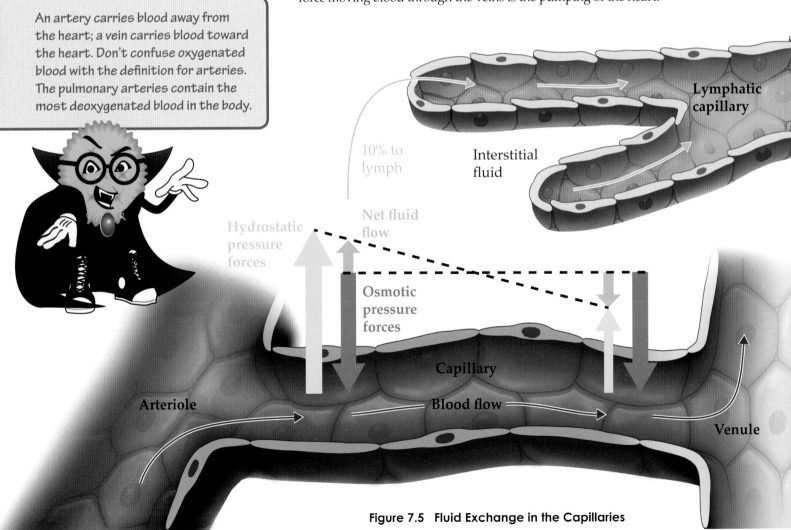

**Figure 7.5  Fluid Exchange in the Capillaries**

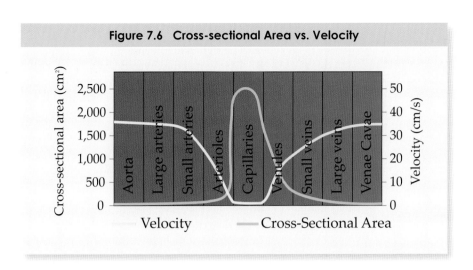

**Figure 7.6  Cross-sectional Area vs. Velocity**

Velocity ———— Cross-Sectional Area

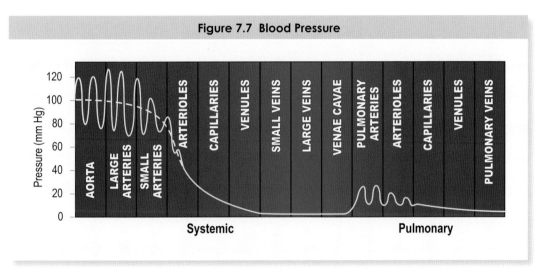

**Figure 7.7  Blood Pressure**

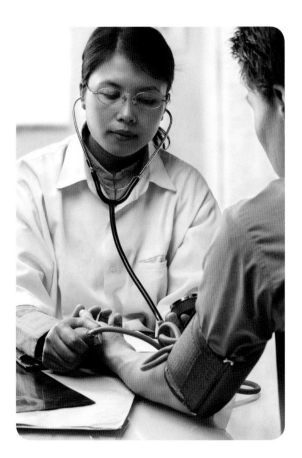

Information on blood pressure, volume, velocity, and cross-sectional area of vessels is more likely to be found in a physics passage. Don't memorize anything, but take a moment here to consider the relationships.

**Pressure:** Blood pressure increases near the heart and decreases to its lowest in the capillaries.

**Velocity:** A single artery is much bigger than a capillary, but there are far more capillaries than arteries. The total cross-sectional area of all those capillaries put together is much greater than the cross sectional area of a single aorta or a few arteries. Blood flow follows the Continuity Equation, Q = Av, reasonably well, so velocity is greatest in the arteries where cross-sectional area is smallest, and velocity is lowest where cross-sectional area is the greatest.

Lecture **7** : The Cardiovascular System; The Respiratory System **167**

**145.** The atrioventricular node:

   **A.** is a parasympathetic ganglion located in the right atrium of the heart.

   **B.** conducts an action potential from the vagus nerve to the heart.

   **C.** sets the rhythm of cardiac contractions.

   **D.** delays the contraction of the ventricles of the heart.

**146.** Cardiac output, which is the product of the heart rate and the stroke volume (the amount of blood pumped per contraction by either the left or the right ventricle) would most likely be:

   **A.** greater if measured using the stroke volume of the left ventricle.

   **B.** greater if measured using the stroke volume of the right ventricle.

   **C.** the same regardless of which stroke volume is used.

   **D.** dependent on the viscosity of the blood.

**147.** Which of the following is responsible for the spread of the cardiac action potential from one cardiac muscle cell to the next?

   **A.** gap junctions

   **B.** desmosomes

   **C.** tight junctions

   **D.** acetylcholine

**148.** In the congenital heart defect known as patent ductus arteriosus, the ductus arteriosus, which connects the aorta and the pulmonary arteries during fetal development, fails to close at birth. This will likely lead to all of the following EXCEPT:

   **A.** equal, or increased, oxygen concentration in the blood that reaches the systemic tissues.

   **B.** increased oxygen concentration in the blood that reaches the lungs.

   **C.** increased work load imposed on the left ventricle.

   **D.** increased work load imposed on the right ventricle.

**149.** Which chambers of the heart pump oxygenated blood?

   **A.** The right and left atria

   **B.** The right and left ventricles

   **C.** The right atria and the left ventricle

   **D.** The left atria and the left ventricle

**150.** Hypovolemic shock represents a set of symptoms that occur when a patient's blood volume falls abruptly. Hypovolemic shock is most likely to occur during:

   **A.** arterial bleeding

   **B.** venous bleeding

   **C.** low oxygen intake

   **D.** excess sodium consumption

**151.** The capillary network comprises the greatest cross sectional area of blood vessels in the body with the highest resistance to blood flow. In a healthy individual, the highest blood pressure would most likely be found in:

   **A.** the aorta

   **B.** the vena cavae

   **C.** the systemic capillaries

   **D.** the pulmonary capillaries

**152.** Gas exchange between the blood and tissues occurs:

   **A.** throughout the circulatory system.

   **B.** in the arteries, arterioles and capillaries.

   **C.** in the systemic arteries only.

   **D.** in the capillaries only.

The respiratory system provides a path for gas exchange between the external environment and the blood (Figure 7.8). Air enters through the nose, moves through the pharynx, larynx, trachea, bronchi, bronchioles, and into the alveoli where oxygen is exchanged for carbon dioxide with the blood. Inspiration occurs when the *medulla oblongata* of the midbrain signals the diaphragm to contract. The **diaphragm** is skeletal muscle, and innervated by the phrenic nerve. When relaxed, the diaphragm is dome-shaped. It flattens upon contraction, expanding the chest cavity and creating negative gauge pressure. (Gauge pressure is measured relative to local atmospheric conditions. See Physics Lecture 5.) *Intercostal muscles* (rib muscles) also help to expand the chest cavity. Atmospheric pressure forces air into the lungs. Upon relaxation of the diaphragm, the chest cavity shrinks (aided by different intercostal muscles and abdominal muscles), and the elasticity of the lungs along with the increased pressure in the chest cavity forces air out of the body.

**Figure 7.8  Respiratory System**

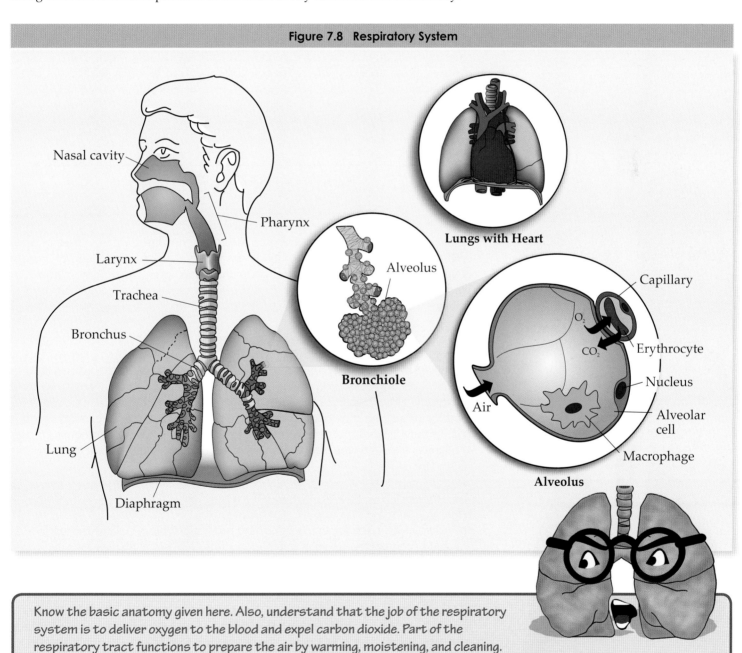

Nasal cavity

Pharynx

Larynx

Trachea

Bronchus

Lung

Diaphragm

Lungs with Heart

Alveolus

**Bronchiole**

Capillary

$O_2$

Erythrocyte

$CO_2$

Nucleus

Alveolar cell

Air

Macrophage

**Alveolus**

Know the basic anatomy given here. Also, understand that the job of the respiratory system is to deliver oxygen to the blood and expel carbon dioxide. Part of the respiratory tract functions to prepare the air by warming, moistening, and cleaning.
Know that since microtubules are found in cilia, and ciliated cells are found in the respiratory tract (and the Fallopian tubes and ependymal cells of the spinal cord), a problem in microtubule production might result in a problem in breathing (or fertility or circulation of cerebrospinal fluid).

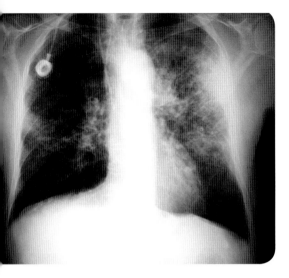

X-ray of a lung cancer.

## Inhalation

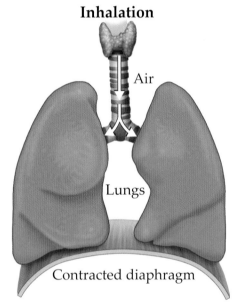

Air

Lungs

Contracted diaphragm

## Exhalation

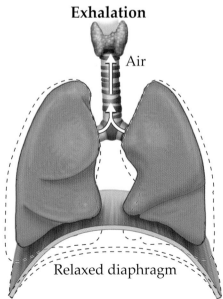

Air

Relaxed diaphragm

**Figure 7.9 Inhalation and Exhalation**

The **nasal cavity** is the space inside the nose. It **filters, moistens,** and **warms** incoming air. **Coarse hair** at the front of the cavity traps large dust particles. **Mucus** secreted by goblet cells traps smaller dust particles and moistens the air. Capillaries within the nasal cavity warm the air. **Cilia** moves the mucus and dust back toward the pharynx, so that it may be removed by spitting or swallowing.

The **pharynx** (or throat) functions as a passageway for food and air.

The **larynx** is the voice box. It sits behind the **epiglottis**, which is the cartilaginous member that prevents food from entering the trachea during swallowing. When nongaseous material enters the larynx, a coughing reflex is triggered forcing the material back out. The larynx contains the vocal cords.

The **trachea** (or windpipe) lies in front of the esophagus. It is composed of ringed cartilage covered by ciliated mucous cells. Like the nasal cavity, the mucus and cilia in the trachea collect dust and usher it toward the pharynx. Before entering the lungs the trachea splits into the right and left **bronchi**. Each bronchus branches many more times to become tiny **bronchioles**. Bronchioles terminate in grape-like clusters called *alveolar sacs* composed of tiny **alveoli**. From each alveolus, oxygen diffuses into a capillary where it is picked up by red blood cells. The red blood cells release carbon dioxide, which diffuses into the alveolus, and is expelled upon exhalation.

## 7.3 | *The Chemistry of Gas Exchange*

Typically, the air we inspire is 79% nitrogen and 21% oxygen, with negligible amounts of other trace gases. Exhaled air is 79% nitrogen, 16% oxygen, and 5% carbon dioxide and trace gases. Inside the lungs, the partial pressure of oxygen is approximately 110 mm Hg, and carbon dioxide is approximately 40 mm Hg. Under these pressures, oxygen diffuses into the capillaries, and carbon dioxide diffuses into the alveoli.

98% of the oxygen in the blood binds rapidly and reversibly with the protein **hemoglobin** inside the erythrocytes forming **oxyhemoglobin**. Hemoglobin is composed of four polypeptide subunits, each with a single heme cofactor. The *heme cofactor* is an organic molecule with an atom of **iron** at its center. Each of the four iron atoms in hemoglobin can bind with one $O_2$ molecule. When one $O_2$ **molecule** binds with an iron atom in hemoglobin, oxygenation of the other heme groups is accelerated. Similarly, release of an $O_2$ molecule by any of the heme groups, accelerates release by the others. This phenomenon is called *cooperativity*.

As $O_2$ pressure increases, the $O_2$ saturation of hemoglobin increases sigmoidally. The *oxyhemoglobin* ($HbO_2$) *dissociation curve* (Figure 7.10) shows the percent of hemoglobin that is bound with oxygen at various partial pressures of oxygen. In the arteries of a normal person breathing room air, the oxygen saturation is 97%. The flat portion of the curve in this region shows that small fluctuations in oxygen pressure have little effect.

The oxygen saturation of hemoglobin also depends upon carbon dioxide pressure, pH, and temperature of the blood. The **oxygen dissociation curve is shifted** to the right by an increase in **carbon dioxide pressure, hydrogen ion concentration, or temperature**. A shift to the right indicates a lowering of hemoglobin's affinity for oxygen. The shift due to pH change is called the *Bohr shift*. 2,3-DPG, a chemical found in red blood cells, also shifts the curve to the right. Carbon monoxide has more than 200 times greater affinity for hemoglobin than does oxygen but shifts the curve to the left. In cases of carbon monoxide poisoning, pure oxygen can be administered to displace the CO from hemoglobin.

Oxygen pressure is typically 40 mm Hg in body tissues. As the blood moves through the systemic capillaries, oxygen diffuses to the tissues, and carbon dioxide diffuses to the blood. Carbon dioxide is carried by the blood in three forms:

1.  in physical solution;

2.  as bicarbonate ion and;

3.  in carbamino compounds (combined with hemoglobin and other proteins).

Ten times as much is carried as bicarbonate than as either of the other forms. The bicarbonate ion formation is governed by the enzyme **carbonic anhydrase** in the reversible reaction:

$$CO_2 + H_2O \rightarrow HCO_3^- + H^+$$

Because carbonic anhydrase is inside the red blood cell and not in the plasma, when carbon dioxide is absorbed in the lungs, bicarbonate ion diffuses into the cell. To balance the electrostatic forces, chlorine moves out of the cell in a phenomenon called the *chloride shift* (Figure 7.11).

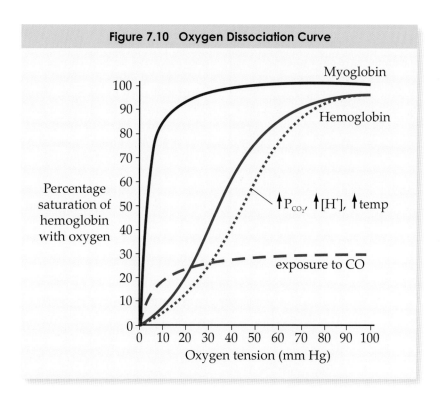

**Figure 7.10  Oxygen Dissociation Curve**

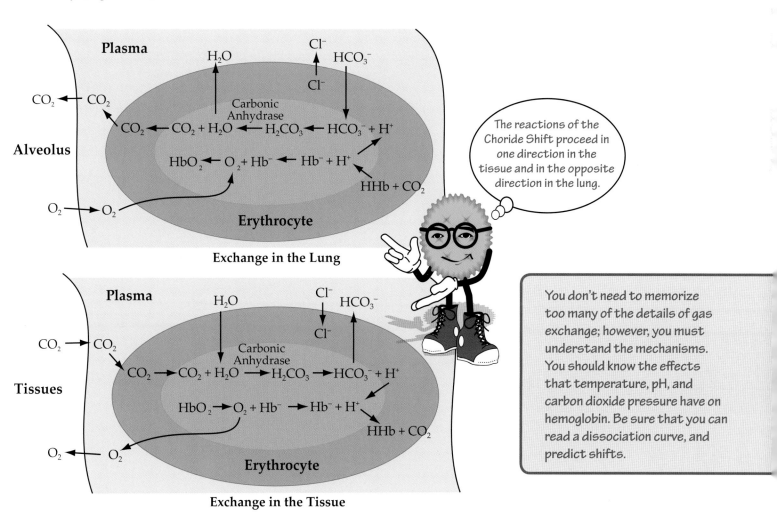

The reactions of the Choride Shift proceed in one direction in the tissue and in the opposite direction in the lung.

**Exchange in the Lung**

**Exchange in the Tissue**

**Figure 7.11  Chloride Shift**

You don't need to memorize too many of the details of gas exchange; however, you must understand the mechanisms. You should know the effects that temperature, pH, and carbon dioxide pressure have on hemoglobin. Be sure that you can read a dissociation curve, and predict shifts.

Carbon dioxide has its own dissociation curve, which relates blood content of carbon dioxide with carbon dioxide pressure. The greater the pressure of carbon dioxide, the greater the blood content of carbon dioxide. However, when hemoglobin becomes saturated with oxygen, its capacity to hold carbon dioxide is reduced. This is called the *Haldane effect*. The Haldane effect facilitates the transfer of carbon dioxide from blood to lungs, and from tissues to blood. Reduced hemoglobin (Hb) (hemoglobin without oxygen) acts as a blood buffer by accepting protons. It is the greater capacity of reduced hemoglobin to form carbamino hemoglobin that explains the Haldane effect.

The rate of breathing is affected by *central chemoreceptors* located in the medulla, and *peripheral chemoreceptors* located in the carotid arteries and aorta. Central and peripheral chemoreceptors monitor carbon dioxide concentration in the blood and increase breathing when levels get too high. Oxygen concentration and pH are monitored mainly by peripheral chemoreceptors.

What about all that nitrogen? What effect does nitrogen have on the body?

Remember your chemistry. Nitrogen is extremely stable due to its strong triple bond. Thus, nitrogen diffuses into the blood, but doesn't react with the chemicals in the blood. However, people that go diving must be careful. As the pressure increases with depth, more nitrogen diffuses into the blood. When divers come back up, the pressure decreases and the gas volume increases. If they don't allow enough time for the nitrogen to diffuse out of the blood and into the lungs, the nitrogen will form bubbles. Among other problems, these bubbles may occlude (block) vessels causing decompression sickness also known as 'the bends.'

*Notes:*

Questions 153 through 160 are **NOT** based on a descriptive passage.

**153.** Alkalosis is increased blood pH resulting in a leftward shift of the oxy hemoglobin dissociation curve. Which of the following might cause alkalosis?

    **A.** hypoventilation
    **B.** hyperventilation
    **C.** breathing into a paper bag
    **D.** adrenal steroid insufficiency

**154.** Which of the following would most likely occur in the presence of a carbonic anhydrase inhibitor?

    **A.** The blood pH would increase.
    **B.** The carbamino hemoglobin concentration inside erythrocytes would decrease.
    **C.** The rate of gas exchange in the lungs would decrease.
    **D.** The oxy hemoglobin concentration inside erythrocytes would increase.

**155.** Which of the following will most likely occur during heavy exercise?

    **A.** Blood pH will decrease in the active tissues.
    **B.** Less oxygen will be delivered to the tissues due to increased cardiac contractions resulting in increased blood velocity.
    **C.** Capillaries surrounding contracting skeletal muscles will constrict to allow increased freedom of movement.
    **D.** The respiratory system will deliver less nitrogen to the blood.

**156.** An athlete can engage in blood doping by having blood drawn several weeks before an event, removing the blood cells, and having them reinjected into her body a few days before an athletic activity. Blood doping is most likely an advantage to athletes because:

    **A.** the increased concentration of immune cells in the blood after reinjection can decrease the chances of becoming ill just before the competition.
    **B.** the increased red blood cell count in the blood after reinjection can facilitate greater gas exchange with the tissues.
    **C.** the increased blood volume after reinjection can ensure that the athlete maintains adequate hydration during the event.
    **D.** the decreased red blood cell count of the blood in the weeks before the competition can facilitate training by decreasing the viscosity of the blood.

**157.** Carbon dioxide partial pressure:

    **A.** increases in the blood as it travels from the systemic venules to the inferior vena cava.
    **B.** increases in the blood as it travels from the pulmonary arteries to the pulmonary veins.
    **C.** is greater in the blood in the systemic capillary beds than in the alveoli of the lungs.
    **D.** is greater in the blood in the systemic capillary beds than in the systemic tissues.

**158.** At high altitude, water vapor pressure in the lungs remains the same and carbon dioxide pressure falls slightly. Oxygen pressure falls. The body of a person remaining at high altitudes for days, weeks, and even years will acclimatize. All of the following changes assist the body in coping with low oxygen EXCEPT:

    **A.** increased red blood cells.
    **B.** decreased vascularity of the tissues.
    **C.** increased pulmonary ventilation.
    **D.** increased diffusing capacity of the lungs.

**159.** In an asthma attack, a patient suffers from difficulty breathing due to constricted air passages. The major causative agent is a mixture of leukotrienes called slow reacting substance of anaphylaxis. During an asthma attack, slow reacting substance of anaphylaxis most likely causes:

    **A.** smooth muscle spasms of the bronchioles.
    **B.** cartilaginous constriction of the trachea.
    **C.** edema in the alveoli.
    **D.** skeletal muscle spasms in the thorax.

**160.** Sustained heavy exercise results in all of the following changes to blood chemistry EXCEPT:

    **A.** lowered pH.
    **B.** raised $CO_2$ tension.
    **C.** increased temperature.
    **D.** decreased carboxyhemoglobin.

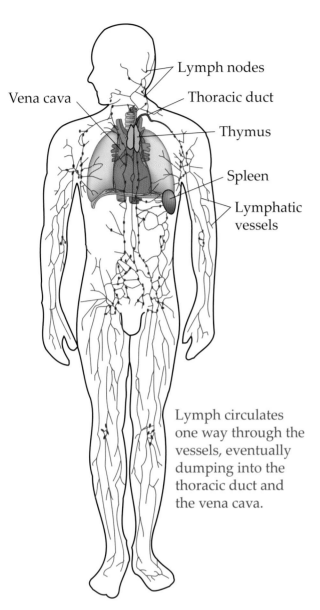

Vena cava

Lymph nodes

Thoracic duct

Thymus

Spleen

Lymphatic vessels

Lymph circulates one way through the vessels, eventually dumping into the thoracic duct and the vena cava.

**Figure 7.12  Lymphatic System**

## 7.4 *The Lymphatic System*

The lymphatic system collects excess interstitial fluid and returns it to the blood. Proteins and large particles that cannot be taken up by the capillaries are removed by the lymph system. The pathway to the blood takes the excess fluid through lymph nodes, which are well prepared to elicit an immune response if necessary. Thus, the lymph system recycles the interstitial fluid and monitors the blood for infection. In addition, the lymph system reroutes low soluble fat digestates around the small capillaries of the intestine and into the large veins of the neck. Most tissues are drained by lymphatic channels. A notable exception is the central nervous system.

The lymph system is an **open system**. In other words, fluid enters at one end and leaves at the other. Lymph capillaries are like tiny fingers protruding into the tissues. To enter the lymph system, interstitial fluid flows between overlapping endothelial cells (Figure 7.13). Large particles literally push their way between the cells into the lymph. The cells overlap in such a fashion that, once inside, large particles cannot push their way out.

Typically, interstitial fluid pressure is slightly negative. (Of course, we mean gauge pressure. See Physics Lecture 5.) As the interstitial pressure rises toward zero, lymph flow increases. Factors that affect interstitial pressure include: blood pressure; plasma osmotic pressure; interstitial osmotic pressure (e.g. from proteins, infection response, etc.); permeability of capillaries. Like veins, lymph vessels are constructed with intermittent valves, which allow fluid to flow in only one direction. Fluid is propelled through these valves in two ways. First, smooth muscle in the walls of larger lymph vessels contracts when stretched. Second, the lymph vessels may be squeezed by adjacent skeletal muscles, body movements, arterial pulsations, and compression from objects outside the body. Lymph flow in an active individual is considerably greater than in an individual at rest.

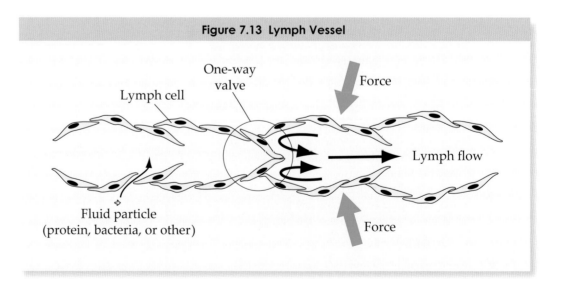

**Figure 7.13  Lymph Vessel**

One-way valve

Force

Lymph cell

Lymph flow

Fluid particle
(protein, bacteria, or other)

Force

The lymph system empties into large veins at the *thoracic duct* and the *right lymphatic* duct. Lymph from the right arm and head enters the blood through the right lymphatic duct. The rest of the body is drained by the thoracic duct.

Throughout the lymphatic system there are many lymph nodes, containing large quantities of lymphocytes.

**Figure 7.14  Flow of Lymphatic Fluid**

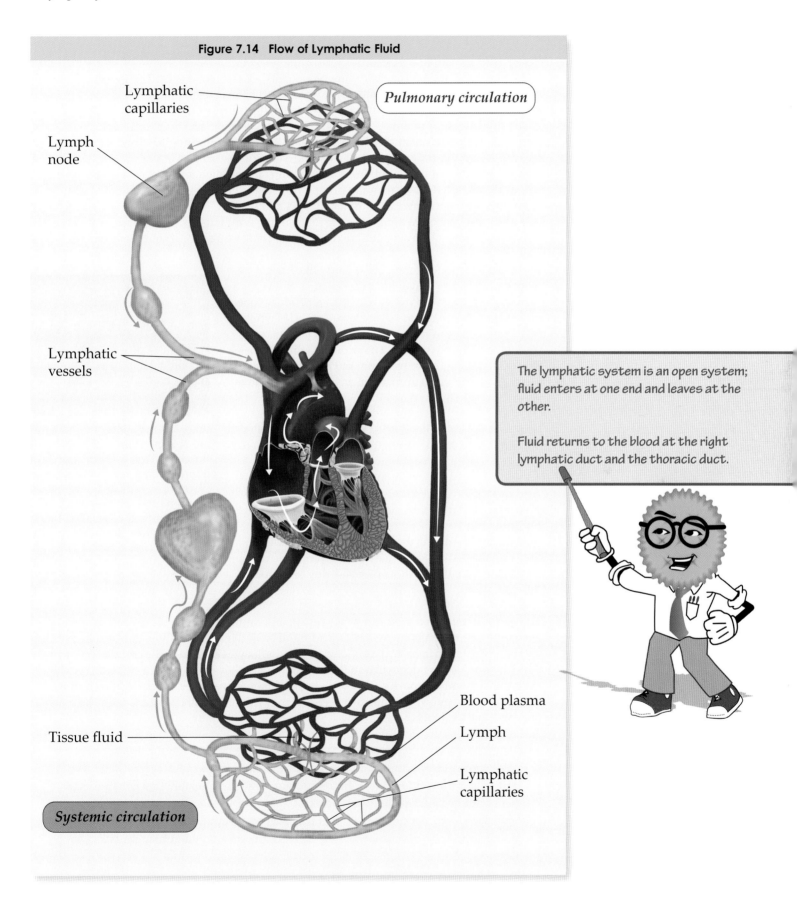

*Pulmonary circulation*

Lymphatic capillaries

Lymph node

Lymphatic vessels

The lymphatic system is an open system; fluid enters at one end and leaves at the other.

Fluid returns to the blood at the right lymphatic duct and the thoracic duct.

Blood plasma

Lymph

Lymphatic capillaries

Tissue fluid

*Systemic circulation*

**Figure 7.15 Blood Composition**

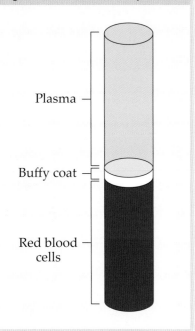

Plasma —

Buffy coat —

Red blood cells —

---

## 7.5 The Blood

The blood is connective tissue. Like any **connective tissue**, it contains cells and a matrix. Blood regulates the extracellular environment of the body by transporting nutrients, waste products, hormones, and even heat. Blood also protects the body from injury and foreign invaders.

When a blood sample is placed in a centrifuge (Figure 7.15), it separates into three parts: 1. the plasma; 2. the buffy coat (white blood cells); 3. red blood cells. The percentage by volume of red blood cells is called the *hematocrit*. Hematocrit is normally 35-50%, and is greater in men than women. Plasma contains the matrix of the blood, which includes water, ions, urea, ammonia, proteins, and other organic and inorganic compounds. Important proteins contained in the plasma are **albumin, immunoglobulins**, and clotting factors. Albumins transport fatty acids and steroids, as well as acting to regulate the osmotic pressure of the blood. Immunoglobulins (also called **antibodies**) are discussed below. Plasma in which the clotting protein **fibrinogen** has been removed is called **serum**. Albumin, fibrinogen, and most other plasma proteins are formed in the liver. Gamma globulins that constitute antibodies are made in the lymph tissue. An important function of plasma proteins is to act as a source of amino acids for tissue protein replacement.

**Erythrocytes** (red blood cells) are like bags of hemoglobin. They have no organelles, not even a nucleus, which means they do not reproduce nor undergo mitosis. They are disk-shaped vesicles whose main function is to transport $O_2$ and $CO_2$. Squeezing through capillaries wears out their plasma membranes in about 120 days. Most worn out red blood cells burst as they squeeze through channels in the spleen or, to a lesser extent, in the liver.

**Leukocytes** (white blood cells) do contain organelles, but do not contain hemoglobin. They function to protect the body from foreign invaders.

All blood cells differentiate from the same type of precursor, a **stem cell** residing in the bone marrow. Erythrocytes lose their nucleus while still in the marrow. After entering the blood stream as *reticulocytes*, they lose the rest of their organelles within 1 or 2 days. Leukocyte formation is more complex due to the many different types.

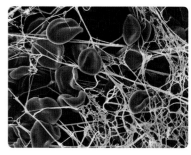

When blood clots, erythrocytes are trapped in a fibrin mesh (brown). The production of fibrin is triggered by cells called platelets, activated when a blood vessel is damaged. The fibrin binds the various blood cells together, forming a solid structure called a blood clot.

The *granular leukocytes* are *neutrophils, eosinophils,* and *basophils*. With respect to dyeing techniques, neutrophils are neutral to acidic and basic dyes, eosinophils stain in acid dyes, and basophils stain in basic dyes. Generally, granulocytes remain in the blood only 4 to 8 hours before they are deposited in the tissues, where they live for 4 to 5 days. *Agranular leukocytes* include monocytes, lymphocytes, and megakaryocytes. Once deposited in the tissues, monocytes become macrophages and may live for months to years. Lymphocytes may also live for years.

> Know that the job of erythrocytes is to deliver oxygen and remove carbon dioxide.

**Figure 7.16 Granulocytes**

Neutrophil

Eosinophil

Basophil

> Notice that granulocytes live a very short time, whereas agranulocytes-other white blood cells-live a very long time. This is because granulocytes function nonspecifically against all infective agents, whereas most agranulocytes work against specific agents of infection. Thus, agranulocytes need to hang around in case the same infective agent returns; granulocytes multiply quickly against any infection, and then die once the infection is gone.

**Platelets** are small portions of membrane-bound cytoplasm torn from megakaryocytes. *Megakaryocytes* remain mainly in the bone marrow. Platelets are similar to tiny cells without a nucleus. They contain actin and myosin, residuals of the Golgi and the ER, mitochondria, and are capable of making protaglandins and some important enzymes. Its membrane is designed to avoid adherence to healthy endothelium while adhering to injured endothelium. When platelets come into conact with injured endothelium, they become sticky and begin to swell releasing various chemicals and activating other platelets. The platelets stick to the endothelium and to each other forming a loose *platelet plug*. Healthy individuals have many platelets in their blood. Platelets The platelet has a half-life of 8-12 days in the blood.

Coagulation occurs in three steps: 1) A dozen or so coagulation factors form a comlex called *protrombin activator*. 2) Protrombin activator catalyzes the conversion of *prothrombin*, a plasma protein, into *thrombin*. 3) Thrombin is an enzyme that governs the polymerization of the plasma protein fibrinogen to fibrin threads that attach to the platelets and form a tight plug. This *blood cot* formation (or coagulation) begins to appear in seconds in small injuries and 1 to 2 minutes in larger injuries.

> Just know that the coagulation process involves many factors starting wth platelets and include the plasma proteins prothrombin and fibrin.

The following is the leukocyte composition in the blood:

- Neutrophils....................................62%
- Lymphocytes.................................30%
- Monocytes.....................................5.3%
- Eosinophils...................................2.3%
- Basophils.......................................0.4%

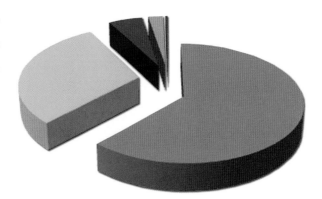

## 7.6 The Immune System

The human body protects itself from infectious microbes and toxins in two ways: *innate immunity* and *acquired immunity*. Innate immunity involves a generalized protection from most intruding organisms and toxins. Acquired immunity is protection against specific organisms or toxins. Acquired immunity develops after the body is first attacked. Innate immunity includes:

1. the skin as a barrier to organisms and toxins;

2. stomach acid and digestive enzymes to destroy ingested organisms and toxins;

3. phagocytotic cells; and

4. chemicals in the blood.

Injury to tissue results in **inflammation**, which includes dilation of blood vessels, increased permeability of capillaries, swelling of tissue cells, and migration of granulocytes and macrophages to the inflamed area (Figure 7.17). *Histamine, prostaglandins,* and *lymphokines* are just some of the causative agents of inflammation that are released by the tissues. Part of the effect of inflammation is to 'wall-off' the affected tissue and local lymph vessels from the rest of the body, impeding the spread of the infection.

Infectious agents that are able to pass through the skin or the digestive defenses and enter the body are first attacked by local *macrophages*. These phagocytotic giants can engulf as many as 100 bacteria. *Neutrophils* are next on the scene. Most neutrophils are stored in the bone marrow until needed, but some are found circulating in the blood or in the tissues. Neutrophils move toward infected or injured areas, drawn by chemicals (a process called *chemotaxis*) released from damaged tissue or by the infectious agents themselves. To enter the tissues, neutrophils slip between endothelial cells of the capillary walls, using an amaeboid-like process called *diapedesis*. A single neutrophil can phagocytize from 5 to 20 bacteria.

**Figure 7.17  The Inflammatory Response**

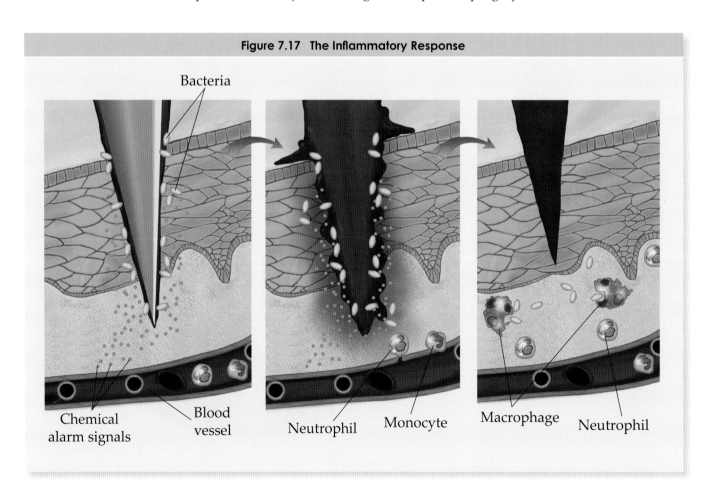

Chemical alarm signals · Blood vessel · Neutrophil · Monocyte · Macrophage · Neutrophil

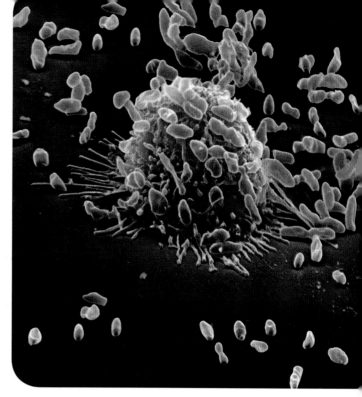

*Monocytes* circulate in the blood until they, too, move into the tissues by diapedesis. Once inside the tissues, monocytes mature to become macrophages.

When the neutrophils and macrophages engulf necrotic tissue and bacteria, they die. These dead leukocytes, along with tissue fluid and necrotic tissue, make up what is known as *pus*.

*Eosinophils* work mainly against parasitic infections. *Basophils* release many of the chemicals of the inflammation reaction.

There are two types of acquired immunity: **humoral** or **B-cell immunity**; **cell-mediated** or **T-cell immunity**. Humoral immunity is promoted by **B lymphocytes**. B lymphocytes differentiate and mature in the bone marrow and the liver. Each B lymphocyte is capable of making a single type of **antibody** or (**immunoglobulin**), which it displays on its membrane. An antibody recognizes a foreign particle, called an **antigen**. The portion of the antibody that binds to an antigen is highly specific for that antigen. The portion of the antigen that binds to the antibody is called an *antigenic determinant*. An antigenic determinant that is removed from an antigen is called a *hapten*. Haptens can only stimulate an immune response if the individual has been previously exposed to the full antigen. Macrophages present the antigenic determinants of engulfed microbes on their surfaces. If the B lymphocyte antibody contacts a matching antigen (presented by a macrophage), the B lymphocyte, assisted by a **helper T cell**, differentiates into **plasma cells** and **memory B cells**. Plasma cells begin synthesizing free antibodies, and releasing them into the blood. Free antibodies may attach their base to *mast cells*. When an antibody whose base is bound to a mast cell also binds to an antigen, the mast cell releases histamine and other chemicals. When other free antibodies contact the specific antigen, they bind to it. Once bound, the antibodies may begin a cascade of reactions involving blood proteins (called *complement*) that cause the antigen bearing cell to be perforated. The antibodies may mark the antigen for phagocytosis by macrophages and *natural killer cells*. The antibodies may cause the antigenic substances to **agglutinate** or even precipitate, or, in the case of a toxin, the antibodies may block its chemically active portion. The first time the immune system is exposed to an antigen is known as the **primary response**. The primary immune response requires 20 days to reach its full potential.

Memory B cells proliferate, and remain in the body. In the case of re-infection, each of these cells can be called upon to synthesize antibodies, resulting in a faster acting and more potent effect called the **secondary response**. The secondary response requires approximately 5 days to reach its full potential.

Humoral immunity is effective against bacteria, fungi, parasitic protozoans, viruses, and blood toxins.

Macrophages ingest bacteria as part of the immune response to infection.

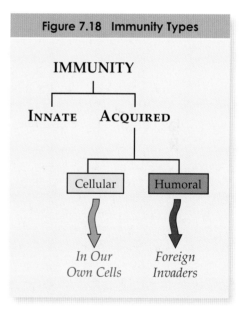

Figure 7.18 Immunity Types

IMMUNITY

INNATE    ACQUIRED

Cellular    Humoral

*In Our Own Cells*    *Foreign Invaders*

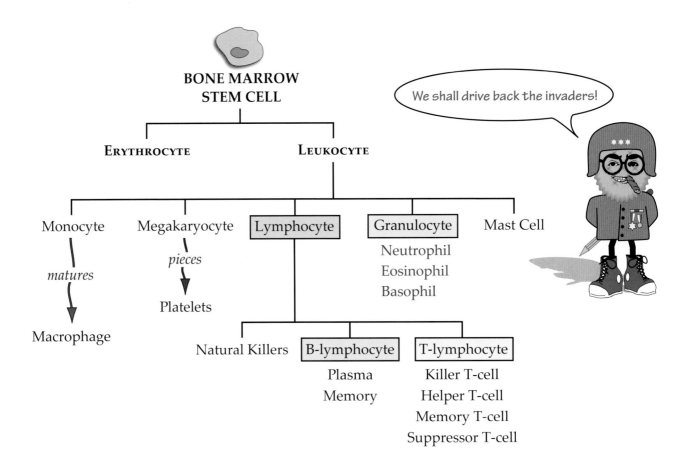

**BONE MARROW STEM CELL**

**ERYTHROCYTE**          **LEUKOCYTE**

Monocyte     Megakaryocyte     Lymphocyte     Granulocyte     Mast Cell

*matures*     *pieces*                          Neutrophil
                                                Eosinophil
Macrophage     Platelets                        Basophil

Natural Killers     B-lymphocyte     T-lymphocyte

Plasma     Killer T-cell
Memory     Helper T-cell
           Memory T-cell
           Suppressor T-cell

*We shall drive back the invaders!*

Cell-mediated immunity involves **T-lymphocytes**. T-lymphocytes mature in the thymus. Similar to B lymphocytes, T lymphocytes have an antibody-like protein at their surface that recognizes antigens. However, T-lymphocytes never make free antibodies. In the thymus, T-lymphocytes are tested against *self-antigens* (antigens expressed by normal cells of the body). If the T-lymphocyte binds to a self-antigen, that T lymphocyte is destroyed. If it does not, it is released to lodge in lymphoid tissue or circulate between the blood and the lymph fluid. T lymphocytes that are not destroyed differentiate into **helper T cells**, **memory T cells**, **suppressor T cells**, and **killer T cells** (also called *cytotoxic* T cells). As discussed above, T helper cells assist in activating B lymphocytes as well as killer and suppressor T cells. Helper T cells are the cells attacked by HIV. Memory T cells have a similar function to Memory B cells. Suppressor T cells play a negative feedback role in the immune system. Killer T cells bind to the antigen-carrying cell and release *perforin*, a protein which punctures the antigen-carrying cell. Killer T cells can attack many cells because they do not phagocytize their victims. Killer T cells are responsible for fighting some forms of cancer, and for attacking transplanted tissue.

Cell-mediated immunity is effective against infected cells.

Let's imagine a bacterial infection. First we have inflammation. Macrophages, then neutrophils, engulf the bacteria. Interstitial fluid is flushed into the lymphatic system where lymphocytes wait in the lymph nodes. Macrophages process and present the bacterial antigens to B lymphocytes. With the help of Helper T cells, B lymphocytes differentiate into memory cells and plasma cells. The memory cells are preparation in the event that the same bacteria ever attack again (the secondary response). The plasma cells produce antibodies, which are released into the blood to attack the bacteria.

You must know that a single antibody is specific for a single antigen, and that a single B lymphocyte produces only one antibody type.

**Figure 7.19  Summary Diagram of Adaptive Immunity**

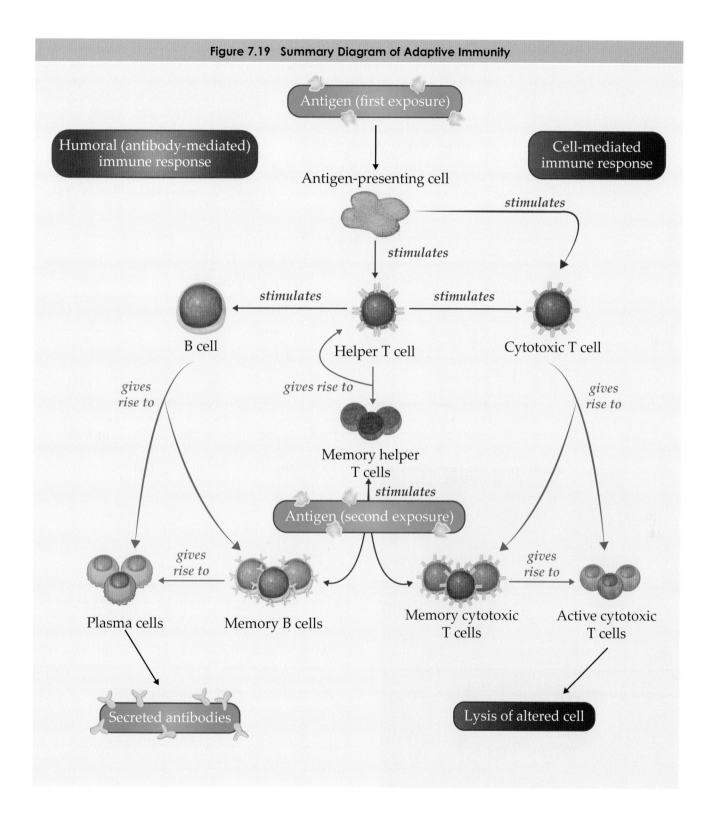

## 7.7 Blood Types

Blood types are identified by the A and B surface antigens. For instance, type A blood means that the red blood cell membrane has A antigens and does not have B antigens. Of course, if the erythrocytes have A antigens, the immune system does not make A antibodies. Type O blood has neither A nor B antigens, and makes both A and B antibodies. Thus, a blood donor may donate blood only to an individual that does not make antibodies against the donor blood. Table 7.1 shows a '+' sign when blood agglutinates (is rejected), and a '−' sign when no agglutination occurs. Notice that an individual with type O blood may donate to anyone (all minuses in the donor column), and an individual with type AB blood may receive from anyone (all minuses in the recipient column).

The genes which produce the A and B antigens are co-dominant. Thus, an individual having type A or B blood may be heterozygous or homozygous. An individual with type O blood has two recessive alleles.

**Table 7.1   Blood Types**

|  |  | Donor | | | |
|---|---|---|---|---|---|
|  |  | **A** | **B** | **AB** | **O** |
| **Recipient** | A | − | + | + | − |
|  | B | + | − | + | − |
|  | AB | − | − | − | − |
|  | O | + | + | + | − |

| Blood type | Genotype |
|---|---|
| A | $I^A I^A$ or $I^A i$ |
| B | $I^B I^B$ or $I^B i$ |
| AB | $I^A I^B$ |
| O | $i\, i$ |

*Rh factors* are surface proteins on red blood cells first identified in Rhesus monkeys. Individuals having genotypes that code for nonfunctional products of the Rh gene are said to be Rh-negative. All others are Rh-positive. Transfusion reactions involving the Rh factor, if they occur at all, are usually mild. Rh factor is more of a concern during the pregnancy of an Rh-negative mother with an Rh-positive fetus. For the first pregnancy, the mother is not exposed to fetal blood until giving birth and problems are rare. Upon exposure, the mother develops an immune response against the Rh-positive blood. In a second pregnancy, the second fetus that is Rh-positive may be attacked by the antibodies of the mother, which are small enough to pass the placental barrier. The problem is life threatening, and treatment usually involves complete replacement of the fetal blood with Rh-negative blood for the first few weeks of life.

## Terms

| | |
|---|---|
| Agglutination | Larynx |
| Albumin | Left Atrium |
| Alveoli | Left Ventricle |
| Antibodies | Leukocytes |
| Antibody | Memory B Cells |
| Antigen | Memory T Cells |
| Aorta | Nasal Cavity |
| Arteries | Oxyhemoglobin |
| Arterioles | Pharynx |
| Atrioventricular Node (AV Node) | Plasma cells |
| B lymphocytes | Platelets |
| Bronchi | Primary Immune Response |
| Bronchioles | Pulmonary Circulation |
| Bundle of His | Purkinje Fibers |
| Capillaries | Right Atrium |
| Carbonic Anhydrase | Right Ventricle |
| Cell-mediated Immunity | Secondary Immune Response |
| Circulatory System | Serum |
| Diaphragm | Sinoatrial Node (SA Node) |
| Epiglottis | Stem Cell |
| Erythrocytes | Superior Vena Cava |
| Fibrinogen | Suppressor T Cells |
| Helper T Cell | Systemic Circulation |
| Hemoglobin | T Lymphocytes |
| Humoral Immunity | Trachea |
| Immunoglobulins | Vagus Nerve |
| Inferior Vena Cava | Veins |
| Inflammation | Ventricle |
| Killer T Cells | Venules |

161. Anemia (decreased red blood cell count) can be caused by over activity of which of the following organs?

   A. Thymus
   B. Thyroid
   C. Spleen
   D. Lymph nodes

162. "Swollen glands" are often observed in the neck of a person with a cold. The most likely explanation for this is that:

   A. blood pools in the neck in an attempt to keep it warm.
   B. lymph nodes swell as white blood cells proliferate within them to fight the infection.
   C. the infection sets off an inflammatory response in the neck, causing fluid to be drained from the area.
   D. fever causes a general expansion of the tissues of the head and neck.

163. Humoral immunity involves the action of:

   A. cytotoxic T lymphocytes.
   B. stomach acid.
   C. pancreatic enzymes.
   D. immunoglobulins.

164. Antibodies function by:

   A. phagocytizing invading antigens.
   B. adhering to circulating plasma cells and marking them for destruction by phagocytizing cells.
   C. preventing the production of stem cells in the bone marrow.
   D. attaching to antigens via their variable portions.

165. Lymphatic vessels absorb fluid from the interstitial spaces and carry it to the:

   A. kidneys, where it is excreted.
   B. large intestine, where it is absorbed and returned to the bloodstream.
   C. lungs, where the fluid is vaporized and exhaled.
   D. lymphatic ducts, which return it to the circulation.

166. Which of the following is true concerning type B negative blood?

   A. Type B negative blood will make antibodies that attack type A antigens but not type B antigens.
   B. Type B negative blood will make antibodies that attack type B antigens but not type A antigens.
   C. Type B negative blood will make antibodies that attack type O antigens only.
   D. Type B negative blood will make antibodies that attack both type A and type O antigens.

167. Which of the following would you not expect to find in a lymph node?

   A. B lymphocytes
   B. proteins discarded by tissue cells
   C. invading bacteria
   D. old erythrocytes

168. An individual exposed to a pathogen for the first time will exhibit an innate immune response involving:

   A. B lymphocytes.
   B. T lymphocytes.
   C. granulocytes.
   D. An individual exposed to a pathogen for the first time must acquire immunity before it can respond.

# MUSCLE, BONE AND SKIN

## 8.1 Muscle

There are three types of muscle tissue:

1. skeletal muscle;

2. cardiac muscle;

3. smooth muscle.

Any muscle tissue generates a force only by contracting its cells. The mechanisms by which muscle cells contract differ between the three types of tissue, and are described below. Muscle contraction has four possible functions:

1. body movement;

2. stabilization of body position;

3. movement of substances through the body;

4. generating heat to maintain body temperature.

> Know the three types of muscle and their four possible functions.

## 8.2 Skeletal Muscle

**Skeletal muscle is voluntary muscle tissue.** It can be consciously controlled.

Skeletal muscle connects one bone to another. The muscle does not attach directly to the bone, but instead is attached via a **tendon**. (A tendon connects muscle to bone; a **ligament** connects bone to bone.) Typically, a muscle stretches across a joint. The muscle *origin* is on the larger bone, which remains relatively stationary, and its *insertion* is on the smaller bone, which moves relative to the larger bone upon contraction of the muscle. Muscles work in groups. The **agonist** (the muscle responsible for the movement) contracts, while a second muscle, the **antagonist**, stretches. When the antagonist contracts, the bone moves

> A muscle uses leverage by applying a force to a bone at its insertion point and rotating the bone in some fashion about the joint. This is a likely MCAT topic because it applies the physics concept of leverage to a biological system. It may seem strange, but most lever systems of the body typically act to increase the required force of a muscle contraction. In other words, a greater force than mg is required to lift a mass m. This is done in order to reduce the bulk of the body and increase the range of movement. If the muscle has a shorter lever arm, it is closer to the body, and thus creates less bulk.

in the opposite direction, stretching the agonist. An example of antagonistic muscles is the upper arm muscles, the biceps and the triceps. In addition to antagonistic muscles, there are usually **synergistic** muscles. Synergistic muscles assist the agonist by stabilizing the origin bone or by positioning the insertion bone during the movement. In this way, skeletal muscle allows for movement and posture.

Contraction of skeletal muscle may squeeze blood and lymph vessels aiding circulation.

Contraction of skeletal muscle produces large amounts of heat. Shivering, controlled by the hypothalamus upon stimulation by receptors in the skin and spinal cord, is the rapid contraction of skeletal muscle to warm the body.

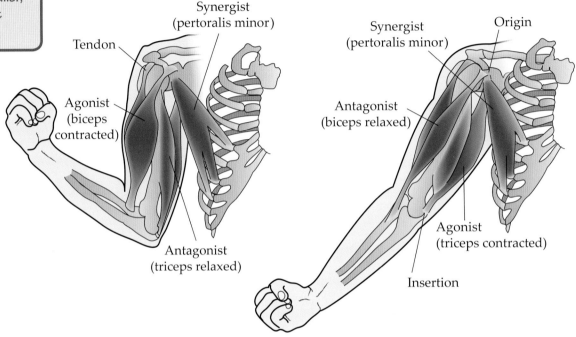

**Figure 8.1  Agonist, Antagonist, and Synergist Muscles**

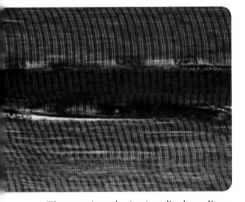

The striated (striped) banding-pattern of skeletal muscle fibers can be seen in this photo. The cross-striations are the arrangement of proteins (actin and myosin) which cause the fibers to contract. Along the junction of the fibers (blue) can be seen multiple nuclei (fuzzy pink); each cylindrical fiber is a single muscle cell.

## 8.3 *Physiology of Skeletal Muscle Contraction*

The smallest functional unit of skeletal muscle is the **sarcomere** (Figure 8.2). A sarcomere is composed of many strands of two protein filaments, the **thick and the thin filament**, laid side by side to form a cylindrical segment. Sarcomeres are positioned end to end to form a *myofibril*. Each myofibril is surrounded by the specialized endoplasmic reticulum of the muscle cell called the sarcoplasmic reticulum. The lumen of the sarcoplasmic reticulum is filled with $Ca^{2+}$ ions for reasons that shall become clear shortly. Lodged between the myofibrils are mitochondria and many nuclei. Skeletal muscle is **multinucleate**. A modified membrane called the **sarcolemma** wraps several myofibrils together to form a muscle cell or muscle fiber. Many muscle fibers are further bound into a fasciculus, and many fasciculae make up a single muscle.

The **thick filament** of a sarcomere is made of the protein **myosin**. Several long myosin molecules wrap around each other to form one thick filament. Globular heads protrude along both ends of the thick filament. **The thin filament** is composed mainly of a polymer of the globular protein **actin**. Attached to the actin are the proteins *troponin* and *tropomyosin*.

**Figure 8.2 Structure of Skeletal Muscle**

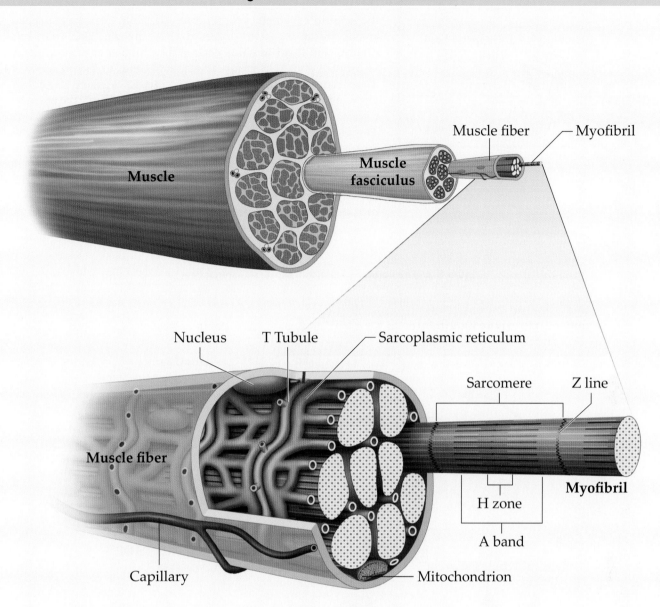

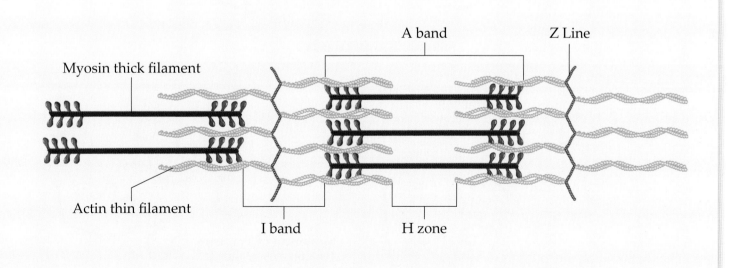

Recognize the importance of calcium in muscle contraction, and be familiar with the functions of the sarcoplasmic reticulum and the T-tubules.

Myosin and actin work together sliding alongside each other to create the contractile force of skeletal muscle. Each myosin head crawls along the actin in a **5 stage cycle** (Figure 8.3). First, tropomyosin covers an active site on the actin preventing the myosin head from binding. The myosin head remains cocked in a high-energy position with a phosphate and ADP group attached. Second, in the presence of $Ca^{2+}$ ions, troponin pulls the tropomyosin back, exposing the active site, allowing the myosin head to bind to the actin. Third, the myosin head expels a phosphate and ADP and bends into a low energy position, dragging the actin along with it. This is called the power stroke because it causes the shortening of the sarcomere and the muscle contraction. In the fourth stage, ATP attaches to the myosin head. This releases the myosin head from the active site, which is covered immediately by tropomyosin. Fifth, ATP splits to inorganic phosphate and ADP causing the myosin head to cock into the high-energy position. This cycle is repeated many times to form a contraction.

## Figure 8.3 Physiology of Skeletal Muscle Contraction

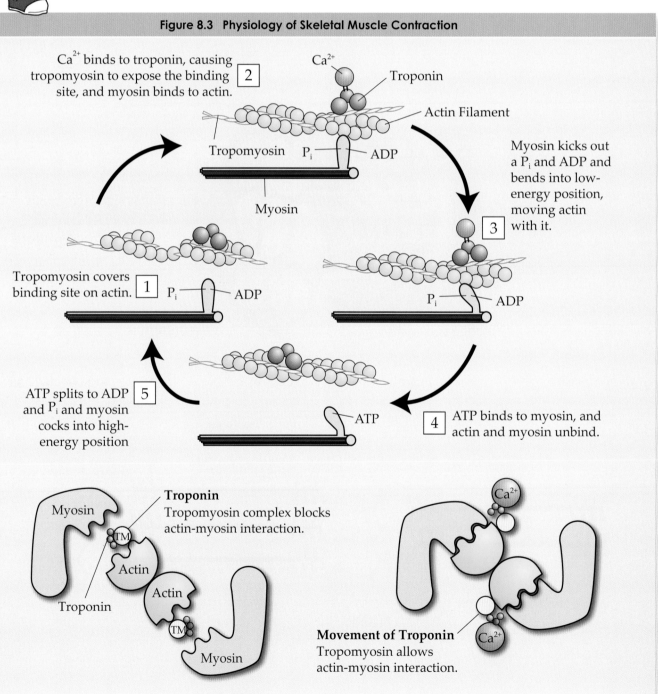

Ca²⁺ binds to troponin, causing tropomyosin to expose the binding site, and myosin binds to actin. [2]

Ca²⁺
Troponin
Actin Filament
Tropomyosin  $P_i$  ADP
Myosin

Myosin kicks out a $P_i$ and ADP and bends into low-energy position, moving actin with it. [3]

$P_i$  ADP

Tropomyosin covers binding site on actin. [1]  $P_i$  ADP

ATP splits to ADP and $P_i$ and myosin cocks into high-energy position [5]

ATP

[4] ATP binds to myosin, and actin and myosin unbind.

**Troponin**
Tropomyosin complex blocks actin-myosin interaction.

Myosin
TM
Actin
Troponin
Actin
TM
Myosin

Ca²⁺
Ca²⁺

**Movement of Troponin**
Tropomyosin allows actin-myosin interaction.

A muscle contraction begins with an action potential. A neuron attaches to a muscle cell forming a **neuromuscular synapse**. The action potential of the neuron releases **acetylcholine** into the synaptic cleft. The acetylcholine activates ion channels in the sarcolemma of the muscle cell creating an action potential. The action potential moves deep into the muscle cell via small tunnels in the membrane called **T-tubules**. T-tubules allow for a uniform contraction of the muscle by allowing the action potential to spread through the muscle cell more rapidly. The action potential is transferred to the sarcoplasmic reticulum, which suddenly becomes permeable to $Ca^{2+}$ ions. The $Ca^{2+}$ ions begin the 5 stage cycle described above. At the end of each cycle, $Ca^{2+}$ is actively pumped back into the sarcoplasmic reticulum.

## 8.4 A Motor Unit

The muscle fibers of a single muscle do not all contract at once. Instead, from 2 to 2000 fibers spread throughout the muscle are innervated by a single neuron. The neuron and the muscle fibers that it innervates are called a *motor unit*. Motor units are independent of each other. The force of a contracting muscle depends upon the number and size of the active motor units, and the frequency of action potentials in each neuron of the motor unit. Typically, smaller motor units are the first to be activated, and larger motor units are recruited as needed. This results in a smooth increase in the force generated by the muscle. Another important point concerning motor units is that muscles requiring intricate movements, like those in the finger, have smaller motor units, whereas muscles requiring greater force, such as those in the back, have larger motor units.

> A motor unit consists of a nerve and all the muscle fibers it synapses with.

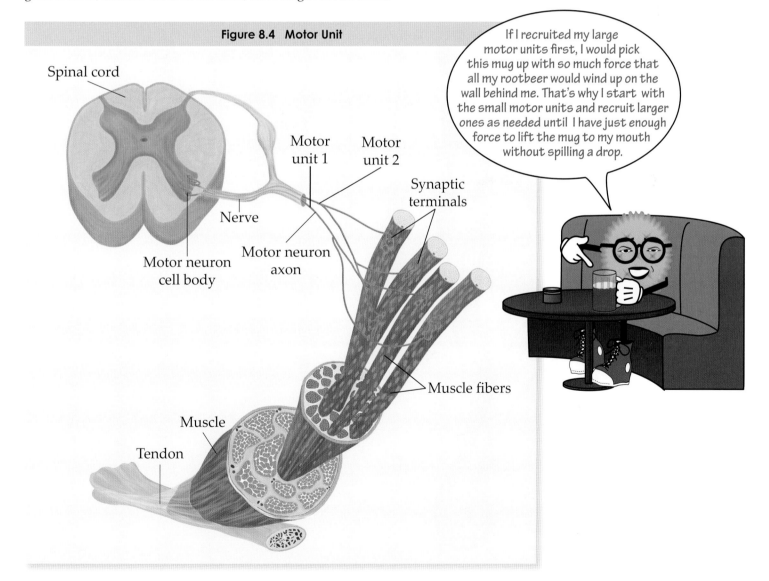

**Figure 8.4   Motor Unit**

> If I recruited my large motor units first, I would pick this mug up with so much force that all my rootbeer would wind up on the wall behind me. That's why I start with the small motor units and recruit larger ones as needed until I have just enough force to lift the mug to my mouth without spilling a drop.

Spinal cord

Motor unit 1

Motor unit 2

Synaptic terminals

Nerve

Motor neuron cell body

Motor neuron axon

Muscle fibers

Muscle

Tendon

# Skeletal Muscle Type

There are three types of skeletal muscle fibers: 1) *slow oxidative (type I) fibers*; 2) *fast oxidative (type II A) fibers*; and *fast glycolytic (type II B) fibers*. Type I or slow-twitch muscle fibers are red from large amounts of **myoglobin**. Myoglobin is an oxygen storing protein similar to hemoglobin, but which has only one protein subunit. Type I fibers also contain large amounts of mitochondria. They split ATP at a slow rate. As a result, they are slow to fatigue, but also have a slow contraction velocity. Type II A or fast-twitch A fibers are also red, but they split ATP at a high rate. Type II A fibers contract rapidly. Type II A fibers are resistant to fatigue, but not as resistant as type I fibers. Type II B or fast-twitch B fibers have a low myoglobin content, appear white under the light microscope, and contract very rapidly. They contain large amounts of glycogen.

Most muscles in the body have a mixture of fiber types. The ratio of the mixture depends upon the contraction requirements of the muscle and upon the genetics of the individual. Large amounts of type I fibers are found in the postural muscles. Large amounts of type II A fibers are found in the upper legs. Large amounts of type II B fibers are found in the upper arms.

Adult human skeletal muscle does not generally undergo mitosis to create new muscle cells (*hyperplasia*). Instead, a number of changes occur over time when the muscles are exposed to forceful, repetitive contractions. These changes include: the diameter of the muscle fibers increases, the number of sarcomeres and mitochondria increases, and sarcomeres lengthen. This increase in muscle cell diameter and change in muscle conformation is called *hypertrophy*.

Myoglobin stores oxygen inside muscle cells. A molecule of myoglobin looks like one subunit of hemoglobin. It is capable of storing only one molecule of oxygen.

Like many cell types, human muscle cells are so specialized that they have lost the ability to undergo mitosis. Only in rare cases does one muscle cell split to form two cells.

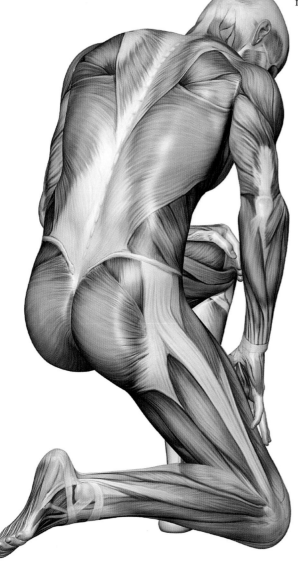

*Notes:*

169. During a muscular contraction:

A. both the thin and thick filaments contract.
B. the thin filament contracts, but the thick filament does not.
C. the thick filament contracts, but the thin filament does not.
D. neither the thin nor the thick filament contract.

170. Irreversible sequestering of calcium in the sarcoplasmic reticulum would most likely:

A. result in permanent contraction of the muscle fibers, similar to what is seen in rigor mortis.
B. create a sharp increase in bone density as calcium is resorbed from bones to replace the sequestered calcium.
C. prevent myosin from binding to actin.
D. depolymerize actin filaments in the sarcomere.

171. Shivering increases body temperature by:

A. serving as a warning that body temperature is too low, prompting the person to seek warmer locations.
B. causing bones to rub together, creating heat through friction.
C. increasing the activity of muscles.
D. convincing the hypothalamus that body temperature is higher than it actually is.

172. Muscles cause movement at joints by:

A. inciting neurons to initiate an electrical "twitch" in tendons.
B. increasing in length, thereby pushing the muscle's origin and insertion farther apart.
C. filling with blood, thereby expanding and increasing the distance between the ends of a muscle.
D. decreasing in length, thereby bringing the muscle's origin and insertion closer together.

173. When one of a pair of antagonistic muscles contracts, what usually happens to the other muscle to produce movement?

A. It acts synergistically by contracting to stabilize the moving bone.
B. It relaxes to allow movement.
C. It contracts in an isometric action.
D. Its insertion slides down the bone to allow a larger range of movement.

174. When undergoing physical exercise, healthy adult skeletal muscle is likely to respond with an increase in all of the following except:

A. glycolysis.
B. the Citric Acid Cycle.
C. mitosis.
D. protein production.

175. The biceps muscle is connected to the radius bone by:

A. biceps tendon.
B. annular ligament of the radius.
C. articular cartilage.
D. the triceps muscle.

176. Skeletal muscle contraction may assist in all of the following EXCEPT:

A. movement of fluid through the body.
B. body temperature regulation.
C. posture.
D. peristalsis.

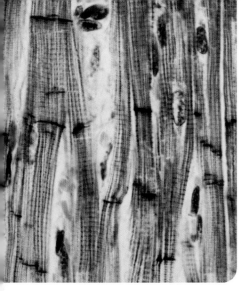

As seen through a light microscope cardiac muscle cells form a net-like structure. The junctions between individual cells are the intercalated discs (dark lines).

## 8.6  Cardiac Muscle

The human heart is composed mainly of **cardiac muscle** (Figure 8.5). Like skeletal muscle, cardiac muscle is **striated**, which means that it is composed of **sarcomeres**. However, each cardiac muscle cell contains only *one nucleus*, and is separated from its neighbor by an **intercalated disc**. The intercalated discs contain gap junctions which allow an action potential to spread from one cardiac cell to the next via electrical synapses. The mitochondria of cardiac muscle are larger and more numerous. Skeletal muscle connects bone to bone via tendons; cardiac muscle, on the other hand, is not connected to bone. Instead, cardiac muscle forms a net which contracts in upon itself like a squeezing fist. Cardiac muscle is *involuntary*. Like skeletal muscle, cardiac muscle grows by hypertrophy.

The action potential of cardiac muscle exhibits a plateau after depolarization. The plateau is created by slow voltage-gated calcium channels which allow calcium to enter and hold the inside of the membrane at a positive potential difference. The plateau lengthens the time of contraction.

Be sure to remember the importance of calcium in the cardiac action potential. Without it, the heart would beat far too quickly to serve as a functional pump, and we would die.

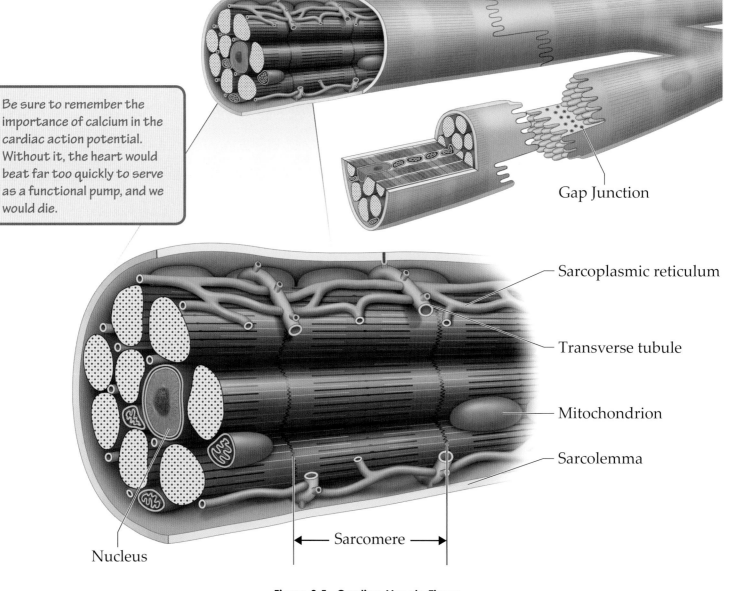

Gap Junction

Sarcoplasmic reticulum

Transverse tubule

Mitochondrion

Sarcolemma

Sarcomere

Nucleus

**Figure 8.5  Cardiac Muscle Tissue**

## 8.7 Smooth Muscle

Smooth muscle is mainly *involuntary*, so it is innervated by the **autonomic nervous system** (Figure 8.6). Like cardiac muscle, smooth muscle cells contain only one nucleus. Smooth muscles also contain thick and thin filaments, but they are not organized into sarcomeres. In addition, smooth muscle cells contain **intermediate filaments**, which are attached to **dense bodies** spread throughout the cell. The thick and thin filaments are attached to the intermediate filaments, and, when they contract, they cause the intermediate filaments to pull the dense bodies together. Upon contraction, the smooth muscle cell shrinks length-wise.

There are two types of smooth muscle: 1. *single-unit* and 2. *multiunit*. Single unit smooth muscle, also called *visceral*, is the most common. Single-unit smooth muscle cells are connected by gap junctions spreading the action potential from a single neuron through a large group of cells, and allowing the cells to contract as a single unit. Single-unit smooth muscle is found in small arteries and veins, the stomach, intestines, uterus, and urinary bladder.

Each multiunit smooth muscle fiber is attached directly to a neuron. A group of multiunit smooth muscle fibers can contract independently of other muscle fibers in the same location. Multiunit smooth muscle is found in the large arteries, bronchioles, pili muscles attached to hair follicles, and the iris.

In addition to responding to neural stimulus, smooth muscle also contracts or relaxes in the presence of hormones, or to changes in pH, $O_2$ and $CO_2$ levels, temperature, and ion concentrations.

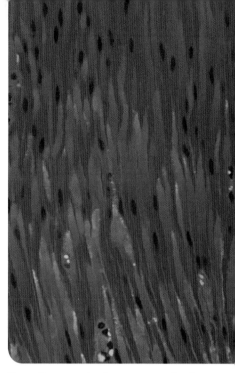

Smooth muscle is composed of spindle-shaped cells grouped in irregular bundles. Each cell contains one nucleus, seen here as a dark stained spot.

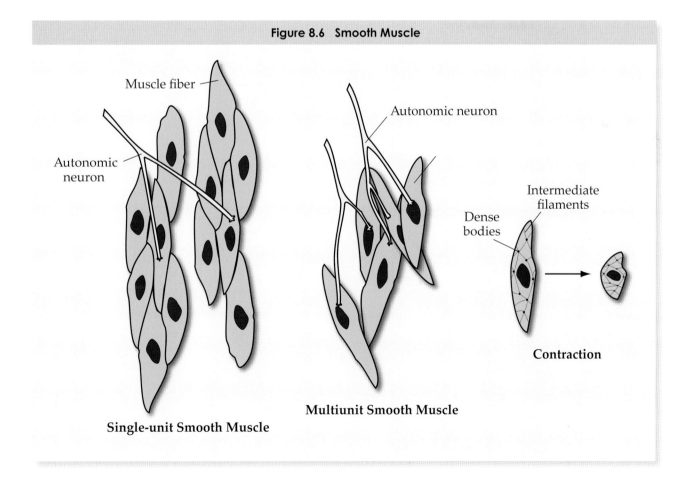

### Figure 8.6  Smooth Muscle

Muscle fiber

Autonomic neuron

Autonomic neuron

Dense bodies

Intermediate filaments

**Contraction**

**Single-unit Smooth Muscle**

**Multiunit Smooth Muscle**

177. The function of gap junctions in the intercalated discs of cardiac muscle is to:

    A. anchor the muscle fibers together.
    B. insure that an action potential is spread to all fibers in the muscle network.
    C. control blood flow by selectively opening and closing capillaries.
    D. release calcium into the sarcoplasmic reticulum.

178. Which of the following muscular actions is controlled by the autonomic nervous system?

    A. the knee-jerk reflex
    B. conduction of cardiac muscle action potential from cell to cell
    C. peristalsis of the gastrointestinal tract
    D. contraction of the diaphragm

179. During an action potential, a cardiac muscle cell remains depolarized much longer than a neuron. This is most likely to:

    A. prevent the initiation of another action potential during contraction of the heart.
    B. ensure that adjacent cardiac muscle cells will contract at different times.
    C. keep the neuron from firing twice in rapid succession.
    D. allow sodium voltage-gated channels to remain open long enough for all sodium to exit the cell.

180. All of the following are true concerning smooth muscle EXCEPT:

    A. Smooth muscle contractions are longer and slower than skeletal muscle contractions.
    B. A chemical change in the environment around smooth muscle may create a contraction.
    C. Smooth muscle does not require calcium to contract.
    D. Smooth muscle is usually involuntary.

181. Which of the following muscles is under voluntary control?

    A. the diaphragm
    B. the heart
    C. the smooth muscle of the large intestines
    D. the iris

182. Cardiac muscle is excited by:

    A. parasympathetic nervous excitation.
    B. constriction of T-tubules.
    C. increased cytosolic sodium concentration .
    D. increased cytosolic calcium concentration.

183. When left alone, certain specialized cardiac muscle cells have the capacity for self-excitation. The SA node is a collection of such cells. The SA node is innervated by the vagus nerve. The frequency of self excitation of the cardiac cells of the SA Node is likely to be:

    A. slower than a normal hearbeat because excitation by the vagus nerve decreases the heart rate.
    B. slower than a normal hearbeat because excitation by the vagus nerve increases the heart rate.
    C. faster than a normal hearbeat because excitation by the vagus nerve decreases the heart rate.
    D. faster than a normal hearbeat because excitation by the vagus nerve increases the heart rate.

184. In extreme cold, just before the onset of frostbite, sudden vasodilation occurs manifested by flushed skin. This vasodilation is most likely the result of:

    A. paralysis of smooth muscle in the vascular walls.
    B. paralysis of skeletal muscle surrounding the vascular walls.
    C. sudden tachycardia with a resultant increase in blood pressure.
    D. blood shunting due to smooth muscle sphincters.

## 8.8 Bone

**Bone** is living tissue. Its functions are *support* of soft tissue, *protection* of internal organs, assistance in *movement* of the body, **mineral storage, blood cell production,** and **energy storage** in the form of adipose cells in bone marrow.

Bone tissue contains four types of cells surrounded by an extensive matrix.

1. *Osteoprogenitor (or osteogenic) cells* differentiate into osteoblasts.

2. **Osteoblasts** secrete collagen and organic compounds upon which bone is formed. Osteoblasts are incapable of mitosis. As osteoblasts release matrix materials around themselves, they become enveloped by the matrix and differentiate into osteocytes.

3. **Osteocytes** are also incapable of mitosis. Osteocytes exchange nutrients and waste materials with the blood.

4. **Osteoclasts** resorb bone matrix, releasing minerals back into the blood. Osteoclasts are believed to develop from the white blood cells called monocytes.

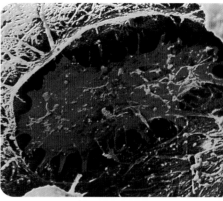

A bone-making osteoblast cell is shown here surrounded by a dense network of collagen fibers.

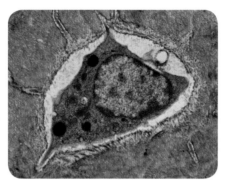

An osteocyte is an osteoblast that has become trapped within a bone cavity (lacuna). Osteocytes are responsible for bone formation, but eventually become embedded in the bone matrix.

> Know the functions of osteoblasts, osteocytes, and osteoclasts.

A typical long bone (Figure 8.9) has a long shaft, called the *diaphysis,* and two ends, each end composed of a *metaphysis* and *epiphysis.* A sheet of cartilage in the metaphysis, called the *epiphyseal plate,* is where long bones grow in length. **Spongy bone** contains **red bone marrow,** the site of *hemopoiesis* or red blood cell development. **Compact bone** surrounds the *medullary cavity,* which holds **yellow bone marrow.** Yellow bone marrow contains adipose cells for fat storage. Compact bone is highly organized. In a continuous remodeling process, osteoclasts burrow tunnels, called **Haversian (central) canals,** through compact bone. The osteoclasts are followed by osteoblasts, which lay down a new matrix onto the tunnel walls forming concentric rings called **lamellae.** Osteocytes trapped between the lamellae exchange nutrients via **canaliculi.** Haversian canals contain blood and lymph vessels, and are connected by crossing canals called **Volkmann's canals.** The entire system of lamellae and Haversian canal is called an **osteon (Haversian system).**

## 8.9 Bone Function in Mineral Homeostasis

Calcium salts are only slightly soluble, so most calcium in the blood is not in the form of free calcium ions, but is bound mainly by proteins and, to a much lesser extent, by phosphates ($HPO_4^{2-}$) and other anions. It is the concentration of free calcium ions ($Ca^{2+}$) in the blood that is important physiologically. Too much $Ca^{2+}$ results in membranes becoming hypo-excitable producing lethargy, fatigue, and memory loss; too little produces cramps and convulsions.

Most of the $Ca^{2+}$ in the body is stored in the bone matrix as **hydroxyapatite** [$Ca_{10}(PO_4)_6(OH)_2$]. Collagen fibers lie along the lines of tensile force of the bone, giving the bone great tensile strength. Hydroxyapatite crystals lie alongside collagen fibers, and give bone greater compressive strength than the best reinforced concrete. Some of the body's $Ca^{2+}$ exists in bone in the form of slightly soluble calcium salts such as $CaHPO_4$. It is these salts that buffer the plasma $Ca^{2+}$ levels. Thus bone acts as a storage site for $Ca^{2+}$ and $HPO_4^{2-}$.

This computer-generated image shows multi-nucleated osteoclasts etching away 0trabecular bone in a process called bone resorption.

Figure 8.7  The Human Skeleton

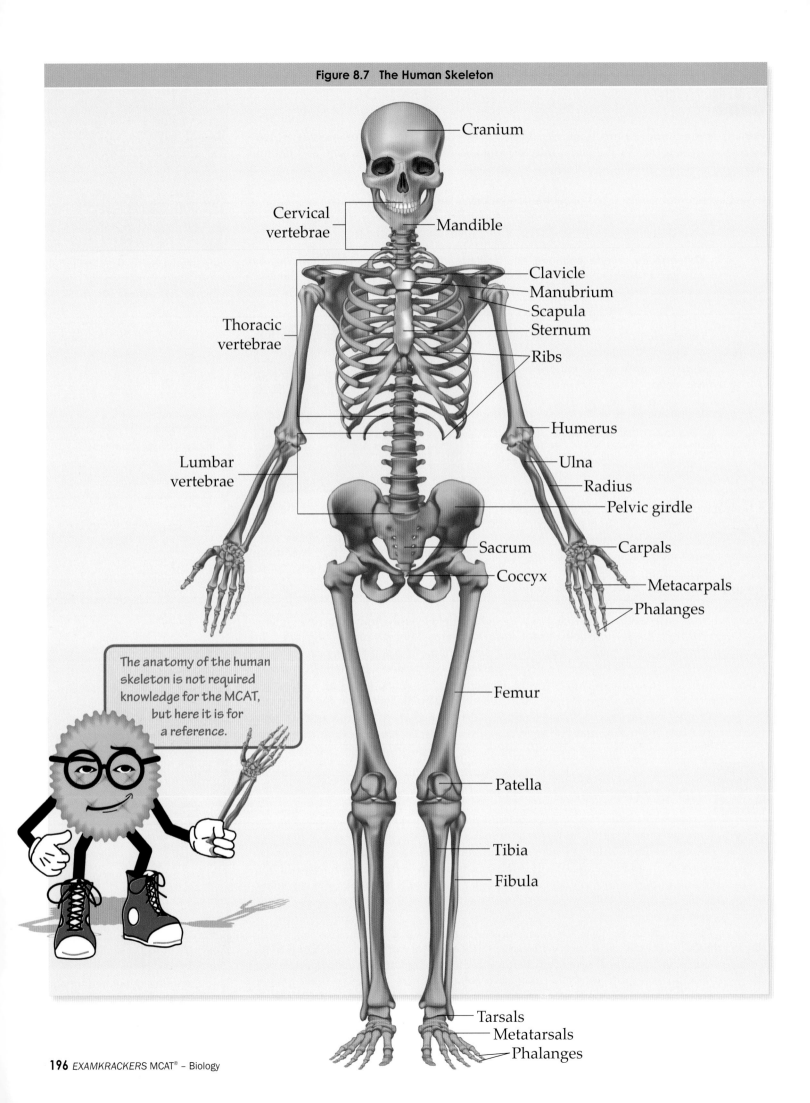

Cranium

Cervical vertebrae

Mandible

Thoracic vertebrae

Clavicle
Manubrium
Scapula
Sternum
Ribs

Humerus

Lumbar vertebrae

Ulna
Radius
Pelvic girdle

Sacrum

Coccyx

Carpals

Metacarpals

Phalanges

The anatomy of the human skeleton is not required knowledge for the MCAT, but here it is for a reference.

Femur

Patella

Tibia

Fibula

Tarsals
Metatarsals
Phalanges

## 8.10 Bone Types and Structures

Most bones fall into one of four types: 1. long, 2. short, 3. flat, or 4. irregular. Long bones have a shaft that is curved for strength. They are composed of compact and spongy bone. Leg, arm, finger and toe bones are long bones. Short bones are cuboidal. They are the ankle and wrist bones. Flat bones are made from spongy bone surrounded by compact bone. They provide large areas for muscle attachment, and organ protection. The skull, sternum, ribs and shoulder blades are flat bones. Irregular bone has an irregular shape and variable amounts of compact and spongy bone. The oscicles of the ear are an example of irregular bones.

Remember that bone is not just for support, protection, and movement. Bone also stores calcium and phosphate, helping to maintain a homeostatic concentration of these ions in the blood. Bone stores energy in the form of fat. Bone is also the site of blood cell formation.

= Long Bone

= Cuboidal Bone

= Flat Bone

= Irregular Bone

**Figure 8.8   Bone Types**

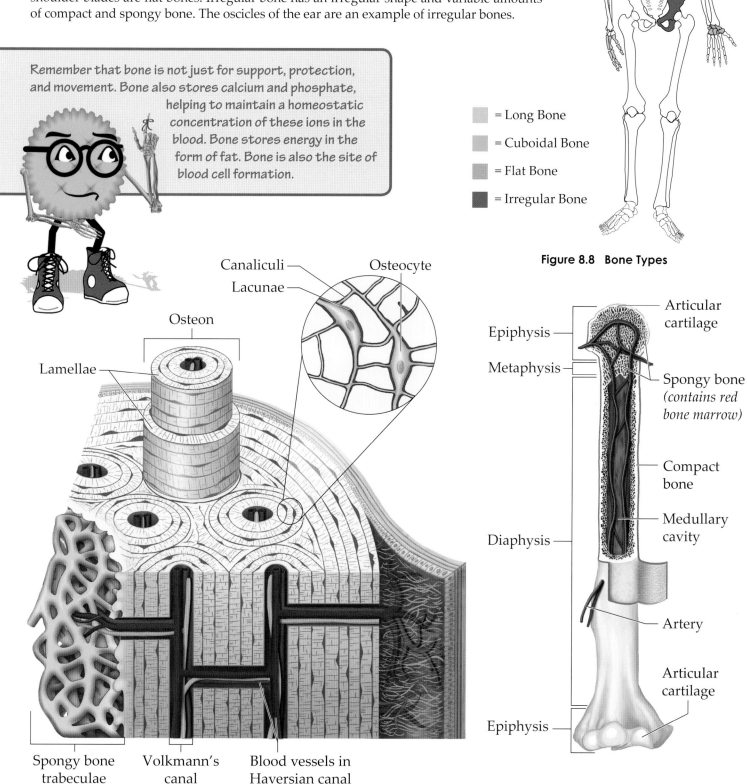

**Figure 8.9   Bone Structure**

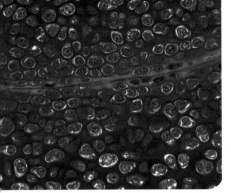

Hyaline cartilage is semi-rigid connective tissue composed of many chondrocytes (cartilage cells, pale purple). These synthesize an extracellular matrix (dark purple) of proteoglycans, collagen and water that keeps them apart from each other in spaces known as lacunae. Hyaline cartilage is strong but compressible due to its high water content. It reduces friction between the bones in the knee joint as they move against each other.

## 8.11 Cartilage

**Cartilage** is flexible, resilient connective tissue. It is composed primarily of collagen, and has great tensile strength. Cartilage contains no blood vessels or nerves except in its outside membrane called the *perichondrium*. There are three types of cartilage: 1. *hyaline*; 2. *fibrocartilage*; and 3. *elastic*. Hyaline cartilage is the most common. Hyaline cartilage reduces friction and absorbs shock in joints.

## 8.12 Joints

Joints can be classified by structure into three types:

1. *Fibrous joints* occur between two bones held closely and tightly together by fibrous tissue permitting little or no movement. Skull bones form fibrous joints with each other, and the teeth form fibrous joints with the mandible.

2. *Cartilaginous joints* also allow little or no movement. They occur between two bones tightly connected by cartilage, such as the ribs and the sternum, or the pubic symphysis in the pelvis.

3. *Synovial joints* (Figure 8.10) are not bound directly by the intervening cartilage. Instead, they are separated by a capsule filled with *synovial fluid*. Synovial fluid provides lubrication and nourishment to the cartilage. In addition, the synovial fluid contains phagocytotic cells that remove microbes and particles which result from wear and tear from joint movement. Synovial joints allow for a wide range of movement.

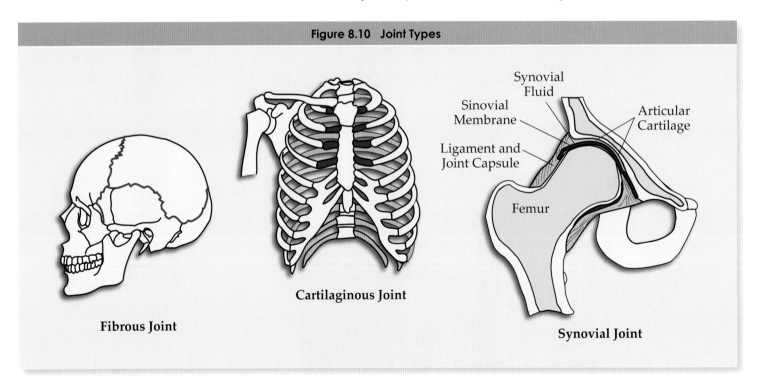

**Figure 8.10 Joint Types**

Fibrous Joint

Cartilaginous Joint

Synovial Joint
- Synovial Fluid
- Sinovial Membrane
- Ligament and Joint Capsule
- Articular Cartilage
- Femur

## 8.13 Skin

The **skin** (Figure 8.11) is an organ, which means that it is a group of tissues working together to perform a specific function. Some important functions of the skin are:

1. **Thermoregulation**: The skin helps to regulate the body temperature. Blood conducts heat from the core of the body to skin. Some of this heat can be dissipated by the endothermic evaporation of sweat, but most is dissipated by radiation. Of course, radiation is only effective if the body is higher than room temperature. Blood can also be shunted away from the capillaries of the skin to reduce heat loss, keeping the body warm. Hairs can be erected (*piloerection*) via sympathetic stimulation trapping insulating air next to the skin. Skin has both warmth and cold receptors.

2. **Protection**: The skin is a physical barrier to abrasion, bacteria, dehydration, many chemicals, and ultra violet radiation.

3. **Environmental sensory input**: The skin gathers information from the environment by sensing temperature, pressure, pain, and touch.

4. **Excretion**: Water and salts are excreted through the skin. This water loss occurs by diffusion through the skin and is independent of sweating. Adults lose one quarter to one half liter of water per day via this type of *insensible fluid loss*. Burning of the skin can increase this type of water loss dramatically.

5. **Immunity**: Besides being a physical barrier to bacteria, specialized cells of the epidermis are components of the immune system.

6. **Blood reservoir**: Vessels in the dermis hold up to 10% of the blood of a resting adult.

7. **Vitamin D synthesis**: Ultra violet radiation activates a molecule in the skin that is a precursor to vitamin D. The activated molecule is modified by enzymes in the liver and kidneys to produce vitamin D.

This is a sample of skin from the back of a human hand.

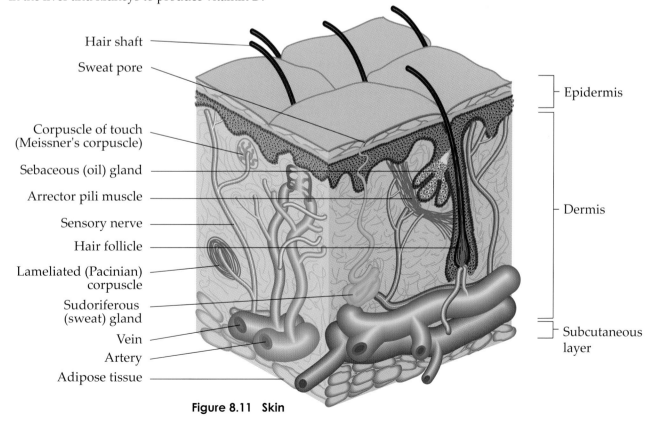

Hair shaft
Sweat pore
Corpuscle of touch (Meissner's corpuscle)
Sebaceous (oil) gland
Arrector pili muscle
Sensory nerve
Hair follicle
Lameliated (Pacinian) corpuscle
Sudoriferous (sweat) gland
Vein
Artery
Adipose tissue

Epidermis
Dermis
Subcutaneous layer

**Figure 8.11 Skin**

The skin has two principal parts: 1) the **epidermis** and 2) the **dermis**. Beneath the skin is a subcutaneous tissue called the *superficial fascia* or *hypodermis*. The fat of this subcutaneous layer is an important heat insulator for the body. The fat helps maintain normal core body temperatures on cold days while the skin approaches the temperature of the environment.

The epidermis is avascular (no blood vessels) epithelial tissue. It consists of four major cell types: 1) 90 % of the epidermis is composed of *Keratinocytes*, which produce the protein keratin that helps waterproof the skin. 2) *Melanocytes* transfer *melanin* (skin pigment) to keratinocytes. 3) *Langerhans cells* interact with the the helper T-cells of the immune system. 4) *Merkel cells* attach to sensory neurons and function in the sensation of touch.

There are five strata or layers of the epidermis. The deepest layer contains Merkel cells and stem cells. The stem cells continually divide to produce keratinocytes and other cells. Keratinocytes are pushed to the top layer. As they rise, they accumulate keratin and die, losing their cytoplasm, nucleus, and other organelles. When the cells reach the outermost layer of skin, they slough off the body. The process of keratinization from birth of a cell to sloughing off takes two to four weeks. The outermost layer of epidermis consists of 25 to 30 layers of flat, dead cells. Exposure to friction or pressure stimulates the epidermis to thicken froming a **callus**.

The **dermis** is connective tissue derived from mesodermal cells. The dermis is embedded by blood vessels, nerves, glands, and hair follicles. Collagen and elastic fibers in the dermis provide skin with strength, extensibility, and elasticity. The dermis is thick in the palms and soles.

The skin, hair, nails, glands, and some nerve endings make up the *integumentary system*. Hair, nails, and some glands are derivatives of embryonic epidermis. Hair is a column of keratinized cells held tightly together. As new cells are added to its base, the hair grows. Most hairs are associated with a *sebaceous (oil) gland* that empties oil directly into the follicle and onto the skin. When contracted, smooth muscle *(arrector pili)*, also associated with each hair, stands hair up pointing it perpendicular to the skin. *Nails* are also keratinized cells. *Sudoriferous (sweat) glands* are found in the skin separate from hair follicles. *Ceruminous glands* produce a wax-like material found in the ears.

**Figure 8.12  Keratinocytes in the Epidermis**

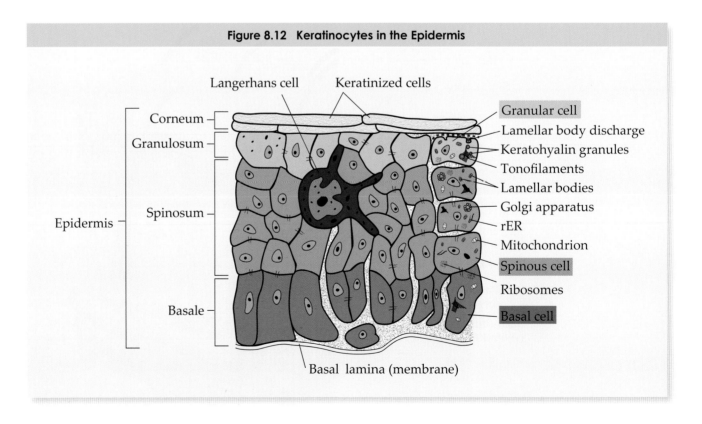

## Terms

| | | |
|---|---|---|
| Acetylcholine | Lamellae | Skeletal Muscle |
| Actin | Ligament | Skin |
| Agonist | Mineral Storage | Smooth Muscle |
| Antagonist | Muscle Contraction | Spongy Bone |
| Bone | Cycle | Striated |
| Callus | Multinucleated | Synergistic Muscle |
| Canaliculi | Myoglobin | T-Tubules |
| Cartilage | Myosin | Tendon |
| Compact Bone | Neuromuscular | Thermoregulation |
| Cardiac Muscle | Synapse | Thick Filament |
| Dense Bodies | Osteoblasts | Thin Filament |
| Dermis | Osteoclasts | Tropomyosin |
| Epidermis | Osteocytes | Troponin |
| Haversian (Central) | Osteon (Haversian | Vitamin D Synthesis |
| Canals | System) | Volkmann's Canals |
| Hydroxyapatite | Red Bone Marrow | Yellow Bone Marrow |
| Intercalated Disc | Sarcolemma | |
| Intermediate Filaments | Sarcomere | |

185.   The production of which of the following cells would most likely be increased by parathyroid hormone?

   A. osteoprogenitor
   B. osteocyte
   C. osteoclast
   D. osteoblast

186.   In a synovial joint, the purpose of the synovial fluid is to:

   A. reduce friction between bone ends.
   B. keep bone cells adequately hydrated.
   C. occupy space until the bones of the joint complete their growth.
   D. maintain a rigid connection between two flat bones.

187.   Surgical cutting of which of the following tissues would result in the LEAST amount of pain?

   A. muscle
   B. bone
   C. cartilage
   D. skin

188.   In a synovial joint, the connective tissue holding the bones together are called:

   A. ligaments.
   B. tendons.
   C. muscles.
   D. osseous tissue.

189.   All of the following are functions of bone EXCEPT:

   A. mineral storage.
   B. structural support.
   C. blood temperature regulation.
   D. fat storage.

190.   All of the following are found in compact bone EXCEPT:

   A. yellow marrow.
   B. haversian canals.
   C. canaliculi.
   D. Volkmann's canals.

191.   Hydroxyapatite is the mineral portion of bone. Hydroxyapatite contains all of the following elements except:

   A. calcium.
   B. sulfur.
   C. phosphate.
   D. hydrogen.

192.   The spongy bone of the hips is most important in:

   A. red blood storage.
   B. red blood cell synthesis.
   C. fat storage.
   D. lymph fluid production.

___

# POPULATIONS

LECTURE 9



## 9.1 Mendelian Concepts

Gregor Mendel was a 19th century monk, who performed hybridization experiments with pea plants. The difference between Mendel and those who had come before him was that Mendel quantitated his results; he counted and recorded his findings. Mendel found that when he crossed purple flowered plants with white flowered plants, the **first filial**, or **$F_1$ generation**, produced purple flowers. He called the purple trait **dominant**, and the white trait **recessive**. Mendel examined seven traits in all, and each trait proved to have dominant and recessive alternatives. When Mendel self-pollinated the $F_1$ generation plants, the $F_2$ generation expressed both the dominant and recessive traits in a **3 to 1 ratio**, now referred to as the **Mendelian ratio** (Fig. 9.1). When the $F_2$ generation was self-pollinated, 33% of the dominants produced only dominants, and the rest of the dominants produced the Mendelian ratio. The white flowered plants produced only white flowered plants. Thus, half of the $F_2$ generation expressed the dominant trait with the recessive trait latent.

**Figure 9.1 Mendelian Ratio 3:1**

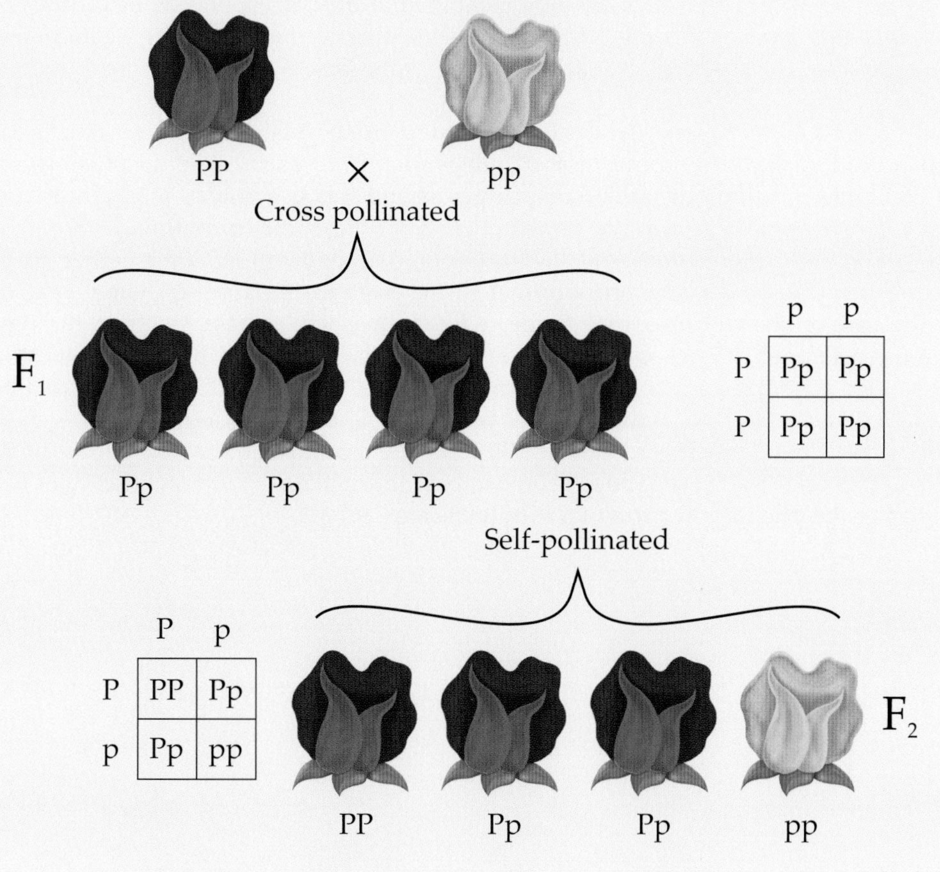


| | p | p |
|---|---|---|
| P | Pp | Pp |
| P | Pp | Pp |

| | P | p |
|---|---|---|
| P | PP | Pp |
| p | Pp | pp |

To test his model, Mendel performed a test cross, where he crossed the heterozygous F₁ generation (purple) with homozygous recessive parent (white). Since there were white offspring resulting from this cross of a purple F₁ plant and a white parent plant, Mendel proved the F₁ generation was heterozygous.

Mendel self-pollinated his pea plants. Mating relatives is called **inbreeding**, and does not change the frequency of alleles, but does increase the number of homozygous individuals within a population. **Outbreeding**, or outcrossing, is mating of nonrelatives which produces hybrids or heterozygotes.

The expression of a trait is the **phenotype**, and an individual's genetic make up is the **genotype**. In Figure 9.1 the phenotypes are purple and white; the genotypes are PP, Pp, and pp. The phenotype is expressed through the action of enzymes and other structural proteins. Which are encoded by genes. In **complete dominance**, exhibited by the flowers in Mendel's experiment, for any one trait, a diploid individual will have two chromosomes each containing a separate gene that codes for that specific trait. These two chromosomes are homologous by definition. Their corresponding genes are located at the same **locus** or position on respective chromosomes. Each gene contributes an **allele** to the genotype. However, only one allele, the dominant allele, is expressed. If both alleles are dominant, then the dominant phenotype is expressed; if both alleles are recessive, then the recessive phenotype is expressed. An individual with a genotype having two dominant or two recessive alleles is said to be **homozygous** for that trait. An individual with a genotype having one dominant and one recessive allele is said to be **heterozygous** for the trait, and is called a **hybrid**.

Mendel's First Law of Heredity, the **Law of Segregation**, states that alleles segregate independently of each other when forming gametes. Any gamete is equally likely to posses any allele. Also, the phenotypic expression of the alleles is not a blend of the two, but an expression of the dominant allele (the principle of complete dominance).

When a heterozygous individual exhibits a phenotype that is intermediate between its homozygous counterparts, the alleles are referred to as partial, or incomplete dominants. Alleles showing partial dominance are represented with the same capital letter, and distinguished with a prime or superscript. For instance, a cross between red flowered sweet peas and white flowered sweet peas may produce pink flowers. The genotype for the pink flowered individual would be expressed as either CC' or Cr Cw. If the heterozygote exhibits both phenotypes, the alleles are codominant. Human blood type alleles are codominant because a heterozygote exhibits A and B antigens on the blood cell membranes.

Figure 9.2 shows a **Punnett square** for predicting genotypic ratios of offspring. The genotypes of all possible gametes of each parent are displayed in the first column and first row respectively. The alleles are then combined in the corresponding boxes to show the possible genotypes of the offspring. Since, according to the law of segregation, each gametic genotype is equally likely, each offspring genotype is also equally likely.

Mendel's Second Law of Heredity, the **Law of Independent Assortment**, states that genes located on different chromosomes assort independently of each other. In other words, genes that code for different traits (such as pea shape and pea color), when located on different chromosomes, do not affect each other during gamete formation. If two genes are located on the same chromosome, the likelihood that they will remain together during gamete formation is indirectly proportional to the distance separating them. Thus, the closer they are on the chromosome, the more likely they will remain together. In Figure 9.2, we use a Punnett square to predict the phenotypic ratio of a **dihybrid cross**. 'W' is the allele for a round pea shape, which is dominant, and 'w' is the allele for wrinkled pea shape, which is recessive. 'G' is the allele for yellow color, which is dominant, and 'g' is the allele for green color, which is recessive. We make the assumption that the genes for pea shape and pea color are on separate chromosomes, and will assort independently of each other. Notice the **phenotypic ratio of a dihybrid cross, 9:3:3:1**.

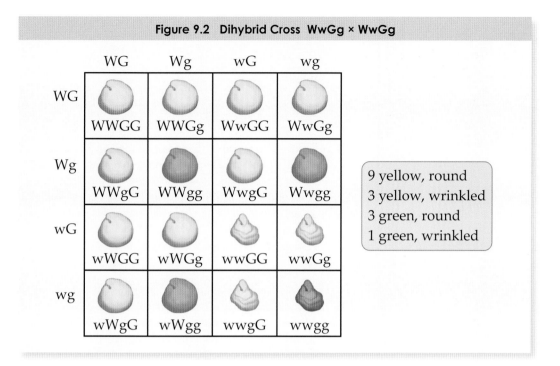

**Figure 9.2 Dihybrid Cross WwGg × WwGg**

|      | WG | Wg | wG | wg |
|------|------|------|------|------|
| WG | WWGG | WWGg | WwGG | WwGg |
| Wg | WWgG | WWgg | WwgG | Wwgg |
| wG | wWGG | wWGg | wwGG | wwGg |
| wg | wWgG | wWgg | wwgG | wwgg |

9 yellow, round
3 yellow, wrinkled
3 green, round
1 green, wrinkled

The chromosomes of males and females differ. In humans, the 23rd pair of chromosomes establishes the sex of the individual, and each partner is called a **sex chromosome**. One of the 23rd chromosomes of a male is abbreviated. Instead of appearing as two Xs in a **karyotype** (a map of the chromosomes), the chromosome pair appears as an X and a Y. All other chromosomes appear as two Xs. When a gene is found on the sex chromosome it is called **sex-linked**. Generally, the Y chromosome does not carry the allele for the sex-linked trait; thus, the allele that is carried by the X chromosome in the male is expressed whether it is dominant or recessive. Since the female has two X chromosomes, her genotype is found through the normal rules of dominance. However, in most somatic cells, one of the X chromosomes will condense, and most of its genes will become inactive. The tiny dark object formed is called a **Barr body**. Barr bodies are formed at random, so the active allele is split about evenly among the cells. Nevertheless, in most cases, the recessive phenotype is only displayed in homozygous recessive individuals. Thus, the female may carry a recessive trait on her 23rd pair of chromosomes without expressing it. If she does, she is said to be a **carrier** for the trait. Such a recessive trait has a strong chance of being expressed in her male offspring regardless of the genotype of her mate.

Hemophilia is a sex-linked disease. The Punnett square shown in Figure 9.3 shows a cross between a female carrier for hemophilia and a healthy male. Since there are two possible phenotypes for the males, and one is the recessive phenotype, the male offspring from such a pairing have a 1 in 2 chance of having the disease.

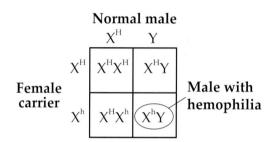

**Normal male**

**Female carrier**

**Male with hemophilia**

**Figure 9.3 Sex-linked Traits**

193. Color-blindness is a sex-linked recessive trait. A woman who is a carrier for the trait has two boys with a color-blind man. What is the probability that both boys are color-blind?

    A. 0%
    B. 25%
    C. 50%
    D. 100%

194. In the pedigree below, the darkened figures indicate an individual with hemophilia, a sex-linked recessive disease. The genotype of the female marked A is:

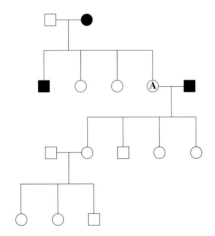

    A. $X^H X^h$
    B. $X^H X^H$
    C. $X^h X^h$
    D. $X^h Y$

195. What fraction of offspring are likely to display both dominant phenotypes in a dihybrid cross?

    A. 1/16
    B. 3/16
    C. 9/16
    D. 15/16

196. In a dihybrid cross, what fraction of the offspring are likely to be dihybrids?

    A. 1/16
    B. 1/4
    C. 1/2
    D. 9/16

197. Sickle cell anemia is an autosomal recessive disease. A male with the disease and a female that is not diseased, but carries the trait, produce two girls. What is the probability that neither girl carries a recessive allele?

    A. 0%
    B. 25%
    C. 50%
    D. 66%

198. The parents of a dihybrid cross:
    A. are genetic opposites at the genes of interest.
    B. are genetically identical at the genes of interest.
    C. are genetic opposites at one gene and genetically identical at the other.
    D. have no genetic relationship.

199. Sex-linked traits in men usually result due to genes located:
    A. on both chromosomes of a pair of homologous chromosomes.
    B. on one chromosome from a pair of homologous chromosomes
    C. on both chromosomes of a pair of nonhomologous chromosomes
    D. on one chromosome from a pair of nonhomologous chromosomes

200. Colorblindness is a sex-linked recessive trait. A woman is born colorblind. What can be said with certainty?

    A. Her father and mother are colorblind.
    B. Her mother and daughter are colorblind.
    C. Her father and son are colorblind.
    D. Her father is colorblind, but her son may or may not be.

## 9.2 Evolution

The **gene pool** is the total of all alleles in a population. **Evolution** is a change in the gene pool. Figure 9.4 shows the eye color alleles for a small population. Even if the ratio of blue eyed to brown eyed individuals temporarily changes, as long as the gene pool remains 30% b alleles and 70% B alleles, the population has not evolved.

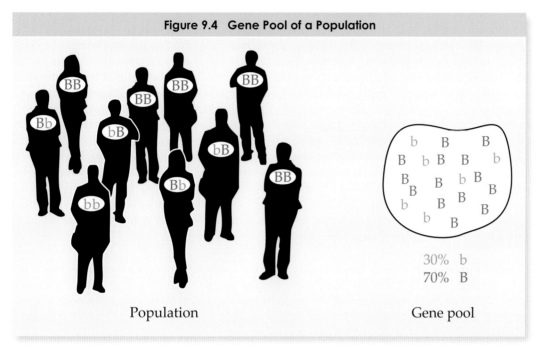

**Figure 9.4  Gene Pool of a Population**

30%  b
70%  B

Population

Gene pool

Most taxonomical classification systems are based upon genetic similarity. The classification system for animals that you must know for the MCAT contains ever more specific groupings in the following order: **Kingdom, Phylum, Class, Order, Family, Genus, Species.** (Plants and fungi use divisions instead of phyla.) Within each group are many subgroups, which are unimportant for the MCAT (except for the subphylum **Vertebrata**, which is in the phylum Chordata). Since organisms within the same group have similar genetic structures, they probably share similar phylogenies (evolutionary histories). For instance, all mammals belong to the class **Mammalia** and the phylum **Chordata**; thus, all mammals probably share a common ancestor that they do not share with birds, which are also in the phylum Chordata, but in the class Aves.

The taxonomy is changing, and for the MCAT you may want to be aware of the new superkingdoms called **domains**. There are three domains: Bacteria, Archaea, and Eukarya. This basically puts the kingdoms of Protista, Fungi, Plantae, and Animalia into the domain Eukarya. It makes the kingdom Monera obsolete dividing it into the domains of Bacteria and Archaea. The two domains of Bacteria and Archaea are divided into several kingdoms each. Archaea is more closely related to Eukarya than is Bacteria.

When naming an organism, the genus and species name are given in order. Typically, they are both written in italics, and the genus is capitalized while the species is not.

**Species** is loosely limited to, but not inclusive of, all organisms that can reproduce fertile offspring with each other. In other words, if two organisms can reproduce fertile offspring, they might be the same species; if their gametes are incompatible, they are definitely not the same species. Another guideline for species (but still an imperfect guideline) is all organisms which normally reproduce selectively fit offspring in the wild. Organisms of different species may be prevented from producing fit offspring by such things as *geographic isolation* (separated by geography), *habitat isolation* (live in the same location but have different habitats), *seasonal isolation* (mate in different seasons), *mechanical isolation* (physically impossible to mate), *gametic isolation* (gametes are incompatible), *developmental*

You should be aware that ontogeny recapitulates phylogeny. In other words, the course of development of an organism from embryo to adult reflects its evolutionary history. For instance, the human fetus has pharyngeal pouches reflecting a gilled ancestor.

*isolation* (fertilized embryo developes improperly), *hybrid inviability or sterility* (hybrid malformed), *selective hybrid elimination* (hybrid is less fit), and *behavioral isolation* (different mating rituals).

In order to survive, the members of the same species will exploit their environment in a unique manner not shared by any other species. The way in which a species exploits its environment is called its **niche**. No two species can occupy the same niche indefinitely. The theory of **survival of the fittest** predicts that one species will exploit the environment more efficiently, eventually leading to the extinction of the other with the same niche. The definition of **the "fittest" organism** in this theory is the organism which can best survive to reproduce offspring which will, in turn reproduce offspring and so on generation after generation. This definition may include living beyond reproduction in order to provide a better chance for offspring to reproduce. In fact, there are two opposing reproductive strategies: *r*-**selection** and *K*-**selection**. *r*-selection involves producing large numbers of offspring that mature rapidly with little or no parental care. *r*-strategists generally have a high brood mortality rate. Their population growth curves are exponential. *r*-strategists are generally found in unpredictable, rapidly changing environments affected by density independent factors such as floods, or drastic temperature change. *K*-selection is the other side of the spectrum. *K*-selection involves small brood size with slow maturing offspring and strong parental care. *K*-strategists tend to have a sigmoidal growth curve which levels off at the carrying capacity. (The *K* comes from an equation variable representing carrying capacity.) The carrying capacity is the maximum number of organisms that an environment can maintain. The carrying capacity is a *density dependent* factor. Most organisms have reproductive strategies somewhere between *K*- and *r*-selections.

**Speciation** is the process by which new species are formed. When gene flow ceases between two sections of a population, speciation begins. Factors which bring about speciation include geographic, seasonal, and behavioral isolation. **Adaptive radiation** occurs when several separate species arise from a single ancestral species, such as the 14 species of Galapagos finches that all evolved from one ancestor.

A species may face a crisis so severe as to cause a shift in the allelic frequencies of the survivors of the crisis. This is called an **evolutionary bottleneck**.

**Divergent evolution** exists when two or more species evolving from the same group maintain a similar structure from the common ancestor (called a *homologous* structure). However, two species may independently evolve similar structures in **convergent evolution**. Such similar structures are said to be *analogous* or *homoplastic*. An example of homoplasticity is the wings evolved by bats and birds; the two do not share a common ancestor from which they received their wings.

Some phenotypic forms vary gradually within a species, such as height. There are short people, tall people and every height in between short and tall. Other forms are distinct, like flower color, either red or white, or chicken plumage, either barred or non-barred. The occurence of distinct forms is called **polymorphism**.

## 9.3 Symbiosis

A **symbiosis** is a relationship between two species. The relationship can be beneficial for both, called **mutualism**; beneficial for one and not affect the other, called **commensalism**; beneficial for one and detrimental to the other, called **parasitism**. There is even a symbiosis called *enslavement* where one species enslaves another.

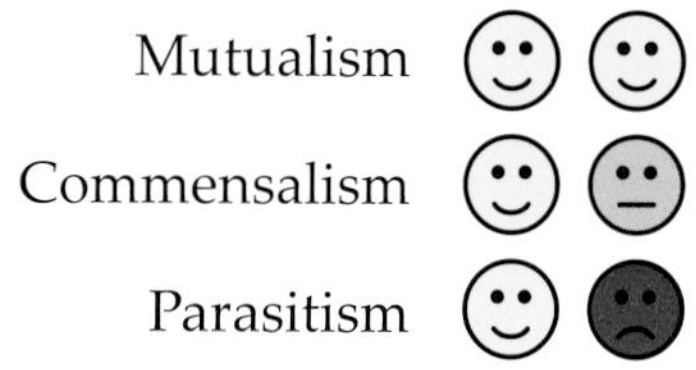

Mutualism
Commensalism
Parasitism

**Figure 9.5  Symbiosis**

## 9.4 Hardy-Weinberg Equilibrium

In the early part of the 20th century, there was some question as to how less frequent alleles might be maintained in the population. Hardy and Weinberg came up with the explanation simultaneously. They showed statistically that there should be no change in the gene pool of a sexually reproducing population possessing the five following conditions:

1. large population;

2. mutational equilibrium;

3. immigration or emigration must not change the gene pool;

4. random mating; and

5. no selection for the fittest organism.

A population with these five characteristics is considered to be in **Hardy-Weinberg equilibrium**. No real population ever possesses these characteristics completely. Small populations are subject to **genetic drift** where one allele may be permanently lost due to the death of all members having that allele. Genetic drift is not caused by selective pressure, so its results are random in evolutionary terms. Mutational equilibrium means that the rate of forward mutations exactly equals the rate of back mutations. This rarely occurs in real populations; however, in the short term, mutations are seldom a major factor in changing allelic frequencies. Any immigration or emigration must not change the gene pool. This condition may occur in some isolated populations and is not typically a major factor in genetic change. The last two conditions probably do not occur in natural populations and are the most influential mechanisms of evolution.

The binomial theorem:

$$p^2 + 2pq + q^2$$

predicts the genotype frequency of a gene with only two alleles in a population in Hardy-Weinberg equilibrium. Imagine that 'A' is the dominant allele and 'a' is the recessive allele, and they are the only alleles for a specific gene. Now imagine that 80% of the alleles are 'A'. This means that 80% of the gametes will be 'A' and 20% will be 'a'. The probability that two 'A's come together is simply $0.8^2 = 0.64$. The probability that two 'a's come together is $0.2^2 = 0.04$. Any remaining zygotes will be heterozygous, leaving 32% heterozygotes. ($2 \times 0.8 \times 0.2 = 0.32$) Using the formula, we represent 'A' as p and 'a' as q. Since there are only two alleles, **p + q = 1**.

201. If a certain gene possesses only two alleles, and the dominant allele represents 90% of the gene pool, how many individuals display the recessive phenotype.

   A. 0%
   B. 1%
   C. 18%
   D. 10%

202. Which of the following would least likely disrupt the Hardy-Weinberg equilibrium?

   A. emigration of part of a population
   B. a predator that selectively takes the old and sick
   C. a massive flood killing 15% of a large homogeneous population
   D. exposure of the entire population to intense radiation

203. Which of the following is most likely an example of two organisms in the same species?

   A. a cabbage in Georgia and a cabbage in Missouri that mate and produce fertile offspring only in years of unusual weather patterns
   B. two fruit flies on the same Hawaiian island with very different courtship dances
   C. two South American frogs that mate in different seasons
   D. two migratory birds that nest on different islands off the coast of England

204. All of the following factors would most likely favor an *r*-selection reproductive strategy over a *K*-selection strategy EXCEPT:

   A. intense seasonal droughts
   B. a short growing season
   C. limited space
   D. large scale commercial predation by humans

205. If two species are members of the same order, they must also be members of the same:

   A. habitat
   B. family
   C. class
   D. biome

206. The wolf, or *Canis lupus*, is a member of the family Canidae. Which of the following is most likely to be true?

   A. There are more living organisms classified as Canidae than as *Canis*.
   B. There are more living organisms classified as *lupus* than as *Canis*.
   C. An organism may be classified as *Canis* but not as Canidae.
   D. An organism may be classified as *lupus*, but not as *Canis*.

207. If, in a very large population, a certain gene possesses only two alleles and 36% of the population is homozygous dominant, what percentage of the population are heterozygotes?

   A. 16%
   B. 24%
   C. 36%
   D. 48%

208. Although human behavior ensures the success of each new generation of corn, selective breeding by humans has genetically altered corn so that it could not survive in the wild without human intervention. Corn population is controlled, and most of the corn seeds are eaten or become spoiled. The relationship between humans and corn is best described as:

   A. commensalism because humans benefit and corn is neither benefited nor harmed.
   B. commensalism because there is no true benefit to either species.
   C. parasitism because humans benefit and corn is harmed.
   D. mutualism because both species benefit.

## 9.5 Origin of Life

The universe is 12 to 15 billion years old. According to the *Big Bang Theory*, the universe began as a tiny spec of highly concentrated mass and exploded outward. In the early moments, only hydrogen gas existed. As the universe cooled, helium was able to form. The explosion was irregular, and gravitational forces created clumping of the mass. Heavier elements, and solar systems formed from these clumps of mass.

Our solar system is approximately 4.6 billion years old. The earth itself is about 4.5 billion years old; however, due to the volatile nature of early earth, there are no rocks on earth older than 3.9 billion years old.

Early earth probably had an atmosphere made mainly from nitrogen and hydrogen gas, and very little oxygen gas. One theory holds that the atmosphere contained clouds of $H_2S$, $NH_3$, and $CH_4$ creating a reducing environment. From this environment, the formation of carbon based molecules that we associate with life required little energy to form. Experiments attempting to recreate the atmosphere of early earth have resulted in the autosynthesis of molecules such as urea, amino acids, and even adenine. **The Urey-Miller experiment** was one of the early experiments to make such an attempt.

The first cells are thought to have evolved from **coacervates**, lipid or protein bilayer bubbles. Coacervates spontaneously form and grow from fat molecules suspended in water.

Organisms may have initially assimilated carbon from methane and carbon dioxide in the early atmosphere.

The earliest organisms were probably heterotrophs subsisting on preformed organic compounds in their immediate surroundings. Fossils of these organisms have been dated at **3.6 billion years old**. As preformed compounds became scarce, some of these organisms developed chemosynthetic autotrophy followed by photosynthetic autotrophy.

Around 2.3 billion years ago, the ancestors of cyanobacteria evolved. They were able to use sunlight and water to reduce carbon dioxide. These were the first oxygen producing, **photosynthetic bacteria**. The atmosphere began to fill with oxygen.

Eukaryotes evolved about 1.5 billion years ago, and did not develop into multicellular organisms until several million years later.

## 9.6 Chordate Features

**Chordata** is the phylum containing humans. Chordata does not mean backbone. All chordates have bilateral symmetry. They are **deuterostomes**, meaning their anus develops from or near the **blastopore**. (Compare protostomes, where the mouth develops from or near the blastopore.) Chordates have a **coelom** (a body cavity within mesodermal tissue). At some stage of their development they possess a **notochord** (an embryonic axial support, not the back bone), **pharyngeal slits, a dorsal, hollow nerve cord**, and a **tail**.

Members from the subphylum **Vertebrata** have their notochord replaced by a segmented cartilage or bone structure. They have a distinct brain enclosed in a skull. Most chordates are vertebrates. Vertebrata is composed of two classes of jawless fish (Agnatha), the cartilaginous fish, bony fish, amphibians, reptiles, birds, and mammals. The agnatha arose first and seperately from the rest about 470 million years ago. Amphibians arose from bony fish. Reptiles arose from amphibians about 300 million years ago. Birds and mammals arose from reptiles. Mammals arose from reptiles about 220 million years ago.

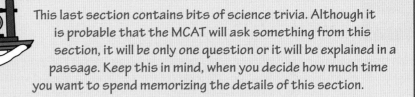

This last section contains bits of science trivia. Although it is probable that the MCAT will ask something from this section, it will be only one question or it will be explained in a passage. Keep this in mind, when you decide how much time you want to spend memorizing the details of this section.

You have now reviewed all the science tested by the MCAT. I suggest that you go back and review all of the tests that you have taken to this point. When you are done, you should pick your weakest area and master it. Then go to your next weakest area, and so on.

Next week is Zen Week. This is an important week of mental preparation. Be sure to attend. If you're not in the class, see the website at www.examkrackers.com for information on Zen Week.

See you!

---

## 9.7 | Equation Summary

| Equations |
|---|

**Hardy-Weinburg Equilibrium**

$$p + q = 1$$

**The Binomial Theorem**

$$p^2 + 2pq + q^2$$

## 9.8 Terms You Need To Know

| Terms | |
|---|---|
| 3 to 1 ratio | Hybrid |
| Adaptive Radiation | *K*-selection |
| Allele | Kingdom |
| Barr Body | Law of Independent Assortment |
| Blastopore | Law of Segregation |
| Carrier | Locus |
| Carrying Capacity | Mammalia |
| Chordata | Mendelian Ratio |
| Class | Mutational Equilibrium |
| Coacervates | Mutualism |
| Coelom | Natural Selection |
| Complete Dominance | Niche |
| Commensalism | Notochord |
| Convergent Evolution | Order |
| Deuterostomes | Parasitism |
| Dihybrid Cross | Phenotype |
| Divergent Evolution | Phylum |
| Domains | Polymorphism |
| Dominant | Punnett Square |
| Evolution | *R*-selection |
| Evolutionary Bottleneck | Random Mating |
| $F_1$ Generation | Recessive |
| Family | Sex Chromosome |
| Gene Pool | Sex-linked Trait |
| Genetic Drift | Sigmoidal Growth Curve |
| Genotype | Speciation |
| Genus | Species |
| Hardy-Weinberg Equilibrium | Symbiosis |
| Heterozygous | Urey-Miller Experiment |
| Homozygous | Vertebrata |

**209.** Which of the following was the earliest to evolve on Earth?

   **A.** plants
   **B.** prokaryotes
   **C.** protists
   **D.** fish

**210.** All of the following are characteristics of members of the phylum Chordata at some point in their life cycle EXCEPT:

   **A.** a tail
   **B.** a notochord
   **C.** a backbone
   **D.** gills

**211.** Which of the following are not members of the phylum Chordata?

   **A.** tunicates
   **B.** apes
   **C.** birds
   **D.** ants

**212.** Which of the following was probably not necessary for the origin of life on Earth?

   **A.** $H_2O$
   **B.** hydrogen
   **C.** $O_2$
   **D.** carbon

**213.** Which of the following is the phylum to which Homo sapiens belong?

   **A.** Mammalia
   **B.** Chordata
   **C.** Vertebrata
   **D.** Homo

**214.** Humans are members of the order:

   **A.** Vertebrata
   **B.** Chordata
   **C.** Primata
   **D.** Homididae

**215.** What do the results of the Urey-Miller experiment demonstrate?

   **A.** the existence of life on Earth
   **B.** that small biological molecules cannot be synthesized from inorganic material
   **C.** that life may have evolved from inorganic precursors
   **D.** that humans have evolved from photosynthetic cyanobacteria

**216.** If the first living organisms on Earth were heterotrophs, where did they get their energy?

   **A.** from eating each other
   **B.** from eating naturally formed organic molecules
   **C.** from the sun
   **D.** from eating dead organisms.

**STOP.**

# STOP!

## DO NOT LOOK AT THESE EXAMS UNTIL CLASS.

**30-MINUTE IN-CLASS EXAM FOR LECTURE 1**

## Passage I (Questions 1-7)

The three dimensional shape of a protein is ultimately determined by its amino acid sequence. The folding pattern itself is a sequential and cooperative process where initial folds assist in aligning the protein properly for subsequent folds. For many smaller proteins, the amino acid sequence alone can direct protein configuration, but for other proteins assistance in the folding process is necessary. Two types of proteins may assist in the folding of a polypeptide chain: enzymes which catalyze steps in the folding process, and proteins which stabilize partially folded intermediates. Proteins in the latter group are called *chaperones*.

An example of an enzyme which catalyzes the folding process is *protein disulfide isomerase*. This enzyme assists in the creation of disulfide bonds. The enzyme is not specific for any particular disulfide bond in a given chain. Instead, it simply increases the rate of formation of all disulfide combinations, and the most stable disulfide formations predominate.

Chaperones also assist in protein folding. As the protein folds, chaperones bind to properly folded sections and stabilize them. Chaperone synthesis can be induced by application of heat or other types of stress, and they are sometimes referred to as *heat shock proteins or stress proteins*.

Although the amino acid sequence determines the configuration of a protein, attempts at predicting protein configuration based upon amino acid sequence have been unsuccessful.

1. Which of the following statements concerning the function of protein disulfide isomerase in the formation of proteins is true?

   A. *Protein disulfide isomerase* increases only the rate at which disulfide bonds are formed.
   B. *Protein disulfide isomerase* increases only the rate at which disulfide bonds are broken.
   C. *Protein disulfide isomerase* increases both the rate at which disulfide bonds are formed and broken.
   D. *Protein disulfide isomerase* increases the rate at which disulfide bonds are formed and decreases the rate at which disulfide bonds are broken.

2. According to the passage, the folding pattern of a protein is determined by the protein's:

   A. primary structure
   B. secondary structure
   C. tertiary structure
   D. quaternary structure

3. Which of the following is the best explanation for why attempts at predicting protein configuration based upon amino acid sequence have been unsuccessful?

   A. It is impossible to know the amino acid sequence of a protein without knowing the DNA nucleotide sequence.
   B. Enzymes and chaperones help to determine the three dimensional shape of a protein.
   C. The three dimensional shape of a protein is based upon hydrogen and disulfide bonding between amino acids, and the number of possible combinations of bonding amino acids makes prediction difficult.
   D. The amino acid sequence of the same protein may vary slightly from one sample to the next.

4. Chaperones assist in the formation of a protein's:

   A. primary structure.
   B. secondary structure.
   C. tertiary structure.
   D. quaternary structure.

5. Natural selection has resulted in increased chaperone synthesis in the presence of elevated temperatures. How might increased *chaperone* production in the presence of heat be advantageous to a cell?

   A. Heat destabilizes intermolecular bonds making protein configuration more difficult to achieve. *Chaperones* counteract this by stabilizing the partially folded intermediates.
   B. Increased temperatures increase reaction rates creating an excess of fully formed proteins. *Chaperones* stabilize the partially folded intermediates and slow the process.
   C. Increased *chaperone* production requires energy. This energy is acquired from the kinetic energy of molecules and thus cools the cell.
   D. Elevated temperatures result in increased cellular activity requiring more proteins. Chaperones increase the rate of polypeptide formation.

**GO ON TO THE NEXT PAGE.**

6. Which of the following bonds in a protein is likely to be LEAST stable in the presence of heat?

   A. a disulfide bond
   B. a hydrogen bond
   C. a polypeptide bond
   D. the double bond of a carbonyl

7. *Protein disulfide isomerase* most likely:

   A. lowers the activation energy of the formation of cystine.
   B. raises the activation energy of the formation of cystine.
   C. lowers the activation energy of the formation of proline.
   D. raises the activation energy of the formation of proline.

---

## Passage II (Questions 8-14)

In *polyacrylamide gel electrophoresis* (PAGE), electrically charged proteins are dragged by an electric field through the pores of a highly cross-linked gel matrix at different rates depending upon their size and charge.

In a SDS-PAGE, proteins are separated by size only. Since different proteins have different *native charges*, the protein mixture is first dissolved in SDS (sodium dodecyl sulfate) solution. SDS anions disrupt the noncovalent bonds of the proteins and associate with the peptide chains, approximately one molecule of SDS for every two residues of a typical protein. The resulting net negative charge on the protein is normally much greater than the charge on the native protein. *Mercaptoethanol* is usually added in the presence of heat to reduce disulfide bonds and complete the denaturization process. This solution is then applied to a porous gel and an electric field is applied. The rate of movement through the gel is inversely proportional to the logarithm of the molecular weight of the protein.

The proteins are then stained with a dye such as coomassie blue. Lines are formed at different points along the gel corresponding to the molecular weight of the proteins.

A second type of electrophoresis, called *isoelectric focusing*, distinguishes proteins based upon their isoelectric points. A permanent pH gradient is established within a polyacrylamide gel by applying an electric field to polyacrylamide polymers with different p*I*s. When the native proteins are applied to this gel in the absence of SDS, each protein moves until it reaches its p*I*.

8. SDS PAGE would be least effective in distinguishing between the masses of different:

   A. carbohydrate-rich glycoproteins.
   B. acidic proteins.
   C. polar proteins.
   D. enzymes.

9. What is the purpose of coomassie blue?

   A. Coomassie blue increases the separation of the proteins by increasing their mass.
   B. Coomassie blue increases the separation of the proteins by increasing their charge.
   C. Coomassie blue allows the results of electrophoresis to be visualized.
   D. Coomassie blue stops further movement of the proteins by increasing their mass.

GO ON TO THE NEXT PAGE.

10. Which of the following proteins would move the most slowly through the gel in SDS PAGE?

    A. a large protein
    B. a small protein
    C. a protein with a high native charge
    D. a protein with a low native charge

11. Electrophoresis is also used to analyze nucleic acids. In electrophoresis of nucleic acids, SDS is unnecessary because:

    A. nucleic acids already contain negatively charged phosphate groups in proportion to their size.
    B. nucleic acids are already large enough to separate appreciably on their own.
    C. nucleic acids don't have a quaternary or tertiary structure to disrupt.
    D. nucleic acids do not contain hydrogen bonds.

12. SDS is a detergent that does not cleave covalent bonds. Which protein structure cannot be disrupted by SDS?

    A. primary
    B. secondary
    C. tertiary
    D. quaternary

13. Which of the following would most likely occur if a multisubunit protein were subjected to the electrophoresis techniques used in SDS PAGE?

    A. The protein would remain intact and separate from other proteins according to its native charge.
    B. The protein would remain intact and separate from other proteins according to its size.
    C. Each subunit would separate independently, according to its native charge.
    D. Each subunit would separate independently, according to its size.

14. Which of the following is most likely a limitation to SDS PAGE in identifying different proteins within a protein mixture?

    A. SDS PAGE is likely to be an expensive process.
    B. SDS PAGE cannot easily distinguish between proteins of similar molecular weight.
    C. Any proteins used in SDS PAGE are denatured.
    D. The native charge on a protein does not always correspond to its size.

## Passage III (Questions 15-21)

Glycolysis is the metabolic breakdown of glucose into the readily useable form of chemical energy, ATP. For some human cells, such as neurons and erythrocytes, glucose is the only source of chemical energy available under typical circumstances.

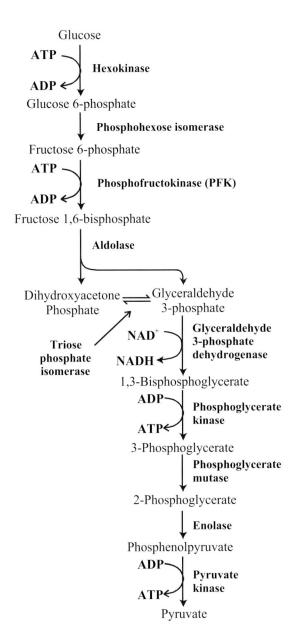

**Figure 1** Glycolysis

Each reaction in the glycolytic pathway is governed by an enzyme. Glucose is phosphorylated as it enters the cell in an irreversible reaction with hexokinase. It is not until the reaction governed by phosphofructokinase (PFK), however, that the molecule is committed to the glycolytic pathway. The PFK reaction is called the *committed step*. PFK activity is inhibited when cellular energy is plentiful, and stimulated when energy is low.

Glycolysis can be interrupted by poisons that interfere with glycolytic enzyme activity. Arsenate, a derivative of arsenic, is a deadly poison that acts as a substrate for *glyceraldehyde 3-phosphate dehydrogenase.*

15. The net result of aerobic respiration can be summarized most accurately as:

    A. the oxidation of glucose.
    B. the reduction of glucose.
    C. the elimination of glucose.
    D. the lysis of glucose.

16. The process of the synthesis of ATP in the glycolytic reaction governed by *phosphoglycerate kinase* is called:

    A. oxidative phosphorylation.
    B. substrate-level phosphorylation.
    C. exergonic phosphate transfer.
    D. electron transport.

17. Which of the following gives the net reaction for glycolysis?

    A. Glucose + 4 ADP → pyruvate + 2 ATP
    B. Glucose + 2 ADP + 2 $P_i$ + 2 NAD+ g 2 pyruvate + 2 ATP + 2 NADH
    C. Glucose + $O_2$ → CO2 + H2O + 2 ATP
    D. Glucose + $O_2$ → 2 pyruvate + 2 ATP + 2 NADH

18. Which of the following would most likely occur inside a cell in the presence of arsenic?

    A. The concentration of glyceraldehyde 3-phosphate dehydrogenase would decrease.
    B. The concentration of glyceraldehyde 3-phosphate would increase.
    C. The concentration of aldolase would increase.
    D. The concentration of 1,3-bisphosphoglycerate would increase.

19. Why is the PFK reaction, and not the hexokinase reaction, the *committed step*?

    A. The hexokinase reaction is irreversible, but the PFK reaction is not.
    B. The PFK reaction requires the hydrolysis of ATP, but the hexokinase reaction does not.
    C. Glucose 6-phosphate is a higher energy molecule than fructose 1,6-bisphosphate.
    D. Glucose 6-phosphate may be converted into glycogen in some circumstances, but fructose 1,6-bisphosphate has only one possible chemical fate in the cell.

20. From the information in the passage, which of the following might be an allosteric activator of PFK?

    A. citrate
    B. insulin
    C. ADP
    D. ATP

21. The action of arsenate on glyceraldehyde 3-phosphate dehydrogenase is best described as:
    A. competitive inhibition.
    B. noncompetitive inhibition.
    C. allosteric inhibition.
    D. negative feedback.

**GO ON TO THE NEXT PAGE.**

22. Cofactors are best described as:

    A. nonprotein substances required for all enzyme activity.
    B. small, nonprotein, organic molecules.
    C. metal ions or coenzymes that activate an enzyme by binding tightly to it.
    D. catalysts.

23. The substrate concentration in a reaction which is governed by an enzyme is slowly increased to high levels. As the substrate concentration increases the reaction rate:

    A. continues to increase indefinitely.
    B. continues to decrease indefinitely.
    C. increases at first, then levels off.
    D. does not change.

---

**STOP.** IF YOU FINISH BEFORE TIME IS CALLED, CHECK YOUR WORK. YOU MAY GO BACK TO ANY QUESTION IN THIS TEST BOOKLET.

---

# 30-MINUTE IN-CLASS EXAM FOR LECTURE 2

## Passage I (Questions 24-28)

The giant amoeba-like *Pelomyxa palustris*, the only member of the phylum Caryoblastea, exhibits one of the most primitive forms of cell division in eukaryotes; it does not undergo mitosis. Instead, the nucleus simply splits into two daughter nuclei. Like most other protists, the nucleus of the *Pelomyxa* is bound by a nuclear envelope. During cellular division, the chromosomes of the *Pelomyxa* double in number and assort randomly to the daughter cells. Multiple copies of each chromosome ensure that each daughter cell maintains the necessary amount of genetic material to specify the organism. *Pelomyxa* has no centrioles or mitochondria; however, it does contain two bacterial symbionts which may function similarly to mitochondria. *Pelomyxa* may represent an early stage in the evolution of eukaryotic cells.

Unicellular protists from the phylum Pyrrhophyta, commonly called *dinoflagellates*, undergo a form of mitosis where the nuclear membrane remains intact. Microtubules extending through the nuclear membrane attach to chromosomes. The nuclear membrane grows between attached chromosomes separating them and creating two daughter nuclei. The dinoflagellate then divides with each daughter cell accepting a nucleus. Most dinoflagellates are photosynthetic, and most are protected by cellulose plates.

Mitosis in diatoms from the phylum *chrysophyta* is similar to that in dinoflagellates, though slightly more advanced.

24. Which of the following is true according to the passage?

    A. Eukaryotes that lack centrioles cannot undergo mitosis.
    B. Some prokaryotes undergo mitosis, while others do not.
    C. Not all eukaryotes undergo mitosis.
    D. All protists lack mitochondria.

25. During mitosis, the nuclear envelope of a mammalian cell:

    A. disintegrates during replication of the chromosomes.
    B. disintegrates while crossing over is taking place.
    C. disintegrates while the chromosomes condense.
    D. remains intact.

26. As presented in the passage, the theory that *Pelomyxa* represents an early stage in the evolution of eukaryotic cells would be most *weakened* by which of the following?

    A. A protist containing mitochondria and undergoing mitosis, proved to be an ancestor to *Pelomyxa*.
    B. Diatoms were found to have evolved from *Pelomyxa*.
    C. New evidence placed dinoflagellates in the kingdom plantae.
    D. A second species belonging to the phylum Caryoblastea is discovered and found to undergo mitosis.

27. The separation of duplicate chromosomes of dinoflagellates most closely resembles which two phases in mitosis?

    A. prophase and metaphase
    B. metaphase and anaphase
    C. anaphase and telophase
    D. anaphase and cytokinesis

28. The bacterial symbionts in *Pelomyxa* most likely:

    A. parasitically infect the *Pelomyxa*.
    B. provide energy for the *Pelomyxa* from the metabolism of absorbed nutrients.
    C. reproduce independently from the *Pelomyxa* through a primitive mitosis.
    D. function in lipid synthesis.

## Passage II (Questions 29-34)

For many genes in eukaryotes, the mRNA initially transcribed is not translated in its entirety. Instead, it is processed in a series of steps occurring within the nucleus. The initial unprocessed mRNA is called pre-mRNA. Just after transcription begins, the 5′ end of the pre-mRNA is *capped* with GTP forming a 5′–5′ triphosphate linkage. The *cap* protects the mRNA from exonucleases acting on its 5′ end, and acts as an attachment site for ribosomes. At the 3′ end, the *polyadenylation signal*, AAUAA, signals the cleavage of the pre-mRNA 10 to 20 nucleotides downstream. Several adenosine residues are added to the 3′ end to form a *poly-A tail*. The poly-A tail wraps tightly around an RNA-protein complex protecting the 3′ end from degradation.

As much as 90% of the pre-mRNA may be removed from the nucleotide sequence as *introns*. The remaining *exons* are spliced together in a single mRNA strand, and leave the nucleus to be translated in the cytosol or on the rough endoplasmic reticulum.

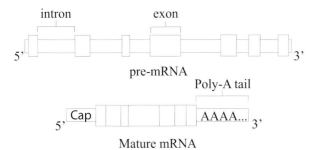

**Figure 1** Post-transcriptional processing of mRNA

In *R looping*, a technique used to identify introns, a fully processed mRNA strand is hybridized with its double stranded DNA counterpart under conditions which favor formation of hybrids between DNA and RNA strands. In this process, the RNA strand displaces one DNA strand and binds to the other DNA strand along complementary sequences. The results can be visualized through electron microscopy and are shown in Figure 2.

In prokaryotes, mRNA is normally translated without modification.

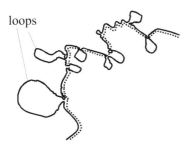

**Figure 2** R looping

---

29. Which of the following would most strongly indicate that the *poly-A tail* is added after transcription and not during transcription?

   **A.** evidence of an enzyme in the nucleus that catalyzes the synthesis of a sequence of multiple adenosine phosphate molecules

   **B.** a sequence of multiple thymine nucleotides following each gene in eukaryote DNA

   **C.** a sequence of multiple uracil nucleotides following each gene in eukaryote mRNA

   **D.** a sequence of multiple adenosine nucleotides following each gene in eukaryote DNA

30. Small nuclear ribonucleoproteins (snRNPs) catalyze the splicing reaction in the post-transcriptional processing of RNA. Based upon the information in the passage, in which of the following locations would snRNPs most likely be found?

   **A.** the cytosol of a prokaryotic cell

   **B.** the cytosol of a eukaryotic cell

   **C.** the lumen of the endoplasmic reticulum

   **D.** the nucleus of the eukaryotic cell

31. The loops in Figure 2 represent:

   **A.** DNA introns.

   **B.** DNA exons.

   **C.** RNA introns.

   **D.** RNA exons.

32. In *R looping* the displaced DNA strand contains the complementary nucleotide sequence for:

   **A.** the entire DNA strand shown in Figure 2.

   **B.** the entire RNA strand shown in Figure 2.

   **C.** the DNA introns only.

   **D.** the RNA introns only.

33. The intron sequences of identical genes in closely related species are often very different. Which of the following is most strongly suggested by this evidence?

   **A.** Identical genes in closely related species may code for different proteins.

   **B.** Changes in the amino acid sequence of a protein do not necessarily change protein function.

   **C.** Intron sequences are heavily characterized by selective pressure.

   **D.** Selective pressure has little or no role in the development of intron sequences.

**GO ON TO THE NEXT PAGE.**

**34.** Which of the following represents the 5′ end of eukaryotic mRNA?

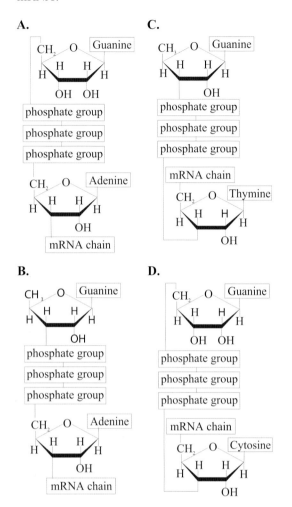

An alteration in cellular DNA other than genetic recombination is called a *mutation*. Mutations can occur in both germ and somatic cells. Germ line mutations are transmitted to offspring and can result in genetic diseases. Somatic mutations lead to *neoplastic diseases*, which are responsible for 20% of all deaths in industrialized countries.

The *basal mutation rate* is the natural rate of change in the nucleotide sequence in the absence of environmental mutagens. Such mutations result mainly from errors in DNA replication. A common error during replication is a *tautomeric shift*. Thymine, in its keto form, pairs with adenine; however, in its enol form, it prefers guanine. Adenine usually exists in an amino form that prefers thymine, and, rarely, in an imino form that pairs with cytosine. Tautomeric shifts result in mismatched base pairs.

Environmental mutagens such as chemicals and radiation can increase the mutation rate. Ionizing radiation, such as gamma rays and x-rays, excites electrons creating radicals inside the cell that react with DNA. Ultraviolet radiation from normal sunlight cannot penetrate the skin nor make radicals; however, it can form pyrimidine dimers from adjacent pyrimidines. Chemicals, such as deaminating agents, can convert adenine, guanine, and cytosine into hypoxanthine, xanthine, and uracil, respectively, which lead to mismatched base pairs and thus errors during replication. Though deamination of adenine and guanine are rare, deamination of cytosine is fairly common.

Because many mutations occur initially to only one strand of a DNA double helix, they can be repaired. In a healthy cell there are specialized enzyme systems which monitor and repair DNA. However, once the DNA is replicated, these enzymes can no longer recognize the mutation and repair becomes very unlikely. For errors occurring during replication there are enzymes called *glycosylases* that can remove mismatches and small insertions and deletions. Glycosylases, which also work on the deaminated bases, must be capable of identifying mismatched base pairs and distinguishing between the old and new DNA strand.

**35.** It has been hypothesized that in ancestral organisms DNA contained uracil and not thymine. Why might DNA that contains thymine have a natural selective advantage over DNA that contains uracil?

A. DNA that contains uracil would be unable to utilize glycosylases that repair mutations caused by the deamination of cytosine.
B. Uracil does not undergo a tautomeric shift and thymine does.
C. DNA that contains uracil cannot form a double helix.
D. Uracil is a purine, and thymine is a pyrimidine.

**36.** Radiation therapy is used to treat some forms of cancer by damaging DNA and thus killing the rapidly reproducing cancerous cells. Why might radiation treatment have a greater effect on cancer cells than normal cells?

A. Normal cells have more time between S phases to repair damaged DNA.
B. Damaged DNA is more reactive to radiation.
C. Cancer cells have lost the ability to repair damaged DNA.
D. The effect of radiation is the same, but there are more cancer cells than normal cells.

**37.** From the information in the passage, which of the following is LEAST likely to be true concerning neoplastic diseases?

A. Tumors may produce neoplastic diseases.
B. Neoplastic diseases are hereditary.
C. Neoplastic diseases begin with the mutation of a normal cell.
D. Exposure to chemical mutagens may lead to a neoplastic disease.

**38.** Ionizing radiation can create double stranded breaks in DNA. Eukaryotes are able to repair some of these breaks, but prokaryotes are not. Which of the following gives the most likely explanation for this difference?

A. Prokaryotes do not possess a ligase enzyme to join separate DNA molecules.
B. Prokaryotic DNA is single stranded.
C. Eukaryotes have matching pairs of chromosomes to act as a template for repair.
D. Eukaryotes contain more DNA making the consequences of a break less severe.

**39.** Which of the following pairs of nitrogenous bases might form a dimer in DNA when exposed to UV radiation?

A. thymine - thymine
B. thymine - adenine
C. thymine - guanine
D. uracil – uracil

**40.** 5-bromouracil resembles thymine enough to become incorporated into DNA during replication. Once incorporated, however, it rearranges to resemble cytosine. If 5-bromouracil were present during the replication of the sense strand shown below, which of the following might be the sense strand formed in the following replication?

5′-GGCGTACG-3′

A. 5′-GGCGCACG-3′
B. 5′-GGCGATCG-3′
C. 3′-CCGCAGGC-5′
D. 5′-GGCGTGCG-3′

**41.** According to the passage, in the absence of *glycosylases*, a *tautomeric shift* would most likely result in which of the following mutations?

A. a frameshift mutation
B. a base pair insertion
C. a base pair substitution
D. a chromosomal aberration

**42.** According to the information in the passage, which of the following is true concerning mutations?

A. Mutations do not occur in the absence of radiation or chemical mutagens.
B. Industrial countries have a higher basal mutation rate than non-industrial countries.
C. Hypoxanthine is an example of a chemical mutagen.
D. Mutations occurring in rapidly reproducing cells are more likely to become a permanent part of the cell genome.

**GO ON TO THE NEXT PAGE.**

Questions 43 through 46 are **NOT** based on a descriptive passage.

43. DNA replication occurs during:

    A. prophase.
    B. metaphase.
    C. telophase.
    D. interphase.

44. Turner's syndrome occurs due to nondisjunction at the sex chromosome resulting in an individual with one X and no Y chromosome. Color-blindness is a sex-linked recessive trait. A color-blind man marries a healthy woman. They have two children both with Turner's syndrome. One of the children is color-blind. Which of the following is true?

    A. Nondisjunction occurred in the father for both children.
    B. Nondisjunction occurred in the mother for both children.
    C. Nondisjunction occurred in the mother for the color-blind child and in the father for the child with normal vision.
    D. Nondisjunction occurred in the father for the color-blind child and in the mother for the child with normal vision.

45. A primary spermatocyte is:

    A. haploid and contains 23 chromosomes.
    B. haploid and contains 46 chromosomes.
    C. diploid and contains 23 chromosomes.
    D. diploid and contains 46 chromosomes.

46. Crossing over occurs in:

    A. mitosis, prophase.
    B. meiosis, prophase I.
    C. meiosis, prophase II.
    D. interphase.

---

**STOP.** IF YOU FINISH BEFORE TIME IS CALLED, CHECK YOUR WORK. YOU MAY GO BACK TO ANY QUESTION IN THIS TEST BOOKLET.

---

# 30-MINUTE IN-CLASS EXAM FOR LECTURE 3

## Passage I (Questions 47-53)

Disease-causing microbial agents are called pathogens. Microbial growth is affected by temperature, $O_2$, pH, osmotic activity, and radiation. Physical methods of pathogen control include chemical, heat, filtration, ultraviolet radiation, and ionizing radiation. Moist heat is generally more effective than dry heat.

*Sterilization* is the removal or destruction of all living cells, viable spores, viruses, and viroids. Sometimes it is only deemed necessary to kill or inhibit pathogens. This is called disinfection. *Sanitation* reduces the number of microbes to levels considered safe by public health standards.

The *decimal reduction time (D)* or *D value* is the time required to kill 90% of microorganisms or spores in a sample at a specified temperature. Environmental factors may affect *D* values. The subscript on the *D* value indicates the temperature at which it applies. Increasing the temperature decreases the *D* value. The *z* value is the increase in temperature necessary to reduce a *D* value by a factor of 10. Table 1 shows *D* and *z* values for some food-borne pathogens.

| Bacteria | Substrate | D value (°C) in minutes | z value (°C) |
|----------|-----------|-------------------------|--------------|
| *C. botulinum* | Phosphate buffer | $D_{121}$=0.20 | 10 |
| *C. perfringens* | Culture media | $D_{90}$=3-5 | 6-8 |
| *Salmonella* | Chicken a la king | $D_{60}$= 0.40 | 5.0 |
| *S. aureus* | Chicken a la king | $D_{60}$= 5.4 | 5.5 |
| *S. aureus* | Turkey stuffing | $D_{60}$= 15 | 6.8 |
| *S. aureus* | 0.5% NaCl | $D_{60}$=2.0-2.5 | 5.6 |

**Table 1** *D* and *z* values for some food-borne pathogens

Like population growth, population death is exponential. However, as the population reduces to very low levels, the proportion of resistant strains increases slowing the overall rate of death.

The food processing industry relies on *D* and *z* values for guidelines in controlling contamination. For instance, after being canned, food must be heated sufficiently to destroy any endospores of *Clostridium botulinum*, the bacteria responsible for botulism. *C. botulinum* is an obligatory anaerobic, gram positive bacterium found in soil and aquatic sediments. When food containing endospores of *C. botulinum* is stored, the endospores may germinate and produce a deadly neurotoxin. Although the disease is fatal to 1/3 of untreated patients, it can be effectively treated with an injection of antibodies produced by horses.

47. Certain eating utensils are treated with a sanitizer. After 3 minutes the number of microbes is reduced from $6.25 \times 10^{12}$ to $2.5 \times 10^{11}$. According to the passage, 3 minutes more exposure to the sanitizer would reduce the number of microbes to:

   A. $1.0 \times 10^{10}$.
   B. $5.0 \times 10^{10}$.
   C. $6.0 \times 10^{10}$.
   D. $1.9 \times 10^{11}$.

48. From Table 1, the *D* value for *Salmonella* in Chicken a la king at 70°C is:

   A. 0.24 seconds.
   B. 2.4 seconds.
   C. 24 seconds.
   D. 40 minutes.

49. If federal regulations require that canned food be heated at 121°C long enough to reduce a colony of *C. botulinum* in a phosphate buffer from $10^{12}$ bacteria to 1 bacterium, how long must canned food be heated?

   A. 12 seconds
   B. 2.4 minutes
   C. 12 minutes
   D. $2.0 \times 10^{11}$ minutes

50. A nutrient rich agar is seeded with a few bacteria, which quickly become a thriving colony. Which of the following most accurately depicts the exponential portion of the population growth on a logarithmic scale?

   **A.** 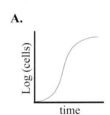 **C.**

   **B.** 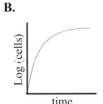 **D.**

**51.** According to the passage, which of the following is true concerning a surface that has been disinfected?

   **A.** No living microorganisms exist on the surface.
   **B.** Some living microbes remain on the surface, but all or most microbes capable of producing disease have been destroyed or reduced.
   **C.** The surface has been cleansed of bacteria, but not necessarily viruses or viroids.
   **D.** All pathogens on the surface are destroyed or removed, while all nonpathogens on the surface remain alive.

**52.** Which of the following statements is best supported by the data in Table 1?

   **A.** A bacterium's resistance to heat is directly related to its $z$ value.
   **B.** *C. botulinum* is more likely to contaminate commercially processed food than *S. aureus*.
   **C.** A bacterium's resistance to heat may vary depending upon its environment.
   **D.** In chicken a la king, *Salmonella* is more resistant to heat than *S. aureus*.

**53.** Which of the following statements does NOT contradict the information in the passage concerning *C. botulinum*?

   **A.** *C. botulinum* thrives in the presence or absence of oxygen.
   **B.** *C. botulinum* has a lipid bilayer outside its peptidoglycan cell wall.
   **C.** A glass containing *C. botulinum* may be disinfected by immersion in boiling water.
   **D.** Animals have no natural defense against the neurotoxin produced by *C. botulinum*.

## Passage II (Questions 54-58)

Even within mature cells, reshuffling of genetic material can take place. The vehicles by which nucleotides move from one position on a chromosome to another, or from one chromosome to another, are collectively termed *transposable genetic elements (TGE)*. TGEs in prokaryotes include *insertion sequence (IS)* elements, and *transposons*.

IS elements are segments of double stranded DNA. Each single strand of DNA in an IS element possesses a nucleotide sequence at one end that is complementary to the reverse sequence of nucleotides at its other end. These end sequences are termed *inverted repeat (IR) sequences*. Between the IR sequences is a *transposase* gene which codes for an enzyme that allows the IS element to integrate into the chromosome. IS elements do not contain entire genes other than the transposase gene. Insertion of an IS element into a gene activates or deactivates that gene, depending upon the location of the insertion and the orientation of the IS element.

The TGEs known as transposons exist mainly as a series of complete genes sandwiched between two opposite oriented IS elements. As well as existing in prokaryotes, transposons are the main type of TGEs found in eukaryotes. They are similar to retroviruses. Both IS elements and transposons are found in bacterial plasmids.

A TGE may move as a complete entity, called *conservative transposition*, or it may move a duplicate copy of itself, called *replicative transposition*.

**54.** One strand of an IS element begins with the nucleotide sequence 5′-ACTGTTAAG-3′. The same strand must end with the nucleotide sequence:

   **A.** 5′-GAATTGTCA-3′
   **B.** 5′-TGACAATTC-3′
   **C.** 5′-CTTAACAGT-3′
   **D.** 5′-ACTGTTAAG-3′

**55.** When the passage states that *transposons* are similar to retroviruses, to what aspect of the life cycle of a retrovirus is the passage most likely referring?

   **A.** reverse transcription of viral RNA
   **B.** proliferation of multiple copies of viral genome leading to the lyses of the host cell
   **C.** capsid formation
   **D.** the procedure by which the viral genome integrates into the host genome

**GO ON TO THE NEXT PAGE.**

56. Which of the following is not typically associated with genetic recombination in prokaryotes?

   A. transduction
   B. TGEs
   C. binary fission
   D. transformation

57. Which of the following mechanisms of genetic recombination between prokaryotes involves plasmids?

   A. transduction
   B. conjugation
   C. meiosis
   D. binary fission

58. Bacterium A is able to live on a histidine deficient medium. Bacterium B is not. After initiating conjugation with bacterium B, Bacterium A is unable to live on a histidine deficient medium. Which of the following statements is most likely true concerning the conjugation?

   A. *Conservative transposition* occurred during conjugation where bacterium A transferred the his+ gene to bacterium B.
   B. *Replicative transposition* occurred during conjugation where bacterium A transferred the his+ gene to bacterium B.
   C. *Conservative transposition* occurred during conjugation where bacterium B transferred the his+ gene to bacterium A.
   D. *Replicative transposition* occurred during conjugation where bacterium B transferred the his+ gene to bacterium A.

**Passage III (Questions 59-65)**

λ phage (pronounced lambda phage) is a double stranded DNA bacteriophage exhibiting both a lytic and a lysogenic lifecycle. The virion injects a single molecule of double stranded DNA containing 40 genes into the host cell. The two ends of the DNA molecule are single strands of DNA that are reverse complements of each other. Once inside the cell, the host cell DNA ligase links the single stranded ends together forming a small circle of DNA. The virus may now enter a lytic phase, or it may insert itself between the galactose and biotin operons. Insertion into the host cell genome requires the viral enzyme *integrase*. Integrase is translated soon after infection of the host cell.

At the same time that integrase is translated, a protein called λ *repressor* is also translated. λ repressor prevents the transcription of all λ phage genes except its own. For as long as the concentration of λ repressor is maintained above a critical limit, the virus remains lysogenic. This can last hundreds of thousands of cell generations.

Damaged DNA activates a cellular protease that degrades λ repressor. When the concentration of λ repressor falls below the critical limit, the gene for *excisionase* is transcribed. Excisionase cuts the viral DNA from the host cell chromosome. The virus then switches from the lysogenic to the lytic pathway which ultimately results in the lysis of the host cell.

59. While integrated into the host cell DNA a λ phage is called a:

   A. virion.
   B. prophage.
   C. chromosome.
   D. plasmid.

60. λ phage most likely integrates into the host cell DNA in the:

   A. host cell nucleus.
   B. host cell mitochondria.
   C. lumen of the host cell endoplasmic reticulum.
   D. cytoplasm of the host cell.

61. Which of the following would most likely lead to lysis of a host cell infected with λ phage in the lysogenic stage?

   A. infection by a second λ phage
   B. binary fission
   C. exposure to ultraviolet radiation
   D. mitosis

62. Which of the following must be true in order for infection with λ phage to take place?

   A. The host cell must be diseased or weakened.
   B. The host cell membrane or wall must contain a specific receptor protein.
   C. Some type of mutagen must be present.
   D. Viral DNA must penetrate the host cell nuclear membrane.

63. Which of the following describes in the correct chronological order the events of an infection with λ phage?

   A. viral DNA is injected into the host cell—viral DNA is translated and replicated—the capsid is formed—the host cell lyses releasing hundreds of viral progeny.
   B. viral DNA is injected into the host cell—viral DNA is transcribed—viral RNA is translated and reverse transcribed—the capsid is formed—the host cell lyses releasing hundreds of viral progeny.
   C. viral DNA is injected into the host cell—viral DNA is transcribed and replicated—the capsid is formed—the host cell lyses releasing hundreds of viral progeny.
   D. viral DNA is injected into the nucleus—viral DNA is transcribed and replicated—the capsid is formed—the host cell lyses releasing hundreds of viral progeny.

64. Which of the following is a likely host cell for a λ phage?
   A. an E. coli bacterium
   B. T-lymphocyte
   C. a paramecium
   D. a neuron

65. Which of the following is never found inside the capsid of a virus?

   A. single stranded RNA only
   B. double stranded RNA only
   C. single stranded DNA only
   D. RNA and DNA

**GO ON TO THE NEXT PAGE.**

66. Bacteria contain all of the following EXCEPT:

    A. membrane bound organelles
    B. double stranded DNA
    C. ribosomes
    D. circular DNA

67. Which of the following statements are true concerning yeast?

    I.    Yeasts are eukaryotic.
    II.   Yeasts are unicellular.
    III.  Yeasts are facultative anaerobes.

    A. I only
    B. I and II only
    C. I and III only
    D. I, II, and III

68. The proteins and glycoproteins which make up the capsid, envelope and spikes of a virus determine the infective properties of that virus. All of the following are true concerning viruses EXCEPT:

    A. Some complex viruses replicate without the synthetic machinery of the host cell.
    B. Animal viruses enter their host via endocytosis.
    C. A bacteriophage sheds its protein coat outside the host cell and injects its nucleic acids through the host cell wall.
    D. A latent bacteriophage consisting only of a DNA fragment is called a prophage.

69. Which of the following is found either in prokaryotes or eukaryotes, but not in both?

    A. a cell wall
    B. ribosomes
    C. RNA
    D. centrioles

---

**STOP.** IF YOU FINISH BEFORE TIME IS CALLED, CHECK YOUR WORK. YOU MAY GO BACK TO ANY QUESTION IN THIS TEST BOOKLET.

---

# 30-MINUTE IN-CLASS EXAM FOR LECTURE 4

## Passage I (Questions 70-76)

Smooth muscle and visceral organs of the body are innervated by the autonomic nervous system, which is controlled mainly by centers within the spinal cord, brain stem, and hypothalamus. The two branches of the autonomic nervous system are the sympathetic and parasympathetic. Most visceral organs are innervated by both branches.

The sympathetic nervous system is composed of motor pathways consisting of two neurons, the preganglionic and the postganglionic. Preganglionic nerve fibers exit the spinal cord between segments T1 and L2. The neuronal cell bodies of the postganglionic neurons are mainly contained in the sympathetic paravertebral chain ganglion located on either side of the spinal cord. One exception to this rule is the nerves innervating the adrenal medulla, which synapse directly onto the *chromaffin cells*. Chromaffin cells are themselves modified postganglionic neurons.

The parasympathetic nervous system is also composed of motor pathways consisting of two neurons; however, the bodies of the postganglionic cells of the parasympathetic system are located on or near the effector organs. Most parasympathetic nerves exit the central nervous system through cranial nerves, the vagus nerve containing 75 percent of all parasympathetic nerve fibers.

The delivery of neurotransmitter to effector organs by the autonomic nervous system is less precise than in neuromuscular junctions of the somatic nervous system.

70. From the information in the passage, it can be presumed that *chromaffin cells* secrete:

    A. cortisol.
    B. epinephrine.
    C. ACTH.
    D. renin.

71. Which of the following is not innervated by the autonomic nervous system?

    A. the arteries of the heart
    B. the iris musculature of the eye
    C. the diaphragm
    D. sweat glands

72. Which of the following cell types most likely contain adrenergic receptors (receptors that respond to epinephrine)?

    A. chromaffin cells
    B. sympathetic postganglionic neurons
    C. parasympathetic postganglionic neurons
    D. cardiac muscle cells

73. Which of the following is not an autonomic response to temperature change?

    A. piloerection
    B. shivering
    C. constriction of cutaneous vessels
    D. sweating

74. Which of the following nervous systems is responsible for the simple reflex arc?

    A. sympathetic
    B. parasympathetic
    C. both sympathetic and parasympathetic
    D. somatic

75. Upon arrival to a high altitude environment, individuals may experience symptoms of nausea and vertigo. These symptoms generally subside after a few days exposure to the environment. The system most likely responsible for acclimatizing the body in this case is:

    A. the somatic nervous system.
    B. the sympathetic nervous system.
    C. the parasympathetic nervous system.
    D. the endocrine system.

76. Amphetamines cause epinephrine to be released from the ends of associated neurons. Which of the following is most likely NOT a symptom of amphetamine usage?

    A. increased heart rate
    B. elevated blood glucose levels
    C. constricted pupils
    D. increased basal metabolism

## Passage II (Questions 77-83)

In a healthy cell, smooth endoplasmic reticulum (ER) performs several functions including carbohydrate metabolism, lipid synthesis, and oxidation of foreign substances such as drugs, pesticides, toxins and pollutants.

The liver maintains a relatively stable level of glucose in the blood via its glycogen stores. An increase of cyclicAMP activates protein kinase A, which leads to the formation of glucose 1-phosphate from glycogen. Glucose 1-phosphate is converted to glucose 6-phosphate, which still cannot diffuse through the cell membrane. Glucose 6-phosphatase, associated with smooth ER, hydrolyzes glucose 6-phosphate to glucose, which is then transported from the cell into the blood stream.

The smooth ER synthesizes several classes of lipids, including triacylglycerols which are stored in the ER lumen, cholesterol and its steroid hormone derivatives, and phospholipids for incorporation into the various membranous cell structures. Phospholipids are synthesized only on the cytosol side of the ER. They are then selectively flipped to the other side by phospholipid translocators.

Most detoxification reactions in the smooth ER involve oxidation. Such reactions usually involve the conversion of hydrophobic compounds into hydrophilic compounds, and are governed by a system of enzymes called *mixed-function oxidases*. Cytochrome P-450, a group of iron-containing integral membrane proteins, is a central component of one mixed-function oxidase system. Mixed-function oxidases also govern the oxidation of steroids and fatty acids. Ingestion of the depressant *phenobarbital* triggers an increase in smooth ER and mixed-function oxidases but not in other ER enzymes.

77. Which of the following tissues would be expected to have especially well developed smooth ER?

   A. skeletal muscle
   B. adrenal cortex
   C. intestinal epithelium
   D. cardiac muscle

78. Where are many of the enzymes necessary for phospholipid synthesis likely to be located?

   A. ER lumen
   B. cytosol
   C. lysosome
   D. Golgi complex

79. Compared to a healthy individual, an individual who ingests large amounts of *phenobarbital* over an extended period of time will most likely:

   A. detoxify dangerous drugs more slowly.
   B. be more able to maintain steady blood glucose levels.
   C. degrade phenobarbital more quickly.
   D. be more responsive to therapeutically useful drugs such as antibiotics.

80. A given type of phospholipid may exist in different concentrations on either side of the same membranous structure. Which of the following enzymes most likely contributes to such an asymmetric arrangement?

   A. glucose 6-phosphatases
   B. phospholipid translocators
   C. cytochrome P-450
   D. protein kinase A

81. The primary structure of *mixed function* oxidases is most likely synthesized at the:

   A. smooth ER.
   B. rough ER.
   C. Golgi apparatus.
   D. cellular membrane.

82. In the final step of the reactions governed by mixed-function oxidases, oxygen is converted to water. In this step, the iron atom in P-450 is most likely:

   A. reduced
   B. oxidized
   C. removed
   D. inverted

83. Some cells, called adipocytes, specialize in the storage of triacylglycerols synthesized by the smooth ER. The primary function of adipocytes is to:

   A. maintain chemical homeostasis of the body.
   B. filter and remove toxins.
   C. provide for cholesterol synthesis.
   D. serve as a reservoir of stored energy.

**GO ON TO THE NEXT PAGE.**

## Passage III (Questions 84-90)

The action potential of cardiac muscle differs from the action potential in skeletal muscle in two important ways. First, depolarization in skeletal muscle is created by the opening of fast Na$^+$ voltage-gated channels; depolarization of cardiac muscle is effected by both fast Na$^+$ voltage-gated channels and slow Ca$^{2+}$–Na$^+$ voltage-gated channels. Fast Na$^+$ voltage-channels exhibit three stages: closed; open; and inactivated. Upon an increase in membrane potential they open for a fraction of a second allowing Na$^+$ ions to rush into the cell, and then immediately become inactivated. Slow Ca$^{2+}$–Na$^+$ voltage-gated channels open more slowly and close more slowly allowing both Na$^+$ and Ca$^{2+}$ to enter the cell. The second major difference between skeletal and cardiac action potentials is that, upon depolarization, the cardiac muscle membrane becomes highly impermeable to K$^+$. As soon as Ca$^{2+}$–Na$^+$ voltage-gated channels are closed, the membrane suddenly becomes very permeable to K$^+$.

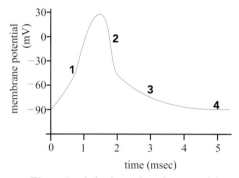

**Figure 1** a skeletal muscle action potential

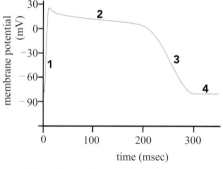

**Figure 2** a cardiac muscle action potential

**84.** Influx of Ca$^{2+}$ ions contribute most to which of the numbered sections from the cardiac action potential in Figure 2?

- **A.** 1
- **B.** 2
- **C.** 3
- **D.** 4

**85.** In Figure 1 the numbered section of the skeletal muscle action potential which best represents depolarization is:

- **A.** 1
- **B.** 2
- **C.** 3
- **D.** 4

**86.** In a lab experiment a student placed a beating frog heart into saline solution. Which of the following is true if the student adds acetylcholine to the same solution?

- **A.** Section number 2 in Figure 2 will lengthen.
- **B.** Section number 4 in Figure 2 will lengthen.
- **C.** Section number 4 in Figure 1 will shorten.
- **D.** Section number 4 in Figure 2 will shorten.

**87.** Which of the following contributes most to section number 3 of the action potential shown in Figure 1?

- **A.** Na$^+$ ions are diffusing into the cell.
- **B.** K$^+$ ions are diffusing into the cell.
- **C.** K$^+$ ions are diffusing out of the cell.
- **D.** Ca$^{2+}$ ions are diffusing out of the cell.

**88.** Between action potentials, a potential difference called the resting potential exists across the neuron cell membrane. All of the following help to establish the resting potential of a neuronal membrane EXCEPT:

- **A.** selective permeability of the cell membrane.
- **B.** the Na$^+$/K$^+$ pump.
- **C.** the Na$^+$ voltage gated channels.
- **D.** the electrochemical gradient of multiple ions.

89. Which of the following cell types most likely contain $Na^+$ voltage gated channels?

    **A.** an epithelial cell from the proximal tubule of a nephron
    **B.** a parietal cell from the lining of the stomach
    **C.** an α-cell from the islet of Langerhans in the pancreas
    **D.** a muscle fiber from the gastrocnemius

90. According to Figure 1, at 2 msec after the action potential begins, $Na^+$ voltage gated channels are most likely:

    **A.** open.
    **B.** closed.
    **C.** inactivated.
    **D.** activated.

---

Questions 91 through 92 are **NOT** based on a descriptive passage.

91. All of the following are true concerning a typical motor neuron EXCEPT:

    **A.** the $K^+$ concentration is greater inside the cell than outside the cell.
    **B.** $K^+$ voltage-gated channels are more sensitive than $Na^+$ voltage-gated channels to a change in membrane potential.
    **C.** $Cl^-$ concentrations contribute to the membrane resting potential.
    **D.** the action potential begins at the axon hillock.

92. In saltatory conduction:

    **A.** an action potential jumps along a myelinated axon from one node of Ranvier to the next.
    **B.** an action potential moves rapidly along the membrane of a Schwann cell, which is wrapped tightly around an axon.
    **C.** an action potential jumps from the synapse of one neuron to the next.
    **D.** ions jump from one node of Ranvier to the next along the axon.

---

**STOP.** IF YOU FINISH BEFORE TIME IS CALLED, CHECK YOUR WORK. YOU MAY GO BACK TO ANY QUESTION IN THIS TEST BOOKLET.

---

**STOP.**

# 30-MINUTE IN-CLASS EXAM FOR LECTURE 5

General hormones which circulate in the blood can be divided into 3 categories. 1) Steroid hormones, synthesized in the smooth endoplasmic reticulum of endocrine glands and secreted from the cell via exocytosis, bind to proteins for transport to their target tissue. They then diffuse through the target cell membrane and normally bind to a large receptor protein in the cytosol, which in turn carries them into the nucleus where they exert their effect directly at the transcriptional level. 2) Peptide hormones bind to membrane bound receptors and act via a second messenger system. 3) Tyrosine derivatives are further divided into thyroid hormones and the *catecholamines*, epinephrine and norepinephrine. Thyroid hormones diffuse through the cell membrane and bind to receptors in the nucleus. They also act directly at the transcription level. The catecholamines act at the cell membrane through a second messenger system.

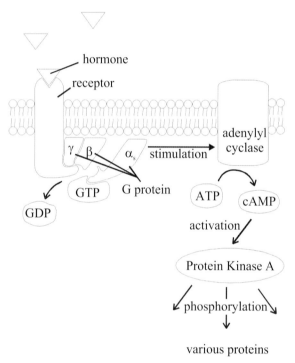

**Figure 1**

One second messenger system, shown in Figure 1, works as follows: the activated membrane bound hormone receptor activates a protein inside the cell, called a *G-protein*. Once activated, the G-protein exchanges GDP for GTP, which causes a portion of the G-protein to dissociate. Depending upon the type of G-protein, the dissociated portion may stimulate or inhibit *adenylyl cyclase*, another membrane bound protein. Inhibitory G-proteins are called $G_i$-proteins; stimulating G-proteins are called $G_s$-proteins. After activating adenylyl cyclase, the dissociated portion of the G-protein must hydrolyze GTP to GDP in order to become inactive and recombine with its other portion. Adenylyl cyclase converts ATP to cyclic AMP. Cyclic AMP activates *protein kinase A*. Kinases are a family of enzymes that catalyze the transfer of $\gamma$-phosphate from ATP to select protein amino acid residues. The biological effects of cyclic AMP are mediated by changes in protein phosphorylation.

In 1957, Earl Sutherland found that liver homogenates incubated with either epinephrine or glucagon would stimulate the activity of glycogen phosphorylase, an enzyme which governs the conversion of glycogen to glucose-1-phosphate. However, if the membranes present in the homogenate were removed by centrifugation, glycogen phosphorylase could no longer be activated by epinephrine or glucagon, but could still be activated by the addition of cyclic AMP.

93. Cortisol most likely binds to a receptor protein:

   A. bound to the cell membrane.
   B. in the cytosol.
   C. on the nuclear membrane.
   D. just outside the cell.

94. Phosphodiesterase breaks down cyclic AMP to AMP. Caffeine, a drug abundant in coffee, suppresses the activity of phosphodiesterase. According to the information in the passage, which of the following would most likely be found in a blood sample of someone who has recently drunk large amounts of coffee?

   A. high ADH levels
   B. low insulin levels
   C. high glucose levels
   D. low glucose levels

95. A certain mutant tumor cell line has normal epinephrine receptors and normal adenylyl cyclase; however, it fails to increase cAMP in the presence of epinephrine. The most likely explanation for this is:

   A. the $G_s$-protein in the cell is either missing or malfunctioning.
   B. the $G_i$-protein in the cell is either missing or malfunctioning.
   C. epinephrine diffuses directly into the cell to act on protein kinase A.
   D. the mutation results in a change in the structure of protein kinase A.

96. Glucagon works via a G-protein system. Which of the following best explains why glucagon stimulates glycogen breakdown in liver cells, but stimulates lipid break down in fat cells?

   A. Fat cells contain a $G_s$-protein while liver cells contain a $G_i$-protein.
   B. Liver cells don't contain *adenylyl cyclase*.
   C. The two cell types contain a different set of proteins phosphorylated by protein kinase A.
   D. Glycogen and lipid breakdown are not governed by cyclic AMP levels.

97. Which of the following was most likely not part of the membrane presence removed by Sutherland during his experiment?

   A. glucagon and epinephrine receptor proteins
   B. adenylyl cyclase
   C. cyclic AMP
   D. G-protein

98. Epinephrine binds to several types of receptors called *adrenergic* receptors. Heart muscle cells contain $\beta_1$-adrenergic receptors, where as the smooth muscle cells of the gut contain many $\alpha_2$-adrenergic receptors. Which of the following is most likely true concerning these two types of receptors?

   A. $\beta_1$-adrenergic receptors activate $G_s$-proteins while $\alpha_2$-adrenergic receptors activate $G_i$-proteins.
   B. $\beta_1$-adrenergic receptors activate $G_i$-proteins while $\alpha_2$-adrenergic receptors activate $G_s$-proteins.
   C. Both $\beta_1$-adrenergic receptors and $\alpha_2$-adrenergic receptors activate $G_i$-proteins.
   D. Both $\beta_1$-adrenergic receptors and $\alpha_2$-adrenergic receptors activate $G_s$-proteins.

99. *Vibrio cholerae*, the bacterium responsible for Cholera, releases an enterotoxin which acts on $G_s$-proteins of the intestinal mucosa inhibiting their GTPase activity. Which of the following is most likely to occur inside an intestinal mucosal cell of an individual infected with cholera?

   A. decreased activation of protein kinase A
   B. increase electrolyte concentration
   C. decreased rate of hormones binding to membrane bound receptors
   D. increased concentration of cyclic AMP

100. Which of the following is the most likely effect of aldosterone?

   A. activation of ion channels via binding to membrane-bound protein channels
   B. increase of cyclic AMP
   C. activation of protein kinase A
   D. increased production of membrane bound protein.

**GO ON TO THE NEXT PAGE.**

## Passage II (Questions 101-106)

Human chorionic gonadotropin (HCG) is secreted by the placenta. It can be detected in maternal plasma or urine within 9 days of conception, which is shortly after the *blastocyst* implants in the uterine wall. Maternal blood levels of HCG increase exponentially for the first 10 to 12 weeks of pregnancy and decline to a stable plateau for the remainder of the pregnancy.

HCG stimulates the *corpus luteum* to secrete estrogens and progesterone until the placenta assumes the synthesis of these steroids. During this time the corpus luteum grows to approximately twice its initial size. After 13 to 17 weeks, the corpus luteum involutes.

HCG acts to stimulate the testes of the male fetus to secrete testosterone. It is this testosterone that accounts for the male sex organs.

HCG acts on a G-protein-coupled receptor on the target cell membrane. LH acts on the same receptor and FSH acts on a very similar receptor. Once activated, the G protein stimulates an increase in cyclicAMP, which activates protein kinase A.

**101.** HCG acts most like which of the following hormones?

    **A.** LH
    **B.** FSH
    **C.** estrogen
    **D.** progesterone

**102.** Which of the following hormones is most responsible for preventing the sloughing off of the uterine wall during pregnancy?

    **A.** FSH
    **B.** HCG
    **C.** estrogen
    **D.** progesterone

**103.** Syncytiotrophoblast cells in the placenta are responsible for manufacture and release of HCG. Which of the following statements most accurately describes this process?

    **A.** HCG is manufactured in the rough ER and modified in the Golgi apparatus before secretion.
    **B.** HCG is manufactured by the smooth ER and diffused into the blood stream.
    **C.** HCG is manufactured in the nucleus and transported via a protein carrier into the blood.
    **D.** HCG is manufactured at the membrane of the syncytiotrophobast and released into the plasma.

**104.** The corpus *luteum* mentioned in the passage is:

    **A.** a permanent functional part of any healthy ovary.
    **B.** the remainder of the follicle which produced the ovum.
    **C.** a gland developed in the fetal ovary during the third trimester of pregnancy.
    **D.** a group of neuronal cells in the hypothalamus.

**105.** Early pregnancy tests use an antibody to bind to a hormone in the urine. Pregnancy is indicated when binding occurs. To which hormone does the antibody most likely bind?

    **A.** progesterone
    **B.** estrogen
    **C.** HCG
    **D.** LH

**106.** Which of the following hormones most likely acts as the substrate molecule for synthesis of cortisol and aldosterone in the fetal adrenal gland?

    **A.** HCG
    **B.** estrogen
    **C.** LH
    **D.** FSH

**Passage III (Questions 107-114)**

Neurons of the hypothalamus secrete gonadotropin-releasing hormone (GnRH), a 10-amino acid peptide which stimulates the anterior pituitary to release the gonadotropins LH and FSH. LH secretion keeps close pace with the pulsatile release of GnRH, whereas FSH changes more gradually in response to long term changes in GnRH levels. Both FSH and LH act by changing intracellular cyclicAMP levels. In women, GnRH secretion occurs monthly guiding the menstrual cycle. In men, GnRH secretion occurs in bursts throughout each day to maintain a relatively steady blood level of the hormone.

Production of spermatozoa occurs in the seminiferous tubules of the testes where a single *Sertoli cell* envelopes and nurtures the developing spermatozoa. FSH stimulates Sertoli cells, which, in turn, secret *inhibin* that acts at the pituitary level to inhibit production of FSH independently of LH. LH stimulates the *Leydig cells* located between the seminiferous tubules to secrete testosterone, which acts on the hypothalamus to inhibit GnRH. Testosterone stimulates spermatogenesis. Both FSH and LH are required for spermatogenesis.

Oogenesis occurs in the ovaries of the female. The oocyte develops surrounded by *theca* and *granulosa cells*. The entire structure is called a follicle. As a follicle develops, granulosa cells secrete a viscous glycoprotein layer, called the *zona pellucida*, which surrounds the oocyte. The granulosa cells remain in contact with the oocyte via thin strands of cytoplasm. Theca cells differentiate from interstitial cells and form a thin layer surrounding the granulosa cells. The follicle does not require FSH to reach this stage. When stimulated by LH, theca cells supply granulosa cells with androgen, which is then converted to estradiol and secreted into the blood along with inhibin. Like testosterone, estradiol inhibits GnRH secretion from the hypothalamus.

107. The follicle in its earliest stages is called a primordial follicle. The primordial follicle most likely contains a:

   A.  haploid, primary oocyte.
   B.  diploid, primary oocyte.
   C.  haploid, secondary oocyte.
   D.  diploid, secondary oocyte.

108. Which of the following two cell types possess the most similar phylogeny (developmental history)?

   A.  theca cells and Sertoli cells
   B.  Leydig cells and granulosa cells
   C.  Leydig cells and theca cells
   D.  granulosa cells and oocytes

109. Androgens are sometimes taken by athletes to improve performance. Which of the following may be a side effect of taking large quantities of androgens?

   A.  infertility due to decreased endogenous testosterone production
   B.  infertility due to decreased secretion of GnRH
   C.  increased fertility due to decreased endogenous testosterone production
   D.  increased fertility due to increased Sertoli cell activity

110. Which of the following hormones would most likely be found in the nucleus of a somatic cell of a pregnant woman?

   A.  GnRH
   B.  FSH
   C.  LH
   D.  testosterone

111. Some post-menopausal women suffer from osteoporosis, a lowering in density of the bones. Administration of estrogens is an effective treatment for this disease. This demonstrates that estrogen most likely inhibits the activity of:

   A.  osteoblasts
   B.  osteoclasts
   C.  osteocytes
   D.  hemopoietic stem cells

112. Which of the following are released into the fallopian tube during ovulation?

   I.   the follicle
   II.  the secondary oocyte
   III. some granulosa cells

   A.  I only
   B.  II only
   C.  II and III only
   D.  I, II, and III

113. Which of the following hormones is most closely associated with ovulation?

   A. estrogen
   B. FSH
   C. LH
   D. GnRH

114. A vaccine that stimulates the body to produce antibodies against a hormone has been suggested as a long term male contraceptive. In order to insure that the vaccine has no adverse effects on androgen production, which hormone should be targeted?

   A. FSH
   B. LH
   C. GnRH
   D. testosterone

---

Question 115 is **NOT** based on a descriptive passage.

115. A competitive inhibitor of TSH binding to TSH receptors on the thyroid would lead to a rise in the blood levels of which of the following:

   A. TSH
   B. Thyroxine
   C. PTH
   D. epinephrine

---

**STOP.** IF YOU FINISH BEFORE TIME IS CALLED, CHECK YOUR WORK. YOU MAY GO BACK TO ANY QUESTION IN THIS TEST BOOKLET.

# 30-MINUTE IN-CLASS EXAM FOR LECTURE 6

Dietary fat is mainly composed of triglycerides and smaller amounts of cholesterol and phospholipids. Lingual lipase secreted in the mouth digests a very small portion of fat while in the mouth and small intestine, but mainly in the stomach. Enterocytes in the small intestine also release tiny amounts of enteric lipase. However, the most important enzyme for the digestion of fats is pancreatic lipase.

Since fats are not soluble in the aqueous solution in the small intestine, fat digestion would be very inefficient were it not for bile salts and lecithin, which increase the surface area upon which lipase can act. In addition, bile forms micelles with the fatty acid and monoglyceride products of enzymatic hydrolysis of triglycerides, and carries these micelles to the brush border of the intestine where they are absorbed by an enterocyte.

Once inside the enterocyte, the fatty acids are taken up by the smooth endoplasmic reticulum and new triglycerides are formed. These triglycerides combine with cholesterol and phospholipids to form new globules called chylomicrons that are secreted through exocytosis to the basolateral side of the enterocyte. From there, the chylomicrons move to the lacteal in the intestinal villus.

Chylomicrons are just one member of the lipoprotein families which transport lipids through the blood. The other members are very low density lipoproteins (VLDL), low density lipoproteins (LDL), and high density lipoproteins (HDL). VLDLs are degraded by lipases to LDL. LDLs account for approximately 60-75% of plasma cholesterol and their levels are directly related to cardiovascular risk. HDLs, on the other hand, account for only 20-25% of plasma cholesterol and HDL plasma levels are inversely related to cardiovascular risk. HDL levels are positively correlated with exercise and moderate alcohol intake and inversely related to smoking, obesity and use of progestin-containing contraceptives.

116. Bile allows lipases to work more efficiently by increasing the surface area of fat. If fat globules are assumed to be spherical, then each time bile decreases the diameter of all the fat globules in the small intestine by a factor of two, the surface area of the fat is increased by a factor of:

    A. 2
    B. 4
    C. 8
    D. 16

117. Most dietary fat first enters the blood stream:

    A. from the right lymphatic duct into arterial circulation.
    B. from the thoracic duct into venous circulation.
    C. from the small intestine into capillary circulation.
    D. from the intestinal enterocyte into the lacteal.

118. Most tests for serum cholesterol levels do not distinguish between HDLs and LDLs. Life insurance rates generally increase with increasing serum cholesterol levels. Which of the following supports the claim that it is important to determine whether HDLs or LDLs are responsible for high serum cholesterol when evaluating a patients risk for coronary heart disease?

    A. The risk from coronary heart disease doubles from an HDL level of 60mg/100ml to 30mg/100ml.
    B. The incidence of coronary heart disease rises in linear fashion with the level of serum cholesterol.
    C. The optimal serum cholesterol for a middle aged man is probably 200mg/100ml or less.
    D. VLDL is the main source of plasma LDL.

119. Lingual lipase most likely functions best at a pH of:

    A. 2
    B. 5
    C. 7
    D. 9

120. Pancreatic enzymes are released from the pancreas in an inactive form called a zymogen. Which of the following activates the zymogen form of pancreatic lipase?

    A. bile salts
    B. trypsin
    C. low pH
    D. high pH

**121.** The process by which bile increases the surface area of dietary fat is called:

    **A.** lipolysis.
    **B.** adipolysis.
    **C.** malabsorption.
    **D.** emulsification.

**122.** A patient that has had his pancreas surgically removed would most likely need to supplement his diet with the following enzymes EXCEPT:

    **A.** lactase.
    **B.** lipase.
    **C.** amylase.
    **D.** proteases.

## Passage II (Questions 123-130)

The rate at which a solute is excreted in the urine is given by the product of the concentration (U) of the solute in the urine and the urine flow rate (V). Dividing this number by the blood plasma concentration (P) of the solute, gives the minimum volume of blood plasma necessary to supply the solute. This number is called the *renal clearance* (C).

$$C = \frac{U \times V}{P}$$

Because almost no solute is completely filtered from the blood in a single pass through the renal corpuscles, the renal clearance does not represent an actual volume of plasma. However, the organic dye, *p*-aminohippuric acid (PAH), is not only filtered but also secreted by the kidney. As a result, 90% of PAH that enters the kidney is excreted. Thus, the clearance of PAH is an approximation of the *renal plasma flow* (RPF) to within 10%.

Due to secretion, resorption, and metabolism in the nephron, the clearance of a solute may not be equal to its rate of filtration by the glomerulus. *Inulin*, a nonmetabolizable polysaccharide, is neither secreted nor resorbed. Thus the clearance of inulin is equal to the glomerular filtration rate (GFR). In a healthy adult, the GFR for both kidneys is approximately 125 ml/min.

The filtration fraction (FF) is the fraction of the plasma that filters through the glomerular membrane. The filtration fraction is given by the equation:

$$FF = \frac{GFR}{RPF}$$

**123.** Which of the following must be true of a solute that has a *renal clearance* greater than the GFR?

    **A.** The solute is being resorbed by the nephron.
    **B.** The solute is being secreted by the nephron.
    **C.** The plasma concentration of the solute must be greater than the plasma concentration of inulin.
    **D.** The solute has exceeded its transport maximum.

GO ON TO THE NEXT PAGE.

124. Since *inulin* is neither secreted nor resorbed, what must also be true about *inulin*, if its clearance is to accurately represent the GFR?

   A. Inulin lowers the renal blood flow.
   B. Inulin raises the filtration rate.
   C. The filtered concentration of inulin is exactly equal to its concentration in the plasma.
   D. 100% of inulin is filtered in a single pass through the kidney.

125. *Inulin* is most likely:

   A. smaller than an amino acid.
   B. the same size as albumin.
   C. the size of a red blood cell.
   D. larger than glucose.

126. Which of the following would LEAST affect the *renal clearance* of a solute?

   A. size and charge
   B. plasma concentration
   C. glomerular hydrostatic pressure
   D. the concentration of PAH

127. Based upon the information in the passage, the renal clearance of glucose in a healthy adult is most likely:

   A. 0 ml/min
   B. 60 ml/min
   C. 125 ml/min
   D. 145 ml/min

128. If a patient has a PAH clearance of 625 ml/min, and an inulin clearance of 125 ml/min, then approximately what percent of plasma is filtered by the patient's kidneys each minute?

   A. 0 %
   B. 0.2 %
   C. 20%
   D. 50 %

129. The blood concentration of creatinine, a naturally occurring metabolite of skeletal muscle, tends to remain constant. Creatinine flows freely into Bowman's capsule, and only negligible amounts of creatinine are secreted or absorbed. A patient with a normal GFR has a urine output of 1 ml/min with a creatinine concentration of 2.5 mg/ml. What is the patient's plasma concentration of creatinine?

   A. 2 mg/100ml
   B. 5 mg/100ml
   C. 2 mg/ml
   D. 5 mg/ml

130. If an individual has a hematocrit of 50%, and a PAH clearance of 650 ml/min, what is his *renal blood flow* (RBF)?

   A. 325 ml/min
   B. 650 ml/min
   C. 1300 ml/min
   D. 2600 ml/min

## Passage III (Questions 131-136)

Like other circulatory systems, renal perfusion is autoregulated. The *juxtaglomerular apparatus* (JGA) assists in regulating the volume and pressure of the renal tubule and the glomerular arterioles. The JGA connects the arterioles of the glomerulus with the distal convoluted tubule of the nephron via specialized smooth muscle cells, called juxtaglomerular cells. Renin, a proteolytic enzyme, is synthesized and stored in these cells. Renin release is stimulated by low plasma sodium, low blood pressure, and sympathetic stimulation via β-adrenergic receptors on the juxtaglomerular cells.

Once released into the blood, renin acts on angiotensinogen, a plasma protein, to form angiotensin I. Angiotensin I, an inactive decapeptide, is cleaved in the lungs to form angiotensin II. Angiotensin II stimulates the release of aldosterone, causes systemic vasoconstriction, enhances neurotransmitter release from sympathetic nerve endings, stimulates ADH release, and acts in the brain to cause thirst. Angiotensin II preferentially constricts the efferent arterioles of the glomerulus.

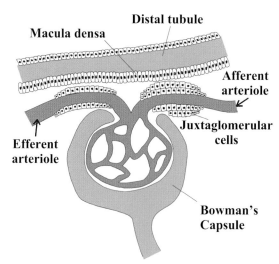

**Figure 1**  A renal corpuscle

Specialized epithelial cells of the distal tubule, called *macula densa*, are contiguous with the juxtaglomerular cells. The presence of low sodium chloride concentration causes the macula densa to signal the juxtaglomerular cells to release renin into the blood, and to lower the resistance of the afferent arterioles. A low resistance in the afferent arterioles increases the glomerular filtration rate.

When functioning properly, the JGA operates to maintain the glomerular filtration rate in the face of large fluctuations in arterial pressure.

131. Amino acids are reabsorbed in the proximal tubule by a secondary active transport mechanism down the concentration gradient of sodium. A high protein diet would most likely lead to:

A. a decrease in glomerular filtration rate and renal blood flow.
B. an increase in glomerular filtration rate and renal blood flow.
C. a decrease in glomerular filtration rate and an increase in renal blood flow.
D. an increase in glomerular filtration rate and a decrease in renal blood flow.

132. Renal artery stenosis (partial blockage of the renal artery) leads to activation of the renin-angiotensin cascade resulting in:

A. high renal blood pressure only.
B. low renal blood pressure only.
C. high systemic blood pressure.
D. low systemic blood pressure.

133. Which of the following is *least* likely to be affected by angiotensin II?

A. the adrenal cortex
B. the thyroid
C. the posterior pituitary
D. the autonomic nervous system

134. The role of renin in the conversion of angiotensinogen to angiotensin I is most likely to:

A. act as a cofactor.
B. bind to angiotensinogen making it soluble in the aqueous solution of the blood.
C. lower the energy of activation of the reaction.
D. add to angiotensinogen in a hydrolytic reaction.

**GO ON TO THE NEXT PAGE.**

135. The renin-angiotensin cascade increases all of the following EXCEPT:

    A. urine volume.
    B. blood pressure.
    C. $Na^+$ reabsorption.
    D. $K^+$ excretion.

136. Angiotensin II most likely:

    A. diffuses into the nucleus of the target cell.
    B. attaches to a receptor on the membrane of the target cell and acts through a second messenger system.
    C. acts on the cells of distal tubule increasing transcription of sodium transport proteins.
    D. creates a chemical reaction in the plasma that increases the permeability of the collecting duct.

---

Questions 137 through 138 are **NOT** based on a descriptive passage.

137. The ability to produce a concentrated urine is primarily based on the presence of functional kidney nephrons. The most important structure involved in concentrating urine within the nephron is the:

    A. glomerulus.
    B. proximal convoluted tubule.
    C. loop of Henle.
    D. Bowman's capsule.

138. Which of the following statements about digestion is NOT true?

    A. Carbohydrate metabolism begins in the mouth.
    B. Most dietary protein is absorbed into the body in the stomach.
    C. The large intestine is a major source of water reabsorption.
    D. The liver produces bile which is stored in the gallbladder.

---

**STOP.** IF YOU FINISH BEFORE TIME IS CALLED, CHECK YOUR WORK. YOU MAY GO BACK TO ANY QUESTION IN THIS TEST BOOKLET.

---

**STOP.**

# 30-MINUTE IN-CLASS EXAM FOR LECTURE 7

## Passage I (Questions 139-145)

The immune system has several methods of selecting and destroying particles that are foreign to the body. One such mechanism works as follows: Large phagocytotic cells called macrophages engulf some antigens and process them internally, ultimately producing antigen fragments that protrude from the outer surface of the membrane of the macrophage. The antigen fragments are held to the membrane by MHC class II molecules. A special type of T-cell, called a *helper T-cell*, recognizes and binds to the MHC class II-antigen complex. The helper T-cell produces protein local mediators called *interleukins* which stimulate the T-cell to divide. A newly formed helper T-cell activates a B-cell capable of producing antibodies that specifically bind to the antigen. The B-cell begins cell division into *plasma cells* and *memory B cells*. Memory B cells resemble unstimulated B cells and do not secrete antibodies. Plasma cells produce antibodies that bind to the antigen. Once bound to the antigen, the antibody may initiate a chemical chain reaction which results in lysis of the antigen carrying cell or, if the antigen is a chemical such as a poison, the antibody may simply inactivate it. In addition, cells with antibodies bound to their surfaces may be engulfed by macrophages or punctured by natural killer cells.

In an effort to discover which cell type creates antibodies, a scientist performed the following experiment. A *nude mouse*, which lacks a thymus and cannot form antibodies, was injected with healthy lymphocytes from the thymus of a donor mouse. The host mouse was then injected with an antigen. Antibodies were produced in the host mouse. Lymphocyte samples were then removed from the spleen of the host mouse and the host cells or the donor cells were selectively destroyed from separate samples. The scientist found that the host cell samples were still able to produce antibodies against the antigen while the donor cell samples were not.

**139.** Which of the following is most likely to create the immune system response mediated by MHC class II molecules?

- **A.** a bacterial infection
- **B.** a cell infected by a virus
- **C.** a tumor
- **D.** a foreign tissue graft

**140.** Which of the following is a cell that a nude mouse would be unable to produce?

- **A.** an antibody
- **B.** a T-cell
- **C.** a B-cell
- **D.** a macrophage

**141.** The experiment demonstrated that:

- **A.** antibodies are produced by T-cells.
- **B.** antibodies are produced by B-cells only after exposure to T-cells.
- **C.** nude mice are unable to produce antibodies.
- **D.** nude mice are unable to produce T-cells.

**142.** *Interleukins* most likely act:

- **A.** via a second messenger by binding to a membrane bound protein receptor.
- **B.** by diffusing through the membrane of the helper T-cell and binding to a receptor in the cytosol.
- **C.** at the transcriptional level by binding directly to nuclear DNA.
- **D.** via the nervous system.

**143.** All of the following arise from the same stem cells in the bone marrow EXCEPT:

- **A.** helper T-cells.
- **B.** B lymphocytes.
- **C.** erythrocytes.
- **D.** osteoblasts.

**144.** Which of the following is a foreign particle capable of provoking an immune response?

- **A.** antigen
- **B.** antibody
- **C.** interleukin
- **D.** histamine

**145.** The function of the *memory B-cell* is most likely to:

- **A.** remain as an immune system reserve against different antigens.
- **B.** attract killer T-cells to the infected area.
- **C.** magnify the immune response by releasing antibodies into the blood stream.
- **D.** allow for rapid production of antibodies in the case of reinfection with the same antigen.

**Passage II (Questions 146-152)**

The function of plasma cells in the immune system is to secrete specific proteins called antibodies, also called immunoglobulins, which bind to antigens and mark them for destruction. One plasma cell can only make antibodies that are specific for a single *epitope* for a single antigen.

Antibodies exist mainly in blood plasma but are also present in tears, milk, saliva, and respiratory and intestinal tract secretions.

Treatment of antibodies with the protease "papain" yields three fragments: two $F_{ab}$ fragments and one $F_c$ fragment. The $F_c$ fragment is nearly identical in all antibodies. *Mercaptoethanol* cleaves disulfide bonds. Treatment of antibodies with mercaptoethanol results in two *light chain* polypeptides (25,000 daltons) and two *heavy chain* polypeptides (50,000 daltons). Both the light and heavy chains possess constant, variable, and hypervariable regions in their amino acid structures. The light chain contains no part of the $F_c$ region.

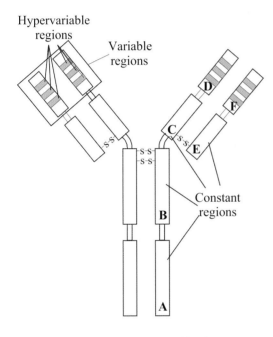

**Figure 1** An antibody

**146.** What level of protein structure is disrupted by mercaptoethanol?

- **A.** primary
- **B.** secondary
- **C.** tertiary only
- **D.** tertiary and quaternary

**147.** Permanent immunity may be imparted to an individual by a vaccine containing:

- **A.** antibodies.
- **B.** antigens.
- **C.** plasma cells.
- **D.** white blood cells.

**148.** The light chain is represented by which of the following labeled segments in Figure 1?

- **A.** A, B, C, and D
- **B.** C, D, E, and F
- **C.** C and D
- **D.** E and F

**149.** Which of the following labeled segments from the antibody in Figure 1 most likely attaches to an antigen?

- **A.** A
- **B.** D and F
- **C.** D but not F
- **D.** C and D

**150.** Which of the following structures in the plasma cell most likely produces antibodies?

- **A.** ribosomes in the cytosol
- **B.** rough endoplasmic reticulum
- **C.** smooth endoplasmic reticulum
- **D.** cellular membrane

**151.** Which of the following statements concerning the immune system is NOT true?

- **A.** Plasma cells which provide immunity against one disease may also provide immunity against a closely related disease.
- **B.** Two antibodies from the same plasma cell must bind to the same antigen type.
- **C.** Plasma cells arise from T lymphocytes.
- **D.** Memory B cells help the immune system to respond to the same antigen more quickly during a secondary immune response.

**152.** Which of the following labeled segments from Figure 1 is part of the $F_c$ region of an antibody?

- **A.** A and B
- **B.** A, B, C, and D
- **C.** A, B, C, and E
- **D.** C, D, E, and F

**GO ON TO THE NEXT PAGE.**

## Passage III (Questions 153-159)

Oxygen in erythrocytes is stored by hemoglobin. In adults, hemoglobin consists of four polypeptide chains, two alpha (α) and two beta (β), each held together by noncovalent interactions. The interior of each folded chain consists almost entirely of nonpolar residues. Each polypeptide chain contains a heme group with a single oxygen binding site. The heme group is a nonpolypeptide unit with an iron atom at its center. The organic portion of the heme, *protoporphyrin*, binds the iron atom at its center with four nitrogen atoms, leaving the iron atom with a +2 or +3 oxidation state and capable of making two more bonds. Carbon monoxide is a byproduct of the break down of the heme group. An isolated heme group binds to CO 25,000 times as strongly as it binds to $O_2$. However, the binding affinity of hemoglobin and myoglobin for CO is only about 200 times as great as for $O_2$.

The oxygen carrier in skeletal muscle tissue is myoglobin. Myoglobin is very similar to hemoglobin, except that it consists of only a single polypeptide chain. Myoglobin does not show a decreased affinity for $O_2$ over a broad range of pH nor in the presence of $CO_2$. Both decreased pH and increased $CO_2$ enhance the release of $O_2$ in hemoglobin. Hemoglobin has a lower affinity for oxygen than does myoglobin, partially due to BPG, a chemical in red blood cells. BPG affects the characteristic sigmoidal oxygen dissociation curve of hemoglobin.

Although the polypeptide chain of myoglobin is identical to the α chain of hemoglobin only at 24 of 141 amino acid positions, the three dimensional shapes of myoglobin and hemoglobin α chains are very similar. Inter-species comparison of the three dimensional shape of hemoglobin reveals this same similarity. A further comparison of the amino acid sequences in the hemoglobin of different species reveals that nine positions are the same in nearly all known species. Several of these invariant residues affect the oxygen binding site.

153. Which of the following most likely acted as the evolutionary selective pressure which led to the decreased affinity of hemoglobin and myoglobin for CO as compared to the isolated heme group?

A. The emergence of industrial societies which significantly increased the level of environmental CO.
B. The products of aerobic respiration.
C. The endogenous production of CO due to the breakdown of heme.
D. Carbonic acid in the blood.

154. Hemoglobin and myoglobin are:

A. similar in their primary and tertiary structure.
B. similar in their quaternary structure but differ in their primary structure.
C. similar in their tertiary structure but differ in their primary structure.
D. similar in their primary structure but differ in their quaternary structure.

155. Which of the following gives the oxygen dissociation curves for hemoglobin H and myoglobin M?

A.

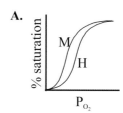

C.

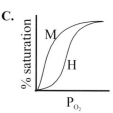

B.

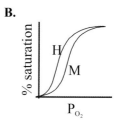

D.

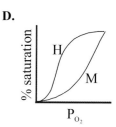

156. Increased concentration of lactic acid due to active skeletal muscle most likely results in which of the following?

    A. increased off-loading of $O_2$ by both hemoglobin and myoglobin

    B. increased off-loading of $O_2$ by hemoglobin but not myoglobin

    C. decreased off-loading of $O_2$ by both hemoglobin and myoglobin

    D. decreased off-loading of $O_2$ by hemoglobin but not myoglobin

157. In a healthy human body, where is BPG likely to have its greatest effect?

    A. in the alveoli
    B. in the capillaries of the lungs
    C. in the muscle cells of the heart
    D. in the capillaries of skeletal muscle

158. The tertiary structure of human myoglobin most likely:

    A. represents a fundamental design for oxygen carriers in nature.
    B. arose relatively late in human evolution.
    C. varies among individuals of the same species.
    D. allows for more than one heme group.

159. Which of the following is LEAST likely to increase the breathing rate of an individual?

    A. increased pH in the blood
    B. low oxygen levels in the blood
    C. increased muscle activity
    D. increased $CO_2$ levels

---

Questions 160 through 161 are **NOT** based on a descriptive passage.

160. Which of the following is NOT true concerning the lymphatic system?

    A. The lymphatic system removes large particles and excess fluid from the interstitial spaces.
    B. The lymphatic system is a closed circulatory system.
    C. The lymphatic system contains lymphocytes that function in the bodies immune system.
    D. Most fatty acids in the diet are absorbed by the lymphatic system before entering the blood stream.

161. Which of the following is a cell that does NOT contain a nucleus?

    A. erythrocyte
    B. platelet
    C. macrophage
    D. B lymphocyte

---

**STOP.** IF YOU FINISH BEFORE TIME IS CALLED, CHECK YOUR WORK. YOU MAY GO BACK TO ANY QUESTION IN THIS TEST BOOKLET.

# 30-MINUTE IN-CLASS EXAM FOR LECTURE 8

**Passage I (Questions 162-169)**

The functional unit of a skeletal muscle cell is the *sarcomere*. The protein polymers actin and myosin lie lengthwise along a sarcomere creating the various regions shown in Figure 1.

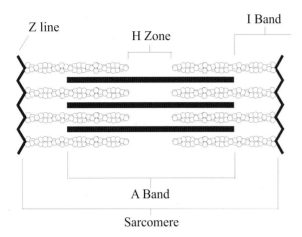

Sarcomere

A group of muscle cells within a muscle may be innervated by a single neuron making up a *motor unit*. The neuron carries an action potential to each muscle cell in the motor unit. The action potential is delivered deep into each muscle cell via tubular invaginations in the sarcolemma or cell membrane called T-tubules. The change in membrane potential is transferred to the sarcoplasmic reticulum, which causes it to become permeable to $Ca^{2+}$ ions and to release its large stores of calcium into the cytosol. Once in the cytosol, the $Ca^{2+}$ ions cause a conformational change in the protein troponin, which in turn acts upon a second protein, tropomyosin, exposing an actin-myosin binding site. Upon binding, the actin and myosin slide past each other shortening the sarcomere and creating a muscular contraction. ATP then binds to myosin releasing it from actin. Myosin immediately hydrolyzes ATP using the energy to return to its ready position. The $Ca^{2+}$ ions are removed from the cytosol by extremely efficient calcium pumps via active transport. Once the $Ca^{2+}$ has been sequestered back into the lumen of the sarcoplasmic reticulum, the $Ca^{2+}$ ions are bound by *calsequestrin*.

Although the direct source of energy for muscle contraction comes from ATP, the ATP concentration in actively contracting muscle remains virtually constant. In addition, it has been shown that inhibitors of glycolysis and cellular respiration have no effect on ATP levels in actively contracting muscle over the short term. Instead, *phosphocreatine* donates its phosphate group to ADP in a reaction catalyzed by *creatine kinase*. Phosphocreatine levels are replenished via ATP from glycolysis and cellular respiration.

For active muscle cells the delivery of oxygen to the cell is far too slow to maintain sufficient energy levels, thus many muscle cells contain large amounts of myoglobin, which along with the cytochromes in the mitochondrial membrane impart a red hue to the muscle.

162. Which of the following proteins is an ATPase?

   A. actin
   B. myosin
   C. phosphocreatine
   D. calsequestrin

163. What is the function of *calsequestrin*?

   A. to lower the free $Ca^{2+}$ ion concentration inside the lumen of the sarcoplasmic reticulum
   B. to raise the free $Ca^{2+}$ ion concentration inside the lumen of the sarcoplasmic reticulum
   C. to make $Ca^{2+}$ for release into the cytosol
   D. to pump $Ca^{2+}$ into the sarcoplasmic reticulum

164. Two types of skeletal muscle are named after their characteristic color, red muscle and white muscle. Which of the following statements is most likely true concerning these muscle types?

   A. Both muscle types contain large amounts of myoglobin and mitochondria.
   B. White muscle contains more mitochondria than red muscle.
   C. White muscle is capable of longer periods of contraction than red muscle.
   D. Red muscle is capable of longer periods of contraction than white muscle.

165. Which of the following concentrations changes the most within the cytosol during the contraction of a muscle cell?

   A. ATP
   B. Myosin
   C. Actin
   D. $Ca^{2+}$

**166.** If a *creatine kinase* inhibitor is administered to an active muscle cell, which of the following would most likely occur?

A. ATP concentrations would diminish while muscle contractions continued.

B. Phosphocreatine concentrations would diminish while muscle contractions continued.

C. ATP concentrations would remain constant while the percent saturation of myoglobin with oxygen would diminish.

D. Cellular respiration and glycolysis would increase to maintain a constant ATP concentration.

**167.** Muscle cell T-tubules function to:

A. create an action potential within a muscle cell.

B. receive the action potential from the presynaptic neuron.

C. deliver the action potential directly to the sarcomere.

D. supply $Ca^{2+}$ to the cytosol during an action potential.

**168.** All of the following are true concerning skeletal muscle cells EXCEPT:

A. skeletal muscle cells contain more than one nucleus.

B. human skeletal muscle cells continue normal cell division via mitosis throughout adult life.

C. skeletal muscle cells contain more than one sarcomere.

D. during muscle contraction, only the H band and the I band change length.

**169.** Which of the following is most likely NOT true concerning the uptake of $Ca^{2+}$ ions from the cytosol during muscle contraction?

A. It requires ATP.

B. The mechanism involves an integral protein of the sarcolemma.

C. It occurs against the concentration gradient of $Ca^{2+}$.

D. It is rapid and efficient.

## Passage II (Questions 170-175)

Connective tissues secrete large molecules that make up their *extracellular matrix*. Specialized cells called fibroblasts play the major role in the formation of the matrix. Three types of molecules characterize a matrix: *proteoglycans*; *structural proteins*; and *adhesive proteins*. Proteoglycans contain hydrated protein and carbohydrate chains, and can be very large. They typically create a gelatinous structure between the cells. Structural proteins add strength and flexibility to the matrix, and the adhesive proteins hold the cells together.

The main component of both bone and cartilage is the matrix. The cellular element of cartilage is called a *chondrocyte*. In their immature form, they secrete the matrix which includes collagen, the most abundant protein in the body. Three polypeptide chains wrap around each other to form the triple helix which gives collagen much of its strength and flexibility. Cartilage is not innervated and has no blood supply.

The human fetus has a cartilaginous endoskeleton which is gradually replaced with bone before and after birth until adulthood. Bone forms within and around the periphery of small cartilaginous replicas of adult bones. Bone forming *osteoblasts* differentiate from *fibroblasts* of the perichondrium. In long bone formation, *periosteum* ossifies around the shaft or *diaphysis* of the bone. Chondrocytes enlarge within the diaphysis and then break down leaving a honeycombed cartilage. Calcium deposits form and vascular connective tissue invades the area. Ossification of the inner portion of the bone proceeds from the center toward each end. *Osteoclasts* differentiate from certain phagocytotic blood cells and begin to burrow through older bone. The osteoblasts line up around the periphery of the newly formed tunnels and deposit concentric layers of bone. Vascular connective tissue and nerves move into these tunnels which are called osteons. In long bones, most *osteons* form along the length of the bone, and the columnar shape of the osteons gives these bones tremendous strength.

**170.** Each concentric layer of bone formed by osteoblasts in an osteon is called a:

A. lacuna.

B. lamella.

C. collagen fibril.

D. diaphysis.

**171.** Osteoblasts which become trapped in small spaces within the bone and mature are called:

A. fibroblasts.

B. chondrocytes.

C. osteoclasts.

D. osteocytes.

GO ON TO THE NEXT PAGE.

172. Which of the following matrix components best describes collagen?

    **A.** structural protein
    **B.** proteoglycan
    **C.** adhesive protein
    **D.** glycosaminoglycan

173. Which of the following hormones most likely stimulates osteoclasts?

    **A.** parathyroid hormone
    **B.** calcitonin
    **C.** epinephrine
    **D.** prostaglandin

174. All of the following statements are true concerning bone EXCEPT:

    **A.** Bone is connective tissue.
    **B.** Bone is innervated and has a blood supply.
    **C.** Yellow bone marrow stores triglycerides as a source of energy for the body.
    **D.** Bone is the only nonliving tissue in the body.

175. Which of the following cells most likely arises from the same stem cell in the bone marrow as an erythrocyte?

    **A.** osteoblast
    **B.** fibroblast
    **C.** osteoclast
    **D.** chondrocyte

**Passage III (Questions 176-182)**

The strength of muscle contraction is directly related to the cross-sectional area of the muscle, with a maximal force of 3 to 4 $kg/cm^3$. The rate at which a muscle can perform work, or the muscle power, varies over time and is given in Table 1.

| Time | Power (kg m/min) |
|---|---|
| First 10 seconds | 7000 |
| Next 1.5 minutes | 4000 |
| Next 30 minutes | 1700 |

**Table 1** Muscle power variance over time

Energy for muscle contraction is derived directly from ATP and ADP. However, a muscle cell's original store of ATP is used up in less than 4 seconds by maximum muscle activity. Three systems work to maintain a nearly constant level of ATP in a muscle cell during muscle activity: *the phosphagen system; the glycogen-lactic acid system*; and the *aerobic system*. *Phosphocreatine* contains a higher energy phosphate bond than even ATP and is used to replenish the ATP stores from ADP and AMP. This is the phosphagen system and it can sustain peak muscular activity for about 10 seconds.

The glycogen-lactic acid system is relied upon for muscular activity lasting beyond 10 seconds but not more than 1.6 minutes. This system produces ATP from glycolysis.

Aerobic metabolism of glucose, fatty acids and amino acids can sustain muscular activity for as long as the supply of nutrients lasts.

The recovery of muscle after exercise involves replacement of oxygen and glycogen. Before exercise, the body contains approximately 2.5 liters of oxygen in the lungs, hemoglobin, myoglobin, and the body fluids. This oxygen is used up in approximately 1 minute of heavy exercise. In a resting adult having just finished 4 minutes of heavy exercise, the oxygen uptake is increased dramatically at first and then levels back down to normal over a 1 hour period. The extra oxygen taken in is called the *oxygen debt*, and is about 11.5 liters. Glycogen stores are replenished in 2 days for individuals on a high carbohydrate diet, but can take several more days for those on a high fat or high protein diet.

176. Based upon the information in Table 1, which of the following are most likely rates of molar production of ATP for the phosphagen system, the glycogen-lactic acid system, and the aerobic system respectively?

A. 1.7 *M*/min, 4 *M*/min, 7 *M*/min
B. 2 *M*/min, 2 *M*/min, 2 *M*/min
C. 4 *M*/min, 3 *M*/min, 2.5 *M*/min
D. 4 *M*/min, 2.5 *M*/min, 1 *M*/min

177. Why is the *oxygen debt* greater than the amount of oxygen stored in the body?

A. Exercise increases the hemoglobin content of the blood so that it can store more oxygen.
B. Heavy breathing after exercise takes in more oxygen.
C. In addition to replenishing the stored oxygen, oxygen is used to reconstitute the phosphagen and lactic acid systems.
D. In addition to replenishing the stored oxygen, oxygen is used to reconstitute the phosphagen, lactic acid system, and aerobic systems.

178. According to the information in the passage, in order for an individual on a high carbohydrate diet to perform at his peak in an athletic event, he should not engage in heavy exercise for at least:

A. 1.6 minutes before the event.
B. 30 minutes before the event.
C. 48 hours before the event.
D. 10 days before the event.

179. Most of the lactic acid produced by muscle activity is reconverted into glucose via the Cori cycle. Which organ plays the major role in the reconstitution of lactic acid to glucose?

A. kidney
B. liver
C. spleen
D. muscle tissue

180. Fast twitch muscle fibers contract with more force than slow twitch muscle fibers. However, slow twitch muscle fibers account for most of the workload in an endurance event. What organelle is most likely more abundant in slow twitch muscle fibers than fast twitch muscle fibers?

A. mitochondria
B. smooth endoplasmic reticulum
C. free floating ribosomes
D. lysosomes

181. In which of the following sports do athletes most likely rely primarily upon the phosphagen system for muscle contraction?

A. tennis
B. boxing
C. diving
D. cross-country skiing

182. Which of the following is depleted first in the body of an athlete performing maximal exercise?

A. phosphocreatine
B. ATP
C. glycogen
D. glucose

**GO ON TO THE NEXT PAGE.**

183. All of the following are true concerning the musculoskeletal system EXCEPT:

    A. Skeletal muscles function by pulling one bone toward another.
    B. Tendons connect muscle to muscle.
    C. Ligaments connect bone to bone.
    D. The biceps works antagonistically to the triceps.

184. Which of the following statements concerning bone is false?

    A. Bone functions as a mineral reservoir for calcium and phosphorous.
    B. Bone contains cells which differentiate into red and white blood cells.
    C. Bone acts as a thermostat for temperature control of the body.
    D. Bone provides a framework by which muscles can move the body.

---

**STOP.** IF YOU FINISH BEFORE TIME IS CALLED, CHECK YOUR WORK. YOU MAY GO BACK TO ANY QUESTION IN THIS TEST BOOKLET.

---

# 30-MINUTE IN-CLASS EXAM FOR LECTURE 9

## Passage I (Questions 185-190)

Two schedules summarize the most important demographic information of a closed population: the *survivorship schedule* and the *fertility schedule*.

The survivorship schedule records the probability that an individual survive to a particular age, and is shown in Figure 1. There are three basic forms of survivorship curves in nature: type I; type II; and type III. Most species in nature exhibit a type III survivorship curve.

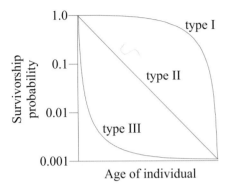

**Figure 1** Survivorship Schedule

The *fertility schedule* records the average number of daughters that will be produced by all the females in the population at each particular age. The *net reproductive rate* is the average number of females produced in the lifetime of a single female. The net reproductive rate can be obtained from the survivorship and fertility schedules as the sum of the yearly products of the probability of survivorship and the average number of females born to a single female during life expectancy.

Any population reproducing in a constant environment (other than species breeding synchronously at a single age) will attain a stable age distribution. In such a population, the proportion of individuals at a given age will remain constant.

**185.** The annual adult mortality of white storks is approximately 21 percent regardless of age. What form of survivorship curve is exhibited by white storks?

A. type I
B. type II
C. type III
D. In order to predict the survivorship curve, the fertility schedule must be known.

**186.** Which of the following could be true concerning a population that has lived in a stable environment for hundreds of years and whose individuals have an average life expectancy of 20 years?

A. The number of individuals that are 13 years old doubles every 100 years.
B. If most of the individuals in the population are over 18 years old, then the population is aging.
C. Most individuals in the population live at least forty years.
D. If 60% of the population is 10 years old, then, in two years, 60% of the population will be 12 years old.

**187.** The net *reproductive rate* is most likely based only on females and not on males because:

A. males reproduce faster than females.
B. females live longer than males.
C. the maximum rate at which a female gives birth is not changed by the number of males in a population.
D. early population scientists designated this as the conventional standard.

**188.** Which form of survivorship curve would most likely be exhibited by a pure *r* strategist?

A. type I
B. type II
C. type III
D. *r* strategists do not exhibit typical survivorship curves.

**189.** Assuming a zero growth rate, the survivorship curve that most closely represents the population of humans in the U.S. during the late 20th century is:

A. type I
B. type II
C. type III
D. The survivorship curve for a zero growth rate population would be flat.

**190.** Which of the following is the LEAST important characteristic for the survival of a species living in a short-lived, unpredictable habitat?

A. large brood size
B. rapid development
C. early reproduction
D. efficient utilization of available resources

## Passage II (Questions 191-196)

*Isogenic* mice are mice that have been inbred until they have nearly identical genotypes. In 1955, Eichwald and Silmser transplanted skin between isogenic mice. *Histocompatibility* is the acceptance of tissue grafts. A Y-linked gene located at the H-Y locus produces the H-Y antigen. Tissue grafts in isogenic mice may be rejected due to the H-Y antigen. In Eichwald and Silmser's experiment, only female mice rejected the skin grafts, and then only from male mice.

In 1984, McLaren bred mice in which the H-Y gene segregated separately from maleness. However, males which lacked the H-Y antigen had a defect in spermatogenesis. Then in 1987, Page mapped a Y-linked gene that coded for a factor important in the development of male genitalia, called the *testis-determining factor (Tdf)*, to a different region on the Y chromosome than that of the H-Y gene.

Not all animals have an X-Y chromosome makeup like that found in mammals. In birds, butterflies, moths, and some fish, the homozygous partner is male, while the heterozygous partner is female.

**191.** In chickens, nonbarred plumage is a sex linked recessive trait. What is the probability that a barred female and a nonbarred male produce a barred chic as their first female offspring?

A. 0
B. 25%
C. 50%
D. 100%

**192.** Which of the following mice do not produce H-Y antibodies?

A. isogenic males of the Eichwald and Silmser experiment
B. isogenic females of the Eichwald and Silmser experiment
C. males of the McLaren experiment that lack the H-Y gene.
D. wild female mice.

**193.** Which of the following is NOT true concerning the H-Y gene and the gene for *Tdf*?

A. They obey the Mendelian Law of Segregation.
B. They obey the Mendelian Law of Independent Assortment.
C. They both code for proteins.
D. They are normally found in males but not in females.

**194.** A human male may inherit all of the following EXCEPT:

A. his mother's mother's X chromosome.
B. his mother's father's X chromosome.
C. his father's father's Y chromosome.
D. his father's mother's X chromosome.

**195.** Colorblindness is a sex linked recessive trait. What are the possible genotypes of the mother of a colorblind female, if the mother's father was not colorblind?

A. homozygous recessive only
B. homozygous dominant only
C. heterozygous only
D. homozygous recessive or heterozygous

**196.** *Isogenic* mice are produced by breeding only siblings for many generations. Which of the following is true concerning the production of a population of isogenic mice?

A. The Hardy-Weinberg law is not violated.
B. It is an example of speciation.
C. Isogenic mice are more likely to have autosomal recessive diseases than are normal mice.
D. Isogenic mice have fewer chromosomes than normal mice.

**GO ON TO THE NEXT PAGE.**

**Passage III (Questions 197-202)**

Gregor Mendel, an Austrian monk, performed the first quantitative studies of inheritance. Using the garden pea, Mendel performed a series of hybridization experiments with lines differing in seven traits. His experiments followed these three basic steps:

1. Pea plants were allowed to self-fertilize for several generations and only plants which faithfully reproduced their original traits in each generation were used.

2. Mendel then cross-fertilized plants having different traits.

3. He allowed the hybrids to self-fertilize for several generations.

These steps had been done before by other scientists with the exception that, this time, Mendel counted and recorded the results.

By chance, each of the traits that Mendel studied followed the Law of Independent Assortment. Each trait also exhibited complete dominance.

197. If the traits that Mendel had studied had not followed the Law of Independent Assortment, how might Mendel's findings have changed?

A. Alleles for the same trait would not have separated independently of each other.
B. Alleles for different traits would not have separated independently of each other.
C. Homologous chromosomes would exhibit alleles coding for different traits at the same loci.
D. Phenotypes of a single trait would resemble both parental phenotypes on the same individual.

198. What was accomplished in step 1 of Mendel's experiment?

A. Pure homozygous populations were created.
B. Pure heterozygous populations were created.
C. Any sick plants were naturally selected against.
D. Recessive alleles were removed from the population.

199. If the red flower trait is dominant and the white flower trait is recessive in garden peas, what is the expected ratio of red flowered plants, pink flowered plants, and white flowered plants when step 3 is performed?

A. 9, 3, 1
B. 3, 0, 1
C. 1, 1, 1
D. 1, 2, 1

200. If the wrinkled pea trait is dominant to the smooth pea trait, which of the following is not possible?

A. The offspring of two pea plants with wrinkled peas has smooth peas.
B. The offspring of two pea plants with smooth peas has wrinkled peas.
C. The offspring of a pea plant with smooth peas and a pea plant with wrinkled peas has smooth peas.
D. The offspring of a pea plant with smooth peas and a pea plant with wrinkled peas has wrinkled peas.

201. Which of the following explains why a cross between a plant with green pea pods and a plant with yellow pea pods results in offspring of plants with either yellow or green pea pods, and does not result in plants with yellowish green pea pods?

A. the Law of Segregation
B. the Law of Independent Assortment
C. the Hardy-Weinberg Principle
D. pleiotropic separation

202. A dihybrid cross is made between individuals with the genotype BbFf. What is the ratio of the following genotypes BBFF, BBff, bbFF, bbff in the progeny?

A. 9, 3, 3, 1
B. 4, 3, 2, 1
C. 1, 3, 3, 1
D. 1, 1, 1, 1

Questions 203 through 207 are **NOT** based on a descriptive passage.

**203.** All of the following habitats would probably favor an r strategist over a *K* strategist EXCEPT:

    **A.** the weedy cover of new clearings in forests.
    **B.** the mud surfaces of new river bars.
    **C.** the bottoms of nutrient-rich rain pools.
    **D.** a cave wall.

**204.** Healthy organisms living in the wild can typically mate and reproduce fertile offspring if they are members of the same:

    **A.** species.
    **B.** genus.
    **C.** family.
    **D.** phylum.

**205.** Colorblindness is a sex-linked recessive trait. If a colorblind man and a woman that is a carrier for the trait have two girls and two boys, what is the probability that at least one of the girls will be colorblind?

    **A.** 0 %
    **B.** 50 %
    **C.** 75 %
    **D.** 100 %

**206.** Sickle cell anemia is an autosomal recessive trait. The ability of homozygous recessives to survive and reproduce is greatly reduced. Which of the following must be true in order for the sickle cell gene to remain in the gene pool indefinitely?

    **A.** Homozygous dominates must have increased fitness over heterozygotes.
    **B.** Heterozygotes and homozygous dominates must have equal fitness.
    **C.** Heterozygotes have increased fitness over homozygous dominates.
    **D.** Heterozygotes must also have decreased fitness.

**207.** All of the following are examples of density dependent factors affecting population growth EXCEPT:

    **A.** competition for resources.
    **B.** catastrophic weather.
    **C.** predation.
    **D.** disease.

**STOP.** IF YOU FINISH BEFORE TIME IS CALLED, CHECK YOUR WORK. YOU MAY GO BACK TO ANY QUESTION IN THIS TEST BOOKLET.

**STOP.**

# ANSWERS & EXPLANATIONS

## FOR

## 30-MINUTE IN-CLASS EXAMINATIONS

# ANSWERS TO THE 30-MINUTE IN-CLASS EXAMS

| Lecture 1 | Lecture 2 | Lecture 3 | Lecture 4 | Lecture 5 | Lecture 6 | Lecture 7 | Lecture 8 | Lecture 9 |
|-----------|-----------|-----------|-----------|-----------|-----------|-----------|-----------|-----------|
| 1. C | 24. C | 47. A | 70. B | 93. B | 116. A | 139. A | 162. B | 185. B |
| 2. A | 25. C | 48. A | 71. C | 94. C | 117. B | 140. B | 163. A | 186. A |
| 3. C | 26. A | 49. B | 72. D | 95. A | 118. A | 141. B | 164. D | 187. C |
| 4. C | 27. C | 50. C | 73. B | 96. C | 119. A | 142. A | 165. D | 188. C |
| 5. A | 28. B | 51. B | 74. D | 97. C | 120. B | 143. D | 166. A | 189. A |
| 6. B | 29. A | 52. C | 75. D | 98. A | 121. D | 144. A | 167. C | 190. D |
| 7. A | 30. D | 53. C | 76. C | 99. D | 122. A | 145. D | 168. B | 191. A |
| 8. A | 31. A | 54. C | 77. B | 100. D | 123. B | 146. D | 169. B | 192. A |
| 9. C | 32. A | 55. D | 78. B | 101. A | 124. C | 147. B | 170. B | 193. B |
| 10. A | 33. D | 56. C | 79. C | 102. D | 125. D | 148. D | 171. D | 194. D |
| 11. A | 34. A | 57. B | 80. B | 103. A | 126. D | 149. B | 172. A | 195. C |
| 12. A | 35. A | 58. A | 81. B | 104. B | 127. A | 150. B | 173. A | 196. C |
| 13. D | 36. A | 59. B | 82. B | 105. C | 128. C | 151. C | 174. D | 197. B |
| 14. B | 37. B | 60. D | 83. D | 106. B | 129. A | 152. A | 175. C | 198. A |
| 15. A | 38. C | 61. C | 84. B | 107. B | 130. C | 153. C | 176. D | 199. B |
| 16. B | 39. A | 62. B | 85. A | 108. C | 131. B | 154. C | 177. C | 200. B |
| 17. B | 40. D | 63. C | 86. B | 109. B | 132. C | 155. C | 178. C | 201. A |
| 18. B | 41. C | 64. A | 87. C | 110. D | 133. B | 156. B | 179. B | 202. D |
| 19. D | 42. D | 65. D | 88. C | 111. B | 134. C | 157. D | 180. A | 203. D |
| 20. C | 43. D | 66. A | 89. D | 112. C | 135. A | 158. A | 181. C | 204. A |
| 21. A | 44. C | 67. D | 90. C | 113. C | 136. B | 159. A | 182. A | 205. C |
| 22. C | 45. D | 68. A | 91. B | 114. A | 137. C | 160. B | 183. B | 206. C |
| 23. C | 46. B | 69. D | 92. A | 115. A | 138. B | 161. A | 184. C | 207. B |

## MCAT BIOLOGICAL SCIENCES

| Raw Score | Estimated Scaled Score |
|-----------|------------------------|
| 22-23 | 15 |
| 20-21 | 14 |
| 19 | 13 |
| 18 | 12 |
| 17 | 11 |
| 15-16 | 10 |
| 14 | 9 |
| 12-13 | 8 |

## MCAT BIOLOGICAL SCIENCES

| Raw Score | Estimated Scaled Score |
|-----------|------------------------|
| 11 | 7 |
| 9-10 | 6 |
| 8 | 5 |
| 6-7 | 4 |
| 5 | 3 |
| 3-4 | 2 |
| 1-2 | 1 |

# EXPLANATIONS TO IN-CLASS EXAM FOR LECTURE 1

## Passage I

1. **C is correct.** Protein disulfide isomerase is an enzyme. The function of any enzyme is to lower the activation energy of both the forward and reverse reactions. Enzymes cannot alter the equilibrium constant of a reaction; they can only increase the rate at which a reaction proceeds towards equilibrium.

2. **A is correct.** The first line of the passage says that folding is dependent upon amino acid sequence, which is the primary structure. The folding pattern itself is the tertiary structure. This question may seem ambiguous, but, especially with the directions "according to the passage", the best answer is A.

3. **C is correct.** Process of elimination is the best technique for this question. To help clarify a question, it is sometimes helpful to restate the question as a statement with "because", and add the answer choices. For example, "Attempts at predicting protein configuration based upon amino acid sequence have been unsuccessful because." Even if A were true, it does not answer the question. B is false because enzymes are catalysts. They do not determine the product; they only increase the rate of the reaction. D is generally false except in rare cases of neutral mutation. C is a direct response to the question and happens to be true.

4. **C is correct.** The folding of a peptide chain is called the tertiary structure of a protein. The passage states that chaperones assist in the "folding process". This is the best answer.

5. **A is correct.** Choice A describes exactly the role of chaperones as explained in the passage. A cell with more chaperones can synthesize proteins more easily, giving it a selective advantage. B is incorrect. Chaperones don't slow the process of protein folding. C is wrong for a number of reasons. For one, the energy for protein synthesis comes from ATP, not heat. For D, chaperones don't affect the rate of polypeptide synthesis; they affect polypeptide folding.

6. **B is correct.** Why does a protein denature in the presence of heat? The hydrogen bonds and other non-covalent interactions in the secondary and tertiary structure are disrupted. Another way to answer this question is to notice that all the bonds are covalent except hydrogen bonds. Although hydrogen bonds are the strongest type of intermolecular bond, they are much weaker than covalent bonds, and will be disrupted before covalent bonds when heat is applied.

7. **A is correct.** This question requires that you know that disulfide bond formation occurs in the synthesis of cystine, not proline, and that you know that an enzyme lowers the activation energy of a reaction. This question is pushing the envelope in how much detail is required by MCAT. In other words, this may be too detailed for MCAT. However, notice that even in this question, the amino acids chosen were ones with which you are likely to be familiar.

## Passage II

8. **A is correct.** This question calls for some speculation. We must assume that carbohydrates do not react with SDS in the same way that proteins do. The passage explains that SDS gives proteins a charge "in approximate proportion to their size." It then says that the rate of movement is related to the molecular weight. The carbohydrates of a glycoprotein increase the mass without reacting to the SDS. Thus, they disrupt the relationship between mass and movement. Process of elimination can help. Acidic proteins are polar, so C can't be correct unless B is also correct. Enzymes include acidic proteins and polar proteins, so D can't be correct unless B and C are correct.

9. **C is correct.** According to the passage, coomassie blue is a dye added to the proteins after they have separated. Thus, it does not affect the results of the experiment. C is the only choice that does not affect the results.

10. **A is correct.** The passage states that SDS separates proteins based upon size only. The native charge is small compared to the SDS. The force on a protein is proportional to the charge, which is proportional to the size. So why wouldn't all proteins move at the same rate? The answer is because large proteins have difficulty fitting through the pores of the gel and thus move more slowly.

11. **A is correct.** The passage explains that SDS gives proteins a charge "in approximate proportion to their size." Only A offers an explanation why this is unnecessary with nucleic acids. C and D are simply false anyway.

12. **A is correct.** Primary structure is the order of amino acids, which is determined by covalent peptide bonds. The question says that SDS cannot disrupt covalent bonds.

13. **D is correct.** Because SDS breaks noncovalent bonds, and mercaptoethanol breaks disulfide bonds, the quaternary structure of a protein is disrupted. Once disrupted, the subunits separate according to their size as explained in the passage.

14. **B is correct.** Since SDS PAGE identifies proteins based upon size, two proteins with similar molecular weight would not be easily distinguished using SDS PAGE. C is true but is not a limitation in identifying the different proteins in a mixture. D is the very reason that SDS is used; to make charge correspond to size.

## Passage III

15. **A is correct.** Aerobic respiration is the oxidation of glucose: glucose + oxygen = carbon dioxide + water. It is also combustion.

16. **B is correct.** Substrate-level phosphorylation is when an energy-rich intermediate transfers its phosphate group to ADP, forming ATP, without requiring oxygen. Oxidative phosphorylation is the production of ATP via the electron transport chain and ATP synthase.

17. **B is correct.** C and D are wrong because glycolysis is independent of oxygen. A has only one pyruvate, no NADH, and isn't balanced.

18. **B is correct.** The passage says that arsenate acts as a substrate for Glyceraldehyde 3-phosphate dehydrogenase. Thus, arsenic would prevent the reaction of glyceraldehyde 3-phosphate to 1,3-bisphosphoglycerate leading to a build up of the former.

19. **D is correct.** D directly explains the word committed. A contradicts the passage. B contradicts the diagram. C is not true and does not answer the question; reactions in chemical pathways do not have to create progressively lower energy molecules.

20. **C is correct.** The passage states that PFK activity is stimulated when cellular energy is low, and inhibited when energy is high. Low cellular energy corresponds to high ADP concentration because ATP has been used. ATP is, itself, an allosteric inhibitor of PFK, and an indicator that cellular energy is high, so D is wrong. (By the way, the concentration of ATP is held relatively constant within a cell, and is usually much higher than the concentration of ADP.) Glucagon is a peptide hormone that doesn't enter the cell, and therefore could not allosterically inhibit PFK, an enzyme of glycolysis, which takes place in the cytosol. Thus, B is wrong. Citrate is a intermediate in the Krebs cycle and actually acts as an allosteric inhibitor of PFK. This makes sense, because if there is an abundance of citrate, then there must be ample energy being produced in the cell. Thus, A is wrong.

21. **A is correct.** Arsenate competes for the active site; this is the definition of competitive inhibition. Arsenate would have to be a product of the glycolytic pathway in order for its action to be considered negative feedback.

## Stand Alones

22. **C is correct.** A is wrong because not all enzymes require cofactors. B is wrong because not all cofactors are organic. D is wrong because cofactors aren't catalysts.

23. **C is correct.** The graph of reaction rate versus substrate concentration for enzymes is shown in Figure 1-8; enzyme activity is saturable.

# EXPLANATIONS TO IN-CLASS EXAM FOR LECTURE 2

## Passage I

24. **C is correct.** According to the passage, the *Pelomyxa* is a eukaryote and does not undergo mitosis. A is not true and not implied in the passage. Fungi lack centrioles and undergo mitosis. B is false. Prokaryotes do not undergo mitosis. They undergo binary fission. D is not true, nor does the passage imply it.

25. **C is correct.** In prophase, the nuclear membrane begins to disintegrate and chromosomes condense. Replication occurs during the S phase so A is wrong. There is no crossing over in mitosis so B is wrong. D is incorrect as well.

26. **A is correct.** The claim that *Pelomyxa* is a primitive eukaryote is based upon its apparently primitive method of nuclear division, and the fact that it has not acquired certain organelles such as mitochondria. Choice A would indicate that *Pelomyxa* underwent mitosis and contained mitochondria at one point and lost the ability and organelles through evolution. This would indicate that *Pelomyxa* was not a primitive eukaryote. B is wrong because it only tells us that Pelomyxa is phylogenetically older than diatoms. C is wrong because it is irrelevant. D is wrong because two species in the same phylum don't necessarily have similar phylogenic age.

27. **C is correct.** Anaphase is the separation of chromosomes. The formation of two daughter nuclei marks telophase. These two phases most closely resemble the separation of chromosomes and formation of the nuclear membrane between chromosomes in dinoflagellates.

28. **B is correct.** The passage states that the symbionts function like mitochondria. Mitochondria provide energy in the form of ATP from the metabolism of nutrients.

## Passage II

29. **A is correct.** Choice A is the only choice that indicates that the poly-A tail is not coded for by DNA but is synthesized separately. It offers a mechanism by which synthesis may take place other than transcription. B seems to indicate that the poly-A tail is transcribed from DNA at the end of the gene. Even if C and D made sense, they would indicate that the poly-A tail was transcribed from a gene.

30. **D is correct.** The question is really asking, "Where does post-transcriptional processing take place?" The obvious answer is in the nucleus. Some (very little) post-transcriptional processing of mRNA does take place within prokaryotes, but snRNPs are not found in prokaryotes. Post-transcriptional processing of rRNA and tRNA commonly takes place in prokaryotes.

31. **A is correct.** Figure 2 is an electron micrograph of R looping. The passage explains that R looping is a technique where DNA and mature RNA are hybridized. Mature RNA has no introns. Therefore, the loops are parts of the DNA that correspond to the removed sections of the RNA; the loops are DNA introns.

32. **A is correct.** The DNA strand that is displaced is the template for the DNA strand shown.

33. **D is correct.** The question says that introns change while the genes that encompass them remain intact. This suggests that the intron plays little or no role in the phenotype. The phenotype is affected by selective pressure. Thus, selective pressure has no apparent mechanism by which to affect introns.

34. **A is correct.** The passage states that the 5′ end is capped forming a 5′-5′ triphosphate linkage. You must understand that the 5′ refers to the carbon number on the ribose. You don't have to know how the carbons are numbered, just that the same carbon on each ribose must be attached to the triphosphate group. This leaves only A or C. C has thymine, so it cannot be RNA. Note: Sometimes, carbon 2 on the first two nucleotides after guanosine has an O-methyl group instead of a hydroxyl group.

## Passage III

35. **A is correct.** The passage says that glycosylases recognize uracil in DNA as a product of deamination of cytosine. After recognizing uracil, the glycosylases change it to cytosine. If DNA naturally contained uracil, glycosylases would have no way to distinguish the good uracil from the uracil that is produced by the deamination of cytosine. B indicates an advantage of having uracil, not a disadvantage. Who knows if C is true or not? If it is, it is knowledge that is beyond that required by the MCAT, and, therefore, cannot be the correct answer. D is a false statement.

36. **A is correct.** Only answer choice A gives a logical reason. The passage says that much DNA damage is not permanent if repaired before replication. The time between S phases (replication) is shorter for rapidly reproducing cells. Cancer cells reproduce rapidly; thus, cancer cells cannot repair the damage as thoroughly as normal cells. B is not true, and we are given no reason to believe that it is. C is not true, and we are given no reason to believe that it is. D is very unlikely; if tumor cells outnumbered normal cells, the patient would have to be dead or near death. Anyway, there is no strong scientific reason that we would know if D is true or not, whereas A is supported by the passage and our knowledge of the cellular life cycle.

37. **B is correct.** The passage states that neoplastic diseases arise from mutations in somatic cells. Thus, they cannot be passed on to offspring. This is not the same thing as saying that susceptibility to neoplastic diseases cannot be inherited. For instance, breast cancer is a neoplastic disease. Susceptibility to breast cancer is inheritable; breast cancer is not.

38. **C is correct.** C is the only choice that answers the question and is true. A and B are false statements; prokaryotes must possess a ligase to connect DNA molecules because they replicate DNA in a very similar fashion to the way eukaryotes replicate; they make Okazaki fragments. Prokaryotic DNA is double stranded. D does not answer the question of why eukaryotes <u>can</u> repair the breaks.

39. **A is correct.** We are looking for two pyrimidines that are both found in DNA. Only A meets this criterion. B and C do not contain two pyrimidines, and D must be RNA.

40. **D is correct.** This is tricky. The sense strand might code for an antisense strand where bromouracil substitutes for T. The next replication, the new antisense strand with bromouracil would code for a guanine at that spot. Thus the new sense strand would be identical to the original except that guanine would replace adenine. (Sense and antisense are ambiguous terms, but their ambiguity is irrelevant to the answer to this question.)

$$\text{original sense strand} = 5'\text{-GGCGTACG-}3'$$
$$\text{new antisense strand in presence of Br} = 3'\text{-CCGCA}\underline{B}\text{GC-}5'$$
$$\text{new sense strand} = 5'\text{-GGCGTGCG-}3'$$

Since there is no answer choice where bromouracil might be present in the second replication, we don't worry about that possibility.

41. **C is correct.** The passage states that a tautomeric shift causes a base pair mismatch. Although this may lead to a deletion upon repair by glycosylases, in their absence, the resulting mutation is a substitution. Choice A requires a deletion or insertion. Choice D is the result of an improper number of chromosomes. There is no mechanism by which a tautomeric shift would result in more or fewer chromosomes.

42. **D is correct.** D is a summary of the last paragraph. Rapidly reproducing cells have less time to repair DNA between replications. A is wrong because there is the basal mutation rate which the rate of mutations in the absence of mutagens. B is wrong because the environmental mutagens simply add to the basal mutation rate, they don't change it. C is wrong because hypoxanthine results from a mutagen; it is not a mutagen itself.

**Stand Alones**

43. **D is correct.** DNA replication takes place during the S stage of interphase. You should memorize the stages of the cell life cycle.

44. **C is correct.** Both children are female because the genotype of Turner's syndrome, as per the question, must be XO. The O came from the parent within whom nondisjunction occurred; the X came from the other parent. The mom only has healthy Xs to pass on, the father has only one colorblind X to pass on. Thus the colorblind child got her X from Dad and her O from Mom, and the healthy child got her X from Mom and her O from Dad.

45. **D is correct.** The primary spermatocyte is the spermatogonium just after DNA replication. Humans never have more than 46 chromosomes. The primary spermatocyte has 92 chromatids but only 46 chromosomes.

46. **B is correct.** Memorize this for the MCAT.

## EXPLANATIONS TO IN-CLASS EXAM FOR LECTURE 3

### Passage I

47. **A is correct.** The passage says that the death rate is exponential. This means that it decreases by the same fraction at even time intervals. In the first three minutes the population dropped to 1/25 of its original size. In the second three minutes it should do this again. $2.5 \times 10^{11}/25 = 1.0 \times 10^{10}$.

48. **A is correct.** The $z$ value for *Salmonella* is 5°C. This means that for each increase of 5°C, the $D$ value is reduced by a factor of 10. Table 1 reports that the $D$ value for *Salmonella* at 60°C is 0.4 minutes or 24 seconds. 70° is 10 degrees more than 60°. 10 degrees is two $z$ values for *Salmonella*. Thus, we divide 24 seconds by 10 twice. We get 0.24 seconds.

49. **B is correct.** In order to go from $10^{12}$ to 1 ($1 = 10^0$), we divide by 10 twelve times. This is 12 $D$ values (a 90% reduction is the same as dividing by 10). One $D$ value is 0.2 minutes, so 12 $D$ values is 2.4 minutes. While answer D may be appealing mathematically, it is logically ridiculous. It is equivalent to 380,500 years. These regulations would be a little stiff.

50. **C is correct.** Exponential growth on a logarithmic scale is a straight line. Get used to reading log scales. They may be on the MCAT.

51. **B is correct.** The passage states that disinfection is the killing or inhibition of pathogens. Pathogens are disease causing microbes (stated in the passage). Disinfection methods (including the controlling methods discussed in the passage) are likely to destroy some nonpathogens as well as pathogens.

52. **C is correct.** The three $D$ values for *S. aureus* vary according to substrate. This supports statement C. A is not true, nor is there sufficient evidence in the table to support it as strongly as C. D is false, and contradicts Table 1. There doesn't appear to be any evidence for B.

53. **C is correct.** *C. botulinum* can be killed by boiling water. However, it takes a long time. Table 1 predicts a $D$ value of 20 minutes for *C. botulinum* at 101°C. A is not true because *C. botulinum* is an obligate anaerobe. B is not true because *C. botulinum* is a gram positive bacterium. D is false because, according to the passage, horses make antibodies to *C. botulinum* toxin.

## Passage II

54. **C is correct.** The passage says that the ends of the strands are reverse compliments of each other. The complement sequence is 5′-TGACAATTC-3′. The reverse of this is 5′-CTTAACAGT-3′.

55. **D is correct.** D is the only choice that is consistent with both viruses and transposons. A, B, and C are all unique to viruses. It should be clear from the passage that transposons are not viruses, they are a form of TGE, which is a vehicle for genetic shuffling.

56. **C is correct.** Binary fission typically produces identical daughter cells. It is not a method of genetic recombination in prokaryotes.

57. **B is correct.** Conjugation is genetic recombination between prokaryotic individuals, which typically involves the F plasmid or some other plasmid. D is not genetic recombination. C does not take place in prokaryotes. A does not typically involve plasmids.

58. **A is correct.** Conjugation is a one way transfer of genetic information from the initiator or F+ to the receiver or F-. The passage says that replicative transposition is when a copy of the gene is transferred. In this case, bacterium A lost the ability to live on histidine lacking medium. Thus the gene must have been completely removed and transferred; conservative transposition.

## Passage III

59. **B is correct.** A virion is the inert form of a virus that exists outside the host cell. A prophage is the name used to describe the virus while it is incorporated into the host cell DNA.

60. **D is correct.** The passage states that λ phage is a bacteriophage. Bacteria don't have nuclei, mitochondria, or endoplasmic reticulum. Their DNA is in the cytoplasm.

61. **C is correct.** You should know that UV light causes DNA damage. The passage states that DNA damage leads to the lytic cycle. A is wrong because the genes of a second λ phage would be repressed by the λ repressor of the first λ phage. B is wrong because the lysogenic stage can last hundreds of thousands of generations. D is wrong because bacteria don't undergo mitosis.

62. **B is correct.** All viruses need a specific protein to bind in order to attach to and infect a host cell. The host cell does not have to be weakened. Mutagens are an entirely separate topic from viral infections. Bacteria don't have nuclei.

63. **C is correct.** A is wrong because DNA is not translated. B is wrong because only some RNA viruses contain reverse transcriptase and lambda phage isn't one of them. D is wrong because bacteria have no nuclei and viruses are never injected into a nucleus.

64. **A is correct.** The passage states that lambda phage is a bacteriophage. This means it attacks bacteria.

65. **D is correct.** No virus has both DNA and RNA.

## Stand Alones

66. **A is correct.** This question should be easy. Bacteria have no complex membrane bound organelles. The MCAT is likely to leave out the 'complex' part.

67. **D is correct.** Yeast is probably the only member of the Fungi kingdom about which you must know anything specific.

68. **A is correct.** All viruses require the host cell in order to replicate.

69. **D is correct.** Only eukaryotes have centrioles. Prokaryotes have peptidoglycan cell walls, and some eukaryotes have cellulose or chitin walls. Of course, both have RNA and ribosomes, so that they can synthesize protein. All living organisms have both DNA and RNA. (Viruses are not living.) By the way, since ribosomes are made from RNA, if you chose B, then C would also have to be true.

## EXPLANATIONS TO IN-CLASS EXAM FOR LECTURE 4

### Passage I

70. **B is correct.** Chromaffin cells are modified postganglionic sympathetic neurons, so they most likely secrete norepinephrine and epinephrine.

71. **C is correct.** The diaphragm is skeletal muscle and is not innervated by the autonomic nervous system. You may be able to eliminate A, B, and D from memory. By the way, sympathetic activity does not innervate skeletal muscle, but its effects increase glycogenolysis in skeletal muscle.

72. **D is correct.** Cardiac cells are innervated by both autonomic nervous systems. Sympathetic neurons release epinephrine onto cardiac muscle cells. A and B would be expected to have similar receptors because chromaffin cells are modified postganglionic sympathetic neurons. All autonomic preganglionic neurons release acetylcholine onto postganglionic neurons.

73. **B is correct.** You should know that A, C, and D are autonomic responses. A and C are autonomic because they have to do with smooth muscle. Sweating is controlled by both the sympathetic and the parasympathetic as well. Shivering is skeletal muscle contraction, which you should know is not controlled by the autonomic nervous system.

74. **D is correct.** The somatic nervous system governs skeletal muscles, which are involved in the simple reflex arc.

75. **D is correct.** The nervous system acts directly and immediately (in seconds or less), while hormones are indirect and require more time.

76. **C is correct.** Epinephrine is a sympathetic neurotransmitter. The sympathetic nervous system dilates the pupils (so you can hunt in the dark [memory aid]).

### Passage II

77. **B is correct.** From the passage, we know that one function of the smooth ER is hormonal synthesis. Thus, B is the best answer.

78. **B is correct.** The passage states that all phospholipid synthesis takes place on the cytosol side of the smooth ER.

79. **C is correct.** The passage states that ingestion of phenobarbital leads to greater production of smooth ER and mixed-function oxidases but not other enzymes. More mixed-function oxidases means more efficiency in degrading phenobarbital. This is why people that take sleeping pills must take increasingly greater doses and are less responsive to antibiotics.

80. **B is correct.** The passage states that phospholipid translocators flip phospholipids from one side of the membrane to the other.

81. **B is correct.** Proteins are synthesized on the rough ER or on ribosomes in the cytosol.

82. **B is correct.** Since oxygen is <u>reduced</u> to water, the iron must be <u>oxidized</u>.

83. **D is correct.** Fat is stored energy.

## Passage III

84. **B is correct.** Although the calcium channels begin opening immediately, they are slow to open and slow to close. The result is the extended plateau of section 2. The sodium channels close very quickly and are the major contributors to depolarization or section 1.

85. **A is correct.** Depolarization is the initial influx of sodium ions.

86. **B is correct.** Acetylcholine is the neurotransmitter used by the parasympathetic nervous system, particularly the vagus nerve innervating the heart. The acetylcholine binds to muscarinic receptors, which stimulate the opening of $K^+$ channels and thus inhibit depolarization. You should know that the time between heartbeats is increased by acetylcholine. Thus, section 4 lengthens.

87. **C is correct.** Near the end of the action potential potassium channels are slow to close while potassium ions exit the cell. Calcium ions are being pumped back into the sarcoplasmic reticulum. Sodium channels are closed.

88. **C is correct.** $Na^+$ voltage gated channels contribute to the action potential but not to the resting potential. They are only open during an action potential. If you removed them, the resting potential would not be affected.

89. **D is correct.** Only cells that experience action potentials contain $Na^+$ voltage gated channels. Muscle cells and neurons are two examples. Since the passage is about action potentials in muscle, this question should be deducible even without this information.

90. **C is correct.** You should know that $Na^+$ channels are shut at the end of section 1 and the beginning of section 2 of the graph in Figure 1. From the passage, you should deduce that they are inactivated not closed.

## Stand Alones

91. **B is correct.** You should know that $Na^+$ channels are more sensitive than $K^+$ channels. That's why they open first.

92. **A is correct.** Choice A describes saltatory conduction.

# EXPLANATIONS TO IN-CLASS EXAM FOR LECTURE 5

## Passage I

93. **B is correct.** Cortisol is a steroid. The passage states, and you should know, that steroids diffuse through the membrane and bind to a receptor in the cytosol, where they are carried to the nucleus.

94. **C is correct.** Caffeine inhibits phosphodiesterase, which leads to an increase in cyclic AMP. This much is derived from the question. Cyclic AMP activates phosphorylase, resulting in breakdown of glycogen to glucose. This is from the last sentence in the passage.

95. **A is correct.** From Figure 1, the only missing link in the chain reaction from hormone to cyclic AMP as explained in the passage is the $G_s$-protein. $G_s$-protein does not activate adenylyl cyclase; it inhibits, so B must be incorrect. C is incorrect as epinephrine binds to plasma membrane receptors. Nowhere in the passage is D discussed; protein kinase A is downstream of the receptor, $G_s$-protein, and adenylyl cyclase.

96. **C is correct.** C describes a mechanism by which the same hormone can stimulate different processes in different cells through increasing cyclic AMP levels. A is wrong because liver cells must contain a $G_s$-protein, since addition of cyclic AMP activates phosphorylase. B is wrong because from the passage we know that liver cells are capable of production of cyclic AMP. D is wrong because the passage says that glucagon works through cyclic AMP levels.

97. **C is correct.** Cyclic AMP is in the cytosol. Look at Figure 1. Cyclic AMP could not be a part of the membrane presence because it is not part of the membrane. It must be the right answer.

98. **A is correct.** Epinephrine is a sympathetic hormone and stimulates the heart while inhibiting smooth muscle of the gut. The answer choices only give the option of a mechanism differing in $G_s$-proteins and $G_i$-proteins. The answer choice must coincide with epinephrine stimulating heart muscle and inhibiting smooth muscle.

99. **D is correct.** Since the Gs-protein can't hydrolyze GTP, it can't turn off. This leads to increased cAMP. A is a bad answer because the passage states that the G-protein must hydrolyze GTP in order to be inactivated. You have no way of knowing about electrolyte concentration so B must be wrong. C is wrong because nothing in the passage mentions any connection between G-proteins and hormone binding to receptors on the outside of the cell.

100. **D is correct.** Aldosterone is a steroid. Its effect is at the level of transcription. It increases protein production.

## Passage II

101. **A is correct.** These two hormones even use the same receptor protein as stated in the passage.

102. **D is correct.** Progesterone prepares the uterus for pregnancy.

103. **A is correct.** The passage states that HCG uses a membrane bound receptor; therefore, HCG is a peptide hormone. It is really a glycoprotein like LH and FSH.

104. **B is correct.** The remaining part of the follicle after it bursts to release the egg is the corpus luteum. The corpus luteum secretes estradiol and progesterone until it degrades into the corpus albicans. You should know this for the MCAT.

105. **C is correct.** Since HCG is produced by the placenta, it is only found when there is a pregnancy. All other hormones normally occur during the menstrual cycle.

106. **B is correct.** Only estrogen is a steroid like all the cortical hormones, so only estrogen could act as a substrate.

## Passage III

107. **B is correct.** Know your mitosis. You should also know that at birth the oocytes are arrested in prophase of meiosis I until puberty.

108. **C is correct.** These two cells arise from the interstitial cells and secret steroids. They are phylogenetically related.

109. **B is correct.** Androgens are male hormones like testosterone. From the passage, testosterone inhibits GnRH. GnRH stimulates FSH and LH which are required for gamete production. Choice A is wrong because, although there would be a decrease in testosterone production, the exogenous production more than makes up for this decrease. Otherwise, there would be no point in taking androgens. C and D are wrong for the reasons that B is correct.

110. **D is correct.** The only steroid choice. Steroids act in the nucleus. Peptides don't enter the cell. Woman produce some testosterone from the adrenal cortex.

111. **B is correct.** Osteoclasts breakdown bone, osteoblasts build bone. This will be covered in Lecture 8.

112. **C is correct.** The follicle bursts on ovulation and remains behind as the corpus luteum. The secondary oocyte and corona radiata are released into the body cavity and swept into the fallopian tubes by fimbriae. The corona radiata consists of the zona pellucida and some granulosa cells.

113. **C is correct.** The LH surge causes ovulation. Yes, this question seems to have more than one answer. Couldn't estrogen also be true? However, read the question closely. It says MOST. LH alone will cause ovulation; estrogen alone will not.

114. **A is correct.** FSH blockage would prevent spermatogenesis by interfering with Sertoli cells and would not interfere with Leydig cells, which produce androgens. The others would affect testosterone production.

## Stand Alones

115. **A is correct.** All hormones work through negative feedback. The negative feedback begins when the effector is overproducing. The effector of TSH is the thyroid. In this case, the effector would be under producing. TSH production would increase to try to correct this.

## EXPLANATIONS TO IN-CLASS EXAM FOR LECTURE 6

### Passage I

116. **A is correct.** The volume of a sphere is $4/3\ \pi r^3$, and the surface area of a sphere is $4\pi r^2$. These equations tell us that while the surface area of a sphere is proportional to the square of the radius, the volume is proportional to the cube of the radius. Since $4/3\ \pi$ and $4\ \pi$ in these equations are just constants, and we do not want to know the exact values of surface area and volume, we can ignore them. For the original fat globule, we will arbitrarily assume its radius = 2; using this radius the volume is 8 while the surface area is 4 (ignoring constants). The problem states that the bile is reducing the diameter (and thus the radius) by a factor of 2. Decreasing the radius by a factor of 2 (new radius = 1) makes the volume = 1, and surface area = 1. Notice that the volume decreased from 8 to 1, while the surface area decreased from 4 to 1. Now you must realize that no fat was lost in this process, so a decrease in volume by a factor of 8 while maintaining the same amount of fat means that the single fat droplet must be divided into 8 smaller fat droplets (each with a volume = 1 and surface area = 1). 8 new fat globules, each with a surface area 4 times as small as the original add up to a total cumulative surface area of 8 (versus the original surface area of 4). The surface area increased by a factor of 2.

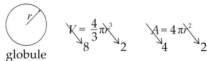

globule

117. **B is correct.** You should narrow this down to A or B from the passage. The thoracic duct delivers lymph to the venous circulation from the lower part of the body and the left arm. This question requires that you know either that the thoracic duct delivers the fat to the blood, or that the lymphatic ducts empty their contents into the veins, not the arteries. This question is on the trivial side for an MCAT question, but it is not impossible that they would ask it.

118. **A is correct.** Only A shows that serum cholesterol level alone might not indicate a health risk to the patient. The HDLs might cause a high serum cholesterol but indicate a healthy patient.

119. **A is correct.** From the passage, lingual lipase works in the stomach.

120. **B is correct.** You should know that trypsin is activated by enterokinase and then activates the other pancreatic enzymes. C and D must be wrong because the duodenum is at a pH of 6.

121. **D is correct.** You should know the word emulsification.

122. **A is correct.** You should know the major pancreatic enzymes, trypsin (works on proteins), chymotrypsin (works on proteins), lipase (works on lipids), and amylase (breaks starch into disaccharides). Disaccharides are broken down by intestinal enzymes. Lactase breaks down lactose, a disaccharide in milk.

### Passage II

This passage offers an opportunity to see some topics that are not required by the MCAT but are likely to be used in a passage. Glomerular filtration rate (GFR) is the rate at which filtrate enters Bowman's capsule. The rate of filtration is affected by: 1) the oncotic pressure difference between the blood and Bowman's capsule (oncotic pressure is osmotic pressure that tends to move fluid back to the blood); 2) the hydrostatic pressure difference between the blood and Bowman's capsule (overpowers the oncotic pressure and moves fluid into Bowman's capsule); and 3) the rate of blood flow (the faster, the greater the GFR). Conventional thinking (MCAT) says that the change in hydrostatic pressure is the regulator of GFR. If we multiply the plasma concentration of solute z ($P_z$) times the GFR, this should tell us the rate at which the solute is excreted. If there is no resorption or secretion, this number should equal the solute concentration in the urine ($U_z$) times the urine volume (V). $GFR \times P_z = U_z \times$

V. If we take into account, secretion, resorption, and change in volume of total filtrate, we can change GFR in the equation to $C_z$: $C_z \times P_z = U_z \times V$. This is the first equation in the passage. Another way to look at clearance is as a type of comparison between the concentration in the urine to the concentration in the plasma. $C_z = (U_z/P_z) \times V$. RBF is the rate at which blood flows through the glomerulae of the kidney. RPF is the rate at which plasma flows through the glomerulae of the kidney. Still another way to look at clearance is as the volume of plasma that must be filtered in order to produce the solute by filtrate alone (i.e. without secretion or resorption).

123. **B is correct.** The GFR is the volume of plasma filtered each minute. The renal clearance of a substance is the minimum volume of plasma needed to be filtered in order to produce that much substance by filtration alone. If clearance is greater than filtration, then the urine must be receiving an additional supply of the substance from some other source. Secretion is the only answer.

124. **C is correct.** To accurately measure GFR you need a substance that is cleared from the plasma solely by glomerular filtration in the absence of any complicating factors that might cause a difference in the concentration of the substance in the filtrate vs. its concentration in the plasma. These substances should not be reabsorbed or secreted by the tubules. It should also not be destroyed, synthesized or stored by the kidneys and pass through the glomerular filtration membrane unhindered. In summary, the substance must not be affected by the nephron (except to be filtered) filtrate should be equal to its concentration in the plasma barring water resorption by the tubules. Choices A and B describe a situation where inulin is affecting the physiology of the kidney, so they must be incorrect. D is incorrect because the passage states that almost no solute is completely filtered in one pass through the renal corpuscles, yet it is possible to measure GFR.

125. **D is correct.** The passage states that inulin is a polysaccharide, so it must be larger than glucose. You should know that a red blood cell is too large to be filtered, so inulin must be smaller. Albumin is just small enough to be filtered but its negative charge prevents filtration. (This knowledge concerning albumin is not required for the MCAT or this question since you know that D must be true of any polysaccharide.)

126. **D is correct.** The renal clearance must be affected by the ability of a substance to filter into Bowman's capsule. This is dependent upon size and charge. The renal clearance is also affected by the filtration rate, which is dependent upon the hydrostatic pressure difference between the glomerulus and Bowman's capsule, and the oncotic pressure difference. PAH is a solute used to measure the plasma flow, and should not significantly affect the clearance of another solute or else its accuracy would be diminished.

127. **A is correct.** You should know that glucose is completely resorbed in the proximal tubule of a healthy adult.

128. **C is correct.** A close reading of the question reveals that it is asking for the filtered fraction. This is equal to GFR/RPF. The clearance of inulin is the GFR, and the clearance of PAH is the RPF. This equals 125/625 = 1/5 = 0.2 = 20%

129. **A is correct.** You must see from the passage that a normal GFR is 125 ml/min. Then you must recognize that creatinine is just like inulin, since neither is absorbed nor secreted. Thus, the clearance of creatinine is equal to the GFR. Now use the equation:

$$\text{GFR} = C = \frac{U \times V}{P}$$

$$\therefore \quad P = \frac{U \times V}{\text{GFR}} = \frac{2.5 \text{ mg/ml} \times \ 1 \text{ ml/min}}{125 \text{ ml/min}}$$

130. **C is correct.** A hematocrit level of 50% means that 50% of the blood by volume is red blood cells and the other 50% is plasma. The renal blood flow, then, is twice the renal plasma flow. The renal plasma flow is equal to the PAH clearance.

## Passage III

131. **B is correct.** Because amino acids and sodium are reabsorbed together in the proximal tubule, less sodium reaches the macula densa cells in the distal tubule. Renin is released, leading to decreased resistance in the afferent arterioles, increased resistance in the efferent arterials, and increased renal blood flow. The increased renal blood flow increases the GFR.

132. **C is correct.** The renin-angiotensin system causes increased systemic blood pressure as per the passage. The renal blood pressure does not increase because blood flow to the kidneys is impeded by the stenosis.

133. **B is correct.** Aldosterone comes from the adrenal cortex; ADH is from the posterior pituitary; and the sympathetic nervous system is part of the autonomic nervous system. The thyroid is not mentioned.

134. **C is correct.** The passage states that renin is an enzyme. An enzyme is a catalyst. A catalyst lowers the energy of activation of a reaction without being permanently altered.

135. **A is correct.** Urine volume is reduced by ADH secretion among other things. Aldosterone causes B, C, and D.

136. **B is correct.** Angiotensin II is a peptide (from the passage). Peptide hormones act via second messenger.

## Stand Alones

137. **C is correct.** Urine is concentrated in the collecting ducts, but the loop of Henle plays the major role in allowing that to happen by establishing a concentration gradient between the collecting duct and the medulla.

138. **B is correct.** The small intestine is the major site for absorption of nutrients.

## EXPLANATIONS TO IN-CLASS EXAM FOR LECTURE 7

### Passage I

139. **A is correct.** Since antibodies are produced, this is an example of humoral immunity. Humoral immunity is directed against an *exogenous antigen* (one found outside the cell) such as fungi, bacteria, viruses, protozoans, and toxins. Cell mediated immunity (T-cells) works against infected cells, cancerous cells, skin grafts, and tissue transplants.

140. **B is correct.** A nude mouse lacks a thymus. T-cells require a thymus for maturation. An antibody is not a cell, so A is wrong. The MCAT may be misleading in this fashion, so read the question closely.

141. **B is correct.** The experiment begins with the premise that nude mice do not produce antibodies or T cells. They do produce B-cells. Since antibodies are produced only after exposure to the donor T cells, either the T-cells or the B-cells are producing antibodies. Since the B-cells continue to produce antibodies after the T cells are removed, B-cells produce antibodies only after exposure to helper T-cells.

142. **A is correct.** Interleukins are protein hormones, so they act through a second messenger system at the membrane surface.

143. **D is correct.** You should know that all blood cells arise from the same stem cells in the bone marrow.

144. **A is correct.** A foreign particle capable of provoking an immune responseis the definition of an antigen. Choices B, C, and D are all molecules being produced by the body (recognized as self) and should not illicit an immune response.

145. **D is correct.** Each B-cell is capable of reproducing only one type of antibody specific to one antigen. When many memory cells are produced, the body will start with many more B-cells that make antibodies against the same antigen, allowing for a faster response in case of a second infection.

### Passage II

146. **D is correct.** Quaternary structure consists of the joining of separate polypeptide chains. From the Figure 1, you should see that the quaternary structure is disrupted when disulfide bonds are broken. You should know that disulfide bonds are also involved in tertiary structure.

147. **B is correct.** If antigens are released within a healthy individual, that individual will make memory B cells for a secondary immune response, often times making the individual immune to infection.

148. **D is correct.** The light chain is the smaller polypeptide. If we break apart the antibody shown in Figure 1 at its disulfide bonds, the passage says that we are left with two heavy and two light chains. Since the light chain contains no part of the $F_c$ region, E and F must mark the light chain. The passage says that the $F_c$ region is constant from antibody to antibody; therefore, it must contain at least, A and B. Since the light chain contains no part of the $F_c$ region, E cannot be in the $F_c$ region.

149. **B is correct.** The variable and hypervariable regions are responsible for antigen binding. Different antibodies have different variable and hypervariable regions that make each antibody specific for particular antigens.

150. **B is correct.** Proteins for secretion are produced at the rough endoplasmic reticulum.

151. **C is correct.** Plasma cells arise from B-cells, not T-cells. A is a true statement. Remember how the vaccine for chickenpox was found through cowpox. This does not contradict the passage. The pathogens or disease carriers may be different but carry similar antigens.

152. **A is correct.** From the passage, the $F_c$ region is constant and not part of the light chain. (See the answer to question 148.)

## Passage III

153. **C is correct.** We want to know why hemoglobin evolved to have less affinity for CO than the heme group has for CO (as explained in the passage). This would only happen if there was some advantage to not binding with CO, and there would only be an advantage if CO were present. So what explains the presence of CO in the cell? Since the passage tells us that the break down of heme produces CO, this is a logical source. Thus **the production of CO by the breakdown of heme, favored the selection of a form of oxygen carrier that had less affinity for CO.** For choice D, there is no simple mechanism that an MCAT test-taker should know that would result in CO from carbonic acid in the blood. Choice A is a far too recent event to account for such broad evolutionary change, and, of course, hemoglobin existed before the Industrial Revolution. For B there is no CO involved.

154. **C is correct.** They differ in their amino acid sequence (primary structure) but have a similar three-dimensional shape (tertiary). Hemoglobin is made from four polypeptides while myoglobin is made from one (quaternary structure).

155. **C is correct.** The passage states that M has a greater affinity for $O_2$. Thus, at a given pressure the M saturation will always be higher. It also states that BPG (in red blood cells) affects the characteristic sigmoidal oxygen dissociation curve for hemoglobin. The M curve should not be sigmoidal because it is not exposed to BPG.

156. **B is correct.** Lactic acid lowers pH. The passage says that only hemoglobin responds to low pH.

157. **D is correct.** The passage states that BPG is found in red blood cells. A and C are not red blood cells, so they must be wrong. As per the passage, BPG affects the characteristic sigmoidal oxygen dissociation curve for hemoglobin. Thus at low pressures of $O_2$ the BPG has the greatest effect. Low levels of $O_2$ would result in the capillaries of skeletal muscle not the lungs.

158. **A is correct.** Since the passage states that the tertiary structure (or three dimensional shape of the polypeptide) does not vary significantly between species it is likely that this shape is fundamental to oxygen transport.

159. **A is correct.** High pH means low $H^+$ concentration and slower breathing so that one doesn't lose too much $CO_2$ (an acid).

## Stand Alones

160. **B is correct.** The lymphatic system is an open system, meaning something goes in one end and out the other. A closed system is like the blood, where fluid doesn't exit or enter the system.

161. **A is correct.** Platelets do not contain a nucleus and they are not cells. Human erythrocytes contain no organelles.

## EXPLANATIONS TO IN-CLASS EXAM FOR LECTURE 8

## Passage I

162. **B is correct.** Myosin hydrolyzes ATP to ADP.

163. **A is correct.** From the passage you know that $Ca^{2+}$ is bound to calsequestrin in the sarcoplasmic reticular lumen. This lowers the concentration inside the lumen, which weakens the gradient that the calcium pumps must work against.

164. **D is correct.** From the passage, we know that the red color comes from myoglobin and cytochromes within the mitochondria. These supply ATP to muscle. Muscle with only small amounts of these, such as white muscle, is capable of only short periods of contraction.

165. **D is correct.** The passage states that ATP levels remain constant. $Ca^{2+}$ concentrations change to create muscle contraction.

166. **A is correct.** From the passage, the function of creatine kinase is to allow phosphocreatine to give or receive a phosphate group to or from ATP. This is what maintains ATP levels during muscle contraction. The passage states that cellular respiration is not fast enough to maintain ATP levels.

167. **C is correct.** T-tubules are invaginations of the sarcolemma which deliver the action potential directly to the sarcoplasmic reticulum along the center of each sarcomere.

168. **B is correct.** This question is a little bit trivial for the MCAT, but is still within the realm of possibility. You should be aware that some cell types in the human body, such as muscle cells and neurons, are so specialized that they have lost the ability to undergo mitosis.

169. **B is correct.** The mechanism involves an integral protein of the sarcoplasmic reticulum not the sarcolemma. The passage says that uptake is active, so it requires ATP and can occur against the concentration gradient of $Ca^{2+}$.

## Passage II

170. **B is correct.** This knowledge may be too trivial to be required on the MCAT. Only one or two questions that require this much detail will be on any given MCAT.

171. **D is correct.** As osteoblasts release matrix materials around themselves, they become enveloped by the matrix and differentiate into osteocytes. This knowledge is required by the MCAT.

172. **A is correct.** The passage mentions strength and flexibility when talking about structural proteins and collagen. This is a hint. The passage also says that collagen is a protein; another hint. You should have some idea that collagen is a structural protein.

173. **A is correct.** Parathyroid increases blood calcium by breaking down bone via stimulation of osteoclasts.

174. **D is correct.** Bone is living tissue containing vascular connective tissue (blood), and nerves.

175. **C is correct.** This question is reading comprehension. The passage says that osteoclasts are differentiated from phagocytotic blood cells. All blood cells differentiate from the same precursor.

## Passage III

176. **D is correct.** These are in the same ratio as the table. Since ATP concentration remains relatively constant within the cell, it makes sense that ATP production rate would mirror muscle power for these systems.

177. **C is correct.** The body must reconstitute the phosphagen system, which requires ATP to make phosphocreatine. Oxygen is required to make ATP. This is the very heavy breathing following exercise. The heavier than normal breathing that follows for approximately 1 hour takes in oxygen to convert most of the lactic acid produced by the glycogen-lactic acid system back into glucose. (This is done principally in the liver.) Choice A is ridiculous because the time frame is to short to make new hemoglobin, and the increase from 2.5 to 11.5 is way too high for the change to be due to hemoglobin. B is not an explanation of why. D is wrong because the oxygen used during aerobic respiration is breathed not stored; the passage states that the aerobic contractions can continue indefinitely or as long as nutrients last. Nutrients are not replenished with oxygen, but with food.

178. **C is correct.** The passage states that glycogen is replenished in 2 days for an individual on a high carbohydrate diet.

179. **B is correct.** The liver makes glucose from lactic acid.

180. **A is correct.** Slow twitch must rely upon aerobic respiration.

181. **C is correct.** Only C is an event that lasts for a period of 10 seconds or less.

182. **A is correct.** ATP levels remain nearly constant. Phosphocreatine is the first thing used to maintain those levels.

## Stand Alones

**183.** **B is correct.** Tendons connect muscle to bone. Muscle pulls on bone not other muscles.

**184.** **C is correct.** Bone does not act as a thermostat for the body.

# EXPLANATIONS TO IN-CLASS EXAM FOR LECTURE 9

## Passage I

**185.** **B is correct.** The best way to answer this is to imagine a simpler example. Imagine 50% died each year. (This is simply the half-life curve. You may already know that a half-life curve is a straight line on a semilog plot.) Now start with a population of 100, record the results for 5 years, and plot them. The amount of adults left alive each year would be: 50, 25, 12.5, 6.25, 3.125. The probability of an individual living to a certain age is simply the number of individuals living to that age divided by total born. This leaves us with 0.5, 0.25, 0.125, 0.0624, and 0.03125. Plotting this on the graph in Figure 1 gives:

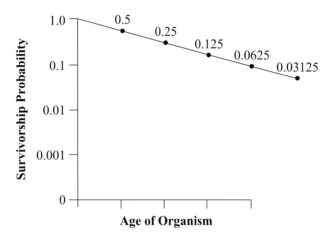

**186.** **A is correct.** As the answer explanation explains, the last paragraph is key; according to the last paragraph, the population in a constant environment attains a stable age distribution (a bell curve) where the proportion of individuals at a particular age remains constant (achieves a steady state). This does not mean that the population is not growing or shrinking; only that the relative number of each age group remains constant. The only way for a particular age class to maintain itself with respect to other age groups is for the birth and death rate to be equal. Choice B does not describe this; instead it describes a situation where the birth rate has plummeted and the population ages due to no great influx of newborns. Remember that the last paragraph said that the proportion of individuals at a particular age remains constant; that means that if 60% of the population is 10 years old now, then 60% of the population should be 10 years old two years from now. Choice D violates this because choice D assigns the same proportion of individuals changing in a two year span of time. Choice C is wrong because if more than half the individuals live to age 40, the average life expectancy must be over 20. A is true only if individuals of all different ages increases proportionally over the same time, and thus could be true, as the question asks.

**187.** **C is correct.** Imagine one female human. In 90 months she could not have more than 10 babies regardless of how many males were in the population. Now imagine one male human. In 90 months, the number of babies he could produce depends only upon the number of females.

**188.** **C is correct.** Remember that an *r* strategist has many babies to ensure the survival of only a few. Thus, many die early on, and type III is the most likely curve.

**189.** **A is correct.** The population growth rate doesn't change the survivorship curve. Humans in the U.S. are expected to live long lives with an increasing expectancy of death later in life.

**190.** **D is correct.** A short-lived, unpredictable habitat is best suited for an *r* strategist. D describes a *K* strategist.

## Passage II

191. **A is correct.** The passage states that male birds are the homozygous partner in the sex chromosomes meaning that they are XX. Thus:

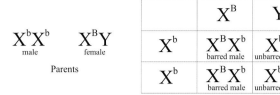

$$X^b X^b \quad X^B Y$$
male     female

Parents

|  | $X^B$ | Y |
|---|---|---|
| $X^b$ | $X^B X^b$ barred male | $X^b Y$ unbarred female |
| $X^b$ | $X^B X^b$ barred male | $X^b Y$ unbarred female |

192. **A is correct.** Those that produce the H-Y antigen will not make the H-Y antibodies. These are the same individuals that have the H-Y gene.

193. **B is correct.** The law of independent assortment does not work for genes on the same chromosome. It says that alleles will separate independently (in a random fashion) during meiosis. The law of segregation says that homologous chromosomes will segregate during meiosis.

194. **D is correct.** D cannot happen because the father cannot pass an X to his son. The Y must come from the father.

195. **C is correct.** If the mother's father was not colorblind, then he gave her one dominant X. If the girl is colorblind, then she inherited a recessive X from her mom. Thus the mother is heterozygous.

196. **C is correct.** Since siblings are more likely to have recessive alleles at the same locus, recessive diseases are more likely.

## Passage III

197. **B is correct.** The Law of Independent Assortment states that alleles for different traits will sort independently of each other. This is only true if the traits exist on separate chromosomes.

198. **A is correct.** Any heterozygotes would have produced both phenotypes when self fertilized. Bb x Bb. When they produced the phenotype opposite to their own, they were removed from the population. Eventually, only homozygotes remained.

199. **B is correct.** This is the Mendelian ratio. BB x bb

200. **B is correct.** bb x bb cannot produce anything but bb. A wrinkle phenotype might be Bb or BB.

201. **A is correct.** The law of segregation states that homozygous alleles segregate independently and do not blend, but show complete dominance.

202. **D is correct.** You can do a Punnett square to figure this out, but why would one genotype be more likely than another? By the way, the phenotypic ratio is 9, 3, 3, 1.

**Stand Alones**

203. **D is correct.** We are looking for a habitat that does not change very often. One in which a species would have to make efficient use of the resources in order to survive. *r* strategists reproduce quickly to take advantage of rapidly changing, short-lived habitats. In longer lived habitats, *K* strategists gain the advantage. The first three answer choices are short-lived habitats.

204. **A is correct.** Members of the same wild species can <u>typically</u> reproduce fertile offspring. There are many exceptions to this rule, but the MCAT tests for the rules, not the exceptions. A wolf and a dog are different species. They can breed and produce fertile offspring. There are cabbage, fish, tobacco plants, and millions of other examples. The rule is "separate species don't <u>normally</u> reproduce fertile offspring in the wild due to a variety of factors."

205. **C is correct.** There is a 50% probability that each girl will be colorblind. This means that there is a 25% probability that both will be colorblind and 25% that neither will be colorblind, leaving 50% that either one or the other might. The boys are irrelevant. We want all situations where at least one is colorblind. 50 + 25 = 75.

206. **C is correct.** If the gene is actively selected against in one form, it must be actively selected for in another form or it will be eliminated from the population.

207. **B is correct.** Density independent factors alter birth, death, or migration rates without having the effects influenced by population density. A storm destroying one half of an island affects all species in the same proportions regardless of density. This is density independent.

# ANSWERS & EXPLANATIONS

## FOR

## QUESTIONS IN THE LECTURES

# ANSWERS TO LECTURE QUESTIONS

| Lecture 1 | Lecture 2 | Lecture 3 | Lecture 4 | Lecture 5 | Lecture 6 | Lecture 7 | Lecture 8 | Lecture 9 |
|-----------|-----------|-----------|-----------|-----------|-----------|-----------|-----------|-----------|
| 1. B | 25. C | 49. A | 73. D | 97. D | 121. C | 145. D | 169. D | 193. B |
| 2. B | 26. C | 50. D | 74. B | 98. C | 122. D | 146. C | 170. C | 194. A |
| 3. A | 27. D | 51. D | 75. A | 99. B | 123. D | 147. A | 171. C | 195. C |
| 4. B | 28. C | 52. A | 76. A | 100. C | 124. A | 148. A | 172. D | 196. B |
| 5. C | 29. A | 53. D | 77. B | 101. D | 125. A | 149. D | 173. B | 197. A |
| 6. D | 30. D | 54. A | 78. D | 102. B | 126. D | 150. A | 174. C | 198. B |
| 7. C | 31. B | 55. D | 79. A | 103. B | 127. A | 151. A | 175. A | 199. D |
| 8. A | 32. D | 56. C | 80. A | 104. B | 128. C | 152. D | 176. D | 200. C |
| 9. B | 33. B | 57. D | 81. B | 105. C | 129. B | 153. B | 177. B | 201. B |
| 10. C | 34. C | 58. C | 82. D | 106. C | 130. D | 154. C | 178. C | 202. C |
| 11. C | 35. D | 59. B | 83. A | 107. D | 131. D | 155. A | 179. A | 203. D |
| 12. C | 36. C | 60. B | 84. D | 108. A | 132. A | 156. B | 180. C | 204. C |
| 13. B | 37. D | 61. D | 85. A | 109. D | 133. B | 157. C | 181. A | 205. C |
| 14. A | 38. B | 62. B | 86. B | 110. A | 134. B | 158. B | 182. D | 206. A |
| 15. D | 39. B | 63. C | 87. C | 111. C | 135. B | 159. A | 183. C | 207. D |
| 16. C | 40. D | 64. B | 88. B | 112. D | 136. A | 160. D | 184. A | 208. D |
| 17. D | 41. B | 65. D | 89. B | 113. C | 137. C | 161. C | 185. C | 209. B |
| 18. B | 42. B | 66. D | 90. A | 114. A | 138. D | 162. B | 186. A | 210. C |
| 19. B | 43. A | 67. D | 91. A | 115. A | 139. B | 163. D | 187. C | 211. D |
| 20. C | 44. A | 68. B | 92. C | 116. C | 140. D | 164. D | 188. A | 212. C |
| 21. C | 45. D | 69. A | 93. D | 117. D | 141. C | 165. D | 189. C | 213. B |
| 22. D | 46. C | 70. C | 94. A | 118. C | 142. B | 166. A | 190. A | 214. C |
| 23. B | 47. C | 71. B | 95. C | 119. C | 143. B | 167. D | 191. B | 215. C |
| 24. C | 48. B | 72. B | 96. A | 120. D | 144. A | 168. C | 192. B | 216. B |

# EXPLANATIONS TO QUESTIONS IN LECTURE 1

1.    **B is correct.** Answers A and C are anabolic reactions. Hydrolysis is used to break down triglycerides, proteins, carbohydrates, and is involved in nucleotide catabolism.

2.    **B is correct.** DNA is a nucleotide polymer. A nucleotide is a ribose sugar, a phosphate group, and a nitrogenous base. The nucleotides in DNA are held together by phosphodiester bonds.

3.    **A is correct.** Plants store carbohydrates as starch. Animals store carbohydrates as glycogen. Glucose is not a polymer. Cellulose is found in plant cell walls and is not digestible by humans.

4.    **B is correct.** This question simply requires that you recognize that protein is the only major nutrient containing nitrogen.

5.    **C is correct.** The bending of the polypeptide chain is the tertiary structure of a protein.

6.    **D is correct.** Fats are a more efficient form of energy storage than carbohydrates and proteins. The phospholipid bilayer membrane is a fatty component of cell structure. Fats such as prostaglandins behave as hormones.

7.    **C is correct.** DNA is double stranded with A, C, G, and T, while RNA is single stranded with uracil (U) replacing T. The 'D' in DNA stands for deoxy-, meaning that DNA lacks a hydroxyl group possessed by RNA at its second pentose carbon atom.

8.    **A is correct.** Both alpha and beta linkages in polysaccharides are hydrolyzed by adding water. The question asks for a reactant; choices C and D are enzyme catalysts which are never reactants.

9.    **B is correct.** Enzymes function by binding the substrates on their surfaces in the correct orientation to lower the energy of activation. The change in free energy for the reaction, $\Delta G$, is the difference in energy between reactant and products and is not changed by enzymes.

10.   **C is correct.** Decreasing the temperature always decreases the rate of any reaction. Lowering the concentration of a substrate will only lower the rate of an enzymatic reaction if the enzyme is not saturated. Adding a noncompetitive inhibitor will definitely lower the rate of a reaction because it lowers $V_{max}$. Changing the pH will increase or decrease the rate of an enzymatic reaction depending upon the optimal pH.

11.   **C is correct.** A high temperature would denature the enzyme.

12.   **C is correct.** Feedback inhibition works by inhibiting enzyme activity and preventing the build up and waste of excess nutrients. Nonenzymatic feedback mechanisms also exist, like the action potential in the neuron.

13.   **B is correct.** Noncompetitive inhibition changes the configuration of the enzyme.

14.   **A is correct.** The implanted, fertilized embryo produces human chorionic gonadotropin, which stimulates the corpus luteum to continue producing progesterone in a positive feedback mechanism; feedback enhancement is made up.

15.   **D is correct.** Peptidases that function in the stomach work at a low pH. Once chyme enters the small intestine, it encounters an alkaline environment, meaning high pH or low hydrogen ion concentration.

16.   **C is correct.** A competitive inhibitor may be overcome by increasing the concentration of substrate.

17.   **D is correct.** Oxygen accepts the electrons (along with protons) to form water.

18.   **B is correct.** The Krebs cycle occurs within the mitochondrial matrix in all eukaryotic cells.

19.   **B is correct.** As electrons flow, the carriers pass along one or two electrons, and are reduced (gain electrons) then oxidized (lose electrons) until the last carrier donates electrons to oxygen.

20. **C is correct.** The electrons from NADH drive protons outward across the inner mitochondrial membrane.

21. **C is correct.** Glycolysis occurs in aerobic and anaerobic respiration.

22. **D is correct.** ATP is a product. Two ATPs enter the reaction to "prime the pump", and four ATPs are produced. Glucose is a reactant and pyruvate is a product. Oxygen plays no role in glycolysis.

23. **B is correct.** The process of fermentation includes glycolysis, which produces two ATPs.

24. **C is correct.** This answer can most easily be found by process of elimination. Choice A is incorrect because ATP synthase is on the *inner* mitochondrial membrane. Choice B and D are poor answers because they mention the specific processes, Glycolysis and Krebs cycle, with which you should be familiar. A change in these processes would indicate a completely different process. Choice C, on the other hand, refers to membrane transport in a more general way allowing for the possibility that a specific mechanism of transport may differ in heart and liver cells.

## EXPLANATIONS TO QUESTIONS IN LECTURE 2

25. **C is correct.** Since A always binds with T and G always binds with C, both the ratio of A/T and the ratio of G/C equal one.

26. **C is correct.** The introns (intervening sequences) are removed during posttranscriptional modification.

27. **D is correct.** This question requires no knowledge of PCR. It requires only that you know that a DNA polymerase replicates from 5′ to 3′, and that you know the complementary bases. (Complementary bases will be covered in this the next section of this lecture. Since DNA is replicated from 5′ to 3′, the primer must be the complement of the 3′ end of the DNA fragment. In other words, the DNA polymerase can only read from 3′ to 5′, so it must start at the 3′ end of the DNA fragment. The complement of the 3′ end of the DNA fragment is answer choice D. (By the way, the primer does not have to start exactly at the end of a DNA fragment in PCR, and a primer is longer than 3 nucleotides.)

28. **C is correct.** DNA replication is semiconservative, which means that both strands are replicated, and each old strand is combined with a new strand.

29. **A is correct.** Introns are removed from the primary trancript during posttranscriptional processing. The number of nucleotides in the mature mRNA would have to be less than the number of base pairs of the gene.

30. **D is correct.** Note that the question asks about complementary strands, which are the two strands in a double strand of DNA.

31. **B is correct.** You should know that mRNA leaves the nucleus in its finished form and that the process of RNA production is called transcription.

32. **D is correct.** Electrophoresis uses an electrolytic cell with a positively charged anode and negatively charged cathode. The phosphate group of the DNA fragment gives it a negative charge that is attracted to the positively charged anode.

33. **B is correct.** The start codon is AUG. mRNA is translated 5′→3′. (Note: You did not need to know that to answer this question correctly.) We are looking for AUG 5′→3′. Only A, B and C have an AUG sequence. However, if there are three codons in C, they must be: AAU, GCG, and GAC. The three in A must be: GAU, GCC, and GGA.

34. **C is correct.** Translation does not take place within the nucleus.

35. **D is correct.** There are $4^3$ possible different codons. There are more codons than amino acids (used in proteins). This means that any amino acid could have several codons. The genetic code is evolutionarily very old, and almost universal. Only a few species use a slightly different genetic code.

36. **C is correct.** The ribosome is made in the nucleolus from rRNA and protein. It does not have a membrane.

37. **D is correct.** The complementary sequence to 5'-AUG-3' is 5'-CAU-3'. Only D contains this sequence in any order. Remember, thymine is only found in DNA, not RNA, so B and C must be wrong.

38. **B is correct.** Only choice B is both true and concerns translation. Ribosomes contain two subunits for both eukaryotes and prokaryotes, so choice A is incorrect. Prokaryotes do contain ribosomes, so choice C is wrong. Translation does not concern DNA, so choice D is incorrect.

39. **B is correct.** The P stands for peptidyl site, where the growing peptide chain attaches to the tRNA.

40. **D is correct.** Signal peptides attach to SRPs to direct the ribosome to attach to a membrane such as the endoplasmic reticulum. The signal peptide is usually removed during translation.

---

41. **B is correct.** A primary spermatocyte has finished the S stage of interphase but not the first meiotic division. Thus, it has 46 chromosomes.

42. **B is correct.** Replication takes place only during the synthesis phase.

43. **A is correct.** In normal meiosis, the only change in the nucleotide sequence of the third chromosome will occur during crossing over. Crossing over occurs in prophase I.

44. **A is correct.** Only germ cells undergo meiosis.

45. **D is correct.** In metaphase I we see tetrads.

46. **C is correct.** Centrioles migrate in prophase of mitosis. Chromosomes align in metaphase; centromeres split in anaphase; cytokinesis usually occurs during telophase.

47. **C is correct.** In prophase I, a tetrad will form and genetic recombination will occur; a spindle apparatus will always form; BUT chromosomal migration describes anaphase.

48. **B is correct.** The life cycle of all oocytes is arrested at the primary oocyte stage until puberty.

---

## EXPLANATIONS TO QUESTIONS IN LECTURE 3

49. **A is correct.** A retrovirus contains RNA which is reverse transcribed to DNA and then incorporated into the host cell genome.

50. **D is correct.** A virus cannot contain both DNA and RNA. Many viruses contain proteins.

51. **D is correct.** The first step in the infection of a host is attachment of the phage tail to a specific receptor on the host cell membrane. The capsid on the bacteriophage does not enter the host cell.

52. **A is correct.** Animal viruses attach by recognizing a receptor protein and entering through endocytosis.

53. **D is correct.** Viruses are not living and do not carry out any type of respiration. They require no nutrients, using energy from their host cell. They cannot reproduce inside nonliving organic matter. Viruses reproduce at the expense of a host. Thus, they most closely resemble parasites.

54. **A is correct.** In the lysogenic cycle of viral infection, a cell harbors inactive viral DNA in its genome.

55. **D is correct.** A bacteriophage has a tail and fibers.

56. **C is correct.** Viruses do not carry ribosomes.

---

57. **D is correct.** Prokaryotes have a cell wall that contains peptidoglycan, ribosomes, and a plasma membrane without cholesterol.

58. **C is correct.** Because DNA is acquired directly from the medium, this is transformation. Transduction is the transfer of DNA via a virus. There is no sexual reproduction in bacteria. Conjugation occurs between two bacteria.

59. **B is correct.** Transduction is the transfer of DNA via a virus.

60. **B is correct.** You should arrive at this answer by process of elimination. You should know that gram negative bacteria do not retain gram stain, so 'A' is wrong. You should know that the membrane is made from phospholipids, so C is wrong. (Remember, archaebacteria are not on the MCAT.) D is wrong because fimbriae allow a bacterium to hold to solid objects. Finally, you should know that a bacterium with an outer membrane is gram negative and protected against certain antibiotics such as penicillin.

61. **D is correct.** The exponential growth in bacteria is due to binary fission—asexual reproduction.

62. **B is correct.** Bacilli are rod-shaped; spirilli are rigid helixes; spirochetes are not rigid; AND cocci are round.

63. **C is correct.** Although this is a simple question, it is a reminder that transduction, transformation, and conjugation are not methods of reproduction in bacteria. They are methods of genetic recombination, which is associated with sexual reproduction in eukaryotics, but is not necessarily associated with reproduction in prokaryotes.

64. **B is correct.** Bacterial plasma membranes are a phospholipid bilayer. Bacteria do not have a nucleus. Ribosomes do not contain peptidoglycans. Bacterial cell walls are made from peptidoglycan.

---

65. **D is correct.** Fungi are unique because they are immotile and have a cell wall (like most plants), but are heterotrophic and not photosynthetic (like most animals).

66. **D is correct.** Hyphae are haploid and lengthen through mitosis.

67. **D is correct.** Fungi are saprophytic. Saprophytes are organisms that break down the dead remains of living organisms.

68. **B is correct.** Fungi are heterotrophs, not autotrophs.

69. **A is correct.** Haploid spores can form and spread faster and more efficiently than diploid zygotes because they don't undergo meiosis.

70. **C is correct.** Because fungus is more like human cells, drugs that attack fungi are more likely to affect human cells.

71. **B is correct.** Similar to the plant kingdom the fungi kingdom is divided into divisions.

72. **B is correct.** Fungi are exodigesters. They put enzymes into their food while it is outside their bodies and then absorb the nutrients. Although dead matter is more susceptible to fungal attack, fungi may attack living or dead matter. Meiosis is associated with sexual reproduction. Yeast is an example of a facultative anaerobe.

---

## EXPLANATIONS TO QUESTIONS IN LECTURE 4

73. **D is correct.** The flagella of bacteria are made from the protein flagellin.

74. **B is correct.** The nucleolus is the site of rRNA transcription not translation. It is not membrane bound and should not be confused with the nucleoid of prokaryotes.

75. **A is correct.** Anytime a compound moves against its electrochemical gradient across a membrane, it is active transport. The sodium electrochemical gradient was established by the expenditure of ATP, making this secondary active transport.

76. **A is correct.** We are looking for the cell that is most active in detoxification, one of the jobs of smooth ER. That would be the liver.

77. **B is correct.** I and II are true, but desmosomes are anchored to the cytoskeleton and are stronger than tight junctions.

78. **D is correct.** Ribosomes are made of RNA and protein. They do not have a phospholipid bilayer.

79. **A is correct.** The nucleus runs the cell and makes nucleic acids; the Golgi body packages materials for transport. The rough endoplasmic reticulum makes proteins for use outside the cell. The smooth endoplasmic reticulum helps to detoxify alcohol in the liver.

80. **A is correct.** The hydrolytic enzymes of lysosomes are activated by a low pH achieved by pumping protons into the interior.

---

81. **B is correct.** A signal is typically transmitted to the dendrites to the cell body and then down the axon; however, synapses are found all along the neuron and a signal may begin anywhere on the neuron. Although an action potential moves in all directions along an axon, the cell body and dendrites do not normally contain enough sodium channels to conduct the action potential for any length.

82. **D is correct.** This question is testing your knowledge of an action potential. The major ions involved in the action potential are sodium and potassium. Blocking sodium channels is the only way given that would block an action potential.

83. **A is correct.** The sodium/potassium pump moves potassium inside the membrane. Potassium is positively charged making the inside of the membrane more positive. The resting potential is measured with respect to the inside.

84. **D is correct.** Acetylcholinesterase is an enzyme that degrades acetylcholine. You should gather this from the name. If this enzyme is inhibited, then acetylcholine will not be catabolized as quickly, and it will bind and release repeatedly with postsynaptic receptors.

85. **A is correct.** White matter is composed primarily of myelinated axons.

86. **B is correct.** This is a knowledge based question. You should know this term.

87. **C is correct.** A negative potential is created inside the cell so excess positive charge is pumped out of the cell.

88. **B is correct.** Invertebrates do not have myelinated axons to accelerate nervous impulse transmission. Instead, they rely upon increased size. Vertebrata is a subphylum of Chordata which is characterized by a dorsal nerve chord at some point in their development.

---

89. **B is correct.** The cerebellum controls finely coordinated muscular movements, such as those that occur during a dance routine. Involuntary breathing movements are controlled by the medulla oblongata. The knee-jerk reflex is governed by the spinal cord.

90. **A is correct.** Every type of synapse in the peripheral nervous system uses acetylcholine as its neurotransmitter except the second (the neuroeffector) synapse in the sympathetic nervous system. You may not have known what a neuroeffector synapse was, but you should have been able to reason that it is an end-organ synapse. An effector is an organ or a muscle, something that responds to neural innervation by making something happen in the body.

91. **A is correct.** Parasympathetic stimulation results in "rest and digest" responses, or responses that are not involved in immediate survival or stress. B is a sympathetic response, as is C. D is mediated by skeletal muscles, which do not receive autonomic innervation.

92. **C is the right answer.** Pressure waves, or sound, are converted to neural signals by hair cells in the organ of Corti in the cochlea.

*Answers & Explanations For Questions In The Lectures* **293**

93. **D is correct.** In order to prevent conflicting contractions by antagonistic muscle groups, reflexes will often cause one muscle group to contract while it sends an inhibitory signal to its antagonistic muscle group. Motor neurons exit ventrally from the spinal cord, not dorsally, so A is out. Reflex arcs (at least somatic ones) are usually confined to the spinal cord; they do not require fine control by the cerebral cortex. This eliminates B. Reflex arcs may be integrated by an interneuron in the spinal cord. C is out as well.

94. **A is correct.** The central nervous system is comprised of the brain and spinal cord. An effector is organ or tissue affected by a nervous impulse.

95. **C is correct.** This is a knowledge based question. The cerebrum is also called the cerebral cortex.

96. **A is correct.** The question describes a simple reflex arc which does not involve neurons in the brain.

## EXPLANATIONS TO QUESTIONS IN LECTURE 5

97. **D is correct.** Aldosterone, as we can tell by its name, is a steroid (any hormone whose name ends in "sterone" or something similar is a steroid). This allows us to eliminate choice A, because steroid hormones do not need cell membrane receptors or second-messenger systems. They simply diffuse across the cell membrane. We can eliminate B because the adrenal cortex is aldosterone's source, not its target tissue. C describes events at a synapse. Aldosterone actually exerts its effect by doing what D says, increasing the production of sodium-potassium pump proteins.

98. **C is correct.** This is a negative feedback question. If another source of aldosterone exists in the body besides the adrenal cortex, negative feedback (through the renin-angiotensin system and increased blood pressure) would suppress the level of aldosterone secreted by the adrenal cortex. A is out because the levels of renin in the blood would decrease, not increase; aldosterone release would increase blood pressure, and renin is released in response to low blood pressure. Oxytocin plays no role in blood pressure (vasopressin does) and would not be affected by this tumor. Now, to choose between C and D: we know that aldosterone from the adrenal cortex would respond to negative feedback, but we aren't sure whether the tumor would. At this point, we know enough to go with C. If we're sure C is a correct response, that must mean D is an incorrect response, and we can eliminate it. In fact, this is a good choice because normally, hormone-secreting tumors will not respond to negative feedback.

99. **B is correct.** All hormones bind to a protein receptor, whether at the cell membrane, in the cytoplasm, or in the nucleus of the cell. Steroids and thyroxine require a transport protein to dissolve in the aqueous solution of the blood. Steroids are derived from cholesterol, not protein precursors.

100. **C is correct.** Acetylcholine acts through a second messenger system, and is not a second messenger itself.

101. **D is correct.** Steroids are lipid soluble. Different steroids may have different target cells. For instance, estrogens are very selective while testosterone affects every, or nearly every, cell in the body. Steroids act at the transcription level in the nucleus, and are synthesized by the smooth endoplasmic reticulum.

102. **B is correct.** Exocrine function refers to enzyme delivery through a duct.

103. **B is correct.** Steroids act at the level of transcription by regulating the amount of mRNA transcribed.

104. **B is correct.** You should know that $T_3$ and $T_4$ (thyroxine) production are controlled by a negative feedback mechanism involving TSH (thyroid stimulating hormone) from the anterior pituitary; parathyroid hormone production is not be affected by thyroxine levels.

105. **C is correct.** Epinephrine release leads to "fight or flight" responses, as does sympathetic stimulation. A is out because insulin causes cells to take up glucose. It is not involved in "fight or flight" responses. B is out because acetylcholine is a neurotransmitter; it has few, if any, known hormonal actions. D is out because aldosterone is involved in sodium reabsorption by the kidney; it has no role in "fight or flight" responses.

106. **C is correct.** The nervous and endocrine systems are, in general, the two systems that respond to changes in the environment. In general, the endocrine system's responses are slower to occur but last longer.

107. **D is correct.** The only important thing to recognize from the question is that high insulin levels exist. Then go to the basics; insulin decreases blood glucose.

108. **A is correct.** This is an important distinction to be made. The hormones of the posterior pituitary are synthesized in the bodies of neurons in the hypothalamus, and transported down the axons of these nerves to the posterior pituitary.

109. **D is correct.** Calcitonin builds bone mass. Menopause contributes to osteoporosis by reducing estrogen levels leading to diminished osteoblastic activity. You are not required to know this, and may have had difficulty in eliminating this answer. Instead, you should answer this question by realizing that D was the exception.

110. **A is correct.** Thyroxine ($T_4$) is produced by the thyroid gland.

111. **C is correct.** Glucagon increases blood sugar, a good thing if you are running a marathon. An increased heart rate and sympathetic blood shunting might similarly be expected in someone who had just run 25 miles.

112. **D is correct.** Parathyroid hormone stimulates osteoclast (bone resorbtion) activity. It also works in the kidney to slow calcium lost in urine. It controls blood calcium levels via these two mechanisms.

---

113. **C is correct.** A looks good (testosterone does stimulate the testes to descend) until you notice that we're dealing with a physically mature male. The testes normally descend during late fetal development. B is out because increased testosterone would cause puberty to occur early, and would not change the timing of puberty if it's already happened (we are, after all, dealing with a physically mature male). D is out because we don't know of any direct mechanism by which testosterone increases body temperature.

114. **A is correct.** Increased secretion of estrogen sets off the luteal surge, which involves increased secretion of LH and leads to ovulation.

115. **A is correct.** The epididymis is where the sperm goes to mature and be stored until ejaculation. Testosterone is secreted by the seminiferous tubules.

116. **C is correct.** Decreased progesterone secretion results from the degeneration of the corpus luteum, which occurs because fertilization of the egg and implantation didn't happen. A is out because thickening of the endometrial lining occurs while estrogen and progesterone levels are high, not while progesterone secretion is decreasing. B is out because increased estrogen secretion causes the luteal surge, and because the luteal surge occurs earlier in the cycle. D is out because, while the flow phase does follow decreased progesterone secretion, it does not occur as a result of increased estrogen secretion.

117. **D is correct.** The layer of cilia along the inner lining of the Fallopian tubes serves to help the egg cell move towards the uterus, where it will implant if it has been fertilized. (Fertilization usually happens in the Fallopian tubes.) A describes what the ciliary lining in the respiratory tract does. B may sound good, but the Fallopian tubes are far enough away from the external environment that protection from its temperature fluctuations is not an issue. C would seem to gum up the whole "continuation of the species" plan. It's not a good answer.

118. **C is correct.** The adrenal cortex makes many other steroid based hormones, as well as testosterone.

119. **C is correct.** Mammalian eggs undergo holoblastic cleavage where division occurs throughout the whole egg. At first glance, this question appears to ask for somewhat obscure knowledge about meroblastic cleavage. However, you should be able to eliminate A, B, and D quite easily as being part of human embryonic cleavage, so it is unnecessary to know meroblastic or holoblastic cleavage.

120. **D is correct.** Generally, the inner lining of the respiratory and digestive tracts, and associated organs, come from the endoderm. The skin, hair, nails, eyes and central nervous system come from ectoderm. Everything else comes from the mesoderm. The gastrula is not a germ layer.

---

*Lecture Question Expls.*

# EXPLANATIONS TO QUESTIONS IN LECTURE 6

121. **C is correct.** Pepsin, whose optimum pH is around 2.0, denatures in the environment of the small intestine, whose pH is between 6 and 7. A is wrong because pepsin isn't working at all in the small intestine; it won't be working synergistically with trypsin. B is wrong because pepsinogen is activated in the stomach by low pH. D is wrong because pepsin is a catalyst, which makes it a protein; amylase digests starch.

122. **D is correct.** The best answer is D because only D is both true and reveals a benefit for enzymes to be inactive while in the pancreas. A may seem logical but would only apply to lipase. B is false. C is true but is not an adequate explanation.

123. **D is correct.** The stomach doesn't digest carbohydrates. If stomach acid secretion is obstructed then: A) fewer bacteria will be killed in the stomach; B) less pepsinogen will be activated; C) the pH will rise.

124. **A is correct.** All macronutrients are digested through hydrolysis, or the breaking of bonds by adding water.

125. **A is correct.** The large intestine absorbs water. Fat is digested in the small intestine. Urea is secreted by the kidney.

126. **D is correct.** Amylases digest sugars; lipases digest fats; and proteases digest proteins.

127. **A is correct.** Pancreatic exocrine function includes enzymes made in the pancreas and secreted through a duct. Bile is not an enzyme. It is made in the liver and stored in the gallbladder.

128. **C is correct.** Most chemical digestion occurs in the first part of the small intestine, the duodenum.

---

129. **B is correct.** Parietal cells secrete HCl. Goblet cells secrete mucus. Chief cells secrete pepsin. G cells secrete gastrin into the blood.

130. **D is correct.** Gluconeogenesis is the production of glycogen from noncarbohydrate precursors. This function is performed mainly in the liver. Glycolysis can be performed by any cell. Fat storage takes place in adipocytes. Protein degradation occurs in all cells.

131. **D is correct.** Most fat digestates enter the lymph as chylomicrons via lacteals. Smooth endoplasmic reticulum synthesizes triglycerides.

132. **A is correct.** 'Essential' means that the body cannot synthesize them. Nonessential amino acids are synthesized by the liver. Amino acids are absorbed by facilitated and active transport. Urea is the end product of amino acid deamination in the liver.

133. **B is correct.** Glucose is absorbed in a symport mechanism with sodium. Sodium is an electrolyte. The absorption of glucose increases the absorption of sodium. Glucose is not an electrolyte. Glucose does not stimulate the secretion of amylase.

134. **B is correct.** Insulin decreases blood sugar levels in several ways. One of the ways is by inhibiting glycogenolysis.

135. **B is correct.** This is a knowledge based question. You should know that blood is an aqueous solution.

136 **A is correct.** Macromolecules are broken down into their basic nutrients.

---

137. **C is correct.** The only process available for the removal of wastes by the Bowman's capsule is diffusion, aided by the hydrostatic pressure of the blood.

138. **D is correct.** Glucose is normally completely reabsorbed from the filtrate and thus does not appear in the urine. When glucose does appear in the urine, the glucose transporters in the PCT (not in the loop of Henle, as stated in answer choice A) are unable to reabsorb all of the glucose from the filtrate. C is wrong because the proximal tubule does not secrete glucose.

139. **B is correct.** The purpose of the brush border is to increase the surface area available to reabsorb solutes from the filtrate. The brush border is made from villi, not cilia, and so has little or no bearing on the direction or rate of fluid movement.

140. **D is correct.** Renin secretion catalyzes the conversion of angiotensin I to angiotensin II, which increases the secretion of aldosterone. If renin is blocked, then aldosterone cannot cause increased synthesis of sodium absorbing proteins, and sodium absorption decreases. Without renin secretion, production of angiotensin II would decrease. Blood pressure would decrease, not increase; A is wrong. Platelets are irrelevant; B is wrong.

141. **C is correct.** This is the correct order of structures.

142. **B is correct.** Vasopressin is antidiuretic hormone increasing water retention. ADH levels will be rise in response to dehydration. Aldosterone is a mineral corticoid released by the adrenal cortex in response to low blood pressure. In a severely dehydrated person, blood volume would be low, likely resulting in diminished blood pressure. Aldosterone levels will rise in response to the low blood pressure.

143. **B is correct.** High blood pressure would result in more fluid being forced into Bowman's capsule.

144. **A is correct.** The loop of Henle concentrates the medulla via a net loss of solute to the medulla. This process is critical to the function of other parts of the nephron; a medulla with a high concentration of solute allows for the passive absorption of water from the filtrate in other areas of the nephron.

## EXPLANATIONS TO QUESTIONS IN LECTURE 7

145. **D is correct.** The atrioventricular node, which sits at the junction between the atria and the ventricles, pauses for a fraction of a second before passing an impulse to the ventricles.

146. **C is correct.** Stroke volume must be the same for both ventricles. If it weren't, we'd have a never-ending backlog of blood in one or the other circulations, ending with the faster circulation running dry. To keep the whole system running smoothly, both halves of the circulation must pump the same quantity of blood with each stroke.

147. **A is correct.** The cardiac action potential is spread from one cardiac muscle cell to the next via ion movement through gap junctions.

148. **A is correct.** Less oxygenated blood will reach the systemic system because some oxygenated blood will be shunted from the aorta to the lower pressure pulmonary arteries. The pulmonary circulation will carry blood that is more oxygenated than normal, since highly oxygenated blood from the aorta is mixing with deoxygenated blood on its way to the lungs. The entire heart will pump harder in order to compensate by with more blood to the tissues.

149. **D is correct.** Oxygenated blood returning from the lungs feeds into the heart at the left atrium. From there, it flows into the left ventricle, which pumps it to the systemic circulation. The right atria and the right ventricle pump deoxygenated blood to the lungs.

150. **A is correct.** Blood loss is likely to be more rapid during arterial bleeding due the greater blood pressure in the arteries.

151. **A is correct.** Don't let the not-so-subtle physics reference fool you. Bernoulli's equation, which would indicate a greater pressure at the greater cross-sectional area, doesn't work here. You should memorize that blood pressure in a human is greatest in the aorta and drops until the blood gets back to the heart.

152. **D is correct.** The capillaries are one cell thick and blood moves slowly to allow for efficient oxygen exchange.

153. **B is correct.** Hyperventilation results in loss of $CO_2$, leading to lower concentrations of carbonic acid in the blood, and an increase in pH. Hypoventilation would result in the reverse. Breathing into a bag would increase the $CO_2$ content of the air and lead to acidosis. <u>Excess</u> aldosterone may lead to metabolic alkalosis due to hydrogen ion exchange in the kidney.

154. **C is correct.** Carbonic anhydrase is a catalyst. Catalysts increase the rate of a reaction. If the catalyst is inhibited, the rate decreases. Since the reaction moves in one direction in the lungs, and the opposite direction in the tissues, answer choice A is ambiguous. Unless one believes that a carbonic anhydrase inhibitor will affect transcription or degradation of hemoglobin, choices B and D are equivalent. If one were true, the other should also be true.

155. **A is correct.** Cellular respiration produces carbon dioxide, which, in turn, lowers blood pH. During heavy exercise, capillaries dilate in order to deliver more oxygen to the active tissues. Nitrogen is irrelevant to respiration.

156. **B is correct.** The increased hemoglobin concentration in the blood after reinjection increases the blood's ability to deliver oxygen to the tissues, often a limiting factor in endurance competitions. A is wrong because, while this may happen, it is not the primary benefit of blood doping. B is a much better answer. C is wrong because, since we are only reinjecting blood cells, we are not increasing the body's hydration status. D is wrong because, while blood is less viscous with fewer red blood cells, we are removing whole blood, not just red blood cells, so we won't be changing the blood's viscosity.

157. **C is correct.** Carbon dioxide is produced in the tissues. It is transported by the blood to the lungs, where it is expelled by diffusing into the alveoli. Since the concentration gradient carries $CO_2$ into the capillaries from the tissues and from the blood into the alveoli, we can reason that there is a higher concentration of $CO_2$ in the tissues than in the alveoli. A is wrong because blood $CO_2$ concentration will not change in the veins; it has nowhere to go. B is wrong because $CO_2$ is expelled into the lungs at the pulmonary capillaries, so $CO_2$ that was present in the pulmonary arteries (before the capillaries) will largely be gone in the pulmonary veins (after the capillaries). D describes the opposite of the concentration gradient that actually exists for $CO_2$ between the systemic tissues and the systemic capillaries.

158. **B is correct.** The person would need increased vascularity to deliver more blood to the tissues because the blood would carry less oxygen.

159. **A is correct.** Constricted air passages is the clue. The bronchioles are surrounded by smooth muscle and small enough to constrict. Cartilage does not constrict, muscle does. The skeletal muscle in the thorax does not constrict the air passages. The alveoli are not part of the air passages.

160. **D is correct.** Heavy exercise manifests increased carbon dioxide production that leads to increased carboxyhemoglobin.

---

161. **C is correct.** Hemolytic anemia can result from abnormalities of the red bloods cells that make them fragile and more susceptible to rupture when they are processed by the spleen. You should know for the test that the spleen destroys old, worn out red blood cells.

162. **B is correct.** "Swollen glands" are actually swollen lymph nodes that are bulging with immune cells gearing up to fight the invasion. A is simply not what's going on here. C is out because an inflammatory response would draw fluid into the inflamed area, not drain it away. D is also just a goofy answer.

163. **D is correct.** Immunoglobulins, or antibodies, are involved in the humoral immune system, or the B cell system. A is out because cytotoxic T cells work in cell mediated immunity. B is out because stomach acid plays a role in the nonspecific innate immunity; humoral immunity is specific and acquired. C is irrelevant.

164. **D is correct.** Antibodies bind to antigens through interactions between the antibody's variable region and the antigen. Antibodies do not phagocytize anything, so A is out. Antibodies are produced by plasma cells, they don't normally bind to them; B is out. Plasma cells are derived from stem cells in the bone marrow. Antibodies will not usually prevent their production. C is out.

165. **D is correct.** Fluid that is picked up by the lymphatic tissues is returned to the circulation at the right and left lymphatic ducts, which feed into veins in the upper portion of the chest.

166. **A is correct.** Type B negative blood carries B antigens and not the Rh factor. It does not carry A antigens. There are no O antigens. Thus type B negative blood makes antibodies that will only attach A antigens and Rh antigens.

167. **D is correct.** Old erythrocytes are destroyed in the spleen and the liver.

168. **C is correct.** The innate immune response does not involve humoral immunity (B-cell) or cell mediated immunity (T-cell). The innate immune system responds to any and every foreign invader with the white blood cells called granulocytes as well as with inflammation and other actions.

## EXPLANATIONS TO QUESTIONS IN LECTURE 8

169. **D is correct.** Neither actin (the thin filament) nor myosin (the thick filament) changes its length during a muscular contraction; instead the proportion of actin and myosin overlap increases.

170. **C is correct.** Permanent sequestering of calcium in the sarcoplasmic reticulum would prevent calcium from binding to troponin, which is what causes the conformational change that moves tropomyosin away from the myosin binding sites on actin. Choice A would occur if calcium were present and ATP were not. Loss of ATP would prevent the myosin from releasing from actin. B is incorrect because a resorption of calcium from bone would result in a decrease in bone density, not an increase. D is incorrect because loss of calcium would not cause depolymerization of actin filaments. If this actually occurred, it would pose a serious problem every time calcium was re-sequestered into the SR after the completion of a contraction.

171. **C is correct.** Shivering results from the increase of muscle tone. When muscle tone increases beyond a certain critical point, it creates the familiar indiscriminate muscle activity typical of shivering. While shivering may serve as a warning, it does more than that, and that is not its primary purpose; A is out. B is simply not the case, nor is D.

172. **D is correct.** Muscles cause movement by contracting (eliminating B and C), bringing origin and insertion closer together, usually by moving the insertion. Neurons cause contractions in muscles, not tendons, and the neural signals are not initiated by the muscle. This eliminates A.

173. **B is correct.** Antagonistic muscles move bones in opposite directions relative to a joint. In order to produce movement, one must relax while the other contracts.

174. **C is correct.** All muscles will need more energy and protein if they are being used rigorously, but in humans, mature skeletal muscle cells do not divide.

175. **A is correct.** MCAT doesn't test anatomy. This question is asking if you know that tendons connect muscle to bone. Ligaments connect bone-to-bone. Tendons are not cartilage.

176. **D is correct.** Peristalsis is a function of smooth muscle only. Shivering is an example of temperature regulation by skeletal muscle. Skeletal muscle may assist in venous blood movement and lymph fluid movement.

177. **B is correct.** Gap junctions allow for the spread of the action potential throughout the heart.

178. **C is correct.** Peristalsis is a smooth-muscle activity, and smooth muscle is innervated by the autonomic nervous system. The skeletal muscles are innervated by the somatic nervous system, so interruption of the autonomic nervous system would not affect the knee-jerk reflex or the diaphragm. An action potential in cardiac muscle is conducted from cell to cell by gap junctions.

179. **A is correct.** The heart requires long steady contractions in order to pump blood. We know we want adjacent heart cells to contract at the same time; B is out. We're not concerned about a neuron here; C is out. Sodium flows into the cell, not out. D is out as well.

180. **C is correct.** Smooth muscle contains thick and thin filaments, so it requires calcium to contract.

181. **A is correct.** This question asks you to recognize that smooth muscle and cardiac muscle are involuntary, and then to recognize muscle types of the different structures. Of the muscles listed, only the diaphragm is skeletal muscle.

182. **D is correct.** All muscles contract in response to increased cytosolic calcium concentration.

183. **C is correct.** You should know that the vagus nerve is a parasympathetic nerve. Heart rate is set by the SA node, and the SA node is innervated by the parasympathetic vagus nerve. The pace of the SA node is faster than the normal heart beats, but the parasympathetic vagus nerve tonically slows the contractions of the heart to its resting pace. Without tonic inhibition from the vagus, the heart would normally beat at 100 – 120 beats per minute.

184. **A is correct.** The word dilation here is the give away. Smooth muscle must be relaxing in order to dilate the vessels.

---

185. **C is correct.** Parathyroid hormone increases blood calcium by increasing osteocyte activity, and increasing osteoclast number.

186. **A is correct.** Synovial fluid acts as a lubricant, decreasing friction between the ends of the bones as they move. Bone cells receive circulation to keep them adequately hydrated; they do not need synovial fluid for this purpose. B is out. Synovial fluid persists in adults, after bones have stopped growing, so we know C is wrong. Synovial fluid is found in synovial joints, which allow movement. Its purpose is not to prevent movement. D is out.

187. **C is correct.** Of the tissues listed, only cartilage does not contain nerves.

188. **A is correct.** Ligaments attach bone to bone. Tendons attach bone to muscle.

189. **C is correct.** Bone does not regulate the body or blood temperature. It does store calcium and phosphate, support and protect the body, produce blood cells, and store fat.

190. **A is correct.** Yellow bone marrow is usually found in the medullary cavity of long bones.

191. **B is correct.** Hydroxyapatite is made up of calcium and phosphate in a compound that includes hydroxyl groups as well. You should know that bone acts as a storage place for phosphate and calcium. The hydroxyl you can get from the name.

192. **B is correct.** Spongy bone contains the blood stem cells important for blood cell synthesis. Red blood cell storage is the job of the liver and spleen. Fat storage is in long bones.

---

## EXPLANATIONS TO QUESTIONS IN LECTURE 9

193. **B is correct.** According to the Punnett square, each time they have a boy, there is a 50% chance that he will be color-blind. The chance that both boys are colorblind is the chance of this happening twice, or $0.5^2$.

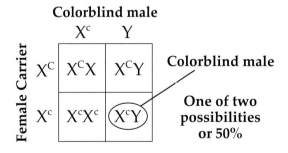

194. **A is correct.** D is a male. Since the mother had the disease, the mother must have been homozygous recessive. The father could not have been a carrier. Thus, female A received an $X^h$ from her mother and an $X^H$ from her father. Since she is only a carrier, it is possible that she passed on only her good X and that all her children are healthy.

195. **C is correct.** From the dihybrid cross Punnett square we have the phenotype ratio 9:3:3:1. Thus, 9 of 16 individuals display both dominant phenotypes.

196. **B is correct.** A dihybrid is heterozygous for both traits. See the dihybrid Punnett square in this chapter and count the dihybrid offspring.

197. **A is correct.** Both girls must carry the trait because they receive their father's recessive chromosome.

**198. B is correct.** A dihybrid cross is when two individuals that are hybrids at two different genes are crossed. i.e. AaBb x AaBb

**199. D is correct.** Sex-linked traits occur on the X or Y chromosomes. The X and Y chromosomes are not homologous.

**200. C is correct.** The woman has two recessive Xs. Her mother gave her one X and her father gave her one X. Her father only had one X to start with, so it must have been recessive and he must have been colorblind. Her son will receive a recessive X from her and a Y from his father so he will be colorblind.

---

**201. B is correct.** First you must recognize that 10% of the gene pool is represented by the recessive allele. Then you must realize that only the homozygous recessives display the recessive phenotype. Now use the binomial theorem to see that homozygous recessives are represented by $0.1^2$ of the population.

**202. C is correct.** Catastrophic events will not cause significant genetic drift to a large homogeneous (well-mixed) population. Emigration, selection, and mutation all affect the HW equilibrium.

**203. D is correct.** Only D does not represent a type of isolation (geographic, seasonal, behavioral) which leads to speciation. The birds are migratory, and thus are not geographically isolated. This makes D the best answer choice.

**204. C is correct.** *r*-strategy is more efficient when the prevailing conditions are governed by density independent factors such as harsh environment, short seasons, etc. Commercial predation methods have a similar effect. *r*-strategists are able to better withstand massive predation from man or others, because they produce so many more offspring than they need to continue the species. *K*-strategists fare better when the prevailing conditions are governed by density dependent factors such as limited resources. *K*-strategists can better exploit limited resources by specializing.

**205. C is correct.** A single class encompasses several orders; two different families can belong to the same order.

**206. A is correct.** Remember: Darn King Phillip Came Over For Good Soup. Domain, kingdom, phylum, class, order, family, genus, species. The epithet *Canus lupus* indicates that the wolf is genus *Canus* and species *lupus*. Family is a broader category than either genus or species, so any organism that is of the species lupus, must also be *Canus* and canidae.

**207. D is correct.** This is an application of the binomial theorem under Hardy Weinberg Equilibrium. $p^2 + 2pq + q^2 = 1$ and $p + q = 1$. So, $p^2 = 0.36$. $p = 0.6$. $q = 0.4$. $2pq = 0.48$.

**208. D is correct.** Corn depends upon humans for its survival as a species. Humans ensure its survival. In return, humans are provided with food. Both species benefit from the relationship.

---

**209. B is correct.** Prokaryotes arose at least 3.6 billion years ago.

**210. C is correct.** Vertebrates, a subphylum of Chordata, contain backbones.

**211. D is correct.** Ants are not chordates. Tunicates, sponge-like creatures that attach to the sea floor, are actually chordates.

**212. C is correct.** Life originated in an atmosphere with little or no oxygen.

**213. B is correct.** The taxonomy of *Homo sapiens* is Domain: Eukarya; Kingdom: Animalia; Phylum: Chordata; Subphylum: Vertabrata; Class: Mammalia; Order: Primata; Family: Homididae; Genus: *Homo*; Species: *Sapiens*.

**214. C is correct.** You need to memorize that the taxonomy of humans is animalia, chordata, mammalian, primata, homididae, *Homo sapiens*.

215. **C is correct.** Urey and Miller demonstrated that organic molecules may be created from inorganic molecules under the primordial earth conditions. Urey-Miller did not prove the existence of life on earth, (you do), nor did they prove that humans have evolved from bacteria, photosynthetic or not.

216. **B is correct.** If you answered A, you would have to explain what the first living organism ate because he had no one else to eat. Even when there were millions of living organisms, they could not survive off each other because one organism would have to eat many others, and there just wouldn't be enough to go around initially.

# Photo Credits

## Covers

Front cover, Anatomical Overlays - Man Running Front View: © LindaMarieB/iStockphoto.com

Back cover, T4 bacteriophage infecting bacterium: © Russell Kightley / Science Source

## Chapter 1

Pg. 1, Body Builder: © Steve Williams Photo/Getty Images

Pg. 2, Dolomedes fimbriatus on black Water: © Alasdair James /iStockphoto.com

Pg. 3, Overhead shot of food containing Omega 3: © Tooga/Getty Images

Pg. 4, Fat cells, TEM: © Steve Gschmeissner/Photo Researchers, Inc.

Pg. 5, Peanuts: © RedHelga/iStockphoto.com

Pg. 6, Picture symbolizing high-protein diet (meat, fish, vegetables): © Ulrich Kerth/Getty Images

Pg. 9, False-color TEM of collagen fibrils: © J. Gross/Biozentrum, University of Basel/Photo Researchers, Inc.

Pg. 10, Glucose level blood test: © Alexander Raths/iStockphoto.com

Pg. 10, Plant Cells (SEM): © Alice J. Belling, colorization by Meredith Carlson/Photo Researchers, Inc.

Pg. 10, Colored SEM of a liver cell (hepatocyte): © Professors Pietro M. Motta & Tomonori Naguro/Photo Researchers, Inc.

Pg. 11, Front view of Holstein cow, 5 years old, standing: © Alexander Raths/iStockphoto.com

Pg. 11, Insect termite white ant: © defun/iStockphoto.com

Pg. 12, DNA molecule: © Sci-Comm Studios/Science Source

Pg. 13, Human Bone, Microscopic View: © David Scharf/Getty Images

Pg. 13, Small child: © Jaroslaw Wojcik/iStockphoto.com

Pg. 15, Hexokinase enzyme with glucose: © Kenneth Eward/Biografx/Science Photo Library

Pg. 16, Vitamin supplements: © Sarah Lee/iStockphoto.com

Pg. 18, Pancreas cell, SEM: © Steve Gschmeissner/Photo Researchers, Inc.

Pg. 21, Sugar in a silver spoon: © Homiel/iStockphoto.com

Pg. 22, Streptococcus viridans: © Biophoto Associates/Photo Researchers, Inc.

Pg. 24, Mitochondrion, SEM: © Dr. David Furness, Keele University/Photo Researchers, Inc.

Pg. 26, Hans Krebs, German-Anglo Biochemist: © Science Source/Photo Researchers, Inc.

## Chapter 2

Pg. 31, Conceptual computer illustration of the DNA double helix: © David Parker/Science Photo Library

Pg. 43, Southern blotting: © James King-Holmes/Photo Researchers, Inc.

Pg. 47, Col TEM of structural gene operon from E. coli: © Professor Oscar Mille/Photo Researchers, Inc.

Pg. 49, Male white lion: © Tony Camacho/Photo Researchers, Inc.

Pg. 52, Cancer cell: © Quest/Photo Researchers, Inc.

Pg. 54, Chromosomes, computer artwork: © SCIEPRO/Science Photo Library

## Chapter 3

Pg. 65, Bacteriophages: © Science Picture Co/Getty Images

Pg. 66, T4 bacteriophages: © Russell Kightley/Science Source

Pg. 68, Close-up of a cold sore on the lower lip: © Dr. P. Marazzi/Photo Researchers, Inc.

Pg. 70, Gut bacterium: © Hazel Appleton, Health Protection Agency Centre for Infections/Photo Researchers, Inc.

Pg. 71, E. coli bacteria: © Andrew Syred/Photo Researchers, Inc.

Pg. 71, MRSA: resistant Staphylococcus bacteria: © K. Lounatmaa/Photo Researchers, Inc.

Pg. 71, SEM of Treponema pallidum on cultures of cotton-tail rabbit epithelium cells: © Science Source/Photo Researchers, Inc.

Pg. 71, Bacterial capsule: © Dr. Kari Lounatmaa/Photo Researchers, Inc.

Pg. 75, Diffusion: © Charles D. Winters/Photo Researchers, Inc.

Pg. 77, Cholera bacteria: © Juergen Berger/Photo Researchers, Inc.

Pg. 79, Gut bacterium reproducing: © Hazel Appleton, Health Protection Agency Centre for Infections/Photo Researchers, Inc.

Pg. 82, False color transmission electron micrograph of a thin section through an endospore of Bacillus subtilis: © Dr. Tony Brain/Photo Researchers, Inc.

Pg. 84, Strawberry Gray Mold disease: © Craftvision/iStockphoto.com

Pg. 84, Trichophyton Interdigitale, or athlete's foot: © Biophoto Associates/Photo Researchers, Inc.

Pg. 84, Athlete's foot: © carroteater/iStockphoto.com

Pg. 84, SEM of Saccharomyces cerevisiae: © SciMAT/Photo Researchers, Inc.

## Chapter 4

Pg. 108, Hand and thumb tack: © Dana Kelley Photos

## Chapter 5

Pg. 127, Atopic dermatitis: © bravo1954/iStockphoto.com

Pg. 128, Third world healthcare: © Scott Camazine/Photo Researchers, Inc.

Pg. 128, Light micrograph of pancreatic islets of Langerhans, stained with H&E (Hematoxylin and Eosin): © Biophoto Associates/Photo Researchers, Inc.

## Chapter 6

## Chapter 7

## Chapter 8

# INDEX

## Symbols

1,25 dihydroxycholecalciferol (DOHCC) 130
2,3-DPG 170
3 to 1 ratio 203, 213
5'→3' 12, 290
5′→ 3′ directionality 33
5′ cap 38
5 stage cycle 188, 189
9+2 93
α-amylase 142
α-cells 129
α-subunit 105
β-cells 129
β-pleated sheet 6, 7

## A

absolute refractory period 103
accommodation 103
acetylcholine 19, 107, 108, 110, 118, 124, 143, 168, 189, 236,
    277, 293, 294
acetyl CoA 21, 24, 26, 27
acid hydrolases 92
acidosis 155, 172, 297
acinar cells 145
acquired immunity 178, 179
acrosome 133, 135
ACTH 121, 125, 126, 131, 138, 139, 234
actin 93, 177, 186, 188, 191, 258, 299
action potential 95, 100-107, 113, 124, 165, 168, 189, 192-194, 236,
    237, 258, 259, 277, 283, 289, 293, 297, 299
activated 18, 36, 37, 82, 85, 91, 104, 129, 133, 143, 145, 148, 176,
    189, 199, 237, 240, 242, 279, 293, 296
activators 19, 36, 37
active site 15-17, 20, 188, 272
active transport 10, 76, 92, 98, 104, 149, 157, 249, 258, 292, 296
Adaptive radiation 208
adenine (A) 33
adenohypophysis 125
adenosine phosphate 33, 223
ADH 14, 121, 123, 126, 127, 138, 139, 158, 240, 249, 281, 297
Adipocytes 3, 28, 92, 116
adrenal cortex 122-124, 126, 127, 138, 140, 158, 235, 249, 278, 281,
    294, 295, 297
adrenal glands 125, 127
adrenaline 110, 128
adrenal medulla 122, 127, 128, 140, 234
adrenergic 110, 234, 241, 249
Adrenocorticotropic hormone (ACTH) 126
Aerobic respiration 24, 272
agglutinate 179
agonist 185, 186

agranular 92
Agranular leukocytes 176
albumin 8, 152, 155, 176, 248, 280
aldosterone 122-124, 127, 158, 162, 241, 242, 249, 294, 297
Aldosterone 124, 127, 131, 138, 139, 156, 158, 278, 281, 294, 297
alimentary tract 22
allele 204-206, 209, 210, 301
alleles 54, 182, 204, 210, 266, 285
all-or-nothing 103, 107
allosteric activators 19
allosteric inhibitors 19
Allosteric interactions 18
allosteric regulation 19
almost universal 45, 290
alveolar sacs 170
alveoli 169, 170, 173, 255, 298
amino acids 5, 6, 18, 21, 27, 31, 35, 45, 46, 53, 62, 77, 91, 126, 127,
    129, 145, 147, 151, 155, 156, 162, 176, 216, 260, 271, 280,
    290, 296
aminoacyl site 46
amphipathic 4, 73, 152
amplified 42, 44
ampulla of Vater 145
amylase 142, 145, 147, 148, 156, 247, 279, 296
amylopectin 10
amylose 10
anabolism 21
Anaerobic respiration 22
analogous 97, 137, 208
Anaphase 56, 60, 61, 273
anaphase II 58, 60
androgen 132, 134, 243, 244
aneuploidy 50
angiotensin 158, 249, 250, 280, 294, 297
Animalia 207, 301
anneal 42
anomers 10
ANS 108-110, 116
antagonist 118, 185
anterior cavity 112
anterior pituitary 121, 125, 126, 128, 131, 134, 140, 243, 294
anterior pituitary hormones 121, 125, 126
antibiotics 157, 235, 277, 292
antibodies 8, 43, 77, 90, 176, 179, 180, 182, 184, 228, 244, 252, 253,
    265, 275, 281, 282, 285, 298
antibody 43, 179, 180, 242, 252, 253, 281, 282, 298
anticodon 46, 53
Antidiuretic hormone (ADH) 127
antigen 179, 180, 252, 253, 265, 281, 282, 285, 298
antigenic determinant 179
antiparallel 6, 33
antiport 157, 162

crypts of Lieberkuhn 144
C-terminus 46
cyclic AMP 12, 105, 124, 240, 241, 277, 278
cystic duct 145
cytochromes 9, 13, 27, 258, 282
Cytochromes 9
Cytokinesis 56, 61
cytoplasmic streaming 84, 93
Cytoplasmic streaming 84
cytosine (C) 33
cytoskeleton 93, 95, 293
cytosol 22, 29, 35, 37, 46, 47, 53, 73, 77, 91, 92, 100, 121-223, 235, 240, 252, 253, 258, 259, 272, 276-278
cytotoxic 180, 184, 298
cytotoxic T cells 180, 298

## D

degenerative 45
dehydration 2, 14, 46, 199, 297
deletion 38, 49, 274
deletions 49, 50, 224
denatured 8, 39, 218
dendrites 100, 105, 107, 108, 293
dense bodies 193
density dependent 208, 267, 301
density independent factors 301
deoxyribonuclease 145
deoxyribonucleic acid 33, 43
depolarization 101, 192, 236, 277
dermis 137, 199, 200
descending colon 141, 146
Desmosomes 95, 116
determination 137
determined 83, 93, 137, 216, 271
Detoxification 155
deuterostomes 211
developmental isolation 207
dextrinase 144
diapedesis 178, 179
diaphragm 169, 194, 234, 276, 299
diaphysis 195, 259
diastole 164
differentiate 134, 137, 176, 179, 180, 195, 243, 259, 262, 283
differentiation 136, 137
diffusion 10, 22, 24, 75, 76, 92, 104, 149, 151, 156, 157, 165, 199, 296
digest 10, 39, 87, 92, 109-111, 135, 145, 147, 148, 293, 296
dihybrid cross 204, 206, 266, 300, 301
dihydroxycholecalciferol 130
diploid 54, 58, 85, 87, 226, 243, 292
disjunction 56, 60
distal tubule 158, 162, 249, 250, 280
disulfide bonds 6, 216, 217, 253, 272, 281
Divergent evolution 208
DNA 12, 14, 28, 31, 33-37, 39-45, 47, 48, 50, 53-56, 58, 61, 62, 65, 67, 71, 79-81, 83, 86, 89, 96, 124, 216, 223-226, 229-232, 252, 273-276, 289-292
DNA ligase 35, 39, 44, 230
DNA polymerase 34-36, 40, 44, 290
DOHCC 130

domains 70, 207
dominant 182, 203-206, 209, 210, 265, 266, 285, 300
dormant 82, 85
dorsal 107, 108, 211, 293
dorsal root ganglion 108
double helix 12, 14, 33-36, 39, 44, 224, 225
double stranded 33, 35, 36, 39, 44, 54, 71, 79, 223, 225, 229-232, 274, 289
duodenum 141, 144, 145, 147, 148, 279, 296
Duplications 50
dynein 93

## E

E. coli 37, 71, 83, 146, 231
ectoderm 137, 140, 295
effector 108, 118, 120, 121, 123, 128, 130, 234, 279, 293, 294
eicosanoids 4
elastic 77, 165, 198, 200
electrical gradient 75
electrical synapses 104, 164, 192
Electrical synapses 104
electrochemical gradient 75, 76, 98, 236, 292
electrolyte absorption 146
electromagnetic receptors 112
electron transport chain (ETC) 27
elements 41, 50, 202, 211, 229
elongation 36, 46
embryonic stem cells 136
emigration 209, 210
Endocrine 119, 123, 138, 139
Endocrine glands 119, 123
endocytosis 90, 92, 232, 291
endocytotic 91, 92
endoderm 137, 140, 295
endoplasmic reticulum (ER) 91, 235
endospores 82, 228
endosymbiont theory 96
endothelium 97, 157, 177
energy storage 14, 92, 149, 152, 195, 289
Enhancers 37
enslavement 209
enterocytes 10, 22, 55, 144-146, 149, 151, 156
enterokinase 145, 279
envelope 47, 65, 77, 84, 89-91, 222, 232, 271
Environmental sensory input 199
enzymes 8, 10, 15-20, 23, 37, 39, 74, 77, 84, 91, 92, 105, 119, 120, 122, 124, 129, 133, 135, 142, 144, 145, 148, 151, 177, 178, 184, 199, 216, 217, 224, 235, 240, 246, 247, 271, 272, 277, 279, 289, 292, 293, 296
enzyme specificity 15
enzyme-substrate complex 15
eosinophils 176
Eosinophils 177, 179
ependymal cells 106, 169
epidermis 199, 200
epididymus 133, 140, 295
epiglottis 170
epinephrine 110, 122, 128, 234, 240, 241, 244, 260, 276-278
Epinephrine 116, 122, 128, 131, 138, 139, 165, 240, 241, 276, 278, 294

gluconeogenesis 21, 127, 129, 131, 138, 151, 155, 156

glucose 10, 11, 14, 15, 19, 22, 23, 27, 29, 37, 76, 77, 92, 98, 100, 123, 126, 127, 129, 131, 138, 147, 149, 151, 155-157, 162, 218, 219, 234, 235, 240, 248, 260, 261, 272, 277, 280, 283, 294, 295, 296

glucose 6-phosphate 22, 92, 235

glyceraldehyde 3-phosphate 22, 219, 272

glycerol 3, 4, 21, 26, 73, 127, 147

glycocalyx 71, 97

glycogen 10, 14, 22, 92, 100, 127, 129, 149, 155, 156, 190, 219, 235, 240, 241, 260, 261, 277, 283, 289, 296

glycogenesis 149, 155

glycogenolysis 14, 21, 129, 149, 156, 276, 296

Glycolipids 4

Glycolysis 1, 22, 28, 29, 218, 219, 290, 296

glycoproteins 74, 217, 232

Glycoproteins 8

glycosaminoglycans 96

glycosidases 92

glycosylated 91

glycosylation 91

goblet cells 144, 156, 170

Golgi 47, 91, 92, 98, 116, 120, 152, 177, 235, 242, 293

Golgi apparatus 91, 98, 120, 152, 235, 242

Golgi complex 91, 235

gonadal hormones 122

gonads 122, 132, 137

G-proteins 18, 105, 240, 278

gradient 10, 22, 27, 29, 75-77, 79, 98, 149, 151, 157, 217, 236, 249, 259, 281, 282, 283, 292, 298

Gram-negative bacteria 77

gram-positive bacteria 77, 82

Gram staining 77

granular 91, 158, 176

granular cells 158

granular leukocytes 176

granulosa cells 134, 135, 243, 278

gray matter 106

guanine (G) 33

gustatory 114

# H

habitat isolation 207

hair cells 114, 118, 293

Haldane effect 172

haploid 54, 58, 60, 84, 85, 87, 226, 243, 292

hapten 179

Hardy-Weinberg 203, 209, 210, 213, 265, 266

Hardy-Weinberg equilibrium 209, 210

Haversian (central) canals 195

HCG 20, 132, 136-139, 242, 278

head 114, 133, 135, 175, 184, 188

heart 97, 105, 109-111, 118, 131, 137, 140, 163, 164, 166-168, 192, 194, 234, 236, 246, 255, 277, 278, 290, 295, 297, 299, 300

helicase 34

helix 6-8, 12, 14, 28, 33-36, 39, 44, 83, 224, 225, 259

helix destabilizer proteins 35

helper T cell 179

helper T cells 180

hematocrit 176, 248, 280

heme 9, 13, 16, 27, 170, 254, 255, 282

heme cofactor 170

hemoglobin 8, 9, 19, 48, 145, 170-173, 176, 190, 254, 255, 260, 261, 282, 283, 298

hemopoiesis 195

hepatic cells 10

hepatic portal vein 154

hepatic sinusoids 154

hepatic vein 154

heterochromatin 31, 54, 55

heterogeneous nuclear RNA [hnRNA] 38

Heterotrophs 86

heterozygous 182, 204, 209, 265, 266, 285, 300

Hexokinase 15, 19, 22

hGH 121, 125, 126, 138, 139

high-density lipoproteins 152

high density lipoproteins (HDL) 4, 246

histamine 143, 179, 252

Histamine 178

histones 54, 71, 96

hollow nerve cord 211

holoenzyme 16

homeostasis 37, 157, 158, 235

homologous 50, 54, 58, 204, 206, 208, 285, 301

homologues 54

homoplastic 208

homozygous 182, 204, 205, 210, 265-267, 285, 300, 301

hopanoids 73, 74

Hormonal communication 99

hormones 4, 8, 14, 75, 90, 99, 119-128, 130-132, 138, 143, 145, 147, 156, 176, 193, 240-244, 260, 276, 278, 279, 281, 289, 294, 295

host 65, 71, 79, 81, 83, 229-232, 252, 275, 276, 291

human chorionic gonadotropin (HCG) 136

Human growth hormone (hGH) 126

humoral 179, 281, 298, 299

hyaline 198

hybrid inviability 208

hydrochloric acid (HCl) 143

hydrogen bond 2, 217

hydrogen ion concentration 20, 170, 289

hydrolases 19, 92

hydrolysis 2, 14, 18, 24, 34, 141, 148, 219, 246, 296

Hydrophilic 2, 28

hydrophobic 2- 4, 6, 44, 156, 235

hydrostatic pressure 77, 158, 164, 166, 248, 279, 280, 296

Hydrostatic pressure 157

hydroxyapatite 13, 195

hyperplasia 190

hyperpolarization 101, 112

hypertonic 77

hypertrophy 190, 192

hyphae 84, 85

hypodermis 200

hypothalamus 110, 111, 118, 125, 126, 131, 186, 191, 234, 242, 243, 295

hypotonic 77

# I

ileum  141, 143, 144, 148
immigration  209
Immunity  181, 183, 199
immunoglobulin  179
immunoglobulins  176, 184, 253
implantation  136, 140, 295
inclusion bodies  71
incus  114
induced  15, 48, 152, 216
induced fit  15
induces  7, 137
inflammation  99, 178-180, 299
inhibin  132, 243
inhibitors  17, 19, 258
inhibitory postsynaptic potential (IPSP)  105
initiation  36, 37, 44, 46, 194
initiation complex  36, 37, 46
initiation factors  36, 46
innate immunity  178, 298
inner ear  114
inner membrane  27, 96
inner mitochondrial membrane  24, 29, 290
insensible fluid loss  199
insertion  49, 185, 186, 191, 225, 229, 274, 299
insertion or deletion  49
insulin  8, 10, 91, 100, 119, 121, 123, 128, 129, 131, 145, 147, 219,
     240, 294, 295
Insulin  10, 129, 131, 138, 139, 156, 296
integral  74, 76, 91, 98, 101, 235, 259, 283
integumentary system  200
interbridge  77
intercalated disc  192
Intercostal muscles  169
intermediate  29, 94, 99, 152, 193, 272
intermediate-density lipoproteins  152
intermediate filaments  94, 193
intermembrane space  27, 29, 96
Interneurons  108, 116
interphase  55, 58, 63, 226, 274, 291
interstitial fluid  99, 143, 152, 174
intracellular second messenger  120
intrinsic factor  143
intrinsic proteins  74
introns  38, 40, 44, 223, 273, 290
inversion  50
involuntary  109, 110, 142, 192, 193, 194, 299
ionophores  104
IPSP  105
iris  113, 193, 194, 234
iron  13, 16, 155, 170, 235, 254, 277
irreversible covalent modification  18
irreversible inhibitors  17
isomerases  19
isotonic  77
isozyme  22

# J

jejunum  141, 144
juxtaglomerular apparatus  158, 249

# K

karyotype  205
Keratinocytes  200
ketone bodies  155
ketosis  155
kidney  10, 22, 95, 124, 127, 131, 138, 151, 155, 157, 158, 247, 248,
     250, 261, 280, 294, 295, 296, 297
killer T cells  180
kinase  18, 19, 219, 235, 240-242, 258, 259, 277, 283
kinetochore  56
kinetochore microtubules  56
Kingdom  87, 207, 213, 301
Krebs cycle  12, 26, 27, 29, 96, 149, 272, 289, 290
K-selection  208, 210, 213
Kupffer cells  155

# L

lac operon  37
lactase  144, 247
lacteal  144, 246
Lactose  22, 37, 147
lacZ  40, 41
lagging strand  35
lamellae  71, 195
Langerhans cells  200
large intestine  141, 146, 148, 184, 250, 296
large population  42, 209, 210
large subunit  46, 53
larynx  128, 132, 169, 170
latent  122, 232
latent period  122
Law of Independent Assortment  204, 213, 265, 266, 285
Law of Segregation  204, 213, 265, 266
leading strand  35
leaflets  73, 74
leakage channels  76
left atrium  164, 297
left ventricle  163, 164, 168, 297
lens  112
Leukocytes  176, 183
leukotrienes  4, 173
Leydig cells  132, 243, 279
LH  121, 125, 126, 132, 134, 138, 139, 140, 242-244, 278, 295
Lieberkuhn  144
ligament  185, 191
ligases  19
lipase  145, 148, 152, 246, 247, 279, 296
Lipase  145, 147, 161
lipases  92, 246, 296
lipid  3, 4, 65, 73-76, 92, 121, 122, 124, 128, 156, 222, 229, 235, 241,
     294
lipid anchored proteins  74
lipopolysaccharides  77
lipoprotein lipase  152
lipoproteins  4, 152, 155, 246

Lipoproteins 4, 74, 152
liposomes 73
liver 10, 14, 22, 26, 29, 55, 92, 98, 127, 129, 131, 137, 145, 149, 151, 152, 154-156, 176, 179, 199, 235, 240, 241, 250, 261, 278, 283, 290, 293, 296, 298, 300
Local mediators 99
lock and key theory 15
locus 204, 265, 285
loop of Henle 157, 158, 162, 250, 281, 296, 297
low-density lipoproteins 152
low density lipoproteins (LDL) 4, 246
lower esophageal sphincter 142
luteal surge 134, 140, 295
lyases 19
lymph 97, 144, 152, 156, 174-176, 178, 180, 184, 186, 195, 202, 279, 296, 298, 299
Lymphatic System 163, 174
Lymphocytes 176, 177, 183
lymphokines 99, 178
lysogenic 230, 231, 275, 291
lysosomes 47, 91, 92, 261, 293
Lysosomes 92, 116
lysozyme 144
lytic 230, 275

# M

macrophages 90, 176, 178, 179, 252
malignant 52
malleus 114
maltase 144
Mammalia 207, 213, 214, 301
mast cells 179
matrix 8, 13, 24, 26, 27, 29, 35, 36, 53, 91, 96, 97, 104, 176, 195, 198, 217, 259, 260, 283, 289
matrix of a mitochondrion 24
mechanical isolation 207
mechanoreceptors 112
medulla 111, 118, 122, 125, 127, 128, 138, 140, 157, 158, 169, 172, 234, 281, 293, 297
medullary cavity 195, 300
Megakaryocytes 177
Meiosis 31, 58, 60, 61, 292
meiosis I 58, 60, 278
melanin 200
Melanocytes 200
melted 39
melting 39
melting temperature (Tm) 39
membrane 4, 8, 9, 22, 24, 26, 27, 29, 42-44, 47, 56, 60, 65, 71, 73-77, 83, 89-93, 95-98, 100-105, 107, 112, 114, 118-122, 124, 126, 129, 144, 151, 152, 157, 158, 177, 179, 182, 186, 189, 192, 198, 222, 231, 232, 235-237, 240-242, 247, 250, 252, 253, 258, 272, 273, 276-278, 280, 281, 289-294
memory B cells 179, 252, 281
memory T cells 180
Mendelian ratio 203, 285
Mendel's First Law of Heredity 204
Mendel's Second Law of Heredity 204
menstrual cycle 126, 134, 140, 243, 278
Merkel cells 200

mesencephalon 111
mesoderm 137, 140, 295
mesosome 71
Metabolism 1, 14, 21, 26, 28
metaphase 56, 58, 60, 63, 222, 226, 291
metaphase II 58, 60
metaphysis 195
methylation 39
micelle 73, 152
Michaelis constant 16
microfilaments 56, 93, 94
microglia 106
microtubule-organizing center 93
microtubules 55, 56, 79, 93, 94, 98, 169
microvilli 93, 114, 118, 144
middle ear 114
midpiece 133
mineral corticoids 122, 127
Minerals 1, 13, 28
mineral storage 195, 202
Minus-strand RNA 86
missense 48
missense mutation 48
Mitochondria 89, 96, 116, 273
mitosis 55, 56, 58, 60, 63, 79, 84, 87, 126, 136, 176, 190, 191, 195, 222, 226, 231, 259, 272, 273, 275, 278, 283, 291, 292
Mitosis 31, 56, 61, 222
mitotic spindle 93
moistens 170
Monera 70, 207
monocistronic 37
Monocytes 177, 179
monosaccharides 10, 21, 22, 145
morula 136, 137, 140
Motor (efferent) neurons 108
motor unit 189, 258
mouth 22, 141, 142, 148, 246, 250
movement 75, 93, 95, 114, 133, 140, 142, 165, 173, 185, 186, 191, 195, 197, 198, 217, 271, 297, 299, 300
mRNA (messenger RNA) 35
mucous 119, 143, 170
mucous cells 143, 170
Mucus 143, 170
multinucleate 186
multiunit 193
Multiunit smooth muscle 193
murein 77
muscarinic 110, 277
Muscle 97, 185-188, 190, 192, 193, 201, 259, 260, 277, 282, 284
muscle tissue 97, 185, 254, 261
mutagens 48, 52, 224, 225, 274
mutation 48-51, 224, 225, 240, 271, 274, 301
mutational equilibrium 209
mutualism 209, 210
mycelium 84
myelin 106
myofibril 186
myoglobin 8, 190, 254, 255, 258, 259, 260, 282
myosin 177, 186, 188, 191, 258, 299

# N

NADH 12, 21-24, 26-29, 219, 272, 290
Nails 200
nasal cavity 170
natural killer cells 179, 252
Negative cooperativity 19
negative feedback 18-20, 123, 126, 140, 180, 219, 279, 294
nephron 157, 158, 162, 237, 247, 249, 250, 280, 297
nerves 97, 100, 108, 111, 198, 200, 234, 259, 283, 295, 300
nervous tissue 97, 106
neural plate 137
neural tube 137
neuroglia 106
neurohypophysis 126
neurolemmocytes 106
neuromuscular synapse 189
neuron 8, 100-102, 104, 105, 107, 108, 118, 189, 193, 194, 231, 236, 237, 258, 259, 289, 293, 299
Neuronal communication 99
neurotransmitter 99, 104, 105, 108, 110, 234, 249, 276, 277, 293, 294
neurotransmitters 99, 105, 110, 119
neurula 137
neurulation 137
neutral mutation 48, 271
neutrophils 90, 176, 178, 179, 180
Neutrophils 177, 178
niche 208
nicked 80
nicotinic 8, 110
nitrocellulose 42, 43
nociceptors 112
nodes of Ranvier 106
non-coding 37
Noncompetitive inhibitors 17
nondisjunction 60, 226, 274
nonsense 46, 49
nonsense mutation 49
noradrenaline 110, 128
norepinephrine 110, 122, 128, 240, 276
Northern blot 43
notochord 137, 211, 214
N-terminus 46
nuclear envelope 47, 84, 89, 91, 222
nuclear pores 35, 46, 89
nucleases 92
nucleic acid hybridization 39, 43
nucleic acids 9, 12, 15, 148, 218, 232, 271, 293
nucleoid 71, 292
nucleolus 35, 46, 56, 89, 98, 290, 292
nucleosidases 144
nucleosome 54
nucleotide derivatives 1
Nucleotides 1, 12, 26, 28, 147
nucleus 4, 35, 36, 38, 44-47, 53-56, 71, 83, 84, 89, 91, 98, 110, 121, 122, 128, 135, 176, 177, 192, 193, 200, 222, 223, 230, 231, 240, 242, 243, 250, 255, 259, 273, 276-278, 282, 290, 292-294

# O

$O_2$ molecule 170
oblongata 169, 293
oils 3
Okazaki fragments 35, 44, 274
olfactory 114
oligodendrocytes 106
oncogenes 52
one nucleus 71, 192, 193, 259
oocyte 58, 60, 134, 135, 243, 278, 291
oogonium 58
Oomycota 84
open system 174, 175, 282
operator 37
operon 37
order 9, 16, 19, 33, 35, 40, 53, 55, 60, 65, 76, 80, 83, 92, 95, 103, 105, 109, 114, 121, 148, 185, 210, 214, 231, 240, 244, 261, 264, 267, 271, 272, 275, 276, 278, 280, 286, 291, 294, 297-301
Order 207, 213, 301
organ of Corti 114, 293
organs 92, 95, 97, 100, 109, 128, 137, 138, 184, 195, 234, 242, 295
origin 34, 39, 47, 79, 185, 186, 191, 214, 299
origin of replication 34, 79
osmotic pressure 77, 149, 157, 166, 174, 176, 279
Osteoblasts 195, 201, 259
Osteoclasts 195, 201, 259, 278
Osteocytes 195, 201
osteon (Haversian system) 195
Osteoprogenitor (or osteogenic) cells 195
outer ear 114
outer membrane 24, 26, 77, 96, 292
oval window 114
oviduct 134
ovulation 58, 134-136, 138, 140, 243, 244, 278, 295
ovum 60, 135, 137, 140, 242
oxidative phosphorylation 22, 27, 219
oxidoreductases 19
oxygen dissociation curve 19, 170, 254, 282
oxyhemoglobin 170
oxyhemoglobin ($HbO_2$) dissociation curve 170
oxytocin 121, 124, 126
Oxytocin 126, 138, 294

# P

palindromic 39
pancreas 22, 98, 119, 124, 128, 129, 137, 140, 145, 147, 154, 237, 246, 247, 296
pancreatic 18, 119, 121, 145, 147, 148, 156, 184, 246, 279
pancreatic amylase 145, 148
pancreatic hormones 121
Paracrine System 4, 89, 99
parallel 6, 110
parasitism 209, 210
parasympathetic 109, 110, 111, 113, 118, 164, 168, 194, 234, 276, 277, 300
parathyroid glands 130
parathyroid hormone 121, 124, 130, 131, 202, 260, 294
Parietal cells 143, 296

parietal (oxyntic) cells  143
partial  170, 173, 249
passive diffusion  76
PCR  38, 39, 42, 44-47, 62, 290
penicillin  77, 87, 292
Penicillin  17, 83
pepsin  8, 18, 142, 143, 148, 296
pepsinogen  18, 143, 296
peptide  5, 6, 18, 47, 53, 119-122, 125-130, 132, 136, 143, 147, 217, 243, 271, 272, 278, 281, 291
peptide bonds  5, 18, 271
peptide hormones  119-122, 125, 128, 147
Peptide hormones  120, 240, 281
peptidoglycan  17, 77, 83, 87, 229, 276, 292
peptidyl site  46, 291
peptidyl transferase  46
perforin  180
perichondrium  198, 259
perilymph  114
Peripheral  74, 116
peripheral chemoreceptors  172
peripheral nervous system (PNS)  108
periplasmic space  77
peristalsis  142, 145, 191, 194
peristaltic action  142
Peroxisomes  92, 116
phagocytosis  79, 90, 92, 93, 179
phagocytotic cells  178, 198, 252
phagosome  90
pharyngeal slits  211
pharynx  169, 170
phenotype  204, 205, 210, 273, 285, 300, 301
pH of 6  145, 279
phosphatases  19, 235
phosphate  4, 12, 22, 33, 34, 44, 46, 73, 92, 130, 157, 188, 197, 202, 218, 219, 223, 228, 235, 240, 258, 260, 272, 283, 289, 290, 300
phosphate group  4, 12, 22, 33, 73, 258, 272, 283, 289, 290
phosphodiester bond  33
phosphodiester bonds  12, 14, 39, 44, 289
phospholipid  4, 53, 73, 75-77, 89, 92, 96, 98, 235, 276, 277, 289, 292, 293
Phospholipids  28, 235
photosynthetic bacteria  211
phototrophs  70
Phylum  207, 213, 301
pigments  112, 113, 157
pili  79, 193, 200
piloerection  199, 234
pinna  114
pinocytosis  90, 92, 165
placenta  122, 132, 136, 137, 242, 278
Plantae  207
Plasma  86, 176, 179, 183, 252, 253, 282, 298
plasma cells  179, 180, 184, 252, 253, 298
plasma membrane  47, 71, 73, 74, 77, 83, 91, 277, 292
plasmid  40, 80, 230, 275
platelet plug  177
Platelets  162, 177, 183, 282, 297
pleated sheet  6, 7

PNS  108, 116
point mutation  48
polar body  60, 135
polarity  75, 101
polyadenylated  38
poly A tail  38
polycistronic  37
polymerase chain reaction (PCR)  42
polymorphic  43
polymorphism  208
polypeptides  5, 46, 47, 126, 145, 151, 156, 253, 282
polyploidy  50
pons  111
porin  24
positive cooperativity  19
Positive feedback  18
postabsorptive state  152
posterior pituitary  14, 121, 126, 131, 249, 281, 295
posterior pituitary hormones  121
postganglionic neurons  110, 234, 276
Post-transcriptional Processing  31, 38
post-translational modifications  46
p + q = 1  209, 212, 301
pre-mRNA  38, 223
preprohormone  120
primary antibody  43
primary follicle  134
primary oocyte  58, 134, 243, 291
primary response  179
primary spermatocyte  58, 63, 226, 274, 291
primary structure  6, 8, 216, 235, 254, 271, 282
primary transcript  38, 44
primary urine  157
Primase  34
primer  34-36, 44, 290
primitive streak  137
prions  67
probe  40, 42, 43
proenzyme  18
progesterone  20, 122, 126, 134, 136-138, 140, 242, 278, 289, 295
prohormone  120
prokaryotes  31, 34-38, 53, 71, 73, 83, 96, 214, 222, 223, 225, 229, 230, 232, 273-275, 291, 292
Prokaryotes  36, 46, 65, 70, 71, 86, 225, 272, 276, 291, 292, 301
Prolactin  121, 126, 138, 139
proline  7, 14, 217, 271
promoter  36, 37
prophage  230, 232, 275
Prophase  56, 62
prophase I  58, 63, 226, 291
prophase II  60, 63, 226
prostaglandins  4, 178, 289
Prostaglandins  99
prostate  133
prosthetic  9, 13, 16, 112
proteases  92, 247, 296
protection  38, 97, 178, 195, 197, 295
Protection  199
protein kinase  18, 235, 240-242, 277
Protein metabolism  155

Proteins 1, 5, 9, 26, 28, 47, 74, 86, 91, 92, 141, 147, 151, 174, 216, 277, 282
proteoglycans 96, 198, 259
Proteolytic cleavage 18
prothrombin 155, 177
Protista 207
proton-motive force 27
proto-oncogenes 52
protoplast 77
protostomes 211
protrombin activator 177
provirus 66
proximal tubule 10, 157, 158, 162, 237, 249, 280, 296
P site 46, 53
PTH 121, 130, 139, 244
pulmonary circulation 164, 297
pulmonary veins 164, 173, 298
Punnett square 204, 205, 285, 300
pupil 113
purines 33
Purkinje fibers 164, 165
pus 179
pyloric sphincter 145
pyrimidines 33, 224, 274
pyrophosphate group 34
pyruvate 21, 22, 24, 26, 29, 219, 272, 290
pyruvic acid 22, 26

## Q

quaternary structure 6- 8, 46, 216, 254, 272, 281, 282

## R

rapid 84, 99, 100, 135, 186, 194, 252, 259, 264, 297
reabsorption 127, 130, 131, 157, 158, 162, 250, 294
receptor 47, 90, 104, 105, 108, 112, 119-121, 124, 129, 231, 240-242, 250, 252, 277, 278, 291, 294
receptor mediated endocytosis 90
receptors 8, 74, 90, 107, 110, 112, 119-122, 186, 199, 234, 240, 241, 244, 249, 276-278, 293, 294
recessive 182, 203-206, 209, 210, 226, 265-267, 285, 300, 301
recognition sequence 39
recombinant DNA 39, 40, 42
rectum 141
red bone marrow 195
reduction division 60
regulated secretion 91
relative refractory period 103
release factors 46
renal calyx 158
renal corpuscle 157, 158
renal pelvis 157, 158
renal pyramids 158
repetitive sequence DNA 31
replication 34-36, 44, 48, 58, 63, 79, 124, 222-226, 273, 274, 290
replication fork 34
replication units 34
replicons 34
replisome 34
repolarization 101

repressors 36, 37
residue 5
respiration 21, 22, 24, 27, 29, 96, 100, 219, 254, 258, 259, 272, 283, 290, 291, 298
resting potential 101, 107, 236, 237, 277, 293
restriction endonucleases 39
Restriction enzymes 39
Restriction fragment length polymorphisms 43
restriction site 39
reticulocytes 176
retina 112, 113, 118
retinal 112
retroviruses 229
reverse transcriptase 40, 276
Reversible covalent modification 18
RFLP 43
Rh factors 182
rhodopsin 112
riboflavin 146
ribonuclease 145
ribosome 44, 46, 47, 53, 71, 98, 290, 291
ribosomes 35, 46, 47, 53, 71, 83, 89, 91, 92, 96, 223, 232, 253, 261, 276, 277, 291, 292
right atrium 164, 168
right lymphatic duct 175, 246
right ventricle 164, 168, 297
RNA 12, 14, 28, 31, 33-36, 38, 39, 42-47, 54, 55, 62, 65, 67, 71, 86, 89, 96, 98, 223, 229, 231, 232, 273, 274, 276, 289-291, 293
RNA polymerase 34, 36
RNA primer 34
rods 112, 113
roughage 146, 149
rough ER 47, 91, 92, 120, 122, 235, 242, 277
round window 114
rRNA 35, 38, 46, 53, 89, 273, 290, 292
rRNA (ribosomal RNA) 35
r-selection 208, 210

## S

saltatory conduction 106, 107, 237, 277
saltus 106
saprophytic 84, 87, 292
sarcolemma 186, 189, 258, 259, 283
sarcomere 186, 188, 191, 258, 259, 283
sarcomeres 190, 192, 193
sarcoplasmic reticulum 186, 188, 189, 191, 194, 258, 277, 283, 299
satellite cells 106
Saturated fatty acids 3
saturation kinetics 16
scala tympani 114
scala vestibuli 114
Schwann cells 106, 107
seasonal isolation 207
sebaceous 119, 200
sebaceous (oil) gland 200
secondary active transport 10, 76, 149, 249, 292
secondary antibody-enzyme 43
secondary follicle 134
secondary oocytes 60
secondary response 179, 180

secondary spermatocytes 60
secondary structure 6, 216
second messenger system 105, 124, 126, 129, 240, 250, 281, 294
secreted 47, 71, 124, 127, 134, 145, 147, 148, 157, 170, 240, 242, 243, 246-248, 280, 294-296
Secretin 147
secretory vesicles 91, 120
Secretory vesicles 91
sedimentation coefficients 46
segmentation 145
selective hybrid elimination 208
selectively permeable 76
self-antigens 180
Semen 133, 139
semicircular canals 114, 118
semiconservative 34, 290
semidiscontinuous 35
seminal vesicles 132, 133
seminiferous tubules 132, 133, 243, 295
semipermeable 75
sense strand 36, 44, 225, 274
Sensory (afferent) neurons 108
septa 84, 165
Sertoli cells 132, 133, 243, 279
serum 156, 176, 246, 279
sex chromosome 205, 226
sex-linked 205, 206, 226, 267
sex-linked disease 205
sex pilus 79, 80
side chains 5, 6
sigmoid colon 141, 146
signal peptide 47, 53, 291
signal-recognition particle (SRP) 47
signal sequence 91
silent mutation 48
Simple epithelium 97
single nucleotide polymorphisms (SNPs) 43
single stranded 35, 39, 42, 225, 230, 231, 289
single-unit 193
Single unit smooth muscle 193
sinoatrial node (SA node) 164
sinusoids 154
size 42-44, 52, 55, 65, 75-77, 103, 126, 136, 140, 145, 165, 186, 189, 217, 218, 242, 248, 264, 271, 272, 274, 280, 293
Skeletal muscle 185, 186, 191, 192, 259, 299
skin 4, 8, 49, 94, 95, 114, 118, 128, 137, 178, 186, 194, 199, 200, 202, 224, 265, 281, 295
slime layer 71, 79
slow oxidative (type I) fibers 190
small intestine 16, 20, 22, 77, 118, 131, 141, 144, 145, 147-149, 162, 246, 281, 289, 296
small subunit 46
smooth endoplasmic reticulum 92, 98, 121, 152, 156, 235, 240, 246, 253, 261, 293, 294
smooth muscle 4, 99, 104, 105, 109, 110, 142, 144, 165, 173, 174, 185, 193, 194, 200, 241, 249, 276, 278, 298, 299
SNPs 43
snRNPs 38, 223, 273
snurps 38
sodium 8, 10, 75, 98, 101, 107, 112, 124, 147, 149, 151, 157, 158, 168, 194, 217, 249, 250, 277, 280, 292, 293, 294, 296, 297

solenoids 54
somatic mutation 48
somatic nervous system 108, 110, 118, 234, 276, 299
Somatostatin 128
somatotropin 126
Southern blotting 43, 44
Speciation 208, 213
Species 207, 213, 301
specific 13, 15, 16, 18, 33, 37, 43, 65, 75, 76, 90, 99, 100, 105, 111, 119, 120, 126, 151, 164, 176, 178-180, 199, 216, 231, 253, 276, 281, 282, 290, 291, 298
sperm 58, 60, 98, 132, 133, 135, 140, 295
Spermatogonia 132, 139
spermatogonium 58, 274
spike proteins 68
spinal nerves 108
spindle apparatus 56, 63, 93, 98, 291
spindle microtubules 56
spirilla 71
spirochetes 71, 292
spliceosome 38
Spongy bone 195, 300
spontaneous 48
sporangiophores 85
spore coat 82
spores 85, 228, 292
SRP 47, 53
SSB tetramer 35
SSB tetramer proteins 35
stapes 114
starch 10, 14, 142, 149, 279, 289, 296
stem cell 176, 260
stem cells 136, 184, 200, 243, 252, 281, 298, 300
stereocilia 114
sterility 208
steroid hormones 75, 119, 122, 124, 127, 294
Steroid hormones 121, 240
Steroids 4, 28, 124, 278, 294
sticky ends 39
stomach 16, 20, 97, 141-145, 147, 148, 154, 156, 178, 184, 193, 237, 246, 250, 279, 289, 296, 298
stratified epithelium 97
striated 186, 192
structural 4, 6, 8, 47, 94, 96, 97, 202, 259, 260, 283
structural proteins 8, 96, 259, 283
substrate level phosphorylation 22, 27
substrate-level phosphorylation 23, 26, 219
substrates 15, 16, 19, 289
sucrase 144
sudoriferous 119
Sudoriferous (sweat) glands 200
Sulfanilamide 17
supercoils 54
superficial fascia 200
superior and inferior vena cava 163
support 96, 97, 100, 106, 108, 126, 195, 197, 202, 275, 300
support tissue 97, 108, 126
suppressor T cells 180
survival of the fittest 208
Svedberg units (S) 46
symbiosis 146, 209

sympathetic 109-111, 113, 118, 128, 138, 165, 199, 234, 249, 276, 278, 281, 293-295

synapse 100, 102, 104, 105, 107, 108, 110, 118, 124, 189, 234, 237, 293, 294

synaptic cleft 104, 189

synaptonemal complex 58

synergistic 186

synergistic muscles 186

synovial fluid 198, 202, 300

Synovial joints 198

synthase 19, 27, 29, 272, 290

synthetases 19

systemic circulation 164, 166, 297

systems 10, 12, 52, 97, 99, 105, 109-111, 132, 185, 224, 234, 249, 260, 261, 276, 283, 294

Systole 164

# T

$T_3$ 122, 125, 126, 128, 138, 139, 294

$T_4$ 122, 125, 126, 128, 138, 139, 294, 295

tail 38, 65, 68, 69, 98, 133, 211, 214, 223, 273, 291, 303

target cell 120, 121, 240, 242, 250

taxonomical classification 207

T-cell immunity 179

Telomerase 35

Telomeres 35, 62

telophase 56, 60, 63, 222, 226, 273, 291

telophase II 60, 63

temperate virus 66

temperature 4, 16, 20, 39, 92, 112, 140, 170, 171, 173, 185, 191, 193, 199, 200, 202, 228, 234, 262, 289, 295, 299, 300

template strand 36

tendon 185, 191

termination 36, 45, 46, 53, 112

termination sequence 36, 53

Terpenes 4

tertiary structure 6, 7, 216, 218, 254, 255, 271, 281, 282, 289

testes 132, 140, 242, 243, 295

testosterone 122, 132, 138, 140, 242, 243, 244, 278, 279, 294, 295

tetrads 58, 60, 291

thalamus 111, 118

thermoreceptors 112

Thermoregulation 199, 201

thiamin 146

thick 71, 77, 91, 97, 165, 186, 191, 193, 200, 297, 299

thick and the thin filament 186

thick filament 186, 191, 299

thin filament 186, 191, 299

thoracic duct 152, 175, 246, 279

threshold stimulus 103, 107

thrombin 177

thromboxanes 4

thymine (T) 33

thyroid 122, 125, 126, 128, 130, 137, 138, 240, 244, 249, 279, 281, 294, 295

thyroid hormones 122, 128, 240

Thyroid-stimulating hormone (TSH) 126

thyroxine 122, 124, 128, 131, 294

Tight junctions 95

tissue 13, 14, 92, 95-97, 106, 108, 119, 122, 123, 126, 127, 129, 131, 132, 134, 136, 137, 144, 145, 152, 165, 176, 178-180, 184, 185, 195, 198, 200, 202, 240, 252, 254, 259, 260, 261, 265, 281, 283, 294

T-lymphocytes 180

totipotent 136

trachea 128, 169, 170, 173

traits 54, 206, 266, 285, 300, 301

transcription 35-38, 47, 48, 53, 63, 89, 105, 121, 122, 124, 126, 129, 137, 223, 229, 230, 240, 250, 273, 278, 290, 292, 294, 298

transduction 79, 81, 83, 230, 292

transferases 19

Transformation 80, 86

transition 48

transition mutation 48

Translation 31, 44, 46, 47, 53, 62, 91, 290, 291

translocation 46, 50

transport 8-10, 13, 24, 27, 29, 75, 76, 90-92, 96, 98, 100, 104, 121, 126, 149, 151, 152, 157, 158, 165, 176, 219, 240, 246, 247, 249, 250, 258, 272, 282, 290, 292-294, 296

transport maximum 157, 247

transposable elements 50

transposons 50, 229, 275

transverse colon 141, 146

transversion 48

transversion mutation 48

Triacylglycerols 3

triglycerides 3, 145, 149, 152, 156, 246, 260, 289, 296

triiodothyronine 122, 128

tRNA 35, 38, 46, 53, 273, 291

tRNA (transfer RNA) 35

tropomyosin 186, 188, 258, 299

troponin 186, 188, 258, 299

trypsin 16, 145, 148, 246, 279, 296

Trypsin 145, 147, 161

TSH 121, 124-126, 128, 138, 139, 244, 279, 294

T-tubules 188, 189, 194, 258, 259, 283

tubulin 8, 55, 93

tumbles 79

tumor 14, 52, 124, 240, 252, 273, 294

Turnover number 16

two fatty acid chains 73

tympanic membrane 114, 118

tyrosine 119, 121, 122, 125, 128

tyrosine derivatives 119, 122, 125, 128

# U

unambiguous 45

unidirectional 104

Unsaturated fatty acids 3

uracil 12, 35, 223-225, 273, 289

urea 148, 151, 155-157, 162, 176

ureter 157, 162

urethra 133, 157, 162

Urey-Miller experiment 211, 214

# V

vaccine 244, 253, 282

vagus nerve 164, 168, 194, 234, 277, 300

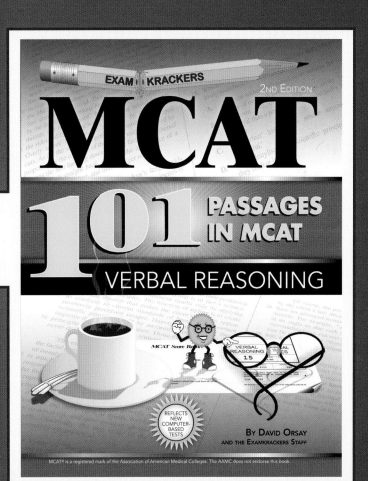

# An Unedited Student Review of This Book

The following review of this book was written by Teri R—. from New York. Teri scored a 43 out of 45 possible points on the MCAT. She is currently attending UCSF medical school, one of the most selective medical schools in the country.

*"The Examkrackers MCAT books are the best MCAT prep materials I've seen-and I looked at many before deciding. The worst part about studying for the MCAT is figuring out what you need to cover and getting the material organized. These books do all that for you so that you can spend your time learning. The books are well and carefully written, with great diagrams and really useful mnemonic tricks, so you don't waste time trying to figure out what the book is saying. They are concise enough that you can get through all of the subjects without cramming unnecessary details, and they really give you a strategy for the exam. The study questions in each section cover all the important concepts, and let you check your learning after each section. Alternating between reading and answering questions in MCAT format really helps make the material stick, and means there are no surprises on the day of the exam-the exam format seems really familiar and this helps enormously with the anxiety. Basically, these books make it clear what you need to do to be completely prepared for the MCAT and deliver it to you in a straightforward and easy-to-follow form. The mass of material you could study is overwhelming, so I decided to trust these books—I used nothing but the Examkrackers books in all subjects and got a 13-15 on Verbal, a 14 on Physical Sciences, and a 14 on Biological Sciences. Thanks to Jonathan Orsay and Examkrackers, I was admitted to all of my top-choice schools (Columbia, Cornell, Stanford, and UCSF). I will always be grateful. I could not recommend the Examkrackers books more strongly. Please contact me if you have any questions."*

*Sincerely,*
*Teri R—*

# About the Author

Jonathan Orsay is uniquely qualified to write an MCAT preparation book. He graduated on the Dean's list with a B.A. in History from Columbia University. While considering medical school, he sat for the real MCAT three times from 1989 to 1996. He scored in the 90 percentiles on all sections before becoming an MCAT instructor. He has lectured in MCAT test preparation for thousands of hours and across the country. He has taught premeds from such prestigious Universities as Harvard and Columbia. He was the editor of one of the best selling MCAT prep books in 1996 and again in 1997. He has written and published the following books and audio products in MCAT preparation: "Examkrackers MCAT Physics"; "Examkrackers MCAT Chemistry"; "Examkrackers MCAT Organic Chemistry"; "Examkrackers MCAT Biology"; "Examkrackers MCAT Verbal Reasoning & Math"; "Examkrackers 1001 questions in MCAT Physics", "Examkrackers MCAT Audio Osmosis with Jordan and Jon".

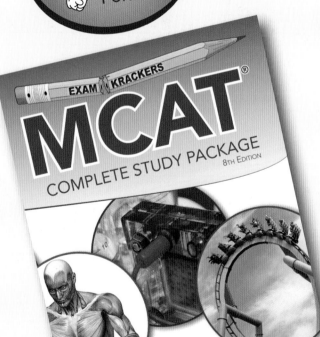

# Physical Sciences
Time: 70 Minutes
Questions 1–52

**PHYSICAL SCIENCES**

**DIRECTIONS.** Most questions in the Physical Sciences test are organized into groups, each preceded by a descriptive passage. After studying the passage, select the one best answer to each question in the group. Some questions are not based on a descriptive passage and are also independent of each other. You must also select the one best answer to these questions. If you are not certain of an answer, eliminate the alternatives that you know to be incorrect and then select an answer from the remaining alternatives. Indicate your selection by blackening the corresponding oval on your answer document. A periodic table is provided for your use. You may consult it whenever you wish.

## PERIODIC TABLE OF THE ELEMENTS

| 1<br>**H**<br>1.0 | | | | | | | | | | | | | | | | | 2<br>**He**<br>4.0 |
|---|---|---|---|---|---|---|---|---|---|---|---|---|---|---|---|---|---|
| 3<br>**Li**<br>6.9 | 4<br>**Be**<br>9.0 | | | | | | | | | | | 5<br>**B**<br>10.8 | 6<br>**C**<br>12.0 | 7<br>**N**<br>14.0 | 8<br>**O**<br>16.0 | 9<br>**F**<br>19.0 | 10<br>**Ne**<br>20.2 |
| 11<br>**Na**<br>23.0 | 12<br>**Mg**<br>24.3 | | | | | | | | | | | 13<br>**Al**<br>27.0 | 14<br>**Si**<br>28.1 | 15<br>**P**<br>31.0 | 16<br>**S**<br>32.1 | 17<br>**Cl**<br>35.5 | 18<br>**Ar**<br>39.9 |
| 19<br>**K**<br>39.1 | 20<br>**Ca**<br>40.1 | 21<br>**Sc**<br>45.0 | 22<br>**Ti**<br>47.9 | 23<br>**V**<br>50.9 | 24<br>**Cr**<br>52.0 | 25<br>**Mn**<br>54.9 | 26<br>**Fe**<br>55.8 | 27<br>**Co**<br>58.9 | 28<br>**Ni**<br>58.7 | 29<br>**Cu**<br>63.5 | 30<br>**Zn**<br>65.4 | 31<br>**Ga**<br>69.7 | 32<br>**Ge**<br>72.6 | 33<br>**As**<br>74.9 | 34<br>**Se**<br>79.0 | 35<br>**Br**<br>79.9 | 36<br>**Kr**<br>83.8 |
| 37<br>**Rb**<br>85.5 | 38<br>**Sr**<br>87.6 | 39<br>**Y**<br>88.9 | 40<br>**Zr**<br>91.2 | 41<br>**Nb**<br>92.9 | 42<br>**Mo**<br>95.9 | 43<br>**Tc**<br>(98) | 44<br>**Ru**<br>101.1 | 45<br>**Rh**<br>102.9 | 46<br>**Pd**<br>106.4 | 47<br>**Ag**<br>107.9 | 48<br>**Cd**<br>112.4 | 49<br>**In**<br>114.8 | 50<br>**Sn**<br>118.7 | 51<br>**Sb**<br>121.8 | 52<br>**Te**<br>127.6 | 53<br>**I**<br>126.9 | 54<br>**Xe**<br>131.3 |
| 55<br>**Cs**<br>132.9 | 56<br>**Ba**<br>137.3 | 57<br>**La***<br>138.9 | 72<br>**Hf**<br>178.5 | 73<br>**Ta**<br>180.9 | 74<br>**W**<br>183.9 | 75<br>**Re**<br>186.2 | 76<br>**Os**<br>190.2 | 77<br>**Ir**<br>192.2 | 78<br>**Pt**<br>195.1 | 79<br>**Au**<br>197.0 | 80<br>**Hg**<br>200.6 | 81<br>**Tl**<br>204.4 | 82<br>**Pb**<br>207.2 | 83<br>**Bi**<br>209.0 | 84<br>**Po**<br>(209) | 85<br>**At**<br>(210) | 86<br>**Rn**<br>(222) |
| 87<br>**Fr**<br>(223) | 88<br>**Ra**<br>226.0 | 89<br>**Ac**⁼<br>227.0 | 104<br>**Unq**<br>(261) | 105<br>**Unp**<br>(262) | 106<br>**Unh**<br>(263) | 107<br>**Uns**<br>(262) | 108<br>**Uno**<br>(265) | 109<br>**Une**<br>(267) | | | | | | | | | |

| * | 58<br>**Ce**<br>140.1 | 59<br>**Pr**<br>140.9 | 60<br>**Nd**<br>144.2 | 61<br>**Pm**<br>(145) | 62<br>**Sm**<br>150.4 | 63<br>**Eu**<br>152.0 | 64<br>**Gd**<br>157.3 | 65<br>**Tb**<br>158.9 | 66<br>**Dy**<br>162.5 | 67<br>**Ho**<br>164.9 | 68<br>**Er**<br>167.3 | 69<br>**Tm**<br>168.9 | 70<br>**Yb**<br>173.0 | 71<br>**Lu**<br>175.0 |
|---|---|---|---|---|---|---|---|---|---|---|---|---|---|---|
| = | 90<br>**Th**<br>232.0 | 91<br>**Pa**<br>(231) | 92<br>**U**<br>238.0 | 93<br>**Np**<br>(237) | 94<br>**Pu**<br>(244) | 95<br>**Am**<br>(243) | 96<br>**Cm**<br>(247) | 97<br>**Bk**<br>(247) | 98<br>**Cf**<br>(251) | 99<br>**Es**<br>(252) | 100<br>**Fm**<br>(257) | 101<br>**Md**<br>(258) | 102<br>**No**<br>(259) | 103<br>**Lr**<br>(260) |

## Passage I (Questions 1–6)

The following experiments were performed using the apparatus shown in Figure 1.

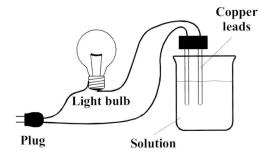

**Figure 1.** Apparatus to measure conductivity

*Experiment 1*

The copper leads were placed into distilled water, and the plug entered into a wall socket. The light bulb did not light. $Ba(OH)_2$ was added to the water until the solution was saturated. The light bulb turned on when the $Ba(OH)_2$ was added. When the indicator phenolphthalein was added to the solution, the solution turned pink. Next 0.2 $M$ $H_2SO_4$ was released drop-wise from a buret into the solution. The intensity of the light emitted from the bulb began to fade. A cloudy white precipitate also began to form. The solution changed to colorless as the light bulb dimmed and then went out. As more $H_2SO_4$ was added, the bulb began to brighten again.

*Experiment 2*

Experiment 1 was repeated substituting 0.2 $M$ NaOH for the saturated solution of $Ba(OH)_2$, and 0.2 $M$ HCl for $H_2SO_4$. The light bulb turned on when NaOH was added. As HCl was added the intensity of the light increased to some maximum, and then remained at that maximum throughout the rest of the experiment. The same color change observed in Experiment 1 was observed in Experiment 2.

1. From the results of Experiment 1, the color of phenolphthalein most likely changes from:

    A.  colorless to pink when going from a pH of 4.4 to 6.2
    B.  pink to colorless when going from a pH of 4.4 to 6.2
    C.  colorless to pink when going from a pH of 7.8 to 9.8
    D.  pink to colorless when going from a pH of 7.8 to 9.8

2. What is the concentration of hydroxide ions in the $Ba(OH)_2$ solution in Experiment 1 before $H_2SO_4$ is added? (Note: the $K_{sp}$ for $Ba(OH)_2$ is $4 \times 10^{-3}$)

    A.  $4 \times 10^{-3}$ $M$
    B.  $4 \times 10^{-2}$ $M$
    C.  $1 \times 10^{-1}$ $M$
    D.  $2 \times 10^{-1}$ $M$

3. Why isn't light emitted from the light bulb when the copper leads are placed into distilled water?

    A.  Pure water is a poor conductor of electricity.
    B.  The plug was not entered into the wall socket.
    C.  Impurities in the water obstructed the current.
    D.  A solution with a neutral pH will not conduct electricity.

4. Why does the light remain on throughout Experiment 2 but dim during Experiment 1?

    A.  The base in Experiment 1 contributes more hydroxide groups per molecule.
    B.  $Ba(OH)_2$ neutralizes the acid in Experiment 1.
    C.  The pH in Experiment 2 is greater than in Experiment 1.
    D.  Electrolytes are removed from solution by the reaction in Experiment 1 and electrolytes are created by the reaction in Experiment 2.

5. If the initial solutions in both experiments have the same pH, which solution has the lowest vapor pressure?

    A.  The $Ba(OH)_2$ solution in Experiment 1 because it contains more hydroxide ions.
    B.  The $Ba(OH)_2$ solution in Experiment 1 because it contains more metal ions.
    C.  The NaOH solution in Experiment 2 because it contains more hydroxide ions.
    D.  The NaOH solution in Experiment 2 because it contains more metal ions.

6. In Experiment 2 why does the intensity of the light bulb stop increasing?

    A.  The NaCl solution becomes saturated, and any additional ions form a precipitate.
    B.  The NaCl solution becomes saturated, and the dissociation reaction reaches equilibrium.
    C.  The solution reaches a point of maximum conductivity where additional ions will no longer increase the current between the copper leads.
    D.  The solution reaches a point of maximum conductivity where additional ions will no longer increase the voltage across the copper leads.

**GO ON TO THE NEXT PAGE.**

**Passage II (Questions 7–12)**

A chemist attempts to estimate Avogadro's number by the following simple procedure.

A watch glass is filled with water. Arachidonic acid, an unsaturated fatty acid with the molecular formula $C_{20}H_{32}O_2$, is deposited slowly on the surface of the water until it has spread over the entire area of the watch glass. (Diagram shown in Figure 1) Because arachidonic acid is largely hydrophobic, it spreads out in a layer one molecule thick.

**Fatty acid layer**

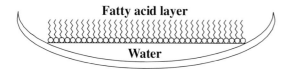

**Water**

**Figure 1** Fatty acid monolayer

Computer-modeling based on valence-shell electron-pair repulsion theory (VSEPR) indicates that the acid can be considered a cylinder with a length roughly three times as long as its diameter. Because the COOH group can bond to the water, these cylinders line up vertically with the hydrophilic COOH group adjacent to the water layer and the large hydrophobic portion projecting upwards.

By measuring the volume of acid used, along with the area of the watch glass, the thickness of the monomolecular layer can be determined. From there, the volume of a single molecule can be estimated, and hence the total number of molecules can be found. If the mass of the acid used to form the monolayer is measured, the number of moles can be found. From this information it is a simple matter to estimate Avogadro's number.

In this particular experiment, the chemist uses a solution of arachidonic acid dissolved in benzene. Benzene is used because it will evaporate rapidly, leaving only the monolayer of acid on the surface of the water. The concentration of the arachidonic acid is adjusted so that, once the benzene is removed, the volume of the arachidonic acid will be 0.01% of the volume of the original solution.

7. The method described in this passage was not the method historically used to make the first estimate of Avogadro's number. Instead the well-known value of the charge on one mole of electrons (1 Faraday = 96,485 C/mol) was used. In addition to this value, what other information had to be known to determine a value for Avogadro's number?

   **I.**   The mass of one electron
  **II.**   The charge on one electron
 **III.**   The mass of one proton
 **IV.**   The mass of one neutron

  **A.**   I only
  **B.**   II only
  **C.**   I, III, and IV only
  **D.**   I, II, III, and IV

8. According to VSEPR theory, what is the shape of $SO_2$?

  **A.**   bent
  **B.**   linear
  **C.**   trigonal planar
  **D.**   trigonal bipyramidal

9. If the watchglass has a diameter of 20.0 centimeters and the volume of the acid solution added is 0.1mL, which of the following represents the approximate thickness of the monolayer in centimeters?

  **A.**   $\dfrac{(0.1)(3.14)(10)^2}{0.0001}$

  **B.**   $\dfrac{(0.1)(0.0001)}{(3.14)(10)^2}$

  **C.**   $\dfrac{(4/3)(3.14)(10)^3}{0.1}$

  **D.**   $\dfrac{(0.1)(20)}{0.0001}$

**10.** What type of bond forms between the COOH group and the water?

    **A.** covalent
    **B.** ionic
    **C.** hydrogen
    **D.** Lewis

**11.** Why does arachidonic acid float on water but dissolve in benzene?

    **A.** The acid group of the arachidonic acid can form hydrogen bonds with the water, but not with the benzene.
    **B.** The molecule is nonpolar, and is therefore more soluble in benzene.
    **C.** Arachidonic acid is less dense than water but about the same density as benzene.
    **D.** Arachidonic acid is ionic, and therefore insoluble in water.

**12.** Which of the following, if true, would introduce the *least* error into the experiment?

    **A.** Not all the benzene evaporated.
    **B.** Surface tension caused the arachidonic acid to form a layer more than one molecule thick before spreading out over the water's surface.
    **C.** Some of the arachidonic acid protonated the water.
    **D.** The arachidonic acid was found to form circular coils rather than vertical columns under the conditions of the experiment.

**GO ON TO THE NEXT PAGE.**

13. A piston is used to apply pressure to an ideal gas inside a cylinder. The gas is warmed from 0° C to 25° C at a constant volume of 10 L. The pressure inside the cylinder increases by 1 atm. How much work is done on the gas?

    A. 0 J
    B. 10 J
    C. 250 J
    D. 500 J

14. The electron configuration of Cu is:

    A. $[Ar]4s^1 3d^{10}$
    B. $[Ar]4s^2 3d^{10}$
    C. $[Kr]4s^2 3d^9$
    D. $[Kr]4s^1 3d^{10}$

15. An ideal fluid moves to the right in a cylindrical pipe shown below. The radius of the pipe at point A is 5 cm, and the radius of the pipe at point B is 10 cm. If the velocity of the fluid is 36 m/s at point A, what is the velocity of the fluid at point B?

    A. 6 m/s
    B. 9 m/s
    C. 18 m/s
    D. 36 m/s

point A          point B

16. If points A and B are connected by a 2 ohm resistor, the power dissipated by the circuit will:

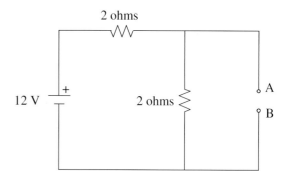

    A. decrease because the current generated by the battery will increase.
    B. decrease because the effective resistance of the circuit will increase.
    C. increase because the current generated by the battery will increase.
    D. increase because the effective resistance of the circuit will increase.

**Passage III (Questions 17–22)**

In 1910, Ernest Rutherford, Hans Geiger, and Ernest Marsden conducted a series of experiments in which alpha particles were projected at a thin gold foil. A schematic of the experimental apparatus is shown in Figure 1:

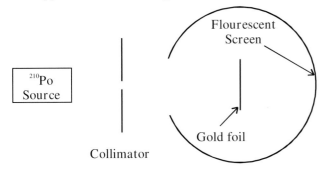

**Figure 1** Experimental apparatus

$^{210}$Po is the most common naturally occurring radioisotope of Polonium. It emits alpha particles with an energy of 5.30 MeV. The half life of this isotope is 138.40 days. The gold foil deflects the alpha particles into the fluorescent screen. By noting the appearance of any flashes on the screen, the angle of deflection of the alpha particle could be found. It was discovered that most particles were deflected very slightly from their original path, but a few were deflected at angles considerably larger, in some cases even returning back in the direction from which they came.

It is interesting to compare the scattering of alpha particles by the gold foil to the scattering of comets entering the solar system. If a comet's path does not happen to bring it near to the sun (or *very* near to a planet) it will only be deflected slightly. If the path ventures near the sun, however, the comet may whip around the sun, perhaps even returning in nearly the direction from which it came.

17. A sealed container holds a 0.20 gram sample of pure $^{210}$Po. After 277 days, what is the composition of the sample?

    **A.**  0.05 grams of $^{210}$Po and 0.05 grams of $^{206}$Pb
    **B.**  0.05 grams of $^{210}$Po and 0.15 grams of $^{206}$Pb
    **C.**  0.05 grams of $^{210}$Po only
    **D.**  0.20 grams of $^{206}$Pb

18. Which of the following is a true statement concerning a comet passing near the sun? (Assume the mass of the comet is negligible when compared to that of the sun. Ignore the effect of planets and any mass loss by the comet.)

    **A.**  The *momentum* of the comet is nearly conserved because the interaction with the sun is similar to an *elastic* collision.
    **B.**  The *momentum* of the comet is nearly conserved because the interaction with the sun is similar to an *inelastic* collision.
    **C.**  The *mechanical energy* (kinetic plus potential) of the comet is nearly conserved because the interaction with the sun is similar to an *elastic* collision.
    **D.**  The *mechanical energy* (kinetic plus potential) of the comet is nearly conserved because the interaction with the sun is similar to an *inelastic* collision.

19. Suppose the alpha particle felt no net force as it traveled through the foil. Which of the following would describe its motion?

    **A.**  It would circle clockwise.
    **B.**  It would circle counterclockwise.
    **C.**  It would slow down.
    **D.**  It would travel at a constant velocity.

20. Before conducting his experiment, Rutherford believed atoms were composed of a uniform positive "jelly" in which electrons were embedded like chocolate chips in a cookie. If this were an accurate structure for the atom, what would the result of Rutherford's gold-foil experiment likely have been? (The alpha particle was known to be much more massive than an electron.)

    **A.**  None of the alpha particles would have been deflected by a large amount.
    **B.**  All of the alpha particles would have been deflected by a large amount.
    **C.**  The alpha particles would have been absorbed by the foil.
    **D.**  The results of the experiment would have been unchanged.

**GO ON TO THE NEXT PAGE.**

**21.** When the alpha particle is emitted by the polonium atom, what energy transfer is taking place?

   **A.** kinetic to potential
   **B.** potential to mass
   **C.** electromagnetic to kinetic
   **D.** mass to kinetic

**22.** Which of the following describes what happens in the experiment when a flash appears on the fluorescent screen?

   **A.** An electron is absorbed, and its energy is transformed into photons.
   **B.** A photon is absorbed, and its energy is transformed into electrons.
   **C.** An alpha particle is absorbed, and its energy is transformed into photons.
   **D.** An alpha particle is absorbed, and its energy is transformed into electrons

---

**GO ON TO THE NEXT PAGE.**

Hess's Law states that enthalpies of reaction are independent of the reaction pathway. As a result, a known enthalpy of a reaction can be used to find the enthalpy of a reaction that cannot be measured experimentally. For example, the enthalpies of the Reactions 1 and 2 are known and can be used to find the enthalpy of formation for CO from graphite and oxygen. This value is $-110.5$ kJ ($\Delta H_2 - \Delta H_1$).

$$CO\ (g) + \tfrac{1}{2}O_2\ (g) \rightarrow CO_2\ (g) \quad \Delta H_1 = -283.0\ kJ$$

**Reaction 1**

$$C_{graphite} + O_2\ (g) \rightarrow CO_2\ (g) \quad \Delta H_2 = -393.5\ kJ$$

**Reaction 2**

A student measured the enthalpy of Reactions 3 and 4 using a coffee cup calorimeter. In the Reaction 3 a small strip of magnesium was placed in HCl solution at room temperature. The magnesium dissolved. The student determined the relevant reaction and change in enthalpy to be:

$$Mg(s) + 2H^+(aq) \rightarrow H_2(g) + Mg^{2+}(aq) \quad \Delta H_3 = -420\ kJ$$

**Reaction 3**

In the Reaction 4 MgO was placed in a fresh solution of HCl. The student determined the relevant reaction and change in enthalpy for this reaction to be:

$$MgO(s) + 2H^+(aq) \rightarrow H_2O(l) + Mg^{2+}(aq) \quad \Delta H_4 = -115\ kJ$$

**Reaction 4**

**23.** At very high temperatures, Reaction 1 will most likely be:

- **A.** spontaneous and exothermic
- **B.** spontaneous and endothermic
- **C.** nonspontaneous and exothermic
- **D.** nonspontaneous and endothermic

**24.** The enthalpy of formation for liquid water is $-285$ kJ/mol. According to the student's experiment, it can be determined that the enthalpy of formation of MgO(s) is:

- **A.** 590 kJ/mol
- **B.** $-47$ kJ/mol
- **C.** $-590$ kJ/mol
- **D.** $-820$ kJ/mol

**25.** Which of the following describes Reaction 3 at STP?

- **A.** exothermic and spontaneous
- **B.** endothermic and spontaneous
- **C.** exothermic and nonspontaneous
- **D.** endothermic and nonspontaneous

**26.** Given that $\Delta H_f$ for $H^+(aq)$ is 0, what is the $\Delta H_f$ of $Mg^{2+}(aq)$?

- **A.** 0 kJ/mol
- **B.** 420 kJ/mol
- **C.** $-420$ kJ/mol
- **D.** $-115$ kJ/mol

**27.** Why can Hess's Law be applied to Reactions 1 and 2?

- **A.** Because temperature is held constant
- **B.** Because enthalpies of reaction remain constant at any temperature
- **C.** Because enthalpy is independent of entropy
- **D.** Because enthalpy is a state function

**28.** Nitrosyl chloride is formed by the following reaction:

$$2NO(g) + Cl_2(g) \rightleftharpoons 2NOCl(g)$$

In a student experiment, this reaction is allowed to reach equilibrium in a sealed 22.4 L container at 0° C. The initial pressure is 10 atm. If the student adds 2 moles of NO gas to the sealed container and allows the reaction to reach equilibrium, the final pressure will be:

**A.** 10 atm because the equilibrium will not shift.
**B.** 12 atm because the equilibrium will not shift.
**C.** less than 12 atm because LeChatelier's principle predicts that the equilibrium will shift to the right.
**D.** greater than 12 atm because LeChatelier's principle predicts that the equilibrium will shift to the left.

**29.** 100 ml of 0.01 $M$ NaCl is mixed in a container with 100 ml of 0.01 $M$ Na$_2$SO$_4$. What is the molarity of Na$^+$ in the final solution?

**A.** 0.010 $M$
**B.** 0.015 $M$
**C.** 0.020 $M$
**D.** 0.030 $M$

**30.** If the voltage across the capacitor is doubled, the net force on the dipole will:

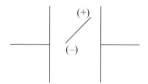

**A.** decrease by a factor of 2.
**B.** remain the same.
**C.** increase by a factor of 2.
**D.** increase by a factor of 4.

**31.** The hydraulic lift below lifts a 1 kg mass 5 cm. If the cross-sectional area of piston 1 is 25 cm$^2$ and the cross-sectional area of piston 2 is 100 cm$^2$, what is the approximate work done by force $F$?

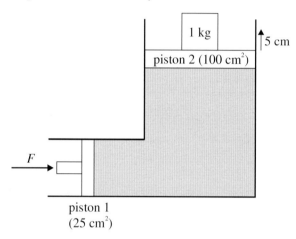

**A.** 0.5 J
**B.** 1.0 J
**C.** 2.0 J
**D.** 4.0 J

Earthquakes are vibrations of the Earth's crust caused by the release of built-up strain. The strain may have accumulated as the result of the movement of tectonic plates, the removal of vast weights when glaciers retreat, or occasionally other sources, such as the added weight of water behind a dam. The vibrations are classified into three broad types. The fastest type consists of the primary waves, or P waves, which are longitudinal waves that travel at approximately 7 km/s through crustal material and about 15 km/s through the Earth's liquid core. The period of P waves is usually short; typically less than one second. The second type is the secondary, or S, waves, which are transverse waves that travel at approximately 4 km/s through the crust. S waves do not travel at all through the Earth's core. The period of S waves is typically a few seconds. The final type of wave travels across the Earth's surface, rather than through the crust. These waves are sometimes referred to as Love waves, and often have periods well in excess of thirty seconds.

The amount of energy released by an earthquake is measured by the Richter scale. The Richter scale is a logarithmic scale similar to the pH scale of intensity, in that an increase of one unit on the Richter scale corresponds to an increase of a factor of ten in energy. Earthquakes of Richter magnitudes below 2.0 are rarely felt; the largest recorded Richter magnitude was approximately 9.0.

**32.** What is the approximate wavelength of an S wave with a period of 2.0 seconds?

   **A.** 0.68 km
   **B.** 2.0 km
   **C.** 8.0 km
   **D.** $6 \times 10^5$ km

**33.** One type of wave created by an earthquake is essentially a low frequency sound wave traveling through the Earth. Which of the following has characteristics most similar to those of a sound wave?

   **A.** Love waves
   **B.** P waves
   **C.** Richter waves
   **D.** S waves

**34.** A seismic station receives waves from an earthquake 200 km away. Assuming the P waves and S waves leave the source at the same time and travel through the crust, which of the following is true?

   **A.** The first P waves arrive less than five seconds after the first S waves.
   **B.** The first P waves arrive about twenty seconds after the first S waves.
   **C.** The first S waves arrive less than five seconds after the first P waves.
   **D.** The first S waves arrive about twenty seconds after the first P waves.

**35.** A building in an earthquake may sway back and forth with gradually increasing amplitude until a collapse finally occurs. This is an example of:

   **A.** destructive interference
   **B.** the Doppler shift
   **C.** resonance
   **D.** Young's modulus

**36.** The ratio of the energy involved in the largest recorded earthquake to the energy involved in one of Richter magnitude 5.0 is:

   **A.** 9:5
   **B.** 4:1
   **C.** 109:1
   **D.** 10,000:1

**11**

**GO ON TO THE NEXT PAGE.**

## Passage VI (Questions 37–42)

The lens system of a normal eye focuses images onto the retina, approximately 2.5 cm behind the lens, to produce sharp vision. The closest distance at which a person can see without blurring or eyestrain is called the *near point*; the furthest distance at which a person can see without blurring or eyestrain is the *far point*.

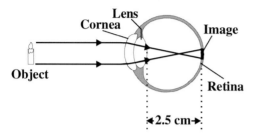

**Figure 1** The eye lens system

Since at least the sixteenth century, lenses have been used to correct vision problems. The most common problems are *myopia* (nearsightedness) and *hyperopia* (farsightedness). Individuals with near points of greater than 25 cm are considered hyperopic. Hyperopia is corrected with a converging lens. The prescription lens and the hyperopic eye together adjust the near-point back to 25 cm. If the far point is any distance short of infinity, the individual is considered myopic. For myopic patients, a diverging lens adjusts light rays from a distant object so that the image is focused onto the retina by the lens system of the eye.

Patients who are both myopic and hyperopic may either obtain two different prescriptions or wear bifocals.

For prescription glasses, it is common to report the reciprocal of the focal length measured in meters. For this purpose, reciprocal meters are referred to as *diopters*.

37. When a nearsighted person uses prescription glasses to view an object on the horizon, the image *formed by the glasses* is:

    **A.**   real, and the image is enlarged

    **B.**   real, and the image is reduced

    **C.**   virtual, and the image is enlarged

    **D.**   virtual, and the image is reduced

38. Light enters the eye through the cornea, and then travels through the anterior cavity, the lens and into the vitreous chamber. The index of refraction for each of these parts of the eye is 1.38, 1.33, 1.4, and 1.34 respectively. Light bends most at the interface between:

    **A.**   air and the cornea.

    **B.**   the cornea and the anterior cavity.

    **C.**   the anterior cavity and the lens.

    **D.**   the lens and the vitreous chamber.

39. Which of the following shows the path of a ray passing through a converging lens?

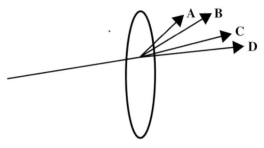

    **A.**   A

    **B.**   B

    **C.**   C

    **D.**   D

40. When a hyperopic individual uses his prescription glasses, the power of his eye lens system:

    **A.**   decreases, because the focal point is moved toward the lens.

    **B.**   decreases, because the focal point is moved away from the lens.

    **C.**   increases, because the focal point is moved toward the lens.

    **D.**   increases, because the focal point is moved away from the lens.

**GO ON TO THE NEXT PAGE.**

**41.** The exterior surface of a prescription lens, whether for myopia or hyperopia, is typically convex. Concentrated light sources sometimes reflect off this surface as if it were a mirror. Which of the following is true of such a mirror image created by glasses?

    **A.** It is reduced in size and on the same side of the "mirror" as the light source.

    **B.** It is reduced in size and on the opposite side of the "mirror" from the light source.

    **C.** It is enlarged in size and on the same side of the "mirror" as the light source.

    **D.** The side of the "mirror" that the image is on depends upon the radius of curvature of the convex surface.

**42.** Which of the following are capable of producing virtual images of an actual object?

    **I.** converging lens
    **II.** diverging lens
    **III.** concave mirror

    **A.** III only
    **B.** I and II only
    **C.** I and III only
    **D.** I, II, and III

---

**Passage VII (Questions 43–47)**

Lewis base strength is determined by several factors. Among them are the electronegativity of the central atom, the size of the central atom, the charge of the compound, and the amount of resonance stabilization.

Atoms that are more electronegative tend to make weaker bases, because they are less likely to donate electron-pairs from other substances. For example, water is a weaker base than ammonia, because oxygen is more electronegative than nitrogen.

Larger atoms are also weaker bases, primarily because an electron pair can spread out over a larger volume on a larger atom. This decreases the charge density, and therefore lowers the Coulombic repulsion between the electrons in the lone pair.

Negatively charged ions are stronger bases than neutral or positively charged ions, primarily because the charge density is higher. Likewise, an ion with a double negative charge tends to be a stronger base than one with a single negative charge. This is the explanation for the increasing base strength as a polyprotic acid dissociates: phosphate is a stronger base than $HPO_4^{2-}$, which is stronger than $H_2PO_4^-$, which is itself a stronger base than phosphoric acid.

Resonance stabilization can enhance the stability of a Lewis base by delocalizing electron-pairs over two or more atoms.

**43.** Which of the following is the best Lewis structure for $HPO_4^{2-}$?

**44.** Based on the $pK_a$ values for phosphoric acid given below, what would be the approximate pH of a 1.0 $M$ solution of $NaH_2PO_4$?

$$pK_{a1} = 2.16$$
$$pK_{a2} = 7.21$$
$$pK_{a3} = 12.32$$

**A.** 3.6
**B.** 7.0
**C.** 7.2
**D.** 11.8

**45.** Which is the stronger Lewis base, nitrate ion or nitrite ion?

**A.** $NO_2^-$, because it is a smaller molecule.
**B.** $NO_2^-$, because it spreads the negative charge over fewer atoms.
**C.** $NO_3^-$, Because it is the conjugate of a strong acid.
**D.** $NO_3^-$, because it is $sp^3$ hybridized.

**46.** If 1.0 mL of 2 $M$ aqueous sulfuric acid solution is added to 100.0 mL of 1.0 $M$ sodium hydroxide dissolved in ammonia, the result is a solution containing primarily:

**A.** $SO_4^{2-}$, $NH^{4+}$, $Na^+$, and water.
**B.** $SO_4^{2-}$, $NH^{4+}$, $NH_3$, $Na^+$, $OH^-$, and water.
**C.** $HSO_4^-$, $NH^{4+}$, $NH_3$, $Na^+$, and $OH^-$.
**D.** $HSO_4^-$, $NH_3$, $Na^+$, $OH^-$, and water.

**47.** Which of the following is NOT a Lewis acid/base reaction?

**A.** The reaction of HCl and NaOH
**B.** The dissociation of $H_2SO_4$ in aqueous solution
**C.** The reaction in which ammonia donates a pair of electrons to $BF_3$
**D.** The reaction in which a fluorine radical extracts a hydrogen atom from methane, resulting in a methyl radical

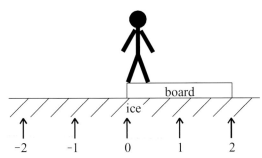

**48.** A 100 kg man stands on the left end of a 100 kg board 2 m long which sits on a frictionless surface as shown below. Where will the left end of the board come to rest if the man walks to the right end of the board and stops?

**A.** −2
**B.** −1
**C.** 0
**D.** 2

**49.** In the diagram below, beaker A contains a volatile solvent, and beaker B contains a 10% solution of a non-volatile solute in the same volatile solvent. Both beakers are placed in a closed environment as shown. Which of the following is true once the closed system has reached equilibrium?

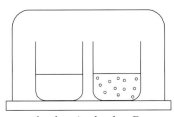

beaker A    beaker B

**A.** Beaker A will contain all the solvent.
**B.** Beaker B will contain all the solvent.
**C.** Beaker B will contain 90% of all the solvent.
**D.** Both beakers will contain the same amount of solvent.

**50.** A student removed an unknown solid substance from a freezer and placed it in a dish on his desk. When he returned, some of the substance had turned to liquid, and the remainder of the solid was floating on the liquid. Which of the phase diagrams might represent the unknown substance?

**A.**

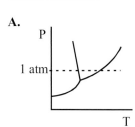

**C.**

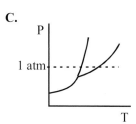

**B.**

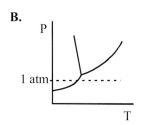

**D.**

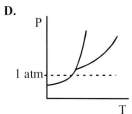

**51.** Approximately how many grams of NaCl must be added to 500 grams of water in order to lower the freezing point by 2° C? (Note: the molal freezing point depression constant for water is 0.51° C kg/mol.)

    **A.**   28.7 g
    **B.**   57.4 g
    **C.**   114.7 g
    **D.**   229.4 g

**52.** In order to lift the 30 kg mass, a force $F$ is applied to the massless meter stick shown below. How much weight must the fulcrum bear if the mass is to be lifted?

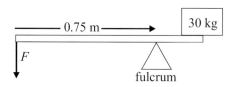

    **A.**   100 N
    **B.**   300 N
    **C.**   400 N
    **D.**   600 N

---

**STOP.** IF YOU FINISH BEFORE TIME IS CALLED, CHECK YOUR WORK. YOU MAY GO BACK TO ANY QUESTION IN THIS TEST BOOKLET.

---

**STOP.**

# Verbal Reasoning
Time: 60 Minutes
Questions 53–92

# VERBAL REASONING

**DIRECTIONS:** There are seven passages in the Verbal Reasoning test. Each passage is followed by several questions. After reading a passage, select the one best answer to each question. If you are not certain of an answer, eliminate the alternatives that you know to be incorrect and then select an answer from the remaining alternatives. Indicate your selection by blackening the corresponding oval on your answer document.

## Passage I (Questions 53–58)

It is generally recognized that shyness is a widespread problem. About 80% of Americans admit to having been shy at some point in their lives. Forty percent consider themselves shy now. …

5   But shyness is not easy to classify. Even self-described "shy" people are not necessarily shy in every social situation. Most are shy only in certain anxiety or stress-producing roles, like public speaking, confronting authority, dating, etc. … Interestingly, even those who don't
10  describe themselves as "shy" may actually experience the same symptoms as those who do. That is, a reticence to speak, blushing, queasiness, self-conscious preoccupation with how one appears to others, negative self-perception, etc. However, the former usually ascribe it to external
15  factors rather than intrinsic shyness. … The difficulty of identifying the "truly" shy is compounded because there is no external test for measuring shyness, other than observers' perceptions. However, these are far from accurate. … One study found that about half of self-described
20  shy people passed as non-shys, while 25% of self-labeled non-shys were actually seen as shy. …

Early theorists found that shyness runs in families, and often concluded that children of shy parent(s) were genetically predisposed to shyness. If this were true, it seems
25  there is little point in seeking effective therapies. But this finding may be flawed. … Today, it is well known that personality is determined by some combination of heredity and environment. But during childhood, heredity and environment tend to converge in the parents, who provide the
30  child with both during the psychologically-formative early years. … Further, some 40% of patients reported overcoming their shyness through various coping tactics. …

Some posit that it is bad parenting itself that causes shyness, especially when the child is made to feel that he is
35  not meeting expectations. Early labeling as "shy" or "underachiever" can lead children to a self-fulfilling prophecy, especially if the label is not periodically re-evaluated based on later achievements. The same is true of early negative experiences in dealing with people, which are
40  often exaggerated by the child's mind into a global phobia of interaction. But parents tread a thin line; nurtured over-achievers tend to have strong expectations of success, and childhood failures can be equally traumatic for them. … Further, parents have little control over the treatment their
45  child receives from teachers, and especially from classmates. … Even if parents created an ideal atmosphere, their children would still be exposed to American society's emphasis on competitiveness and self-reliance, and its habit of judging people by beauty, money, and status. … If such
50  early traumas are the root of shyness, then psychotherapy should be most effective in treating shyness, by allowing

the patient to understand the childhood trauma and avoid generalizing it into all situations. …

The noted shyness therapist … Zimbardo also pos-
55  tulates that certain modern lifestyle trends perpetuate shyness. For example, the ease of travel combined with job mobility exposes children following their parents' job relocations to the stress of moving to unfamiliar environments and losing old networks of friends. … In the inner cities,
60  fear of crime isolates neighbors. … Perhaps most importantly, children's frequent turning to television rather than social games as a recreation tends to acclimatize them to passive watching, rather than participation.

Finally, it may be that shy people lack social skills,
65  and would benefit from conversation skills training, which would allow them to make better social impressions. But again, the data is mixed. If a shy person is so inhibited that he cannot bring himself to join in a conversation, no amount of social skills will make any difference. Indeed, some
70  small-scale studies suggest that shys' negative self-evaluations are a worse impediment to socializing than any lack of skills. …

**53.** According to information in the passage, in the past, it was believed that a behavior based solely on genetics:

   **I.**    would be likely to respond to treatment.
  **II.**    would be unlikely to respond to treatment.
 **III.**    This information is not provided.

  **A.**   I only
  **B.**   II only
  **C.**   III only
  **D.**   I, II, and III

**54.** What distinction is implied in the passage between self-described shy people and self-described non-shy people, respectively?

- **A.** Shyness and non-shyness was perceived by others
- **B.** Genetically predisposed
- **C.** Poor and strong social skills
- **D.** Feels and does not feel shy

**55.** Suppose it is discovered that severe stutterers rarely suffer from negative self-images. Does this discovery support the author's argument?

- **A.** Yes; it confirms it.
- **B.** No; it does not affect it.
- **C.** No; it weakens it.
- **D.** No; it disproves it.

**56.** The passage suggests that some of the difficulty of classifying shyness derives from the fact that:

- **A.** "truly" shy people avoid these types of studies.
- **B.** suffering from the symptoms of shyness does not mean one feels shy.
- **C.** there are no external tests for shyness.
- **D.** shyness is blamed on society.

**57.** Which of the following assertions does the author support with an example?

- **I.** Shyness is not easy to classify.
- **II.** Shyness is a widespread problem.
- **III.** Certain modern lifestyle trends perpetuate shyness.

- **A.** I only
- **B.** I and II only
- **C.** II and III only
- **D.** I, II, and III

**58.** Which of the following statements is the most reasonable conclusion that can be drawn from the author's description of American society (line 47)?

- **A.** Parents should protect their children from exposure to American society.
- **B.** American society nurtures overachievers.
- **C.** American societal emphasis is the root cause of shyness.
- **D.** American society is not an ideal atmosphere for raising children.

**GO ON TO THE NEXT PAGE.**

**Passage II (Questions 59–63)**

Economists usually aim to improve systems' rationality, based on principles of efficiency and proper incentives. … Our modern system of criminal justice was influenced in part by such logical planning, but mostly by historical
5   factors which were founded more on abstract notions of "morality," "justice," and "vengeance" than on rational analysis. Not surprisingly then, the justice system which developed is largely inefficient from an economic standpoint. Any competent economist could devise the means to
10  reform it dramatically. Yet would the public, or the legislature, accept his suggestions? …

For example, when a perpetrator commits a crime, like burglary, we punish him, and only him. We feel he is the one who should be "punished", because he alone is
15  "morally blameworthy". Yet from an efficiency standpoint, also fining robbery *victims* a portion of the losses might be desirable; it would encourage them to take greater precautions against becoming victims of crime. Sometimes (though not always), victims abet criminals through their
20  "contributor negligence" (to use a legal term which reduces legal compensation for careless civil plaintiffs, but is never applied in criminal trials). This is often apparent in swindles, where a victim's gullibility and greed allows con men to get away with objectively preposterous, double-your-
25  money-overnight pitches. … Of course, fining victims is effective only if some precaution is actually possible against the specific crime, and not prohibitively expensive.

Occasionally, the victim is more blameworthy than the felon. For example, the crime of "statutory rape" means sex
30  with an underage woman. (Despite the name, it does not imply any force, and is almost always applied to consensual sex. Nor is it a defense that the man honestly believed the woman was older, even if she lied about her age.) Economists might debate whether consensual sex imposes
35  any societal harm which should be prevented. But it is certain that statutory rape, whether harmful or not, would occur less often if the woman were also punishable, since she would bear some cost of, and thus have incentives not to participate in, statutory rape. In those cases where the
40  man is truly unaware the woman is underage, the woman is actually the least-cost preventer, because she always knows her true age, so it would be more efficient to assign liability to her than to him.

Morally, however, such a rule would be unpalatable
45  for most people committed to the archaic conception of "justice", because such a "comparative negligence" rule implies that the criminal is not fully responsible for (or even "guilty" of) his/her crimes. Thus, the law would seem to blame the victim. … This is especially unpopular for crimes
50  such as forcible rape, for which the proper degree of bilateral precaution is unclear, and often mired in sexist/feminist dogma.

Another regime which makes little sense to economists is jailing criminals. The cost of imprisonment is, at last tally, over forty thousand dollars per year, which just happens to be the average American income. Assuming this
55  median income is subject to a tax rate of about one-third, it takes 3 people, working a total 6,000 hours, to support one criminal in a state of enforced unproductivity, for every year of incarceration. One of several ways to avoid this vast societal waste is not to jail minor felons for petty violations. …
60  But more broadly, serious felons should be required to pay their own way, which imposes added incentives to stay legal. … Of course, since many felons are indigent, this would require forced labor, which is not the most unproductive use of jail time. … Yet owing to our nation's
65  experiences with slavery and the ensuing civil war, the Supreme Court usually refuses to tolerate forced prison labor, and most of society would agree.

**GO ON TO THE NEXT PAGE.**

**59.** Which of the following assertions is the most effective argument *against* the author's concept that, from an economic standpoint, "forced labor … is not the most unproductive use of jail time" (lines 63–64)?

   **A.** It is even more expensive to pay for the guards which would be required to force prisoners to work.

   **B.** It is less expensive to simply fine the prisoners for their unproductive use of jail time.

   **C.** Forced labor is tantamount to slavery and was abolished during the Civil War.

   **D.** Forcing the prisoner to pay his own way is the most productive use of jail time.

**60.** On the basis of the passage, it is reasonable to conclude that:

   **A.** a competent economist could devise the means to successfully reform the criminal justice system.

   **B.** a competent economist would not be able to successfully reform the criminal justice system.

   **C.** the author recognizes that his economic perspective would not be widely accepted.

   **D.** the author fails to recognize that his economic perspective would not be widely accepted.

**61.** The author argues that, it is debatable whether consensual sex imposes any societal harm that should be prevented. Which of the following claims, if true, would most WEAKEN the argument?

   **A.** Young boys and older men should not be allowed to have consensual sex.

   **B.** Young women who become pregnant frequently take the lives of their newborn babies.

   **C.** Consensual sex involving a minor more frequently results in conception.

   **D.** Consensual sex among several partners results in a marked increase in sexually transmitted disease.

**62.** The author most likely believes that one of the main purposes of the criminal justice system should be to provide society with:

   **A.** an economically efficient system of preventing crime.

   **B.** an economically efficient system for housing and caring for incarcerated prisoners.

   **C.** a more modern system, based less upon archaic notions.

   **D.** a more equitable system for determining punishment.

**63.** The passage suggests that its author would probably *disagree* with which of the following statements?

   **A.** It might be worth jailing minor offenders if their sentences were slightly reduced.

   **B.** Statutory rape should not really be considered rape.

   **C.** A young person is able to make up their own mind regarding what is right and wrong.

   **D.** A woman can bear no fault for being forcibly raped.

**GO ON TO THE NEXT PAGE.**

## Passage III (Questions 64–69)

Today, most Western-looking political theorists view the democratically elected republic as virtually the only viable form of government. No doubt, this is partly due to the late 20th Century's bitter experience with Communism
5 and Fascism, and the United States' economic preeminence. … Yet for much of human history before the turn of the century, people experimented with various systems, from small tribal councils dominated by elder "wise men" and shamans, to dictatorship, to absolute and then constitutional
10 monarchy, etc. … Accordingly, most early political theory would posit that the *form* of a nation's government is not the prime determinant of that nation's success or virtue.

… During the Hellenic period, the most comprehensive treatment of political philosophy remains Aristotle's
15 *Politics*, which is a virtual catalog of all possible governmental types, with commentary on each one's features. … In *Politics*, Aristotle wrote, "those men may be expected to lead the best life [and] who are governed in the best manner *of which their circumstances admit*", … He then goes on to
20 define the "good" life as one where the individual has sufficient property, health, and morality. He clearly holds the government responsible for the material and even moral condition of its people. For example, in his criticism of an existing Hellenic city-state's constitution … he concluded
25 that unwisely framed property laws and civil codes had caused dissent, avarice, militarism, and arrogant feminism in an originally moral populace. … Aristotle recognized that there are three viable government types, which were created to strive for the public good, and can succeed in
30 giving the ruled good laws and a good life, to varying degrees. The most perfect of the three forms, the "polity" – essentially a representative republic with frequent elections – holds its preeminence because it is based on the just principle that all citizens should govern, and provides freedom
35 (or, at least, the chance to dominate) by revolving leadership among the citizens. In addition, this power sharing minimizes class struggle, resulting in a stable and moderate (Golden Mean) government with a large middle class, which tends to gravitate toward the Golden Mean in its policies.

40 However, Aristotle recognized that democracy and oligarchy were also viable systems, though not as universally applicable. … The democracy was "direct" democracy, with each person voting directly and equally, instead of through an elected representative. While this
45 system was definitely fair, it becomes impractical in any polis larger than a small town. … Also workable is the oligarchy, where a small ruling class determines governmental policy. But this system is valid only to the extent the ruling class is merit-based, and avoids entrenchment and
50 self-serving legislation. … For Aristotle, the only flatly unacceptable systems are those which are initially designed to favor one class over another; he claims they can only produce legislation that is either bad, or worse. …

Much later in history, Briton John Locke became the
55 preeminent representative of enlightened English political theory. … Locke, in his *Second Treatise*, repeatedly stressed that in a natural state, men had freedom and a right to property, and that "the chief end...of men's uniting into commonwealths...is the preservation of their property."
60 (The term "commonwealth" is meant to represent any independent, self-governing community, rather than a particular governmental type.) Locke stresses flexibility; while the legislative power is supreme, it can be given to the many, the few, or the one, depending on which works best for a
65 given people. In any case, Locke reasons, there is another reason the form of government is not critical. If the people are ever dissatisfied with it, they always retain their "natural" right to dissolve the government and choose another configuration, or a return to the natural state. The only limi-
70 tations on a government is that it must abide by popular consent, always act in the best interests of the community as a whole, and avoid depriving any innocent man of his property …. Clearly, these safeguards suggest a government is generally well ruled, regardless of its form. …

**64.** The author claims that Aristotle's idea of "power sharing minimizes class struggle, resulting in a stable and moderate (Golden Mean) government with a large middle class, which tends to gravitate toward the Golden Mean in its policies" (lines 36–39). The support offered for this conclusion is:

- **A.** strong; the acceptance of this system is based upon unreasonable assumptions.
- **B.** strong; the author outlines one of the suggested methods for peacefully transferring power.
- **C.** weak; there is no information provided regarding 'how' power sharing would take place.
- **D.** weak; there is no information provided regarding 'how' minimizing class struggle would result in a large middle class.

**65.** Author Aldous Huxley wrote that "Morality is always the product of terror; its chains and strait-waistcoats are fashioned by those who dare not trust others, because they dare not trust themselves, to walk in liberty". Based upon passage information, it is most likely that Aristotle would have:

- **A.** disputed that morality could be related to liberty or laws.
- **B.** argued that morality actually contributed to stability through good laws.
- **C.** concurred that laws concerning morality were the result of the minority inflicting its will on the majority.
- **D.** agreed that this might be so, but that it is not related to passage information.

**66.** Which of the following statements most strongly *challenges* one of the assertions made in the passage?

- **A.** A dictatorship is one of the most oppressive forms of government.
- **B.** In one form of democracy, the people actually vote for representatives.
- **C.** The best and most stable forms of government cannot be overthrown from within.
- **D.** A popular uprising is an acceptable result of a form of government gone awry.

**67.** The author is primarily concerned with demonstrating that the form a government takes is less important than:

- **A.** the people who are ruled by that government.
- **B.** the rulers of that government.
- **C.** has ever been theorized in the past.
- **D.** western political theorists think that it is.

**68.** The existence of which of the following prevalent situations would most strongly CHALLENGE the information in the passage?

- **A.** Irrefutable evidence that a monarchy was the most successful and virtuous form of government.
- **B.** The simultaneous existence of several forms of oppressive governments.
- **C.** The simultaneous existence of several forms of successful governments that were neither successful nor virtuous.
- **D.** Strong evidence indicating that no government can satisfy all of its citizenry.

**69.** Which of the following conclusions about Aristotle can be inferred from the passage?

- **A.** Aristotle was apparently renowned in his time and ours as a great philosopher.
- **B.** Aristotle's Hellenic period was predominantly characterized by small towns.
- **C.** Aristotle was not a supporter of what we today might refer to as "women's rights".
- **D.** By "dominate" (line 38), Aristotle meant that the leadership's decisions should never be questioned.

---

**Passage IV (Questions 70–75)**

A recent psychological experiment by Drs. Alloy, Abramson and Viscusi examined the relationship between depression and subjects' realism in judging the degree of their personal control over external events. Basically, the
5 experiment assembled people who showed signs of being depressed. They were given various mechanisms whereby they could win money, all of which were random in nature. The most transparent was a coin flip; heads they kept the quarter, tails they did not. More complex permutations had
10 them go through different ritualistic behaviors which might superstitiously be believed to influence luck. ... The two aspects of the study that could raise questions are its ecological validity (i.e. the extent to which the conditions of the study mimic reality, and thus are amenable to general-
15 ization in the real world) and its baseline assumptions that depressed patients tend to exhibit more "realism."

The procedure was well described, and most confounding factors were ruled out. However, ... the better the experimental design and the more well-controlled the
20 study is, the less ecologically valid it becomes. This is a problem with any experimental study that has well-defined experimental conditions; in the real world, situations like keeping flipped quarters ... rarely occur. This problem is so common that psychological experimenters are willing to
25 admit this limitation on their work.

The operational definitions of "depressed" or "elated" mood were specific, and appeared reliable. The investiga-tors evaluated a subject's mood by using scores from common questionnaire tests, like Beck's Depression
30 Inventory (BDI), the Multiple Affect Adjective Checklist, and writing speed. Although depressed persons usually exhibit lower scores on the BDI, it does not attempt to define depression clinically. Therefore, this study does not necessarily deal with depression in the clinical sense.
35 However, the study never purports to do so, using the term "depressed mood" throughout the article. This makes the experiment repeatable/verifiable. It also diminishes human error, as anyone can administer BDI and score it properly. ...Yet this prevents the investigators from making the more
40 powerful analogy between true depression and perceived control, since "depressed mood" may not be "clinical depression." Nonetheless, the symptoms of depression never expressly contradict any recognized symptom of clinical depression, allowing some speculation about their
45 similarity.

The investigators took other steps to bolster this comparability. For example, since decrease in writing speed is commonly found in clinically depressed individuals, the experimenters tested subjects' writing speed to help assess
50 their mood. As one experimenter pointed out, in the clinical world, there are so many influences at work that we cannot rule out a third variable influencing mood and perception of self-control. This study shows very well that one's mood often determines one's perception of self-efficacy, but only
55 under specific conditions.

The other aspect ... that readers may question is the assumptions that underlie the study. In their introduction, the investigators review the theoretical idea of "realism," and other researchers' hypotheses that non-depressives
60 often succumb to an "illusion of control," sometimes believing their actions can influence objectively-random outcomes. The experimenters argue that non-depressives' tendency to attribute successful outcomes to themselves and failure to outside factors resembles their predisposition
65 to form an "illusion." For depressives, their opposite at-tributional style should counteract such illusions. The term "realism" carries certain connotations that are only valid in this particular experiment. ... In this experiment, subjects really have *no* control over how much they win. But this is
70 not necessarily true for all situations, many of which do depend on internal factors rather than luck. This experi-ment does not suggest whether the depressive relinquishes control in all contingencies, or in realistic accordance with the circumstances. One cannot argue that depressives'
75 attributional style resembles realism, but only in some circumstances. ... Also, the experimenters tested only an event without the possibility of negative outcomes. ...

**GO ON TO THE NEXT PAGE.**

70. Which of the following scientific conclusions would most *compromise* the research reported in the passage?

   A. Depressed patients frequently believe that a failure on their part was not their fault.
   B. When offered additional opportunities to win, the depressed patients tended to refuse.
   C. Illusions are more commonly found among those who are not depressed than those who are.
   D. Non-depressives easily distinguish any random event from that over which they have control.

71. The author's primary purpose in the passage is apparently:

   A. to question the experiment described therein.
   B. to clarify further what the experimenters expected to find out regarding depression.
   C. to evaluate the type of experimentation used by Abramson and Viscusi..
   D. to justify the premise that those who are depressed have a negative outlook.

72. According to the passage, one of the author's arguments is that:

   A. the experiment does not consider whether depressives might believe that they have no control when they actually do.
   B. the operational definitions of the experiment were vague and did not appear reliable.
   C. the subjects of the experiment were never proven to conclusively be 'clinically depressed'.
   D. handwriting speed is an inexact method of gauging depression.

73. According to information in the passage, depressive moods would be likely to exist when an individual:

   I. believes that she never has control over positive random events.
   II. believes that she never has control over negative random events.
   III. believes that she never has control over any events in her life.

   A. I only
   B. II only
   C. I and II only
   D. I, II, and III

74. In order to distinguish the nature of the experiment's subjects, the author of the passage draws a distinction between:

   I. random and realism.
   II. the BDI and the Multiple Affect Adjective Checklist.
   III. depressed mood and clinical depression.

   A. I only
   B. I and II only
   C. II and III only
   D. III only

75. According to passage information, which of the following situations would the non-depressive inaccurately attribute to her own abilities?

   A. Controlling her vehicle during a long skid on an icy road
   B. Remembering the birth date of an acquaintance's sister
   C. Helping the neighbor to locate his lost car keys
   D. Choosing the winning numbers in the California state lottery

**GO ON TO THE NEXT PAGE.**

**Passage V (Questions 76–81)**

Southeast Asia is a region strongly influenced by colonialism. Colonialism is the drive toward creating and expanding empires. Virtually the entire region was colonized by the Dutch, French, Spanish, and Americans. The
5 British colonized Malaysia. … Although many countries were colonized, it is Malaysia that has been influenced the most, having had its political and cultural atmosphere altered forever.

To understand colonialism's impact on Malaysia, its
10 geography and history must be understood. Malaysia today consists of two parts. In the west is the Malay Peninsula, which contains Kuala Lumpur, the nation's capitol. … To the east, across the South China Sea, is the island of Borneo. On Borneo are the two provinces Sarawak and
15 Sabah. Together, they comprise the other half of Malaysia. …

Malaysia's colonial history began in 1511, when Portuguese explorer Alfonso de Albuquerque sailed into the port of Malacca on the Malay Peninsula. There, he forcibly seized control over the natives. By 1641, the Dutch gained
20 control of Malacca. At this point, colonization was nonexistent. This changed in 1785, when the British took control of Malacca. The British controlled Malacca and the other major port, Singapore, through the 1860s. They intervened in the Malayans' local wars, and thereby obtained the
25 Pangkor Agreement, which allowed Britain to obtain a stronger foothold in the region. The British ruled this land exclusively until 1957. The disruption of British rule came from an independence movement …. In 1961, Malaya, Sarawak, Sabah and Singapore joined to form the
30 Federation of Malaysia. Yet after only a few years, Singapore left the federation. … Although this officially ended Malaysia's colonial period, the effects of colonialism remain.

After England's rule ended, Malaysia acted atypically.
35 De-colonization is the usual process whereby colonies attempt to free themselves from their mother nation's customs. Malaysia did the opposite, to its advantage. Malaysia exploited the powerful economy England had created. Colonial Britain based Malaya's economy on
40 rubber, mining, and its strategic trade location. The British controlled the Malay Peninsula's Strait of Malacca, a key access point for many countries to trade with Southeast Asia, including the bustling Singapore. … Today, the Malaysian government maintains its old colonial trade ties,
45 building upon British groundwork. … Consequently, the region prospered due to British colonizers' political-economic ventures.

Neo-colonialism is the continued use of economic and political power in retaining influence over former colonies.
50 England never strove to control Malaysia politically, but still retains economic influence as its major trade partner.

Its large contribution to Malaysian businesses' revenues ensures that its interests are articulated often by local concerns mindful of maintaining friendly trade relations. …

55 Another political aspect of Malaysia affected by England is its regional boundaries. Malaysia consists of thirteen states, two of which are not on the same continent as the others. The British colonial rulers established most of these borders, which endure today.

60 Malaysia contains diverse groups that create a mixed culture. … Historically and presently, Malaysia contains many different ethnicities. The native Malays of the Malay Peninsula are … Muslims. Today, they constitute 58% of Malaysia's population. The Chinese, who are Buddhists,
65 are another prominent group. Many Chinese immigrated to the Malay Peninsula and Borneo during Malaysia's colonial period. The Chinese people have sometimes been threatened by discrimination from Malays. A third important group is the Indians, who comprise 10% of Malaysia's
70 population, and are mostly Hindu. The British colonizers also added their own values, creating a distinct culture.

**GO ON TO THE NEXT PAGE.**

**76.** The author of the passage would be most likely to agree with which of the following ideas expressed by other historians detailing the colonization of Malaysia?

A. Without the colonial impact of the Dutch, it is doubtful that Malaysia's economy could compete in today's markets.

B. It is quite clear that the major port cities were significant to controlling Malaysia during its colonial periods.

C. Singapore's unique ethnic mix allowed Malaysia to prosper well beyond other countries in the region.

D. In Southeast Asia, colonialism has, for the most part, served to improve and strengthen the region's politics and culture.

**77.** One can infer from the passage that the underlying goal of the British in colonizing Malaysia was:

A. to exert political and cultural control in order to further monetary goals.

B. to achieve cultural and physical control in order to further profitable goals.

C. to gain physical control in order to further economic goals.

D. to apply political control in order to further money-making goals.

**78.** Elsewhere, the author of the passage states that, "Today, Malaysia remains heavily influenced by England; a carryover from the British colonial occupation of the late 18th and early 19th centuries". This statement most directly supports the passage assertion that:

A. Large economic contributions to Malaysia ensure that British interests are still strongly considered.

B. The British colonialism of Malaysia strove for political and economic control.

C. Due to British efforts to control Malaysia politically, Malaysia remains influenced by England.

D. Because of early British influence, Singapore remains Malaysia's most widely used port city.

**79.** According to the author, the provinces of Sarawak and Sabah:

A. contain Kuala Lumpur, the nation's capital.

B. are located on Borneo and the Malay Peninsula, respectively.

C. comprise the eastern half of Malaysia.

D. are port cities.

**80.** Based upon passage information, it is safe to assume that:

A. colonization has proven to be a boon to many heretofore underdeveloped countries.

B. post-colonization, most nations divest themselves of the vestiges of their colonizers.

C. the long-term effects of colonization are poorly understood.

D. Malaysia's prosperity is an anomaly in the litany of post-colonized nations.

**81.** According to passage information, Malaysia's history includes control by Portuguese, Dutch, and finally British subjects. Yet the Dutch differed in that:

A. they were more concerned with trade than colonization.

B. under their control, there was no colonization.

C. Singapore became the focus of the colonization efforts.

D. they were able to obtain the Pangkor Agreement.

**GO ON TO THE NEXT PAGE.**

## Passage VI (Questions 82–87)

The "Governed Market Development State" model of economic development contends that government intervention can improve on the free market and spur faster than average growth. This model is credited for the rapid growth
5 of Asia's emerging economies, like Hong Kong, Taiwan, and Singapore.

There are two requirements for the developmental state: it must be relatively autonomous from the influence of business, and efficient and coordinated enough to imple-
10 ment a unitary policy. (Obviously, it also must have the money to intervene.) … However, the effectiveness of a government's developmental promotion programs is usually judged by actual results, so the explanation easily becomes circular. A more objective, proactive measure of a
15 government's efficiency is still needed. …

Policy tools available to a state include: lowering bank interest rates, manipulating currency exchange rates, controlling tariffs, deficit spending (borrowing from abroad for domestic investment), and printing more money at the
20 risk of inflating the currency. … Interestingly these are the same instruments neoclassical economists always warn governments to *avoid* manipulating, at the risk of disrupting the free market's efficiency. … If neoclassicists point to examples where state intervention in these variables slowed
25 development, and 'statists' point to others where intervention aided growth, it is logical to conclude that government intervention *can* change the course of development, for better or worse. Logically, then, advocating a minimalist approach for the state, instead of finding and pursuing those
30 policy instruments found to be effective, is dogmatic rather than pragmatic.

For more mature economies, further policy tools of a more visible nature are available. … Nations can improve technical expertise through control of state college curricula
35 and national patent laws. They can implement land reform. Through their influence with the banking sector, they can guide credit availability. Socialist economies may attempt to privatize their inefficient state-owned enterprises, and avoid wasteful social welfare legislation.

40 "Explicit" tools are those policies reached by negotiation between industry and government leaders, or incentive programs publicly offered to all interested firms. Those imposed by the state without consultation, or those that are secret or not available to all firms on a competitive basis are
45 "implicit." … Industrial policy is classifiable into functional or industry specific programs; the former promote an intended effect across all industries (e.g., a customs rebate on exports encourages all industries to export), while the latter are targeted to benefit certain industries. … When
50 policies "lead the market," they are proposed by government and implemented (with assistance) through business; when they "follow the market," they are adopted by governments on the advice of private business leaders. …

Economist Prof. Wade suggests the proper methodol-
55 ogy to objectively study state policies should look to the lobbying efforts which led up to them, with the assumption that the party proposing any measure is the one expecting to gain the most from it. This returns the focus of industrial policy to political economy, rather than efficiency econom-
60 ics, and underscores the heterogeneity of interests that contribute to the making of it, rather than viewing policy as a monolithic construct. If lobbying records are unavailable, we can … determine agency by studying the effects of intervention and reconstructing the goals. If they lead to
65 short-term profits, they are probably industry-led, but if they address long-term government goals, they can be assumed to be state led.

82. According to the passage, which of the following is most likely to be true about the relationship between the government and the economy of a state?

   A. It is generally a poor idea to print more money in an effort to manipulate a state's economy.
   B. State-owned enterprises are generally more efficient than privately-owned enterprises.
   C. The neoclassical economic model has been largely disproved.
   D. It has proven difficult to evaluate a government's efficiency and success in economic intervention.

83. According to the passage, if government involvement can change the course of development, then:

   A. the state should carefully minimize this intervention in a dogmatic fashion.
   B. intervention in most areas of economic development is pragmatic.
   C. studies should be conducted prior to the involvement in order to avoid disruptions.
   D. the government should intervene using those policy instruments which have been found effective.

**84.** According to the passage, one of the requirements for the developmental state is that "it must be relatively autonomous from the influence of business" (lines 8-9). Based upon this information, it would generally be mistaken for the state to:

A. "lead the market".
B. "follow the market".
C. use "explicit" tools.
D. use "implicit" tools.

**85.** Suppose it is discovered that independent, privately owned colleges in the former Soviet Union produced more graduates with greater technical expertise than did the colleges with a state-mandated curricula. How would this information affect the author's claims about controlling college curricula?

A. It would *support* the claim that nations *cannot* improve technical expertise through control of state college curricula.
B. It would *support* the claim that independent, privately owned colleges are *more* efficient than those that are state-run.
C. It would *weaken* the claim that nations *can* improve technical expertise through control of state college curricula.
D. It would *weaken* the claim that independent, privately owned colleges are *less* efficient than those that are state-run.

**86.** The existence of which of the following situations would most strongly CHALLENGE the information in the passage?

A. Discovery of an accurate diagnostic tool for evaluating the usefulness of government economic intervention
B. Evidence that the usefulness of policy tools varies depending upon the maturity of the economy
C. Proof that the neoclassical economic theories are the most valid
D. Verification that Soviet and Red Chinese economies compare poorly with those of the free world

**87.** Which of the following opinions would the author be most likely to endorse?

A. The ability to allocate money within an economy should be spread among several governmental agencies.
B. The managers of a governmental agency tasked with economic intervention should come from the industries themselves.
C. A blend of the neoclassicist and statist approaches is required for the most effective results.
D. A completely reliable and accurate method of gauging the effectiveness of government intervention has not yet been developed.

**GO ON TO THE NEXT PAGE.**

## Passage VII (Questions 88–92)

Early political theory commonly advocates that individuals reject private property for the good of the state. But more modern theories elevate property, often maintaining that the concept of government was imposed largely to
5 protect individual property.

Plato's *Republic* is fairly demonstrative of the older outlook. Its analysis is unconcerned with citizens' material comforts or financial prosperity, so that property is at best unnecessary. To ensure the republic's continuation, its most
10 immediate need is unity, and Plato holds to the proverb that extremes of both wealth and poverty should be avoided. Ancient philosophers and theologians often maintained that material property is incompatible with cardinal virtues like discipline, intelligence, wisdom, and justice, because
15 "money is the root of all evil." *Republic*, as well as the Bible, is filled with stories of how luxury inevitably ruins the body and soul. Thus, to prevent corruption among the guardian class/caste (rulers and soldiers) upon whom the fate of the city rests, Plato advocates that "no one [among
20 them] must have any private property whatsoever, except what is absolutely necessary." When asked is it fair to deprive a section of the populace of material comforts, Plato replies that a penniless class is needed for the good of the entire state, which takes precedence over the happiness
25 of any one class, and the guardians will sacrifice good living for assured virtue, deriving satisfaction from fulfilling their essential role. This is done not with the final aim of helping the guardians themselves attain personal virtue (as is the intent in Christian renunciation of riches), but
30 rather because virtuous guardians are necessary for the city to prosper. Were Plato interested in the moral perfection of every citizen, he would not allow any class to accumulate wealth, but he sees no point in trying to stop it, since the strength of the city (i.e., its military defense) does not rely
35 on the lower classes.

The new, pro-property ideology arose, appropriately enough, in mercantile England, that "nation of shopkeepers". It is typified by Jorf Belle, who said property is not an impediment to the efficient state; rather it is to preserve
40 property that governments were formed. In nature, he claimed, men have the right to their own bodies and, by extrapolation, the products of their labor. In addition, they had the right to stop infringement upon their property, through retaliation. In consenting to join a governed so-
45 ciety, they gave up the latter, agreeing to be bound by civil laws in addition to natural ones "for their comfortable, safe, and peaceable living [and] a secure enjoyment of their property". Property is outside the sphere of government, not because it is not instrumental, but because the right to prop-
50 erty is an intrinsic right of man which precedes government and continues after it. A governing body which "invade[s] the property of the subject" has betrayed its purpose and its trust, and Belle advocates dissolving it. Property is even

presented by Belle as a divine boon; natural resources were
55 given by God, "[for] the greatest conveniences of life [men] were able to draw …. He gave it to the industrious and rational, (and labor was to be [their] title to it)."

However, though these two credos are in fundamental disagreement about property, both agree that excess prop-
60 erty can be the cause of harm. Plato notes that luxury corrupts the individual, while Belle argues that it will harm the community by creating waste, which is theft from someone who could have used it more wisely. It seems that no matter which of these two systems is accepted, it becomes
65 a duty of the government to limit property. In the Platonic republic, the masses can accumulate unlimited wealth, but can never gain political control, while the ruling class is kept without private property. But in Belle's ideal commonwealth, it would seem that the state should limit every
70 individual's possessions to the point where they do not cause any waste.

88. The claim that "it is to preserve property that governments were formed" (lines 39–40), necessitates which of the following conclusions?

   A. The concept of property existed before governments.
   B. Governments were formed based upon greed.
   C. England should be considered the first true form of government.
   D. Belle had probably been studying the theories of Plato.

**89.** According to one of the positions presented, Plato held "to the proverb that extremes of both wealth and poverty should be avoided" (lines 10–11), and "the masses can accumulate unlimited wealth" (line 66). If both of these premises are true, what conclusion is most reasonable?

- **A.** Plato most likely believed that his theories should not be forced upon the guardians of the state.
- **B.** Plato probably felt that it was most important for the rulers to adhere to these tenets.
- **C.** Perhaps Plato felt that the military defense of the city relied upon the masses.
- **D.** Plato doubtless understood that unlimited wealth would eventually destroy them.

**90.** What distinction is implied in the passage between Belle and Plato, respectively?

- **A.** Limit and limit
- **B.** Deprive none and deprive some
- **C.** Early and modern
- **D.** Unnecessary and natural right

**91.** Apparently, both Plato and Belle assume that luxury is:

- **A.** a necessity.
- **B.** natural.
- **C.** wasteful.
- **D.** harmful.

**92.** According to the passage, Belle believed that if a citizen's right to property were infringed upon by his government, then:

- **A.** that citizen had the right to retaliate.
- **B.** that citizen had given up the right to retaliate.
- **C.** that government could no longer bind him through civil laws.
- **D.** that government should be disbanded.

---

**STOP.** IF YOU FINISH BEFORE TIME IS CALLED, CHECK YOUR WORK. YOU MAY GO BACK TO ANY QUESTION IN THIS TEST BOOKLET.

---

# Biological Sciences
Time: 70 Minutes
Questions 93-144

## BIOLOGICAL SCIENCES

**DIRECTIONS.** Most questions in the Biological Sciences test are organized into groups, each preceded by a descriptive passage. After studying the passage, select the one best answer to each question in the group. Some questions are not based on a descriptive passage and are also independent of each other. You must also select the one best answer to these questions. If you are not certain of an answer, eliminate the alternatives that you know to be incorrect and then select an answer from the remaining alternatives. Indicate your selection by blackening the corresponding oval on your answer document. A periodic table is provided for your use. You may consult it whenever you wish.

## PERIODIC TABLE OF THE ELEMENTS

| 1 H 1.0 | | | | | | | | | | | | | | | | | 2 He 4.0 |
|---|---|---|---|---|---|---|---|---|---|---|---|---|---|---|---|---|---|
| 3 Li 6.9 | 4 Be 9.0 | | | | | | | | | | | 5 B 10.8 | 6 C 12.0 | 7 N 14.0 | 8 O 16.0 | 9 F 19.0 | 10 Ne 20.2 |
| 11 Na 23.0 | 12 Mg 24.3 | | | | | | | | | | | 13 Al 27.0 | 14 Si 28.1 | 15 P 31.0 | 16 S 32.1 | 17 Cl 35.5 | 18 Ar 39.9 |
| 19 K 39.1 | 20 Ca 40.1 | 21 Sc 45.0 | 22 Ti 47.9 | 23 V 50.9 | 24 Cr 52.0 | 25 Mn 54.9 | 26 Fe 55.8 | 27 Co 58.9 | 28 Ni 58.7 | 29 Cu 63.5 | 30 Zn 65.4 | 31 Ga 69.7 | 32 Ge 72.6 | 33 As 74.9 | 34 Se 79.0 | 35 Br 79.9 | 36 Kr 83.8 |
| 37 Rb 85.5 | 38 Sr 87.6 | 39 Y 88.9 | 40 Zr 91.2 | 41 Nb 92.9 | 42 Mo 95.9 | 43 Tc (98) | 44 Ru 101.1 | 45 Rh 102.9 | 46 Pd 106.4 | 47 Ag 107.9 | 48 Cd 112.4 | 49 In 114.8 | 50 Sn 118.7 | 51 Sb 121.8 | 52 Te 127.6 | 53 I 126.9 | 54 Xe 131.3 |
| 55 Cs 132.9 | 56 Ba 137.3 | 57 La* 138.9 | 72 Hf 178.5 | 73 Ta 180.9 | 74 W 183.9 | 75 Re 186.2 | 76 Os 190.2 | 77 Ir 192.2 | 78 Pt 195.1 | 79 Au 197.0 | 80 Hg 200.6 | 81 Tl 204.4 | 82 Pb 207.2 | 83 Bi 209.0 | 84 Po (209) | 85 At (210) | 86 Rn (222) |
| 87 Fr (223) | 88 Ra 226.0 | 89 Ac= 227.0 | 104 Unq (261) | 105 Unp (262) | 106 Unh (263) | 107 Uns (262) | 108 Uno (265) | 109 Une (267) | | | | | | | | | |

| * | 58 Ce 140.1 | 59 Pr 140.9 | 60 Nd 144.2 | 61 Pm (145) | 62 Sm 150.4 | 63 Eu 152.0 | 64 Gd 157.3 | 65 Tb 158.9 | 66 Dy 162.5 | 67 Ho 164.9 | 68 Er 167.3 | 69 Tm 168.9 | 70 Yb 173.0 | 71 Lu 175.0 |
|---|---|---|---|---|---|---|---|---|---|---|---|---|---|---|
| = | 90 Th 232.0 | 91 Pa (231) | 92 U 238.0 | 93 Np (237) | 94 Pu (244) | 95 Am (243) | 96 Cm (247) | 97 Bk (247) | 98 Cf (251) | 99 Es (252) | 100 Fm (257) | 101 Md (258) | 102 No (259) | 103 Lr (260) |

## Passage I (Questions 93–99)

Christian De Duve was first to identify lysosomes in the early 1950s with a series of subcellular fractionation experiments. Only after their biochemical properties were revealed were lysosomes recognized in electron micrographs. De Duve was monitoring acid phosphatase as a control for an entirely different experiment when he made the discovery. Upon analyzing the products of centrifugation of liver cells, he found that only 10 percent of the expected acid phosphatase was revealed. Assuming an error in his experiment, he refrigerated his samples for later analysis. Upon reanalysis a few days later he found a 10-fold increase in acid phosphatase. He soon discovered other treatments besides storage which delivered the same increase in acid phosphatase, such as homogenizing in a blender, freezing and thawing, heating, and treating with detergents. From this, De Duve postulated that the acid phosphatase was contained in a membrane bound organelle. He named this organelle the lysosome.

Lysosomes contain several dozen other enzymes, all of which are hydrolytic and attain maximum activity at pH 5. These enzymes are synthesized on the rough endoplasmic reticulum and tagged with mannose when they enter the endoplasmic matrix. They are moved from the smooth endoplasmic reticulum to the cis-golgi via a transfer vesicle. In the cis-golgi the mannose is phosphorylated to mannose 6-phosphate targeting the lysosomal enzymes to their destination in the lysosome. In contrast, secretory and plasma proteins, although glycosylated, are not targeted by carbohydrate markers. From the cis golgi the lysosomal enzymes move to the trans golgi where mannose-6-phosphate binds to a membrane bound receptor. Vesicles containing the enzymes in this form break free from the trans golgi and fuse with other vesicles which have been made more acidic by ATP-dependent proton pumps in their membranes. The low pH causes the enzyme to separate from the receptor, and a phosphorylase cleaves the phosphate group from the mannose group. New vesicles containing the active lysosomal enzymes bud off from these *sorting vesicles*, and deliver their contents to lysosomes via vesicle fusion. The mannose 6-phosphate receptors are returned to the golgi via a different set of vesicles. The mature lysosome is capable of degrading all types of macromolecules found in the cell.

93. From the information in the passage, homogenizing in a blender, freezing and thawing, heating, and treating with detergents probably:

  A. activate acid phosphatase.
  B. denature acid phosphatase.
  C. destroy the chemical identity of all components in the cell.
  D. disrupt a phospholipid bilayer membrane.

94. *Mucolipidosis* is a hereditary disorder characterized by an inability to phosphorylate mannose. An individual afflicted with mucolipidosis would most likely:

  A. possess lysosomal enzymes that are more active than normal.
  B. have cells with large cytoplasmic vesicles containing undigested macromolecules.
  C. be unable to manufacture lysosomal enzymes on the rough ER.
  D. lack the DNA sequences which code for lysosomal enzymes.

95. According to the passage, which of the following is a reactant in the enzyme catalyzed degradation of macromolecules within a lysosome?

  A. $H^+$
  B. $H_2O$
  C. ATP
  D. acid phosphatase

96. In the original experiment performed by De Duve, only 10 percent of the acid phosphatase was revealed. Which of the following best explains these results?

  A. De Duve performed the assaying techniques improperly.
  B. The assaying techniques used by De Duve disrupted the quaternary structure of acid phosphatase.
  C. The techniques were not designed to reveal acid phosphatase.
  D. The assaying techniques used by De Duve did not disrupt the lysosomal membrane.

**GO ON TO THE NEXT PAGE.**

**97.** In I-cell disease, eight lysosomal enzymes essential for the degradation of glycosaminoglycans and glycolipids are found in high concentration in the blood and urine. Which of the following most likely occurs in the cells of I-cell disease patients?

   **A.** The eight enzymes are degraded prematurely by the low pH within the lysosome.
   **B.** A mutation prevents the translation of these enzymes at the rough endoplasmic reticulum.
   **C.** Mannose is not phosphorylated in the cis-golgi for these enzymes.
   **D.** The vesicles containing lysosmal enzymes are unable to fuse with the lysosome.

**98.** Glycosylation of integral proteins takes place in the lumens of the endoplasmic reticulum and the golgi. Carbohydrate groups of glycoproteins in the plasma membrane are always found on:

   **A.** the extracellular surface only.
   **B.** the intracellular surface only.
   **C.** the extra and intracellular surfaces.
   **D.** The side of the membrane on which the glycoproteins are found depends upon the cell type.

**99.** Tunicamycin blocks glycosylation of proteins. If present in the cell, how might tunicamycin affect the targeting of proteins?

   **A.** Both proteins normally targeted for secretory vesicles and for lysosomes are found in lysosomes.
   **B.** Both proteins normally targeted for secretory vesicles and for lysosomes are found in secretory vesicles.
   **C.** Proteins normally targeted for secretory vesicles are found in lysosomes, while proteins normally targeted for lysosomes are found in secretory vesicles.
   **D.** Tunicamycin should not affect the targeting of proteins in the golgi because the signal sequences are synthesized in the rough endoplasmic reticulum.

**Passage II (Questions 100–103)**

The structure of Taxol is shown in Figure 1. This natural product has been used in the fight against breast cancer. Taxol can be isolated from the bark of the Pacific yew trees; however, the tree is sacrificed during the process. The treatment of one cancer patient requires the bark of at least three 100 year old trees.

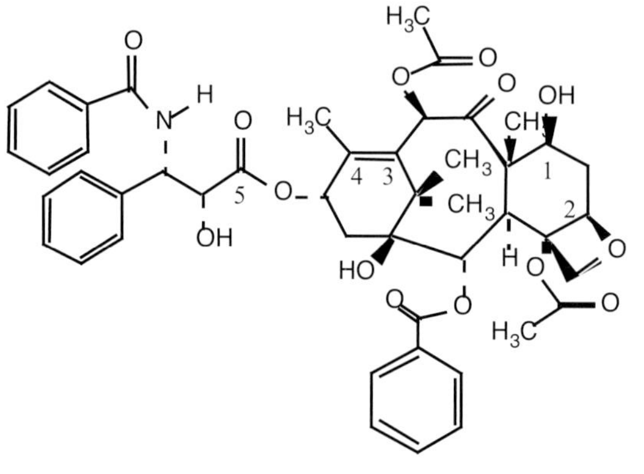

**Figure 1** Taxol

One solution to this difficult problem is a partial synthesis of taxol starting with a compound which can be isolated from the leaves of the yew tree, which can regenerate. A group of French scientists published the scheme for the synthesis of taxol shown below in the Journal of the American Chemical Society (1998, *110*, 5917–5919).

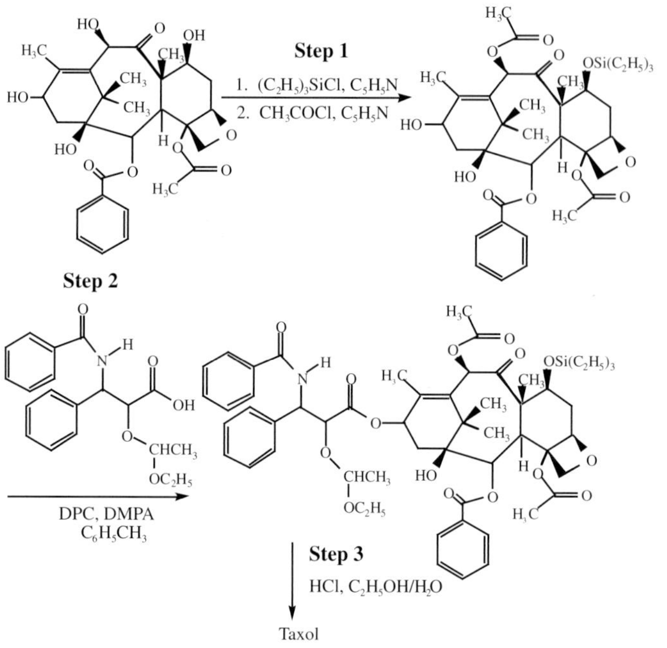

**Scheme 1** Partial synthesis of taxol

**GO ON TO THE NEXT PAGE.**

**100.** What is the hybridization of the carbon labeled 4 in Figure 1?

**A.** sp

**B.** $sp^2$

**C.** $sp^3$

**D.** $sp^3d$

**101.** Molecule A is added in step 2 of the synthesis. What is the relationship between molecules A and B?

**A.** epimers

**B.** structural isomers

**C.** diastereomers

**D.** enantiomers

**102.** Step 2 of Scheme 1 is which of the following reaction types?

**A.** hydrolysis

**B.** esterification

**C.** alkylation

**D.** oxidation

**103.** In Figure 1, how do the absolute configurations of the carbons labeled 1 and 2 compare?

**A.** They have opposite absolute configurations.

**B.** They have the same absolute configuration.

**C.** The carbons are both achiral.

**D.** The absolute configurations cannot be determined without a polarimeter.

**Passage III (Questions 104–109)**

The adult hemoglobin molecule (Hb A) consists of 2 pairs of polypeptide chains designated α and β. Fetal hemoglobin (Hb F) does not contain β chains but contains γ chains instead. Hb F in the blood is replaced by Hb A gradually over the first few months of life.

Defects in the polypeptide chains may arise through mutation of the chromosomes creating a genetic disease. Sickle cell anemia is one such disease. It is believed that sickle cell anemia is caused by an A → T transversion in the gene coding for the β chain of adult hemoglobin. The resulting sickle cell hemoglobin (Hb S) contains the amino acid valine in the sixth position rather than the normal glutamic acid found in Hb A. This single change in the amino acid sequence produces a protein that is less soluble in aqueous solution under low oxygen conditions. Under such conditions, Hb S may cause erythrocytes to take on a sickle shape possibly leading to the blocking of blood vessels (thrombosis) and necrosis of surrounding tissue (infarction). In addition, Hb S erythrocytes are more delicate and thus more likely to lyse resulting in severe anemia.

Sickle cell disease has an autosomal recessive mode of inheritance. Homozygotes rarely live beyond age 40. Although heterozygotes do not experience anemia, they do enjoy increased resistance to malaria, a potentially lethal tropical disease caused by the protozoan *Plasmodium falciparum*.

Sickle cell disease can be diagnosed by electrophoresis or hematologic methods; however, since the chromatic abnormality occurs in an otherwise palindromic nucleotide sequence, a more definitive diagnosis may be obtained through treatment with restriction enzymes and application of Southern blotting.

**104.** A section of the DNA template strand that codes for the Hb A β chain is given below:

5′ CTC CTC AGG 3′
Glu – Glu – Pro

The codon for valine created by the Hb S β chain is most likely:

**A.** GAG

**B.** GTG

**C.** GUG

**D.** CAC

**GO ON TO THE NEXT PAGE.**

**105.** Which of the following, by itself, would allow for a diagnosis of sickle cell disease:

  **I.** a blood sample
  **II.** a skin sample
  **III.** a blood pressure reading

  **A.** I only
  **B.** II only
  **C.** I and II only
  **D.** I, II, and III

**106.** What is the probability that the first child of two individuals heterozygous for the sickle cell trait will have sickle cell disease?

  **A.** 0 %
  **B.** 25 %
  **C.** 50%
  **D.** 100%

**107.** According to the passage, under normal oxygen levels Hb A and Hb S differ in their:

  **A.** primary structure
  **B.** secondary structure
  **C.** tertiary structure
  **D.** quaternary structure

**108.** Which of the following is least likely to be found in *plasmodium falciparum*?

  **A.** a nucleus
  **B.** a ribosome
  **C.** centrioles
  **D.** a chitin cell wall

**109.** One approach to the treatment of sickle cell disease is to induce increased production of Hb F. This approach is most likely effective because:

  **A.** the defective peptide chain is not found in Hb F.
  **B.** fetal hemoglobin is smaller than adult hemoglobin decreasing the risk of thrombosis.
  **C.** Hb F has a higher affinity for oxygen, and lowers the oxygen concentration in the blood.
  **D.** Hb F has a lower affinity for oxygen, and raises the oxygen concentration in the blood.

---

Questions 110 through 113 are **NOT** based on a descriptive passage.

**110.** Which statement about enzymes is NOT true?

  **A.** Many enzymes show a distinct pH optimum.
  **B.** Enzymes show a linear increase in reaction rate with increasing temperature.
  **C.** Competitive inhibitors compete with substrate for binding at the enzyme active site.
  **D.** The binding of noncompetitive inhibitors outside the active site distorts the active site.

**111.** Which of the following proteins is not found in blood serum?

  **A.** albumin
  **B.** fibrinogen
  **C.** immunoglobulin
  **D.** transferrin

**112.** All of the following have cellular organelles EXCEPT:

  **A.** Escherichia coli
  **B.** tetrahymena
  **C.** erythrocytes
  **D.** monocytes

**113.** An artificial increase in blood calcium levels would most likely be followed by a blood level increase in:

  **A.** PTH
  **B.** calcitonin
  **C.** TSH
  **D.** ACTH

---

**GO ON TO THE NEXT PAGE.**

## Passage IV (Questions 114–117)

Electrical impulses are transferred from one neuron to another via a synapse. Synapses can be electrical or chemical. In response to an electrical stimulus such as an action potential, the presynaptic neuron in a chemical synapse releases a neurotransmitter across a small space between the two neurons known as a *synaptic cleft*. Neurotransmitters may have excitatory or inhibitory effects depending upon the type of membrane bound protein receptors possessed by the postsynaptic neuron. For instance, the neurotransmitter acetylcholine binds to nicotinic acetylcholine receptors creating a conformational change which allows small cations to rush into the cell through the receptor. The receptor remains open only for a fraction of a second. The greatest number of cations flowing through the receptor are $Na^+$ ions, since they have the largest electrochemical gradient. Once the receptor is closed, acetylcholine is released and then degraded to choline and acetic acid by acetylcholinesterase in the basal lamina. The choline is then taken up by the presynaptic cell and recycled.

A second type of acetylcholine receptor, the muscarinic acetylcholine receptor, works more slowly through the activation of a G protein which in turn opens $K^+$ channels in the postsynaptic membrane. An action potential in the post synaptic cell is then inhibited.

The G protein contains three subunits, α, β, and γ. A proposed mechanism of the G protein is shown in Figure 1.

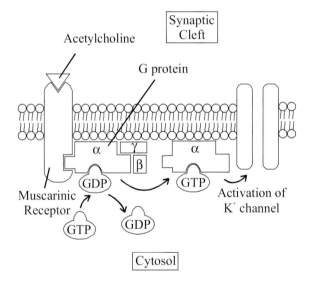

**Figure 1** Mechanism of a G protein

114. Cardiac muscle cells transfer electrical signals from one cell to another via:

    **A.** tight junctions
    **B.** desmosomes
    **C.** chemical synapses
    **D.** gap junctions

115. The inhibition of an action potential via muscarinic acetylcholine receptors is most likely the result of:

    **A.** an influx of $K^+$ depolarizing the postsynaptic neuron.
    **B.** an efflux of $K^+$ depolarizing the postsynaptic neuron.
    **C.** an influx of $K^+$ hyperpolarizing the postsynaptic neuron.
    **D.** an efflux of $K^+$ hyperpolarizing the postsynaptic neuron.

116. Where are muscarinic receptors most likely to be found?

    **A.** cardiac muscle cells innervated by parasympathetic neurons
    **B.** synapses between the preganglion and postganglionic neurons of the sympathetic nervous system
    **C.** synapses between the preganglion and postganglionic neurons of the parasympathetic nervous system
    **D.** within membranes of skeletal muscle tissue at neuromuscular junctions

117. Communication from one neuron to another across a chemical synapse is:

    **A.** unidirectional.
    **B.** bidirectional.
    **C.** reversible.
    **D.** more rapid than across an electrical synapse.

**GO ON TO THE NEXT PAGE.**

**Passage V (Questions 118–123)**

Caffeine is a stimulant found in coffee, tea and cola nuts. It has also been added to some commercial pain relievers to help in the reduction of headaches. Increased respiration, heart rate, and stimulation of the central nervous system are a few symptoms of caffeine consumption. The structure of caffeine is shown in Figure 1.

Caffeine is in the class of compounds known as alkaloids. All alkaloids have basic nitrogens, and form salts. Other well known alkaloids include nicotine, cocaine, and morphine.

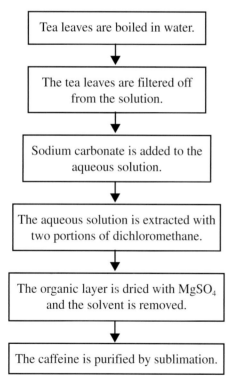

**Figure 1** Caffeine

The crystalline white solid of caffeine can be isolated from tea leaves and the brown tannin impurities by following the scheme shown in Figure 2.

> Tea leaves are boiled in water.

> The tea leaves are filtered off from the solution.

> Sodium carbonate is added to the aqueous solution.

> The aqueous solution is extracted with two portions of dichloromethane.

> The organic layer is dried with $MgSO_4$ and the solvent is removed.

> The caffeine is purified by sublimation.

**Figure 2** Procedure for isolating caffeine from tea leaves

118. How many chiral carbons are present in caffeine?

    **A.** 0
    **B.** 1
    **C.** 2
    **D.** 3

119. Why is sodium carbonate added to the aqueous solution before the extraction with dichloromethane?

    **A.** to protonate caffeine making it soluble in dichloromethane
    **B.** to remove the proton from caffeine making it soluble in dichloromethane
    **C.** to degrade the tannin impurities
    **D.** to catalyze the extraction

120. The tannin impurities have the general structure shown below. After the addition of $Na_2CO_3$, in which extraction layer will the tannins be found?

    **A.** the aqueous layer
    **B.** the organic layer
    **C.** both layers
    **D.** The layer cannot be determined from the structure.

121. In Figure 2, after drying the mixture with $MgSO_4$, which process would be most efficient in separating the solvent from the caffeine?

    **A.** distillation
    **B.** sublimation
    **C.** liquid-liquid extraction
    **D.** vacuum filtration

**122.** Which of the following must be true in order to use dichloromethane as an extraction solvent in the procedure shown in Figure 2?

    **I.** Dichloromethane and water must be immiscible.
    **II.** Dichloromethane must have a greater density than water.
    **III.** Dichloromethane must have a higher affinity than water for caffeine.

    **A.** I only
    **B.** III only
    **C.** I and III only
    **D.** I, II, and III

**123.** Which of the following phase changes describes sublimation?

    **A.** solid to liquid
    **B.** liquid to gas
    **C.** gas to solid
    **D.** solid to gas

---

> Questions 124 through 127 are **NOT** based on a descriptive passage.

**124.** Carbonic anhydrase catalyzes the production of carbon dioxide to carbonic acid in the first step of the following reaction:

$$H_2CO_3^- + H^+ \rightarrow H_2O + CO_2$$

Which of the following statements is true concerning this reaction?

    **A.** This reaction takes place mainly in the plasma outside red blood cells.
    **B.** This reaction demonstrates one mechanism for increased blood pH as the blood enters the lungs.
    **C.** Heavy muscle activity pushes this reaction to the left in the tissues.
    **D.** The reverse of this reaction is one step in the Kreb's cycle.

**125.** All of the following are true concerning smooth muscle EXCEPT:

    **A.** The main contributor to depolarization of the cell membrane during an action potential is $Ca^{2+}$ voltage-gated channels.
    **B.** Smooth muscle does not contain sarcomeres.
    **C.** Smooth muscle contains actin and myosin.
    **D.** Smooth muscle is striated.

**GO ON TO THE NEXT PAGE.**

**126.** Which of the following compounds has the lowest solubility in aqueous solution?

    **A.**  $CH_3(CH_2)_{10}COOH$
    **B.**  $CH_3(CH_2)_{16}COOH$
    **C.**  $CH_3(CH_2)_{22}COOH$
    **D.**  $C_6H_{12}O_6$

**127.** The propagation step in the radical reaction between propane and the chlorine is exothermic. The energy diagram for this reaction is shown below.

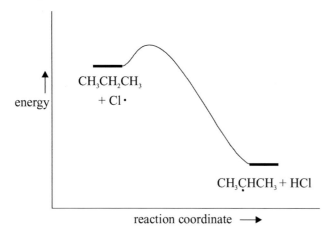

According to the Hammond postulate, which of the following most closely resembles the transition state?

    **A.**  $-\overset{|}{\underset{|}{C}}---Cl\cdots\cdots H$

    **C.**  $-\overset{|}{\underset{|}{C}}---H\cdots\cdots Cl$

    **B.**  $-\overset{|}{\underset{|}{C}}\cdots\cdots Cl---H$

    **D.**  $-\overset{|}{\underset{|}{C}}\cdots\cdots H---Cl$

---

**Passage VI (Questions 128–133)**

Elimination occurs when a substrate loses two atoms or groups, usually accompanied by the formation of a pi bond. Elimination can be first order or second order depending upon the reagents and conditions involved. Competing substitution reactions often accompany eliminations.

**Equation 1**

Equation 1 shows a first order dehydrohalogenation reaction. The procedure is not stereospecific and may be accompanied by rearrangement of the carbon skeleton.

**Equation 2**

Equation 2 shows the competing $S_N1$ reaction to first order dehydrohalogenation. This procedure is also not stereospecific and may also be accompanied by rearrangement. Polar solvents heated to reflux increase the rate of both reactions.

**Equation 3**

Equation 3 shows a second order dehydrohalogenation reaction. This procedure is stereospecific and no rearrangement is possible. The proton and the leaving group must be trans and both be axial.

**Equation 4**

Equation 4 shows the competing $S_N2$ reaction to second order dehydrohalogenation.

**128.** Which energy diagram most accurately depicts an E1 dehydrohalogenation?

**A.**
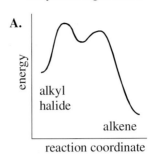

**B.**
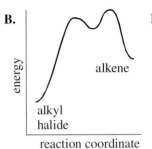

**C.**
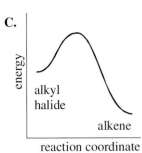

**D.**
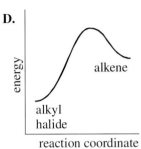

**129.** Reactions with alkylhalides often result in a mixture of substitution and elimination products. All of the following conditions favor elimination over substitution except:

A. a strong base
B. a bulky base
C. high temperatures
D. a highly polarizable base

**130.** Which of the following is the intermediate leading to the minor product in Equation 1?

**A.**

**B.**

**C.**

**D.**

**131.** What is the most likely major product of the following reaction?

$$CH_3CH_2 - \overset{\overset{\displaystyle CDH_2}{|}}{\underset{\underset{\displaystyle CH_3}{|}}{C}} - Br \xrightarrow[CH_3OH]{NaOCH_3}$$

**A.** $CH_3 - HC = C \overset{\diagup CDH_2}{\diagdown CH_3}$

**B.** $CH_3 - CH_2 - C \overset{\diagup CDH_2}{\diagdown CH_2}$

**C.** $CH_3CH_2 - \overset{\overset{\displaystyle CDH_2}{|}}{\underset{\underset{\displaystyle CH_3}{|}}{C}} - CH_2CH_3$

**D.** $CH_3O - \overset{\overset{\displaystyle CDH_2}{|}}{\underset{\underset{\displaystyle CH_3}{|}}{C}} - CH_2CH_3$

**GO ON TO THE NEXT PAGE.**

**132.** What is the only E2 dehydrohalogenation product for the reaction shown below?

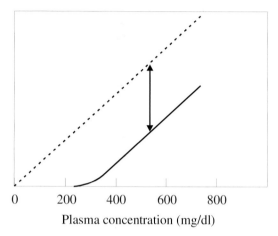

**133.** In Equation 1, methyl alcohol behaves as:

    **A.**   a base attacking a carbon.
    **B.**   a base removing a proton.
    **C.**   a nucleophile attacking a carbon.
    **D.**   a nucleophile removing a proton.

---

**Passage VII (Questions 134–139)**

The primary function of the kidney is to stabilize the composition of the body fluids. The kidney accomplishes this task by adjusting the solute concentrations of the blood plasma flowing through the renal vasculature. As blood flows through the kidney, a portion of the plasma is filtered into the renal tubules as filtrate. The tubules remove and add solute to the filtrate. The removed solutes are returned to the blood, leaving the remaining filtrate to be washed out as urine.

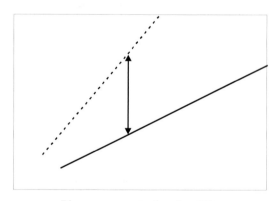

**Figure 1** The transport maximum system

Plasma concentration (mg/dl)

**Figure 2** The Gradient-time system

     **··** Filtration
     **—** Excretion

There are two patterns of transport that take place across the membranes of the epithelial cells of the tubule: the *transport maximum system* and the *gradient-time system.* Figures 1 and 2 demonstrate both systems respectively. The dashed line represents filtration, and the solid line represents excretion. Typically, the transport maximum pattern is followed by solutes that are actively reabsorbed, while the gradient-time pattern is followed by substances that passively diffuse across the tubule membrane. Sodium is an exception because the maximum rate of the sodium-potassium ATPase pump is much greater than the rate of sodium reabsorption. Sodium ions follow the gradient-time system.

**134.** Filtrate moves through the tubule to the renal pelvis via which of the following pathways?

   **A.** Bowman's capsule, the proximal tubule, the collecting duct, the distal tubule, the loop of Henle
   **B.** the proximal tubule, the loop of Henle, the distal tubule, the collecting duct, Bowman's capsule
   **C.** Bowman's capsule, the distal tubule, the loop of Henle, the proximal tubule, the collecting duct
   **D.** Bowman's capsule, the proximal tubule, the loop of Henle, the distal tubule, the collecting duct

**135.** The process by which a solute is released into a renal tubule from tubular epithelial cells is called:

   **A.** excretion
   **B.** secretion
   **C.** clearance
   **D.** filtration

**136.** The two headed arrow in both Figure 1 and 2 represents the rate of:

   **A.** excretion
   **B.** secretion
   **C.** clearance
   **D.** reabsorption

**137.** In the proximal tubule, glucose is carried across the tubule cell membrane by a symport mechanism that relies on the concentration gradient of sodium. Which transport pattern does glucose most likely follow?

   **A.** The transport maximum system because glucose is actively transported across the tubule membrane.
   **B.** The transport maximum system because glucose is transported across the tubule membrane by facilitated diffusion.
   **C.** The gradient-time system because glucose is transported across the tubule membrane by facilitated diffusion.
   **D.** The gradient-time system because glucose passively diffuses across the tubule membrane.

**138.** As the plasma concentration of sodium increases in a healthy individual, the amount of sodium excreted:

   **A.** remains constant up to a certain point, and then increases at the same rate as filtration.
   **B.** increases at the same rate as filtration.
   **C.** increases at a lower rate than filtration.
   **D.** increases at a greater rate than filtration.

**139.** Substance A follows the *transport maximum system.* If the concentration of substance A in the filtrate is greater than its transport maximum, and the plasma concentration of substance A is increased, which of the following is true?

   **A.** Reabsorption of substance A will increase.
   **B.** Reabsorption of substance A will decrease.
   **C.** Reabsorption of substance A will remain the same.
   **D.** Excretion of substance A will remain the same.

**GO ON TO THE NEXT PAGE.**

Questions 140 through 144 are **NOT** based on a descriptive passage.

**140.** Which of the following structures arises primarily from endoderm?

**A.** the femur
**B.** the heart
**C.** the brain
**D.** the liver

**141.** All of the following are true concerning a peptide bond EXCEPT:

**A.** A peptide bond joins two amino acids.
**B.** The carbonyl carbon and an amine are free to rotate about the sigma bond that joins them.
**C.** A peptide bond is broken by hydrolysis.
**D.** A peptide bond forms an amide.

**142.** All of the following are true concerning taxonomic classifications EXCEPT:

**A.** Two species may not occupy the same niche indefinitely.
**B.** Two animals capable of reproducing fertile offspring must be the same species.
**C.** Animals of the same genus are more closely related than animals of the same family.
**D.** A single species may evolve divergently into two separate species.

**143.** Which of the following acts as a coenzyme in fermentation?

**A** $NAD^+$
**B.** pyruvate
**C.** lactic acid
**D.** ethanol

**144.** What is the probability of an individual being homozygous recessive in both traits of a dihybrid cross?

**A** 1/16
**B.** 1/8
**C.** 1/4
**D.** 1/2

---

**STOP.** IF YOU FINISH BEFORE TIME IS CALLED, CHECK YOUR WORK. YOU MAY GO BACK TO ANY QUESTION IN THIS TEST BOOKLET.

---

# Examkrackers MCAT Simulated Exam #1H Answer Key

| Physical Sciences | | Verbal Reasoning | Biological Sciences | |
|---|---|---|---|---|
| 1. C | 28. C | 53. C | 93. D | 124. B |
| 2. D | 29. B | 54. D | 94. B | 125. D |
| 3. A | 30. B | 55. B | 95. B | 126. C |
| 4. D | 31. A | 56. B | 96. D | 127. C |
| 5. D | | 57. D | 97. C | |
| 6. C | 32. C | 58. D | 98. A | 128. A |
| | 33. B | | 99. B | 129. D |
| 7. B | 34. D | 59. A | | 130. A |
| 8. A | 35. C | 60. C | 100. B | 131. A |
| 9. B | 36. D | 61. B | 101. D | 132. A |
| 10. C | | 62. A | 102. B | 133. B |
| 11. B | 37. D | 63. D | 103. A | |
| 12. C | 38. A | | | 134. D |
| | 39. D | 64. D | 104. C | 135. B |
| 13. A | 40. C | 65. B | 105. C | 136. D |
| 14. A | 41. B | 66. C | 106. B | 137. A |
| 15. B | 42. D | 67. B | 107. A | 138. C |
| 16. C | | 68. A | 108. D | 139. C |
| | 43. C | 69. C | 109. A | |
| 17. B | 44. A | | | 140. D |
| 18. C | 45. B | 70. D | 110. B | 141. B |
| 19. D | 46. B | 71. A | 111. B | 142. B |
| 20. A | 47. D | 72. A | 112. C | 143. A |
| 21. D | | 73. C | 113. B | 144. A |
| 22. C | | 74. D | | |
| | 48. B | 75. D | 114. D | |
| 23. C | 49. B | | 115. D | |
| 24. C | 50. A | 76. B | 116. A | |
| 25. A | 51. B | 77. C | 117. A | |
| 26. C | 52. C | 78. A | | |
| 27. D | | 79. C | 118. A | |
| | | 80. B | 119. B | |
| | | 81. B | 120. A | |
| | | | 121. A | |
| | | 82. D | 122. C | |
| | | 83. D | 123. D | |
| | | 84. B | | |
| | | 85. C | | |
| | | 86. C | | |
| | | 87. D | | |
| | | 88. A | | |
| | | 89. B | | |
| | | 90. B | | |
| | | 91. D | | |
| | | 92. D | | |

# RAW SCORE CONVERSION

| Physical Sciences | | Verbal Reasoning | | Biological Sciences | |
|---|---|---|---|---|---|
| Raw Score | Estimated Scaled Score | Raw Score | Estimated Scaled Score | Raw Score | Estimated Scaled Score |
| 50-52 | 15 | 40 | 15 | 51-52 | 15 |
| 47-49 | 14 | 39 | 14 | 49-51 | 14 |
| 45-46 | 13 | 38 | 13 | 47-48 | 13 |
| 41-44 | 12 | 35-37 | 12 | 45-46 | 12 |
| 38-40 | 11 | 31-34 | 11 | 42-44 | 11 |
| 35-37 | 10 | 28-30 | 10 | 39-41 | 10 |
| 31-34 | 9 | 25-27 | 9 | 36-38 | 9 |
| 26-30 | 8 | 23-24 | 8 | 32-35 | 8 |
| 22-25 | 7 | 21-22 | 7 | 30-31 | 7 |
| 18-21 | 6 | 18-20 | 6 | 26-29 | 6 |
| 15-17 | 5 | 16-17 | 5 | 23-25 | 5 |
| 14 | 4 | 15 | 4 | 22 | 4 |

**For explanations to the exam questions, please check out website at www.examkrackers.com.**

**GO ON TO THE NEXT PAGE.**